THE SHORTER
ENCYCLOPEDIA OF REAL ESTATE TERMS

The Shorter
ENCYCLOPEDIA
of
REAL ESTATE
TERMS

BASED ON ENGLISH AND NORTH AMERICAN PRACTICE,

including Australian, Canadian, New Zealand, Scots Law,
Civil Law and Latin terms.

DAMIEN ABBOTT
BSc FRICS CDip.AF

London   Kimball, MI
DELTA ALPHA PUBLISHING

DELTA ALPHA PUBLISHING LIMITED

London   Kimball, MI

www.deltaalpha.com

While every care has been taken in the preparation of the material contained in this book, it is not intended to be a substitute for professional advice. If legal advice or other expert assistance is required, the services of a competent professional adviser should be sought.

None of the material set out in this book should be construed as being either official or unofficial policy of any of the governmental bodies or any organisations referred to herein.

This book is sold on the understanding that neither the publisher, nor author, nor any contributor is engaged in rendering legal, financial or other professional advice or services.

Acknowledgments of permission to quote from previously published works are made on pages xi-xii.

Library of Congress Control Number: **2003099971**

British Library Cataloguing in Publication Data

Abbott, Damien
  The shorter encyclopedia of real estate terms
  1. Real property - Dictionaries   2. Real estate business - Dictionaries
  I. Title   333.3'3'03

Includes bibliographical references

ISBN 0-9668946-1-8

Printed in the United States of America on recycled and acid free paper

To Maurice Hurrell

who provided invaluable comments and suggestions on the First and Second Editions of the
ENCYCLOPEDIA OF REAL ESTATE TERMS

Cover design by **Deborah Lloyd**

Photographs by **Damien Abbott**

CONTENTS

PREFACE

The First Edition of the Encyclopedia of Real Estate Terms was started over 30 years ago. It was followed by the Second Edition, published in 2000 – now it is time for The Shorter Edition. This book is based on the Second Edition of the Encyclopedia, but excludes the French terminology and many of the detailed reference sources. However, as the number of terms continues to grow, the Shorter version is still longer than the First Edition.

The Shorter Encyclopedia retains my original three aims: (i) to provide a clear and precise explanation of the meaning of a particular word or phrase; (ii) to help the user find answers to many of the questions that occur in real estate today (if not directly, then by a ready reference to other sources); and (iii) to identify where a problem might occur upon which, when required, further advice and counsel should be sought.

The Shorter Edition continues to be definitional, but goes much further. It chronicles that which has been said relating to a particular term – or, to be more precise, over 7,500 terms – with extensive cross-referencing. In addition, the text sets out many of the aspects of real estate that follow from the explanation of the meaning and significance of a particular word or phrase; endeavoring to suggest answers to many of the questions that arise on a given subject. In total, there are more than 1,600 sources for further reference (including over 600 cases, 500 statutory or code references and over 400 bibliographical references). Thus, it is a comprehensive reference book on real estate – a dictionary, a thesaurus and an *Encyclopedia*, all in one book. The terminology is drawn from all areas of the real estate and related areas of business: accounting, appraisal, development, finance, insurance, investment, law, surveying, taxation, valuation and zoning.

The Shorter Edition is international in scope drawing on material from the United Kingdom, the United States, Canada, Australia and New Zealand, as well as Latin and Civil Law terms. Every effort has been made to distinguish between the different sources, so that the user may readily identify a source relevant to his area of practice or concern and to identify similarities and differences in the application of a word or phrase in various countries. This should serve to assist those who practice in the increasingly international business of real estate.

This book is a distillation of the work that went into the First and Second Editions of the Encyclopedia of Real Estate Terms and would not be as it is without the help of all those who assisted me in the preparation of those versions and I should like to repeat my appreciation to all those who helped on those endevours.

I should also like to thank Kate Robinson and Liz York who have been responsible for proof reading much of the text of this version, finding numerous errors, and making many suggestions that have improved the content no end.

In addition, I should like to express my appreciation to John Knox, Deborah Lloyd and Andrew Zoltowski who have offered advice and in other ways helped me put this book together.

As far as possible, entries are current as at the end of 2003 and every care has been taken to ensure accuracy.

Finally, I must accept full responsibility for all errors and omissions in the text.

Damien Abbott

Comments and suggestions from users for alterations or revisions are welcome and can be sent to shortersuggestions@deltaalpha.com.

ACKNOWLEDGEMENTS

The author and publisher would like to acknowledge all those whose works are quoted in this book. In particular, the following who have granted their permission to reproduce definitions or extracts from the following publications to which they, or the authors, *own the copyright:*

The American Law Institute for permission to reproduce extracts from the Restatements of the Law, especially the *Restatement of Contracts; Restatement of Property;* and the *Restatement of Torts.*

The American Law Institute and National Conference of Commissioners of Uniform State Law for permission to reproduce extracts from the *Uniform Commercial Code.*

The Appraisal Foundation for extracts from its *Uniform Standards of Professional Appraisal Practice* (2004 edition).

The Australian Property Institute and the Property Council for Australia for extracts from its *Glossary of Property Terms* (2000).

The Building Owners and Managers Association International for the extracts from its *Standard Method for Measuring Floor Area in Office Buildings* (1996) in respect of 'gross building area' and 'rentable area'.

Butterworths for the use of extracts from: *The All England Law Reports; Cheshire and Burn's Modern Law of Real Property* (16th ed. 2000); *Cheshire, Fifoot & Furmston's Law of Contract* (14th ed. 2001); *Halsbury's Law of England* (4th ed. Reissue); Lord Denning's *The Discipline of Law* (1979); *Maudsley & Burn's Land Law. Cases and Materials* (7th ed. 1998).

The Incorporated Council of Law Reporting for England and Wales for extracts from its *Law Reports* and *Weekly Law Reports.*

The International Council of Shopping Centers for extracts from definitions of 'gross leasable area', 'merchants association', 'neighborhood shopping center' and 'shopping center'.

LexisNexis™ for the use of extracts from *American Jurisprudence 2d*, which are reproduced with permission.

Matthew Bender & Company, Inc. for an extract from Corbin on Contract (1993-).

Merriam-Webster, Inc. for extracts from the definitions of 'basement', 'exterior', 'forest', 'meadow', 'obligation', 'occupant', 'parish' and 'shopping center' contained in *Webster's Third New International Dictionary*,®, *Unabridged* ©1993 (www.Merriam-Webster.com)

Oxford University Press for extracts from the definitions of 'alienation, 'assent', 'neighbour', 'possession', 'puff', and 'storey' contained in *The Oxford English Dictionary* (2nd ed. 1989).

Routledge & Kegan Paul for extracts from the entries for 'adjacent, adjoining, contiguous'; 'border, boundary'; 'offer, bid, tender, propose'; 'gain, profit, emolument, lucre'; 'outwards, external, exterior'; 'occupancy, occupation'; and 'place, spot, site' contained in *Crabb's English Synonyms* (1816, reprinted 1982).

The Royal Institution of Chartered Surveyors for extracts from the definitions of 'existing use value', 'market value', 'willing buyer' and 'willing seller' contained in the *Appraisal & Valuation Standards* (5th ed. 'The Red Book' 2003); and definitions of 'effective floor area', 'gross external area', 'gross internal area', 'gross site area', 'net internal area' and 'retail area' contained in the *Code of Measuring Practice: A Guide for Surveyors and Valuers* (5th ed. 2002).

Sweet & Maxwell for extracts from: *Gale on the Law of Easements* (17th ed. 2001); *Megarry & Wade's Law of Property* (6th ed. 1999); *Exclusion Clauses in Contracts* (2nd ed. 1985); *Williams' Contract for the Sale of Land and Title to Land* (4th ed. 1975); and *Woodfall's Landlord & Tenant* (28th ed. ©1978).

West Group for extracts from the definitions of 'trust company', 'vacant possession', 'writing' contained in *Black's Law Dictionary* (6th ed 1990); and for extracts from *Corpus Juris Secundum* ©1985-1999 which are reproduced with permission.

USER GUIDE

Alphabetical order

Words are placed in word-by-word order. In this respect, hyphenated words are treated as separate words, unless there is an optional spelling that creates one word.

Thus, **at-risk rule** comes before **at sight**, **cooperator** comes before **co-ownership**; **coal** comes before **co-assurance**; and **package-deal contract** comes before **package insurance policy**. Where two similar or derivative words or terms are used together (as with **dominant estate** or **dominant tenement**), these also are in alphabetical order, unless one spelling or form of usage predominates over another.

Cross-references

Cross-references are marked in **boldface type**. Such entries may be in the body of the text or at the end where they are prefaced by 'cf.', 'See' or 'See also'. These cross-references are an integral part of the Encyclopedia. Such terms need to be understood and, if necessary, referred to for a complete understanding of any particular entry. The insertion of a cross-reference is based on various criteria: related meaning, related subject matter, entries that contain other supporting (or contradictory) material, or entries that contain additional sources of reference. In many cases, the significance of the points surrounding any word or phrase are only fully appreciated by understanding a cross-referenced term, e.g. **trade fixture** requires an understanding of **fixture**; **commission** is dependent on **procuring cause** or **ready, able and willing**; **exclusionary zoning** should be contrasted with **inclusionary zoning**; and a **lease** compared to a **licence**. Boldface is used to emphasize a term only the first time it appears in an entry, but the importance of that term's meaning is equally important in any subsequent usage.

Gender pronouns

Pronouns that are used in a general context are usually in the masculine form. This follows common historical practice and no offence is intended, and, it is hoped, none is taken. It can only be pleaded that 'he or she' may be considered unnecessarily verbose in some contexts; in other contexts, the use of 'she' may be taken as gender specific.

National or linguistic references

Many terms are marked to indicate that they are more applicable to a particular country, or have a linguistic meaning that derives from, or may be applied to, one country more than another. However, as real estate investment becomes more international, many terms creep into usage elsewhere – especially terms of financial usage (e.g. collateralized mortgage obligation). On the other hand, terms that were once used in one country (e.g. 'conditional fee' in England) have now become obsolete there, but remain in use, for example, in some jurisdictions in the United States.

The abbreviations are used to indicate the country of primary (but not necessarily exclusive) usage:

(BrE) Terms or spellings that are used in British English. Such terms or spellings are also used in other English-speaking countries (although there may be local variants that are not included in this book). However, these terms are not generally used in the United States and in many cases the alternative use is indicated as a cross-reference.

(Eng) Terms that originate from and are used wholly or predominately in English law (in particular terms of English statutory derivation). Such terms may be used in other English-speaking countries (especially those that have adopted the common law), but they are not generally used in the United States. Many of these terms are also applicable in the rest of the United Kingdom, but in some instances the statutory law provisions differ; accordingly the entry in its entirety may be applicable only in England and Wales. In most cases, tax terms are equally applicable to Scotland and Northern Ireland, although there may also be local variations.

(AmE) Terms or spellings that are used in American English. Such terms, or spelling, may be used also in other English-speaking countries (and there may be local variants that are not included in this book). However, these terms are not widely used in the United Kingdom and in many cases the alternative use is indicated as a cross-reference.

(US) Terms that are used wholly or predominately in the United States; especially in a legal or a particular business context. Such terms may be used in other English-speaking countries (especially in the context of finance and commerce). Generally the most commonly used definition is included, with reference to some of the differences between jurisdictions; but space does not permit for the inclusion of all variations (in this respect the complete edition of the **Encyclopedia of Real Estate Terms** provides more comprehensive coverage).

(Aus) Terms used wholly or predominately in Australia.

(Can) Terms used wholly or predominately in Canada.

(Civ) Terms of civil law derivation.

(HK) Terms that are used wholly or predominately in Hong Kong.

(Ire) Terms that are used wholly or predominately in Irish land law.

(NZ) Terms that are used wholly or predominately in New Zealand.

(Scot) Terms that are used wholly or predominately in Scots law.

Case citations

Cases from non-US sources are in *italics* (including cases from English, Scots, or other Commonwealth courts), with the year after the name of the parties, e.g. *O'Brien v Robinson* (1984) 13 HLR 7 (HL). United States cases are in Roman type, with the year of the decision at the end, e.g. Village of Euclid v. Amber Realty Co., 272 US 365, 47 S Ct 114, 71 L Ed 303, 314 (1926).

Parenthetical designations after cases (such as (Aus) (Can) (Scot) (NZ)) indicate the appropriate jurisdiction. In most instances an indication is given if the decision is from an appellate court. (See Appendix D for a list of Abbreviations.)

Statutory references

United States statutes are set out in the following form:

Fair Housing Act of 1968, Real Estate Settlement Procedure Act of 1974, Comprehensive Environmental Response, Compensation, and Liability Act of 1980, generally followed by the reference to the United States Code Annotated (USCA).

English statutes are set out in the following form:

Housing Act 1985, Law of Property Act 1925, Town and Country Planning Act 1990, and in most instances the references are abbreviated, e.g. HA 1985, LPA 1925, TCPA 1990. (See Appendix D for a list of Abbreviations.)

Spelling

Spelling is based predominately on *The Oxford English Dictionary* or *Webster's Third New International Dictionary, Unabridged*. A list of some of the major spelling differences that arise in the Encyclopedia are set out below:

American	**British**
acknowledgment	acknowledgement
amortization/amortize	amortisation/amortise
authorization	authorisation
bylaw or byelaw	by-law
capitalization/capitalize	capitalisation/capitalise
center	centre
check	cheque
collateralization	collateralisation
color	colour
defense	defence
dwelling house	dwelling-house
fulfill	fulfil
installment	instalment
-ize	-ise
-ized	-ised
judgment	judgement
license	licence
meter	metre
neighbor	neighbour
organization	organisation
realization	realisation
securitization	securitisation
sublease	sub-lease
unitization	unitisation

In entries that relate predominantly to usage in Great Britain (especially those based on current English law), British spelling is preferred, and in entries that relate predominantly to the United States, American spelling is preferred. It is hoped that, in this way, the spelling will correspond to that which is more familiar to the user when referring to a particular entry.

A

a fortiori(Lat)   'Much more'; 'by or with stronger reason'.

à prendre   See **profit à prendre**.

a priori(Lat)   'From before'. As deduced by reasoning from the general to the particular or from cause to effect.

AAA rating   See **triple A rating**.

ab extra(Lat)   'From without'; 'from outside'. See **contract**.

ab initio(Lat)   'From the beginning'. See also **adverse possession**, **rescission**, **trespass**, **void contract**.

ab intestato(Lat)   'From an intestate', i.e. succession to property from a person who has left no will. See **intestacy**.

abandonee   One who takes over the right to a property that has been abandoned. See also **abandonment**.

abandoned property   **Property** that has been voluntarily surrendered or vacated, or to which title has been relinquished, without any intention of reclaiming it or transferring it to another. See also **escheat**, **abandonment**, *res nullius*, **treasure trove**, **vacant**.

abandonment   **1.** The act of giving up or proscribing completely. Yielding, ceding or giving up totally, especially ceding permanent control to another.   **2.** The voluntary relinquishment or surrender of property without any intention of resuming enjoyment or possession, or of vesting it in anyone else. The disclaiming of a right, expressly or by implication, without leaving any evidence of an intention to reclaim that right.

Abandonment is a voluntary and wilful act and may thus be distinguished from **eviction** and **forfeiture** either of which can arise as a result of either an illegal act or an omission.

The ownership of a **fee** title to land may be given away or sold, and it may be lost by the **adverse possession**; but it cannot be abandoned. Simply not using an **easement** does not of itself constitute abandonment. There must be a clear intention to abandon, or an overt act that is repugnant to the right of user (*Swan v Sinclair* [1924] 1 Ch 254, 266, aff'd [1925] AC 227 (HL)); 28A C.J.S., Easements, § 126). A **lease** cannot be abandoned unilaterally during its term. However, if a tenant leaves the premises that are leased to him empty, or demonstrates a manifest intention not to occupy the premises, and then permits the landlord to re-enter (or, more precisely, the tenant has offered, and the landlord has accepted a **surrender** of the possession), a tenancy may be said to have been abandoned. cf. **laches**, **repudiation**. See also **constructive eviction**, **escheat**, **estoppel**, **frustration**, **lapsed land**(US), **release**, *res nullius*. **3.** The discontinuance of a use of land for a considerable period of time, especially a **non-conforming use**, so that the use may not legally be resumed.

In English planning law, the abandonment of a use produces the result that the resumption of that use may constitute **development** and, therefore, requires planning permission. In this connection factors to be considered are: (i) the condition of the property; (ii) the period of time for which the use is discontinued; (iii) whether there is any intention to re-establish the discontinued use, which may be judged from the state of the property or any elected action on the part of the party seeking to re-establish the use; and (iv) any intervening user (*Pioneer Aggregates (UK) Ltd v Secretary of State for the Environment* [1985] AC 132, [1984] 2 All ER 358 (HL); *Hughes v Secretary of State for the Environment, Transport and the Regions* [2000] JPL 826, (2000) The Times, February 18 (CA). See also **completion notice**(Eng). **4.** The act of relinquishing damaged property or salvage to an insurer with the aim of claiming a total loss. See also **subrogation**.

abatement   **1.** A reduction or decrease in that which is due. A diminution in value. The act of reducing something in size or value. A suspension of a continuing payment; for example, a tenant may receive an abatement of rent, or an owner an abatement of taxes, because of limitations placed on the full use of the property, or a purchaser may receive an abatement of purchase price because he has not received that for which he contracted. A court may grant an abatement of the purchase price when it is considered appropriate for the sale should to proceed, but at a reduced price, because the loss to the purchaser is not substantial. The abatement is granted together with a decree of **specific performance**. Such a decision arises especially in cases of **misdescription**. See also **frustration**, **rent concession**, **set-off**, **termination**.   **2.** A termination, removal or extinguishment of a **nuisance** or a potential hazard. See also **abatement notice**(Eng), **self-help**.   **3.** A reduction in the entitlement to the payment of a debt when a person has insufficient assets to satisfy his creditor in full. A reduction of a tax obligation.   **4.** The proportional reduction in a pecuniary legacy when there are insufficient funds to pay the beneficiaries in full.

abatement notice(Eng)   A notice, served by a local authority, that requires a person to desist from, restrict, or terminate, a statutory **nuisance**, e.g. to cease creating noise, or air or river pollution (Public Health Act 1936, s. 93; Environmental Pollution Act 1990, s. 80). cf. **prohibition notice**. See also **nuisance order**, **wasteland**.

abeyance   In suspense or expectation. Undetermined and not fully settled. Depending on a contingent event. A freehold estate cannot be in abeyance, as there must always be a holder of the freehold (*Freeman d Vernon v West* (1763) 2 Wils KB 165, 95 Eng Rep 745). A future estate is not in abeyance, but merely a right that follows on from a preceding estate. Although an estate may be said to be in abeyance when it is unclear who should take it (Illinois Central Railroad Co. v. Bosworth, 133 US 92, 10 S Ct 231, 33 L Ed 550, 553 (1889)). In the US, in those states that provide a **statutory**

right of redemption, title to the property may be said to be 'in abeyance' when the property has been sold by order of the court, but the party who will eventually take title is still to be ascertained. See also **remainder**, **inchoate interest**.

able ready and willing   See **ready able and willing**.

able to purchase   See **ready able and willing**.

abode   A temporary stay. A place where one lives, or intends to live. A place for dwelling. Although a **residence** is an abode, an abode generally includes a place where one stays for a shorter period. For the purpose of service of a process or notice, an abode is generally the place where one presently has a place of residence, or a place of **domicile**. See also **home**.

Aboriginal land rights(Aus)   Statutory title to land granted to a group of Aboriginal people (e.g. Aboriginal Land Rights (Northern Territories) Act 1976, s. 3(1)). Such rights may be granted to a group of Aboriginal people that has a common spiritual affiliation with a site on the land. See also **native title**.

aboriginal title(Aus/NZ)   See **native title**.

abrogation   **1.** The act of annulling, cancelling or abolishing by formal action. See also **derogation from grant**.   **2.** The action of abolishing, terminating or repealing a formal act or deed, especially a statute, law or regulation. The making of a new law may abrogate an old one. cf. **subrogation**.

absentee landlord or **absentee owner**   A landlord or owner who resides away, usually at some distance, from the property to which he holds title. A landlord or property owner who leaves the management and running of a property almost entirely at the discretion of an agent, making rare or no visits for the purpose of supervision or inspection.

absolute   Without any condition, limitation, qualification or restriction. See also **absolute estate, fee simple absolute, fee simple absolute in possession**(Eng), **term of years absolute**(Eng).

absolute assignment   An absolute or unconditional **assignment** of the whole of a chose-in-action or debt, as distinguished from an assignment by way of security. For example, if a building contractor transfers to a lender his rights to all money due, or to become due, under a building contract as security for a debt, and empowers the lender to settle all accounts under the contract, he absolutely assigns the debts of the contract (*Hughes v Pump House Hotel Co* [1902] 2 KB 190 (CA)). See also **legal assignment**.

absolute auction(US)   See **without reserve**.

absolute covenant   See **covenant**.

absolute conveyance(US)   1. A conveyance that transfers property without any condition. In particular, a deed that transfers an unconditional fee simple.   2. In those jurisdictions that recognize the 'title theory' of mortgages, 'absolute conveyance' (or such terms as 'absolute deed of conveyance' or 'absolute conveyance with instrument of defeasance) may be used to refer to a transfer of title to property to a mortgagee as security for a debt, with a **reconveyance** when the debt is repaid. (The use of terms such as 'absolute conveyance' or 'absolute deed' without words of qualification in this context can be confusing, as strictly speaking an 'absolute conveyance' is as in **1**. above and in this respect is used in contradistinction to a **conditional conveyance**.) See also **defeasible conveyance, mortgage**.

absolute deed   See **absolute conveyance**.

absolute estate   1. A right to real property without condition or qualification. An **estate** in land that is not liable to be determined or modified in any way and therefore may well continue forever. An estate may be 'absolute' even though it is subject to the rights of another, e.g. a mortgagee. cf. **qualified estate**. See also **fee, fee simple absolute in possession**(Eng), **ownership, term of years absolute**(Eng).   2.(US)An estate that is equivalent to a **fee simple** estate, being the most absolute right to land. In particular, an estate that is not qualified in any way and is not held in trust.   3. An **estate** that comprises an entire property and the unconditional power of disposition during the lifetime of the holder.

absolute fee simple   See **fee simple absolute**(US), **fee simple absolute in possession**(Eng).

absolute leasehold(Eng)   An **absolute title** to the rights arising out of a lease that has been registered at the Land Registry (LRA 2002, s. 10). cf. **good leasehold, possessory leasehold**. See also **term of years absolute**.

absolute liability   See **strict liability**.

absolute net lease(AmE)   See **triple net lease**.

absolute ownership   See **absolute title, ownership**.

absolute sale   A sale that is made when there are no conditions or limitations that affect the subject matter. In particular, a sale of fee title that is indefeasible. In the case of real property, the actual sale takes place when a **deed of grant** or **conveyance** is executed, i.e. on **completion** of the sale; although for some purposes (especially in relation to a liability to taxation) the sale may be deemed to take place when the agreement is no longer subject to any conditions. cf. **conditional sale**.

absolute title   1. A **title** to property that is good against any third party's claim and, therefore, cannot be defeated by any other claim. An unlimited right of **ownership**. In general, an absolute title is one that is as good as can be held, which may be considered as the title held by the owner of an unencumbered **fee simple**. In English common law, there is no such right as an absolute title, or absolute ownership, as all rights to land are based on the relative strength of the titles proved by the rival claimants (*Ocean Estates Ltd v Pinder* [1969] 2 AC 19, 25 (PC)). cf. **possessory title**. See also **absolute estate, doctrine of estates, good title, legal estate**.   2.^(Eng)A title to land that is registered at the Land Registry (after appropriate investigation as to its validity) and is guaranteed by the state as valid against all comers. An absolute title may be freehold or leasehold and represents the best form of such title that can exist. A person may be registered with absolute title "if the registrar is of the opinion that the person's title to the estate is such as a willing buyer could properly be advised by a competent professional adviser to accept", LRA 2002, ss. 9(2), 10(2); and in the case of a leasehold title "the registrar approves the lessor's title to grant the lease", LRA 2002 s. 10(2)(b). In either case "the registrar may disregard the fact that a person's title appears to him to be open to objection if he is of the opinion that the defect will not cause the holding under the title to be disturbed", LRA 2002, ss. 9(3), 10(5). The first registered proprietor of an absolute freehold estate is granted a **fee simple** in possession, together with all rights, privileges or appurtenances thereto, but subject to: encumbrances or other entries appearing on the register; any interest that overrides the first registration, such as a legal easement or profits à prendre, customary rights and public rights, local land charges and coal mining rights (unless the register expressly excludes such an interest); and any interest acquired under the Limitation Act 1980, as when person is in possession of land or when the first registered proprietor has notice of claim by adverse possession. In the case of a leasehold interest, absolute title is subject to all the same rights or obligations as affect the freehold estate, as well as: all express and implied covenants, obligations and liabilities incident to the registered estate; any encumbrances or entries that are protected by an entry on the register; and all covenants and obligations of the lease (LRA 2002, s. 12). cf. **qualified title, possessory title**. See also

freehold absolute, land certificate, land registration, overriding interest.

absorption rate   1. The number of units of property that will be leased or sold in a given period of time, e.g. 500,000 square feet of offices may be 'absorbed' per year in a particular office market. In the UK, generally called the 'take-up rate'.   2. The time taken for a given number of units to be absorbed (let or sold) in a particular market, e.g. the absorption rate for a new 10,000 sq. ft. building may be six months, or the annual 'absorption rate' may be forecast as 50%, i.e. half the building is expected to lease in one year.

absque hoc^(Lat)   'Without this'.

absque impetitione vasti^(Lat)   'Without impeachment for **waste**'.

abstract   An abridgement, summary or epitome. In particular, an extract from, or a shorten form of, an **abstract of title, epitome of title**.

abstract company^(US)   See **abstractor**.

abstract fees^(US)   The fees and expenses paid to an abstractor for the preparation of an **abstract of title**.

abstract of title   A chronological summary of all the deeds, grants, conveyances, transfers, wills, instruments or any other documents that represent evidence of the **title** to a particular interest in real property, together with details of all relevant events (including marriages and divorces) or encumbrances (e.g. easements, restrictions, mortgages, liens, judgements, pending lawsuits, or other claims or releases) that may reinforce or impair that title. Such a resume is prepared before the execution of a contract of sale to indicate the rights to that property as held by the seller and any encumbrances that may affect the buyer.

In the US, an **abstractor** (an attorney, a public officer, or more usually a specialist company) generally prepares an abstract of title and certifies that it is a full record of the documents that relate to a particular property. The abstract indicates the public records that have or have not been searched, and lists the recording date and book and page number where the deed may be located in the office of the county recorder or registrar or in any other appropriate public record. A reference to a transfer will refer to the grantor and grantee, and a reference to a mortgage will state the names of the borrower and lender, together with an indication of whether the loan has been repaid or, if not, the amount of outstanding debt. An abstract of title does not provide any guarantee or insurance as to the validity of the title, but it is issued as an opinion on the title and the abstractor may be liable for any loss arising as a result of his negligence as to the information contained in the abstract. However, an abstract of title may be used to obtain **title insurance**.

In English legal practice, an abstract is prepared by a vendor's solicitor prior to the transfer of property; usually to show evidence of at least 15 years of continuous ownership (LPA 1925, ss. 10, 44(1); LPA 1969, s. 23). It is then submitted to the purchaser's solicitor for his review. The abstract starts with a good **root of title**; sets out all transfers to date that affect the title to the land, such as wills and deeds of conveyance; and provides details of any event, such as a marriage or death, that affected the title during that period. In legal practice, the abstract is generally written in a form of shorthand, with the vowels of words omitted. An abstract of title provides no guarantee as to the validity of the title, but represents the best evidence of the validity of an unregistered title. In practice, the abstract may not be made up of the original documents, but may be prepared as an 'epitome', comprising photocopies of all deeds, instruments or other written documents (e.g. birth, death or marriage certificates) that are relevant to a proper proof that someone has title to land, together with a list in chronological order of those documents, signed by the solicitor as an authentic list. A party who has contracted to sell an estate or interest in land is under an obligation to prove that he has a good title to that which he has contracted to sell

and an abstract represents the best available evidence of that title. A vendor must, at his own expense, produce a proper abstract of title for the prospective purchaser, unless there is an agreement to the contrary. Also, when a **land certificate** for a parcel of registered land shows that the title is 'qualified', an abstract of title may be produced in an endeavour to remove the qualification.

In Australia, sometimes called a 'statement of title'. See also **beneficial owner**, **certificate of title**[US], **chain of title**, **constructive notice**, **epitome of title**, **requisition**, **title report**.

abstracted in chief   That which has been set out in full, e.g. a deed or event set out in full, and not merely in resume as, usually, in an **abstract of title**.

abstracter[AmE]   See **abstractor**.

abstracter's certificate[US]   See **abstractor's certificate**.

abstracting   A term in **quantity surveying** for the process (undertaken after **taking-off**) of collecting together similar items that are to be costed, usually according to trade, prior to preparing a **bill of quantities**. See also **billing**.

abstraction approach or **abstraction method**[AmE]   The process of determining the value of land by using the sale prices of comparable properties and then deducting, or 'abstracting', the value of buildings or improvements to ascertain the value of the land alone. Also called 'appraisal by abstraction', 'extraction approach', 'extraction method' or the 'allocation method'. See also **appraisal**, **land residual technique**.

abstractor or **abstracter**[AmE]   A person who specializes in examining titles to land, preparing abstracts of title and issuing certificates indicating his view on a purported title to land. An abstractor is not necessarily a lawyer but specializes in real estate law and issues relating to title insurance.

An abstractor's certificate, as a rule, does not guarantee any form of title and, except in a case of negligence, there is no recourse against an abstractor for a defect in the title he has investigated. See also **abstract of title**.

abstractor's certificate or **abstracter's certificate**[US]   A certificate set out at the end of an **abstract of title**, as prepared by an **abstractor**, stating which documents of title to a parcel of land have, or have not, been examined and the date on which the abstract is valid. Generally, the abstractor will certify that he has examined all the matters of public record that relate to the particular parcel of land. See also **certificate of title**.

abusus[Lat]   In the civil law, the absolute right to dispose of, or otherwise deal with, property – *jus abutendi* – whether by grant or sale, or by destruction. See also **ownership**.

abut   To adjoin or border on; usually but not necessarily, physically **contiguous**. Abutting implies a closer proximity than **adjacent**; the former is used frequently when land borders a highway. See also **abutting owner, adjoining, frontage**.

abutendi[Lat]   See *jus abutendi*.

abuttal   A land boundary, especially the point or points at which two areas of land are in physical contact. Commonly used in the plural, 'abuttals' being the parts of land that adjoin those of a neighbour – the 'buttings and boundings' of land. In particular, the abuttal is the section of land that abuts a highway; or the front of a parcel of land, as in the expression 'abuttals and sidings'. See also **abut, boundary line**.

abutter   See abutting owner.

abutter's rights   See **access, party wall, right to support**.

abutting owner   An owner of **contiguous** or abutting lands. One whose property abuts, or is contiguous or adjoins, the boundary of another property. An owner whose land abuts the highway. Sometimes called an 'abutter'. See also **abut, neighbor**[AmE]/**neighbour**[BrE].

abutting foot[US]   See frontage.

accelerated depreciation   A method of allowing for **depreciation** by which in the earlier years a higher amount is written-off, than would be done using **straight-line depreciation**. For example, the allowance may be calculated by deducting a fixed percentage from the outstanding capital each year, termed **declining-balance depreciation** or 'diminishing balance depreciation'. Other forms of accelerated depreciation include **sum-of-the-years digits depreciation**; 'double declining balance depreciation'; or 'double diminishing balance depreciation', by which the amount deducted is doubled each year (or, for that matter, by any other increasing amount). In the US, accelerated depreciation is called the 'Accelerated Cost Recovery System' (ACRS) (for properties placed in service between 1981 and 1986), or for properties placed in service after 1986 the 'Modified Accelerated Cost Recovery System' (MACRS) (or the 'General Depreciation System' (GDS)), which allows double the straight-line method in the early years based on depreciation allowance tables that are applied according to the type of property (26 USC, Internal Revenue Code, § 168; Tax Reform Act of 1986).

acceleration clause   **1.** A clause in a contract or deed that brings forward the right to the enjoyment of an estate in land on the happening of a particular event. In particular, a provision which specifies that on the happening of a given event an interest in land may become vested in another; or a clause in a **conditional sale contract** or an **installment land contract** which provides that the purchaser is obliged to pay the outstanding purchase monies, for example if the property is mortgaged or sold. An acceleration clause may be inserted in a lease to provide that in the event of a default in the payment of rent, the entire rent for the residual term of the lease becomes due. Such a clause is generally unenforceable as it amounts to a provision for the payment of a **penalty** and is not an amount of 'liquidated damages' based on the true loss suffered by the landlord. However, if it is considered as a reasonable payment that has been agreed by the parties as payable in the event of a breach of covenant, it may be enforceable (especially on the principle that the parties can agree in advance how and when rent is to be payable) (*Rolfe v Peterson* (1772) 2 Bro PC 436, 1 Eng Rep 1048 (HL); Fifty State v. Pioneer, 46 NY.2d 573, 415 NYS.2d 800, 389 NE.2d 113, 116). See also **conditional interest, penal rent**. **2.** A clause in a mortgage, deed of trust or promissory note that permits the borrower or, more usually, the lender to advance the date for the repayment of the principal so that either party may seek to terminate a loan. An acceleration clause is most commonly brought into effect when a mortgagor is in default in complying with a term of the mortgage agreement (especially the non-payment of interest or real estate taxes). The mortgagee 'accelerates' the date on which the entire loan becomes due and payable, and if the debt is not then repaid in full he may take steps to foreclose the mortgage or exercise his power of sale. Such a right may be exercised only if expressly provided for in the mortgage deed; in the absence of an acceleration clause the mortgagee merely seeks payment of any overdue amounts. An acceleration clause may be 'automatic' or 'optional'. An 'automatic' clause provides that on the happening of a specified event, e.g. a sale of the property or a default, the entire loan advances to maturity, although it is not a forfeiture clause. An 'optional' clause gives the mortgagee the right to demand the repayment of the entire loan if a specified event or default arises. Also called as a 'call provision' or, in the US, if the provision applies in the event the property is sold, a **due-on-sale clause**, 'due-on-transfer clause' or 'alienation clause'; or if the property is encumbered, as by a second mortgage, a 'due-on-encumbrance' clause. See also **foreclosure, unconscionable bargain**.

acceleration of an estate   The advancement of the time when a future estate becomes an estate in possession by reason of the failure of the preceding estate. See also **contingent remainder, future estate**.

acceptance   The positive act of agreeing to an **offer**. "An engagement of one party to the proposition of the other", *Jeune v Ward* (1818) 1 B & Ald 653, 659, 106 Eng Rep 240, 242. In order for an acceptance to create a binding **contract**, it must be communicated to the offeror, expressly or impliedly; it must be made unconditionally while the offer remains open; it must correspond with terms of the offer in its mode, time and place of operation; and there must be an understanding as to what has been accepted. Acceptance need not be in any particular form (unless required by the offer), but there must be a *consensus* between the parties based on evidence of an intention to be bound to an agreement (*Brogden v Directors of the Metropolitan Ry Co* (1877) 2 App Cas 666, 672 (HL); United States v. Braunstein, 75 F Supp 137 (SD NY 1947)). Thus acceptance may be implied by the actions of the grantee, such as entry onto a property or the payment of money. Acceptance takes effect when communicated to, or brought to the attention of, the offeror. It must be unconditional, and the means of acceptance must accord with the terms required by the offer; otherwise it normally constitutes a **counter offer** – which, in turn, requires acceptance. See also **auction, estoppel, mistake, subject to contract, time is of the essence, writing**.

access   A means or right to enter and leave a property; such as a right of access to a public highway, or a landlord's right of access to his property to inspect its state of repair. See also **access land**(Eng), **easement of access**(US), **easement of necessity, entry, landlord's access, neighbor**(AmE)/**neighbour**(BrE), **right of entry, right of way, riparian rights**.

access agreement(Eng) An agreement between a local authority and an owner of open country, by which the general public is permitted access to an area of land for recreational purposes (National Parks and Access to Countryside Act 1968, s. 180). Upon entering into such an agreement a landowner is compensated for costs incurred by him, such as providing surfacing to a footpath, fencing, signs, etc., and for any diminution in the value of land resulting from the permitted access. See also **access order, footpath, right of way**.

access land(Eng) Land over which there is a statutory right of access for the public on foot for the purpose of open-air recreation (Countryside and Rights of Way Act 2000, s. 2). This statute (CROW) provides rights of access for the public to designated areas of **open country**, registered **common land**, land over 600 metres above sea level, land that has been dedicated under a voluntary access agreement, and land over which there are statutory rights of access (such as a metropolitan common, manorial waste land). Certain lands are excluded from this provision ("excepted land") such as ploughed land, quarries, gardens, land within the curtilage of buildings, and livestock pens.

access order(Eng) **1.** An order that is made by a local planning authority and confirmed by the Secretary of State when a landowner is unwilling to permit the public to have access across his land (National Parks and Access to the Countryside Act 1949, s. 65 (as amended)). The order produces the same effect as an **access agreement** and the same provisions for compensation apply. **2.** An order made by a court to enable a landowner to obtain access to adjoining or adjacent land in order to carry out work that is "reasonably necessary" to preserve or repair his own property when the work cannot be carried out (or would be substantially more difficult to carry out) without entry onto the adjoining land (Access to Neighbouring Land Act 1992). cf. **easement of necessity**.

accessio cedit principali(Lat) 'An accessory thing follows the principal thing'. See **accession**.

accession Additions to property that increase the whole. A principle derived from the civil law that an owner of property is entitled to all it produces and any thing that is added to it, either naturally or artificially. Property can be acquired by accession based on the principle, *accessio cedit principali* – 'an accessory thing follows the principal thing'. Accession may arise from natural growth, i.e. by **accretion**; or by artificial improvement as by annexing a **fixture**, or the carrying out of building work on land. See also **annex, compensation for improvements, reliction**.

accessory building A subordinate building that is used in conjunction with a main building, e.g. a workshop or outhouse. A building that is in some way detached, but is part of the same lot and is used as an accessory to the main building, may be an accessory building. However, a building that is an integral part of the main building is not an 'accessory' thereto. Also called an 'ancillary building'. See also **appurtenance, curtilage**.

accessory contract A contract that is subordinate to an existing contract but is made to secure performance of the main contract, as with a contract of **surety**.

accessory instrument See **supplemental deed**.

accessory property See **accession, fixture**.

accessory use(US) A use that is incidental and subordinate to the principal use of a building. A use of property that is secondary to a permitted use. Examples of accessory uses may include servant's quarters, a home office in a residential property, a parking area for a restaurant, or a retail store in a large hotel. An accessory use is incident to the principal use and as such is normally permitted as accessory to the principal use of a property. The determination of what constitutes an accepted accessory use, unless expressly set out in a **zoning ordinance**, is a matter of fact for determination on a case-by-case basis by the courts. Also called an **incidental use**.

accident insurance   Insurance against an occurrence that results from an accident (a fortuitous or unexpected event or an act of God), but not against an inevitability such as death. A term that normally excludes **indemnity insurance**, e.g. fire and marine insurance, as well as life insurance (from natural causes), but includes injury, disability and public liability insurance. Also referred to as 'personal accident insurance' or 'casualty insurance' (although the former term may apply to insurance against bodily injury to the insured, as well as damage to others, and the latter term strictly applies to any insurance other than life or fire and marine insurance and is used to refer to many specialist forms of accident insurance such as health, automobile liability, and worker's compensation insurance). See also **contingency insurance, professional liability insurance**.

accommodation agent(Eng)   An **agent** who deals with the letting of residential property, especially an agent who acts for tenants who are seeking to rent residential property. Generally, an 'accommodation agent' merely maintains a register of property to let and of tenants seeking such accommodation. An accommodation agent is not permitted to charge for merely registering, or undertaking to register, the requirements of any person seeking to rent residential property; nor for supplying details of properties that are available to let (Accommodation Agencies Act 1953).

accommodation density   See **residential density**.

accommodation land   1. Land held for future development or for an intended permanent use, but in the meantime used on a temporary basis such as for the grazing of cattle or for recreation

purposes.   2. Land obtained or improved in order to increase the value of other land, or for the more convenient use of other land. For example, land acquired in order to improve the development potential of another parcel of land.   3.(US)Land upon which a builder or speculator has erected houses in order to obtain the benefit of increased ground rents.

accommodation party   A party who is a signatory to a **negotiable instrument**, in order to provide additional security for the maker, acceptor or endorser, but receives no consideration for the note. An accommodation party has no liability on the instrument until it is negotiated, discounted or it passes to the holder for value. See also **guarantor**.

accommodation value(HK)   See **floor area ratio**.

accommodation work(Eng)   Work carried out by a public authority to accommodate an owner or occupier of land that is affected by the operations or undertakings of that authority. For example, work carried out following the compulsory purchase of part of an owner's land in order to reduce the severance damage. Accommodation work may include such matters as the provision of new boundary fences, accessways, drains, bridges, etc. Accommodation work is carried out frequently *in lieu* of **compensation for severance**, when an authority compulsorily acquires part of an owner's land, or to reduce the amount of **compensation for injurious affection**. See also **mitigation work**.

accord and satisfaction   The purchase of a **release** from an obligation by the payment of an amount that is less than, or different from, the **consideration** required to fulfil the obligation. An arrangement by which a party to a contract accepts that, instead of insisting on his complete rights under the contract, he will enter into a substituted agreement and take a payment or benefit that differs from his full entitlement. 'Accord' is the substituted agreement or **consent** thereto, and 'satisfaction' is the consideration, or that which is given, to support that agreement. Accord and satisfaction create a new contract with new consideration in substitution for the old contract. The creation of the new contract completely discharges the original. However, the payment of a sum of money that is less than the full amount due to a creditor is not of itself sufficient consideration to prevent the creditor from pursuing a later claim for the full debt; payment of a lesser sum can be no satisfaction for a greater sum (*Pinnel's Case* (1602) 5 Co Rep 117a, 77 Eng Rep 237). The substituted consideration may be small or unusual, but it may still be adequate to support a claim that the obligation has been discharged, for the creditor may have a special reason to accept that which is proffered: "the gift of a horse, hawk or robe etc., in satisfaction is good, for it shall be intended that a horse, hawk, or robe etc., might be more beneficial to the plaintiff than the money, in respect of some circumstance, or otherwise the plaintiff would not have accepted it in satisfaction", *Foakes v Beer* (1884) 9 App Cas 605, 616 (HL), per Lord Blackburn quoting Lord Coke. "The American decisions that accord with *Foakes v Beer* are innumerable ..." although "in some states the contrary rule has been adopted by statute, either providing that the payment of an overdue debt shall operate as full satisfaction if accepted by the creditor, or that it shall so operate if the creditor gives a full receipt or other written acknowledgment of full satisfaction", 6 *Corbin on Contracts* (1993-), § 1281. There must be a proper assent to support the accord and satisfaction of the parties, which cannot be achieved by a mere pretence of a bargain, by a gratuitous promise, or by **duress** or **undue influence**. cf. **novation**, **rescission**.

accountant's rate of return   See **average annual return**.

accounting net yield   The net rate of interest received by an investor from a securitized loan, i.e. the return after the fees paid to the loan servicer.

accounts method of valuation   See **profits method of valuation**.

accretion   1. The gradual, slow and imperceptible increase to an area of land as a result of natural causes, as by alluvial deposits left by changes in the course of a river or stream. Accretion can be caused by **alluvion** – the washing up of mud, silt, sand or sediment in such a way as to create new *terra firma*; **dereliction** – retreat of the water below its normal level; **reliction** – a permanent but gradual withdrawal or recession of the water-level. (Strictly speaking, the term 'accretion' signifies the process and alluvion is the material deposited, although the words are used synonymously and the word 'dereliction' is more generally used than reliction for the lowering of the water level or a change in the course of a river.) Land created by the natural process of accretion normally belongs to the owner of the land to which it is annexed; the boundary in the center of a river or stream being adjusted accordingly, even though the original boundary may still be ascertainable (*Southern Center of Theosophy Inc. v State of South Australia* [1982] AC 706, 716, [1982] 1 All ER 238 (PC); Jefferis v. East Omaha Land Co., 134 US 178, 10 S Ct 518, 33 L Ed 873 (1890)). cf. **avulsion**. See also **accession**, **riparian rights**.   2. An addition to value or a loan over time; an increase in a sum of money or a fund by the addition of interest. Also called an 'accrual'. In particular, an increase in the amount of principal owed under a loan when the actual interest paid is less than the face rate on a note or bond.   3. An increase in the value of an asset over time, especially by an external addition. cf. **depreciation**.   4. The increase in an inheritance or legacy arising when a co-heir, or joint legatee, dies.   5.(Scot)The perfection of a title to property as a result of the perfection of the title held by a predecessor in title. Thus, in the event that a party who has conveyed land to which he does not have a perfect title subsequently acquires that title, there is no need for a new conveyance.

accrual   See accretion.

accrual accounting   The preparation of accounts so that income and expenditure items are brought into the accounting period in which they are earned or incurred, rather than the period in which they are actually paid or received as cash. cf. **cash accounting**.

accrue   **1.** To come into existence by an increase in something held. To occur as a natural result. See also **accretion**.   **2.** To accumulate periodically or gradually, for example as an increase in a profit or loss. See also **sinking fund**.

accrued depreciation   **1. Depreciation** that has already been accumulated in a company's financial statement. Also called 'accumulated depreciation'. cf. **future depreciation**.   **2.**(AmE) The difference between the current cost of replacing a building and the present appraised value of that structure, i.e. a loss in value due to obsolescence up to the date of an appraisal. Also called 'diminished utility'.

accrued estate or **accrued interest**   An estate, or interest, in land that will come into effect with the passage of time; the interest 'accrues' when the instrument creating it becomes operative. See also **future interest, remainder, vest**.

accrued income   Income earned but not yet received.

accrued interest   **1. Interest** due. Interest earned but yet not received. Interest that is not paid at its due date but is added to the outstanding principal. Interest that has been 'rolled-up' or added to the principal balance owed. Future interest is paid on the aggregate of the principal and the 'rolled-up' or accrued interest. Also called 'rolled-up interest' or 'deferred interest'. See also **compound interest**.   **2.** See **accrued estate**.

accumulated depreciation   See **accrued depreciation**.

accumulation   Increase by growth or addition. The reinvestment of **interest** as it accrues. The addition of interest to capital in order to provide an ever-increasing sum of money that will be payable or receivable at a future date. cf. **amortisation**. See also **accrued interest, compound interest, rule against perpetuities, sinking fund**.

accumulation of one per period   See Appendix C, **Financial Formulae**.

accumulative rate   A low-risk rate of return that is considered appropriate to provide for the replacement of a capital asset at its historic cost. A rate of return incorporated in a **dual-rate capitalization factor**(AmE)/**dual rate years' purchase**(BrE), to provide a sinking fund to replace the cost of a wasting asset. Thus, if an investor acquires a wasting asset, or an investment with a limited life, he may set aside a portion of the income receivable therefrom to be reinvested at an 'accumulative' rate of interest in order to replace the original cost of the investment. The rate may be expressed before or after the investor's liability for tax. cf. **remunerative rate**. See also **sinking fund rate**.

acid-test ratio   See **liquidity ratio**.

acknowledgement(BrE) or **acknowledgment**(AmE)   An admission that an act or document is legally binding, that a debt is still due, or that an obligation subsists. In particular, a formal declaration made before a notary public, authorised officer or court of law, that a particular document is genuine and is being entered into freely and voluntarily by the person who is signing it. An acknowledged document must normally contain the name of the person making it; the capacity in which that person is acting (e.g. trustee, corporate officer); and the date of the signature. As a rule, an acknowledgment can only be made before a party who is independent of any transaction resulting from the document. 'Acknowledgment' may also refer to a separate certificate produced by a notary public and attached to the main document. A testator, who has not attested his will, i.e. signed it in the presence of two witnesses, may later 'acknowledge' his signature in the presence of two witnesses and thereby validate the will. cf. **affidavit, attestation, jurat**. See also **assent, attest**.

acquiescence   A passive compliance, either by silence or tacit acceptance. A tacit or passive **agreement** or **consent** to a course of action, especially when there already exists a degree of active consent. A failure to enforce a right or avail oneself of a privilege so that another may assume that the right or privilege has been waived or relinquished, especially as distinguished from an avowed consent.

In the case of acquiescence on the part of one party in the use of his land by another (as when the other party is claiming of a right by prescription) a person cannot be said to 'acquiesce' if that use if it is enforced by violence or fear, when the acquiescing party has no knowledge of the use, or when he is paid a recurrent consideration for the use. cf. **assent, laches**. See also **estoppel, waiver**.

acquiring authority(Eng)   A public body that acquires, or is empowered to acquire, property by **compulsory purchase**.

acquisition   1. The act or process by which something is acquired, gained or procured, especially as a consequence of a positive act. A term of no legal import but, in common usage, acquisition may refer to the taking or acquiring of title or ownership of property as a result of **purchase** (voluntarily or compulsorily); **succession; accession; assignment; adverse possession;** *bona vacantia* or **escheat;** or **dedication**. It is a positive act with a permanent result and in that strict sense may preclude a gift, descent or inheritance, or similar fortuitous gain. cf. **requisition**. See also **compulsory purchase**(BrE), **eminent domain**(AmE),

expropriation.   2. That which is acquired, whether by purchase or other means.

acquisition cost   The total expenditure incurred by a purchaser of property, i.e. the actual price paid (taking into account the net value of any exchange of properties), plus fees or commission paid to agents or brokers, attorney's and legal fees, transfer taxes, title insurance and any other incidental costs directly related to the acquisition. 'Acquisition cost' and 'purchase cost' may be used synonymously, although the latter term refers usually to the amount paid as consideration for the purchase of a property, excluding any additional or associated costs. See also **purchase price, closing costs**(AmE), **completion costs**(BrE).

acquittance   1. A written discharge of a debt or obligation. It may take the form of a **receipt** or a formal contractual **discharge**. 'Acquittance' may also refer to the act of clearing a debt or obligation. See also **accord and satisfaction**.   2. A document that provides written evidence of the discharge of a debt.

acre   See **sale by acre**; Appendix B, **Table of Measurements**.

acre foot   The quantity of water that is sufficient to cover one acre of land to a depth of one foot, i.e. 43,560 cubic feet, 1,232.75 cubic meters or 325,693 US gallons (271,193 imp. gallons). The term may also be applied to an area of mineral deposits as with a coal seem.

acre right(US)   A share in the common lands of a town in New England. This amount was fixed for each town, but varied from town to town, being an area that was considered appropriate for public usage.

acreage zoning(US)   See **exclusionary zoning**.

act of God   A sudden or extraordinary act arising directly and exclusively from natural causes, and that cannot reasonably be foreseen or controlled by man, e.g. earthquake, hurricane, lightning, volcanic eruption. An 'act of God' is generally one that is: (i) abnormal or unusual; (ii) strictly natural in origin with no human assistance or influence; and (iii) inevitable, so that it could not have been reasonably prevented or provided against by the exercise of ordinary human foresight. An act of God cannot be avoided by human care, skill, foresight or any reasonable measures; it is different from an inevitable accident, even though it may have happened at least once before. An act of God, therefore, is not the liability of a party in a claim for damages or insurance – it is said to 'prejudice no one'. An act of God may preclude parties from meeting a contractual obligation; thus an owner of building or improvements that are destroyed by act of God is not normally responsible for the failure to complete their sale (unless there is an agreement to the contrary) and the purchaser may be required to take the land in its 'damaged' state. Accordingly, when a contract is executed for the sale of land and buildings the prospective purchaser should obtain insurance against any damage to the buildings that may arise from an act of God. 'Act of God' and *force majeure* are sometimes used interchangeably, although strictly speaking the latter is more comprehensive as it may encompass an act brought about by the hand of man. See also *damnum fatale*, **fire insurance**, **frustration, strict liability**, *vis major*.

actio in personam(Lat)   An **action** *in personam*.

actio in rem(Lat)   An **action** *in rem*.

actio personalis moritur cum persona(Lat) 'A personal action dies with the person'. A principle of common law that an **action** *in personam* (an action against the person) cannot subsist after the death of the individual concerned. This rule does not generally apply to an action resulting from a contract, an action arising from the misappropriation of property, or most actions in a tort.

action   A civil claim for one's right brought against another in a court of law. A judicial proceeding, either in law or in equity, to enforce a right, or to obtain relief or satisfaction at the hands of a court for a wrong or injury. In particular, an action in law, as distinguished from a suit in equity. See also **action** *in personam*, **action** *in rem*, **chose, forcible entry and detainer, foreclosure, forfeiture**, *lis pendens*, **quiet title action, real action, recovery**.

action area(Eng)   An area that a local planning authority considers should be included in a 'local plan' because it requires "comprehensive treatment by development, redevelopment or improvement (or partly by one and partly by another method)", TCPA 1990, s. 36(7). See also **development plan, housing action area**.

action *ex contractu*   See *ex contractu*.

action *ex delicto*   See *ex delicto*.

action for double rent(Eng)   See **double rent**.

action for double value   See **double rent**.

action for quiet title(US)   See **quiet title action**.

action *in personam*   An action against a person, involving his personal rights as distinguished from his rights to property. Also called a 'personal action'. cf. **action** *in rem*. See also **personal action, tort**.

action *in rem*   An action for the recovery of a thing itself, rather than an action against a person. An action by which a person seeks an interest in a specific thing, but not to create a direct personal liability. An action *in rem* is brought against any claimant to the property, not merely a particular individual; thus, it is said to be taken 'against the whole world'. cf. **action** *in personam*. See also **ejectment, foreclosure, real action**.

action price(AmE)   The price at which a deal is

likely to be agreed. cf. **asking price**.

active income(US)   The income that a taxpayer receives for an activity in which he or she materially participates, such as salary, wages and commission. cf. **passive income**.

active partner   See **general partner**.

active trust   A **trust** in which the trustees have active and substantial duties and powers of management, control and disposition of the trust property, as set down in the instrument that created the trust. An active trust may be regarded as a 'real trust', as distinguished from a **passive trust** which does not impose on the trustee any responsibility, other than to hold a title to the trust property. An active trust is the most common form of trust. Sometimes called a 'live trust'. See also **special trust**, **trust for sale**(Eng).

actual age   The age of a building based on its chronological date of construction. cf. **effective age**.

actual authority   The **authority** given by a principal to his agent, either (a) expressly or intentionally or (b) by implication, i.e. by reasonably allowing the agent to believe himself to possess such authority or by the custom or normal course of business between the parties. The extent of an agent's actual authority may be implied from the terms or nature of the appointment, i.e. those duties or powers that are expected from the agent based on written authority, from **usage** or **custom**. cf. **ostensible authority**.

actual cash value   **1.** The **market value** that should be received when a property is offered for sale, for cash. cf. **forced-sale value**.   **2.** The fair or reasonable price paid for a property when it is sold entirely for cash in the normal course of business, as distinguished from a price obtained on compulsory purchase or condemnation, or at a forced sale.   **3.** In insurance, the current value of a property in terms of cash at the time it is destroyed or stolen. Actual cash value insurance is provided on the basis that the insured will receive no more than the actual loss, after due account has been taken of physical wear and tear. See also **reinstatement cost**.

actual cash value insurance(AmE)   See **reinstatement cost**.

actual cost   See **acquisition cost**.

actual eviction   The physical expulsion or removal of a tenant from possession of a property. cf. **constructive eviction**. See also **eviction**.

actual interest rate   See **effective interest rate**.

actual knowledge   See **actual notice**, **knowledge**.

actual notice   Notice that has been received by direct communication, whether oral or written, i.e. notice that has been brought expressly to a person's attention. Although strictly speaking, actual notice means actual **knowledge** of the facts, the term is given a broader meaning in law. Thus, actual notice may include such information as a person is likely to glean, or be aware of, by the nature of a transaction; notice implied from the knowledge and circumstances of a transaction. A person does not have actual notice if he makes reasonable and diligent enquiries, although he may still be affected by **constructive notice** if he fails to make the relevant inquiries that would solicit such information (e.g. an examination of the public records). Actual notice may not be inferred from general negotiation, nor casual conversation, nor by proof that a person had constructive notice; it must be brought to the mind of a person so that he might have an intelligent apprehension of the relevant issue. cf. **imputed notice**. See also **implied notice**.

actual occupation   See **occupation**.

actual possession   See adverse possession, possession, exclusive possession.

actual rate   The rate at which interest is earned on a loan, whether or not it is paid currently. cf. **pay rate**. See also **annual percentage rate, effective annual interest rate**.

actual value(US)   1. The **fair market value** as used when referring to the value of property in condemnation proceedings. See also **value**.   2. For the purposes of real estate taxation 'actual value' is equivalent to or synonymous with **market value**.

actual yield   See **running yield**.

actuarial rate of return   See **internal rate of return**.

actum(Lat)   'A deed'; 'something done'.

ad coelum usque ad centrum or ***ad coelum usque ad inferos***(Lat)   'From heaven to the center of the earth (or to hell)'. An historical view of the limits for the ownership of **land**. However, this principle has been rejected in most countries or overruled by statute law as an unreasonable extension of the right to private property. See also **air rights**, *cujus est solum*, **mineral rights**.

ad filum viæ(Lat)   'To the center of a way'. See *ad medium filum*.

ad filum aquæ(Lat)   'To the center of a stream'. See *ad medium filum aquæ*.

ad hoc(Lat)   'For a special purpose'. 'For the purpose of the matter concerned'. See **overreached interest, trust for sale**.

ad idem(Lat)   'Of the same mind'; 'to the same effect'; agreed. See **agreement**, *consensus ad idem*, **contract, mistake**.

ad medium filum or ***ad medium filum viæ***(Lat)   'To the center line'; 'to the center thread of a way'. Used in defining a **boundary line** between two parcels of land on opposite sides of a road. It is generally assumed (unless there is evidence to the contrary) that the land under a street or highway is owned to the center of the way by the adjoining owner, the surface being vested usually in the highway authority (a rule that does not normally apply to a railway). See also *ad medium filum aquæ*.

ad medium filum aquæ(Lat)   'To the middle of a stream or river'. At common law, unless there is evidence to the contrary, where a non-tidal stream or river forms the boundary between two parcels of land, in separate ownership, the bed of the stream or river belongs to the land owners *usque ad medium filum aquæ*. See also **accretion, boundary line, riparian rights, water rights**.
Cole, George M. *Water Boundaries*. New York: Wiley, 1997.

ad opus sum(Lat)   'For his own use', as where land is placed in **trust** for the use of the beneficiary. See also **use**.

ad valorem(Lat)   'According to value'. An *ad valorem* tax is one assessed according to the value of a property, or as a percentage of its cost. See also **registration duty, valued added tax**.

adaptive re-use(US)   Adapting a building to another productive use. This new use, which is more suitable for current demand, may be called an 'adaptive use'. See also **rehabilitation**.

add-on factor(AmE)   See **loss factor**.

add-on interest rate   See **annual percentage rate**.

addendum   An appendix or **rider** to an agreement, contract or other written document. In the US, such language is sometimes referred to as 'amendatory language'. The main agreement or document should refer to any addendum, or addenda, in order that it may form an integral part thereof and the addenda should be dated and signed or initialed in the same way as the principal document. See also **codicil, joinder**.

addition   Something added or joined to another, especially something in the nature of an **improvement** to a property that permanently increases or improves its value. What constitutes an addition to an existing building, as distinguished from the creation of something new, is a matter to be determined by looking at all of the circumstances. An addition to a building normally comprises something physically annexed to a building or, at least, something used in connection and closely associated with an existing building. The construction of a new building separately from an existing building or to replace an old building is not an addition. See also **accession, fixture**.

additional premium   A payment required from a mortgagor for the privilege of repaying the entire principal in advance and thus avoiding the payment of further interest.

additional rent   1. Any amount paid to a landlord by his tenant over and above the principal sum fixed as **rent** at the start of the tenancy. In particular, a sum paid as an **operating expense**(AmE)/**service charge**(BrE). Thus, a lease may stipulate that certain charges and expenses if not paid when due shall be 'additional rent' and, in that case generally the payment may be recovered in the same way as any other rental payment (provided the payment is not purely personal in nature). See also **indexed rent, overage, percentage rent, reddendum**.   2.(Eng)A sum stipulated as payment, in the form of **rent**, for a breach of a condition of the tenancy. Where a covenant in a lease stipulates that if the tenant does a prohibited act he is to pay additional rent then, as a rule, the tenant can commit the act and

merely pay the additional rent. But if the prohibition is absolute, mere payment of the additional rent does not necessarily permit a breach of the covenant. See also **penalty**.

ademption   The **revocation** or extinction of a **legacy** by an act of the testator, as by making a lifetime gift of the same property so that the provision of the will can no longer be carried out. Ademption and 'revocation' are used interchangeably in relation to a will, although strictly speaking ademption arises from an act of the testator and revocation from an external act, especially as a result of a statutory provision.

adequate compensation(US)   See **just compensation**.

adequate consideration   An amount of **consideration** that represents a fair and reasonable value for a benefit received. Adequate consideration may be distinguished from 'good consideration', which has no value but represents a motive for a contract; and from 'valuable consideration', which has pecuniary value but is not necessarily adequate for, or equal to, the benefit received. See also **market value**.

adhesion contract   A contract that is very one-sided, generally favouring the party who drafted it. A contract that is offered based on 'take it or leave it'. A contract established upon terms set down by the offeror, with little or no variation by the acceptor. Such a contract may be voidable if the party who was obliged to accept it can demonstrate that it does not provide what a reasonable person would accept, or if the contract is unconscionable or brought about by **undue influence** or **duress**. An adhesion contract commonly takes the form of a standard document that is presented as representing the only basis upon which a contract can be entered into, or as setting down the 'normal' terms for the form of agreement being made. See also *contra proferentem*, **standard-form contract, unconscionable bargain**.

adjacent In close proximity but not necessarily touching; near to but not necessarily next to. Adjacent is a relative term, unlike abutting. It can mean **contiguous**, adjoining or close by. Its precise and exact meaning however is determined principally by the context in which it is used. "Adjacent means close to or near by or lying by: its significance or application in point of distance depends on the circumstances in which the word is used", *English Clays v Plymouth Corp'n* [1974] 2 All ER 239, 243. See also **abut**.

adjacent support See **lateral support**.

adjoining Bounding or actually touching. In its legal and primary sense 'adjoining land' touches in some part the land that it is said to adjoin. In some instances, adjoining may mean near by, next door but one, or 'just across the way', but it generally means that there is some form of annexation. However, 'adjoining' is a word that is liable to misinterpretation and should be avoided in contracts for the transfer of land. "There are three words, 'adjoining', **adjacent**, and **contiguous**, which lie not far apart in the meaning which they convey. But of no one of them can its meaning be stated with exactitude and without exception. As to 'adjoining' the expression 'next adjoining' or 'immediately adjoining' is common and legitimate. This expression at once conveys that two things may adjoin which are not next to each other", *Cave v Horsell* [1912] 3 KB 533, 544 (CA). It may be said that "lands are adjacent to a house or a town; fields are adjoining each other; and houses contiguous to each other", George Crabb, *Crabb's English Synonyms*. 1816. Reprint, London: Routledge, 1982. See also **abut**, *ad medium filum*, **adjoining landowner**.

adjoining landowner The owner of **adjoining** or **contiguous** land. The owner of lands separated by a common boundary. See also **boundary line, encroachment, party wall, tree, right to support**.

adjudication 1. The legal act or process of resolving a dispute. A decision as reached by a court of law, tribunal, or other judicial power, on a matter that is in dispute. The determination of a dispute.

In England and Wales, 'adjudication' refers in particular to a process that may be employed to resolve construction-related disputes (excluding building work commissioned by a homeowner). A party to a construction contract may refer any dispute arising under the contract to an independent adjudicator, either as named in the construction contract or nominated by an independent body (an 'adjudicating nominating body' (ANB)) such as the Royal Institute of British Architects or the Official Referee's Solicitors Association (Housing Grants, Construction and Regeneration Act 1996, s. 108). cf. **arbitration**. See also **mediation**.

Caller, Russell (editor). *ADR and Commercial Disputes* London: Sweet & Maxwell, 2001.

Stevenson, Robert, and Peter Chapman. *Construction Adjudication*. Bristol: Jordans, 1999.

Redmond, John. *Adjudication in Construction Contracts*. Oxford: Blackwell, 2001.

2.(Scot)A formal attachment of a **heritable estate** as security for a debt.

adjunction The process of adding or annexing something, especially as a subordinate part. See also **accession, subordination**.

adjustable-mortgage loan (AML) Any form of mortgage loan that provides for the mortgagor's regular payments to vary or be changed during the term of the mortgage. In the US, 'adjustable-mortgage loan' is used especially to refer to an **adjustable-rate mortgage** made by a federal savings and loan association. Also the term may be used to refer to a **flexible-payment mortgage**.

adjustable rate class(US) See **real estate mortgage investment conduit**.

adjustable-rate mortgage (ARM) 1. A mortgage granted at a rate of interest that varies during the term of the loan based upon a base rate, index or formula. The rate may be increased or reduced in line with an autonomous interest rate, such as a rate determined from time to time by market conditions, e.g. a bank rate, prime rate, or Treasury bill rate, (plus an agreed margin). In such cases, the rate is subject usually to a ceiling on annual adjustments or may be subject to a ceiling on the total increase permitted over the term of the loan. The variations may also be set out in the mortgage agreement, as when the rate is reduced to a stipulated rate during the initial term of the loan to assist the borrower in making the necessary payments and increased during the later period to compensate. In the latter instance, if the rate is adjusted at set stages during the period of the loan the arrangement is more usually called a 'graduated-rate mortgage' or if the rate may be varied as agreed between the parties, or as determined by the lender from time to time, a 'renegotiable-rate mortgage'. Also called a 'variable-rate mortgage'. cf. **variable-payment mortgage, renegotiable-rate mortgage**. See also **convertible-rate mortgage, price-level-adjusted mortgage, step-rate mortgage**. **2.**(US)A mortgage loan that provides that the mortgagee may vary the interest rate by up to 1 per cent at fixed intervals, without changing the amount of the mortgagor's regular repayments.

adjusted basis(US)   See **basis**.

adjusted book value(US)   See **book value**.

adjusted funds from operations (AFFO)(US) See **cash available for distribution**.

adjusted internal rate of return (AIRR) See **internal rate of return**.

adjusted gross income (AGI)(AmE)   **1.** See **effective gross income**.   **2.** The income upon which federal income tax is payable. Generally, gross income less allowable trade and business deductions.

adjusted market price   See **adjusted sale price**.

adjusted sale price   **1.** The sale price of a property adjusted by deducting the vendor's costs (e.g. commission, closing costs, attorney's costs, etc.); that is, the true consideration received for a property. See also **purchase price**.   **2.** A price paid for a real property, increased or reduced to take account of extraneous aspects such as the inclusion of personal property, need of repair, provision of financing, date of sale, etc., and thus used as a suitable comparable when preparing a valuation. Also called 'adjusted market price'. See also **comparable property, market price, sales comparison approach**(AmE).

adjusted tax basis(US)   See **basis**.

adjusted value(US)   See **book value**.

adjustment board(US)   See **board of adjustment**.

adjustment cap   See **interest rate cap**.

adjustment of income and charges   See **apportionment, closing costs**(AmE)**, completion statement**(BrE).

adjustment sheet(AmE)   See **settlement statement**.

admeasurement   The process of dividing, allotting or assigning a person's just share. 'Admeasurement' of **dower** was a common law remedy by which upon achieving majority an heir could rectify the share of an inheritance when the doweress had received more than her legal entitlement.

administration of an estate   The procedure by which the property of a deceased person is dealt with in an orderly manner by the **administrator, executor** or **personal representative**, including the payment of debts and the distribution of any surplus property to the persons beneficially entitled. See also **intestacy, probate, will**.

administrative charge or **administrative expense**   A charge or item of expenditure, incurred by a property owner, that is not directly related to ownership of a property, e.g. a company administration expense. cf. **service charge**.

administrator (f. **administratrix**)   A person appointed by a court to administer the affairs of a person who dies without leaving a will, or when no one has been nominated or is willing and able to act as an executor of a will. The position of administrator is derived from the court appointment, as distinguished from that of executor, which is derived from a will. See also **personal representative**.

adopted highway or **adopted street**   See **adoption, dedication**.

adoption   1. The act of agreeing to be bound to a contract or obligation especially one entered into by another. For example, the taking over, by a trustee in bankruptcy or a liquidator, of the right to complete a contract that remains incomplete at the time of bankruptcy or liquidation; or the acceptance by a corporation of a contract initially entered into by the founder or promoter of the corporation after the corporation has been formally incorporated. cf. **novation, ratification**.   2.(Eng)The taking over, by a public authority, of the responsibility for the maintenance of a **highway** or **sewer** (Public Health Act 1936, ss. 17, 18; Highways Act 1980, ss. 37, 38). See also **dedication**.

advance   1. A payment made before the due date. A pre-payment or payment on account, especially a payment under a contract made before the obligations have been completed or before legally due. See also **deposit, interim payment, premium, rent in advance/rent in arrears**.   2. A sum of money granted for a specific purpose, especially as a loan, or as part of a loan; including additional funds granted under an **open-end mortgage**. A disbursement of capital to a developer under a **construction loan**. See also **tacking**.   3.(US)Money paid by the beneficiary of a trust deed, to meet real estate taxes, insurance premiums, etc., in order to protect the beneficiary's interest in the subject matter of that deed.   **4.** A rise or increase in value.

advance bid(US)   A bid made after a **judicial sale** in order to reopen the sale. As a rule, the bid must be at least ten per cent over the previous highest bid.

advance commission   See **advance fee**.

advance commitment   See **commitment**.

advance factory   A factory built before there is a known tenant or occupier, especially when this is done to entice industry to a particular area or district.

advance fee   A fee paid in anticipation of a service, but before the service is rendered, e.g. a fee paid to an agent or broker before a property is offered for sale or lease. The acceptance of such a fee may be contrary to the **code of conduct** of a professional organisation.

In California, it is illegal for a real estate broker or salesperson to demand or collect an 'advance fee' for listing, advertising or offering to sell or lease property, other than in a newspaper of general circulation, unless approved by the Department of Real Estate (California Business & Professional Code §§ 10026, 10085).

In English law, an **accommodation agent** is not permitted to charge a fee merely for supplying details of property that is available to let; for placing the name of a tenant on a register; or issuing any advertisement or list of premises to let without proper authority (Accommodation Agencies Act 1953, s. 1).

advance obligation   See **future advance**.

advance refinancing   See **refinancing**.

advance rent   See **premium**.

advance service charge(BrE)   An advance payment made by a tenant towards his estimated share of the service charge for a building. Generally, this payment is made, in addition to the rent, when a tenant takes possession of the demised premises, or at the start of the landlord's financial year. A balancing payment is paid, or repaid, when the tenant's actual service charge liability is ascertained. See also **primary and secondary rental**(US).

advancement   **1.** A gift of part of his assets, made by a parent to his child (or sometimes to a presumptive heir), with the intention that, in the event the parent subsequently dies intestate, the gift should be treated as part of the child's (or heir's) entitlement. Advancement may also take the form of expenditure incurred by the parent for the benefit of the child and in that respect may be distinguished from a **gift** or loan. See also **hotchpot**.   **2.**(Eng)A sum of money that may be advanced to a minor by the trustees of a **settlement** for the 'advancement', i.e. assistance with self-improvement, of the child. The right to make such payments is called the 'power of advancement'.

adverse claim   See **adverse possession**.

adverse gearing or **adverse leverage** See **reverse leverage**.

adverse land use(US)   See **non-conforming use**.

adverse occupation   See **squatting, trespass**.

adverse possession   Actual **possession** of land without the licence or consent of the true owner. The open, continuous, notorious and peaceful possession of real property in a manner that is inconsistent with the rights of a true owner, or of a person entitled to possession as of right; especially when that possession is maintained in order to bar the true owner's right to recover his land. Adverse possession requires an intention to oust the true owner – an *animus possidendi*. It requires an action that is inconsistent with the rights to enjoyment by the true owner; not merely the causing of inconvenience as by minor act of trespass. However, in the final analysis, what constitutes that intent is a question of fact and degree.

Adverse possession may be distinguished from **prescription**, which is concerned with the acquisition of incorporeal rights over the land of another, such as easements and use restrictions, and not the acquisition of title or a possessory right to land itself. Land must ultimately belong to someone, therefore, the Statutes of Limitation effectively provides for the recognition of a tacit change of ownership; whereas a prescriptive right is newly created.

Title to property may be acquired, or at common law a person's title to property may be extinguished, by a period of unchallenged and adverse possession for a period of time prescribed by the **Statutes of Limitation**. The principle behind the law is to reinforce the possessor's ultimate title to property; *adversus extraneos vitiosa possessio prodesse solet* – 'prior possession is a good title of ownership against all who cannot show a better'. Nonetheless, adverse possession does not defeat a better title, so that an adverse possessor of a leasehold does not ipso facto defeat the holder of the freehold. This is no more that an extension of the principle that a tenant cannot deny his landlord's title. Also, an adverse possessor takes the land subject to any existing encumbrances that would bind the ousted possessor. Furthermore, adverse possession must be claimed against a possessor of land and not against a party who has a future right to possession, i.e. it cannot be exercised against a remainderman.

Adverse possession may arise *ab initio*, as when someone enters onto land as a squatter; it may arise when the paper owner apparently relinquishes possession and another takes up possession; or it may arise when a person remains in possession after his legal right has come to an end, or after entry under an imperfect title. However, adverse possession cannot arise merely because land is vacant; a person must have taken possession of the land against the right of the legal possessor. It should arise from a **dispossession** and not a 'discontinuance of possession'; it does not arise merely by reason of trivial acts of trespass or user.

The period of limitation does not start to run until the true owner has been effectively dispossessed by the intentional taking of possession by another, and therefore the possession must be continuous. Although occupation by a succession of persons, i.e. **tacking** of successive periods of possession, may be counted, provided there is a period of continuous occupation, and the successive persons are claiming one from another. In addition, the possession must be held without **fraud**, **mistake**, or deliberate concealment, but with a clear intention that the courts will uphold.

In English law, "no action shall be brought by any person to recover any land after the expiration of twelve years from the date on which the right of action accrues to him or, if it first accrued to some person through whom he claims, to that person", LA 1980, s. 15(1). Such a right generally accrues from "the date of dispossession or discontinuance" of the dispossessed party (LA 1980, Sch. 1, Part I). (In cases of claims by the Crown or certain public bodies, the period is longer.) With effect from October 13 2002, a person claiming a title by adverse possession must register that claim at the Land Registry, which can be done after a period of 10 years' adverse possession (LRA 2002, Sch. 6).

In the US, where such possession is also called 'hostile possession' or 'distinct possession', the claim must be: (i) actual; (ii) continuous; (iii) open and notorious; (iv) exclusive; and (v) hostile, all for the period prescribed by law, and there must be an intent to exclude the possessor. In this context, 'hostile' does not mean ill will or malevolence, but only that the person in possession of land is claiming an exclusive right thereto. In most jurisdictions, the function of the statutes is to go beyond the common law view of barring an existing right; it aims to confer ownership on the adverse possessor by limitation. Most states require 10, 15 or 20 years continuous, open, hostile and uninvited possession before a person can claim a **possessory title**, and the onus of proof is placed on the party claiming title by adverse possession. In a few states, the period is as short as 5 or 7 years, and, in some states, a different period is prescribed depending on whether the possession starts as a **claim of title** by an adverse possessor, or starts from possession taken under a defective conveyance, i.e. with **color of title**. The period may even be affected by the payment, or not, of real estate taxes. Nonetheless, adverse possession is usually a mixed question of law and fact, depending on the circumstances and conduct of the parties.

In the US, adverse possession cannot be applied to acquire title to **public lands**. See also **encroachment**, **hostile possession**, **quiet title action**[(US)], **squatting**, **Statutes of Limitation**.
Jourdan, Stephen. *Adverse Possession*. London: Butterworths, 2003.

adverse possessor   A person who is in **adverse possession**. One who has taken **possession** of land in a manner that is inconsistent with the rights of a true owner, or of a person entitled to possession as of right; especially when that possession has been long enough to bar the true owner's right to recover his land or an interest in the land. See also **squatter**.

adverse use or **adverse user**[(US)]   A use and enjoyment of property without the licence or consent of the owner. In particular, a use that is open, notorious, and continuous and is hostile to the rights of the true owner and is a precursor to a claim to a right over land, such as an easement. Adverse use is a form of **prescription** and may be distinguished from **adverse possession**, which is a 'possession' of land in such a way as to bar an owner's ownership or title to the land. See also **hostile possession**, **squatting**.

adversus extraneos vitiosa possessio prodesse solet[Lat] 'Prior possession is a good title of ownership against all who cannot show a better title'. See **adverse possession**.

advertisement A note, sign, label, showcard, billboard, panel, announcement, representation, exhibit or any other similar format used to call attention to, or warn someone (usually the general public) of, an item, product, fact or even a fiction. An advertisement may be transmitted orally, in writing, in print, by sound or by light waves.

In England and Wales the display of an advertisement on the external part of a building not normally used for such display is considered a "material change of use" and, therefore, **development** for which planning permission is required (TCPA 1990, s. 55(5)). However, the placing of outdoor advertisements is controlled primarily by regulations made in accordance with the Town and Country Planning Acts and planning permission is deemed to be granted for an advertisement that is displayed in accordance with such regulations (TCPA 1990, ss. 220-222; Town and Country Planning (Control of Advertisement) Regulations 1992, as amended). These regulations state that certain forms of advertisement are exempted from the operation of the regulations and that other forms of advertisement, are "deemed" to be authorised (unless or until the authority seeks to revoke that deemed authority "in the interests of **amenity** or public safety" by the service of a discontinuance notice, a practice sometimes known as a 'challenge procedure'). Consent to all other forms of advertisement must be obtained from the local planning authority. Certain types of advertisement are specifically excluded from the regulations such as advertisements inside a building or not readily visible from the outside of an enclosed area of land; certain short-term advertisements, such as election notices. However, all such advertisement must comply with Standard Conditions set down in the Regulations. Consent is "deemed" to be granted by the regulations for a number of minor advertisements such as functional advertisements of a local authority; various temporary signs, such as estate agent's boards; business name plates; hotel or inn signs; advertisements on the forecourt of business premises; flags identifying a business owner; provided these are within specified limits as to size. Stricter rules apply in an **area of special control**, or in a **conservation area**, where, as a rule, no advertisements may be displayed.

In the US, regulations to restrict the erection or maintenance of advertisements, signs, or billboards are considered a reasonable exercise of **police power**, unless the municipal ordinance or regulation is clearly unreasonable or arbitrary. See also **billboard**[AmE], **general offer**, **invitation to trade**[AmE]/**invitation to treat**[BrE], **tender**, **purchase notice**[Eng].

aedificare in tuo proprio solo non licet quod alteri noceat[Lat] 'One is permitted to build on one's own land as long as it does not interfere with the rights of others'. See **ancient lights**, **natural rights**.

aedificatum solo, solo cedit[Lat] 'That which is built on the **land** goes with the land'. See also **fixture**.

aedificia solo cedunt[Lat] 'Buildings go with the land'. See **fixture**.

aedificium[Lat] A **building**.

aesthetic A word, derived from the Greek *aisthetikos*, 'things perceptible by the senses'. A term used widely in architecture and town planning for that which is pleasing, or is considered by common opinion to be pleasing to the eye; especially that which is in unison with the environment, i.e. with natural rather than purely man-made features.

In English **town and country planning**, an authority that is in a position to grant planning permission for a new development is expected to have regard to that which is aesthetic, which may include ensuring that development is in harmony with the general architecture or design of the immediate area.

In the US, the protection of the "aesthetic" appearance of an area may be considered to be a reasonable exercise of **police power**. However, a zoning ordinance based solely or predominately on aesthetic considerations may well not find support, especially if it constitutes an "unreasonable device of implementing community policy", or what is being sought is no more than "artistic conformity or nonconformity". Whereas, an ordinance based on such criteria as 'design compatibility' or 'variety of architectural design', and not purely aesthetic considerations, is more likely to be upheld as a valid exercise of police power for the benefit of the community.

affected valuation basis(Aus/NZ)   The value of a property taking into account works or plans that would have a detrimental effect on the property, especially public works such as the construction of a motorway or airport. See also **blight**.

affidavit   A statement confirmed by oath; a written declaration sworn before a notary public, or a public official with authority to administer an oath, of a known or believed fact or of an expert opinion. In the US, for example, a seller or grantor of land may provide an 'affidavit of title' affirming that he is the true owner; that to his knowledge the property is free of any **cloud on title**; and that the seller has enjoyed possession of the property for a stated period of time, or that there has been no change in the status of the title since the agreement to sell. See also **attestation, statutory declaration**(Eng).

affiliate broker(AmE)   See **salesperson**.

affirmation   **1.** A declaration or signification of what is, as a statement of fact rather than opinion. Acceptance, concurrence or agreement as when a person affirms or accepts a voidable contract. Affirmation of a contract occurs in particular when a contract is entered into as a consequence of a misrepresentation and the party entitled to rescind the contract accepts, either expressly or impliedly, but in full knowledge of the facts, that he will forego his right to rescission of the contract. See also **ratification**.   **2.** A formal declaration that a statement is true. See also **affidavit**.

affirmative easement(US)   See **easement**.

affirmative covenant(US)   A **covenant** by which someone undertakes that something will be done. In particular, a covenant that commits someone to carry out work for the repair, maintenance or improvement of land. cf. **restrictive covenant**.

affirmative waste   See **waste**.

affixed to land   See **fixture**.

affordable housing(US)   Housing provided for those whose income is at or below the average for a particular area. The level of income appropriate for someone to qualify for affordable housing is determined by the U.S. Department of Housing and Urban Development (HUD). Affordable housing is generally built with government assisted funding.

affordability index   An index that measures the relationship between household income and the median cost of a mortgage. Generally, this index is based on the monthly income before tax of a median-income family and the monthly cost of servicing an **amortization mortgage**.

afforestation   The turning of open land into forest or woodland. cf. **assart**(BrE).

after   See **time**.

after-acquired clause(US)   A clause in a mortgage deed which provides that any property acquired by the mortgagor, or any improvements added to a mortgaged property, while the mortgage debt is outstanding, will become additional security for that debt. In some jurisdictions, such a provision is considered as only capable of creating an equitable lien on the additional property. In other jurisdictions, an after-acquired clause may only apply to property attached to mortgaged real estate, i.e. to a fixture or property that is appurtenant to the mortgaged property. In other cases the provision may be limited in its effectiveness against third party creditors of the mortgagor in respect of property that is not appurtenant to the existing mortgaged property. Also called an 'after-acquired property clause'.

after-acquired title(US) An interest or estate in land that a seller acquires to the same land after a transfer of title has taken place. As a rule, where real property is transferred by **warranty deed**, or where the seller has stated that he has title to land, even if he does not, the seller cannot retain any after-acquired title. An after-acquired title does not normally pass under a quitclaim deed. See also **covenant for further assurance, estoppel by deed**.

after taking(US) See **before-and-after method**.

after-tax cash flow (ATCF)(US) See **cash flow**.

age-life method of depreciation See **straight-line depreciation**.

agency A relationship by which one person (a **principal**) appoints or authorises another (an **agent**), expressly or impliedly, to act on his behalf with the aim of bringing about an agreement or a transaction affecting a third party so as to alter the legal position of the principal. Agency is a relationship that goes beyond mere employment, because the consequence of the agent's action is to create a legal relationship (whether in the form of a contract or a transfer of an interest in property) between the principal and a third party.

A contract of agency is one that requires **good faith**; it is a **fiduciary** relationship. It may be considered more analogous to a trust, rather than a mere contract, in view of the type of relationship created (although a trustee is not the beneficiary's representative and, in most respects, is under a stricter duty to account for all his actions to the beneficiary).

The relationship of agency may be terminated when the agent has fulfilled the duties for which he was appointed; the expiration of an agreed time limit for **performance**; by mutual agreement; by the death or incapacity of either party; if the performance of the agent's duties is frustrated; or by an express **revocation** of the agent's authority (provided the agency is not coupled with a subsisting interest). See also **agency coupled with an interest, agency of necessity, dual agency, exclusive agency, authority, listing, ratification, respondeat superior, time is of the essence, undisclosed agency**. **2.**(US)An affiliated arm of the government, e.g. **Federal National Mortgage Association**.

agency agreement An agreement by which the relationship of **agency** is expressly brought into effect. An agreement by which one party (an **agent**) is appointed to represent another (a **principal**) in negotiations or other business discussions with a third party. In particular, an agreement that sets out the terms for the appointment of an agent. An agency agreement need not be in **writing**, although some jurisdictions in the US require that an agency or **listing agreement** for real property must be in writing. However, an agent cannot execute an agreement that must itself be in writing, unless the agent's authority is given in writing. See also **contract, power of attorney**.

agency by estoppel See **estoppel, ostensible authority**.

agency by necessity See **agency of necessity**.

agency by ratification See **ratification**.

agency contract See **agency agreement**.

agency coupled with an interest   An **agency** relationship where the agent has an interest in the property that forms the subject matter of the relationship. Such a relationship cannot be automatically revoked, at least as long as the agent retains his interest. Also, it does not terminate automatically on the death of principal, but may subsist until the agent has fulfilled his duties in respect of the property under the terms of his appointment. A real estate agency under an exclusive listing agreement is not an 'agency coupled with an interest'. See also **authority**.

agency of necessity   An action taken by one person, on behalf of another, on the grounds of urgent necessity so as to bring into existence a relationship that is akin to **agency**; especially where there is already a relationship between the parties. In particular, when, on behalf of his principal, an agent takes an action that is considered to be in the best interest of the principal, but for which he has no **actual authority**; such as an action taken in an emergency and in **good faith**, when an agent is unable to communicate with his principal, as from a ship in peril. Agency of necessity may also arise where there is no relationship between the parties but a mere stranger acts out of positive necessity, in a manner similar to an authorised agent, in order to prevent a loss by another. For example, an action taken to prevent damage or deterioration to another's property, especially when the person taking the action has some right or interest in the property such as a bailee who sells perishable goods to preserve the monetary worth entrusted to him. The necessity should arise out of something stronger than mere inconvenience; it should arise as the only reasonable and prudent course to follow combined with a necessity to spend money. As a rule, the courts prefer to construe an act of an agent that binds his principal as an extension of his authority, by implication, rather than accepting that a new authority has been created 'as of necessity'. Also called an 'agency by necessity'. See also **quasi-contract**.

agency in fact   See **agent**.

agency to sell   See **broker, exclusive agency, exclusive right to sell**.

agent   A person (the agent) authorised by another (the **principal**) to act on the latter's behalf, or in his place, in establishing a legal relationship, with a third party. Someone appointed, expressly, impliedly, or ostensibly, to act for another, and who is authorised to act within the limits of the terms of that appointment. An agent may even be a person who acts for another, initially without an **actual authority**, provided that other party ratifies his actions subsequently. An agent may be: (i) 'universal' – when the authority covers all matters relating to the principal's business; (ii) 'general' – when the authority applies to a group of related matters especially when those matters arise in the ordinary course of a business or profession or out of an appointment to act for the benefit or profit of a principal in a certain area of business, e.g. the duties of a **managing agent**; or (iii) 'special' or 'specific' – when the agent is appointed to perform a specific task designated by the principal, e.g. an agent appointed to sell a particular property.

An act of an agent, done within the limitation of his authority (express or implied), is binding on his principal. However, once an agent has established an agreement on behalf of his principal, he drops out and leaves the principal as the sole contracting party. The rule is that the principal has entered into the contract made by his agent, and that the principal may sue or be sued upon that contract. (Exceptions to this rule may arise when there is a contrary intention; when the agent intends to be bound; or when there is an undisclosed principal or, possibly, if there is an unnamed principal.)

An agent's **authority** may arise by the mutual consent of the principal and agent (an 'agency in fact'); or it may arise by implication; by **estoppel**; or sometimes as a matter of sheer necessity – an **agency of necessity**. The express authority of an agent is to be found within the instrument by which the authority is granted, "either in express terms or by necessary implication", *Bryant, Powis, and Bryant, Limited v La Banque du Peuple* [1893] AC 170, 177 (HL).

This instrument is called an **agency agreement** or **power of attorney**. An agent's implied authority may arise from a matter that is incidental to the proper performance of his duties; from the very nature of his position; from the **custom** or trade **usage** of the business in which he is involved; or when it is implicit in the nature of appointment. A person who purports to have authority to act as an agent and enters into a contract cannot later endeavour to prove that there is no contract merely because he had no authority. If the agent has such authority, express or implied, the principal is bound, but if the agent enters into a contract outside his authority without the knowledge of his principal, normally the agent is liable to fulfil that contract.

An agent's responsibility to his principal extends beyond that of a normal contract, there is a **fiduciary** relationship; one based on trust. An agent is responsible for keeping his principal informed of any matter that affects the authority entrusted to him and he is obliged by the nature of his position to avoid any conflict of interest; any form of self dealing; or making any secret profit that may be at his principal's cost. An agent should inform his principal if he (the agent) is acting for another party who may be involved in a transaction for which the agent is appointed to act; as a rule he should not act for both sides on a sale of property (although see **dual agency**); and he must inform his principal of any other matter that is relevant to the proper performance of his duties. An agent owes a special duty of care to his principal similar to that due from any professional advisor to his client, and an agent cannot escape a liability for his own **tort** by claiming that he is acting on behalf of another. Any money received by an agent, unless there is an agreement to the contrary, is the property of the principal and must be handed over to the principal. cf. **independent contractor, stakeholder, trustee**. See also **accommodation agent, agency, auctioneer, broker, developer**(US), **estate agent**(BrE), **factor, land agent, subagent**.

agent of necessity   See **agency of necessity**.

agglomeration   An urban or built up area, especially a massing of urban development. A group of buildings, villages or towns that have merged together to form one mass or whole. In particular, a number of urban areas or districts that have merged into one by organic growth. See also **conurbation, urbanization**.

aggregation   The adding together of units to make a whole, such as adding the value of assets together for taxation purposes. See also **component valuation, hotchpot**.

aggregate retail value (ARV)(AmE)   The value of all the units in a subdivision on the basis that they are all complete and available for sale. This value assumes that the lots are sold as a whole and takes no account of any premium obtained by individual sales.

agistment or **egistment**   1. An arrangement by which a land owner, or agister, takes in live stock to pasture on his land in return for a payment, usually at a rate per head, and upon the understanding that the animals will be returned to the owner on demand. Agistment is a form of **bailment** for the purpose of grazing and feeding of animals and conveys no interest in land.   2. An obligation to maintain a bank or wall in order to keep out the sea.

agrarian   Relating to land, especially **agricultural land**.

agreed notice(Eng)   See **notice**.

agreement   An arrangement made between two or more parties by which they signify their assent, whether in writing or otherwise, to a course of action, or to a distinct intention, that affects the parties. A common understanding on an objective **cause**. Agreement is said to be reached when there is a meeting of minds – a *consensus ad idem*. An agreement may be **express** or may be **implied** from the conduct of the parties. An agreement may be implied also from other circumstances, such as the normal course of dealing or trade usage.

An agreement may be distinguished from a **contract**, because the former is only one element in the legal relationship created by the latter and, although every contract is an agreement, not every agreement is a contract. An agreement is a broader term than a contract, and an even broader term than a **bargain** or a **promise**. See also **agreement for sale**, **agreement for a lease**, **agreement to sell**, **contract for sale**, **gentlemen's agreement**.

agreement for a lease   A **contract** entered into between two parties by which one party promises to grant and the other to accept a **lease**, but no formal lease is brought into existence. "An agreement for a lease is to be distinguished from a lease, because a lease is actually a conveyance of a legal estate in land, whereas a contract for a lease is an agreement that such a conveyance shall be entered into at a future date. ... Like any other legally binding agreement, an agreement for a lease must constitute a contract in accordance with the ordinary law of contract ...", 1 *Woodfall's Law of Landlord and Tenant,* para. 4.001. Thus, an agreement for a lease must: (i) identify the parties to the proposed lease; (ii) establish the premises to be leased; (iii) have a determined, or determinable commencement date and duration; and (iv) establish the rent or other consideration to be paid. In addition, in many cases the agreement must be made in writing.

In common law, since the **Statute of Frauds** of 1677, a lease for more than three years that was not made in writing only created a **tenancy at will**. However, such an agreement may be enforceable in **equity** (and is thus called an **equitable lease**) provided: (i) there is a definite agreement between the parties (not merely an agreement to agree) on all the matters relevant to a lease (the commencement date, term, parties, property and rent); and (ii) there is a **memorandum** or **note** in **writing** evidencing the agreement, or an act of **part performance** suggesting unequivocally that an agreement has been reached. However, an agreement for a lease is considered to have certain shortcomings when compared with a formal lease: (a) it is dependent upon the courts exercising their discretion in granting a decree of **specific performance** to enforce the agreement; (b) it is enforceable only between the original parties to the agreement and, as there is no **privity of estate**; (c) a tenant at will cannot normally recover the land if he is dispossessed (the remedy being damages, unless he has some form of statutory rights protecting his occupation of the premises); and (d) a landlord cannot levy **distress** under an agreement for a lease. Further, an agreement for a lease may not be enforceable if it ought properly to have been made by deed, as with a lease by a corporation; a lease without consideration; or a lease of an incorporeal hereditament (e.g. an easement).

In English law, (i) any **implied easement** and other benefit granted to a tenant under a formal lease (being a **conveyance**), is not granted under an agreement for a lease; and (ii) the agreement may not be enforceable against a *bona fide* **purchaser** for **value** of a **legal estate**, i.e. it may not be enforceable against the purchaser of the landlord's interest or another lessee, unless the tenant's right is protected by registration as a **land charge** against unregistered land, or by registration as a **minor interest** in the case of registered land.

In English law, on or after September 27, 1989 a lease for more than three years must be made in writing and must incorporate all the terms which the parties have expressly agreed in one document, or by reference to some other document (or if the leases are to be exchanged between the landlord and tenant, in both lease documents) (LP(MP)A 1989, s. 2). Thus, for such leases, the distinction between an agreement for a lease and a formal lease is no longer of much significance as such a lease cannot be made orally and, therefore, cannot be partially performed.

In the US, as a general rule, where the agreement contemplates the execution of a formal lease at a future time, the instrument is an agreement for a lease, rather than a lease itself. However, if the agreement defines the property granted and the terms are definite and explicit, the instrument is generally an actual lease rather than an agreement for a lease. In the US an agreement for a lease may also be called a 'contract for a lease' or a 'contract for a tenancy'. See also **usual covenant**.

agreement for sale 1. An **agreement** upon the principle terms for the sale of real property, but one that has not been put into a legally binding form. In the US, in most jurisdictions, an agreement for the sale of real property must comply with the **Statute of Frauds** to be enforceable, i.e. most agreements must be in **writing**.

In English law, on or after September 27, 1989 an 'agreement for sale' in respect of most real property transactions must be made in writing, and in all other respects comply with the LP(MP)A 1989, s. 2, otherwise it is not enforceable (*viz.* **writing**). cf. **conditional contract**. See also **binder**, **estate contract**(Eng), **subject to contract**. 2. See **executory contract**.

agreement for sale and purchase(US) See **contract for sale and purchase**.

agreement of sale 1. See **contract of sale**. 2.(US)See **contract for deed**.

agreement to agree See **conditional contract**.

agreement to negotiate See **conditional contract**.

agreement to sell See **contract of sale**.

agreement under seal See **contract under seal**.

agricultural building allowance(Eng) A form of **capital allowance** permitted in respect of expenditure incurred on the construction of farm buildings.

agricultural building(Eng) A building that is statutorily defined as one that is exempt from a liability for non-domestic rates. Essentially the building must be occupied together with **agricultural land** and be used solely in connection with agricultural operations on the land. It does not include a dwelling (General Rate Act 1967, s. 26(4); Local Government Finance Act 1988, Sch. 5, ss. 3-5).

agricultural charge(Eng) A **charge** created by a farmer on his farming stock or other agricultural assets as security for a sum advanced to him by a bank. Such a charge must be registered at the **Land Registry** (in the 'register of agricultural charges') within seven days of its execution or it will be void against any person other than the farmer (Agricultural Credits Act 1928, ss. 5, 9).

agricultural charges register(Eng) See **agricultural charge**.

agricultural fixture See **agricultural tenant's fixture**(Eng), **emblements**, **fixture**.

agricultural holding(Eng) In ordinary usage, an area of land used for agricultural or pastoral purposes. In particular, "the aggregate of the land (whether **agricultural land** or not) comprised in a contract of tenancy which is a contract for an **agricultural tenancy**, not being a contract under which the said land is let to the tenant during his continuance in any office, appointment or employment held under the landlord", AHA 1986, s. 1(1). Agricultural leases granted on or after September 1, 1995 take the form of **farm business tenancies** and, therefore, the term 'agricultural holding' is no longer applicable to such tenancies. See also **agricultural property**.

Densham, H. A. C., and Della Evans. *Scammell & Densham's Law of Agricultural Holdings*. 8th ed. London: Butterworths, 1996, with supplement 2001.

Muir Watt, James, and Joanne R. Moss. *Agricultural Holdings*. 14th ed. London: Sweet & Maxwell, 1998.

Smith, Graham. *Agricultural Law*. 2nd ed. Welwyn Garden City: EMIS Professional Publishing, 1997.

agricultural land 1. Land used for the trade or business of **agriculture**, including arable, pasture and meadow land and land used for keeping and breeding of livestock or poultry. Land used as commercial woodland, for forestry, or as a commercial orchard or market garden, is generally considered as agricultural land, but not land that is used for sport or recreation, nor land that is used as a private garden. 2.(Eng)"Land used for **agriculture** which is so used for the purposes of a trade or business", AHA 1986, s. 1(4). The trade or business need not itself be agriculture. Land used for a non-commercial (i.e. not for a trade or business) purpose is not agricultural land under this statutory definition.

In connection with the exclusion of agricultural land and buildings from liability for non-domestic rating, agricultural land is "(a) land used as arable meadow or pasture ground only, land used for a plantation or a wood or for the growth of saleable underwood", as well as land used for poultry farming (exceeding 0.10 hectares), a **cottage garden** (exceeding 0.10 hectares), **market garden**, nursery grounds, orchards or land used as an **allotment** (including an **allotment garden** as defined by the Allotment Act 1922), but does not include land occupied together with a house as a park, gardens (other than as previously mentioned), pleasure grounds, or land kept or preserved mainly or exclusively for purposes of sport or recreation, or land used as a racecourse, and for the purposes of this paragraph the expression 'cottage garden' means a garden attached to a house occupied as a dwelling by a person of the labouring classes; and (b) includes land occupied with, and used solely in connection with the use of, an **agricultural building** (GRA 1967, s. 26(3)(a); Local Government Finance Act 1988, Sch. 5, s. 2(1)(2)). The same definition is applied to a tenancy that cannot be an **assured tenancy** because it is a tenancy of dwelling-house let with "agricultural land" that in total exceeds two acres (HA 1988, Sch. 1, s. 6(2)). Land or buildings used for fish farming is also not liable for rates (GRA 1967, s. 26A). See also **agricultural holding, agricultural property**.

Agricultural Lands Tribunals(Eng) Tribunals that have been established to deal with disputes relating to agricultural tenancies that are given statutory protection, including the termination of such tenancies; the fixing of rent; and such landlord and tenant disputes as claims of bad husbandry or tenant's requests to carry out improvements. See also **agricultural tenancy**.

agricultural lease(US) A lease of agricultural property. In several jurisdictions, agricultural leases are limited by statute as to their maximum duration, usually as short as 50 years or even 25 years.

agricultural licence(Eng) See **grazing licence**.

Agricultural Mortgage Corporation (AMC)(Eng) A body established in 1929, under the Agricultural Credits Act 1928, whose principal objective is making long-term mortgage loans for the purchase or improvement of agricultural property, and for providing working capital secured on agricultural property. Loans granted by the AMC are restricted to farmers and are granted for terms of 5 to 40 years in the case of farms, and up to 60 years for forestry purposes. See also **Lands Improvement Company**.

agricultural tenancy 1.(Eng)A "contract of tenancy" of an **agricultural holding**. In substance, a tenancy of **agricultural land** (which includes buildings thereon) used for **agriculture** and "which is so used for the purposes of a trade or business", AHA 1986, s. 1(4). An agricultural tenancy may arise from "a letting of land, or from an agreement for the letting of land, for a **term of years** or from year to year", AHA 1986, s. 1(5)). For this purpose any letting, or agreement to let agricultural land, for an interest that is less than a **tenancy from year to year** (including a licence, provided the occupier has exclusive use of the land), is deemed to be a tenancy from year to year (AHA 1986, s. 2(2)). In the case of a tenancy for two years or more, then *prima facie* it continues at the end of the term as a tenancy from year to year, unless either party has given proper written notice to quit not less than one year nor more than two years before the date of expiration. Thus, apart from a letting for more than one year but less than two years (which is not a tenancy "for a term of years or from year to year", as a general rule, any other letting, or agreement for letting (or licence), of an agricultural holding is an 'agricultural tenancy' and continues as a tenancy from year to year, until terminated by a notice to quit. Instead of the common law period of six months that would be required to terminate a **tenancy from year to year**, an 'agricultural tenancy' can only be brought to an end by at least one years notice to expire on the anniversary of the commencement of the tenancy (AHA 1986, s. 25(1)). Such a notice will only operate to terminate the tenancy if at the time of the notice the landlord has a right to terminate the tenancy in accordance with the statutory provisions (AHA 1986, s. 26). The tenant has a right to serve a counter notice objecting to the landlord's notice and, in that case, the Agricultural Land Tribunal must decide the matter. If an agricultural tenancy is brought to an end, the tenant may have a right to **compensation for disturbance**. The landlord and tenant are free to agree to any rent level for an agricultural tenancy, but either party may demand that the rent for a new tenancy be fixed by arbitration. See also **agricultural lease**(US), **agricultural tenant's fixture, compensation for improvements, emblements, good husbandry, implied covenant, tenant-right**.   2.(Aus)A tenancy of agricultural land. In particular a tenancy that is regulated by statute (e.g. Agricultural Tenancies Act 1990 (NSW); Property Law Act 1974, ss. 153-167 (QLD); Agricultural Holding Act 1891 (SA)). In the States where these statutes apply the holder of such a tenancy may be entitled to compensation for improvements to the land carried out during the course of the tenancy.

agricultural tenant's fixture(Eng)   A chattel or building that has been fixed to land by a tenant of an **agricultural holding**, but does not become the landlord's property at the end of the tenancy as by law it may be removed. At common law, an agricultural tenant's fixture was not considered a **trade fixture** (farming not being considered a 'trade') and, therefore, it could be removed at the end of a lease even though it was affixed solely for the purpose of farming the land. However, by statute law, the tenant of an agricultural holding has a right to remove certain items – 'agricultural tenant's fixtures' – up to two months after the end of his tenancy (Agricultural Holding Act 1986, s. 10). This right is limited to certain defined fixtures and the tenant must give the landlord notice of his intent to remove the fixtures. Upon receipt of the tenant's notice the landlord has a right to purchase the fixtures at their "fair value". In addition, any tenant under a "**farm business tenancy**" may remove any fixture (of whatever description) and any building affixed or erected by the tenant (Agricultural Tenancies Act 1995, s. 8). The tenant may not remove any fixture or building erected pursuant to some obligation; if it was a replacement for a fixture or building of the landlord; or if it is a building for which he has a statutory right to compensation. See also **compensation for improvements**.

agricultural tied cottage(Eng)   See **tied accommodation**.

agriculture   Derived from 'acre' (a field) and 'culture', the science or art of cultivating the soil. The process, science or art of cultivating and tilling the soil; including the planting of seeds, the raising and harvesting of crops and plants, the rearing, feeding and management of livestock, poultry and other animals for eventual human use or consumption, as well as preparing and delivering such produce to market.

In English statute law, in connection with the use of land as part of an **agricultural holding**, agriculture "includes horticulture, fruit growing, seed growing, dairy farming and livestock breeding and keeping, the use of land as grazing land, meadow land, osier land, market gardens and nursery grounds, and the use of land for woodlands where that use is ancillary to the farming of the land for other agricultural purposes", AHA 1986, s. 96(1). For a farm business tenancy the same definition is applied and "agricultural" is construed accordingly (Agricultural Tenancies Act 1985, s. 38(1)). In the case of a **protected occupier** who is employed full time in "agriculture" the term is defined to include "(i) dairy-farming and livestock keeping and breeding (whether those activities involve the use of land or not); (ii) the production of any consumable produce which is grown for sale or for consumption or other use for the purposes of a trade or business or of any other undertaking (whether carried on for profit or not); (iii) the use of land as grazing, meadow or pasture land or orchard or osier land; (iv) the use of land for market gardens or nursery grounds; and (v) **forestry**", Rent (Agriculture) Act 1976, s. 1.

In English planning legislation, the use of land (and buildings associated therewith) for agriculture (including forestry and afforestation) is not considered as **development** and, therefore, does not require planning permission (TCPA 1990, s. 55(1)(e)). In this connection "'agriculture' includes horticulture, fruit growing, seed growing, dairy farming, the breeding and keeping of livestock (including any creature kept for the production of food, wool, skins, fur, or for the purpose of its use in the farming of land), the use of land as grazing land, meadow land, osier land, market gardens and nursery grounds, and the use of land for woodlands where that use is ancillary to the farming of land for other agricultural purposes", AHA 1986, s. 96(1) (TCPA 1990, s. 336(1)). See also **agricultural land**, **allotment**, **agricultural property**.

air-conditioning (a/c) The treatment of air for the ventilation and temperature control of a room or building, including air filtration and humidity control. See also **central heating**.

air easement See **right to air**.

air lease[US] A lease of air-space, i.e. the lease of an **air right** over land.

air lot[US] A specific air-space over a parcel of **land**. See also **air right**.

air rights 1. The right to use the air space over a parcel of **land**. Technically the ownership of land extends *ad coelum* – 'to the heavens'. Thus, an owner controls the space above his land; he has 'air-rights' over his land that enable him to make reasonable use of the land. However, this right means that no other person can acquire any title or exclusive right to any space above another's land without an agreement. Any use of the air or space that is injurious to the use of a person's land, or which constitutes an actual interference with the possession or beneficial use of land constitutes a **trespass**. However, this right is limited to such height as is necessary for the ordinary use and enjoyment of the land and the structures upon it (United States v. Causby, 328 US 256, 36 S Ct 365, 90 L Ed 1206 (1945); *Bernstein of Leigh (Baron) v Skyviews & General Ltd* [1978] QB 479, 488, [1977] 2 All ER 902). A landowner may cede a right for another to occupy or take possession of a part of the air space above his land. This 'air right' may take the form of an outright sale or the grant of a lease of a strata of land, e.g. the disposal of an apartment; but the term air right is more usually applied to the grant of an easement or a mere licence to use the space, e.g. a right for the job of a tower crane to pass over land during the period of building construction on adjoining land.

In common law, a landowner can prohibit the placing of any object, such as a billboard, shutter or eaves, that projects onto his property by taking an action in **trespass**; or he may prevent aircraft consistently flying low over his land by taking an action for **nuisance**. However, statute laws recognise the right of aircraft to fly over land above a certain height. cf. **right to air**. See also **avigation easement**[US], *cujus est solum*, **inverse condemnation**[US], **tree**. 2.[US]See **transferable development right**.

aircraft (trespass by) See **air rights**, **avigation easement**[US], **inverse condemnation**[US], **trespass**.

air space An expanse of space above **land**, especially a cube (or similar shape) of space that is held in different ownership to the surface of the land. See also **air rights**, **condominium**, **flying freehold**[(Eng)], **partial ownership**.

aisle 1. A gangway, or passageway, as in a retail store or warehouse. 2. The passage or way by which cars enter and leave parking spaces.

aleatory contract 1. A contract that is dependent on an uncertain event or chance; in particular a fortuitous or hazardous event. Accident and fire insurance contracts are aleatory. See also **conditional contract**. 2. A wagering contract.

alienation "The act of transferring the ownership of anything to another", *The Oxford English Dictionary*. 2nd ed., 1989 (1 *Co Litt* 118). The voluntary transfer of ownership, title, an estate or interest in property from one party to another, whether during a lifetime or on death. The act, or power, by which a person 'divests' himself of an interest in **land** and 'vests' that interest in another. In particular, alienation is used to refer to the absolute conveyance of an interest in real property, as distinguished from a transfer by operation of law. Also, the mere grant of a personal right, without the grant of a right to property is not 'alienation'.

The term 'alienation' may be used to refer to any transfer or disposition of an estate or interest in real property, as distinguished from (i) a transfer by operation of law; (ii) the transfer of a lease; (iii) the transfer of an incorporeal right (such as an easement or restrictive covenant); (iv) the transfer of a debt or mortgage.

In the US, a transfer of an interest in property against the owner's will, as with a foreclosure sale, a tax sale, adverse possession or eminent domain, may be referred to as an 'involuntary alienation'. See also **conveyance, forfeiture, mortmain, restraint on alienation, rule against perpetuities, statutory alienation**.

alienation clause 1. A clause in a contract setting out the rights of transference, e.g. the rights of a lessee to assign or to sub-let or any prohibition of assignment or sub-letting. See also **restraint on alienation**. 2.[(US)]A clause in a mortgage, deed of trust or promissory note that provides that in the event of an alienation of the property secured by the mortgage or note the entire outstanding debt becomes due and payable. In this context, alienation is usually defined broadly to include the sale or other form of transfer of the property, or any interest in the property, to any third party, including the grant of another mortgage. cf. **assumption clause**. See also **acceleration, due-on-sale clause**. 3. A clause in an insurance policy that provides for the policy to terminate automatically if the owner disposes of, or changes the title to, the property that is the subject-matter of the policy without the consent of the insurer.

alienee One to whom property is transferred. A person to whom a property is transferred by **alienation**. cf. **alienor**.

alienor One who transfers property to another. Generally called a **grantor** or **assignor**. See also **alienation**.

aliquant or **aliquot** An aliquant is a number that if divided into another leaves a remainder and an aliquot is a number that leaves no remainder. Thus, 6 is the aliquant of 19, but the aliquot of 18. As applied to a **resulting trust** or the division of an estate, 'aliquot' means a definite share or any fraction.

alimentary trust See **protective trust**.

all-in contract See **package-deal contract**.

all-inclusive deed of trust (AITD)[(US)] See **wraparound mortgage**.

all-inclusive mortgage (AIM)[(US)] See **wraparound mortgage**.

all-loss insurance[(AmE)] See **all-risks insurance**.

all monies mortgage   A mortgage which provides that it acts as security for all monies advanced by the lender to the borrower, both present and future. See also **deficiency judgment**(US), **further advance**(Eng)/**future advance**(US), **recourse**.

all right, title and interest(US)   See **conveyance**.

all-risks insurance   Insurance against all hazards, e.g. fire, smoke, explosion, lightning, storm, flood, collision or impact, breakage, collapse, except those expressly excluded in the policy. The term 'all-risks insurance' is misleading because it does not cover 'all risks' but only those risks not expressly excluded, or arising from fraud or wrongdoing by the insured; as compared with **comprehensive insurance**, which stipulates a large range of risks or perils that are covered by the insurance policy. The policy does not cover damage or loss resulting from an inevitable event, e.g. physical deterioration, or commercial risks such as a consequential loss of profit. In American English, also called 'all-loss insurance'. cf. **extended-perils insurance**. See also **builder's risk insurance**, **contractor's all-risks insurance**, **householder's insurance**.

all-risks rate (ARR) or **all-risks yield** (ARY)   A single **capitalisation rate** (or a single yield) that takes account of all the risk factors and prospects that are relevant to a particular investment; usually a rate (or yield) derived from an analysis of the return obtained on comparable investments. cf. **component capitalization rate**. See also **composite rate**, **overall capitalization rate**, **remunerative rate**, **years' purchase**.

all the estate   See **conveyance**.

all the title   See **conveyance**.

allegans contraria non est audiendus(Lat)   'He who makes statements mutually inconsistent is not to be listened to', i.e. a person cannot 'blow hot and cold'. See **election**, **estoppel**.

alley or **alleyway**   A narrow passageway or street; especially a right of way that runs between buildings to provide access to the rear. An alley is generally wide enough for the passage of only one vehicle. It may be a private right of way, but more usually is a public means of access. An alley may be a **street** but can be distinguished therefrom by serving only a limited area or number of properties and generally being narrower than a regular street in a town or city. In particular, an alley may run between street blocks, either linking parallel streets or as a dead-end street or cul-de-sac.

alligator(AmE)   An investment that generates a substantial **negative cash flow** or loss, or requires continual expenditure.

alligator clause(US)   A clause in a lease that is structured in such a way that it substantially reduces the economic benefit that one of the parties anticipates. For example, a provision that allows the tenant to terminate the lease in the event of fire or destruction when the consequent damage is not of a 'substantial nature'. A provision that does not enable the landlord to pass through the normal operating expenses he incurs in respect of the leased property; or a provision that requires the tenant to pay for major structural repairs, or the cost of any environment clean up, even though it is not necessarily a result of his own activities.

allocated loan amount   See **partial release clause**.

allocation method(AmE)   See **abstraction method**.

allodial system   A system of land tenure by which an individual may hold land in his own right, as opposed to the **feudal system** where all land is vested in the Sovereign or land is held subject to the acknowledgment of a superior right. See also **bundle of rights theory**, **ownership**.

allodium or **alodium**   Derived from the Latin *allodium*, 'entire property'. Land held in absolute ownership; land held under the **allodial system**, as distinguished from land held as a servient right.

allonge   A strip of paper attached to a **promissory note** or **negotiable instrument** to enable endorsements to be added or to enable the document to be assigned.

allotment   **1.** A share or portion; a division. That which is allotted, as with part ownership of a property or a company that is granted by the party having effective control of the whole. In particular, the apportionment of newly issued securities between the subscribers by the investment house or syndicate that is arranging for the issue.   **2.** The **subdivision** of a larger area of land. One of a number of parcels of land into which a larger area of land has been subdivided. **3.** Funds made available by an institutional mortgage company for lending during a given period of time, i.e. the amount it intends to lend, or makes available to purchase mortgages in a secondary market, during that period. cf. **commitment**.   **4.**(Eng)An area of land that has been subdivided, usually into small parcels, and let to individuals for horticultural cultivation either for food or pleasure. Allotments are defined by statute as having an area of around (Allotments Act 1922, s. 3, s. 22(1); Allotment Act 1925, s. 1). A tenant of an allotment is provided with **security of tenure** and an entitlement to compensation in the event of a termination of his tenancy. A local authority also has a statutory duty to provide adequate allotments for local residents. For planning purposes an allotment is treated as land used for **agriculture** and, therefore, does not require planning permission. See also **compensation for improvements, enclosure, smallholding**.

alluvion or **alluvium**   Derived from the Latin *alluvius*, 'washed against'. Sand, silt, clay, gravel or similar material washed up by the sea or a river so as to add to the extent of the bordering land; especially when the material is deposited as a gradual and imperceptible increase. Strictly speaking, 'alluvion' is the process by which the material is washed up and 'alluvium' or 'alluvial deposits' the material. In common usage, 'alluvion' refers to the material that is added to land by **accretion**. cf. **dereliction**.

alodium   See **allodium**.

along a highway(US)   A means of describing a parcel of real estate that fronts a highway and which indicates that, unless expressed to the contrary, the boundary extends to the center of the highway.

alteration   **1.** The act or process of changing the character, fabric or constitution of a building, without making something that in essence is totally different. In particular, the making of changes or modifications that affect the form or structure of a property and constitute more than mere repair or cosmetic change. Strictly, an alteration does not change the external dimensions of a building, as that would be an **addition**; nor does it amount to building anew. A change of a thing from one form or state to another, making it different from what it was but without destroying its identity. Generally, an alteration is something permanent and substantial, not merely casual, short lived or *de minimus*. Alteration used alone means any change that is more than *de minimus*; whereas 'structural alteration' goes further and means a substantial change, generally one that changes the nature or integrity of the building or includes a physical change to the structural or supporting elements, such as the bearing walls, columns, beams, girders or external elements. See also **improvement**. **2.** A material change in an instrument or deed, e.g. a change of the **date**. An alteration of a deed is presumed to have been made before or at the time of execution. A subsequent alteration may be considered a **fraud** and invalidate the deed (unless there is an agreement of all the parties and the delivery of a new deed). cf. **rectification**. See also **codicil, endorsement, supplemental deed**.   **3.** An alteration to an entry at the **Land Registry**, pursuant to an order of a court or at the instigation of the registrar to correct a mistake; to bring the register up to date; to give effect to any estate right or interest that has been excepted from registration; or alter the register to remove a superfluous entry (LRA 2002, ss. 20, 21, Sch. 4, paras. 2, 5).

alternative accommodation(Eng)   See suitable alternative accommodation.

alternative cost   See opportunity cost.

alternative dispute resolution (ADR) See arbitration, adjudication, expert.

alternative mortgage loan (AML) or **alternative mortgage instrument** (AMI)(US)   A term that may be applied to any form of mortgage loan that differs from the traditional form of loan, i.e. from one for a fixed term of thirty years, at a fixed interest rate, with equal monthly repayment to pay interest and repay the principal over the term of the loan. Examples are the **adjustable-rate mortgage**; the **dual-rate mortgage**; the **variable-payment mortgage**, 'graduated-payment mortgage' or variants thereof; the **reverse annuity mortgage**; and the **equity-participation mortgage**. Under the Alternative Mortgage Transaction Parity Act of 1982 which was passed to resolve conflicts between state and federal regulation of alternative mortgage instruments and to permit state chartered lenders to make such loans, an "alternative mortgage" includes adjustable-rate loans, re-negotiable loans with balloon payments, and loans "involving any similar type of rate, method of determining return, term, repayment, or other variation not common to traditional fixed rate, fixed term transactions, including without limitation, transactions that involve the sharing of equity or appreciation", 12 USC § 3802(1). See also **amortization mortgage**, **flexible loan insurance plan**, **growing-equity mortgage**, **shared-equity mortgage**.

alternative use value (AUV)   The value of land or buildings on the assumption that they are or may be put to a use that is different from the current use. In order to assess the **highest and best use** of a property the alternative use should be considered, provided that it is not inconsistent with a requirement for the continuation of the 'existing use'. For example, the value of a property for an alternative use cannot be considered in isolation if that would require the closure or relocation of an existing business. cf. **current use value**. See also **certificate of appropriate alternative development**(Eng).

altius non tollendi or *non altius tollendi*(Lat)   In the civil, French or Scots law, a **servitude** by which a restriction is placed on the height above which a building can be erected on a parcel of land. A term that may also be used to refer to a similar restriction imposed by a public authority. See also *non aedificandi*.

alvei mutatio(Lat)   A term of Roman or Scots law for the advance and retreat of water. The result of *alvei mutatio* is that the proprietor of the land on one bank of a river or stream gains land and the proprietor on the other bank loses land to the water.

alveus   The bed or channel of a river. A term used primarily in Roman or Scots law for the land under a defined channel of water that belongs to the adjacent proprietor in the case of a non-tidal river and to the Crown or State in the case of tidal waterway. See also *ad medium filum aquæ*.

ambiguity   Uncertainty of meaning. Ambiguity may be patent, as when it is apparent on the face of a document (e.g. a blank space in a document); or latent, as when it is uncertain of the effect until it is applied to the circumstances. For example, a latent ambiguity may be applicable to a will when property is left to "my cousin John" and the testator has two cousins called John. Wording is not ambiguous merely because it is difficult to determine the intent. See also *contra proferentem*, **equivocation**, **habendum**, **rectification**, **reddendum**, **words**.

ambiguitas contra stipulatorem est(Lat) 'An ambiguity is construed against the stipulator'. Doubtful words are construed most strongly against the party using them. See also *contra proferentem*.

ambiguum pactum contra venditorem interpretandum est(Lat) An ambiguous contract is interpreted against the seller. See also ambiguity, *contra proferentem*.

ambulatory Subject to change; capable of being altered. See also **accretion, floating charge, will**.

ameliorating waste See **waste**.

amelioration The act of improving or making something better. See also **betterment, improvement**.

amendatory language(AmE) See **addendum**.

amenity 1. The attractiveness, utility and **aesthetic** attributes of land or building, as distinguished from monetary or economic value. In England and Wales, for the purpose of the power of a local authority to make regulations "in the interests of amenity" for the control of an **advertisement**, the amenity of the area should take into account "the general characteristics of the area, including the presence of any feature of historic, architectural, or cultural interest", Town and Country Planning (Control of Advertisements Regulations 1992, reg. 4(1). See also **advertisement, amenity societies**(Eng), **area of special control**(Eng), **building of special architectural or historic interest**(Eng), **compensation for improvements**(Eng), **conservation area**(Eng), **development plan**(Eng), **discontinuance order**(Eng), **negative easement, planning, town and country planning, tree preservation order**(Eng), **wasteland**(Eng). 2. A facility that adds to the desirability of a property such as a health club, swimming pool or restaurant in a residential project. 3. See **negative easement**.

amenity land Land that is used for public enjoyment or recreation. Land that acts as an amenity for other land. See also **accommodation land, open space**.

amortisation(BrE) or **amortization**(AmE) or **amortizement**(AmE) 1. The gradual extinguishing of a debt or liability; especially by means of equal periodic payments at stated intervals which, in total, are sufficient to repay the capital or principal at the end of a given period, and to pay interest on the outstanding balance throughout the period. In the context of an **amortization mortgage**, 'amortisation' means that the payments are *equal* and are calculated to pay the accrued interest and a portion of the capital, so that the entire principal is repaid over the term of the loan. However, amortisation can be made under any schedule that is determined in such a way that a debt or loan is extinguished over a given period of time. The extinguishing of a debt by a single payment derived from an accumulated fund, e.g. from the proceeds of a **sinking fund**, may also be called amortisation. Amortisation is sometimes used synonymously for **depreciation**. However, amortisation is a deduction to allow for deterioration; whereas depreciation is a decline or reduction and is a more subjective process. See also **amortisation rate, debt service, negative amortisation, redemption, standing loan**. 2. The transfer of property in perpetuity to a corporation or charity, i.e. a transfer or alienation in **mortmain**. 3.(US)In zoning, the gradual elimination of a **non-conforming use**. 4. The gradual writing down of the cost of an asset, especially an intangible asset (such as goodwill, a patent or a copyright), by periodic charges against a profit and loss account or as an expense. 5. The periodic reduction of the premium paid for a bond bought above par value in order to bring the investment or book value into line with par at maturity.

amortise(BrE) To gradually pay off a debt or liability. To write down the cost of an asset by periodic charges to expense or a profit and loss. In American English, spelt 'amortize'. See also **amortisation**(BrE)/**amortization**(AmE).

amortization fund(AmE)   See **sinking fund**.

amortization loan or **amortization mortgage**   A loan, or mortgage, that provides for interest and principal to be repaid by means of level, or equal, annual instalments, i.e. by a constant **annuity**. These level payments are calculated so that, at the start, the annual instalment is sufficient to pay interest charged in the year on the entire loan, together with a small payment of capital. As the amount of outstanding capital decreases, so the proportion of the constant payment that goes to pay interest decreases and the capital proportion increases. At the end of the period of the loan, the entire capital, together with accrued interest on the outstanding balance, is totally repaid. This is a common method for repaying a residential mortgage loan. (For the formula for calculating the level payments see the **annuity one will purchase**.) Also called a 'level-payment mortgage', 'constant-payment mortgage', 'annuity mortgage', 'amortizing mortgage', 'amortized mortgage', 'fully-amortizing mortgage', or a 'standard fixed-payment mortgage'. It may also be called a 'flat-rate mortgage', although that term is best reserved for a mortgage in which the interest rate is fixed for the term of the loan. cf. **direct reduction mortgage**. See also **amortization**.

amortization profit(AmE)   See **equity build-up**.

amortisation rate(BrE) or **amortization rate**(AmE)   The rate at which a loan, excluding any interest appertaining thereto, is repaid. The rate used for the **amortisation** of a loan or a sum of money. Generally, regular payments expressed as a percentage of a loan or capital. A term used synonymously with **sinking fund rate**, 'accumulative rate' and 'recapture rate'. See also **annuity one will purchase**, **depreciation rate**.

amortisation schedule(BrE) or **amortization schedule**(AmE)   **1.** A schedule to a mortgage loan agreement that sets out the rate at which the debt is to be repaid. In the US,

sometimes called a 'curtail schedule', although to 'curtail' implies repayment earlier than anticipated. See also **amortization loan**.   **2.** See also **amortization term**.

amortization term   The period of time over which a loan is repaid. In particular, the period of time over which a loan would be fully amortized under a level-payment mortgage. In the latter case sometimes called the 'amortization schedule'.

amortize(AmE)   See **amortise**(BrE).

amortized loan(AmE)   See **amortization loan**.

amortizement(AmE)   See **amortization**.

amortizing mortgage(AmE)   See **amortization loan**.

amotion   The removal of someone from **possession** of land. The **eviction** of a tenant. See also **ouster**.

amount of one   See Appendix C, **Financial Formulae**.

amount of one per period or **amount of one per annum**   See Appendix C, **Financial Formulae**.

anaconda mortgage(US)   A mortgage that provides that in the event of default the mortgagee may foreclose on any loans that are owed by the mortgagor to the same mortgagee, whether incurred before or after the execution of the mortgage, in addition to the specific debt secured by the mortgage. The actual clause that contains such a provision may be called a **dragnet clause** or 'Mother Hubbard clause'. See also **consolidation of mortgages**.

ancestral estate or **ancestral property**(US)   **1.** An **estate** that is acquired by descent, especially an estate that is intended to be limited to lineal descendants. cf. **non-ancestral estate**.   **2.** Land that has been allotted to members of an Indian tribe or their ancestors (McDougal v. McKay, 237 US 372, 385, 35 S Ct 606, 607, 59 L Ed 1001 (1915)). See also **ancestral land**(NZ).

ancestral land(NZ)   In connection with a rezoning of land to accommodate a destination tourist resort, 'ancestral land' is lay land that was the original home of a Maori tribe, even though it has been sold to a European settlor.

anchor lease   A lease, usually for a long term, of part of a shopping center to an **anchor store**.

anchor store   A major department or chain store in a **shopping center** that acts as a magnet for other stores. In a neighbourhood or district center, the anchor store may be a supermarket, junior department, variety store or drug store. In a regional center, there will normally be more than one anchor store and at least one of the anchors would be a **department store**. Anchor stores are considered the lynchpins to the success of a major retail center development and are located normally at the extremes of the mall in order to draw the visitors through the center. Sometimes called a 'magnet store'. cf. **satellite store**.

anchor tenant   A tenant who occupies an **anchor store**.

ancient boundaries(US)   Boundary markers of a property such as trees, hedges or stones that have been in existence beyond living memory and are established as representing the evidence of a limit of ownership.

ancient lights(Eng)   A **right of light** acquired by **prescription**. Under common law, a right that had existed from 'time immemorial', but since the Prescription Act 1832, s. 3, one that has existed for more than 20 years; unless it has been granted expressly (in certain cases this period may be extended to 27 years (Right of Light Act 1959, s. 1)). See also **easement, spite fence**.

ancient map or **ancient survey**(US)   An authenticated **map** (or **survey**) that has been in existence for a considerable period of time can be used to prove the location of a boundary line.

ancient monument(Eng)   1. A building, structure or site of considerable architectural, archaeological or historic interest that is included in a list prepared by the Secretary of State for the Environment as being considered worthy of preservation (Ancient Monuments and Archaeological Areas Act 1979). The list includes over 12,000 monuments in Britain ranging from major national monuments to archaeological sites, excavations, and even caves. An ancient monument may also be any other monument which the Secretary of State thinks is "of public interest by reason of the historic, architectural, traditional, artistic or archaeological interest attaching to it", AMAAA 1979, ss. 61(1), (12)(b); as well as "any structure, work, site, garden or area which in the [Historic Buildings and Monuments] Commission's opinion is of historic, architectural, traditional, artistic or archaeological interest", National Heritage Act 1983, s. 33(8). These definitions are broad enough to include any building structure, or a site of archaeological interest. It is an offence to destroy, alter, repair or carry out most forms of building works to a scheduled monument or any other ancient monument without obtaining the consent of the Secretary of State. If 'scheduled monument consent' is refused, compensation may be payable in limited instances for any resultant loss or expenditure incurred by a person having an interest in the monument (AMAAA, s. 27). The Secretary of State has powers to acquire any ancient monument, or to place it under his own or a local authority's guardianship, to ensure its proper control and management (AMAAA 1979, ss. 10-12). See also **English Heritage**(Eng), **historic building, historic sites**(US), **listed building**.

ancient rent   An old term for the best or **rack rent** obtainable under a lease.

ancient survey(US)   An official survey that has been recorded as a public document for a substantial period of time and may be produced as evidence of the location of a boundary line.

ancient wall(US)   A **party wall** that has prescriptive rights attached thereto, e.g. a wall that has a right to support from a neighbor's building and, as a result of the length of time that the support has been enjoyed, has fulfilled the requirements of time needed to acquire that right by **prescription**.

ancient window   See **ancient lights**.

ancillary building   See **accessory building**.

ancillary easement   1. A right that is ancillary but reasonably necessary to the exercise or enjoyment of an **easement**.   **2.** A right in the nature of an easement that is necessary in order to fully enjoy a **profit à prendre**. For example, a right to pass over land in order to extract minerals from the adjoining land. cf. **secondary easement**. See also **easement of necessity**.

ancillary use   See **accessory use, planning unit**(Eng).

and his heirs   See **heir**.

animals   See **damage feasant, game, negligence, nuisance, profit à prendre,** *res nullius*, **strict liability, trespass**.

animus contrahendi(Lat)   'The intention to enter into a contract'. Intention that the language of conduct of the parties should result in a contract.

animus domini(Lat)   'The intention to hold as owner'. See **ownership**.

animus possidendi(Lat)   'The intention to have possession'; 'the intention of possessing'. The intention of excluding the owner of land, as well as others, as a prerequisite to a claim to **adverse possession**.

animus revertendi(Lat)   'Intention to return'. See **occupation**.

annoyance   See **harassment, nuisance**.

annual   Recurring once a **year** or each year; happening yearly. See also **annuity, per annum**.

annual capital charge   A yearly sum (annuity) that is sufficient to provide interest on an investment of capital and repay or recapture the amount of invested capital. A sum obtained as the product of a capital sum and an **annuity one will purchase** (or obtained by dividing that sum by the **present value of one per period**, i.e. by a **years' purchase**).

annual constant   See **mortgage constant**.

annual crop   See **emblements, way-going crop**.

annual debt service (ADS)   See **mortgage constant**.

annual equivalent   The capital cost, or value, of an asset converted into an annual figure which if invested, over the economic life of that asset, will compound to the capital figure. An annual equivalent may be assessed simply by dividing the capital sum by the number of years for the economic life of the asset (although that method takes no account of compound interest), or by dividing the capital sum by a **capitalisation factor** or **years' purchase** (i.e. the reverse of capitalisation – sometimes called 'decapitalisation'). See **annuity, virtual rent**.

annual gross income   See **gross income**.

annual interest rate   See **annual percentage rate, effective annual interest rate**.

annual loan constant   See mortgage constant.

annual percentage rate (APR)   The true annual interest rate payable for a loan over a period of one year taking account of all charges made to the borrower, including compound interest, discount points, commitment fees, mortgage insurance premiums and taking into account the time at which the principal is repaid (especially when payments of principal are made by instalments throughout the year, but interest is charged on the outstanding principal at the beginning of the year), but not the actual expenses incurred by the lender in making the loan and recharged to the borrower. Credit purchase agreements and bank personal loans are frequently made on the basis that a nominal interest rate is charged on the original principal as if the whole balance were outstanding throughout the term of the loan, but the loan and interest is made repayable by equal instalments, usually monthly. Thus, the borrower is paying interest on capital he has effectively repaid. For example, on a loan of $100 at a nominal interest of 8% the borrower may pay 12 instalments during the year of $108/12 = \$9.00$ per month, in arrears; on this basis the nominal or 'add on' interest rate of 8% produces an APR of 14.45%. The APR may be calculated by assessing an **internal rate of return**. cf. **effective annual interest rate**. See also **usury**.

annual rent   1. The **rent** payable for one year. 2.(Scot)A payment of **interest**; so called because when usury was illegal a payment was made as a right to land.

annual sinking fund (a.s.f.)   A sinking **fund** calculated on an annual basis.

annual value   The value or monetary worth to be derived from a property over a period of one year; the yearly rent or income to be derived from property as a result of ownership. See also **market rent, rateable value**.

annulisation(BrE) or **annualization**(AmE)   The conversion of a capital sum into an annual equivalent; the reverse of capitalisation. See also **annuity**.

annuitant   One entitled to receive, or one who receives, an **annuity**.

annuity   1. A series of specified or determined sums of money payable or receivable yearly (or at fixed intervals during a year); whether for a particular period of time (a life or a number of years) or even in perpetuity. Although an annuity may be said to be payable "in perpetuity", it may be more correct to say that it is payable for an indeterminable period, as with a government bond, until the payee elects, at its option, to repay the principal. An annuity may be payable for a predetermined duration, or it may be made 'conditional' or 'contingent', e.g. 'until A marries'. The payment may be of equal amounts each year – a 'level annuity'; or may increase or decrease each year – a 'variable (increasing or decreasing) annuity'. The actual amount may be paid every month, quarterly, half yearly, yearly or by any other regular instalments. Annuity may also be used to refer to the purchase of an annual income, especially from an insurance company. An annuity differs from **rent** (or a **rentcharge**), which is a burden imposed on or issuing out of land and is therefore enforceable as a claim against the land. See also **deferred annuity, general equitable charge**(Eng), **land charge**(Eng), **mortgage constant, reverse annuity mortgage**.   2. A sum of money paid annually so that it will accumulate over a given number of years, together with accrued interest, to a specified capital sum.

annuity capitalization(AmE)   A method of valuing a future income stream or annuity, receivable for a limited period of time, by taking the sum of the present values of the projected periodic incomes; i.e. capitalization by applying a factor based on the **present value of one per period** (called an **Inwood factor** in the US and a 'years' purchase for a term of years' in the UK).

Also called the 'annuity method of valuation' or 'yield capitalization'. cf. **straight capitalization**. See also **discounted cash flow, dual-rate capitalization factor**.

annuity factor   See Appendix C, **Financial Formulae**.

annuity method   1. A method of analyzing the worth of a capital investment by comparing the annual income generated by that investment with the amount required to provide a suitable rate of return on the investment to cover interest on the capital and repay, or recapture, the capital over the life of the investment (i.e. to provide for an **annual capital charge**). Expressed another way, the annuity method may be applied by comparing the annual income generated by the investment with the **annual equivalent** cost of the capital invested (i.e. with the capital invested divided by an appropriate capitalisation factor). Also called the 'equivalent annual value method'.   2. A method of allowing for **depreciation** by writing-off each year, over the anticipated life of an asset, an amount based on the **annuity one will purchase**.   3.[AmE]See **annuity capitalization**.

annuity mortgage   1. See **reverse annuity mortgage**.   2. See **amortization loan**.

annuity of one per period or **annuity of one per annum**   See Appendix C, **Financial Formulae**.

annuity one will purchase   See Appendix C, **Financial Formulae**.

annul   To nullify or declare void; to abrogate. See also **voidable contract**.

ante[Lat]   'Before'; 'prior'.

anticipation privilege[US]   See **prepayment privilege**.

anticipatory breach   See **breach of contract**.

anti-deficiency legislation[US]   See **deficiency judgment**.

apartment   A place of residence, comprising a room or suite of rooms, usually on one level, in a building that contains two or more dwelling units that are divided from one another horizontally. An apartment is generally a self-contained unit that is leased to the occupier with the landlord having an obligation for the upkeep of the **common areas** and for the provision of common services, such as maintenance of the technical equipment (elevators, heating, lighting, etc.). See also **apartment house**[AmE], **community apartment, cooperative, condominium, dwelling house, efficiency apartment, flat**[BrE], **garden apartment, house, maisonette, service apartment, studio apartment, tenement, walk-up apartment house**[AmE].

apartment building[AmE]   A building that contains three or more dwellings or apartments. See also **apartment, block of flats**[BrE].

apartment hotel   A building that resembles an **hotel** but is laid out with accommodation for guests that is more akin to an **apartment**, for example by the provision of a sitting room and kitchen facilities, but without the full housekeeping services found in an hotel. In many cases, an apartment hotel may have all or most of the facilities of an hotel, but with the important distinction that some of the units are granted out on short-term leases (usually from week to week or from month to month) and not by the night. cf. **boarding house, lodging house**.

apartment house[AmE]   A building that comprises a number of apartments that are deigned for separate living, but with certain mechanical conveniences, such as heat, light, or elevator services, provided as common facilities for all the occupiers of the building. Such apartments are normally occupied on short-term rental agreements and in that respect may be distinguished for an **apartment hotel**. Sometimes called a 'flat house'. 'Apartment building' and 'apartment house' are frequently used synonymously, although the latter is generally a smaller building and may be less salubrious. In British English called a **block of flats**. See also **apartment**.

apparent authority   See **ostensible authority**.

apparent easement(US)   An **easement** that can easily be ascertained to exist, as by a careful inspection of the properties affected. For example, a right of way over a well-beaten track leading from one parcel of land providing a right of way to another parcel; a drain taking water from the eaves of a house or the drain that, even though not visible, patently takes the water away from the house. An apparent easement may be distinguished from a non-apparent easement whose existence can only be ascertained because of the document by which it is expressly created. In the US, sometimes called an 'open and visible easement' if it is so apparent that it can be seen by a person who is ordinarily conversant with the property, such as a path or a sewer line where there is a manhole. In some states, an apparent easement passes by implication upon a **grant** of land, unlike a non-apparent easement, which does not pass if it is not expressly referred to in the deed of transfer. Sometimes called an 'open easement'. See also **notice**, **quasi-easement**.

apparent servitude(US)   A **servitude** that may be perceived by external works, such as a roadway, door, window, or aqueduct (La CC, art. 728; Quebec CC, art. 1180). See also **apparent easement**.

apparent title(US)   See **color of title**.

appendant   1. Something that is adjunct, or is an accessory to another thing and passes with it, especially by inheritance. See also **power of appointment**.   2. Annexed to land by operation of law, as a result of use from 'time immemorial'. An appendant right is assumed to have existed since living memory and, therefore, may arise only

by **prescription**, i.e. personal usage for a long time, unlike a right **appurtenant** which may be acquired by prescription or by grant. Once a thing appendant has been separated from the property to which it is annexed (the principal hereditament), so as to be independent or in gross, it cannot become appendant again, although it may become appurtenant. See also **annex**, **appurtenance**, **profit à prendre**.

appointment   1. A **fixture**, item of furnishing, equipment and any fitting installed in a building, especially a decorative item installed with the intention of improving its value to an occupier (but not necessarily the owner).   2. The act of specifying the destination of a property, as in a will. See also **power of appointment**.

apportionment   1. The act or process of dividing or assigning rights or liabilities proportionately. The giving by way of a portion for a particular purpose. For example, the allocation of costs, rent, rates, service charges, etc., equitably or proportionately, between different owners or occupiers of a property. The costs of occupying a property are commonly apportioned according to the area occupied, although they may be apportioned by 'value' or on a 'per unit' basis.

At common law, **rent** does not accrue from day to day, but is due on a particular rent day so that if a lease is terminated between rent payment days, unless there is anything expressed to the contrary, the lessor could not obtain any rebate for any rent paid in advance. However, in many jurisdictions, there are statutory provisions that require rent to be treated as accruing from day to day. In English law, if rent is payable on one of the **quarter days** (March 25, June 24, September 29, December 25), as is common in leases of commercial property, and a lease commences 'on' May 10 with rent payable in advance, the tenant is obliged to pay rent for the period May 10 (inclusive) to June 23 (inclusive), i.e. 45/365ths of the annual rent (Note: if the lease commenced 'from' May 10 the first per diem payment is not due until May 11.) On a sale, if an annual rent of £10,000 is payable on the 'usual quarter days' in advance, and a property is sold on the August 20, the purchaser will be entitled to 39/365 × 10,000 = £1,068.49 as rent for the period from August 21 to September 28 inclusive (not 39/97 × 2,500 = £1,005.15). See also **closing costs**(AmE), **completion costs**(BrE), **day**. **2.** The allocation of the receipts and expenses of an estate between income and capital, in particular with due regard to the beneficiaries of income and capital.

apportionment clause See **contribution clause**.

appraisal(AmE) An expert opinion on the value of a property. A **valuation** carried out by a person who is suitable qualification, or has the experience, to judge the value of a property. An estimate of value carried out by an impartial, independent and suitably qualified person who opines on the worth of a property based on his or her professional experience and knowledge of the market place for such property. "An analysis, opinion, or conclusion relating to the nature, quality of specified interests in, or aspects of, identified real estate", Code of Professional Ethics of the Appraisal Institute. Normally this opinion is substantiated by a full written report on the factors underlying the opinion of value, as assessed by the **appraiser**, incorporating all the relevant data (zoning, comparable information, area measurements, etc.) relating to the property at the date of the appraisal.

In the US, the principal methods or 'approaches' used by appraisers to estimate the value of a property (with the equivalent British terms for 'methods of valuation') are: (i) the **sales comparison approach**, 'direct sales comparison approach', 'market comparison approach' or 'market-data approach' ('comparison method of valuation'); (ii) the **income approach** or net income capitalization approach ('investment method of valuation'); (iii) the **cost approach** or replacement cost approach ('reinstatement method of valuation'); and (iv) the **abstraction approach** or **land residual approach** ('residual method of valuation')—although in the US this approach is generally considered to be part of the 'cost approach' as it is based essentially on the assessed cost of a replacement property.

The term 'appraisal' is more commonly used in the American English for that which is called 'valuation' in British English. See also **appraisement, appraisal report, before-and-after method, building residual approach, land residual technique, estimate**.

Appraisal Institute. *The Appraisal of Real Estate.* 12th ed. Chicago: Appraisal Institute, 2001.

appraisal certificate(US) See **appraisal report**.

appraisal clause(US) A clause in an insurance policy which provides that, in the event of loss or damage being occasioned to the insured property, the insurer or the insured may call for an independent appraisal to determine the indemnity payable. See also **unvalued policy**.

appraisal correlation(US) See **correlation process**.

appraisal date(US) The date at which a valuation is placed on a property, i.e. the date applicable to an **appraisal report**. Also called the 'effective date', especially when referring to the date at which the appraiser makes his assessment rather than the date of the final report. See also **valuation date**.

appraisal fee schedule(US) See **scale fee**.

Appraisal Foundation(US) See Appendix A, Real Estate Associations, Appraisal Foundation.

Appraisal Institute(US) See Appendix A, Real Estate Associations, Appraisal Institute.

appraisal report(AmE) A detailed report, set out in writing, together with an 'appraisal certificate' signed by an **appraiser**, that describes a particular interest in a parcel of real estate, the appraiser's opinion of value and the facts and analysis that support that opinion. The report outlines the purpose of the appraisal; (e.g. insurance, sale value, loan collateral); describes the property in detail and the interest being appraised; sets down any factors and assumptions that affect its value; incorporates a summary of the appraisal process carried out by the appraiser, together with details of all comparables; and sets out the value of the property being appraised and the effective date of the appraisal. In addition, the report will generally contain such supporting information as a location map, floor plans and photographs. The certificate should state that the statements in the report are correct to the best of the appraiser's knowledge; that the report is based only on the assumptions and conditions set out therein; that the appraiser has no interest in the subject property and that he has or she has no reason for bias or special relationship with any parties for whom the appraisal is addressed; that the appraiser's fee is not dependent on any aspect of the report; that the appraiser has (or has not) personally inspected the property; that only those referred to in the report have been involved in its preparation; and, in most cases, that appraisal has been performed in accordance with the **Uniform Standards of Professional Appraisal** (USPAP). If the appraiser is a member of a particular professional organization, the appraisal must also state that it complies with the requirements of that organization. See also **market value, restricted appraisal report, self-contained appraisal report, summary appraisal report, valuation report**(BrE).

Appraisal Standards Board. *Uniform Standards for Professional Appraisal Practice (USPAP)*. Washington, DC: The Appraisal Foundation, 2004 edition.

Akerson, Charles B. *The Appraiser's Workbook*. 2nd ed. Chicago: Appraisal Institute, 1996.

Himstreet, William C. *Communicating the Appraisal: The Narrative Report*. Chicago: Appraisal Institute, 1991.

appraisal review(US)   See **review appraiser**.

appraisal standards(US)   See **Uniform Standards of Professional Appraisal Practice**.

appraisal surplus   An increase in value arising from an increase in the **appraised value** of an asset or assets. In particular, an increase in an owner's or shareholder's equity value that arises from the reappraisal of a company's assets.

appraised value(AmE)   The value of a property as assessed by a qualified **appraiser**. See also **appraisal, appraisal report, market value**.

appraisement   The act or procedure of carrying out an **appraisal**, especially when required under a court order; for example, prior to an award of compensation, or by a person selected by parties to a dispute. In such instances two appraisals are frequently made and the value fixed by the average. Appraisement for taxation purposes is also called **assessment**. cf. **arbitration**. See also **expert**.

appraiser   A professionally skilled, trained, and experienced person who provides an estimate or opinion on the quality, worth or value of real or personal property. One who is appointed to carry out an **appraisal**. See also **certified appraiser, fee appraiser, review appraiser, staff appraiser, valuer**.

appraiser's certification(US)   See **appraisal report**.

appreciation   **1.** An increase in the **value** of a property over its purchase price or book cost. An increase that may arise as a result of an increase in demand for, or a reduction in the supply of, such property; or as a result of a reduction in the purchasing power of money, i.e. due to inflation, but not as a direct result of an improvement or addition to the property. Appreciation may be actual or realised, when a property is sold for a profit; or estimated or unrealised, when it results from a reappraisal or revaluation. cf. **depreciation**. See also **capital gain**.   **2.** An assessment of the value, or the process of assessing the value, of a property. See also **appraisal**.

appreciation-participation mortgage
See **equity-participation mortgage**.

approaches to appraisal[(AmE)] See **appraisal**.

approbate and reprobate To approve and reject. To accept one part and reject another. The doctrine of approbation and reprobation requires that a person elect one of two alternatives; one cannot approbate (select) and reprobate (reject) a mutually exclusive course of action – *quod approbo non reprobo*. See also **election, estoppel**.

appropriate alternative development[(Eng)]
See **certificate of appropriate alternative development**.

appropriation 1. The act or process of taking as one's own. The claiming or using of something as if one has a pre-eminent right, even though not authorised by the true owner. The taking of a thing into private ownership, possession or use. The taking of something without proper authority and converting to one's own use. Accepting a gift from someone who is in a vulnerable position or a position of trust may amount to appropriation.
In the US, appropriation may be used, in contradistinction to the taking of land by exercise of the power of **eminent domain**, to signify a taking of land for public use; although, whether land is appropriated or expropriated, it is still taking of private property into public hands entitling the owner to **just compensation**. cf. **expropriation**. See also **assumption**. 2. The setting aside or application of something to a particular purpose, such as setting a specific property against a specific debt or setting land aside for a particular purpose. See also **dedication**. 3. The use of land acquired by expropriation, or compulsory purchase, for a different purpose to that originally intended. 4. The allocation of public funds for a specific purpose. 5. The taking of real property into

perpetual ecclesiastical use or ownership. cf. **impropriation**. 6.[(US)]The taking of something in public use for private use, especially the taking of water where there was no prior user. The doctrine of appropriation, which is applied in some jurisdictions (especially western states), may enable someone to take unappropriated water from a watercourse or any other body of water, provided it does not interfere with a prior claim to that water and is used for a reasonable beneficial purpose (Arizona v. California, 283 US 423, 51 S Ct 522, 75 L Ed 1154, 1168 (1931); Nebraska v. Wyoming, 325 US 589, 65 S Ct 1332, 1349, 89 L Ed 1815 (1935)). However, this doctrine is now generally restricted by statute. 'Appropriation' may also be used to refer to the taking of water when a right thereto is being claimed by **prescription**. See also **water rights**.

appurtenance That which belongs to something else as an inherent part thereof. An adjunct or accessory. A right or privilege that is incidental or an adjunct to the ownership of a property, especially that which is necessary for the enjoyment of the property and passes with it. For example a right of access that is necessary to the enjoyment of land. In the US, appurtenances that are used and enjoyed with land at the time of a conveyance pass with land, unless expressly excluded (Humphreys v. McKissock, 140 US 304, 11 S Ct 779, 35 L Ed 473, 476 (1891)). In English law, a **conveyance** of land is deemed to include (by the statutory insertion of 'general words' into the conveyance) various rights, privileges or advantages "appurtenant to the land or any part thereof", LPA 1925, s. 62. cf. **appendant**. See also **accession, covenant running with the land, right of common**.

appurtenant Belonging or incidental thereto. That which is joined as an **appurtenance**. See also **easement appurtenant**.

apron[(AmE)] An extensive hard-standing surface around a building used for parking, circulation and loading or unloading.

arbiter   1. One who makes a decision on matters in dispute, e.g. a referee. Originally one who was governed by the rules of law and equity, unlike an **arbitrator** who is governed primarily by his personal judgement.   2.^(Scot)An **arbitrator**.

arbitrage   1. The movement of funds from one market to another to take advantage of price differences. The simultaneous purchase of something in one market and sale in another with the intention of making a profit on the different prices prevailing in the respective markets. A spread, or difference, between interest rates for similar loans but in different situations. 2.^(AmE)The difference between the rate on a first mortgage loan and on a corresponding **wraparound mortgage**.   3. The rendering of a judgement, or the making of an **arbitration**.

arbitration   The hearing and adjudication of a difference, or dispute, between two parties by referring their differences to an independent and impartial third party, who is acceptable to those involved in the dispute, rather than to a court of law. The essence of arbitration is that a matter in dispute is submitted to some body or person (**arbitrator**), chosen by the parties, to make a final decision or award based on the evidence presented by the parties. An arbitrator listens to the submissions of both parties and determines the issue on the evidence; his decision is final and normally accepted as binding on the parties to the dispute. Arbitration is usually used to determine disputes on matters of fact, rather than law, although an arbitrator may have authority to express an opinion on a point of law or he may submit a matter of law to a court for its decision. Although an arbitration is not a part of the judiciary, an arbitration procedure remains within the ambit of the law (such as, in English law, the Arbitration Act 1996; or, in the US, the Federal Arbitration Act (FAA) of 1947 (9 USC § 1 et seq.); and ordinary legal defenses remain open to the parties, in particular a right of appeal to a court on a point of law, either when both parties request a hearing or with the leave of the court.

When a matter is submitted to a body or person who is requested to settle the dispute, usually with each party making representations, that is an arbitration; but if that party is required to fix a price using his own knowledge that is not an arbitration, but a submission to an **expert** who is required to use his professional judgement i.e. to make a **valuation** or **appraisal**. A submission to arbitration may arise from an arbitration agreement or, in certain cases, from statute law. See also **adjudication, interim award, rent review clause**^(Eng).

Bernstein, Ronald, et al. *Handbook of Arbitration Practice*. 3rd ed. London: Sweet & Maxwell, 1998.

arbitration agreement   A written agreement by which the parties mutually agree to submit an existing or future difference to **arbitration**, whether an arbitrator is named in the agreement or not. An arbitration clause in a contract is normally a mandatory provision and is intended to avoid the cost of litigation.

arbitration award   See award.

arbitration clause   See **arbitration agreement**.

arbitrator   A person appointed to settle a matter by **arbitration**. An arbitrator is a judge appointed by individuals rather than by a government. He is a judge who acts in a private court (called an arbitral tribunal) and makes a private judgement (called an **award**). An arbitrator, unlike an **expert**, does not act without receiving submissions or evidence from the parties (although he relies also on his own expertise). Normally, if he refuses to accept submissions or evidence, his award may be set aside for misconduct. An arbitrator's function is governed by statute law, but he is not normally liable for negligence when arriving at his award. However, his decision should lie between the extremes represented by the parties. cf. **appraiser**.

arcade   1. A covered passageway or pedestrian

thoroughfare, commonly with rows of shops or stalls along the sides. Strictly speaking, the 'arcade' should have an *arched* roof, although any covered or colonnaded parade of shops set along or on either side of a pedestrian way may be called a shopping arcade, especially where it links two distinct areas such as two buildings or two open streets. **2.** A series of arches forming a building or gallery.

archaeological area(Eng) An area of land designated by the Secretary of State or a local authority as being of archaeological importance (Ancient Monuments and Archaeological Areas Act 1979, s. 33). It is an offence to disturb the ground of such an area, or to flood or tip on the area, without previously notifying the local district council. Upon receipt of such notification the Secretary of State, or certain other bodies, have powers to enter and carry out investigatory work on such an area.

architect Derived from the Greek *architekton*, 'chief artificer', 'master builder'. A person who is skilled in the art of building; one who specialises in the design of buildings and in the control, supervision and methods for the execution of building work. An architect is employed by a client to interpret and advise on that person's requirements; to convert those requirements into plans and then into a building; to supervise the erection of that building and ensure that it is sound and complies with all codes and legal requirements; and as far as possible, to make the building aesthetically pleasing. An architect who is engaged by a building owner to supervise a contract acts as an **agent** for that purpose and has no authority to act beyond the strict terms of his engagement. An architect is responsible for exercising skill, commensurate with the standard expected of this profession, when performing his professional duties and he owes a reasonable **duty of care** to his employer. See also **defects list**, **certificate of completion**(AmE), **certificate of practical completion**(BrE), **certificate of valuation**, **professional negligence**, **progress certificate**(AmE), **punch list**(AmE); Appendix A, **Real Estate Associations, American Institute of Architects, Royal Institute of British Architects**.

Chappell, David, and A. Willis. *The Architect in Practice*. 8th ed. Oxford: Blackwell, 2000.

architect's instruction (AI)(BrE) A written instruction issued under a building contract by an **architect** (or, if applicable, another professional appointed under the contract – a 'contract administrator') to a building contractor changing, varying or clarifying the provisions of the contract. The instruction may cover, for example, such matters as discrepancies in the documentation, divergences between statutory requirements and the contract documents, nomination of subcontractors or suppliers, or variations or modifications to the design, quality or quantity of the work. In the latter instance, the instruction may also be called a **variation order** or 'variation instruction', especially when it requires the addition, omission or substitution of any work or a change to the kind or standard of any materials and has financial implications. See also **change order**(AmE).

architect's lien See lien.

archive **1.** A chamber or room for storing documents or records. A part of a building set aside as a repository, especially for formal, historical or legal purposes. **2.**(US)An original of a deed or other document that is placed in a public record store as evidence of title.

area **1.** The horizontal surface of a defined unit of land, or a building or defined part of a building. A flat, or relatively flat, surface, especially one that is enclosed, bounded, or set aside for a particular purpose. See also **area of comprehensive development**(Eng), **common areas, conservation area**(Eng), **development area, gross external area**(BrE), **gross internal area**(BrE), **gross leasable area**(US), **net internal area**(BrE), **renewal area**(Eng), **rentable area**(US), **retail area**(BrE), **site area, special**

area(Eng).   **2.** A clear open space. In particular, an open area within a house or an adjoining enclosure. **3.**(BrE)A sunken enclosure, especially one that gives access to the basement of a building. See also **areaway**(AmE).

area concept(US)   A principle that in an area that is to be redeveloped because it contains substandard housing, the entire designated area may be acquired and assembled by **eminent domain**, even though some of the properties may not be substandard or blighted.

area of comprehensive development(Eng) An area of land that is to be developed or redeveloped as a whole, either by a private or by a public body. See also **urban development area**.

area of outstanding natural beauty (AONB)(Eng)   An area in England designated by the Countryside Commission, or in Wales the Countryside Council for Wales, under the provisions of the National Parks and Access to the Countryside Act 1949, s. 87, as requiring strict standards of development control and measures to conserve or enhance its natural beauty, such as the removal of eyesores. Such an area is similar but smaller than a **national park**. See also **article 4 direction, conservation area**.

area of special control(Eng)   An area in England or Wales where the display of most forms of **advertisement** is strictly controlled, so that only special classes or specifically authorised advertisements are permitted (TCPA 1990, s. 221, and regulation made thereunder). These areas, sometimes called special areas, are mostly rural; although orders have been made in respect of other areas that appear to the Secretary of State "to require special protection on the grounds of amenity", TCPA 1990, s. 221(3).

area of special scientific interest(Eng)   See **site of special scientific interest**.

area research   See **feasibility analysis**.

area variance(US)   See **zoning variance**.

area zoning   See **zoning**.

areaway(AmE)   A passage or space underground intended to be used to provide access to, or light or ventilation to, the basement of a building. A cellar or room under the sidewalk of a street. See also **area**.

argentum Dei(Lat)   'God's money'. Money paid to secure a bargain, i.e. **earnest money**.

arles   Money given to secure a bargain; **earnest money**.

arm's-length transaction   An agreement between parties who do not have a particular or special relationship or obligation to one another (for example, associated companies, landlord and tenant, husband and wife). A transaction may be said to have been conducted at arm's length when both parties are unrelated and unaffiliated; have acted independently and in their own best interest; and when neither party has an advantageous bargaining position or is able to exert an **undue influence** on the other. See also **special purchaser, market value, vested interest**.

arrearages(AmE)   See **arrears**.

arrears   A debt that is due but not yet paid. Payments (e.g. rent or interest payments) that have not been made at the appointed time, i.e. on the due date. A sum of money that is in arrears remains in arrears until there is proper **payment**. In the US, sometimes called 'arrearages' or 'delinquent payments'. See also **rent in advance/rent in arrears, tender**.

arrent(BrE)   To let land annually. To let land at a rental. In particular, the grant by the Crown of an area of forest that could be enclosed subject to the payment of an annual rent.

arrogation   Derived from the Latin *arrogare*,

'to lay claim to'. The act or process of taking over something without the least right or title. Claiming or assuming a right to which one is not entitled. See also **appropriation**.

artesian well   A narrow and usually deep well from which water rises out of an underground stratum under hydrostatic pressure, especially after the stratum has been pierced or broken by drilling. The term is sometimes used to refer to any underground water supply where water is pumped to the surface through a deep bored well. See also **water rights**.

article 4 direction(Eng)   A Direction issued by the Secretary of State for the Environment (in respect of England) or the Secretary of State for Wales (in respect of Wales), or the local planning authority (with the approval of the Secretary of State), restricting the carrying out of development that would otherwise be 'permitted development' under the provisions of a **General Development Order** (Town and Country Planning (General Permitted Development) Order 1995, article 4). See also **area of outstanding natural beauty, compensation for planning restrictions, conservation area**.

article of roup(Scot)   See **roup**.

artificial person   An entity, other than a human being, that has a legal status, e.g. a **company, trust** or cooperative. An institution created by law for the purposes of society or government; a corporation or body politic. In the US, also called a 'juristic person'. See also **partnership**.

as-built drawings or **as builts**   Drawings of a building that represent the finished structure and the layout of the floor spaces. Such drawings are usually prepared by the architect or a surveyor to show all or a part of a completed building for such purposes as rent or sale price determination or for use in a maintenance manual, especially as buildings are frequently constructed with variations from the original design and development drawings.

as, if and when clause   A clause in a broker's or real estate agent's agreement that **commission** will be paid to the agent 'as, if and when' a purchaser is introduced who is **ready, willing and able**, to purchase; although the phrase 'as, if and when' could just as easily be replaced by 'when'.

'as is' or **'as it stands'**   Accepting a property in its existing condition. 'As is' implies that the purchaser must satisfy himself by his own inspection, "for better or worse, for less or for more". Generally, the vendor who sells a property 'as is' gives no **warranty** as to the condition or suitability of the property and the purchaser takes it at his own risk, usually upon the implication that there may be a some defect known to the purchaser, but he trusts his own judgement. On the other hand, a sale of a property 'as is' does not eliminate any express warranty that may be given; nor does it vitiate a claim for fraudulent **misrepresentation**; or intentional concealment of facts. See also *caveat emptor*, **fit for the purpose, latent defect, warranty of habitability**.

as of right   See **custom, enjoyment**.

as of right zoning(US)   See **permitted zoning use**.

as soon as possible   Within the shortest possible time. 'As soon as possible' requires that something is done with all possible expediency, using the greatest diligence and not just in a reasonable period of time. cf. **as soon as practical**. See also **time is of the essence**.

as soon as practical or **as soon as practicable**   As soon as one is able in all the circumstances. 'As soon as possible', 'as soon as able', and 'as soon as practical or practicable' may all be considered as requiring a similar degree of urgency by requiring diligence and persistence, but allowing for extraneous circumstances;

whereas 'immediately' presupposes no such eventualities. However, in the order as set out they denote slightly higher levels of patience or realism on the part of the recipient or beneficiary. See also **time is of the essence**.

asked price(AmE)   The lowest price at which an investor or dealer declares that he will sell a security or commodity. See **asking price**.

asking price   1. The price at which a seller indicates that his property may be acquired. In particular, the price at which someone makes an invitation to negotiate, but not intended as an **offer** to be bound for acceptance. A term that generally implies a willingness to accept a lower price. Also called an 'asked price', especially when used with reference to a security or commodity. cf. **action price**(AmE), **reserve price**. See also **invitation to trade**(AmE)/**invitation to treat**(BrE).   2. The price at which a landowner lists his property for sale with a real estate broker. Also called the 'listing price'.

assart(BrE)   The removal of trees by the roots so that they will not grow again, in particular when converting woodland or forestry into arable or pasture land. Assart differs from **waste** where trees are cut but may grow again. Sometimes spelt 'essart'. cf. **afforestation**.

assemblage   The consolidation of two or more parcels of land into single ownership or common use, especially in order to increase the usefulness or value of the whole. In the US, also called 'plottage', although that term refers more to the outcome than the process of assemblage. In Australia, also called 'consolidation'. cf. **parceling**. See also **plottage value**(AmE), **marriage value**(BrE).

assemblage value(US)   See **plottage value**.

assembled land   See **assemblage**.

assent   1. Derived from the Latin *assentio*, which is compounded of *ad* and *sentio*, signifying to bring one's mind or judgement to something. General approval; an expression of a willingness to accept a course of action. Concurrence or **acquiescence** in, or compliance with, something. Assent arises when one has indicated a willingness to accept or concur. Assent generally requires an act or expression of consent, as distinguished from 'acquiesce', which signifies compliance, without effective opposition or resistance. In particular, assent may be considered as an essential element to the creation of a contract or a change in the conditions of a valid contract and in this respect requires some overt act or conduct that confirms a mental concurrence. cf. **acceptance**. See also **consent, election, estoppel, ratification, waiver**. 2.(Eng)A document in **writing** or under seal, signed by a **personal representative**, that vests property in the beneficiary, in accordance with the wishes of a deceased person or according to the rules of entitlement on intestacy. An assent to be effective in passing a **legal estate** must be in writing (but need not be by deed); signed by the personal representatives; and must state the name of the person in whom the estate is to be vested (AEA 1925, s. 36(4)). An assent must be executed even if the personal representatives are to hold land on trust. An assent represents the valid title of a *bona fide* **purchaser** for **value**; he need not concern himself with the will, he need only concern himself with the grant of probate or letters of administration. Generally, the effective date of transfer relates back to the testator's death. See also **vesting document**.

assessable value or **assessed value**(US)   1. An official value placed on a property for state taxation. In particular, an estimate of the value of a property made for the purpose of levying an **ad valorem** tax. A value that is considered fair and reasonable, or is determined as such, by an assessor on behalf of a taxation authority; but not necessarily the fair market value. An assessed value is determined as "the highest price the property would bring, free of encumbrances, at a fair and voluntary private sale thereof for cash, or, in other words its fair cash market value, is ordinarily a just criterion of its value; but, unless otherwise provided by constitution or statute, market value is not a conclusive criterion, and many factors affecting value must be considered", 84 C.J.S., Tax, pp. 783-4. In particular, the assessed value of all the properties in a particular tax district must be determined on a uniform basis, especially as the system of assessment must not violate the 'equal protection' provision of the Fourteenth Amendment to the Constitution of the United States (Allegheny Pittsburgh Coal Co. v. Webster County, W. Va., 488 US 338, 109 S Ct 633, 102 L Ed 688 (1989)). See also **assessment, board of equalization, highest and best use. 2.** The value placed on a property for **condemnation** purposes.

assessment 1. An evaluation, or the result of an evaluation, made in order to determine the amount of tax to be paid by an individual; in particular by an owner or occupier of land or buildings. **2.**(US)A determination of the **assessed value** of real property. An official valuation made for the purpose of a local tax that is to be levied on the basis of the assumed market value of a property. 'Assessment' may also refer to a species of tax that is raised from the owners of specific properties to pay for specific expenditure, unlike general taxation, which is levied on all properties in a prescribed area. It may be called a 'local assessment' when levied against all or most properties in a given town or area; or, a 'special assessment' when levied against an owner or owners of properties to pay solely for the cost of public work or public services that benefits those particular properties. A special assessment is usually levied only against the properties in a 'special assessment district', based on a measure such as a property's foot frontage or land area. A special assessment must relate to local works or improvements, otherwise it would be a 'tax', which is levied against the community in general. See also **improvement district**.
Eckert, Joseph K., et al. *Property Appraisal and Assessment Administration.* Chicago: International Association of Assessing Officers, 1990.
3. A tax levied on the basis of the value of a

property. In particular, a charge levied for the purpose of paying for an improvement to one or a number of properties, as distinguished from a tax that is levied for general public purposes.

When a tenant is obliged to pay 'assessments' that will cover property taxes levied against the property as leased, but not an obligation to pay for any increase arising from an improvement required of the landlord, or any other special burden placed on a landlord such as a tax levied for special purposes. Similarly, a tenant is obliged to pay "taxes", and no more, he is not obliged to pay assessments, i.e. the obligation is to pay the tax directly imposed on the tenant, but not the taxes levied on the property. See also **assessed value, rateable value**(BrE), **lien. 4.** The act or process by which a **tax, rate** or **duty** is levied by law, especially by a local or municipal authority. **5.** The amount allocated to an individual unit in a property that contains several similar units, such as a property held in some form of co-ownership (including a condominium or cooperative). The process by which operating costs or expenses are apportioned between the occupiers of a building. See also **apportionment. 6.** An **appraisal** or **estimate**. In particular, an official determination of the amount of **just compensation** payable to a property owner when his property is taken by the exercise of the power of eminent domain.

assessment appeal board(US) A local government body that considers appeals against the **assessed value** placed on a property. See also **board of review**.

assessment district(US) An area or territory that is designated so that all the properties therein should be the subject of a particular form of **assessment** or local tax. In particular, an area or district that benefits from a public improvement that is specific to that area and, therefore, is made subject to a local or special assessment to pay for that improvement.

assessment ratio The ratio of the **assessed value** of a property to its **market value**. At the time that an **assessment** is made it should be based on the market value, although the assessed value may be lower than the market value for a number of reasons such as the date fixed for making the assessment, a discount or partial exemption allowed by law, or an allowance or factors taken into account by the assessing officer.

assessment roll(US) An official list or roll, maintained in a local tax district, setting out a legal description of all the taxable properties in the district, the **assessed value** of each property, the party billed and the amount levied against each property (which is usually a percentage of the assessed value). Also called a 'tax list', 'tax roll' or 'tax book'. See also **rating list**(BrE).

assessment map(US) See **cadastral map**.

assessor **1.** An **expert** called upon to provide an opinion of value, especially in a dispute. In Roman and the civil law an assessor is also a person called on to give legal advice or assistance. **2.**(Scot)A person who assesses the annual value of a property for rating taxation purposes. **3.**(US)A public official, or officer of the executive branch of government, who determines the **assessed value** of a property for taxation purposes. Usually called a 'tax assessor'. **4.** An adjudicator, or adjuster, called on to determine the loss suffered subsequent to an insurance claim. In the US, generally called an 'adjuster'.

asset Derived from the Norman French *assetz*, 'enough'. Any **property** that is owned and has value. That which is available to meet a debt or liability. Property, real or personal, tangible or intangible (including an interest in property, a chose-in-action, debt or even goodwill) that is available, or may be made available, to meet a debt of a person or corporation. cf. **liability**. See also **asset value, capital asset, current asset, farm assets**(AmE), **fixed asset, floating asset, goodwill, intangible asset, wasting asset, working capital**.

asset-backed security (ABS) A security, or similar form of obligation, that is collateralized by a pool of loans secured by a group of assets or receivables, such as residential or commercial mortgages, consumer loans, trade receivables, automobile loans, credit card loans, or corporate or municipal bonds. See also **mortgage-backed obligation**.

Baums, Theodor, and Eddy Wymeersch (editors). *Asset Backed Securitization in Europe*. The Hague, London & Boston: Kluwer, 1996.

asset life See **economic life**.

asset management The administration, operation and management of one or more assets, especially the real estate assets owned by a corporation or institution, in order to maximise the return on the investment made in those assets. Asset management includes, but goes further than, **property management** as it requires a general overview of the investment criteria of the owner of the asset and involves a continuous and proactive process of review to determine areas where action can be taken to improve the return and reduce the risk of the investment. Asset management may be considered to fall within the ambit of **facility management**. See also **portfolio management**.

asset stripping Purchasing a company in order to sell all or a significant part of the assets at a profit, without regard to the viability of the company as a going-concern. See also **asset value, break-up value, going-concern value**.

asset value The total net realisable value of the assets of a company after all debts (excluding the ordinary shareholders funds) have been paid. In particular, 'asset value' may be taken to mean 'tangible value' as distinguished from 'market value' or 'earning value'. cf. **net asset value**.

assign **1.** To transfer or make over to another; the process of **assignment**. To grant, especially a *chose in action*. Assign is used in particular to refer to the transfer of the entirety of a lease, as distinguished from 'sub-let' which is used to refer to a transfer a portion of the interest. **2.** An **assignee**. A person who succeeds to or in whom a property is vested as a result of a voluntary act of another.

assigns   See **assignee**.

assignable lease   A lease that can be transferred, or assigned by the lessee without the permission from, or consent of, the lessor. See also **assignment, restraint on alienation**.

assignation   **1.** The transfer of a right to property. An **assignment** of a right. A term used especially in Scots law.   **2.**(Scot)A written deed that is used to transfer incorporeal property.

assignee   A transferee or grantee. The party who benefits from the **assignment** of an interest. An assignee may be the party to whom a landlord or a tenant assigns his interest, but the term is more commonly applied to tenant's assignee. A person is not an assignee of the land unless he takes the entire estate of the assignor and upon identical terms. See also **privity of estate**.

assignment   **1.** The **transfer** of a right, title or interest in property to another. The transfer of the liabilities or rights under a contract to a person or body that is not a party to the original contract, whether as an act of a party to the contract or by operation of law. Assignment may be used to refer to the transfer of any kind of property. However, the term is used in particular to refer to a transfer of a debt, contract or option, as well as personal property (including a lease) or a chattel. The transfer of a freehold interest is more strictly speaking a **conveyance**, because at common law such a transfer was required to be made by **deed**; whereas an assignment need only be made in **writing**. An assignment may be made as a **gift** or for **consideration**. In the context of a lease, an assignment may refer to the transfer of the term, as held by the lessee, or the reversion, as held by the landlord. Usually it refers to the latter.

Assignment of the term of a lease means parting with the entire interest held, not merely a part thereof; in particular a transfer of the lease without the retention of a **right of re-entry**, or retention of a **reversion**. The retention of any of the transferor's interest in the property (but not necessarily a part of the demised premises), no matter how short, would create an underlease or **sub-lease**.

As a rule, either party to an executed contract (but not an offer that has not been accepted) may assign his rights or obligations, unless expressly prohibited, or unless the performance of the contract calls for the participation of the original party as with most contracts of personal service. Thus, if a lease is silent on the matter, the tenant is entitled to assign his interest. However, in the US, a few states require that the landlord's consent be obtained for an assignment, even if the lease does not expressly so require; although this requirement applies mostly to tenancies for less than two years. Nonetheless, a lease commonly contains a covenant in some form limiting assignment, or otherwise parting with possession of the demised premises, at least without the lessor's consent. In the event of an assignment of a lease, the assignee becomes liable for the payment of rent, as there is **privity of estate** between new parties to the lease. On the other hand, the assignor is generally not relieved of his obligation under the lease, as there is still **privity of contract** between the original parties.

A covenant not to assign or otherwise part with the premises is broken by a sub-lease, whereas a covenant not to 'assign or transfer would not necessarily prevent a sub-letting, provided the assignor retains a reversionary interest in the leased premises. A covenant against subleasing may well restrain an assignment, the principle being that an assignment carries with it the constituent of a sub-lease, although much depends on the actual words used in each covenant. The grant of a mortgage may be considered as an assignment of a lease, although the form of the mortgage will determine whether this is an assignment or a lesser right such as the grant of a lien or charge. cf. **novation**. See also **absolute assignment, alienation, equitable assignment, estoppel certificate**(US), **legal assignment, restraint on alienation**.   **2.** A task or job. An appointment to carry out of a task, duty or service. In particular, the provision of a consulting service in accordance with an agreement between a client and a professional advisor, such as the preparation of an **appraisal, valuation** or the carrying out of a **survey**.

assignment of rents(US)   An agreement by which a mortgagor assigns the rights to all rents and profits receivable from the mortgaged property to the mortgagee. Such a right is not normally exercisable until the mortgagor is in default, at which stage the mortgagee can direct the tenant or tenants to pay all income to him, or to a receiver, to be applied to make payments of interest or principal due under the loan agreement. Generally, such payments continue to be made, until the mortgagor is able to make good the deficiencies; the loan is repaid in full; or, if applicable, the mortgagee forecloses on the loan, or the property is sold following an exercise of the mortgagee's power of sale. See also **issues and profits, rent**.

assignment *pro tanto*   See *pro tanto*.

assignor   A party who assigns an interest. One who makes an **assignment**.

assigns   An assignee. A person substituted for another. In particular, one who will or may take an assignment of an interest in property that has been granted to another by will, conveyance or descent. See also **heirs and assigns, novation**.

assisted area(BrE)   A generic term for an area or region of the United Kingdom that benefits from government financial assistance to industry aimed at improving economic activity, in particular the provision, maintenance and safeguarding of employment and to assist with the furtherance of the government's regional policy for the UK. Such an area may be classified as a **development area**;

special development area, or **intermediate area**, depending on the extent of the aid available (Industrial Development Act 1982, Part I).

associate broker(AmE)   See **salesperson**.

associate licensee(AmE)   See **salesperson**.

association   A body of persons who come together for a common purpose, but without a formal charter. An association is not strictly a legal entity, but the word is commonly used to refer to a **company, corporation, partnership** or a **society**. See also **homeowners' association**.

assumable mortgage   See **assumption**.

assumed life   See **holding period**.

assumption   **1.** Laying claim to, or taking possession of, something. The act of taking upon oneself a debt or obligation, e.g. the obligations of a lease or mortgage. In particular, taking over of a liability for a mortgage debt or the obligations of a deed of trust. The term 'assumption' in relation to a mortgage debt is used primarily in the US to draw a distinction from the purchase of the property **subject to mortgage**. With a purchase 'subject to mortgage', the purchaser accepts that the property is mortgaged, but does not take over any personal liability for the mortgage debt. Whereas a person who 'assumes' a mortgage becomes the principal debtor under the mortgage, with the liability extending, if necessary, beyond the extent of the loss of the mortgaged property. Generally, the original mortgagor remains liable for the debt in the event of the failure of the purchaser to abide by his obligations, unless there is an express release by way of an assumption or **novation** agreement. An assumption of the mortgage is generally made by an express tripartite agreement, but in a few cases may be implied from the terms of the agreement, especially from the price paid. See also **appropriation, due-on-sale clause, recourse**.   **2.** The acceptance of a **risk**.   **3.** A promise or undertaking not under **seal**. See also *assumpsit*.

assumption clause(US)   **1.** A clause in a mortgage deed prohibiting the transfer of the mortgage contract by the mortgagor without the consent of the mortgagee. Most mortgage deeds contain an assumption clause prohibiting the transfer of the mortgage debt without the mortgagee's consent and, if such consent is given, the mortgagee frequently charges an 'assumption fee' to cover his costs or to reap part of any benefit that might accrue to a new party to the loan. See also **acceleration clause, due-on-sale clause**.   **2.** A clause in a deed, lease or other document for the transfer of property by which the transferee assumes an obligation of the transferor in respect of the property being transferred. In particular, a clause in an agreement for the transfer of a mortgage loan which stipulates that the transferee or grantee accepts the personal liability for the mortgage debt. See also **assumption**.

assumption fee(US)   A charge levied by a mortgagee or lender for granting consent to his debt or liability being transferred to another. See also **assumption**.

assumptions as to planning permission(Eng) See **planning assumptions**.

assurance   **1.** The act of transferring property; or something that operates as a transfer of property. An old word for a **conveyance**. Any written instrument evidencing a title to real property. See also **alienation, beneficial owner, disentailing assurance, further assurance**.   **2.** Synonymous with **insurance**; although generally used, especially in the UK, with reference to life assurance or a contract of indemnity that is based on a known occurrence or fixed date of payment. **3.**(Aus)"A **conveyance** or other instrument by which an estate in land is disposed of, otherwise than by will", Conveyancing Act 1919, s. 7(1) (NSW) (Similar definitions are given in other property law statutes (s. 18(1) (VIC); s. 4 (Qld); s. 7 (SA); s. 7 (WA); s. 2 (Tas); s. 4 (NT)).

assured   See **insured**.

assured shorthold tenancy (AST)(Eng)   A tenancy of a dwelling-house where, after the expiry of an initial period of six months, a landlord may obtain possession as of right by giving at least two months notice in writing. The notice may be given before or any time after, the expiry of the initial period (HA 1988, s. 19A, as added by HA 1996, s. 96)). Before the Housing Act 1996 came into force an assured shorthold tenancy had to be granted for an initial fixed term of six months, but this is no longer required. With a few exceptions, any **assured tenancy** becomes an 'assured shorthold tenancy', unless the tenancy agreement states otherwise or the landlord serves notice to the same effect before the tenancy commences. A tenancy cannot be an assured shorthold tenancy, if immediately before the grant of the tenancy the tenant was an 'assured tenant'. An assured shorthold tenancy may be converted into an assured tenancy if the agreement so provides, or by the landlord giving notice to the effect. A tenant of an assured shorthold tenancy may apply to the **Rent Assessment Committee** to determine the appropriate level of rent that "the landlord might reasonably be expected to obtain under the assured shorthold tenancy" for the initial fixed term (HA 1988 Act, s 22(1)). The tenant may only make such an application once and the power to make such an application does not apply to tenancies of the same premises made between the same parties.

assured tenancy(Eng)   A **tenancy** of a **dwelling-house** let as a "separate dwelling" to an individual who occupies the dwelling-house as his "only or principal home", and one that is not excluded under the provisions of the Housing Act 1988, s. 1. If the dwelling is let to joint tenants, at least one individual must occupy the dwelling as his only or principal home. An assured tenancy is the basic form of residential tenancy for new letting subsequent to the passing of the HA 1980. An assured tenancy may be a periodic tenancy or one granted for a fixed term. In either case, the landlord cannot obtain possession of the dwelling-house without a court order and, unless the tenant voluntarily gives up possession, or the parties agree to a new tenancy, at the end of the initial term, the tenancy continues automatically as a periodic statutory tenancy. To obtain a court order the landlord must first serve a notice on the tenant in the prescribed form specifying the ground or **grounds for possession** and must then apply for an order for possession within the prescribed time limits (HA 1988, s. 8, Sch. 2). There is no statutory control on the level of rent that may be agreed upon under an assured tenancy, although upon renewal of an assured tenancy, if the tenant disagrees the terms proposed by the landlord, the tenant may apply to the **Rent Assessment Committee** to determine the terms that are appropriate for such a tenancy. In that case the rent is to be determined in accordance with the statutory provisions. In addition, a rent increase under a periodic tenancy can only be effected by service of a prescribed notice and the rent cannot be increased within one year of the commencement of the tenancy nor earlier than twelve months after such a rent increase takes effect (HA 1988, s. 6).

The principal exclusions in section 1 are that the tenancy is: (i) granted by the same landlord to the same holder of a previous **protected tenancy** or **statutory tenancy**; (ii) granted at a **low rent**, which primarily applies to tenants who hold the property under a long-term ground lease; (iii) a **business tenancy**; (d) let as on-licensed premises; (iv) a letting of **agricultural land** exceeding two acres, together with a dwelling-house; (v) an **agricultural holding** and the tenant is in control of the farming; (vi) a student letting; (vii) a letting as a holiday home; (viii) one granted by a **resident landlord** (although such a letting may be a **restricted contract**); or (ix) the landlord is one of a number of expressly exempt bodies. In the event of the death of an assured tenant, the tenancy passes to the surviving spouse provided he or she occupied the dwelling-house immediately before the death as his or her only or principal home (HA 1988, Sch. 1). Only a single succession to an assured

tenancy can occur. See also **assured shorthold tenancy, protected occupier.**

Bridge, Stuart. *Assured Tenancies.* London: Blackstone Press, 1999.

Fancourt, Timothy. *Megarry's Assured Tenancies.* London: Sweet & Maxwell, 1999.

Fox-Andrews, James, and Del Williams. *Assured Tenancies* 3rd ed. London: Estates Gazette, 2002.

at arm's length   With care; without being imposed upon or obligated to someone; without restraint or favour. See also **arm's-length transaction.**

at law   See **common law, legal estate.**

at least   See **clear day.**

at par   See **par value.**

at-risk rule[US]   An Internal Revenue Service rule that tax deductions for investment credits on real estate are only allowed in respect of investments that are considered 'at risk' for the investor, which generally means the cash contributed to the investment and loans for which the investor is personally responsible. Non-recourse debt may be considered 'at risk' provided it is made by an unrelated lender who is regularly engaged in commercial lending and no more than 80 per cent of the financing for the property is non-recourse (26 USC, Internal Revenue Code, § 49).

at sight   A payment of a **bill of exchange** or **promissory note** upon its presentation, i.e. on demand.

at-the-money option   An **option** to purchase a secured property at a price that equals its current market value at the time the option is exercised.

attach   1. To add, fix or fasten one property to another, generally by some form of physical means. To bind, fasten or join. See also **annex, attached.**   2. To take by legal authority; to seize by a writ of **attachment.**

attached Connected to, or forming part of, something, usually on a permanent basis. Fixed or fastened to something. Two objects are usually 'attached' by some physical means, especially where one becomes an adjunct of the other and cannot readily be separated, at least without causing damage to the property to which the object is attached or affixed. However, a property that is affixed to land only by its own weight, but one that is difficult to remove may be said to be attached to the land, especially if it has become an inherent part of the land. See also **attach**, **fixture**.

attachment 1. A legal process or writ used for taking or seizing custody of real or personal property pending settlement of a debt. Generally used against an absconding, evasive or fraudulent debtor by a creditor who has already received a direction from the court that a debtor must meet his obligations (i.e. by a **judgement creditor**); or used prior to a formal court hearing to prevent a debtor removing property from the appropriate jurisdiction. In English law, a writ of attachment, or a 'garnishee proceeding' or 'attachment of debts', is used to prevent a judgement creditor from paying any creditors until the 'attached debt' has been settled. See also **distress**, **garnishment**, **lien**. 2. The action of attaching; fixing or fastening one thing to another. See also **annex**, **attached**, **fixture**. 3. A document that is added to another. See also **endorsement**, **codicil**, **rider**.

attendance(Eng) The provision of personal services by a landlord to a tenant, as distinguished from services of a more general nature (e.g. heating, lighting, etc.). It means "service personal to the tenant performed by an attendant provided by the landlord ... for the benefit or convenience of the individual tenant in his use and enjoyment of the demised premises", *Palser v Grinling* [1948] AC 291, 310 (HL). Attendance may include such matters as cleaning the interior of a flat, or providing linen, but it does not cover general property maintenance or upkeep of any common parts of a building. A tenant who is provided with attendance, the cost of which forms a substantial proportion of his rent, cannot claim a right to a **protected tenancy** (Rent Act 1977, s. 7), although he may have a **restricted contract**. See also **board**, **service tenancy**.

attest To bear witness to a fact. To certify formally that a document is true (i.e. freely entered into or a true copy) by **signature**, or to signify that another's signature on a deed has been freely made. At common law it was not essential to attest a **deed** (unless it was a **will**, **bill of sale**, or a **transfer** of registered land), although it was common practice.

In the US, in some jurisdictions, any signature to be valid must be attested, and, in a few jurisdictions, two witnesses must attest a conveyance. In most jurisdictions attestation, or **acknowledgment** before a notary public, is required before recording a deed. A will must be attested by two witnesses (or in some states by three witnesses).

In English law, on or after July 31, 1990 although a deed need no longer be under seal, it must be attested in the presence of one witness (or, if a grantor directs another to sign a deed, as when he is incapacitated, in the presence of two witnesses) (LP(MP)A 1989, s. 1). See also **certified copy**.

attestation The act of bearing witness to the signature of a written document in order to demonstrate that it has been freely made. The act of a third party who witnesses the actual execution of an instrument. cf. **acknowledgment**. See also **attest**, **will**.

attestation clause The clause in a **deed** or **will** that contains the signature of the witness or witnesses, or declares that the document has been duly executed. An attestation clause uses such words as 'signed, sealed and delivered by XY in the presence of AB'. In common law, a **testator** must sign, or acknowledge his or her signature to a will, in the simultaneous presence of two witnesses (in a few jurisdictions in the US three witnesses are required). See also **attest**, **testimonium**.

attorney   1. An **agent** or person who acts in another's place or stead. In a general sense, an attorney is anyone who acts in another's place and a 'private' attorney is also called an 'attorney-in-fact'. However, the term is more commonly understood to refer to an attorney-at-law. See also **power of attorney**.   2. A lawyer. An individual or a professional law association, corporation, or partnership authorized under applicable law to practice law (US Bankruptcy Code § 101). In England and Wales, a term originally applied to someone who was permitted to practice in the superior courts (in particular the courts of common law); today called a barrister.

attorney-at-law or **attorney at law**   A person who is admitted to practice in a particular jurisdiction. A lawyer. See also **attorney**.

attorney-in-fact   A person authorised to act on behalf of, or in the place of another person. In particular, one who is granted a limited or special power to act in someone's stead. Someone who is vested with a **power of attorney**; an **agent** with specified authority. An attorney-in-fact may, but need not be, a lawyer or 'attorney-at-law'. See also **attorney**.

attornment   The acceptance of the coming into existence of a legal relationship; such as when a tenant recognises that another landlord, or a mortgagee (or a receiver), has acquired the immediate reversionary interest, i.e. has effectively become that tenant's immediate landlord.

An attornment agreement may be made between a subtenant and the superior landlord to the effect that if the intervening, or intermediate, lease is terminated the subtenant becomes the direct tenant of the superior landlord. A mortgagee may enter into such an agreement especially to protect a subtenant in the event of foreclosure on the superior landlord's interest. An attornment to a landlord does not normally create a new tenancy, but is a mere acknowledgement of the relationship of a tenant to his landlord; or it merely substitutes the new landlord on the same terms and conditions of the original lease.

An attornment clause may be inserted in a mortgage as a means by which the mortgagor acknowledges that he is the tenant of the mortgagee (thereby giving the mortgagee the extra right to distrain for unpaid interest), although such a provision is not absolutely essential.

In the US, a lease frequently requires that a tenant formally accepts or 'attornes' the existence of a new owner as landlord; in that event, the original landlord is generally released from any future liability. An 'attornment clause' may be inserted in a lease by which the tenant accepts that he will be bound by the lease even after a foreclosure, or the sale of the property subsequent to foreclosure. In the case of a mortgage an attornment clause may be inserted in the mortgage deed to the effect that the mortgagor attornes or acknowledges that the **mortgagee** may have a right not only to the mortgaged property, but also the 'rents and profits therefrom'. If a mortgagee enters into possession and accepts rent from a tenant that 'attornment' removes any right of the mortgagee to deny that tenant's rights and generally relieves the mortgagor of the obligation to collect the rent. In the US, 'attornment' may be used to refer to a demand for rent as made by a new owner of property.

'Attornment' may also arise when a bailee (one who holds goods in **bailment**) acknowledges to the person for whom he was holding goods that he is holding them on behalf of another party. See also **estoppel**, **non-disturbance clause**, **sub-lessee**.

attornment agreement(US)   See **subordination, non-disturbance and attornment agreement**.

attractive nuisance doctrine(US)   See **negligence, trespass**.

auction   A public sale of land by seeking open oral bids and accepting the highest offer. A method of selling property by which a potential vendor, or his agent (auctioneer), invites open and unconditional offers, in stages, from the public at large (or, at least, from that sector of the public that attends the sale) and then accepts the highest price bid, usually by striking a hammer or gavel on a board (hence a 'sale under the hammer'). In a Dutch auction (sometimes called a Chinese auction) the property is put up for sale, usually at a price that is greater than its estimated value, and then this price reduced in stages until the first bid is made and this bid is then automatically accepted.

An advertisement that a property is to be offered for sale by auction is an **invitation to trade**(AmE)/ **invitation to treat**(BrE), and the property may be withdrawn before the auction sale without obligation. When a property is put forward at an auction sale the auctioneer continues to make an invitation to treat and is at liberty to reject any bid until he signifies acceptance by the fall of his hammer, or any other proper signification of acceptance. Similarly, a bidder may retract his bid up to the same stage. However, if a property is auctioned **without reserve** the property is offered for sale and cannot be withdrawn by the auctioneer once the sale process has commenced. See also **bidding agreement, buy-in, mock auction, particulars of sale, reserve price**.

7 *Am.Jur.2d.*, Auctions and Auctioneers, §§ 1-86.

7A *Cor.Jur.Sec.*, Auctions & Auctioneers, §§ 1-27.

Carpenter, C., and S. Harris (editors). *Property Auctions.* London: Estates Gazette, 1988

Fancourt, Timothy. *Megarry's Assured Tenancies*. London: Sweet & Maxwell, 1999.

auction ring   See **bidding agreement**.

auction with reserve or **auction with reservation**   See **reserve price**.

auction without reserve or **auction without reservation**   See **without reserve**.

auctioneer   A person instructed to sell a property by auction; effectively a vendor's **agent**, who is authorised by law to submit a property for sale on a specific occasion (or a second or further occasion if the objective is not achieved on the first occasion) and then to seek the highest offer or bid. An auctioneer may have express instructions regarding the conduct of the auction sale. Nonetheless, as part of the nature of the role, he has an implied authority to effect a sale of the property entrusted to him (unless expressly instructed to the contrary, as when there is a reserve or upset price set by the seller below which the property is not to be sold) and, at common law, has the authority to make representations about that property. The auctioneer is employed primarily to bring about a sale of the property and, therefore, it is in the nature of his responsibility to his client to see that a sale takes place at the best price possible. The auctioneer must not act in any way to prevent a fair, free and open sale, as that can be considered contrary to public policy and can vitiate the sale. See also **chilling a sale, puffer, misrepresentation, reserve price, without reserve**.

augmentation   The act of increasing or making larger. A term used in Scotland to refer to an increase in a periodic payment such as a rent, feu-duty or stipend.

author(Scot)   The party that grants title to another by sale or gift.

authorised development(Eng)   Development carried out with the benefit of **planning permission**. cf. **permitted development**. See also **discontinuance order, non-conforming use**.

authorization to sell(AmE)   See **listing, exclusive right to sell**.

authority   1. A power or right conferred on a person or body. Approval or sanction to make a representation or to receive a submission on behalf of another. Authority is founded only on right, unlike a **power**, which may exist independently of right; authority is given but a power may be taken or usurped. Authority may be 'bare', 'naked' or 'mere'; or 'coupled with an interest'. A bare authority usually may be revoked at will. An authority coupled with an interest may be revoked only after the interest is revoked An authority may be 'express' or 'implied'. Express authority is that which is contained within the four corners of the contract by which the authority is granted, or is directly granted or conferred on the agent. Implied authority extends to acts that are ordinarily necessary to the exercise of the agent's express authority. In particular, implied agency may arise from the words and conduct of the parties and the facts and circumstances affecting the transaction in question, or from that which is required to carry out the express requirements of the contract. Implied authority embraces matters that are incidental to the agent's express duties, as distinguished from 'apparent' or **ostensible authority**, which has the pretence of being granted, as when a principal allows a third, party to believe an agent possesses a particular authority. See also **actual authority, agency of necessity, agent, estate agent**[(BrE)], **ostensible authority.   2.** A public body or administration having local or quasi-governmental powers. A body vested with delegated power. See also **planning authority**[(BrE)], **highway authority**[(BrE)], **highway commission**, *ultra vires*.

authority coupled with an interest   See **agency coupled with an interest**.

automatic reinstatement clause   See **reinstatement basis**.

autre vie[(Lat)]   'The life of another'. See **life estate**, *pur autre vie*.

avail   An old word for the profit from the sale of property.

average   See average clause.

average annual return (AAR)   The return from an investment calculated by taking the total return over the life of the investment, dividing that sum by the number of years the investment is held, and taking the resultant as a percentage of the initial cost of the investment. The return may

be based on income, capital appreciation (or depreciation) or the combination of both. For example, if an investment costs $100,000, produces a total income over three years of $40,000 and is sold then for $120,000 the average annual return would be:

$$\frac{40,000 + 20,000}{100,000} \times \frac{100}{3} = 20\%$$

This rate of return takes no account of the time at which the income is received or the capital appreciation (or depreciation) occurs, i.e. it is a non-discounted rate of return. Also called a 'book rate of return', an 'accountant's rate of return', an 'average rate of return' or an 'unadjusted rate of return'. cf. **internal rate of return**. See also **pay-back method**.

average clause   1. A condition in an insurance contract that the insured amount is 'subject to average', i.e. if the insured property is worth more than it is insured for (the property is underinsured) then, in the event of a partial or total loss, the insurer will only pay the proportion that the amount of cover bears to the actual cost of replacement. In some policies the contract may state that the amount payable will not exceed a stated percentage of the actual cash value of the loss suffered by the insured. Sometimes called a co-insurance clause as the insured is considered a co-insurer for part of the risk.   2. A clause in a **blanket insurance** policy which provides that in the event of a loss the payment attributed to an individual building will be in the same proportion that the value of the building bears to the total value of all the properties covered by the policy.

average daily room rate (ADR)   The total revenue received by an **hotel** from the charges made for the rooms per night divided by the number of rooms. This rate is for the room occupancy only and excludes other charges made to guests (food & beverage, phone calls, etc.). The rate may be based on the rack rate that could be charged for the rooms, but is normally based on the 'effective rate' after allowing for discounts granted to guests. Also called the 'average room rate' or the average daily rate'. See also **room yield**.

average rate of return (ARR)   See **average annual return**.

aversionem(Lat)   See **sale** *per aversionem*.

aviation easement(US)   See **avigation easement**.

avigation easement(US)   An **easement in gross** for the unobstructed passage of aircraft. See also **air rights**.

avoid   **1.** To shun or keep away from.   **2.** To set aside, cancel or make **void**.

avoidable   See **voidable**.

avoidance   The act or process of withdrawing from a **voidable contract**.

avulsio(Lat)   'tearing off'; 'avulsion'.

avulsion   The sudden and identifiable change in the limits of land at a water's edge due to natural causes, e.g. a change in the course of a river due to the collapse of a river bank or a flood. A change due to avulsion does not affect property ownership boundaries; unlike the gradual and imperceptible process of **accretion** (State of Nebraska v. State of Iowa, 143 US 359, 12 S Ct 396, 36 L Ed 186 (1891); *A-G of Southern Nigeria v John Holt and Co (Liverpool) Ltd* [1915] AC 599 (PC)).

award   **1.** The decision arrived at by an **arbitrator** or referee following a submission to **arbitration**. See also **interim award**.   **2.** The amount adjudged in court as an appropriate level of **damages**.

away-going crop   See **way-going crop**.

azimuth   **1.** An arc that extends from a fixed point (such as true north), the zenith, in a horizontal circle passing through an object (such as the earth's horizon).   **2.** The angular distance between the direction of an object and the direction of a fixed point. The direction of a boundary line relative to the meridian or north-south line, expressed as a number of degrees of deviation from the meridian. A line of course or bearing.

B

back-bond or **back-letter**   1. A **bond** or instrument that qualifies another deed; especially an instrument in which an **indemnity** is given to a person who is in turn a surety or guarantor. 2.(Scot)See **counter letter**.

back of the house(AmE)   The area of a retail store that is not used for selling, such as administrative offices, stockrooms or bathrooms. Also called the 'back room'.

back room(AmE)   See **back of the house**.

back title letter(US)   A letter given to an attorney by a title insurance company setting out details of the status of a title at a particular point in time. The attorney may then use such a letter to start his preparation of the **abstract of title**.

back-to-back escrow(AmE)   See **dual escrow**.

back-to-back house   A house that forms part of a row or terrace of similar houses, joined together at the rear as well as the sides. The essential characteristic of a 'back-to-back' house is that it has only one external wall (the front wall), except for the house at each end of the terrace, which also has an external gable-end wall.

back-to-back lease   An arrangement by which an owner of one building agrees to take over the liabilities for an existing lease from a tenant in another building and in exchange, the tenant agrees to enter into a lease of accommodation in the owner's building.

back-to-back loan   1. An assignment of security to one bank, or in one jurisdiction, in exchange for a loan from another bank, or a bank in another jurisdiction. In particular, an arrangement by which a loan made in one country is guaranteed by security held in another. This arrangement, which is usually made through the medium of a bank in each country, may be used, for example, when the security offered is real estate that the borrower holds in a different country from that in which the loan is made.   2. An agreement by which a company or financial institution in one country guarantees a loan made to a company or institution in another country, where the domestic borrower or guarantor may not wish to be known to the ultimate lender; or where, to avoid foreign exchange control, reciprocal guarantees are given by the respective organisations.   3. A loan made to finance a series of related transactions so that the loan will eventually be granted exclusively to the final purchaser of a property.

backhanded rent(Scot)   Rent reserved in a lease that is to be paid at a specified future date falling after the end of the period that the rent is intended to cover. cf. **forehand rent**.

backland   Land that is situated behind an established development and generally has inadequate access for the purpose of development. See also **easement of necessity**.

backside   An ancient term for **premises**, or a yard, at the rear of a house.

backup offer   An offer made by a third party to purchase a property, so that if a prior, or higher, offer proves to be unacceptable or unsupported by action, the third party's offer is available for acceptance by the seller. See also **conditional contract, gazump, subject to contract**.

bad faith   An intention to deceive or misrepresent. A state of mind that applies to one who acts without honesty of purpose. A failure to comply with an undertaking without any reasonable excuse. (An act done negligently is not necessarily one done in bad faith.) cf. **good faith**. See also **fraud, misrepresentation, secret profit**.

bad title   A title that is so defective that it conveys no interest to the purchaser or holder of a property. In particular a title that, due to missing or defective documents, cannot be used to establish a sufficient **chain of title**. cf. **good title**, **marketable title**.

badges of fraud[(US)]   Circumstances that overhand or cast suspicion on the legality of a transaction. In particular, indications that there has been fraudulent intent surrounding a conveyance of property. Badges of fraud are signs or marks of **fraud**, but are not in themselves sufficient to constitute fraud. Badges of fraud include such matters as inadequacy of consideration; secrecy or haste of sale; or a special relationship between the grantor and grantee.

bailee   A person who, under an expressed or implied contract, temporarily retains personal property, which will be returned to the rightful owner when the purpose for which it was granted no longer applies, i.e. a person who holds goods under a process of **bailment**.

bailiff   **1.**[(BrE)]An officer of a court who is engaged to serve and enforce its orders. A sheriff's officer or a person employed by a sheriff to serve writs or to execute similar legal procedures. In particular, an officer employed to levy **distress**.   **2.** A person appointed to manage landed property on behalf of another; in particular to collect rents. One who manages and acts as the landlord's steward for a large estate or farm.   **3.**[(US)]A court officer whose principal duties are to act as an usher for witnesses and spectators, to announce the entrance of the judge, to maintain custody of the jury and the prisoner, and to keep order in the court room.

bailment   A delivery of **possession** of goods from the owner (bailor) to another (bailee), on trust, and on condition that they will be handed back when a period of safekeeping, or use, has elapsed. Bailment must be accompanied by a transfer of actual or constructive possession of the goods; it does not arise merely because a person is given permission to leave goods on or in another's property. Bailment may take several forms such as: (i) a deposit of goods for safekeeping or repair;

(ii) a means of assisting or giving an advantage to the bailee (as with goods in transit); (iii) to enable the bailee to use the goods, e.g. for **hire** ('bailment for hire'); or (iv) a **pawn** or **pledge**. See also **deposit**, **hire-purchase agreement**[(BrE)], **leasing**.

bailment lease[(US)]   See **leasing**.

bailor   A person who hands over goods under a process of **bailment**. A bailor passes possession of the goods to another for a specific purpose, and usually for a specified period of time, but retains ownership or title.

balancing allowance or **balancing charge**[(Eng)]   Where an asset is disposed of (whether as an outright sale, on receipt of compensation or insurance monies, as a result of a lease that expires, or any other form of disposal) and that property has been the subject of a capital allowance, a balancing allowance may be made if the proceeds of sale of the property are less than its written-down value (the 'expenditure unallowed'). Conversely, if the proceeds exceed the written-down value, a charge may be made on that excess, although the charge cannot exceed the total of the allowances given (Capital Allowances Act 1990, ss. 128-130).

balloon loan or **balloon mortgage**   A loan, or mortgage, granted on the basis that payments of principal will be deferred until the end of the loan period and only interest will be payable during the loan period. Alternatively, only part of the principal is repaid by a number of equal regular instalments and the balance is repaid, at the end of the mortgage term, by a single sum that substantially exceeds those regular instalments. For example, a mortgage of $10,000 may be granted for a term of 10 years with a provision that the capital is repaid, or amortized, by nine annual instalments of $800 and one final payment – a 'balloon payment' – of $2,800. In the US, this type of arrangement is sometimes called 'ballooning' a loan. Also called a 'bullet loan', especially where there is no prepayment provision and all, or virtually all, of the principal is repayable at the end of a short-term loan; the final payment being called a 'bullet payment'. cf. **standing mortgage**. See also **instalment loan**.

balloon payment   See balloon loan.

ballooning(AmE)   See balloon mortgage.

Baltimore method of appraisal(US)   A method of valuing a **corner lot**, i.e. a lot that has a frontage to two streets, by which it is assumed that such a lot has a value equal to the value of two ordinary lots.

band-of-investment rate(AmE)   An **overall capitalization rate** derived from a weighted average of (i) the current cost of debt service (based on an appropriate **mortgage constant**), and (ii) an appropriate rate of return on the equity invested in a property (a **cash-on-cash return**). As an example, assume that a mortgage can be obtained to finance 80 per cent of the cost of acquiring a property investment and the 'debt-service constant' (the constant rate required to repay interest and principal by equal instalments over the term of the loan) is 15%, and also assume that an investor requires an 8% return on his 20 percent equity investment. Then the overall capitalization rate would be four-fifths of 15%, plus one-fifth of 8%, i.e. 13.6%. A band-of-investment rate may be applied, in the same way as any other capitalization factor, to ascertain the capital value of a projected or anticipated income from an investment. The procedure may be reversed to ascertain the required rate of return on equity by taking away the cost of debt finance from an appropriate overall capitalization rate deduced from comparable investments. For example, if the overall rate is assessed as 9% and a 75 percent mortgage can be repaid by an 8% mortgage constant, then the **cash-on-cash return** ('equity-dividend rate') is:

$$\frac{(1 \times 0.09) - (0.75 \times 0.08)}{0.25} = 0.12 \ \text{ or } \ 12\%$$

A band-of-investment rate calculated using only the interest rate on the mortgage (and not a debt-service constant) is also called a 'basic rate'. Also called a 'synthetic capitalization rate'. See also **weighted average cost of capital**.

bank check(AmE) or **bank cheque**(BrE)   See bank draft.

bank draft or banker's draft   A **cheque**, **draft**, or other form of payment drawn by one bank on a deposit held to its account by another bank. A cheque drawn by a bank on its own account and payable on demand, as when a branch bank draws a cheque on an account at its head office. A **bill of exchange**, where the drawer is a bank, being a negotiable instrument that is as good as cash when it is presented. A bank draft is usually used to pay for a property when the vendor requires a guaranteed payment at the time of completion. Also called a 'bank cheque' when drawn on funds at the bank's own account, or a 'cashier's cheque' as it is generally signed by the cashier of the bank. cf. **certified cheque**.

bankruptcy   In general, the condition of being unable to meet one's debts because of a lack of sufficient property or funds. The effect of a failure to have, or be able to obtain, assets to pay one's debts as they fall due. The debtor is known as a 'bankrupt'. Bankruptcy may be 'voluntary', as when a person applies to a court of his own accord; or 'involuntary', as when a creditor seeks to force payment of a debt. cf. **liquidation**. See also **disclaimer, inhibition, insolvency**.

bankruptcy remote corporation (BRC)   See **special purpose corporation**.

bare agency   An **agency** that is not coupled with an interest and is generally terminable at will. cf. **agency coupled with an interest**.

bare expectancy   A right to land that is based on a possibility of inheritance, as distinguished from a **vested interest** that is not dependent on any contingent or uncertain event, and a **contingent interest** that will come into effect on the happening of a particular event.

bare licence(BrE) or **bare license**(AmE)   See **licence**.

bare title   See **naked title**.

bare trust(BrE)   1. A **trust** under which the trustee has no other responsibility or interest in a property other than to hold a nominal or 'paper' title, generally pending its transfer to the *cestui que trust*, or beneficiary, who is of full age and sound mind. A 'bare trust' commonly comes into existence when a beneficiary reaches the age of majority and, being without disability, is able then to require the trustee to deal with the trust property as demanded. Also called a 'naked trust'. cf. **active trust**, **trust for sale**. See also **passive trust**(US), **simple trust**.   2. A **trust** that is created when land is left to one person to be held in trust for another, but with no further instruction, so that the operation of the trust is left to the construction of the law.

bargain   An arrangement or undertaking negotiated between two or more parties by which the parties accept a mutual undertaking; the terms upon which parties propose to enter into contract. "A bargain is an **agreement** to exchange promises or to exchange a promise for a performance or to exchange performances", The American Law Institute, *Restatement Second, Contracts* § 3 (1981). See also **agreement for sale**, **damages**, **earnest money**, **subject to contract**.

bargain and sale   1.(Eng)An ancient method used to convey land. In English law, all transfers by bargain and sale were abolished in 1926. All transfers of land must now be made by **deed of grant** (LPA 1925, s. 51). In the US, a transfer by 'bargain and sale' is still recognized in a few jurisdictions, although to become effective, consideration must have been paid over. See also **bargain and sale deed**(US).   2.(US)A contract for the sale of property (especially personal property)

by which an executory contract is first entered into (the bargain) and then the actual 'sale' is completed. The words 'bargain and sale' are sometimes used to refer to an **executed contract**, as when the contract was made (bargained for) and then the sale is completed or executed.   3.(US)Words that, when used in a deed, are considered in some jurisdictions as sufficient to convey a **fee simple** title. Words such as 'grant, bargain and sell' or 'grant, bargain, sell, and release' have similar effect. Although such words continue to be used, in most jurisdictions they are no longer necessary to convey a fee simple. See also **words of grant**.

bargain and sale deed(US)   1. A **deed** for the sale of land that contains only the minimum essentials of a contract and stipulates the consideration but, unlike a **warranty deed**, contains no covenants of title. The seller implies that he has an interest in the land to be conveyed and has done nothing to impair the title to the land. However, he implies that he is transferring only the interest set out in the deed. A deed of bargain and sale is now rarely used.   2. A deed that effects a **bargain and sale**.

bargain money(US)   Money paid to secure a **bargain**; **earnest money**.

bargain sale(US)   A sale of a property for less than its **fair market value**. Such a sale may create a tax liability for the benefit received by the recipient.

bargainee   The recipient or grantee of a bargain. In particular, the acquirer of property under a **bargain and sale deed**.

bargainor   The grantor of a bargain. In particular, the transferor of property under a **bargain and sale deed**.

barrier fence(Aus)   A fence that is erected as an impediment to noxious animals, especially rabbits, and is declared to be such a fence. The Crown, a rural protection board, or any other person may erect a barrier fence. The rights and obligations for the repair and maintenance vary from State to State. See also **dividing fence, dog fence**.

barring the entail   See **base fee, entailed interest**.

base date or **base period**   1. The point, or period in time, used as a reference in the future; such as in an indexation process, being either the date at which the index is first compiled, or the starting point for assessing an increase in an item relative to an index.   2. The start date of a lease, or construction contract, when used as a reference point for determining a future revision or escalation of the rent, or contract price. See also **base year**.

base estate   An estate in land that is less than a **fee simple** because it comes to an end on the happening of a contingent event. In general, a base fee is any estate that is not assured of lasting forever, i.e. it is a **qualified fee**. It is the uncertainty as to when, or if, the estate will come to an end that makes the estate a base estate and not an **absolute estate**. See also **base fee**.

base fee   1.(Eng)An estate in land that arises when the holder of an **entailed estate**, who is not in possession, or has not obtained the consent of the **protector of the estate**, executes a **disentailing assurance** (i.e. any conveyance or transfer of a fee simple estate), thereby seeking to bar the rights of succession. In that event, the recipient of the estate receives a 'base fee'. "That estate in fee simple into which an estate in tail [entailed estate] is converted where the issues in tail are barred, but persons claiming estates by way of remainder or otherwise are not barred", Fines and Recoveries Act 1833, s. 1. In other words, a base fee would be an absolute estate in fee simple, except that the holder of that estate risks the possibility that the person who is entitled to the immediate **remainder** (or, if he is dead, the person entitled to his estate) may be entitled to regain the fee

simple. A base fee may be enlarged into a fee simple by: (i) the tenant in tail in remainder executing a new disentailing deed, either with the consent of the protector of the protector or after the protectorship has ceased (e.g. after the death of the holder of the life estate) (FRA 1883, ss. 19, 35); (ii) the base fee and the fee simple absolute in remainder being united in the same person, as by the holder of the entailed interest (or anyone to whom he has conveyed his base fee) acquiring the successor's fee simple interest (FRA, s. 39); (iii) by lapse of time (LA 1980, s. 27); or (iv) in certain circumstances, by a gift by will by the holder of the entailed estate, provided he is in possession of the land (LPA 1925, s. 176(1)(3)). See also **determinable fee, qualified fee, strict settlement**. 2.(US)A **fee** interest in land that may last forever, but must come to an end on the occurrence of some event or act specified when the interest is created. 'Base fee' may also be used to refer to a **conditional fee** or a **determinable fee**.

base lands(US)   See **lieu lands**.

base line(US)   1. A line on a map or plan drawn parallel to the equator to show the east-west orientation of property on a government survey of a township. See also **government survey system**. 2. A horizontal survey line that indicates the direction or route of a thoroughfare, such as a highway or railroad.

base map   A map, showing the existing physical pattern of land use, used for superimposing planning proposals or survey information. Usually it shows limited information such as property boundaries, communication routes, etc., and the superimposition is in the form of a transparent overlay.

base period   See **base date**.

base rent   1. The amount of rent payable under a lease that provides for a **percentage rent**. Sometimes called a 'basic rent'. See also **dead rent**. 2. The minimum rent payable under a lease. A term used especially to refer to the rent payable at the start of the lease, being the rent payable before any increase due to **operating expense** escalations. See also **escalation clause**.   **3.** The initial rent payable under a lease that provides for an **indexed rent** and is used as the point of reference for calculating the indexation increases.

base right(Scot)   A subordinate right.

base services(Eng)   See **villeinage**.

base tenure   See **base fee**.

base year(US)   The year fixed in a commercial lease as the reference point for the operation of an **escalation clause**, generally being the start year of the lease. In most commercial leases, an increase in operating expenses or real estate taxes over and above that established at the base year may be recharged to the tenant. Thus, if expenses are $8 per sq. ft. in 2004 (the base year) and $8.50 per sq. ft. in 2005, the tenant pays $0.5 per sq. ft. as expenses in 2004. The amount of expenses in the base year may be referred to as the 'expense stop', being the level above which the expenses are passed through to the tenant. See also **full service lease**.

basement   **1.** The substructure or pedestal of a building. In particular, a part of a building of full storey height that is wholly or substantially below ground level or the finished grade of a building. A basement floor is normally wholly below ground level, but in most building regulations a storey that has more than half its height below ground is considered as a basement. cf. **cellar**. See also **sub-basement, superstructure**.   **2.**(US)"The interior at ground level in a **basement house** or in a building having a basement facade", *Webster's Third New International Dictionary*®, *Unabridged*, ©1993.

basement house(AmE)   A dwelling in which the principal sitting rooms are at least one story above ground level, with the main entrance reached directly from ground level or one story

above ground level and reached by steps. The area of the building at ground level that is normally used for storage or as a garage.

basic capitalization rate(AmE)   See **basic rate**.

basic rate(AmE)   **1.** A term used in the **mortgage-equity capitalization technique** for the capitalization rate that is applied when no allowance is made for mortgage amortization (i.e. for capital repayments), or for equity build-up (i.e. for projected changes in capital value).   **2.** The rate of return on equity, before any allowance is made for the repayment or recapture of capital, and before capital appreciation (or depreciation) is brought into account; as distinguished from the **overall capitalization rate** which allows for capital repayments and equity build-up (or the loss of equity value).   **3.** See **band-of-investment rate**.   **4.** See **safe rate**.

basic rent   See **base rent**.

basis(US)   The cost of a property as used when assessing a liability to tax on a sale or taxable exchange of that property. The ordinary 'basis' is usually the original cost to the taxpayer (which may include assumed liabilities). This cost may then be 'adjusted' by adding the cost of capital improvements (plus permitted carrying costs and assessments) and deducting any allowed or allowable depreciation (26 USC, Internal Revenue Code, §§ 1011, 1012). In addition, in the case of a residence, this basis is reduced by any untaxed gain that has been carried over from the sale of a former residence. Capital gains tax is payable on the difference between the net proceeds of sale (or **adjusted sale price**), taking account of any property received in exchange, and the 'adjusted basis'. See also **book value**.

basis point   One hundredth of a point, i.e. 1/100 of one per cent. An increase in an interest rate from 7% to 7.5% is an increase of 50 basis points. See also **point**.

batable land or **batable ground**   Land that is the subject of a dispute or debate as to its true ownership, especially land on the border of two states or nations.

batture   Deposits of sand, silt, stone or rock that are mixed together and washed up along the sides of a river under the water. This material when exposed at low tide becomes part of the bank of the river. The material is **alluvion**, when it rises above the surface of the river it is known as 'batture land' and may come to form part of the bank or levee of the river. A term used especially for part of the bed of the Mississippi river that is uncovered at low tide but is covered by water at high tide.

bazaar store   See variety store.

beach   An area of land over which the sea flows between ordinary high and low water marks. In this technical sense, a beach comprises, or is a part of, the **shore**, or is more akin to the **foreshore** than the hinterland (*Tito v Waddell (No. 2)* [1977] Ch 106; Am.Jur.2d., Waters, § 375, p. 813). In more common usage, the shore is an area, usually of sand, shingle or pebbles, that is used for bathing, boating and leisure activities connected with the ocean or sea and in that respect is predominately above the ordinary high-water mark (although for part of the time it will extend to the low water mark) and is defined or limited to the rear by a natural boundary or sea wall beyond which is the 'upland'.

bearing   An angle, between 0° and 90° measured in a horizontal plane that fixes the course of a line in relation to true north or south.

bed   A flat or level surface. A flat piece of ground on which anything lies. A layer or stratum. A horizontal course of a distinct form or material. The bottom of a lake, sea or **watercourse**; especially the land that is covered by water in its ordinary low stage. The bed does not extend to the soil along the edge of the river where grasses, shrubs and trees usually grow. See also **littoral land, shore, water rights**.

bedroom community   A residential district that offers little industrial or social life. In particular, an area where the residents sleep and conduct personal activities, but from which the majority of the working population commute to places of employment or business and to find cultural activity. Also called a 'dormitory suburb' or 'dormitory town'. See also **suburb**.

bedsitting room or **bedsitter**(BrE)   A flat or **apartment** that consists of one room that serves as both a sitting room and bedroom.

before-and-after measure(US)   See before-and-after method.

before-and-after method   A means of determining the increase or deterioration in the value of a parcel of land (or a building); especially as used to ascertain the loss or damage caused by the actions of a public authority as when part of an owner's land is acquired, work is carried out on adjoining land, or a partial interest (e.g. an easement) is acquired by the authority. The land is valued before and after the change and the difference represents the loss or gain to the landowner. This method is used in particular when assessing a compensatable loss (or a taxable gain) in the value of land.

In the US, when part of an owner's land is taken by eminent domain, **just compensation** is normally assessed on the basis of the 'before and after' method. In federal cases, this method is sometimes called the 'federal rule', on the basis that the Fifth Amendment to the Constitution only provides for just compensation when land is "taken"; as distinguished from the 'state rule' which applies when the state legislation provides that just compensation is payable when land is 'damaged' by the actions of a state. The before-and-after method may also be applied to ascertain whether a regulatory action amounts to a 'taking', even though "such a comparison is by no means conclusive", Keystone Coal Associates v. DeBenedictus, 480 US 470, 107 S Ct 1232, 94 L Ed 472, 492 (1987). This method is sometimes called the 'before-and-after measure'.

In the UK, the 'before-and-after method' of valuation is the most commonly used method for assessing **compensation for injurious affection** or **compensation for severance**. See also **severance damages**(US).

before-and-after rule(AmE)   See **before-and-after method**.

before-tax cash flow   See **cash flow**.

before-tax income   See **income**.

below par   At a price that is less than the face or nominal value, or below the **par value**. A discounted price.

belt highway(AmE)   An urban by-pass or a highway that encircles a city.

bench mark or **bench-mark**   An official mark on a fixed or permanent object (usually in the form of a brass plaque or metal post set into the sidewalk or the base of a major building) indicating the level of the ground relative to a given base level, usually mean sea level, or an official **datum** level. In particular, a surveyor's mark cut into rock, or similar material, as a reference point in **topographical surveying**. See also **geodetic surveying**.

benefice   See **ecclesiastical benefice**.

beneficial enjoyment   Enjoyment of the benefits that real property affords a person in his own right, i.e. enjoyment as a **beneficiary** rather than as a trustee for another. The benefit to be enjoyed from owning property, without necessarily having legal title. See also **beneficial owner**, **benefit**.

beneficial estate   An **estate** in land that is held by someone who has the right to the benefits and profits, but the right to possession does not arise until a future date. A beneficial estate is usually held in **trust** and the beneficiary may have a present or future right to receive the income that is derived therefrom. See **beneficial interest, use**.

beneficial interest   1. An interest in property that is held by a person for his own use, advantage or benefit; as opposed to an interest held for the use or benefit of another, e.g. as by a trustee. The right to the enjoyment of property where one party holds the legal title and the benefit of use is held by another. The interest held by a **beneficiary** for whom property is held in **trust**. See also **beneficial owner**, **equitable interest**.   2.(US)An interest in a real estate investment trust.   3. An interest that arises as a result of an insurance policy and is available to the insured.   4. An interest of value, worth, advantage or use. A term that is used especially in relation to a liability for tax. See also **bundle of rights theory**. 5.(US)An interest in a tract of government-owned land held by someone who has completed all the formalities required to obtain ownership, i.e. someone who is entitled to a **patent** but has not yet had title transferred to him.

beneficial occupation(Eng)   See **rateable occupation**.

beneficial owner   1. One who has the enjoyment and benefit of **ownership**, but not necessarily possession or title. When a property is held in trust, the beneficial owner is the person entitled to the financial rights and other benefits from the property itself, i.e. the **beneficiary**, rather than the trustee.

In English law, a person who conveys land for valuable **consideration**, and is stated to be a "beneficial owner", gives certain **implied covenants** that are set down by statute (LPA 1925, s. 76, Sch. 2, Part I). An owner of a legal estate in land who does not profess to be the beneficial owner implies only that he has not himself created any encumbrance that he has not expressly declared to the purchaser. See also **equitable interest**, **equitable owner**.   2.(Eng)A mortgagor who has been granted a mortgage in the form of a **charge by way of a legal mortgage**.

beneficial use   1. The right to the **use** and **enjoyment** of the benefit and profit arising from property, as distinguished from a mere right of possession or physical occupation. A right to use property that is granted to one person when another holds the legal title. See also **beneficial interest, trust**.   2.^(Eng)See **reasonably beneficial use**.   3.^(US)The right to use water; a right that is **appurtenant** to the ownership of land. See also **riparian rights**.   4. In **water rights**, in the arid and semi-arid states west of the one-hundredth meridian, a right to appropriate water based on a prior or customary use, provided that the water taken is applied to a preferred use.

beneficiary   1. A person for whom a property is held in **trust**. One who is entitled to property for his own benefit and not as a **trustee**. A beneficiary includes any person who has a right to the use or benefit of property, whether as a holder of a present or future interest, or a vested or contingent interest. In English law, in connection with a **trust of land**, a beneficiary is any person who has an interest in property subject to the trust, including a trustee or personal representative who holds such an interest in his own right (Trusts of Land and Appointment of Trustees Act 1996, s. 22). See also **beneficial owner**.   2. A person who is named in a **will** to receive property in accordance with its provisions. If a beneficiary receives real property he is called a 'devisee', and if he receives personal property, a 'legatee'.   3. A person who is in possession of an **ecclesiastical benefice**.   4. The person named in an insurance policy as the one who will receive any proceeds or benefits that may be paid out under the provisions of the policy.   5.^(US)A lender who has obtained a right to a property that is being held as security under a **deed of trust**.   6.^(US)One who is entitled to the use and profits from a property that is held under a **deed in trust**.

beneficiary statement^(US)   See **reduction certificate**.

benefit   1. An advantage or gain. A natural or financial advantage received without need of restitution; aid or assistance received without obligation. In relation to real property, a benefit may be considered as an enhancement of value, especially when arising from public works or improvements. See also **beneficial enjoyment, benefits**^(US), **betterment, consideration, profit, scheme of development**.   2. An advantage obtained from having a right or restriction over adjoining land, especially an advantage that arises from the enjoyment of an **easement, restrictive covenant**, or **profit à prendre**. See also **covenant running with the land**.

benefit-cost analysis   See **cost-benefit analysis**.

benefited tenement^(US)   See **dominant tenement**.

benefits^(US)   An advantage or increase in the value of land that accrues to the owner as a result of the activity of an authority that acquires part of an owner's land by the exercise of the power of **eminent domain**. In assessing the amount of compensation payable for the acquisition of the land, the claimant should be compensated for "the loss caused to him by the appropriation – and this involves consideration of damages on the one hand and of benefits on the other", Aaronson v. United States, 79 F.2d 139, 140 (1935). See also **consequential damages, set-off, severance damages**.

benigne faciendæ sunt interpretationes chartarum, ut res magis valeat quam pereat^(Lat)   Literal interpretations should be given to an instrument, so that the purpose may stand rather than fall. See also **ambiguity**, *contra proferentem*, **exception**.

bequeath   See **bequest**.

bequest or **bequeath**   A transfer of property by **will**. A gift by testamentary disposition. In particular, a transfer of **personal property** by will.

'Bequest', and the verb 'bequeath', is sometimes used when referring to real property in a will, but **devise** is the correct word for that purpose. However, if the context clearly indicates that the intention is to make a testamentary gift of real estate, and the word 'bequeath' is used, the word is considered as synonymous with devise and is sufficient to pass real and personal property. See also **legacy**.

best and highest use   See **highest and best use**.

best bid   1. The highest bid at a sale by **auction**. 2. The lowest price submitted in response to a request for bids for construction work or the provision of services.

best rent   The highest **rent** at which a property might reasonably be expected to let. A term used in English statutes to refer (among other conditions) to the rent at which a mortgagor in possession may grant a lease that will be binding on the mortgagee. Such a rent is not defined, except as that which can "reasonably" be obtained "regard being had to the circumstances of the case" and one that is to be obtained "without taking a fine", LPA 1925, s. 99(6). See also **rack rent**.

betterment   1. An **enhancement** in the overall value of land, or buildings thereon, brought about by positive changes, such as road improvements, the provision of public services, the grant of consent for a new form of development, a change of use, etc., and by the restrictions imposed on the use or development of other land; or by the prospect or expectation of such changes or restrictions.
Betterment of land, especially when realised, is considered an appropriate subject for taxation as, in many cases, it is brought about by the actions, or at the expense, of the community. As a corollary, **compensation** may be paid for depreciation in the value of an individual's land when it is brought about by an action for the betterment of the community, e.g. the construction of a new airport or sewage works. See also **planning gain**(Eng), **recoupment, set-off, special suitability or adaptability**(Eng)**, windfalls and wipeouts**.   2. An increase in the value of a property produced by expenditure of time or money, especially when that increase is brought about by a physical **improvement** or alteration to the property and not merely as a result of repair. See also **mistaken improver**.   3. In insurance, an improvement in the value of a property following its reinstatement, as a better or more modern equivalent, after damage or destruction. See also **indemnity**.

betterment acts(US)   See **mistaken improver**.

biannual   Occurring twice a **year** or semi-annually. cf. **biennial**. See also **half a year**.

bid   1. An **offer** to enter into a contract, especially when made by a willing buyer. An offer of a specified sum of money made by a prospective purchaser of a property, especially at an **auction** or a foreclosure or judicial sale. A bid is a particular mode of offer, it is anticipatory, and aspires for acceptance; "one *bids* with the hope that one's offer will be accepted", George Crabb, *Crabb's English Synonyms*. 1816. Reprint, London: Routledge, 1982. 'Bid' is used especially in commerce to refer to an offer to conduct or to enter into business. See also **acceptance, best bid**.   2. The price submitted by a contractor or supplier in response to a request for a **tender** for work. A bid does not create any form of contract until accepted. See also **quotation**.

bid bond   1. A **bond**, or form of **surety**, provided on behalf of a bidder for a building contract, especially for the construction of public improvements, to guarantee that the bidder will enter into a building contract if his bid is accepted. Also called a 'proposal bond' or, if the requirement is merely to pay a deposit to show the seriousness of the bid, a 'bid security'.   2. A bond given by a contractor, in conjunction with a bid to carry out building works, by which the contractor agrees to pay damages if he is awarded the contract but fails to enter into the contract or fails to provide the requisite **performance bond**. The commitment by the contractor may take the form of a bond issued by a bank or insurance company, or may be in the form of a cash deposit.

bid in   See **buy in**.

bid price   The price at which a prospective buyer is prepared to acquire a property. A term used especially with reference to a security or commodity.

bid security(AmE)   See **bid bond**.

bidder   A person who makes a **bid**. One who makes an offer to buy at a stated price, especially at an auction. See also **puffer**.

bidding agreement   An arrangement by which a group of potential bidders agree that only one of them will put forward bids at a sale by **auction**, in order that the members of the group can acquire a property at a lower price than would prevail if there were truly competitive bidding by the members. If the property is acquired successfully, then either the spoils are divided between those parties to the agreement on a predetermined basis, or a second auction is held with only the parties to the agreement present and any profit resulting from that sale is divided amongst the group in an agreed proportion. Such an arrangement is generally illegal or may make the sale void. Also called a 'knock-out agreement'. See also **chilling a sale**, **mock auction**.

biennial   Occurring or appearing once every two years; existing or lasting for two years (the latter meaning is the less common, except in the sense of an ability to regenerate every two years). cf. **biannual**.

bilateral contract   A term originating from the civil law for a **contract** that creates a reciprocal obligation – a **promise** exchanged for a promise, i.e. one where each party has rights and obligations both as promisor and promisee. For example, a

contract of sale where one party undertakes to deliver property and the other to pay over money or a brokerage contract by which the broker undertakes to seek a suitable purchaser for a property and the principal undertakes to pay a commission for the successful resulting sale. Most business contacts are bilateral contracts. Also called a 'synallagmatic contract' or, in Louisiana, a 'commutative contract'. cf. **unilateral contract**.

bi-level house(AmE)   See **split-level house**.

bill   A document that evidences either a transaction in personal property or an agreement to pay money; an account rendered for goods sold, services provided, or work done. See also **bill of exchange**, **note**.

bill for specific performance(US)   A complaint requesting someone to perform the duties required of them under a court order for **specific performance**.

bill of exchange   A written demand by which one party requires another to pay a stipulated sum of money to a third party on demand or at a fixed or determinable future date. The demand may require the payment to be made to a specified party or to the bearer of the bill. The person making the order is called the drawer, the person to whom it is addressed the drawee, and the person to whom payment is made the payee. A valid bill normally requires a date, a clearly specified value, a place to be specified where it is drawn or payable and must be signed by the drawer. The term bill of exchange may be used synonymously with 'draft', although bill of exchange is more commonly used in connection with foreign transactions and the 'draft' is used in connection with domestic transactions. See also **bank draft**, **check**(AmE)/**cheque**(BrE), **discount**, **endorsement**, **negotiable instrument**.

bill of quantities(BrE)   A detailed schedule setting out the quantity of materials required for each trade and describing the constituent parts of the work to be undertaken by a building contractor. A document that is used essentially to arrive at the price for a building or construction contract, especially one that is to be based on competitive tenders, and normally forms part of that contract. See also **abstracting, billing, quantity surveying**(BrE)**, schedule of quantities**(AmE)**, taking-off**.

bill of sale   A written instrument evidencing the transfer of the ownership of personal property, usually in exchange for monetary consideration. cf. **receipt**. See also **chattel mortgage, conditional sale, sale**.

bill of specific performance(US)   See **specific performance**.

bill of variations(BrE)   A schedule of all the variations made during the course of a building contract setting out details of changes in the quality or quantity of any items altered or modified and the resultant price variation. See also **variation**.

billboard   A panel, board, fence or similar structure on which notices or advertisements are posted or printed; especially a large panel mounted near the highway or a public place to carry outdoor advertisements.

In the US, the display of billboards and other signs may be regulated in the interests of safety or health. Aesthetic considerations alone are not adequate grounds for the exercise of **police power** to control outdoor advertisements. However, billboards may be regulated to ensure safety on the highway, to prevent accumulation of trash, to preserve the benefits of an area for tourists, to protect scenic beauty or historic sites, or to maintain the natural features of a parkland; but, in most jurisdictions, not solely to please the aesthetic considerations of the municipal authority. See also **advertisement, aesthetic**.

billing(BrE)   The writing up of a **bill of quantities**, i.e. copying out the quantities and describing in detail the work required for a building contract. Billing is carried out after the process of **abstracting**; it divides the required work into its related constituent parts and is used then to price the building contract.

binder   1. A written statement of the principal terms of an agreement. In particular, a statement of the terms of an agreement for sale as prepared by a broker and executed by the parties to the agreement. A receipt for the payment of earnest money or a deposit may also be termed a 'binder', which in itself constitutes a simple, but 'binding', form of contract. Thus, a binder represents the right to buy property that may be bought and sold as with an option agreement. See also **conditional contract, open contract**.   2.(US)A written acknowledgment that an insurance policy has come into existence, issued when the formal policy cannot be immediately submitted to the insured. The binder sets out the principal terms of the policy and a summary of the risks covered (although it may be subject to the verification of certain details such as the value or condition of the property covered). The insurance policy may still be rejected after the binder is issued if the risk is not as originally represented to the insurer. Also called, especially in the UK, a **cover note**. 3.(US)A summary of the title to a property issued before the grant of a **title insurance policy**. Usually a 'title binder' is only valid for a short period of time and excludes any liens or encumbrances that come into effect after the date of issue.

bird-dog   1. A person who acts as a **middleman** in a transaction, especially someone who merely seeks out or locates prospects for business. Generally, a 'bird-dog' does not take an active part in seeing transactions through to completion.   2. A **commission** paid to a middleman.

blacklist   A list of firms or individuals to be avoided, discriminated against, or with whom business should not be conducted. See also **boycott, void contract**.

blanket deed of trust(US)   See **blanket mortgage**.

blanket insurance   Insurance that covers all the properties specified in the insurance policy, or a number of specified risks, up to an agreed limit. The policy has the advantage that the terms and conditions are standardised, except where specifically varied by a schedule or a rider to the policy.

blanket lien or **blanket mortgage**   A lien or **mortgage** secured on two or more properties. A form of mortgage that may be used to finance the development of building lots or a condominium so that, as individual lots or units, are sold they are released from the mortgage. In the US, where the use of blanket mortgages is more common than in the UK, a **deed of trust** secured on two or more properties, or all the assets or properties of a debtor, may be referred to as a blanket mortgage or a 'blanket trust deed'. Also called a 'bulk mortgage', or a 'general mortgage' when it is subordinate to one or more other mortgages. See also **after-acquired clause**, **consolidation of mortgages**, **floating charge**, **partial release clause**.

blanket policy   See **blanket insurance**.

blanket trust deed   See **blanket mortgage**.

blended rate(AmE)   1. See **band-of-investment capitalization rate**.   2. See **wraparound mortgage**.

blight   1. A change in the economic or social conditions of a property, area or neighbourhood. In particular, a change in an area that results in a significantly reduced level of prosperity or economic activity. Blight may arise from an increase in noise, congestion, crime, disease, etc. It may also result from the introduction of non-conforming or undesirable uses into an area. cf. **betterment**. See also **derelict land**, **development area**, **slum**.   2.(BrE)A condition, factor or

influence that causes decay and stultifies growth. An external factor that causes a reduction or decline in real property values, especially when the reduction is brought about by local or central government proposals to carry out building work, such as the construction of a new highway that will affect directly the property or the surrounding area, or a proposal to compulsorily purchase land. Blight may also arise from planning proposals, such as the coming into effect of a **development plan**, when it is generally called 'planning blight'. See also **blight notice, blighted land, compulsory purchase compensation, condemnation blight**(US).

blight notice(Eng)   A notice that may be served on an appropriate authority by an owner-occupier of 'blighted land' when that land has become hard or impossible to sell, except at a substantially reduced price (TCPA 1990, ss. 149-171, Sch. 13). The land must be 'blighted' by one of the statutorily defined circumstances and not merely be affected within the general sense of the word. The owner of the land may also have to comply with various statutory conditions, such as having made efforts to sell the property before serving the notice. A blight notice may be distinguished from a purchase notice, as the latter may be served following an adverse planning decision (generally a refusal or conditional grant of planning permission) while the former arises from positive and adverse planning proposals. See also **compulsory purchase compensation, inverse condemnation**(US).

blighted area   An area of a town or city that has become unsightly and of sufficiently reduced economic value as to warrant clearance and rebuilding. An area, usually in a city, that is in transition from a state of relative civic health to the state of being a **slum**. In particular, an area that is considered substandard and in need of **urban renewal** or redevelopment, even though not all the buildings in the area may be substandard. See also **slum clearance**.

blighted land(Eng)   Land that is affected by one of 23 categories of 'planning proposals' as set out in the TCPA 1990, Sch. 13. An owner-occupier of such land may be entitled to serve a **blight notice** on the authority that has made such proposals requiring that authority to purchase the land.

blind-pool offering(US)   An arrangement by which money is raised initially from a number of investors (i.e. the investors put their 'stakes' into a pool) and then those funds are invested in property. The investors do not know which properties will be acquired when making their commitment to the funding. Normally the investors appoint a **general partner** who is given full discretion to acquire properties on their behalf. This arrangement is illegal in certain states (notably New York), where only a **specified-property offering** is permitted. Sometimes called a 'non-specified property offering'. See also **open-end fund**.

block   **1.** An area in a town or city, between two sets of intersecting streets or avenues. A space in a city that is usually rectangular, enclosed by streets, and used for or intended for use as an area for building. Also, the distance along one side of this area. In the US, where used as a measurement of distance, a block was considered to be about 300 feet. See also **lot and block system**(US).   **2.** An integrated set of buildings, or a large building that contains a number of smaller units. A group of terrace or row houses. A large building, or building complex, especially a commercial building that has been or is capable of subdivision into a number of units for separate use and occupation. See also **block of flats**(BrE).   **3.** A sector of a **neighbourhood**.

block of flats(BrE)   A building that incorporates a large number of residential units or flats that are occupied, or are intended to be occupied, separately, but with common facilities, such as an entrance hall, lift, staircase, parking, etc. See also **apartment house**(AmE), **flat**.

block-income approach   See **term and reversion method**.

block plan   A small-scale plan that shows, in broad outline, an existing or proposed building or buildings, or a part of a neighbourhood.

block policy   See **blanket insurance**.

blockbusting(US)   A method of deflating property values by introducing neighbors of a different race or class, or creating or spreading rumors to play on prejudices. The properties are then bought at a reduced price with the intention that they will be resold later at a profit when the prejudice is either removed or accepted by the newcomers. An illegal practice under the Fair Housing Act, Title VIII of the Civil Rights Act of 1968 (42 USC § 3604).

blot on title   See **cloud on title**.

blue chip   A valuable asset. An investment, a company, or shares in a company, of the highest financial standing, especially a company that has a long established record of stable growth and profit, good management and consistent dividends. Derived from the colour of the highest-value poker chip. See also **triple A rating**.

blue-sky laws(US)   State laws passed to protect the public against fraud in the sale of securities. Statutes that provide for the regulation and supervision of investment companies and are intended to prevent the sale of fly-by-night concerns and other fraudulent practices. These laws particularly relate to stocks, bonds, debentures and similar instruments and, in most states that have adopted such laws, to mortgages. 'Blue-sky laws' may also require that a lender set out details of the terms of a proposed mortgage, in order to ensure that the mortgagor is fully aware of the conditions of the commitments he is entering into, especially the **effective rate of interest** being charged. In some states such laws also prohibit the making of a **blind-pool offering** to the public. See also **real property security**.

board   The provision of daily meals, usually for

reward; especially the provision of meals in an inn, hotel, lodging or boarding house. Without qualification 'board' means the provision of sufficient meals for a day; but may be qualified as the provision of one main meal a day (half board), or two main meals (full board), in either case including breakfast. 'Board' may also be used to refer to the provision of sleeping accommodation, as well as the provision of meals; although that is more strictly **board and lodging**.

In English law, when deciding whether a tenancy is precluded from being a **protected tenancy**, **assured tenancy**, or **restricted contract**, 'board' generally means a provision by the landlord of such food as would ordinarily be consumed at daily meals and would be obtained and prepared by the tenant himself, if it were not provided by somebody else.

board and lodging   The provision for compensation of some or all meals and also sleeping accommodation, generally as a combined package. See **board, boarding house, lodging**.

board of adjustment(US)   An administrative body appointed by the local municipality to hear zoning appeals from decisions of the local zoning administration. Such appeals may be against a refusal to grant a variation to a **zoning ordinance**; to grant a zoning exception; or to agree to a request for a conditional or **special-use permit**. A board of adjustment also interprets the local zoning ordinances and maps. In some states called a 'board of zoning appeal', 'board of review', 'board of standards and appeals', 'zoning board of appeals' or sometimes an 'adjustment board'. See also **zoning variance**.

board of appeals(US)   A non-judicial authority that is responsible for hearing appeals from decisions of an administrative body or tribunal. See **board of adjustment, board of equalization, board of review**.

board of equalization(US)   A quasi-judicial body whose function is to consider the **assessed value** of individual properties and the general level of assessed values in a county or other tax district, in order to make all assessments as equal and fair as practicable In particular, the board adjusts the assessed value of properties to bring value into line with a common or uniform base to ensure that one county or district does not set its level of values low in order to reduce its tax contributions to the state or another tax district or to avoid discrimination between different classes of property. Also called an 'equalization board'.

board of review(US)   A board authorized to hear cases of error or improper assessments and valuations of real estate as submitted by individual property owners. In some jurisdictions, such a body may be called a 'board of tax review' or may be referred to as an 'assessment appeal board'. See also **board of equalization**.

board of zoning appeals(US)   See **board of adjustment**.

boarding house   1. A building to which guests may come to obtain meals, lodging, and sometimes entertainment, at a cheap or moderate price. A place where a guest may seek rest and refreshment (**board**) for the night, but not somewhere that can be classified as an **inn** or **hotel**. cf. **apartment hotel**. See also **lodging house**.   2. A house, or a small hotel, which provides board and lodging for holiday purposes.

boatel(AmE)   A building that is an integral part of a marina and is used to provide accommodation and services similar to those provided in an **hotel**.

bodily heirs   See **heirs of the body**.

boiler plate or **boiler-plate language**(AmE)   A fixed or standardized language, or form of wording, that is common to a particular form of agreement or contract. For example, the common language used in a **standard-form contract** or similar documents. Boiler plate may also refer to any clause in a document that is considered standard to the form of transaction. See also **adhesion contract, usual covenant.**

bona fide(Lat) 'In good faith'. Without intention to deceive or defraud. Genuinely and with honesty. Originally the term was used adverbially, meaning in good faith, but *bona fide* is now commonly used adjectivally as in a '*bona fide* contract'. The noun (which is singular) is *bona fides*. cf. *mala fide*. See also *bona fide* **purchaser, fraud, utmost good faith.**

bona fide **purchaser** (BFP)   One who acquires land (or an interest in land) in **good faith** and, in particular, one who also pays 'valuable' **consideration** and does not have **notice**.

In English common law, a 'bona fide purchaser for value of a **legal estate** without **notice**' acquires a legal estate to unregistered land free of any equitable claims against the land – provided he has acted genuinely, honestly and without fraud; has no notice (express, constructive or imputed) that there is any third party who has a right or interest in the land; and has paid value (which means a sum of money, money's worth – land, chattels, stocks or shares – or marriage, but not necessarily the market value) for the land. A *bona fide* purchaser acquires the most absolute estate in land (a 'legal estate') and can enforce his right against the whole world. In other words, a party who (a) purchases a legal estate in land; (b) pays some consideration (which may even be nominal (*Midland Bank Trust Co Ltd v Green* [1981] AC 513, 531-2, [1981] All ER 153 (HL)); and (c) makes reasonable and genuine enquiries to establish the existence of those interests that are likely to bind him (including inspecting the property, searching for matters of which he would have constructive notice, e.g. registered land charges, and taking steps to be informed of matters which have come to the attention of his agent or solicitor), is not bound by any **equitable interest** that affects the land and of which he has not become aware. In this context, a **purchaser** includes a **mortgagee**, as well as a **lessee**. In the US, sometimes called an 'innocent purchaser'. See also **bill of exchange, land charge**(Eng), **overreachable interest**(Eng).

bona fidei emptor(Lat)   A '*bona fide* purchaser'.

bona vacantia   Personal property that has no apparent owner. Unclaimed goods or personalty. In common law, when a person dies intestate and without an heir, or there is no claimant following a liquidation, the estate becomes *bona vacantia*. See also *res nullius*.

bond   **1.** A formal promise binding one person (an obligor) to pay a specified sum of money to another (an obligee) on a specified date or during a specified period of time. Written evidence of a debt, especially when made by a **deed** (which is itself called a bond or, sometimes, an **obligation**). A contract under seal acknowledging a present or future debt. A certificate or instrument of indebtedness issued by a company or government by which the issuer promises to pay a specified amount of interest for a stipulated duration and to repay the principal debt at the expiration date. Alternatively, the bond may provide for the repayment of debt in the form of a series of payments through the duration of the loan. Bonds may be classified according to the nature of the security; the method of repayment of the debt; the issuing party; or their purposes. For example, a 'development bond' – issued to finance the development of property, or a 'mortgage bond' – secured on specified property. The term 'bond' is commonly used to refer to a long-term debt of a company, a **debenture**. It may also be used in contrast to a certificate of ownership, a **share** or **stock**. Most bonds are conditional, i.e. they come to an end on the happening of a given condition such as the performance of an obligation or repayment of a debt. See also **bid bond, collateral mortgage bond, completion bond, deep discount bond, deposit, first and general mortgage bond, interest-only bond, junk bond, maintenance bond, mortgage-backed obligation, obligation**

bond, payment bond, performance bond, promissory note, property bond(BrE).   **2.** An insurance policy that provides that the insurer will become a surety for a specified financial loss. Also called an 'indemnity bond'. See also **indemnity insurance**.

bond by tenant(NZ)   A sum of money payable or paid by a tenant under security for the observation or performance of the obligations of the tenant. Payment of such sums is strictly controlled by statute as to the amount and the obligations of the landlord to return the payment at the end of the lease (Residential Tenancies Act 1986, ss. 18-22 (NZ)). See also **deposit**, **security deposit**.

bond for deed(US)   See **contract for deed**.

bond for title(US)   **1.** See **contract for deed**. **2.** A **bond** granted to indemnify a purchaser against a defect of title. For example, an agreement to pay a fixed sum of money in the event that a pending suit does not grant certain rights to a purchaser of land. See also **title insurance**.

bond net lease(AmE)   See **triple net lease**.

bonus(US)   A lump sum payment made under an **oil and gas lease** merely for the right to enter into the lease and independent of any other rental or royalty payment. Such a payment is usually a cash obligation, but it may take the form of an oil or royalty bonus. cf. **delay rental**.

bonus clause   **1.** A clause in a building contract that provides for the payment of a bonus to the contractor if work is completed in its entirety on, or before, a specified date. The bonus may be a fixed sum, a percentage of the contract price, or paid at a given rate per day, per week or per month. cf. **penalty clause**. **2.**(US)A clause in a mortgage deed, or deed of trust, that provides for a 'bonus' to be paid to the borrower in the event that the loan is repaid, in whole or in part, before the due date.

bonus deposit(US)   A payment given by a tenant to a landlord in consideration for the grant of a lease. See also **deposit**, **key money**.

bonus zoning(US)   See **incentive zoning**.

book cost   See **book value**.

book rate of return (BRR)   See **average annual return**.

book value   **1.** The value of an asset as shown in a book of accounts or balance sheet. Usually the original cost of the asset, plus the cost of any additions or improvements, less any allowance made for depreciation. The book value may be adjusted to take account of any revaluation of the asset (in the US, also called 'adjusted value' or the 'adjusted book value'). A book value before any allowance for depreciation or revaluation may be referred to as the book cost and after such an allowance as the 'net book cost' or 'net book value'; although after such an adjustment it is no longer a true cost. cf. **asset value**. See also **basis**, **equity**, **going-concern value**.   **2.** The difference between the value of the total assets (excluding depreciation or amortisation) and the total liabilities of a business or enterprise, as shown in the balance sheet or financial statement. A book value of a corporation is generally expressed as a price per share of common stock, although it may not be equivalent to the price of the shareholder's stock as quoted on a stock market. Also called the 'net book value'.

boom   A period when economic activity is accelerating or expanding rapidly. The stage when an economy nears the peak of the business **cycle**. In the real estate market, during a boom demand exceeds supply, rents and capital values rise, and investment and development activity increases. The likely consequence is that property values and new building work outstrip the level that can be sustained for any length of time, financing costs exceed the income that can sustain such costs, demand for accommodation becomes inadequate to absorb the available supply, confidence wanes and the brakes are applied to the detriment of the unwary.

boosey pasture(Eng)   Literally, pasturing on hay. A right to leave cattle on pasture land to enable them to feed on the past year's hay or straw, after the expiration of an agricultural licence or tenancy.

boot(US)   **1.** Additional cash, or other consideration, paid over to make up the difference between the values of two exchanged properties, especially when paid as part of a 'tax-free exchange'. Boot may take the form of securities, release of a mortgage obligation, or any form of property, provided it is of a different kind from the property being exchanged. In particular, liquid assets or 'cash to boot' paid as part of an exchange of shares under a corporate reorganization; a mere exchange of stock or security not being a recognizable tax loss or gain (26 USC, Internal Revenue Code, § 354(a)(1)).   **2. See bote.**

border   An 'outer edge' or 'limit'. A defined edge. In particular, a strip or tract of land that demarcates a frontier, especially between two countries. A border is an outer edge and may be distinguished from a **boundary** that serves to indicate a limit of a property. "The *border* is the outer edge or tract of land that runs along a country as the borders of England and Scotland ... The boundary is that which bounds or limits, as the boundaries of countries or provinces ... The term *border* may be extended in its application to any space, and boundary to any limit", George Crabb, *Crabb's English Synonyms*. 1816. Reprint, London: Routledge, 1982.

bote(Eng)   A profit or advantage, or something given as compensation; the term being a progenitor of **boot.**

bottle shop(Aus)   "Premises whose main business is to sell packaged liquor for consumption off the premises", Australian Property Institute and Property Council for Australia, *Glossary of Property Terms* (2000). See also **licensed premises.**

bottom land(AmE)   Land situated near a river or lake and that is liable to flooding, but not the bed of a river.

bound   A landmark. A limit or boundary. See also **bounds**, **metes and bounds system**(US).

boundary   The perimeter of a parcel of land. In particular, a dividing line (real or imaginary) that represents the legal demarcation between two **contiguous** parcels of land. Something that indicates the limit of two adjoining properties. A land boundary that starts 'from' a particular object or monument excludes that item, unless the context or custom indicates to the contrary. cf. **border**. See also **bounds**, **boundary line**.

boundary line   A line that **bounds** or limits. A line that demarcates the **boundary** of a space or area. An imaginary or natural line that divides, or marks the limit of, two **contiguous** parcels of land. A boundary line may be delineated horizontally, vertically or in any direction that parties choose to divide land (or buildings). In the US, generally called a 'lot line' where it is an imaginary limit of ownership. See also **abuttal**, *ad medium filum*, *ad medium filum aquæ*, **description**, **enclosure**, **encroachment**, **fence**, **foreshore**, **government survey system**(US), **hedge and ditch presumption**(Eng), **march**, **metes and bounds system**(US), **mistake**, **party wall**, **rectification**, **tree**, **trespass**.

Anstey, John. *Boundary Disputes and How to Resolve Them.* 2nd ed. London: RICS Books, 1998.

Barlow, John R., and Donald M. VonCannon. *The Legal Elements of Boundaries and Adjacent Properties.* Charlottesville, VA: Lexis Publishing, 1997.

Cole, G. M. *Water Boundaries.* New York: Wiley, 1997.

Hanbury, William. *Boundary Disputes.* Welwyn Garden City: EMIS Professional Publishing, 2003.

Robillard, Walter G. and Donald A. Wilson. *Brown's Boundary Control and Legal Principles.* 5th ed. New York: Wiley, 2003.

Sara, Colin. *Boundaries & Easements.* 2nd ed. London: Sweet & Maxwell, 1996.

boundary point   A point that marks the extremity of a **boundary line**. See also **monument**.

bounds   The external limiting lines of a space. The natural or predetermined limits of a part of the earth. "*Bounds* and **boundary**, from the verb *bound*, signify the line which sets the *bound* or marks the extent of which any spot of ground reaches. *Bounds* is employed to designate the whole space, including the outer limit that confines: *boundary* comprehends only this outer line. *Bounds* are made for local purposes; … *Bounds* are temporary and changeable; *boundaries* are permanent and fixed: … We speak of setting *bounds* or keeping within *bounds*, but to know a *boundary*", George Crabb, *Crabb's English Synonyms*. 1816. Reprint, London: Routledge, 1982. See also **close**, **metes and bounds system**[US].

bow-tie loan   A loan that provides for the cash payments of interest, the **pay rate**, to be lower than the actual rate of interest charged on the loan. The difference is accrued and added to the principal. The reduced rate of cash payment is generally limited to the early years of the loan and in some cases the pay rate may increase during the later years to compensate for the reduced rate of loan amortisation.

bracketing[AmE]   An appraisal technique whereby comparable sales values are grouped together into those that probably have a higher value than the subject property and those that probably have a lower value. These groups of values may then be used to establish a range within which the value will lie.

breach of condition   See **condition**.

breach of condition notice (BCN)[Eng]   A notice served in respect of a breach of a **planning condition** (or limitation) requiring the person responsible for that breach to comply with the condition, or conditions, as specified in the notice (TCPA 1990, s. 187A). See also **enforcement notice**.

breach of contract   A material failure, without legal cause or excuse, to perform the promise or promises that forms a part, or the entirety, of a **contract**; including the refusal of a party to recognise the existence of the contract or the doing of something inconsistent with its existence. To constitute a breach of contract, in order to enable the injured party to claim repudiation of the contract, the default must be major or 'fundamental' and thus go to the root of the contract and not be just a minor failing. cf. **breach of covenant**. See also **deposit**, **election**, *quantum meruit*, **rectification**, **rescission**, **specific performance**, **time is of the essence**.

breach of covenant   The failure to perform or observe a **covenant**, or acting in a manner that is inconsistent with a covenant. In particular, the failure of a tenant to comply with a term or terms of his lease. cf. **breach of contract**. See also **forfeiture**, **grounds for possession**[Eng], **repairs notice**[Eng], **restriction**.

breach of duty of care   See **duty of care**, **negligence**.

breach of warranty   **1.** The giving of false information that forms an essential part of a **warranty**, or a substantial failure to comply with the requirement of a warranty.   **2.** A failure to comply with an executory condition of a deed. See also **executory contract**.

breach of warranty of authority   An action by an **agent** that is outside his powers or the **authority** granted by his principal. Generally, the agent, and not the principal, is liable to a third party for the consequences of any such action. A material disregard for the authority granted to an agent may deprive the agent of his commission or make him liable to the principal for damages. See also **power of attorney**.

break an entail   See **barring the entail**.

break clause   A clause in a lease that sets out

a 'break point'; i.e. a date or condition on which either party, or both parties, may have a right to determine a tenancy (especially a **tenancy for a fixed term** before it has run its full term). The clause may be included, for example, to permit a landlord to regain possession of a property for demolition or redevelopment, or to permit a tenant to terminate a lease at the time of a rent review, or simply to enable either or both parties to terminate a long-term lease at given dates. cf. **rent review clause**. See also **security of tenure, termination**.

break-even point or **break even point** The stage at which an investment produces an income that is just sufficient to cover recurring expenditure. For an investment in real property, the point at which effective gross income is equal to normal operating expenses, including debt service, i.e. the stage at which **cash flow** becomes positive. Sometimes called the 'default point'.

break point 1. See **break clause**. 2. In a turnover lease, the amount of sales required before a percentage or **turnover rent** is charged.

break-up value The value of a company if it were to cease operations and its assets were to be sold independently of the business. In the US, also called the 'gone-concern value'. cf. **going-concern value**. See also **intrinsic value**.

breaking the entail(US) See **barring the entail**.

bridge financing See **bridge loan**.

bridge loan or **bridge-over loan**(AmE) A short-term loan granted to cover an intermediate stage in business. For example, a loan that is made to cover all or part of the cost of purchasing a property before the proceeds from the sale of another property are available to the buyer. In the British English, usually called a 'bridging loan' or 'bridging finance'. See also **financing, gap financing, interim finance**.

bridging finance or **bridging loan** See **bridge loan**.

bridleway or **bridlepath** or **bridleroad** or **bridle trail** A path or track along which it is permitted to ride or lead a horse (i.e. by a bridle), as well as to pass on foot or by bicycle, but from which motorised or vehicular traffic is generally excluded. Sometimes called a 'droveway' or 'horseway' (although strictly speaking the latter would only be for horses and would exclude other animals). cf. **footway**.

brief of title(US) See **abstract of title**.

bring-down search(US) A continuation or update of a **title search**, usually undertaken at the time of closing a sale to ascertain whether there have been any changes affecting the title since the time of an earlier search. Also called a 'continuation search' or a 'take-down search'.

broad-form insurance(US) See **all-risks insurance**.

brochure A pamphlet or advertising document, such as one that sets out details of properties being offered for sale or lease. See also **particulars of sale**.

broker One who, in the normal course of his business, for a **commission** or fee, negotiates to bring parties together and assists in negotiations between the parties. The commission or fee is normally contingent on success. Thus, a broker is sometimes referred to as a 'commission agent' – one whose business is to bring buyers and sellers together and thereby be remunerated.

Although a broker normally acts for one party, and in that respect he is an **agent**, his primary aim is to bring both parties to a meeting of the minds and in that way earn his remuneration. An agent's terms of reference are essentially to represent a principal, but without necessarily having to effect a transaction in order to be remunerated. An agent acts solely for the principal, whereas a broker is more concerned with bringing about an agreement between two parties. A broker may be distinguished from a **middleman** (colloquially called a 'bird dog'), as the middleman only brings the parties together, but takes no part in the negotiations.

In all states in the US and the District of Columbia, a 'real estate broker' must hold a **real estate license** from the state in which he operates or, in some cases, the state in which the property is located. cf. **commission merchant, factor**. See also **authority, deposit, estate agent**(BrE), **fiduciary, listing agreement, procuring cause, salesperson, utmost good faith**.

Burke, D. Barlow. *Law of Real Estate Brokers*. 2nd ed. Looseleaf. Frederick, MD: Aspen, 1992.

broker-associate(AmE)   See **salesperson**.

broker price opinion (BPO)(AmE)   The price at which a broker considers a property could be sold in the open market within a reasonable time frame. A BPO is a limited form of appraisal carried out by a licensed broker. See also **market value**.

broker salesperson(AmE)   See **salesperson**.

brokerage **1.** The service provided by a **broker**. A process by which two parties to a transaction are brought together under the auspices of a third party, who is called a broker.   **2. Commission** payable to a broker. In particular, a commission that is contingent on success and not dependent on the amount of work done. Also called 'brokerage commission'. See also **bird-dog**.

brokerage listing(AmE)   See **listing**.

broker's commission(AmE)   See **commission**.

broker's license(AmE)   See **real estate license**.

broker's lien(AmE)   See **lien**.

brownfield site   An unused or undeveloped area of land that contaminated as a result of previous, but discontinued, industrial or commercial use. An area of land that is unsuitable for development due to environment pollution or soil contamination. In particular, a derelict industrial site that requires an environmental assessment report and may well require subsequent remediation. See also **derelict land, environmental audit**.

Koselar, A. L., and J. M. Kovilaritch, *Buying and Selling Brownfield Properties: A Practical Guide for Successful Transactions*, 27 N. Ky. L. Rev. 467 (2000) – includes a checklist.

budget   A financial or quantitative statement of the planned income or expenditure (or both) for a given period. An itemised list of the estimated income and expenditure for a person, public body or financial scheme, over a period of time; a statement of how it is planned to obtain or spend money over a given period (usually a year). A budget that shows the income and expenditure for a particular property may be referred to as the 'operating budget' and is intended as a forecast and guide to the planned running of that property. See also **operating expense**(AmE), **operating statement, service charge**.

budget mortgage(US)   A mortgage loan agreement that provides for the mortgagor to pay not only interest and principal, but also the tax and insurance that is related to the ownership of the mortgaged property. A budget mortgage is intended to enable the **mortgagee** to exercise greater control over the mortgagor's total property expense budget. An arrangement more commonly used for mortgages secured on residential property, especially loans insured by the Federal Housing Administration or VA-approved loans. See also **piti payment**.

buffer area or **buffer-strip** or **buffer-zone**   An area of land that is used or reserved for planting, fencing or landscaping in order to separate conflicting users, e.g. an area between a residential area and a major highway or between a residential district and an industrial zone. In particular, an area that is used to create a sound barrier between a highway or industrial park and adjoining property. See also **building line**, *non aedificandi*, **setback**.

build-operate-transfer contract　A form of building contract where the cost is paid from the revenue generated by the completed project. In effect the builder or contractor finances the project and agrees to accept payment as and when it produces income. Alternatively, the contractor may agree to be paid only when the completed building is sold.

build-to-suit contract　A building contract by which the contractor undertakes to erect a building according to the design and specification of the end user. The building may be constructed on the user's owned land (in which case it is merely a 'building contract'); or on land that is owned by the developer and will be sold or leased to the user upon completion of the construction work (in which case there is a building contract and a sale, or lease, contract). Such a lease may be referred to as a 'build-to-suit lease' and the building as a 'build-to-suit' for short. cf. **design-and-build contract**, **turnkey contract**. See also **lump-sum contract**.

build-up method(AmE)　See **component capitalization rate**.

buildable area　The area of land over which buildings may be erected after all allowances for circulation space, set backs, yards, etc. That part of an area of land that is intended to be covered with buildings, as distinguished from any part that is to be left for landscaping, service roads, car parking, etc. See also **floor area ratio**(US), **plot ratio**(BrE).

builder　One who constructs, rebuilds, alters, repairs, improves or erects a building or other form of structure, whether on his own or another's land, usually for profit. In particular, one who enters into a **building contract** for construction, repair,

maintenance or any form of building work. A company or individual whose occupation is to control and direct the process of construction or alteration of a building or other form of structure. See also **building operations**(Eng), **contractor**, **developer**.

builder's bond(AmE)　　See **bid bond**, **performance bond**.

builder's lien　See **lien**.

builder's risk insurance　Insurance provided to cover risks associated with a building that is in the course of construction. Normally such insurance is purchased by the contractor but it may be taken out by the building owner, usually with the contractor being specified as an 'interested party'. See also **contractor's all-risks insurance**.

building　Something constructed or erected for a purpose, especially a house or similar structure erected for a useful purpose. An edifice constructed of substantial material and permanently fixed to, and generally above, the soil. In particular, a structure that encloses a space within its walls, and usually, but not necessarily, is covered with a roof. A building may be no more than a wall (provided it is of some stature), an underpass or underground structure or even a roof with lateral supports. The word 'building' generally does not extend to a fence, gate, post or any similar structure; an erection that is not intended to stay in one place, such as a caravan; or machinery and equipment, whether forming part of a building or not. However, where there is a **restrictive covenant** that prohibits 'building' or 'a building', it is necessary to look at the form and intent of the restriction, and in some cases a fence, billboard, sign or similar structure, or an extension to a building, may be deemed a building.

In English planning law, a building includes "any structure or erection, and any part of a building, as so defined, but does not include plant and machinery comprised in a building", Town and Planning Act 1990, s. 336(1) (Building Act 1984, s.

121(1)). See also **agricultural building, building operations**[(Eng)], **erection, fixture, industrial building, listed building**[(Eng)], **messuage, obstructive building**.

building agreement An agreement, between an owner of land and a builder, by which the builder is granted a **licence** to enter the land in order to erect a property or properties to an agreed specification, particularly houses, which then are sold or leased to the ultimate purchaser or lessee (who may be the builder himself). In English law, this form of agreement constitutes an **estate contract**. Sometimes called a 'building licence'. See also **building lease**.

building and loan association[(AmE)] A quasi-public corporation chartered to accept funds or savings from its members in order to assist those members to build or purchase homes, or other forms of real property, with loans from the corporation. In most states, building and loan associations are not banks or savings institutions and have now been replaced by **savings and loan associations**, or reclassified as a special form of savings and loan association. Such associations were also called 'building associations', 'homestead associations' (in Louisiana and southern and western states), and 'cooperative banks' (in New England). See also **building society**[(BrE)].

building area The total floor area of a building measured to the limits of the external structure. cf. **buildable area**. See **gross building area**[(AmE)]/ **gross building area**[(Aus)], **gross external area**[(BrE)].

building association[(US)] See **building and loan association**.

building capitalization rate[(AmE)] **1.** The capitalization rate used in the **building residual technique**. The ratio of the income that is deemed to be derived from a building and the capital value of the building. Building capitalization rate may be expressed by the symbol R_B. See also **capitalization rate**. **2.** A capitalization rate

that provides an adequate return to cover the risk of an investment in building work or improvements.

building certificate See **certificate of occupancy**[(US)], **certificate of practical completion**[(BrE)], **certificate of valuation**[(BrE)].

building code **1.**[(US)]A set of rules or codes established by a state or municipal authority to regulate the design and construction of buildings and equipment installed therein; to set out standards as to the quality of materials; to control the use and occupation; and to ensure public health and safety in buildings, as well as the provision of light and air to the occupiers of buildings. See also **building permit, certificate of occupancy, police power, Uniform Building Code**.
Hageman, Jack M. *Contractor's Guide to the Building Code.* Carlsbad, CA: Craftsman Book Co., 1998.
International Code Council. *International Building Code.* Looseleaf. Country Club Hills, IL: International Code Council, 2003.
Parish, Scott. *Uniform Building Code Compliance Manual.* New York: McGraw-Hill, 1999.
2.[(BrE)]A set of regulations prepared to control the standard of construction, reconstruction, and other building work. In Great Britain, the British Standards Institute produces codes of practice for building work based on its research and expertise, but unlike the **building regulations**, these are only recommendations and have no legal application. See also **building controls**.

building consent[(NZ)] Consent to carry out building work, as issued by a local authority.

building contract A **contract** for the erection or extension of any building or other structure, usually containing details of the specification and plans to indicate to the contractor or builder how the work is to be performed. See also **bill of quantities, cost-plus contract, fixed-price contract, Joint Contracts Tribunal**[(BrE)], **lump-sum contract, package-deal contract, remeasurement contract, turnkey contract**.

Chappell, David. *Understanding JCT Standard Building Contracts*. 6th ed. London: E. & F. N. Spon, 2000.

Clough, Richard H., and Glenn A. Sears. *Construction Contracting*, 6th ed. New York: Wiley, 1994.

building contractor   See **contractor, main contractor**.

building controls   Statutory controls over the design, development, construction and use of a building. See also **building code, building regulations, bylaw, fire certificate**[(Eng)], **listed building consent**[(Eng)], **negligence, overcrowding, planning permission**[(Eng)], **zoning ordinance**[(US)].

building coverage   See **site coverage**.

building density ratio[(Aus)]   See also **plot ratio**.

building efficiency ratio[(Aus)]   See **efficiency ratio**.

building finance   See **construction finance**.

building footprint   The horizontal outline or impression of a building as represented at ground level. The area of a building lot that is covered with the buildings. See also **floor area ratio**[(US)], **plot ratio**[(BrE)].

building height plane[(Aus)]   A plane that runs at an angle from the boundary of a site and is prescribed to control the height and setback of building on the site. Also called 'envelope control'. See also **bulk envelope**.

building inspector   A local government officer who is charged with inspecting buildings or other structures to ensure that they are constructed in accordance with local building codes or regulations.

building land   Land that is capable of being built on and that is likely to be developed within a reasonable period of time. Land that is ripe for building. See also **development land**.

building lease   A long-term **lease** of unimproved land on which the lessee covenants to erect a new building or to substantially improve, alter or add buildings. Commonly the lease is for at least 99 years, although it may be as short as 50 years or as long as 999 years. Usually a building lease is granted at a fixed **ground rent**, or at a ground rent with reviews at intervals such as 25 or 33 years. See also **building agreement, ground lease, ground rent lease**[(US)], **emphyteotic lease, leasehold enfranchisement, restraint on alienation, tenant for life**.

building licence[(BrE)] **or building license**[(AmE)]   **1.** A generic term for a licence or permission granted to allow building work to proceed. See also **building controls, building permit**[(US)], **building regulations**[(Eng)], **licence**[(BrE)]/ **license**[(AmE)], **planning permission**[(Eng)]. **2.** See **building agreement**.

building lien   See **lien**.

building line   **1.** A line on a plan that shows the existing, or permitted, limit of an outer wall or the major external surface of a building. **2.** An established line by a local law or ordinance beyond which an owner of land is not permitted to build. In particular, a line fixed by law, or private covenant, in front of which a landowner is not permitted to build. Sometimes called a 'setback line' or, in the US, a 'front line' or 'yard line'. cf. **improvement line**. See also **compensation for injurious affection, setback, zero-lot line**[(US)].

building loan   See **construction finance**/ **construction loan**.

building lot or building site   **1.** A parcel or tract of land that is suitable for the construction of a new building, which may be a virgin site or a site that has been cleared of buildings or other structures but is serviced ready for new development. See also **lot, site area**.   **2.** An area of land upon which a building is being erected. A 'building site' generally includes not only the land that is covered by buildings, but also the ancillary land that forms part of the project. In the US, more commonly called a 'construction site'.

building maintenance   See **maintenance**.

building mortgage   See **construction mortgage**.

building of special architectural or historic interest(BrE)   See **listed building**.

building operations(Eng)   In determining what constitutes **development** for the purpose of deciding whether an operation requires **planning permission**, building operations include: "(a) **demolition** of buildings; (b) rebuilding; (c) structural alterations of or additions to buildings; and (d) other operations normally undertaken by a person carrying on business as a builder", TCPA 1990, ss. 55(1A), 336(1)). In general, preparation work such as is necessary merely to prepare an estimate would not be a building operation, nor is the carrying out of minor repair or decoration. On the other hand, ancillary **demolition**, such as would be carried out in connection with rebuilding, is a building operation if it amounts to the form of work normally undertaken by a person 'carrying on business as a builder' (*London County Council v Marks and Spencer* [1953] AC 535 (HL)). See also **engineering operations, mining operations**.

building ordinance(US)   See **ordinance, zoning ordinance**.

building permit(AmE)   Written consent, granted by a local government body or municipal corporation, for the erection of a new building, or for a major alteration or extension to, or demolition of, an existing structure. The proposed building work must be drawn up so that it conforms with any local **zoning ordinance** and the **building code** before a building permit will be granted. Also, any such authorized

building must comply with the plans and specifications submitted with the application for the permit. A fee is normally payable before such a permit is issued and, in most jurisdictions, a copy of the permit is required to be posted on the construction site while the authorized work is being carried out. Also called a 'zoning permit' or a 'building and zoning permit'. See also **certificate of occupancy, special-use permit**.

building plot   See **plot of land**.

building preservation notice (BPN)(Eng)   A notice served by a local planning authority on any owner and any occupier of a building (or in the case of an emergency affixed to some object on the building) that is *not* a **listed building**, to the effect that in the opinion of the authority the building "(a) is of special architectural or historic interest and (b) is in danger of demolition or of alteration in such a way as to affect its character as a building of such interest", P(LBCA)A 1990, s. 3(1). The notice makes demolition, extension, or alteration, without consent, an offence.

building regulation   Any form of regulation that controls the type of building work that may be carried out, including alterations that can be carried out to a building, as well as the means of carrying out such building work. See also **building code, building permit**(US)**, building regulations, planning, town and country planning, zoning ordinance**.

building regulations   1.(Eng)A code that sets out the methods of construction and types of material to be used in building work in England and Wales. These regulations (which are now made in accordance with the provisions of the Building Act 1984) are currently contained in the Building Regulations 2000 (SI 2000/2531, as amended). See also **fire certificate**.

Billington, M. *Manual to the Building Regulations*. London: The Stationary Office, 1999.

Billington, M., et al. *The Building Regulations Explained and Illustrated*. 12th ed. Oxford: Blackstone, 2003.

Stephenson, John. *Building Regulations Explained*. 6th ed. London: E. & F. N. Spon, 2000.
2.(US)Regulations that govern the construction of new buildings and the use to which they may be put. In particular, regulations that control the height of new buildings and their mode of construction. Such regulations are made by legislative enactment for the safety, comfort, or convenience of the people, and for the benefit of property owners generally (Welch v. Swasey, 29 214 US 91, S Ct 567, 53 L Ed 923, 930 (1909)). See also **building code, zoning ordinance**.

building residual technique(AmE)   A method used to determine the appraised value of a building, or an improvement, separately from the land on which it stands by using a variant of the **income approach** to the appraisal. An assessment is made of the income that represents a reasonable return on the land alone, i.e. a market ground rent, and this amount is deducted from the total net income receivable from the property, including the buildings. The difference is multiplied by an appropriate capitalization rate, such as a rate that would amortize the building cost over its economic life. cf. **land residual technique**. See also **property residual technique, residual method of valuation**.

building restriction(US)   **1.** See **building code, ordinance**.   **2.** A private restriction placed upon the use of land or on the type or form of building that can be erected on land, i.e. a **restrictive covenant** against a use or building on the land, being a **covenant running with the land**.

building scheme   See **scheme of development**.

building site   See **building lot**.

building society   An organisation established by statute, with a fixed set of rules, to make long-term loans for the purchase of property, by means of mortgages secured thereon. Building societies receive money from the general public who then become members of the society. Building societies are established for the purpose of "raising, by subscriptions of the members, a stock or fund for making advances to members out of the funds of the society by way of mortgage of freehold or leasehold estate", Building Societies Act 1962, s. 1(1). In the US, building societies were the forerunner of the **savings and loan associations**.

building standard(AmE)   The level or standard of building work that a landlord proposes to provide as part of the **tenant improvement allowance**. A landlord may provide, or pay the equivalent contribution to the tenant, for 'building standard' work or may agree to pay for 'over standard work'. See also **work letter**.

Building Trust(BrE)   A form of **equity-participation mortgage** where a 'Building Trust' is formed to receive capital from approved pension funds and then the trust grants mortgages to purchasers of dwelling-houses at an interest rate that is set at two-thirds of the rate for comparable mortgage loans. In return, the trust retains a right to receive a half-share of any increase in the capital value of any of the houses as and when they are sold. The house owner retains the remaining half-share in the increase in equity.

building-type restriction(US)   A restrictive **covenant** that limits the type of property that may be erected on a parcel of land, usually to a dwelling-house or residential property.

building unit lot(Aus)   A building lot shown on a **strata title** plan. The term may also be used to refer to an allotted unit of a building shown on the strata plan.

building value   The value of a building, excluding the land on which it stands. See also **building residual technique**(AmE).

built area   The total constructed area of a building, generally measured as the gross external area. See **gross building area**(US).

built-up capitalization rate(AmE) See **component capitalization rate**.

built-up district(US) A zoning term for a part of a town or city that is almost entirely developed with buildings and in which there are few if any vacant lots.

bulk envelope The three-dimensional space within which a structure can be built on a zoning lot. See also **floor area ratio, zoning ordinance**.

bulk mortgage 1. See **blanket mortgage**. 2. A mortgage secured on all personal property (furniture, chattels, etc.) owned by a mortgagor. In particular, a mortgage secured on a mortgagor's place of business and any personal property at the same place.

bulk zoning(US) See **zoning ordinance**.

bullet loan See **balloon loan**.

bundle of rights theory(AmE) A theory that propounds that ownership of real estate is made up of a number of rights, the sum total of which constitute absolute ownership. The theory holds that, because land cannot be transferred as a physical entity, it is represented by a set of distinct and separate rights and benefits (sometimes called 'beneficial interests') each of which is capable of separate transfer. These rights include the right to use, to profit from, to occupy, to sell, to charge, to bequeath, to lease, to develop or to build on, and to encumber land. The holder of an unencumbered **fee simple** possesses all such rights. These rights are not unqualified, but are limited by the power of the State in the form of its right to raise taxes; to exercise the power of **eminent domain** (to take private property by condemnation); **escheat** (to take property that has no known owner or if taxes are not duly paid); and what are colorfully called the State's **police power** (the regulation of new building, zoning ordinances, health regulations, etc.). See also **partial ownership**.

bungalow A term originating from the Hindi word *bangla*, a house built in a Bengal or Kashmir style, that is, of a single-storey construction with a low sweeping roof and surrounded by a veranda. A residential building of which the main walls are no higher than one storey, although the building may incorporate gable projections in the roof to accommodate an additional half storey The term may also be applied to any detached house or cottage that is intended for summer or vacation use, especially one with a veranda.

burden Something taken or accepted as a duty or obligation. An **encumbrance**. A restriction imposed upon a freedom to use land. cf. **benefit**. See also **notice, restrictive covenant**.

burdened tenement(US) See **servient tenement**.

bureau A specialised administrative office or unit, especially one that is responsible for public administration. A department or subdivision of an executive branch of government. See also **Bureau of Land Management**(US).

Bureau of Land Management (BLM)(US) A bureau created in 1946 as part of the U.S. Department of the Interior (as a result of the consolidation of the General Land Office and the Grazing Service) that is responsible for the survey, engineering, classification, administration, improvement, conservation and use of public lands and natural resources (including timber, fish and wildlife habitat, minerals, water resources, historical and archeological sites and wilderness areas). The BLM is responsible for managing 264 million acres of land – about one-eighth of the land in the United States – and about 300 million additional acres of subsurface mineral resources. Most of the lands the BLM manages are located in 12 western states. The BLM administers public lands within a framework of numerous laws, the most comprehensive of which is the Federal Land Policy and Management Act of 1976. See also **Land Department of the United States, public lands**. (www.blm.gov)

business Derived from Old English *bisignis*, 'being officiously, actively or fully occupied'. An activity engaged in as a means of gaining a livelihood, especially an enterprise that involves a commercial or mercantile activity. Work in which a person or firm is regularly or usually engaged for profit or gain. Transactions or dealings of any kind where time and effort are utilised toward a particular end; generally, but not exclusively, to make a profit. Business is a general term that includes a **trade**, but a person who is involved in business is not necessarily involved in trade. A **profession** may be conducted as a business, and employment may involve a business activity; but neither a profession nor employment need be pursued as a business. Business is conducted by a person's own volition, not as a consequence of a calling; it requires no special learning but only an independence of judgement and decision. Business may even include the renting or leasing out of premises (especially as serviced offices), or the taking in of lodgers, provided the business is a commercial activity.

In English statute law, in relation to a **business tenancy**, business includes "a trade, profession or employment and includes any activity carried on by a body of persons, whether corporate or unincorporate", L&T Act 1954, s. 23(2). See also **business premises**.

business cycle See **cycle**.

business day A normal working **day**. Any day upon which business is normally conducted, but generally excluding Saturday, Sunday or any legal holiday. The term 'business day' has no all-embracing meaning and typically refers to a day during which business is conducted in the activity or business to which the term is applied.

business enterprise value The value of the intangible assets of an ongoing business, which includes the value of the **goodwill** and other aspects that contribute to the business such as management and work force skills that cannot be sold separately from the enterprise.

business homestead(US) A place of business that is established as part of a person's **homestead** rights. In some jurisdictions, 'homestead' may include "a place where the head or members of the family may pursue such business or avocation as may be necessary for the support and comfort of the family", 40 Am.Jur.2d., Homestead, § 29, p. 134.

business improvement district (BID) A district where the owners of two or more private properties or businesses work together to share the cost of solving common problems or realizing common economic opportunities associated with their location. A BID may be managed by a public agency or a non-profit corporation and may be responsible for performing a wide variety of services ranging, for example, from cleaning to consumer marketing. In the UK, such districts are more commonly referred to as 'town centre management programs'. See also **improvement district**.
Schwanke, Dean. *Mixed-Use Development Handbook.* 2nd ed. Washington, DC: Urban Land Institute, 2003.

business interruption insurance See **consequential loss insurance**.

business invitee See **invitee**.

business, loss of See **compensation for disturbance**(BrE), **consequential damages**(US).

business park A large area of land that is developed to provide high-quality low-density buildings in a park or campus-like setting. The buildings are intended to provide for a range of associated uses, including offices, light manufacturing and assembly, research and development, and ancillary facilities. The 'park' is normally developed in accordance with a **master plan** with extensive landscaping and designed to provide an attractive working environment. A single developer normally undertakes the development. The developer may subdivide the land into separate lots for sale to individual owner-occupiers, or the developer may construct the buildings, either for rent or for sale, in accordance with the specific requirements of the end users. The entire development is subjected to covenants and restrictions that are enforced to ensure that the park is maintained to a high standard. A similar form of development that contains only office buildings is called an 'office park'. See also **covenants conditions and restrictions**(US), **scheme of development**.

Frej, A.nne, et al. *Business Park and Industrial Development Handbook.* 2nd ed. Washington, DC: Urban Land Institute, 2001.

business premises   1. Any premises (land, houses, buildings, etc.) occupied for the purpose of **business** or **trade**.   2.(Eng)Premises that, when let, may form the subject matter of a **business tenancy**, and therefore be subject to the protection afforded by the Landlord and Tenant Acts, including any premises occupied for the purpose of a 'business' which, in turn, "includes a trade, profession or employment and includes any activity carried on by a body of persons, whether corporate or unincorporate", L&T Act 1954, s. 23(1). Thus, one person can carry out a trade, business or employment and the premises may be classified as business premises, but the "activity" must be carried on by a "group of persons". For the purposes of this statutory interpretation, occupation by a business that is merely incidental to residential occupation is not occupation for the purposes of a business (*Cheryl Investments Ltd v Saldanha, Royal Life Saving Society v Page* [1979] 1 All ER 5 (CA)). In the case of a right to **compensation for improvements** the holding to which the L&T Act 1927 applies means any premises held under a lease, other than a mining lease, and "used wholly or partly for carrying on thereat any trade or business", L&T Act 1927, s. 17(1). This section expressly includes "premises regularly used for carrying on a profession", It excludes any part of an agricultural holding; premises let by reason of an office appointment or employment for the landlord; and premises used for the business of sub-letting residential flats. See also **commercial property**, **holding**.

business property(US)   Commercial **property**, especially when used for the retail trade, including banks, hotels and theatres.

business tenancy(Eng)   A **tenancy** of **business premises**, i.e. "any tenancy where the property comprised in the tenancy is or includes premises which are occupied by the tenant and are so occupied for the purposes of a **business** carried on by him or for those and other purposes", L&T Act 1954, s. 23(1)). It must be a tenancy in the strict sense of the word; a **licence** cannot qualify under this definition; nor does a **tenancy at will**, whether created by implication of law or expressly. An **underlease** or an **agreement for a lease** may be a business tenancy. The premises may be partly residential provided the business purpose is the predominate user.

The following are expressly excluded from the provision of the L&T Act 1954: (i) a tenancy of an **agricultural holding**; (ii) a **mining** lease; (iii) certain tenancies of on-licensed premises (a public house or the like); (iv) a **service tenancy**; (v) any tenancy granted for a term certain not exceeding six months, unless there is an arrangement to extend or renew the term beyond six months from the commencement of the tenancy, or when the tenant (including his predecessor in the business) has been in occupation for a period which exceeds twelve months; (vi) an **extended lease** as granted under the Leasehold Reform Act 1967, s. 16; and (vii) premises that are certified as being required in the public interest by certain public bodies, or for national security (L&T Act 1954, ss. 43, 57-60, as amended by the LPA 1969, s. 12). The holder of a business tenancy is entitled to **security of tenure** in that the tenancy may not come to an end unless terminated in accordance with the provisions of the L&T Act 1954, Part II. In the event that a business tenancy is brought to an end in accordance with the statutory provisions, the tenant may have a right to: (a) to **compensation for disturbance**; and (b) **compensation for improvements**. In the latter instance, the right applies to any premises held under a lease, other than a mining lease, and "used for any trade or business", including premises used for a profession or used as an on-licence; but excluding an agricultural holding, premises where the tenant carries on the business of letting residential flats, as well as any premises let to a tenant as holder of any office, appointment or employment, from the landlord (L&T Act 1927, s. 17).

The methods by which a business tenancy may be brought to an end under the L&T Act 1954 are: (i) a landlord's notice to terminate (L&T Act, s. 25); (ii) a tenant's request for a new tenancy (L&T Act, s. 26); and (iii) a tenant's notice to terminate (L&T Act, ss. 24(2), 27). The tenant may terminate the tenancy by the service of notice to quit in the usual way for a periodic tenancy; or, if the tenancy was granted for a fixed term, by the service of three months prior written notice that he does not wish the tenancy to continue at the end of the term (or, if the tenancy has been allowed to continue after the end of the term, by three months notice of his intention to quit the premises to expire on any of the **quarter days**). The tenancy may come to an end also by the following common law methods: (i) a **surrender** of the tenant's interest to his immediate landlord; (ii) **forfeiture** due to a breach of covenant, provided there is a proviso for re-entry in the terms of the tenancy; or (iii) forfeiture of a superior tenancy (L&T Act, s. 24(2)). A landlord's notice to terminate does not take the form of a common law notice to quit, but must be given in accordance with the statutory provisions and in a prescribed form (L&T Act 1954 Part II (Notices) (Amendment) Regulations 1989, as amended) or "substantially to the like effect". See also **interim rent**.

Aldridge, Trevor M. *Letting Business Premises.* 7th ed. London: Pearson, 1996.

Hilditch, Brian, et al. *Renewing Business Tenancies* 3rd ed. Bristol: Jordans, 2003.

Lewison, Kim. *Drafting Business Leases.* 6th ed. London: Sweet & Maxwell, 2000.

Williams, Del. *Fox-Andrews on Business Tenancies.* 6th ed. London: Estates Gazette, 2002.

Williams, Del., et al. *Handbook of Business Tenancies.* Looseleaf. London: Sweet & Maxwell, ©1985.

business trust   A **trust** established to hold property for the profit or gain of the beneficiaries. In particular, a trust in which the trustees are also the managers who deal with the trust property for the use and benefit of the beneficiaries and are remunerated for their services. The beneficiaries receive transferable certificates of participation or shares in the trust. In the state of Massachusetts (where corporations were limited in their powers to hold and deal in real estate) a trust, or 'mutual fund', that invests in real estate is referred to as a 'Massachusetts trust'. Also called a 'common law trust' as it was originally formed under the common law trust laws by which title to the property was held by the trustees, but the rents and profits were available to the beneficiaries. See also **discretionary trust**, **real estate investment trust**.

butt   To join end to end. See also **abut**.

butts and bounds system(US)   See **metes and bounds system**.

buy-and-sell agreement or **buy-sell agreement**   1. An agreement between two parties, especially members of a **joint venture** or **partnership**, which provides that in certain circumstances (e.g. on the termination of the partnership) one party may purchase the assets, or an interest in those assets, from the other. Frequently a reciprocal arrangement, by which one party, usually the larger shareholder, has the first right to buy assets from the other and, if this right is not exercised, it is available then to the other party. The price is determined usually by reference to the agreed market price or is sometimes fixed in advance.   2. An arrangement by which a lender who has granted an interim loan, secured on a property that is to be constructed, agrees to sell or assign that loan to a permanent lender who, in turn, agrees to buy the loan on satisfactory completion of the project (which may include conditions such as a stipulated level of leasing or sales).   3.(US)See **contract for sale**.

buy-down(AmE)   An arrangement by which a lender provides for a reduction in the interest rate actually payable during the early period of a loan (usually the first two or three years) in exchange for an additional fee or **discount points** payable at the start of the loan. In particular, a reduction in the interest rate for a residential loan where the cost of this 'buy-down' is met by a developer, builder, or seller, who wishes to assist a buyer with his initial monthly payments. See also **deferred-interest mortgage**.

buy in **1.** The purchase of a property offered for sale by **auction** by the vendor himself or by an interested party (commonly the auctioneer acting as the vendor's agent) if the final bid is inadequate; or the purchase of a property at auction by a mortgagee or lienee who has an interest in the subject property. In the US, in some jurisdictions, if a mortgagee states the amount of the loan outstanding (plus allowable costs), any amount bid above that amount is payable to the borrower. Also referred to as 'bid-in'. See also **reserve price**(BrE)/**reserved price**(AmE). **2.** To purchase a junior or subordinate interest in a property in which the purchaser already has an interest, e.g. the purchase of a leasehold interest by a freeholder of the same property. See also **marriage value**(BrE).

buy-out See **takeout commitment**.

buy-out rate The **capitalisation rate** agreed as appropriate for the sale of a development property at the time of its completion. Generally, 'buy-out rate' refers to the capitalisation rate that is agreed between the developer and a purchaser who has made a commitment to acquire the development on completion. This agreed rate is normally applied to the net income that is receivable at the time the building is fully leased. See also **takeout commitment**.

buyback agreement See **repurchase agreement**.

buyer A **purchaser**, especially one who exchanges money for goods or services. See also *caveat emptor*, **ready able and willing**.

buyer's concession See **concession**.

buyer's equity(AmE) See **down payment**.

buyer's market A market for a commodity or property where there are significantly more sellers than buyers so that prices are bid down; a condition in a market when the buyer is in a stronger position than the seller because supply exceeds demand. cf. **seller's market**.

buyer's option See **purchase option**.

by See **time**.

by-bidder(AmE) See **puffer**.

by-bidding(AmE) See **puffing**.

by the whole and not by the moiety See **tenancy by the entirety**.

bylaw or **by-law** or **byelaw** **1.** A local law. An **ordinance** or **code** that is applied in a specific area, such as a town or county, i.e. a code of restriction on the residents in the locality to which the law applies.
  In the US, 'bylaw' and 'ordinance' may be used interchangeably, although an ordinance is enacted by public officers under a legislative authority and applies to the citizens, residents and visitors within the legislative jurisdiction. Whereas a bylaw is a private rule or code, especially one adopted by a corporation, and applies to the officers or members of that corporation (or anyone who expressly or impliedly assents to be so bound). In Canada (and in the UK before the advent of **building regulations**), 'building by-laws' refer to regulations that control the construction of new buildings. See also **building regulations**(Eng), *ultra vires*. **2.** A rule or regulation made to govern the running of a corporation, an unincorporated organisation, association (such as a **condominium owners' association, homeowners' association**, or a **housing association**), a society or a business trust and the rights and duties accepted by the shareholders or members. cf. **covenants, conditions and restrictions**. See also **commonhold community statement, condominium declaration, restraint on alienation, strata title**.
  Note: Meaning 2. is more common to the US where the spelling 'bylaw' or 'by-law' is more usual.

cabin **1.** A simple lodging, generally under one roof and containing one room, built of logs, mud or similar material. A small single-storey dwelling, usually of basic design and construction, commonly used for vacation purposes (although in North America the word was used to refer to the same type of structure as would have been constructed by the early settlers). **2.** Sleeping accommodation that forms part of a larger complex and is adjoined to a **motel**. **3.**(US)In the Southern States, a simple structure that formed the home of a family or worker on a plantation.

cadastral map or **cadastral plan** An official map or plan used to register land for taxation purposes. A map or plan produced to show, as a public record, the boundaries of all property ownerships and the assessed value of each property. The cadastral map (or plan) is normally accompanied by a description of the property, by reference number, area, etc., but does not necessarily show physical features that appear on the ground, unless these correspond with the ownership boundaries. Land ownership as shown on the official cadastral map is based on historically recorded land ownership details. In the US, when used to record property tax assessment sometimes called an 'assessment map' or 'tax map'. See **cadastral survey**.
Dale, Peter F. *Cadastral Surveys in the Commonwealth*. London: Her Majesty's Stationery Office, 1976.
Larsson, Gerhard. *Land Registration and Cadastral Systems*. Harlow, Essex: Longman, 1991.

cadastral register A public register of the quality, value and ownership of immovable property in a country, compiled primarily to serve as a basis for recording property tax assessments. Also called a 'cadastre'. See also **cadastral map**, **Torrens title system**.

cadastral survey A survey made to determine and record the position of property boundaries, especially for the purpose of preparing an official register of land ownership for taxation purposes. See also **cadastral map**, **surveying**.

cadastre Derived from the Latin *capistratum*, 'poll tax'. A register of land compiled for tax purposes. A **cadastral register**. See also **cadastral map**.

caducary or **caduciary** Relating to **escheat**, lapse or **forfeiture** of property. A caducary estate being one that is transferred by such means.

caeteris paribus(Lat) 'Other things being equal'.

calendar day See **day**.

call **1.** A demand for, or right to demand, payment of money or delivery of goods, immediately or on a specified date. In particular: (a) a demand for payment of a loan when a major condition of the loan has not been complied with; or (b) a demand to subscribe for stock in a company. See also **call option**, **demand loan**. **2.**(US)A reference to a course, distance, monument, marker, or natural object, made where a **boundary** of a property is being described or 'run'. An identifying mark or line on a survey plan, or on a plan attached to a deed of conveyance, that corresponds to an object, landmark, natural object (e.g. a tree) or a natural boundary (e.g. a stream) on the land, or the limit of the land, to which the plan refers. The line is sometimes called a 'running line'.

call clause(US) See **due-on-sale clause**.

call loan See **demand loan**.

call money An interest bearing deposit that may be withdrawn at 24 hours notice. See **demand loan**.

call option **1.** An **option** or short-term contract

which gives the beneficiary the right, but not the obligation, to purchase property, stock or a commodity at an agreed or pre-arranged price (an 'exercise' or 'striking' price) within a specified period of time. Normally a certain sum of money (a **premium**) is paid for the right to the call option. A provision in a contract that grants one party a call option is sometimes called a 'call provision'. cf. **put option**. See also **purchase option**.   **2.** A right to purchase a stipulated quantity of a commodity, stock or securities on a predetermined basis. Generally, the price for one call option is based on an accepted quantity of the item to which the option applies, e.g. the price for one call option represents the right to purchase 100 shares or one ounce or one ton of a commodity.

call provision(US)   **1.** See **acceleration clause**. **2.** See **call option**.

call rate   The rate of interest charged on a loan that is payable 'at call' or on demand.

called-in planning application(Eng)   An application for **planning permission** that is considered sufficiently important for the Secretary of State to make a direction that it be referred to the Secretary, instead of being dealt with by the local planning authority. A similar action may be taken in respect of an approval of a proposal under a development order. If required by either party, the Secretary of State must hold a hearing or public enquiry before deciding whether to grant or refuse an application that has been 'called in' (TCPA 1990, s. 77). Such an action is not compatible with the European Convention on Human Rights, Art. 6(1) which provides that "everyone is entitled to a fair and public hearing within a reasonable time by an independent and impartial tribunal established by law" (*Holding & Barnes plc v Secretary of State for the Environment Transport and the Regions* [2003] 2 AC 295, 295 (HL)). See also **planning inquiry**.

Canadian mortgage   An amortization **mortgage** that provides for interest to be compounded half yearly but payments to be made monthly.

Canadian rollover mortgage   A mortgage loan provided on the basis that all or part of the principal may remain outstanding for the term of the loan, which is generally 20 to 25 years, but the interest rate can be adjusted at fixed intervals, usually by renegotiation at five-year intervals. Unlike a conventional **renegotiable-rate mortgage** if the revised rate is not agreed the parties have a right to terminate the loan agreement.

canal   An artificial channel or cutting through land used for the flow of water from one source to another. A man-made **watercourse** built for navigation, or for the transportation of water for the drainage or flood control, or for the irrigation of land. As a man-made watercourse a canal does not carry any of the **riparian rights** appertaining to a river. A navigable canal may be considered as a form of **highway**. See also **drain**.

cancellation   The act of bringing to an end. **Termination** of a contract by agreement of the parties. The **abrogation** of an instrument, usually made by writing words of revocation across the face, or defacing or physically destroying it. The term cancellation may also be used in the specific sense of "the right of one contracting party to unilaterally terminate a contract because of its breach by the other party. cf. **forfeiture**. See also **discharge, rescission, revocation**.

cancellation clause   **1.** See **termination clause**.   **2.**(US)A clause in a lease that permits the landlord to terminate the lease upon the occurrence of a specified event, in particular in the event of a sale of the leased property. cf. **acceleration clause**.

Candlemas   See **quarter day**.

canon   **1.** An old term for a rent or tribute payable to a church.   **2.** A rule of discipline or a principle accepted as a guideline by members of an association, e.g. a **code of conduct** accepted by professional valuers.

cap   See **interest rate cap**.

cap rate   See **capitalisation rate**.

capital   1. A stock of accumulated and material **wealth**. The surplus of production over consumption at a particular time, especially of goods, plant, equipment, inventories or real assets retained for the purpose of further production, reinvestment and ultimate profit. Capital is required because production is not an instant process; it is a non-permanent resource that is used to produce or maintain income for all or a sector of mankind. In classical economics capital is one of the factors of production, the others being labour and **land**. Capital may be classified broadly as **fixed capital** which is retained intact throughout the production process and includes buildings, plant and machinery; **working capital** which is added or reduced according to fluctuations in production levels and includes stocks and work in process; and **real capital** which is that which is finally produced. See also **capital value**, **fixed asset**.   2. The total **estate** of an individual or a body, including money, goods, land and buildings. See also **capital money**, **chattel**.   3. The total assets of a corporation. The **net worth** (excess of assets over liabilities) of a company as owned by the proprietor(s) (sometimes called the proprietor's or owner's capital), which may be the 'authorised', 'issued' or 'paid-up' capital. See also **equity capital**, **investment**.   4. **Money** available or retained to run a company. The amount invested in a business for the purpose of making a profit or fair return to the investors. See also **capital money**.   5. The **principal** due under a loan, as distinguished from the interest payable thereon. See also **debt capital**.

capital allowance[BrE]   Allowances that may be offset against the taxable profit of a person carrying on a trade, profession, vocation or employment who have incurred capital expenditure. Capital allowances are given on the cost of plant and machinery and most agricultural and industrial buildings (including expenditure on extensions and improvements) and on some hotels (Capital Allowances Act 1990, as amended). See also **balancing allowance**.

capital appreciation   See **appreciation**.

capital asset   1. An **asset** of a permanent nature; an asset intended for continuous use or to provide an income, rather than for trade, sale, conversion, or consumption. In particular, an asset that is held for long-term investment or continuous use in a business. See also **capital**, **fixed asset**.   2.[US] All property held by a taxpayer (whether or not held in connection with his trade and business) that is not expressly excluded as 'capital assets' under the tax code. Items that are not 'capital assets' primarily include inventory or items that are used in the taxpayers trade or business of a character which is subject to depreciation as provided in the code. In particular, stock-in-trade, copyright, accounts receivable, certain short-term securities, and property held by the taxpayer primarily for sale to customers in the ordinary course of his trade or business and property used in his trade or business, which generally includes property held for rental, but not land that is acquired for subdivision and resale (26 USC § 1221).

capital depreciation   See **depreciation**.

capital expenditure   1. Expenditure incurred to acquire property for the long term, or to increase the permanent value of property. Expenditure on a **fixed asset**, as distinguished from expenditure on a current or liquid asset or 'revenue expenditure' incurred in the day-to-day running of an enterprise. In determining whether expenditure is of a capital nature it is more appropriate to determine what the money is spent on rather than where the money comes from. In general, money spent on **improvement**, **alteration** or **renewal** is capital expenditure, but money spent on repair and maintenance is not. **2.**(US)Certain forms of expenditure that are classified as not being allowed in computing taxable income, In particular expenditure on building improvements (26 USC, Internal Revenue Code, § 263).

capital gain 1. An increase or gain in the value of a **fixed asset** or property from its original cost to its current value. A capital gain may be notional, or 'unrealised', when the asset is still held; or 'realised' when a disposal has taken place and an actual profit has been obtained. In particular, capital gains arise from an isolated transaction, as distinguished from profits or gains that arise in the normal course of business. When recorded in the financial statement of a company or when realised, it may be called a 'capital profit' or when the subject for taxation a 'taxable gain'. cf. **income**. **2.**(US)The profit realized from the sale or exchange of a **capital asset** (26 USC, Internal Revenue Code, § 1201). This profit is the difference between the cost, or adjusted **basis**, of the asset and the net proceeds from the sale or exchange of the asset.

capital gains tax A tax levied on an increase in the value or profit from the sale of a **capital asset**. A tax arising on the sale or exchange of an asset (including an estate or interest in land). See also **capital tax**, **market value**, **principal private residence**(Eng), **principal residence**(US).

capital gearing See **gearing**, **leverage**.

capital grant See **grant**.

capital improvement 1. Any **improvement** that increases the value, or extends the useful life, of real property. Expenditure that is incurred on making a simple **repair** is not a capital improvement; there must be an element of betterment or amelioration. However, the replacement of damaged or worn out property may be a capital improvement, especially when the expenditure is substantial or amounts to a renewal of all or part of the property. See also **capital expenditure**. 2. An expense that is

charged against the principal and not the income of a **trust**.

capital investment An investment made to acquire a **capital asset**, fixed asset or a long-term security as distinguished from the acquisition of a liquid or short-term asset. Money or resources invested in a business or enterprise for the assiduous benefit of that entity; money paid out to acquire something of permanent use or value to a business. Money expended to increase the value of an asset. See also **capital expenditure**.

capital lease See **finance lease**.

capital loan A loan secured on a **capital asset**.

capital messuage(Eng) The principal **mansion house** of an estate. See also **messuage**.

capital money 1. Money arising from the sale of a **fixed asset**, or expended on the purchase or improvement of such an item. Money that amounts to **capital expenditure**, as distinguished from expenditure that occurs on a regular or recurring basis. See also **capital gain**. **2.**(Eng)Money received and held by the trustees of a **settlement**. In particular, money that is received by trustees from the sale of, or other dealings in, **settled land**; as distinguished from income received from settled land retained by the **tenant for life**. Capital money must be retained for the benefit of those entitled under the settlement; it must be invested either to meet a particular purpose for which money was raised from the settled land, or in accordance with one or other of the twenty-one forms of investment or applications for the money stipulated in the (SLA 1925, ss. 67(2), 73-84).

capital profit See **capital gain**.

capital recapture See **recapture**.

capital recapture rate(US) See **recapture rate**.

capital recovery   See **recapture rate**.

capital tax   Any tax on a change in capital value (including **capital gains tax**, **estate tax** or **inheritance tax**), as distinguished from a tax on income.

capital valuation   See **capitalisation**, **investment method of valuation**.

capital value   **1.** The **value** of a property ascertained at one particular time bringing into account all future income and benefits. The value of an asset ascertained by the **capitalisation** of income. See also **asset value**, **capitalised value**, **market value**.   **2.**(Aus)"The amount that an unencumbered **fee simple** in land might reasonably be expected to realise upon sale", Valuation of Land Act 1971, s. 5(1) (SA) i.e. the **market value** of an unencumbered fee simple (*CSR Ltd v Valuer General* (1977) 17 SASR 446, 450-451, 42 LGRA 52 (Aus)).   **3.**(NZ)See **land value**.

capitalisation(BrE) or **capitalization**(AmE)   **1.** The conversion of a series of anticipated income instalments into a single current or **capital value**. The discounting of the net income (all income less all outlays) to arrive at a single value. The anticipated or projected income from an investment is discounted at a rate of interest that takes account of the risk of obtaining that income in the future. Capitalisation involves ascertaining the market value of a future income stream as if that income were receivable at a single moment in time.

The capitalisation process may apply a single multiplier or capitalisation factor to the current income – called direct or **straight capitalization**, or 'capitalisation in perpetuity'; or it may apply a present value factor (such as the present value of one per annum) to a future income stream – called, yield or **annuity capitalization** or 'capitalisation for a limited period of time'. See also **income approach**(AmE), **investment method of valuation**(BrE), Appendix C, **Financial Formulae**.   **2.** The total of all securities issued by a corporation, including common and preferred stock, bonds and additions to reserves. See also **net worth**.   **3.** In accounting, a term used to refer to additions to **capital** or reserves created in a financial statement or balance sheet. Also, the act of recording **capital expenditure** in a book of accounts.   **4.** In finance, additions of unpaid or **accrued interest** to a total indebtedness or to the principal outstanding on a loan – the interest so added, in turn, bears interest until paid. See also **compound interest**.

capitalisation table(BrE) or **capitalization table**(AmE)   See Appendix C, **Financial Formulae, Bibliography**.

capitalisation rate(BrE) or **capitalization rate**(AmE) (CAP rate)   **1.** A rate of discount or percentage selected as appropriate for the conversion of income into capital, i.e. for **capitalisation**. A rate that is sufficient to provide a return to an investor for accepting the risk of a capital investment as well as a return, or recapture, of the capital invested. Such a rate may be divided into 100 to produce a **capitalisation factor** for 'straight capitalisation' (i.e. multiplication by the current income). Thus, in the formula $I \times R = CV$, where I = the income and CV = capital value, R = capitalisation factor; or $100/R$ = the capitalisation rate. A capitalisation factor may also be applied in a formula, such as the **present value of one per period**, or the **Inwood factor**, to provide a factor for 'annuity capitalization'. In the US, 'capitalization factor' is more commonly referred to as a 'capitalization rate' or 'CAP rate', i.e. if an income is capitalized at a 'factor' of 20 the CAP rate is 5%. When this rate expresses the ratio between a single year's income and the equity invested in a property it is also called the 'equity yield rate'. See also **band-of-investment rate**(US), **component capitalization rate**(AmE), **discount rate**, **income approach**(AmE), **investment method of valuation**(BrE), **overall capitalization rate**(AmE), **yield**.   **2.**(US)See **recapture rate**.

capitalise(BrE) or **capitalize**(AmE)   **1.** To convert a series of income instalments into a single capital sum; to divide income by a percentage rate (expressed as a decimal) to obtain a capital value. **2.** To charge expenditure to a capital or reserve account. See also **capitalization**. **3.** To provide capital to a corporation, association or partnership, especially equity capital for a new venture.

capitalised value[BrE] **or capitalized value**[AmE]   **1.** A capital value obtained by the **capitalisation** of the anticipated income from a property, i.e. the value obtained by multiplying the projected income by an appropriate capitalisation factor (or dividing by a capitalization rate). See also **income approach**[AmE], **investment method of valuation**[BrE]. **2.**[Aus]"The amount that an unencumbered **fee simple** in land might reasonably be expected to realise upon sale", Valuation of Land Act 1971, s. 5(1) (SA), i.e. the **market value** of an unencumbered fee simple.

capitalisation table[BrE] **or capitalization table**[AmE]   See Appendix C, **Financial Formulae**, Bibliography.

capitalization[AmE]   See **capitalisation**[BrE].

capitalization approach[AmE] **or capitalization method**[AmE]   The application of a **capitalization factor** to the projected future net income receivable from an investment as used to arrive at the capital value. See also **capitalization**, **income approach**.

capitalization factor[AmE]   A factor or multiplier used to convert an income stream into a **capital value**. The reciprocal of a **capitalization rate** multiplied by 100, thus a capitalization rate of 5% is a capitalization factor of 20. See also **capitalization rate**, **dual-rate capitalization factor**, **single-rate capitalization factor**, **years' purchase**[BrE].

capitalize[AmE]   See **capitalise**[BrE].

capitalized-income approach[AmE]   See **income approach**.

capitalized value[AmE]   See **capitalised value**[BrE].

capper[AmE]   See **puffer**.

caption[AmE]   The introductory part of a deed, instrument, pleading, or any similar formal document. See also **premises**.

captive brand store[AmE]   A retail store that sells only brands of goods that are not traded anywhere except in stores within the same chain.

capture rate[AmE]   See **catchment area**.

caravan   **1.**[BrE]A covered vehicle for carrying people, especially one that can be used as a residence or place of business. A house on wheels, which is normally towed by a motorised vehicle, but may itself be motorised. A structure designed or adapted for human habitation that can be moved from one place to another by being towed or transported.

In English law, the installation of a caravan on land may be **development** and require **planning permission**. In addition, an occupier of land must obtain a **site licence** from the local authority before he can use that land as a 'caravan site' (Caravan Sites and Control of Development Act 1960). For this purpose a caravan is defined as: "any structure designed or adapted for human habitation which is capable of being moved from one place to another (whether by being towed, or by being transported on a motor vehicle or trailer) and any motor vehicle so designed or adapted, but does not include: (a) any railway rolling stock which is for the time being on rails forming part of a railway system, or (b) any tent", Caravan Sites and Control of Development Act 1960, s. 29(1). This definition was extended in 1968 to exclude 'twin-unit caravans' above a certain size (Caravan Sites Act 1968, s. 13(1)). Exemption to the requirement for a site licence is granted for the use of land as a caravan site within the curtilage and as an incidental use of a dwelling-house; certain short-term stays; and for certain exempt authorities

(Caravan Sites and Control of Development Act 1960, Sch. 1). See also **mobile home**. **2.**(US)A covered vehicle that is equipped with living quarters for use when traveling. A motor vehicle that is in tow of another motor vehicle, especially a vehicle that is being transported for sale. See also **mobile home**. **3.**(US)A group tour of a number of listed properties made by a group of brokers, or members of a broker's sales staff.

care See **duty of care**.

caretaker One who is put in charge of something. A person who is responsible for the upkeep and maintenance of a building. In particular, a person who fulfils such functions on a part-time basis or in the absence of the day or full-time manager. A caretaker may have limited responsibility for day-to-day maintenance and repairs, but not for the general management of the building. See also **janitor**.

carport A covered area of hard standing, usually abutting a dwelling-house, intended to be used for the parking of an automobile or automobiles. Unlike a garage, a carport is not entirely walled-in and commonly takes the form of a lean-to or roofed extension to a building that is open at least at the front end.

carriageway(BrE) A **highway** over which there is a right to drive vehicles, as well as (unless prohibited by statute) a right to drive or ride animals or to pass and repass on foot. The term 'carriageway' is presumed at common law to include a **bridleway**, but not necessarily a **driftway** (*Suffolk County Council v Mason* [1979] AC 705, 727, [1979] 2 All ER 369, 384 (HL)). A carriageway may incorporate a **footway**, but a footway is not a carriageway. A carriageway is defined by statute as "a way constituting or comprising a highway, being a way (other than a cycle track) over which the public have a right of way for the passage of vehicles", Highways Act 1980, s. 329(1). Sometimes called a 'cartway', especially when restricted to wheeled vehicles.

carried interest A partial **interest** that is retained by the vendor after the sale of a property. See also **equity participation**.

carry-over clause(US) See **extender clause**.

carryback financing(US) An arrangement by which the seller of a property agrees to defer receipt of all the purchase monies and takes back a promissory note for the unpaid balance, usually secured by a lien or mortgage on the property. See also **installment land contract**.

carrying charge or **carrying cost** **1.** The recurring costs of holding a vacant property, or a property under development or construction. For example, the interest charges on a loan. See also **front money**. **2.**(US)The regular costs of running a property. A term that may also be used to refer to the apportioned **closing costs**.

carrying rental(US) See **delay rental**.

cart-bote See **estovers**.

cartway A way for the movement of wheeled vehicles. An unmade track that serves as a means of access to a private property for a wheeled vehicle, although the public at large generally has a right thereover. See also **carriageway**, **highway**.

carve out(US) To exclude from an agreement or contract, especially in favor of another. In particular, an exclusion of specified liabilities from a blanket loan provision, as with an exclusion of a borrower from personal liability for environmental defects to a mortgaged property.

cash That which readily circulates as **money**. A term that normally has a more restricted meaning than money. Cash primarily means coins and bank notes or any **legal tender**. However, in economics it may also extend to negotiable checks and a credit balance at a bank. In particular, cash may be considered the antonym of cheque and, therefore, it includes a cashier's or certified cheque, but it does not normally include a **promissory note** (except in the form of a bank note that is legal tender). In accounting, cash may be defined as anything that a bank will accept as a deposit to be credited to a person's account.

A provision in a lease that a tenant will 'pay' or 'yield and pay' a sum of money as **rent** means payment must be made in cash, in its restricted sense (i.e. legal tender), and not by a personal cheque (although rent can be agreed to be payable in any form acceptable to the parties). In common law, if a landlord accepts a personal cheque, or indicates that he will accept a cheque in payment of rent, thereafter he cannot refuse such means of payment; provided the cheque is honoured as soon as it is presented.

cash accounting　The method of preparing accounts under which income and expenditure items are recorded when they are actually received or paid. Thus, rent, for example, is recorded when paid, rather than when legally due. Also called the 'cash basis', the 'cash receipts method', or the 'disbursement method' of accounting. cf. **accrual accounting**.

cash allowance(US)　See **prime-cost sum**.

cash available for distribution (CAD)(AmE) The cash that is available for distribution by a **Real Estate Investment Trust** to its shareholders. The CAD is determined by deducting from the **funds from operations** (FFO) the normal recurring real estate-related expenditure to maintain the REIT's properties and its revenue stream, as well as other non-cash expenses to arrive at the 'adjusted funds from operations' (AFFO), and then deducting the nonrecurring expenditures. In this calculation the rents are 'straight lined', i.e. it is assumed that the rents are received at the same average rate through the term of the lease. Also called the 'funds available for distribution' (FAD).

cash back　A financial inducement, in the form of a cash payment, or a reduction of a tenant's future obligations under a lease, granted by a building owner to a prospective tenant as an inducement to sign a lease of vacant property. See also **rent concession**, **reverse premium**.

cash basis　See **cash accounting**.

cash discount　A reduction in a price or a consideration due under a contract for early or prompt payment. cf. **trade discount**.

cash down(US)　1. See **deposit**.　2. See **cash out**.

cash flow　1. The actual movement of **cash** in and out of an enterprise, as distinguished from the earnings of the enterprise. A term also used for the difference between the income and expenses resulting from an investment, particularly when these sums are accounted for as and when paid or received (as in cash accounting), rather than when due (as in accrual accounting). cf. **net profit**. See also **net cash flow**.　2. The cash generated by an investment after all payments have been made that are necessary to sustain that investment. In the case of a real estate investment 'cash flow' generally refers to the **income** available to the owner, after the payment of all operating expenses, but before depreciation and tax. Cash flow may be before or after debt service (principal and interest), although when used without qualification it generally refers to the latter; the actual cash available to the building owner. However, cash flow is income received before taking any account of the investor's personal outgoings, i.e. before management overheads and tax, and before depreciation. Sometimes cash flow may refer to the cash available after tax, but this should be referred to expressly as 'after-tax cash flow' or **net after-tax cash flow**. In the US, cash flow is also called 'cash throw-off'. cf. **net income**, **spendable income**.

cash-flow analysis　The financial analysis of **net cash flow** to be derived from a real estate investment or a development project. Cash-flow analysis considers the total of all cash outflows and inflows for the investment or project. In particular, cash flow analysis is carried out to ascertain the debt or equity requirements at any stage in the anticipated life of the investment or at any stage during the development, from its inception to completion. In addition it ascertains the income that may be generated from the investment. See also **discounted cash flow, feasibility analysis**.

cash-flow mortgage(US)   A mortgage that provides that the repayments will be made based entirely on the cash flow from the property. Such an arrangement is more common on workouts where the income is insufficiently predictable to meet a fixed rate of interest.

cash-flow rate of return(US)   See **cash-on-cash return**.

cash market value   See **cash value, market value**.

cash method   See **cash accounting**.

cash-on-cash return or **cash-on-cash yield**   The relationship, expressed as a percentage, between **cash flow** (i.e. the net income receivable after debt service but before tax) and the total **equity** outlay on an investment. In determining such a return the cash flow includes the **effective gross income** less all outgoing (real estate taxes, operating expenses and interest and principal on financing); but no account is taken of capital appreciation (or depreciation) or 'equity build-up' resulting from repayments of principal on any loan secured on the property. Also called the 'equity-dividend rate' (especially when expressed on the basis of after-tax cash flow), 'cash-flow rate', 'cash-flow return' or 'cash-on-cash rate'. In the UK also called the 'equity yield' (this latter term should be distinguished from the **equity yield rate**, which is used in the US to refer to a return that takes into account increases in the equity value of a property). See also **free and clear return**.

cash on the barrel head or **cash on the line**(US)   See **front money**.

cash out(US)   The requirement by a seller to take the entire proceeds of a sale in cash, i.e. to require 'cash down' rather than granting a **purchase money mortgage** or accepting an **installment contract**.

cash receipts method of accounting   See **cash accounting**.

cash rent   1. A fixed or **base rent** payable under a lease when there is no provision for any additional payment as a contribution towards operating costs, nor any payment based on a share of the tenant's business operations such as a **percentage rent**. cf. **share rent**. See also **escalation clause, primary and secondary rental**.   2. An amount of rent payable, in **cash**; usually in advance. See also **cash tenant**.

cash tenant   A tenant who pays rent as cash. In particular, a farm tenant whose rent is based solely on a monetary payment, as distinguished from a tenant who pays rent wholly or partly on the basis of a share of his crops. cf. **share tenant**. See also **cash rent**.

cash throw-off(US)   See **cash flow**.

cash value   The **market value** of a property on the basis of a private sale with no exchange of properties, transfer of debt or deferred payments, i.e. on the basis of an all-cash transaction. The value that could be received in cash for a property when it is sold in the normal course of business and there is no compulsion to sell. cf. **forced-sale value**. See also **actual cash value, cash out**.

cashier's check(AmE) or **cashier's cheque**(BrE)   See **bank check**.

casualty insurance   See **accident insurance**.

catching bargain   An **unconscionable** bargain. In particular, an agreement to lend or pay money, made on unreasonable or oppressive terms, usually because the borrower or payer is at a distinct bargaining disadvantage relative to the other party. A term which originally referred to a loan made to someone who had expectations of receiving property, especially as an heir expectant, when the lender hoped to receive a share of the property or inheritance, thereby rendering the loan unconscionable. See also **usury**.

catchment area   The area from which a business or retail center is assumed to derive its trade; the area over which a public service, e.g. a school, cinema, etc., exerts an influence; or the area from which any new development project is likely to draw significant demand. The limits of this area may be assessed by considering population mobility; competitive influences on consumer demand; socio-economic trends; and factors that affect accessibility, whether physical or psychological. The constituents of a catchment area may be analysed on the basis of population (size, family units, age, etc.); income levels; and other economic data (car and durable goods ownership, consumer preferences, housing, etc.). For a **shopping center**, this area is determined primarily by travelling time (the attraction of a center decreases in geometric proportion to the travelling time for a consumer); the dynamic attraction of the center; natural barriers, such as intervening high land, a river or railroad, and the influence of competitive retail units. According to Reilly's Law "the competitive influence of any two retail centers will be in direct proportion to the square of the size of those centers and in inverse ratio to the square of the distance from any unit of population", W. J. Reilly, *The Law of Retail Gravitation*. 2nd ed. New York: Pillsbury, 1953. Also called a 'market area', 'retail trade area' or 'trade area'. In the US, the percentage of the population that is likely to be drawn to a retail center from the catchment area is referred to as the 'capture rate'. See also **feasibility analysis**.

causa causans(Lat)   'The causing cause'; 'the immediate cause'. The effective cause of **damage**;

the last link in the chain of events that causes injury or loss.

causa mortis(Lat)   'In expectation of death'. See **gift** *causa mortis*.

causa proxima et non remota spectatur(Lat)   'It is the immediate, not the remote cause, that should be considered'. See **damages**.

cause   1. Something or somebody that brings about an action, effect or event. An act that precedes, and brings about, a result. See also **commission**.   2. A ground for a legal **action**; a court action.   3. The justification for the making of a promise; the reason or motive for an action or condition. In the civil law, a cause is one of the principal requirements for a valid contract; but the common law requires more than a cause, it requires a motive and **consideration**.

caution   1.(Eng)A temporary means of protecting an interest in, or a charge on, registered land by which the person seeking protection (the cautioner) enters his claim on the Proprietorship Register (if against the land) or the Charges Register (if against a charge) at the Land Registry. The effect of a caution is to enable the cautioner to take steps to protect his interest, but it does not of itself create any interest in land. The Land Registrar must notify a cautioner of any proposal (**dealing**) affecting the subject land, thereby giving him the opportunity to raise an objection to a proposed first registration or a dealing (LRA 1925, ss. 53-56, as amended). With the repeal of the LRA 1925, 'cautions against dealing' can no longer be entered on the Register (LRA 2002, Sch 13). 2.(Eng)An entry on the Land Registry made in respect of unregistered land by a person who claims to be the owner of a "qualifying estate" or an "interest affecting a qualifying estate". A qualifying estate is a legal estate which relates to the land that is the subject of the caution; and is an interest of any of the following kinds: "(i) an estate in land, (ii) a rentcharge, (iii) a franchise, and (iv) a profit a prendre in gross" LRA 2002, ss. 15, 132(1). A caution is entered on the register to protect a claimant's rights against the first person to register his land, but is not intended to be a substitute for registration and may not be used to protect an estate that should itself be registered. **3.**(Aus)An entry that is recorded against land to indicate that there are rights against the subject land that have not yet recorded. Used especially when land is first recorded under the **Torrens title system**. See also **caveat**.

caution money(US)   See **earnest money**.

caveat   **1.** A caution or warning. A notice that is filed with a court to stay proceedings until a person's claim is heard. In particular, an entry on a register that is intended to notify someone of a charge or claim to land. See also **caution**, **land charge**.   **2.**(Aus/NZ)A document that, when lodged with the **Land Titles Office**, protects an existing right, or establishes an existing claim, against land. A caveat is intended to protect an interest in land temporarily, either when that interest is not recordable or has not yet been recorded. A caveat is not intended to be **notice** of the existence of the interest, but is recorded so that the holder of the interest is notified before any **dealing** takes place in the subject land. In Australia, the system for the recording of caveats varies according to the State. In New Zealand, caveats are registrable in accordance with the provisions of the Land Transfer Act 1952. See also **caveatable interest**.
Lindsay, S. *Caveats Against Dealing in Australia and New Zealand*. Annandale, NSW: The Federation Press 1995.

caveat emptor(Lat)   'Let the buyer beware'. A principle derived from Roman law on the sale of **goods** and now a general principle of common law that a buyer of goods should make all reasonable enquiries before effecting a purchase.
The principle of *caveat emptor* is considered to have limited application to contracts for the sale of real property. A seller is not bound to draw attention to a **patent defect**, in that respect the buyer is expected to make his own enquiries and

investigations. Nonetheless, a vendor of property is obliged to disclose any **latent defect** of which he is aware; must not misdescribe or misrepresent any facts; and in certain cases has a statutory obligation to adequately describe or represent the condition of the property. The principle does not apply if an enquiry is made and the vendor does not supply a reasonable and accurate response; when there is a fiduciary relationship between the parties; or in cases of **fraud**. It does not excuse a seller in cases of passive concealment or **misrepresentation**. Nonetheless, *caveat emptor* generally applies in the case of a sale by auction, or to a **judicial sale**, where the purchaser must take the risks of his own inquiry and there is usually no 'warranty' as to title.
In English law, it is a criminal offence to make a "false or misleading statement" about property matters in the course of estate agency business or property development business, unless the person making the statement can show that he took all reasonable steps and exercised all due diligence to avoid the offence (Property Misdescription Act 1991, ss. 1, 2). cf. *caveat venditor*. See also **as is**, **constructive notice**, **exclusion clause**, **fit for human habitation**(Eng), **fitness for the purpose**, **misdescription**, **negligence**, **notice**, **undue influence**, **warranty of habitability**(US).

caveat venditor(Lat)   'Let the seller beware'. A maxim primarily of the civil law. cf. *caveat emptor*. See also **fit for human habitation**(Eng), **implied term**, **misrepresentation**, **negligence**, **puffing**, **warranty of habitability**(US).

caveatable interest(Aus/NZ)   An interest that can be the subject of a **caveat** in respect of land that is recorded under the **Torrens title system**. Such an interest must relate to land itself and not merely be the subject of a personal contract. Caveatable interests includes an equitable lease; an equitable mortgage; the benefit an easement or a restrictive covenant; a purchaser's right under a contract for the sale of land; and the right to the proceeds of sale from land held in trust. See also **trust for sale**.

cease and desist order(US)   An order issued by a court or regulatory authority commanding a party to refrain from, or to take, a certain course of action. See also **injunction**.

cede   To give up, yield, or **surrender**. To grant or **transfer**. See also **assignment, cession**.

ceiling loan   The maximum amount that a mortgagee agrees to advance as a loan against the security of a particular property or properties. Used especially to refer to the maximum amount that will be advanced when certain conditions have been met, e.g. when a building is fully let. Also called a 'top loan'. cf. **floor loan**. See also **holdback, mortgage loan**.

ceiling price   1. The highest price that a purchaser will bid or pay for a property.   2. The highest price that can be obtained for a property, or the highest price that a vendor seeks to achieve before he will conclude a bargain. A ceiling price may be equivalent to the **market value** or, if the parties agree, it may exceed that value.

cellar   A vault or underground room. An area of a building, entirely or predominantly below ground level, usually used for storage purposes. A cellar may be distinguished from a **basement** by reason of its use; the former, normally, is left as a bare shell and is used primarily for storage, whereas the latter is generally decorated in some way and used for any purpose for which other floors in a building can be used.

center line   See *ad medium filum, ad medium filum aquæ*, **boundary line, party wall**.

central assessment(US)   An **assessment** that is made in respect of a property that is held by a single owner but is located in more than one assessment district.

central business district (CBD)   The center of the 'downtown' area of a town or city; the core of an urban area where generally there is the greatest concentration of administrative and financial offices, retail establishments, entertainment facilities and hotels. In the US, the CBD is the area that historically was the center of a town or city for business and shopping and was the area of highest land values, i.e. the area where economic activity is at its highest. (Based on the theory that land will tend to be used for those purposes that yield the highest net return—the **highest and best use**, the CBD is the area where competition for land is at its greatest; although in some towns and cities the CBD is no longer the areas of highest property values as the most valuable users have moved to decentralized or new suburban locations.) cf. **civic center**. See also **location theory, prime location**.

central core   See **service core**.

central heating   A system for heating all or most of a building from one heat source, without any means of artificial air treatment. Usually hot water or steam from the source is circulated through pipes, or hot air through ducts, to radiators or air outlets around the building. cf. **air-conditioning**.

CERCLA(US)   Commonly known as 'Superfund'. The Comprehensive Environmental Response, Compensation, and Liability Act of 1980 (42 USC §§ 9601 to 9675) as amended by the Superfund Amendments and Reauthorization Act of 1986 (SARA), that imposes obligations on owners, occupiers, users or operators and lenders involved with hazardous materials and environmental remediation of land. The Act, and its related regulations, provides powers for the **Environmental Protection Agency** to limit the spread of hazardous waste from an area of land or to clean up a contaminated site and recover the cost from the owner or operator of a contaminated site or any party who generated the contamination. All parties are jointly and severally liable for the cost of complying with the EPA's requirements and have a strict and retrospective liability for any contamination.

certain price   See **price**.

certain rent   See dead rent.

certain term   See term.

certainty of rent   See rent.

certificate as to title(Aus/NZ)   A certificate that evidences a title to land. See **Torrens certificate of title**.

certificate   1. See **building certificate**.   2. See **appraisal report**(US), **certificate of valuation**(Eng), **interim payment**.   3. See **land certificate**.   4. See **tax certificate**.

certificate for value(Eng) A statement, usually at the end of a conveyance, certifying within which band of values for **stamp duty** a transaction falls. Also called a 'certificate of value'.

certificate of abstracter(US)   See abstracter's certificate.

certificate of acknowledgment(US)   See acknowledgment.

certificate of appraisal(US)   See **appraisal report**.

certificate of appropriate alternative development(Eng)   A certificate that may be issued, to assist in determining the amount of **compulsory purchase compensation**, which indicates a specified form of development that would have been permitted if the land concerned were not to be acquired compulsorily (Land Compensation Act 1971, s. 17, as amended by the Planning and Compensation Act 1991, s. 65). Such a certificate is sought when no specified form of use or development that has a market value is laid down for the area of land to be acquired. The application for the certificate represents a form of application for planning permission. Also called a 'section 17 certificate'. See also **planning assumptions**.

certificate of charge(Eng) See charge certificate.

certificate of classification(Aus) A certificate issued by a local council upon completion of a building setting out the type of construction used and the uses that are permitted for the building.

certificate of completion (CC)(US)   A certificate issued by the architect (or sometimes the engineer) responsible for building work confirming that the construction work has been completed in accordance with the plans and specification and that final payment under the contract is due and payable. Also called a 'completion certificate'. See also **certificate of practical completion**(BrE), **certificate of occupancy**(US).

certificate of completion of making good defects   See **certificate of practical completion**.

certificate of compliance(US) See **certificate of zoning compliance**.

certificate of deposit (CD) A receipt issued by a bank or trust company as an acknowledgment that funds have been received on deposit and will be repaid to the depositor or some other person specified in the certificate. The deposit may be repayable on 'demand' (a 'demand certificate') or after a stated period of time (a 'time deposit').

certificate of eligibility(US)   A certificate issued by the Veterans Administration confirming that a prospective mortgagor will qualify for a **Veterans Administration loan**.

certificate of estoppel(US)   See **estoppel certificate**.

certificate of fair rent(Eng)   See **registered rent**.

certificate of headright(US)   See **land scrip**.

certificate of insurance   See **cover note**, **insurance certificate**.

certificate of indebtedness 1. A short-term **promissory note** issued by a corporation or statutory body as an acknowledgment of a **floating charge**. cf. **debenture**. 2. In banking another term for a **certificate of deposit**.

certificate of interest(US) A certificate issued to a participant in a **joint venture** evidencing the extent of the bearer's participation or interest in a property held by the venture.

certificate of lawfulness(Eng) A certificate issued by a local planning authority to a person who has made a request to know if: (a) any existing use of land or buildings, (b) any operation that has already been carried out, or (c) any other matter constituting a failure to comply with a planning condition is "lawful"; or if any proposed operation or use of land or buildings is "lawful" (TCPA 1990, ss. 191-193). If granted, a certificate of lawfulness demonstrates that the proposed, or the existing development, is lawful. It does not act as a grant of **planning permission**. An appeal against a refusal, or a failure to issue a certificate may be made within eight weeks to the Secretary of State (TCPA 1990, s. 195). Also called a 'certificate of lawfulness of existing use or development' (CLEUD); or a 'certificate of lawfulness of proposed use or development' (CLOPUD). See also **abandonment**.

certificate of no defenses(US) See **estoppel certificate**.

certificate of non-completion(BrE) A certificate issued in accordance with the provisions of a **building contract** by the architect (or if appropriate the 'contract administrator') certifying that the contractor has failed to complete the contract works by the completion date. The certificate usually fixes a new completion date and may enable the employer to levy liquidated and ascertained damages against the contractor. See also **liquidated damages**.

certificate of non-listing(Eng) See **listed building**.

certificate of occupancy (CO)(US/Aus) A document issued by a local municipality or council confirming that a new building meets the zoning and building ordinances of the state, city or town and, therefore, that it may be occupied. A certificate of occupancy is a complement to the **building permit**, or in Australia a building approval, as it confirms that the building conforms to the provisions of that permit. In some areas called a 'completion order'. Also called an 'occupancy certificate' or 'occupancy permit'. See also **certificate of zoning compliance**.

certificate of partial completion See **certificate of practical completion**.

certificate of partial possession See **certificate of practical completion**.

certificate of payment See **certificate of valuation**.

certificate of practical completion(BrE) A certificate issued by the architect, engineer or other professionally appointed party (a 'contracts administrator') confirming that a building contract has reached the stage of **practical completion**. The effect of the certificate is to hand over responsibility for the building works from the contractor to the employer. The certificate is normally accompanied by a statement that the employer is liable for the final instalment of the contract price, less any agreed **retention sum**. The certificate may be issued in conjunction with a schedule or certificate of outstanding defects and fixes the commencement date for the **defects liability period**. The certificate also ends the period for **liquidated damages**. The certificate of practical completion transfers responsibility for the works to the employer and thereby ends the contractor's liability for insurance. When the defects have been made good to the satisfaction of the contracts administrator a 'certificate of completion of making good defects' is issued and any outstanding payment is released to the contractor. A 'certificate of partial possession' (also called a 'certificate of partial completion') may be issued when the employer is granted possession of only part of the work and before completion of the whole. In that event, the certificate has the same effect, but only in respect of the completed part.

In Australia, also called a 'notice of practical completion'. See also **certificate of completion**(US).

certificate of purchase(US)   See **certificate of sale**.

certificate of reasonable value (CRV)(US) A certificate issued by the Veterans Administration confirming the appraised value of a property and the maximum loan amount that the VA will guarantee against the security of that property. See also **Veterans Administration loan**.

certificate of redemption(US)   A certificate issued by the sheriff after a judgment debtor has exercised a **statutory right of redemption** confirming receipt of the full amount due, including interest, and that the property has been released from the mortgage or lien.

certificate of reduction(US)   See **reduction certificate**.

certificate of sale(US)   A certificate issued subsequent to a **tax sale** or a **judicial sale** confirming that title to property will pass to the designated purchaser, after any statutory period allowable for redemption by the former debtor or mortgagor. Only after the expiration of the period of redemption is a **tax deed** delivered confirming the transfer of title. Prior to that stage the purchaser has merely an inchoate right or lien, which ripens into title upon compliance with the statutory requirements that govern such sales. Also called a 'certificate of purchase', or in the case of a tax sale a 'tax certificate'.

certificate of satisfaction(US)   See **satisfaction certificate**.

certificate of search(Eng)   See **official certificate of search**.

certificate of title   1.(US)A formal certificate that gives an opinion on the status of an owner's or mortgagee's title to a parcel of land based on an examination of the public records. Usually issued by a title company, attorney, a licensed abstractor, or a government-appointed Registrar of Titles. Certificates of title are used mostly in southern and eastern states. The certificate is issued after recorded documents of title have been examined in detail and it stipulates who is understood to be the true owner of the land in question, the status of the title, and sets out details of any charges, encumbrances, liens, etc. affecting the land. The certificate deals only with matters of public record, it is an 'opinion' and as such does not guarantee the title nor does it exonerate a purchaser against any defect of title of which he has **notice** or against fraud, forgery or similar 'hidden defects'. The issuer of the certificate is only responsible for any negligence in the search and preparation of the certificate. (Not to be confused with a **title insurance** document, which warrants the validity of the title.) In some states called a 'title opinion' or 'opinion of title'. cf. **abstract of title**. See also **abstractor's certificate**, **marketable title**.   2. A certificate that evidences a title to land. See **land certificate**(Eng), **Land Transfer land**(NZ), **Torrens certificate of title**(Aus/NZ/US).

certificate of valuation   1. See **valuation certificate**.   2.(Eng)A certificate, issued by an architect, engineer, or other suitably qualified third party (the 'contract administrator' or 'owner's representative'), confirming the value of the work carried out under the terms of a building or construction contract. The certificate states the value of the work carried out up to a particular point in time and confirms to the client the amount of any payment due to the contractor. An 'Interim Certificate' is generally issued at regular intervals (usually monthly) during the term of the building work, confirming the value of work done and the amount of the 'progress payment', if any, due at that stage. A 'Penultimate Certificate' may be issued along with the **certificate of practical completion**, which apart from providing for the 'penultimate payment' requires the reduction of the **retention sum**, generally from 5 to 2½ per cent. A 'Final Certificate' is issued when all the obligations of the building contract have been fulfilled and any **defects period** has passed. The Final certificate is intended to inform the employer that all work has been carried out, to the certifier's satisfaction, and that payment should be made in full (or as agreed between the parties), including the release of the balance of the retention sum. Also called (as appropriate) an 'architect's certificate' or 'engineer's certificate'. See also **progress certificate**.

certificate of value(Eng) **1.** A formal certificate, issued by the **Lands Tribunal**, stating the value of a property when land is to be sold to a body with compulsory purchase powers. **2.** See **certificate for value**. **3.** A certificate produced by a **valuation officer** setting out the **rateable value** of a particular **hereditament** at a given point in time (Non Domestic Rating (Chargeable Amounts) Regulations 1994, reg. 35).

certificate of zoning compliance or **certificate of zoning ordinance compliance**(US) **1.** A certificate that is issued by an authorized representative of the local municipality confirming that all the zoning regulations have been complied with. See also **certificate of occupancy**. **2.** A certificate issued by a local municipality indicating the areas in which a building fails to comply with the local zoning regulations and, therefore, may be considered a **non-conforming use**. Such certificates are only applied in a few jurisdictions.

certified appraiser(US) An appraiser who is certified by the appropriate state agency to value real estate in accordance with the provisions of the Federal Institutions Reform, Recovery, and Enforcement Act (FIRREA). Only a certified appraiser may appraise property in connection with federally related transactions, as well as most properties that are to be used as security for federally insured loans or loans to be made by federal agencies.

A certified appraiser is required to comply with the Appraisal Qualification Criteria promulgated by the Board of the **Appraisal Foundation**. A certified appraiser is generally a member of one of the major appraisal organizations in the US. See also Appendix A, **Real Estate Associations**.

Certified Assessment Evaluator(US) See Appendix A, **Real Estate Associations, International Association of Assessing Officers**.

certified check(AmE) or **certified cheque**(BrE) A personal check/cheque that the bank upon whom it is drawn has certified will be honoured when it is presented for payment. The check is stamped on the face 'certified' or 'accepted' and signed by an officer of the bank and funds are then set aside (or frozen) to meet the liability. Also called a 'marked check'. See also **bank draft**.

certified copy A copy of a document or instrument that is signed and certified as being a true copy by the person having custody of the original, e.g. by a lawyer or an officer of a public records office. See also **attest, conformed copy**(US), **office copy**.

Certified Property Manager (CPM)(US) See Appendix A, **Real Estate Associations, Institute of Real Estate Management**.

certum est ...(Lat) See *id certum est quod certum reddi potest*.

cessation clause(US) A clause in an **oil and gas lease**, which provides that the lease will not terminate if operations cease after the failure to find oil or gas or if production ceases, provided new drilling or operations restart within a specified period, or if a specified payment of a fixed rental is made. See also **dead rent**.

cesser **1.** The ending of a term, annuity or similar continuing right. In particular, the **determination** of an interest in land due to the ending of a term of years. See also **termination**.

2. The ending of a liability, annuity, or the like. **3.**(Eng)The coming to an end of a mortgage term on repayment of the mortgage debt (LPA 1925, s. 116). See also **equity of redemption, satisfied term.**

cession The **transfer** or **relinquishment** of a right of action or a claim. The yielding or ceding of property to another. In international law, the yielding up of territory by one state or government to another. In ecclesiastical law, the vacating or surrendering of a **benefice**. See also **cede.**

cession deed(US) **1.** A deed used to transfer a right or a claim to a debt, obligation, or property. Equivalent to a deed of assignment in English law. **2.** A deed by which a property owner expressly dedicates a street to a government or municipal authority. See also **dedication.**

cessment An **assessment** or tax.

cestui que trust (pl. **cestuis que trust**) Pronounced 'ses'twe-ker-trust' and derived from Norman French *cestui à que trust*, 'he for whom is the trust' (held). The **beneficiary** of a trust; the party in whose name a property is held in trust. cf. *cestui que use.*

cestui que use or **cestuy que use** Pronounced 'ses'twe-ker-use'. A shortened form of *cestui à que oes le feoffment fut fait*, being Norman French for 'he to whom the use of the **feoffment** is made', i.e. the person to whom the true benefit of land is conveyed. In modern law when a trust is established to hold land for another's benefit the **beneficiary** may be referred to as the *cestui que trust.* See also **use.**

cestui que vie **1.** Pronounced 'ses'twe-ker-vie' and derived from Norman French *cestui à que vie*, 'he for whose life'. A person whose life determines the duration of an estate or interest in land, especially when another holds that interest. See also *pur autre vie*, **tenant for life.** **2.** A person against whose life an insurance policy is written.

ceteris paribus(Lat) 'All other things being equal'.

chain of title The succession of deeds or other instruments that establish a **root of title**. The history of a title to land as traced from conveyance to conveyance, or through conveyances and other documents of transfer. In particular, the documents that prove title to land where there is no established or recorded title; as opposed to a **certificate of title**(US), or a **land certificate**(Eng), which evidences title to registered or recorded land.

In the US, a chain of title may be ascertained from the public recorder's office and may well go back to a patent granted by the federal government (or in colonial states to a grant from the British Crown or the French or Spanish governments), or some other official grantor of titles, or its "original source". However, in practice the abstractor may not consider it necessary to go back more than 60 years (or in some jurisdictions 50 or even 30 years) to establish a good 'root of title'.

In English law, as a rule, a chain of title is now only required to go back 15 years (LPA 1969, s. 23), although it may be desirable to go back up to 30 years to allow for the discovery of all rights that may affect the land and to allow for fraud or a mistake in one of the previous documents.

In Australia and Canada, in most jurisdictions, good chain of title must go back at least 30 years. In New Zealand, it must go back at least 20 years. See also **abstract of title.**

chain store One of a group of stores, in common business ownership, management or supervision, selling similar merchandise under a uniform policy. The trading outlets may be a series of small stores, supermarkets, department stores, or any other form of **retail** store. See also **shop, store.**

chalet **1.** A Swiss French derivative of the Old French *chasel*, 'farmstead' or 'cottage' A small wooden house or cabin with an A-frame style of construction, originally found in the Alpine regions of Europe (especially Switzerland). The house is characterised by large overhanging eaves that provides protection from heavy snowfalls. **2.** A small hut on a beach or holiday camp.

challenge procedure(Eng) See **advertisement**.

chance bargain A **bargain** made when both parties recognise the risks entailed, or a contract made on the basis of supposed facts that the parties acknowledge might have limited veracity.

change in interest A term used in insurance policies to refer to a change in the nature or quantity of the interest held in a property, especially a change that affects the risk to the insurer such as a division of the interest in a property between a husband and wife.

change of use 1. A change in the use to which a property is put, especially a substantial change of use or a significant intensification of the use of land or a building. As a rule, such a change is considered a breach of the planning or zoning regulations and requires authorisation. However, what constitutes a 'change of use' is a matter of degree, in general the change should be material and extend beyond a mere intensification of use. See also **material change in the use**(Eng). **2.** A change in the use to which a leased property is put. If a lease contains no restriction as to the use to which the demised premises may be put, the tenant is at liberty to make whatever use of the premises, he chooses, provided the use is consistent with the design and construction of the property, is lawful, and is consistent with the general terms of the lease (*Gas Light and Coke Co v Turner* (1840) 6 Bing NC 324, 133 Eng Rep 127; 49 Am.Jur.2d., L & T, §§ 484, 506). However, a lease normally stipulates, in the **use clause**, the purpose for which the demised premises may, or may not, be used. This covenant may take the form of an absolute prohibition of any change of use; it may specify one or more uses to which the premises may be put; it may prohibit certain types of use; or it may prohibit uses that cause a nuisance, or

are offensive, noxious or dangerous, or in some other way affect the value of the property or adjoining property. The covenant may provide also that the landlord's consent is to be obtained to any change of use, giving the landlord either an absolute right to refuse such consent or giving him the right to refuse consent on 'reasonable' grounds. In the event of a breach of such a covenant, the landlord may obtain an award of damages or apply for an injunction to restrain the tenant. This type of covenant runs with the land and binds any assignee or subtenant.

Under English statute law, a landlord is prohibited from requiring a **fine** (in the form of any increased rent or otherwise) merely for granting consent to a change of use (L&T Act 1927, s. 19(3)). A landlord may restrict any change of use in accordance with the express terms of the lease and, unlike a **restraint on alienation** (a covenant not to assign or sub-let), there is no statutory introduction of words such as 'not to unreasonably withhold consent' in the case of such a restriction. On the other hand, if the covenant expressly provides that the landlord's consent shall not be unreasonably withheld, then the landlord may not refuse consent in order to obtain a collateral advantage. For example, he may not refuse consent because of the effect that a change of use might have on the value of an adjoining property that is also owned by him. However, if the lease provides that a change of use may be refused when that is considered to be in the best interests of 'good estate management' of adjoining property and the landlord can demonstrate a genuine policy in that respect, such refusal may be upheld.

In the US, any restriction imposed by the landlord on the tenant's free right to use the demised premises is generally construed against the landlord. In addition, the courts may look to the normal business practices and the limitations on the tenant's ability to trade freely. As a rule, a lease clause that sets out a particular use to which the premises may be put sanctions that use, but does not necessarily limit the tenant to that use alone (*Forman v. United States*, 767 F.2d 875, 880-

881 (Fed. Cir. 1985)). See also **restrictive covenant, usual covenant**.

change order(AmE)   A properly authorized request, submitted by the owner, architect, or sometimes an engineer, to a contractor, to make a change in the work to be carried out under a building contract or to change a term or provision of that contract. Such an order may permit the contractor to demand a change in the contract price or the date for completion if the change warrants extra cost for new work or fundamentally affects the construction program. Most construction contracts provide that any change order must be submitted in writing and, if not so ordered, they will not be binding on the employer. However, an order made by the owner may be binding provided it is clear what changes the owner requires; especially when the changes require an immediate decision. Sometimes called a 'modification order' or 'proceed order', according to the form of instruction issued. See also **variation order**(AmE).
Cushman Robert F., and Stephen D. Butler. *Construction Change Order Claims*. New York: Wiley, 1994 with 1996 supplement.
O'Brien, James. *Construction Change Orders*. New York: McGraw-Hill, 1998.

channel   A passageway between well defined banks through which water is intended to flow. The bed of a river, stream or other **watercourse**, especially the hollow bed of the river where the main stream of water flows. See also *ad medium filum aquæ*, **canal**.

charge   1. An obligation or liability to pay money, supported by an agreement in which property is bound as **security** for the performance of that obligation, but where there is no corresponding transfer of possession, title, or an interest in the property. 'Charge' is a word of general meaning and as such may include a **mortgage**, **lien**, or any similar claim against property, although it does not have as broad a meaning as **encumbrance**. In a more restricted sense, the term may be applied to any loan that includes a right to hold property, or a right over property, as security for a debt, and, therefore, any loan that is more effective than a personal debt. The principal difference between a charge and a common law mortgage is that a chargee cannot foreclose (i.e. acquire ownership of the property), as he has no title that can be converted into a right to own the property nor may he take any form of action for possession. The chargee has no ownership interest in the property proffered as security, but he may apply to a court for an order that the property be sold as satisfaction for the discharge of the debt, or he may appoint a **receiver** to collect any rents and profits generated by the property. See also **charge by way of a legal mortgage**(Eng), **charging order**, **equitable mortgage**, **fixed charge**, **floating charge**, **land charge**(Eng), **limited owner's charge**(Eng), **rentcharge**.   2. "Any mortgage, charge or lien for securing money or money's worth", LRA 2002, s. 132(1).   3. An expense incurred or due; a price required or demanded for something. A pecuniary liability for property, which may include any expense related to the property, including real property tax. See also **cost**, **expenditure**, **liability**, **service charge**.   4. To impose a burden or claim against a property.

charge by way of a legal mortgage(Eng)
One of the two ways in which **legal mortgage** may be created (LPA 1925, s. 85). In the case of a freehold, the mortgagee is granted the same protection, powers and remedies (including the right to take proceedings to obtain possession from the occupiers and the persons in receipt of rents and profits, or any of them) as if a mortgage had been created by a lease for a term of 3000 years; and in the case of a mortgage for a term of years absolute, the mortgagee is granted the same rights as if the mortgage had been created for a term that is one day less than the mortgagor's term (LPA 1925, s. 87; *Regent Oil Co v J.A. Gregory (Hatch End) Ltd* [1966] Ch 402, 431, [1965] 3 All ER 673, 681). In practice, a 'charge by way of a legal mortgage' is the most common way of creating a legal mortgage because: (a) the form is simpler than granting a lease for a term of years; (b) the

mortgagor retains his interest in the land which he may sell, provided he redeems the loan; (c) it can be applied in the same way to a freehold or a leasehold interest in land (or to combined interests, if so required); and (d) the mortgagor is free usually to sub-let his property without being bound by the formalities incumbent on a tenant. Although strictly a charge (being called a **legal charge**), in substance a 'charge by way of a legal mortgage' is a mortgage; the creditor being treated in law as if he has an interest in the land rather than a mere claim to the proceeds of sale of the secured property. In particular, in the event of a default, the mortgagee has the same right to take proceedings to obtain possession (the **right of re-entry**) as a lessor. In the case of registered land, it is not necessary to use the expression 'by way of a legal mortgage'; although the right does not take effect as a 'legal charge' until it is registered. See also **charge certificate**, **legal interest**, **registered charge**.

charge certificate(Eng)   A certificate issued by the **Land Registry** after a mortgagee of registered land has entered his charge on the Charges Register. The certificate has the original mortgage or charge deed annexed, but in other respects it takes the same form as the **land certificate**. It is issued in favour of the chargee and is generally retained by the chargee, or it can be deposited at the Land Registry to be held for as long as the charge subsists (LRA 1925, ss. 63, 65). With the advent of electronic conveyancing, a charge certificate will no longer issued by the Land Registry and a 'title information document' will be provided as a copy of the register to the **registered proprietor** (LRA 2002, s. 67). See also **legal charge**, **registered charge**.

chargeable gain   See **capital gains tax**.

Charges Register(Eng)   See **Companies Charges Register, Land Charges Register, Land Registry, local land charges register**.

charging clause(US)   A clause in a trust document that states that a trustee may charge for his services.

charging lien(US)   See **lien**.

charging order   1.(Eng)An order, made by the High Court or any county court for the purpose of enforcing a judgement or an order of either of those courts, for the payment of money by a debtor to a creditor. In particular, such an order is made against the stock of a publicly quoted company. A charging order may impose a charge on any land, or interest in land, of the debtor as specified in the order (Charging Orders Act 1979, s. 1(1)). See also **caution**, **equitable charge**.   2.(Eng)An order, made by a local authority, which creates a charge on a property and is granted for the benefit of a tenant who has been obliged to carry out repairs in accordance with the provisions of a **repairs notice**. The order is a means by which a tenant can secure the recovery of those costs that are the responsibility of his landlord.   3.(US)An order by which a creditor of a judgment debtor, who in turn is a partner, is able to obtain a right to the debtor's beneficial interest (Uniform Partnership Act, § 28).

charity shop(BrE)   A **shop** used for the sale of goods received by a charity. The occupier of such shops is entitled to relief from the liability to pay rates (Local Government Finance Act 1988, ss. 43, 47).

chartered surveyor   See Appendix A, **Real Estate Associations, The Royal Institution of Chartered Surveyors**.

chase   Derived from the Latin *captare*, 'to take' or 'to hunt'. An area of open land set aside for keeping wild beasts of chase, with a right to hunt thereover either exclusively or in common with others, or as a game preserve. Historically, an area of enclosed land stocked with wild beasts of chase and granted as a liberty or franchise for hunting by select individuals, either as a sole right or a joint right with the owner of the land. A **forest** may be a chase but, as a rule, a chase is smaller and is left in a more natural state than a forest. A chase is bigger, less enclosed and less formal than a **park**.

chattel   Derived from mediaeval Latin *capitale*, 'principal' or 'wealth', or the Old French *chatel*, 'goods' or 'property' (from which comes the Norman French *cattel* or cattle which were a primary form of wealth and an early means of exchange). Any kind of goods, property or right to property, other than a freehold interest in land. Chattels include goods, but also living things such as horses, cattle, dogs, cats, poultry, etc. In particular, a right to property that is not of unlimited duration, either because of the temporary nature of the property or of the right. Chattels are classified as 'chattels real' – those associated with land or realty; and 'chattels personal' – a broad category of movable and tangible property or personal effects, e.g. furniture, jewellery, stocks, shares, horses, beasts, as well as intangible property such as copyright. Trees and crops that are part of the realty before cutting, i.e. non-annual crops, are sometimes referred to as 'chattels vegetable'. In modern usage the term 'chattel' is more commonly used to refer to 'chattels personal'.

Chattels real includes a **leasehold**, which in common law is not strictly 'real property', but merely a source of income rather than a right to land per se. The term may also include a **mortgage**.

'Chattels personal' or personal chattels may be divided into choses-in-action, e.g. a debt, copyright, etc. and choses-in-possession, e.g. goods and money. Choses-in-action primarily consists of rights to things that produce a mere claim or income. Chose-in-possession are tangible movables (e.g. furniture) that can be transferred or held by physical possession— in common usage it is in this latter sense that the term chattel is understood.

Upon intestacy in English statute law personal chattels means "carriages, horses, stable furniture and effects (not used for business purposes), motor cars and accessories (not used for business purposes), garden effects, domestic animals, plate, plated articles, linen, china, glass, books, pictures, prints, furniture, jewellery, articles of household or personal use or ornament, musical and scientific instruments and apparatus, wines, liquors and consumable stores, but do not include any chattels used at the death of the intestate for business purposes nor money or securities for money", AEA 1925, s. 55(1)(x).

In modern English land law, and in most jurisdictions in the US, the 'estate' of freehold and the 'interest' of leasehold (especially a term of years absolute) have moved closer together and in most respects the latter is treated as a right to real property. Thus, although a leasehold interest is technically personal property, in modern practice it has little in common with 'chattels personal'. cf. **fixture**. See also **chose**, **personal property**, **treasure trove**.

chattel fixture(US)   See **fixture**.

chattel mortgage   A contract by which a **chattel**, or a right to a chattel, is transferred as security for the payment of a debt, subject to a right to reclaim the chattel when the debt is repaid. A **mortgage**, or more usually, a **charge** on a chattel; in particular on pure personalty or goods. A chattel mortgage usually applies to a specific item or items of personal property. A chattel mortgage may be distinguished from an **assignment** in payment of a debt as the assignee parts entirely with the property, whereas the chattel mortgagor retains possession of the property and can recover his unencumbered right thereto upon repayment of the debt. In effect, a **bill of sale** may create a chattel mortgage if there is a clear intent that the property is intended as security for a loan, or if there is a right of defeasance annexed thereto, i.e. a separate agreement that if a stipulated sum is paid the property will be returned. A charge on 'chattels real' (a leasehold) is called more commonly a **leasehold mortgage**.

Under the United States Uniform Commercial Code § 9.102, a chattel mortgage is classified as a "security interest" and, therefore, a **financing statement** must be filed to perfect the mortgagee's claim. cf. **conditional sale**, **pledge**. See also **promissory note**.

chattels personal   See chattel.

chattels real   See chattel.

chattels vegetable   See chattel.

check(AmE) or **cheque**(BrE)   A written order from one party, the drawer, to a banker, demanding the payment of money to another specified person or to the bearer of the order. A form of **bill of exchange**, drawn on a bank, that does not require acceptance by the party to whom it is submitted, but requires payment on demand (Bill of Exchange Act 1882, s. 73). A **draft** drawn upon a bank and payable on demand, signed by the maker or drawer containing an unconditional promise to pay a sum of money certain to the order of the payee (UCC § 3-104(2)(b)). A check/cheque may be distinguished from a bill of exchange by being payable on demand and purportedly being drawn against a deposit of funds. A check is the principal means of transferring money from one individual's bank account to the bank account of another or of withdrawing cash from the drawer's own account. However, a check is not a valid form of payment until it is honoured by the issuer's bank. See also **commercial paper**, **payment**.

cheque(BrE)   See **check**.

chilling a sale   A bargain or conspiracy made at an **auction** sale by potential bidders, or sometimes the auctioneer, with the aim of suppressing fair competition, or with the aim of enabling one of the bidders to acquire the property for less than its fair value. For example, by telling potential bidders that a property is defective or encumbered, when that is not the case, or forming a ring to reduce the number of potential bidders. Any sale that results from such activity is normally invalid. As a rule, any contract arising therefrom may be rescinded and usually a court will not award a decree of **specific performance** to enforce

such a sale. In the UK also called 'damping a sale'. See also **bidding agreement**.

Chinese auction   See **auction**.

chirograph   An instrument written out and subscribed by the hand of the maker. A **deed** written by hand in duplicate on the same sheet of paper or parchment. The duplicate parts are divided by a line on which the inscription *chirograph* is made and the two parts are then separated along that line and a part given to each party.

chose   Derived from the French **chose**, 'thing'. Property; in particular an item of **personal property** – a 'chattel personal'. 'Chose' in the common law has a similar meaning to **res** in the civil law being any 'thing'. A chose may be 'in possession' representing anything that is tangible, movable and can be taken by physical possession, e.g. goods, animals; or 'in action' representing anything that may be claimed or recovered only by an action in law, and is not physically held, e.g. a debt, the benefit of an obligation arising out of a contract, the beneficial interest of a trust, an option to purchase land, an insurance policy, a negotiable instrument, stocks and shares in a company or the right of an heir to an interest in the estate of a deceased. A right to a chose-in-possession means that a person has a physical right of user or of holding something as security; whereas a chose-in-action is essentially a right to income or capital.

chose in action   See **chose**.

chronological age   See **actual age**.

church land or **church property**   Land that belongs to a church or ecclesiastical body, or land used for church buildings and land reasonably incidental thereto. Land and buildings required for the use of the church, and used primarily for religious worship and instruction. This does not normally include property owned by a church but not held for the purposes of worship or instruction or property that is held for investment purposes.

churning   **1.** Moving the tenants or occupiers of a building for financial advantage. For example, moving tenants between floors to improve the appearance of leasing activity or in order to generate extra commissions for a broker.   **2.** The rapid turnover of tenants in a building, as in a newly opened shopping center where the retailers may change until the trade pattern becomes more stabilised.

circulating capital   See **floating capital**.

circulation space   The communication areas within a building. The space on the floor of a building that is used by the occupiers to move from one area to another, especially between one normally occupied part and another. Circulation space includes halls, lobbies, foyers, corridors, and space that provides access to stairs, elevators or lifts. The stairway and elevator or lift is generally considered part of the circulation space, but may be referred to as vertical circulation space as distinguished from the horizontal circulation areas. See also **apron**, **common areas**, **net internal area**(BrE), **usable area**.

citizen-participation(US)   See **public participation**.

city lot(US)   See **lot**.

city region   See **urban region**.

civic center(AmE) or **civic centre**(BrE)   An area of a town or city where the principal public buildings are grouped together, in particular the town or city hall, law courts, municipal offices and other civic buildings. The civic center commonly forms part of, or adjoins the **central business district**, but may be established as a separately developed entity.

Civic Trust(Eng)   A body founded in England in 1957 by Duncan Sands to promote the highest standards of architecture, civic design and town planning and encourage public interest in the appearance of towns and villages (for example, by means of the renowned Civic Trust Awards). The Civic Trust is a registered charity, "with the mission – and the passion – to improve those places where people live, work and relax: the everyday 'built environment' in Britain's cities, towns and villages". It has pioneered effective regeneration in all sizes of town and city using The Civic Trust's Regeneration Unit as a spearhead. The Civic Trust's ultimate objective is to improve the quality of the environment in which people live and work. (**www.civictrust.org.uk**).

civil day   See **day**.

claim   **1.** A demand for a **right** or **privilege**. A demand for money or property. A demand as of right or supposed right, such as a demand for compensation. In connection with US bankruptcy law a claim has been defined as "(A) right to payment, whether or not such right is reduced to judgment, liquidated, unliquidated, fixed, contingent, matured, unmatured, disputed, undisputed, legal, equitable, secured or unsecured; or (B) right to an equitable remedy of **specific performance** if such breach give rise to a right to payment, whether or not such right to an equitable remedy is reduced to judgment, fixed, contingent, matured, unmatured, disputed, undisputed, secured, or unsecured", 11 USC, Bankruptcy, § 101(5).   **2.** An assertion of a **title**, e.g. by staking out the boundaries of an area of land. The process of asserting a right to ownership of property by taking possession and subsequent action that precludes any challenge to that right. A claim is an assertion of a right to that which belongs to another, whether legally or illegally. In particulaire, a right to a tract of land that has been obtained by a settler on government owned land. See also **adverse possession**, **quitclaim deed**.   **3.** See **mining claim**.

claim form(Eng)   The principle means of starting legal proceedings in English law. Since 1999, the claim form has replaced the **writ** or summons for most cases. A claim form must contain a concise statement of the nature of the claim; specify the remedy claimed, including any claim for interest on the judgement and the grounds for claiming any aggravated or exemplary damages; and contain a statement of the value of the claim (Civil Procedure Rules, effective April 26, 1999).

claim of right or claim of title(US) A claim to the ownership or a right over property by adverse or hostile possession. A claim of a right to property by someone who has no legal title but is claiming a title to land by **adverse possession**. 'Claim of title' may be used synonymously with **color of title**, although etymologically a 'color' of title is a semblance or appearance of a right (even though no such right may exist) and a 'claim' of title arises from an entry or holding of land so as to establish a right or title by adverse possession. 'Claim of right' may also refer to a claim to a right (such as an easement) by **prescription**.

claimable Crown land(Aus) Crown land that may be claimed by Aboriginal people as theirs by virtue of use and custom. Such land is primarily land outside a town or city in which no person, other than the Crown, has an interest and that is not needed for development or public purposes. Such land may then be allocated as available for claim by a group of Aboriginal people or, in Queensland, by Torres Strait Islanders. See also **granted land**.

clam, vi, aut precario(Lat) 'Stealth, violence and entreaty'. See *nec vi, nec clam, nec precario*.

clandestine mortgage or clandestine charge A **mortgage**, or charge, entered into secretly. In particular, a mortgage or charge entered into in respect of land that is already affected by a mortgage or charge, when the mortgagor does not declare the existence of the prior claim.

In English law, the concealment of any instrument or encumbrance affecting a title to property that is disposed of for money or money's worth with intent to defraud, is a punishable

misdemeanour; the purchaser may claim damages for the resultant loss from the person (or, if applicable his agent or solicitor) who disposed of the property (LPA 1925, s. 183). See also **fraudulent conveyance**.

Class A office building An **office** building of the highest quality in terms of location, design, building standards and efficiency. In particular, Class A office buildings are those that command the best rent in a particular market. Office buildings that fall short of this standard may be classified as Class B or Class C as the particular attributes fall short of the Class A qualities. See also **prime property, trophy building**.

class gift A **gift** of property, or an aggregate sum of money, to a group of persons of a defined category, but so that the total number of recipients is not known at the time of the gift. For example, a gift "to my grandchildren" or "to all my children who reach 18 years of age". Under a class gift the number of such persons will not be ascertained until a future time, so that the share received by each will not be known until all the members of the class are ascertained. When the persons who are to receive the property are known, they receive the gift as 'one divisible subject' in equal or other defined proportions, the share of each recipient being dependent for its amount upon the ultimate number of persons.

clause 1. A section or paragraph of a legal document, such as a contract, deed or statute. See also **covenant**. 2.(Eng)A section of a parliamentary bill.

claw back or clawback To reclaim a benefit that has been granted but has wholly or partially surrendered. To claim back money that has allocated elsewhere. In particular, an arrangement by which a tax benefit or relief is retaxed under a separate tax provision.

clear lease(Eng) A lease in which the tenant bears "all the costs and risks of repairing, maintaining and running the building ... so that the rent payable reaches the landlord clear of all the expenses and overheads [associated with the demised premises]", *O'May v City of London Real Property Co Ltd* [1983] 2 AC 726, 748, [1982] 1 All ER 660, 671 (HL). See also **full repairing and insuring lease, triple net lease**.

clear title A **title** to land that is free of any **encumbrance, lien, burden**, claim or defect, except those agreed to by the purchaser. A title that is free of any material or palpable defect. Generally, 'clear title' is considered to be synonymous with **good title**, being a title that is free of doubt in law and fact and may be sold, or used as security for a mortgage, without doubt on the part of a prudent purchaser or lender. See also **free and clear title**.

clearance area(Eng) An area that the local housing authority considers should be cleared of all buildings because the authority is satisfied that the dwelling-houses or houses in multiple occupation in the area "are **unfit for human habitation** or by reason of their bad arrangement, or narrowness or bad arrangement of the streets, dangerous or injurious to the health of the inhabitants of the area" Housing Act 1985, s. 289(2)(a). Clearance areas are now rarely declared as such, the preference being to improve areas of poor housing whenever possible by declaring them to be part of a **renewal area**. See also **redevelopment area, rehabilitation order, urban renewal**.

clearance easement(US) See **avigation easement**.

clerk of works or **clerk of the works**(BrE) A person appointed to represent the owner or employer on a building site, usually on the recommendation of the **architect** to whom he normally reports. The clerk of works is responsible for regular supervision of building work to ensure that it complies technically with the building contract. In particular, he is responsible for keeping a factual record of building work; inspecting the quality of workmanship; and resolving detailed problems on site, subject to regular reference to the architect.

client's money(BrE) See **commingling**.

clog A **fetter**, restriction or impediment, especially such an impediment on a mortgagor's **equity of redemption**. A stipulation or provision in a mortgage deed that prevents the mortgagor from recovering his property unencumbered, after repayment of all the monies due to the mortgagee or performance of all the obligations for which the property was given as security. Any fetter or clog on the mortgagor's right to redeem his property is void as being alien to the nature of a mortgage (*Noakes & Co Ltd v Rice* [1902] AC 24, [1900-3] All ER Rep 34 (HL); Williams, Clogging the Equity of Redemption, 40 W Va LQ 31, 49 (1933); *Hoar v Mills (No. 2)* [1935] 1 WWR 433, 434 (Sask. CA Can)). However, this rule is less stringently enforced today than ever before and a limitation or restriction on the right of the mortgagor to repay the loan is less likely to be construed as a fetter where both parties are business persons, represented by lawyers, and are clearly aware of the consequences of the agreement. See also **once a mortgage always a mortgage, option, redemption, unconscionable bargain**.

close 1. A parcel or tract of land. In particular, an area enclosed by a bank, fence, hedge or any similar enclosure. Also, the grounds immediately surrounding a religious house or place of worship. See also **adjacent, boundary, bounds, cul-de-sac, enclosure**. 2. See **metes and bounds system**(US). 3. To complete a real estate transaction; the act of **closing**.

closed contract(Eng) A contract for the sale of land that automatically incorporates terms set out in a **standard-form contract** (e.g. the Law Society's Conditions of Sale) except where expressly varied. cf. **open contract**. See also **conditions of sale**.

closed-end investment company An **investment company** that has a fixed share capital and trades its shares like any other company, the price of which is based on the performance of the company; as distinguished from an **open-end investment company** which buys and sells its own shares as the investors increase or reduce their holding in the company.

closed-end investment trust See **closed-end trust**.

closed-end mortgage or **close-ended mortgage**[US] A mortgage under which neither the properties secured by the mortgage nor the amount of the indebtedness may be changed before maturity. A mortgage that limits the mortgagor's ability to raise additional finance on the security of the mortgaged property. Also called a 'closed mortgage'. See also **open-end mortgage**.

closed-end trust or **close-ended trust**[US] An **investment trust** that has a fixed capital or has a fixed number of shares. Generally, such an entity is not a 'trust' as such, but is more usually incorporated. However, it takes in funds to invest in a diverse range of investments 'on trust' for the shareholders. Once formed a closed-end trust does not issue new shares, but its shares are bought and sold on the open market; as distinguished from an **open-end trust** or **mutual fund** in which shares are bought and sold by the trustees or managers as investor demand dictates.

closed mortgage[US] 1. A mortgage that cannot be repaid until its date of maturity. See also **fetter**. 2. See **close-ended mortgage**.

closer[US] A representative of a title insurance company who attends the closing of a real estate transaction and performs all the clerical duties relevant to the closing, such as preparation of the **settlement statement**; preparation of documents for insurance and taxation purposes; assembling all documents required to record the transaction and arranging for the disbursement of funds between the parties. A payment made to that representative for his attendance is also called a 'closer'. See also **title insurance**.

closing[US] 1. The **completion** of the transfer of the ownership of property (or the completion of the documentation for the entering into a mortgage). Closing takes place when all the consideration is paid, if applicable, mortgages secured, and the title is transferred to the purchaser by the **delivery** of the deed (or when the mortgage deed or deed of trust is executed). The execution of an agreement of purchase and sale, or any similar document, strictly speaking does not constitute a closing. However, the execution of such a document in unconditional form and the placing of it in **escrow** may be referred to as 'closing the sale'. The 'legal closing' takes place when the escrow is consummated, or when all monies are paid and title is transferred. The disbursement of the monies in accordance with the closing statement may be referred to as the 'financial closing'. 2. See **metes and bounds system**.

closing adjustment[US] See **apportionment**, **settlement statement**.

closing costs or **closing charges**[AmE] The costs incurred in consummating a real estate transaction, whether paid by the vendor, purchaser, lessor, lessee, mortgagor, or mortgagee. In particular, those costs paid at the time of **closing** over and above the purchase price, or the loan amount. The costs incurred by a purchaser may include: any transfer or conveyance tax, title examination or abstract preparation costs, costs of notarizing or recording a deed (including a mortgage deed, if applicable), any title insurance premium, attorney fees, and any mortgagee's commitment fee or loan assumption fees. Against these costs any **earnest money** paid by the purchaser is brought into account. The costs incurred by the seller may include: attorney fees, brokerage commission, transfer tax (although this is borne usually by the purchaser), and any mortgage release fee or prepayment penalty. In addition, variable expenses associated with the property (real estate taxes, property insurance premiums, rents, security deposits, operating expenses, utility charges and, if applicable, any mortgage loan payments or condominium owners' association fees) must be prorated between the purchaser and vendor as at the date of closing. In the case of a loan closing the costs incurred by the borrower may include a loan origination fee, discount points, attorney's fees (usually including the lender's attorney fees), survey fees, mortgage insurance premium, and any loan transfer of assumption fees. The closing costs are set out usually in the **settlement statement** (or 'closing statement') prepared by the seller's (or mortgagee's) attorney (or sometimes the sellers' broker) or by the title insurance company. Broker's fees may be payable by the seller at or after closing, while survey fees, appraisal fees and public search fees may have to be paid prior to closing, although such amounts may be set out on the settlement statement. See also **apportionment, friction costs**.

closing date   The **date** upon which a **closing** takes place. The date upon which **completion** of a transfer or mortgage of property takes place, i.e. the day upon which the deed of sale is executed, final settlement is made of the sale or loan proceeds, and delivery of title is effected. See also **completion date**.

closing fees(AmE)   See **closing costs**.

closing order   1.(Eng)An order served by a local authority upon a person having control of a dwelling-house, or a house in multiple occupation, specifying that the house may no longer be used for any purpose, other than a purpose approved by the authority (Housing Act 1985, ss. 264, 267). A closing order may be served when the local authority is satisfied that the house is **unfit for human habitation**. A closing order may be made when the authority considers it is the most appropriate course of action, as when a **demolition order** would not be appropriate; for example, if the building is listed as being of special

architectural or historical interest or it is required for support to an adjoining property. Once a house has been made fit for habitation the local authority is bound to lift the order and there is a right of appeal against a refusal to so end the order (HA 1985, s. 278). The owner of the property may be entitled to compensation for the diminution in the value of his interest in the property arising as a result of the order (HA 1985, s. 584A).   2.(Aus/NZ)An order issue by a court upon the owner of a property that is considered unfit for human habitation and as a consequence a nuisance is being caused.

closing statement(US)   See **settlement statement**.

cloud on title(US)   A defect, or potential defect, on an owner's title to property that could prevent an owner from providing **marketable title**; especially an instrument, claim, lien or deed that if valid would impair a title to land, even though after careful examination it may turn out to be invalid or unenforceable. A defect that prevents an owner from providing a good or marketable title. A cloud on title produces an apparent title or casts doubt on the owner's title. A cloud on title produces a semblance of title, although the title, in fact, is invalid, or it is a title that it would be inequitable to enforce without modification. For example, an option that has passed the date by which it should have been exercised but still remains on a public record; a claim for a breach of covenant that has been rectified; an attachment of record for a debt that has been paid or a recorded mortgage that has been repaid in full; or a defectively executed deed. A cloud on title is usually revealed on a title search or a search of a public record. A cloud on title can normally be removed by a **quitclaim deed** or a **quiet title action**; a process sometimes known as 'perfecting title'. Sometimes called a 'blot on title'. See also **chain of title, encumbrance,** *lis pendens*.

cluster development(US/Aus)   A development in which buildings are grouped together to a higher density than normal, in order to provide extra space for recreation, common open space, areas that are environmentally sensitive or other amenity areas. The overall zoning density for the district is not changed, but buildings are sited closer together or clustered onto smaller lots as compared with the conventional layout for the area. Also called a 'cluster subdivision', especially when the permitted development does not allow for an increase in the number of units or an increase in the overall density, but substitutes smaller lot sizes with more open space. See also **contract zoning**, **planned unit development**.

cluster housing(US)   A housing development where the buildings are grouped together with limited yard space, especially where the development is planned to increase the amount of common areas compared with a more conventional development. See also **cluster development**.

cluster zoning   See **cluster development**.

co-agent(US)   See **joint agent**.

coal   See **mineral rights**.

co-assurance   See **co-insurance**.

co-broker(AmE)   See **cooperating broker**, **joint broker**.

code   A written compilation of laws, especially a systematic preparation or consolidation of legal ordinances on a given subject. A set of rules or regulations produced to regulate or guide a particular group of persons, or to provide uniformity in a field of activity. See also **building code**, **code of conduct**, **ordinance**, **rules of conduct**.

code of ethics(AmE)   A body of rules, principles and regulations established and accepted by a professional body for the conduct of their activities. In particular, a code accepted by real estate brokers, appraisers, or property managers.

A code of ethics, supported by disciplinary action for a breach of the rules, is accepted by most professional bodies: Members of the **Appraisal Institute** accept Regulation 10 of that Institute as their code of ethics, and the Code of Ethics of the **National Association of REALTORS**® has been adopted by several states as the basis for granting licenses to REALTORS®. See also **canon**, **rules of conduct**.

codicil   An instrument made by a testator that adds to, supplements, expands, or alters a **will** in some way. "An addition or supplement added into a will or testament after the finishing of it, for the supply of something which the testator had forgotten, or to help some defect in the title", *Termes de la Ley*. A codicil, which may be endorsed on the will or may form a separate document, must be executed and attested in the same way as the will to which it is adjunct; it then forms part of that will and the two documents are read together.

coercion   The act of compelling someone to do something against their will. The application of force (whether physical or mental), or a sanction, in order to produce an agreement or bring something or someone into conformity. Coercion may be actual or physical; or it may be 'constructive' as where a person exerts any form of pressure, or uses a position of influence, to prevent another from acting of their own free will. **Duress** may be considered as a form of coercion, but a limited form of coercion may not amount to duress. cf. **consent**. See also **duress**, **harassment**, **undue influence**.

co-heir   One of two or more persons who receives property by inheritance as if he or she were a single **heir**. An heir who takes property as a **joint tenant** with another, or other heirs. See also **coparcenary**.

co-insurance or **coinsurance** or **co-assurance**   **1.** The acceptance of part of the insurance risk by the insured. A responsibility on the part of the insured to maintain his own insurance for a specified amount or a percentage of the actual value of the property insured, failing which he becomes a co-insurer to the extent of the omitted insurance. In the event that the amount of coverage at the time of loss is below the fair value of the property insured, the insurer is not liable for any greater proportion of the loss than the ratio of the face amount of the policy to the specified percentage of the actual value of the property at the time of the loss. See also **average clause**.   **2.** The provision of insurance by different insurers of the same risk on the same property. For example, when a building policy covers the contents that are also covered by a separate contents policy. The effect of such co-insurance is that the insured is effectively over insured and can only recover from one of the policies. Sometimes called 'double insurance'. See also **contribution clause, over-insurance**.   **3.** The division of responsibility for a risk between two or more insurers. Normally a lead insurer accepts the risk and then brings together other insurers, each of who accepts a percentage of the risk.

co-insurance clause   A clause in an insurance policy which provides that there will be an element of **co-insurance**. See also **average clause**.

cold calling or **cold canvassing** Contacting a person who has expressed no prior interest in a product, or the purchase of a property, in order to solicit new business.

co-lessee   See **joint tenant**.

collar   See **rate cap**.

collateral   Derived from the Latin *con* or *co*, 'with', *latus*, 'side'; that which is granted alongside another undertaking to secure its performance, but has an independent existence. Assets (property, bonds, stock, money, etc.) pledged as security for a loan. 'Collateral' may mean something that is intended to stand side by side and not as a secondary obligation, i.e. a collateral obligation is

made along with the main undertaking and is enforceable because the main undertaking is enforceable. However, 'collateral' is used more commonly to refer to any security granted to insure the performance of an agreement or pledge, but as a secondary or subsidiary line of defence. For example, collateral property is property, or a claim to property, granted to a lender as concurrent affirmation that the loan will be repaid so that if the primary obligation to the lender is not duly satisfied, the property is forfeited. On the other hand, the collateral obligation is discharged when the primary obligation is discharged. See also **collateral contract, collateral security, defeasance, guarantee, warranty**.

collateral advantage   See **equity of redemption**.

collateral agent   The party that holds **collateral** on behalf of the borrower or grantor of the collateral. In particular, in securitized financing, the financial institution that holds the documents relating to the pooled loans or mortgages in trust for bondholders. Also known as the 'custodian'.

collateral agreement   See **collateral contract**.

collateral assurance(US)   An assurance (conveyance) made for the purpose of confirming or perfecting a title that has previously been conveyed, but was lacking or defective in some respect. See also **collateral, covenant for further assurance**.

collateral contract   A contract that runs side by side with a principal contract. A contract that is **collateral** to another contract and which reinforces that other contract. A collateral contract may be one that arises out of negotiations before a formal contract and comes to fortify the main contract. However, it is an independent contract, but one that is consistent with the contract it supports. See also **guarantee**.

collateral covenant   A **covenant** in a conveyance or deed of transfer of real property that does not directly relate to the property, but one that is personal to the parties.

collateral guarantee   A tautology because a **guarantee** is essentially **collateral**. However, the term is sometimes used to emphasise that an agreement is strictly a guarantee, i.e. an accessory contract, and not a **surety**, which connotes a simultaneous, and not a successive, obligation to accept a commitment. cf. **collateral warranty**.

collateral heir   An **heir** who is descended from a common ancestor, but not in a direct line to another heir.

collateral limitation   See **conditional limitation**(US), **limitation**.

collateral mortgage bond   A bond or note that is designed not to directly secure an existing debt, but one that is secured by another mortgage note that is pledged as collateral security for a debt or a succession of debts. A bond that is secured by the deposit of mortgage bonds and, therefore, is indirectly secured by a mortgage or a pool of mortgages. cf. **mortgage-backed obligation**. See also **collateralized mortgage obligation**.

collateral security   Something of monetary value given as additional **security** for the performance of a contract, as distinguished from personal security. A separate obligation attached to another contract to guarantee performance. In particular, security for a debt in the form of a separate asset or some commitment provided by a third party. Collateral security for a debt is provided in addition to, rather than in lieu of, the borrower's personal liability. Collateral security is intended to remain as security unless or until the principal obligation is performed. See also **collateral**, **mortgage**.

collateral value   The value of a property held as **collateral security** for a loan; the value as determined for the purpose of granting a loan against the security of a property. The amount advanced against the security of a property is generally less than its loan value (which in most instances would be the same as the **market value**). Many lending institutions are restricted by law as to maximum percentage of the loan value of a property they may advance against the security of that property. Also called the 'loan value', or sometimes in the US, when the property is to be held as security for a lien or mortgage, the 'hypothecary' or 'hypothecatory' value. See also **loan value, mortgage value**.

collateral warranty   An undertaking that stands alongside one given by another party. In particular, a **warranty** by which a third party or stranger to a contract undertakes to perform the principal obligations if the principal party fails to fulfil his obligations. In real estate, a collateral warranty generally refers to a warranty given by a stranger to the title; an obligation that is personal to the covenantee and does not pass to a purchaser of the land. See also **surety**.

Fearon, W. *Collateral Warranties*. 2nd ed. Oxford: Blackwell Science, 2000.

collateralized mortgage   A mortgage that is secured by **collateral**, such as a letter of credit or cash deposit, in addition to the real estate.

collateralized mortgage obligation (CMO)   A debt obligation that is a form of 'pass-through' **mortgage-backed obligation** by which payments received from the underlying mortgages are pooled and payments to the holders of the CMOs are made on a class-by-class basis. The holder of a CMO has a right to certain payments based on interest and principal received, but does not have any ownership interest in the underlying assets. CMOs are amortizing debt instruments, collateralized by mortgages, with the principal characteristic that the instruments provide for different cash flows and different maturities, called 'tranches'. For example, CMOs may be divided into short-, medium-, and long-term. The short-term holders receive distributions based on the repayment of the mortgages until they are repaid in full; after that payments are made to the medium-term holders and only after they have been repaid in full are payments of principal made to the long-term holders. In each case the CMO holder receives interest payments at a certificate rate. CMOs may be packaged in a variety of other ways. Thus, one group of holders may receive only interest payments and another only repayments of principal. The obligations may also be secured by a package of different mortgages, with different coupon rates, different types of secured property, differing mortgage terms, etc. Unlike a conventional mortgage-backed obligation, where the holder may receive repayments of his investment as and when the mortgagor repays his loan (if he moves or refinances), the holder of a CMO has a more certain cash flow. CMOs may well be backed by a specific class of mortgage securities, for example Freddie Mac participation certificates (PCs), Fannie Mae mortgage-backed securities (MBS), Ginnie Maes, a combination of such securities or by conventional mortgage loans. See also **real estate mortgage investment conduit**(US).

Davidson, Andrew S., et al. *Collateralized Mortgage Obligations*. Chicago: Probus Publishing, 1994.

Fabozzi, Frank J., and Chuck Ramsey. *Collateralized Mortgage Obligations: Structure and Analysis*. 3rd ed. New York: McGraw-Hill, 1999.

collective ownership(BrE)   The ownership of one (or more) units that form part of a group of properties, combined with a right to use and enjoy, in common with others, certain property that is essential to the proper enjoyment of the individual units. This is not strictly speaking a term of English law, but may be used to make a distinction from **co-ownership**, which is a joint right to the whole of a property. Collective ownership covers such forms of ownership as a **flying freehold**; **cooperative ownership**; and the holding of all the units in trust for a number of persons with proprietary rights to individual units, as in a **housing trust**. See also **commonhold, condominium, housing association.**

color of title(US)   A semblance of title. A **title** that appears and is believed to be good but, due to some defect, cannot or does not transfer the right to land to which it purports. For example, when the transferor lacks the proper title due to a defect in his chain of title, or does not effect a proper transfer due to a failure of the correct formalities (e.g. a defective deed). A title that has all the appearance of a valid title, but where one or more of the transfers in the chain of title may be irregular, although generally not to such an extent that there is a complete *hiatus* in the chain.

In some jurisdictions, a title by **adverse possession** may be established in a shorter period if there is a 'color of title', i.e. if the possessor is claiming through a title that appeared valid, provided the claim is made in **good faith**. In that context, 'color of title' may be considered to be synonymous with **claim of title**. Sometimes called 'apparent title', or in Canada 'colourable title'. See also **just title, quitclaim deed, paper title.**

colourable title(Can)   See **color of title.**

combination loan or **combination mortgage**   A loan, or mortgage, that combines, in the same agreement, different progressions for the payment of the interest or the principal. For example, a loan which provides initially for a variable interest rate and then, after a stated period of time, a fixed interest rate; or a loan that provides for the principal to be repaid in the same way as in an **amortization loan** and then, after a stated period, for it to be repaid by equal instalments. See also **drop-lock debenture, variable-rate mortgage.**

combination trust(US)   See **real estate investment trust.**

combined insurance   See **package insurance.**

combined residential density   The **residential density** of a mixed housing development, e.g. flats, houses and bungalows;

generally expressed as persons or habitable rooms per acre.

comfort letter   See **letter of comfort**.

commendation(Eng)   A process by which a person who had a right to land ceded that right to a feudal lord and relegated himself to the status of vassal or feudal tenant, in exchange for protection from an invader or a common enemy. See also **feudal system**.

commercial   Of or relating to **trade** or commerce. In the context of real property, commercial generally means an activity that involves a **business**, trade or merchantile activity. In particular, wholesale or retail sales or distributions, or a business that is carried on as a regular activity. 'Commercial' is used also to refer to property that is not used for residential, agricultural, forestry or industrial purposes. The renting or leasing of property may well be a commercial activity, although a property that is rented or leased is not *ipso facto* a **commercial property** (especially when the term is used in the context of planning, zoning or building regulations).

commercial acre(US)   The area of subdivided land, per acre, that is available for development after allocating land for streets, sidewalks, parking and other such ancillary uses; the area from one acre left for development or sale.

commercial hotel   See **hotel**.

commercial loan(US)   **1.** A loan granted against the security of **commercial property**.   **2.** A loan granted for a commercial business purpose. In particular, a **short-term loan** or **overdraft** granted to finance a business on a day-to-day basis.

commercial mortgage-backed security (CMBS)   See **mortgage backed security**.

commercial paper   A short-term unsecured promise that may be a negotiable or non-negotiable instrument. In particular, 'commercial paper' includes short-term notes or instruments that are used to raise debt capital for a business and may be traded, including a **bill of exchange**, **negotiable instrument**, **promissory note**, **certificate of deposit**, **check**(AmE)/**cheque**(BrE) or **draft**. Commercial paper generally has a maturity of three to six months.

commercial property   **1.** Real estate used for a **trade**, **business**, or **profession** including an office, retail property, shopping center, hotel, restaurant, or industrial property, but excluding residential and agricultural property and any property used for public purposes, e.g. a school or hospital.

In English statute law, in relation to a **capital allowance**, a commercial building or structure is defined as "other than an industrial building or structure, or qualifying hotel, which is used for the purpose of a trade, profession or vocation or, whether or not for such a purpose, as an office or offices, but does not include any building in use as, or as part of, a dwelling house", Finance Act 1980, s. 74. See also **business premises**, **office**, **shop**.   **2.** Any form of income-producing or investment property, or property intended to be used for profitable purposes, other than property held for use and occupation.

commercial rent   See **market rent**, **rack rent**.

commingled fund   See **commingling**, **commingled trust fund**.

commingled trust fund(US)   A trust established to permit a number of investors, such as pension funds or insurance companies, to make common investments. Also called a 'common trust fund'. See also **property unit trust**(BrE).

commingling   The placing of funds from different, and usually conflicting sources, into the same account. For example, placing a client's funds in the same account as an agent's or broker's personal funds.

In the US, most states require that a real estate broker maintain separate accounts into which he must place funds entrusted to him, whether as a broker (such as a deposit), as an escrow agent or similar custodian. Such accounts may be interest bearing and in many states the interest must not be retained for the benefit of the broker.

In English law, any money received by an estate agent as a contract or pre-contract deposit ("client's money"), whether held in his capacity as an agent, bailee, stakeholder, or in any other capacity, is held on trust for the party who may rightfully be entitled to the return of the money. Thus, the funds must be kept apart from the agent's funds and placed in a "client's account" (Estate Agent's Act 1979, ss. 12-17; Estate Agent's (Accounts) Regulations). See also **deposit**.

commission 1. Remuneration paid to an **agent** or **broker** for his services in conducting a specific duty, such as introducing a purchaser of a property, effecting a sale of a property to a third party, or obtaining a loan facility. The compensation or reward paid to an agent or broker for successfully transacting business for the principal, the amount of which is generally based on a percentage of the value of the transaction, or sometimes the profit resulting to the principal as a result of the agent's or broker's actions. Usually this remuneration is made payable only on the successful conclusion of the specified function, e.g. on **completion** of a sale; or the introduction of a person who is **ready**, **willing and able** to purchase a particular property. No commission is payable unless there is a contract, express or implied, between the agent and the principal and commission is generally only payable for carrying out the task with which the agent has been entrusted (*Toulmin v Millar* (1887) 58 LT 96, 3 TLR 836 (HL); *Hodges & Sons (G. T.) v Hackbridge Park Residential Hotel, Ltd* [1940] 1 KB 404, [1939] 4 All ER 347 (CA); Bianchi v. Vere, 17 F.2d 22 (1st Cir. Puerto Rico 1927); 12 C.J.S., Brokers, § 143; *Dolphin v Harrison, San Miguel Pty Ltd* (1911) 13 CLR 271, [1911] ALR 444 (Aus)). Generally, for this

purpose, an option is not the same as a sale (or similar transaction), unless the option is exercised. Finding a party to take a lease is not the same as finding a purchaser. However, a broker who is retained to find a purchaser, but introduces a party who takes a lease, should be entitled to a commission commensurate with the benefit obtained by the property owner.

Commission is not intended as a payment for work done, but as a reward for achieving that which the principal required of the agent or broker. Commission is not payable until the particular result required by the principal has been achieved, strictly in accordance with the terms by which the broker was appointed. However, in the absence of an express stipulation as to the act that would entitle the agent or broker to a commission, a payment is normally due upon the completion of a transaction to the party who was the **procuring cause** thereof.

Normally commission is only paid to an agent or broker when the transaction that he was employed to bring about is concluded or, at least, brought to an irrevocable stage. On the other hand, the principal cannot ordinarily avoid payment of commission by, for example, refusing to consummate a transaction, or by cancelling the broker's agreement and selling through another agent. If a vendor undertakes to pay commission to an agent or broker on completion of a 'sale', that payment is due, as a rule, when a binding and unconditional contract is executed. If the vendor then withdraws in breach of contract, he may still remain liable to pay commission as a form of damages for loss suffered by the agent, the agent having performed the duty required of him (*Luxor (Eastbourne) Ltd v Cooper* [1941] AC 108, 142 (HL) *obiter*; 12 ALR4th 1083: Recovery of Real Estate Commission, §§ 18, 19). In any event, there may be an agreement (express or implied) to pay for work done, or expenditure actually incurred by the agent, in the event of a termination of the appointment. In some cases this may amount to payment of the full commission.

An agent must act with the **utmost good faith** and loyalty in order to receive a commission; "it is only an honest agent who is entitled to any commission", *Andrews v Ramsay & Co* [1903] 2 KB 635, 638. The agent is expected to keep the principal fully informed of any information that might affect the principal's decision to sell or otherwise deal with the subject property; to obtain the best possible terms for the principal or, at least, to present the best terms for the principal's consideration; and to disclose any other relevant information regarding the prospective purchaser and any other information know to him that may affect the terms of sale.

In the US, in most states, a real estate broker must be licensed at the time the service was performed and be employed under the terms of a written agreement, otherwise he may be unable to bring an action to recover any commission due. cf. **fee**. See also **bad faith, brokerage, deferred commission, dual agency, exclusive right to sell, extender clause, finder's fee, multiple agency, option,** *quantum meruit.* **2.** An **authority**, or request, given to another to carry out some act or duty. In particular, a formal written authority given to one party to act in place of another. See also **agency**. **3.** A payment, based on a percentage of an insurance premium, made by an insurer to an agent or broker for introducing business. For property insurance, the percentage is generally between 5 per cent and 20 per cent. When insurance is arranged directly by the insured, the premium may be reduced proportionately to reflect the commission saved by the insurer.

commission agent An agent who earns his **commission** based on repeat orders or similar repeat business. See also **broker**.

commission merchant One who buys and sells for profit as well as selling on commission. One who receives goods for sale on commission. A commission merchant is a **factor** who takes possession of the goods that he intends to sell, as distinguished from a **broker** or 'merchandise broker' who acts as an agent for the sale of property, but does not take actual possession of the goods.

commissive waste(US)   See **waste**.

commitment An **agreement** to do something. A pledge or engagement. For example, an agreement by a lender to accept an application for a loan, usually subject to certain conditions such as timing. A loan commitment may be 'firm' or 'stand-by'. With a firm commitment the intention is that the loan will be made when certain conditions have been met, for example when it has been established that the borrower's financial rating is adequate and any collateral has been appraised or assessed. A stand-by commitment is intended as a source of finance of the last resort and, usually, is taken only if a contingent event occurs, such as when expenditure exceeds a budgeted cost, as a form of interim financing, or the borrower takes up an option to purchase a property. cf. **letter of comfort**. See also **commitment fee, conditional contract, forward commitment, open-end commitment, permanent commitment, promise, takeout commitment, title commitment**(US)**, top-line bottom-line commitment**(US).

commitment fee A charge made by a lender to an applicant for a loan at the stage when the application is accepted, i.e. at the time a **commitment** is made. The fee, which is usually a small percentage of the total amount that is to be lent, is paid to cover the cost to the lender of holding funds available. The lender normally retains such a fee if the borrower fails to perform his part of the bargain. cf. **standby fee**. See also **commitment letter**.

commitment letter A written offer or promise to make a **commitment**, especially to provide a loan at some future time. A letter of commitment to make a loan contains the essential terms for the proposed loan – the parties, amount of the loan; interest rate; period for which the funds will be available; property required as security – and normally specifies a date for acceptance. If the prospective borrower accepts the terms of the commitment letter, a **commitment fee**

may well be payable. Also called a 'facility letter'. See also **forward commitment**.

common   1. Held by two or more parties. In particular, belonging or pertaining to the community at large. cf. **several**. See also **right of common, tenancy in common**.   2. Usual, habitual; that which is accepted in the regular course of events. See also **common law, custom**. 3. An area of land in a village, town or city set aside for common and public usage; especially land that has been left unenclosed and, usually, in its natural state or for common pasture by local inhabitants. See also **park**.   4.(Eng)"[A]ny land subject to be enclosed under the Inclosure Acts of 1845 to 1882, and any town or village **green**", TCPA 1990, s. 336(1). See also **common land, enclosure**.   5. A right held by one person in conjunction with one or more others to enjoy the profits, or take the produce, from the land of another. A **profit à prendre** enjoyed by several persons over **common land**. See also **tenancy in common**.

common at large(Eng)   See **common in gross**.

common appendant   See **appendant, right of common**.

common appurtenant   See **appurtenant, right of common**.

common area charges   The expenses borne by the landlord for the upkeep of the **common areas** of a property or the expenses borne by the condominium owners' association for the **common elements** of a condominium. In particular, those operating expenses that are recharged to the tenants or owners for the maintenance and repair of those areas. In a shopping center such charges are usually referred to as 'common area maintenance' (CAM) charges. See also **operating expense**(AmE), **service charge**(BrE).

common area maintenance (CAM)   The cost of operating and maintaining the **common areas** of a property. Common area maintenance does not normally cover expenditure on capital improvements. See **common area charges**.

common areas   1. Those areas of a building that are not allocated to a particular occupier, but are available for common use by all owners, tenants and visitors. In particular, those parts of a property that are shared between the occupants of a multi-let property, or a building held in some form of collective ownership, such as hall areas, lobbies, atrium spaces, concierge areas, stairways, elevators, plant rooms, fire control areas, common toilets, means of access to or egress from the property, landscaped areas, some service bays, and common or visitor parking areas; but specifically excluding any areas leased to or used by one occupier to the exclusion of others. Sometimes called the 'common parts'. See also **implied covenant**. 2.(US)The areas of a **condominium** or a **planned unit development** that are used in common by the individual unit or landowners. See also **common elements**.

common building scheme   See **scheme of development**.

common chase   See **chase**.

common covenant   See **usual covenant**.

common duty of care   See **duty of care**.

common elements(US)   Those parts of a building held in **condominium** ownership that are shared between the individual unit owners, such as hallways, lobbies, elevators, staircases, janitorial areas, plant rooms or water tanks, washrooms, meeting rooms, means of access to or egress from the property and, if applicable, outside yards, decks, pools or recreational areas that are common to all the owners; but specifically excluding any areas deeded to one owner to the exclusion of others. Any part of the property included in the condominium declaration that is not part of an individual unit, or not held in several ownership by the condominium owners' association, may be considered as a common element, including the structural walls, floors, roof of a building, as well as the land on which the building stands. The condominium owners' association may own the common elements and grant easements and other rights to the unit owners; or the common elements may be held as a **tenancy in common** (in jurisdictions that recognize such a common law form of co-ownership), with the owners of condominium units having an undivided interest in those areas. These elements may be common to all the owners, such as the hallways, stairway, corridors, etc.; or may be limited to certain owners ('limited common elements') to the exclusion of all others, e.g. parking spaces, decks, terraces. The surface areas that constitute common elements, such as the hallway, corridors, etc., are usually called the 'common areas'. See also **apportionment**.

common field(US)   A small and unusually shaped tract of land situated outside a village, usually fenced off and used by occupants of the colonial French towns or villages for common cultivation and pasturage. Due to the unusual shape and use of the land, a common field was recognized for such continued use by Act of Congress rather than being taken, for example, as State owned land under the Louisiana Purchase (Glasgow v. Hortiz, 1 Black 595-600, 66 US 595, 17 L Ed 110, 113 (1861)).

common gables(Scot)   A shared division wall between two separate but connected buildings. The owner of a house who built it with a gable wall may be obliged to permit the owner of an adjoining parcel to build against that wall, subject to the payment of half the cost of the wall. Similar to a form of **party wall** as found in English law. Also called 'mutual gables'.

common in gross(Eng)   See **right of common**.

common interest   1. An interest in property held in common with others. In common law, a term

of no legal significance, but one that may be used to refer to any form of **co-ownership**. See also **common property**.   2. A joint interest in a business venture. See also **joint venture partnership**.   3.(US)An interest in the **common elements** of a property. In particular, the percentage share that an individual unit owner in a **condominium** owns in the common elements. See also **apportionment**.   4.(Scot) An interest in property held by different people in separate units of the same property, but sharing a common concern. In particular, the ownership of a load-bearing wall in a tenement building or the rights in a non-tidal river held by the proprietors on each side.

common interest development(US)   A term that may be used to refer to "any of the following: (1) A **community apartment** project. (2) A **condominium** project. (3) A planned development project. (4) A stock **cooperative**", Cal CC, § 1351(c). See also **planned unit development**.

common land   1. Land held in separate or several ownership, but used in common. Land over which a **right of common** exists. In particular, in England and Wales common land is a remnant of the **feudal system** of land tenure by which, although all land was owned by the Sovereign or held therefrom by a subordinate lord of the **manor**, large areas of uncultivated wasteland or woodland were used by the tenants of the manor in common and in a manner recognised by custom or common law. Today common land may be part of a manor; be owned privately, whether in common or severalty; or have been acquired by a public authority such as a parish council, with the rights of common exercisable by 'commoners' (who are usually members of the local community).

All common land in England and Wales, as well as "rights of common" over such land and the owners or persons claiming to be the owners of such land, must be registered with a county or metropolitan council or the council of the London borough, in the 'register of common land' (Commons Registration Act 1965). For this purpose 'common land' means: (a) "land subject to rights of common (as defined in this Act) whether those rights are exercisable at all times or only during limited periods"; or (b) "waste land of the manor not subject to rights of common"; but not "a town or village **green** or any land which forms part of a highway", CRA 1965, s. 22(1). (A separate register is maintained of town or village greens.) After July 1970, any such land that is not so registered cannot be deemed to be common land and no rights of common can be exercised over unregistered land. However, new commons may arise by grant or prescription, and may then be registered (S.I. 1969 No. 1843, r. 3(1), n. 5). However, commons that arise in this way do not cease to be common land, nor do the rights of common cease to be exercisable, if the land is not registered.

In the US, lands over which there are rights of common existed from before the War of the Revolution. However, the local municipality now generally owns such lands or statutes have been passed to provide that such lands are held by incorporated proprietors. The term may also be used to refer to land that has been dedicated for public use, as with a public common or open public ground. See also **common field**(US), **enclosure**.

Ubhi, Navjit, and Barry Denyer-Smith. *Law of Commons and of Town and Village Greens.* Bristol: Jordans, 2003.

common law The system of unwritten law that derived its authority from ancient **usage**, **custom** and **precedent**. Law that is not created but develops by successive decisions of the courts under the principle of *stare decisis* – 'to abide by a decided case'. In different contexts, common law can have the following meanings: (i) unwritten law, especially the Anglo-American traditions of law-making, as distinguished from a written code of law (whether a civil code or statute law); (ii) law that was administered by the English Courts of Common Law prior to the Judicature Acts 1873-75, as distinguished from the rules of **equity** administered in the Court of Chancery; (iii) law that is common to an entire realm, as distinguished from local rules or customs accepted by a group of individuals; (iv) an evolving judge-made law, as distinguished from ecclesiastical, admiralty or statute law; (v) law that was shaped in England, based on Anglo-Saxon and Norman laws, became the basis of law in the Commonwealth and formed the basis of law in most states in the US, as distinguished from law based on a Constitution or statute adopted by a particular nation or state; (vi) specific to the US, the law adopted by each state and applied as local law, based on local usage, subject to alteration by statute; there being no common law of the United States as a whole, different states having adopted the 'common law' in a different manner and at a different time.

English common law has formed an important element in establishing the foundations of modern land law so that even today, as a result of this established body of law, all land is considered to be held from the Crown; there is no absolute form of land **ownership** recognised in common law; a leasehold interest is considered **personal property** (a 'chattel real'); distinct legal and equitable interests can, and in certain cases must, be held in the same land; and the modern form of **trust** stems from the former conflict of common law with equity.

The term 'at law' or 'law' is frequently used, especially in English statutes, to refer to rules derived from common law as distinguished from principles established 'in equity'; thereby making them actionable as of right and not merely at the discretion of the court (this distinction is noticeable in the English LPA 1925). 'At law' may also mean in all courts of law, as distinguished from 'in equity', which means in a court of equity with the element of discretion appertaining thereto.

In this book, unless the context indicates to the contrary, the expression 'common law' or 'the common law' refers to the body of law built up by the precedents of the courts since the reign of Henry II and applied throughout England and Wales and many other jurisdictions that adopted the same legal system (including the American colonies before the American Revolution).

common-law dedication See **dedication**.

common-law lien See **lien**.

common law title(Aus)   See old system title.

common-law mortgage   The traditional form of **mortgage** made on the basis that title to land was transferred to the mortgagee and could only be reclaimed when the debt was paid in full. Under such a mortgage, if the debt was not repaid in full when due, the land was ceded to the mortgagee. Also called a 'dead pledge'. See also **strict foreclosure**.

common-law trust(US)   See business trust.

common listing   See open listing.

common lodging-house(Eng)   A **lodging house** in which the poor are housed and boarded communally for a night, or for a short stay, normally for a modest charge. "[A] house [other than a public assistance institution] provided for the purpose of accommodating by night poor persons, not being members of the same family, who resort thereto and are allowed to occupy one common room for the purpose of sleeping and eating", Housing Act 1985, s. 401. The premises that constitute a common lodging-house may be part of a building, as long as there is a communal use of accommodation for sleeping and eating. The occupation of the premises by some residents on a weekly basis does not necessarily preclude them from being a 'common lodging-house'. The keeper of a common lodging-house must be approved and registered as such with the local authority and must fix a notice that the premises are a registered common lodging-house to the outside of the house. Common lodging-houses are subject to local by-laws covering such matters as overcrowding, sanitation, water supply, fire escape, and general standards of hygiene and must be inspected regularly by the local authority (HA 1985, Part XII). See also **control order, overcrowding**.

common mistake   See mistake.

common nuisance(US)   See nuisance.

common of fishery   See right to fish.

common of pasture   See right of common.

common of piscary   See right to fish.

common of turbary(Eng)   A right to dig turves (peat, but not green turf) from the land of another for use as fuel. Turbary may be granted or acquired by prescription; it may be a right **in gross** (as a **profit à prendre**), or it may be **appurtenant**.

common open space   Land that forms part of a development and is left open for enjoyment by the residents and owners in that development. **Open space** that is common to a group of individuals, or sometimes the public at large. See also **common land**(Eng), **planned unit development**.

common ownership   The ownership of all the means of production by those responsible for the production process, as distinguished from **co-ownership**, which applies especially to ownership of real property. See also **common property**.

common partition wall(US)   A **party wall** between two units held in **condominium** ownership.

common parts   See common areas.

common plan of development(US)   See scheme of development.

common property   1. Property held in public ownership for the common benefit, such as a national park. cf. **private property**.   2. Property held by all the members of a community without separate or private forms of ownership. Common property is said to exist when there is a usufructuary right to property but no absolute or individual ownership of property. Also called 'communal property'. See also **collective ownership**.   3. Property in which one or more parties have rights in common, either apart from or together with the owner. See also **common land**, **right of common**, **tenancy in common**. **4.**(Scot)A right to the ownership of property as held by two or more persons in an undivided state. Common property is held *pro indiviso* and may not be disposed of except with the mutual consent of all the parties, although each co-owner may sell or otherwise dispose of his or her *pro indiviso* share. Any one of the co-owners may realise his or her share by having the property physically subdivided or, if that is not practicable, by having the property sold and the proceeds divided rateably. A form of ownership that is similar to a **tenancy in common** in English law. cf. **joint property**. **5.**(US)Property that is not held by any person and is considered common to all. Rights to oil and gas may be considered common property "title to which becomes absolute when they are captured and reduced to possession", Ex parte Wood, 34 Cal App.2d, 93 P.2d 1058, 1061 (1939). **5.** In a **condominium**, or jurisdictions (notably Australia and New Zealand) that recognise **strata ownership**, the areas that are held in common ownership, as distinguished from the private units or lots. See also **common elements**. **6.** The parts of a building that are used by all the tenants of a multi-let property. See also **common areas**.

common recovery(Eng) See **recovery**.

common right of way A right of way available to two or more parties in common. See also **common areas**.

common scheme of development(US) See **scheme of development**.

common source of title doctrine(US) See **deraignment of title**.

common trust fund See **commingled trust fund**.

common wall See **party wall**.

commonable land(Eng) Land to which a **right of common** is attached. In particular, land owned in severalty but over which a commoner could pasture beasts for part of the year (usually after the severalty crop has been removed); especially land subject to such rights as **cattlegate**. See also **common land**.

commoners See **common land**.

commonhold **1.**(Eng)The separate freehold ownership of a 'unit' in a building, that contains two or more such units, together with an interest in a **commonhold association** that owns the **common parts** of the building. The building may be a residential property (a **flat** or **house**), or a commercial property (a **shop**, **office** or a light industrial building (but not an area of agricultural land). Commonhold is a new form of tenure that has been established by statute to enable each unit holder to have a freehold title (an estate in **fee simple**) to his property and, along with the other owners of units in the building, a title to the common parts, which are vested in the **commonhold association**. Thus, the owner of a commonhold has an absolute right to an enclosed space or 'unit' and a right in common with others to the use of **common parts**, which includes (as applicable) the hallways, staircases, roadways, open spaces, etc. This "community of freeholders" is bound by a 'local law' called a **commonhold community statement** (CCS). The exact extent of each unit is delineated by plans attached to the CCS. Under the provisions of the CCS each owner is bound by the same rights and obligations, as is every new owner, and the CCS regulates the rights and duties of the commonhold association and the unit holders. It also specifies the percentage of the common charges payable by each owner by means of a 'commonhold assessment'. This assessment should be sufficient to cover the cost of maintaining and repairing the common parts of the property, as well as such matters as insurance, cleaning, refuse collection, lighting, heating or air-conditioning, security, staff costs, property management expenses or fees, and an appropriate contribution to one or more "reserve funds" to finance the repair and maintenance of common parts. The community of owners is controlled by the members through the commonhold association established for the purpose. The Association may be made up entirely from owners or may include professionals appointed to assist in the running of the association. The Association is responsible for the management of the common parts and ensuring that the owners comply with the provisions of the CCS, including enforcing the payment of the commonhold assessment.

A commonhold can only exist where the entire property is a freehold and that property is registered as a second 'commonhold' title over the underlying freehold title. In order to register a condominium title there must be a CA and a CCS. The property must be in touch with the land so that a flat over a ground floor shop is excluded. Each unit owner has an equal interest in the property and has one vote at meeting of the commonhold association (regardless of the size or value of the unit). The owner of each unit has an absolute right to transfer their unit, although the association may impose restrictions on the right of a unit-holder to grant leases and any tenant of a unit-holder may be made subject to regulations made in accordance with the CCS, including the payment of charges levied against the applicable unit-holder (Commonhold and Leasehold Reform Act 2002 Act, ss. 17-19). See also **condominium**, **flying freehold**.

Aldridge, Trevor M. *Commonhold Law*. London: Sweet & Maxwell, 2002.

Clark, D. N. *Commonhold. The New Law*. Bristol: Jordans, 2002.

Furber, John, et al. *The Commonhold and Leasehold Reform Act 2002*. London: Butterworths, 2002.

Fetherstonhaugh, Guy, and Edward Peters. *Commonhold. Law & Practice*. London: Lexis Publishing, 2002.

2. A generic term for the form of ownership by which the owner has the separate or several ownership (a fee title or equivalent) of an individual unit in a building that contains a number of similar units and has a right to the use of designated common areas. In addition, the owner is a member of the association or 'syndicate' that has the overall responsibility for management of the building and for the upkeep of the common areas. This term can encompass **condominium** ownership, as found in the North America and other countries that have adopted this form of common ownership; and **strata ownership**, as found in Australia and New Zealand. See also **flying freehold**.

commonhold assessment(Eng)   See **commonhold**.

commonhold association (CA)(Eng) A private company limited by guarantee that has been established to own the **common parts** of a **commonhold**. The commonhold association owns the freehold of all the common areas of a commonhold property and is responsible for setting the annual 'commonhold assessment' (Commonhold and Leasehold Reform Act 2002, ss. 34-36). The commonhold association has the responsible of collecting the assessed amount from each unit holder and for the insurance, repair, maintenance and upkeep of all parts of the property, except the individual units (CLRA 2002, s. 26). Where there are a large number of units the CA may be responsible under the provisions of the **commonhold community statement** for the insurance and structural repair of the entire building. In most respects normal company law governs the CA.

commonhold community statement (CCS)(Eng)   A document that sets out the rights and duties of the **commonhold association** and of the unit-holders in a **commonhold** property (Commonhold and Leasehold Reform Act 2002, ss. 32-33). This statement represents a form of local law for all the properties in the commonhold and must be prepared by the **commonhold association** before the 'commonhold title' is registered. It is prepared in accordance with regulations set out under the provisions of the CLRA 2002. The CCS also delineates the limits of each individual unit in the building and the percentage of the common charges payable by each owner by means of a 'commonhold assessment'.

commons See **common land**.

communal property See **common property**.

community apartment(US) An apartment building held by means of a **tenancy in common**, with a right of occupancy of one or more apartments granted to each co-owner. cf. **cooperative ownership**. See also **co-ownership**.

community association(US) An association created to manage or protect a neighborhood or commonly owned property. See also **condominium**, **condominium owners' association**.

community center See **shopping center**.

community estate(US) See **community property**.

community house(US) **1.** A building used as a social center in a town or district. **2.** A house occupied by two or more families, in particular where there are shared facilities. See also **apartment house**, **tenement house**.

community property **1.** A civil law basis for holding **marital property** by which certain property (real or personal) is held by the spouses jointly but apart from, and under a different regime to, property held by either spouse in their own right. In countries or states in the US that recognize community property, ownership of any property held by the partners to a marriage may be: (a) the husband's separate property; (b) the wife's separate property; or (c) community property. The separate property of the husband and wife consists of any property owned by them at the time of their marriage, and any property either received in his or her own right by gift, devise, legacy or descent – sometimes called property acquired by 'lucrative title'. Any other property, including property given to both of the partners, is considered to have been acquired by the joint efforts of both parties and to be community property. In the US, community property is found in nine states: Arizona, California, Louisiana, New Mexico and Texas, which adopted the civil law (or Spanish) tradition in this respect; and Idaho, Nevada, Wisconsin and Washington state which adopted community property by statute. See also **homestead**, **marital property**, **tenancy by the entirety**.

McClanahan, W. S. *Community Property Law in the United States.* Rochester, NY: Lawyers Co-operative, 1982.

Mennell, Robert L., and Thomas M. Boykoff. *Community Property in a Nutshell.* 2nd ed. St. Paul, MN: West, 1988.

Reppy, William A. Jr. *Gilbert Law Summaries on Community Property.* 18th ed. St. Paul, MN: West Publishing, 2002.

2.(Aus)The property in a **community scheme** that is held as common property.

community scheme(Aus) A scheme that is established for the **subdivision** of a large area of land into lots that may be used in subsidiary schemes. A community scheme takes the form of a traditional subdivision, but the subdivided areas of land are intended to be further subdivided into areas that are to be used for subsidiary schemes. A community scheme commonly takes the form of a traditional subdivision, combined with the rules that will govern a **strata plan** for the use of the divided lots. See also **precinct scheme**.

community shopping center See **shopping center**.

community unit plan(US) See **planned unit development**.

commutation **1.** The **exchange** or substitution of one form of payment, remuneration, or charge for another. Money substituted for a service, for example where a rent or tithe became payable in money and not in produce. **2.** The conversion by law of a periodic sum of money into a fixed or single sum, e.g. the conversion of an annual **tithe** into a tithe redemption annuity. See also **capitalisation**. **3.**(US)A cash payment made by a homesteader to obtain title from the government on public lands in lieu of remaining on the land for the requisite statutory period. See also **homestead**.

commutative contract(US)   See **bilateral contract**.

commuted value   The value of the gift of a future interest reduced to its **present value**.

Companies Charges Register(Eng)   A register maintained by the Registrar of Companies that contains details of charges created by all companies registered in England and Wales. In the case of a **fixed charge** on land created by a company before January 1, 1970 or a floating charge created at any time, registration at the Companies Charges Register is a sufficient alternative to registration at the **Land Charges Register** (LCA 1972, s. 3(7)). Since January 1, 1970 any charge on land (other than **floating charge**) created by a company must be registered at the Land Charges Register to be binding on a **purchaser** of that land. If the charge is to bind creditors and liquidators, it must also be registered in the Companies Charges Register within 21 days of its creation (Companies Act 1985, ss. 395-399, as amended by Companies Act 1989). A company must also keep a register of charges at its registered office (1989 Act, ss. 406-409, as amended). Also called the 'companies register' for short (not to be confused with the 'register of company charges' which must be maintained by every limited company at its registered office). See also **land charge**.

McCormack, Gerard. *Registration of Company Charges*. London: Sweet & Maxwell, 1994.

company   An association or collection of individuals formed together for some common purpose or business, which carries on that business separately and distinctly from those individuals, but leaves each individual generally free to dispose of his interest in that association to any other individual. A company may be incorporated or unincorporated. An incorporated company or corporation has at law an existence and rights and duties distinct from those of the individual persons whom from time to time form or make up that entity. From the moment of its incorporation it has perpetual succession; a common **seal**; it is an 'artificial person', i.e. it has no mind or soul; it may acquire or dispose of property in its own name; and it may sue or be sued in that name. An unincorporated company has no separate existence and is not distinct from its members, but in other respects it carries on its business like an incorporated company and, unlike a **partnership**, the individuals remain free to transfer their shares, subject to the regulations adopted by the company. The terms 'company' and 'corporation' are frequently used interchangeably, although the former has a far wider significance and the latter is normally incorporated.

In the US, a 'company' may be "a corporation, a partnership, an association, a joint-stock company, a business trust, or an organized group of persons, whether incorporated or not, or any receiver, trustee, or other liquidating agent of any of the foregoing in his capacity as such", 15 USC § 79(b)(2). See also **firm**, *ultra vires*.

company letting(Eng)   A letting of residential property to a corporate body, usually for occupation by its employees. A term used to refer to such a letting that may be excluded from any one of a number of statutory controls because the property is not let to an 'individual'. However, if the intention is not to let the premises to the company, but the arrangement is merely a sham and the true tenant is the employee, it may be construed by the courts as in reality a direct letting to that person. See also **assured tenancy, assured shorthold tenancy, protected occupier, protected tenancy**.

comparable property   A property that has been the subject of a recent transaction and is sufficiently similar that it can be used to measure the value of another property. A comparable property should be the subject of a recent arm's-length transaction and ideally should be similar in location; age and design; construction and condition; and size and layout to the subject property, i.e. what is or has been available in a similar market. In practice, an ideal comparable property hardly ever exists; instead a valuer or appraiser extrapolates information on values from similar properties, makes adjustments and allowances, and uses his judgement to apply the resultant figure to the property he is seeking to value. Also called 'comparables', or 'comps' for short. See also **comparison method of valuation**(BrE), **sales comparison approach**(US).

comparables   See **comparable property**.

comparative market analysis (CMA)(AmE) See **sales comparison approach**.

comparison approach or **comparison method**(US)   See **sales comparison approach**.

comparison method of valuation or **comparative method of valuation**(BrE)   A method of assessing the **value** of a property by reference to the actual price obtained for similar properties. The prices paid for any comparable properties are analyzed and adjusted for differences (as applicable) in location, condition, size, age, tenure, time of sale, 'special suitability', and any other relevant factors. The 'adjusted prices' for all comparable properties are then used as the basis for estimating the market value of the property under consideration. The 'adjusted-price' may be reduced to a unit cost or rate, e.g. price per square foot or square meter, per room, per car space, (i.e. devalued) and that rate applied to the property being valued (i.e. revalued); the principle of this method being 'as one devalues so one revalues'. This method is used when there is adequate evidence of comparable sales in the market place for recent and directly comparable property. It is especially used for residential property and for the types of property that are regularly bought and sold in an open market. When it can be applied it is the most direct and reliable method of determining the value of a property.

However, in the final analysis, the opinion of the value arrived at is dependent on the valuer's skill and experience rather than any scientific formulation. Also called the 'direct comparison method'. See also **sales comparison approach**(US), **unit cost, valuation**.

comparative-unit method(US)   See **unit-in-place method**.

compensation   **1.** Something paid, or rendered, to make good a loss or injury. A payment made as an equivalent or substituted value to that which has been lost. A return or recompense for a loss or for damage suffered, especially when the party making the payment has acted lawfully. Compensation may be distinguished from **damages**, the former being a payment to which a person is entitled in recompense for property taken from him, whereas damages is a sum of money that is recoverable as a consequence of an actionable wrong.

In relation to real property, 'compensation' is commonly used to refer to a payment made for the condemnation, taking or compulsory purchase of property. In the US, where the right to compensation for the 'taking' of land is enshrined in the Fifth Amendment to the Constitution, the term used is **just compensation**. In this respect, 'compensation' and 'damages' may be considered to be synonymous. In English law, the term generally used is **compulsory purchase compensation**. In other countries the term used may be 'compensation for condemnation'. See also **just terms**(Aus).   **2.**(Scot)A right to **set-off**.

compensation for condemnation(US)   See **just compensation**.

compensation for disturbance(Eng)   **1.** Compensation paid to a person whose interest in property is acquired by compulsory purchase for the loss of use or profit as a result of having to vacate the property. It is paid by the acquiring authority for such items as the cost of moving to new premises; adapting fixtures to new premises; loss on forced sale of stock; professional fees;

business loss or injury, i.e. loss of **goodwill** (whether a partial or total loss, depending on the circumstances); and such other loss and expense resulting directly from the dispossession. "[A]ny loss sustained by a dispossessed owner (at all events one who occupies his house) which flows from a compulsory acquisition may properly be regarded as the subject of compensation for disturbance provided, first, it is not too remote and, secondly, that it is a natural and reasonable consequence of the dispossession of the owner", *Harvey v Crawley Development Corporation* [1957] 1 QB 485, 494, [1957] 1 All ER 504, 507 (CA). (The *Harvey v Crawley* case approved the payment of costs associated with the buying of a new house: surveyor's fees, legal costs, travelling expenses, which are colloquially called 'Crawley' costs. However, if a dispossessed owner acquires another property at a higher price he is not compensated for that extra expenditure because he would be presumed to have got value for money.) There is no separate statutory right to compensation for disturbance (although it is referred to in the LCompA 1961, s. 5(6)). Compensation for disturbance is assessed separately, but forms part of the total amount of **compulsory purchase compensation** payable by the acquiring authority. See also **consequential damages**[US], **ex gratia payment, farm-loss payment, home-loss payment. 2.** Compensation paid in accordance with a statutory provision when a tenant is no longer permitted to renew his tenancy. In the case of a **business tenancy**, in the event that the landlord, upon certain grounds, successfully opposes the grant of a new tenancy, a tenant may be entitled to compensation based the rateable value of the premises (L&T Act 1954, s. 37; L&T (Appropriate Multiplier) Order 1990). A holder of an **agricultural tenancy**, upon being required to vacate the holding may be entitled to compensation of between one and four year's rent (AHA 1986, s. 60). See also **tenant-right**.

compensation for improvements

1.[Eng]Compensation paid to an outgoing tenant for an **improvement**, carried out by the tenant, or at the tenant's expense, to the leased premises during the term of the expired tenancy. In common law, any improvement in the value of a property made by the tenant accrues to the landlord, without compensation, at the end of a tenancy.

In the case of a **business tenancy** a tenant is entitled to compensation for any improvement, not being a trade or other fixture, that the tenant is by law entitled to remove, whether carried out by him or his predecessors in title, upon the **termination** of his **lease** and upon quitting the premises, subject to a number of statutory prescribed conditions (L&T Act 1927, Part I, as amended by the L&T Act 1954, Part III). In the case of an **agricultural tenancy**, a tenant upon the termination of his tenancy is entitled to compensation when he quits the holding. This right was originally granted by custom, on the principle that a tenant was entitled to compensation based on any increase in the value of the holding available to an incoming tenant as a result of the outgoing tenant's improvements. This right is now governed entirely by statute (AHA 1986, ss. 64-70, Sch. 9). A tenant who holds a **farm business tenancy** is entitled to compensation based on any increase in the value of the holding at the termination of the tenancy (Agricultural Tenancies Act 1995, s. 20). A tenant of a **market garden** has a similar, but more extensive, right to compensation for improvement than a tenant of an agricultural holding, including a right to compensation for any improvement previously paid for as an incoming tenant (AHA 1986 ss. 79-81, Sch. 10). See also **allotment, completion certificate, emblements, tenant right. 2.**[US]As a rule of common law, adopted by most jurisdictions in the US, absent any agreement or statute to the contrary, a tenant is not entitled to compensation for an **improvement** that he has made of his own volition to the demised premises. However, equity may provide that where a landlord is seeking to recover possession from a bona fide occupier of land or makes a claim for **mesne profits** as a result of the tenant's continuing occupation of the demised premises after a lease has expired, then the tenant may be able to set-off the value of the improvements that are left for the benefit of the landlord against the claims of the landlord. This is sometimes called the equitable doctrine of 'melioration' "It is a maxim suggested by nature, that reparations or meliorations bestowed upon a house, or on land, ought to be defrayed out of the rents", Green v. Biddle, 8 Wheat 82, 21 US 82, 5 L Ed 547, 567 (1823) (*Coulter's Case* (1598) 5 Co Rep 30a, 77 Eng Rep 98). However, this is an equitable right and is only accepted at the discretion of the courts See also **mistaken improver, unjust enrichment**.

compensation for injurious affection(Eng) Compensation paid for depreciation in the value of land as a result of either: (i) the acquisition of part of an owner's total land holding and a consequent reduction in the value of the land retained due to the contributory nature of the work carried out on the land acquired; or (ii) the carrying out under statutory powers of work on adjoining land in separate ownership, when no part of an owner's land is taken. In the first case, compensation is paid not only for the land taken, but also for any damage sustained by the owner of the land as a result of the **severance** of land purchased from the other land of the owner, as well as for any **injurious affection** (noise, dirt, smell, etc.) caused by the acquiring authority (Land Clauses Consolidation Act 1845, s. 63; Compulsory Purchase Act 1965, s. 7). In addition, if the injurious affection arises from work carried out partly on the land acquired and partly elsewhere the amount of compensation shall be assessed "by reference to the whole of the works and not only the part situated on the land acquired or taken", Land Compensation Act 1973, s. 44. In the second case, when no land is taken, but injurious affection is caused by work on adjoining land, the right to compensation is analogous to damages paid for a private nuisance, but it extends to cover damage caused by any act of the statutory authority acquiring the land that results in a physical deterioration in the value of the land. The amount of compensation payable for injurious affection is based on the reduction in the **market value** of the land affected and is measured usually by means of the **before-and-after method** of valuation. If the damage is temporary, the loss is assessed for the period that the claimant has suffered a reduction in the value of his land (*Wildtree Hotels Ltd v Harrow LBC* (2000) 150 NLJ 984 (HL)). See also **compensation for severance, set-off, severance damages**(US).

compensation for planning restrictions(Eng) Compensation paid for the depreciation in the value of land resulting from the loss of a right to carry out development or a right to use and enjoy land. As a general rule, in English law, a landowner is not entitled to any recompense for being prohibited from carrying out development by virtue of a parliamentary enactment. However, compensation may be payable to a landowner when there has been a limit placed on an existing right to use land. In particular: (i) when a planning permission is varied or withdrawn by a modification or **revocation order** including the modification or revocation of planning permission that was granted, or deemed to be granted, by a **General Development Order**; (ii) following the service of **discontinuance order** requiring the removal or alteration of an authorised development from land; (iii) following the issuing and subsequent withdrawal of a **stop notice**; (iv) when there has been a refusal of consent to cutting of trees affected by a **tree preservation order**, or a requirement to replant trees affected by such an order; (v) when the owner is required to remove an **advertisement** that has been in existence since the 1948; (vi) following the making of a **pedestrian precinct order**; (vii) following a revocation or modification of a **listed building consent**, or a modification of consent to the demolition of an unlisted building in a conservation area; (viii) when a **building preservation notice** is issued but the building to which it related is not subsequently listed; (ix) in the event of a revocation or modification of a 'Hazardous Building consent'. Such compensation is based on the reduction in the **market value** of the interest held in the subject property resulting from the restriction. Such a reduction of market value is generally measured by the **before-and-after method** of valuation. Compensation may be payable also for expenditure incurred for authorised work that has had to be aborted as a result of the restriction. See also **blight notice, compensation notice, just compensation**(US)**, police power**(US)**, purchase notice.**

compensation for severance(Eng) Compensation for damage caused "by reason of the severing of the land purchased from the other lands of the owner", Compulsory Purchase Act 1965, s. 7. It may be damage following a compulsory purchase order that results either in the total loss of part of an owner's holding or the separation of one part of an owner's land from the rest of his land by the construction of works, such as a new highway. Thus, when land is acquired compulsorily, compensation is paid not only for the land taken, but also for losses caused by **severance**, provided the severance results in either: (i) a reduction in the market value of the land retained; or (ii) other incidental losses resulting from the compulsory purchase, e.g. increased costs of running a farm, inefficiencies of scale, damage during construction work undertaken by the acquiring authority and the need for subsequent reinstatement. The amount of compensation paid for severance is based on the reduction in the **market value** of the land affected and is measured generally by the **before-and-after method** of valuation. However, it is more technically correct to determine the value of the land taken and then add the loss in value of the retained land. See also **accommodation work, apportionment, compensation for injurious affection, compulsory purchase compensation, severance damages**(US)**.**

compensation notice(Eng) Notice of a charge against land that has been registered in favour of a local authority that has paid compensation for a planning restriction that has been revoked or modified (TCPA 1990, s. 110; Local Land Charges Act 1975, s. 1). This compensation must be repaid in the event that the restriction is lifted. See also **compensation for planning restrictions, local land charge.**

competent landlord(Eng) See **landlord.**

complete appraisal(US) An **appraisal** that is carried out in accordance with the **Uniform Standards of Professional Appraisal Practice** and is not limited or restricted by adopting the **Departure Rule**, which permits an appraisal to fall short of the full standard in certain circumstances. cf. **limited appraisal**. See also **self-contained appraisal report.**

completion 1. The bringing of a transaction for the sale of land, or an interest in land, to finality. Completion of a sale takes place when all legal documentation is signed, the final account is settled between the vendor and purchaser, and, in particular, there has been **delivery** of the title and of possession (whether vacant possession or possession of the rent and profits); "the complete conveyance of the estate and final settlement of the business", *Lewis v South Western Ry* (1852) 22 LJ Ch 209, 212 (*2 Bl Comm* 199; *Dingey v. Paxton*, 60 Miss 1054; *Killner v France* [1946] 2 All ER 83, 85, aff'd (1947) 1949 EG 92 (CA)). Generally, completion takes place on the **date** on which good title is transferred, the actual transfer of possession takes place, and the purchase money is paid in full. See also **acquisition, closing**(US)**, completion date, specific performance, time is of the essence**. 2. See **practical completion, substantial performance**. 3.(Eng)See **completion notice.**

completion bond A bond posted by a landowner or developer, usually in favour of a lender, which provides a **guarantee** that proposed building work or development will be completed in accordance with the plans and specification, free of all liens or third party claims. A completion bond is provided to ensure that the work is carried out, even if the contractor is not paid, due to a dispute with the developer or landowner, and in that respect it may be distinguished from a

performance bond which only ensures the execution of a contractual obligation. Generally, a completion bond is drawn on only if and when the landowner or developer has failed to complete the project. A completion bond may take the form of an insurance bond, or a **letter of credit** taken out in favour of the lender. cf. **payment bond**.

completion certificate   1. See **certificate of practical completion**(BrE), **certificate of completion**(US), **certificate of occupancy**(US). 2.(Eng)A certificate issued to a tenant who holds a tenancy of business premises and has carried out authorised improvement work for which he intends to claim **compensation for improvements** at the end of the tenancy. If the tenant has made a request for a certificate, after the works are duly completed, and the landlord fails to issue one, the tenant can apply to the court for such a certificate (L&T Act 1927, s. 3(6)).

completion costs(BrE)   The costs incurred in consummating a property transaction; expenses incurred by a party to a transfer of an interest in land, whether as a vendor, purchaser, lessor, lessee, mortgagor, or mortgagee. In particular, expenses incurred by either party to a transaction over and above the consideration set out in the contract. The costs incurred by a purchaser may include: stamp duty, Land Registry search fees, cost of registering a deed (including a mortgage, if any), a title insurance premium (if required), legal fees, and any mortgage commitment fee. The costs incurred by a vendor may include: legal fees, estate agent's fees, and any mortgage release fee. In addition, variable expenses associated with the property (rent, rates, insurance premiums, service charges, and other income and expenses related to the ownership of the property) must be prorated between the purchaser and vendor as at the date of completion. These costs are set out usually in the **completion statement** prepared by the vendor's solicitor. Estate agent's fees may be payable after completion (and are generally billed separately by the agent), while property survey fees and search fees may have to be paid prior to exchange of contract. See also **apportionment**, **closing costs**(AmE).

completion date   1. The **date** upon which a transaction is completed in its entirety. See also **completion**, **delivery**.   2. The date fixed for completion of a building work, or the date upon which building work is actually completed. See also **certificate of completion**(US), **certificate of practical completion**(BrE), **performance**, **practical completion**, **time is of the essence**.

completion notice(Eng)   1. Notice served by a local planning authority on a property owner, occupier or any other party involved in the development of property, when the authority considers that development, for which the authority has granted **planning permission**, will not be completed within a prescribed period of time that related to the original permission (TCPA 1990, s. 94).   2. Notice served upon one of the parties to a contract for the sale of land requiring **completion** of the contract and thereby making time of the essence from the date the notice is deemed to take effect. See also **time is of the essence**.   3. Notice that may be served on the owner of a newly completed building, by a local (billing) authority, specifying that in the opinion of the authority the building is complete and, therefore, the owner is liable for the payment of rates (Local Government Finance Act 1988, s. 46, Sch. 4A, as amended). The authority may also serve a completion notice, specifying a completion date, when it is of the opinion that the work remaining to be done can reasonably be completed within three months. See also **valuation tribunals**.

completion order(US)   See **certificate of occupancy**.

completion statement(BrE)   A cash accounting statement of all the costs and expenses of a property transaction. In particular, a 'completion statement' may be either: (i) an account prepared by the vendor's solicitor on completion, and agreed with the purchaser's solicitor to show the amount due to the vendor from the purchaser (with the rents, service charges, etc. duly apportioned); or (ii) the account prepared by a solicitor after completion showing how the solicitor has dealt with the money he has handled and any balance due to the client, or to the solicitor. The statement shows also an **apportionment** of all income and expenses between the purchaser and vendor and the resultant sum due or paid by one party (usually the purchaser) to the other. See also **completion costs, settlement statement**(US).

component capitalization rate(AmE) A **capitalization rate** that is made up by adding different rates to reflect the various elements of risk for an investment. For example, the appropriate 'risk rates' for an investment may be considered to be:

safe rate (based on the safest form of investment)	2.5%
general risk (general risk of the specific investment)	3.5%
illiquidity risk, especially for real property (risk of finding a ready purchaser)	2.0%
leasing void risk (risk of lost income from non-letting)	<u>1.0%</u>
producing a 'component rate' of	9.0%

Also called the 'summation rate'. The application of a component capitalization rate to an income is sometimes called the 'built-up capitalization method'. cf. **band-of-investment rate**. See also **all-risks rate, overall rate**.

component depreciation Depreciation applied at different rates to different parts of, or interests in, the same property. For example, the structure of a building may be depreciated on a straight-line basis over 30 years and the services, equipment and other fixtures depreciated over 10 years. When different rates or methods of depreciation are applied to different engineering components of a building, such as the elevator, air-conditioning plant, etc., this method of depreciation may also be called 'engineering breakdown depreciation'. cf. **composite depreciation**.

component financing See **split financing**.

composite depreciation Depreciation applied at a single rate to an entire property, land and buildings, as distinguished from **component depreciation** where different rates are applied to different parts of the property.

composite hereditament(Eng) A **hereditament** part of which comprises domestic property (Local Government Finance and Valuation and Finance Act 1991, s. 64(9)). The entirety of a composite hereditament is entered in the rating list, but the rateable value for the purpose of levying the **Uniform Business Rate** is determined on the basis of the annual value to be derived from the non-domestic element. The domestic accommodation is assessed separately and occupation of that element creates a liability for **Council Tax**.

composite rate A rate of return on an investment that provides a yield to the investor that is adequate for the risk entailed and provides for the recapture of the initial capital cost. See also **all-risks rate, dual-rate capitalization factor**(AmE).

composition See **compound** (a debt).

compound (a debt) To agree to terms for a payment. A lender may compound a debt by agreeing to receive a smaller sum in settlement of the debt in discharge of the full liability. Such an agreement is called a 'composition'. See also **accord and satisfaction, compound interest**.

compound amount of one See Appendix C, **Financial Formulae**.

compound interest Interest payable or earned on both the original principal and subsequent accrued interest, i.e. on interest already due or earned. If a sum of money P is invested at a compound interest rate of i per period, then at the end of n periods that sum will accumulate to a total of $A = P(1 + i)^n$.

In the US, in some states, a distinction is made in **usury** laws between 'compound interest' where interest is added on overdue installments of interest or the interest is added to the principal and a new loan comes into effect with the borrower having the opportunity in the intervening period to repay the loan, and 'interest on interest' where any unpaid interest is automatically added to the principal and interest assessed on the total balance. cf. **simple interest**. See also **discount rate**.

compound settlement(Eng)   A **settlement** of the same land effected by two or more documents over a period of time. For example, a settlement followed by a resettlement. Such documents are read as if they were one settlement and normally the tenant for life is the same under both documents. See also **joinder**.

comprehensive development   The redevelopment of an area as a whole under a comprehensive planning scheme; frequently where an area has been brought into common ownership. See also **action area, area of comprehensive development**.

comprehensive development area   See **area of comprehensive development**.

comprehensive insurance   Insurance against a broad range of specified risks, as compared with **all-risks insurance**, which covers risks (but not certainties) not specifically excluded by the policy. Also called 'named-perils insurance' (when the policy sets out the exact risks or perils that are covered) or sometimes 'multiple-perils insurance', or in the US, 'comprehensive liability insurance' or 'broad-form insurance'. See also **package insurance policy**.

comprehensive liability insurance(US) See **comprehensive insurance**.

comprehensive plan or **comprehensi[ve] zoning plan**(US)   A plan that is intended to regulate the physical growth and development of a community and to cover all aspects of development, including land use, public facilities and transportation. A comprehensive plan includes a zoning map for the area and a descriptive text of the basis for its implementation. The term 'comprehensive zoning plan' refers especially to a plan that shows existing uses and aims to confine related buildings and uses to designated areas or districts; to limit the growth of non-conforming uses; to ensure that any rezoning conforms broadly with the plan and the municipalities decisions in this respect are not arbitrary, unreasonable or discriminatory. Such a plan is sometimes referred to as a **master plan**; however, 'master plan' is a more generic term and a comprehensive plan is made for the specific purpose outlined above. See also **zoning**.

compromise   To settle by mutual agreement. Settlement of a dispute upon terms that are between those desired by all parties; a mutual yielding of opposite claims. See also **accord and satisfaction, novation**.

compromise sales agreement(US)   A compromise agreement, entered into when a borrower is deeply in debt, by which the lender agrees to take the proceeds of sale of the borrower's assets in exchange for an agreement not to proceed through the foreclosure process.

comps   See **comparable property**.

compulsory listing(US)   See **multiple listing**.

compulsory purchase or **compulsory acquisition**(BrE)   The purchase of property against the will of the owner, subject to the payment of proper compensation. In particular, the purchase of an interest in land for public purposes by a body possessing statutory powers, e.g. for highway construction; comprehensive redevelopment; or a statutory undertaking.

Compulsory purchase is initiated by the service of a **notice to treat** (or the issue of a **general vesting declaration**), following authorisation obtained under a **compulsory purchase order**, and is completed when **compensation** is settled and the interest in land transferred to the acquiring authority.

In England and Wales the land acquisition powers of public authorities are wide ranging so that land may be acquired not only for a specific statutory purpose, e.g. to facilitate the construction of a new highway, but merely for "the proper planning of an area", Local Government, Planning and Land Act 1980, s. 91. However, no minister or public authority can acquire any land compulsorily except when the power to do has been given by Parliament; and Parliament grants it, or should grant it, only when it is necessary in the public interest, and then only on the condition that proper compensation is paid (*A-G v De Keyser's Royal Hotel* [1920] 1 AC 508 (HL); *Prest v Secretary of State for Wales* (1983) 266 EG 527, 528.).

Compulsory purchase requires an authorising statute; in most cases is made in accordance with the procedures contained in the Acquisition of Land Act 1981; is carried through in accordance with the provisions of the Compulsory Purchase Act 1965; and compensation is paid upon the basis laid down primarily in the Land Compensation Act 1961.

In the US, compulsory purchase is referred to as the exercise of the power of **eminent domain**, or **condemnation proceedings**. (The term eminent domain is hardly ever used in English law, although it may be used to refer to the right of the Sovereign to acquire land, as distinguished from compulsory acquisition, which comprehends such a right being obtained with the consent of Parliament.) See also **blight notice, compulsory purchase compensation, expropriation, leasehold enfranchisement, purchase notice,** *ultra vires*.

compulsory purchase compensation (Eng)

A single sum of money paid to an individual with an interest in land, for the loss of that interest as a result of its purchase by an authority possessing powers of **compulsory purchase**. The amount of compensation is intended to put the party in the same position financially as if the land had never been taken – the principle of 'equivalence'. However, the determination of compensation payable as a result of the compulsory purchase of land is not entirely a matter for negotiation between the parties, supported by resort to an independent expert or arbitrator, but is a subject governed by statutory rules. Such rules are now incorporated in the Land Compensation Act 1961, ss. 5, 6 and Schedule I (as amended). See also **compensation for injurious affection, compensation for planning restrictions, compensation for severance, just compensation**(US), **notice of entry, notice to treat, valuation date**.

Brand, Clive M (general editor). *Encyclopedia of Compulsory Purchase and Compensation*. 2 vols. Looseleaf. London: Sweet & Maxwell.

Denyer-Green, Barry. *Compulsory Purchase and Compensation*. 6th ed. London: Estates Gazette, 2001.

Hawkins, David., and Sir John Boynton. *Boynton's Guide to Compulsory Purchase and Compensation*. 7th ed. London: Sweet & Maxwell, 1994.

Hayward, Richard. *Handbook of Land Compensation: Law and Valuation*. Looseleaf. London: Sweet & Maxwell, 1995.

compulsory purchase order (CPO) (Eng)

An order, made or confirmed by a Minister of State, in accordance with statutory authority (e.g. Compulsory Purchase Act 1965), by which a body or authority is authorised to purchase land compulsorily for a specified purpose, subject to the payment of proper **compensation**. A compulsory purchase order derives its power from an enabling statute and an authority cannot extend its powers beyond those expressly conferred by the appropriate statute. Once a CPO has been obtained, the powers of the acquiring authority are usually exercised under the Compulsory Purchase Act 1965. See also **blight notice, compulsory purchase, general vesting declaration, purchase notice,** *ultra vires*.

compulsory resumption(Aus)   The **compulsory purchase** of land by the Commonwealth. The term is based on the principal that the Crown owns all land and that it is exercising its right to regaining an area of land, subject to the payment of reasonable compensation (Commonwealth of Australia Constitution Act 1900, s. 51(xxxi)). See also **Crown land, just terms**.

concession   1. Something given or yielded to achieve an objective. See also **surrender, yield**.   2. A reduction in a price made to induce someone to enter into a contract. A sum of money or other consideration granted to a special buyer or a wholesaler. In particular, an unusual payment or special terms granted to a buyer (a 'buyer's concession') to induce him to pay a higher amount for property than might otherwise be the case (in appraising the property such an inducement must be excluded). See also **abatement, cash back**(US), **grant, rebate, rent concession**.   3. The grant of a right or privilege. In particular, the grant, either by lease or more usually by **licence**, of a right to use all or part of another's property for a specific purpose, especially for a purpose that is supplemental to another. For example, a right granted to a seller of branded goods to use part of a retail center or departmental store to display and sell his goods. Also, the space allocated for such a purpose may be referred to as a concession. See also **assent, franchise**.

concessionaire   One who has been granted a **concession**; a person who has been granted a right in the nature of a **licence** or privilege. One who operates a business within another's premises under licence. See also **licensee**.

concierge   A person who is responsible for the control of the entrance of a building. See also **caretaker, janitor**.

concurrent condition or **concurrent covenant**   A **condition** or **covenant** that is mutually dependent on another condition or covenant. A condition, or covenant, that is to be performed at the same time as another condition or covenant. A condition of a contract the performance of which is dependent on the performance of a condition by the other party, usually at the same time. The sale of land for a price may be considered to create concurrent conditions, the payment of the price and the transfer of title to the property. See also **bilateral contract, condition precedent**.

concurrent estate or **concurrent interest**   An estate or interest in land held by two or more persons at one and the same time, i.e. an estate in land that exists when ownership or possession is held by two or more persons at the same time. In particular, an interest in land as held under a **joint tenancy**, **tenancy in common**, **tenancy by the entirety**, or **coparcenary**. A grant of land 'to A and B in fee simple' creates a concurrent interest, but a grant 'to A for life, and thereafter to B in fee simple' creates several and successive interests. An interest held in **community property** or in **partnership property** may also be called a concurrent interest. cf. **several estate**. See also **co-ownership, cotenancy**.

concurrent insurance   Insurance effected, under separate contracts, to cover the same risk, on the same property, at the same time and in favour of the same person. cf. **co-insurance**.

concurrent lease   A lease granted by an existing landlord, of all or some part of the same premises, to a party other than an existing tenant, to run for at least part of the term of the existing lease, i.e. both leases run for some common period of time. A concurrent lease usually grants the third party a lease of the landlord's **reversion**, i.e. the landlord is assigning a right to part of his reversionary interest. Thus, if A has granted a lease to B for a term that has five years remaining, A may grant a concurrent lease to C, which commences immediately, or before the expiry of the lease to B, and continues for all or part of the remaining five years. B takes over the place of A and receives the rents payable by C under the initial lease and may then obtain a right to exclusive possession. Immediately the concurrent lease comes into effect, **privity of estate** exists between the lessee who holds the initial term and the lessee who holds the reversion. It is possible to have any number of concurrent leases of the same premises. cf. **reversionary lease**. See also **intermediate lease**.

concurrent negligence(US)   See **contributory negligence**.

concurrent ownership   See **concurrent estate**.

condemnation   1.(US)An enforced sale of property. The procedure by which private property is taken against the will of the owner by the exercise of the power of **eminent domain**, i.e. the sovereign right of the State or any authorized government authority to acquire property for public use against the will of the individual. The US federal government can exercise its power of eminent domain under one of various Congressional enactments authorizing such taking, or, rarely, by taking possession without formal proceedings. A municipal authority or a county can only condemn land when authorized by its charter or by its own statutory authority. In some cases a public utility, public service company, or even a private corporation, may be authorized, usually by delegated authority from the state, to take or cause damage to private property, provided the property is being taken for a public use or purpose (United States v. Carmack, 329 US 230, 67 S Ct 252, 91 L Ed 209 (1946)). In all cases the taking of property must be made with 'due process' and subject to the payment of **just compensation**. cf. **appropriation**. See also **compulsory purchase**(BrE), **excess condemnation**, **inverse condemnation**, **police power**.   2. An act or process by which a property is declared unfit for use or occupation and only suitable for closure or demolition, unless the property is substantially repaired or reconstructed.

condemnation blight(US)   A reduction in the value of a property resulting from the threat or prospect of **condemnation**. In determining the amount of **just compensation** payable in eminent domain proceedings, any increase or decrease in the 'fair' market value of a property resulting from the imminence of eminent domain proceedings, or attributable to the project for which the property is being acquired, is to be disregarded (United States v. Virginia Electric & Power Co., 365 US 624, 81 S Ct 784, 81 L Ed 784, 849 (1961)). See also **blight**, **inverse condemnation**.

condemnation proceedings(US)   The process by which property is taken for public use by the exercise of the power of **eminent domain** and the payment of due compensation.

condemnee(US)   One whose property is to be taken by **condemnation**.

condemnor(US)   A public or quasi-public authority that acquires private property by **condemnation**.

condition   1. A provision or stipulation, especially one that is a prerequisite to something else. Something that must occur or not occur before a right comes into existence; or something that if it occurs, or does not occur, enlarges or brings an estate, right or interest to an end. A provision in a contract that limits or modifies the rights or obligations under the contract. In particular, it denotes a component of, or clause of restraint in, a contract that is essential to the operation of the contract, whether to bring the contract into effect or bring it to an end. A condition may be contrasted with a **warranty** or a **covenant**, as the latter may be considered subsidiary to the main purpose of the contract. The breach of a condition of a contract (or strictly speaking the 'occurrence' of a breach), gives rise to a right to repudiate the contract and sue for damages; as opposed to a breach of covenant, which gives only a right to a claim for damages. Similarly, a breach of a condition cannot give rise to a decree of **specific performance** for, as a rule, there is no contract left to perform, whereas a breached covenant can generally be rectified, usually subsequent to such a decree.

A condition may be an **express term**, i.e. set down by the parties (in the US sometimes called a 'condition in deed'); or an **implied term** based on the action or intention of the parties or implied by law to give efficacy to an agreement (in the US sometimes called a 'condition in law'). cf. **representation**. See also **breach of contract, condition precedent, condition subsequent, conditional contract, conditional interest, planning condition**(Eng), **repudiation, time is of the essence.** **2.** A qualification, limitation or restriction annexed to an **estate** in land that is intended to cut down or limit the estate granted. A qualification or restriction annexed to a conveyance of land that has the effect of bringing the estate into effect, that enlarges or defeats an estate, or vests that estate in another person, upon the happening, or not happening, of an event described in the conveyance. Such a condition may be 'neutral' if it takes effect in the event that a particular event does, or does not, happen; or 'personal' if the grantee does or does not do a particular act. A condition may be 'precedent', 'subsequent' or 'inherent'. A condition precedent must occur before an estate or interest in land is created, enlarged, or vested in someone. A condition subsequent changes or defeats an estate if a particular event happens, or does not happen, or if the grantor or grantee does, or does not, do a particular act. An inherent condition is an intrinsic and pre-existing part of the provision, so that it qualifies or restrains the estate. A condition may be compared with a **limitation** in that the former cuts short a precedent estate, whereas a limitation specifies how long an estate will last and a condition is only for the benefit of the grantor of an estate, whereas a limitation may benefit a third party. 'Condition' may be considered to be synonymous with 'qualification' in relation to an estate in land, so that a **qualified fee** and a **conditional fee** are to all intent and purpose the same. See also **defeasance, vest.** **3.** A clause or term in a lease that is essential to the existence of the contract. If the intention of the clause or term is that the lease shall be brought to an end in the event of a failure of the requirement, it is a condition: the lease can no longer exist because of the failure. In any other case it would be construed as a **covenant**, providing rights between the parties other than bringing of the contract to an end. Merely calling a provision a 'condition', or using words to that intent, does not necessarily create a condition; the provision must be essential to the proper continuation of the agreement between the parties. See **right of re-entry**.

condition concurrent   See **concurrent condition**.

condition of sale   **1.** A **condition** or **term** upon which an offer for sale is made and accepted. **2.** An express condition upon which a property is sold. See also **conditions of sale**.

condition precedent   See **condition**.

condition subsequent   See **condition**.

conditional acceptance   An **acceptance** of an offer subject to a condition or conditions. Such an acceptance does not normally create a binding contract but, in effect, amounts to a **counter offer**, which in turn requires acceptance by the original offeror; even though it was not be intended to amount to a rejection of the original offer. See also **conditional contract**.

conditional agreement   See **conditional contract**.

conditional contract   A **contract** made subject to a **condition**, i.e. a contract that is entirely dependent upon the fulfilment of a condition or contingency. Whether a conditional contract is enforceable depends primarily on the certainty with which it can be put into effect.

In English law, a contract made 'subject to the purchaser obtaining a satisfactory mortgage' may well be void for uncertainty. Whereas, a contract subject to a 'price to be agreed by the parties', with an arbitration provision failing such agreement, is likely to be binding.

In the US, in most jurisdictions, the courts will seek to enforce a conditional contract (more commonly called a 'contingent contract') wherever the condition can be made certain. A contract at a price that is to be based on the 'appraised' value of the subject property may be considered too vague, unless a clear mechanism is available to determine that price.

A conditional contract may be distinguished from an **option** or a **right of pre-emption**, because the latter forms of agreement depend on the wishes of one of the parties, whereas a conditional contract depends on some outside event. cf. **escrow, executory contract**. See also **contract of sale, conditional sale, negotiation, subject to contract, subject to finance, subject to survey**.

conditional conveyance(US) **1.** A conveyance that provides that the estate being transferred will be defeated or reconveyed in the event that a stipulated condition occurs. **2.** A **mortgage** may be called a 'conditional contract', the condition being that the property is held as security until the loan is repaid in full. cf. **conditional sale**. See also **absolute conveyance**.

conditional delivery   See **delivery**.

conditional estate   See **conditional fee, conditional interest, estate on condition**.

conditional fee   1.(Eng) See **conditional fee simple**.   2.(US) A **fee** estate that is limited to a specified donee and a given class of heirs, exclusive of others, and which reverts to the original donor of the estate, or his heirs, in the event of a failure of the requisite issue. The conditional fee estate is only recognized now in Iowa, Oregon, and South Carolina and in most other states a conditional fee, if granted, is automatically converted into a fee simple or if an estate is granted subject to such a condition it grants no more than a life estate. 'Conditional fee' is sometimes used

synonymously with **base fee**. See also **fee simple conditional**.

conditional fee simple(Eng)   An interest in land that is equivalent to a **fee simple**, but may be cut short if a specified event or condition occurs. A fee simple estate that comes to an end on the occurrence of a **condition subsequent**. For example, a grant of land 'to A as a fee simple on condition that he does not become a Doctor of Philosophy' continues unaffected, unless A becomes a Doctor of Philosophy, at which stage it is brought to an end. A conditional fee simple is intended to be enjoyed in the same way as any other fee simple, provided that the condition does not occur. A conditional fee simple is created by the use of such words as 'on condition that', 'provided that' or 'but if', as distinguished from a **determinable fee simple** which is created by such words as 'while', 'until', 'during' or 'for as long as'. In particular, a conditional fee simple does not automatically terminate upon the happening of the conditional event, but must be brought to an end by the exercise of a **right of re-entry**. Also called a 'fee simple upon condition', 'fee simple defeasible by condition subsequent' a 'fee on condition subsequent' or an 'estate in fee on condition'. (Where the term is used to refer to such an interest arising under a **strict settlement** the suffix, 'simple' is not used in that context: see **settlement**.) See also **base fee, conditional fee, qualified fee**.

conditional interest   **1.** An interest in land that is conveyed subject to a **condition subsequent**, i.e. an interest that may be brought to an end if a particular event does or does not happen, or if the grantor or grantee does or does not do a particular act. A conditional interest is created by the use of such words as 'on condition that', 'provided that'; the intention being to restrict the benefit of the interest at the outset if the prescribed event does or does not occur. A conditional interest, or 'interest on condition subsequent', may be distinguished from a **determinable interest** in that the specified interest is granted, whereas a determinable interest grants something less than the interest specified. In particular, following the creation of a conditional interest the occurrence of the event itself does not automatically terminate the interest; the grantor (or his heirs) must reclaim the estate by exercising a **right of re-entry** to reclaim the land from the grantee. Also called an 'interest subject to a condition'. cf. **contingent interest**. **2.** An interest that may be determined upon the occurrence of an event specified by the grantor. In particular, an interest in land that may be terminated by an exercise of a **right of re-entry**, as with a right reserved upon the grant of rentcharge. See also **conditional fee simple**.

conditional limitation　1.(US)A **condition** specified upon the grant of an estate which, if it occurs or fails to occur, terminates or 'limits' the estate and automatically vests it in a third party. For example, a grant 'to A until B returns for Xanadu' provides that the estate will pass to B in the event of his return. Also called an 'estate upon conditional limitation'; or sometimes a 'collateral limitation', especially when the estate is granted for a specified period, but the right to continue the enjoyment of that estate is dependant upon a contingent event. (Note: The American Law Institute, *Restatement of Property* (1936) considers the use of the term 'conditional limitation' undesirable, preferring to refer to an estate so created as an estate in **fee simple defeasible**.) cf. **special limitation**. See also **conditional interest**, **limitation**. **2.** A provision in a lease that provides for the lease to be brought to an end immediately in the event the tenant fails to meet an agreed obligation (for example obtaining consent to a particular user within a defined period of time), as distinguished from a **condition subsequent** where the landlord may have a right of re-entry in the event of a default by the tenant.

conditional purchase tenure(Aus)　A statutory right that granted a right to occupy Crown land under a long-term or perpetual lease, subject to a fee. The occupier was required to improve the land and had a right to purchase the land. In some cases the occupier entered into a conditional contract by which he paid for the land under an instalment sale. Such forms of tenure are no longer granted.

conditional sale　A **sale** that is made subject to the fulfilment of a **condition** or conditions. Strictly speaking a contradiction in terms because a sale subject to a condition is not a 'sale', but an agreement that sets out the terms for a sale in a **conditional contract**. However, 'conditional sale' may be used to refer to the sale of a chattel where possession and use is transferred, but the transfer of title is subject to the fulfilment of a condition, usually the payment of the full price. cf. **absolute sale**. See also **agreement for sale**, **contract for sale**, **contingent sale contract**, **contract of sale**.

conditional sale contract(US)　A contract in which the seller retains title to the subject property until a condition is met (usually payment of the entire purchase price), but possession and use of the property is given to the purchaser, provided he continues to make payments under the terms of the contract. A term that is generally used in connection with a contract for personal property. Sometimes called an 'executory contract of sale'; or a 'purchase money security agreement' (UCC § 9-105(h)). When a similar form of contract relates to real estate, it is usually called an **installment land contract**, a 'land contract', or a 'contract for deed'. See also **escrow**, **executory contract**, **instalment contract**.

conditional upon　See **subject to**.

conditional use permit(US)　See **special-use permit**.

conditional zoning(US)　A zoning ordinance that authorizes a particular use, but sets out certain conditions that must be complied with. A zoning approval that is granted subject to the owner complying with certain provisions that are set out in the zoning ordinance. Conditional zoning is intended to bring some flexibility to an otherwise rigid system of control. cf. **contract zoning**. See also **special-use permit**.

conditions of sale   1. The conditions upon which a property is to be sold by **auction**. Such conditions are normally provided along with details of the proposed auction and displayed in the auction room at the time of the sale.   2.(Eng)The conditions set down by the parties to a contract for the sale of land. In particular, conditions provided by statute law or an independent body. The sets of conditions in most common use are: The Law Society's Standard Conditions of Sale (SCS) (3d edition, 1984 Revision) and the Standard Commercial Property Conditions (First Edition) (SCPC) (both of which are produced by the Law Society and the Solicitors' Law Stationary Society for use by solicitors); the National Conditions of Sale (20th edition); and the Conveyancing Lawyers' Conditions of Sale. These general conditions of sale are supplemented, or varied, by 'special conditions' set down by the parties as relevant or required for the property being sold. See also **auction, National Conveyancing Protocol, particulars of sale, precedent, special conditions**(US)**, standard-form contract**.

condo   Short for **condominium**.

condohotel or **condotel**(US)   A building held in **condominium** ownership and used as an **hotel**, i.e. the owner holds a condominium interest in all or several units in a building and lets out those units for use as in a regular hotel. See also **apartment hotel**.

condominium   Derived from the Latin *condominium*, 'joint dominion' or 'co-ownership'. The separate ownership of part of a building – in substance, a space within the confines of a wall, floor and ceiling – together with an undivided share in the **common elements** that are used by all the other owners and usually an undivided share in the ownership of the land. A condominium is part of a multi-unit building. Thus, the condominium owner has (1) a separate interest in the 'unit' or apartment, and (2) an undivided interest with the other unit owners (usually as a **tenancy in common**) in a portion of the building called the 'common elements', e.g. corridors, stairways, elevators, community facilities and the like, as well as the foundations, main walls, floors, roof, etc.; and an undivided interest in the land. A condominium can be held as a fee simple, leasehold, or even as a life interest. The owner of a condominium has the same rights to alienate, charge, or otherwise deal with his individual property as an absolute owner, being restrained only by the law, the terms and conditions upon which he bought the property, and any restriction or covenants imposed by agreement with other condominium owners in the same building. All 50 states, the District of Columbia, Puerto Rico and the US Virgin Islands have adopted condominium statutes (called variously a 'Condominium Act', 'Condominium Property Act', 'Condominium Ownership Act', 'Horizontal Property Act', 'Unit Property Act', 'Unit Ownership Act' or 'Apartment Ownership Act'). Also, all the provinces of Canada have adopted condominium statutes.

In the US, in most jurisdictions, upon completion of a condominium project (or prior to the conversion of a building to condominium ownership) the developer or owner of the building is required to submit a document (a **condominium declaration**) to the authority responsible for controlling condominium ownership and once this declaration is approved and recorded the property takes on the condominium form of ownership. Normally a **condominium owners' association** or **homeowners' association** is formed by the condominium owners to manage and maintain the common elements and to decide on other matters that affect the owners collectively. cf. **cooperative**. See also **bylaw, covenants conditions and restrictions, co-ownership, enabling declaration, flying freehold**(Eng)**, lollipop condominium, master deed, planned unit development, strata title**.

Freedman, Warren, and Jonathan B. Alter. *The Law of Condominia and Property Owners' Associations*. New York: Quorom Books, 1992.

Institute of Real Estate Management. *Condominiums and Cooperatives*. Chicago: Institute of Real Estate Management, annual.

Woodson, R. Dodge. *The Condo & Co-Op Handbook: A Comprehensive Guide to Buying and Owning a Condo or Co-Op*. New York: Macmillan, 1998.

Wyatt, W. S. *Condominium and Homeowner Association Practice*. 3rd ed. Philadelphia, PA: ALI-ABA Committee on Continuing Education, 2000.

condominium association(US)   See **condominium owners' association**.

condominium bylaws(US)   See **bylaw**.

condominium conversion(US)   The change of a property from being let as individual units, or held in cooperative ownership, to ownership in the form of a **condominium**. In most jurisdictions, a tenant of a property that is to be converted to a condominium must be given an opportunity to find alternative accommodation (usually by providing for a notice period prior to the conversion or a right to an extended period of occupation) and a right of first refusal on his unit when it is converted to condominium ownership. In several jurisdictions certain tenants, notably senior citizens and handicapped tenants, are given a right to remain as tenants in the condominium project. Once converted the project, or an individual unit, may be referred to as a 'condominium conversion' or sometimes a 'conversion condominium'.

condominium declaration(US)   The basic document for the establishment of a **condominium**; the 'constitution' of a condominium. The condominium declaration is a detailed document that is filed with the appropriate regulatory authority (which may be the Attorney General's office or the state's or city's Department of Real Estate or Real Estate Commission) by the owner of a proposed condominium. The declaration stipulates such matters as the name of the condominium; the name of the **homeowners' association**, or **condominium owners' association**, and its proposed constitution, **bylaws** and voting rights. It details the physical boundaries of each unit of ownership; the rights and liabilities of each unit owner; the basis for levying assessments on each unit; every component of the **common elements** and the rights thereover; as well as the percentage share of liability for the cost of upkeep of each of these elements as imposed on each unit owner. Also, the declaration contains a copy of the pro-forma deed (the **master deed**) that will be used to transfer title to each owner. In addition, the declaration sets out the **covenants**, **conditions and restrictions** that will affect the use and occupancy and transfer of units; any other information pertinent to the property; and formally declares that the property will be subject to the provisions of the local Condominium Act. Once this document is approved and recorded the condominium comes into existence. The condominium declaration is one of the principal documents that must be made available to a prospective purchaser of a condominium unit. Also called a **declaration of condominium**, 'declaration', 'enabling declaration', or prior to its recordation a 'condominium offering document' or a 'condominium public offering document'. In some jurisdictions the declaration in its entirety is called the 'master deed'. See also **bylaw**, **condominium map**, **declaration of restrictions**.

condominium map(US)   A plan of a condominium project that details the location of every element of the project, including the dimensions of each individual unit and the **common elements**. The condominium plan is usually prepared by the architect responsible for the project and is filed as part of the condominium offering documents. It subsequently forms an essential part of the **condominium declaration** and is used as the basis for the allocation of **common area charges**. See also **apportionment**.

condominium owners' association(US)   A non-profit association that is formed by the owners of the units in a **condominium** and is responsible for the running of the project. In particular, the association is responsible for the enforcement of the deed restrictions that apply to the individual unit owners; the enforcement of the condominium bylaws; and for the upkeep, maintenance and repair of the common elements. Each unit owner is automatically made a member of the association upon completion of his purchase and has voting rights based on either a 'per unit' basis or on his percentage share of ownership in the project. The association in turn elects a board of directors to be responsible for the general management of the association. Also called a 'condominium association'. See also **homeowners' association**. Dunbar, Peter, M., and M. W. Dunbar. *The Homeowners Association Manual.* 4th ed. Tallahassee, FL: ARAS Publishing, 1999.

condominium plan(US)   See **condominium map**.

conduit   **1.** A pipe, tube, or similar channel used to conduct a liquid, electricity, fibre optic, telephone or telegraph wires or cables, or other material, from one point to another. See also **canal, culvert, drain, pipeline, sewer**.   **2.** A person who acts as an intermediary or nominee for the transfer of real estate. For example, someone who acquires a property and immediately contracts to sub-sell it to another. See also **subcontractor, sub-sale**.   **3.** An agency or private company that purchases pools of mortgages and resells them to other investors.   **4.** In the secondary mortgage market the means by which funds flow from the actual borrower to the current lender or investor. See also **securitization**.   **5.** The transfer of an income stream from one party to another so that the recipient is liable for tax on that income.

confirmation of an estate   The transfer of an estate in land to someone who has possession or another interest in the same estate in order to validate a voidable estate or to enlarge a **particular estate**. Confirmation of an estate can make good a voidable estate but cannot change an estate that is already void.

confirmatory deed(US)   See **deed of reformation**.

confiscation   See **appropriation**.

conflict of interest   See **dual agency, fiduciary, utmost good faith**.

conformed copy(US)   An exact copy of a legal document that is made out or certified to comply with the original. Similar to a **certified copy** except that a conformed copy may have notations attached thereto relating to the veracity of the document.

conforming loan(US)   A loan that is acceptable for funding or purchase either by the **Federal Home Loan Mortgage Corporation** or the **Federal National Mortgage Association**.

conforming use   In land-use planning, a use that conforms to the permitted classification for an area or zone. cf. **non-conforming use**.

conjoints   A married couple. In particular, persons who own property jointly. See also **community property**.

conjunct and several liability(Scot)   See **joint and several liability**.

conjunction agent(Aus)   See **joint agent, cooperating broker**(US).

consensus ad idem(Lat)   'Agreement as to the same thing'. See **acceptance, contract, mistake**.

consent   Derived from the Latin *consentire*, 'to agree', or the French *con sentire*, 'with' 'feel'—hence 'perceive'. A reasoned and deliberate **agreement** to, or active **acquiescence** in, an act. Consent is that which is given actively, and not taken on an understanding of another's intent, as is commonly understood by mere acquiescence. Consent may be unilateral or bilateral, and in the former sense differs from agreement, although it is a prerequisite to agreement. Consent cannot be said to exist when there has been **fraud, coercion, duress, undue influence** or, in certain cases, a **mistake**. See also **accord and**

satisfaction, assent, ratification, restraint on alienation.

consent authority[Aus]   An authority that grants approval to a development or planning application.

consequential damages   **1. Damages** that arise as a natural, but indirect, consequence of an action. In particular, damages that arise from a breach of contract and, at the time of making the contract, should reasonably be contemplated to arise therefrom.   **2.** Damages that do not arise as a direct result of an action or breach of promise, but follow on as a result or consequence of a principal act, e.g. loss of business resulting from fire damage to a building. Damages awarded as recompense for a loss suffered indirectly as a result of a tort or a breach of contract – sometimes called 'special damages' or 'constructive damages'. See also **consequential loss insurance**.   **3.**[US]Damages paid for a loss resulting from the exercise of the power of **eminent domain**, but not the compensation paid for the actual loss of land. 'Consequential damages' refers, in particular, to loss of business, goodwill, profits, removal expense, or similar disturbance caused by taking or damaging of land in condemnation proceedings. In the event of a federal acquisition of land "the Fifth Amendment does not require any award for consequential damages arising from a condemnation", United States v. 50 Acres of Land, 469 US 24, 33, 105 S Ct 451, 83 L Ed.2d 376, 385 (1984); (Bothwell v. United States, 54 US 231, 41 S Ct 74, 65 L Ed 238, 240 (1920)) (although damages may be payable as a result of any act that amounts to a tort or trespass). On the other hand, many state statutes provide that compensation may be payable in the event of 'damage' or 'taking' of property, including consequential damages or such losses as temporary loss of profit as a result of a forced relocation. The entitlement to such compensation, or consequential damages must be considered according to the state statute. 'Consequential damages' may also be used to refer to losses to the remainder of a condemnor's property in the event of partial taking; although such losses are strictly speaking **severance damages**. See also **compensation for disturbance**[Eng], **injurious affection, inverse condemnation, just compensation, partial taking**.

consequential loss insurance   Insurance against a loss that is not the direct result of the destruction of an insured property, but arises as a subsequent result, such as a loss of profit for a business; increased working costs; cost of renting alternative premises; or the payment of expenses for a property that cannot be fully utilised. Depending on the risk covered such insurance may also be called 'loss-of-profits insurance', 'use and occupancy insurance'[BrE], 'use and occupation insurance'[AmE], 'extra business expenses insurance', or 'business interruption insurance'. Cloughton, David. *Riley on Business Interruption Insurance.* 8th ed. London: Sweet & Maxwell, 1999.

consequential loss of rent   See **rent-loss insurance**.

conservation   The preservation of property against damage, misuse or **waste**. In particular, the protection of the natural environment against the ravages of use by the population in general. See also **amenity, amenity societies**[Eng], **conservation area**[Eng], **environmental impact report**[US], **Environmental Protection Agency**[US].

conservation area[Eng]   An area designated as being of "special architectural or historic interest the character or appearance of which it is desirable to preserve or enhance", P(LBCA)A 1990, s. 69(1)(a)). A conservation area may cover any area, from a town centres to a group of buildings. It is the character of area rather than individual buildings that is the major consideration. Open spaces, trees, an historic street pattern, a village green, or features of archaeological interest may also contribute to the special character of the area. The effect of designating a conservation area is to impose an obligation on the local authority to publish proposals and to take steps to preserve and enhance the character and appearance of any parts of their area that are conservation areas; to strictly control all forms of new development; to restrict building demolition, so that no building may be demolished without a 'conservation area consent'; and to require the preservation of most trees in the area. In particular, the grant of planning permission, or the exercise of any similar function, in a conservation area must pay special attention to "the desirability of preserving or enhancing the character or appearance of that area", P(LBCA)A 1990, s. 72. See also **area of outstanding natural beauty, listed building, permitted development, tree preservation order**.

Campbell, Gordon. *Heritage Law & Policy: Listed Buildings and Conservation Areas.* Isle of Wight: Palladian, 2001.

Mynors, Charles. *Listed Buildings and Conservation Areas.* 3rd ed. London: Sweet & Maxwell, 1999.

conservation easement(US)   An **easement** that is created in order to protect or conserve the environment, a building, or a view that is of particular interest. Such easements are created usually by a conveyance of a right over land to a government or non-profit entity, either voluntarily or subsequent to condemnation. See also **easement in gross, facade easement, scenic easement**.

Diehl, Janet, and Thomas S. Barrett. *Conservation Easement Handbook.* Washington, DC: Land Trust Alliance, 1988.

Gustanski, Julie Ann, and Roderick H. Squires. *Protecting the Land: Conservations Past, Present, and the Future.* Washington, DC: Island Press, 2000.

conservator(US)   A person put in charge of property by a court as a temporary custodian when the true owner is incompetent, insane, or missing.

consideration   Remuneration or recompense given in exchange for a benefit or advantage conferred on one person by another under the provisions of a contract. It is the legal motive, cause or reason for a contract; the *quid pro quo*. The common law requires that a contract should comprise more than an undertaking by one party to another; a bargain when struck should have a motivating reason that goes beyond a moral obligation. Consideration is the reason, or in a commercial sense the price, for which the promise, that constitutes a contract, is bought (*Dunlop Pneumatic Tyre Co Ltd v Selfridge Co Ltd* [1915] AC 847, 855 (HL); 17A Am.Jur.2d., Contracts, § 113, p. 129). A promise to pay money (but not the promise *per se*) is sufficient consideration to support a contract; as is the foregoing of a claim or right. Consideration is something that would not be given, done, or foregone, but for the promise it supports.

Consideration may be **valuable consideration**, which is something that is real, not nominal or illusory; something that is of some value in the eyes of the law; or **good consideration**, which refers to a motive that has no tangible value, such as love and affection or a strong moral obligation. Good consideration may be a reasonable or moral cause for the making of a contract, but, in common law, it will not support an executory contract. Valuable consideration is that which is required for a valid contract (unless the contract is made by **deed**, in which case good consideration will suffice). "Some right, interest, profit or benefit accruing to one party, or some forbearance, detriment, loss, or responsibility, given, suffered, or undertaken by the other", *Currie v Misa* (1875) LR 10 Ex 153, 162, aff'd (1876) 1 App Cas 554 (HL) (The American Law Institute, *Restatement Second, Contracts* (1981), §§ 17(1), 71).

Consideration may be 'executed' or 'executory'. 'Executed' consideration is that which is actually given before or at the time of the making the contract; consideration made in return for the performance of an act. Executory consideration is a promise to do something in exchange for a counter-promise; consideration that has not yet been performed. Consideration may be expressly stipulated in the contract; or the amount due may be implied from the act or conduct of the parties, as when it is clear from the surrounding circumstances that a fair market value has been paid. In common law, it is not essential to the enforceability of a contract for the amount of consideration to be adequate recompense, provided it is 'real' (not vague) and 'sufficient' to support the bargain made. However, consideration must move from the promisee to the promisor in order to give effect to that contract, i.e. the consideration must be paid over, not merely promised or paid to a total stranger to the contract. Consideration must be co-existent with the promise given, or be related to the transaction; so that 'past' consideration, e.g. a mere expression of gratitude for a past act or consideration in respect of a past benefit, is insufficient to support an action on a contract. In the event that there is no consideration, as in a transfer by **gift**, a contract may still be valid, provided it is made by **deed**. See also **accord and satisfaction, adequate consideration**, *bona fide* **purchaser, estoppel, rent, price, simple contract, value**.

consolidation   1. See **assemblage**.   2. The uniting of at least two mortgages on two or more properties, granted to a single mortgagor, into a single (i.e. jointly redeemable) mortgage. Where a mortgagee holds mortgages on several properties that are mortgaged to one mortgagor, the mortgagee may reserve the right to consolidate; that is, he may not permit any one mortgage to be redeemed without the redemption of one or more of the other mortgages. In English law, a mortgagor is entitled to redeem any one mortgage without paying money under any other mortgage, provided there is no contrary intention expressed in the various mortgage deeds or in any one of them. In addition the mortgagee cannot insist on consolidation until the legal date for redemption of all of the relevant mortgages has passed (LPA 1925, s. 93; *Pledge v White* [1896] AC 187, 198 (HL)). In the US, in most jurisdictions, the doctrine of consolidation has no application because the mortgagor can only be required to pay the debt secured by the individual mortgage. However, some jurisdictions consider that if the same person holds a first and second mortgage on the same property, the mortgagor may be required to redeem the first mortgage before the second. In Canada, the doctrine has also been abolished in several provinces. In Australia, it has also been abolished in most States; although a provision in a particular mortgage that all amounts due by a

mortgagor to a mortgagee are secured by that mortgage may be enforceable (*Katsikals v Deutsche Bank (Asia) AG* [1988] 2 Qd R 641, 653 (Aus)). In New Zealand, a mortgagor who seeks to redeem any one mortgage may do so without paying any money due under a separate mortgage (Property Law Act 1952, s. 85 (NZ)). cf. **tacking**.

consolidation loan(US)   A loan that is taken out to repay an existing loan and to add that debt to another loan in order to create a single and more manageable financial arrangement for the debtor. See also **refinancing**.

consolidated metropolitan statistical area (CMSA)(US)   See **metropolitan area**.

constant(US)   See **mortgage constant**.

constant annual per cent(US)   See **mortgage constant**.

constant-payment mortgage   See **amortization loan/amortization mortgage**.

constant prepayment rate (CPR)   The rate at which the principal balance is repaid on a pool of mortgages. In particular, the rate at which principal is repaid on the assumption that a constant portion of the outstanding mortgages is paid each month.

constant-rent factor(BrE)   A factor that may be applied to the rent payable in the open market to take account of the benefit of a longer than normal interval between one rent review and the next. Thus, if a tenant has a lease with 14-year intervals between reviews to market rent and the accepted pattern of rent reviews is 5 years, then a tenant is likely to be prepared to pay a different rent at the outset because his initial rent is fixed for a longer period of time. A higher rent if he anticipates rising rental values and a lower rent if he anticipates falling rental values. This differential is represented by the 'constant-rent factor', which can be obtained from the following formula:

$$\frac{(1+r)^n - (1+g)^n}{(1+r)^n - 1} \times \frac{(1+r)^t - 1}{(1+r)^t - (1+g)^t}$$

Where:

r = lessor's required return on capital

g = annual rate of rental growth (or decline)

n = number of years between rent reviews in the actual lease

t = number of years between normal rent reviews.

Sometimes called an 'uplift factor' (assuming that rents are expected to rise). If this formula is applied to the market rent payable under a lease with conventional rent review periods it produces the 'equated rent' that the tenant may be prepared to pay at the start of the lease. See also **interim rent**.

construction   The act or process of **building**, especially a thing out of its constituent parts. The creation or extension of a building or **structure** so as to create something new, either in its entirety or as an **addition** or substantial **alteration** to that which exists. Construction includes the bringing together and assembling of materials in order to erect a building or structure; it requires more than maintaining the *status quo*. The making of an alteration or addition to a building may constitute construction, but mere repair, maintenance, or renovation of an existing building does not. See also **building operations**.

construction allowance(US)   See **tenant improvement allowance**.

construction area(US)   See **gross building area**.

construction bond   See **bid bond, performance bond**.

construction contract   A contract, including plans and specifications, by which one party undertakes to carry out construction or building

work for another. See also **building contract, management contract**.

Circo, Carl J., and Christopher H. Little (editors). *Construction & Design Law, A State-by-State Guide.* Chicago: ABA Publications, 1998.

Bartlett, Andrew (general editor). *Emden's Construction Law.* 5 vols. Looseleaf. London: Butterworths, 1992.

Murdoch, John, and W. Hughes. *Construction Contracts: Law and Management.* 3rd ed. London: Spon Press, 2000.

Ramsey, Vivian, and Stephen Furst. *Keating on Building Contracts.* 7th ed. London: Sweet & Maxwell, 2000.

Wallace, Ian Duncan. *Hudson's Building and Engineering Contracts.* 11th ed. London: Sweet & Maxwell, 1994.

construction finance or **construction loan**   A loan that is made to provide funds to enable an owner of land to construct improvements thereon. Short-term or **interim finance** granted for the period and for the purpose of financing development or construction work. A loan that is granted on the basis that it will be replaced by more permanent finance on, or soon after, completion of the construction work. Generally, construction finance is advanced as building work progresses and is limited to a percentage of the total expenditure incurred by the borrower at any stage of the building work. An initial advance may also be made to cover all or part of the cost of land acquisition and predevelopment expenses. Interest is charged, usually at a variable or floating rate, upon the outstanding principal and may be payable at regular fixed intervals or sometimes when the entire loan is repaid. The loan is normally secured by a mortgage on the land and buildings construction thereon. Also called a 'building loan'. See also **finance, takeout commitment**.

construction interest   Interest payable on a **construction loan**, in particular that part of the interest that specifically relates to the cost of the building or construction work.

construction lien   See **lien, mechanic's lien**.

construction loan   See **construction finance**.

construction management (CM) or **construction project management** A method used for the management of construction work where the owner employs a representative to advise and administer the entire process from design and planning through to completion of the project. "The provision of professional management services to the owner of a construction project with the objective of achieving high quality at minimum cost", Richard H. Clough and Glenn A. Sears, *Construction Contracting*, 6th ed. New York: Wiley, 1994. A construction manager provides value engineering and project coordination services; makes recommendations on the selection and terms of appointment of the general contractor; and, if necessary, advises on the appointment of subcontractors. During the construction work, the construction manager helps control costs and expedite the delivery of materials and endeavours to keep the work on schedule. The construction manager may be a contractor, project manager, architect, or specialist construction professional. The construction manger does not enter into any direct contractual obligation with the suppliers, contractors or subcontractors, although he may be appointed to negotiate with the general contractor on behalf of the owner. The construction manager is remunerated by a fee that is usually based on a percentage of the contract value.

Under a 'construction management contract' or 'management contract', the owner may enter into any form of contract that he considers to be appropriate for the work (either with a single contractor or a number of subcontractors) but, unlike a conventional building contract, the construction manager receives a fee and does not normally share in the profit (or loss) of the construction work. See also **project management**.

Halpin, Daniel W., and Ronald W. Woodhead, *Construction Management*. 2nd ed. New York: Wiley, 1998. Loulakis, Michael C., et al. *Construction Management: Law and Practice*. New York: Wiley, 1995 with 1996 supplement. Nunnally, S. W. *Construction Methods and Management*, 6th ed. Upper Saddle River, NJ: Prentice-Hall, 2004.

construction manager See **construction management**.

construction mortgage A mortgage secured for a **construction loan**. As a rule, such a mortgage only secures the amount advanced and not the total loan facility that may be made available, although the **priority** of the loan for the total amount advanced usually dates back to the date of the initial advance. Also called a 'building mortgage'. See also **mechanic's lien, tacking**.

construction permit See **building permit, building controls**.

construction operation and reciprocal easement agreement (COREA)(US) See **reciprocal easement**.

construction retainage(US) See **retention sum**.

constructive adverse possession(US) A form of **adverse possession** that is recognized by some state statutes when a person, under **color of title** (i.e. one who believes he has a title to a property), pays real estate taxes; as distinguished from *actual* adverse possession.

constructive annexation The fixing of something to land by reason of its purpose or nature. For example, lifting tackle that forms part of a gantry that in turn is fixed to a building may be said to be constructively annexed to the building and, therefore, to form part of the land on which the building is erected. See also **fixture**.

constructive condemnation(US) See **inverse condemnation**.

constructive condition A **condition** that will be imported into a contract to give fairness or justice to the terms of the contract. In particular, a condition that is imputed by a court of law. In the US, also called a 'condition-in-law', as distinguished from a 'condition-in-fact', or an implied **condition**, which is an essential part of the contract and can be implied from the surrounding facts or custom.

constructive contract(US)   See quasi-contract.

construction conversion   See conversion.

constructive damages   See consequential damages.

constructive delivery   See delivery.

constructive entry   See entry.

constructive eviction   Interference with a tenant's proper enjoyment of a property by the landlord, or anyone under his authority, without necessarily depriving the tenant of physical possession. Such an act or omission if it renders the leased premises substantially unsuitable for the purposes for which they are leased, or which seriously interferes with the beneficial enjoyment of the premises, is a breach of the covenant of **quiet enjoyment** and constitutes a constructive eviction of the tenant. Constructive eviction may arise when a landlord deliberately permits a property, or makes a property, fall into a state so that it is unfit for the purpose for which it was let; or when the tenant is deprived, for a substantial period of time or in a material manner, of beneficial use or enjoyment of the demised premises. For example, restricting proper and free access to the property, cutting off utilities or other services, allowing vermin infection, defective drainage, odour, dampness, noise, etc., or a failure of the landlord to carry out his repairing obligations so that the tenant is no longer able to use the property. Constructive eviction actually takes place when the tenant vacates or abandons the premises, provided that was a direct consequence and arises within a reasonable time of the landlord's act. As a rule, once a tenant has suffered constructive eviction, he is relieved of his obligation to pay rent from the date he leaves the property. cf. **actual**

eviction. See also **abandonment, eviction, fit for habitation, fit for the purpose, harassment, landlord's access.**

constructive fraud   See fraud.

constructive knowledge   See constructive notice.

constructive mortgage(US)   See equitable mortgage.

constructive notice   Notice that is implied or imputed by law to have been given, even though a party may be ignorant of the fact or information that would be imparted if they had **actual notice**. Knowledge that is imputed to a person, either because it would have come to his attention on further enquiry or because a person has wilfully omitted to make enquiry to avoid being put on notice. 'Constructive notice' is sometimes used synonymously with **implied notice**, although the latter term is best reserved for the form of notice that a person would glean from his knowledge of the facts or the nature of the business. Constructive notice is a presumption of law (thus it is also called 'legal notice'); whereas implied notice is a presumption of fact.

If a person has 'actual' knowledge of a document, such as one that is not recorded, or is defectively recorded, he is affected by the common law doctrine of constructive notice and therefore is still bound by that document, i.e. that person cannot be said to be a *bona fide* purchaser 'without notice' in respect of that document. The doctrine of constructive notice requires that a purchaser should inspect the property; make proper inquiries as to the basis of any occupation, or apparent occupation, of the property; make inquiries of any land registration or recording office (including any local government office) and, if possible, where the title is not recorded take possession of and examine carefully the title documents, either personally or preferably through a professionally qualified advisor. In particular, constructive notice applies to unregistered land, as in the case of registered land the system of registration gives notice of most interests affecting land. cf. **imputed notice**. See also *caveat emptor*, **land charge**[(Eng)], **overriding interest**[(Eng)], **requisition**, **title search**.

constructive possession   A right to **possession** as recognised by law or based on intent, as distinguished from 'actual possession'. Possession as exercised by someone who has the ability to control a property, but without actual possession. A mortgagee may have constructive possession if he has served notice on a tenant of his right to collect the rents, but has not entered into physical possession. See also **constructive adverse possession**.

constructive re-entry   An action by a landlord that by implication amounts to **re-entry** and **forfeiture** of a lease. In particular, letting another party into possession of the leased property and permitting him to remain there, or allowing an existing sub-tenant to take occupation in place of the direct tenant, so as to unequivocally indicate that the existing lease has come to an end. Constructive re-entry may also be inferred when a landlord, possessing a right of re-enter, accepts rent for the demised premises from a party other than his tenant. See also **abandonment**, **constructive eviction**.

constructive trust   A **trust** that arises when an owner has acquired property as a result of enrichment by another and it is only equitable for the owner to hold the property, subject to the acknowledgment of the beneficial right of that other. In particular, a trust that arises by operation of law when property has been obtained by **fraud**, **duress**, abuse of confidence, or any similar unconscionable conduct or questionable means, so that the true owner is not deprived of the beneficial right to the property and, in particular, the right to have the property conveyed to another. The owner is considered to hold the property as a trustee for the **beneficiary**, or *cestui que trust*, who made the enrichment. A constructive trust does not arise merely out of any express or presumed intention of the parties; in that respect it may be distinguished from an **implied trust** or a **resulting trust** either of which arise from the implied aim or supposed intention of the parties. Thus, an implied or resulting trust may be said to be a true trust in that it creates a fiduciary relationship between the parties, whereas a constructive trust is essentially a vehicle to circumvent an **unjust enrichment**, fraud or violation of a fiduciary relationship. A constructive trust commonly arises when one person contributes towards the cost of a property that is held by another, expecting in the course of time to derive some benefit from, or obtain some interest in, the property.

An **agent** who makes a profit as a result of performing the duties entrusted to him by his principal is a constructive trustee for those monies and must account to his principal in full. Similarly, a constructive trust would arise if the principal were induced to transfer property to the agent at a price well below its true value. A constructive trust is also considered to exist when a binding contract for the sale of a legal estate has been executed; the vendor then holds the estate upon trust for the purchaser pending completion of the sale. Sometimes called an 'involuntary trust'. See also **license by estoppel**, **matrimonial home**[(Eng)], **power of sale**, **strict settlement**.

Oakley, A. J. *Constructive Trusts*. 3rd ed. London: Sweet & Maxwell, 1996.

constructive trustee   See **constructive trust**.

consuetudo est altera lex[(Lat)]   'A **custom** has the force of law'.

consummate   To carry out, an agreement; to bring (a transaction) to **completion**. A real estate transaction is generally consummated upon the **closing**, i.e. on the payment in full of the consideration and the transfer or delivery of title.

consumer price index (CPI)   An official index of consumer prices, usually compiled and published by a government agency (in the US the

Bureau of Labor Statistics of the federal Department of Labor, and in the United Kingdom, where it is called a 'retail price index', the Department of Employment). Commonly used as an objective reference for adjusting the price in a contract, such as a lease rent, to keep it in line with inflation. In common parlance called a 'cost-of-living index'. See also **cost-of-living clause**, **indexation**.

consummate dower   See **dower**.

contamination   See **brownfield site**, **environment audit**, **environmental impact assessment**[BrE], **environmental impact report**[AmE].

contiguous   Derived from the Latin *contiguus*, 'to touch closely'. In close proximity and usually, touching. Meeting at a common boundary, so that there is no intervening land. Two properties on opposite sides of a road or river may be 'contiguous', because in such cases the ownership boundary extends *ad medium filum*, 'to the center of the way', or *ad medium filum aquæ*, 'to the center of the river', unless there is evidence to the contrary, or unless it is clear that the land under the road or river does not belong to the parties. See also **abut**, **adjacent**, **adjoining**.

contingency   A possibility of coming to pass. An event that may or may not occur. Something related to an uncertain event. See also **conditional contract**, **contingent interest**, **contingent liability**.

contingency contract[US]   A contract the performance of which is dependent on the occurrence of a contingent event. See also **conditional contract**, contingent fee.

contingency insurance   Insurance against a fortuitous, or contingent, liability. Insurance against a specific and foreseeable event that can be described in the policy (although the event may never happen), rather than against risks of a general nature. For example, insurance against loss

due to a known defect in the title to a property, or insurance against loss arising from an infringement of a long standing easement where the beneficiary is unknown. The amount of payable in the event of a loss under such a policy is normally quantified in the policy. In general, all insurance is based on a contingent event, but the term contingency insurance is more applicable to insurance against a specified loss – the insured is covering the event and the possible loss if the event occurs, rather than a property, person, or object. Also called 'contingent liability insurance'. cf. **endowment insurance policy**. See also **title insurance**, **valued policy**.

contingency listing[US]   A listing given to a **multiple-listing service** that is made upon terms that differ from those normally provided by the members of that service. For example, a listing given to only one member of the service, i.e. an **office exclusive**, or a listing granted for a shorter term than is normal for such listings.

contingency reserve   See **retainer**.

contingency sum   A provision for a cost that is likely to be incurred, but cannot be ascertained when an **estimate** is prepared for the cost of building work. For example, an allowance included for delays due to inclement weather. See also **contingent liability**, **provisional sum**.

contingent business interruption insurance   See **consequential loss insurance**.

contingent contract   See **conditional contract**, **contingent sale contract**.

contingent debt   See **contingent liability**.

contingent estate or **contingent interest** An **estate** or **interest** in land that comes into effect only upon the happening of a 'contingent' event, i.e. an event that may or may not happen. A right to property that is uncertain, either as to who will enjoy the right to possession or as to when possession will be enjoyed. For example, a fee simple estate granted 'to A for life and then to B, or if B is not then living to C', provides B with a contingent estate, or a 'contingent fee simple', which is dependent upon B outliving A. A contingent interest represents a prospect of having an interest in land, as contrasted with a **vested interest**, which is a present or future right to land, but one that will arise with the passage of time. In other words, if the condition upon which the interest depends is precedent, the interest is contingent; but if the condition is subsequent, i.e. can be defeated or is 'subject to defeasance', it is a vested interest. For example, an interest granted 'to A and upon his death to X or Y, X taking in preference to Y, unless at that time Y has obtained an MBA', grants X a contingent interest. Also called a 'springing interest' as the interest 'springs up' or is vested if the future event occurs. cf. **conditional interest, determinable interest**. See also **remainder, rule against perpetuities**.

contingent fee   1. See contingent estate.   2. See **commission**, *quantum meruit*.

contingent fee simple   See **contingent estate**.

contingent finance offer   See **subject to finance**.

contingent interest   1. See contingent estate. 2. Interest on a loan that is dependent on a contingent event. For example, interest that is payable only when a building produces a stipulated net operating income. See also **equity participation**.

contingent liability or **contingent debt** A potential liability. A **liability**, or **debt**, that is not considered to be a definite obligation (in terms of its amount or its existence), but one that arises if a given event occurs. A liability that may or may not accrue. In accounting, a contingent liability refers to a sum set aside as a reserve against the possibility that an event that would require a payment might occur in the future. For example, a liability to pay rent as provided by a surety on behalf of a lessee; or a payment arising as a result of an adverse decision on a legal action. There need be no certainty of the event occurring, only that a payment would be required if it occurs. See also **contingency insurance, guarantee**.

contingent liability insurance   See **contingency insurance**.

contingent remainder   See **remainder**.

contingent sale contract   A contract of sale that is dependent upon a contingent event. In particular, a contract for the sale of a property made upon the basis that the final price or consideration will depend upon a future, uncertain, event. See also **conditional contract**.

continuation search[US]   See **bring-down search**.

continued occupancy clause[AmE]   A clause in a lease of retail premises that stipulates that the tenant will only be obliged to continue to trade if a particular tenant or tenants occupy other premises in a shopping center, usually a tenant of an **anchor store** in the center. Also called a 'continuing occupancy clause'. cf. **continuous operation clause**.

continuing contract   See **executory contract**.

continuing covenant   See **covenant**.

continuing occupancy clause[AmE]   See **continued occupancy clause**.

continuous and uninterrupted use   See **prescription**.

continuous drilling clause[US]   See **continuous operation clause**.

159

continuous easement   See easement.

continuous occupation   See adverse possession.

continuous operation clause   1. A clause in a lease of retail premises which specifies that the tenant is required to keep the demised premises open for business during normal business hours or during hours specified in the lease. As a rule, there is no implied covenant in a lease of retail property that the premises should be maintained open for business, although most leases of retail premises expressly provide hours for 'continuous operation' and provide the landlord with a right of **right of re-entry** in the event of non compliance. A court may agree to a termination of a lease in the event that the tenant closes his business (even though the tenant continues to pay rent), especially if that severely impacts the other properties owned by the landlord. However, a court would be reluctant to grant a decree of **specific performance** to force the tenant to reopen, because that would require the continuous supervision of the court.

In the US, some jurisdictions consider that where there is a **percentage rent** there is an implied obligation on the tenant to use and operate the premises as profitably as possible for the intended purpose. Nonetheless, the courts are reluctant to imply conditions into leases and will not normally imply a continuous operation clause if it considers that the base rent is reasonable recompense to the landlord, or the landlord clearly accepted the percentage rent risk to induce a tenant into a center. Also called a 'go dark' provision or, strictly speaking a 'not-go-dark' provision, a 'dark store clause', a 'keep-open' clause', or a 'stay-open clause'. cf. **continued occupancy clause**.
Austin Hood, *Continuous Operation Clauses and Going Dark.* Real Prop.Prob. & Tr.J. 365-390 (Summer 2001).
2. A clause in an **oil and gas lease** that permits the term of the lease to be extended, even if production has ceased, provided that drilling operations are still in operation. Also called a 'continuous drilling' clause.

continuous possession   See adverse possession

contour line   A line on a map that joins up points of equal elevation. See also **topographical surveying**.

contra bonos mores(Lat)   'Against good conscience'; 'against public morals'. See **void contract**.

contra proferentem(Lat)   'Against the person who proffers.' A rule that provides for an uncertainty or ambiguity in an instrument, or a term of a contract, to be construed more strongly against the person who stipulated for, or will benefit most from, the provision. One of the cardinal rules of interpreting an express contract is "that in order to escape from the consequences of one's own wrongdoing, or that of one's servant, clear words are necessary", *Photo Production Ltd v Securicor Transport Ltd* [1980] AC 827, 846 (HL) (United States v. Seckinger, 397 US 203, 90 S Ct 880, 206, 25 L Ed.2d 224, 233 (1970)). See also **adhesion contract, ambiguity**, *benigne facienda sunt...*, **exclusion clause, forfeiture clause**.

contract   Derived from the Latin *contrahere*, 'to draw together' or make a **bargain**. A deliberate promise or mutual agreement, between two or more parties, to do or not to do something, that is intended to be legally binding and enforceable. In order for an **agreement** to constitute a contract enforceable at law there must be an **offer**; an **acceptance** of that offer with the intent to bind the parties, i.e. a *consensus ad idem*; a legal **consideration** for the agreement; and the agreement must not infringe any rule of law. In summary, a legally binding contract should contain the following elements: (i) at least two parties, all of whom have a legal capacity to contract; (ii) a clear identification of the parties; (iii) an ascertainable subject matter; (iv) an offer and unqualified acceptance; (v) an agreement that demonstrates *consensus ad idem* and an intention to be legally committed by both parties; (vi) free and genuine consent; (vii) consideration of some value (however small), unless the contract is made by **deed**; (viii) an aim or intent that is legal, and not negated by **fraud**, **duress** or **undue influence**; (ix) terms that are certain or capable of being rendered certain; and (x) an ascertainable date or time to the contract, i.e. ascertainable dates of commencement and termination of the obligation(s) of the contract.

A contract, and the terms of the contract, may be **express**, that is clearly evidenced (either in **writing** or orally) by the parties; **implied** by the actions or conduct of the parties; or inferred from the known facts, circumstances, **custom**, or general language of the parties. A contract may also be a 'constructive contract' or **quasi-contract**, which arises in law (although it may not be considered a true contract) to create the effect of a contract where one party might obtain an unjust benefit or 'enrichment'. (In the US, 'implied contract' and 'quasi-contract' are generally considered to be synonymous, taking on the latter meaning; whereas in English law the tendency is to prefer to construe an implied contract from the actions or relationship of the parties – implied from the facts rather than writing.)

A contract may be simple (parol); formal (specialty); or of record. A **simple contract** may be in writing, oral or implied. A **formal contract** is made by deed. A **contract of record** is one imposed upon parties *ab extra*, 'from outside', as by a court of law. A contract may be unilateral or bilateral. With a **unilateral contract** the promisor undertakes to pay consideration to the promisee provided the latter performs, or does not perform, some action; with a **bilateral contract** (a synallagmatic contract) both parties accept or undertake obligations to each other. See also **adhesion contract**, **assignment**, *assumpsit*, **breach of contract**, **building contract**, **contract for sale**, **contract of sale**, **covenant**, **executed contract**, **executory contract**, **illegal contract**, **misrepresentation**, **novation**, **open contract**, **oral contract**, **performance**, **privity of contract**, **repudiation**, **rescission**, **signature**, **specific performance**, **subject to contract**, **termination**, **void contract**, **voidable contract**.

Calamari, John D. and Joseph M. Perillo. *Hornbook on Contracts*. 4th ed. St. Paul, MN: West, 1998.
Furmston, M. P. *Cheshire, Fifoot & Furmston's Law of Contract*. 14th ed. London: Butterworths, 2001.

contract administrator   A person who is responsible for administrating a building or **construction contract**. The construction manager may be an architect, engineer or project manager and is usually the agent of the proprietor. The contract administrator is responsible for the assessment, valuation and certification of the work as it is carried out.

contract default[US]   See **breach of contract**.

contract for a lease   See **agreement for a lease**.

contract for deed[US]   A contract by which a seller undertakes to transfer a deed of title to property when certain conditions have been met, usually the payment of the entire purchase price. An **executory contract** to convey title when the consideration is paid (Hicks v. Dunn, 622 So.2d 914, 915 n., 918 (Ala 1993)). Also called a 'bond for title', or a 'bond for deed' as it may be considered an agreement to execute a deed of sale in the future. See also **contract for sale**, **escrow**, **installment land contract**.

contract for sale   1. A **contract** made for the sale or other disposition of land or an interest in land. A **contract** in which parties agree the essential terms for a future **sale** of property, especially the subject matter (its extent or quantity) and the price, by which the parties acknowledge that there is a clear intention to complete a transfer of title when the necessary formalities are complete. In English law and most jurisdictions that followed the common law, since the **Statute of Frauds** 1677, most contracts for the sale of land have required greater formality than many other contracts. Such a contract is required to be in **writing**, although the doctrine of **part performance** may enable an oral contract to be enforced in equity.

In English law, on or after September 27, 1989 (with a few minor exceptions), "a contract for the sale or other disposition of an **interest** in land can only be *made* in writing and only by incorporating *all* the terms which the parties have expressly agreed in one document or, where contracts are exchanged, in each", LP(MP)A 1989, s. 2(1). The terms can be incorporated by reference to some other document, but the document, or documents, must be "signed by or on behalf of each party to the contract", LP(MP)A 1989, s. 2(2)(3). The doctrine of part performance no longer applies to such contracts, as there is *no* oral contract that can be partially performed.

In Australia, a contract for sale of land must be recorded in writing to be enforceable, although the doctrine of part performance may enable an oral contract to be enforced in equity. Also most States have adopted a standard form of contract that is required for contracts relating to real property.

A 'contract for sale' may be distinguished in particular from a contingent or **conditional contract** that is made subject to a condition and may not therefore form a true contract at law or may never come into effect. A 'contract for sale' may also be referred to as a 'purchase contract', an 'agreement of sale', or a 'sales contract'. The term **contract of sale** is frequently used interchangeably with 'contract for sale'. However, the former term is more usually used to refer to an agreement that relates to goods, and the later in respect of land transactions. cf. **lease**, **option**. See also **beneficial owner**, **conditions of sale**, **contract for deed**, **contract for sale**, **conversion**, **estate contract**(Eng), **executory contract**, **fire insurance**, **livery of seisin**, **mortgage**, **open contract**(Eng), **specific performance**, **Statute of Frauds**, **subject to contract**(Eng). **2.**(US)An agreement in **writing** specifying the parties, price (and the manner of payment), an adequate description of the property,

an expression of intent, and signed by the parties. A binding commitment by the parties which, after investigation of title, proceeds to a **completion** at which time the purchase price, or the balance of the purchase monies, are due in full and the seller usually delivers a deed of title. An **option** to purchase is not a contract for sale as the optionee is not a purchaser, but merely has a right to purchase. A contract should also state any exclusion, exception, covenant, condition, restriction, or encumbrance that the parties intend to be binding when title is transferred. In the US, also called a 'real estate contract', 'purchase contract', 'purchase and sale agreement', a 'buy-and-sell agreement', an 'earnest money agreement' (especially when it is a simple agreement that recognizes the receipt of **earnest money**), or simply an 'offer and acceptance'. See also **binder**, **conditional contract**, **contract for deed**, **deposit**, **installment contract**, **sale**.

contract for sale and purchase(US)   A contract by which the buyer and seller agree to be bound to transfer property, even though the full price may not be paid until a later date. Such a contract is more than an **option** and, as a rule, would entitle a broker to a payment of a commission as the **procuring cause** of the sale. See also **contract for sale** (of land), **installment contract**.

contract implied by law(US)   See **quasi-contract**.

contract of adhesion   See **adhesion contract**.

contract of agency   See **agency**.

contract of indemnity   See **indemnity**, **insurance**.

contract of insurance   See **insurance policy**.

contract of record   **1.** A contract that results from an adjudication of a court of law and not from any agreement between the parties, such as a judgement of a court that a debt is owed by one party to another. The enforceability of a contract of record depends entirely on the records of the court and not on the parties' own understanding. **2.** A contract that has been recorded at a public record office.

contract of sale A **contract** in which parties agree the essential terms for a future **sale** of property, especially the subject matter (its extent or quantity) and the price, by which the parties acknowledge that there is a clear intention to complete a transfer of title when the necessary formalities are complete. A 'contract for sale' may be distinguished in particular from a contingent or **conditional contract** that is made subject to a condition and may not therefore form a true contract at law or may never come into effect. A 'contract of sale' may also be referred to as a 'purchase contract', an 'agreement of sale', or a 'sales contract'. cf. **lease**, **option**. See also **contract for sale**, **executory contract**, **mortgage**.

contract of tenancy See **agreement for a lease**, **tenancy agreement**.

contract of surety See **surety**.

contract price **1.** The actual **consideration** paid under a contract. In a contract for the sale of real property, the contract price is usually the price received by the vendor, before deducting any associated costs of effecting the sale. See also **sale price**. **2.**(US)A tax term for the total price realized under an **installment sale**, being the total selling price, less the net amount of any mortgage debt assumed, i.e. the equivalent to the amount of the seller's equity in the property.

contract rent The **rent** stipulated as actually payable under an existing lease. A term used to distinguish the lease rent from an **economic rent**, or from the **market rent** that could be obtained if the property were vacant and available for lease in the open market.

contract sum See **contract price**.

contract to sell(US) A contract by which a party agrees to transfer property for a consideration called the price. An **executory contract** for the transfer of real estate. In particular, a contract that is provisional (e.g. an earnest money contract), conditional, or executory. Also called an 'agreement to sell', as distinguished from a **sale** or an **option**. See also **contract for sale** (of land), **installment contract**.

contract time See **time is of the essence**.

contract under seal A contract made by **deed**. See also **contract for deed**, **seal**, **specialty**.

contract zoning(US) An arrangement by which a municipal authority agrees to an amendment of the local zoning map or ordinance in respect of a particular area of land in exchange for the agreement by the landowner to accept certain conditions that are not imposed on other areas of the same classification. Contract zoning is considered illegal in many states as it represents the bargaining away of **police power**. However, it may be considered a valid arrangement when, for example, it can be shown that the municipal authority is maintaining its independent right to impose conditions that benefit the community, or, in some jurisdictions, where such arrangements are authorized by statute. Such an arrangement may be considered a form of **conditional zoning**, although strictly speaking the latter term is applied to a change in the zoning that will be permitted only when a specified condition has been fulfilled, especially a condition that aims to alleviate a loss of value to neighboring property. Whereas 'contract zoning' requires that the property owner provide some consideration for the change in the zoning or ordinance. Also called a 'development agreement'. See also **incentive zoning**, **special-use permit**, **spot zoning**, **zoning**.

contracted-out tenancy(Eng) A business **tenancy** that is 'contracted out' of the provisions of the Landlord and Tenant Act 1954 and, therefore, the tenant is not given protection under the Act (L&T Act 1954, s. 38, as incorporated by the LPA 1969, s. 5). Any provision that purports to preclude the tenant's rights under a business tenancy is void. However, the landlord and tenant can apply jointly to the court for an agreement between them to be excluded from the rent and renewal provisions of the L&T Act 1954. Such an agreement must be entered into freely; be endorsed by the court before it commences; and be for a "**term of years** certain". The court will generally grant its approval to an exclusion in the case of a lease for five years or less when a joint application is made by parties who are legally represented.

contractor   Any person who enters into a **contract**. In particular, one who contracts to provide a service, to supply labour, or to perform building works for a definite price. Thus, a contractor, unlike an employee, is not controlled (except as required under the terms of the contract) as to the means by which he achieves the object of the contract. cf. **agent**. See also **builder, general contractor, independent contractor, subcontractor**.

contractor's all-risks insurance **Insurance** that is provided to cover all risks associated with building, engineering or construction work, including claims made against the contractor and any subcontractor. A form of **all-risks insurance** that covers all building works, plant, equipment, tools and machinery, as well as injury to employees, other third parties and members of the public who may be injured by the building or engineering work. Normally such insurance is purchased by the contractor, but it may be taken out by the building owner, usually with the contractor being specified as an 'interested party'. Also called 'contractor's liability insurance', although that term may be used to refer to **comprehensive insurance** that covers specified risks rather that the broader 'all-risks insurance'. See also **public liability insurance**.

contractor's basis or **contractor's method**[Eng]   A method of valuing specialist properties, especially a method of **rating valuation** by which an 'effective capital value', or 'adjusted reinstatement cost', is estimated for the buildings, to which is added the capital value of the site of the property, and an annual value is then assessed by applying to that total value a percentage rate of return considered appropriate for the particular type of property. The capital value of the building is based on the cost of constructing a suitable alternative, after allowing for depreciation or obsolescence and the current cost of acquiring a suitable alternative site. The principle behind this method of valuation is to ascertain the cost of a similar substitute property and then to apply an appropriate factor (to 'decapitalise' that figure) to arrive at a hypothetical rental value, which is then adjusted to take account of any special factors that affect the subject property. The contractor's basis is used especially when comparable rental evidence is not available, as with a property that has a limited or no ready market value, e.g. a church, school, hospital. This method is referred to sometimes as a method of last resort because it is used when no other method of valuation is suitable or can be applied to the type of property involved; although in some cases it may be the only method available. Referred to sometimes as a 'contractor's test' valuation. See also **depreciated replacement cost, reinstatement method of valuation**.

Brown, Peter. *The Contractor's Law and Practice*. London: Institute of Revenues, Rating and Valuation. 2003.
RICS Books. *The Contractor's Basis of Valuation for Rating Purposes: A Guidance Note*. London: RICS Books, 1996.

contractor's bond   See **performance bond**.

contractor's liability insurance   See **contractor's all-risks insurance**.

contractor's lien   See **lien, mechanic's lien**.

contractor's method   See **contractor's basis, reinstatement method of valuation**.

contractual licence   See **licence**.

contractual tenancy   A **tenancy** that arises from a contract between the parties, orally or in writing, as contrasted with a **statutory tenancy, which** arises by force of law. A contractual tenancy may be terminated in accordance with the terms of the contract, unless these are themselves superseded by statute. See also **express contract, lease**.

contribution clause   1. A clause in an insurance policy that provides for the liability to be divided equitably between the insurers when there is more than one insurer covering the same risk. Thus, if a policy on a building includes cover for third-party liability, which is covered also by a separate policy with a different insurer, the insured may not recover his entire loss under both policies. Also called an 'apportionment clause', especially when the clause sets out a basis for such apportionment. See also **co-insurance, double insurance**.   2.(US)See **average clause**.

contribution to service charge(BrE)   See **apportionment, service charge**.

contributory mortgage   See **joint mortgage**.

contributory negligence   A careless act or omission that contributes substantially to a person's own loss or injury and acts as a defence or mitigation to a claim of **negligence** brought by another. Contributory negligence is not a complete defence (especially in a case of intentional negligence), but damages recoverable for negligence may be reduced where the court considers the defendant has contributed to his own loss. Contributory negligence requires a lack of reasonable care and a degree of connection between that lack of care and the injury suffered.
Under common law, the principle was that a plaintiff who had contributed to his damage by his own negligence was totally barred from recovering damages. In English law, this principle has been replaced by the principle that the partial fault of the defendant only acts to reduce the amount of damages that may be awarded to the plaintiff "to such an extent as the court thinks just and equitable having regard to the claimant's share in the responsibility for damage ...", Contributory Negligence Act 1945, s. 1(1). (This statute does not apply to contracts, nor to matters of **utmost good faith**.)
In the US, also called 'comparative negligence', especially in states that have replaced the original common law principle of contributory negligence, which provided that contributory negligence was a bar to any rights of the plaintiff, by statutes that provide that a claim for negligence is not barred by the plaintiff's negligence, but may be reduced by the percentage contribution to the loss caused by the defendant. The strict common law principle is now only adopted in a few states. See also *volenti non fit injuria*.

control order(Eng)   An order that enables a local housing authority to take over "control" of a house in multiple occupation when it is considered necessary to do so in order to protect the "safety, welfare or health of persons living in the house" (Housing Act 1985, ss. 379-394). The order permits the local authority to take possession of the house, to control the management, and receive income from the occupiers of the building. The authority is required to prepare a 'management scheme' for capital expenditure that it considers necessary to improve the living conditions of the occupiers. Such an order may take effect for a period of up to five years. At the end of the period for which the order is effective the net cost incurred by the authority may be recovered from the dispossessed proprietor and, if unpaid, any balance becomes a **charge** on the property. See also **local land charge**.

conurbation   A loosely integrated urban area, comprising a number of towns or villages that are not totally integrated, but form a single socio-economic unit. A continuous grouping of parcels of built-up land, which may encompass parks and rural land, but are not delimited by a significant area of agricultural land. See also **urban region**.

convenience lease(US)   A lease entered into solely to provide an income for the landlord as compared with one granted to an intending occupier. In particular, a lease to a credit-worthy tenant that is entered into in order to provide a form of guaranty to a mortgagee. See also **component financing, head lease, synthetic lease**.

convenience shopping center   See **shopping center**.

convenience store   A local retail store that sells a variety of goods that are purchased mainly for immediate consumption, such as candy, magazines, newspapers, basic foods and household goods. A convenience store is usually situated in a residential neighbourhood and is smaller than a **variety store**.

conventional estate(US)   An **estate** in land created by the parties to a transaction, such as a fee simple, life estate or an estate for a term of years, as distinguished from an estate created by operation of law, such as dower or curtesy. cf. **legal life estate**.

conventional loan or **conventional mortgage**(US)   A loan or mortgage that is secured on real estate, but is not collateralized by any third party; especially a loan that is not secured or guaranteed by a federal agency, such as the Federal Housing Administration or the Veterans Administration. Conventional loans are generally made at higher interest rates and lower loan-to-value ratios to those that have the higher security of the extra guarantee. A 'non-conventional mortgage' is one that is insured or guaranteed by a federal agency. See also **surety**.

conversion   **1.** An intentional and unjustifiable retention or use of another's goods, which amounts to a denial or contradiction of that person's right to the goods. Conversion may be 'actual' as when the goods are taken into possession or 'constructive' as when someone deprives the owner of the use of the goods, provided in both instances there is an intention to claim dominion over the goods. See also **market overt**.   **2.** The process of turning property into money, i.e. the sale of real property for money. The exchange of **real property** for **personal property**, or *vice-versa*. (Strictly speaking the process of changing money into property is **reconversion**.) In equity, certain rights to real property are regarded as a right to the proceeds of sale of real property, rather than to the property *per se*, i.e. the property is deemed to be converted from one form to another even though no actual conversion has taken place. In particular, conversion may take place to satisfy the requirements of a will so that real property is regarded only as a right to the income or proceeds of sale. Also, conversion is considered to arise when a contract is executed for the sale of real property. At that stage the vendor's interest is 'converted' into a right to the money proceeds and, therefore, an interest in personal property. This doctrine follows from the maxim that 'equity looks on that as done which ought to be done'. This process is called the 'equitable doctrine of conversion' or merely 'equitable conversion'. See also **overreachable interest**(Eng).   **3.** The sale of real property on the instruction of a court in order to satisfy a debt.   **4.** A change in the nature of a property, either by a substantial change of use, or by structural works that change its function, e.g. from a warehouse to a retail store or from a single dwelling to apartments. See also **material change in the use**(Eng).   **5.** A change in the form in which the ownership of property is held, e.g. from several ownership to co-ownership or from a rental property to condominium ownership. See also **condominium conversion**.   **6.** A change in the quality of a **title** to land, as with a change from a **qualified title** to an **absolute title**.   **7.** A change of the means by which an investment is held, for example the conversion of debt into equity, or the conversion of the right to hold property as security for a debt into an equity interest in the property. See also **convertible mortgage**.   **8.** The substitution of one form of guaranty, surety or means of financing for another. See also **refinancing**.   **9.** The addition of accrued interest to the outstanding principal on a loan so that the total debt then bears interest. See also **compound interest**.

convertible ARM   See **convertible-rate mortgage**.

convertible mortgage   A mortgage loan that enables the lender to acquire an **equity** share in the property held as security in place of accepting repayment of the principal due under the loan. A convertible mortgage agreement may provide that the mortgagee has an option, at certain intervals, to buy an ownership interest in the mortgaged property or even to buy the property outright, either by investing his own funds or by forgiving part of the debt. After these intervals interest is payable on the outstanding principal, if any, and normally the mortgagee receives a **preferred return** on the amount of equity he has invested. A convertible mortgage is a form of joint venture between the mortgagee and the owner of the property. The arrangement frequently starts entirely as **debt financing** and is converted at a later stage into **equity participation**. The enforceability of the mortgagor's right to convert his debt into an ownership position may be restricted if the arrangement is considered a **fetter** or **clog** on the mortgagor's **equity of redemption**. See also **convertible-rate mortgage, equity-participation mortgage, leveraged buyout**.

convertible-rate mortgage   An **adjustable-rate mortgage** that provides the borrower with the right to convert to a **fixed-rate mortgage** during the term of the loan, usually at a specified time, such as after a specified number of years. Also called a 'convertible ARM'.

convertible security   Preferred stock or a debenture that can be converted into shares of common stock in a corporation. A **security** that can be converted into an ownership or 'equity' position in the property secured.

convey   To transfer property from one party to another, in particular by means of a written instrument. A term that is used especially in relation to real property.

In the US, in some jurisdictions, the use of the word 'convey' in a deed has the same effect as 'grant' and implies that the estate is free from any encumbrances, except as expressly stated in the deed. See also **conveyance, operative words**.

convey and warrant(US)   Words used in a **conveyance** or **deed of grant** to indicate that the grantor is transferring a fee simple interest and to import the 'usual' **covenants for title**, i.e. covenants to the effect that there are no encumbrances, there is a grant of seisin and warranty of title, and a grant of quiet enjoyment; except as stipulated to the contrary.

conveyance   1. The creation or transfer of an interest in **land**, especially the transfer of a real interest in land by a written instrument or **deed**. 2. A document (usually a **deed**) that is used to transfer, voluntarily, a title to land from one living party to another. 'Conveyance' means the action of transferring ownership (in the strict sense of a positive act of acquisition and not through descent) and the instrument that effects the transfer may be referred to as a **deed of grant**, a 'deed of conveyance', or simply a 'conveyance'. (Other voluntary transactions to transfer real property may be made by a 'deed of gift', 'devise' or a 'settlement' – according to the circumstances; although such instruments are all sometimes called conveyances.) Historically, a conveyance was a sealed document that was required to transfer a legal title to land. However, in modern usage conveyance is used to refer to any formal document or instrument that transfers a legal or equitable interest in land by the voluntary act of a living person. It may be a deed of sale, or a **lease**, **mortgage** or similar instrument. In particular, 'conveyance' is frequently used to refer to an instrument that is used to effect a **sale** of real property, although a sale is not necessarily a conveyance. Generally, a will is not a conveyance. The terms 'deed', 'conveyance' and 'deed of conveyance' are frequently used interchangeably to denote the same legal concept. Each is commonly understood to mean an instrument in writing whereby the grantor conveys to the grantee some right, title or interest in real property. A deed of conveyance may be described according to the form of title granted by the vendor, such as a **quitclaim deed, grant deed, warranty deed** or **bargain and sale deed**.

In the US, a conveyance may be defined broadly as "an act by which it is intended to create one or more property interests, irrespective of whether the act is effective to create such interests", The American Law Institute, *Restatement of Property* (1936), § 11(1) and this definition includes "attempted testamentary dispositions as well as inter vivos transactions", § 11(1), Comment b.

In English statute law, 'conveyance' is defined to include "a mortgage, charge, lease, assent, vesting declaration, vesting instrument, disclaimer, release and every other assurance of property or an interest therein by any **instrument** except a will", LPA 1925, s. 205(1)(ii). Neither an **agreement for a lease** nor an oral lease is a 'conveyance' within this definition (*Rye v Rye* [1962] AC 496, [1962] 1 All ER 146 (HL)). (The Land Charges Act 1972, s. 17(1) contains a similar definition, but excludes "disclaimer".)

A conveyance may contain, inter alia, the following clauses: (i) a **recital** (introduction); (ii) a **testatum**; (iii) a description of the parties; (iv) an **operative clause**, or **granting clause**(US) (which effects the transfer); (v) a **parcels clause** or **premises clause** (describing the property); (vi) a **habendum, tenendum**, and, in a lease, a **reddendum** (limiting the estate, or interest, and setting forth the rent); (vii) a **testimonium** or **testimonium clause** (witnessing clause); (viii) an **attestation clause** (signature, and acknowledgment if required); and (ix) a **date**. In addition there may be conditions or covenants set out in the instrument.

In English law, since 1925, a 'conveyance' of land is deemed to include "all buildings, erections, fixtures, commons, hedges, ditches, fences, ways, waters, watercourses, liberties, privileges, easements, rights and advantages whatsoever, appertaining or reputed to appertain to the land, or any part thereof, or, at the time of conveyance, demised, occupied or enjoyed with, or reputed or known as part or parcel of or appurtenant to the land or any part thereof", and land with buildings thereon conveys the buildings and houses, as well as "all outhouses, erections, fixtures, cellars, areas, courts, courtyards, cisterns, sewers, gutters, drains, ways, passages, lights, watercourses, liberties, privileges, easements, rights, and advantages whatsoever, appertaining or reputed to appertain to the land, houses, or other buildings, conveyed", and anything **appurtenant** thereto, unless any of these things are expressly excluded (LPA 1925, s. 62(1)(2)). cf. **assignment**. See also **absolute conveyance**(US), **alienation, beneficial owner, contract for sale, convey, covenants of title, delivery, demise, fraudulent conveyance, general words, grant, voluntary conveyance**.

Friedman, Milton R. *Contracts & Conveyances of Real Property*. 2 vols. 5th ed. New York: Practicing Law Institute, ©1991 with annual supplements.

Thompson, Professor M. P. *Barnsley's Conveyancing Law and Practice*. 4th ed. London: Butterworths, 1996.

Butt, Paul. *Conveyancing*. 10th ed. Bristol: Jordans, 2002.

3.(Eng) A **transfer** of property or a means by which property is transferred from one person to another. In particular, a transfer of a **legal estate**, but not the creation, or means for the creation, of a new interest or right to property. **4.**(Aus) A **disposition** or **alienation** of land under the **old system title** (a common law transfer or 'common law title'), especially as distinguished from a transfer under the **Torrens title system**. **5.**(NZ)"'Conveyance' includes any deed of assignment, appointment, lease, settlement, or other assurance by deed of any property; and 'convey' has a corresponding meaning", Property Land Act 1952, s. 2.

conveyance tax(US)   A state tax imposed on the transfer or conveyance of an interest in real property. Also called a 'transfer tax'. See also **registration duty**.

conveyancer   A person who undertakes work

in relation to the transfer of interests in real property. In particular, someone who is authorised by law to provide details of titles, prepare deeds and mortgages and other documents relating to the transfer of estates and interests in real property. In English law a conveyancer or 'authorised practitioner', must hold a licence issued by the Authorised Conveyancing Practitioners Board that is in force to allow him to provide "conveyancing services", Court and Legal Services Act 1990, s. 37. See also **conveyancing**.

conveyancing 1. The creating or transferring of estates and interests in land. The process of arranging for a **conveyance** of an interest in land. The process of effecting a transfer of title to real property, including verification of title, drawing up the necessary documentation (including wills, mortgages, leases, etc.), and the entire process associated therewith, through to arranging the completion of a transaction.
Coates, Ross M. *Practical Conveyancing: Residential Commercial and Agricultural*. 13th ed. London: Pearson, 1995.
Silverman, Frances. *Conveyancing Handbook*. 10th ed. London: Law Society, 2003.
2.(Aus) The process of effecting a transfer of title to real property, including investigating title and drawing up the necessary documentation. A term that is used in the context of both 'old system' titles and transfers under the **Torrens title system**.

convivium(Eng) A form of feudal **tenure** by which a tenant was bound to provide food and drink to his lord at least once a year. See also **feudal system**.

co-obligor One who has a joint obligation with another, such as a joint party to a promissory note.

cooling-off period(Aus) A period of time during which a purchaser of land is allowed to terminate a contract for the purchase of land. In Victoria after a purchaser has signed a contract for the purchase of land he has three business days from the execution of the agreement to terminate the contract; and in South Australia the same right

may be exercised within two business days after receipt from the vendor of certain statutorily prescribed information. In New South Wales the parties to the purchase of a residential property may enter into a preliminary agreement in a prescribed form, with the final contract attached. The vendor is tied to the agreement, at least until the prescribed period has elapsed. The parties then have a prescribed number of days to complete this contract or terminate the agreement. If this right is exercised the purchaser may loose his preliminary deposit. These provisions do not apply to sales by auction or, as a rule, if the purchaser has had the benefit of independent legal advice.

cooperating broker(US) A **broker** who agrees to work with an appointed broker (generally the 'listing broker') to effect the transaction for which the listing broker has been appointed. Generally, a cooperating broker is the broker that introduces a prospective client to the listing broker on the basis that he will receive a share of the commission that will be payable to the listing broker if a successful transaction is concluded. A cooperating broker does not have any direct contract with the client, but may be considered a **subagent** of the listing broker. Also called a 'participating broker' or 'co-broker', or in Australia a 'conjunction agent'. See also **joint agent, multiple-listing, procuring cause**.

cooperative (co-op) or **cooperative ownership** A means of holding a property, such as an apartment, by which a corporation (or trust) is formed to hold the land and buildings and the stockholders (or beneficiaries) have a right to occupy part of the property. A legal hybrid in that the 'owners' have a personal interest in stock and a right to an occupancy or **proprietary lease**, which is entered into between the owning corporation (or trust) and the shareholder (or beneficiaries) permitting them to have exclusive occupation of a part (usually one unit) of the property and common rights over other parts of the property, e.g. entrance areas, staircases, lifts, etc. Unlike any form of **co-ownership**, or the ownership of a **condominium**, the shareholders (or beneficiaries) have no right of ownership to any part of the property as ownership is vested in the corporation (or trustees). Likewise any mortgage on the property is granted by the owning entity over the entire property (although in certain cases the tenant may be able to obtain a second mortgage on his leasehold interest). Thus, the owning entity is responsible for taxes levied on the property and all other outgoings, including any mortgage payments, and then recovers such expenditure from the shareholders (or beneficiaries) in accordance with the terms of their occupancy leases. In the event of any deficiency in making such payments by the corporation or trust, the tenants or beneficiaries risk losing the entire property to a mortgagee or lien holder. As a rule, the holders of an interest in a co-op building do not have the ability to offset mortgage interest from their income for taxation purposes. Also, the owner of a co-op may require the consent of the other shareholders, or the board of directors, of the building prior to a sale or transfer of their lease. Accordingly, a 'co-op' is generally considered a less advantageous form of ownership to a condominium (although the occupiers may benefit from a more exclusive from of occupation as a result of the ability of the shareholders to choose the occupiers of the building). If a cooperative occupier wishes to dispose of this interest he sells his shares (or assigns his beneficial interest) and assigns his proprietary lease, which in some jurisdictions requires the consent of the board of the cooperative corporation or trust.

Cooperative ownership is uncommon in the UK, although it is encountered in the form of a 'housing cooperative' that owns, in the form of a company (or trust), a group of houses or flats and the shareholders (or beneficiaries) are granted occupancy leases. However, in a housing cooperative the occupiers do not necessarily participate in any growth in the capital value of the houses as generally this is retained by the owning company (or trustees) and the loss of this benefit is reflected in the rent charged to the occupiers. cf. **property trust**. See also **restraint on alienation**, **timesharing**.

Institute of Real Estate Management. *Condominiums and Cooperatives*. Chicago: Institute of Real Estate Management, annual.

Woodson, R. Dodge. *The Condo & Co-Op Handbook: A Comprehensive Guide to Buying and Owning a Condo or Co-Op.* New York: Macmillan, 1998.

cooperative bank(US)   See **building and loan association**.

cooperator(US)   A shareholder or beneficiary in a **cooperative** apartment. Also called a 'tenant cooperator' as the shareholder or beneficiary is generally a tenant of the property.

co-ownership   A generic term for the ownership of an interest in the same property held by two or more persons at the same time. In particular, 'co-ownership' may be used to include a **joint tenancy** or a **tenancy in common**, as well as **coparcenary** and a **tenancy by the entirety**; although coparcenary is obsolete for all practical purposes, and any remaining tenancy by the entirety was abolished in English law in 1925 (although it still exists in a few jurisdictions in the US). Co-ownership essentially is a right to the use and possession by two or more owners of the whole of the subject property at the same time, as distinguished from successive rights to ownership of the same property, i.e. rights, which follow one another, to an estate in the same land. The term may sometimes be used to refer to ownership of a **community property** and sometimes for an interest in a **condominium**. Also called 'joint ownership', ownership of a **concurrent estate**, or sometimes in the US 'multiple-ownership'. cf. **collective ownership**(Eng). See also **commonhold**, **cotenancy**, **partnership**, **strata title**, **trust for sale**.

co-ownership tenancy(Eng)   A tenancy granted to a person who also has a share in the capital value of the property that is the subject of the tenancy. In particular, a tenancy of a dwelling-house granted by a **housing association** to a member of the association who, upon ceasing to be a member of the association, receives a share in the capital value resulting from a sale of the property (HA 1990, Sch. 10, para. 1(4)). See also **housing trust, shared ownership**.

coparcenary or **coparcenery** An interest in land that arose either when land descended on intestacy to two or more persons as if they constituted one heir ('parceners', 'coparceners' or 'co-heirs), or because of the local custom of **gavelkind**. The former applied only to daughters (for whom there was no hereditary rule of primogeniture) and the latter to sons. In English law, gavelkind and most similar forms of tenure by which land descended to heirs on intestacy have been abolished (AEA 1925, s. 45(1)). In the US, in most jurisdictions, no new interests can be created in coparcenary and any interest held by coparcenary has been converted into a tenancy in common. Also called a 'tenancy in coparcenary' or, in the US, an 'estate in coparcenary'. Sometimes spelt 'coparceny'. See also **joint tenancy**.

coparcener See **coparcenary**.

coparceny See **coparcenary**.

coppice or **copse** A small wood left to grow with the underwood in order to provide trees for felling, usually for fuel or to provide fencing or similar material. As a rule, the trees are intended to be cut at intervals of less than 20 years so that new growth springs again from the stubs and underwood. See also **tree preservation order**(Eng).

copyhold See **feudal system**.

core See **service core**.

core space See **service core**.

corner lot(AmE) or **corner plot**(BrE) A plot of land or a property situated at an intersection and thereby having a frontage to two streets. See also **Baltimore method of appraisal**(US), **zoning method**(BrE).

corner stakes(US) Points at which there is a change of direction, as set out by a surveyor when preparing a survey using the **metes and bound system**.

corporation An association or artificial succession of individuals formed together by written articles of association, under one name, in such a way that they are incorporated by law into an entity that has an existence independent of the individuals who, from time to time, make up that entity and that is capable of existing (although it need not necessarily exist) forever. A corporation may be made up of one person who holds an office that has a right of perpetual succession and is independent of the individual (a Secretary of State or Public Trustee) – a 'corporation sole', or two or more persons who have established a means by which they will be followed by a perpetual succession of members – a 'corporation aggregate'. A corporation has the same capacity as an individual to acquire, hold and dispose of property in its own name. In the US, corporations sole are virtually extinct, except for those that may be held by ecclesiastical bodies. cf. **partnership**. See also **company, mortmain**.

corporation mortgage bond A bond issued by a corporation and secured as a mortgage on the fixed assets of that corporation. See also **debenture, fixed charge**.

corporate real estate (CRE) Real estate that is held by a corporation for its own use. Corporate real estate includes property that is used for the operation of the business, as distinguished from property that is held solely for investment. See also **fixed asset**.

corporeal hereditament Any tangible property, including **land** and any physical object annexed and that which is capable of passing by inheritance. An inheritable right to immovable or real property, including any building or **fixture** attached to land. A right to land, if accompanied by possession, may be considered as a corporeal hereditament; but a partial right to land that is not accompanied by possession is an **incorporeal hereditament**. Corporeal hereditaments are said to **lie in livery**, i.e. are transferred by physical possession; whereas incorporeal hereditaments **lie in grant**, i.e. are transferred by a written document or deed. See also **corporeal property, hereditament, land**.

corporeal property or **corporeal things** Literally **property** that has a *corpus* or bodily form. Property, or **things**, that have a material existence, i.e. are tangible and palpable, such as land or goods, as distinguished from **incorporeal property** which is merely a right to property that exists in contemplation, such as a right to receive rent. The term corporeal property is more of civil law derivation; in the common law the equivalent term is a **corporeal hereditament**. See also **chattel, fixture**.

corpus(Lat) 'Body'. The **capital** or principal of an estate, as distinguished from the interest or income derived therefrom. The entire body or subject matter of a trust.

corpus possessionis(Lat) Actual **possession** of a thing, especially as distinguished from legal possession which must include an intention to possess – *animus possidendi*. See also **occupation**.

correction deed(US) See **deed of reformation**.

correction lines(US) Lines that are set out under the **government survey system** to compensate for the curvature of the earth. Lines at 24-mile intervals (i.e. at every fourth Township) are used as correction lines.

correlation 1. The relationship between two variables. If one variable (price) increases as another variable (population) increases there is a positive correlation, and if the price increases as

the population decreases there is negative correlation. If there is no change in the one variable as the other changes there is said to be 'independence'. A perfect positive correlation is represented by a coefficient of $+1$, and -1 indicates a perfect negative correlation. A 'correlation coefficient' (coefficient of correlation) of 0 indicates that there is no linear correlation. A correlation coefficient of $r = 0.6$ indicates that 60% of the y variable is related to variations in the x variable. **2.**(US)See **reconciliation**.

correlative water rights(US) A principle, adopted in some states, that one who has a common riparian right to take water may only take such quantities as are reasonable having regard to the 'needs of all' who might share that water. See also **riparian rights, water rights**.

correspondence Communication by an exchange of letters or the letters so exchanged. See **open contract, writing**.

corridor valuation(US) The valuation of a corridor of land, such as a road, railroad, or an oil pipeline. This valuation may be based on the value of the land on either side of the corridor ('across the fence value') adjusted for the limitation of the use of the subject land; the cost of providing an alternative route; or a comparison approach (where comparables are available); an income approach; or a replacement cost basis. See also **before-and-after method**.

cost The amount given, exchanged, or bartered for that which is acquired. The total amount expended or laid out to acquire a property, whether as money or a monetary equivalent. In particular, the **price** paid or expended for property received or services rendered. Generally, cost is measured in pecuniary terms; but it may be measured in any way that reflects the disutility or endeavour of acquiring something. A cost may be said to precede a price, because theoretically it is necessary to consider the cost before determining a price, and an **expense** succeeds both (George

Crabb, *Crabb's English Synonyms*. 1816. Reprint, London: Routledge, 1982). The cost of a property may be based on an amount of **money** parted with in order to acquire some thing – **acquisition cost** – or may be based on the amount that needs to be parted with in order to acquire some thing – **reinstatement cost**. A sum of money or outlay that has been incurred is a cost, but when that amount is allocated to a person, fund or object it becomes a **charge** or 'expense'. cf. **value**. See also **basis, book cost, expenditure, historic cost, reinstatement cost, reproduction cost**.

cost approach(US) A method or approach used to estimate the value of an improved property by which the **reinstatement cost** of the buildings is assessed (after an appropriate allowance for depreciation), and the market value of the land is added based on comparable sales data. The sum total is the estimated 'value' of the property. The land is assumed to be vacant and available for development for its existing use. This approach to the appraisal of a property is based on the presumption that a purchaser is prepared to pay the same sum for a property as he would pay to acquire a site and reproduce or build a similar alternative – the 'principle of substitution'. However, this presumption has limited validity and the method should be used as a last resort, i.e. when no other approach is considered applicable.

When assessing the amount of **just compensation** payable in condemnation proceedings, the cost approach may be used when there is no comparable sales information available and no other method of appraisal is applicable to the subject property. Nonetheless, in this context the cost approach is considered to be "one of the least reliable indicia of market value", United States v. Certain Interests in Property in Champaign County, 271 F.2d 379, 382 (7th Cir. Ill 1959), cert. den. 362 US 974. Also called the 'replacement cost approach', the 'reinstatement cost approach', or the 'summation approach'. See also **contractor's basis, reinstatement method of valuation**(Eng).

cost basis(US) See **basis**.

cost-benefit analysis (CBA) An analytical technique for assessing the benefits to be derived from a project, taking account of monetary and social advantages, and setting those benefits against the total financial and social cost (the **opportunity-cost**) that arises from undertaking that project. All gains and losses, arising directly or indirectly from the project, are given a unit of value (in terms of money or on a scale of importance) and are either weighed against each other or applied in a **discounted cash flow** analysis. A technique commonly applied to major government schemes or planning proposals, such as a new airport or a new town development; although the result tends to be dependent on the value-judgement of the party applying this method of analysis or the governing body of the day. See also **feasibility analysis**.

Boardman, Anthony E., et al. *Cost-Benefit Analysis: Concept and Practice*. 2nd ed. Upper Saddle River, NJ: Prentice-Hall, 2000.

Layard, Richard, and Stephen Glaister. *Cost-Benefit Analysis*, 2nd ed. Cambridge University Press, 1994.

Nas, Tevfik F. *Cost-Benefit Analysis: Theory & Application*. Thousand Oaks, CA & London: Sage Publishing, 1996.

Schofield, John A. *Cost Benefit Analysis in Urban & Regional Planning*. London: Routledge, 1990.

cost estimating See **quantity surveying, valuation**.

cost-in-use The cost of a property measured according to its total recurring cost of use and occupation. Determining the cost-in-use is a means of comparing the financial implications of alternative projects by which all costs are reduced to an annual figure. The 'cost-in-use' is assessed especially to compare the cost of alternative building designs – the development costs are converted to an **annual equivalent** over the anticipated economic life of the building and the annual running costs added to arrive at the total annual cost. Alternatively, the total cost of a building or project may be ascertained over a given period of time, taking into account the capital cost and all future recurring costs, and then the present annual value ascertained by means of a **discounted**

cash flow analysis. See also **carrying charges, occupancy cost, virtual rent**.

cost-less-depreciation approach   See **depreciated replacement cost, reinstatement method of valuation**(BrE).

cost of capital   See **weighted average cost**.

cost-of-living clause   A clause in a contract, especially a lease, that provides for the price or rent to be varied in line with a **consumer price index**, 'retail price index' or 'cost-of-living index'. See also **indexation, rent escalation**.

cost-of-living index   See **consumer price index**.

cost of replacement method   See **reinstatement cost, reinstatement method of valuation**(BrE),

cost of reproduction   See **reproduction cost**.

cost-pass-through clause(US)   See **escalator clause**.

cost-plus contract   A form of a **building contract** in which the price is based on the actual cost (the prime cost of labour, materials and plant) as incurred by the contractor in the performance of his contractual duties, plus a fixed fee, or a fixed percentage, added for overheads and profit. If a fixed fee is added the contract is called a 'cost-plus-fixed-fee contract'. Such a form of contract is used especially when the extent of the building work is unknown or difficult to ascertain at the outset. In this form of contract the employer bears the risk of virtually all increase in the cost of labour and materials; although he may still benefit from any cost savings. A variant of the cost-plus contract is the 'target-cost contract(BrE)' or 'upset-cost contract(US)' by which a 'target' cost, or 'upset' price, is stipulated and on completion the difference between the actual cost and the target

cost is apportioned between the employer and contractor on the basis of an agreed formula. Alternatively, if the total cost (including the fee) exceeds the target no fee is payable on the excess; or the fee may be based on a percentage of the contract price, but with a ceiling on the amount payable. Generally, a provision is made to take account of variations required by the employer and such matters as building regulations, as well as for agreed price fluctuations. As a further variant, the fee may vary according to the cost actually expended so that the amount or percentage decreases as the cost exceeds certain agree levels (a 'value-cost contract'). As a rule, under a cost-plus contract the contractor is reimbursed for all the costs that he incurs in good faith on the project and, except where specified in the contract, is not required to prove that the costs are reasonable, although he cannot spend any amount he sees fit. Sometimes called a 'cost-reimbursement contract' or a 'prime-cost contract', although such terms do not propound that there is to be a payment over and above the actual cost and would imply that the contract provides for a specified fixed amount as profit. cf. **fixed-price contract**.

cost-plus-fee contract   See **cost-plus contract**.

cost-plus-maximum contract   A contract (in particular a building contract) that provides for payments to the contractor to be based on the actual costs he incurs, as with a **cost-plus contract**, subject to an agreed maximum.

cost recovery(US)   See **depreciation**.

cost-recovery method(US)   See **deferred-payment method**.

cost-reimbursement contract   See **cost-plus contract**.

cost rent   See **economic rent**.

cotenancy   A form of **co-ownership** where two

or more persons have an undivided interest in the same property; ownership of property as held by two or more persons so that they have an undivided right to possession of the same property. 'Cotenancy' is a term of broad usage and may refer to a **tenancy in common**, a **joint tenancy**, a **coparcenary**, or a **tenancy by the entirety**. In addition, it may sometimes be used to refer to holding of a lease by two or more persons (a 'joint tenancy' or '*co*tenancy'). See also **concurrent estate**.

cottage   1. A small **dwelling-house** situated in the country or in a village, generally with little or no land (other than in some instances a small garden) attached to it; especially a house of some antiquity. A small, and usually old or quaint, country or village dwelling-house, especially a dwelling that would at one time have been occupied by an agricultural labourer. 2. A small dwelling used for vacation purposes and, generally, detached and of no more than two stories.

cottage garden   A small **garden** or **allotment** attached to a cottage. See also **agricultural land**, **cottage holding**.

council house(BrE)   A dwelling-house owned by a local government body to meet the special housing needs of the area under its administration. Council houses are built and generally retained by local authorities for letting to approved tenants (generally families with low incomes or special requirements). See also **public housing, secure tenancy**.

Hughes, David, and Stuart Lowe. *Hughes & Lowe: Public Sector Housing Law.* 3rd ed. London: Butterworths, 1999.

Council Tax(Eng)   A tax levied on the owners and occupiers of domestic property (Local Government Finance Act 1992, Part I). Council Tax is levied partly on the value of the dwelling and partly on the residents. The value of any property that is used wholly for the purpose of private dwelling is assessed based on one of eight bands of capital value. This value is assessed on certain statutory assumptions, including that the property has been sold (i) in the **open market**; (ii) as a freehold, or in the case of a flat as an interest held for 99 years at a nominal rent; (iii) by a **willing seller**; (iv) free of any rentcharge or encumbrance; (v) in a state of reasonable repair; (vi) with the benefit of vacant possession; and (vii) on the basis of its use as a private dwelling, without any consent to carry out development other than "permitted development" (Council Tax (Situation and Valuation of Dwellings) Regulations 1992). The value is assessed by the local 'Listing Officer' (the **valuation officer** with responsibility for the area) who is responsible for maintaining the valuation list for the properties in the appropriate billing area. Council tax is then levied by the local (billing) authority at its determined rate in the pound.

Slater, Ed, and Bill Lovell. *Council Tax Law and Practice.* London: Institute of Revenues, Rating and Valuation, 1998, updated annually.

Counselor of Real Estate (CRE)(US)   See Appendix A, **Real Estate Associations, American Society of Real Estate Counselors**.

counter notice(Eng)   A formal response to a **notice** given in accordance with a statutory provision. For example, notice given by a holder of a **business tenancy** in response to a landlord's notice to terminate the tenancy; or a notice served by a local authority stating that it objects to a **purchase notice** or a **blight notice**. Frequently the server of the counter notice is claiming certain rights, such as a right to a new tenancy, or not to be bound by the original notice.

counter offer   A response to an **offer** proposing one or more conditions or terms that are at variance with the basis of the offer. Strictly speaking a counter offer has the effect of rejecting the original offer and, therefore, does not constitute an **acceptance**, unless there is a clear intention to the contrary (*Hyde v Wrench* (1840) 3 Beav 334, 49 Eng Rep 132; *Cullen v Bickers* (1878) 12 SALR 5 (Aus); The American Law Institute, *Restatement Second, Contracts* § 39 (1981)). A counter offer may be an offer in its own right and, in turn, must be accepted by the original offeror to create a binding contract. However, the counter offer may not necessarily amount to a rejection of the original offer, but may be considered part of the haggling process and should not be taken as leaving the original offeror free to deal elsewhere, at least not without clear notice to the party making the counter offer that the original offer is no longer open for acceptance. A 'conditional acceptance', because it does amount to an acceptance of the offer as made, is in effect a form of counter offer. See also **conditional acceptance, subject to contract**.

counter-cyclical development process

The tendency for property development to be out of phase with general economic **cycles** due to the time lags of the planning and building processes. A developer starts planning a new project during an up-turn or recovery in the economic cycle, but may not complete the building process until the cycle has ebbed; thus new buildings may continue to arrive on the market during the down turn in the cycle. Also, as the economy reaches its peak pressures such as higher interest rates are likely to reduce demand for new property at the stage that many new buildings are nearing completion. Both of these factors push the real estate market out of phase with the general economy and not infrequently result in a real estate crisis. See also **boom, slump**.

counter-letter   1. An instrument that qualifies another instrument that in turn is unqualified as to its effect. A separate deed or written document executed simultaneously with another deed for the transfer of property, whereby the grantee undertakes to transfer the property back to the grantor when certain terms and conditions set out in the counter-letter have been fulfilled. For example, a deed by which a party acknowledges that another transaction does not, as may appear, transfer an absolute right of ownership, but is merely a transfer of a right to a surety or mortgage against the subject matter. The signatory to the deed normally declares that he is only a trustee or mortgagee and not an absolute owner of the subject matter. In Scotland called a 'back letter'.   2.(Civ)A document made, in secret, to defeat, as between the parties, another instrument, especially when the intention is to reduce a tax liability. See also **simulation**.

counterpart   Historically, one of the two parts of an **indenture**, but nowadays the principal copy of a deed used when a document is executed in duplicate, especially a copy of a conveyance or lease. The original and counterpart of a document are signed and then exchanged between the parties, the grantee (or tenant) retaining the original (which was prepared by the grantor) and the grantor (or landlord) the counterpart. In common law, the original of a deed prevails as the correct document, unless there is clearly a mistake in the original and then the counterpart may be brought into account. However, where one or more copies are signed by all the parties, which is more common in North America than in English legal practice, all the documents may be considered as originals.

Countryside Agency(Eng)   A statutory body that are responsible in England for making life better for people in countryside and improving the quality of the Countryside for everyone. (**www.countryside.gov.uk**).

Countryside Council for Wales   The Government's statutory advisor on sustaining natural beauty, wildlife and opportunities for outdoor enjoyment in Wales and its inshore waters. (**www.ccw.gov.uk**).

county matter(Eng)   See **planning authority**.

coupled with an interest   See **agency, authority, licence**.

coupon rate   The stated annual interest rate on a bond or security. The interest rate shown on the face of a **negotiable instrument**, such as a bond or promissory note. Sometimes called the 'nominal rate' or 'nominal yield', or the 'face rate' or 'note rate'. See also **nominal interest rate**.

court See **courtyard**.

courtesy See **curtesy**.

courtesy fee(US) A fee paid by a listing broker, or owner, to a buyer's broker for introducing a prospect who completes the purchase of the listed property. See also **cooperating broker**.

courtyard or **court** A term derived from **curtilage**, but generally limited to an enclosed area, commonly walled-in and hard surfaced, around a dwelling-house. Structures or buildings within the courtyard of a building are normally **appurtenant** to that building.

covenant 1. A promise or agreement by which two or more parties accept an obligation to do, or not to do, something; acknowledge that a certain state of affairs exists; or one or more parties stipulates the truth of certain facts. Covenant may mean the promise, or in law it more usually refers to the agreement, or part of the agreement, that contains the commitment. In particular, 'covenant' is frequently used to refer to any solemn agreement or stipulation, especially any fundamental provision of a conveyance, lease, mortgage, or other instrument dealing with real property. A covenant may be considered as no more than a formal **condition**; however a condition is a mutual agreement of the parties and is binding on both, whereas a covenant is an assurance by one party that something will be done.

In a lease, or other form of agreement for the grant of an interest in real property, the breach of a condition may result in the automatic termination or **forfeiture** of the estate, whereas the breach of a covenant does not automatically terminate the estate, but will only subject the breaching party to a liability for damages. Although whether a clause is a covenant or a condition depends in the final upon the intention of the parties, based on the overall interpretation of the entire agreement.

A covenant may be **express**, whether set down in writing or inferred by the construction of the entire agreement; or **implied** by law from the nature of the transaction. It may be 'absolute' if it is not limited or qualified; or it may be 'conditional'. A covenant may be 'positive' or 'affirmative' as when it requires the performance of some act or payment of some consideration; or 'negative' or 'restrictive' when it imposes an obligation that prevents some act. In the US, a covenant may also be categorized as 'affirmative' when the covenantor stipulates the veracity of certain facts. A covenant may also be 'continuing' as when the obligation persists for the term of an agreement or it requires performance as often as the occasion arises, for example an obligation to pay rent. See also **affirmative covenant**(US), **breach of covenant**, **covenants conditions and restrictions**(US), **express covenant**, **implied covenant**, **positive covenant**, **privity of contract**, **real covenant**(US), **restrictive covenant**, **seal**, **servitude**, **usual covenant**, **warranty**. 2. A provision or clause in a **lease** that governs the relationship of the lessor and lessee. A covenant between landlord and tenant is generally called a 'leasehold covenant'; as distinguished from a restrictive covenant between owners of freehold land, which may be called a 'vendor and purchaser covenant' as it arises upon the sale of land. See also **agreement for a lease**, **covenant running with the land**, **equitable lease**, **personal covenant**, **privity of contract**, **privity of estate**, **usual covenant**.

Kenny P., and R. Hewitson. *Blackstone's Guide to Landlord and Tenant Covenants*. London: Blackstone, 1996.

Parson, Andrew. *Tenant Default under Commercial Leases*. 3rd ed. Welwyn Garden City: EMIS Publishing, 2000.

3. The financial standing or credit rating of a tenant or guarantor. A strong financial tenant (especially a company with a **triple A rating**) may be referred to as a 'prime covenant' or in North America as a **credit tenant**).

covenant affecting the subject-matter of the lease(Eng) See **covenant running with the land**.

covenant against alienation See **restraint on alienation**.

covenant against assignment or **subletting** See **restraint on alienation**.

covenant against encumbrances(US) A covenant in a conveyance, or other deed of transfer of real estate, that there are no encumbrances, or outstanding rights, burdens, charges or claims, that will diminish the value of the estate being transferred, other than those specified. Such a covenant provides a form of indemnity by the grantor and requires the payment of damages for any consequential loss suffered by the grantee as a result of a breach of the covenant. Some jurisdictions take the view that such a covenant is not breached by a visible or open and notorious encumbrance, such as a public right of way. As a rule, a covenant against encumbrances is personal to the parties and does not 'run with the land'. See also **beneficial owner**(Eng), **encumbrance**.

covenant against grantor's acts(US) See **warranty deed**.

covenant appurtenant(US) See **appurtenant**, **covenant 'running with the land'**.

covenant charge(Aus) A charge that is recorded against land by a public authority when the land owner has failed to comply with a **positive covenant**, such an obligation to maintain a building or provide services to the land.

covenant for further assurance A covenant that a grantor of real property will do everything that is necessary to perfect a **conveyance**. The covenantor undertakes to execute any additional conveyance (assurance) that may be necessary to make good or to perfect the title obtained by the grantee, his heirs or assigns. Such a covenant affects not only the instrument by which the property is transferred, but also any document by which the vendor has acquired title. A covenant for further assurance runs with the land, unless there is a statutory provision to the contrary. Also called a 'covenant of further assurance' or, sometimes, a 'covenant of further assistance'. See also **beneficial owner**(Eng), **covenant for title**(US), **covenant of warranty (of title)**(US), **full title guarantee**(Eng), **limited title guarantee**(Eng).

covenant for possession(US) A covenant by which a seller of land undertakes to grant possession upon completion of the transfer of title. See also **covenant of quiet enjoyment**.

covenant for quiet enjoyment(Eng) or **covenant of quiet enjoyment**(US) A covenant by which a grantor of land undertakes, expressly or impliedly, to give **quiet enjoyment**, i.e. that the grantee will not have his proper possession and enjoyment fettered, or substantially interrupted, by any act of the grantor or anyone claiming title though him. A covenant for quiet enjoyment does not require any particular wording, but arises from the intention of the parties based on the overall construction of the instrument used to transfer title to land. See also **beneficial owner**(Eng), **covenant for title**, **warranty deed**.

covenant for right to convey(Eng) See **full title guarantee**, **limited title guarantee**.

covenant for seisin(US) See **covenant of seisin**.

covenant for title or **covenant of title 1.**(US)A covenant set out in a deed by which a grantor of real property gives an undertaking as to the quality of the title to the property. In particular, the 'usual' covenants for title are: (i) that the grantor will provide 'seisin' of the land conveyed, i.e. he is the owner of the estate being granted and will provide possession thereof – the **covenant of seisin**; (ii) that the grantor will defend the title he purports to convey – **covenant of warranty**; (iii) that there are no adverse encumbrances, except as expressed – **covenant against encumbrances**; and (iv) that the grantor will not disturb the right to possession of the property being conveyed – **covenant of quiet enjoyment**. Such covenants are usually inserted in a **conveyance**, or deed of grant, or they may be implied where such words as 'convey and warrant' are used in the conveyance. A **covenant for further assurance**, i.e. to secure the execution of such other deeds or instruments as are necessary to perfect the title may also be given, although this is less common. In the majority of jurisdictions a **warranty deed**, substantially in the form required by state statute, implies the usual covenants for title without the need for them to be expressly set out. Also, in some jurisdictions, the 'covenant of seisin' implies that the grantor is the owner of an indefeasible estate in fee simple (following the common law). Alternatively, the grantor may only give a **covenant of right to convey** by which the grantor undertakes that he has the right to the property he purports to convey. In a few jurisdictions there are no implied covenants of title. Sometimes called 'warranties for title'. **2.**(Eng)A promise or covenant made, by the vendor to a purchaser of land, concerning the title that is to be transferred. A covenant for title is normally set out in a **conveyance**, or 'deed of grant', confirming that the seller has a **good title** to the property, or is selling as **beneficial owner**.

In Australia a similar provision applies in all States where a vendor sells as 'beneficial owner'. See also **demise, full title guarantee, limited title guarantee, implied covenant, usual covenant, warranty deed**.

covenant in gross(US) A **covenant** that does not run with the land. See also **privity of estate, restrictive covenant**.

covenant not to compete See **non-competition clause**.

covenant of further assistance See **covenant for further assurance**.

covenant of quiet enjoyment(US) See **covenant for quiet enjoyment**(Eng).

covenant of non-claim(US) A covenant to the effect that neither the seller, nor any party claiming through the seller, will claim any title to a property being conveyed.

covenant of right to convey(US) A covenant by which a grantor of land stipulates that he has the right to the property that he purports to convey, but does not necessarily have an absolute right to possession of the land. For example, a covenant that the grantor is not restrained by a trust or similar restraint that prohibits a transfer of the subject property. Thus, such a covenant is personal to the covenantee and does not run with the land. Sometimes called a 'covenant of good right to convey'. See also **covenant for title**.

covenant of seisin or **covenant of seizin**(US) A covenant by which a grantor of an interest in land claims to have and to transfer **seisin** to another. 'Seisin' corresponds to **possession** and, therefore, by this covenant the grantor should transfer a 'right of possession' of the land, as well as the complete legal title. In particular, a covenant which implies that the title is an 'indefeasible' fee simple, i.e. it will not come to an end as a right to possession upon the occurrence of some condition attached to the estate. Such a covenant is breached if the grantor states that he is selling a fee simple, but only holds a life estate; or, if he has no title to the land in question, as where he is claiming by adverse possession, but the claim has not been substantiated. A covenant of seisin may be contrasted with a **covenant of right to convey** as the latter does not stipulate that the grantor has an absolute right to possession of the estate, although in most jurisdictions the covenants are considered to be synonymous, both giving a right of ownership and possession. As a rule, a covenant of seisin is personal and does not 'run with the land'. See also **covenant for title, warranty deed**.

covenant of title(US) See **covenant for title**.

covenant of warranty(US)   A covenant or assurance by the grantor of an estate that in the event of a failure, in whole or in part, of **good title** he will take any necessary steps to perfect the title, or will insure that the grantee, or his heirs and assigns, will not be deprived of possession. A covenant of warranty of title is generally the only one needed and, in the event such an undertaking cannot be maintained, the grantor undertakes to pay compensation for any loss suffered by the grantee as a result of the defect of title. In some jurisdictions, the provision may be a 'covenant of general warranty', when the assurance is against claims of title superior to that of the grantor; or a 'covenant of special warranty', when the assurance is against anyone claiming through the grantor. See also **covenant for title, warranty deed**.

covenant running with the land   A **covenant** that is considered to benefit the parcel of land to which it relates, as distinguished from a covenant that is strictly personal to the parties to a contract, or is merely collateral to the parties' interest in the land. A covenant that runs with the land is one that affects the nature, quality, mode of use or value of the land *per se* and, therefore, is one that may be binding on an assignee of an interest in the land. However, the covenant is only binding if it 'touches and concerns' the land, i.e. it has direct reference to the land or it lays down something that is to be done upon the land; "if the thing to be done be merely collateral to the land, and doth not touch and concern the thing demised in any sort, there the assignee shall not be charged", *Spencer's Case* (1583) 5 Co Rep 16a, 16b, 77 Eng Rep 72, 74. "If the covenant has direct reference to the land, if it lays down something which is to be done upon the land, or, and perhaps this is the clearest way of describing the test, it affects the landlord in his normal capacity as landlord or the tenant in his normal capacity as tenant, it may be said to touch and concern the land; *Cheshire's Modern Law of Real Property*, 13th ed. p. 430-431", *Hua Chiao Commercial Bank Ltd v Chiaphua Industries Ltd* [1987] AC 99, 107, [1987] 1 All ER 1110, 1112 (HL) (Greenspan v. Rehberg, 56

Mich App 310, 224 NW.2d 67, 73 (1974)). Covenants that 'touch and concern' land include, for example, covenants to pay rent; to repair; to provide services such as heat, light, water; to insure *and* rebuild in the event of fire; not to assign or sub-let the lease; to use the premises only for a specified purpose; and a covenant for quiet enjoyment. (The expression 'touch and concern' is slightly misleading as physical annexation is not an absolute necessity.) Covenants that are merely personal include, for example, an obligation to pay money to a third party; a covenant relating solely to personal property or to land other than the demised property; a covenant that relates only to a specified tenant; and a covenant to employ certain personnel on the premises. This rule is especially applicable to the enforceability of the burden of an affirmative or **positive covenant**. See also **alienation clause, privity of estate, real covenant**(US), **restrictive covenant, solus agreement**(Eng), **use clause**.
Fancourt, Timothy. *Enforceability of Landlord and Tenant Covenants*. London: Sweet & Maxwell, 1997.

covenant to repair   See repair.

covenant touching and concerning the land   See **covenant 'running with the land'**.

covenantee   The person to whom a promise is made by a **covenant**, i.e. the party that has the benefit of the covenant.

covenantor or **covenanter**   The maker of a **covenant**; the person who makes the promise. One who is bound by the terms of a covenant, i.e. the party that is bound by the burden of the covenant.

covenants, conditions and restrictions (**CC&Rs**)(US)   Conditions and limitations, such as easements, user restrictions and restrictions on the rights of transfer, placed upon the use and enjoyment of a property. In particular, such benefits or burdens that will be contained in a conveyance or deed of transfer of a unit in a **condominium**. In a condominium, the CC&Rs usually form part of the

condominium declaration and cannot be altered without the approval of the authority that governs the creation of condominiums in the particular jurisdiction, as compared with the **bylaws** or regulations, which may be altered by the **condominium owners' association**. In some jurisdictions CC&Rs are simply called 'restrictions'. See also **reciprocal easement**.

cover   1. Security, or funds, held against a liability.   2. A factor by which one income exceeds another that is dependent on it. For example, if the interest payable on a mortgage is $100,000 p.a. and the net income (before depreciation) derived from the property held as security for the mortgage is $300,000 p.a., the interest is covered by a factor of three. See also **debt-coverage ratio, loan value, margin, secured ground rent**.   3. The risks or contingencies for which an insurer is liable under an **insurance policy**. See also **risk**.   4. The monetary value of a potential loss against which an **indemnity** has been obtained through an insurance policy. In the US, the policy itself may sometimes be called a cover and the indemnity called 'coverage'. See also **unvalued policy, valued policy**.

cover-all clause(US)   See **Mother Hubbard clause**.

cover note   A memorandum of the terms of a provisional contract of insurance. The note may be signed by the insurer, or an insurance agent, and provides evidence of interim cover while the insurer considers details of the required insurance and prepares a formal insurance policy. A cover note is not an insurance policy as such but the insurer accepts to provide cover for the risks set out in the note, subject to the results of his inquiries. A cover note may be issued also to confirm that an existing policy has been transferred into the name of the person to whom the note is addressed. Also called a 'certificate of insurance' or 'memorandum of insurance' or in the US, especially when such a memorandum is prepared by the insurer, a **binder** or sometimes a

'binding slip'. See also **utmost good faith**.

cover ratio   See **debt-coverage ratio**.

coverage   See **cover, site coverage**.

covered area   The total area of a site that has been covered with buildings or structures. See also **buildable area, floor area ratio**(AmE), **plot ratio**(BrE).

coverture   A term derived from the common law for the condition of a woman during marriage. The term was particularly applied during the time in English law, prior to Married Woman's Property Act 1882, s. 1(1) and the Law Reform (Married Women and Tortfeasors) Act, 1935, when a woman could not own property in her own right. See also **dower**.

cramdown or **cram down**   An arrangement by which creditors, usually under a bankruptcy reorganization, are required to accept a dilution of their position either in favour of new creditors or providers of new capital. Such an arrangement generally requires the consent of all the creditors.

cratered property   A property investment that is a financial disaster. See also **distressed property**.

crawl space(US)   A space with limited headroom between two floors in a building, especially between the ground level and the first floor, in place of a basement, or between the top floor ceiling and the roof, in place of an attic. Such space is generally intended to provide limited storage room.

Crawley costs(Eng)   See **compensation for disturbance**.

created ground rent   A rent that is fixed at a level between the value of undeveloped and developed land, i.e. between the **unimproved ground rent** and the **market rent** of land and buildings.

creative financing(US)   1. Financing obtained

other than from a conventional source, such as seller financing, a sale-and-leaseback, or a mortgage-backed security or similar form of financing. See also **collateralized mortgage obligation, purchase money mortgage**. **2.** Any form of financing that differs from a conventional loan. 'Creative mortgage financing' generally refers to any mortgage that is not granted with a provision for payment of interest and capital throughout the term of the loan. In particular, any mortgage loan that is not granted for 30 years with equal monthly payments calculated to repay interest and all principal over the term of the loan. See also **alternative mortgage loan**.

credit **1.** The ability to borrow money. The ability to buy with a promise to pay in the future. The actual delivery of goods or title subject to payment at a future date. In banking, the ability to obtain credit is commonly measured by the four C's, character (the moral risk or nature of the borrower); capacity (the business risk or ability to pay); capital (the property risk or security for the debt); and collateral (as may be made available to secure a loan in the event of default). **2.** That which is due to a person or entity. The right of one party to defer making payment to another. In accounting, credits increase the liabilities, equity and revenues, and correspondingly decrease the assets and expenses of an entity, and are shown in the right hand side of a **financial statement**. cf. **debit**. See also **letter of credit, line of credit**.

credit bargain See **usury**.

credit enhancement A form of collateral that is provided to reduce the risk of a security or investment. Credit enhancement may take the form of a letter of credit, guarantee, cross-collateralization, or any similar contractual obligation that may be called on in the event of a default. In particular, any form of financial support (additional capital, guarantees, insurance, reserve account, etc.) added to a mortgage-backed security by the issuer. See also **mortgage-backed obligation**.

credit life insurance See **mortgage insurance**.

credit line See **line of credit**.

credit rating The opinion of traders, banks or rating agencies on the financial standing, net worth and the ability of a firm or individual to pay its obligations, especially to pay for items brought on any form of loan or credit. A credit rating may be obtained from a reputable organization, such as a bank or financial institution or from a credit-rating agency that specializes in such rating work, such as Standard & Poor's Corporation or Moody's Investors Service. The strength of the credit rating of a tenant has an effect on the value of a property investment to an owner. See also **covenant, triple A rating**.

credit report A written report on an individual's or a company's creditworthiness or **credit rating**.

credit sale[US] A sale in which the seller is a creditor. The term includes "any contract in the form of a **bailment** or **lease** if the bailee or lessee contracts to pay as compensation for use a sum substantially equivalent to or in excess of the aggregate value of the property and services involved and it is agreed that the bailee or lessee will become, or for no other or a nominal consideration has the option to become, the owner of the property upon full compliance with his obligations under the contract", 15 USC § 1602(g).

credit-sale agreement[BrE] An agreement for the sale of goods whereby part or all of the purchase price is paid by instalments, after the date of transfer; but one that is not a **conditional sale agreement** (Consumer Credit Act 1974, s. 189(1)). A term generally applied only to personal property. A credit sale means that title to the property has been transferred (unlike a conditional sale agreement or a **hire-purchase agreement**) so there is no statutory right to terminate the transaction and the creditor has no right to retake possession if the debtor falls into arrears; the only remedy is an action on the debt. Also called an 'instalment sale'. See also **agreement for sale**.

credit tenant(AmE)   A tenant that has a strong credit rating. In British English, generally called a 'prime covenant' See also **prime tenant**.

credit union(US)   A non-profit cooperative organization that takes deposits from a closed group of members (a labor union, club, etc.) and makes loans to the same members. A credit union is democratically managed and normally makes loans on more favorable terms, or pays higher rates of interest, to its members as compared with other financial institutions.

criterion rate of return   See **target rate of return**.

critical path analysis (CPA) or **critical path method**   A method of analyzing a project by breaking it down into its component parts, or required actions, and developing a program showing each part or action in sequence; the relationship between the various parts or actions; and the time required to complete the whole sequence. For example, a chart is prepared which endeavours to set out all the stages in a building or development process, in order to assist in monitoring the critical actions that will affect the timing of completion. The critical path is the one that shows the optimum period required to complete the process and the parts of the process that are critical to its completion.
Antill, James M., and R. W. Woodhead. *Critical Path Methods in Construction Practice.* 4th ed. New York: Wiley, 1990.
Lockyer, K., and James Gordon. *Critical Path Analysis & Other Project Network Techniques.* 5th ed. London & Philadelphia: Pitman, 1991.
O'Brien, James. *CPM in Construction Management.* 5th ed. New York: McGraw-Hill, 1999.

croft   A small area of enclosed land, used for pasture, arable, or horticultural use, usually with a dwelling-house. A small farm. See also **close**.

crop rent(US)   See **sharecropping lease**.

crop-share lease(US)   See **sharecropping lease**.

cropper(US)   See **sharecropping lease**.

crops   See **emblements, way-going crop**.

cross collateralization   See **cross-default clause**.

cross-default clause   A provision in any one of a number of mortgages granted to the same mortgagor to the effect that, in the event of a default on one of the mortgaged properties, the mortgagee has a right of action against some or all of the mortgaged properties. Such a provision is commonly found in a **blanket mortgage**. Similarly, a **wraparound mortgage** generally provides that a default on the senior mortgage is a default on the wraparound or junior mortgage. The provision of such a facility is known as 'cross collateralization'. See also **collateral, marshalling**.

cross easement   An **easement** that provides reciprocal rights of user, e.g. a joint access road or a right to use one parking lot at one time of day in exchange for the use of another at alternative times. See also **party wall, reciprocal easement agreement**.

cross remainder(US)   An estate in land that is held by two or more persons so that the survivor (or survivors) obtains the right to the land as a **remainder**. For example, if an estate is granted to A, B, and C jointly with cross remainder to each of them, the estate passes on the death of one of the parties to the other two and thereafter to the sole survivor.

cross-use agreement(US)   An agreement, which usually takes the form of an **easement**, that provides a property occupier with a right to use or cross over an adjoining property for the benefit of the occupier's property and normally provides for restrictions on the use of the adjoining property. For example, a tenant of a shopping center may be granted vehicular access over an adjoining center to provide additional access to the surrounding streets, or a tenant may be granted a right to shared use of parking facilities. Generally, such agreements are limited as to the time and quantity of use that can be made of the shared facilities, for example the roadway and parking areas may not be used for employee parking or delivery trucks. See also **reciprocal easement agreement**.

Crown Estate(BrE)   The lands and other rights, including minerals and certain incorporeal hereditaments, that the monarch enjoys in the political capacity as the right of the Crown and that are now managed by the Crown Estate Commissioners. The Crown Estate is held for the use of the Crown, but in the monarch's public capacity so that it passes by succession to the next monarch. The term 'Crown land' may be used to include other lands that are held by the Crown, including the royal palaces and royal parks, that do not come under the management of the Crown Estate Commissioners, as well as land held by the Sovereign in her natural capacity. In relation to the exemption of the Crown from the need to obtain planning permission 'Crown land' means land belonging to Her Majesty in the right of the Crown or belonging to a government department or held in trust for Her Majesty for the purposes of a government department and an interest in land belonging to Her Majesty in right of the Duchy of Lancaster or belonging to the Duchy of Cornwall (TCPA 1990, s. 293(1)). See also *bona vacantia*, **demesne land**, **escheat**, **foreshore**, **forfeiture**.

Crown Estate Commissioners(BrE)   See **Crown Estate**.

Crown grant   A grant of land by the sovereign (especially in former British colonies) whereby the Crown divests itself of land and transfers title to a private party, but does not normally grant any of the privileges that were enjoyed by the sovereign, such as the right to minerals. A Crown grant represents the original evidence of **title**. Such early grants were generally made subject to the payment of a **quit rent**. Such forms of transfer are now replaced in most jurisdictions by an outright sale or lease of the land, as with any private sale.

Crown land   **1.** See **Crown Estate**(BrE).   **2.**(Aus)In general, any land that is the property of the Commonwealth, a State, or a Territory (Lands Acquisition Act 1989, s. 6). Such land may or may not be dedicated to public use, but does not include land that has been dedicated to any person by the government. Following the British claim to Australia in 1788 all of the land was deemed to be vested in the Crown as it was considered that the Continent was not held or owned (in the common law sense) by anyone. It was *res nullius*. Until 1992 all land was viewed in law to be derived form this Crown 'title' and no rights to land could exist unless ceded by the Crown, either as a grant, by sale or by the right of a squatter. The High Court of Australia has rejected this legal doctrine and ruled that the acquisition of Sovereignty by Britain did not, *ipso facto*, extinguish Aboriginal Australian's land rights – **native title** (*Mabo v Queensland (No 2)* (1992) 175 CLR 1, 107 ALR 1). Crown land is thus subject to any established native title. Several State statutes defined Crown land to be estates or interests in land held by the Crown, even though another holds such land on lease, licence, or other such right. Crown land may also be defined as any land that has not been alienated by the Crown, other than land dedicated for public purpose. **3.**(NZ)Land that is held by the Crown and that is permanently set aside for national park and reserves; that is leased to individuals for farming or other purposes; that is being subdivided for settlement by individuals; or land that is vested in the Crown, but is not set aside for public purposes, is not held by a person in fee simple or on lease or licence, or is not under development by the Commissioners of Crown Lands (Land Act 1948, s. 2; Reserves Act 1977, s. 2; Conservation Act 1987, s. 2; Crown Minerals Act 1991, s. 2 (NZ)).

Land (other than Maori customary land and Crown land reserved for Maori) that has not been alienated from the Crown for a subsisting estate in fee simple (Te Ture Whenua Maori/Maori Land Act 1993, s. 129 (NZ)).

Crown lease(Aus) **1.** Land held under a lease from the Crown. A Crown lease may be for a term of years or may be granted in perpetuity. Such a lease frequently contains a right to convert it to a freehold or a right to a **conditional purchase tenure**. **2.** A lease granted by the Commonwealth or the Federal Capital Commission in the Australian Capital Territory, where all land is held under a lease from the Crown rather than by freehold. See also **pastoral lease**.

CTS system(US) A system for classifying residential property. A property may be classified as to its Class (single-family, two-family, detached, row house, etc.); its Type as determined by the number of floor levels; and its Style (contemporary, ranch, colonial, etc.).

cubing An estimation of the cost of building work by reference to the volume of the quantities of materials required.

cujus est solum, ejus est usque ad coelum et ad inferos(Lat) 'Whose is the soil, his is also that which is above and below it (literally from heaven to hell)'. An expression that has limited application to modern land law. See also **air rights**, **land**.

cul-de-sac A **street** or alley that is closed at one end, but usually has an area for turning at the closed end. A street that is only open at one end. In British English, also called a 'close'. In the US, commonly called a **dead-end street** or 'blind alley'. See also **highway**.

culvert An underground channel or arched passageway built for carrying water, especially to channel a river or to carry storm water under a road or railroad, but not as part of the road drainage system. cf. **watercourse**. See also **drain, sewer**.

cum testamento annexo(Lat) 'With the **will** annexed'.

curable obsolescence or **curable depreciation** Deterioration or depreciation to a building that can be repaired or made good at an economical cost, especially depreciation that is normally repaired, or should be repaired, by a prudent owner or occupier. Most physical or functional obsolescence is curable, but economic obsolescence is not readily curable. cf. **deferred maintenance, incurable obsolescence**.

currency **Money** that passes from hand to hand and is readily accepted for transacting business or as a medium of trade. Coins or notes issued by the government. See also **cash, legal tender**.

current asset Cash or an **asset** that is fairly readily converted into cash, e.g. stocks, debtors, accounts and notes receivable, or an asset that is intended to be resold in the normal course of business or can be sold for cash within a short period of time (usually within less than one year). Sometimes called a '**liquid asset**' when the item can readily be converted to cash. cf. **fixed asset**. See also **illiquid asset, working capital**.

current debt See **current liability**.

current liability or **current debt** A liability, or **debt**, that must be met or paid for within a short period, which is generally taken as the operating cycle of a business or a financial year. See also **current ratio**.

current market value **Market value** at a specified point in time. The best price that can reasonably be obtained by negotiation at the present time.

current price See **market price**.

current ratio The ratio of the current assets

to the current liabilities of an enterprise based on the figures in its financial statement. The ratio is a measure of a firm's liquidity or ability to meet its debts.

current use value (CUV) The **market value** of an interest in land assuming that it will not be used for any purpose other than that to which it is currently put, or that which is authorised by an existing planning permission or zoning regulation. cf. **alternative use value**.

current yield or **current return** The present yield from an investment, calculated on the basis of the current **net income** as a percentage of the **cost** or current **market value** of the investment. Sometimes called the 'passing yield'. cf. **equated yield**, **initial yield**, **redemption yield**. See also **running yield**.

curtail schedule See **amortisation schedule**.

curtain principle(Eng) See **trust instrument**.

curtesy See **tenancy by the curtesy**.

curtilage Derived from the Latin *cortile*, 'court' or 'yard' or Old French *courtillage*, 'courtyard'. A small **courtyard** or parcel of land attached to a dwelling-house and forming an integral part of the dwelling, especially an area that is fenced or enclosed with the dwelling-house. A small area around a building (United States v. Romano, 388 F Supp 101, 104 (DC Pa 1975); *Dyer v Dorset CC* [1989] 1 QB 346, 351 (CA)). A curtilage may include a court, garden, yard, or vacant land and buildings ancillary to a house, but generally excludes such land as a separate orchard or land held under a separate tenure. The 'curtilage' of a house is the land that is clearly part and parcel thereof. It is not essential that the land is marked off or enclosed provided it can be seen, in all the circumstances, as an integral part of the dwelling-house. See also **messuage**.

custodian One who holds something in **custody**. A person or institution that holds specific documents on behalf of another. See also **collateral agent**, **trustee**.

custody The care and control of a property or person. The retention of property for another but not for the possessor. Possession that arises as a result of a lawful process or authority, but not necessarily physical possession. See also **bailment**, **distress**.

custom A practice or course of action that has been long established in a particular place or country; something that becomes established from frequent repetition of an action or from what is done generally. **Usage** that has continued from time immemorial and, therefore, is recognised as having force of law without having been enacted as such. A business custom, or trade usage, is the generally accepted way of conducting a trade, business or profession. A business custom must be certain, reasonable and generally acknowledged as such in the business, trade or profession to which it relates. A custom may establish an **implied term** in a contract, provided it does not conflict with an express term or the general tenor of the contract. Thus, the local custom may determine the way in which an agent is expected to conduct his or her business, the extent of an agent's **authority**, or the arrangements for the splitting of **commission**, when such matters are not clearly set down in the terms of appointment. See also **agent**, **alienation**, **authority**, **customary right**, **precedent**, **prescription**, **tenant right**.

custom building or **custom-built property** A building designed to the specific requirements of the intended occupier. cf. **speculative building**. See also **package-deal contract**.

customary right(Eng) A right over land acquired by **custom**. A right to use another's land as acquired by an undefined and fluctuating group of persons, such as the residents of a village. For example, a right to hold an annual fair; a right of way to a church; a right to hold a sporting activity on land; or a right to enter on land to draw water.

Such a right is also called a 'local customary right' because it is generally enjoyed by the members of a local community. Such a right is deemed to have existed from time immemorial and to have continued without interruption. However, a customary right must be certain, confined to a particular area and be a reasonable right. It is a right that, although similar to **easement**, cannot be an easement because it is not appurtenant to any dominant parcel of land and, because it benefits a class of persons, it cannot be the subject matter of **grant**. However, a customary right, once acquired, cannot be lost merely by non-user or waiver. See also **dedication**, *jus spatiandi*.

cut-off notice(US) A notice given by a mortgagor to the mortgagee stipulating that any **future advance** that may be made under the mortgage loan agreement will no longer have priority over subsequent lenders or lien holders. Several states provide a statutory right, when there is a 'future advances clause' in the loan agreement, for the borrower to limit the priority of such advances, after the date of a cut-off notice, in order to limit the discretionary right of the lender to make future advances with equal **priority** to the initial advances. The purpose of this provision is to allow the borrower to raise additional funding from a third party, or obtain credit from a supplier, without that party having the risk of his priority being significantly deferred by the first mortgagee's further advances. The cut-off notice only applies to discretionary advances and does not affect the priority of mandatory advances such as are required under a construction loan.

cy-pres doctrine A doctrine by which a court can vary the arrangements for a charitable trust when the intent is clear, but the arrangements were inadequately made or the original object is now inadequate. The new arrangement must be considered '*si près*' – so near' or proximate to the donor's intent.

cycle A periodic space of time. A phase or swing in economic activity that fluctuates between expansion, possibly leading to a **boom**, and then contraction, possibly leading to a depression or **slump**. Movements in an economy may be considered as analogous to a roller coaster so that each haul to the top is followed by the gravitational pull to the bottom. Property development, being a particularly dynamic process, tends to follow a cyclical trend: as general economic activity expands, demand for property increases, and consequently property values rise. The response is an initiation of new development; a process that tends to accelerate as further investment takes place. Eventually supply exceeds demand, values ease, new development becomes less viable and the resulting uncertainty leads to a reduction in activity. The recession in building activity is reversed only when the excess of supply is absorbed and a new phase of activity can start again. See also **counter-cyclical development process**.

D

damage Derived from the Latin *damnum*, 'loss'. Harm or **injury** (physical or economic), to a person or an object; especially when arising from a wrongful act, default or negligence of another. A loss or deterioration of property due to impact, collision, an act of God, fire, etc. A loss that may be redressed by an amount equal to the cost of restoring the property to its original condition. It has been said that "neither in common parlance nor in legal phraseology is the word 'damage' used as applicable to injuries done to the person, but solely as applicable to mischief done to property … We speak indeed of '**damages**' as compensation for injury done to the person, but the term 'damages' is not employed interchangeably with the term 'injury', with reference to mischief wrongfully occasioned to the person", *Smith v Brown* (1871) 40 LJ QB 214, 218. Therefore, in the context of property the word 'damage' should be used to distinguish it from personal 'injury' inflicted, or 'loss' suffered, especially as a result of a tort or breach of contract; 'injury' being the illegal invasion of a legal right; and 'damages' the recompense or compensation awarded for the damage suffered. There is a tendency in both common and legal phraseology for the terms 'damage', 'damages' and 'injury' to overlap. However, injury is the illegal invasion of a legal right; damage is the loss, hurt, or harm that results from an injury; and **damages** are the recompense or compensation awarded for the damage suffered. There can be damage suffered, but it may not be recognised by the law as a violation that leads to the payment of 'damages'. See also **destroy, injurious affection, insurance**.

damage feasant or **damage faisant**(Eng) 'Doing **damage**'. Damage caused to grass, corn, wood, etc. by another's beasts, cattle or fowl trespassing onto one's land. A common law right to seize and detain such animals until compensation is paid for the damage, 'distress damage feasant', has been abolished in English law. However, in certain cases, an occupier of land may detain and, after 14 days (if they are not claimed), sell livestock that has strayed onto his land and is not under control (Animals Act 1971, s. 47). See also **strict liability**.

damages 1. A sum of money paid as compensation for the infringement of a right or neglect of a duty. In particular, pecuniary recompense awarded by a court of law, on a once and for all basis, to a person for a wrong or injury done to him or her (whether directly, or to his or her rights or property), either as a result of a breach of an obligation, or a breach of a **duty of care** owed by one person to another. The obligation, or duty, may be one that is imposed by general law, by statute, or under the terms of a contract.

Entitlement to damages may arise because of a **breach of contract** or a **tort**. The common law principles for the award of damages are: (i) there should be no damages awarded in the absence of 'legal' wrong, *damnum sine injuria*; (ii) the claimant or plaintiff must have suffered injury or loss; (iii) a person is entitled only to such damages as might have been expected to arise consequentially or naturally, i.e. in the normal course of events, or such an amount as the person causing wrong might reasonably contemplate could result from his or her acts, with the burden of proving such damages being on the person claiming them (unless a statute dictates otherwise) (*Hadley v Baxendale* (1854) 23 LJ Ex 179, 9 Exch 341, 156 Eng Rep 145; Brayton v. Chase, 3 Wis 456, 1854 WL 3451 (1854); *Victoria Laundry (Windsor) Ltd v Newman Industries Ltd* [1949] 2 KB 528); in other words, the loss should be foreseeable or not too remote; or colloquially, it should be 'on the cards' – other factors considered in this respect include the sequence of cause and effect; natural and probable result; and any intervening act in the chain of causation; (iv) The damage should restore, as nearly as possible by monetary recompense, the injured party to the same position as if no wrong had been suffered – the principle of *restitutio in integrum* (or in the case of a breach of contract, to the same position as if the contract had been performed); (v) The person claiming damages is under a duty to mitigate or minimise his claim; (vi) The award may be reduced by a failure on the part of the claimant, as when the plaintiff contributes to his own loss or does not take proper care for his own safety, usually amounting to **contributory negligence**.

Damages may be classified as: (a) 'nominal' – a token payment awarded when there has been a wrong suffered but no actual financial loss or damage, as with a technical breach of contract; (b) 'general', 'actual' or 'compensatory' – based on the actual loss judged to have been suffered as a direct result of the wrong (sometimes called 'substantial', being something worth having as distinguished from merely nominal or token, or from exemplary or punitive which go further); or (c) 'special' – those losses that do not flow directly or as an inevitable result of the wrong, but can be proved to have been suffered as a natural result and which should have been contemplated by the offender as likely to arise. In exceptional cases of tort, a court may award 'aggravated' damages for extreme or malicious behaviour by the offender, such as may affect a person's feelings or dignity; or 'exemplary', 'vindictive' or 'punitive' (or 'punitory') damages as a punishment to the wrongdoer for reckless, wanton or malicious acts, or whenever it is necessary to teach him or her that the 'tort does not pay' or to deter the wrongdoer from committing similar acts (for example, in a case of **nuisance** arising from oppressive harassment by a landlord or gross or deliberate negligence), rather than merely awarding recompense to the wronged party. The amount may be referred to as 'contemptuous' if the award is derisory.

When determining the damages payable for a breach of contract, the amount to be paid to the party who suffers a loss may be based on a pre-estimate agreed when the contract was entered into – **liquidated damages**; or may be awarded at the discretion of a court – **unliquidated damages**.

In common law, the amount of compensation for damage to real property, or from contracts involving real property, should be compensatory, measured by the loss to the injured party. For example, in the event of a negligent valuation, the amount of compensation is based on the difference between the valuation and the price that the property was most likely to fetch in the open market at the time of the valuation (*Banque Bruxelles SA v Eagle Star* [1997] AC 191, 221 (HL)). On the other hand, where there has been **negligence** in the design or construction of a building, the cost of making good the property, subject to limits based on the reduction in the value of the injured party's property, is a more appropriate measure of the loss suffered. In English law, since 1989, if the seller is at fault by failing to complete a contract for the sale of land (as when he is unable to make a good title), the damages are based on the loss of the bargain. Thus, if the property is worth more than the purchase price, the purchaser is able to recover the difference. If the property is worth less, he can recover any **deposit** paid (with interest) and seek damages for the cost of investigating the title.

In the US, in most cases the measure of damage to real property is based on the difference between the fair market value of the property immediately before and immediately after the injury. There is a wide range of views on the appropriate level of damages for a failure of the vendor to complete the transfer of land. Most jurisdictions take the view that the damages should be based not merely on the costs incurred, but on the loss of the bargain. In some jurisdictions, the measure of recovery depends on the cause of the failure, so that in the event of bad faith or fraud, substantial damages may be payable and in some cases, notwithstanding the reason for the failure, the purchaser is entitled to recover damages for the loss of the bargain. Similarly, if the vendor conveys a property based on a fraudulent representation, the amount of damages may be based on the actual expenses incurred by the purchaser, but many jurisdictions will award damages based on the loss of the benefit of the bargain.

As a rule, at the end of a lease the amount of damages payable for a failure to **repair** a property is the cost of putting the premises into the state of repair specified in the lease, or the reasonable cost of carrying out the necessary repairs, excluding deterioration due to normal wear and tear during the term of the lease. However, during the term of the lease, such damages are generally restricted to the loss suffered by the landlord at the time of the want of repair, which is normally measured as the diminution in the value of the landlord's reversion at the time of the want of repair (*Conquest v Ebbetts* [1896] AC 490 (HL); 51C C.J.S., L & T, § 375(5)(b)).

In English law, this principle is reinforced by a provision that, if the premises are to be pulled down or structurally altered so as to make the repairs valueless, no damages are recoverable by the landlord (L&T Act 1927, s. 18(1)).

In the US, in a minority of jurisdictions, during the term of the lease the lessor can recover the actual cost of carrying out the repair and, at the end of the lease, the damages are based on the deterioration in the value of the demised property. cf. **indemnity**. See also **consequential damages, deposit, injunction,** *quantum meruit*, **mesne profits, specific performance, penalty, penalty rent, restitution.** 2.(US)Compensation paid for a loss in the value of land as a result of the taking of an owner's land by the exercise of the power of **eminent domain**. Such compensation may be referred to as **severance damages** when it arises as a result of the severance of one area of land from another, or **consequential damages** when only part of an owner's land is taken but the remainder is reduced in value as a result of works carried out on the taken land. See also **before-and-after method, just compensation, partial taking**.

damnum(Lat)   'Damage'; 'loss'.

damnum absque injuria(Lat)   'Damage without wrong'. Loss without legal **injury**. A principle of law which states that a court will not award **damages** unless there is an injury suffered or a loss sustained for which there is a legal redress.

damnum sentit dominus(Lat)   'Injury falls

on the owner'. A principle of the common law which states that the owner of real property is liable for its loss if it is destroyed by fire or a similar casualty, even though he may have contracted to dispose of it to another. Until the purchaser takes possession, he is not normally considered to be the owner of the property (*Paine v Meller* (1801) 6 Ves Jun 350, 31 Eng Rep 1088, 1089). See also **property insurance**.

damnum fatale(Lat)   'Damage from fate'. An action that is unavoidable or is beyond human control. A term used in the civil law for acts that are unusual and which may be considered similar to acts of God in the common law, although *damnum fatale* generally extends to any irresistible force. See also **act of God**, *force majeure*.

damnum sine injuria esse potest(Lat)   **'Damage** may arise without injury'. A principle that damage or loss may be inflicted, but the law may not consider such an injury as the subject for an award of compensation.

damping a sale(BrE)   See **chilling a sale**.

dangerous premises   Premises that present an inherent risk or danger to an occupant. Land or buildings upon which there are hidden dangers or pitfalls, especially to a **visitor** or even a trespasser. See also **invitee, negligence, repair, strict liability, trespass**.

dark store clause(AmE)   See **continuous operation clause**.

data   See **datum**.

date   Derived from the Latin *datus*, 'given'. The **time** at which an action takes place, is given or specified, or is in some way ascertained or fixed. In particular, the **time** (**day**, **month** and **year**) as set out in a written document, either to show when it was executed (or when it comes into effect) or to show when an action is to be performed. In a deed, the 'date' expresses the year, month and day on which the document was made. Stating just the year, or even the month and year, is insufficient to constitute a date, especially as '10, 1912' may refer to the 10th month, or the tenth day of an undefined month in that year. (Note: in North America, dates are usually written as month, day, year and sometimes, especially in Canada, year, month, day, such as 12-10-1999 or 1999-12-10 for December 10, 1999; but in Britain and most other English speaking countries the day is traditionally placed first so 10-12-1999 is that same date.) The date stated in a deed is presumed to be the day on which that instrument takes effect, although strictly (unless there is a clear intention that the instrument should take effect on a date different from the delivery date) the time of its **delivery** is the correct date on which a deed takes effect. The date of a deed, or of delivery, is not judged by reference to the hour or minute, but the day of delivery – a day being an indivisible time for that purpose, unless it is essential to determine priority between deeds (*Pugh v Duke of Leeds* (1777) 2 Cowp 714, 720, 98 Eng Rep 1323; Burnet v. Willingham Loan & Trust Co., 282 US 437, 51 S Ct 185, 75 L Ed 448, 450 (1931); Husebye v. Jaeger, 534 NW.2d 811, 815 (ND 1995)). However, the precise meaning of the date of an agreement or an action depends upon context, as there are numerous instances when it means actual as distinguished from any conventional time.

When time runs 'from' a particular date, as a rule, it begins to run at the end of that day (as the law makes no provision for fractions of a day, 3 *Co Inst* 53). However, the particular day may be included if any other construction would defeat the purpose of a contract, or there is parol evidence to indicate that the contract should take effect so as to include the first day. A lease for a period 'beginning with' a particular date would normally include the first day. However, to avoid ambiguity, it is preferable to use such language as 'commencing on and including [January 1]'.

When something is to be done during a period that spans given dates, the entirety of the last day is included, especially when the first day is excluded, unless there is evidence to the contrary.

See **time**, especially if the time starts 'on' a specified date. See also **maturity date**, **valuation date**.

date of acquisition   See date, completion.

date of appraisal$^{(AmE)}$ or **date of valuation**$^{(BrE)}$ See **appraisal date**$^{(AmE)}$; **valuation date**.

datum (pl. **data**)   **1.** A point, level or line used as a point of reference, e.g. a reference point indicating the height of a specific place above mean sea level. In some cities in the US, a datum is established at the same level throughout the city as a reference point for determining the ownership of a building in a horizontal plane, e.g. the vertical plane of a condominium unit. See also **bench mark**. **2.** Any kind of detailed information, such as may be collected to assist in preparing an **appraisal report** on a property; including 'general data' covering economic, demographic and social facts; 'specific data' covering details of the subject property; and 'comparative data' or comparables of similar property. See also **comparable property**.   **3.** That which is delivered; a first principle; a **date**.

day   A period of 24 hours. A day, unless expressed to the contrary or implied by custom or context, may be any day of the week. As a rule, a day runs from one midnight to the subsequent midnight (a natural day). In common law, two fractions of a day cannot make one day; a day is an indivisible period of time. However, in most dealings, a day may be any span of 24 consecutive hours, but in some dealings it may be limited to certain hours. 'Days' means consecutive or 'running days' and include Sundays and public holidays (sometimes called 'calendar days'), unless there is a custom to the contrary, or the word is qualified as 'working days', 'business days', or in a similar way. In most business operations, a day means a usual 'business day', i.e. a day when business is normally done and excludes Saturday, Sunday, and legal holidays. Thus, if a negotiable instrument or loan is due for payment on a Sunday or a legal holiday, it is payable on the next business day (except in a few states in the US, where it is payable on the preceding business day). See also **clear day**, **date**, **law day**, **time**.

day-to-day loan(BrE)   See **demand loan**.

day work or **day-work**   In relation to a building contract, work that is to be paid for on the basis of time and materials, plus an agreed percentage for profit and overhead. A method of paying for building or construction work on the basis of the **prime cost** (actual cost to the builder or contractor, less any trade discount) of labor, materials and plant and a percentage addition for the profit of the builder or contractor. Day work is used to assess the cost of work that cannot be readily be measured, such as specialist work it is not possible to quantified at the outset.

daylight factor(Eng)   A measure of the amount of natural light reaching a room, whether as direct sunlight or reflected from the walls of other buildings. In particular, a factor that is measured in order to determine whether a **right of light** has been breached. Generally, a daylight factor is expressed as a percentage relationship between the light at an outside windowsill on a clear day and the light three feet above the floor in the darkest working area of a room. See also **plot ratio**.

days of grace   1. Days allowed as a matter of favour for the performance of some act or the making of a payment. In particular, days allowed for the payment of a debt after the due date for curing a default without penalty, or days allowed for the renewal of a contract. Normally an express number of days, although custom may dictate the permitted period. Also called a 'grace period'.   2. A specified period, after the renewal date, during which the premium to renew an insurance policy must be paid. Generally, insurance remains in effect during this period, unless it can be shown that there is no intention to renew the policy, as when the insured has effected an alternative policy.

daywork   See **day work**.

de cujus(Lat)   'From whom'. A person from whom another claims. An attestor.

de die in diem(Lat)   'From **day** to day'.

de facto(Lat)   'In fact'. A *de facto* corporation is one that has been formed but may not have come into existence in law. A *de facto* contract is one that purports to pass title to another, but is defective in some way. cf. *de jure*. See also **possession**.

de jure(Lat)   'By right'; 'by legal **title**; 'valid in law'. cf. *de facto*.

de minimis(Lat)   'Minute'; 'insignificant'; 'concerning trifles'.

de minimis non curat lex(Lat)   'The law does not concern itself with trifles'. See **substantial performance**.

de minimis PUD(US)   A **planned unit development** in which the common amenities do not have a significant effect on the market value of the unit in the development, in particular when the charges for upkeep of the common amenities are minimal.

de novo(Lat)   'Anew'; 'from the beginning'.

dead-end street(US)   A street with only one entrance. A **cul-de-sac** without an adequate turning circle at the closed end.

dead hand   See **mortmain**.

dead loan   A permanent or **long-term loan**, as distinguished from an interim loan.

dead pledge   1. A **mortgage** of land or goods whereby the property itself is transferred as security for the loan. cf. **living pledge**. See also **common-law mortgage**, **mortgage**.   2.(US)A mortgage that is paid on time as required or pledged.

dead rent   A rent fixed independently of any **royalty** paid for a mining right; a sum that does not vary with the yield from the mine and is payable even when the mine is not worked. Also called a 'certain rent', 'sleeping rent' or simply a 'minimum rent'. cf. **bonus**.

dealer   A person who regularly buys and sells property (whether by wholesale or retail), especially one who so trades on his own account. A person who purchases property at an auction with a view to an early resale at a profit is generally considered a dealer.

dealer disposition(US)   In relation to a potential liability to taxation, "any disposition of real property held by the tax payer for sale to customers in the ordinary course of the taxpayer's trade or business", 26 USC, Internal Revenue Code, § 453. This term excludes most timeshare and installment sales.

dealing   1.(Eng)A transfer of title, or a transaction in respect of registered land, that requires registration at the **Land Registry**. See also **caution, inhibition, registered disposition**. 2.(Aus)An instrument that affects land under the **Torrens title system** and that is capable of being registered or that the Registrar is able to accept for registration. A dealing may include a deed of transfer, a mortgage, a lease or a sub-lease, but not a **Crown grant** or a **caveat**. A dealing is the only means by which a title can pass and the benefit of the registration is obtained by the transferee. A dealing is noted on the certificate of title.

death duty or **death tax**   A generic term for a tax levied or payable on the value of a deceased's estate and levied on his or her death. See also **estate tax**(US), **inheritance tax**.

debenture   An **instrument** that acknowledges a long-term debt. A document, made usually but not necessarily under seal, that acknowledges a debt owed by a corporation or public body to the registered holder or bearer, i.e. written evidence that a loan (normally long-term) has been made. A debenture is not part of the **capital** of a company. A debenture may be a simple recognition of a debt – a 'naked debenture'; or accompanied by a charge on one or more properties of the corporation – commonly called a 'mortgage debenture'. A debenture may be distinguished from a **bond** in that a debenture is an unsecured corporate obligation whereas a bond is secured by a lien or mortgage on corporate property. However, the word 'bond' is often used to cover both bonds and debentures. Generally, a debenture is an unsecured instrument providing no legal title or similar right of ownership, and at the most it confers only an equitable right on the holder. In the event that there is security for the debt, the debenture holder may have a **fixed charge** on certain assets of the corporation. However, the holder more usually has a **floating charge** on all, or an agreed part, of the assets of the corporation.

In English statute law (unless a contrary intention is stated) a 'debenture' is defined to include "debenture stock, bonds and any other securities of a company, whether constituting a **charge** on the assets of the company or not", Companies Act 1985, s. 744; or "debenture stock, loan stock, bonds, certificates of deposit or other instruments creating or acknowledging indebtedness", Financial Services Act 1986, Sch. 1. cf. **mortgage**. See also **drop-lock debenture, redemption**.

debenture trust deed   A **trust deed** that vests specific property in trustees in order to give a holder of a **debenture** greater security or priority over other lenders.

debenture with warrants   A form of **debenture** that provides the debenture holder with a right to a share in the equity of a company or in a property investment held as security. See also **convertible mortgage, equity participation, warrant**.

debit   That which is due or owed by a person or entity. In accounting, debits are amounts that result from an increase in the assets and expenses and are shown on the left side of the **financial statement**. cf. **credit**.

debt Derived from the Latin *debere*, 'to owe'. Something of value, usually money, owed by one person to another, whether contingent or not. An **obligation** by a person or organisation to pay money, or something of monetary value, to another at present or in the future. Generally, an obligation to repay a **loan**, render a service, or supply goods. 'Debt' may refer to the obligation to pay money or the money owed. Strictly speaking, neither a **mortgage** nor a **lien** is a debt, but only a form of security to pay a debt. See also **accord and satisfaction**, **bond**, **chose**, **interest**.

debt capital Finance for an enterprise (e.g. for a business or property investment) that is derived from a source other than the owner or owners of the enterprise. A loan, generally on a long-term basis, to finance capital expenditure; for example, money provided by a **bond**, **debenture**, or a **mortgage loan**. A provider of debt capital does not receive, or accept, a share in the profit (or loss) to be derived from the enterprise to which it lends money; the reward for the provision of debt capital is the receipt of **interest**, plus repayment of the debt. A provider of debt capital has priority over the owner of the enterprise – the provider of **equity capital** – in the event of the liquidation of the enterprise. Debt capital may be secured by a charge or mortgage on the assets of the borrower. Also called 'loan capital' or, when the loan is granted by means of a debenture, 'debenture capital'.

debt-coverage ratio (DCR) The number of times the effective annual **net operating income** from a property exceeds the annual cost of **debt service**. Lenders frequently require a minimum debt-coverage ratio of 1.1:1 to 1.25:1 before considering a loan on an income-producing property. Also called the 'debt-service cover ratio'. See also **default ratio**.

debt-equity ratio or **debt-to-equity ratio** The ratio of total liabilities to stockholders' equity or capital. The ratio of the **debt capital** to the **equity capital** of a corporation or of an investment, i.e. the number of times the amount lent to a corporation, or secured against a property, exceeds the amount of owner's capital including reserves, or exceeds the equity invested in the property. Also called the 'leverage ratio'. The reciprocal is called the 'capital-to-debt ratio'.

debt financing The use of **debt capital** to acquire property; the payment in whole or in part for an investment with borrowed funds. cf. **deficit financing**. See also **financing**.

debt ratio 1. The ratio of debt capital to the asset value of an organisation. This ratio indicates the security in terms of the assets available to the lender of debt capital in the event of a liquidation of the organisation. cf. **debt-equity ratio**. See also **margin**. 2. The ratio of a borrower's debt service expenses (especially mortgage outgoings) and other property related outgoings to his income. See also **debt-coverage ratio**.

debt retirement The repayment of a loan, especially the repayment of a medium-term or long-term loan by a corporation.

debt service 1. The periodic payment required to pay a debt or mortgage loan, including interest and capital repayment. See also **amortisation**, **debt-coverage ratio**. 2. The cost of **debt capital** over a given period of time, usually a year.

debt-service constant See **mortgage constant**.

debt-service cover ratio (DSCR) See **debt-coverage ratio**.

debt-to-equity ratio See **debt-equity ratio**.

debtor One who owes a **debt** to another. cf. **surety**. See also **mortgagor**.

decapitalisation(BrE) or **decapitalization**(AmE) The conversion of a capital sum into an annual income or **annual equivalent** – the reverse of capitalisation. See also **contractor's basis**(BrE).

deceit A fraudulent or deceptive representation made by words or actions, with the intention that another will act on it, so that prejudice or harm may result therefrom. Mere silence cannot amount to deceit. Deceit is a **tort** when the representation is untrue; is known so to be or is made recklessly without regard for the truth; is made with the intention that another will act thereon to his or her detriment; and when that party did act thereon and suffered damage or injury as a result. cf. **misrepresentation**. See also **bad faith, fraud, misdescription**.

decentralisation(BrE) or **decentralization**(AmE) Dispersal from a center. A process by which population, commerce or industry is redistributed from an urban center, usually from a congested area, to the surrounding or suburban area. Decentralisation is an active process (unlike **overspill**) which is encouraged by central or local government with the object of: (a) redistributing employment opportunities; (b) reducing population and economic pressures in an existing area, especially when this is aimed at assisting the redevelopment of that area; and (c) improving the general use of land and reducing the density of development. The term 'decentralisation' is also used to describe a movement from an established business center, especially when made in order to reduce property occupation costs. Decentralization may be considered as a means of countering economic or market forces in order to achieve a political objective, for example decentralizing a particular business activity in order to provide employment and thereby retain the population in another area. See also **new town**.

declarant(US) The party that is responsible for the 'declaration' of a condominium. See also **condominium declaration**.

declaration of condominium(US) See **condominium declaration**.

declaration of covenants and restrictions(US) A document that sets out the restrictions and rights of the lot owners on a tract of land that has been subdivided for sale to a number of separate purchasers under a **scheme of development**. The declaration acts as a form of local zoning regulation that is intended to bind all future landowners for their mutual benefit. The declaration sets out, in particular, such matters as all **covenants**, **conditions and restrictions** that affect the entire development and will be binding on the individual lot purchasers and their successors. The declaration also describes the entire project and the individual lots or units; the common elements or areas; the powers of the **homeowners' association**; and the rights and obligations of the unit owners. Such a declaration is normally prepared for any **planned unit development** by the subdivider and must be recorded before any sales of individual units can take place. The declaration then forms part of any deed of conveyance and runs with the land to bind all future buyers. In some states, the declaration must be drawn up in accordance with the statutes regulating such developments. Due to the extensive nature of such a declaration, it may also be called a 'declaration of restrictions, easements, liens and covenants'. A similar declaration is normally required for any condominium development where it is usually referred to as the **condominium declaration**. See also **master deed**.

declaration of homestead(US) A declaration by the owner of a property by which he avails himself of the statutory right to declare his property the subject of a **homestead** exemption from creditors. Such a right must be filed, usually with the county recorder, to have legal effect. Some states require an annual filing to protect the homestead exemption.

declaration of no defenses(US) See **estoppel certificate**.

declaration of restrictions(US)   See **declaration of covenants and restrictions**(US).

declaration of title(US)   A judicial procedure by which a person obtains a court declaration as to the validity of a **title** to land.

declaration of trust   A statement or other means by which a person acknowledges or declares that property is held in **trust**. In particular, a declaration made when the holder of property confirms himself to be the trustee of property that is to be held for the use or benefit of another. Equity will treat such a declaration as constituting a transfer of property, even though there is no transfer of the subject matter. See also **express trust**, **implied trust**, **vesting declaration**(Eng), **trust instrument**(Eng), **writing**.

declining-balance depreciation   A method of calculating **depreciation** by which a fixed percentage of the total outstanding balance of the cost of a property is deducted, or written-off, each year. A form of **accelerated depreciation** that provides for the absolute amount of depreciation to be higher in the early years and decline gradually at a later stage. For example, if a cost of 100 is depreciated at an annual rate of 10%, then the outstanding balance would reduce to 90 at the end of year 1; 81 at the end of year 2; 72.9 at the end of year 3; and so on until the cost is reduced to a scrap or residual value, or to nil. Also called 'diminishing-balance depreciation' or 'reducing-balance depreciation'.

decorative repair   See **tenantable repair**, **relief**.

decoy duck(US)   See **puffer**.

decree of foreclosure   See **foreclosure**, **strict foreclosure**.

decree of specific performance   See **specific performance**.

decrement   The process of reducing in value. A decline in property values due to economic or social factors in the area. cf. **increment**. See also **blight**.

dedication   The grant or donation (expressly or tacitly) by a private landowner of a public right of user; such as a grant, or giving over of land or an interest in land, for a public **right of way**, **highway**, **green**, **park** or a similar public use. The dedication may be made in the form of an easement retaining title to the underlying land. Alternatively, the owner may 'dedicate' title to the land, usually as a fee interest. Dedication may arise by an express grant, by agreement, by appropriation, or it may arise by implication. Dedication may also arise by **estoppel** so that, if a person evinces an intention that his land is to be used for a public purpose, he may be estopped from denying that he had dedicated the land for that purpose. However, to constitute a dedication the owner must evidence a clear intention that the land is to be used by the public at large and not just a group of individuals or a section of the public. Dedication may also arise following a statutory taking of the right for which compensation would be payable as in any taking of land. See also **abandonment**, **cession deed**(US), **compulsory purchase**(Eng), **eminent domain**, **foreshore**.

deducing title(Eng)   The process by which a vendor of an interest in land establishes the validity of his **title** to that interest for the benefit of a prospective purchaser. See also **abstract of title**, **good title**.

deductible   See **excess**.

deed   A written or printed document, **signed**, **sealed and delivered**, that conveys or confirms an interest in real property; passes some right or title (not being a **will** or codicil); or creates or affirms a claim or obligation, or an agreement between two or more parties. Historically a deed had to be under **seal**, although sealing is no longer essential for an instrument to be considered a deed.

A deed transfers a right to property at the moment of **delivery**. In that respect it differs from a will, which is essentially an instrument that is not to take effect until after the death of the testator. The instrument that creates a **lease** may be referred to as a deed, especially when such a lease must be made by the formality of a deed; but an instrument that transfers a lease is generally called an **assignment** or 'deed of assignment'.

In the US, a deed for the transfer of an estate or interest in land may be described according to the form of title granted by the vendor, such as a **warranty deed, grant deed, bargain and sale deed, quitclaim deed**, or a **deed of gift**. A mortgage may be considered a deed, especially in a jurisdiction that recognizes the 'title theory' by which a mortgage is considered to grant title to land to the mortgagee as security for a loan, with a reconveyance when the debt is satisfied. In other jurisdictions, a mortgage may be considered as merely a lien, without a transfer of title to the mortgagee. Alternatively a mortgage may be created by a **deed of trust**, which transfers the property to a third party as security for the loan.

In English statute law, any deed may be described as "a deed simply or as a **conveyance**, deed of exchange, **vesting deed**, **trust instrument**, **settlement**, **mortgage**, charge, transfer of mortgage, appointment, lease or otherwise according to the nature of the transaction intended to be effected", LPA 1925, s. 57. On or after July 31, 1990 a deed can be on any permanent substances and a seal is no longer essential for the transfer of real property by an individual (LP(MP)A 1989, s. 1). However, "an instrument shall not be a deed unless – (a) it makes clear on its face that it is intended to be a deed by the person making it or, as the case may be, by the parties to it (whether by describing itself as a deed or expressing itself to be executed or signed as a deed or otherwise); and (b) it is validly executed as a deed by that person or, as the case may be, one or more of those parties", LP(MP)A 1989, s. 1(2). "An instrument is validly executed as a deed by an individual if, and only if – (a) it is signed – (i) by him in the presence of a witness who attests the signature; or (ii) at his direction and in his presence and the presence of two witnesses who each attest the signature; and (b) it is delivered as a deed by him or a person authorised to do so on his behalf", LP(MP)A 1989, s. 1(3)). Thus, a deed may be referred to as a 'formal instrument': the form in modern English law being a **signature**, **attestation**, and **delivery**. In English law, a deed is required in the following real property transactions: (i) A conveyance of land, or any interest in land, that is intended to convey or create a **legal estate**, except for: (a) an assent by a personal representative; (b) a disclaimer by a trustee in bankruptcy; (c) the grant of a lease that is not intended to be a **legal lease** (basically a lease that does not exceed three years); (d) a vesting order of the court; and (e) a receipt that need not be made under seal; and a surrender or conveyance which takes effect by operation of law (LPA 1925, ss. 52, 54(2)). (ii) The grant or assignment of any lease of an **incorporeal hereditament**. (iii) A contract made without **consideration**. (iv) An express release of a right to land (including the express **surrender** of most leases: LPA 1925, s. 52) or of a right of action. (v) In most cases, for the appointment of new trustees under the Trustee Act 1925. (vi) The grant of a lease of **settled land** for a term exceeding three years (SLA 1925, s. 42). (vii) To effect a **transfer** of title to registered land, in the same way as a conveyance of unregistered land. (viii) The grant of a **power of attorney** when an agent is to be authorised to execute a deed on behalf of his principal. (ix) In most cases, a conveyance of land, lease, assignment or surrender of a lease made by a company. cf. **contract for deed**[US]. See also **acknowledgment, cession deed**[US]**, charge by way of a legal mortgage**[Eng]**, contract for deed, date, deed poll, escrow, indenture, mortgage deed, operative part, specialty contract, release deed, tax deed**[US]**, witness**.

Lefcoe, George. *Real Estate Transactions.* 4th ed. Newark, NJ: LexisNexis, 2003.

Friedman, Milton R. *Contracts & Conveyances of Real Property.* 2 vols. 5th ed. New York: Practicing Law Institute, ©1991 with annual supplements.

deed absolute(US)   A **deed** that transfers an absolute title to land, as distinguished from a **defeasible deed** which transfers title to a mortgagee subject to a condition that title will be transferred back to the mortgagor when the debt is repaid in full.

deed-in-lieu of foreclosure(US)   A **deed** by which a borrower, who is seriously in default, agrees to transfer a mortgaged property to the lender instead of going through the process of **foreclosure**.

deed in trust(US)   A **deed** used to transfer legal title to land to be held in trust, generally with full power over the land being vested in the trustee. See also **land trust**.

deed of arrangement(Eng)   A formal agreement that sets out in writing the arrangements for the control of the property of a debtor for the benefit of his creditors made when no bankruptcy order has been made, but the debtor is insolvent. Although such an agreement must be in writing, it not need necessarily be made in the form of a **deed** for it to be called a 'deed of arrangement'. See also **Land Charges Register**.

deed of assignment   1. A **deed** that effects an **assignment** of a right or interest. In particular, a deed that effects the assignment of a lease. A deed by which an insolvent debtor undertakes to transfer his assets to his creditors in settlement of their claims against him.   2. A **deed** that is used to appoint an assignee, usually in the form of a trust company, to take charge of the affairs of an insolvent business; the deed usually states the rights and duties of the assignee.

deed of bargain and sale(US)   See **bargain and sale deed**.

deed of conveyance   See **conveyance**.

deed of confirmation   A deed by which something that is defective, imperfect or void is ratified or rendered valid. Also called a 'correction deed'. See also **deed of reformation**.

deed of enlargement   See **enlargement**.

deed of gift   A **deed** executed and delivered without **consideration**, i.e. a deed that conveys property as a **gift**. A gift of real property is generally unenforceable at law unless made by deed. See also **conveyance, unenforceable contract, voluntary conveyance**.

deed of grant   A formal written instrument that is signed and delivered and expresses the intention of the grantor to pass an interest in land to the grantee. A **deed** that is used to effect a **grant** of real property. See also **conveyance, grant deed**.

deed of lease(US)   See **deed**.

deed of partition   A deed executed for the purpose of partitioning a right to property, i.e. a deed that provides for two or more parties to take separate and distinct interests in a property. See also **partition**.

deed of priorities   1. A deed executed by a lender, who has a **floating charge** over the assets of a corporation, in which it is agreed that the corporation may grant a fixed charge over certain assets to another lender and that the first lender will defer his priority in respect of those assets. 2. A deed that affirms a **subordination**.

deed of quitclaim(US)   See **quitclaim deed**.

deed of reconveyance(US)   See **release deed**.

deed of rectification(Eng) or **deed of reformation**(US)   A **deed** that is used to rectify or correct a previous agreement or deed; a deed that is used to correct an instrument made in writing in order to express the true intention of the parties, as when a mistake or fraud has occurred. A deed of rectification, in effect, creates a new agreement. In the US, also called a 'reformation deed', 'correction deed', 'deed of confirmation' or a 'confirmatory deed'. See also **rectification, reformation**(US).

deed of reformation(US)   See **deed of rectification**(Eng)/**deed of reformation**(US).

deed of release(US)   See **release deed**.

deed of restriction(US)   See **restrictive covenant**.

deed of satisfaction(US)   See **release deed**.

deed of surrender   See **surrender**.

deed of title   A **deed** that represents a claim, or forms part of a claim, to a **title** to land. The term 'deed' is frequently used alone to refer to a document that evidences, or is used to transfer, title to land. In English law, such a document is generally called a **title deed**. See also **abstract of title**.

deed of transfer   See **transfer deed**.

deed of trust(US)   **1.** A **deed** that grants title to property to a third party (a trustee) to be held in **trust** until a particular obligation has been performed. In particular, the transfer of title to a property owned by a borrower to a trustee, on condition that it is held until a loan has been repaid in full. Although similar in purpose to a **regular mortgage**, a deed of trust differs in form by transferring power over the secured property to a disinterested third party, rather than directly to the lender or mortgagee. In practice the powers of the trustee are similar to those of a mortgagee who has a **power of sale**. In the event of default by the mortgagor, the trustee is required to exercise its power of sale; but if and when the debt is paid in full the trustee is obliged to transfer the property unencumbered to the borrower by means of a 'release deed' or 'deed of reconveyance'. Also, under a deed of trust there is no statutory right of redemption available to the mortgagor after the

power of sale has been exercised and generally no right to a **deficiency judgment** in favor of the mortgagee. Sometimes called a 'trust deed mortgage'. The terms 'deed of trust' and 'trust deed' are generally used interchangeably, although 'deed of trust' is a more generic term for any deed that creates a trust or transfers property to a third party as trustee. See also **land trust, mortgage, power of sale, trust deed**.   **2.**(Eng) See **trust instrument**.

deed poll   **1.** A **deed** made by one party only. A term derived from a practice of 'polling', or cutting a deed evenly at the top (rather than indenting or cutting with serration), to signify that there is only one party to the deed. A **power of attorney** is generally granted by means of a deed poll. cf. **indenture**.   **2.**(Eng)A form of conveyance used by an authority possessing compulsory purchase powers to vest land in itself when an owner is unable or unwilling to convey title to a property that has been included in a compulsory purchase order. See also **general vesting declaration**.

deed restriction(US)   A restriction or enjoyment of land that is contained in a deed. See also **restrictive covenant**.

deep discount bond   **1.** A bond that is issued at a price that is substantially below its face value, usually at a discount of 25% or more.   **2.** A zero-interest bond that is sold at a discount and provides that the entire interest is payable at maturity.

deemed disposal(Eng)   A disposal of property that is assumed to take place when the owner carries out a certain activity, or when a given event occurs such as the death of the owner. A term that is used especially to refer to a stage at which a tax liability arises.

deemed planning permission(Eng)   See **development**.

default   A failure to perform a legal obligation, e.g. a failure to perform a **condition** of a contract, or a failure to pay a sum of money when it falls due. The default of a mortgagor (or tenant) to make payment when due may give a mortgagee (or a landlord) a right to possession of the property held as security (or of the leased property). See also **breach of contract, cross-default clause, forfeiture, foreclosure, right of re-entry**.

Parson, Andrew. *Tenant Default under Commercial Leases.* 3rd ed. Welwyn Garden City: EMIS Publishing, 2000.

default clause   A clause in a contract that permits one of the parties to terminate the contract if a particular condition is not complied with, such as a provision in a building contract that permits termination in the event of insolvency of the contractor. Sometimes called a 'forfeiture clause'. See also **breach of contract, cross-default clause**.

default point   See **break-even point**.

default ratio(US)   The ratio of the **effective gross income** to be derived from a property to the total annual cost of holding that property, including debt service, operating expenses and direct real estate taxes. A ratio that indicates the point at which there is a risk of default in the payment of a mortgage secured on the property.

defeasance   1. The rendering of a right null and void. Defeasance makes a previous deed, action or condition void. In particular, defeasance of an **estate** is the termination of that estate upon the occurrence of a condition stipulated when the estate was granted.   2. An **instrument** that can have the effect of defeating the terms or provisions of another deed. A provision in a contract that, if fulfilled, may weaken or defeat another agreement, or bring an estate in land to an end. If a defeasance is contained in the principal deed it is in effect a **condition**. A grant of property 'subject to partial defeasance' means that the number of recipients may increase or decrease, for example a grant "to A for life and then to B's children", where B has children but may have more (or less) before A's death.   See also **defeasance clause**.   3. The retirement of a debt in substance, but not in practice, as with the

substitution of one form of security for another.

defeasance clause(US)   A clause in a mortgage deed which provides that the mortgagee's right to the mortgaged property will come to an end, or be terminated, if and when the mortgage debt is repaid in full, i.e. a provision in a 'title theory' state which states the terms and conditions upon which the **mortgage** ceases to be security for the debt and the title is to be transferred back to the mortgagor. See also **defeasance, defeasible interest, equity of redemption, partial release, shifting clause**.

defeasible   Subject to **defeasance**. Capable of being made void or undone. See also **defeasible fee simple**.

defeasible conveyance or **defeasible deed**(US)   A conveyance or deed that creates a **defeasance**, i.e. transfers title to property subject to a condition that, if it occurs, transfers the property back to the grantor or to a third party. In some jurisdictions, a **mortgage** may be considered a 'defeasible conveyance' because it transfers title to the mortgagee on the basis that the title will be reconveyed when the secured debt is repaid. See also **absolute conveyance, mortgage deed**.

defeasible fee simple(US)   An estate in land that is equivalent to a **fee simple** but may be brought to an end on the happening of an event that is specified in the document that created the estate, but (unlike death) is not certain to occur. Thus, a defeasible fee simple may last forever, but it is not a **fee simple absolute**, nor is it a **life estate**. 'Defeasible fee simple' is used sometimes to refer to a **fee simple determinable**, although the former is a generic term that covers any fee simple that may be cut down (including a **fee simple conditional** and a fee simple subject to an **executory limitation**). See also **fee simple defeasible**.

defeasible interest   An interest in land that may be defeated or come to an end by the happening of a future event or the operation of a **condition subsequent**, e.g. an owner's interest that may be defeated by the exercise of an option to purchase. A mortgage is said to be defeasible because of the existence of the mortgagor's **equity of redemption**. cf. **indefeasible interest**. See also **defeasance**.

defeasible title(US)   A title that can be defeated or rendered void by the claim of another; but one that is not already void. cf. **indefeasible title**.

defect   1. A fault or failure of something. An imperfection or deficiency. See also **defect of title, negligence**. 2. An absence of something required for completeness. A failure to provide that which is required. A fault or deficiency in design, material or construction that leaves a building or product incapable of being used for its intended purpose, or that does not comply with the standard that was agreed upon. In particular, an inadequate standard of workmanship as required under a building or construction contract. See also **defects list, inherent defect, latent defect, patent defect**.

defect of record(US)   Any encumbrance or defect against a title that is a matter of public record, especially one that prevents a landowner from providing **clear title**.

defect of title   A **title** that does not provide what a purchaser requires or expects because of, for example, an incomplete document. For example, e.g. a deed that has not been properly signed or that does not cover all the property to be conveyed; a damaged or lost document; a document that has been signed by a party that does not have the proper authority or capacity; or a prescriptive right that has not been exercised for the requisite length of time. In English law, the deliberate concealment of any instrument, or encumbrance, or the falsification of any document relevant to the title, is a criminal offence (LPA 1925, s. 183).

In common law, a vendor of property is under an obligation to point out to a purchaser any **latent defect** of title, i.e. a defect that cannot readily be ascertained by reasonable enquiry, but it has been said that the vendor cannot be held responsible for "the carelessness of the purchaser who does not care to inquire", *Oldfield (or Bowles) v Round* (1800) 5 Ves Jun 509, 31 Eng Rep 707. "Since a vendor's title to land is exclusively within his own knowledge, he is bound to disclose all latent defects in his title to an intending purchaser. ... The vendor's disclosure should be frank and full, and it is not sufficient for him to make ambiguous or misleading statements. If he wishes to prevent a purchaser from objecting to a defect he must do so in plain terms, stating clearly the exact nature of the defect to which the purchaser is not to make objection", *Halsbury's Laws of England*, Sale of Land (4th ed. Reissue), para. 55, p. 52. Thus, if a vendor of land is unable to convey a fixture (i.e. an item that is so annexed to the land that it has become a part thereof and any purchaser would expect it to be included in the sale), for example because another party has a lien on it, he is obliged to notify the purchaser. If he does not make a material disclosure, and the property that can be conveyed is materially different from that which he contracted to convey, the vendor is unlikely to be able to obtain a decree of **specific performance** to enforce completion of the transaction. See also **constructive notice, contingency insurance, defective title, good title, title insurance**.

defective title(US)   A title that is not a **marketable title**. A defective title may be considered as no title because it does not pass that which has been bargained for. cf. **good title**.

defective premises   See **duty of care, negligence, implied covenant, repair**.

defects liability period   A period, stipulated in a building contract, during which a builder is obliged to make good any defect of workmanship or materials in order to comply with the terms and conditions of the contract. Usually this period is six months from **practical completion** of the building work (or twelve months for mechanical and electrical work) and generally the employer keeps part of the **retention sum** (commonly half of the amount that had been retained during the contract period) to ensure that the outstanding work is completed satisfactorily. However, this is not the entire period during which the contractor can be liable for building defects; he may be liable for negligent workmanship or a **latent defect** until such an obligation is barred by statute. See also **certificate of completion**(US), **certificate of practical completion**(BrE), **negligence**.

defects list   A list of matters that have not been completed in accordance with the terms of a building contract, especially defects of workmanship and materials. Usually the architect prepares a defects list when the building contractor requests the architect or contract's administrator to certify **practical completion**. The owner may then accept that the contract has been 'substantially performed', subject to completion of the items on the defects list. Sometimes called a 'snagging list' or, in the US, a 'snag list' or **punch list**. See also **substantial performance**.

defeneration   The lending of money on **usury**.

defer   To delay in time; to put off. To delay or postpone to a future date, but not with the intention of giving up or abandoning. See also **deferred value**, **present value**.

deferred annuity   An annuity or annual payment that does not come into effect or start until a future time or date, e.g. a pension right arising at a person's set age. An annual income that will be paid in the future, but is provided for by the payment of a present capital sum.

deferred charge or **deferred expense**   An expense incurred, or payment made, for a benefit that will be received in a later accounting period. An item of expenditure incurred in one accounting period, but which is to be written off over a longer period of time, e.g. company formation costs that may be spread over the initial years of a company's profit and loss account. See also **prepaid expense**.

deferred commission   A **commission** that has been earned but not yet received. In the US, sometimes called a 'residual commission'.

deferred income   1. The **present value** of an anticipated future income.   2. A sum of money the payment of which has been postponed to a time after the due date. See also **deferred annuity**. 3.(AmE)Income received in advance of its due date. Income that has been received but not earned. Deferred income is shown in a company's balance sheet as a liability and is entered as an asset only when it is earned or becomes due. See also **rent in advance/rent in arrears**.

deferred interest   1. Interest the payment of which has been postponed, as with a bond issued at a discount whereby the interest is payable at maturity. See also **accrued interest, discount points**.   2. An interest in land that comes into effect only in the future, either on the termination of a prior estate or upon the occurrence of a contingent or conditional event. See also **executory interest, future interest**.

deferred-interest mortgage (DIM)(US)   A mortgage loan that provides for a lower interest rate to be payable in the early years, with the difference being paid by a third party (such as a government agency or a seller) or added to the principal balance owed by the borrower. See also **adjustable-rate mortgage, alternative mortgage loan, buy-down**.

deferred liability   A liability that has been deferred beyond a specific date. A long-term liability, in particular one that does not have to be met in a current accounting period or financial year.

deferred maintenance(US)   **Maintenance** or **repair** of a property that is due but has not yet been incurred, especially physical deterioration that arises primarily from a neglect of good management. Work that has been left to be carried out as part of a scheme of **rehabilitation** or renovation may also be referred to as 'deferred maintenance'. See also **curable depreciation**.

deferred-payment method(US)   A method of accounting by which taxable income is reported when it is received, especially in the case of an **installment sale** (26 USC, Internal Revenue Code, § 453). Also called the 'cost-recovery method' or the 'return-of-capital method'.

deferred-payment mortgage (DPM)   A mortgage loan that provides for lower repayments of capital in its earlier years, generally to assist first-time house buyers. A form of **variable-payment mortgage**. In Britain, also called a 'low-start mortgage', especially when the mortgage is granted to a first-time homebuyer.

deferred-payment sale(US)   See **installment sale**.

deferred value   A value that has been reduced to take account of the passage of time until it can be realised. The **present value** of a property.

deferred yield   An increase in an owner's **equity** that will not be realised until a property is sold, especially the return from property produced by loan repayments and capital appreciation. See also **equity build-up**, **redemption yield**.

deficiency   A lack of something; an insufficiency. In connection with a mortgage, a deficiency may be used, in the event of a default, to refer to any part of the debt that is not repaid following the sale of the mortgaged property. A deficiency may be a personal liability of the former mortgagor. See also **deficiency judgment**, **recourse**.

deficiency decree or **deficiency judgment**(US)   The imposition of a personal liability on the mortgagor when, following a **foreclosure sale**, the proceeds of sale are insufficient to meet the full amount of the underlying debt. A deficiency judgment may be obtained in certain circumstances when, in the event of default, the mortgaged property is sold and the proceeds are less than the outstanding mortgage debt (including delinquency interest and foreclosure costs). Many states have 'anti-deficiency legislation' that sets out strict procedures to be followed before a deficiency judgment can be levied and that limit the mortgagee's right to levy a deficiency judgment in certain cases, such as a private home. In addition, several states have a 'one action' or 'security first' rule, which provides that, in the event of default, the mortgagee may bring only one claim against the mortgagor, and in that claim he must seek foreclosure or a judicial sale; only if that provides insufficient funds can he seek recourse to the personal obligation of the mortgagor. See also **non-recourse mortgage**.

deficit financing   1. Finance obtained to pay for a deficit, i.e. the excess of current liabilities over current assets. In particular, the issuing of government securities to provide funds to cover the budgeted excess of current expenditure over revenue.   2. A loan obtained to finance an investment in property when the **cash flow** is insufficient to cover the cost of the existing **debt service**, i.e. a loan required to finance a negative cash flow, 'negative gearing', or 'to feed an alligator'. A high risk form of loan that is generally granted only when there is a good prospect of increases in cash flow (from early rent increases or improved property management) or to avoid liquidation of the company owning the property. The provision of such finance is sometimes called 'pump priming'.

deflating a mortgage(AmE)   Reducing the principal balance or amortization rate on a mortgage loan and increasing the interest payable by the same amount in order to enable the borrower to obtain a greater tax deduction.

deforcement   1. The wrongful retention of possession of land to which another is entitled.

See also **tenancy at sufferance**. 2. The ejecting of someone from possession of property by force. See also **disseisin**.

delay See **laches**.

delay rental[US] A rental payment that may be made under an **oil and gas lease** for the privilege of delaying the start of drilling or other operations during the primary term of the lease. Once drilling work has commenced, a similar 'shut-in royalty' may be made to permit a delay in exploration and production. Failure to make either of these payments usually results in automatic termination of the lease. Sometimes called 'carrying rental'. cf. **bonus**, **royalty**.

delayed completion See **completion, time is of the essence**.

delegatus non potest delegare[Lat] 'A delegate cannot himself delegate'; a person to whom power has been delegated cannot delegate further. See **subagent**.

delict A civil wrong or misdemeanour that causes injury to another but does not arise from a breach of covenant or a strict liability. A term used in Roman law, Scots law and civil law jurisdictions (including Louisiana). Delict is analogous to **tort** and covers matters of negligence (including occupiers and vicarious liability) and nuisance, as well as trespass, fraud, defamation, passing off, and breach of confidence. However, it also covers matters that in the common law would be classified as a criminal offence, such as certain forms of theft and robbery.

McManus, Francis, et al. *Delict: A Comprehensive Guide to the Law*. Chichester, Sussex & New York: Wiley, 1998. Walker, David M. *The Law of Delict in Scotland*. 2nd ed. London: Sweet & Maxwell, 1981.

delinquent payment A sum of money that is unpaid when due either under the terms of a contract (e.g. rent, mortgage interest, payment under a promissory note), or by law (e.g. a tax). A payment that has fallen into arrears. See also **rent in advance/rent in arrears**.

delinquency ratio The ratio of loans that are past due to the total number of loans held by a bank or institution. In particular, the same ratio when a number of mortgage loans have been pooled or 'securitized' and sold to one or more lenders in a secondary market.

delivery 1. The act of placing something in the legal or constructive **possession**, or control, of another. The actual surrender and handing over of property from one party to another. A legal act whereby control or possession of property is transferred voluntarily to another party in such a way that there is no possibility or intention that it will be recalled. Delivery may be 'actual' when physical possession is handed over to the other party or to his authorised agent; or it may be 'constructive' when the law deems that possession of something has been transferred, as when a document evidences that possession has been transferred without right of recall. Constructive delivery requires a clear demonstration on the part of the grantor, by his words or deeds, that he has given up control or ownership of the property in favour of the grantee. Delivery may also be described as 'symbolic' when something that represents a right to possession is transferred, such as documents of title or keys to a property. Delivery may arise from an act of 'attornment', as when a third party acknowledges that he holds goods on behalf of a new owner or possessor. See also **escrow**. 2. The final stage in the formalisation of a **deed** when the document is handed over and accepted by the other party, thus delivery establishes the **date** on which the deed becomes valid. Delivery is an essential element to complete a **conveyance** of real property; "after a deed is written and sealed, if it be not delivered, all the rest is to no purpose", *Termes de la Ley* (*Xenos v Wickham* (1866) LR 2 HL 296, 312 (HL); 3 Am.L.Prop. § 801). Delivery may be effected in words or by conduct and, although not essential, should be acknowledged by the recipient. Delivery does not have to take the form of a 'handing over' of the deed, provided there are acts, words, or circumstances which clearly indicate that the grantor intends to be bound thereby. Delivery may be (a) 'conditional', so that it does not take effect unless or until a specified event occurs or a condition subsequent has been complied with; or (b) 'unconditional', taking effect without reservation or delay, or at least without possibility of recall. Under a conditional delivery the grantor may reserve the right to revoke the deed, in which case there is no delivery until the condition has occurred or been complied with. Also a deed may be delivered 'in **escrow**' when it is transferred to a third party and is held until a specified condition is performed or a stipulated event occurs. See also **acquisition, completion, livery of seisin, signed sealed and delivered, surrender.**

delivery as an escrow   See **escrow.**

delivery in escrow   See **escrow.**

demand for rent   See **rent.**

demand loan   A loan repayable by the borrower upon the demand of the lender. A loan that has no fixed maturity date and which may be terminated by either party at will. Also referred to as a 'call loan' or sometimes in Britain a 'day-to-day loan'. See also **acceleration clause.**

demand note   A debt instrument, such as a **bill of exchange** or **promissory note**, that allows the lender to call for the payment of the balance due at any time without prior notice, i.e. a note that provides for payment 'on demand'.

demesne land(Eng)   **1.** See **manor. 2.** "Land belonging to Her Majesty in right of the Crown which is not held for an estate in fee simple absolute in possession", LRA 2002, s. 132(1).

deminimis PUD(US)   See **de minimis PUD.**

demise   Any **transfer** or **conveyance**, especially a transfer of land in fee simple, fee tail, or for a term of years, or for life. Demise is generally used to refer to the grant of a **lease**; 'demise' being used synonymously with 'lease'. A lease may be considered as a 'conveyance by demise' (or, as a verb, 'to demise' is a more legalistic term for 'to lease' or 'to let'). The use of the words 'demise' or 'grant and demise' in a lease imply a covenant for **quiet enjoyment** during the term of the grant, as well as a **covenant for title** (i.e. the lessor has the power to grant a lease, even if not the power to grant the lease he purports to grant); unless there is an express stipulation limiting the implication. 'Demise' may also be used to refer to a transfer upon death, whether under a will or by bequest or descent. See also **demised premises, grant, implied covenant, let.**

demised premises   Land that is the subject of a **demise**; any real property that is transferred by means of a conveyance. The term 'demise' is used more usually to refer to the subject matter of a lease, i.e. the exact extent of the property that is leased to a tenant. Also called the 'leased premises'. See also *falsa demonstratio*, **plan, premises.**

demising partition or **demising wall**   A wall or partition that divides the area between two leased properties. See also **demise, party wall.**

demolition   The act of completely pulling down, tearing down, or destroying (as a building or structure). A reduction to ruins or to a mass. The scattering of all the component parts.

In English planning law, strictly speaking the demolition of a building is a 'building operation' and therefore amounts to **development** for which planning permission is required (Town and Country Planning Act 1990, s. 55(1)(a)). The partial demolition of a building may be development if it amounts to a structural alteration and therefore constitutes **building operations**, or it amounts to **engineering operations** (Town and Country Planning (Demolition—Description of Building) Direction 1995). See also **conservation** area(Eng), **destruction**, **listed building**(Eng), **permitted development**(Eng).

demolition clause See **break clause**.

demolition order 1.(Eng)An order by which a local housing authority requires the demolition of a dwelling-house, or house in multiple occupation (but not a flat) that is considered to be unfit for human habitation when the authority considers that the demolition is the most satisfactory course of action (Housing Act 1985, ss. 265, 267-275). The owner of the property that is required to demolish a property in conformity with a demolition order retains the cleared site and may be entitled to compensation for the diminution in the value of his interest in the property arising as a result of the order (HA 1985, s. 584A). See also **clearance area**, **closing order**. 2.(Aus)An order issued by a local council requiring the demolition of a building that is considered unsafe or a danger to the public; or when a building has been erected without the requisite approvals.

denial of title See **quiet enjoyment**, **tenancy by estoppel**.

density The mass of buildings or people per given area of land. A ratio that expresses the relationship between a number of units – houses, rooms, persons, etc. – and the space occupied by those units, e.g. houses per acre (or hectare), employees per square foot (or square meter). See also **floor area ratio**(US), **floor space index**(BrE), **land-use planning**, **plot ratio**(BrE), **population density**, **residential density**, **site coverage**.

density bonus(US) See **incentive zoning**.

density transfer(US) See **cluster zoning**, **transferable development right**.

density zoning(US) A form of residential zoning that is designed to limit the density of new development in a particular area and to encourage the maintenance of a high level of green or open space. Generally, the zoning regulations specify the percentage of land that can be used for open space and the percentage that may be used for dwelling units. See also **cluster development**, **exclusionary zoning**, **zoning ordinance**.

Fader, Steven. *Density by Design: New Directions in Residential Development*. 2nd ed. Washington, DC: Urban Land Institute, 2000.

department lease(US) See **leased department**.

Department of Housing and Urban Development (HUD)(US) A cabinet department of the federal government established under the provisions of the Housing and Urban Development Act of 1965 (42 USC § 3531-3537) with responsibility for urban affairs and for federal housing programs. In particular, HUD administers the **Government National Mortgage Association** (GNMA or 'Ginnie Mae') and other **Federal Housing Administration** (FHA) insurance policies, as well as being responsible for programs of urban renewal, public housing, the registration of subdivisions with the Office of Interstate Land Sales, and for the provision of equal housing opportunities for every individual. (**www.hud.org**).

department store A large retail store selling a broad range of merchandise under one roof such that it is not identified with any one line of goods; although, for the purpose of promotion, advertising, control and accounting, it is divided into separate departments. A department store aims to provide a wide range of consumer goods, including apparel, shoes, jewellery, cosmetics, stationery, gifts, furniture, appliances, electrical goods, etc., while maintaining a single system of service, control and management. A store that provides a more limited range of merchandise, but more than a **variety store**, may be called a 'junior department store'.

departmentalized specialty store(US) A retail store that specializes in one basic line of goods, e.g. clothing or furniture, and has been subdivided into different departments such as men's and women's apparel, or kitchen and bedroom furniture, and generally has a separate area for promotion and marketing.

departure provision(US) A provision of the **Uniform Standards of Professional Appraisal Practice** that permits the appraiser to make limited departures for sections of the Standard, provided the appraiser to set out any ways in which his appraisal falls short of a complete report. For example, the appraiser should set out that he is carrying out a more limited form of report given the use to which it is to be put. The appraisal clearly state it calls for less than would be required form a complete appraisal; it must remain credible and not mislead or confuse; and be appropriate to the purpose for which the client will use it. The Departure Rule does apply to the preamble to the report; the ethics and competency provisions; and the definitions that are set out in the Uniform Standards (Uniform Standards of Professional Appraisal Practice, Departure Provision, which contains a detailed explanation of these requirements). See also **limited appraisal**, **self-contained appraisal report**.

dependent covenant A promise or **covenant** that is intended to be performed or complied with concurrently with another promise or covenant. A covenant that is dependent upon the fulfilment of a condition or contingency. A 'dependent covenant' in a contract for the sale of land is one that depends upon the prior performance of an independent act or the compliance with a prior condition. See also **condition precedent**, **conditional contract**, **subject to**.

depending on See **subject to**.

depleting asset See **wasting asset**.

deposit 1. Something given for safe keeping, as security, or as an act of good faith. A sum of money, generally deemed to be a part payment of the purchase price, usually lodged with the vendor's agent, broker or lawyer, before or at the time of the signing of a contract for sale, to show the purchaser's earnest intentions. In the case of a contract for the sale of land, a deposit may be made as a 'pre-contract' payment, popularly called **earnest money**, or it may be paid as a **condition** of a contract. In either case the deposit is intended to demonstrate that the purchaser means business.

In common law, and in some jurisdictions in the US, if the purchaser fails to complete a contract for the sale of land, without good reason, then he forfeits any deposit paid as security for the performance of the contract (*Howe v Smith* (1844) 27 Ch D 89), unless the deposit amount is excessive, i.e. it can be considered as a **penalty** (*Workers Trust & Merchant Bank Ltd v Dojap Investments Ltd* [1993] AC 573, [1993] 2 All ER 370 (PC)—where a deposit of 25% was considered an unreasonable amount for the particular contract. However, whether a party has a right to recover a payment made under the provisions of the contract for sale depends primarily on the nature and terms of the contract, in particular whether the payment is intended as a genuine and reasonable guarantee of performance, or whether it is intended to be a part payment for the property (*Lozcal Holdings Ltd v Brassos Developments Ltd* (1980) 111 DLR (3d) 598 (Can); *Hyundai Shipping & Heavy Industries Co Ltd v Papadopoulos* [1980] 1 WLR 1129 (HL); The American Law Institute, *Restatement Second, Contracts* § 356 (1981)). On the other hand many US courts have been reluctant to enforce forfeiture of deposit provisions.

In common law, as a rule, if the vendor was unable to complete, as where he cannot make a **good title**, the purchaser can recover his deposit (together with interest thereon), as well as the expenses of investigating title; but could not recover **damages** resulting from his loss of the bargain (*Bain v Fothergill* [1874] LR 7 HL 158 (HL)). However, in English law, for contracts made after 1989 the rule in *Bain v Fothergill* has now been abolished (LP(MP)A 1989, s. 3) so that, if the vendor knew that he could not provide good title at the time of completion, he may be liable for the consequential loss suffered by the purchaser. The rule in *Bain v Fothergill* has also been much criticised in several Commonwealth jurisdictions, and a number of exceptions to this rule now exist. In English law, if a court refuses to grant a decree of **specific performance**, or "in any action for the return of a deposit", the court may order the repayment of any deposit (LPA 1925, s. 49(2)).

In the US, some jurisdictions follow the common law that a deposit may be recovered by the purchaser if the vendor fails to provide good title, but not damages for the loss of the bargain. However, the common law rule will not normally be upheld if the vendor simply refuses to make a good title (even though he has the same), has not acted in good faith, or if there is misrepresentation or a similar action by which the vendor seeks to avoid making a good title. By the same token, if the purchaser fails to complete through his own fault, the vendor will normally be able to keep the deposit, especially if the court considers the amount is a reasonable determination of the amount of **liquidated damages** for the breach of contract and not a **penalty**.

A third party who receives a deposit may hold it as an **agent** or as a **stakeholder**. An agent (who may be, for example, a lawyer, real estate agent, broker or auctioneer) usually holds the deposit on behalf of the seller and, to all intent and purpose, the deposit is held as if it were the property of the seller. In such an instance, if the agent fails to return the deposit when the depositor is rightly entitled to receive it back, technically an action must be brought against the vendor, and not the agent, for the return of the deposit. However, the agent may be enjoined if he has failed in his duties to act on the instruction of the seller. More commonly the person holding the deposit acts as a stakeholder or trustee, is responsible to both parties and, therefore, is solely responsible for the money and must account for the deposit based on the terms of the agreement between the parties. Nonetheless, if there is no condition set down in a contract as to how the deposit is to be held, the third party usually holds the monies as an agent and, accordingly, action for its recovery is against the principal, unless there is evidence of any wrong doing by the agent, or circumstances indicate that the agent assumed responsibility for his principal's actions. An exception to this rule applies to an **auctioneer**, who receives any payment after the fall of the hammer as a part payment of the purchase price and, therefore, holds any deposit as a stakeholder, unless there is a clear indication that he will hold any money as agent for the vendor alone. See also **escrow**.   **2.** An amount of **collateral**, or a **premium**, paid at the start of a lease. See also **security deposit**.   **3.** A sum of money entrusted to a bank or other financial institution for safekeeping, and usually for the purpose of earning interest. cf. **investment**. See also **certificate of deposit, principal**.   **4.** The placing of title deeds with a lender as **security** for a loan. See also **charge by way of a legal mortgage**(Eng), **equitable mortgage, puisne mortgage**.   **5.** See **bailment**.

deposit receipt   A written acknowledgment of receipt of a **deposit** or **earnest money**. This **receipt** may contain the elements of a valid **contract** and thus can create a legally binding contract, or at least an 'agreement for sale' or an 'agreement for a lease'. See also **binder**.

depreciable life   The period of time over which a property is depreciated or its cost is recovered. cf. **economic life**.

depreciated cost   The cost of a property, less accrued depreciation, as shown in a financial statement. See also **basis**(US), **book value**.

depreciated replacement cost (DCR)(BrE) The cost of replacing a property based on the value of an alternative site that could be used for the same purpose, plus the estimated cost of a replacement building (including all site works) after an allowance has been made for the age, condition and the economic or functional obsolescence of the building, i.e. the cost of the building after allowing for **depreciation**. This method is used for the valuation of specialised property for which there is no ready market (e.g.

an oil refinery, hospital or museum), but when a 'valuation' is required for financial reporting. See also **contractor's basis, cost approach**[US], **reinstatement method of valuation**.

The Royal Institution of Chartered Surveyors. *Appraisal & Valuation Standards*. 5th ed. London: RICS Books, 2003, PS 3, Appendix 3.1.

depreciation   1. A loss in value due to use, physical wear and tear, or the effects of time and neglect. A reduction in the worth of an asset over a period of time due to deterioration and/or **obsolescence**. 'Deterioration' is that which is caused by physical changes in the state of a property, i.e. it arises from use or consumption (depletion), or from **wear and tear**; whereas 'obsolescence' is that which is caused by functional changes such as changes in design and style, or by economic or environmental changes such as external changes in the neighbourhood. Depreciation may be considered as 'curable', i.e. it can be made good economically by repair and maintenance; or 'incurable', i.e. it is produced by changes that are beyond the control of the property owner and cannot be made good economically. See also **component depreciation, deferred maintenance, injurious affection**.   2. The writing down, and eventually writing off, of the cost of an asset over its useful or estimated economic life, in the profit and loss account of an organisation, especially for taxation purposes. The provision for depreciation in a valuation, a financial statement or an assessment of a liability for tax, is referred to as a 'depreciation allowance' or 'depreciation provision'. The principal methods of allowing for depreciation are: **straight-line depreciation**; the **annuity method**; **sinking-fund method**; and the **sum-of-the-years-digits depreciation**. See also **accrued depreciation, capital allowance**[BrE], **tax shelter**.

Baum, Andrew. *Property Investment Depreciation and Obsolescence*. London: Routledge, 1991.

3. See **depreciated replacement cost**.

depreciation allowance or **depreciation provision**   See **depreciation**.

depressed area   See **development area**.

deprival value   The value of a property to an occupier based on the cost of finding a suitable alternative building to continue in business. This 'value' is generally applied to a property when it is not possible to readily ascertain the market value of that property and the occupier needs to ascertain the cost of acquiring alternative premises in order to maintain his business or operations. The value is based on the assumption that the replacement is similar in age, size and construction to the subject property. See also **depreciated replacement cost, reinstatement cost**.

depth factor[US]   A factor used in appraisal to adjust the unit price of comparable lots that have different depths. The price of a lot is adjusted by the appraiser using a percentage rate in order to reflect the effect on the value of the plot of its depth relative to the depths of other comparable plots. The rate of adjustment may not be proportional to the depth; as a lot with a very narrow frontage, with a relatively large depth, is likely to be less sought after than a more regular shaped lot. In particular, a 'depth factor' may be obtained from 'depth tables' that show the percentage adjustment considered appropriate for the depth of a particular lot relative to a standard lot. The application of such a factor is used especially in order to provide uniformity in tax assessments. See also **four-three-two-one rule, zoning method**[BrE].

depth tables   See **depth factor**.

deraignment of title[US]   To prove **title**. In particular, to prove better title than a defendant against whom title is claimed by tracing each of the contestants' titles to a common source, such as a government grant or an entry by adverse possession, or by proving a better source of title than the other party. Under this doctrine the claimant must prove the strength of his own title, and not the weakness of his adversary. See also **quieting title**.

derelict   Abandoned; left by the possessor. In particular, personal property that has been wilfully abandoned by the owner and thereby left to be claimed by the first possessor. See also **abandonment, derelict land**.

derelict land   Land that has been neglected or damaged by man's intervention. Land gutted of use or devoid of purpose. In particular, land that has been damaged by mineral working or industrial development so that it is no longer capable of beneficial use within a reasonable time without considerable expenditure. Land that has been intentionally abandoned or neglected after the former use has become uneconomic, or when the former user is no longer required, as with a mine, quarry, airfield, railroad line or dock land. 'Derelict land' does not include land that may have a similar appearance, but has been lain waste by natural causes, such as a desert, marsh land, disused farmland, or land that has now blended into, or has become part of, the landscape and is no longer detrimental to the local amenity. Derelict land is likely to be unsightly and may well give rise to a public **nuisance**. See also **brownfield site, urban decay, wasteland**.

dereliction   The recession of the water of the sea or a navigable river so as to increase the dry land on the shore or foreshore. Land created by **reliction**. In the event of sudden dereliction the land boundaries remain unaltered. However, if the change is gradual and imperceptible, the derelict or dry land belongs to the riparian owner from whose shore or bank the water has so receded. Also called 'diluvion'. cf. **alluvion**. See also **accretion, riparian rights**.

derivative   See **derivative security**.

derivative conveyance   A **conveyance** that presumes the existence of another conveyance and serves to alter, enlarge, modify or confirm that conveyance. A conveyance that transfers or modifies an interest in land that has been transferred by another conveyance, for example an assignment, surrender, release or defeasance.

derivative lease   See **sub-lease**.

derivative mortgage   See **sub-mortgage**.

derivative possession   The type of **possession** that one holds by virtue of another's right to possession such as that held by a tenant or licensee. cf. **paramount possession**.

derivative or **derivative security**   A financial instrument that is a by-product of, is dependent on, or is created from another instrument or the movement of a financial market. For example, a forward contract or future, financial **option**, **swap**, or **warrant**. Derivatives are used primarily to hedge against future changes in the value of the underlying form of asset or as a means of leveraged speculative investment.

derivative settlement   A **settlement** created out of the beneficial interest of one of the beneficiaries of another settlement.

derivative title   Title held as an accessory or dependence of another's title, such as is held by a subtenant. A title that is inferior to another's. The common law principle of derivative title states that, when a person acquires a title, that right cannot be better than that of the grantor. cf. **paramount title**. See also *nemo dat qui non habet*.

derogation from grant   Diminishing, or militating against, a right or interest that has already been granted, i.e. doing something that takes away, grants to another, or interferes with a benefit that one person has contractually conferred on another. In particular, upon the grant of a lease a landlord implies that he will not take away the rights that he has given the tenant to enjoy. Derogation from the grant includes such matters as carrying on a noisy activity next to residential property; permitting a retail unit in a shopping center to be used in such a way that it deters visitors to an adjoining shop. The derogation must be substantial; it does not normally include an act that merely inconveniences a person's privacy or amenity; or an action such as allowing adjoining retail premises to be used for a competing purpose (unless there is a separate express provision against such an activity). Derogation may also arise when the grantor of an easement takes a course of action that limits the beneficiary's proper or full enjoyment of that easement, e.g. periodically placing obstructions over a right of way or building in order to obstruct a right of light. cf. **quiet enjoyment**. See also **frustration, implied covenant, quasi-easement**.

descent Hereditary succession. The result of a transfer of property by **inheritance**. 'Descent' refers normally to inheritance by operation of law and not as a result of the provisions of a will. Strictly speaking 'descent' applies to real property, but in common parlance the term is used to refer to a hereditary succession to any form of property. See also **curtesy, dower, heir, issue**, *per capita, per stirpe*s.

description 1. A statement of the boundaries or limits of a right to property, usually made by reference to survey or a detailed description of the site dimensions; by reference to a **map, plat** or **plan**; or merely by a statement of the postal or other known address. See also **boundary, government survey system**(US), **lot and block system**(US), **metes and bounds system**(US), **Mother Hubbard clause**(US), **plat map**(US), **sale in gross**(US). 2. The part of a deed or conveyance that describes the subject matter. See also **parcels clause, plan, premises**. 3. A representation given by one person that tells another, as clearly as possible, what a thing is. A description is adequate if it gives a view that enables the thing to be recognised when seen or when sensed in another appropriate way. See also **misdescription, particulars of sale, schedule of condition**.

design-and-build contract A building contract that provides for the contractor to be responsible for all the professional design services

(architectural, engineering, etc.) as well as the building work. Under this form of contract the person for whom the work is carried out accepts the completed building according to the contractor's design and specification. Also called a 'design-and-construct', 'all-in', or a 'package-deal contract', especially if the employer has virtually no involvement in the design and the contractor accepts all risk of changes as the work progresses. cf. **build-to-suit contract, turnkey contract**.

Chappell, David, and Vincent Powell-Smith. *The JCT Design and Build Contract*. 2nd ed. Oxford: Blackwell Science, 1999.

Turner, D. F. *Design and Build Contract Practice*. 2nd ed. Harlow, Essex: Longman Scientific, 1995.

design-and-management contract(US) See **turnkey contract**.

designated area(Eng) An area of land delineated as liable to be purchased by a local authority or public body. An area designated for a specific form of future development, e.g. for a **new town**. See also **area of comprehensive development, area of special scientific interest, urban development area**.

desist To refrain or resist from an action. See also **abandonment, cease and desist order, remit**.

destroy 1. To tear down or demolish a property. To rend something useless or of negligible value. A property may be considered to be 'totally destroyed' for insurance purposes when it ceases to exist as a building, even though a portion of the foundations remain that might be used for rebuilding. A property may be destroyed but not demolished if it is reduced to such a state that it cannot be used in any reasonable manner for its intended purpose. See also **demolition, frustration**. 2. To take away all reasonable use or value. A property may lose its value and be destroyed economically, without being physically destroyed, for example by the rerouting of a highway. See also **condemnation**. 3. To revoke all or part of a **will** by tearing up, burning or otherwise defacing it to evidence an intention that it is no longer to have any effect. To be truly effective the destruction should be made in the presence of a witness. See also **revocation**.

detached dwelling or **detached house** A dwelling-house that has no party wall in common with another building. A dwelling-house that stands apart from any other house or non-associated building. A house separated from others and usually surrounded by unbuilt land on all sides. In the US, also called a 'single family detached' (SFD) when such a property is intended to be occupied by one family. cf. **semi-detached house, row house**(AmE), **terrace house**(BrE).

detailed planning permission(Eng) See **planning permission**.

detainer The act of unlawfully withholding property from someone who is legally entitled to possession. In particular, the unlawful retention of goods, even though possession might originally have been obtained legally. See also **conversion, forcible entry and detainer**.

deterioration A reduction or degeneration in the quality or value of a property due to wear and tear, usage, or any other physical cause. Deterioration is the primary physical factor that causes **depreciation**, i.e. loss in value. cf. **obsolescence**. See also **fair wear and tear**(BrE), **physical deterioration, waste, wear and tear**(AmE).

determinable fee 1.(Eng)See **determinable fee simple**. 2.(US)A fee **estate** that is granted to a person and his heirs, but subject to a qualification that the duration of the estate must end upon the occurrence of an event that may, or may not, happen. For example, a **fee** held for as long as the property is used for a particular purpose, e.g. as a school. A determinable fee may be distinguished from a life interest as the former *may* last forever, whereas the latter will come to an end. It may be distinguished from **conditional fee** as the person entitled to the subsequent estate must re-enter and

take possession, whereas the 'determinable fee' automatically reverts to the grantor or the person designated to take the estate if the specified event occurs. In some jurisdictions, the terms 'determinable fee', '**base fee**' and '**qualified fee**' are used synonymously for any fee that expires on the occurrence of a specified event. Also called an 'estate on limitation' or 'limited fee'. See also **fee simple determinable, possibility of reverter**.

determinable fee simple(Eng) An estate in land that is equivalent to a **fee simple**, except that it will automatically come to an end upon the occurrence of some act or event that is specified at the time the interest is created, but is an event that is unpredictable and may never happen, e.g. a fee simple granted 'to A until she marries' or 'to B for so long as the land is used as a school'. A determinable fee is limited by a contingency and is created by such words as 'for so long as', 'while', or 'until'. If the words limit or demarcate the utmost duration of the estate, then those words create a determinable fee simple; but if the words are intended merely to defeat the estate before it reaches its boundary then the estate is a **conditional fee simple**. With a determinable fee simple the limiting circumstances are integral to the duration of the estate, whereas with a conditional fee simple the limiting condition operates to cut short the estate before the end of its normal duration. See also **possibility of reverter**, a **right of re-entry**.

determinable interest 1. An interest that is terminable upon the happening of a contingent event. A modern example of a determinable interest is a grant of land to a highway authority with a provision that the land will revert to the original grantor within 50 years if the land ceases to be a public highway. cf. **conditional interest, executory interest**. See also **determinable fee simple**(Eng), **protective trust, rule against perpetuities, tenancy determinable with a life**. 2. An interest in land that is granted for a fixed period of time, but which may be brought to an end by a prescribed event, e.g. a lease that is granted for ten years but may be terminated "if the property is no longer used as a medical center". In the US, also called a 'tenancy upon special limitation'. See also **determination, tenancy for life**.

determinable limitation   A limitation on an estate in land that creates a **determinable interest**.

determination   1. A bringing or coming to an end, usually by some deliberate act. The bringing or coming to an end of a contract, or an estate or interest in property; especially by notice as expressly provided for in a contract or as a consequence of a fundamental breach of a condition of the contract. 'Determination' is used more commonly to convey the same meaning as **termination**, i.e. the deliberate ending of an interest, rather than **expiration** due to effluxion of time. Nonetheless, determination may be used to signify the coming to an end in any way whatever. It is necessary to look at the context to ascertain whether 'to determine' or 'determination' is intended to require an act by someone to bring the contract to an end, or whether effluxion of time suffices. cf. **rescission**. See also **breach of contract, lease**.   2. A definitive decision by a court or an administrative body, as with a judicial decision or an arbitration adjudication. The fixing of a rent tax assessment or a similar value for a property by an independent **expert** or **arbitrator**.

detrimental reliance   See **constructive trust, estoppel**.

developer   1. One who organises and supervises a project of development from inception to completion. A person or body that carries on the **development** of land or buildings. A developer is usually responsible for both the development or building works, as well as for the subsequent leasing or sale of the completed project. In particular, a developer has a financial involvement in a development and in that respect may be distinguished from a professional advisor or consultant. A developer generally has definite plans for the use of his property, and in that respect may be distinguished from a **speculator** who has no specific plans for property he acquires, but holds it in anticipation of a short-term rise in value. See also **entrepreneur, property developer**. 2.[US]In connection with the subdivision and sale of land lots, the person who initially subdivided and platted the land, and "any person who directly or indirectly sells or leases, or offers to sell or lease, or advertises for sale or lease any lots in a subdivision", Interstate Land Sales Full Disclosure Act (15 USC § 1701(5)). This role is extended to an "agent" who, in this context, is defined as "any person who represents, or acts for or on behalf of, a developer in selling or leasing, or offering to sell or lease, any lot or lots in a subdivision; but shall not include an attorney at law whose representation of another person consists solely of rendering legal services", 15 USC § 1701(6). 3.[US]The party that acquires land or a building in order to develop or convert it for sale as a **condominium**. In particular, the party that makes the initial **condominium declaration** and is actively involved in the marketing and selling of the condominium units, and usually establishes and is the founding member of the **condominium owners' association**. See also **declarant, promoter**.

developer's residual approach[US]   See **residual approach**.

development   1. Carrying on an activity that changes the nature of land or buildings. The carrying out of substantial **improvement** or **alteration** to land or buildings. An activity that changes the basic character or use of land. The making of changes in the physical environment. In particular, the opening up, laying out, or changing and improving the potential of land or buildings thereon; including any change in the use, or intensity of use, of land or buildings. 2.[Eng]In English statute law, for planning control purposes, 'development' means "the carrying out of building, engineering, mining or other operations in, on, over or under land or the making of any **material change in the use** of any **building** or other **land**", TCPA 1990, ss. 55(1), 336(1). Unless a particular activity is exempt by statute, the carrying out of any form of development requires **planning permission**. Anything that materially or permanently affects the appearance of land or the exterior of a building is likely to be considered as development. The 1990 Act sets out matters that are 'development' such as the use of a single dwelling-house for the purpose of two or more separate dwellings and the display of an **advertisement** on the external part of any building not normally used for such purposes. On the other hand, certain "operations or uses of land" are deemed not to be 'development', such as maintenance, improvement or alteration that affects only the interior of the building; incidental changes to the use within the **curtilage** of a dwelling-house, provided such changes are incidental to the enjoyment of the dwelling; and changes within the same 'use class'. Certain minor matters (generally related to a change of use or a temporary use), although classified as development, are deemed not to require planning permission, i.e. planning permission (conditionally or unconditionally) is granted for such 'development' by virtue of a **General Development Order**. See also **advertisement, demolition, building operations, certificate of lawfulness, enforcement notice, engineering operations, listing building, mining operations, permitted development, redevelopment, subdivision, Use Classes Order.**

Cadman, David, and R. Topping. *Property Development.* 4th ed. London: E. & F. N. Spon, 1995.

Millington, A. F. *Property Development.* London: Estates Gazette, 2000.

Colley, B. C. *Practical Manual of Land Development*, 2nd ed. New York: McGraw-Hill, 1993.

Miles, Mike E., et al. *Real Estate Development.* 3rd ed. Washington, DC: Urban Land Institute, 2000.

Peiser, Richard B., et al. *Professional Real Estate Development.* Washington, DC: Urban Land Institute, 2003.

development agreement   See **contract zoning**[US], **planning obligation**[Eng].

development analysis   A financial analysis made in order to ascertain the total cost and return from a proposed development project. See also **feasibility analysis, land residual technique**[US], **residual method of valuation**[BrE], **residual process**[US], **sensitivity analysis**.

development application[Aus]   A formal request to a local authority or planning body for consent to construct a new building, create a land subdivision, or carryout major building works.

development appraisal   See **appraisal, development analysis**.

development approach[US]   See **residual process**.

development area   1.[BrE]An area suffering from adverse economic conditions, especially from high levels of unemployment and the consequent adverse migration of its population. An area that is considered to be in need of central government assistance or other inducements. See also **enterprise zone, special area, special investment area, urban development area**.   2.[US]See **distressed area**.

development consent[Aus]   Permission that is granted by a local government council to carry out development. Similar to **planning permission** in the UK.

development control   1.[US]See **billboard, cluster development, planned unit development, zoning, zoning classification, zoning ordinance**. 2.[Eng]See **advertisement, building controls, discontinuance order, conservation area, enforcement notice, listed building consent, planning permission, revocation order, tree preservation order**.

development control plan (DCP)[Aus]   A **plan** prepared by a local government authority showing the proposed basis for the future use and development of the area within their control. A development plan acts as a control for future development of the area and is used as the basis for the consideration of any **development application**.

development cost   The total cost of a project of development, including all land acquisition costs, building or construction costs (including demolition and site preparation costs), professional fees and financing costs. See also **feasibility analysis**, **hard cost**, **soft cost**, **residual method of valuation**(BrE).

development district(Eng)   See **development area**.

development fee or **development impact fee**(US)   A fee payable to a local municipality by a developer to meet some or all of the environmental costs of a new development. The fee is intended to pay for additional services such as police, community facilities, utilities, etc., that will be needed as a result of the new development. Such a fee may be distinguished from a 'special assessment', which is levied against the owners of existing properties to pay for improvements. A 'development fee' may be levied as a condition of the approval of a new development; but, as a rule, the monies must be used to meet the cost of providing additional facilities necessitated by the new development, i.e. there should be a 'nexus' between the fee and the impact of the new development. See also **assessment**, **incentive zoning**, **police power**.
National Association of Home Builders. *Impact Fee Handbook*. Washington, DC: Home Builders Press, 1997.

development land   Land held for planned future development. See also **development property**, **land bank**.

development finance or **development loan**   A loan obtained, or finance used, for any project of development. The term may also be used to refer to a short-term or interim loan granted to a developer to cover the cost of land acquisition and preliminary development expenditure. See also **construction finance**.

development management   See **project management**.

development order(Eng)   See **General Development Order**, **Special Development Order**.

development permit(Can)   A permit that is required for the 'development' of land, unless the development is expressly exempt by statute or a land use bylaw.

development plan   1. A **plan** that is prepared for a given area to show proposals for the use and development of land. A development plan shows the existing and future communication network; acts as a control for future development of the area; indicates proposals to improve the physical environment; and sets down private and public development and redevelopment priorities. Also called a 'general development plan' (GDP), especially when it is intended to show the development intentions in outline. See also **master plan**, **planned unit development**(US), **zoning**, **zoning ordinance**(US).   2.(Eng)A plan prepared by a local planning authority that sets out the framework for the making of planning decisions. In particular, a 'unitary development plan' that is in force in Greater London or a metropolitan county (TCPA 1990, s. 54, 54). Also, 'development plan' may refer (especially outside Greater London and the metropolitan counties) to: (a) a 'structure plan'; (b) a 'local plan'; or (c) a 'unitary development plan'. A structure plan is prepared by a county council (or in some cases two or more 'unitary councils') and comprises a written statement, together with diagrams, illustrations or other descriptive matter, as required in order to set out its strategic policies and proposals "in respect of the development and use of land" in the area under the council's jurisdiction (TCPA 1990, s. 31). A structure plan is intended as a statement of the 'general policies' for the development of the area showing trends and tendencies; it is not intended to set down any specific land use maps or similar strictures. A local plan takes the form of a written statement prepared by the local authority of the 'detailed policies' in respect of the development and use of land in the authority's area, together with a map (the 'proposal map'), diagrams and illustrations and such other descriptive or explanatory matter as is required. A local plan is required to be in general conformity with the structure plan. The local plan may also designate an area within the authority's area as an **action area**. In some cases a more detailed 'general local plan' may be prepared by the local council to expand the requirements of the structure plan for a given district; or a 'subject plan' may be prepared to deal with a particular planning issue over an extensive area, such as a green belt policy or land reclamation. A local plan may also take the form of (a) a 'minerals local plan' detailing policies for the winning and working of minerals in the area; or (b) a 'waste local plan' setting out policies for the depositing of refuse or waste material. In the London boroughs and metropolitan districts, the functions of the structure plan and the local plan are combined into a 'unitary development plan'. See also **enforcement notice**, **public participation**.

Walton, David, and Stanley Kenyon. *Development Plans: Law & Practice.* London: Sweet & Maxwell, 1997.

development property　Property held, or capable of being used, for **development**. Property held for future development or redevelopment purposes. Property that can be increased in value by capital expenditure, especially by the construction of new buildings. See also **residual method of valuation**(BrE), **residual process**(US).

development rights transfer (DRT)(US) See **transferable development right**.

development scheme　See **scheme of development**.

development valuation　See **residual method of valuation**(BrE), **residual process**(US).

development value　1. The **latent value** of a property that can be realised by carrying out development work. See also **hope value**.　2. An increase in the value of land that results from the grant of consent to a revised zoning or change of the permitted use. See also **betterment**.

devise　1. Derived from the Latin *divisio*, 'division'. The transfer of, or the act of transferring, property. In particular, the transfer of **real property** as a gift by **will**, i.e. the effective transfer of property from a dying to a living person. Devise is strictly speaking used only for the transfer of real property and **bequest** to refer to personal property, although the terms are sometimes used interchangeably (or even together) and in interpreting a will the intent, or general context, can be as important as the actual word used. Thus, devise "when used as a noun, means a testamentary disposition of real or personal property and when used as a verb, means to dispose of real or personal property by will", United States Uniform Probate Code § 1-201(8) (Caracci v. Lillard, 7 Ill.2d 382, 130 NE.2d 514 (1955)). Similarly, The American Law Institute, *Restatement of Property* (1936) uses 'devise' to refer to the disposition by will of real and personal property. A devise may transfer or '**vest**' the property immediately, or the transfer may be contingent on a future event such as the death of another party. It may also be a 'general devise' which transfers all the deceased's property; a 'specific devise' which transfers only specified property; or a 'residuary devise' which transfers the remaining property after one or more specific devises. It may also be an 'executory devise' if it creates an **executory interest**, i.e. a future interest that does not revert to the original grantor or his or her heirs. See also **descent**.　2. To give land by a **will** that is duly attested by law.

devisee　A person who receives property by **devise**, i.e. by will.

devisor   A person who grants or bequeaths property by **devise**, i.e. by will.

devolution   The transfer of property, or a right, title or interest in property, from one person to another, especially by operation of law, as on death or bankruptcy. See also **disposition**.

devolve   To pass property by transmission or succession. To transfer property from a dying person to a living person, especially by the operation of law. See also **devise**, **disposal**.

dicta(US)   See *obiter dictum.*

dictum(Lat)   'A saying'; a statement. See *obiter dictum.*

differential rent   A rent based on a tenant's ability to pay for the use or benefit of the leased premises rather than a **market rent**. See also **profits method of valuation**.

dilapidation   Derived from the Latin *di*, 'tear down', plus *lapis*, 'stone'; literally to tear down stone. The act of wastefully destroying any building or letting it slide into ruin and decay by neglect of reparation. Dilapidation may give rise to a legal right as a result of (a) waste; (b) a tort, e.g. **negligence** through failure to make a property safe for visitors; (c) a **breach of covenant**, e.g. failure to comply with an obligation to **repair** as contained in a lease; or (d) a failure to comply with statute law, e.g. the Housing Acts. See also **fair wear and tear**(BrE), **forfeiture, schedule of dilapidations**(BrE), **wear and tear**(AmE).

Dowding, Nicholas, and Kirk Reynolds. *Dilapidations, The Modern Law and Practice.* 2nd ed. London: Sweet & Maxwell, 2000.

Royal Institution of Chartered Surveyors. *Dilapidations: A Guidance Note*, 4th ed. London: RICS Books, 2003.

Smith, P. F. *West & Smith's Law of Dilapidations.* 11th ed. London: Estates Gazette, 2001.

Williams, Del., et al. *Handbook of Dilapidations.* Looseleaf. London: Sweet & Maxwell, ©1992.

dilapidations survey(BrE)   See **schedule of condition, schedule of dilapidations**.

diluvion   See **dereliction**.

diminishing asset   See **wasting asset**.

diminishing-balance depreciation   See **declining-balance depreciation**.

diminution of a claim   See **set-off**.

diminution of damages   See **damages**.

diminution of value   See **depreciation, injurious affection**.

DINK(AmE)   'Dual income, no kids'. A term used to refer to those with high disposable income who represent good prospects for home sales.

direct capitalization(AmE)   See **straight capitalization**.

direct labour   Labour employed directly by the owner of a property, for maintenance or building work, rather than by an **independent contractor**.

direct reduction mortgage (DRM)(AmE)   A mortgage loan that provides for the borrower to repay the principal by fixed regular amounts. Under a direct reduction mortgage each payment goes, at least in part, to reduce the outstanding principal balance, so that the amount of interest, and hence the total amount payable, reduces throughout the term of the loan. 'Direct reduction mortgage' is sometimes used as synonymous with **amortization mortgage**, but the basis for calculating repayments of interest and capital under an amortization mortgage is very different from that for a DRM, as the former provides for equal payments that cover interest and principal

direct sales comparison approach(AmE)   See **sales comparison approach**.

direct value comparison   See **comparison method of valuation**(BrE).

disabling restraint   See **restraint on alienation**.

disaffirm   To repudiate or revoke. To disclaim a previous action or transaction. See also **repudiation**.

disbursement   **1.** The payment of money, especially in settlement of a debt. In particular, **expenditure** incurred to defray the cost of a current asset.   **2.** A payment made as part of the amount to be advanced under a loan, in particular a **construction loan**.

discharge   To complete or execute a duty or obligation in full. To make an agreement that has the effect of bringing a contract to an end. To release from a burden or obligation, such as by the making of a settlement that extinguishes a loan or debt. 'Discharge' may be used to cover any one of a number of arrangements that bring a binding agreement or contract to an end including **accord and satisfaction**, **repudiation**, **rescission**, **release**, **performance** or **frustration**. The notable feature of discharge is that the agreement is totally ended; there is no residual commitment between the parties. The term discharge is used more commonly to refer to the ending of a contract when all the obligations have been fulfilled, or when it has been agreed that the parties have no further obligation, debt or commitment, but not when there has been a **breach of contract**. See also **estoppel, laches, merger, novation, restrictive covenant, waiver**.

discharge deed(US)   See **release deed**.

disclaimer   **1.** The **repudiation**, **renunciation** or rejection of a claim, right or obligation. For example, an agent or broker may insert a **disclaimer clause**(US) or **exclusion clause**(Eng) in the particulars of sale of a property, renouncing liability for the accuracy of the information contained in the particulars, or stating that the particulars do not constitute an offer or form part of any contract. See also **abrogation**.   **2.** A statement in a **valuation report**(BrE) or an **appraisal report**(AmE) that the report does not cover or relate to a particular condition. For example, that the report does not amount to a structural or environmental survey. **3. Renunciation** of a title to, or an interest in, property. A formal means by which someone states that an estate or interest in property is not to pass to them. A disclaimer by a tenant is a denial of the existence of any relationship of landlord and tenant, and effectively means that no tenancy came into existence. See also **estoppel, implied covenant, repudiation, tenancy by estoppel**.   **4.**(Eng) The notification by a trustee in bankruptcy (of an individual) or a liquidator (of a company) of his refusal to be bound by an onerous contract, or to accept the ownership of onerous property, especially a property that is not readily saleable. The purpose of such an action is to prevent future claims, for example those of a landlord, from defeating the present claims of other creditors.

disclaimer clause(US)   A clause in a contract that seeks to define and limit the extent of the promisor's liability or obligation under the contract. For example, a clause that stipulates that the promisor will not be liable for such matters as a defect in goods offered for sale; for providing any **warranty** as to the quality or condition of the subject matter of the contract; or for any damage that is suffered by the promisee as a result of negligence or misrepresentation on the part of the promisor. A disclaimer clause may be regarded either as an attempt to clarify that which is set out in the contract, or as a means of circumventing the contract. It is in the latter sense that the term is more commonly used. In the US, also called an 'exoneration clause'. See also **exclusion clause**(Eng), **exculpatory clause**.

disclosed principal   A **principal** whose identity is made known to any party with whom an agent is dealing. cf. **undisclosed principal**.

disclosure   See **disclosure statement, misdescription, utmost good faith**.

disclosure statement(US)   A statement that is required by law to be submitted to a prospective customer or consumer before a transaction is consummated. In particular, a statement that must be given under the federal Truth-in-Lending Act before entering into a consumer credit agreement. See also **condominium declaration, settlement statement, statement of record**.

discontinuance   1. The termination or cessation of a right, privilege or course of action. See also **dispossession**.   2. The cessation of a use of land, especially when made for a short period of time. The termination of a use of land, in particular the abandonment of a **non-conforming use**. Discontinuance may be used as synonymous with **abandonment** in connection with a use of land, both connoting a voluntary and affirmative act, although discontinuance denotes a gap, or a 'failure for the time to use it' and may imply that the use will be continued later. Discontinuance may also be an act that amounts to an abandonment of possession and is thus a precursor to the act of **adverse possession**. See also **discontinuance order**(Eng).

discontinuance notice(Eng)   See **advertisement**.

discontinuance order(Eng)   An order made by a local planning authority requiring a use of land to be discontinued, imposing a condition on the continuation of a use of land, or requiring a building or works to be altered or removed (TCPA 1990, ss. 102, 103). Compensation is payable to any person who has suffered damage as a result of a discontinuance order. If appropriate, the order may grant **planning permission** for an alternative use or development of the land. cf. **enforcement notice**. See also **compensation for planning restrictions, purchase notice**.

discontinuous easement   See **easement**.

discount   1. A reduction in the value of something. A reduction or abatement of a face value or price. A reduction in the amount of principal granted for the early repayment of a loan. A discount is a reduction given or made in advance, as distinguished from a **rebate** which is an amount given back after payment in full. A discount may be granted on the presumption that something is worth more at present than it may be in the future, or to take account of the risk of receiving, or not receiving, it in the future. See also **discounted cash flow, present value**.   2. A reduction from face value made when a third party buys a **bill of exchange**. The purchaser 'discounts' or buys the bill of exchange (i.e. the right to receive the face value on maturity) at a price that is reduced by an amount that takes into account the time to maturity and the financial standing of the debtor. The discount or charge made by the purchaser of the bill is usually expressed as an annual percentage rate applied to the face value of the bill, i.e. a **discount rate**.   3. A reduction in the amount advanced under a loan, or expressed in a note, which effectively represents an advance payment of interest on the amount that is payable at maturity. In effect, such advance interest is levied at a higher rate than the normal loan rate, because the borrower is paying interest before he has use of the funds so the discount is compounded at the outset. Called 'bank discount', as distinguished from 'true discount' which is calculated so that there is no compounding or 'interest upon interest'. See also **discount points**.

discount department store   See **discount store**.

discount house(US)   See **discount store**.

discount points   A percentage reduction in the amount of a loan, so that the amount actually advanced to the borrower is less than the nominal amount of the loan; consequently resulting in an increase in the true annual interest rate. For example, a loan of $10,000 is established upon which interest is charged at 9% per annum and that is repayable at the end of the loan term, but only $9,800 is advanced. The lender has adjusted the loan by two discount points. (The true interest rate for one year is 11.22% instead of the nominal rate of 9%.) Similarly, a lender may increase the loan amount for the purpose of calculating the interest rate; for example, the principal loan amount is increased to $10,200 but only $10,000 is advanced (the true annual interest rate then becomes 11.18%). cf. **origination fee**. See also **annual percentage rate, front loading, point**.

discount rate   1. The amount of a **discount** expressed as an annual percentage.   2. The rate of return used in the application of a **present value** factor in discounting future income. A term that may be used synonymously with **capitalisation rate**.   3. The rate at which a note or bill of exchange is discounted, i.e. the amount, expressed as a percentage, by which the price paid to the holder of a bill of exchange falls short of the **face value**.   4.(US)The annual rate at which the district Federal Reserve banks lend money short term to eligible banks. cf. **Federal funds rate**.   5. An annual rate of interest deducted from a loan before the capital is advanced. See also **discount points, discounted-interest loan**.

discount store or **discount warehouse** A retail store, or warehouse, that offers goods for sale at prices lower than those pertaining in the standard high street or downtown store or in a regular **department store**. A discount store is normally divided into departments; provides more limited customer service; uses self-service techniques; and usually sells non-branded goods, frequently in quantities that are larger than those offered by a standard retail store. A discount store may sell hard goods or soft goods, but generally provides limited or no food sales. Called a 'discount department store' if the store sells an appropriate range of goods. See also **variety store**.

discounted cash flow (DCF) The **present value** of the estimated future **cash flow** to be derived from an investment in a capital asset over a given period of time (the anticipated 'economic life' or 'holding period' of the investment). The term 'discounted cash flow' can also be applied to the technique for analyzing the viability of a capital investment project by discounting all budgeted, or projected, income and expenditure flowing from or into a project, including the initial outlay and any residual value. This type of analysis can be used either: (i) to find the difference between the present value of all income and the present value of all expenditure, i.e. to determine the **net present value** or 'net discounted revenue'; or (ii) to find a single discount rate that makes the present value of the estimated future income equal to the present value of all expenditure over the life of an investment, i.e. to determine the **internal rate of return**. The discounted cash flow technique is the basis for most forms of financial analysis over time, especially as a method of comparing alternative forms of investment over the same time span. Also called 'present value analysis'. cf. **pay-back method**. See also **capitalisation**; Appendix C, **Financial Formulae**.

discounted-interest loan   A loan upon which the interest charge is deducted from the amount of the loan before the capital is advanced, e.g. a loan subject to **discount points**. See also **annual percentage rate, discount rate**.

discounted loan or **discounted mortgage** A loan, or a mortgage, sold by the lender, or mortgagee, for an amount that is less than the principal due under the loan, i.e. a loan sold at a **discount**.

discounted rate of return or **discounted-cash-flow rate of return** See internal rate of return.

discounted value   The present value of a future payment or income, calculated at a given rate of interest.

discounting   1. The process of ascertaining the **present value** of a sum of money that is receivable in the future. **2.** The application of a **discount** to the value of something or on the amount of money advanced on loan. **3.** The process of selling a **bill of exchange**, before its maturity date, for a sum of money that is less than the face value of the bill.

discretionary trust **1.** A trust that provides for the investment of the funds and the distribution of any income or principal to be left to the discretion of the trustee; although the trust deed may limit the extent of that discretion. A discretionary trust may require the trustees to distribute the entire trust property, leaving a discretion as to how the proceeds are to be distributed – an 'exhaustive trust'; or the trustees may have discretion as to whether to make a distribution at all – a 'non-exhaustive trust'. cf. **passive trust**. See also **protective trust**. **2.** An **investment company** that is not restricted to one form or class of investment. See also **open-end trust**.

discrimination See **blockbusting**(US), **redlining**(US).

discumberment(US) The release of a property from an **encumbrance** or **lien**.

disentail(Eng) To bar or free an estate from the constraint of being an **entailed estate** and convert it to a fee simple. See also **barring the entail**.

disentailing assurance(Eng) A deed, or a provision in a will, that has the effect of converting an **entailed estate** into a fee simple absolute, i.e. a deed that removes the possibility of an estate passing to a specified or restricted line of direct descendants and enables the estate to pass without limitation. See also **base fee**.

disentailing deed(Eng) See **disentailing assurance**.

disintermediation A reduction in savings and consequently in investment. In particular, a reduction in net deposits with savings or other conventional financial institutions in favour of other forms of investment that provide a more attractive rate of return, or the transfer of funds from low-interest to high-interest bonds. Disintermediation can result in a reduction in the availability of mortgage funding. cf. **intermediation**.

dismortgage(US) To redeem a property from a mortgage. See also **redemption**.

dispone(Scot) To dispose of property in particular, to convey formally or in proper legal form.

disponee(Scot) A person to whom a property is transferred.

disponer(Scot) A person who transfers property. In particular, a person makes a **disposition**.

disposal The act of transferring something form one person to another. Disposal of real property is generally taken to mean the transfer of a party's entire interest, by any means (including barter or exchange), as well as all acts by which a wholly new interest is created in a property. See also **disposition**, **dispose**.

dispose To transfer something from the control of one person to another, whether by an act of the parties or by operation of law. 'Dispose' and 'disposal' are words of wide meaning, which may extend to include any transfer of property, including a **sale**, **exchange**, **gift**, **lease**, **pledge**, or **mortgage**, as well as a **grant** of any interest, easement, right or privilege over property. In particular, 'dispose' and 'disposal' are used to refer to a transfer between living persons, as distinguished from **devise** which refers to a transfer upon a person's death. However, if the context so admits, 'dispose' may be used to refer to a disposition by will. See also **alienation**, **assignment**, **disposition**.

disposition **1.** The act of getting rid of or

transferring ownership of property. Disposition is a word of broad meaning and may encompass any means by which a person parts with something, especially in an absolute way. The surrender of an existing interest, such as a tenancy for years or for life, may be a 'disposition'. Disposition is used sometimes in tax statutes as a 'catch all' for any alienation of property, even including discharging a debt. In particular, disposition covers a transfer of property by act of the parties, as distinguished from **devolution** which is a transfer by act of law.

In certain English statute law, a 'disposition' "includes a **conveyance** and also a devise, bequest, or an appointment of property contained in a will", LPA 1925, s. 205(1)(ii); or in connection with settled land "'disposition' and 'conveyance' include a mortgage, charge by way of a legal mortgage, lease, assent, vesting declaration, vesting instrument, disclaimer, release and every other assurance of property, except a will", SLA 1925, s. 117(1)(v). In the case of a registered estate [one registered on the register of estates at the **Land Registry**], a 'registrable disposition' is essentially: (a) a transfer of the freehold; (b) a grant of a lease for a term of seven years, or an assignment of a lease with more than seven years to run (as well as certain shorter lease, such a 'discontinuous lease' – e.g. a right under a timeshare where the landlord's interest is registered, and a reversionary lease that gives the tenant a right to possession within three months); and (c) in most cases, a transfer of a right to a legal mortgage, a legal charge, a legal easement or a restrictive covenant (LRA 2002, s. 27).

In Australia, disposition is defined to include "a conveyance … vesting instrument, declaration of trust, disclaimer, release and every other assurance of property by any instrument except a will, and also a release, devise, bequest, or an appointment of property contained in a will; and **dispose** has a corresponding meaning", Conveyancing Act, 1919, s. 7(1) (NSW). See also **disposal**. **2.**(Scot)A deed by which a right to property is conveyed. A written deed of conveyance.

disposition fees   Fees paid to a servicer of a

mortgage-backed security (MBS) for making a loan current or dealing with a foreclosed property. The fee may cover administration costs, late fees on the mortgage or fees for modifying the loan agreement. The general level of such fees is established when the MBS is created.

dispositive power   See **power of appointment**.

dispossession   The regaining of **possession** of real property by legal process, especially by a landlord on termination or expiration of a lease. The act of depriving or ousting someone from a right to possession of land, whether rightly or wrongly. By dispossession one person comes in and drives out another from possession, as distinguished from a 'discontinuance' or **abandonment** of possession which arises when someone gives up possession and is followed in by an other. cf. **deforcement, disseisin, expropriation**. See also **abatement, disturbance, ejectment, eviction**.

dispute resolution   See **arbitration, adjudication, expert**.

disregards(Eng)   Factors to be ignored when assessing the market value of a property. In particular, factors to be ignored when assessing the market rent on the renewal of a **business tenancy**; the **fair rent** for a regulated tenancy; or the rent for an **agricultural tenancy**.

disrepair   The state of being in need of **repair**, either due to general decay or as a result of neglect in complying with the terms of a lease or other contractual obligation. See also **dilapidation, negligence, repairs notice**(Eng)**, waste**.

disseisin or **disseizin**   1. The act of depriving someone of a right of **seisin**, i.e. wrongfully dispossessing or ousting the person entitled to a freehold. In the US, used sometimes to describe any wrongful exclusion of a person from possession, especially the injurious or forcible removal of a tenant from possession by his landlord. cf. **dispossession**. See also **deforcement**. **2.**(US)The act that starts a claim for **adverse possession**. An old term for an actual expulsion of the true owner from land for the period of time prescribed by statute.

disseisor   A person who effects **disseisin**. One who wrongfully dispossesses someone from property, especially a person who ousts a freeholder.

distinct possession(US)   See **adverse possession**.

distrainor or distrainer   One who distrains on property. The party that takes property by the process of **distress**.

distraint   The taking of another's personal property and holding it as a pledge or security until a debt has been satisfied. The act or process of levying **distress**.

distress   A common law remedy of 'self-help' that permits someone (the distrainor) to remove and, after a period of time and due notice, to sell the goods of another as a means of enforcing the payment of a debt (especially the payment of **rent**). The distrainor may take actual possession of the goods and remove them from the premises, or prepare a list of the distrained articles and leave them in situ condition that they are not removed from the premises (the latter procedure being called 'walking possession'). However, the person exercising the right of distraint, or a party employed by him, must not use force to enter premises to obtain the goods.

Distress for rent is rarely used as it must be carried out strictly in accordance with the common law and applicable statutes and the landlord may be liable for excessive, irregular or wrongful distress. In addition, the UK the levying of distress may be considered a contravention of the Human Rights Act 1998, especially if carried prior to an application for a court order or if there is a dispute

as to the rent owed (*viz*: Rook, Deborah. *Property Law & Human Rights*. London: Blackstone Press, 2001, pp. 180-191). The levying of distress may also be considered a contravention of the European Convention on Human Rights, which requires "a fair and public hearing" when determining a persons civil rights (Art. 6(1)).

In the US, distress was never recognized in some states and has been abolished in many other states; or it is deemed unconstitutional as not being a procedure that is carried out by the "due process of law". Where it is permitted, distress must generally be carried out in accordance with rules of the state statutes. Distress has been abolished in all States in Australia, except South Australia and Tasmania.

Sometimes called the 'issue of a landlord's warrant'. The goods distrained upon may themselves be called 'distress'. See also **additional rent, attachment, damage feasant**.

Magor, David L. *Distress for Local Taxation and Rent*. London: Institute of Revenues, Rating and Valuation, 1999.

Rook, Deborah. *Distress for Rent*. London: Blackstone Press, 1999.

distress damage feasant(Eng)   See **damage feasant**.

distressed area(US)   An area that suffers from adverse economic conditions, especially from high unemployment or deprived social conditions. An area that is considered by the federal government to be in need of financial assistance or other inducements, with the aim of stimulating new development, attracting further investment and thereby increasing potential employment. Also, an area that has been severely damaged by a natural disaster. See also **development area**(Eng).

distressed property(US)   A property that has become an unprofitable investment for the owner, especially when the owner is faced with action by a mortgagee. Distressed property is not inherently unsatisfactory, unusable or damaged in any way, but the term is used predominately to refer to property that is unsuitable to the owner (as when it is overleveraged), or property that has been mismanaged by its owner.

distressed sale   See **forced sale**.

distributee(US)   A person who by law receives all or part of the estate of a deceased who has left no **will**. In particular, a person who receives personal property from someone who dies **intestate**. See also **beneficiary**.

distribution trust(Eng)   See **trust for sale**.

district plan(Eng)   See **development plan**.

district shopping center   See **shopping center**.

district valuer (DV)(Eng)   An employee of the Commissioner of the Inland Revenue who is responsible for providing valuation advice, particularly for property taxation purposes; for assisting local authorities with matters relating to compensation; for advising on the valuation of property for rating purposes; and for providing other advice to local government bodies on financial matters, including terms for development, acquisition and disposal of land and buildings, especially when central government grants or loans are involved. See also **valuation officer**.

disturbance   **1.** Interference with the legal enjoyment of a right. A reduction in the proper or full enjoyment of real property by the act of another, whether arising by menaces, force, persuasion or otherwise. Disturbance of a right to possession may arise from any act that prevents the possessor from enjoying his right of possession peaceably. It may arise from **trespass** or **nuisance**, or in any other similar manner. In the case of an incorporeal right, e.g. an easement or profit à prendre, disturbance means an act that prevents the exercise of that right, such as by blocking up an ancient light or obstructing a right of way. The legal remedy for the disturbance of a right to

property may take the form of an **injunction** or an award of **damages**. See also **adverse possession**, **constructive eviction**.   **2.**(Eng)An action of an authority possessing compulsory purchase powers that gives rise to a claim for **consequential damages**, as when the exercise of those powers leads to the termination or reduction of the profits of a business, or when a person is relocated against their will. See also **compensation for disturbance**.

disturbance damages   See **compensation for disturbance**.

disturbance payment(Eng)   A payment made to a person who is displaced from land (other than agricultural land) when the dispossessed party does not have an interest in land, but is displaced by an authority possessing compulsory purchase powers (Land Compensation Act 1973, ss. 37-38). Such a payment is made when the dispossessed party has no other means of claiming compensation for being disturbed. The amount of compensation is determined at the discretion of the authority and is intended to cover the reasonable expenses of moving and the loss sustained by the disturbance to a trade or business. See also **compensation for disturbance, farm-loss payment, home-loss payment**.

ditch   A trench or narrow open passage running through the ground, whether naturally occurring or man made, that acts as a conveyance for water, for either drainage or irrigation purposes. A ditch may also act as a dividing line or barrier between contiguous parcels of land. See also **boundary line, channel, drain, fence**.

divest   **1.** To deprive someone of a right or title. To take away an estate or interest in property. To annul. cf. **vest**. See also **devest**.   **2.** To sell something as a result of a court order. See also **alienation**.

divided agency   See also **dual agency**.

divided interest   See **partial interest**.

dividend yield The yield obtained by calculating the relationship of the dividend payable on a share to the current share price. Similar to the 'equity-dividend rate' or **cash-on-cash return** from a real estate investment, being the net return on the cash invested. cf. **earnings yield**.

dividing fence(Aus) A boundary **fence** between two properties. In particular, a fence that is required by statute to be erected between owners of adjoining land. All States have enacted legislation in respect of a 'dividing fence' (e.g. Dividing Fences Act 1981 (ACT); Dividing Fences Act 1991 (NSW); Fences Act 1972 (NT); Dividing Fences Act (Qld); Fences Act 1975 (SA); Boundary Fences Act 1908 (Tas); Fences Act 1968 (Vic); Dividing Fences Act 1961 (WA)). Such legislation provides a procedure for the sharing of fencing costs; rights of access to repair a dividing fence; and a system for the resolution of disputes in the local courts. This legislation may not apply if there is an express agreement between adjoining land owners as to the liability for the dividing fence, or the owner plans to erect a fence that is of a higher standard than that considered by statute to be 'sufficient'. See also **barrier fence**.

dividing wall See **party wall**.

divisible contract See **severable contract**.

division wall See **party wall**.

divot(Scot) See **feal and divot**.

doab A tract of land between two rivers. In particular, the area of land formed by the sediment deposited by two converging rivers.

dockominium(US) A boat slip that is sold as a condominium.

doctrine of adhesion See adhesion contract.

doctrine of estates A principle of common law that a person does not own land outright, as with a chattel, but has a mere right to an **estate**, i.e. a right to hold land for a period of time. This doctrine enables land ownership to be divided into successive holdings, but in such a way that different holdings can exist at the same time in the same piece of land. For example, one person may hold a fee simple estate with an immediate right to possession, another an estate that comes into possession if a particular condition is fulfilled, and another an estate for life. The word 'estate' denotes the duration of a person's ownership of land, as compared with **tenure** (or, in modern terms, tenancy), which denotes the length of time for which a person may use another's land.

The doctrine of estates was based originally on **seisin**, i.e. the principle that one person only has a right to land that is superior or inferior to another, there being no absolute right to the **ownership** of land in common law. The highest right to land that a person may possess is a **freehold** (which in itself was held from the Crown). Freeholds may be subdivided into freeholds of inheritance, and freeholds not of inheritance, i.e. life interests. All other rights to land are of fixed or determinable duration, i.e. leaseholds, which could not be recovered by real actions and therefore are strictly **personal property** or 'chattels real'. Each estate in land can have a separate marketable value – a value that is essentially deferred in time. The doctrine of estates is a unique and fundamental feature of common law, that although recognized in the US as of historical significance in the formulation of rights over land, is now superseded in most jurisdictions by the **bundle of rights theory** as to the division of the various rights to the ownership and possession of land. See also **doctrine of tenure, property, real property, remainder, reversion**.

doctrine of laches See laches.

doctrine of lost modern grant See lost modern grant.

doctrine of notice   See *bona fide* purchaser, notice.

doctrine of part performance   A doctrine that seeks to enforce a contract when an action is taken that is of such a character that it would be performed only if it were done in reliance on an intended contract. In particular, the doctrine provides that, although an agreement for the sale or other disposition of land, or an interest in land, has not been put into **writing**, or evidenced in writing, and duly signed, and therefore would not be enforceable by an action 'at law', if one of the parties to the agreement acts to his detriment, based on a reasonable presumption that there is an enforceable agreement, the other party cannot accept the benefit of that action and then claim the agreement is unenforceable merely because it is not in writing.

A common instance of the application of the doctrine of part performance arises when a prospective tenant enters into **possession** of a property, pursuant to an oral contract, and carries out valuable and permanent improvements thereto. If the only reasonable explanation for that action is the existence of an oral contract, and the performance is consistent with that agreement, the court will normally enforce the contract.

It is fundamental to the application of the doctrine of part performance that: (a) there is evidence of the essential terms of the contract; (b) the intention of the parties can be clearly ascertained; (c) the action that has been performed unequivocally refers to, and is consistent with, the alleged contract; and (d) the terms of the contract must relate to land. In addition, the contract in question must be capable of enforcement, i.e. it must not be illegal or arise from fraud or misrepresentation (*Steadman v Steadman* [1976] AC 536, 2 All ER 977 (HL); *Starlite Variety Stores Ltd v Cloverlawn Investments Ltd* (1978) 22 OR (2d) 104, 92 DLR (3d) 270, 275 (Can); Pelletier v. Stuart-James Co., Inc., 863 F.2d 1555 n. 6 (5th Cir. Ga 1989)). The doctrine of part performance is applied frequently to support a request for a decree of **specific performance** when there appears to be a proper and justifiable contract to support.

In the US, some jurisdictions accept that delivery of possession alone may be sufficient 'part performance' to support an oral contract, but most jurisdictions require possession and at least the payment of money or, more usually, improvements to the property by a purchaser or tenant; or substantial actions, or a significant change in the situation, by the prospective purchaser or tenant, to indicate that it was reasonable to assume that it is intended that the parties would complete a sale or lease of the subject property. Some jurisdictions require that the claimant demonstrate that he has so changed his position in reasonable reliance on the contract that injustice can be avoided only by specific enforcement of the contract. A few states do not recognize the doctrine of part performance and a party who has altered his position in reliance on an oral contract for the sale or other disposition of land may have to rely on the doctrine of **estoppel** or the establishment of a **constructive trust** to enforce that contract.

In English law, on or after September 27, 1989, "a contract for the sale or other **disposition** of an interest in land can only be made in **writing** and only by incorporating all the terms which the parties have expressly agreed in one document, or where contacts are exchanged, in each", LP(MP)A 1989, s. 2. Thus, the doctrine of part performance now has little or no application to contracts for the sale or other disposition of land. As in the US the remedy may be to rely on estoppel or a constructive trust where money has been paid in respect of the sale or disposition of land, but the matter has not been properly set down in writing and signed by the parties. See also **agreement for a lease, unjust enrichment**.

doctrine of stale demands(US)   See **laches**.

doctrine of substantial performance   See **substantial performance**.

doctrine of tenure   An ancient principle of common law that all land is held in subordination to another, subject to the performance of certain obligations by the holder or 'tenant', with the ultimate ownership of land being vested in the Crown. A principle that is more applicable to the **feudal system** of land tenure than modern land law. In the US, since the Declaration of Independence, this doctrine is primarily of historical significance, although many aspects of modern land law may be understood only by looking at the ancient forms of **tenure**. See also **manor**.

doctrine of unjust enrichment   See **unjust enrichment**.

doctrine of worthier title   See **worthier title doctrine of**.

document   An **instrument** used for the purpose of recording any matter in an appropriate form, which may include printing, engraving or photocopying. In particular, an instrument or **writing** that may be used as a form of legal evidence, including a letter, contract, **receipt**, **bill of sale**, **conveyance**, **deed** or a **will**.

document of title   See **title document**.

documentary stamp tax(US)   See **stamp tax**.

documentary transfer tax(US)   See **transfer tax**.

dog fence(Aus)   A fence that runs from South Australia to Queensland and is intended to prevent the entry of dingoes and dogs onto pastoral land (Dog Fence Act 1946).

domain   1. The total and absolute **ownership** of real property or the property so owned. Landed property held in one's own right, as distinguished from property held subject to a superior lord. See also **doctrine of estates**, **dominion**.   2. A territory over which an authority exists as of right, especially a sovereign or government authority. 'National domain' or 'public domain' is all the land owned by the government. See also **eminent domain**.

domestic fixture(AmE)   A chattel that has been fixed to a dwelling house for the comfort and convenience of the tenant, such as a light fitting, a refrigerator, or demountable shelving. A domestic **fixture** is not considered to be part of the real property because, although it may be affixed to the property, the purpose of such annexation is not such that it is intended to become part of the realty, unless it is so fixed that it would cause material damage to the realty if removed.

domicile   1. Derived from the Latin *domus*, 'home'. A person's true and permanent home. The place to which someone is most likely to return; to regard as his or her ordinary place of dwelling; or intends to be his or her fixed home, unless or until something shall occur to induce him or her (unexpectedly) to adopt some other permanent home. A domicile once acquired is presumed to continue until it is shown to have changed both in terms of an actual change and in terms of an intention to change. A person may have a number of places in which to reside, but he or she may have only one domicile at any one time. The place of a person's domicile is dependent on the acts or deeds that lead to a conclusion as to where that person has voluntarily established a permanent place of habitation. cf. **residence**.   2. The place where a **bill of exchange** or other form of negotiable instrument is made payable.

dominant estate or **dominant tenement** The land or tenement that benefits from an **easement**, **restrictive covenant**, or any other form of **servitude**. In the US, also called the 'dominant premises', or sometimes the 'benefited tenement'. cf. **servient estate**. See also **easement appurtenant**(US).

dominant premises(US)   See **dominant estate/ dominant tenement**.

dominant tenement   See **dominant estate**.

dominion   The absolute right to the **ownership** of something, including both title and possession. Absolute property. See also *dominium*.

dominium(Lat)   Absolute **ownership**. In Roman law *dominium* represents the absolute and exclusive right to property, whether land or movables – the right to use; the right to enjoy and profit from; and the right to alienate or even destroy property – *jus utendi*, *jus fruendi*, *jus abutendi* – subject only to the restraints imposed by law. *Dominium* may be distinguished from **possession**, because possession may be absolute but represents no more than a personal entitlement to property, whereas dominium is a real right. Possession may entitle a person to a right that is protected by law, but does not, of itself, give that person a right to mastery over property.

In Scots law, land was held in *dominium utile*, a right to hold land as a vassal, i.e. in recognition of a superior landowner. The superior holding a *dominium directum*, or superiority of the land. The estate of *dominium utile* as a feudal estate has now been abolished, and the estate of *dominium utile* is now the "ownership" of land (Abolition of Feudal Tenures etc. (Scotland) Act 2000, s. 2).

donatio mortis causa(Lat)   'A **gift** on account of death'. A gift made in anticipation of death, with the intention that it shall take effect on the donor's death. See also **gift** *causa mortis*.

donation   A charitable **gift**. The voluntary transfer of something without receiving any reward or tangible benefit in exchange. A voluntary and gratuitous transfer of title or possession of property without contemplation or expectation of consideration. See also **exaction**, **gift** *causa mortis*.

donee   1. The recipient of property transferred as a **gift**; one who receives property without valuable consideration.   2. One to whom a **power of appointment** is granted.

donor   1. A person who transfers property as a **gift** to another, i.e. without receiving consideration in exchange.   2. One who grants a **power of appointment**.

dormant partner   See **silent partner**.

dormant title   A claim of title to property that is unasserted, such as a claim by **adverse possession**.

dormitory suburb or **dormitory town** See **bedroom community**.

dotard   A tree that is not suitable for **timber**, normally because it is dead or dying. As a rule, dotards may be removed by a tenant for life without constituting an act of **waste**.

double agency(US)   See **dual agency**.

double annual value   See **tenancy at sufferance**.

double conversion(US)   The sale of real property and its conversion into money combined with a simultaneous transaction to purchase other real property with the proceeds. See also **conversion**.

double declining balance depreciation See **accelerated depreciation**.

double diminishing balance depreciation   See **accelerated depreciation**.

double decking(US)   The illegal sale of the same property to different purchasers.

double escrow(US)   See **dual escrow**.

double house(US)   A single building comprising two or more floors that contains two or more residential units that are divided from each other vertically and are intended for occupation by two separate households with independent means of ingress. Also called a 'two-family house'. cf. **duplex house**. See also **semi-detached house**.

double insurance See co-insurance.

double net lease(AmE) See net lease.

double rent 1.(Eng)Rent payable by a tenant who has given a valid notice to quit but does not then deliver possession at the time mentioned in the notice and as a result the tenant becomes a trespasser and is treated as such by the landlord. Such **rent**, at twice the rate payable under the expired tenancy, is recoverable like any other amount of rent, but ceases when the tenant vacates without the need for further notice to quit. The landlord's right to recover this amount is a statutory right and is called an 'action for double rent' (Distress for Rent Act 1737, s. 18). **2.** A sum payable, at "double the yearly value", by a tenant who remains in possession of property, without legal or statutory authority, after being given due notice. A tenant who 'wilfully' holds over after notice to quit and a demand for possession in writing is liable for such 'double rent' under English law (L&T Act 1730, s. 1) and in some jurisdictions in the US (1 Am.L.Prop. § 3.36 n. 15). The landlord must give notice of such a claim before the expiration of the tenancy or thereafter. The tenant is not liable for such double payment if he holds over in good faith and belief that the retention of possession is justified, as where he is expecting to be granted a new lease. Such a payment is strictly not rent (as with **1.**) but an amount of damages for a failure to vacate the premises. Also called an 'action for double value'. See also **holding over**, **mesne profits**, **penalty rent**(US), **tenancy at sufferance**.

double sinking-fund method(BrE) A method of capitalising a variable income from a property investment with a limited life, such as a leasehold interest. Unlike the application of a **dual-rate years' purchase**, which capitalises the income by allowing for a new sinking fund to start each time there is a change in the rent receivable, the double sinking fund method allows for a single sinking fund for capital recoupment during the entire period for which the income is capitalised.

double value See double rent.

double waste The causing of **waste** to a property in such a way that a double injury is caused. For example, unlawfully felling trees for the purpose of using the timber therefrom to carry out repairs that the tenant is obliged to carry out, and then not making the repairs. See also **waste**.

doubtful title(US) A title that is open to reasonable doubt. A title that would expose the purchaser to the possibility of litigation in order to defend it. A title that cannot be considered a **marketable title**. cf. **good title**. See also **unmarketable title**.

dower A common law right of a wife to a life interest in a third of the freehold property owned by her husband at any time during the marriage, in particular the property that her issue, if any, might inherit (*Magna Carta*, Ch. 7; 25 Edw. I (*Magna Carta*) 1217). The right to dower has been abolished in English law (AEA 1925, s. 45(2)). In the US, in most jurisdictions, dower has been abolished, although the term may be used for a statutory right that a widow (or widower) may have to claim a share of her husband's (or his wife's) estate from his (or her) testamentary disposition. See also **tenancy by the curtesy**, **matrimonial property**.

down payment **1.** A sum of money paid as a **deposit** on the signature of a contract for sale. A sum of money paid as **earnest money**. In the US, the total cash paid for a property, excluding any monies borrowed upon the security of that property, is sometimes referred to as the down payment or the 'buyer's equity'. The term 'down payment' may also be used to refer to money paid as **earnest money**, although earnest money is generally a pre-contract payment, whereas a down payment generally refers to a payment made to secure a contract or agreement. cf. **instalment**. **2.** A payment made at the time that a property is acquired, especially the cash payment made under an **instalment contract**.

downREIT(US)   See **umbrella partnership REIT**.

downside leverage(US)   See **leverage**.

downside risk   The ultimate **risk** of bankruptcy or of a project reaching a position of total loss. The risk of a loss occurring. A downside risk may be contrasted to the possible gain, or 'upside potential', from an investment. See also **leverage**.

downstroke(US)   The total cost of acquiring an investment; the amount of **equity** required to acquire a property, including closing costs.

downzoning(US)   A change in the **zoning** of an area in order to limit the use or development that can be carried out in that area. This may be achieved, for example, by reducing the **floor area ratio** or the number of permitted units per acre; substituting single-family residences for multi-unit buildings; limiting the type or range of use permitted; or changing the permitted use completely. Downzoning is normally considered valid if it is to correct an inconsistency with the general plan for the area or if it is temporary. For example, when the downzoning is made while there is a lack of adequate services to the area. However, a downzoning that completely takes away, or substantially reduces, the value of an area of land may amount to a form of expropriation, entitling the owner of the affected land to **just compensation**. See also **inverse condemnation, rezoning, spot zoning**.

dowry   Property, real or personal, that a wife brings to her husband on marriage. A payment or gift made by a wife, or usually her father, to her husband as recompense for obligations he is assumed to have accepted on marriage. A similar type of property existed in Roman law, called *dot*, or **dotal property**, although such property was brought into the marriage to assist the husband with the marriage establishment expenses. See also **dower, matrimonial property**(Eng), **separate property**.

draft   1. A written order from one person (the 'drawer') to another (the 'drawee') to pay a sum of money to a named person or the bearer of the order (the 'payee'), either on demand or at a future time. In many cases the drawer and payee are the same party, the draft being made payable to 'ourselves'. A draft may take the form of a **bill of exchange** or a **check**(AmE)/**cheque**(BrE); although 'draft' more usually refers to an order drawn on a bank, i.e. a **bank draft**. Also, a bill of exchange must be negotiable, whereas a draft may be non-negotiable. cf. **note**.   2. An outline drawing or sketch of a proposed land or building development scheme. 3. See **draft agreement**.

draft agreement   A document in writing (but not the final version) setting out details of an **agreement** and prepared by one side, such as a seller or landlord, for consideration by the other side. Commonly referred to simply as a 'draft'. See also **subject to contract**.

dragnet clause(US)   An omnibus or blanket clause in a mortgage note which provides that, in the event of default, the mortgagee may foreclose on any other loans that are owed to him by the mortgagor, whether incurred before or after the execution of the mortgage, in addition to the specific debt secured by the mortgage. In some jurisdictions, dragnet clauses are unenforceable because the courts will enforce only mortgages that are tied to specified collateral; or the clause may not be enforceable in respect of an advance made before the mortgage has been effected. In several jurisdictions, a dragnet clause will be enforced only if it is clear that, at the time the mortgage was granted, the mortgagor was fully aware of its potential effect. Also called an 'open-end clause', an 'omnibus clause', or colloquially (and more commonly) a 'Mother Hubbard clause'. See also **anaconda mortgage, future advance**.

drain   An artificial ditch, channel or conduit designed to discharge surface or ground water from land. In particular, a channel or pipe that is built to run water from one property to another, especially to discharge surface or foul water. Generally, a drain conducts liquid and some solids from one property, as distinguished from a **sewer**, which is a large drain that serves several properties or an entire district. A sewer is, in every case a drain, but not every drain is a sewer. A drain is frequently considered as a conduit for surface and rain water, whereas a sewer collects discharges from drains and takes away waste matter, effluent or similar noxious matter. A drain may carry off rain water, but the word does not normally extend to a gutter.

In the US, a drain may be defined to include "any water course or ditch, opened or proposed to be opened, and improved for the purpose of drainage, and any artificial ditch or drain, levee, dyke or barrier, or tile drain proposed or constructed for such purpose", Act No. 316 of the Public Acts of 1923.

In English statute law, a 'drain' may be "used for the drainage of one building or of any building or yards appurtenant to buildings within the curtilage", Public Health Act 1936, s. 343(1). See also **easement, watercourse**.

drainage ditch   A **ditch** dug for the purpose of draining land. Strictly speaking a drainage ditch is not a **watercourse**, although it is sometimes encompassed within that term.

draw-down or **draw down**   1. The amount of money actually borrowed, i.e. used rather than available under a loan facility.   2. To take an **advance** under a loan agreement. Also called 'take down'. See also **draw request, tranche**.

draw request   1. A request for the advance of money under a loan agreement, especially for a further advance under a **construction loan**. See also **future advance**(BrE)/**further advance**(AmE). 2.(US)A schedule, prepared by a real estate developer or his architect or project manager, showing the stages at which he is likely to require to draw down cash from a loan facility.

drawing area   See **catchment area**.

driftway   A common way for driving cattle or horses, especially to market. Also called a 'droveway'. In common law, a driftway may be permitted within a **carriageway** or a **bridleway**. See also **highway**.

drip   See **easement of drip**.

drop-lock debenture or **drop-lock FRN**   A form of debenture loan, or floating rate note (FRN), that provides for the interest rate to be fixed if it falls below a specified level. Advances under the loan are made at the floating rate, unless or until the rate falls below the predetermined rate, at which stage the entire loan is 'locked in' at the fixed rate.

dry closing(US)   See **preclosing**.

dry mortgage(US)   A **mortgage** in which the mortgagor has no personal liability and the mortgagee must look solely to the secured property as security for the debt. See also **non-recourse mortgage**.

dry trust   See **passive trust**.

dual agency   An agency where the same **agent**, who is seeking to be remunerated by both sides, is representing both parties in a transaction. As a rule, dual agency is contrary to the principle of agency because an agent owes a **fiduciary** responsibility to his principal and is unlikely to be able to fulfil that responsibility on behalf of opposing principals. Most professional real estate associations discourage their members from accepting or seeking dual agency. For an agent or broker to be able to claim two commissions he must fulfil the two conditions: (i) make a full disclosure to each party of the exact nature of his position before he enters into any agreement; and (ii) obtain the consent of each party in the clearest possible terms and with the clearest possible information to each of his principals. As a rule, unless an agent or broker makes it clear to both sides that he is acting solely as an intermediary (or **middleman**) and is seeking to be remunerated by both parties simply for establishing a common business interest, the principal may declare the agreement void and not be obliged to pay any commission.

Similarly, an arrangement by which the agent or broker agrees to a fee split with the party he does not directly represent, or that party's broker, will make the commission agreement voidable unless it is made known to all the parties. However, splitting a fee with a participating broker who has assisted by introducing a third party to the appointed broker is fairly common and usually enforceable. Many state licensing laws prohibit dual agency, unless the principal gives his written consent to such an arrangement. Also called a 'double agency', 'divided agency', or sometimes in the US 'multiple agency'. cf. **joint agency**. See also **in-house sale**, **subagent**, **voidable contract**.

dual contract(US) An arrangement whereby a buyer and a seller of property agree to terms different from those of the true or original contract, generally in order to benefit fraudulently from some form of commission or payment. For example, a contract that is made at a higher price than the true contract to enable the buyer to obtain a larger mortgage. Such a contract is a federal crime, and may also be a state offence. See also **counter-letter**, **fraud**.

dual escrow(AmE) An arrangement by which two related escrow agreements are entered into. For example, when **escrow** is established for the sale of two properties that are to be closed simultaneously and the proceeds of one are to be used for the purchase of the other. Also called a 'back-to-back escrow', or a 'double escrow', when the monies held in one escrow account are to be used to purchase property held in the other escrow. See also **sub-sale**.

dual-rate capitalization factor(AmE) See Appendix C, **Financial Formulae**.

dual-rate mortgage (DRM) A mortgage loan that provides for actual payments of interest to be made based on a short-term market rate (the 'effective rate'), but with the true rate calculated on the basis of a medium to long-term rate (the 'payment rate'). The loan is fully amortising during its term. The actual payments due are assessed on the outstanding principal at the end of each year (based on the effective rate) and this is deducted from the regular amortisation payments (based on the payment rate), any difference being used to adjust the outstanding principal balance. See also **adjustable-rate mortgage**.

dual-rate years' purchase(BrE) See Appendix C, **Financial Formulae**.

due compensation(US) See **just compensation**.

due date The **date** upon which an obligation or payment falls due, for example the date upon which a promissory note falls due for payment. See also **days of grace**, **maturity date**, **rent in advance/rent in arrears**.

due diligence Reasonable inquiries, surveys, searches and investigations made to ascertain information relating to a property prior to entering into a contract or purchase. Such diligence as a reasonable and prudent man would exercise in the conduct of his own affairs, in order to ascertain such facts as may be discovered to be material to a transaction. The term is also used in modern real estate practice to refer to inquiries that are made between a preliminary agreement, or an option agreement, and the execution of a binding commitment. For example, due diligence includes physical and environmental surveys, income and expense verification, financial and market analysis, and such matters as would lead a purchaser to ascertain that the proposed transaction is worth the proposed formal commitment. See also **inquiry**, **notice**, **survey**.
Siedel, George J., and Janis K. Cheezem. *Real Estate Law*. 4th ed. Cincinnati, OH: West Educational Publishing, 1999, Appendix A, "Checklist for Use in Real Estate Transactions".

due-on-alienation clause(US)   See **due-on-sale clause**.

due-on-encumbrance clause(US)   See **due-on-sale clause**.

due-on-sale clause or **due-on-transfer clause**(US)   A clause in a mortgage deed that gives the lender the power to demand repayment of the entire loan if the mortgaged property is sold or otherwise transferred without the mortgagee's consent. Some jurisdictions consider such a provision as unenforceable, because it represents an unreasonable restraint on the alienation of real estate, whereas other jurisdictions do not consider it unreasonable for the mortgagee to be repaid when the mortgaged property is sold, especially if the mortgagee can demonstrate that there is an increased risk that the mortgage will be repaid by the new owner. Also called an 'alienation clause', 'due-on-alienation clause', 'due-on-transfer clause', 'non-assumption clause', 'call clause' or, if the provision applies to the creation of a new encumbrance, a 'due-on-encumbrance clause'. cf. **acceleration clause**. See also **assumption clause**, **restraint on alienation**.

Dumpor's Case(Eng)   See **partial release**.

duplex   **1.** A self-contained apartment on two levels, forming part of a building that contains other separate apartments.   **2.** One of the two units, spread over two floors, situated in a two-family apartment building.   **3.**(AmE)A residential unit that is divided horizontally from a similar unit in the same building but has a separate means of access. 'Duplex' may also be used to refer to a unit that is divided vertically from a similar unit, but that is more commonly called a **double house** – or in British English a **semi-detached house**. See also **duplex house, maisonette**.

duplex house   A building with two separate apartments, or containing accommodation for two families, usually on different floors, with separate entrances to each unit; especially a building that would otherwise be one private residence and has the appearance of one house. A building that contains two dwellings both of which comprise two stories. A building designed and used for residential purposes and containing two dwelling units separated by a common party wall or otherwise structurally separated. cf. **double house**. See also **duplex**.

duration   **1.** The span from the beginning to the end of a period of **time**. A period of time for which an estate or interest in property exists, e.g. the **term** of a lease. In particular, a period of successive days. A duration may be varied according to the custom of the business being conducted, so that a period of "60 days' duration" may be 60 consecutive days, but in some cases it may be 60 working days, exclusive of Sundays and legal holidays. A lease is always granted for successive days (unless clearly expressed to the contrary) and rent is payable accordingly, but a licence or franchise may be based on working days. See also **day, estate, quantity**.   **2.** The time for which an agreement is made. In particular, the term of a loan or the time period for which a loan is outstanding. See also **time value of money**.

duress   Actual or threatened violence. An unlawful coercive act that vitiates consent. An action or threat of an action against a person or his property, especially when used to compel someone to enter into a contract or to discharge a contract. Duress implies feebleness on one side and overpowering strength on the other. It may also arise from economic pressure or financial stress. A contract entered into under duress is usually of no legal effect and is voidable at the instigation of the sufferer; or, in extreme cases, it may be void at the outset. See also **coercion, harassment, unconscionable bargain, undue influence, voidable contract**.

during   See **time**.

Dutch auction   See **auction**.

duty 1. An **obligation** to do something or refrain from doing something. cf. **power**. See also **debt**, **duty of care**. 2. Something owed to another, especially to a government. 3. A levy or **tax** payable to a government on the importation of goods into a country.

duty of care A term predominately of the English law of **negligence** which is based on the principle that it is incumbent upon any person to take reasonable care not to cause damage or injury to another who is likely to be in proximity to his or her actions or, in one word, not to cause damage or injury to one's **neighbour** (*M'Alister (Donoghue) v Stevenson* [1932] AC 562, 580 (HL)). A principle founded on the ethic of 'mutuality of behaviour' and imbedded in modern law in the form of a requirement that a person should have in mind those in reasonable, and legal, proximity to his or her daily conduct and that such a person should avoid actions that might deliberately harm others. "A legal duty so called is nothing but a prediction that if a man does or omits certain things he will suffer in this or that way by judgment of the court", Oliver Wendell Holmes, *Collected Legal Papers* (1920).

A duty of care may be considered, in many instances, to arise in two stages. First, to determine if there is a sufficient degree of proximity between the parties that carelessness by one may be likely to cause damage to the other. Second, whether there are any considerations that might limit the scope of the duty or the class of persons to whom the duty may be owed. Thus, the duty may be limited with respect to a trespasser on land or when the offended party can be shown to have contributed, in whole or in part, to his own downfall. However, the duty must be looked at in all the circumstances to see if there is such a close and direct relationship that the action of one party may cause a potential loss or danger to another.

A duty of care arises in particular between anyone who claims to be, or is held out to be, an expert in an area where others acknowledge far less proficiency. If a person has a particular skill or ability and takes it upon himself to give information or advice to, or allows his information or advice to be passed on to, another person whom he knows, or should know, will place reliance upon it, then a duty of care is owed to that other person (*Hedley Byrne and Co Ltd v Heller & Partners Ltd* [1964] AC 465, 503 (HL)).

In English law, a landlord who has an obligation to repair or maintain leased premises, or has a right of entry to repair and maintain leased premises, and therefore should reasonably be aware of any defect in the **premises**, owes a duty of care to any person who might be affected by that defect (Defective Premises Act 1972, s. 2). Also, a landlord of multi-let premises has an obligation (unless there is an express provision to the contrary) to keep the common parts in a reasonable state of repair and maintenance and thereby owes a similar duty of care. See also **constructive eviction**, **invitee**, **occupier**, **professional negligence**, **trespass**, **visitor**.

duty to convert See **conversion**, **trust for sale**.

dwelling house or **dwelling-house** A building that is used, constructed or adapted for residential use and is lived in, or is capable of being physically used wholly or principally for human habitation. A house occupied or intended to be occupied as a residence. A **house** where a person (or persons) lives, i.e. eats, sleeps and rests; especially a place where one has established a **home**. A dwelling-house may be a single room or a mansion; or it may form part or the entirety of a building, including rooms that are not actually lived in but form part of the whole, e.g. a cellar or outhouse; but it is commonly understood to refer to a single dwelling, as opposed to a building that contains a number of dwellings.

The fact that a house is rarely lived in does not preclude it from being a dwelling-house, as long as the potential occupier has an intention to return, the *animus revertendi*, and the legal ability to return to the house. A house does not cease to be a dwelling-house solely because the law prohibits its use for dwelling purposes, especially if it possesses the basic characteristics expected of such a house. Generally, 'dwelling-house' refers to premises with a reasonable degree of permanence (and thus it excludes most caravans), but it may be part of a building used for other purposes. An **hotel** is not normally considered to be a dwelling-house.

In English law, in the case of a **protected tenancy** or an **assured tenancy**, a dwelling-house may be an entire house or part of a house, which includes a flat or even accommodation in a hotel, provided the premises form a separate dwelling (*Luganda v Service Hotels Ltd* [1969] 2 Ch 209, [1969] 2 All ER 692 (CA)) (but generally not a **caravan**). The premises must be used for "dwelling", which may be defined to include "all the main activities of life, particularly sleeping, cooking and feeding"

and there should be some degree of continuity and purpose (*Curl v Angelo* [1948] 2 All ER 189, 190 (CA)).

In the US, the Fair Housing Act of 1968 defines a dwelling as "any building, structure, or portion thereof which is occupied as, or designed or intended for occupancy as, a residence by one or more families, and any vacant land which is offered for sale or lease for the construction or location thereon of any building, structure, or portion thereof", 42 USC § 3602(b). Note: dwelling-house is generally hyphenated in British English (as in *The Oxford English Dictionary*), but not in American English (as in *Webster's Third New International Dictionary, Unabridged*). See also **abode**, **apartment**, **apartment house**(AmE), **flat**(BrE).

E

early redemption charge See **prepayment penalty**.

early retirement mortgage See **growing-equity mortgage**.

earn-out(AmE) **1.** A share of the profit realized on the sale of a property by a holder of a charge or mortgage secured on that property. For example, a mortgage agreement may provide, that in the event of a sale of the mortgaged property, the mortgagee will receive a share of the proceeds above a previously agreed price. See also **equity participation**. **2.** A share of the profit received by a vendor of property after it has been sold, usually as a result of a management agreement or a joint venture entered into with the purchaser.

earnest A part payment made to secure a **bargain**. A sum paid as an instalment. See also **earnest money**.

earnest money **1.** An initial payment made to secure a **bargain**. A sum of money, or something tangible, paid as a token of good faith by a prospective purchaser upon the execution of an agreement of sale.

In English legal usage, earnest money may be described as a sum paid under a provisional agreement to show that the parties are serious and as a restrain on the seller from dealing elsewhere. It may also be used as synonymous with the term **deposit**; but it generally refers to a smaller, e.g. 0.5% or 1% per cent of the total consideration, rather than 5% or 10% which is more usual as a 'deposit'. (For a history of earnest money see *Howe v Smith* (1844) 27 Ch D 89, 101.)

In the US, 'earnest money' and 'deposit' (or 'down payment') are generally used interchangeably. In any event, the intention of the payment is that it will be forfeited to the seller if a contract does not arise from the provisional agreement, as the purchaser can then no longer be considered 'in earnest'—unless that failure is a direct result of an action or default of the seller.

In some cases the earnest money may be given to the seller's broker, and the broker then has a responsibility to deposit the money in a client trust account, unless both parties agree to an alternative arrangement. Upon completion of a sale the money is paid to the vendor as part of the purchase consideration. If the vendor is unable to complete the sale through his own fault (especially when he is unable to provide proper title) the money should be returned to the purchaser. On the other hand, if the purchaser fails without valid cause to complete the transaction, generally the earnest money should be paid over by the broker to the vendor. As a rule, a broker has no claim on the earnest money for his commission, unless there is an agreement to the contrary, although some jurisdictions take a counter view. Also called 'bargain money', 'good faith money', 'good faith deposit', 'hand money', 'caution money' or 'binder'. See also **commingling, consideration, handsel, stakeholder**. **2.** A **down payment** made as a condition to purchasing a property at an auction.

earnest money contract or **earnest money agreement**(US) See **contract of sale**.

earnings Something obtained, usually in the form of money, in return for labour or the use of capital. The price of services performed. The revenue received over a period of time after deducting directly related expenses, i.e. net income received from an investment. cf. **profit**. See also **cash flow, income**.

earnings approach(AmE) See **income capitalization approach**.

earnings multiplier See **price-earnings ratio**.

earnings yield The percentage relationship between the net profits or earnings that a company could make available for distribution as dividends to the ordinary shareholders and the current share price. The earnings yield is calculated as follows:

$$\frac{\text{earnings per ordinary share after tax} \times 100}{\text{market price per ordinary share}}$$

The earnings yield is the reciprocal of the **price-earnings ratio**. The earnings yield available to an ordinary shareholder in a company is comparable with the **cash-on-cash return** available to an investor in real estate, as both measure the total return on equity (before the investor's personal liability for tax). cf. **dividend yield**.

easement   A right or privilege that the owner of one area of land enjoys over land owned by another for a particular purpose that does not amount to taking anything off the land. The owner of the one parcel derives a benefit from the use of other land, such as a **right of way**, **right of light** or a **right of support**. The land that has the benefit of this right is called the dominant land or 'dominant tenement' and the land that is subjected to the burden is called the servient land or 'servient tenement'. The owner of the servient tenement retains full dominion over his land, subject only to the limitation imposed by the easement. The right to use the other person's land does not grant a right to retain possession, or a right to take any profit from the land. Normally an easement is enjoyed for a specific purpose, is a permanent interest over the land of the other, but is not inconsistent with the ownership of the servient tenement. It is not a right that is personal to the owner of the land, but is said to be **appurtenant** or incidental to the land affected.

An easement is an **incorporeal hereditament**, i.e. it creates no **estate** in land because the dominant tenement does not derive any right of ownership over the servient tenement. It does not confer any right to possession, as with a **lease**, but is merely a right to impose proprietary restrictions. However, it is an **interest** in land and an easement may continue even if there is a change in the ownership of the land; it is said to

'run with the land', although it is extinguished if both tenements come into the same hands.

In common law, the essential requirements of an easement may be summarised as follows: (i) there must be an identifiable dominant and servient tenement; (ii) the easement must accommodate or benefit the dominant tenement and there must be a *nexus* between the right enjoyed and the user of the dominant land (it must do more than simply benefit the owner of that land as a personal right); (iii) the owners or occupiers of the dominant and servient tenements must be different parties (an easement is a right *in alieno solo* – 'against another's land'); (iv) the easement must be capable of forming the subject matter of a **grant**, whether express, implied or presumed, i.e. it is a right that is sufficiently definite (both as to the parties and the subject land) that it is capable of being (although it need not be) set down in a **deed** (*Re Ellenborough Park* [1956] Ch 131 (CA); *Canadian Pacific Ltd v Paul* (1988) 53 DLR (4th) 487 (Can)). The dominant and servient lands need not be contiguous, although they frequently are, but they must be proximate so as to enable the dominant land to derive benefit from the easement. The right should not amount to the exclusive use or possession of the servient tenement (or a joint use with the owner of the servient tenement). The right to exclude others from the servient tenement extends only so far as it permits the owner of the dominant tenement from preventing an interference with the permitted right that is enjoyed over the servient tenement.

An easement may be classified as 'continuous' or 'discontinuous'. A continuous easement does not require the interference of man for its existence, as with a right of light; whereas a discontinuous easement requires the intervention of man, as by the exercise of a right of way.

In the US, many jurisdictions do not consider that the existence of the dominant tenement is an essential element to an easement, and a similar irrevocable right, which does not benefit another parcel of land, is considered to be a valid easement and is called an **easement in gross** (3 Tiffany on Real Property (3rd ed. 1939), § 758, p. 204).

An easement may be distinguished from a **profit à prendre** as the latter allows someone to take something physically from the land or benefit from the profits of the soil, whereas an easement does not. Also, a profit à prendre may and usually does exist 'in gross', i.e. it does not need to benefit another parcel of land. It may be distinguished from a **licence**, which as such does not create any interest in land but is merely a privilege that is personal to the parties. On the other hand, a licensee may be granted a right to occupy land, or may be granted a right that is combined with an easement. An easement may be distinguished from a **customary right**, which may be used by a specific class of persons and benefits no defined area of land.

An easement may be granted as an indefinite right, or it may be limited for a period of time, or even for a life. It can be created by statute (as by appropriation by a public authority); by an **express grant**, i.e. a written agreement (the most common way); by express **reservation** or by **implied reservation**; by **implied grant** based on the intention of the parties, especially when it arises out of the existence of a **quasi-easement**; by 'presumed grant' or **prescription**; or even by **estoppel** when it would be unconscionable to deny that such a right exists. An easement may arise as 'of necessity' (an **easement of necessity**), as when a parcel of land is 'landlocked'. However, whether created expressly or by implication, an easement is always granted; it cannot arise purely as an amenity or privilege, enjoyed by virtue of an informal understanding or custom.

An easement may be extinguished by an express **release**, usually by deed (but not by unilateral revocation); by an implied and clear intention on the part of the dominant owner not to resume his right, i.e. **abandonment**; by the **merger** of the dominant and servient tenements into common ownership and possession (called 'unity of seisin'); by expiration of a period of time, or purpose, stipulated in the original grant; by an alteration in the dominant tenement in such a way that the easement is unnecessary, as when the dominant tenement is a building that is destroyed; by losing it to another by prescription; or by statute, as when a statutory authority uses its powers to extinguish a right of way (effectively by expropriation). An easement may be temporarily suspended if there is merely **unity of possession** between the holders of the dominant and servient tenements.

An easement can be 'positive' or 'affirmative', or it can be 'negative'. A positive easement is a right to do something positive on the servient land, but not a right to demand anything from the owner of that land; it is enjoyed for a specific purpose. Examples of positive easements are: a right of way; a right of support; a right to share a **party wall**; a right to water, i.e. to enter land to extract it; a right of access for the purpose of facilitating repair to a building; a right to run utilities across land; or even a right to use a letter box on another's land. A **negative easement** is a privilege by which the servient owner may be obligated to refrain from certain uses, or actions, on the servient tenement for the benefit of the dominant owner, e.g. not to build above a given height so as to obstruct the access of light to a house on the dominant tenement. cf. **servitude**. See also **apparent easement**, **conservation easement**[US], **conveyance**, **easement appurtenant**[US], **equitable easement**, **general words**, *jus spatiandi*, **legal easement**[Eng], **natural rights**, **overburdening**[US], **right of light**[BrE]/**right to light**[AmE], **right to air**, **right to view**, **riparian rights**, **scenic easement**[US], **water rights**, **wayleave**[BrE], **writing**.

Bruce, Jon W., and James W. Ely Jr. *The Law of Easements and Licenses in Land*. Looseleaf. St. Paul, MN: West, 2001. Thomas, David (editor-in chief). *Thompson on Real Property, Second Thomas Edition*. Newark, NJ: LexisNexis, 1994 with cumulative supplements, Ch. 60 "The Law of Easement". Gaunt, Jonathan, and Paul Morgan. *Gale on the Law of Easements*. 17th ed. London: Sweet & Maxwell, 2002.

easement appurtenant[US]   A common law or true **easement**, i.e. one that is a burden on one parcel of land (the servient tenement) for the benefit of another (the dominant tenement). An easement appurtenant attaches to and runs with the land and, unlike an **easement in gross**, is not a purely personal right. It is appurtenant to the land

and, therefore, cannot exist separately and apart from the land to which it is annexed. Sometimes called a 'pure easement'. See also **appurtenance**.

easement by estoppel An **easement** over land that arises by **estoppel**, as when a party allows another to exercise a right over his land and acts or takes actions that convey the clear impression that the right may be exercised (25 Am.Jur.2d., Easements and Licenses, § 17). For example, when a vendor represents to a purchaser of a property that a right of way exists over land retained by the vendor and then the easement is not expressly granted; or when someone is allowed to connect a new building to a sewer by means of a drain that crosses another's land. In such cases, the owner of the burdened land may be estopped from denying the right if he has acquiesced in its existence or continuation.

easement by implication See easement, quasi-easement.

easement by implied grant See easement of necessity.

easement by implied reservation See quasi-easement.

easement by necessity(US) See easement of necessity.

easement by prescription See prescription.

easement for batter An **easement** that grants the owner of land above a sloping wall, terrace, or bank (a batter) a right of access to the land below the batter for the purpose of repair or maintenance. Such a right does not necessarily oblige the higher land owner to maintain the batter.

easement in gross(US) A right over another's land that in all respects is an **easement**, except that there is no dominant land, i.e. it is a right or privilege that the owner of one parcel of land enjoys over another parcel – but there is no separate parcel of land that benefits from that right. In particular, it is a right over land that does not benefit another parcel of land but is personal to the beneficiary. For example, a public utility or services easement, a highway easement, a railroad easement, or a right to draw water given personally to the owner of neighboring land. An easement in gross is personal to the beneficiary, thus as a rule it cannot be assigned and it cannot last beyond the life of the holder. However, there is an increasing tendency to regard an easement in gross, such as a utility easement, as a real right and, therefore, no different from an easement appurtenant. In English law, it is generally considered that an easement cannot exist 'in gross', because as such it would then be a personal right and by definition it cannot be a true easement. cf. **easement appurtenant**. See also **scenic easement, usufruct, wayleave**(Eng).

easement of access(US) A right that an abutting owner of land has to ingress and egress from his property to a public highway. As a rule, an abutting owner has an 'easement of access' from his land for ingress and egress to a public highway that adjoins his land. Easement of access may sometimes be used to refer to the right of an owner of land that abuts a highway to enjoy the free flow of light and air to his land from a public highway. See also **easement of necessity, right of access**.

easement of air See easement, right to air.

easement of convenience(US) See easement of necessity.

easement of drainage An **easement** by which the owner of one parcel of land (the 'dominant tenement') is permitted to discharge water onto adjoining land (the 'servient tenement'). Such a right is generally acquired as a result of continuous use, i.e. by **prescription** – although, as with any other form of easement it may be acquired by express or implied grant or reservation.

easement of drip(US) See **easement of eavesdrop**.

easement of eavesdrop or **easement of eavesdropping**   An **easement** by which an owner of land is permitted to discharge rainwater from the eaves of his house onto adjoining land. An owner of land has a natural right for rainwater to flow from his land onto an adjoining property. However, if he erects a building on the land, the right is no longer natural and water that is channelled or thrown off the roof requires an easement to permit it to fall onto adjoining land; although such a right is commonly acquired by implication or long user. In Scots law, such a right is called a **servitude** of 'eavesdrop' and in the US an 'easement of drip'.

easement of light   See **right of light**.

easement of necessity   **1.** A right of way or **easement** that arises when two parcels of land that were held in common ownership are separated by a conveyance and access over one of the parcels of land (the servient tenement) is *essential* to the proper enjoyment of the other parcel (the dominant tenement). For example, access from one parcel to another in order to gain access to a highway when the land would otherwise be landlocked. "A way of necessity, strictly so called, arises where, on a disposition by a common owner of part of his land, either the part disposed of or the part retained is left without any legally enforceable means of access", Jonathan Gaunt & Paul Morgan, *Gale on the Law of Easements*. 17th ed. London: Sweet & Maxwell, 2002, p. 149. An easement of necessity arises when the property retained could not otherwise be used; it does not grant a right that is merely necessary to the reasonable or better enjoyment of that property. The means of access should be by the most convenient route for the beneficiary and the least onerous for the owner of the land over which it is exercised. Once a route has been adopted, the owner of the dominant tenement cannot change or intensify the use without a new grant. In the US, also called an 'easement by necessity'; or a 'way of necessity'. cf. **implied easement**, **quasi-easement**. See also **easement of access**[US].   **2.** An easement

that is considered essential to the proper enjoyment of land or a building, such as a right of lateral support to the land or a wall. See also **natural rights**, **party wall**, **right of support**.

easement of support   See **right of support**.

easement of view   See **right to view**.

east half or **E2**[US]   The eastern half of a **section** of land as set out under the government survey system.

ecclesiastical benefice[Eng]   Property owned or effectively controlled by an ecclesiastical authority, namely the established Church of England, which may include a rectory or parsonage house.

ecclesiastical property[Eng]   Where notice is to be served under any provisions of the TCPA 1990 on the owner of 'ecclesiastical property', that term is defined as "land belonging to an **ecclesiastical benefice**, or being or forming part of a church subject to the jurisdiction of a bishop of any diocese or the site of such a church, or being or forming part of a burial ground subject to such jurisdiction or being diocesan **glebe land**", TCPA 1990, s. 318(6). In such cases notice must also be served on the Church Commissioners.

economic   age-life   method   of depreciation   See **straight-line depreciation**.

economic depreciation   See **depreciation**.

economic impact statement   A report on the effect that a major development project will have on the local economy, including such factors as employment, business activity, taxation and market conditions. cf. **environmental impact report**.

economic interest   **1.** An interest in land that has an economic value.   **2.**[US] The possibility of profit from the extraction and sale of oil or gas as held by the grantor of an **oil and gas lease** which entitles the beneficiary to a depletion tax allowance.

economic life   The period of time for which something may be used profitably. The time span for which a building is expected to yield a return in excess of that obtainable from the bare land; the period for which it is economic to maintain a capital asset or an improvement. The economic life cannot exceed the **physical life** although, due to external factors such as changes in the neighbourhood in which the building is situated, it may be shorter. Also called the 'useful life' or sometimes the 'service life'. See also **depreciation**, **effective age**.

economic obsolescence   See **obsolescence**.

economic rent   **1.** The **market rent**, as distinguished from the contract rent payable under the terms of a tenancy agreement or lease. The economic rent may equal, exceed, or fall short of the contract rent. See also **profit rent**[(BrE)].   **2.** Rent that is just sufficient to cover all the costs of running a property, including interest charges, operating expenses, service charges, management fees, etc., i.e. a 'break-even' rent to the landlord. Also called a 'cost rent'.   **3.** In economics, any sum earned by a factor of production (especially capital) that exceeds the minimum amount required to keep that factor in its existing use, i.e. any sum that exceeds the **opportunity-cost** of maintaining that factor in production. Accordingly, economic rent is 'unearned' income because it is derived merely from the ownership or control of the factor of production with no direct effort made by the recipient of the income. When received from land, this sum is also called 'land rent', being the surplus or profit over and above the minimum cost of keeping land in operation. In theory, such an amount of 'economic rent' can be sustained only in the short-term because, in the long-term, alternatives will be produced that result in a reduction in earnings to a level that barely covers the cost of production. Based on that theory,

economic rent as produced by machinery or other factors of production was called by Alfred Marshall 'quasi-rent' (*Principles of Economics* (1890)). See also **marginal land**.

economic value   **1.** The value of a property as assessed by capitalising the future anticipated net operating income for the **economic life** of the property.   **2.** The value of a property based on its earning potential. See also **economic rent**.

edifice   Derived from the Latin *ædificium* or the Old French *ædificare*, 'to build', 'to construct' or 'to make a house'. A large **structure**; an imposing **building**.

effective age   The age of a building taking into account such factors as design, layout, standard of maintenance, equipment and amenities; rather than the age based on the building's actual date of construction. A well-designed and maintained building may have a lower (i.e. younger) effective age than its actual age and thus have a longer **economic life**. The effective age of a building can be reduced by improvement or renovation. For example, a 100-year old building that was completely· renovated to modern standards ten years ago may be regarded as having an 'effective age' of ten years (or less) and would be valued accordingly.

effective annual interest rate   The true interest rate payable over one year when interest is compounded at intervals of less than a year. The formula for converting a **nominal interest rate** to an effective annual rate is:

$$I = [1 + \frac{i}{m}]^m - 1$$

Where: $i =$ nominal interest rate (expressed as a decimal)

$m =$ number of compounding periods per annum

$I =$ effective annual interest rate.

Thus, a nominal interest rate of 8% per annum would be an effective rate of 8.3% when interest is compounded monthly. Also called an 'effective rate' or, when the same conversion is made to arrive at the rate of return on an investment that produces an income at intervals of less than once a year, the 'effective rate of return'. See also **annual percentage rate, internal rate of return**.

effective capital value (ECV)   See **contractor's basis**.

effective cause   See **commission, procuring cause**.

effective date   The date upon which an agreement or action takes effect. For example, the date from which an insurance policy provides cover. See also **appraisal date**(AmE), **valuation date**(BrE).

effective floor area(BrE)   The floor area that is considered usable or to have value for an occupier. Although there is no single accepted method of measuring residential property for valuation purposes, the area of such a property may be referred to as the 'effective floor area', which may be defined as "the usable area of the rooms within a building measured to the internal face of the walls of those rooms. INCLUDING (1) Living rooms, dining rooms, bedrooms, kitchens and the like; (2) Areas occupied by fitted cupboards within those rooms; (3) A floor area which contains a ventilation/heating grille; (4) Areas occupied by skirting; EXCLUDING (5) Bathrooms, showers and toilets; (6) Stairwells, liftwells, halls, landings and balconies; (7) Corridors and the like whether formed by structural walls or not; (8) Internal walls whether structural or not, columns, piers, chimney breasts, vertical ducts, and the like; (9) Areas with headroom less than 1.5m; (10) Fuel stores, lift rooms, tank rooms, plant rooms, cupboards, etc.; (11) Areas under the control of service or other external authorities including meter cupboards and statutory service supply points", The Royal Institution of Chartered Surveyor, *Code of Measuring Practice*. 5th ed.

London: RICS Books, 2002. Areas such as (9) may be better stated separately (Note: this definition is accompanied in the *Code* by diagrams and detailed notes for amplification. The *Code* is intended for use in the UK only and is intended to aid understanding of area measurements.) A measurement used in council tax banding of flats and maisonettes. See also **net internal area, usable area**.

effective gross income (EGI)(US)   The **gross income** (including all rental and miscellaneous income) that can be anticipated from a property when it is fully leased and after making allowance for vacancies and defaulting tenants (or 'collection loss'), but before deducting operating expenses. See also **income**.

effective gross income multiplier (EGIM)(AmE)   See **income multiplier**.

effective interest rate   See effective annual interest rate.

effective lease rate or **effective rental rate**   The true lease rate payable by a tenant, after taking into account allowances made by the landlord such as a free rent, contributions made to meet the cost of any improvements above the building standard made by the tenant and, if appropriate, the cost of assuming the tenant's existing lease. Also called the 'net effective rate', 'rental equivalent' or **equivalent rent**, especially in the UK. cf. **virtual rent**.

effective possession(US)   Actual occupancy of part of a tract of land, which may qualify as sufficient to support a claim for **adverse possession** of the whole. Also called 'virtual possession'. Sometimes used synonymously with **constructive possession**, although the latter does not include actual occupation but merely a claim to **possession**.

effective procuring cause(US)   See **procuring cause**.

effective rate   1. See effective annual

interest rate.   2.(AmE)The **effective lease rate** based on the area of the building occupied, i.e. per sq. ft.   **3.** See **average daily room rate**.

effective rate of return or **effective yield** **1.** The return or yield from a bond, or other instrument, based on the actual price paid and taking full account of the date income is received, or interest paid, and the date the investment matures or is sold; as opposed to the **nominal rate of return** which is based on the 'face value' or 'par value' of the bond or instrument. In the case of a real estate investment, the 'effective rate of return' takes into account the actual stages at which the rent is paid; thus if the rent is payable monthly in advance it will have a higher effective yield than if the rent is payable quarterly in arrears. See also **annual percentage rate**, **equivalent yield**, **redemption yield**.   **2.** The rate of return on an investment based on the actual rent receivable, i.e. based on the **effective lease rate**, and taking into account any immediately pending vacancies or defaulting tenants. See also **internal rate of return**. **3.** See **effective annual interest rate**.

effective rent   **1.** See **effective lease rate**.   **2.** The total rent payable by a tenant of a retail store, including the **base rent** and any **percentage rent**.

effective rental rate   See **effective lease rate**.

effective yield   See **effective rate of return**.

effects   Movable property, especially movable or **chattel** property of any kind. 'Effects' is commonly used as synonymous with **goods**, but strictly speaking it is less extensive in meaning than goods, being only that which a person has and that is capable of effecting, producing or creating money – usually by sale. 'Effects' is frequently used in a restricted sense, as in the expression of 'furniture and effects' or 'household effects', to refer to items that contribute to the use and ornament of a house; or as in 'personal effects' which embraces such tangible property as is worn or carried about the person. The term 'effects' used in a will *simpliciter*, without further qualification or amplification, is understood to mean goods, movables and personal estate, i.e. it passes the entirety of a person's **personal property**. On the other hand, if the context so admits, it may encompass real and personal property. Thus, 'real and personal effects' or 'all the remainder of my effects whatsoever, both real and personal' when used in a will may embrace the testator's entire estate. Nonetheless, the meaning of the word 'effects' must be collected from the context and the particular sense in which the testator has intended to use it. See also *ejusdem generis*, **movable**, **personal effects**.

efficiency apartment or **efficiency unit**(AmE)   A small dwelling unit that comprises a single habitable room together with a kitchen and bathroom. (In British English such a unit would commonly be called a 'bedsitting room'.) See also **studio apartment**.

efficiency frontier(Aus)   "A line plotted on a risk/return chart which shows the highest investment return that can be expected for any given level of **risk**", Roger Goldsmith et al., *The Dictionary of Australian Investment Terms*. 6th ed. Oxford University Press, 2003.

efficiency ratio   **1.** The ratio of the **net internal area**(BrE) or **rentable area**(AmE) of an office building to the **gross internal area**, i.e. the ratio of the area for which the tenant pays space and the area that has been built. In Australia the 'building efficiency ratio' or 'space efficiency ratio' is defined as the ratio of the **net lettable area** of a floor to the total area of that floor, or the ratio of NLA of the building to the **gross building area** (GBA) of the building (Property Council of Australia, *Glossary of Property Terms* (2000)).   **2.**(AmE)The ratio of the **usable area** to the **rentable area** of a building or a floor in a building. For example, if the usable area of an office floor is 8,000 sq. ft. and the rentable area is 10,000 sq. ft. the efficiency ratio is 80%. See also **loss factor**.

effluxion of time   See **expiration**, **lease**.

egistment   See **agistment**.

egress   The exit or means of exit from a property. cf. **ingress**. See also **easement of access**.

ejection(Scot)   A remedy to recover land against a person who has taken adverse possession. An action that may be used when the possessor has taken the land by *vi, clam, aut precario* (by force, stealth or precariously). Ejection is a remedy that is used predominately in cases where the defender had no right of possession to land, as distinguished from removal which is used against a person who had a right to possession that has come to an end, as with a tenant. Ejection may be used against a squatter or a seller who has not vacated land.

ejectment   1.(Eng)See **mesne profits**, **recovery**. 2.(US) A right based on the common law action that may be used to reclaim possession of land from someone who is holding the land under an invalid title. "To recover the possession of real property in an ejectment action, either the plaintiff must have title to the property and a present right of possession, or the plaintiff must have actual possession of the property, together with a right to maintain possession, when ousted by the defendant and a present right to possession when the action was begun", 25 Am.Jur.2d., Ejectment, §§ 1, 6. Ejectment cannot be used in a case of mere trespass. A similar process called 'equitable ejectment' may be brought in some jurisdictions to enforce **specific performance** of a contract for the sale of land when the seller fails to deliver possession. Such an action is now brought by summary proceedings in accordance with statutory regulations and may be referred to as an 'action to recover possession of land', an 'action for summary possession of land', an 'action for **forcible entry and detainer**', or (especially when applied in landlord and tenant proceedings) an 'action for eviction'. See also **adverse possession**, **ouster**. 3.(US)A remedy used by a landlord to recover possession of leased property from a tenant. In most jurisdictions, there are statutes that enable a landlord by summary proceedings to recover possession from a tenant, especially when he is holding over at the expiration or termination of a lease or the tenant is in breach of a condition of the lease. Similar proceedings are known in different jurisdictions as '**forcible entry and detainer**', 'dispossessory warrant proceedings', 'unlawful detainer', or 'landlord and tenant proceedings'. See also **eviction**, **dispossession**, **mesne profits**.

ejusdem generis(Lat)   'Of the same kind or nature'. The *ejusdem generis* rule is applied when there is a particular or class description of property followed by some general or all embracing description; it is assumed that items covered by the general description are of the same kind or nature as the particular. For example, an insurance policy may cover things that are of a similar nature or *genus* to those set out in the contract, even if they are not specifically referred to in the policy. On the other hand, the policy does not cover things of a different *genus*. In construing a statute, the rule is that if the Legislature had intended the general words to be used in their unrestricted sense, they would have made no mention of the particular classes and general words may be restricted to the same genus as the specific words that precede them. cf. ***noscitur a sociis***. See also **words**.

election   A choice, in particular between a plurality of alternatives. There may be an election between rights or an election between remedies. For example, a person who is induced into a contract by misrepresentation may either exercise his right to affirm the contract (and claim damages for the loss suffered by the misrepresentation), or he may seek to rescind it – he cannot do both. If a person has knowingly done an unequivocal act that demonstrates that he has taken a particular course, he cannot elect to take another course that by his act he has rejected. In particular, the third party to a contract, upon discovering the identity of an

undisclosed principal, may elect to take an action against that principal, in place of the agent, but his election in that respect may preclude any right of action against the agent with whom he has contracted (*United Australia Ltd v Barclays Bank Ltd* [1941] AC 1, 30, [1940] 1 All ER 20 (HL)). cf. **abandonment**. See also **approbate and reprobate**, **forfeiture**, **waiver**.

elective share(US)   The share of an estate that a surviving spouse may claim by statute if he or she is omitted from the **will** of the other spouse, or is left less than he or she would otherwise receive by statute. See also **tenancy by the curtesy**, **dower**.

elevation   1. The height above a fixed level, especially the height above sea level.   2. The façade or side view of a building.

Ellwood capitalization rate(AmE)   A **capitalization rate** for appraising investment property, named after L. W. Ellwood MAI, which takes into account the financing used to purchase an investment and, thus, the effect of **gearing**. The principle behind this method of arriving at the capital value of an investment is based on the theory that the value of an investment is a function of: (i) the amount of **debt capital** that can be obtained to acquire that investment at current mortgage rates; and (ii) the amount of equity capital that would be invested at a required rate of return on that equity, i.e. value = loan available + present value of equity, where the present value of equity is the present value of the before-tax cash flow, plus the present value of the future selling price, minus the present value of the balance due on the mortgage at the time of sale. L. W. Ellwood produced a series of tables to provide a single capitalization rate given: (i) the mortgage coefficient at the appropriate interest rate (the **mortgage constant** calculated at the **equity yield rate**); (ii) the term over which the amount of equity invested is to be recaptured; (iii) the period of the mortgage; (iv) the ratio of debt to equity; (v) the required **equity yield rate**; (vi) the projected appreciation or depreciation in the property over its investment life; and, if required, (vii) the tax rate of the investor. The application of the Ellwood capitalization rate represents an extension of the **mortgage-equity capitalization technique**, having been developed to take account of all the above variables.

Ellwood, L. W. *Ellwood Tables for Real Estate Appraising and Financing*. 4th ed. Cambridge, MA: Ballinger Publishing for American Institute of Real Estate Appraisers, 1977.

Wood, Ernest. *Property Finance: Evaluating Its Effects* (1973) 277 EG 1425.

emblements   Pronounced em-blem-ents. Derived from Old French *emblaer* or *emblaement de bled*, 'to sow with grain'. An annual crop produced by the labour of cultivation. Emblements include such crops as corn, wheat, rye, flax, potatoes, melons and garden vegetables, but not perennials or the fruits of trees. Emblements are crops that may be considered by a tenant of land as personal property. The common law doctrine of emblements provides a right for a tenant who holds an uncertain interest in agricultural land – e.g. from year to year, for life (and sometimes at will if the tenant does not terminate the tenancy), or one whose interest was granted for a fixed term, but is unexpectedly brought to an end – to reap ripened crops he has previously sown, even after his tenancy has ended, except when the termination is a consequence of the tenant's own actions (2 *Bl Comm* 123); *Haines v Welch & Marriott* (1868) LR 4 CP 91. This doctrine does not apply to a tenancy for a fixed term that expires by normal effluxion of time because such a tenant is supposed to be able to plan his husbandry to cultivate and harvest crops before the term ends.

At common law, a personal representative of a **tenant for life** may enter land after the estate has come to an end and reap crops that had been sown by the life tenant. This applies only to artificially grown crops, such as corn, hemp, flax, carrots or potatoes; the personal representative may not return to collect fruits from seeds or plants that do not produce a crop within one year of sowing or planting, and he may only reap a single crop (1 *Co Litt* 55b; 2 *Bl Comm* 122; *Graves v Weld* (1833) 5 B & Ad 105, 119, 110 Eng Rep 731). In English law, the common law doctrine of emblements no longer has any application to periodic tenants, because an agricultural tenancy must be terminated by 12 months notice to quit to expire at the end of a year of the tenancy, thereby allowing the tenant ample time to reap his annual crops (AHA 1986, s. 21).

In the US, some states have statutes that regulate the taking of emblements at the end of an estate for life, and some jurisdictions take a more favorable view of the entitlement to fruits on trees to that postulated by the common law (American Law Reports, *Annotations and Cases*, Anno: 47 ALR3d 784, Emblements—Respective Rights). See also **compensation for improvements**, **way-going crop**.

eminent domain　Literally, 'superior dominion' over land. The right of a sovereign authority (nation, state or municipality) to take private property for a public use. A term coined in the 17th century by Dutch jurist Hugo Grotius to describe the inherent power of a sovereign state, government, or a public body (or even a duly authorized private person) to take private property, for public use, without the owner's consent. The process or proceedings for settling this action is known as **condemnation** or **expropriation**. The power of eminent domain is considered an "incident of sovereignty, and ... requires no constitutional recognition", United States v. Jones, 109 US 513, 3 S Ct 346, 27 L Ed 1015, 1017 (1883) (Kohl v. United States, 1 Otto 367, 91 US 367, 23 L Ed 449 (1875); i.e. it is the right of the state to take back property over which it is considered to have sovereign authority. A power that may be delegated to private corporations, such as railway or utility companies, in order to provide a public service (Stoebuch, *A General Theory of Eminent Domain*, 47 Wash. L. Rev. 553, 588-599).

In the US, the exercise of the power of eminent domain is limited by the Fifth Amendment to the Constitution, which states that no private property shall be "taken for public use, without just compensation", and the Fourteenth Amendment which states that no person shall be deprived of property "without due process of law". The taking of private property for 'private use', without the payment of just compensation, or without due process of law, is a violation of the Constitution of the United States, unlike **police power** which is an action taken under regulations designed to conserve the community at large from injury (Panhandle Eastern Pipeline Co. v. State Highway Comm'n, 294 US 622, 79 L Ed 1095 (1935)). Several states also provide in their constitution or by statute (absolutely or subject to certain qualification) that private property shall not be 'taken' or 'damaged' for public use without just compensation. The power of eminent domain may be exercised to acquire any interest in land, as well as a right over land such as an easement or a profit, although the taking must be for a public purpose and not merely for a private benefit.

The term 'eminent domain' is not used in English law, except to describe a process recognised in international law. The corresponding process in the United Kingdom is called **compulsory purchase** and in Canada 'expropriation'. Strictly speaking, eminent domain is a form of natural power vested in the state, the superior dominion, to acquire land for public use, whereas compulsory purchase is a right obtained from parliamentary decree or statute. In Louisiana the process is also called 'expropriation'. See also **severance damages**.

Eaton, James D. *Real Estate Valuation in Litigation.* 2nd ed. Chicago: Appraisal Institute, 1995.

Interagency Land Acquisition Conference. *Uniform Appraisal Standards for Federal Land Acquisitions.* Chicago: Appraisal Institute in cooperation with U.S. Department of Justice, 2000 rev. ed.

Sackman, Julius L. (editor). *Nichols on Eminent Domain.* 18 vols. 3rd rev. ed. Looseleaf. San Francisco: Matthew Bender.

emphyteotic lease　A form of long-term lease found in the civil and French law and legal systems based on the Napoleonic Code. An emphyteotic lease may be described, for example, as "a contract by which the proprietor of an **immovable** conveys it for a time to another, the lessee subjecting himself to make improvements, to pay the lessor an annual rent, and to such other charges as may be agreed upon", Civil Code of Lower Canada, art. 567 (a similar definition is contained in the Quebec CC, art. 1195). The essential elements of this form of lease are: (i) the lease is long-term (between 18 and 99 years); (ii) the lessee is obliged to maintain the property (including being responsible for the structural repair of any building on the land) and is usually obliged to make improvements to the land or erect new buildings thereon; and (iii) the lease is a real right and it may be alienated or charged as security (subject to any restraints contained in the lease), but it cannot be abandoned. The lease may be renewed by agreement, but there is no automatic right of renewal. Although originally intended as a form of lease of agricultural land, an emphyteotic lease can now be granted (as it often is) for the use of land for residential, commercial or industrial building.

emphyteusis   In Roman and civil law, a contract by which land was leased for a long term of years (or indefinitely) subject to the payment of an annual rent or *canon* upon a condition that the land is improved by cultivation, building or otherwise. The lease is alienable and can be transferred by inheritance. This was a 'real' right to the land entitling the holder to a full right of **possession**, and the grantor cannot recover the land, except in the case of non-payment of rent. This form of contract is the forerunner of the **emphyteotic lease**.

emphyteutic lease   See **emphyteotique lease**.

emptor (f. *emptrix*)(Lat)   'Buyer'; 'purchaser'. See *caveat emptor*.

empty nester(US)   A couple whose children have grown up and left home, thereby leaving the couple with a home that may be too large for their needs.

en ventre sa mere   'In the mother's womb'; *in utero*. An unborn child. See **rule against perpetuities**.

enabling declaration(US)   See **condominium declaration**.

enagenacion(US)   A Spanish-American term for a transfer of a fee title. The term may also be used to refer to the transfer of any interest in land, i.e. alienation.

enclosure or **inclosure**   1. An area of land that is fenced off, especially when this is done in order to keep something or someone from entering or escaping from the land, or in order to demarcate or assert a right to **possession** of land. See also **adverse possession**, *animus possidendi*, **strict liability**, **trespass**.   2. The fencing in of an area of land in order to restrict or contain its use. In particular, in England the closing in of an open field in order to prevent its use as **common land**. The enclosure of common land is now rare because any such enclosure must be established as being "of benefit to the neighbourhood as well as the private individual", Commons Act 1876, s. 7.
 In British English, 'enclosure' is normally used to refer to the surrounding of land with a fence or wall, and 'inclosure' is used to refer to the legal process of appropriation. However, the spellings are interchangeable. See also **fence**, **manor**.

encroach   1. Derived from the Old French *encrochier*, 'to seize' or 'to fasten upon'. To intrude beyond defined limits. In particular, to intrude gradually onto another's land. See also **encroachment**.   2. To seize or acquire wrongfully.

encroachment or **incroachment**   A gradual or partial intrusion onto the land of another, especially by the shifting of a property boundary or the erection of a building that intrudes onto another's land. An illegal entry or intrusion onto the land of another, normally by an adjoining owner, especially when made in such a way that it does not give the appearance that any title is being claimed beyond the true boundary. Encroachment may include such acts as physically taking away land or exercising a right to land; or building over land, whether on, above, or below the surface. Such action normally constitutes a **trespass**. It may also involve an intrusion or interference with the proper use of land, especially onto adjoining land, in such a way as to cause a **nuisance** to an owner of land. An encroachment may also arise if a beneficiary of an **easement** extends or enlarges his rights over the servient land. An encroachment, if acquiesced in, may ripen by **adverse possession**, or by **prescription**, into a title to, or a permanent right to, an interest in land. In the US, 'encroachment' may also be used in the confined sense of an intrusion onto a highway (such as by a fence, building, or other fixture), as distinguished from an 'obstruction', both of which require different statutory processes for their removal. See also **ejectment, strict liability, tree.**

encumbrance or **incumbrance**   Derived from the Old French *encombrer*, 'to block out' or 'to hamper'. A **burden, claim, lien,** or other impediment on property, especially one that depreciates the value, impairs the use, or limits the transferability of the property. Although an encumbrance may limit or restrict the use or value of property, it does not necessarily prevent the transfer of property. An encumbrance on real property has no strict technical meaning, but is interpreted according to the context. It is most commonly used to refer to an impediment on title, or to a financial restriction, such as a **mortgage, charge** or lien. Thus, encumbrances may be classified broadly as: (a) those that limits a title or right to full enjoyment of a property, e.g. a mortgage, lien, charge, pending legal action (*lis pendens*) or judgement to secure a debt; and (b) those that restrict the physical use of property, e.g. the burden of an **easement** or a **restrictive covenant**.

In English statute law, an 'incumbrance' over land is defined to include "a legal or equitable mortgage and a trust for securing money, and a lien, and a charge of a portion, annuity, or other capital or annual sum", LPA 1925, s. 205. See also **adverse possession, cloud on title, covenant against encumbrances, encroachment, land charge**[(Eng)], **minor interest**[(Eng)], **overriding interest**[(Eng)].

encumbrancer   1. The party who holds property that is the subject of an **encumbrance**, such as a **mortgagor** or **lienor**. Sometimes spelt 'incumbrancer'.   2. The party who has the benefit of the impediment over another's land, such as a **mortgagee** or **chargee**. (This usage of the term is unusual, the definition in **1.** being the more usual.)

end allowance   A deduction or provision made to a valuation after the basic assessment has been made, in order to take into account special factors, such as a particular impediment or locational disability. See also **adjusted sale price, comparison method of valuation**[(BrE)], **sales comparison approach**[(US)].

end loan[(US)]   See **takeout commitment**.

end money   A sum of money that is borrowed if the actual cost of a project exceeds the estimated cost. Especially a sum drawn from a contingency fund. Also called 'over-and-above money', especially when used in relation to Federal Housing Administration projects.

endorsement or **indorsement**   1. Derived from the Latin *in-dorsum* 'on the back'. The act of the payee, holder or drawee of a bill, cheque/check, or other negotiable instrument, of writing, usually on the back, in order to transfer or assign the benefit to another. A signature placed on a document, in order either to ratify it, and any alterations thereto, or to transfer rights under the document. In the US, generally spelt 'indorsement' as in the Uniform Commercial Code (UCC § 3-202 et seq.), although the reverse of a check/cheque usually says 'endorse here'.   2. A **rider** or **memorandum** to a document, especially to an insurance policy, to clarify or give effect to an alteration of the terms. For example, an alteration to an insurance policy stating that a particular person has contracted to purchase the property that is the subject of the policy, and therefore that he has an interest in the property.

endowment   **1.** Derived from the Old French *en-douer*, 'to give a dowry'. The furnishing of someone with an income. The transfer, generally as a **gift**, of an income from property. See also **dower, endowment mortgage, portion**.   **2.** Property or money given as a permanent provision to a school, hospital, college, library or similar institution for its administration or support. Any property held permanently by a charity or benevolent society, which is also called an 'endowment fund'.

endowment insurance policy or **endowment policy**   A form of insurance policy that provides for investment as well as life insurance. The premium under the policy in effect provides a form of compulsory savings contribution. The policy provides that the insurer will pay an income, or a fixed sum, to a designated person (usually the policyholder, or the beneficiary of his estate) at a future date, such as when that person reaches a specified age, or on the policyholder's death if that occurs earlier. Unlike most other insurance policies that take the form of **contingency insurance**, which provides that a payment will be made only if a specified event occurs, an endowment policy provides that a payment will be made when the specified event occurs. See also **endowment mortgage**.

endowment mortgage   A **mortgage loan** coupled with an **endowment insurance policy** so that the policy will guarantee payment of the mortgage debt, either on the death of the insured or when the debt falls due for redemption. The mortgagor does not repay any part of the principal he has borrowed during the term of the loan but pays only interest to the mortgagee. However, coincidental with the commencement of the loan, he takes out an endowment insurance policy

(usually for the same period as the loan). Unlike a regular insurance policy, the 'premiums' include a payment towards a regular insurance policy and towards an investment policy to repay the loan. This endowment policy may be 'non-profits', 'full-with-profits', or 'low-cost'. A non-profits policy merely provides a guarantee to repay the loan on maturity, or on the death of the mortgagor if that occurs beforehand. A full with-profits scheme provides insurance for the amount of the loan and additionally the insurance company pays periodic bonuses, based on its investment performance, so that at maturity the insured is likely to receive more than the amount borrowed. A low-cost scheme provides that, if the policyholder should die before the date set for repayment of the loan (the redemption date), the loan will be paid in full. However, if the policyholder survives until the redemption date, the policy guarantees the payment of an amount that covers only part of the sum borrowed. It is assumed that the difference will be provided from bonuses allocated to the scheme based on the insurance company's investment performance. (The low-cost scheme is cheaper than a full with-profits policy; however, there is a risk that the bonuses may not reach expectations, leaving the borrower to find the difference.)

enforcement notice(Eng)   A notice served (or strictly speaking 'issued' with copies served) by a local planning authority upon the **owner** and **occupier** of land (and any other person who has an interest in the land which in the opinion of the authority would be materially affected by the notice) when it appears to the authority that there has been a "breach of planning control" and the authority considers it expedient to issue the notice taking into account the provisions of any local **development plan** and any other "material considerations". The notice requires the breach to be remedied. A breach of planning control may be the carrying out of **development** without the required planning permission or a failure to comply with any condition or limitation imposed on the grant of a planning permission. An enforcement notice requires the removal of the unauthorised development and the restoration, as effectively as possible, of the property to the condition that would have existed if the breach had never occurred. The enforcement notice, in effect, grants planning permission for the use or development it is seeking to restore. An enforcement notice is valid only if it is served in accordance with strict statutory rules. A person served with an enforcement notice may appeal to the Secretary of State on one of a number of statutorily prescribed grounds. Failure to comply with a valid enforcement notice is an offence making the convicted party liable to a fine (TCPA 1990, s. 172-182). cf. **discontinuance order**. See also **breach of condition notice, stop notice**. **2.**[Aus] A notice served by a local council or statutory authority upon an owner or occupier of land stipulating that there has been a breach of a planning, environmental or agricultural regulation and requiring the occupier to take steps to remedy that breach.

Bourne, Felix. *Enforcement of Planning Control: A Practitioners Guide*. London: Sweet & Maxwell, 1992.

Millichap, Denzil. *The Effective Enforcement of Planning Control*. 2nd ed. London: Butterworths, 1995.

Harwood, Richard. *Planning Enforcement*. Welwyn Garden City: EMIS Professional Publishing, 1996.

enfranchisement   Literally to 'set free', in real property, from the payment of rent. The enlargement of a lesser interest in land into a **freehold** interest, usually upon the payment of a fixed sum. See also **leasehold enfranchisement**[Eng], **secure tenancy**.

engineering breakdown depreciation[US]   See **component depreciation**.

engineering insurance   Insurance of items situated in a property, e.g. boilers, lifts, electrical plant and mechanical equipment. In particular, engineering insurance covers breakdown, collapse and explosion, as well as resulting damage to other property and to third parties. Such insurance is usually provided on condition that the insurance company undertakes regular inspections to ensure the proper upkeep and safety of the plant and equipment.

engineering operations or **engineering works**   Any works of construction, especially of a structural nature. In general, works for the creation of a road, highway, railway, canal, dock, harbour, or bridge and works for laying a sewer or other public utilities, including earthworks required for such purposes.

In English town and country planning law, 'engineering operations', which is a form of **development**, includes "the formation or laying out of means of access to highways", TCPA 1990, s. 336(1); and 'means of access' includes "any means of access, whether public or private, for vehicles or for foot passengers, and includes a street", TCPA 1990, s. 336(1). See also **operations**.

English auction   See **auction**.

English covenants of title[US]   See **beneficial owner, covenant of title**.

English Heritage   Formally the 'Historic Buildings and Monuments Commission for England'. A corporate body established in 1984 to take over the advisory role of the Ancient Monuments Boards with duties to secure the preservation and repair of ancient monuments and historic buildings in England; to promote public knowledge and interest in such properties; to preserve and enhance the character and appearance of any conservation area in England; and to promote the public's enjoyment and knowledge of ancient monuments and historic buildings (National Heritage Act 1983, ss. 32-33). See also **ancient monument, building preservation notice, historic building, listed building**. (www.english-heritage.org.uk).

English Nature (EN)[Eng]   The Nature Conservancy Council for England (more commonly known as 'English Nature' replaced the 'Nature Conservancy Council' (NCC) in 1991. English Nature champions the conservation of wildlife, geology and wild places in England. It is a government agency set up under the

Environmental Protection Act 1990, ss. 128-139. English Nature owns and manages many National Nature Reserves. It is also responsible for **sites of special scientific interest**. In addition, EN works throughout the countryside, and in urban areas and the marine environment, to restore degraded and impoverished habitats in order to improve their life-supporting functions. In Scotland and Wales similar responsibilities have been transferred to the Scottish National Heritage and the Countryside Council for Wales. (**www.english-nature.org.uk**).

English Partnership A national regeneration agency that was first established in 1961 (New Towns Act 1959, Part II). A 'new' English Partnership was created in May 1999 with the merger of the **Commission for the New Towns** and the **Urban Regeneration Agency** (New Towns Act 1981, Part II, as amended). The English Partnership has taken over the properties of the New Towns and the Urban Regeneration Agency. The English Partnership remediates sites and aims to bring new jobs to areas of the country in need of economic development. The English Partnership focuses on sustainable development; working with the **Housing Corporation** to assist registered housing associations and self-build societies provide affordable housing; development of brownfield sites; and urban regeneration and development. (www.englishpartnerships.co.uk).

enhancement An increase in **worth** or **value** by any cause. A change or action that makes something better or larger. Improving the quality or obtaining approval for an improved use or development of the building, or improving the area, may enhance a building. See also **betterment**, **improvement**.

engrossment or **ingrossment** The preparation of a **deed** in final form for execution (i.e. signing and sealing) by the parties thereto, or a deed that is prepared for execution. 'Ingrossment' is a virtually obsolete spelling of the word.

enjoin To order something to be done. To prohibit or regulate, especially by a court order. See also **injunction**.

enjoy See **enjoyment**.

enjoyment The receipt or retention of a benefit, advantage or reward. The exercise of a legal **right** or beneficial use. The deriving of an economic benefit or advantage; in particular, the benefit of the use of land. Enjoyment of a right over land may be had by consent or agreement, but not necessarily by occupation or possession. One may 'enjoy' or have the advantage of using an incorporeal right (such as an **easement**) in the same way as one takes possession or uses a corporeal property. Enjoyment 'as of right' – in relation to a prescriptive claim to an easement – means an enjoyment had *nec vi, nec clam, nec precario* (not by force, not by stealth, not by permission), and not as a result of regular consent (*Tickle v Brown* (1836) 4 Ad & E 369, 111 Eng Rep 826; *R v Oxfordshire County Council, ex parte Sunningwell* [2000] 1 AC 325, [1999] 3 All ER 385 (HL)).

In the context of a 'right to **quiet enjoyment**', the word 'enjoy' "is a translation of the Latin word '*fruor*' and refers to the exercise and use of the right and having the full benefit of it, rather than to deriving pleasure from it [*Kenny v Preen* [1963] 1 QB 499, 511 (CA)]", *Southwark L.B.C. v Mills* [1999] 4 All ER 449, 455 (HL). Thus, it does not necessarily mean enjoyment that is free of noise. See also **acquiescence**, **beneficial enjoyment**, **occupation**, **prescription**.

enlargement 1. An increase in a right to real property. For example, an enlargement of a leasehold into a freehold by **enfranchisement**; the enlargement of a **base fee** in possession into a fee simple; the enlargement of the right of a **mortgagee** in possession, after the expiration of the statutory limitation period, into a right to the mortgagor's interest; the enlargement of a life estate by the **remainderman** transferring his interest to the tenant for life; or the enlargement of a lease for a term of years by the landlord granting a longer lease or transferring his interest to the tenant. See also **ground rent lease**[(US)], **leasehold enfranchisement**[(Eng)], **merger**. **2.** To make larger by **addition.** To increase or expand the space allotted to a building (horizontally or vertically) by improvement or alteration. See also **extension**.

entail **1.** An estate that is a **fee** interest, but the right of inheritance is limited to a designated class of issue. Also called a **fee tail**, as distinguished from a fee simple, which may be transferred to any issue of the holder of the estate as long as such subsist. See also **entailed estate**. **2.** To create an estate in tail (a 'fee tail'), i.e. an estate limited to a person and his or her particular heirs, but not to heirs in general.

entailed estate or **entailed interest** An interest in land that has been limited to a person and his or her lineal descendants or to designated issue, i.e. an interest that is given to a person and after his or her death passes to a restricted line of direct descendants or a specified class of heirs (as to male children only). If the interest cannot go to further descendants, the estate normally reverts to the original donor or his or her heirs. Thus an entailed estate lasts as long as the original grantee or recipient (the 'tenant in tail') or any of his or her (specified) lineal descendants is alive. An entailed estate is a **fee** interest, but it is less than a **fee simple**: the old name for such an estate 'fee tail' being derived from *feudum talliatum* – a fee that has been 'cut down' or 'truncated'. An entailed interest or 'entail' is intended to have a longer duration than a **life interest**, but is enchained for a number of lives. The estate descends to successive generations in direct line of descent, but not to relatives from any other bloodline. If the line runs out, the estate returns to the grantor's successors. An entailed estate is not intended to pass out of the specified direct line of issue without first returning to the effective control of the donor. It differs from an intestate succession by which, if the direct line dies out, the land passes to a related line, e.g. a brother and his heirs.

An entailed estate may be: (a) a 'general entail' or 'tail general' which descends without further restriction, e.g. 'to A and the heirs of his body' regardless of the spouse of that person or the sex of the descendants; (b) 'special entail' or 'tail special' which descends only to the heirs through a particular spouse, e.g. 'to A and the heirs of his body begotten by him upon X'; or (c) an entail limited to a particular sex (whether from any wife of the recipient or from one specified wife), whether a 'tail male' or 'tail female', e.g. 'to A and the male (or female) heirs of his body'. The person entitled to the ownership of the land at any point in time is called a 'tenant in tail', or if there is no appropriate issue born before the recipient dies, a 'tenant in tail after possibilities of issue extinct'.

In English law, an entailed interest, like any other fee estate, can be transferred to a third party but in principle, that party's interest remains liable to be extinguished by an issue of the transferor after his or her death. However, that risk may be removed or reduced by the tenant in tail disentailing or, 'barring the entail', i.e. by conveying a fee simple. Although the holder of the entailed estate must be in possession of the estate, or obtains the consent of the **protector of the estate**, otherwise he merely creates a **base fee**. The tenant in tail in possession disentails by creating a deed (a **disentailing assurance**) that immediately grants a fee simple estate. Whereas a tenant in remainder, or one who does not have the consent of the protector, has to create a further disentailing assurance when the protector's consent is obtained, or when he comes into possession of the estate.

The terms 'estate in tail', 'estate tail', 'entail', 'entailed interest', and 'fee tail' may be used interchangeably. However, in English law since 1925, an 'entailed interest' (or an 'estate tail') is an entail that can be alienated, but exists only as an **equitable interest**, and can only take effect under a **strict settlement** as governed by the SLA 1925. An entailed interest may be created in personal property in the same way as real property (LPA 1925, s. 130). In practice, due primarily to the level of inheritance taxes, an entailed estate is now rarely created under English law. Since January 1, 1997 if an attempt is made to create an entailed estate, the property is held in trust absolutely for the person to whom the property was purportedly granted (Trusts of Land and Appointment of Trustees Act 1996, Sch. 1, para. 5).

In the US, the terms **fee tail** and 'estate tail' are more commonly used than 'entailed estate', 'entailed interest', or 'entail'. However, in most states, the interest of 'fee tail' (however it is called) has been abolished or converted to a fee simple. See also **conditional fee, disentailing assurance, estate in tail after possibility of issue extinct**(Eng), **freehold, quasi-entail, rule against perpetuities, words of limitation**.

enter   See **entry**.

enterprise zone(BrE) **or enterprize zone**(AmE) **(EZ)**   An urban area where it is considered that special government assistance is required to generate economic activity. In particular, an inner-city area that has suffered from 'urban decay' and requires substantial new development to encourage new business, employment and improved social and economic conditions. The intention is to restore incentives for private investment by fiscal policies and an easing of planning constraints.

In the US, enterprize zones have been proposed for a number of areas of high unemployment, low economic activity and general distress. These zones are intended "to create a free market environment in depressed areas through relief from taxes, regulations and other government burdens, privatization of some city services and involvement of private neighborhood organizations", Department of Housing and Urban Development, *The Administration's Enterprise Zone Proposal: Fact Sheet* (1982).

In England and Wales, the Secretary of State may designate an area as an Enterprise Zone following a submission by a local government body that a particular area is appropriate for economic assistance. Such Enterprise Zones are intended to

be experimental and they retain their status for 10 years (Local Government, Planning and Land Act 1980, Part XVII; TCPA ss. 6, 88). See also **capital allowance**(Eng), **special area**(Eng), **urban development area**(Eng).

entire contract   1. A contract in which all the terms are contained in one document.   2. A contract which provides that the entire fulfilment of the promise – the completion of all the parts of the contract – is a **condition precedent** to the fulfilment of any part of the contract. A contract where the intention of the parties is that full and complete **performance** of the contract is required before the price is paid. For example, a building contract that provides for all the building work to be completed satisfactorily before any payment is made. As a rule, a contract will generally be construed as several and not as entire, with payments being due for performance as the contract progresses. However, if the contract provides only for a lump-sum payment, after the duties and obligations are performed in their entirety, the contract will normally be enforced in its entirety. Sometimes called an 'indivisible contract'. cf. **severable contract**. See also **lump-sum contract, part performance, substantial completion**.

entire tenancy   See **several estate**.

entireties   See **tenancy by the entirety**.

entirety   See **tenancy by the entirety**.

entirety clause(US)   A clause in an **oil and gas lease** which provides that if the lessor transfers part of the leased land to another party, or the land is owned as separate tracts, then the royalties are to be pooled as if the land were still held as one undivided parcel. The receipts are then apportioned according to the area of land held by the separate land holders. Sometimes called a 'royalty apportionment clause', which may be considered a more apt description.

entitled   To be furnished with, or have a right to, a **title**. A term that has no strict legal meaning, but usually means a right to immediate **possession** and not merely a right in reversion or remainder. 'Entitled' may apply to any right that will come into possession; but it does not normally apply to a right to a **contingent interest**, i.e. a right that may never come 'into possession' or may be defeated.

In English law, 'entitled to possession' (in respect of a landlord seeking possession under the Rent Acts) means a legal right to possession, not simply a right to enforce that right through an order of the court. Thus a landlord is entitled to obtain possession when he has served a valid notice to quit and acquired a legal right to possession; he has no need to wait until a court, at a later date, grants an order for possession (*Hill v Hasler* [1921] 3 KB 643). See also **beneficiary**.

entitlement(US)   **1.** The right to a benefit, title or estate. The right to use or enjoy land in a specific way. In particular, the right to use or develop land in accordance with a zoning or building approval. See also **entitled, private property, vested right**.   **2.** The right to benefit from a particular authorization, as with a right of a veteran to obtain a VA loan.   **3.**(Aus)See **lot entitlement**.

entry   **1.** "'The act of going onto land, or doing something equivalent, with the intention of asserting a right in the land.' Rap. & L. Law Dict. tit, 'Entry'", Johnson v. Cobb, 29 SC 372, 7 SE 601, 605 (1888). Obtaining possession or occupation of a property when exercising a legal right. In particular, **taking possession** of a property at the commencement of a lease; exercising one's legal right to regain possession of land; or the act of going onto land to assert some other legal right thereover. Entry may be 'physical or actual entry', or 'constructive entry'. Constructive entry arises as a result of the exercise of a right under the law, as when a mortgagee exercises his right to collect the rent and profits from the property held as security.

Entry may be made onto land only by peaceful means, a principle first enacted into English law by the Forcible Entry Act 1381: "none from henceforth may make any entry into any land or tenements, but in the case where entry is given by law; and in such case not with strong hand, nor with multitude of people, but only in peaceful and easy manner". See also **forcible entry and detainer, landlord's access, notice of entry**(Eng), **possession, right of entry, right of re-entry, trespass, writ of entry**(Eng).   **2.** An alley or path leading up to, or into, a house or other building. A covered way between a pair of houses.   **3.** The act of making or setting something down in a formal record, or something entered into a record. See also **land recordation, land registration**.

entry and possession(US)   See **foreclosure**.

entryman(US)   One who enters onto public lands under a right of **homestead**.

enure   See **inure**.

envelope control   See **building height plane**(Aus), **bulk envelope, zoning ordinance**(US).

environment   The surrounding circumstances or influences. All external conditions and influences that affect the quality of life. The social, economic, aesthetic, and cultural conditions that affect people and the way they live, work and play. "Environmental means the surrounding conditions, influences or forces [that] influence or modify ... Webster's New International Dictionary", United States v. Amadio, 215 F.2d 605, 611 (7th Cir. Ind 1954). In particular, the environment is concerned with climate, pollution, health and safety, wildlife, vegetation, ecology and hydrology, as well as adverse factors such as crowding, squalor and crime. The term is also used to refer to all the social, economic, physical and political factors that affect the development, use and value of a property, including traffic, noise and pollution of the air or land.

In the US, the National Environmental Policy

Act of 1969, § 11049 defines 'environment' to include "water, air, and land and the interrelationship which exists between water, air, and land and all living things" (42 USC, § 11049); thus it "encompasses all the factors that affect the quality of life ...", Jones v. United States Dept. of Housing and Urban Development, 390 F Supp 579, 591 (1974).

In English law, 'environment' "consists of all, or any, of the following media, namely, the air, water and land; and the medium of air includes the air within buildings and the air within other natural or man-made structures above or below ground", Environmental Protection Act 1990, s. 1(2). The European Commission Directive 79/111, art. 2 defines it to mean "the relationship of human beings with water, air, land and all biological forms".

In economic or business terms, the entire context in which business is conducted – embracing, profitability, market structure, government regulation, taxation, finance, and the state of the economy. See also **aesthetic**, **environmental impact assessment**[BrE], **environmental impact report**[US], **police power**[US].

Bell, Stuart, and Donald McGillivray. *Environment Law.* 5th ed. Oxford: Oxford University Press, 2000.

Campbell, Gordon. *Environmental Liability.* Welwyn Garden City: EMIS Professional Publishing, 1998.

Environment Agency[Eng]   A body set up in 1985 as a non-departmental public body to provide high quality environmental protection and improvement in England and Wales. The principal aim of the Agency is "... to protect or enhance the **environment**, taken as a whole ... [and] to make the contribution towards attaining the objective of achieving sustainable development ...", Environment Act 1985, s. 4(1). The Agency's functions include the regulation of air quality; conservation and ecology, especially along rivers and wetlands; prevention of land pollution and removal or containment of contamination; flood protection; acting as the navigation authority for inland rivers, estuaries and harbours; encouraging the enjoyment of the use of inland and coastal waters and land around them; regulation of waste management and waste disposal; the control of fresh, marine, surface and underground water quality; and the monitoring of water resources, including the issuing of 'abstraction licenses'. The Agency has power to serve improvement and prohibition notices under the Health and Safety at Work Act 1974. It is also responsible for the monitoring the disposal of radioactive material. The Agency's emphasis is on education and prevention of environmental damage, with the ability to use enforcement power where necessary. The Environment Agency is sponsored largely by the Department of the Environment, Food & Rural Affairs and the National Assembly for Wales. (www.environmental-agency.gov.uk).

environmental assessment   See **environmental impact assessment**[BrE], **environmental impact report**[US].

environmental audit   An investigation of a property to ascertain if it is affected by any environmental problems, such as soil contamination, the existence of underground storage tanks, hazardous waste or toxic substances on the property, or the use of deleterious materials in the buildings, for example, asbestos, polychlorinated biphenyl (PCB) and high alumina cement.

In the US, an environmental audit is made in three phases. Phase I is a preliminary inspection of the property and examination of all historical and public records to ascertain if any problem exists. Phase II includes a detailed survey and the development of a remediation plan, generally in conjunction with the appropriate agency. Phase III is the actual remediation through to certification that the property is no longer affected by any deleterious substances. Sometimes called an 'environmental site assessment'. See also **due diligence**, **environment**, **environmental impact assessment**[BrE], **environmental impact report**[US].

Harwood, Richard. *Contaminated Land: Property Transactions and the New Regime.* Welwyn Garden City: EMIS Publishing, 2000.

environmental impact assessment[BrE]   A systematic analysis and the presentation of information on a planned development project prepared to enable the public to assess the impact of the project on the **environment** (traffic, noise, pollution, use of resources, etc.) and to enable a local authority to insist upon measures to mitigate or modify the effects of the project prior to the granting of the requisite approvals. This process generally results in the production of an 'environmental statement' (ES) (similar to an **environmental impact report** in the US), which is a document or series of documents that provides a statement of the environmental information relating to the development project, compiled for the purpose of assessing the likely effect of the project on the environment. Such an assessment is mandatory for major projects such as oil refineries and airports, and may be required for large-scale developments such as new industrial estates or marinas (European Council Directive 85/337 June 27, 1983). It is also required in the case of most major developments, especially for commercial and industrial schemes.

Morris P., and R. Terival. *Methods of Environmental Impact Assessment.* 2nd ed. New York: Spon Press, 2001.

Weston, Joe (editor). *Planning and Environmental Impact Assessment in Practice.* Harlow, Essex: Longman, 1997.

environmental impact report (EIR)[US]   A report prepared by a landowner and submitted to a federal, state or local agency that indicates the likely effect or change that a major project may have on the immediate **environment** or region. The report usually addresses such matters as traffic, noise, air pollution and demand for utilities, and may be required to address such issues as the effect on employment, schools and other community matters. The report must set out measures that are to be taken to alleviate any detrimental impact on the environment, as well as the alternatives forms of development that have been considered. In some cases, a municipal authority may determine beforehand that a proposed development will have no impact on the environment and will then issue a 'negative declaration'. Also called an

'environmental impact statement', especially when filed by a federal agency that proposes "to take a leading role in activity affecting the environment", National Environmental Policy Act of 1969, § 102 (42 USC § 4332, Note 121). In addition, the term 'environmental assessment' may be used to refer to a 'rough-cut, low budget' environmental impact statement that is designed to show whether a full-fledged environmental impact statement is necessary (Hoosier Environmental Council, Inc. v. U.S. Army Corps of Engineers, 105 F Supp.2d 953, 959 (SD Ind 2000)). See also **Environmental Protection Agency**.

Burchell, Robert W., et al. *Development Impact Assessment Handbook.* Washington, DC: Urban Land Institute, 1994.

Canter. Larry W. *Environmental Impact Assessment*, 2nd ed. New York & London: McGraw-Hill, 1996.

Kreske, Diori L. *Environmental Impact Statements*, New York: Wiley, 1996.

Sullivan, Thomas F. P. (editor). *Environmental Handbook.* 14th ed. Rockville, MD: Government Institutes, 1997.

environmental impact statement (EIS)[US]   See **environmental impact report**.

Environmental Protection Agency (EPA)[US]   A federal agency established pursuant to the Reorganization Plan 3 of 1970 (National Environmental Policy Act of 1969, Section 1; 42 USC § 4321) to monitor, control and seek to abate environmental problems; in particular, all forms of pollution and similar risks to human health. The mission of the U.S. Environmental Protection Agency is "to protect human health and to safeguard the natural environment—air, water, and land—upon which life depends". The EPA programs include air pollution and water quality control; solid waste, toxins and pesticide management; solid waste disposal; marine protection; noise control; control of radiation; and land disposal of toxins and hazardous wastes. The agency sets standards of acceptable pollution, carries out extensive environmental research programs, and provides advice and assistance to state, regional and municipal environmental control agencies. In particular, the Agency is responsible for the administration of the Comprehensive Environmental Response, Compensation, and Liability Act of 1980, as amended by the Superfund Amendment and Reauthorization Act of 1986. See also **environmental impact report**. (www.epa.gov).

environmental site assessment (ESA) See **environmental audit**.

environmental statement (ES)   See **environmental impact assessment**.

eo instante or ***eo instanti***(Lat)   'At that instant'; 'immediately'; 'instantly'.

epitome of title   A brief summary or resume of the documents of title to land. In English legal practice, an 'epitome of title' is generally prepared by the use of photocopies of all the appropriate documents, or marked abstracts thereof. See **abstract of title**.

equalization of assessments(US)   The adjustment of the general level of assessments as between different tax districts to ensure that no one tax district shall bear an unreasonable share of the taxes collected by the county, city or state. The adjustment, by a **board of equalization**, of the **assessed value** of properties in order to apportion more equitably the values, and hence the tax burdens, in an administrative area.

equalization board(US)   See **board of equalization**.

equated rent   See **constant-rent factor**.

equated yield(BrE)   A discount rate that when applied to the total income from an investment, taking into account the current income and the projected income when the current rental levels are reviewed to market value (either at the time of any rent review provision, or on the renewal of any lease), equals the initial cost of the investment. The equated yield is determined to provide a single yield for a property that is let below the market rent so that it can be directly compared with an investment that is let at the current market rent. When an equated yield is determined based on values current at the date of the valuation, i.e. taking no account of increases in rental value due to inflation, this yield is called the **equivalent yield**. Sometimes called an 'effective yield'. See also **discounted cash flow**, **internal rate of return**, **redemption yield**.

equation of rents theory   A theory that a tenant is prepared to pay only a fixed sum for the cost of occupying a property. According to this theory if property taxes or occupancy costs increase, then the rental value of a property will decrease.

equitable annuity(Eng)   An annuity secured on land which because it is a life interest cannot be a legal interest and, therefore, must be an **equitable interest**. See also **general equitable charge**.

equitable assignment   1. An assignment that, although not strictly valid in law, will be enforced in **equity**. For example, an assignment that is not made in accordance with statute law (as when it should be, but is not, made in writing), and therefore, cannot constitute a **legal assignment**; or the assignment of a debt or choses-in-action that is not made as an **absolute assignment** (i.e. it is made subject to a condition that restricts the present transfer).   2.(Eng)An assignment that is not made with the correct formality required to pass a legal interest and, therefore, passes only an **equitable interest**. In particular, an assignment of a lease that is only enforceable 'in equity' because it is not, as required by statute, made by **deed** (LPA 1925, s. 52(1)); or the assignment of an **equitable lease**. An equitable assignment requires no particular formality, provided the intention to transfer the lease is clear. The assignment may be evidenced in **writing**, or by some act of **part performance** (such as the assignee taking possession of the demised premises and paying rent to the lessor). An equitable assignment is enforceable between the assignor and assignee at the discretion of the court, provided it can be satisfied that, based on the actions of the parties, it would be equitable to do so. Even though there is a lack of a requisite formality, the court will apply the maxim 'equity looks on that as done which ought to be done'. See also **specific performance**.

equitable charge   1. A **charge** over property that is created when the property is transferred (either physically for personal property or by the deposit of deeds of title for real property) as a security for a debt, but without a grant of any true right to ownership or possession. A transfer that gives beneficial interest to the transferee and grants a security interest to a third party. An equitable charge usually arises when property is transferred with no formal documentation, but with the clear intention that it is to be held as security for the debt. cf. **trust**.   2.[Eng]A **charge** on land created when a lender has a right to have his debt satisfied from the proceeds of sale of the land, or to have a receiver appointed in the event of a default by the debtor; but has no right to foreclose on, nor take possession of, the charged land, nor an automatic right to obtain the grant of a **legal mortgage**. An equitable chargee has no interest in the land charged as security for the loan and he has fewer powers than an equitable mortgagee. An equitable charge does not create a **legal estate**, but grants only an **equitable interest** to the creditor. It entitles the holder to have the land sold by an order of the court to raise the money charged, or it may carry the right to have a legal mortgage created. It may be distinguished from an **equitable mortgage**, which is founded on a right to possession of the property and technically carries the right to foreclosure. An equitable charge need not designate specific property to be used to discharge an unpaid debt and, although it must be made in **writing**, it need not be created by the use of any particular form of wording, provided there is a manifest intention to charge property. On the other hand, a formal agreement to transfer title to property as security for a loan creates an equitable mortgage rather than an equitable charge. An equitable charge is frequently created by the use of such words as "on condition that" implying that the right does not arise until the debt remains unpaid when due. cf. **charge by way of a legal mortgage**. See also **general equitable charge**.

equitable doctrine of conversion   See **conversion**.

equitable doctrine of notice   See **notice**.

equitable easement[Eng]   An **easement** that is an **equitable interest**, i.e. one that is enforceable only in equity because: (i) it is not created by the proper formalities (which usually means by deed or will, or sometimes by statute); (ii) it is granted by a landowner who holds only an equitable interest in the servient land (for example, a landowner who holds only a life interest or a periodic lease); or (iii) it is not granted as an interest that is equivalent to **legal estate**, i.e. it is not held as "an easement … in or over land for an interest equivalent to an estate in fee simple absolute or a term of years absolute", LPA 1925, s. 1(2)(a). The LPA 1925 states that "any easement, liberty, or privilege over or affecting land and being merely an equitable interest" is referred to in that Act as an "equitable interest" LPA 1925, s. 2(3)(iii). This definition should be interpreted strictly, as the term 'equitable easement' does not embrace such 'mere equities' as an equitable right of entry or re-entry, a right of access for repair, or any other right that resembles an easement but arises in equity or, in particular, by **estoppel**. An equitable easement is registrable as a **land charge** if land comprising the servient land is unregistered, or protected by a **notice** or **caution** if title to the land is registered. cf. **legal easement**, **quasi-easement**.

equitable ejectment[US]   See **ejectment**.

equitable estate   1.[Eng]An **estate** in land that

is enforceable only in a court of equity, as distinguished from a **legal estate**, which is enforceable 'at law', i.e. against anyone without the element of discretion that can be applied in equity and that may be dependant on how the estate came into the claimant's ownership. "A legal estate is a right *in rem*, an equitable estate is a right *in personam*, that is to say the former confers a right enforceable against the whole world, the latter one which can be enforced only against a limited number of persons", E. H. Burn, *Cheshire and Burn's Modern Law of Real Property*. 16th ed. London: Butterworths, 2000, p. 56. An 'equitable estate' is one that is considered not to be enforceable against someone who purchases the 'legal estate' (which since 1925 has been designated by English statute law as the most absolute right to land); acts in good faith; pays valuable consideration; and does not have the requisite legal knowledge or notice that the equitable estate exists (a '*bona fide* **purchaser** for **value** without **notice**'); although it may be enforceable against all other purchasers.

In English law, since 1925, an equitable estate may be considered, by exclusion, to be any estate that is not a 'legal estate', i.e. one that is "capable of subsisting or of being conveyed or created at law" because it is either: (a) "an estate in **fee simple absolute in possession**"; or (b) "a **term of years absolute**", LPA 1925, s. 1(1). (These two estates, which are expressed by the LPA 1925, s. 1(1) to be the only estates capable of existing as, and usually are, legal estates, may be equitable estates; for example if they are not created by the requisite formality, which usually means they are not created by deed.) Accordingly an equitable estate includes any estate (including an easement or rentcharge) for a life, an entailed estate, or an equitable charge, as well as a fee simple that is neither 'absolute' (such as a determinable fee simple or a conditional fee simple), nor 'in **possession**' (such as a future right to a fee simple, i.e. an interest in reversion or remainder), and a leasehold estate that is not a term of years 'absolute' (e.g. a term of years terminable with a life or a term of years created by an agreement for a lease). However, the term 'equitable estate' is no longer

generally used – any estate that is not a legal estate is termed an **equitable interest** (LPA 1925, s. 1(3)). See also **estate contract**[Eng]. **2.**[US]An **estate** that is recognised only by a court of **equity**. In particular, an estate that is held in trust by a third party who holds the **legal estate**. **3.**[US]The value of a property excluding all debts or charges against it. See also **equity**.

equitable estoppel   See estoppel.

equitable interest   **1.** An **interest** in land that is enforceable only in a court of **equity**.   **2.** The interest held by a beneficiary under a **trust**. See also **equity**, **equitable title**.   **3.**[Eng]An interest in land, originally recognised by the Court of Chancery, as enforceable against only a limited number of persons – as distinguished from a **legal interest**, which is enforceable against the world at large. An equitable interest is defined in English statute law, by exception, as "Estates, interests, and charges in or over land which are not legal estates", LPA 1925, s. 1(8). An equitable interest is one that depends for its continued existence on the 'equitable doctrine of notice', i.e. it is enforceable against everyone, except a purchaser acting in good faith (a *bona fide* **purchaser**) who acquires a **legal estate** in unregistered land for **value** (which includes money, money's worth or even a promise of future marriage), and does not know, nor could reasonably have known, i.e. does not have **notice**, of the existence of the equitable interest. (As a rule, knowledge of the existence of the interest is dependent on its registration at the Land Registry and diligent inspection and search.) An equitable interest is referred to merely as a right *in personam*, i.e. a contractual obligation enforceable only against certain persons, which does not grant any right to the ownership of land, as compared with a legal interest which is a right *in rem*, i.e. a right to take the land itself. However, as this suggests that an equitable interest is not a proprietary right, capable of being assigned or inherited, it may be preferable to describe an equitable interest as a right *in personam ad rem* – a right to **real property**, which is limited because it binds any person, except a particular form of purchaser of the affected land and one who claims through such a purchaser.

Equitable interests may be subdivided into: (a) interests that depend for their existence on a right over land; and (b) interests that can just as well exist as a claim to the proceeds of the sale of land. The former type of interest must be registered to be enforceable against a purchaser of an interest in the land; registration being automatic notice to the purchaser of the existence of the interest. The latter type of interest cannot be registered and is 'overreached' by the purchaser of a legal estate, i.e. the beneficiary's right is transferred from the land to the proceeds of sale.

Equitable interests include any estate in land that is not by definition a 'legal estate', i.e. an **equitable estate** (in English law since 1925 the term 'equitable estate' is no longer generally used, any estate that is not a legal estate is termed an 'equitable interest' (LPA 1925, s. 1(3)). In addition, equitable interests include any interest of a beneficiary under a **trust**; as well as an **estate contract** (which includes a contract to purchase or an option to purchase; but not a right of pre-emption, which may be considered to be a personal contract between the parties – even though a right of pre-emption may be registered as an 'estate contract'); an **equitable lease** (including an interest arising from an **agreement for a lease**); a **right of re-entry** under an equitable lease or under an equitable rentcharge; **licence by estoppel**; an **equitable mortgage**; an **equitable charge**; an **equitable lien**; an **equitable easement**; a **restrictive covenant**; a **profit à prendre** created in respect of an equitable interest in land; and a mortgagor's **equity of redemption**.

An equitable interest should be distinguished from a **mere equity** which is a right enforceable in equity, such as a right to have a mistake corrected, a right to an injunction, or a right to specific performance (*Shiloh Spinners Ltd v Harding* [1973] AC 691, 721, [1973] 1 All ER 90, 99 (HL)). A mere equity does not bind a bona fide purchaser for value of a legal estate, nor a purchaser of an *equitable interest*, who does not have notice of the

mere equity; whereas an equitable interest is binding on any party other than a bona fide purchaser of the legal estate without notice of that equitable interest (*National Provincial Bank v Ainsworth Ltd* [1965] AC 1175, 1237-1238, [1965] 2 All ER 472, 488 (HL)). See also **equitable estate**, **land charge**, **minor interest**, **overreachable interest**, **tenancy in common**.

equitable land burden(US)   See **equitable servitude**.

equitable lease   1. See **agreement for a lease**. 2.(Eng)A **lease** that is not capable of being enforced 'at law', because it has not been made with the proper formalities – a lease that in all other respects would be a **legal lease**.   3.(Eng)A lease granted by a lessor who holds an **equitable interest** in land, e.g. by a landlord who has a right to land held under an **estate contract**. The holder of such an 'equitable lease' retains the tenancy subject to the equitable right of his landlord to enforce his right to the land. See also **tenancy by estoppel**.

equitable licence   See **licence**.

equitable lien   See **lien**.

equitable mortgage   1.(Eng)A **mortgage** that is enforceable in **equity** because: (i) the mortgagor has only an **equitable interest** in the mortgaged property (e.g. a beneficial interest under a trust for sale, a life interest under a settlement, or a contract for a lease); (ii) the mortgage is of a legal interest, but is not created with the formalities required for a legal mortgage (sometimes called an 'informal equitable mortgage'); or (iii) in the case of registered land, there has been a failure to register a legal mortgage. The holder of an equitable interest in land may grant a mortgage by assigning the interest to the mortgagee with a proviso that the interest will be reassigned on repayment (redemption) of the mortgage debt. Such an assignment, if not made by will, must be made (and not merely evidenced) in **writing** and signed by the person making the assignment (LPA

1925, s. 53(1)(c)). Similarly, if the grantor of the mortgage does not have the legal estate, or the power to charge the legal estate, but in either case he considered that he had the power to do so, the purported grant of a legal estate would create an equitable mortgage. An informal equitable mortgage may arise when the parties enter into an agreement to execute a legal mortgage, monies are advanced, but the legal mortgage is not formalised by deed as required under the LPA 1925, ss. 85 or 86. On or after September 27, 1989 an equitable mortgage has to be *made* in "writing", signed by or on behalf of both the mortgagor and the mortgagee, and the written document must incorporate *all* the terms that the parties have expressly agreed in one document, or by reference to some other document; or, where documents are exchanged, by setting out the details in each document (LP(MP)A 1989, s. 2). The most common means of creating an equitable mortgage is by a deposit of the title deeds, or for registered land, a deposit of the land certificate or charge certificate, accompanied (on or after September 27, 1989) by an agreement in writing, signed by both parties, confirming the intention to grant the mortgage and setting out the terms of the mortgage.

An equitable mortgagee has similar rights to the holder of a legal mortgage except that, when the mortgage is not made by deed, a **receiver** may only be appointed by the court, and the equitable mortgagee has no strict right to possession of the rent and profits (as there is no lease of the property which grants such a right), unless expressly permitted by the mortgage deed. If an equitable mortgagee forecloses on an equitable interest, theoretically he acquires the more restricted right to the mortgaged property; but the court may insist on the mortgagor conveying a legal title to the mortgagee in order to complete the process of foreclosure. If an equitable mortgagee exercises a power of sale the purchaser acquires an equitable interest only. However, if an equitable mortgage is made by deed (which is rarely the case for such mortgages) then the mortgagee normally has a right to require the legal estate to be transferred to the purchaser. An equitable mortgage of unregistered land created without the deposit of the title deeds must be registered as a **land charge** to protect the mortgagee against a subsequent mortgagee (LPA 1925, s. 97; LCA 1972, s. 2(4)) and the mortgagee should protect himself by giving written notice of the equitable mortgage to the holder of the legal estate (the trustees or the estate owner) (the rule in *Dearle v Hall* (1828) 3 Russ 1, as extended to real property by the LPA 1925, s. 137). In the case of registered land, if the land certificate is not deposited with the mortgagee, it must be protected as a **minor interest**. cf. **equitable charge, legal mortgage**. See also **general equitable charge, priority**.   **2.**[US]An arrangement by which a debt or obligation is created with the intention that the creditor should have the same rights to a property as if a formal mortgage had been made, but due to the lack of such formalities the mortgage would only be enforced in a court of **equity**. In particular, an agreement that is intended to create a mortgage or lien on real property, but is defective by not complying with the requisite statutory requirements, e.g. is not made in **writing**, or not properly recorded. For example, a **promissory note** or similar document that expresses an intention that a particular property should be held as security for a debt or obligation. An equitable mortgage may also arise when a person transfers a deed of title to property before consideration is paid in full for the property on the understanding, express or implied, that the grantor of the deed will have a lien on the property until payment is made in full. However, in most jurisdictions a mere deposit of title deeds as security for a debt does not create an equitable mortgage (59 C.J.S., Mortgages, § 19). In some jurisdictions, an **installment land contract** is treated as a form of equitable mortgage giving the seller a right to foreclosure or a power of sale in the event of non-payment. Sometimes called a 'constructive mortgage'. See also **equitable charge**.

equitable owner   **1.** The holder of an **equitable interest** in land. cf. **legal owner**. See also **beneficial owner, conversion**.   **2.**[US]A person to whom another agrees to convey real property and has placed the deeds in escrow with the intention that they are to be held pending completion of the transaction. See also **equitable title**.

equitable redemption   See **redemption**.

equitable relief   See **relief**.

equitable restriction(US)   See **equitable servitude**.

equitable right of redemption   See **equity of redemption**.

equitable rights   See **equity**.

equitable servitude(US)   A restriction on the use of land, or on the ability to build on land, that is enforceable in equity. In particular, a limitation or restriction that arises as a result of a **scheme of development**. Equitable servitudes are essentially the reciprocal benefits and burdens that are considered to be enforceable subsequent to the English Court of Equity decision in *Tulk v Moxhay* (1848) 2 Ph 774, 41 Eng Rep 1143, which acknowledged that it would be inequitable for a party to accept a restriction on the use of his land and then to escape that obligation as soon as the land is sold to another (Parker v. Nightingale, 6 Allen 341 (Mass 1848)). Such servitudes do not require there to be **privity of estate** between the parties; they are enforced on the principle *qui sentit commodum sentire debet et onus* – 'he who assumes the burden ought to assume the benefit'. An equitable servitude, or 'equitable restriction', is enforceable by or against a subsequent assignee of the land provided that: (a) it 'touches and concerns the land'; (b) it is intended by the parties who accepted the restriction that it would be binding on future assignees; (c) it is negative (in particular it does not require the expenditure of money); and (d) the purchaser or assignee has **notice** of the restriction. Unlike a **real covenant** (which must be made in writing), in most jurisdictions an equitable servitude may arise by implication. For

example, the right to use the common areas and accessways that form part of a subdivision or planned unit development. In effect, an equitable servitude is more than a right enforceable between the parties; it is an interest in land. Also called an 'equitable land burden', or sometimes a **negative easement**. See also **equitable easement, reciprocal negative easement, restrictive covenant**.

equitable title   A claim to have a title to property that may be enforced only in equity. For example, a claim to a property that a purchaser holds by virtue of a **conditional contract** for sale or an **instalment contract**. A title to property that can be enforced only by **specific performance**.

In English law, 'equitable title' may be used in particular to refer to: (a) an interest held by a beneficiary under a **trust for sale**; or (b) a right to land held by virtue of an unregistered **estate contract**. See also **agreement for sale, deed of trust**(US), **equitable interest**.

equitable waste   See **waste**.

equitization(US)   See **securitization**.

equity   1. Derived from the Latin *æquitas*, 'equality' or 'levelling'. Administration according to the rules of fairness and natural justice and not solely by the application of a universal set of rules. Equity is enshrined in the maxim *jus est ars boni et æqui*, 'law is the art of what is good and fair'. Equity is the soul of a civilised legal system and is intended to mitigate the rigors of the body of law encased in books and statutes. The function of equity is to find reason, right and remedy when it is not apparent in the written law; it avoids the extreme righteousness of the letter of the law – in a way it overrides the rigors of law.

In English law (and systems derived therefrom), 'equity' has a specialised meaning. It refers to a body of rules derived from the Court of Chancery, rather than from the courts of **common law**. Equity was intended to qualify, moderate and "reform the rigour, harshness, and edge of the law" and "to support and protect the common law from shifts and crafty contrivances against the justice of the law. Equity therefore, does not destroy the law, nor create it, but assists it", Lord Cowper, LC in *Dudley (Lord) v Dudley (Lady)* (1705) Prec Ch 241, 244, 24 Eng Rep 118, 119.

The remedies and procedures developed by equity have left a number of notable components that have become an integral part of modern real property law, in particular, the **equity of redemption**; the permitted enforceability of a **restrictive covenant** against a successor in title; provisions for bringing an action on certain informal contracts, particularly an **agreement for a lease**; **relief** granted against **forfeiture** and against the charging of a **penalty** on a contract; and the determination of the **priority** of non-recorded mortgages. The distinction between the legal and **equitable interest** in land; the **trust**; and the doctrine of **estoppel** are vestiges of the inherent strife between common law and equity. In addition, the **injunction**, **rectification**, **rescission** and **specific performance** are equitable remedies, being discretionary and granted only when damages would prove an impossible or unreasonable remedy.

In the US, in most jurisdictions, common law and equity have been merged and are dealt with in the same courts and legal and equitable remedies have been commingled. However, a few jurisdictions still have separate courts to administer remedies 'at law' and 'in equity'. See also *bona fide* **purchaser**, **resulting trust**, **use**. **2.** The amount of an investor's own funds paid over to acquire a property, or the difference between the present market value of a property and the amount of debt or mortgage loans outstanding against the net worth of an owner's interest in a property. See also **debt-equity ratio**, **equity build-up**, **loan value**. **3.** In accounting and finance, the **equity capital** of a company, enterprise or business. The term 'equity' is commonly used to refer to the ordinary share capital of a company, i.e. the capital that is provided by the owners of the company. The 'equity' in a company or an investment has no secured position and is repayable only after all loans or **debt capital**; accordingly it is the riskiest form of capital. Hence, it is sometimes referred to as 'top-slice capital' or 'top-slice finance'.

equity accrual See **equity build-up**.

equity-adjusted mortgage(US) See **equity-participation mortgage**.

equity appreciation See **equity build-up**.

equity build-up or **equity appreciation** An increase in the owner's **equity** in a property resulting from the repayment by the owner of a loan, or an increase in the market value of that property. The term 'equity build-up' generally refers to the former and 'equity appreciation' to the latter, although 'equity appreciation' may be used to refer to a combination of both. Upon sale of the property, the 'profit' that has resulted purely from repayment of the loan is sometimes called 'amortization profit'. Also called 'equity accrual'. See also **equity yield rate**.

equity capital The amount of **capital** available to the owners of an enterprise after all other liabilities have been allowed for or paid and upon which the owners expect to receive a return in the form of a share of the profits. The capital that belongs to the true owners of a company, i.e. the ordinary shareholders of that company, rather than capital loaned by creditors, namely **debt capital**. It comprises the amount of capital originally contributed by the shareholders, plus retained earnings minus any losses. See also **equity**, **net worth**, **risk capital**.

equity capitalization rate(AmE) The rate that expresses the relationship between the current cash flow from an investment and the **equity** invested in that investment. The equity capitalization rate is generally based on the per-tax cash flow. Equity capitalization rate may be expressed by the symbol R_E. See also **capitalization rate**, **equity yield rate**.

equity conversion See **reverse annuity mortgage**.

equity-debt ratio   See **debt-equity ratio**.

equity dividend rate or **equity dividend yield**(US)   See **cash-on-cash return/cash-on-cash yield**.

equity financing   **1.** The provision of a loan on the basis that the lender will receive a right to a share of the profit or **equity** to be derived from the project for which the loan is used. See also **equity capital**.   **2.** The sale of shares or an ownership interest of a company in order to raise capital. In real estate one of the primary sources of equity financing is the sale of stock in real estate companies, or in the US, the sale of stock in a real estate limited partnership or in a **real estate investment trust**.

equity fund(US)   See **equity trust**.

equity investment value(AmE)   The value of a property based on the amount of **equity** required by an investor in order to obtain a given rate of return over the life of the investment, after allowing for any mortgage loans or debt capital available to the investor. The equity investment value represents the capitalized value of the net income after debt service; or the capital value of the total net income less the amount of debt capital that can be secured on the property. See also **Ellwood capitalization rate**, **mortgage-equity capitalization technique**.

equity kicker   See **equity participation**.

equity-linked mortgage   See **equity-participation mortgage**.

equity loan   See **home equity line-of-credit**.

equity of redemption or **equitable right of redemption**   A mortgagor's equitable right to the **redemption** of the mortgaged property. The right of a **mortgagor** to have his property released to him without hindrance after he has performed his obligations under the mortgage, in particular the repayment of the outstanding debt, including principal, interest and costs to the mortgagee. The equity of redemption may also represent a right to compel the mortgagee to release the mortgaged property, even after the mortgagor has defaulted, at any stage before **foreclosure**, or an exercise of a **power of sale**, and before any consequent transfer from the mortgagor of an unencumbered title to the mortgagee. An equity of redemption is a proprietary right that may be bought, sold, or even mortgaged (although the mortgagee's consent to any such action may well be required), but it never passes to the mortgagee (unless he acquires it in good faith and pays what it is worth). The right to get back the mortgaged property, unencumbered, when the mortgagor has complied with the terms of the mortgage deed is sometimes called, especially in the US, the 'legal right of redemption', or simply the right of redemption; the right to redeem even after there has been a breach of a condition of the mortgage or after the contractual date for complying with the terms of the loan, may be called the 'equitable right of redemption'. These rights together represent the mortgagor's equity of redemption. In common law, the mortgagor's equity of redemption cannot normally be waived and any covenant in a mortgage that unreasonably prevents redemption, for example by giving inadequate time to repay the debt, is regarded as a **clog** or **fetter** on the equity of redemption and is unenforceable (*Noakes & Co Ltd v Rice* [1902] AC 24, [1900-3] All ER Rep 34 (HL); Peugh v. Davis, 6 Otto 332, 96 US 332, 24 L Ed 775, 776 (1877).

In English law, although a clog or fetter on the equity of redemption is void, the right to redeem may be postponed so that the mortgagor is not permitted to repay the principal before the time stipulated in the mortgage deed; provided the postponement is not for an unreasonable length of time and is not unconscionable nor oppressive to the nature of a mortgage – especially when both parties are knowledgeable, acting at arm's-length and are independently advised (*Knightsbridge Estates Trust Ltd v Byrne* [1939] Ch 441, [1938] 2 All ER 444 (CA), aff'd [1940] AC 613, [1940] 2 All ER 401

(HL)). Thus, 'clogs and fetters' on the equity of redemption do not preclude fair business dealing between the parties; the doctrine is not intended to be totally preclusive.

In the US, most jurisdictions follow the common law view that a clog or fetter on the equity of redemption should not make the mortgage irredeemable, nor should the mortgagee seek to gain an unfair collateral advantage (Clark v. Reyburn, 8 Wall 318, 75 US 318, 19 L Ed 354, 356 (1869); Humble Oil and Refining Co. v. Doerr, 123 NJ Super 530, 303 A.2d 898, 908 (1973)). However, several jurisdictions take a more free market approach to collateral advantages, so that "in the absence of usury statutes being violated, a collateral, even though it outlasts redemption, will be relieved against only on general doctrines of oppressiveness and unconscionable advantage", Casner, James A. (editor-in-chief). *American Law of Property,* Boston, Mass.: Little Brown, 1952, Vol. 4, § 16.60, p. 112.

An **option** to purchase, granted simultaneously with the execution of the mortgage, is likely to be construed as an unreasonable fetter on the equity of redemption as it changes the transaction from a true mortgage into a form of sale (*Samuel v Jarrah Timber and Wood Paving Corp'n Ltd* [1904] AC 323 (HL); 4 *American Law of Property* (1952), § 16.57, p. 105, § 16.59, p. 108; Humble Oil & Refining Co. v. Doer, *supra* at 906-8). In the US, in some jurisdictions, if a mortgage of commercial property is entered into between sophisticated parties who are represented by legal counsel, an option may be enforceable, even though it forms part of the main mortgage transaction, provided it is not dependent on an event of default under the terms of the mortgage agreement (Uniform Land Security Interest Act 1986 § 211; New York General Obligations Law 1986, § 5.334; California Civil Code (1984) § 2906; 60 St. John's Law Review, pp. 492-497).

The equity of redemption may be lost by: (a) a release or effective transfer of the right to the mortgagee; (b) a sale of the property following the exercise by the mortgagee of his power of sale; (c) a decree of foreclosure, i.e. a court decree that the property should be transferred to the mortgagee free of the mortgagor's equity of redemption (in the US known as **strict foreclosure**); or (d) the mortgagee entering into possession and enlarging his interest after the expiry of the time allowed under the Statute of Limitations. In the US, the mortgagor's equity of redemption is also called a 'right of redemption', or sometimes an 'equity of tardy redemption'. cf. **statutory right of redemption**(US). See also **consolidation of mortgages, once a mortgage always a mortgage, prepayment penalty, reconveyance, restrictive covenant, solus agreement, unconscionable bargain, undue influence, usury.**

equity participation   A share of the profit or **equity** of a business or venture. In particular, a right obtained by the grantor of a loan to share in the profits of a business, or the income from an investment, or a share in the borrower's equity acquired by a supplier of **debt capital**. Generally, a provider of debt capital (or a mortgage loan) receives only interest on his money; however, the borrower may agree to provide the lender with a share of the profits, sometimes referred to as 'contingency interest', in exchange for a lower interest rate or as a means of obtaining a loan when funds are in short supply. For example, a **joint venture** is established between the equity partner or 'active partner', and the lender or 'passive partner', by which the passive partner receives a **priority yield**, or an agreed rate of interest. In addition, a share in any profit or equity received by the joint venture (after payment of the priority yield) is divided between the participants according to an agreed formula. The formula is based on the ratio of debt to equity and an assessment of the participants' respective risks.

Real estate equity participation may take a variety of other forms such as: (i) rental or 'income participation' – the lender receives a share in the income received from a property, usually over and above an agreed base level; (ii) sale proceeds or 'capital-value participation' – the lender receives a share in the proceeds resulting from a revaluation of the property (in book form or as part of a refinancing arrangement), or the proceeds resulting from a sale of the property—in the US called an 'earn-out'; or (iii) 'option to participate' – an option for a lender to purchase the mortgaged property at a future date at a previously agreed price or at a percentage of the then current market value. A loan that provides for a share of the equity may be referred to as a 'kicker loan' or as providing an 'equity kicker' for the lender, i.e. a benefit that kicks in at a later date. See also **equity-participation loan**, **equity sharing**, **gearing**, **sale-and-leaseback**.

equity-participation loan or **equity-participation mortgage** A loan or mortgage agreement that provides for the mortgagee to receive a share of the income or profits to be derived from the mortgaged property, i.e. the mortgagee is entitled to share in the appreciation in the value of the property or to benefit from **equity participation**. Usually the mortgagee or lender grants the loan at a rate of interest that is lower than the market rate and, in return, has a right to a share of the income, capital profit (in the event of a sale), or any refinancing proceeds to be derived from the property, generally above an agreed level or base. The lender may obtain the participation by taking an ownership interest in the property or by receiving an incremental interest rate that is contingent on the income or sale value of the property. The latter form of participation may result in a significant increase in the obligation of the borrower if there is a substantial increase in the value of the property. Equity appreciation or 'shared-appreciation mortgages' are commonly granted for a long term with a significant prepayment penalty in the early years.

In common law, an equity-participation mortgage may not be enforceable if it is intended to create a **clog** or **fetter** on the mortgagor's **equity of redemption**, as where the profit share relates to a period after the debt has been redeemed (*Bradley v Carritt* [1903] AC 253 (HL)). On the other hand, a commercial profit-sharing agreement may be enforceable if the profit share is merely part of the price for the mortgage loan and is not unconscionable or oppressive (*Santley v Wilde* [1899] 2 Ch 474 (CA); *Browne v Ryan* [1901] IR 653 (CA)).

In the US, the 'shared-appreciation mortgage', or the mortgagee's right to purchase some or all of the mortgaged property, is not generally considered to fall foul of the principle that they are an impediment to the equity of redemption. In particular, the American Law Institute considers that the adoption of a shared-appreciation mortgage as posing an unfair collateral advantage "should not be permitted to pose obstacles to socially useful financing transactions", The American Law Institute, *Restatement Third, Property (Mortgages)* § 3.1, Comment *g* (1997).

Also called an 'equity-adjusted mortgage'; 'equity-linked mortgage'; equity-sharing mortgage'; 'appreciation-participation mortgage'; 'shared-participation mortgage'; 'participation mortgage', a 'kicker mortgage loan', or sometimes a 'hybrid mortgage'. cf. **shared-equity mortgage**. See also **alternative mortgage loan**[US], **Building Trust**[Eng], **convertible mortgage**.

equity purchaser[US] One who acquires the value of the **equity** in a property, without necessarily assuming liability for any loan secured on the property. See also **non-recourse mortgage**.

equity rate of return[US] See **cash-on-cash return**.

equity ratio The ratio of the **equity** invested in a property and the market value, or purchase price, of that property. cf. **debt-equity ratio**, **loan ratio**.

equity REIT[US] See **real estate investment trust**.

equity rent A rent payable to a head landlord which is assessed on the basis of a proportion of the income received by the tenant from the subtenants or occupiers of a property; a rent that provides **equity sharing** for the head landlord. See also **gearing**, **sale-and-leaseback**.

equity risk premium An additional rate of return that is required over and above that generated by a risk-free or low-risk investment to reflect the additional risk of a particular investment. See also **component capitalization rate**.

equity sharing   An arrangement by which two or more participants share, or take a stake, in the **equity** obtained from a real estate investment. A common example arises when a landowner agrees to lease a site to a developer at a nominal ground rent in return for a share in the return from the completed development. The term 'equity-sharing lease' may be used to refer to a lease that is granted at a rent that is below the current market value thus enabling the lessee to obtain a **profit rent** by sub-letting the premises, i.e. to receive a share of the equity available from the property. See also **equity participation**, **equity-participation mortgage, equity rent, lease-and-leaseback financing, leverage**.

equity-sharing lease   See **equity sharing**.

equity skimming(US)   The practice of assuming a mortgage secured on an income-producing property and then not applying the rents received to repay the mortgage debt. Normally such a practice is illegal or contrary to the terms of the mortgage loan and entails fraud or deception on the part of the party that has acquired the mortgage. Also called 'rent skimming', or sometimes 'equity stripping', especially when the equity in a property is used to pay the debt.

equity stake   See **equity sharing**.

equity trust(US)   See **real estate investment trust**.

equity value   The value of the **equity** invested in a property. The difference between the present market value of a property and the amount of debt secured against that property.

equity yield(BrE)   See **cash-on-cash return**.

equity yield rate(US)   The rate of return on equity capital. In particular, the rate of return over a period of time represented by the ratio of (i) the **present value** of the future anticipated **cash flow** from a property, plus **equity build-up** expressed as an annual figure to (ii) the total initial cash (or **equity**) invested in that property. This return is assessed after debt service, but before any allowance for depreciation. The rate is equivalent to the **internal rate of return** from an investment, after debt service, including the discounted value of any capital gain (or loss); or the **cash-on-cash yield** (or equity dividend yield) plus the present value of capital appreciation (or depreciation). The equity yield rate corresponds to a **redemption yield**, after taking into account the effect of debt repayments, but before tax. Also called the 'investment rate'. See also **Ellwood capitalization rate, mortgage-equity capitalization technique**.

equivalent annual value method   See **annuity method**.

equivalent reinstatement(Eng)   A method of assessing **compulsory purchase compensation** based on the cost of replacing or providing an equivalent property (Land Compensation Act 1961, s. 5, Rule 5). This method is applied primarily when determining the amount of compensation payable for special purpose properties for which there is no ready market value, e.g. a church, school, hospital, theatre, private railway (*Birmingham Corporation v West Midland Baptist (Trust) Association (Inc.)* [1970] AC 874, [1969] 3 All ER 172 (HL)). The compensation is based on the **reinstatement cost**, i.e. the cost of acquiring an alternative site and constructing an equivalent building thereon, after due allowance for depreciation. Also called 'rule 5' compensation. See also **valuation date**.

equivalent rent(BrE)   The rent adjusted to take into account inducements, incentives or concessions given to a tenant. cf. **headline rent**. See **effective lease rate**.
Davidson A., and Clive Darlow. *The Boston Gilmore Rental Equivalent Tables and Lease Incentives*. London: Estates Gazette, 1993.

equivalent yield(BrE)   The single yield from an investment property taking into account the total income receivable from the property, including any increases in rent due to rent revisions. The equivalent yield is based on current values; thus, if the property is rented at the current rack rent, the nominal yield is the same as the equivalent yield. When there is a single rent review, the equivalent yield on an investment may be obtained from the formula:

$$P_0 = \frac{r}{e} + \frac{(R-r)}{e(1+e)^n}$$

Where: P_0 = initial investment or cost
       r = initial rental income
       R = estimated market rental value
       n = number of years to the next market rent review
       e = equivalent yield.

If the rent is receivable at regular, but not annual, intervals in advance (such as quarterly or monthly in advance) the yield taking into account this timing is referred to as the 'true equivalent yield'. The 'equivalent yield' may be contrasted with the 'nominal yield' which is calculated based on the direct ratio of the total annual rent to the capital value of the investment. See also **equated yield**.

equivocation   The use of a word or expression in a way that can have two different meanings, especially in order to mislead. The use of a word that has a double or doubtful meaning or sense. See also **ambiguity**.

erection   Derived from the Latin *erigere*, 'to put up straight'. The putting up or setting up of a **structure** or **building**; including putting up of walls, fences, scaffolding, or even the construction of a driveway serving a building.

In English planning law, "erection" is defined to include "extension, alteration and re-erection" TCPA 1990, s. 336(1).

ERISA(US)   The Employment Retirement Income Securities Act of 1974. A federal statute passed to establish standards for the administration of retirement plans ("employee benefit plans"); to regulate investments made by private pension funds and other retirement benefit plans; to ensure disclosure and reporting to the beneficiaries of such plans as to the manner in which the institution invests the funds it holds; and to ensure that the plan funds are administered equitably and that the retirement plan beneficiaries are not disadvantaged in such matters as discrimination or unduly restrictive forfeiture provisions. This statute requires diversification and prudence in pension fund investment. In particular, the statute requires that the administrator of the plan will publish an annual report, which must be filed with the Secretary of State, that includes a "financial statement" containing inter alia a statement of the assets and liabilities of the plan.

erosion   The gradual wearing away of soil due to the action of nature. The wearing away of the bank of a stream or river, usually by the action of the flowing water which slowly takes away the substance of the bank and deposits it elsewhere. A part of the land lost through erosion no longer belongs to a riparian or littoral owner, unless it is restored by **accretion**; unlike land lost by the sudden process of **avulsion**. See also **riparian rights**.

error   A failure to achieve or set out that which is intended. That which deviates from truth or correct meaning, especially as a result of human failing. A **mistake** is an error of choice or an error that arises from ignorance. An error may arise may the performance of an act – an 'error of commission' or by a failure to perform an act – an 'error of omission'. See also **rectification**.

errors and omissions insurance (E. & O. insurance)   Insurance that is provided to cover the insured against liabilities for errors, mistakes or oversights in the performance of a business or profession. In particular, this term is used to refer to coverage that is of a limited scope as compared with a comprehensive **professional liability insurance**.

escalation clause or **escalator clause**   **1.** A clause in a contract that provides for an increase in the price or consideration to take account of a change that is not a direct function of the subject matter of the contract. For example, a clause that provides for the price to be adjusted in line with the retail price index. In particular, a provision in a building contract that provides for the contract price to be increased in the event of an increase in the cost of labour or materials, based upon a pre-agreed formula.   **2.**(US)A clause in a lease that enables the landlord to increase the rent to cover increases in **operating expenses**, or real estate taxes or assessments (when it is called a 'tax escalation clause' or 'tax participation clause'). The amount by which the rent is altered is usually based on actual variations in expenditure, but it may be based on fixed periodic variations, or sometimes some form of indexation. This rental variation is intended to be related to changes in operating expenses rather than changes in the market value of the property. Also called a 'cost pass-through clause', 'pass-through clause', 'increase clause', 'step-up clause' or sometimes a 'contribution or participation clause' as the tenant is required to contribute to increasing cost of building maintenance and occupancy. See also **expense stop**, **net lease**, **tax**, **tax-stop clause**.   **3.** A clause in a lease that provides for rent to be increased (or even decreased), usually at fixed intervals during the term of the lease, in accordance with an agreed formula, e.g. an **indexed rent** or a 'stepped' or **graded rent**. cf. **rent review clause**.   **4.**(US)A clause in a lease that provides for the landlord to increase the rent in accordance with the prescribed law, in the event that rent control regulations are lifted during the terms of the lease.   **5.** A clause in a mortgage deed that permits the mortgagee to alter the interest rate on the mortgage loan in line with the market rate of interest or any other specified rate of interest. See also **variable-rate mortgage**.   **6.**(US)A clause in a mortgage deed or land contract that provides that the stipulated rate of interest may be increased if the maximum permitted rate under prevailing usury laws is increased. See also **usury**.

escalation lease(US)   See **index lease**.

escalator clause or **escalator lease**(US) See **escalation clause**.

escape from land   See **strict liability**.

escape clause   **1.** A clause in a contract that permits one of the parties to modify or repudiate that contract, usually on the occurrence of a specified condition, e.g. a clause which permits a tenant to break his lease if the rent is increased at the date of a rent review. cf. **exclusion clause**. See also **break clause**, **conditional contract**.   **2.**(US)A clause in a lease of a cooperative apartment that enables the tenant to surrender his interest to the cooperative association without compensation and then to be relieved of all future payments to the association.

escheat   **1.** The passing of land to the State (or in the United Kingdom to the Crown) in the event that there is no owner, as when a person dies leaving no competent heir or claimants. Escheat is derived from the **feudal system** of land tenure, whereby upon determination of a right of **tenure** (due primarily to a lack of blood succession) land tacitly went back to the lord of the manor, or ultimately the Sovereign, to whom the landholder was beholden (known as escheat *propter defectum saguinis*). In English law, since 1925, escheat has been abolished and such property is said to pass *bona vacantia* to the Crown (or in certain cases to the Duchy of Lancaster or the Duchy of Cornwall) (AEA 1925, ss. 45, 46). However, the result is similar.

In the US, any property that has no owner escheats to the state or county if an owner dies intestate and no heirs can be traced. In most states the escheat of property is regulated by statute. An estate that passes to a sovereign body or state in this way is also called an escheat.   **2.**(Scot)The forfeiture of the right of a holder of a **liferent** to his superior if the vassal commits a serious crime or is adjudged an outlaw. This form of escheat has fallen into desuetude.

escrow The delivery of a **deed** to a third party subject to a proviso that when a specified condition occurs the deed will take full effect, but if that **condition** does not occur the deed has no effect, i.e. until the condition is fulfilled the deed is in suspense. A written instrument that is deposited by the seller, grantor, or 'escrower' of property with a third party ('escrow holder' or 'escrowee') to be held until a **condition** (express or implied) has been fulfilled, at which stage the property is transferred to the buyer or grantee. A document, property, or money delivered to a stranger or an independent third party, to be held by that party as escrow agent, with the intention (express or implied) that it will be delivered, or take full effect as a deed, upon the performance of some condition, or the happening of some specified event (such as the payment of a purchase price or the establishment of a proper title).

If the condition is performed, an instrument becomes absolute as a deed; but until then it remains in suspense or 'in escrow' and does not operate to convey title. However, the grantor cannot recall a deed delivered in escrow, unless the grantee fails to fulfil the relevant condition. A deed delivered subject to a condition that it can be withdrawn is not an escrow, but merely a deed awaiting delivery. One of the most common forms of escrow arises when a deed is delivered by a seller (grantor) of property to a third party, an attorney or title company, on the basis that it will be handed over to the purchaser (grantee) when the purchase monies are paid in full. Strictly speaking an escrow is not a deed as it does not transfer any interest in property, it becomes a deed only when all the conditions are fulfilled and delivery has taken place. However, when the escrow agreement relates to a subject that requires a deed (e.g. real property), it should contain the minimum requirements for a valid deed and operates as such when the conditions are satisfied. A deed need not be expressed as 'delivered in escrow, providing it can be shown that there is an intention to hold delivery in suspense. Also, even though a document is drawn and expressed for immediate delivery, if delivery of the property is not to be made until a condition is fulfilled, it will nevertheless operate as an escrow.

Title to property is not transferred until delivery and accordingly, unless there is an agreement to the contrary, the vendor remains the owner of the property; is responsible for its insurance (or loss in the event of fire); for the payment of expenses and taxes; and is entitled to the rents and profits until completion or execution of the deed (and the grantee is not entitled to lease or determine leases of the subject property until after final delivery). However, when it is necessary to give efficacy to the transaction, to put into effect the intention of the parties, or to avoid a patent injustice, the final deed may 'relate back' to the date of the escrow agreement; i.e. an escrow takes effect at the time of the original conditional delivery and not the date on which the condition is satisfied (*Butler and Baker's Case* (1591) 3 Co Rep 25a, 76 Eng Rep 684; 28 Am.Jur.2d., Escrow, §§ 29-3639-43). For example, if a judgement is issued against the grantor, or the grantor dies or is impaired during the intervening period, this does not necessarily affect the grantee.

In the US, real estate is frequently sold by means of an 'escrow closing' whereby a contract for the sale of land, together with an **escrow agreement** or escrow instructions, are entered into prior to verification of title and the title deeds are held and verified by an escrow agent. An escrow closing is used especially to ensure that all the funds are available, including mortgage funds, before the title is transferred or recorded. When the escrow agent is satisfied, he transfers the title deed to the purchaser, and pays the purchase monies he has been holding on behalf of the grantor in accordance with the escrow agreement. When the purchase price for a property is to be paid over a period of time and the title deeds are to be held in escrow until the final payment is made, an escrow agreement may be referred to as a 'contract for deed' or an 'installment contract' (although those terms also have separate meanings in most other contexts). See also **piti payment, relation back**.

escrow agent   A third party or **agent** to whom a contract is delivered in **escrow** and who takes on the responsibility for executing the transaction and performing the instructions of the parties to the contract. The agent is usually an attorney, or a specialised corporate entity (an 'escrow company'), which may be a department of a bank, that acts with integrity to ensure that the interests of both parties are considered in the complete performance of the contract. In particular, the escrow agent gathers all the documents required for the closing of a sale or loan, holds the deeds of title to the property that is the subject of an escrow transaction until the requisite conditions of the transaction are fulfilled (or not as the case may be) and, if necessary, is responsible for handling the **closing** of such transactions including arranging for the recording of any requisite documents. Also called an 'escrow holder' or 'escrowee'.

escrow agreement   An agreement that sets out the terms upon which an instrument is to be held in **escrow**, as distinguished from an agreement or instrument that is itself placed in escrow (Home v. Wilson, 210 Ky 237, 275 SW 691 (1925); 30A C.J.S., Escrows, § 3).

escrow closing(US)   See **escrow**.

escrow company(US)   See **escrow agent**.

escrow costs(AmE)   The **closing costs** paid upon completion of a transaction carried out by means of an **escrow**.

escrow overage or **escrow shortfall**(US)   The monies that are surplus to, or insufficient for, that which is required to complete a transaction that is held in **escrow**.

escrow payment(US)   See **piti payment**.

escrowee   A party to whom a contract is

delivered in **escrow**. See also **escrow agent**.

escrower   The party, or grantor, who delivers a deed to a third party, or escrowee, to be held on the former's behalf in **escrow** until certain specified conditions have been met.

essart(Eng)   See **assart**.

essence of a contract   See **condition, time is of the essence**.

established use   A use of land that has been in existence for a period long enough to establish that planning consent is not required for its continuation. See **certificate of lawfulness**(Eng), **existing use**, **non-conforming use**.

established use certificate(Eng)   See **certificate of lawfulness**.

estate   **1.** A right to **land** of defined (but not necessarily ascertained) duration; the degree, quantity, nature or extent of a person's interest in real property. The word 'estate' is derived from 'status' and thus it represents in essence the right to land of one person in preference to others; the standing that one person has in relationship to the ownership, possession or control of his property. In particular, an estate is the right to possess land for a duration. 'Estate' is used in place of ownership to refer to the right to hold land, because in common law there was no absolute right to the ownership of land, but merely a right to land for a greater or lesser duration. A fee simple estate is the most complete estate in land, with all other estates providing lesser rights of use and occupation. An estate may be of unknown duration, a **freehold**: an estate in **fee simple**, in **fee tail** (an entailed interest), or a **life estate**. It may also be of known or ascertainable duration – a **leasehold**, whether for a term of years, any other fixed duration, or from year to year. Also, 'estate' may be used to denote any form of property, whether **real estate** or **personal estate**. An estate may be classified also as contingent or conditional; in possession or remainder; in severalty or in common; or as a **legal estate** or an **equitable estate**.

In the US, the term estate is also used when **tenancy** would be used in English law, e.g. an 'estate for a term of years', a 'joint estate', an 'estate in coparcenary', thereby extinguishing or reducing the common law classification of a leasehold as personal rather than real property. See also **doctrine of estates**, **estate owner**, **future estate**.   **2.** The aggregation of an individual's property (real and personal), especially of a deceased person when considered for taxation purposes. In a will 'estate', unless the context indicates to the contrary, acts to pass all the testator's real and personal estate.

In English law, in the context of administering the estate of a deceased, estate means all property, which "includes a thing in action and any real or personal property", AEA 1925, s. 55(xvii). See also **estate tax**[US], **inheritance tax**.   **3.** An extensive area of land or a large farm, usually encompassing a substantial residence. See also **manor**.   **4.** A person's **domain**.

estate agent[BrE]   A person, firm or association that deals in real property on behalf of another. In particular, an **agent** who, "in connection with the acquisition or disposal of any land or other premises, brings together or takes steps to bring together the person wishing to dispose thereof and a person prepared to acquire it, or undertakes to do either of those things, or who acts or undertakes to act as **auctioneer**, or, in the case of a proposed transaction, negotiates or undertakes to negotiate as to the terms on behalf of either party", Restriction on Agreements (Estate Agents) Order 1970 art. 2(1). The Estate Agents Act 1979, s. 1(1) defines estate agency work, with certain exceptions, as comprising "things done by a person in the course of a business (including a business in which he is employed) pursuant to instructions received from another person (in this section referred to as 'the client') who wishes to dispose of or acquire an interest in land—(a) for the purpose of, or with a view to, effecting the introduction to the client of a third person who wishes to acquire or, as the case may be, dispose of such an interest; and (b) after such

an introduction has been effected in the course of that business, for the purpose of securing the disposal or as the case may be, the acquisition of that interest". The Director General of Fair Trading has power to make an order to prevent an unfit person from doing estate agency work (Estate Agents Act 1979, s. 3). An estate agent may also undertake the letting, management, surveying and valuation of all forms of property for another, and may seek to raise finance secured on property held by another.

An estate agent is usually given a general **authority** in relation to a property and that authority includes the right to describe the property truly, to represent its actual situation, and normally an authority to represent its value. Such representations, as a rule, are not warranties (unless made with the clear authority of the principal) and should be verified. Although an estate agent is liable for a **misrepresentation** that forms part of a contract of sale and may be criminally liable for a **misdescription**.

An estate agent is employed normally to find and introduce suitable candidates or prospects for a property, but is not normally responsible for making the contract of sale and is not usually authorised to sign a contract. However, an estate agent may be given a special authority and in that capacity may be authorised, upon stipulated terms, to bind his principal. Unless so clearly appointed, a principal may accept or reject any person introduced by the agent; although, as a result, he may not necessarily avoid a liability to the agent to pay **commission**. An estate agent owes a duty to act on behalf of his principal until his duties are fulfilled, or until his authority is withdrawn, and he must communicate to his principal any offer received for a property that he is offering for sale, until or unless a binding contract for sale has been entered into (*Keppel v Wheeler* [1927] 1 KB 577, 586 (CA)).

In Australia, an estate agent (or as they are normally called in NSW and Qld a **real estate agent**), must be licensed by State law. See also **accommodation agent, broker, deposit, puffing, subagent, surveyor**.

Murdoch, John. *The Law of Estate Agency and Auctions*. 4th ed. London: Estates Gazette, 2003.

The Royal Institution of Chartered Surveyors. *Manual of Estate Agency Law and Practice* London: RICS Book, 1998.

estate agent's fee(BrE)   See **commission, scale fee**.

estate at will(US)   See **tenancy at will**.

estate at sufferance(US)   "An estate at sufferance is an interest in land which exists when a person who had a possessory interest in the land by virtue of an effective conveyance, wrongfully continues in possession of the land after the termination of such interest, but without asserting a claim to a superior title", The American Law Institute, *Restatement of Property* § 22 (1936). See also **tenancy at sufferance**.

estate by entirety or **estate by entireties**(US)   See **tenancy by the entirety**.

estate by purchase(US)   See **purchase**.

estate by sufferance(US)   See **tenancy at sufferance**.

estate by the curtesy(US)   See **tenancy by the curtesy**.

estate by the entirety(US)   See **tenancy by the entirety**.

estate clause(Eng)   An express clause in a **conveyance** which stated that the grantor was transferring 'all his estate, right, title and interest' in the property. Such a clause is now implied in any "conveyance" (LPA, 1925, s. 63).

estate company   A private company formed to hold real estate, especially one formed to enable the beneficiaries to reduce their liability to taxation.

estate contract(Eng)   An enforceable contract (whether oral or in writing) by which a person has the right, at the date of the contract, to have a **legal estate** (which may include a legal interest or a legal charge) conveyed to him or created for his benefit. An estate contract may take the form of a **contract for sale**; an **agreement for a lease**; a contract to grant a mortgage, easement or profit; or any like agreement (whether relating to corporeal or incorporeal property) that places a person in a position to acquire a legal estate – including a contract for the purchase of a legal estate from a person who has himself a contract for the purchase of that interest from the existing estate owner. An estate contract grants an **equitable interest** for the benefit of the intended purchaser or lessee; the legal estate remains with the grantor, who holds it as trustee until an actual conveyance or lease has been executed. An estate contract affecting unregistered land may be registered as a Class C(iv) **land charge** – in this context an estate contract includes a valid **option** to purchase, a **right of pre-emption,** or any other like right (LCA 1972, s. 2(4); *Philips v Mobil Oil Co Ltd* [1989] 1 WLR 888 (CA)). If the estate contract is not registered, it is void against a subsequent *bona fide* **purchaser** of a legal estate for **value** without **notice**. In the case of registered land, it can be protected by registration as a **minor interest**. cf. **agreement for sale.** See also **overreachable interest.**

estate for life(US)   An **estate** in land which, although equivalent to a **freehold**, is limited for the life of a person and thus carries no right of inheritance. "An estate for life is an estate which is not an estate of inheritance, and (a) is an estate which is specifically described as to duration in terms of the life or lives of one or more human beings, and is not terminable at any fixed or computable period of time; or (b) though not so specifically described as is required under the rule stated in Clause (a), is an estate which cannot last longer than the life or lives of one or more human beings, and is not terminable at any fixed or computable period of time or at the will of the transferor", The American Law Institute, *Restatement of Property* § 18 (1936). (In English law, such an estate in land is generally called a **life estate** or a 'life interest'.)

estate for years An interest granted under a lease for a fixed term of one or more years, or for a period that is fixed as part of a **year**. "An estate for years is an estate, the duration of which is fixed in units of a year or multiple or divisions thereof", The American Law Institute, *Restatement of Property* § 19 (1936). See also **tenancy for years, term of years**.

estate from period to period(US) "An estate which will continue for successive periods of a year, or successive periods of a fraction of a year, unless it is terminated", The American Law Institute, *Restatement of Property* § 20 (1936). See also **periodic tenancy**.

estate from year to year(US) See **tenancy from year to year**.

estate in common(US) See **tenancy in common**.

estate in community(US) See **community property, concurrent estate**.

estate in coparcenary(US) See **coparcenary**.

estate in entirety(US) See **tenancy by the entirety**.

estate in expectancy See **future estate**.

estate in fee(US) See **fee, fee simple**.

estate in fee conditional(US) See **conditional fee simple**.

estate in fee simple(US) See **fee simple**.

estate in fee tail(US) See **fee tail**.

estate *in futuro* See **future estate**.

estate in joint tenancy(US) See **joint tenancy**.

estate in pledge(US) See **mortgage, pledge**.

estate in possession See **vested interest**.

estate in remainder See **remainder**.

estate in reversion See **reversion**.

estate in severalty(US) The ownership of real or personal property without anyone else sharing that right. Also called a 'tenancy in severalty', although the use of the term 'tenancy' refers to a right of ownership and not in the more modern sense of a relationship of landlord and tenant. See **several estate**.

estate in tail See **entailed estate/entailed interest, fee tail**.

estate in tail after possibility of issue extinct(Eng) An **estate** that represents a virtual life interest when an interest in land cannot pass, as was intended, to a special class of heir(s) owing to the premature death of a spouse who is intended to beget the heir(s). Thus, when an interest in land has been given to a man and his wife, or to either of them solely, with the intention that the interest (which is called a 'tail special' or 'special tail', i.e. a form of **fee tail** that is limited to issue of a particular union) should pass only to *their* issue and either of them dies without leaving such issue (or the survivor outlives any issue) then the surviving party is termed a 'tenant in tail after possibilities of issue extinct' – the terminology vividly demonstrating that the surviving owner of the land holds it for his or her life, but thereafter the estate returns to the grantor (or his or her heirs). Also called a 'tenancy in tail after possibility of issue extinct' ('tenancy' in this context indicating a right of ownership of land and not a relationship of landlord and tenant).

estate in tenancy in common(US) See **tenancy in common**.

estate manager A person retained to

manage real estate, in order to ensure that the best use, profit or benefit is derived therefrom. The role of an estate-management surveyor has been defined as "to advise upon the process for which land can be used to its best advantage, and to manage landed estates – large or small – primarily for the business purpose of getting the best income out of them, but at the same time having due regard to the duties of the owner towards his tenant, his neighbours and the community, local, regional and national", Lord Justice Scott, *Principles and Practice of Land Use: estate management lecture*, University of London (1948). See also **land agent, property manager**.

estate management   The science of directing, administering, planning, supervising and coordinating the responsibilities of those who own, lease, finance, occupy or use real estate in order to achieve a predetermined objective, usually the maximisation of the use and benefit to be derived therefrom. The means and activity by which land is maintained and controlled, including the study of all matters that affect land as a factor of production, in order to ensure that the best use and benefit is derived therefrom. Estate management includes control of the daily running of the property (**property management**); the planning and analysis of the present and future economic benefits to be obtained from ownership of real estate; and coordination of the responsibilities of those involved in real estate and, where applicable, the maintenance of good landlord and tenant relations. See also **facility management, highest and best use, land economics, portfolio management**.
Stapleton, Tim. *Estate Management Practice*. 3rd ed. London: Estates Gazette, 1994.

estate of freehold(US)   See **freehold**.

estate of inheritance   An estate that is capable of descending to an **heir** by operation of law. All **freehold** estates are estates of inheritance, as the holder may enjoy the estate not only for his life but it can pass to an heir or heirs *in perpetuum*. Estates of inheritance may be 'absolute' – a **fee simple**, which descends to lineal and collateral heirs; or 'limited'–a **fee tail**, which descends only to lineal heirs. See also **entailed estate**.

estate on condition(US)   An **estate** in land that may be created, enlarged, or destroyed, upon the happening of an event that may or may not arise. An estate on condition, although liable to come to an end, does not do so until the party that has the right to take the estate enters and determines the prior estate. An 'estate on condition' may be distinguished from an estate on limitation or **conditional limitation** which ends on the mere happening of the event. See also **conditional fee simple**(Eng), **fee simple conditional, shifting interest**.

estate on condition subsequent   See **fee simple conditional**.

estate on limitation(US)   See **determinable fee**.

estate owner(Eng)   The owner of a **legal estate** (LPA 1925, s. 205(1)(v)). An estate owner may be the beneficial owner of the legal estate in his own right, i.e. as an absolute owner (including a mortgagor, even though if the mortgagee exercises his power of sale he may have the legal estate conveyed to the purchaser); or, if land is held in trust for a beneficiary, the estate owner is the trustee (a **bare trustee**) who holds the legal estate and whose function is to give effect to the equitable interest of the beneficiary. If land is the subject of a strict settlement, the estate owner is the tenant for life or a statutory owner. If the land is held under a trust for sale the estate owner is the trustee for sale. Also a **personal representative** may be an estate owner on an interim basis.

estate *pur autre vie*   An estate 'for the life of another'. See also **life estate**.

estate rentcharge(Eng)   See **rentcharge**.

estate tail   See **entailed estate, fee tail**.

estate tax(US)   A tax levied on the value of a deceased's estate, regardless of the estate's destination, but payable before the estate can pass. An estate tax accrues at the time the estate vests, i.e. upon the death of the decedent, and is payable on the entire value of the estate less allowable deductions. An estate tax is levied on the estate, unlike a **succession tax** which is levied on those who succeed to the estate. Some states also levy a 'death tax' or **inheritance tax** (legacy or succession tax) which is payable by the beneficiaries and is levied according to the value of the benefits received. See also **gift tax**.

estate terrier   See **terrier**.

estate upon conditional limitation(US) See **conditional limitation**.

estate upon condition subsequent(US) See **conditional fee simple**.

estimate   The probable cost of a project. An assessment or evaluation of the cost or value of something. An estimate in terms of the cost of a building or project is intended only as an opinion based on the best available information; as a rule it based on the reasonable cost of a building erected in accordance with the plans and specifications set out in the estimate. An estimate is not an actual bid for the work to be carried out until agreed as such. An estimate by a contractor does not normally represent an **offer**; it is merely a proposal to do business (an **invitation to trade**(AmE)/ **invitation to treat**(BrE)). Although, if the general tenor of the document, even if called an 'estimate', indicates that the proposal is a clear basis upon which business can be done, it may be an offer, and **acceptance** thereof will create a binding contract. See also **bill of quantities**(BrE), **quantity survey method**(AmE), **quantity surveying**(BrE), **valuation, quotation, tender**.

estimated rental value (ERV)(BrE)   The best rent at which a property might reasonably be expected to let. Also called the 'full rental value' (FRV), especially when a property is currently leased at below its market value. See also **market rent, open market rental value, rack rent**.

estimator   A person who prepares an **estimate**. One who makes an assessment of the cost or value of a property. In particular, a person who estimates the cost of constructing a new building. See also **quantity surveyor, valuer**.

estopped certificate(US)   See **estoppel certificate**.

estoppel   A principle established by the English courts of **equity** that it would be inequitable for a person to go back on his word, or to act inconsistently with his previous representations or deeds (whether express or implied) when another has acted thereon to his detriment. Estoppel may even prevent a person from stating that something is true and, therefore, should be now acted on with a legal consequence, if that statement is inconsistent with a previously accepted statement. In summary, estoppel "is a principle of justice and of equity. It comes to this when a man, by his words or conduct, has lead another to believe that he may safely act on the faith of them – and the other does act on them – he will not be allowed to go back on what he has said or done when it would be unjust or inequitable for him to do so", Denning, The Rt. Hon. Lord. *The Discipline of Law*. London: Butterworths, 1979, p. 223. Estoppel is a rule of evidence and not a cause of action per se.

Estoppel takes many forms, but may be classified broadly as: (A) 'promissory estoppel' – which arises when a person makes a promise not to insist on, or enforce, his legal rights against another. (B) proprietary estoppel, or 'estoppel by encouragement and acquiescence' – which arises when a person takes a certain action that is to his detriment or prejudice, such as taking possession of property to carry out work therein, and another clearly accepts or acquiesces in that action. (C) 'legal estoppel', estoppel as a 'matter of fact' – which arises when there is a material fact that induces an action. (D) 'equitable estoppel' or 'estoppel *in pais*' – when it is not based on a deed or contract but on an action or conduct, or representation ('estoppel by representation'), or when a person remains silent ('estoppel by silence or by inaction'), especially when a person observes an action by another that is based clearly on a misapprehension or a mistaken understanding by that other party. A similar form of estoppel may be referred to as estoppel 'by convention', where the convention for dealing between two parties clearly indicates that one party will allow a reasonable period of time to elapse before relying on his rights. Equitable and promissory estoppel (also called 'quasi-estoppel') are akin and may be distinguished from estoppel based on a deed, or a record or judgement of a court. **Estoppel by deed** may arise when a seller does not have title at the time he purports to convey a property, but if he subsequently acquires title to that property, he would be estopped from then denying that title and transferring it as originally represented.

In the US, estoppel may be categorized as: (i) 'estoppel by record'; (ii) 'estoppel by deed' or 'estoppel in writing'; or (iii) 'estoppel in pais' or 'equitable estoppel'. (i) covers matters arising from the records of the courts and applies to such matters as probate and crime; (ii) is the denial of a formal intent of a deed or such aspects as recitals and powers to convey; and (iii) covers the 'quasi', 'promissory' and 'proprietary' estoppel referred to above, all of which arise from the *conduct* of a party. (The term 'promissory estoppel' is to be preferred to 'equitable estoppel' as the remedy is itself equitable.)

Estoppel may be distinguished from **ratification** as the former induces a prejudicial action by another and is an equitable right, whereas ratification occurs after the event and is a matter of law. Estoppel is closely allied to waiver. However, it may be distinguished from **waiver** as the latter generally refers to an intentional surrender or relinquishment of a known right for a consideration, whereas estoppel creates a restraint or inhibition on an inconsistent action. cf. **misrepresentation, quasi-contract, waiver**. See also **dedication, estoppel by deed, estoppel certificate, licence by estoppel**[Eng], **mistaken improver, ostensible authority, recital, tenancy**

by estoppel, vested right.

Magor, D. L. *Distress for Local Taxation and Rent*. London: Institute of Revenues, Rating and Valuation, 1999.

Kingcome-Turner, The Rt. Hon. Sir Alexander. *Spencer-Bower and Turner: The Law relating to Estoppel by Representation*. 4th ed. London: Butterworths, 2003.

estoppel by deed[US]   An extension of the principle of **estoppel** to an **after-acquired title**. In most jurisdictions, if a grantor of land by means of a **warranty deed** has no title at the time of the conveyance, but subsequently acquires title to that land, he is estopped from denying that he had title and the 'after-acquired title' inures to the benefit of the original grantee or his successors. See also **tenancy by estoppel**.

estoppel by lease[US]   See **tenancy by estoppel**.

estoppel certificate or **estopped certificate**[US]   An attestation that prevents a person from later acting inconsistently with that which he has previously affirmed. A written statement or certificate that creates an **estoppel** upon the action or representations of the maker, e.g. a certificate from a lender or the vendor of a property showing the amount of mortgage loan outstanding at the date of transfer of a mortgage (and, usually, details of future interest and principal repayment due under the loan).

An estoppel certificate is normally obtained from the tenant or tenants of a building prior to sale or mortgage, setting out the terms of the tenant's lease and such details as the current operating expense levels payable. It may also confirm (or otherwise) that there are no offset payments due from the landlord and no disputes with the landlord. Also called a 'waiver of defenses', a 'no set-off certificate', a 'certificate of no defenses' or, when it relates to an encumbrance or lien on a property, as issued by an owner or lender, an 'offset statement'. If issued in the form of a letter, called an 'estoppel letter'. See also **reduction certificate**.

estoppel letter[US]   See **estoppel certificate**.

estoppel licence(Eng) See **licence by estoppel**.

estoppel statement(US) See **estoppel certificate**.

estovers Timber or wood that a tenant for life or a tenant for a term of years is allowed to take for essential purposes from land that is demised to him. The equivalent Saxon word was *bote*, so estovers may be *fuelbote* or *firebote*, for fuelling a house; *housebote*, for repairing a house; *ploughbote* or *cartbote*, for making and repairing agricultural implements; or *haybote* or *hedgebote*, for repairing existing fences, ditches and walls (1 *Co Litt* 41b; 2 *Bl Comm* 35). A tenant is not permitted to take more timber than is immediately required for the necessary repair or maintenance, nor to fell growing trees for fuel if there is adequate dead wood for the purpose, as that would constitute **waste**. See also **right of common**.

estray A tame animal that is found wandering without an owner, especially an animal that has escaped from the control of its owner. See also **waifs and estrays**.

estrepement or **estrepment** The needless destruction or aggravated **waste** of land by a tenant for life. The common law remedy for such waste was a 'writ of estrepement'.

et al(Lat) Abbreviation of *et alii* or *et alia(e)*; 'and others'; 'all others'.

et uxor or ***et ux***(Lat) 'and wife'.

et vir(Lat) 'and husband'.

Euclidean zoning(US) A term derived from *Village of Euclid v. Amber Realty Co.*, 272 US 365, 47 S Ct 114, 71 L Ed 303, 314 (1926) which decided that the application of use or density zoning was a legal exercise of **police power**, unless "clearly arbitrary and unreasonable, having no substantial relation to the public health, safety,

morals, or general welfare". See also **inverse condemnation**.

every quarter See **quarterly**.

eviction Derived from the Latin *evincere*, 'to conquer'; to recover by judicial process. Eviction may refer to any form of expulsion, whether by process of law or forcible re-entry, and any action of expulsion exerted against a tenant, trespasser or squatter. Eviction may also be used to refer to: (i) the **recovery** of possession of land by process of law; (ii) the **dispossession** (legally or illegally) of a tenant by his landlord (it is more commonly used in this sense); or (iii) dispossession by **paramount title** (as when a tenant is dispossessed by a person who has a superior right to that of the tenant's landlord). Eviction may be 'actual' or 'constructive'. **Actual eviction** occurs when a tenant is physically deprived of possession, especially when the landlord retakes possession. **Constructive eviction** occurs when the landlord restricts the tenant in his proper enjoyment of the property and compels the abandonment of the demised premises.

In particular, eviction refers to a wrongful act, being something of a grave and permanent nature done by the landlord with the intention of depriving the tenant of the enjoyment of the whole or part of the demised premises. Nevertheless, to relieve the tenant of his obligation to pay rent, the landlord's act must be (i) of a 'permanent character', and (ii) done with 'particular intent and effect', namely preventing the tenant from continuing to 'hold' the demised premises, or depriving him of the 'use and enjoyment' of the thing demised, or some part thereof.

In English law, it is an offence to unlawfully deprive, or to attempt to unlawfully deprive, a person who is a legal occupier of a residence (a **residential occupier**) of possession of that residence, unless it can be shown that the person seeking the eviction can prove that he believed, and had reasonable cause to believe, that the residential occupier had ceased to reside in the premises (Protection from Eviction Act 1977, s.

1(2)). Such an offence includes "acts likely to interfere with the peace or comfort of the residential occupier or members of his household", as well as withdrawing or withholding services "reasonably required for the occupation of the premises as a residence" when the landlord knows, or has reasonable cause to believe, that such acts are likely to cause the residential occupier to give up or refrain from enjoying the whole or any part of the leased premises (PEA 1977, s. 3A, as inserted by HA 1988, s. 29). A landlord who commits such an offence, or is aware that such an offence is being committed, may be liable to summary conviction and may be obliged to pay compensation based on the financial gain accruing to him as a result of the eviction (PEA 1977, s. 1(4), as amended). When a tenancy of a dwelling comes to an end, even though it does not then become a statutory tenancy, the owner cannot enforce his right to recover possession without proceeding in court (PEA 1977, s. 3). In addition, a residential tenant who is a victim of unlawful eviction can sue a landlord for damages (HA 1988, s. 27). Thus, any landlord (or his agent) is well advised to proceed with caution before seeking to evict or dispossess any person in occupation of a residential property.

In the US, any act of a landlord by which he seeks to recover possession of leased premises, without "due process of law" and against the wishes of the tenant, is a misdemeanour; although some jurisdictions permit a landlord to 'peaceably' re-enter a property if the tenant is holding over, but has physically vacated the property. cf. **abandonment**. See also **dispossession, ejectment, harassment, ouster, quiet enjoyment, security of tenure, self-help**.

Arden and Partington's Guide to Remedies for Harassment and Illegal Eviction. 5th ed. London: Legal Action Group, 1998.

eviction by title paramount See **paramount title**.

evidence of title A document that evidences a right to the ownership of property, especially to real property. See also **abstract of title, title document, certificate of title, title**.

evidenced in writing See **contract, memorandum, unenforceable contract, writing**.

ex causa(Lat) 'From or with cause'; 'by right'; 'by title'.

ex contractu(Lat) 'Arising out of **contract**', e.g. an action *ex contractu* arises from a contractual obligation that has not been performed or has been breached.

ex debito(Lat) 'As of right'. cf. *ex gratia*.

ex delicto(Lat) 'Arising out of **tort**', e.g. an action *ex delicto* arises from a breach of a duty owed to others by a particular class of people.

ex gratia(Lat) 'Out of grace'; 'as of favour'. Not by legal right; especially without admission of liability. cf. *ex debito*. See also **ex gratia payment**.

ex gratia payment A payment made without admission of liability or obligation. A payment made out of 'empathy' and not as a result of any contractual or other legal liability for damages. An ex gratia payment is based entirely on the discretion of the payer and need bear no relation to any loss suffered by the payee. An ex gratia payment may be made to avoid the cost of further dispute and litigation, especially as a result of an insurance claim. See also **home-loss payment**(Eng).

ex hypothesi(Lat) 'From the hypothesis'; 'upon the supposition'. See **hypothetical**.

ex nudo pacto non oritur actio(Lat) 'A right of action cannot arise out of a bare pact'. See **naked contract**.

ex parte(Lat) 'On the one side'; 'on behalf of'. An action by one party in the absence of another.

ex post facto(Lat) 'By a subsequent act'; 'after the act'.

ex turpi causa non oritur actio(Lat) 'An action does not arise from a base cause', i.e. an action cannot be brought at law on the basis of an immoral or **illegal contract**.

ex via termini(Lat)   See **right of way** *ex via termini*.

exact interest or **exact-day interest**
Interest calculated on the basis of 365 (or 366) days in a year, in particular when so calculated and quoted as a per diem rate.

exaction(US)   An amount taken without right. The demanding of some benefit that is not lawfully due. Also used to refer to a fee or other requirement demanded of a developer in exchange for a building permit or approval of a variation to the permitted form of development. For example, a requirement that a developer dedicate land or a right over land to public use. An exaction may amount to a 'taking' requiring the payment of **just compensation**, unless what is required mitigates some harm that would be done to the community (Nollan v. California Coastal Commission, 483 US 835, 838, 107 S Ct 3141, 97 L Ed.2d 677 (1987). See also **dedication, donation, development fee**.

examination of title   The process of checking that a person has **good title** to a property. Normally carried out by an attorney before the exchange of contracts for the sale of land. See also **abstract of title, abstractor, searches**.

examiner of titles(Aus)   A barrister or solicitor who assists the Registrar-General with the examination of titles that are to be registered under the **Torrens title system**. See also **Torrens certificate of title**.

excambion(Scot)   A contract by which one parcel of land is exchanged for another, in particular **heritable property**.

excambiator(Scot)   An agent who arranges for an exchange of real property.

excepted risk   **1.** A risk that is not expressly covered in an insurance policy. Also called an 'exception'. See also **all-risks insurance, special perils**.   **2.** In a building contract, a risk that is excluded from the contractor's liability and, therefore, one against which he does not have to insure.

exception   In a deed of conveyance, an exclusion of part of a property, or a particular thing, from that which is the subject of a **grant**. In particular, the exclusion of part of the land or estate granted that would otherwise pass under the general description in the deed. An exception must be something that is severable from that which is to be granted; a particular thing out of a general one – as a room out of a house, ground out of a manor, timber out of land, etc. An 'exception' is a taking out immediately of some part of what has been granted so that it does not pass with the grant, as distinguished from a **reservation** which is the taking out or creating of something new from that which is being granted; although the words are frequently used together and sometimes interchangeably. The words 'excepting and reserving', or sometimes 'subject to', in a contract for sale of property or in a lease, are followed either by: (i) those things that are excluded from the grant and do not pass at all, e.g. minerals; or (ii) any part of the demise that is taken back or reserved, e.g. profits or sporting rights. Although no specific technical words create an exception, it must be expressed clearly and unambiguously, and words of exception are construed, *prima facie*, against the grantor who has drafted or caused the words to be drafted. See also **excepted risk**.

exception clause   See **exclusion clause**.

excess   The first portion of a loss, being a specified sum, that the insured agrees to bear himself before any claim is paid by the insurer. Usually an excess is a small percentage of the total sum insured; thus it avoids the insurer having to administer small claims and should result in a reduced premium for the insured. Sometimes called 'deductibles'. See also **first-loss insurance**.

excess condemnation[US] The exercise by a public authority of the power of **eminent domain** to acquire more land than is required for a development scheme or public works. A process that may be used to enable the authority to recoup part of its cost by selling off the surplus land at an increased price when the development work is complete. See also **condemnation, recoupment**.

excess liability policy See **umbrella insurance**.

excess rent **1.** An amount of rent that exceeds the current market rental value, in particular when the contract rent under a lease exceeds the market rent. Such rent is normally considered more risky than the market rent and, therefore, if capitalised a higher capitalisation rate is used. See also **premium**. cf. **profit rent**[BrE]. **2.** In economics, the return from cultivated land over the minimum return required to keep the land in use, i.e. the return over and above the 'marginal cost of cultivation'. See also **economic rent**.

exchange The giving or receiving of one thing for another when those things are considered to be of equal or similar worth. The reciprocal **transfer** of properties; a trade, barter or swap. A transfer or conveyance of one property for another like property, especially when there is no payment of money or its equivalent. An exchange is an action that must be completed, i.e. it must result from an **executed contract**. An exchange may be distinguished from a **sale** by the lack of consideration (or the payment of money), other than as represented by the value of the properties transferred. An exchange of interests in land must be evidenced in the same way as any contract for the sale of property. See also **bill of exchange**, **exchange of contract**[Eng], **tax-free exchange**[US], **writing**.

exchange of contract[BrE] The stage at which a contract for the sale of land comes into formal effect. Exchange takes effect when each part of the contract, signed by the vendor or the purchaser as the case may be, is in the actual or constructive possession of the other party or his solicitor. Exchange may take place: (a) 'face to face', usually in the office of the vendor's solicitor; (b) by post, which means it takes place when the last part is actually posted; or (c) by telephone, after both the vendor and the purchaser sign contracts in identical form and the parties confirm (usually through their solicitors) that they are holding the copies of the contract for the order of the other party. The latter practice should take place only when partners or proprietors of the respective solicitors have agreed and recorded identical attendance notes confirming that their respective clients have duly executed a contract. See also **writing**.

exchange value See **value**.

excheat See **escheat**.

excluding and limiting terms See **exclusion clause**.

exclusion clause[Eng] A clause in a contract that seeks to define and limit the extent of the promisor's liability or obligation under the contract. For example, a clause which stipulates that the promisor will not be liable for such matters as a defect in goods offered for sale; for providing any **warranty** as to the quality or condition of the subject matter of the contract; or for any damage that is suffered by the promisee as a result of negligence or misrepresentation on the part of the promisor. An exclusion clause (also called an 'exception clause' or an 'exemption clause') may be regarded either as an attempt to clarify that which is set out in the contract, or as a means of limiting the liability of one or other parties for damages to the other in specified circumstances, whether quantitatively or by limiting the time for action. It is in the latter sense that the term is more commonly used.

An exclusion clause that refers to the substance

of the contract must be 'fair and reasonable' and, as a rule, a person cannot negate the effect of a representation by words that are placed in the small print. The exclusion clause must be an integral part of the contract to which it refers, not merely something to which the promisor may point to escape an obligation, but which was not at all evident when the promisee entered into the contract. An exclusion clause is intended to safeguard against inaccuracies, errors and mistakes, but not to exclude a liability for fraud (*Pearson v Dublin Corporation* [1907] AC 351, 365 (HL)). In addition, the clause must be signed by or clearly brought to the notice of the affected party; it must not be ambiguous nor totally devoid of applicability to the contract; and it may not be relied upon by a party to a contract who is fundamentally in breach of a condition of the contract in order to negate that condition.

English statute law has further intervened to limit the effect or to control the use of exclusion clauses especially for the purpose of consumer protection. In particular, the Misrepresentation Act 1967, as amended by the Unfair Contract Terms Act 1977, which applies to contracts affecting 'business liability' – including the occupation of premises used for business purposes (but not an occupation that is purely for recreational or educational purposes). Furthermore, a clause seeking to exclude or restrict a liability to **misrepresentation** must be "fair and reasonable … having regard to the circumstances which were, or ought reasonably to have been, known to or in the contemplation of the parties when the contract was made", Misrepresentation Act 1967, s. 11, and "it is for those claiming that the term satisfies that requirement to show that it does", Misrepresentation Act 1967, s. 3. Therefore, the enforceability of an exclusion clause depends on the nature of the contract. Nonetheless it must be fair and reasonable; must not of itself be the result of a misrepresentation as to its scope; must be brought to the notice of the party against whom it is seeking to operate; must not run against the fundamental intent of the agreement; and is best used to clarify, and at the same time to encase, the terms of an agreement, rather than as a means to seek to bar the fulfilment of an undertaking – a ploy used when one party to a contract becomes aware of that which he should have been aware at the outset. Also called an 'exemption clause'. In the US, generally called a **disclaimer clause**. cf. **escape clause**. See also *contra proferentem*, **exculpatory clause**[US], **particulars of sale**, **puffing**.

Yates, David. *Exclusion Clauses in Contracts*. 2nd ed. London: Sweet & Maxwell, 1982.

Lawson, Richard. *Exclusion Clauses and Unfair Contract Terms*. 6th ed. London: Pearson, 2000.

exclusionary zoning[US]   Land use control regulations or zoning ordinances aimed at excluding a particular category of persons or a type of user from a given area. Exclusionary zoning may be aimed at excluding persons of a particular income level or economic class, or excluding a use or form of development that will not prove to be a net contributor to local government revenue (the latter form of exclusion is also called 'fiscal zoning') or is intended to limit the pressures on public services. Exclusionary zoning may take the form of restrictions on such matters as high-density development, low-cost housing, recreational facilities for low-income groups (e.g. communal halls, state crèches), or may stipulate minimum lot-size requirements ('acreage zoning' or 'large-lot zoning'), minimum floor space requirements, number of houses per acre, or the 'gross density' for a subdivision or a similar density requirement (called 'density zoning'). If such regulations are made for the general public good, or are intended to improve or maintain the appearance or character of the area, and they are not arbitrary or capricious, they are normally considered to be valid (Construction Industries of Sonoma County v. City of Petaluma, 375 F Supp 574, 583 (DC Cal 1975); Village of Belle Terre v. Boraas, 416 US 1, 94 S Ct 1536, 39 L Ed.2d 797 (1974)). However, they are invalid or may be considered unconstitutional if they are discriminatory on the grounds of race, religion, sex, handicap, familial status, or national origin, or if the municipality is clearly endeavoring to avoid accepting its 'fair share' of the constituents of the community, i.e. it is legitimate to require a fair provision of low-cost housing (South Burlington County NAACP v. Mount Laurel Tp., 93 NJ 158, 456 A.2d 390 (1983)). Exclusionary zoning that requires a residential development to have large building lots is sometimes called 'acreage zoning' or 'large-lot zoning'. Sometimes called 'snob zoning'. cf. **inclusionary zoning**.

exclusive agency An agency agreement by which a specified **agent** is appointed to sell (or otherwise dispose of) a property on the understanding that the principal will not enter into an agreement with any other agent in respect of the subject property (usually for a given period of time and/or in a given district). However, the agency may be exclusive or sole to that agent, but it does not preclude the principal from also seeking to find an interested party and, thereby, not being obliged to remunerate the agent for his services. In the UK, this arrangement is generally called a **sole agency**, as the agent is the 'sole' party appointed. An exclusive agency may be contrasted with an **exclusive right to sell** or **sole selling right** where the principal is liable to pay a commission even though he sells the property himself.

In the event of a successful transaction, a payment is due to the appointed agent, even if the purchaser is introduced by another agent or broker (the assumption is that the 'exclusive agent' was appointed to negotiate with all prospective purchasers to the exclusion of other agents or brokers and in all probability would have concluded the 'bargain' with the taker). If the owner appoints another agent or broker during the term of an existing exclusive agency agreement and that agent or broker makes a sale, the principal may be obliged to pay both parties, or at least the appointed agent or broker may recover the commission he might have earned as damages and the principal will have to pay the second party whatsoever was agreed. On the other hand, if a transaction results directly from a contact and the efforts of the principal, the agent or broker is normally precluded from receiving any payment.

However, if the agent procures a purchaser (or any other appropriate party to the transaction) who is **ready**, **willing and able** to proceed *before* the owner concludes his transaction, payment is normally due to the agent. In English law, in such an instance it has been held that the agent may not be entitled to the same **commission** as if he had concluded the transaction unaided – the agent's entitlement to commission depending on the precise terms of the appointment and the extent of the duties performed (*Hampton and Sons Ltd v George* [1939] 3 All ER 627).

An 'exclusive agent' normally accepts that he will 'use his best endeavours' to sell, or otherwise dispose of the property as required by the principal, and is generally appointed for a fixed period of time. During the period of appointment he is responsible for marketing the property; negotiating with prospective purchasers; reporting fully to his principal; and, usually, making every effort to introduce a person who is 'ready, willing and able' (or a similar person) to acquire the property upon the terms agreed as acceptable to the principal. Also called a 'sole selling agency' or, in the US, an 'exclusive agency to sell'. cf. **exclusive right to sell**, **multiple agency**. See also **broker**, **exclusive agency listing**, *quantum meruit*, **listing**.

exclusive agency listing or **exclusive listing**(AmE) A right granted, usually in writing and for a specific period of time, to a broker to sell or otherwise dispose of a particular property to the exclusion of any other broker during the term of the agreement. The listing may take the form of an **exclusive agency** (or 'exclusive agency listing') if the principal (seller) is not precluded from using his own efforts to find a buyer so that, if a sale results from those efforts, no commission is payable to the broker. Alternatively the listing may be granted as an **exclusive right to sell** if the principal is obliged to pay a commission to the agent even if the principal finds the buyer. Generally, an 'exclusive listing' takes the form of an exclusive agency. cf. **open listing**. See also **listing**.

exclusive agency to sell(AmE)   See **exclusive agency**.

exclusive clause(AmE)   See **non-competition clause**.

exclusive dealing agreement(BrE)   See **solus agreement**.

exclusive listing(AmE)   See exclusive agency listing.

exclusive occupation   The sole right to occupy a property; "a person has a right to 'exclusive occupation' of a room when he is to occupy it himself, and no one else is entitled to occupy it", *Luganda v Service Hotels Ltd* [1969] 2 Ch 209, 219, [1969] 2 All ER 692, 695 (CA). 'Exclusive occupation' and '**exclusive possession**' are similar terms, the former denoting primarily a question of fact and the latter more a question of law; any further distinction depends primarily on the difference between **occupation** and **possession** and the context in which the term is used. Exclusive occupation grants a right to physically occupy premises to the exclusion of others, but does not give the exclusive right to possession as a legal right. Thus, one in 'exclusive occupation', as with the occupier of a room in an hotel or students in a hall of residence, does not have overall control of the premises; whereas a tenant who has 'exclusive possession' may bar anyone in much the same way as an owner, unless there is agreement or legal authority to the contrary.

In English law, in the case of a **restricted contract**, which essentially requires a right of exclusive occupation, a person who is given an exclusive right to a room is generally in exclusive occupation, notwithstanding the fact that the landlord retains a key to the room or an employee of the landlord comes to clean the room on a daily basis, but the use of accommodation in a hostel where rooms are shared is not a right to exclusive occupation (*AG Securities v Vaughan, Antoniades v Villiers* [1990] 1 AC 417, [1988] 3 All ER 1058 (HL)).

A party may be said to have exclusive occupation as an essential element of **rateable occupation** if he has paramount control. On the other hand, where access is more limited, as when it is shared with the owner, then it is less likely to create 'exclusive occupation' (*Smith v Lambeth Assessment Committee* (1882) 10 QBD 327 (CA); *Channel Shipping (Newport) v Newport Borough Council* [1988] 16 EG 87). See also **beneficial occupation, lodger, occupation**.

exclusive possession   The right to **possession** of a property as one's own to the exclusion of any other person or persons. The obtaining of an exclusive claim over land and its appropriation to one's own use and benefit, and not for another. "The expression 'exclusive possession' in relation to the occupier of a property may be used in more than one sense. It may ... be used to mean that, as a factual matter, the occupant, alone or together with his family, occupies the premises and does not share them with any other person ... Or the expression may be used to mean that the occupant has a right to exclude the owner from the premises", *Heslop v Burns* [1974] 1 WLR 1241, 1247. 'Exclusive possession' does not preclude the right of the landlord, upon notice, to enter onto the premises to view them or to carry out repairs; but if a landlord or his servants have unlimited access to the premises, for example to provide attendance and services, or if the occupier is clearly a **lodger**, the occupant cannot be said to have exclusive possession.

In common law, it is one of the primary features of a **lease** (as distinguished from a **licence**) that the lessee has 'exclusive possession' of the entire leased premises, even against the owner of the fee (unless there is an agreement or a statutory provision to the contrary) (*Street v Mountford* [1985] AC 809, 816B-C, [1985] 2 All ER 289 (HL); United States v. 15.3 Acres of Land, 154 F Supp 770 (DC Pa 1957)). If a person is not granted a right of exclusive possession as against the landlord, then in effect there can be no lease, but only a licence. However, a right to exclusive possession does not of itself create a tenancy, there must be more. A person in exclusive possession may be "an owner in fee simple, a trespasser, a mortgagee in possession, an object of charity or a service occupier. To constitute a tenancy the occupier must be granted exclusive possession for a fixed or periodic term certain in consideration of a premium or periodic payments", *Street v Mountford, supra* at 818. (However, a 'service occupier' in exclusive occupation is, to all intent and purpose, a tenant – see **service tenancy**). In the US, also called 'sole possession' or 'open possession'. See also **exclusive occupation**.

exclusive rent(BrE)   A rent that is paid excluding rates, i.e. the tenant accepts the liability under the tenancy to pay rates, or similar property taxes, direct to the local authority. cf. **inclusive rent**. See also **net rent**.

exclusive right of sale(AmE)   See **exclusive right to sell**.

exclusive right to sell(AmE)   An arrangement by which an agent or broker is given sole responsibility for negotiating the sale of a property, so that for the term of the appointment the principal agrees not to appoint any other agent or broker and is obliged to pay a commission to the agent even if a purchaser is procured by another party. An exclusive right to sell is similar to an **exclusive agency** (or 'exclusive agency to sell'); except that, with an 'exclusive *right* to sell', the broker receives a **commission** (or, at least, damages for his time and expenses or loss of revenue), even if the sale results from the intervention of the principal. A listing or agency agreement will normally be construed as an exclusive agency, and not an exclusive right to sell, so that if the principal sells the property himself he is not liable to pay a commission, unless the agreement clearly stipulates to the contrary. Also called an 'exclusive right of sale', 'exclusive authority to sell', 'sole selling right', or in the UK a 'sole right to sell'. See also **extender clause**.

exclusive use   1. The **use** of a property to the exclusion of others. In particular, in the US, the use of a property in order to exclude the rights of the holder of the legal title as a means to set up a prescriptive right. In this context, 'exclusive use' does not mean that no other person has used the right in question, but only that the right is not dependent upon a similar right held by another. See also **prescription**.   2.(US)The use of property for its primary purpose. cf. **accessory use**.

exclusive use zoning(US)   Zoning that restricts a particular area to only one use. For example, zoning of an area only for residential purposes or only for industrial purposes. cf. **pyramid zoning**. See also **zoning classification**.

exculpate   To free from blame. To be without liability or recourse. See also **non-recourse mortgage**.

exculpatory clause(US)   1. A clause in a contract by which one party holds himself blameless from damage or injury arising out of certain circumstances relating to that contract. For example, a clause in a lease which states that a landlord is not liable for damage to any person, whether a tenant or a third party, due to any act of the landlord or his agent, or for his or the tenant's failure to repair the property. Such conditions may be difficult to enforce at law, especially when it can be shown that there was a disparity of bargaining power between the parties at the time that the contract was entered into. In many jurisdictions, such clauses are considered contrary to public policy and, therefore, not enforceable, especially in the case of residential leases. In addition, several states have enacted statutes prohibiting or severely limiting the enforceability of such clauses. In addition, the Uniform Residential Landlord and Tenant Act (which has been adopted in some 20 states) provides that an exculpatory clause should have limited application. In those jurisdictions that do recognize the validity of exculpatory clauses, they are strictly construed, generally against the landlord. Also called a 'hold-harmless clause'. See also **exclusion clause**.   2. A provision in a trust instrument by which the trustee is relieved from liability for any act carried out in accordance with the trust instrument in good faith. Also called a 'hold-harmless clause'. **3.** A clause inserted in a mortgage deed by which the mortgagee agrees not to take a personal action against the mortgagor if the mortgaged property provides insufficient security for the debt, i.e. language that creates a **non-recourse mortgage**.

executed consideration Consideration that has been actually given in satisfaction of a contract.

executed contract A contract that has been completed in its entirety according to its terms leaving no party with any residual duty or obligation to perform. An executed contract of sale of land is one that has been performed by both the vendor and purchaser, the purchase price has been paid and the deed has been executed and delivered. An executed contract cannot be frustrated, unlike an **executory contract** where something is still left to be done. See also **delivery**.

executed trust A trust that is completed and is irrevocable. A trust arising from a settlement that can take full effect on the basis of the document by which it is established, as compared with an **executory trust** which requires further documentation to give full effect to the settler's intentions.

execution 1. The carrying of an obligation through to **completion**. The performance of the duties and obligations of a contract, such as the carrying out and completion of building work by a contractor. See also **practical completion**. 2. The effecting of an instrument in the form required by law. In English law, a deed is said to be executed by an individual when it has been signed or, if appropriate, the individual has placed his mark (LPA 1925, s. 73(1)). See also **delivery**, **executed contract**. 3. The putting into effect of a judgement of a court, such as for possession of property.

execution sale(US) See **judicial sale**.

executor (f. **executrix**) A person (an individual or trust company) appointed in a will to administer the affairs of the deceased (the testator) and carry out the provisions of the will. An executor is responsible for such duties as collecting together all the testator's property, contacting all beneficiaries named in the will, arranging for the payment of all debts and taxes of the estate and disposing of the residue of the estate as directed in the will. If there is no executor, as in the case of intestacy, a court will appoint an **administrator** to perform the same effective duties. See also **personal representative, probate**.

executor's deed A deed of transfer that is executed by an **executor**.

executory consideration See **executory contract**.

executory contract A contract that is still to be brought into effect, in whole or in part, or executed by the action of the parties or by an external event; as distinguished from an **executed contract** which has been wholly performed. An executory contract still requires performance and therefore may be frustrated, unlike an executed contract that cannot. An executory contract of sale of land leaves something to be done by one or other of the parties before **delivery** and passing of title, such as the payment of the balance of the purchase price. Consideration to be paid under such a contract may be referred to as 'executory consideration'. Sometimes called a 'continuing contract'. cf. **conditional contract**. See also **contract for sale, estate contract, good consideration, lien**.

executory devise A devise of a future estate; a devise that takes effect upon the occurrence of a future event, i.e. a grant of property by will made subject to a condition that has to be satisfied before the transfer takes effect. If the condition occurs before the death of the devisee, the estate goes to the heir at the time of the event, and not to the heir at the time of the death. With an executory devise, no estate vests at the death of the devisee, but it vests only on the occurrence of the condition. An executory devise differs from a **remainder** in that: (a) there needs be no particular estate to support it; (b) a fee simple or a lesser estate may be limited after a fee simple; and (c) an estate for years may be limited to take place after an estate for life, whereas a life estate once granted vests the entire estate without a remainder. See also **executory interest, executory limitation**.

executory interest   A **future interest** held by a third person, other than the grantor, which either 'shifts' from one person to another, or 'springs up' as a right to possession, after the natural termination of the preceding estate. An executory interest is not a **remainder**, i.e. it does not return to the original grantor or his or her heirs, but takes effect as a present interest upon the occurrence of a contingent event that divests (cuts short) an existing interest in the same land. An executory interest takes effect in possession by cutting off the preceding estate prematurely, as distinguished from a remainder which takes effect in possession at the *expiration* of the preceding estate. A shifting interest (sometimes called a 'shifting use' or 'secondary use') abruptly cuts short the interest of another person who might have obtained a right to possession of the land. For example, if A grants White House to B "for as long as it is used as a medical center, and if not, to C", then C has a shifting interest. A springing interest cuts short the interest of the grantor. For example, if X grants Green Acres "to his daughter Y, if she marries", then Y has a springing interest. cf. **determinable interest**. See also **contingent interest**.

executory interval(US)   The time in a transaction for the sale of land between the agreement or execution of the contract and the transfer or delivery of title. See also **conversion, executory contract**.

executory limitation   A limitation that defines when a future estate or interest may come into effect. In particular, a limitation set out in a deed or will that states when a future interest may vest in someone other than grantor. For example, a grant by A of an estate in fee simple "to B and his heirs, but if B dies without issue surviving at the time of his death, then to C and his heirs". The limitation does not stipulate for the return of the estate to A (or his or her heirs) and it defines a future event when C would receive the estate. If the limitation is contained in a will it is generally called an **executory devise**. cf. **special limitation**. See also **conditional limitation, determinable fee**.

executory remainder(US)   See **remainder**.

executory trust   A **trust** that cannot take effect on the basis of the document by which it has been established, but requires further documents or clarification in order to achieve legal effect, to fulfil the purpose of the trust or give effect to the creators intent. An executory trust may be distinguished from an **executed trust** which gives immediate effect to the settler's intentions.

executory use(Eng)   See **shifting use**.

exemplary damages   See **damages**.

exempli gratia (e.g.)(Lat)   'For example'. 'For instance'.

exemplify   To make an official copy of a document, especially as made by a court of law or authenticated by a court seal. See also **certified copy, conformed copy**(US).

exemption clause   See **exclusion clause**.

existing use   1. The use to which land is put at a particular point in time.   2. An actual use of land that existed before the enactment of a zoning or planning ordinance or regulation and, therefore, one that may continue without causing a legal infraction. See also **established use, nonconforming use**.

existing use rights(Eng) **1.** All those rights to use property that may be exercised without the need for planning permission; any use that may be undertaken without constituting **development**. See also **certificate of lawfulness, General Development Order, highest and best use, permitted development, purchase notice, Use Classes Order.** **2.** See **compensation for planning restrictions**.

existing use value (EUV) The value of a property on the basis that it will continue in its current use, without taking into account any potential future development or redevelopment of the land on which the property is situated, although any potential to expand the existing property may be brought into account.

"The estimated amount for which a property should exchange on the date of valuation between a **willing buyer** and a **willing seller** in an **arm's-length transaction**, after proper marketing wherein the parties had acted knowledgeably, prudently and without compulsion, assuming that the buyer is granted vacant possession of all parts of the property required by the business and disregarding potential alternative uses and any other characteristics of the property that would cause its **Market Value** to differ from that needed to replace the remaining service potential at least cost", The Royal Institution of Chartered Surveyors, *Appraisal & Valuation Standards*. 5th ed. London: RICS Books, 2003, UKPS 1.3. EUV is used only to estimate the value a property that is owner-occupied by a business, or other entity, for inclusion in a Financial Statement. A detailed Commentary on this definition, and on the definition of 'market value', is set out in the *Appraisal & Valuation Standards*. This value is based essentially on the price the business would have to pay in the open market to replace the property. Where there is a significant difference between the existing use value and the market value the valuer should provide an opinion on both bases and explain the reasons in the valuation report. cf. **depreciated replacement cost**. See also **current use value**.

exoneration clause See **disclaimer clause**.

exor(Lat) 'Executor'.

expansion An increase in the extent, size or scope of something. In particular, an **enlargement** of a building. See also **development, extension, non-conforming user**.

expedit reipublicæ ne sua re quis mal utatur(Lat) 'It is for the public good that no one use his property badly' (or 'so as to injure others'). A maxim of Roman law. See also **negligence, nuisance**.

expendable cash after tax (ECAT)(Aus) The cash return available to an equity investor, after tax. See also **cash available for distribution**(AmE), **cash-on-cash return**.

expenditure See **expense**.

expenditure on land See **compensation for improvements, estoppel, licence by estoppel**(Eng).

expense Derived from the Latin *ex-pensus*, that which is paid out or given up. Money, or its equivalent, that is spent to acquire a benefit. That which is used up, consumed or forborne in order to achieve an objective or bring about a result. An expense is represented by actual disbursements. In particular, a sum of money that has been laid out in return for a benefit. Expenses that relate to real estate include repair and maintenance costs; taxes or assessments; insurance premiums; management fees; and any other **operating expense**(AmE)/**service charge**(BrE) arising from ownership of property and the consequent need to maintain the use and value of that property. Generally, a provision for depreciation and the cost of debt service (principal and interest) is not an expense, as it does not form any part of the direct cost of maintaining the property. However, money paid into a sinking fund for the replacement of capital equipment is usually considered as an expense in the year in which it is paid out and is offset in the year in which it is incurred. See also **charge, payment.**

expense stop(US)   The expense level of a commercial building above which a tenant agrees to pay increases in operating expense. In effect, this is the expense level to which the landlord's obligation is limited. An expense stop is generally expressed as a rate per square foot and the tenant undertakes to pay all operating expenses above that rate. See also **base year, escalator clause.**

expense ratio(US)   The ratio of expenditure to income. In particular, the ratio of **operating expenses** (excluding debt service) to **effective gross income.** See also **operating expense ratio.**

expert   1. A person who is knowledgeable in a particular field, from experience or by study, education or qualification. An expert is required to be experienced and actively engaged in the field in which he expresses competence and, in order that his opinion should be credible, there should be no possibility, or appearance, of bias in the views on which he is expressing expertise. See also **expert witness.   2.**(Eng)One who is appointed by parties to a dispute to use his knowledge, experience and independent judgement to express an opinion on the basis for the settlement of the dispute. A person appointed as an expert in a dispute is not limited to the information provided to him by the parties (or their advisors), but also uses his own experience or knowledge in order to determine the basis for the settlement of that dispute. As a rule, his decision is binding on the parties who have sought his opinion (for that is what they normally asked for); unless there is clearly an error on the face of that opinion or negligence, fraud or collusion on the part of the expert (*Mercury Communications Ltd v Director General of Telecommunications* [1996] 1 WLR 48, [1996] 1 All ER 575 (HL)). An expert is required to make his own investigations and searches to ascertain the facts that affect the matter on which he is acting. In some instances he may receive submissions or evidence from the parties to a dispute on which he is to express his expert opinion but, unlike an **arbitrator**, his opinion may be outside the extremes maintained by the parties to the dispute if his own investigations and knowledge leads to that conclusion. See also **arbitration, professional negligence.**

RICS Books. *RICS Guidance to Surveyors Acting as Arbitrators & as Independent Experts in Commercial Rent Reviews.* London: RICS Books, 2002.

Kendall, John, and Clive Freeman. *Expert Determination.* 3rd ed. London: Sweet & Maxwell, 2001.

expert witness   A person called at a judicial or quasi-judicial proceeding to give evidence based on specialist knowledge, experience, professional qualifications, or careful study. An expert witness must have a special knowledge in a particular field, obtained by means of a course of study or habit, which surpasses that of an inexperienced person or layman and, therefore, makes him or her better equipped to express an informed opinion. Whether a person is qualified or sufficiently knowledgeable to give evidence as an expert witness is dependent on the judge of the court; it does not depend necessarily on professional qualification (*R v Silverlock* (1894) 2 QB 766); The Congress and Empire Spring Company v. Edgar, 99 US 645, 25 L Ed 487, 490 (1879)).

Matson, Jack V. *Effective Expert Witnessing.* 2nd ed. Boca Raton, FL and London: Lewis Publishers, 1994.

Reynolds, Michael P., and Philip S. D. King. *The Expert Witness and his Evidence.* 2nd ed. Oxford: Blackwell Scientific, 1992.

Hall, Jean, and Gordon D. Smith. *The Expert Witness,* 2nd ed. Chichester: Barry Rose, 1998.

RICS Books. *RICS Guidance to Surveyors Acting as Arbitrators & as Independent Experts in Commercial Rent Reviews.* London: RICS Books, 2002.

expiration or expiry   1. Cessation. Strictly speaking the coming or bringing to an end, due to lapse of time. For example, the coming to the end of a lease for a term of years. The 'expiry date' or 'expiration date' of an option is the last **day** upon which the option can be exercised. A lease or contract may also be said to come to an end or expire by 'effluxion of time'. See also **term, termination**. **2.** The extinction of a right by the voluntary action of the parties: that is, when the right is not forcibly brought to an end by such means as **forfeiture** or **surrender**. cf. **determination**.

expiry   See **expiration**.

exploding guarantee   A form of guarantee that is entered into when a new loan is granted but will not be called on unless or until one of a number of specified, and usually major, events occurs, such as the bankruptcy of the borrower or the exercise of an injunction against the lender that prevents enforcement of the loan. Such guarantees are more usually encountered in conjunction with the workout of an existing loan and may well terminate if the loan is paid in full or the property is sold. Usually, if one of the specified events occurs the guarantee is due in full.

exponent   A symbol that represents a mathematical operation to be performed on a the number or function immediately before it. For example, a symbol that represents a power or the times a number or base is multiplied by itself. Thus y^3 is equivalent to $y \times y \times y$ and 3 is the exponent.

exposure   The extent to which a property has been offered for lease or for sale on the open market. See also **market value**.

express   Clearly evidenced or stated. Set forth in words. That which is stated clearly and definitely; the communication of information in such a way that it is indubitable, unambiguous and does not require inference or any support in order to ascertain what is conveyed. An express statement may be made orally or in writing, provided that what has been said can be clearly established. See also **contract, covenant, express term**.

express authority   See **authority**.

express condition   See **express term**.

express contract   See **contract**.

express covenant   See **covenant, express term**.

express grant   A **grant** of a right over land in writing, especially a right incorporated in a **conveyance**.
   In English law, in addition to the rights that are set out in the conveyance, **general words** are deemed to be incorporated into any conveyance of land so as to transfer various rights, privileges, easements, buildings, fixtures, etc., that appertain, or are **appurtenant**, to the land conveyed (LPA 1925, s. 62) – provided those words do not conflict with the express words of the conveyance. cf. **implied grant**. See also **general words**.

express reservation   See **reservation**.

express trust   See **trust**.

express term or **express condition**   A **term** or **condition** of a contract that is clear and definite, whether given by word of mouth or set out in writing. A contract wholly in writing is taken to be expressed within the pages of the written instrument. Accordingly, such a term or condition cannot be varied by an oral evidence or agreement, except in cases of fraud or rectification and except, in certain circumstances, as a defence in actions for specific performance. However, a condition or a covenant may be treated as express if it can be 'inferred' from the written text as forming part of the express intention of the parties or when there is an ambiguity in the contract. An express condition is sometimes called a 'condition in deed' or 'condition in fact' (from the Law French, *condicionem fait*), i.e. one declared in the terms of a deed or instrument, as distinguished from an **implied condition** or 'condition in law' (1 *Co Litt* 201a). See also **merger clause, oral contract, usual covenant, writing**.

expressio unius est exclusio alterius(Lat) 'The express mention of one thing implies the exclusion of another'. When a person or things of a class are expressly referred to in a contract, statute or document, it may be inferred that the intention is to exclude any others of a similar nature; or, when one exception is made to a general rule, other exceptions are excluded. "A valuable servant but a dangerous master in the construction of statutes or document", *Osborn's Concise Law Dictionary*, 8th ed. London: Sweet & Maxwell, 1993.

expressum facit cessare tacitum(Lat) 'That which is expressed puts an end to that which is implied (or that which is silent)'. An express declaration puts an end to that which silence may signify. See also **express term**.

expropriation   The taking of property for public use or benefit, usually by a government agency. The taking of property by the State, especially when there is no payment of compensation. In English law, expropriation generally refers to the power exercised by a government over foreign-owned assets, rather than to the process of acquiring real property against the will of the owner, subject to the payment of proper compensation, or **compulsory purchase**, although it may be used in the latter senses. "'Expropriation' generally is used to mean a taking which conforms with the requirements of international law; 'confiscation' is used to describe a taking which is unaccompanied by compensation: 'nationalisation' is commonly used to denote an expropriation of major resources as part of a general program of social or economic reform; and 'requisition' usually means a taking for a temporary purpose", 18 *Halsbury's Laws of England*, Foreign Relation Law, 4th ed., para. 1728, note 2.

In the US, **eminent domain** is the most common term for any taking by the State, subject to the payment of **just compensation**. In Canada, expropriation is the term more commonly used for the same process.

extended coverage insurance(US)   See **extended-perils insurance**.

extended lease   1. See **extension**.   2.(Eng) A lease that may be acquired by the tenant of a **house** that has been occupied as his or her residence under a lease that was originally granted for a term of not less than 21 years at a **low rent** (a **long tenancy**). The tenant must have been the occupier of the house, or a part thereof, for the past three years, or a total of three of the past ten years. In addition, this right may be exercised only by the occupier of a "house and premises" that falls within certain rateable value or other statutorily specified limits. A tenant who qualifies under the Act may be entitled to an extended lease of fifty years from the expiry of his existing lease on similar terms, but at a **modern ground rent** (Leasehold Reform Act 1967, ss. 1-4, 14-16, as amended).   3.(Eng) A lease that may be acquired by the tenant of a **flat** that has been occupied as his or her residence under a lease that was originally granted for a term of not less than 21 years at a **low rent**. The tenant must have occupied the premises for at least three years, or three years out of the last ten years, as his only or principal home before being able to exercise this right. A lease for a further term of 90 years at a peppercorn rent may be acquired by a qualifying tenant of a flat, i.e. a lease of a flat that is held on a long lease (not less than 21 years) at a low rent by a tenant who would otherwise qualify to have a right of **leasehold enfranchisement** (Leasehold Reform, Housing and Urban Development Act 1993, Chapter II, as amended). The tenant may acquire an extended lease when his existing lease comes to the end of its term, or the tenant may surrender his existing lease and acquire a new lease from the same landlord. The new lease is acquired for a premium which is based in the aggregate of the diminution in the value of the landlord's interest in the leased property, and the landlord's interest in any other property, arising as a result of the grant of the extended lease, plus a share of the **marriage value** (as statutorily defined) (1993 Act, Sch. 13, para. 2, as amended by HA 1996, s. 110). In other respects the new lease is granted on the same terms as the old lease.

extended-perils insurance 1. A form of property insurance that extends beyond a 'standard' policy for fire cover to include such risks as impact damage, storm, lightning, explosion, riot, smoke, aircraft and vehicular impact and similar perils. The policy may be extended as far as the contract specifies but, unlike **all-risks insurance**, the perils covered are effected by inclusion rather than exclusion. In the US, also called 'extra or extended coverage insurance'. See also **comprehensive insurance, special perils**. 2.(US)A title insurance policy that covers such aspects as encumbrances, rights of occupancy, easements, etc. See also **contingent liability insurance**.

extender clause or **extension clause**(US) A provision in a broker's **listing agreement** to the effect that the principal will pay a **commission**, even after the term of the agreement has ended, provided that a sale is made to a prospective purchaser who was introduced by the broker during the subsistence of the agreement. The listing agreement may provide that the extension provision applies to a purchaser who was 'negotiating' with the broker, or who had submitted an offer or a proposal during the term of the agreement, and with whom a binding sales contract is entered after the agreement has expired. Also, the extender clause may be made to apply only when the broker had 'introduced' the purchaser to the seller, or only if the purchaser has made an 'offer' during the term of the agreement. As a rule, although the broker does not have to be involved throughout the entire negotiation process, there is a requirement that there is some connection or relationship between the broker's role and the ultimate transaction, not just a single contact. An express extender clause is usually limited to a fixed period of time after the end of the agreement, commonly six to twelve months. If no period of time is expressed in the agreement, then a court will normally limit the extension to a 'reasonable' period of time from the expiration of the agreement. Although some courts may view the arrangement as an open listing as soon as the agreement has expired, unless clearly expressed to the contrary. As a matter of good practice, most brokers supply details of all parties with whom they are in negotiation during the term of the agreement, and unless a party is included in such a list, the broker cannot claim to have been negotiating with that party under the provisions of most extender clauses. Also called a 'carry-over clause' or an 'override'. See also **procuring cause**.

extension 1. The prolonging of a right, especially for an additional period of time. The extension of a lease generally means to continue the lease for a further period of time, but upon the same basic term, except usually for the rent. Although 'extension' and 'renewal', in some contexts, may be used synonymously, strictly speaking an extended lease is considered to have been granted for the full duration of both the expired and the extended term, but a renewed lease creates a lease for the new term usually with new conditions. The 'extension' of a mortgage may prolong the maturity, or may mean an extension of the security to cover additional indebtedness or a **future advance**. See also **extension agreement, option to renew**. 2. The act or process of increasing a space or adding a structure to a building. An **enlargement** in size or space. See also **development**(Eng), **improvement, material change in the use**(Eng). 3. An increase in the allotted time for completion of a contract. See also **delay, time is of the essence**.

extension agreement or **extension clause** An agreement, or clause in an agreement, that provides for the prolongation of a right when it comes to its end. For example, an agreement to continue a tenancy beyond its expiry date; a loan or mortgage after its maturity date; or a building contract after the completion date. See also **extender clause, time is of the essence**.

extension clause See **extender clause, extension agreement**.

exterior See **external**.

external Situated or connected with the outside; out of doors. Generally, the external part of a building is that part of the building exposed to the atmosphere, or not enclosed but forming the enclosure of the premises. An outer or external wall is one where at least one face is exposed to the outside elements or to view. A wall that rests upon the wall of an adjoining property, and would be exposed to the atmosphere if the adjoining wall were to be demolished may be considered as a wall that is 'external' to the demised premises – the wall *in extremis* to the building. On the other hand, windows are not *prima facie* an external part of a building, unless they form part of the external cladding, e.g. as a curtain wall; or are looked upon as forming part of the outside frame of the building. In order to emphasize that the intention is to refer to a part of a structure that is truly on the outside, 'exterior' may be preferred, being that which is "esp. situated at and forming the outer surface or limit … capable of withstanding normal wear and tear of weather conditions for a considerable period of time", *Webster's Third New International Dictionary®, Unabridged*, ©1993. "When we speak of anything which has two coats, it is usual to designate the outermost by the name of 'exterior'; when we speak simply of the surface, without reference to anything behind it is denominated external; as the 'exterior' coat of a walnut, or the external surface of a thing", George Crabb, *Crabb's English Synonyms*. 1816. Reprint, London: Routledge, 1982. See also **repair**.

external valuer(BrE) A **valuer** who is not employer or directly associated with the client for whom a valuation is being carried our. See also **fee appraiser**(US).

external wall See **external**.

extinction The bringing to an end. The discharging of a right or claim. cf. **release**. See also **merger**, **termination**.

extinguishment The act or process of putting to an end or causing to end. The **termination** or cancellation of a right. The destruction of a right or contract; the act by which a contract is made void or no longer enforceable or of no legal effect. A debt is extinguished when paid; although strictly it may be said to be discharged or released by the act of the payer, in contradistinction to an extinguishment 'by operation of law'. A right to real property may be extinguished by a **merger** of interests, e.g. the purchase of a leasehold by the freeholder or the **unity of possession** of the dominant and servient tenements associated with an easement. An easement may be extinguished also by **release**, **abandonment**, by express or implied notice, or by statute. A tenant obligation to pay rent may be extinguished by a **surrender** or **frustration** of the lease or tenancy; by a merger of the landlord's and tenant's interests; or upon the expiration of a lease that was granted for a fixed term; by eviction of the tenant under due process of law; or occasionally by **abandonment** of the leased premises and re-entry by the landlord. See also **accord and satisfaction**.

extortionate credit bargain See **usury**.

extra coverage insurance(US) See **extended-perils insurance**.

extraction approach(US) See **abstraction approach**.

extraordinary repair(Scot) Repairs that result from structural and **latent defect** and that are normally the responsibility of the landlord, unless the tenant is clearly and expressly made liable for such repairs. See **inherent defect**, **repair**.

extrinsic Arising from an external act or cause; not inherent. Derived from outside. See also **latent defect**.

exurbanisation(US) The growth of a town or city beyond its present suburbs. See also **ribbon development**.

fabric Something that has ben put together, constructed or manufactured for a special purpose. The 'fabric' of a **building** is the main structure or framework of the building; the carcass or load-bearing part of the building, but generally excludes the doors, windows, internal partitions, equipment, services and finishings. See also **structure**.

façade or **facade** That which is made or appears as the face or front of a building, especially a face that is given a special architectural feature. The wall, or walls, of a building that demonstrate its primary external architectural appearance. See also **elevation**.

facade easement(US) An **easement** (or, more strictly speaking, a **restrictive covenant** or 'private zoning') by which an owner of land is prohibited from altering the façade, or exterior, of an existing building. A municipal authority may impose a façade easement on a building or structure of historic significance in order to preserve its external appearance. See also **historic building**, **negative easement**.

face interest rate See **nominal interest rate**.

face rate 1. See **nominal interest rate**. 2. See **coupon rate**.

face value 1. The value stated on the face of a negotiable instrument or on an insurance policy, i.e. the amount of principal that the issuer of the instrument or the insurer undertakes to pay when the instrument or policy matures. The nominal or **par value**, rather than the market value. The face value is used as the basis for calculating interest on a mortgage, bond, debenture or other form of security. In some instances the face value of an interest-bearing note may be stated as the principal amount, plus any accrued interest. 2. The apparent value of a property, i.e. the value on first impression. cf. **book value**, **intrinsic value**.

facilitator Someone who assists or promotes business; a **middleman**. See also **agent**, **broker**.

facilities management (FM)(BrE) or **facility management**(AmE) The function that is required to manage buildings and their components for the benefit of the users. "Facility management is a profession that encompasses multiple disciplines to ensure functionality of the built environment by integrating people, place, process and technology", International Facility Management Association (www.ifma.org/about/org). Facility management may include facility planning, forecasting and budgeting facility needs, interior space planning, preparation and review of workplace specifications, architectural and engineering planning and design, managing environmental health and safety, maintaining physical plant and equipment, as well as real estate acquisition, disposal and management. See also **property management**.

Cotts, David G. *The Facilities Management Handbook*. 2nd ed. New York: American Management Association, 1999.
Fielder, Ian R. (general editor). *The Complete Guide to Facility Management*. London: LexisNexis UK, 2003.
Kaiser, Harvey. *The Facilities Manager's Reference: Management, Planning, Building Audits, Estimating*. Kingston, MA: R. S. Means Company, Inc., 1989.
Rondeau, Edmond P., and Robert Kevin Brown. *Facility Management*. New York: Wiley, 1995.
Seth, Anand K. *Facilities Engineering and Management Handbook: Commercial, Industrial and Institutional Building*. New York: McGraw-Hill, 2001.

facility 1. A service that is built into or installed in a building to ensure that it functions for the use intended; a service or appliance that is available or essential to the running of a home or business. For example, heating or air-conditioning, elevators, toilets or restrooms. The 'facilities' of a building may refer to anything that is not an integral part of the main frame or structure; or the term may be used to refer to the additional services that one building is able to offer to an occupier, such as 'telecommunication or computer facilities'. See also **facilities management**(BrE)/**facility management**(AmE), **services**. **2.** A service made available by a financial institution or bank to assist a customer. In particular, an undertaking to provide a loan or overdraft up to a stipulated amount and on stipulated terms. See also **commitment**.

fact sheet(AmE)   See **property brief**.

factor **1.** Any number that divides exactly into another. A number that multiplied by one or more numbers forms a product. A percentage figure expressed as a decimal, or the reciprocal of a **rate of return**. If i = income, c = capital value, the factor $F = c/i$. **2.** A number used in the **capitalisation** of an income. See also **capitalisation factor**. **3.** A commercial **agent** who is entrusted with possession of another's goods for the purpose of selling them; usually in his own name. A factor is a restricted or special agent who is only involved, on behalf of another, in the buying and selling of goods. See also **lien**. **4.** A bank or financial institution that specialises in credit supervision and book keeping services. In particular, an institution that specialises in the purchase of book debts (accounts receivable) and the granting of loans secured against debts. Upon the purchase of a debt by a factor, the creditor receives an immediate cash payment, but the amount of that payment is discounted, i.e. the creditor receives a smaller sum than is due from the debtor, to take account of the risk to the factor of recovering the debt in full. The bank or institution then retains the right to keep any amount that it recovers against the debt and, by using its more specialised debt collection capabilities, thereby endeavours to profit. **4.** In the case of a securitized mortgage, the ratio of the outstanding principal to the original securitized loan. **5.** Except in Scotland, an obsolete term for a land agent or bailiff.

factorage   See **factor**.

factoring process(US)   See **garnishment**.

factory A building, part of a building, or a group of buildings, usually covered, used for the manufacture, processing, assembly or repair of goods or products. A place where goods are fabricated, processed or assembled. The term factory may be used to refer to a **mill** or a **workshop**, although 'mill' is a more specific place where material is pressed, cut, spun, woven, rolled, ground or similarly processed, usually requiring a significant supply of water; and a workshop is a smaller establishment usually fitted with powered equipment for crafting, moulding, turning or similarly processing goods.

In English statute law, a factory is defined as "any premises in which, or within the close or curtilage or precincts of which, persons are employed in manual labour in any process for or incidental to any of the following purposes, namely, (a) the making of any article or of part of any article; or (b) the altering, repairing, ornamenting, finishing, cleaning or washing or the breaking up or demolition of any article; or (c) the adapting for sale of any article …", Factories Act 1961, s. 175(1). The Factories Act also includes premises used or associated with slaughtering animals, and section 175(2) sets out a list of premises "in which persons are employed in manual labour" which also come within the statutory definition of a factory. cf. **commercial property**, **store**, **warehouse**. See also **industrial building**, **flatted factory**, **overcrowding**.

factum est(Lat)   'It is done'.

fair A place where people gather at particular times for the purpose of displaying, buying or selling goods. A fair is similar to a **market**, except that a market is held at more regular and frequent intervals, usually once or twice a week, whereas a fair is generally held monthly, semi-annually, annually, or at intervals determined by custom or statute. A fair, therefore, is a market, but every market is not a fair (2 *Co Inst* 406). In modern usage a fair is a place, usually licensed for the purpose, where people meet to exhibit goods, wares and services; to buy and sell local produce; to display artistic or craft works; or to set up a temporary bazaar for such purposes, commonly coupled with the provision of food, entertainment and amusement. The term may also be used in the form of a 'trade fair', where firms or companies gather to demonstrate to other businesses, or associated trades, the availability of their products, which may or may not entail the sale of displayed items.

fair actual value(US)   See **fair market value.**

fair and reasonable value   See **fair market value.**

fair annual value   See **full annual value.**

fair cash value   See **fair market value.**

fair consideration   An amount of **consideration** that is deemed to represent the reasonable price for the subject matter of a contract. In particular, a fair price paid for a property between parties acting in good faith. See also **fair value, fraudulent conveyance.**

fair housing laws(US)   Laws that have been passed to prevent discrimination in the provision of housing. In particular, the Fair Housing Act of 1968 (42 USC §§ 3601-3631), which makes it illegal to discriminate on grounds of "race, color, religion, sex, or national origin" as well as "familial status or mental or physical handicap" when dealing with the sale or rental of residential property or land for housing (most sales or rentals of commercial property are exempt from the provisions of the Act). The FHA also prohibits discrimination in mortgage lending and makes such practices as **blockbusting** and **redlining** illegal. It expressly prohibits a refusal to represent, deal or negotiate with any person on discriminatory grounds or to use discriminatory forms of advertising, representation or misrepresentation. The Act prohibits the practice of 'racial steering', whereby racial and ethnic groups are encouraged to acquire homes in areas occupied by other members of the same group and discouraged from areas occupied predominately by different racial or ethic groups. The **Office of Equal Opportunity** is responsible for the administration of the Federal Housing Acts. Further anti-discrimination provisions are contained in other Civil Rights Acts, notably the Civil Rights Act of 1866 and the Civil Rights Act of 1964 (Title VI, Nondiscrimination in Federal Assisted Programs).

fair market rent   See **economic rent, market rent.**

fair market value (FMV)   1.(US)A value that would be paid in an open market and is considered fair and reasonable for the property concerned. In particular, the value of property as ascertained in order to determine the amount of **just compensation** upon condemnation or 'taking' of property – 'fair market value' being the value as determined "by what a willing buyer would pay in cash to a willing seller, in a transaction at arm's length, with a bargained price freely arrived at", 27 Am.Jur.2d., Eminent Domain, § 299. In this context, 'fair market value' and **market value** have the same meaning, being based on the value of the property for the **highest and best use** to which the owner might reasonably be able to put his property at the time of the taking and that a reasonable time would be allowed to find a purchaser who is aware of all the uses to which the property could be put. "Just compensation includes all elements that inhere in the property, but it does not exceed market value *fairly* determined [emphasis added]", Olsen v. United States, 292 US 246, 54 S Ct 709, 78 L Ed 1236, 1244 (1933). In particular, the term *fair* market value indicates that any special value, brought about solely by the proposals or activities of the condemning authority, is to be disregarded; in other words, by ignoring any such increase in value, the price paid is considered fair to the condemning authority (United States v. Miller, 317 US 375, 63 S Ct 276, 87 L Ed 336, 147 ALR 55 (1943) – although in that case it was said that 'fair' "hardly adds anything to 'market value'", at 343). In such proceedings the value of the condemned property should be determined, if possible, on the basis of the **sales comparison approach**, but the **income approach** may be accepted when direct comparables are not available (or in the case of an investment property); or, the **cost approach** may be adopted for 'special use' property, but only when there is no market information available and 'reproduction' of the property is a valid alternative (United States v. Toronto, Hamilton & Buffalo Navigation Co., 338 US 396, 70 S Ct 217, 403, 94 L Ed 195, 201 (1949); United States v. 50 Acres of Land, 469 US 24, 105 S Ct 451, 83 L Ed.2d 376 (1984)). Expressions such as 'fair actual value', 'fair cash value' or 'full cash value', 'fair value', 'fair and reasonable value' and 'full market price' convey a similar meaning. cf. **forced-sale value**. See also **assessed value, economic rent**. **2.**(Can)The sum of money that can be obtained for a property by a willing, but not anxious, seller under normal market conditions. A term that is used in tax assessments and has a similar meaning to that referred to in **1.** above. "[T]he highest price available estimated in terms of money which a willing seller may obtain for the property in an open and unrestricted market from a willing knowledgeable purchaser acting at arm's length", *Minister of National Revenue v Northwood Country Club* [1989] 1 CTC 2230 (Can). See also **market value, open market value**(BrE).

fair rates and prices(Eng)   A term used in a **bill of quantities** for the basis of assessing the amount to be paid for variations. The price of work is based on 'fair rates and prices' or a 'fair valuation' when the work is not similar to, or is not executed under similar conditions to, other work required under the building contract. In such instances the amount to be paid cannot be based on other provisions of the contract. In such cases a 'fair valuation' is based on cost plus a reasonable percentage for profit. If there is proof of a general market rate for comparable work it may be taken into consideration or applied completely.

fair rent   **1.** A rent that is considered fair and reasonable. A **market rent** as contrasted with an exorbitant or **rack rent**. (Terms such as 'fair rent',

'reasonable rent' should be avoided in leases as they are subjective; what is fair to one is not necessarily fair to another. 'Market rent' or 'open market rental value' is preferable.)   **2.**(Eng)A rent that is assessed by dint of the Rent Act 1977 as being reasonable for a tenancy of a dwelling-house that comes within the ambit of that statute, i.e. rent that has been fixed under the statutory provisions that apply to a **regulated tenancy**. Since 1989 no new regulated tenancy can be created and, therefore, few tenancies are subject to the payment of a 'fair rent' as determined under the provisions of the 1977 Act. See also **premium**.

Prophet J. *Fair Rents: A Practical Guide.* 3rd ed. London: Shaw & Sons, 1985.

fair value   A price paid that is considered fair and reasonable for that which has been obtained. In particular, the price paid between a willing buyer and a willing seller in an **arm's-length transaction**. When such a price is the **consideration** payable for something that is transferred under a contract, it may be referred to as 'fair consideration'. See also **fair market value, fair rent**.

fair wear and tear(BrE)   Deterioration to the fabric of a property due to aging – "the natural operation of time flowing on effects" – or normal and reasonable tenant use. A clause in a lease exempting a tenant from 'fair wear and tear' "exempts a tenant from liability for repairs that are decorative and for remedying parts that wear out or come adrift in the course of reasonable use, but it does not exempt him from anything else. If further damage is likely to flow from wear and tear, he must do such repairs as are necessary to stop that further damage", *Regis Property Co v Dudley* [1959] AC 370, 410 (HL) Thus, a tenant is required to carry out work to prevent further damage to a property, for example to replace a tile that has fallen off a roof in order to prevent rain penetration. See also **dilapidation, repair, wear and tear**(US).

fait(Lat) A deed.

fallout risk(AmE) The risk that even though all the terms have been agreed a borrower will not close on a loan or that a purchaser will not close on a sale. See also **conditional contract**.

fallow land Land that has been ploughed and then left unseeded, usually between crop rotations.

falsa demonstratio non nocet cum de corpore constat(Lat) 'A false description does not vitiate a document when the thing is described with certainty'. Thus, if there is an adequate and sufficient definition of what is intended to pass by a deed, any subsequent erroneous addition does not impair the entire deed. Similarly, if there is more than one description of land in a conveyance or lease a court may reject one or more of the descriptions, unless it is manifestly inaccurate or absurd so to do; but it need not reject the entire document.

false representation See **misrepresentation**.

Fannie Mae(US) See **Federal National Mortgage Association**.

farm 1. A tract of land used for agricultural purposes, either for the raising of crops or pasturage, or both; as well as land used for dairy, poultry, stock raising, fruit production, fish farming and allied industries. A tract of land, including water, used for tillage, artificial cultivation, rearing of animals, fish, or pasture, especially when such items are to be sold. In common usage, a farm is an area of land used for **agriculture**, usually including a farmhouse and buildings. Farm' is a word of broad meaning and when used in a conveyance includes a farm house, farm buildings, all arable and pasture land, woods, etc. used as a part of a farm or for purposes incidental to the running of the farm, unless there is something expressed to the contrary. In many contexts, especially land planning, zoning and taxation, a dwelling-house that is within the confines of an area that would otherwise be considered a farm, but is used solely as a domestic unit, is not considered a part of the 'farm'. See also **agricultural land**, **farm assets**(US). 2.(Eng) Historically, land held subject to the payment of money or the rendering of services to the owner. 3. To let out or demise for a fixed rent.

farm assets(AmE) All the assets of a farm or ranch, including the land, personal residence, and buildings used for farming or ranching, pipelines, any irrigation system, livestock and any unharvested crops. Such assets are given special tax treatment for income tax purposes in the event of a sale.

farm business tenancy(Eng) A tenancy of land that is used for agricultural purposes, that has been created on or after September 1, 1985, and that is not subject to the security of tenure provisions that are applicable to an **agricultural tenancy** (Agricultural Tenancies Act 1995, ss. 1-2). A farm business tenancy arises only if it meets the statutory "business conditions together with the agriculture conditions or the notice conditions". The business conditions require that all or part of the land comprised in the tenancy is farmed for the purpose of a trade or business and has been so farmed since the beginning of the tenancy. The agricultural conditions require that (having regard to the terms of the tenancy and other relevant circumstances) the character of the tenancy is primarily or wholly agricultural, i.e. the land is used for **agriculture**. The notice conditions require an exchange of notices between the landlord and tenant acknowledging that the tenancy is to be, and remain, a farm business tenancy. Notwithstanding any agreement to the contrary, a farm business tenancy granted for a term of more than two years continues at the end of that term as a **tenancy from year to year**, unless terminated by not less than twelve nor more than twenty four months prior written notice. A tenancy from year to year must be terminated by a similar period of notice. However, unlike an 'agricultural tenancy', there is no automatic right of renewal provided to the tenant. The parties may freely fix the initial rent payable under the tenancy, although either party may refer the level of rent to arbitration (1995 Act, ss. 10-13). See also **compensation for improvements**.

Barr, William, et al. *Farm Tenancies*. 2nd ed. London: Sweet & Maxwell, 1997.

Sydenham, Angela, and Neil Mainwaring. *Farm Business Tenancies*. Bristol: Jordans, 1995.

farm land   See **farm**.

farm-loss payment(Eng)   A form of disturbance compensation paid to the holder of an "owner's interest" (a freeholder or the holder of a tenancy from year to year or greater interest) in an "agricultural unit" of land, for a loss of profit arising as a consequence of the compulsory acquisition of his interest in the whole, or a 'substantial part', of the agricultural unit, when that "owner" is displaced from the land and obliged to take a new farm (LCA 1973, ss. 34-36, as amended). See also **compensation for disturbance**.

Farmer's   Home   Administration (FmHA)(US)   A federal agency that is part of the US Department of Agriculture and was established under the Farmers Home Administration Act of 1946 (7 USC § 1001, note). The agency primarily provides mortgage loans to farmers or owners of rural homes who may have difficulty in obtaining loans on reasonable terms elsewhere. FmHA also provides **mortgage insurance** and guarantee programs for rural properties in marginal areas. The agency now operates under the Consolidated Farmers Home Administration Act of 1961 (7 USC § 1921); Title V of the Housing Act of 1946 (42 USC § 1471); and Part A, Title III of the Economic Opportunity Act of 1964 (42 USC § 2851).

farmworker's house(Eng)   See **protected occupier**.

fashion center   See **specialty shopping center**.

fast track system or **fast tracking**   Any system of project delivery that aims to reduce the overall time frame for the project in comparison with a more traditional system of delivery. Fast track construction involves carrying out certain stages of the work before all of the working drawings or other construction documentation is complete and the overlapping of various stages of the construction work. The objective is to carry out the entire project in the shortest possible time. Fast tracking aims to save time and money, but entails an increase in the risk as materials may be delivered before they are required, and work may be carried out before detail designs are complete or may be delayed if the drawings and specifications are not finalised for a particular stage of construction.

faubourg(US)   In Louisiana, a suburban town or residential community.

feal and divot(Scot)   A right to take sods or turf from land to make fences or for roofing of cottages. This may be granted as a **servitude** or may be a right of common (similar to a **common of turbary** as found in English law).

feasant   See **damage feasant**.

feasibility analysis or **feasibility study** 1. A financial and economic study of the viability of a planned project. "A study of the cost-benefit relationship of an economic endeavor", Appraisal Standards Board, *Uniform Standards for Professional Appraisal Practice (USPAP)*. Washington, DC: The Appraisal Foundation, 2004 edn., 'Definitions'. A feasibility analysis usually aims to show the yield or profit from the project by relating the projected revenue (net income or proceeds of sale) to the total cost and balancing these factors against the **risk** criteria of the prospective investor. The analysis or study generally takes the form of a detailed report that assesses the risks and gains to be made from the proposed project; sets out details of competitive projects; provides estimates of supply and demand for the project; and usually includes a **sensitivity analysis** of the returns under different conditions or criteria. cf. **market survey**. See also **appraisal, cost-benefit analysis, residual method of valuation**[(BrE)]. **2.** A survey or study carried out to ascertain whether a given area or neighbourhood will support a proposed development project, such as a new shopping center. See also **catchment area, market survey**. Barrett, Vincent G., and John P. Blair. *How to Conduct and Analyse Real Estate Market and Feasibility Studies*. 3rd ed. Upper Saddle River, NJ: Prentice-Hall, 1999.

Federal Agricultural Mortgage Corporation (FAMC or Farmer Mac)[(US)]   A federal agency established under the Agricultural Credit Act of 1987 to assist in raising capital in the secondary mortgage market for loans secured on farms and agricultural-based property. In particular, Farmer Mac provides guarantees on mortgage-backed securities that represent interests in a pool of farm mortgages.   (**www.farmermac.com**).

Federal Deposit Insurance Corporation (FDIC)[(US)]   An independent executive agency originally set up under the provisions of the Banking Act of 1933 to insure savings held by federally regulated banks and savings associations. The FDIC is now regulated by the Federal Deposit Insurance Act of 1950. The FDIC is required to promote sound banking practices and accordingly has supervisory and examination powers over the major financial institutions of the United States. In particular, the FDIC administers the nationwide deposit insurance system ('mutual guaranty of deposit') for US banks. (**www.fdic.gov**).

federal funds rate[(US)]   The rate of interest at which eligible banks borrow from the Federal Reserve. Generally, this rate is at or below the **discount rate**, but in periods of tight money supply it may exceed the discount rate as banks are forced to increase their borrowing from the Federal Reserve.

federal grant[(US)]   The transfer of title to an area of **public lands**, whether by act of Congress,

by treaty, or by patent under general law.

Federal Home Loan Bank Board (FHLBB)[(US)]   See **Federal Housing Finance Board**.

Federal Home Loan Mortgage Corporation (FHLMC or Freddie Mac)[(US)]   A federally-chartered and publicly-traded corporation established in 1970, to acquire residential mortgages from federally-regulated commercial banks, mortgage banks, savings institutions and credit unions, as well as other financial institutions whose deposits are federally insured, and thereby improve the secondary market for such loans. In particular, the corporation buys mortgages from lenders and then sells participation certificates (PCs) secured on a pool of such mortgages to investors, with the benefit of its own guarantee. It may also purchase FHA-insured and VA-guaranteed loans, as well as conventional home loans, but does not provide loans directly to homeowners. The Corporation has established its Loan Prospector® as an automated underwriting service to provide lenders with the information they need to make consistent, fair, and reliable lending decisions and thereby ease the processing of loans that may be purchased by Freddie Mac. Loans that are acceptable for purchase by FHLMC are called 'conforming loans'. The Federal Home Loan Mortgage Corporation is known colloquially as 'Freddie Mac' or sometimes 'The Mortgage Corporation', 'Mortgage Corp.' or merely 'The Corporation'. See also **collateralized mortgage obligation, participation certificate**. (**www.freddiemac.com**).

Federal Housing Administration (FHA)[(US)]   A wholly-owned government corporation established under the National Housing Act of 1934 to: (i) improve housing standards and conditions; (ii) maintain and expand homeownership, rental housing and healthcare opportunities; (iii) stabilize the mortgage market;

and (iv) provide an adequate home financing system through mortgage insurance. FHA was consolidated as a division of the newly established Department of Housing and Urban Development (HUD) in 1965. The FHA is now increasingly involved in providing insurance for private home loans, with 100 per cent guarantees, and providing loans at higher than average loan-to-income and loan-to-value ratios. In particular, a 'FHA loan' is one granted by a private bank, insurance company, savings and loan association, or any other approved lender, which is insured by the Administration. Such loans are provided primarily to low or moderate-income families and minorities for the purchase, construction or improvement of moderately priced properties, in one to four-family housing units, especially first-time buyers. In addition, the FHA has a 'Home Equity Conversion Mortgage' program that allows elderly homeowners in need of income to draw on the equity of their home by obtaining a **reverse annuity mortgage** and thereby avoiding the sale of their home. See also **mortgage insurance**. (**www.hud.gov/fha/fhahome.html**).

Federal Housing Finance Board (FHFB)(US)   An independent agency of the executive branch that was empowered by the Financial Institutions Reform, Recovery, and Enforcement Act of 1989, to take over the functions of the Federal Home Loan Bank Board. The Federal Housing Finance Board (or the 'Finance Board') is responsible for regulating the twelve Federal Home Loan Banks and the Office of Finance to ensure that they, and other members of the Federal Home Loan Bank System, operate in a financially sound and safe manner and also for supervising the banks and ensuring that they are adequately capitalized and able to raise sufficient funds in the capital markets. The Finance Board also establishes policy for the Community Investment Cash Advances program (including the Affordable Housing and Community Development Investment programs) and the Community Support Program. The Finance Board is responsible also for statistical data relating to the housing industry. (**www.fhfb.gov**).

federal intermediate credit bank(US)   One of 12 banks first established in 1923 under the Federal Farm Loan Act. Such banks provide loans for farmers, ranchers, rural residents and others involved in farming and discount agricultural paper from financial institutions. These banks now operate in accordance with the consolidating provisions of the Farm Credit Act of 1971.

federal land(US)   Land owned by the Government of the United States.

federal land bank (FLB)(US)   A federally chartered bank that specializes in the provision of long-term, low-cost, mortgages for rural properties. There are 12 federal land banks set up around 'farm credit districts' into which the US is divided for the Bank's lending purposes.

Federal National Mortgage Association (FNMA or Fannie Mae)(US) A corporation established in 1938 originally as a federal agency, but now partly owned by private shareholders, whose principal function is to improve the secondary mortgage market for housing loans, particularly by buying and selling existing mortgage loans and raising money by issuing government-backed debentures. In 1968, under the Housing and Urban Development Act, Fannie Mae was divided into two entities, the **Government National Mortgage Association** and the privately owned Fannie Mae. Fannie Mae has two major lines of business, portfolio investment and mortgage-backed securities. The company buys home mortgages from banks, trust companies, mortgage companies, savings and loans, and insurance companies for its investment portfolio, and earns a spread between the yield on portfolio investments and the cost of debt funding those investments. Fannie Mae also receives pools of mortgage loans from lenders and exchanges them for mortgage-backed securities, which the company guarantees. Loans that are acceptable for purchase by Fannie Mae are called 'conforming loans'. Fannie Mae is regulated by the Secretary of Housing and Urban Development. See also **mortgage-backed obligation**. (www.fanniemae.com).

federal rule(US)   See **before-and-after method**.

financially related transaction(US)   See **real estate-related financial transaction**.

fee **1.** Derived from the Old English *fief* or Latin *feudum*. Historically, the right of a tenant or vassal to hold land, subject to the acknowledgement of a superior owner or lord. 'Fee' has a similar derivation to 'fief', 'feud', or 'feodum' and signified a feudal benefice, i.e. land held of a superior lord, or the Crown, subject to the rendering of a payment in kind, such as crops or services. In modern usage, unless qualified by other wording, a fee is an **estate** of inheritance, i.e. an estate that endures until the person entitled to it 'for the time being' dies intestate and leaves no heirs (1 *Co Litt* 1a, 1b, 18a; 2 *Bl Comm* 105). In particular, the largest estate in land that a person can hold.

As the **feudal system** of land tenure in England evolved into the modern system of landownership, a 'fee' came to signify an absolute estate, in perpetuity, which on the death of the owner was capable of being transferred unconditionally to his or her heirs. A fee can be qualified or limited. The annexation of the word 'simple' signified that the inheritance was unrestricted, but the use of a suffix, such as 'tail', 'tail male', 'tail female', indicated that there was a limitation on the line of inheritance.

In the US, in several jurisdictions, a 'fee estate' or an 'interest in fee' is equivalent to a **fee simple**, the more limited estate of a **fee tail** having been abolished or severely curtailed, or, as in some states, it was never recognized. In most jurisdictions the holder of the fee estate is the absolute owner of the land and the use of the word 'fee' without qualification usually refers to a **fee simple absolute**. See also **allodial system**, **base fee**, **conditional fee**, **manor**, **qualified fee**, **movable**

fee. **2.**(Scot)A right to hold land from another under a form of feudal tenure subject to the payment of a **feu-duty**. The holder of a 'fee' or 'feu' is virtually the owner of the land, and this right may be distinguished from the holder of land subject to a **liferent**. With the effective abolition of the feudal system, the holder of a fee or a 'fiar' is now an owner of land having a right of *dominium*. In particular, 'fee' is a right to own land, as distinguished from other real rights to land such as a servitude or a lease. See also **heritable property**. **3.** A recompense, normally in the form of a fixed sum of money, paid for the rendering of a service, especially for an official or professional service or for any other service demanding a special talent or skill, such as a charge for preparing an appraisal or valuation report. A fee may be distinguished from a **commission**, which is contingent upon success. See also **commitment fee**, **contingency fee**, **finance fee**, *quantum meruit*, **scale fee**.

fee appraiser(US)   An independent **appraiser** who carries out appraisal services in return for a fee, as opposed to a 'staff appraiser' who is an employee of the company that commissions the appraisal. See also **review appraiser**.

fee conditional(US)   See **conditional fee**, **fee simple conditional**.

fee estate   See **fee**.

fee farm rent(Eng)   A form of perpetual **rentcharge**, i.e. an annual sum payable upon the purchase of a fee simple interest, generally in lieu of all, or part, of the purchase price. Such payments are now only found in a few parts of England, notably Manchester, Bath and Bristol. Most forms of fee farm rents were abolished in 1935; the remainder are being phased out so that they will all be extinguished no later than 2037. See also **ground rent lease**(US), **quit rent**, **right of re-entry**.

fee insurance(US)   See **title insurance**.

fee on condition subsequent(US)   See **conditional fee simple**.

fee simple .   Derived from the term *in feodo simpliciter*. In common law, the most absolute and unqualified **estate** that can be held in land. The highest **freehold** estate that a person can hold, i.e. a 'freehold estate in fee simple'. '**Fee**' indicates that the owner is free to hold the land for a potentially indefinite duration and transfer it without hindrance, and if the estate is not disposed of during the owner's lifetime, that it can pass without constraint to the heirs of the owner. 'Simple' indicates that the estate is inheritable by any of the **heirs** of the owner; without condition, limitation, or restriction as to the heir who can take the land ('heirs general'); as opposed to a **fee tail,** which can be inherited only by specified descendants (but not ascendants or relatives who are not in a direct line). Under the common law a fee simple is the most dominant form of ownership that may be held by a private party.

In the US, fee simple is a generic term and may be subdivided into a **fee simple absolute** (usually called a 'fee simple'); a **fee simple determinable**; and a **fee simple conditional**. In several jurisdictions, the terms 'fee', 'fee simple,' and 'fee simple absolute' are considered to be synonymous being the most absolute estate that can be held in land.

In modern English law, an estate in fee simple may be: (i) 'absolute' (in particular a **fee simple absolute in possession**); (ii) subject to a 'condition subsequent' (a **conditional fee simple**) that creates a condition by which the holders interest can be brought to an end; or (iii) subject to a determining event or 'executory limitation' that, if it occurs, automatically brings the holder's interest to an end (a **determinable fee simple**).

A fee simple owner, unless curtailed in some way, has the **natural rights** to **land**; a right of **alienation** (except as limited by the **rule against perpetuities**); and the right to **use** his land, within the confines of the law. On the other hand, there are limitations placed on any right to land. In particular: (i) statutory restrictions or regulations, such as are imposed by zoning, planning and public health laws – in the US called the **police power** over land; (ii) a liability for any **nuisance**, as well as a **strict liability** to a neighbour; (iii) limitations on the right to take certain property from land, such as **treasure trove** and, in some cases, to extract **minerals** from land; (iv) rights of others over the land, e.g. the beneficiary of an **easement** or a **lease**; (v) any **encumbrance**, including a **mortgage**, **lien**, or **charge** on the land; (vi) **covenant** that restricts the use of the land in favour of another landowner; (vii) limitations on **water rights**; (viii) no entitlement to *res nullius*, i.e. things that are incapable of ownership such as air, water in natural channels, and wild animals; (ix) any requirement that a disposal by will may be subject to a reasonable provision being made for certain relatives of the owner.

fee simple absolute   1. A **fee** interest in land without limitation as to its duration or right of inheritance. A perpetual **fee simple**, i.e. a fee that is not limited as to the heirs who may succeed to that right and is not likely to be cut down by a conditional or contingent event. In the US, the terms 'fee simple' and 'fee simple absolute' are generally used interchangeably to refer to the highest estate in land that can be held. cf. **fee simple defeasible**, **fee tail**.   2.(Eng)See **fee simple absolute in possession**.

fee simple absolute in possession(Eng)   A term of English statutory derivation, being the largest unqualified **freehold** estate in land. The only one of two estates (the other being a term of years absolute) that is "capable of subsisting or of being conveyed or created at law", LPA 1925, s. 1(a), i.e. a **legal estate** – any other estate being an **equitable estate**. In theory the owner of this interest has the unrestricted – or absolute – right, in perpetuity, to transfer this estate as long as he lives, and thereafter as long as there are heirs capable of taking and then transferring the estate. The word **fee** denotes that the estate can be inherited and consequently is capable of lasting forever, even though it *may* be brought to an end.

'Simple' denotes that the estate will descend to any heirs of the owner, as distinguished from **fee 'tail'**, which is limited to designated heirs. 'Absolute' denotes that the estate is not limited in time or capable of being cut short by the occurrence of a certain specified event, i.e. it will continue in perpetuity, as distinguished from a **qualified fee** which is capable of coming or may be brought to an end upon a given condition or the occurrence of some event. A fee simple that is subject to a condition that has become impossible of performance is a fee simple absolute. Also, 'absolute' does not mean that there are no other rights over the land; for example, it may be subject to a mortgage or charge. **Possession** means the right to the present enjoyment of land, not merely the right to actual possession, as distinguished from a right to a **reversion** or **remainder**. Also, 'possession' for this definition includes "receipt of rent and profits or the right to receive the same, if any", LPA 1925, s. 205(xix) (SLA 1925, s. 117(1)(xix)). Trustees may hold a legal estate even though they do not enjoy physical occupation. Thus, there is a holder of the 'fee simple absolute in possession' for every parcel of land, whether as a landlord if the property is leased, or a trustee if the land is subject to a life interest, entail, or any other form of limited estate. Both a **flying freehold** and a **movable fee** can be a fee simple absolute in possession. See also **absolute estate**, **freehold absolute**, **possession**, **right of re-entry**.

fee simple conditional   An interest in land that is equivalent to a **fee simple**, but may be enlarged or destroyed upon the occurrence of an event that may or may not arise. For example, an estate that lasts "as long as" land is used for a particular purpose; continues indefinitely "provided that" a specified event does not occur; or continues "on condition that" some stated event does not occur. A fee conditional (or a 'fee simple subject to a condition subsequent') may be distinguished from a **fee simple determinable** as the latter ends automatically on the mere happening of the event, whereas the former

continues unless or until the condition occurs and then may be brought to an end by the grantor exercising his **right of re-entry**. Although not essential at common law (*Mary Portington's Case* (1613) 10 Co Rep 35b, 42a, 77 Eng Rep 976), in most jurisdictions in the US, the right of re-entry must be expressed in the deed of grant in order to transfer a fee simple subject to a condition. An **estate** in fee simple conditional may be described as an estate of "potentially infinite duration inheritable only by issue of the first taker", The American Law Institute, *Restatement of Property* § 17 (1936). Thus, in the grant of an estate "to B and the heirs of his body", B is the first taker and the estate may be cut short if there are no heirs. The fee simple conditional may be regarded as the predecessor of the **fee tail**, and it is still recognized by the original terminology in Iowa, Oregon, and South Carolina. Also called a 'fee on condition subsequent' or an 'estate on condition subsequent'. See also **conditional fee**, **conditional fee simple**(Eng), **estate on condition**, **fee simple defeasible**(US).

fee simple defeasible(US)   A fee simple estate that may last forever, but is granted subject to a provision that may defeat it. A fee simple that may come to an end on the occurrence of a specified event. 'Fee simple defeasible', or as it is also called a 'defeasible fee', is a generic term for any form of fee simple estate that may come to an end as a result of a condition or a limitation specified for when the estate is created. A fee simple defeasible may be a **fee simple conditional** (or 'fee simple subject to a condition subsequent'); a **fee simple determinable**; or a 'fee simple subject to an executory limitation'. If either of the first two estates is defeated they return to the party who created them (or their successors), whereas an estate on executory limitation goes to a third party.

"An estate in fee simple defeasible is an estate in fee simple which is subject to a **special limitation**, a **condition subsequent**, or an executory limitation or a combination of such restrictions", The American Law Institute, *Restatement of Property* § 16 (1936). A defeasible fee may also be referred to as a 'base fee', determinable fee' or a **'qualified fee'** – although those terms also have separate and distinct meanings in some jurisdictions.

fee simple determinable(US)   An estate created by a conveyance that contains words that are effective to create a **fee simple** and in addition words that will automatically bring that estate to an end upon the occurrence of a stated event (Selectmen of Town of Nahant v. United States, 293 F Supp 1076, 1078 (DC Mass 1968)). For example, an estate that exists 'while', 'for so long as', or 'during' a stated period. "An estate in fee simple determinable is created by any limitation which, in an otherwise effective conveyance of land, (a) creates an estate in fee simple; and (b) provides that the estate shall automatically expire upon the occurrence of a stated event", The American Law Institute, *Restatement of Property* § 44 (1936). cf. **fee simple conditional**. See also **determinable fee**, **determinable fee simple**(Eng), **possibility of reverter**.

fee simple subject to a condition subsequent   See **fee simple conditional**.

fee simple subject to executory limitation(US)   See **executory limitation**.

fee tail   A 'fee cut down'. An 'estate tail' or **entail**, i.e. an interest in property (real or personal) that is limited as a right of inheritance to lineal heirs. A fee tail is a **freehold**, i.e. it is an **estate** of inheritance that may last forever, but it passes to a specified line of heirs, unless or until that line dies out. A fee tail may be limited to the 'heirs of the body', all 'issue', or certain issue; but not to all heirs (collateral and lineal), otherwise it would be a **fee simple**. "The expression *fee tail* or *feodum talliatum*, was borrowed from the feudists ... among whom it signified any mutilated or truncated inheritance,

from which the heirs general were cut off", 2 *Bl Comm* 112 n. (Strictly, the line of heirs is called the 'entail'; the land is said to be 'entailed'; the estate is an 'entailed estate'; and the holder of that estate is the 'tenant in tail'.) A fee tail may be unlimited passing to any lineal heirs of the grantee – 'tail general'; it may be limited to the one or specified heirs of the body, such as from a particular marriage -'tail special'; also a tail general or a tail special may be limited to the male heirs only – 'tail male', or to the female heirs only – 'tail female'. 'Fee tail' is used frequently as synonymous with an entailed interest; however a fee tail was a form of legal estate in land that existed in English law prior to 1925 and was abolished as such by the LPA 1925, s. 1. The term **entailed interest** is now used in English law, as it was in the LPA 1925, s. 130(1) – although that section has been repealed. Since January 1, 1997, no new fee tail interest can be created and if an attempt is made to create an entailed estate the property is held in trust absolutely for the person to whom the property was purportedly granted (Trusts of Land and Appointment of Trustees Act 1996, Sch. 1, para. 5).

In the US, 'fee tail' or 'estate in fee tail' is a more common term than entailed interest or entail. An estate in fee tail "is created by an otherwise effective conveyance which (a) is made in favor of a natural person as to whom the conveyance contains **words of inheritance**; and (b) in specific words confines the succession to the issue of the first taker or to a designated class of such issue", The American Law Institute, *Restatement of Property* § 59 (1936). The estate of fee tail has been abolished in most jurisdictions, having been converted into a fee simple or 'fee estate'. In the US, sometimes called an 'estate tail', an 'estate in fee tail' or a 'tenancy in tail'. See also **base fee**, **conditional fee**, **remainder**.

fee tail after possibility of issue extinct   See **estate in tail after possibility of issue extinct**.

fee tail female   See **fee tail**.

fee tail general   See **fee tail**.

fee tail male   See **fee tail**.

feed the estoppel   See **tenancy by estoppel**.

felling direction(Eng)   An order from the Forestry Commission, requiring an owner to fell certain trees in order to improve the productivity of a forested area (Forestry Act 1967, s. 18).

fence   A barrier or division designed entirely, or partially, to enclose land or any other space, usually to prevent intrusion from without or straying from within. A barrier or structure intended to act as a means of enclosure, protection or to mark a **boundary** line. A fence may be any visible, tangible obstruction, made of wood, boards, rails, iron, palings, masonry, stone, chain, wire, or other suitable material. 'Fence' may sometimes be used to refer to any barrier designed for similar effect; anything placed or constructed around land or a building to guard against intrusion or prevent escape. It may be a **hedge**, a **wall**, or a **ditch** or any similar structure that is sufficient to define or act as an enclosure.

At common law, there is no obligation to erect or maintain a fence around a property. However, a landowner may have a statutory obligation or there may be a local custom that requires him to fence the land to keep livestock (or other animals) from straying onto adjoining property; or it may be clearly essential to fence the land to keep animals from straying and causing injury or damage to other people, their property or land. In addition, a landowner may have an obligation by virtue of an agreement with an adjoining landowner that he will fence his land. In the US, most states have statutes as to what constitutes a 'legal fence' or an 'adequate fence' for the purpose of keeping livestock from straying onto neighbour's land. In Australia, all States have enacted legislation in respect of a "dividing fence". Such legislation provides a procedure for the sharing of fencing costs; rights of access to repair a dividing fence; and a system for the resolution of disputes in the local courts. This legislation does not apply if there is an express agreement between landowners as to the liability for the dividing fence. In New Zealand, the occupiers of adjoining lands that are not divided by a sufficient fence are required to contribute equally to the cost of "work on a fence", Fencing Act 1978, s. 2. See also **barrier fence**(Aus), **boundary line**, **dividing fence**(Aus), **dog fence**(Aus), **easement**, **enclosure**, **encroachment**, **fence in/ fence out**(US), **fixture**, **party wall**, **restrictive covenant**, **spite fence**(US), **strict liability**, **trespass**.
Aldridge, Trevor M. *Boundaries, Walls and Fences*. 8th ed. London: FT Law & Tax, 1997.
Mynors, Charles. *The Law of Trees, Forests and Hedgerows*. London: Sweet & Maxwell, 2002.

fence in or fence out(US)   The status in terms of the liability of a landowner for damage as a consequence of fencing, or not fencing, his land to keep cattle from trespassing. In some jurisdictions the common law principle is accepted by which a landowner is required to fence in his animals to prevent them straying and causing damage to another's land. In other jurisdiction, a landowner has no strict obligation to fence his land to keep cattle in and, therefore, another landowner is expected to 'fence out' if he wishes to avoid damage from stray cattle. Sometimes the terms are used in reverse, so that a landowner 'fences in' his land to keep cattle from straying thereon, but the principle is the same. The 'fence out' rule does not sanction willful trespass, but puts a greater duty on the landowner to protect his own land. The 'fence in' rule generally applies in states where stock raising is not of major importance. See also **trespass**.

feræ naturæ(Lat)   'Of a wild nature'. Animals that are by nature wild, e.g. lions, as distinguished by *domitae naturæ* – domestic animals. See **strict liability**.

festival shopping center   See **specialty shopping center**.

fetter   To prevent someone doing some thing.

A fetter or **clog** on a mortgage prevents the mortgagor exercising his **equity of redemption**, i.e. repaying the loan and taking back an unencumbered right to the property, and is considered anathema to the concept of a mortgage. See also **once a mortgage always a mortgage**.

feu 1. See **fee**. 2.(Scot)A form of feudal tenure by which land was held subject to the payment of a rent or duty. The feudal system of land tenure has now been abolished in Scotland (Abolition of Feudal Tenures etc. (Scotland) Act 2000). See also **feu-duty**.

feu-duty or **feuduty**(Scot) An annual payment for land. Similar to a perpetual **rentcharge** in England. A term that derived from an amount that was made payable for the right to hold land from a feudal or superior lord. Feuduties have now been abolished (Abolition of Feudal Tenures etc. (Scotland) Act 2000). However, certain similar duties or burdens may continue in effect such as those that are imposed as "a facility benefiting other land. For example, duties that are imposed to meet the cost of maintenance of common parts of a building. See also **fee**, **feud**.

feudal system or **feudalism** A socio-political and economic system that is found in many early societies and was common in Europe from at least the time of the Roman Empire to the Middle Ages. The system is based on the strength given to a privileged class by permitting them an absolute right to land, and the bond or allegiance required from a weaker majority who are permitted to hold or use land only at the will of the privileged class. The feudal system depends essentially on the maintenance of the relationship of 'fiefs' and 'vassals'. The fiefs or lords are the sole landowners and the vassals or tenants have a right or privilege to hold land only for as long as they perform services for the landowner. The feudal system is, primarily, a means by which political power is exerted through the control of the primary source of wealth and production in a rural society, namely **land**, combined with the subordination of one group of people to another. The services rendered may be the provision of goods, acts of reverence, maintenance and improvement of the land or service in arms.

The English system of feudal tenure came into its own after the conquest of 1066 when William, Duke of Normandy, granted to his barons land obtained as a result of his conquest in recompense for their assistance. The barons were obliged to render services to the king, such as to supply knights to keep up his standing army but these 'tenants in chief' were permitted in return to grant any number of a right of tenure to inferior or 'villein tenants' of their own – a process known as 'subinfeudation'. Thus, the holding of land from a superior lord, and ultimately from the Sovereign became the foundation of the feudal relationship. In time the rights of tenure came to be classified according to the type of service rendered. There was 'free tenure', i.e. non-servile tenure, which included knight service and spiritual tenure; common socage (i.e. the performance of certain and fixed agricultural services); and 'unfree tenure' or **villeinage** granted to the common peasant in return for servile work. Gradually the superior services were abolished; military and socage tenures were commuted for money payment; and by the Statute of *Quia Emptores* 1290 subinfeudation was prohibited, so that new tenures could no longer be created and only existing rights were capable of alienation. The Tenure Abolition Act 1660 converted free tenures into 'free and common socage' or **freehold** tenure in socage. The Law of Property Act 1922 finally swept away from England and Wales the vestiges of the feudal system, converting any remaining copyhold tenure to freehold and leaving the **fee simple absolute** as tantamount to absolute ownership of land. Nonetheless, the feudal system has left its roots in the English system of land law. The ancient principles are so interwoven with every part of the modern that to attempt to entirely eradicate the past would make aspects of modern land tenure less comprehensible.

In the US, the feudal system was inconsistent with the Declaration of Independence and after that time it was rapidly dismantled, although several of the doctrines of modern landownership are explicable solely by their feudal origins.

In Scotland, the entire feudal system of land tenure has been abolished, along with all feuduties and similar perpetual periodic payments (Abolition of Feudal Tenures etc. (Scotland) Act 2000). cf. **allodial system**. See also **doctrine of tenure**, **doctrine of estates**, **manor**, **tenure**.

FHA mortgage(US)   A mortgage that is insured by the **Federal Housing Administration**.

fi. fa.(Lat)   Abbreviation for *fieri facias*.

fiar(Scot)   One who held a **fee** or **feu**. A term used under the **feudal system** for the person who would now be considered the owner of land.

fiction of a lost grant(US)   See **lost grant**.

fictitious document(US)   See **form document**.

fictitious bid   See **puffer**.

fictitious sale(US)   **1.** A sale that a broker reports as having taken place even though it has not been completed.   **2.** See **simulation**.

fidelity bond   See **fidelity insurance**.

fidelity guarantee   A **guarantee** that is good only up to a specified amount.

fidelity guarantee insurance or **fidelity insurance**   **1.** **Insurance** against the default or dishonesty of another person, e.g. an employee or a person in a position of trust (such as a property management company or an escrow company). Fidelity insurance provides a form of insurance and a **surety** for the insured; in a broad sense there is insurance against loss, but in a particular sense if a loss arises there is a surety to cover that loss. Sometimes called 'surety insurance'. A similar form of surety granted in the form of a bond is called a 'fidelity bond'. See also **utmost good faith**.

2.(US)Insurance provided to a residential project as a whole (e.g. to a condominium or cooperative building or a planned unit development), as opposed to a policy that applies to only one unit in the project. In particular, such insurance covers risks associated with the use of the common areas and employee dishonesty. Also called a 'fidelity bond' or sometimes a 'surety bond' as such a policy takes the form of a bond.

fiducia(Lat)   'Trust'. In Roman law, an agreement that provided for property to be held as security for a debt, but without any actual ***traditio*** or delivery of title to the property.

fiduciary   **1.** Derived from the Latin *fiducia*, 'trust', or the French *fidere*, 'to trust', which in turn is related to *fides*, 'faith'. A relationship where one party acts in **good faith**, **trust**, and confidence on behalf of another. A person acting in a fiduciary capacity has a special position of trust which requires loyalty, care and diligence; full disclosure of all matters that may be relevant to any transaction; and a duty to account for all monies arising or paid in connection with a transaction. In particular, a fiduciary should not make a personal profit as a result of his position, but should act primarily for the benefit of the party represented. "It is quite clear that if an **agent** uses *property*, with which he has been entrusted by his principal, so as to make a profit for himself out of it, without his principal's consent, then he is accountable for it to his principal, see *Shallcross v Oldham* (1862) 2 Johns & Hem 609, 70 Eng Rep 1202. So also if he uses a *position of authority*, to which he has been appointed by his principal, so as to gain money by means of it for himself, then also he is accountable to the principal for it, see *Reading v A-G* [1951] AC 507, 516 (HL). Likewise with *information* or *knowledge* which he has been employed by his principal to collect or discover, or *knowledge he has otherwise acquired*, for the use of his principal, then again if he turns it to his own use, so as to make a profit by means of it himself, he is accountable …", *Phipps v Boardman* [1965] Ch 992, 1018-9 (CA). See also **agency**, **broker**, constructive trust, dual agency, misrepresentation, undue influence, utmost good faith. 2. An individual, corporation, or association that is in a position of trust, or has power and authority, with respect to another person or another's property. The term originates from Roman law where a fiduciary was a person who had authority to act on trust for another. In general usage, a fiduciary may be an **executor**, **administrator**, **agent**, **trustee**, **receiver**, or guardian. In particular, a fiduciary is a party appointed by an express trust and not merely as a result of a right or duty springing out of contract.

fiduciary loan   An unsecured loan; a loan based entirely on **trust**. See also **fiduciary**, **good faith**.

field   1. A tract of land, especially open land or land cultivated for pasture or tillage. Generally, a tract of some size, such as a quarter acre or more. 2. An area of ground set out for some purpose and usually bounded or marked out as such. An area of land set out for sporting events.

field book   A book used by a surveyor to set down his work in the field and containing a description of the bounds, courses, marks, measurements, etc. that will be used when setting down a map or plan of a property. 'Field notes' are notes set down by the surveyor in his field book.

field garden allotment(Eng)   A small patch of land turned over to domestic horticulture and gardening. In particular, land that was appropriated as a form of **allotment** for the use of the labouring poor following the **enclosure** of lands or the regulation of an area of common land under an Inclosure Act (Inclosure Act 1845, s. 31; TCPA 1990, s. 336(1)). Historically, a field garden allotment was land that formed part of the **wasteland** of a manor and had been cultivated as a garden or fuel allotment. After the enclosure of the wasteland, this land was let to the poor of the parish usually in plots of under a quarter of an acre.

field notes   See **field book**.

fieri facias(Lat)   'Cause (it) to be made'. A writ *fieri facias* (or *fi. fa.*) is a writ of execution requiring a sheriff to whom it is addressed to levy **distress** on goods and chattels for the amount owed by a judgement debtor. "Derived from the words in the writ by which the sheriff is commanded, *quod fieri faciat de bonis*, that he cause to be made of the goods and chattels of the defendant the sum or debt recovered", 3 *Bl Comm* 417.

figuring(AmE)   **Taking-off** quantities or estimating costs from a drawing. See also **bill of quantities**.

file   To deliver a document to an authorised official for the purpose of its registration or public recording. See also **archive**, **land recording**(US).

filed plan(Eng)   A **plan** used for the registration of the title to a particular parcel of land and on which the general boundaries of the subject land are usually edged red. The filed plan is sewn up with a **land certificate** or **charge certificate** and forms a part thereof. On the face of the certificate it is referred to as the 'official plan'. It is not intended to show the exact boundaries of the land, but only to support the written description of the registered land. Other matters affecting registered land are by the convention of the Land registry coloured in different ways, e.g. green edging for land excluded from the title but within the boundary of the registered land, brown tint for land for a right of way over other land but used by the registered land, blue tint for a right of way over the registered land for use by other land.

filling station   A place, usually located abutting a street or highway, at which gasoline (or as it is called in British English 'petrol'), motor or lubricating oil and some motor vehicle accessories are stored and supplied to the public for immediate use in motor vehicles. Commonly such facilities also have a retail outlet for travellers, selling such items as soft drinks, snacks and magazines. Also a filling station may serve as, or form part of, an area for the repair, service or washing, or for the sale of motor vehicles or spare parts. In American English commonly called a 'gas station' or 'gas filling station' and in British English a 'petrol station' or **garage**. See also **service station**.

filum(Lat)   See ***ad medium filum***.

filum aquæ(Lat)   See ***ad medium filum aquæ***.

final certificate   See **certificate of valuation**.

final completion   See **substantial performance**.

final title(Aus)   See **radical title**.

finance   Payment of a debt or settlement of a business. Money or credit supplied for a business or enterprise. The **capital** provided as a loan to a corporation or individual. The use of borrowed **capital** or funds for a project, enterprise, company or individual. Any one of several methods used to obtain or supply money or credit for a business or venture. In real estate, finance may be categorised as 'direct' or 'indirect'. Direct finance is related to property itself and may be secured by a charge or mortgage on the property. Such finance may take the form of: (i) a **bridge loan**, **interim loan** or **gap finance**; (ii) a **construction finance**; (iii) a loan secured by a **mortgage**, **charge** or **deed of trust**; (iv) a 'forward' or **takeout commitment**; (v) a **sale-and-leaseback** (and variations thereon), or an **instalment sale**, or it may be made available as a combination of such forms of finance. Indirect finance may be obtained as **equity capital** subscribed to a partnership, corporation or any other vehicle that acquires or invests in real estate; or as **debt capital** that is loaned to such an enterprise.

Barter, Stephen L. *Real Estate Finance*. 2nd ed. London: Butterworths, 1997.
Clauretie, Terence M., and G. Stacy Sirmans. *Real Estate Finance: Theory and Practice*. 3rd ed. Upper Saddle River, NJ: Prentice-Hall, 1998.
Brueggerman, William B., and Jeffrey Fisher. *Real Estate Finance and Investments*. New York: McGraw-Hill, 2002.
Nelson, Grant S., and Dale A Whitman. *Real Estate Finance Law*. 3rd ed. St Paul, MN: West, 1994.
Madison, Michael T., et al. *The Law of Real Estate Financing*. St. Paul, MN: West, 1994, with updates and CD-ROM.
Sirota, David. *Essentials of Real Estate Finance*. 9th ed. Chicago: Real Estate Education Company, 1998.

finance charge   Any fee, commission or charge made in connection with the grant of a loan. In particular, a charge that must be brought into account in assessing the **annual percentage rate** of interest payable on the loan. See also **usury**.

finance fee or **finance procuration fee**   A **commission** paid to an agent or broker for arranging terms for a suitable loan, i.e. a fee paid to a middleman for procuring equity or debt capital. Variously referred to as a 'mortgage service charge', a 'mortgage brokerage fee' or a **finder's fee**. cf. **origination fee**. See also **finance charge**.

finance house(BrE)   A type of company that specialises predominately in making short-term loans and loans for more speculative investments, e.g. hire purchase, property development, leasing. 'Finance house' may be used to refer to any merchant bank, although strictly it should be applied only to members of the Finance Houses Association.

finance lease   1. A **lease**, generally of plant, equipment or machinery, that is used as a form of financing so that substantially all the benefits and risks associated with ownership are transferred to the lessee. Under a finance lease, there is effectively a deferred sale of the asset, with the lessee paying the purchase price over the term of the lease and automatically acquiring ownership at the end of the lease. The lessee is granted the right to the asset for a non-cancellable term that extends for the major part of its economic life, at a rent that is sufficient to amortize the capital cost (return *of* the capital invested) and pay interest (return *on* the capital invested) over the term of the lease. As a rule, the 'lessee' is responsible throughout the term of the lease for the repair, servicing and maintenance of the asset, as well as its insurance.

Under the US Statement of Financial Accounting Standards No. 13 (SFAS 13) such a lease is called a "capital lease" and may be classified as such if it meets any one of the following criteria: (i) ownership (title) to the property will pass to the lessee by the end of the lease term; (ii) the lessee has a "bargain purchase option" (i.e. pays a relatively nominal sum) to purchase the asset, usually at the end of the lease term; (iii) the lease term is equal to or greater than 75% of the estimated economic life of the asset; and (iv) the net present value of the lease payments (excluding payments for maintenance, insurance, taxes or similar payments) equals or exceeds 90% of the fair market value of the asset at the start of the lease. If the lease fails to meet any one of these criteria, it is an **operating lease**. As the finance lease is strictly a form of financing, the subject property is recorded as a purchase of the asset by the lessee (even though, at least until the end of the lease, there may be no legal transfer of title); as distinguished from property held under an operating lease, where the asset remains an asset of the lessor. For the lessor to maintain this accounting treatment, one of the above criteria must remain in place, and (i) the collection of the lease payments must be reasonably predictable, and (ii) there must be no significant uncertainty as to the basis for the payment of any remaining non-reimbursable costs by the lessor. **2.** A lease by which the lessor expects to obtain a return of the full amount invested, including interest and profit costs, over the term of the lease. The lessor's return of capital is derived from the rental income (the **finance rent**), estimated tax benefits, and the residual value of the property at the end of the lease. The lease may provide that the total investment is recovered over a 'primary period' and then the lease continues for a secondary period with the lessee paying only a nominal rent. Also called a 'full-payout lease' of a 'fully-amortized lease'. See also **leasing**.

finance procuration fee See **finance fee**.

finance rent A rent that is calculated as being sufficient to repay, or amortise, the cost of a property or any other asset, together with accumulated interest, over the period during which the rent is payable, i.e. a rent calculated on the basis of a **sinking fund**. See also **leasing**, **finance lease**.

financed out A situation where a property is used a security for a 100% loan, i.e. one that has no **equity value**.

financial institution An organization established by law to conduct the business of receiving funds from depositors or investors and granting finance. A private or publicly-owned business organization that is firmly established and provides a wide range of financial services. The term 'financial institution' may be used to refer to any one of a number of major finance organizations, including a commercial bank; investment or merchant bank; **building society**(BrE), **building and loan association**(US), **savings and loan associations**(US), or **credit union**(US); an **investment company** (including an 'investment trust' or 'mutual fund') or a **trust company**; **pension fund** or insurance company; **mortgage company**; securities brokerage house or securities dealer, or any other major institutional investor that provides capital for business or enterprise. See also **real estate investment trust**(US).

financial leverage The use of borrowed money to increase the size of investment that can be acquired, i.e. pure **leverage**, as distinguished from **operating leverage**.

financial management rate of return See **internal rate of return**.

financial statement **1.** One or more reports issued by an enterprise that show the financial position of the enterprise at a particular point in time. In particular, a statement showing the **balance sheet**, or net worth, and the profit and loss position of the enterprise at the end of its financial year. An independent accountancy firm generally certifies a financial statement as being a fair and reasonable statement of the enterprise at the time it is prepared. See also **operating statement**.   2. A statement of the assets and liabilities and the net worth of an individual at a specified date, especially as submitted with a loan application.

financing   Funds provided to acquire a property, exclusive of the **equity**. See **debt capital**, **finance**.

financing charges   Interest charges, but not capital repayments, incurred in purchasing or developing property. See also **carrying charges**.

financing statement(US)   A document that sets out details of **goods** or other personal property that have been granted by way of security for a loan. In particular, a public record that a person has a security interest or claim to goods to secure a debt (Uniform Commercial Code, § 9-402). A Financing Statement (on Form UCC-1) must be filed with the appropriate government agency to 'perfect' a lien on personalty (chattels). Once filed the statement will protect any subsequent claimant (even in respect of an item that has been affixed to real property so as to become a **fixture**, but still readily removable) as it acts as **constructive notice** to any lender or third party who provides finance secured on such goods. A mortgage may constitute a financing statement if it sets out details of the goods that are not covered by the mortgage security.

finder's fee   1. A fee or **commission** paid by a banker for the introduction of business from which the bank makes money.   2. A fee or commission paid to an agent or broker for introducing a party to a property or a source of finance, especially introducing a buyer or seller of property. In particular, 'finder's fee' refers to a payment to

someone who assists in finding a party to a transaction, but leaves the ultimate negotiation and consummation of the business to the principals. Also called a 'referral fee' or a 'procuration fee'. See also **brokerage**, **finance fee**, **kickback**, **middleman**, **procuring cause**, **prospective purchaser**, **ready, willing and able**.

fine   1. A sum paid as a penalty for an infringement or failure to meet a legal obligation. An amount of valuable consideration given or required as the price for something.   2.(Eng)The price paid for consent to the grant, renewal or assignment of a lease. A fine is usually a single payment of a lump sum paid over and above a regular payment such as rent. A fine may include "a **premium** or **foregift** and any payment, consideration, or benefit in the nature of a fine, premium or foregift", LPA 1925, s. 205(1)(xxiii).

finite life real estate investment trust (FREIT)(US)   See **real estate investment trust**.

fire certificate(Eng)   A certificate issued by a Fire Authority (the London Fire and Civil Defence Authority, a metropolitan fire and civil defence authority or a combination of county councils) confirming that commercial premises comply with the authority's requirements on such matters as user, means of escape and access thereto in case of fire; fire fighting equipment; fire alarms; and number of occupiers on the premises at any one time. A fire certificate is required for any premises put to a "designated use". That includes a factory, shop, office or railway property, where more than 20 people work, (and any factory where inflammable materials or explosives are kept); most hotels, hostels or similar establishments; cinemas, theatres, exhibition halls, dance clubs and the like; hospitals, residential homes and similar institutions; schools and other training establishments; and dwelling-houses where the occupants may be subject to a greater than normal risk in case of fire, e.g. boarding houses. A fire certificate must be obtained by an occupier of such premises (or the owner in the case of multi-occupied premises) and displayed on the premises. The fire authority may exempt premises from the need for a fire certificate if it thinks fit, or in certain specified cases (although the premise must still be provided with fire fighting equipment and adequate means of escape). Regular occupiers of the premises must be made familiar with the means of escape from the premises in case of fire and a record kept of their instruction or training for that purpose. The certificate is intended to safeguard the day-to-day use of a property by members of the public rather than to impose controls on building construction (Fire Precaution Act 1971, as amended). See also **building regulations**.

Osliff, F. *Knight's Guide to Fire Safety Regulation.* Looseleaf. Croydon, Surrey: Tolley, 1999.

fire clause(US)   A provision in a lease which provides for termination in the event the demised premises are destroyed by fire and, usually, if the landlord decides not to rebuild. See also **reinstatement clause**.

fire insurance   Insurance that provides protection against damage or loss of property caused by fire. Fire insurance is one of the principal forms of insurance provided in respect of real estate. It provides an indemnity against the cost of repairing or replacing a building that is destroyed or damaged by an accidental fire and, usually, includes any consequent damage to the property of a third party. See also **consequential loss insurance, conversion, insurance rent, property insurance, reinstatement cost**.

fire sale   A sale made under conditions of compulsion or distress. Derived from the sale of property after a fire or a similar catastrophe. See also **forced sale**.

firebote or **fire-boot**   See **estovers**.

firm   An unincorporated organisation or business association; usually a **partnership**. In English statute law, defined as "persons who collectively entered into partnership with one another [are for the purpose of this statute] collectively called a firm", Partnership Act 1890, s. 5(b). cf. **corporation**. See also **company**.

firm commitment   See **commitment**.

firm-price contract   See **fixed-price contract**.

first and general mortgage bond(US)   A mortgage bond secured as a **first mortgage** on certain properties of a corporation (usually a railroad) and as a general charge on the other properties. Also called a 'first lien and general mortgage bond'.

first delivery(US)   The delivery of a deed into **escrow**. The 'second delivery' being the delivery out of escrow to the grantee.

first floor   In British English, the first level, being at least one full floor height above the ground floor. In American English, the 'first floor' generally refers to the first level of a building situated at, or immediately above, ground level. See also **ground floor**.

first in time   See **priority**.

first lien   See **first mortgage**.

first-loss insurance   Insurance that covers for losses only up to a maximum specified amount, which is less than the insured's total potential loss. The insurer is informed of the full value of the property that is the subject of the insurance policy and this is taken into account in assessing the premium, but the insurer provides an **indemnity** for only the most vulnerable percentage of the potential loss. First-loss insurance may refer also to insurance that is provided on the basis that the indemnity is not reduced to take account of depreciation – although such insurance is more commonly called 'new-for-old insurance'. See also **excess, valued policy**.

first mortgage   A mortgage that has **priority** over all other mortgages or liens, whether taken out before or after the grant of another mortgage. Also called a **senior mortgage**, although that term may be used for any mortgage that has priority over another. cf. **second mortgage**. See also **mechanic's lien**.

first refusal   See **right of first refusal**.

first right to buy   See **right of first refusal**.

fiscal year   A **year** as used for taxation, accounting or business purposes A fiscal year may, but does not necessarily correspond, to a calendar year, but it is a period of twelve consecutive calendar months.

fiscal zoning(US)   See **exclusionary zoning**.

fish   See **right to fish**, **piscary**.

fit for habitation or **fit for human habitation**(Eng)   Intended to be, or capable of being lived in, without having any serious effect on the occupier's health or safety. Accommodation that is 'fit for habitation' usually provides a reasonable degree of comfort, essential facilities for living, and proper sanitary amenities.

A landlord who lets a **house** at a **low rent** is obliged to ensure that it is "fit for human habitation". In this context regard is to be had to the following matters: "repair; stability; freedom from damp; internal arrangement; natural lighting; ventilation; water supply; drainage and sanitary conveniences; facilities for preparation and cooking of food and for the disposal of waste water"; and the house shall be regarded as unfit for human habitation "if, and only, if it is so far defective in one or more of those matters that it is not reasonably suitable for occupation in that condition", L&T Act 1985, s. 10.

A person who takes on work for provision of a dwelling (whether by erection, conversion or enlargement of a building) is under a duty to see that the work he takes on is done in a workmanlike and professional manner, with proper materials and that, in respect of the work done, the dwelling is fit for habitation upon completion (Defective Premises Act 1972, s. 1). This liability lies with the builder and all building professionals involved in the work, and the person undertaking the work is liable for the work of independent sub-contractors. cf. **unfit for human habitation**. See also **fit for the purpose, furnished tenancy, implied covenant, implied warranty, repair, warranty of habitability**(US).

fit for the purpose or **fit for the use**   A provision that **premises** are made or provided in a manner that is appropriate for the intended purpose or the proposed use. As a rule, in common law, there is no **implied term** in a lease that premises are fit for the purpose or use for which they are let; the tenant is presumed to have made his own enquiry and to take the premises as he finds them (*Baxter v Camden, Baxter v Camden LBC* [1999] 4 All ER 449, 453, 461, 45 EG 179, 180 (HL); Hatfield v. Palles, 537 F.2d 1245, 121247-8 (4th Cir. 1976)). In the US, several jurisdictions take the view that there may be an implied term that arises from the nature of the premises and the tenant's inability to use them for that purpose. In effect, this implied obligation amounts to a recognition that a failure of the landlord to maintain such a minimum standard amounts to a form of **constructive eviction** of the tenant; or constitutes a breach of the landlord's covenant for **quiet enjoyment**. See also **fit for human habitation**(Eng), **repair, implied warranty, warranty of habitability**(US).

fit-out allowance(BrE)   See **tenant improvement allowance**.

fit-out cost   The cost of fitting out a property to an agreed specification. In particular, the cost of converting a shell into premises that is available for occupation. See also **tenant improvement allowance, work letter**.

fitness for habitability(US)   See **warranty of habitability**.

fitting   An item of furniture, an appliance, or other equipment installed in a building. An item attached to property, but not so that it necessarily becomes a part thereof. The term is commonly used to refer to an item that is merely a **chattel** (such as curtains, a free standing kitchen appliance, bookcase, hanging cupboard or mirror); but it may be used to refer to an item that has been installed to improve or 'fitting out' a building (such as a door handle, fitted bookshelf, air-conditioning unit) and has become a **fixture**. See also **fixtures and fittings**.

fitting-out allowance(BrE)   See **tenant improvement allowance**.

five unities   The common rights or 'unities' that may be said to exist with a **tenancy by the entirety**; i.e. the four unities (title, time, interest and possession) that exist with any other form of **joint tenancy**, plus the unity of the husband and wife who hold such an estate (United States v. Jacobs, 306 US 363, 59 S Ct 551, 83 L Ed 763, 768 n. 12 (1938)).

fixed asset   An **asset** of a company that is acquired for the running of a business and is intended to be retained for the ongoing operations of the company. An asset that is used on a continuing basis for the normal operating activities of a company. In particular, a fixed asset is not intended to be readily converted into cash without affecting the normal operation of the enterprise. An asset that is required permanently for the running of a company, as distinguished from a **current asset** that is intended primarily for trading or for resale in the normal course of business. Real property, plant, fixtures, tools, machinery, etc. are all generally classified as fixed assets. A fixed asset is not necessarily immobile and may include aircraft, heavy movable equipment, etc. A fixed asset is generally tangible; but an intangible asset, such as goodwill, a patent or development costs,

may be classified as a fixed asset. Any investment that is retained as part of a company's long-term reserves may also be categorised as a fixed asset. See also **capital asset**, **depreciation**, **fixed capital**.

fixed capital   Capital acquired by a company and retained in the form of assets that are not intended to be used up, but are employed to produce the profit or income for which the capital has been subscribed. Capital that is permanently invested in a business and is not intended to be used up in the normal running of that business (*Ammonia Soda Company v Chamberlain* [1918] 1 Ch 266, 286, [1916-7] All ER Rep 708, 713 (CA)) cf. **floating capital**, **working capital** See also **fixed asset**.

fixed charge   1. A **charge** on a specified property. A charge on a parcel of land, or a particular asset, especially the land or assets of a company. Any mortgage or charge over the assets of a company may be referred to as a fixed charge, as distinguished from a **floating charge** which is secured over all or some of the assets (including land, stock in trade, chattels, as well as future property). See also **debenture**.   2. See **fixed expense**.

fixed expense   An expense of running a property that does not vary with its degree of use or occupancy and must be paid when it falls due, e.g. rent, insurance premium, debt service and most real property taxes. Depreciation may also be accounted for as a fixed expense, although strictly speaking it is not expended. Sometimes called a 'fixed charge'. cf. **variable operating expense**. See also **operating expense**.

fixed-fee contract   See **cost-plus contract**.

fixed instalment mortgage   See **fixed-principal-payment mortgage**.

fixed lease(US)   See **gross lease**.

fixed option   An **option** to buy a property at a

price that is fixed for a given period of time from when the option is granted. See also **call option**, **put option**.

fixed-payment mortgage See amortization loan.

fixed period tenancy See **tenancy for a term of years**.

fixed periodic estate See **tenancy for a term of years**.

fixed-price contract A contract to provide goods or services at a definite predetermined price. For example, a building contract in which the contractor accepts an obligation to complete work at an agreed, determinable or unalterable sum. A fixed-price contract may be either a single 'lump-sum contract' or a 'measurement contract'. A lump-sum contract normally provides that there will be no variation in the price, although the term may be used to refer to a contract in which the price fluctuates according to an external indicator, e.g. a construction price index. A 'measurement contract', 'scheduled contract' or 'measurement and value contract' provides a schedule of agreed prices or rates that are applied on completion of the contract to the measured quantity of work done. Also called a 'firm-price contract' when there is no provision for any fluctuation in the price, or in the quantities that are considered to have been used. cf. **cost-plus contract**. See also **design-and-build contract**, **measured contract**, **turnkey contract**.

fixed-principal-payment mortgage A mortgage loan that provides that repayments of principal are fixed at a constant amount, with interest payable on the declining balance. With a fixed-principal-payment mortgage as the principal reduces so the total amount payable as principal *and* interest reduces. A fixed-principal-payment mortgage may be contrasted to an **amortization mortgage**, which provides for the payment of a constant amount throughout the term of the loan,

which is calculated to pay interest and to amortize the principal by the end of the term. Also called a 'fixed instalment mortgage'. cf. **flexible-payment mortgage**.

fixed-rate loan or **fixed-rate mortgage (FRM)** A mortgage, or loan, on which interest is charged at the same rate throughout the term of the loan. If a mortgage contains an **assumption clause** or a **due-on-sale clause**, and the mortgagee has a right to adjust the interest rate in the event that another borrower assumes the mortgage, then strictly the mortgage may not be considered as a 'fixed-rate mortgage'. Also called a 'flat-rate mortgage' or a 'fixed-rate interest mortgage'. cf. **adjustable-rate mortgage**. See also **amortization loan**.

fixed rent See **base rent, dead rent, flat rent**.

fixed-term tenancy[Eng] A tenancy for a specified period of time, e.g. a tenancy for a **term of years**. A tenancy that cannot be brought to a premature end by notice. cf. **periodic tenancy**. See also **tenancy for a fixed period**.

fixed trust See **passive trust**.

fixer-upper A property that requires a lot of repair or renovation work and is generally sold in its existing state with the purchaser accepting the want of repair. See also **as is**, *caveat emptor*.

fixture An article of personal property that has been so attached or wrought into **land** (or a **building** on land) that it becomes part and parcel of the land and may only be removed with the consent of the owner of the land. An article of personalty that has been so attached to real estate as to become a part thereof, even though it may retain its separate physical identity. Any chattel that has been so affixed to land that, in the view of the law, it has taken on a nature that makes it part of the land, loses its character as a **chattel**; it becomes a part of, and passes with, the ownership of land (thus, in the US, a fixture is sometimes referred to as a 'chattel fixture'). Ultimately a fixture becomes the property of the owner of the freehold or fee interest, unless there is clear evidence to the contrary. The principle that an item secured to the land may become part of the realty is recognised in Roman law (by *accessio*); in the civil law; and, since the 16th century, has been part of the common law. Once an item becomes a 'fixture', it may not be removed by an occupier or a tenant of land, even though initially it was the property of that party; unless the consent of the owner, or a person who has contracted to be the owner, has been obtained or unless there is a statutory provision which overrules the dictum *quidquid plantatur solo, solo cedit*, 'whatever is affixed to soil, belongs to the soil'.

At common law, in determining whether an item has become a fixture, it is necessary to consider (a) the purpose, intent or object of the annexation; and (b) the degree or manner of annexation to the land or a building thereon (*Holland v Hodgson* (1872) LR 7 CP 335; *D'Eyncourt v Gregory* (1866) LR 3 Eq 382). There must be a union between the chattel and the land; a lack of physical attachment mitigates against an item being considered a fixture. However, an object resting on the ground by its own weight alone can be a fixture, provided it is clearly intended to form an adjunct to the soil or a building thereon. When the intention is to improve the property permanently the personal property becomes a fixture, but if it is well secured purely to ensure its proper safety, use or better enjoyment it is likely to remain a chattel. Nonetheless, the onus must be on the person who affixed it to show that it was intended all along to continue as a chattel, or (especially if the chattel is fixed only by its own weight) for the owner of the land to show that it has ceased to be a chattel. In the final analysis, what constitutes a fixture is a question to be determined by the facts in each case.

In English law, items that have been held to remain chattels include light bulbs; a valuable tapestry fixed with battens to the wall of a private residence solely for its protection; an ornamental chimney piece; ornamental panelling; seats bolted in the auditorium of a theatre; an army hut bolted in sections to a concrete foundation. A plumbed-in washing machine, a gas fire, and a bedroom headboard must each be fixed for its proper enjoyment, but none of these is normally intended to enhance, or become an essential part of the freehold. Items held to have become fixtures include a tapestry set into the wall as part of the design and decoration of a house; seats secured to the floor of a cinema hall; 436 power looms installed in a mill; door and window fastenings; gratings to sinks and gullies; and statues and stone garden seats secured by their own weight but forming part of a formal garden design. Thus, there are no hard and fast rules that may be used to decide if a chattel has become a fixture, as Lord Lindley said in *Reynolds v Ashby & Sons* [1904] AC 466, 473-74 (HL): "My Lords, I do not profess to be able to reconcile all the cases on fixtures, still less all that has been said about them. In dealing with them attention must be paid not only to the nature of the thing and to the mode of attachment, but to the circumstances under which it was attached, the purpose to be served and … to the position of the rival claimants to the thing in dispute". However, since that date the common law precedents have established five rules that can generally be applied to determine if an item has become a fixture: (i) articles attached only by weight are not fixtures, unless intention or purpose indicates otherwise; (ii) annexation favours the determination that an item is a fixture; (iii) degree and object of the annexation may patently show the change in the nature of a chattel; (iv) intention is important where it flows from (v); and (vi) the tenant has a right to remove a trade fixture (*Belgrade Nominees Pty Ltd v Barlin-Scott Airconditioning (Aust.) Pty Ltd* ([1984] VR 947, 951 (Aus); *MacMillan Bloedel Ltd v Sunshine Coast Assessor* (1982) 19 MPLR 204, 210 (BC Can)).

In the US, as a rule, the principles have followed the common law, although the courts have tended to place more emphasis on the question of intention as a test in deciding whether an item has become a fixture and the mere fact of annexation to land or buildings has lost some of its primacy. In most jurisdictions, the factors for determining whether an item has become a fixture may be summarised as: (i) the mode and sufficiency of annexation; (ii) the purpose and intent behind the annexation, especially whether annexation is necessary for the proper use of the item; (iii) the degree to which the item has become adapted to be used as part of the property; and (iv) the ease with which the article may be removed without injury to the premises. American courts increasingly give greater significance to modern expectations and accepted practices than to the older English rules of 'fixing'. Thus, such items as a kitchen cabinet, an air-conditioning unit or a gas or electric range (even though such items may be easily removed) are usually installed as an essential item to an apartment and, therefore, are clearly intended to remain as fixtures. Wall-to-wall carpeting is not necessarily a fixture, provided it can be removed without damaging the property and was not intended to become part of the property. Other items that have been held to be fixtures include: chairs fixed to the floor of a theatre; wall beds; a chair lift at a ski resort; and a solar water heater panel. Most jurisdictions accept that the tenant can remove items fixed for trade or manufacture at the end of the lease (35 Am.Jur.2d., Fixtures, § 1 et seq.; 36A C.J.S., Fixtures, § 1 et seq.)

Even when a chattel has been so affixed to premises that it may be classified as a fixture, it may be possible for the person who fixed it to remove it because of: (a) a covenant or agreement with the landowner; (b) a common law rule, as with a **trade fixture**; or (c) a statutory provision. Items that a tenant has a right to remove (either because they are installed for convenience, as a trade fixture, or as an agricultural tenant's fixture) may be referred to as 'tenant's fixtures', and those that he may not remove, whether fixed by the landlord or the tenant, may be referred to as 'landlord's fixtures'.

At common law, any fixtures that a tenant has a right to remove must be taken out of the premises during the term of the lease, unless there is an agreement with the landlord to the contrary. However, if the tenant holds over (either by agreement or statutory right), or if the tenancy is renewed, as a rule, the tenant has a right to remove his fixtures until he finally gives up possession. At common law, (a view still supported reluctantly by the English courts) once a lease has expired all rights of the tenant to remove any fixture also expires. In the US, in some jurisdictions, after the end of a tenancy that was held for an uncertain duration (such as a tenancy at will), a reasonable period of time is allowed for the removal of fixtures; but not if a notice to vacate is of sufficient duration that the tenant could have removed the items during that period.

A freeholder may remove any item from his property; but once he has contracted to sell the land he may only remove items that are clearly chattels, unless he expressly agrees to the contrary. English statute law provides that a **conveyance** of land is deemed to pass all fixtures (but not chattels) to the purchaser, unless an item is expressly reserved by the vendor (LPA 1925, s. 62(1)).

In the US, a sale of land generally includes any permanent fixtures, unless an item is expressly excluded, although consideration should be given to intent of the parties and any correspondence or other matters that have passed between them.

A mortgagee's right to land includes fixtures annexed thereto, even though they are not specified in the mortgage deed, and the mortgagee acquires a right to items annexed by the mortgagor whether annexed before or after he takes possession; although this rule normally excludes items that would be 'tenant's fixtures'.

In the US, the Uniform Commercial Code (which deals primarily with commercial transactions and **goods** and not real estate) stipulates that "goods are 'fixtures' when they become so related to particular real estate that an interest in them arises under real estate law", UCC § 9-313(1)(a). The Code deals with the priority of "security interests" in goods and the position when they become fixtures. However, the code expressly excludes "ordinary building materials incorporated into an improvement on the land", UCC § 9-313(2). The Code provides that goods may retain their chattel nature in respect of chattel financing, and therefore their priority as regards creditors, if they are not integrally incorporated into the real estate. Also, the code sets out priority requirements as between a real estate mortgagee and a holder of a purchase-money security interest in the 'chattel' that has been attached to the realty. This provision of the Code has been statutorily adopted in some states, although it has been significantly modified in many states. See also **accession, agricultural tenant's fixture**(Eng), **appurtenance, compensation for improvements, constructive annexation, emblements, financing statement**(US), **mobile home**.

fixtures and fittings A term commonly used in a contract for the sale of land, or a lease to refer to items that are included with the property that is the subject of the transaction, either because they are considered to be fixtures, or it has been expressly agreed that these items will be included as part of the property to be transferred. The term 'fittings' may be used to refer to chattels that are not part of the real property (but pass when it is transferred) and fixtures to things that are, or have become, part of the real property (and must by definition, pass when it is transferred). However, the words are used interchangeably and jointly for any property that is considered or intended to be part of the realty. See also **fitting, fixture**.

Fixtures, Fittings and Contents Form(Eng) See **Property Information Form**.

flag lot(US) An L-shaped lot that resembles an extended flag and pole. The narrower part of the lot, or the pole, is generally the entrance to the site.

flat 1. A floor or storey in a house, especially one that forms a complete residence or apartment. 2.(Eng)A separate set of premises, usually but not necessarily on the same floor, constructed or adapted for use as a dwelling in a building that comprises other similar premises that are divided horizontally one from another. A dwelling constructed on top or below another similar dwelling, occupying all or part of the floor of a building that contains two or more units of a similar type. The living accommodation may be entirely self-contained or certain facilities within the building may be shared. In British English, a flat generally refers to a residential property that occupies all or part of a floor, regardless of the form of ownership, and corresponds to **apartment** as used in American English (the latter in British English generally being more spacious and luxurious). 'Apartment' in American English usually refers to a rented property. See also **flying freehold**(Eng), **house, maisonette, tenement**. 3. An **apartment** or floor of a residential building used for rental purposes. A suite of rooms, forming all or part of one floor of a building, used for housekeeping purposes or for housing of part of the family, visitors or friends. See also **apartment house**(AmE). 4. A level tract of land, especially the area of land that is alternatively covered and left bare by the ocean. The **shore** of the sea or a lake. See also **flats**.

Aldridge, Trevor M. *The Law of Flats*. 3rd ed. London: Longman, 1994.

flat cost The cost of labour and materials, but not overheads or profit, as applied in a building estimate or contract. See also **cost-plus contract**.

flat house(AmE) See **apartment house**.

flat lease(US) See **flat rent, gross lease**.

flat loan See **standing loan**.

flat ownership See **condominium**.

flat-rate mortgage See **fixed-rate mortgage**.

flat rent A rent that is fixed at the same amount for the entire term of the lease or for a stipulated term during the lease. Sometimes referred to as a 'fixed rent', although a flat rent may be fixed for only part of the lease term, whereas a fixed rent usually remains as such for the entire term of the lease. In the US, a lease containing a flat rent is referred to as a 'flat-rental lease' a 'level-payment lease', or sometimes a 'flat lease'.

flat-rental lease(US)   See **flat rent**.

flat scheme(Eng)   See **scheme of development**.

flat yield   See **running yield**.

flatted factory(Eng)   A factory forming part of a building that is constructed or adapted by horizontal subdivision for multiple occupation or for use as separate industrial units. Each unit or factory occupies all or part of a floor of the multi-storey building and may enjoy the use of other areas in the building in common with other occupiers. Also called a 'tenement factory'. See also **common parts**, **tenement building**.

flats   An area of land covered with tidal waters from time to time, but too shallow for commercial navigation. Land that is covered by tidal waters along a river, lake or the ocean. 'Flats' may also be considered to be synonymous with **shore**.

flex space   Space in a building that is designed for a variety of uses. In particular, space in a building that is primarily designed as a warehouse or industrial property, but can easily be adapted to office use.

flexible loan insurance plan (FLIP®)(US) A mortgage that provides for the payments to be graduated during the term of the loan, with a pledged reserve account to supplement the payments in the early years. For example, the mortgage payments may be reduced from the amount due under a conventional amortization mortgage by up to 20 per cent for the first year and then gradually increased to the normal level over the next five years. The pledged account (which is normally interest bearing) is then drawn on by the lender to supplement the shortfall in the initial payments, especially to avoid negative amortization; or the pledged amount may be used

to reduce the principal on the loan in the event of default. See also **pledged-account mortgage**, **variable-payment mortgage**.

flexible-payment mortgage (FPM)   See **variable-payment mortgage**.

flexible-rate mortgage   See **variable-rate mortgage**.

flexible zoning(US)   A **zoning** plan that sets out general regulations for an area and leaves final details for each development to be decided when a decision is made to proceed with that development. See **conditional zoning**, **floating zone**, **incentive zoning**.
Porter, Douglas R., et al. *Flexible Zoning: How it Works.* Washington, DC: Urban Land Institute, 1988.

flight easement(US)   See **avigation easement**.

flip-sale(AmE)   **1.** See **sub-sale**.   **2.** The sale of a property concurrently with its purchase, but at a higher price, with the aim of defrauding a lender or investor.

float   **1.** The range within which a variable interest rate on a mortgage loan may be permitted to change. For example, a rate may be fixed at 3% above a given base rate, but have a floor of 8% and a ceiling of 15%. A rate that has no such limits is called a 'full float'. See also **variable-rate mortgage**.   **2.**(US)A **grant** of land by the government of the United States, especially in the western states, giving a right to a certain amount of land within a particular tract or territory, such as a quarter square mile, but without designating the final location of the land to be granted. The grantee receives a 'float certificate' and the actual area of land is conveyed at a later stage.

floating asset   An asset that is continually changing or is consumed in the course of the operation of a business, e.g. money, stocks. cf. **fixed asset**. See also **current asset**.

floating capital   Capital used by a company to meet current or recurring expenditures. Capital used to acquire a **floating asset**, as distinguished from capital invested in a fixed asset. Sometimes called 'circulating capital', especially when used to acquire a current asset. cf. **fixed capital**. See also **working capital**.

floating charge or **floating lien**   A charge or lien that does not only secure property given as collateral at the time the charge or lien is created, but one that secures a class of property such as the assets of a corporation. A floating charge normally covers the existing, as well as the future or after-acquired assets of the debtor. However, with a floating charge the debtor is free to deal with the charged property in its normal course of business. Nonetheless, in certain circumstances (such as bankruptcy), the security holder may intervene to enforce his claim, at which stage the charge is said to 'crystallize'. Thereafter, the debtor no longer has authority to deal freely with the property. In particular, a floating charge may be converted to a specific or **fixed charge** if the corporation ceases to be a going-concern; acts outside its usual course of business; or if the party holding the charge has a right to intervene and take steps to pin down its charged assets. Also called a 'floating security'. See also **debenture**, **deed of priorities**.

floating easement(US)   An **easement** by which a right of way is granted over another's land, but the exact location or limits of that right are not defined. An easement must be sufficiently defined that the rights can be set down in a deed of grant, but in a few cases the exact limits of that right may not be set down. See also *jus spatiandi*.

floating interest rate   A rate of interest that varies at short-term, even daily, intervals according to money market conditions. See also **float**, **variable-rate mortgage**.

floating security   See also **floating charge/floating lien**.

floating zone(US)   A form of zoning provision that is not fixed as to its location, but only as to its use or density. For example, an area zoned for residential development may include a 'floating zone' for a filling station, with the basic parameters for the size, set back, access requirements, etc. being laid down in the zoning ordinance. The exact location of the filling station is left to be determined as the development of the surrounding area progresses, or when an application is made to carry out the particular development. Such forms of zoning are more generally found in a **planned unit development** to allow for flexibility in the allocation of particular uses to specific lots. Generally, the special use is considered to be legislatively pre-approved, subject only to the approval of the details. cf. **spot zoning**.

floor   **1.** The bottom or lower surface of a room or usable area of a building. See also **ground floor**, **storey**(BrE)/**story**(AmE).   **2.** A lower limit. See **rate cap**.

floor area   The total enclosed area of a particular building measured at one level, or the aggregate of all such levels, usually as measured to the surface of the external wall. See also **gross building area**(US), **gross external area**(BrE), **gross internal area**(BrE), **gross leasable area**(US), **net internal area**(BrE), **rentable area**(US), **retail area**(BrE), **usable area**.

floor area index(US)   See **floor area ratio**.

floor area ratio (FAR)(US)   The ratio of the total **gross floor area** of a building (excluding areas below ground level that are used only for storage and utilities) to the total area of the lot allocated to the building. A ratio that is used for zoning purposes. The FAR may be expressed as a ratio, e.g. 3 to 1; or, if the built area is less that the land area, as a decimal or percentage, e.g. 0.45 or 45%. Thus, a lot area of 20,000 sq. ft. with an FAR of 5:1 would permit the construction of up to 100,000 sq. ft. In Hong Kong, called the 'accommodation value'. Sometimes called a 'floor area index', 'floor lot ratio' or in Australia, the 'floor space ratio'. See also **plot ratio**(BrE), **zoning ordinance**.

floor area restriction(US) A zoning restriction on the total floor area that may be constructed in a particular area or district.

floor loan(US) An amount of money that a lender agrees to advance, but not to exceed, until a given condition, or conditions, have been met by the borrower. For example, a lender may make a 'floor loan' towards construction of a building, but will not make any further advances until a stipulated percentage of a building has been leased or the building has achieved a stipulated level of cash flow. cf. **ceiling loan**. See also **gap finance**, **holdback**.

floor lot ratio(US) See **floor area ratio**.

floor plan A **plan** showing the detailed layout of a building or part of a building at one particular level. See also **floor area**.

floor price The lowest price at which a vendor will contract to sell a property. cf. **asking price**, **ceiling price**. See also **reserve price**(BrE)/**reserved price**(AmE).

floor space index (FSI)(BrE) The ratio of the **gross external area** of a building above ground to its total 'site area' extended to include half the width of surrounding roads, i.e. the **gross site area**. An index established to control the density of new development on a given site, especially for high-rise buildings. cf. **plot ratio**. See also **floor area ratio**(US).

floor space ratio(Aus) See **floor area ratio**.

floor-to-ceiling loan(US) A loan that contains a stipulated amount that will be advanced initially, a **floor loan**, and an amount that will be advanced when a particular condition has been met, a **ceiling loan**. Usually such a loan is made at two distinct stages that involve two separate loan closings.

flowage easement(US) 1. The common law right for water from higher land to flow over lower land. See also **natural rights**. 2. A right or **easement** acquired by the federal government or state to flood an area of land, either as a permanent **easement in gross** or as temporary right for water to flow over the land for the benefit of adjoining land. The water does not have to flow in a defined watercourse and may vary its course or level from time to time. Sometimes called an 'overflow right'.

flow-through(US) See **pass-through**.

fluctuation clause(US) See **escalator clause**.

flume A stream or river. In particular, an artificial channel in which water is conducted to an industrial user or mine. A channel in which water is run to facilitate the transport of logs and lumber.

flying freehold(Eng) A **freehold** interest in a part of a building, usually excluding any right to ownership of the ground, e.g. a freehold flat at an upper floor level. In common law, the ownership of **land** may extend above, or below, the ground to include different stories of a building and, therefore, the right to a freehold may be granted in stratas of a property, such a right being referred to as a 'flying freehold'. "A man may have an inheritance in an upper chamber though the lower buildings and soil be in another", 1 *Co Litt* 48b. The owner of the 'flying freehold' unit must have right of access, support and shelter in respect of the rest of the building and usually enters into a **scheme of development** (or 'flat scheme') whereby the other owners of the building accept mutual positive covenants, such as to repair and maintain the building, and restrictive covenants regarding user, rebuilding, etc. Flying freeholds are rare because of the difficulty in traditional common law of enforcing covenants between successive owners of adjoining property. See also **collective ownership, commonhold, co-ownership, quasi-easement, right of support, strata ownership**.

folio number 1.(US)See **grantor-grantee index**. 2.(Aus)See **certificate of title**.

foot frontage See frontage.

foot-frontage method See frontage method.

foot-frontage rule(US) See frontage method.

footpath A path trodden down or established by constant usage on foot. A path, track or part of a **highway** over which the public has a **right of way** on foot only. English statutory law draws a distinction between a 'footpath' that crosses privately owned land and a **footway** that is incorporated in a highway (Highways Act 1980, s. 329(1)). In common usage, these terms are used synonymously; although in the US the path incorporated in a highway is called a **sidewalk**.

footway 1.(BrE)A **right of way** on foot whether for the public at large or a group of private individuals. "A way comprised in a **highway** which also comprises a carriageway, being a way over which the public has a right of way only", Highways Act 1980, s. 329. A footway generally means a paved way set alongside a highway and reserved for foot passengers, but not for vehicles, carriages or animals. A way that crosses private ground is not normally a 'footway'. See also **footpath, walkway**. 2.(AmE)A way for pedestrians. A **sidewalk** or path. cf. **carriageway**.

for sale by owner (FSBO)(US) Colloquially called a 'fizz-bow'. A situation where a property is offered for sale directly by the owner without the appointment of a broker. In such a situation, a broker is only entitled to a commission if he directly introduces a prospective purchaser and is the **procuring cause** of a sale. See also **open listing**.

for value See *bona fide* purchaser, **value**.

forbearance The act of holding back or abstaining from a course of action, especially a delay in taking legal action. The act of refraining from claiming a debt when it has fallen due for payment. Forbearance to pursue a debt is sufficient **consideration** to support a contract. See also **unilateral contract, valuable consideration**.

forbearance agreement(US) See **workout agreement**.

force majeure(Civ) Literally a 'superior force'. A term that is used more in civil or French law, as well as in insurance, to refer to a physical or material act that is uncontrollable or beyond human capacity to prevent, such as lightning, storms, earthquake, or sudden death. *Force majeure* in the civil law resembles that which causes **frustration** as found in common law. In particular, *force majeure* is used to refer to conditions that hinder performance of a contract, especially a building contract. *Force majeure* is sometimes compared to an **act of God**, however, *force major* includes any event that is outside the contemplation of the parties to a contract and cannot be avoided by due care and attention, including acts of God and acts of man. See also ***vis major***.

McKendrick, Ewan (editor). *Force Majeure and Frustration of Contract*. 2nd ed. London: Lloyds of London Press, 1995.

Treitel, Professor Guenter H. *Frustration and Force Majeure*. London: Sweet & Maxwell, 1994.

forced sale 1. A sale made against the will of the owner. A sale made when there is a compulsion as to its time or place. In particular, a sale that has to be made within a period that is inadequate to find a buyer who will pay the best price, usually because the potential buyers know that the seller is under an obligation to sell. A sale conducted against the wishes or best interests of the owner of a property, e.g. a sale by a mortgagee, or under an order of a court, to satisfy a debt. Also called, especially in the US, a 'distressed sale'. See also **forced-sale value, foreclosure sale, power of sale**. **2.** A sale to an authority that has the power to acquire that property against the wishes of the owner. See also **compulsory purchase, condemnation, eminent domain, expropriation**. **3.**(US)In Louisiana, a term that is synonymous with **judicial sale**, a sale made before a court of competent jurisdiction.

forced-sale value or forced sale value

The value of a property on the basis that the vendor is under a compulsion to sell; especially when the sale must be completed within a period of time that is not reasonable or adequate to negotiate a sale with all prospective purchasers, or to await a recovery of the property market in a period of depressed values. The value assuming that the vendor is not a **willing seller**, as when the property is being sold to meet an imminent debt. cf. **fair market value**(US), **market value**. See also **power of sale**.

forcible detainer   See **forcible entry and detainer**.

forcible entry   See **ejectment, eviction, forcible entry and detainer, harassment**.

forcible entry and detainer   A common-law offence of violently taking (by entry) and keeping (by detainer) possession of land "with menaces, force and arms, and without the authority of the law", 4 *Bl Comm* 148. The term is commonly used as a conjunct – the common element being the use of force – although the offences of forcible entry and forcible detainer rarely occur together. The offence is essentially a disturbance of the public peace. The Forcible Entry Acts 1381-1623 were abolished in English law in 1977. It has now been made a criminal offence to use violence, or threaten violence, to secure entry to premises without lawful authority. Also, a trespasser who refuses to leave when requested to do so by a "displaced residential occupier" or a "protected intending occupier" may commit a criminal offence (Criminal Law Act 1977, ss. 6-11, 13(1)); although it may be a defence that the occupier was a displaced **residential occupier** (1977 Act, ss. 6(7), 12(3-5)).

In the US, in several jurisdictions, forcible entry and forcible detainer remain separate and distinct wrongs and have been re-enacted as such. However, in many jurisdictions, the term However, in many jurisdictions, the term 'forcible entry and detainer proceedings' is used to refer to the remedy that seeks the recovery of possession of real property with the intention of preventing "disturbances of public peace, and to forbid any person righting himself by his own hand and violence", 36A C.J.S., Forcible Entry & Detainer, § 3. It is no longer considered a common law remedy, but is authorized and controlled entirely by statute. The essence of the action is to reclaim the property peacefully, but not necessarily to decide on the merits of the opposing claims. See also **ejectment**.

foreclosure   The process of barring, closing out or taking away. A judicial remedy that technically brings a **mortgage** to an end and vests the mortgagor's estate or interest in land in the mortgagee. The action of barring or precluding the mortgagor's **equity of redemption**, i.e. barring his right to reclaim the mortgaged property. Strictly speaking foreclosure is the process by which a mortgagee has a right to claim title to the property when a mortgagor is in default in paying the mortgage debt (but not before), and may be distinguished from any other procedure by which the mortgagee may seek to have the property sold and merely lay claim to the proceeds of sale. Nonetheless, 'foreclosure' may be used to refer to any process by which the mortgagee seeks to cut off, beyond recall, the mortgagor's right to the mortgaged property, including the process by which a mortgagee may seek a sale of the property by recourse to a court order, or by exercising his **power of sale**; as well as taking possession of the mortgaged property and holding possession for the period allowed for redemption (in the US called 'foreclosure by entry and possession' or

'foreclosure by writ of entry'). Foreclosure is a remedy available to any legal or equitable mortgagee (whether the original mortgagee or an assignee, and to any first or subsequent mortgagee); but not to a chargee, because a **charge** does not grant a right to any interest in land.

In English law, foreclosure may be instigated only by application to the High Court and the action must involve all parties interested in the mortgaged property. The court initially may issue a decree of 'foreclosure nisi' and give the mortgagor time to pay (usually six months). At that stage all subsequent mortgagees also have the right to repay the delinquent mortgage, or else lose their security, i.e. be foreclosed by the prior mortgagee – hence the expression **redeem up, foreclose down**. If the debt is not repaid by a time specified by the court, the court may then grant a 'foreclosure absolute' which vests the mortgagor's fee simple, or term of years, in the mortgagee, free of the mortgagor's right to redeem and the rights of all subsequent mortgagees, although any prior or superior mortgages remain in place (LPA 1925, ss. 88(2), 89(2)). However, between the order nisi and the order absolute the mortgagor may apply to the court for a sale of the property in place of foreclosure (LPA 1925, s. 91(2)). Even after a foreclosure absolute, the court has, for a reasonable period of time, a discretionary right to decree that the mortgagor may redeem and thus keep the property. In addition, if the mortgaged property is a dwelling-house (which includes ant building or part thereof which is used as a dwelling), the court has a discretionary right to stay proceedings if it considers that the mortgagor can remedy the default that gave rise to the foreclosure action within a reasonable time (AJA 1970, s. 36, as amended by AJA 1973, s. 8). If a mortgagor in possession refuses to vacate the mortgaged property after the fee simple has been vested in the mortgagee then the mortgagee must obtain an order for possession from the court, as it is a criminal offence to physically oust a person from property. The court is empowered to direct that the property be sold, especially when requested so to do by a party who has an interest in the mortgaged property, rather than grant a foreclosure absolute, if that is considered more equitable. This is commonly done, particularly when the property is worth significantly more than the unpaid debt, or when there is a rising property market. The sale of the mortgaged property may be made on such terms as the court thinks fit, "including the deposit in court of a reasonable sum fixed by the court to meet the expenses of the sale and to secure performance of the terms", LPA 1925, s. 91(2).

In the US, foreclosure may take a number of different forms depending on the jurisdiction. It may be (i) **strict foreclosure**; (ii) foreclosure by a **writ of entry and possession**; (iii) foreclosure by action; or (iv) foreclosure under a 'power of sale'. In most jurisdictions, the law does not sanction strict foreclosure, i.e. the taking of the property by the mortgagee. Under foreclosure by entry and possession, upon a mortgagor's default the mortgagee enters onto the property (actually or constructively) and retains possession during the period allowed for redemption. This procedure is only available in some New England states. The most common procedure against a delinquent mortgagor is by an action of foreclosure or a 'foreclosure suit', whereby a decree of foreclosure is obtained after the mortgagor has failed to pay the debt on time, and then a sale of the property in accordance with that decree. In some jurisdictions, after a public sale, the mortgagor may be entitled to exercise a **statutory right of redemption**. Thus, 'foreclosure' may be used in a more generic sense for the finalization of the process of depriving the mortgagor of his right to reclaim the mortgaged property. Foreclosure by exercise of a power of sale may also be classified as: (i) **judicial foreclosure**, which is carried out under an order of a court when there is no power of sale set out in the mortgage document; or (ii) non-judicial foreclosure (which is permitted in only a few jurisdictions) whereby the mortgagee can proceed with a sale of the property without recourse to a court of law, provided such a process is allowed for in the mortgage document or deed of trust. See also **deed of trust**(US), **deficiency judgment**(US), **foreclosure sale**.

Beaumont, Marc. *Effective Mortgage Enforcement*. Welwyn Garden City: EMIS Professional Publishing, 1998. Nelson, Grant S., and Dale A Whitman. *Real Estate Finance Law*. 3rd ed. St Paul, MN: West, 1994.

foreclosure absolute   See **foreclosure**.

foreclosure by entry and possession or **foreclosure by writ of entry**(US)   See **foreclosure**.

foreclosure by sale   See **foreclosure sale**, **power of sale**.

foreclosure nisi   See **foreclosure**.

foreclosure payment   A payment made to the holder of a **mortgage-backed obligation** following on from a **foreclosure** on property held as security.

foreclosure sale(US)   The sale of property made to enforce a mortgage, lien or deed of trust, whether as a **judicial sale** or by the exercise of the **power of sale**. In most jurisdictions **strict foreclosure**, i.e. taking the mortgaged property in satisfaction of the debt, is prohibited and the foreclosure sale procedure has been adopted in its stead. In the event of a default by the mortgagor, a mortgagee may have a right to sell the mortgaged property in accordance with the provisions of state laws regulating such a sale. Up to the time of the sale the mortgagor, any junior mortgagee, or any other party that has an interest in the property to protest, may pay off the outstanding debt and prevent the sale proceeding. At the foreclosure sale the first mortgagee may be permitted to bid up to the amount of the outstanding debt without putting up any money. If the mortgagee is successful, he effectively forecloses. However, if a higher bid is made, the bidder receives title to the property. On the other hand, if the property is sold to a third party for less than the mortgage debt, the net proceeds of the sale are set against the debt and in some cases the mortgagee has a right of recourse against the mortgagor on his personal debt by way of a **deficiency judgment**. In some jurisdictions, the mortgagee may pursue a foreclosure on the property and concurrently or consecutively sue for any deficiency that may be realized from the sale of the property. However, in other jurisdictions the mortgagee may have to elect to accept only one form of satisfaction. cf. **statutory foreclosure**. See also **forced sale**, **foreclosure**, **judicial foreclosure**, **statutory right of redemption**.

forecourt   An open area, enclosed or marked off, in front of a building or group of buildings.

foregift   A **premium** paid for the right to a lease; especially a payment that must be made before a tenant is allowed into possession. See also **fine**(Eng).

forehand rent(US)   Rent paid in advance or paid as a **premium** upon the taking of a lease. See also **rent in advance/rent in arrears**.

foreign investor   See **absentee owner**.

foreign real estate dealer(US)   A real estate **broker** who is licensed in one state to deal in real estate in another state. In most jurisdictions, a broker (or the salesperson who is employed by the broker) is not entitlement to a **commission** unless, at the time the broker is hired, he has a licence to operate in the state where the property being sold is situated. However, in some states, if the broker is a "foreign real estate dealer" (i.e. a broker licensed in a state to act as a broker in respect of real estate in another state) he may be able to claim a commission in the state where he is licensed in respect of a transaction in another state. Such a broker should be distinguished from a broker who is licensed in another state, but has no right of action in respect of property in a state in which he is not licensed. Nonetheless, some states do permit the payment of a commission to a broker from a foreign state (a 'foreign-licensed broker'), provided he has a current license in that state. See also **real estate license**.

forensic appraisal(AmE)   An **appraisal** that is made for use in litigation proceedings.

foreshore   The **shore** of the sea, or of any tidal water, that lies between the limits of the high and low water marks at 'ordinary tides'. Land that is alternately wet and dry according to the flow of tides based on the medium high-water mark between springs and the neaps. An area of land that may extend into creeks, channels, bays, estuaries or up navigable rivers as far as the tide flows; as well as the 'seashore' as understood in common usage. The boundary of land bounded by the foreshore may well vary in accordance with the position of the median high water mark. When used in a conveyance the words 'seashore' and 'foreshore' have the same extensive meaning, unless it is clear that only land bounding the open sea is being referred to.

In English law, the foreshore of the sea is *prima facie* vested in the Crown; the adjoining landowner's boundary ceasing (in the absence of evidence to the contrary) at the median high water mark (land along freshwater rivers belonging to the riparian owner). The foreshore is subject to certain public rights of fishery, navigation and such rights as access for walking, bathing, and taking seaweed, shingle, sand and shells.

In the US, some jurisdictions follow the common law and accept that the ownership of land abutting the sea or tidal waters stops at the mean high water mark, with the land below that point being vested in the individual state; although a dry beach may belong to the abutting landowner, subject to the public rights of fishing and navigation. However, several states have decided that the general public should enjoy the foreshore or beach, either because it has been enjoyed by **custom**, or as a right arising by **dedication**, as when a landowner has permitted the public on a beach over an extended period of time. See also **accretion, dereliction**.

forest   An area of land densely covered with trees and undergrowth and usually of substantial acreage. A dense growth of trees and underbrush covering a large tract of land; "...*specif.*: an extensive plant community of shrubs and trees in all stages of growth and decay with a closed canopy having the quality of self-perpetuation or of development into an ecological climax", *Webster's Third New International Dictionary®, Unabridged*, ©1993. cf. **chase, park**. See also **forestry, woodland**.

Mynors, Charles. *The Law of Trees, Forests and Hedgerows*. London: Sweet & Maxwell, 2002.

Forest Service[(US)]   The United States Department of Agriculture (USDA) Forest Service is a federal agency with authority over National Forest Areas, National Grasslands and other such special areas. The USDA Forest Service's primary mission is "to achieve quality land management under the sustainable multiple-use management concept to meet the diverse needs of people". This includes, amongst other duties, advocating a conservation ethic in promoting the health, productivity, diversity, and beauty of forests and associated lands; providing technical and financial assistance for the protection, management and use of forests and rangelands; and encouraging State and private forest landowners to practice good stewardship and quality land management. The Forest Service is empowered through the Secretary of Agriculture to acquire land for National Forests and may make arrangements to facilitate access to forest land. It may also control and limit the use of forest lands. (**www.fs.fed.us**)

Several states have Forest Services to carry out similar duties in respect of forest land within the jurisdiction of that state.

In Canada, the Canadian Forest Service aims to "promote the sustainable development of Canada's forests and competitiveness of the Canadian forest sector for the well-being of present and future generations of Canadians". The Canadian Forest Service has ten national networks dealing with such matters as forest health, fire management, landscape management and socio-economic research. (**www.nrcan-rncan.gc.ca/cfs-scf/national**).

forestry   **1.** Land set aside for the growing of trees and wooded plants. See also **forest, Forestry Commission**[(Eng)], **Forest Service**[(US)]. **2.** The science or art of growing and cultivating forests or nursery grounds for trees. The management of growing trees, including the felling and replanting of trees. See also **timber**.

Forestry Commission(Eng)   A body established in the UK in 1919 to promote the interests of forestry, the development of afforestation and the production and supply of timber. The Commission owns and maintains large areas of forestry land, especially Crown owned forests. (**www.forestry.gov.uk**).

forestry lease(Eng)   A lease of forest land that is granted to the Minister of Agriculture by a **tenant for life** in respect of settled land. Such a lease may be one granted for any purpose for which the Minister is authorised to acquire forestry land. It may also be granted at a nominal rent for up to ten years, or at a rent that is based on the timber cut in any one year, or on any other basis where the profit of the land is shared (SLA, s. 48). A tenant for life may grant a forestry lease for up to 99 years (SLA, s. 41).

forfeiture   **1.** The loss of the right to a property as a result of some negligent or illegal act or omission, or a failure of performance. The loss of an estate, privilege, benefit or right, without compensation, due to a failure to fulfil a condition or comply with a legal obligation. cf. **abandonment, rescission**. See also **condition subsequent, deposit, earnest money.   2.** The loss of a right to a **lease** that arises when the landlord exercises his right to regain possession of the demised premises against the wishes of the tenant. A landlord may exercise this right, his **right of re-entry**, either: (i) if there is a breach of a **condition** of the lease by the tenant; or (ii) if there is a breach of a **covenant** (i.e. a provision that is not essential to the operation of the lease) *and* there is also a **forfeiture clause** or 'proviso for re-entry' inserted in the lease.

In the US, the forfeiture of a lease to the landlord is not favored by the courts and, as a rule, can only be applied if there is an express provision in the lease or, in some jurisdictions, in accordance with a statutory provision. In many jurisdictions, forfeiture is applied only in cases of non-payment of rent or an illegal use of the property. In any event, unless the lease expressly provided otherwise, the landlord must give a clear and unequivocal statement of his intention to forfeit the lease, usually by a written notice to that effect followed by the procedure required of the local law.

If there is no such proviso in the lease, then the lessor's only recourse for a breach of covenant is to seek some other form of remedy (e.g. **damages** or an **injunction**) or, in the case of a periodic tenancy, to serve a **notice to quit**. However, most modern leases contain a provision that the lessor may exercise a right of re-entry in the event of a breach of any covenant contained in the lease, normally by issuing and serving a writ for possession. Forfeiture renders a lease **voidable** and not void and any act by the landlord that indicates that he does not intend to follow through on his rights (such as accepting rent) may act as a **waiver** of his right of re-entry.

In English law, forfeiture of a lease for breach of a covenant can only be enforced in accordance with statute. In the case of a breach of a covenant or condition, in most leases a right of re-entry or forfeiture "shall not be enforceable, by action or otherwise, unless and until the lessor serves on the lessee a notice – (a) specifying the particular breach complained of, and (b) if the breach is capable of remedy, requiring the lessee to remedy the breach; and (c) in any case, requiring the lessee to make compensation in money for the breach; and the lessee fails, within a reasonable time thereafter, to remedy the breach, if it is capable of remedy, and to make reasonable compensation in money, to the satisfaction of the lessor, for the breach", LPA 1925, s. 146(1). (Such a notice is sometimes called a 'section 146 notice'.) A number of exceptions apply to this requirement. However, in all other cases, only when this procedure has been followed can the lessor proceed with a re-entry. In addition, the tenant has a right to apply to the court for **relief** from such an action and the court may grant or refuse relief as it thinks fit, having regard to the circumstances and the conduct of the parties (LPA 1925, s. 146(2)). Also, the court may grant an alternative form of remedy, such as an injunction to force the tenant to comply with the covenant in the lease or damages, if that is considered more appropriate. Forfeiture is a remedy that is considered by common law as a form of penalty; it is enforced against the will of the losing party, and generally is permitted only when there is a wilful act or omission that the defaulting party has not attempted to remedy. In the case of a breach of a covenant to repair, contained in a lease (other than one of an agricultural holding) granted for seven years or more with three or more years left to run, the tenant must be given a right to serve, within 28 days, a counter notice to the 'section 146 notice' if he considers the landlord's notice unreasonable (Leasehold Property (Repairs) Act 1938, s. 1). Forfeiture of a lease for non-payment of **rent** must normally be preceded by a formal demand for the exact sum due, unless the lease exempts the landlord from this requirement. In addition, (a) there is at least half a year's rent in arrears; (b) there are insufficient chattels on the premises to provide a landlord who distrains with a possibility of recovering the arrears; and (c) the landlord has reserved a right of re-entry for non-payment of rent (Common Law Procedure Act 1852, s. 210). Further, if the tenant pays all arrears of rent and costs before the trial the court will normally not proceed with the grant of an order of forfeiture. cf. **rescission**. See also **determination, dilapidations, election, eviction, grounds for possession**(Eng), **sub-lessee, waiver**. 2. A loss, especially as a result of a default or an offence. See also **deposit**.

forfeiture clause 1. A clause in a lease that enables a landlord, in certain specified circumstances, to terminate the lease and re-enter the demised premises. A forfeiture clause is generally construed against the landlord and in favour of the tenant – based on the *contra proferentem* rule. Also called a 'proviso for re-entry', a 'right of termination' or a 'power of termination'. See also **condition, forfeiture, right**

of re-entry.   2.(US)A clause in an **installment land contract** which provides that, in the event of a default in payment by the purchaser, the seller may retain as liquidated damages all payments that have been made before the default and has no further obligation to the purchaser for the transfer of title. In some jurisdictions, such a provision may be unenforceable and, if a substantial amount has already been paid, a court would generally construe that amount as a **penalty** and require that only a fair amount be retained to compensate the seller for his actual loss.   3. See **default clause**.

forfeiture restraint(US)   See **restraint on alienation**.

forgery   Falsification or alteration of a document or writing (or a signature to a document) with the intention that it shall appear genuine, or with an intent to defraud or deceive another person. A forged deed will not transfer title to real property and **title insurance** may be arranged to safeguard an innocent purchaser against forgery by a predecessor in title. See also **fraud, rectification**.

form document(US)   A model or outline of a document in which the general terms and conditions are set out so that it may be used for any number of transactions relating to similar business. Form documents are produced usually by authoritative bodies, together with drafting guides, to assist those that use such documents by being time saving, consistent and, theoretically, less liable to misinterpretation. A form document may be recorded in order to set out the terms that will apply to a series of similar or related transactions, such as deeds of trust or mortgages, thereby avoiding the necessity of repeating language in the subsequent deeds. Such recorded documents are called 'fictitious documents' as they are not the true documents of title. A **short-form document** is then executed in which is set out the essential terms of the transaction (parties, property, price, date) and, in turn, the short-form document may refer to the fictitious document for the details. The recording of the short-form document (combined with the fictitious document) represents the true document of title. See also **boiler plate**(AmE), **precedent**(Eng), **standard-form document**(Eng).

form of contract　See **deed, writing**.

Form UCC-1(US)　See **financing statement**.

formal contract　A contract in **writing**, as distinguished from an oral or informal contract. Historically, a contract under **seal** (although a seal is no longer essential in English law, nor in most jurisdictions in the US, to real estate contracts). cf. **open contract**. See also **attestation, conditions of sale**(Eng), **deed, simple contract**.

formation　The act of creating a binding contract.

forms and precedents　See **precedent**.

formula method(Eng)　A method used to value certain types of property, owned by a statutory undertaker (such as a gas, water, or railway undertaker), for the purpose of assessing the **rateable value**, by applying a formula laid down by statute and Statutory Orders (e.g. Electricity Supply Industries (Rateable Values) Order 1994). Following the privatisation of many of these enterprises, this method is being phased out and the value of such properties is being assessed by reference to the 'profit's basis'. See also **profits method of valuation**.

forty(US)　A forty acre tract of land. A quarter of a quarter of a **section of land** (640 acres); or a half of a half of a quarter section of land (160 acres). A measure used especially in the mid-west and west for land that is the subject of a government grant.

forty-five degree rule(Eng)　See **daylight factor**.

forum-shopping clause(US)　A clause in a contract that specifies which state's legal jurisdic-tion will apply to any dispute. The doctrine of *forum non conveniens* originated in Scotland and 'forum shopping' is the seeking of a court of jurisdiction that is likely to give a plaintiff the most favorable judgment. See also *lex loci*.

forward commitment　1. See **takeout commitment**. 2. An agreement or commitment between a lender and borrower to close on a loan and advance funds when certain specified **due diligence** has been completed and the requisite legal documentation has been formalised. Also referred to as a 'pre-funding commitment'.

forward delivery　A binding arrangement to transfer ownership of, or title to, a property at a future date. In particular, the transfer of a bill of sale for a commodity or a right to a security document. A sale under a forward delivery agreement affords the purchaser an opportunity to sell the property, or the right to the security, before he is committed to take delivery.

forward letting　See **pre-let**.

forward sale　See **takeout commitment**.

four-three-two-one rule(US)　A method of valuing a plot of land by applying a **depth factor** to four assumed depths in the ratio of 4:3:2:1. The front depth having four times greater value than the rear depth. See also **zoning method**(BrE).

four unities　See **joint tenancy**.

fraction of a section(US)　See **section of land**.

fractional appraisal(US)　The **appraisal** of part of a property. For example, the appraisal of a fractional or **partial interest** in land, excluding buildings or improvements; or an appraisal of parts of a building (such as the structure) for fire insurance purposes.

fractional assessment(US)　An assessment

that is made at a discount to the full value, as where an assessment is based on a percentage of the market value. cf. **full-value assessment**.

fractional area(US)   See **fractional section**.

fractional interest(US)   A **partial interest** in land. This may be a physical part of a building, such as a condominium unit; a right to use a section of land, including an air or mineral right; or a partial estate, such as a leasehold or life interest. See also **bundle of rights theory**.

fractional section(US)   A parcel of land that is less than a conventional **section**. The true measure of a parcel of land may differ from the more conventional measurement (which is usually an even part of a square mile – one 'section') due to the inclusion of land that is submerged by water (as by a river or lake), or because of an error or as a result of the land being cut off by an overlapping survey.

fractionalized mortgage(US)   See **participation loan**.

fragmentation of ownership   The division of the right to the ownership of property into its component parts, i.e. into the right to use, enjoy, manage, possess, transfer or alienate, charge or mortgage, or even to destroy that right. See also **estate, partial ownership, tenure**.

franchise   A right, privilege or licence granted or sold to an individual, or group of individuals, to market or distribute goods, or services, or to use the name of another (e.g. a brand name) on terms and conditions that are mutually agreed upon. Historically, a privilege or liberty conferred in England by Royal prerogative, or in the US, by legislative grant or government authority, permitting an individual or corporation a right that is not available to the public at large. Although the grantor may differ, the modern principle of franchise remains the same. Generally, the grantor of the franchise (the franchiser) agrees to provide assistance to the beneficiary of the franchise (franchisee) in the form of marketing assistance, promotion, advertising, etc., and sometimes the goods to be sold by the franchisee. The franchise is normally restricted to a clearly defined territory or market. The payment made for the privilege, which may take the form of a flat fee or a percentage of gross sales, may also be called a franchise.

Real estate brokers may use a franchising system which provides that member firms, who hold the franchise, will receive details of properties that are available on a **multiple listing** basis. The participating brokers receive assistance with advertising, sales techniques, publicity, etc. They pay a fee as members of the franchise organization and usually a fee based on their gross sales income. In addition, franchised firms refer a prospect to firms holding the same franchise in other parts of the defined territory. See also **royalty**.

fraud   An intentional act of **deceit** or moral turpitude. A false representation by word or deed that in some way wilfully coaxes, tricks or cheats someone into a course of action that brings an unfair advantage to the person making the representation. In particular, fraud may arise when one party takes advantage of superior knowledge or a position of trust, or acts knowing of a deception, so as to cause injury or loss. A deliberate omission or concealment of a fact with the intention to deceive may constitute a fraud (a 'constructive fraud'). However, generally it is not a fraud to take advantage of legal rights. A contract that is entered into by a fraudulent inducement is voidable at the instigation of the wronged party; but if the contact that is entered into contains a fraudulent element, or if it would never have been entered into without the fraud, it is void and unenforceable.

In English law, the concealment of any instrument or encumbrance that is material to a title, or the falsification of the pedigree of any matter upon which a title depends, by any person who is disposing of property for money or money's worth, with intent to defraud, is a criminal offence (LPA 1925, s. 183).

In the US, in several jurisdictions, statutes have

been enacted to make it a criminal offence to defraud a party to a sale, mortgage or lease of real estate, especially to defraud creditors, or when property is sold without title or an attempt is made to sell the same property twice. See also **alteration, blue-sky laws**(US)**, clandestine mortgage, constructive trust, damages, deed of rectification**(Eng)**/deed of reformation**(US)**, equity skimming**(US)**, exclusion clause, fraudulent conveyance, inhibition**(Eng)**, misrepresentation, puffer, rectification, repudiation, rescission, statement of record**(US)**, unconscionable bargain, undue influence**.

fraudulent assignment   See **fraudulent conveyance**.

fraudulent alienation(US)   See **fraudulent conveyance**.

fraudulent conversion   Lawfully receiving possession of money or property of another and then fraudulently withholding it, or converting or applying it to one's own use. An offence that is now treated in English law as theft (Theft Act 1968, s. 1) or in the US, is an element of the crime of embezzlement. See also **conversion**.

fraudulent conveyance   The transfer or **conveyance** of real or personal property, or any contract for the sale of property, made with the intention of depriving another of his proper claim, as when a company sells assets (particularly in anticipation of a financial failure) and distributes the proceeds in order to reduce a creditor's chance of satisfying his debt. A transfer of property in order to prevent, frustrate, hinder or otherwise place that property beyond a rightful or potential claimant. A transfer of property made without fair and reasonable consideration may constitute a fraudulent conveyance, especially when there is a close relationship between the parties or it is made by one who is in a position of trust.

In English law "every voluntary disposition [i.e. a gift] of land made with the intent to defraud a subsequent purchaser is voidable at the instance of the purchaser", LPA 1925, s. 173(1). Also, it is a misdemeanour to seek to conceal or falsify a disposition of property or an interest in property (LPA 1925, s. 183). In addition, a bankrupt is guilty of an offence if he makes a gift or transfer, or makes a charge on, his property, or conceals or removes any part of his property (Insolvency Act 1986, s. 357).

In the US, in most jurisdictions, a conveyance is fraudulent when its object or effect is to defraud another, or the intent is to avoid some duty or debt owed by the person making the transfer. Also called 'fraudulent assignment' or 'fraudulent alienation', especially when the property is assigned or transferred other than by outright sale. See also **clandestine mortgage, Mareva injunction, misrepresentation, undervalue, undue influence**.

fraudulent misrepresentation or **fraudulent representation**   See **fraud, misrepresentation**.

fraudulent preference   A transfer or conveyance of property that is made with the intention of changing the **priority** of creditors. The act of an insolvent debtor of granting one or more creditors preference over other creditors with the intent to hinder or defraud the other creditors.

Freddie Mac(US)   See **Federal Home Loan Mortgage Corporation**.

free and clear return(US)   The relationship, expressed as percentage, between the **net operating income** receivable from a property and the total cost of the property, whether paid as debt or equity, i.e. the return based on the assumption that the property is acquired 'all cash' or with 100 per cent equity. Also called the 'overall yield rate'. cf. **cash-on-cash return**.

free and clear title(US)   A title to property that is free of any defect and not encumbered by any mortgage, lien or other encumbrance. Usually a fee simple property sold without debt ('free' signifying the condition of the title and 'clear' the lack of debt). See also **marketable title**.

free conveyance(US)   A **conveyance** whereby the purchaser of real estate is freed of any expense of the conveyancing.

free rent   See **rent free period**.

freeboard(Eng)   A strip of land that runs around an ancient park, which is not necessarily owned with the park but over which the park owner can exercise rights such as the imposition of a restriction on building.

freehold   An **estate** in land held for a described but uncertain duration. In common law, 'estate' represents the duration of a right to the ownership of land and a freehold estate represents a right to possession of land for a time span that is incapable of exact determination. (Any estate that is for a definite period, even 999 years, is technically not a freehold but a leasehold.) A freehold may be in **possession**, **reversion**, or **remainder**. A freehold may be classified as 'of inheritance', i.e. one that passes so long as there are heirs; or 'not of inheritance', i.e. one that lasts only for a life. A freehold 'of inheritance' may be a **fee simple** (whether absolute, conditional or determinable), i.e. it passes to a person and any class of heir (as long as they persist); or a **fee tail** (or **entailed estate**), i.e. it passes to specified heirs. A freehold 'not of inheritance' is a **life estate**, either for the life of the holder, or for the life of another – *pur autre vie*. In common usage, the term 'freehold' is used to refer to an estate of inheritance, i.e. a fee interest (especially a fee simple absolute) and 'life interest' or 'life estate' is used to refer to an estate for a life. A freehold estate may be contrasted with a **leasehold** or leasehold estate (commonly called a tenancy), which arises from the relationship of landlord and tenant and is technically not a real right to land, but strictly speaking a personal right arising from contract. See also **dower, freehold absolute**(Eng), **tenancy by the curtesy, tenure**.

freehold absolute(Eng)   A **freehold** interest in land that has been registered with an absolute title. A registered interest in land that is equivalent to a **fee simple absolute in possession** of unregistered land. A freehold absolute title is granted by the Land Registrar when he is satisfied that an applicant's interest cannot be challenged. It guarantees to the owner that the title is the most absolute recognised in English law. Such a title is subject only to any entries shown on the register; any **overriding interest** (unless stated to the contrary on the register); and any **minor interest** of which the freeholder has **notice**. See also **land registration**.

freehold estate(US)   An **estate** in land that is a **freehold**. A freehold estate may be 'of inheritance' or 'not of inheritance'. A freehold 'of inheritance' lasts as long as there are heirs; although it may be conditional, determinable or otherwise defeasible, or is limited to a particular gender of heir (a fee tail). A freehold 'not of inheritance' lasts only for the life of the holder or the life of a designated third party.

freeholder   The holder of a **freehold** interest in land.

freestanding store(US)   A retail store that is not physically attached to any other retail store. A 'freestanding store' may be totally separated from any other retail property and operate in all respects independently. On the other hand, it may be physically detached but form part of a **shopping center** or mall and operate with shared facilities such as car parking.

fresh tenancy   A tenancy granted to a tenant who is not the same party as held the tenancy that has come to an end.

FRI lease(BrE)   See **full repairing and insuring lease**.

friction cost   A cost of doing business or completing a transaction that exceeds the amount that is normal or clearly ascertainable. In particular, a cost that reduces an investment return beyond that which may have been predicted or expected, e.g. unexpected commissions or taxes. 'Friction costs' may be used to refer to **closing costs** that are paid over and above the purchase price, especially the costs that are not expected or readily ascertainable. See also **completion statement**(Eng), **settlement statement**(US).

frictional vacancy   See **vacancy rate**.

from   See **boundary, date, time**.

front-end fee   See **commitment fee**.

front-end money   See **front money**.

front-ending   See **front loading**.

front foot(AmE)   See **frontage**.

front loaded or **front loading**   A financial arrangement or investment that provides for a significant share of the cost to be payable or recognised at the start. A front-loaded investment provides for all or most of the management fees to be paid on the initiation of the investment, thereby significantly affecting the return over the total investment period. A front-loaded loan may provide that all or a significant part of the interest is payable by the borrower at the start of a loan; or merely that a significant **commitment fee** or **discount points** are charged by the lender so as to increase the true annual interest rate. Sometimes called 'front-ending', especially when a significant share of the profit of a venture is recognised before it is actually earned. See also **annual percentage rate**.

front money   1. The cash required by a developer prior to starting development works to meet the cost of land acquisition, fees, survey costs, etc., Sometimes called 'front-end money', 'start-up money', 'seed money', 'cash on the barrelhead', or 'cash on the line'. See also **end money**. 2. **Short-term finance** for the development of land.

frontage   1. The distance that a parcel of land or building abuts a street, river or similar demarcation. This distance when measured in feet is called the 'foot frontage'. In the US, also called 'abutting foot', 'running foot', or when used with reference to the **assessed value** of a property (especially when making a special assessment based on the portion of a property that abuts a street), the 'front footage'. The means of making such proportional charge is called the 'front foot method' or the application of the 'front foot rule'. See also **abut**. 2. The **boundary line** of a property immediately abutting a highway or street. The side of a building that faces onto a street, road, footpath or highway, or the side upon which the main entrance is situated.

frontage line   1. A line defined on a plan by a local authority beyond which no new building work is permitted to encroach. See also **building line, improvement line**. 2. The line that represents the limit of a landowner's property where it fronts a public highway or footpath.

frontage method   A method of valuing a plot of land or a building based on its frontage to a street, mall, footway, etc. Also called the 'foot-frontage method' or, in the US, when used to determine the amount of a local assessment payable in respect of a particular property, the 'foot-frontage rule' or the 'front-foot method'. See also **comparison method of valuation**.

frontager   A landowner who has a boundary line that abuts a highway, street, river, etc. See also **riparian owner**.

frustration   An event or incident that prevents an action being performed, or a purpose being achieved, as anticipated; such as one that renders a contract incapable of performance. In particular, an event or instance that goes to the foundation of a contract, such as the destruction of the subject matter or an interruption or delay that in effect creates a different contract. A contract may be frustrated if: (a) the subject-matter totally disappears; (b) a particular thing or factor required in order to fulfil the contract is not and cannot be made available; (c) the whole underlying business reason is removed by circumstances that could not have been anticipated by the parties; or (d) performance of the contract is subsequently but unexpectedly made illegal. In common law, a contract relating to land is unlikely to be frustrated; most land (but not necessarily the buildings thereon) being considered indestructible in law. See also **fit for the purpose, reinstatement clause, warranty of habitability**(US).

McKendrick, Ewan (editor). *Force Majeure and Frustration of Contract*. 2nd ed. London: Lloyds of London Press, 1995.

Treitel, Professor Guenter H. *Frustration and Force Majeure*. London: Sweet & Maxwell, 1994.

frustrum terræ(Lat)   A piece of **land** that stands alone.

fuel allotment(Eng)   See **allotment**.

full annual value   The **best rent** or **market rent** of a property. Sometimes called a 'fair annual value'. See also **annual value, rack rent**.

full cash value   The **fair market value** assuming a wholly cash transaction. See also **cash value**.

full covenant and warranty deed(US)   See **warranty deed**.

full float   See **float**.

full floor rentable area(US)   See **rentable area**.

full market value   See **fair market value**.

full-payout lease or **full payout lease**   See **finance lease**.

full-payout loan   A loan that will be fully repaid (including all interest and capital) over its term. See also **amortization loan**.

full rent   See **rack rent**.

full rental value (FRV)(BrE)   See **estimated rental value**.

full repairing and insuring lease (FRI lease)(BrE)   A lease that requires all running costs including property taxes, repairs and maintenance costs, and insurance premiums, to be paid by the lessee. Sometimes called an **institutional lease** because an institutional investor in real property normally requires a lease of commercial property to be made on an FRI basis, although such a lease may require other conditions that are favourable to the landlord. See also **net lease, triple net lease**.

full security(Eng)   See **security of tenure**.

full service gross (FSG)(US)   See **full service lease**.

full service lease(US)   A lease that provides that the landlord is responsible for all operating expenses during the first year of the lease. After that the tenant is responsible for its prorated share of increases in the operating expenses above the level at the **base year** (first year), in addition to the base rent. For example, the base rent may be fixed at $24.00 ('full service gross') per square foot per annum, which includes operating expenses. If the 2000 operating expenses are $12.00 per square foot per annum and 2001 operating expenses are $12.45 per square foot per annum, then the tenant pays his prorated share of $0.45 per square foot in 2001, plus the base rent of $24.00, for a total lease obligation of $24.45.

full title guarantee(Eng)   A form of title to land that, if expressed as such, contains implied covenants for title. The grant of land "with full title guarantee" implies that the person making the disposition of the property (a) has the right to dispose of the property as he purports to, with the concurrence of any other person conveying the property (a 'covenant for right to convey'); (b) will at his own cost do all that is possible to give the title he purports to (a 'covenant for further assurance'); and (c) (except for matters to which the disposition is expressly made subject) will convey the property free (i) of all charges and encumbrances (whether monetary or not); and (ii) from all other rights exercisable by third parties (other than those charges, encumbrances or rights that are not or could not be reasonably known to exist) (LP(MP)A, ss. 1-5). In the case of a disposition of a leasehold interest (whether or not made for valuable consideration) it is implied also that: (a) the lease is subsisting at the time of the disposition; and (b) there is no subsisting breach of the lease or anything that would render the lease liable to forfeiture (LP(MP)A 1994, ss. 1(1)(2), 4(1)). cf. **limited title guarantee**. See also **covenant for title**.

full covenant and warranty deed(US) See **warranty deed**.

full-value assessment(US) An **assessment** that is made at the market value without any discount, as distinguished for a **fractional assessment** that allows for a discount to the full value.

fully-amortized lease(AmE) See **finance lease**.

fully amortizing mortgage(AmE) See **amortization mortgage**.

fully-modified mortgage-backed security A mortgage-backed security that allows the investor to receive the full amount of interest and principal receivable on the underlying security with the issuer being responsible for making up any delinquent payments of the mortgagors.

fully-net lease(AmE) See **triple net lease**.

functional depreciation See **depreciation**.

functional inutility See **obsolescence**.

functional obsolescence See **obsolescence**.

fund 1. A sum of money, in cash or cash equivalent (cheques, drafts, money orders). In particular, a fund is a financial resource or capital that is set aside for a special purpose, such as to replace an asset or provide a pension. See also **sinking fund**. 2. An investment in a range of liquid investments; a group of investments or a **portfolio** that is managed by a financial institution. See also **investment trust, mutual fund, real estate investment trust**.

fundamental breach See **breach of contract**.

fundamental term See **condition, exclusion clause**.

funding 1. The provision of a sum of money to meet a future contingency or a known debt. See also **sinking fund**. 2. Obtaining a loan, especially a long-term loan to replace a short-term loan. See also **financing**. 3. The conversion of **debt** into **equity**. See also **convertible mortgage**.

funding date The date upon which funds are first advanced under a loan, which may or may not correspond to the **closing** date.

funds available for distribution(AmE) See **cash available for distribution**.

funds from operations (FFO)(AmE) The **net income** of a **Real Estate Investment Trust**, excluding gains or losses from sales of property or debt restructuring, and before depreciation. See **cash available for distribution**.

fungible goods or **fungibles** Derived from the Latin *fungi*, 'perform' or 'discharge'. Goods that can be measured so that they can be substituted by a similar quantity, e.g. cash, grain, sugar, oil.

Land or real estate is essentially non-fungible as each parcel or property is unique. Goods that are fungible may be substituted under most contracts, but one cannot substitute one parcel of land for another as a means of satisfying a contractual obligation for the sale of land.

furnished premises(Eng)   See **furnished tenancy**.

furnished tenancy(Eng)   The grant of a tenancy of a dwelling-house that is partly or fully furnished; in particular when a substantial proportion of the rent includes payment for the use of furniture.

In common law, in a lease of furnished residential premises, there is an **implied covenant** that the property is **fit for human habitation** at the start of the tenancy, although the landlord is not under any obligation to keep the premises fit throughout the term of the lease, unless required by the terms of the lease. Matters that make premises unfit for human habitation include: the presence of rats, bugs, disease, germs, etc.; defective drains containing stagnant filth; and dampness from condensation.

further advance(Eng) or **future advance**(US)
A second or subsequent advance of money under an existing mortgage, usually against the security of the property already held by the mortgagee, but sometimes against the security of another property. Interest not paid when due, i.e. accrued and added to the outstanding principal balance, may be considered as a further advance.

In English law, a further advance may be added onto an existing advance so that the total loan has equal **priority** if: (i) there is an agreement of the subsequent mortgagee; (ii) if, at the time the further advance is made, the mortgagee does not have **notice** of the subsequent mortgage; or (iii) if there is a 'further advances clause' by which the mortgagee is bound to make further advances, as would normally be the case with a **construction loan** (LPA 1925, s. 94).

In the US, a future advance may be categorized as 'mandatory' or 'optional'. A mandatory advance

is one that was included as an essential part of the original mortgage deed as where the mortgagee contracts to advance monies as building work progresses. A mandatory advance normally maintains the same priority as the initial advance. An 'optional clause' in a mortgage permits the mortgagee to advance additional funds at his discretion. An optional advance does not normally maintain the same **priority** against third party creditors as the initial advance, unless there is an agreement to the contrary or the advance is made to protect the existing loan. See also **accrued interest, cut-off notice**(US), **open-end mortgage, tacking, usury**.

further assurance   See **covenant for further assurance**.

future advance(US)   See **further advance**.

future advances clause   See **further advance**.

future depreciation   Depreciation that it is assumed will accrue over the life of an asset and for which a provision has or will be made. cf. **accrued depreciation**.

future estate   An **estate** that does not bestow a right to possession until a future time, i.e. the right to the enjoyment of the benefits (including receipt of the rents and profits) arises in the future. An estate that comes into existence at the time of creation, but is not immediately vested in the grantee. Sometimes called an 'estate in expectancy'; estates in expectancy may be classified as of two sorts, "one created by the acts of the parties, called a **remainder**; the other by act of law, called a **reversion**", 2 *Bl Comm* 163. See also **future interest**.

future interest   An **interest** in land that the owner holds now but does not take effect, as a right to **possession** or enjoyment, until a future time or until the happening of a future event. An interest that represents a right to the possession of property at a future date. Thus, if Green Fields Mall (or the income to be derived therefrom) is granted to A for life and thereafter to B, then A has a present interest and B, a future interest. A future interest can be classified as one that returns to the grantor, or one that passes to a person other than the grantor. Also, as the creator of a future interest has not conveyed all that he owns, there are 'pieces of ownership' that are left for the future. These pieces may be classified as: (i) a right in **reversion** – an interest that returns to a grantor who parted with an interest for a shorter duration than that which he held, as with a lease or a life interest; (ii) a 'fee simple determinable' (also called a 'determinable fee', or one of a number of similar terms) – an interest that is granted as if it were a fee, but subject to a contingent event which, if it arises, would automatically return the fee to the grantor or his heirs, known as the **possibility of a reverter**; or (iii) a 'fee simple on condition subsequent' (also called a 'conditional fee', or any of a number of similar terms) – an interest that will return to the grantor if a stipulated condition occurs, but only if it is retaken by the exercise of a **right of re-entry** (or a 'right of entry' or 'right of entry for condition broken'). A future interest may also be a **remainder** – an interest that does not revert to the original grantor.

A future interest may be either: (i) a 'vested remainder' or **vested interest**; or (ii) a 'contingent remainder' or **contingent interest**. A vested interest is one that passes to a person who is ascertained when the interest is granted, but does not pass unless or until a specified event occurs. A contingent interest is one that passes to someone who is not ascertained when the right is first granted, or is an interest that is dependent on a contingent or uncertain event. The final classification of a future interest is an **executory interest** – an interest that does not return to the present property owner but, upon the occurrence of a contingent event, cuts short the present interest and transfers the right to possession to a third party. The holder of a future interest is not guaranteed future enjoyment, but it is a presently existing interest in that it may be alienated and the holder can restrain the present holder of possession from committing **waste**. See also **conditional fee**, **executory interest**, **rule against perpetuities**.

future lease   See *interesse termini*, **reversionary lease**.

future value or **future worth**   The value of a capital sum at a future date, or after a given period of time, after allowing for income or interest earned thereon. cf. **present value**.

future worth of one per period   See Appendix C, **Financial Formulae**.

G

gain   An increase in resources, possessions or advantage that results from business dealings or transactions. An advantage or benefit obtained keeping what one has or from getting what one has not. An increase in the value or worth of a property, whether realised or unrealised; especially as measured by the cost, or income, at one point in time and the increase in value at a subsequent point in time. Gain is a general term that may include a **profit**, advantage or benefit received by an individual or group of individuals. In particular, a gain is that which accrues to a person, whether of a pecuniary nature or otherwise and in that respect may be distinguished from a 'profit' which results from a thing, usually by buying or selling. "*Gain* and *profit* may be extended to other objects, and sometimes are opposed to each other; for as that which we *gain* is what we wish only, it is often the reverse of *profitability*", George Crabb, *Crabb's English Synonyms*. 1816. Reprint, London: Routledge, 1982. cf. **loss**. See also **capital gain, chargeable gain**.

gale   1.(Eng)A form of **gavel**, i.e. a periodic payment based on the produce of land. The term 'gale' is derived from 'gavel' – a rent or duty. See also **gale-day**.   2.(Eng)An amount due to a superior. A payment of **rent**, tax or similar annual sum due as a form of consideration for a licence or right to land, in particular for a mining right. The word gale may be used to refer the grant itself of a right to mine; to refer to the licence conferred by the grant, or more frequently to refer to the defined property that is the subject of the grant. 'Gale' is used particularly to refer to such a grant made by the Crown, or to the subject matter of such a grant.   3. In Ireland, a common term for rent.   4. See **rental period**.

game   Wild birds or wild animals that are hunted for sport, in particular, hares, pheasants, partridges, grouse, heath or moor game, black game, bustards, woodcocks and snipes. 'Game' includes all game birds, game fowl, and game animals; but, ordinarily, it does not include domesticated animals or birds. As a rule, unless they have been tamed or are too young to escape, game belongs to nobody absolutely. The right to hunt, catch and appropriate game is part of the right to the ownership of land (subject to any statutory restriction, especially as to the time for such pursuits). If land is leased the right to hunt or catch game belongs basically to the tenant; although a landlord may well reserve such a right to himself. See also **profit à prendre**.

gangway   A way over which people pass and repass in the course of their work. A passageway in a building, especially a way opened for a particular and generally temporary purpose. See also **aisle, mall**.

Gantt chart   A bar chart used in **project management** or production scheduling to show the tasks involved against time. A horizontal bar is used to depict each task, with the left end showing the start date and the right shows the scheduled completion date. A bar can than be marked alongside to show the proportion of the tasks that has been completed. The bars can also be interrelated by marking the start of a task against the completion of a task upon which it is dependent. See also **project evaluation and review technique**.

gap finance   Finance that is made available to cover a temporary need. In particular, finance provided to cover the difference between funds that can be drawn on immediately, either as equity or under a loan facility (a **floor loan**), and the total cost of a development or building project. Usually gap finance takes the form of a short-term loan secured by a second mortgage, obtained independently of any interim or **construction finance**, and replaced, upon completion and letting of a project, by more permanent finance or by an increase in the floor loan. See also **bridge loan, commitment, holdback, interim finance**.

garage   A building or structure used for the storage, shelter and protection of motor vehicles. An enclosed area of land that is mainly covered and used for the cleaning, servicing, or repairing of motor vehicles. A 'garage' may be (a) a building or place where motor vehicles (in particular automobiles) are left or stored, or a place where vehicles are taken for servicing and repair, or kept prior to sale or hiring; or (b) a building or structure used to store a private vehicle, especially one that is appurtenant to a private residence or apartment building – a 'private garage'. In American English, 'garage' generally refers to a structure or building used for the covered storage by an individual of an automobile or automobiles, usually adjoining or as an integral part of a residence – a 'private garage'; or a large covered or a multi-story building for the storage of automobiles- a 'public garage'. In British English, the latter building or structure is commonly called a 'multi-storey car park'. See also **carport**, **filling station**, **service station**.

garden   A piece of land used for raising plants, flowers, fruits, herbs or vegetables. A parcel of land, usually enclosed and commonly forming part of the curtilage of a dwelling-house, used for the cultivation of flowers, fruit, ornamental trees, vegetables and lawns, and generally used for the pleasure of the inhabitants of the house. A garden is usually a small tract of land, but it may be any area of land laid out for formal display and for horticulture. A garden may be used for profit, although unlike a nursery ground, that is not the principal objective. In American English such an area is generally referred to as a **yard**, especially when forming part of a private residence. See also **allotment**, **cottage garden**, **field garden**, **horticulture**, **market garden**.

garden apartment(AmE)   An **apartment** situated in a multi-unit apartment building with an open area usually in the form of a court that can be used by the occupants as a predominately private garden. In some areas a garden apartment may be one that is situated in a building that is no more than two or three stories in height above grade. See also **condominium**.

garden city   A form of town designed to provide pleasant living and working conditions, surrounded by a rural belt, and large enough to provide a balanced community. This form of town was intended as a marked contrast to the paleotechnic urban jungles that grew up during the Industrial Revolution. "A Garden City is a town designed for healthy living and industry; of a size that makes possible a full measure of social life, but not larger; surrounded by a rural belt; the whole of the land being in public or held in trust for the community", Garden City Association (1919). A. T. Thomas first applied the term to a design in 1869 for an estate on Long Island, New York. In Great Britain, the term is more commonly associated with model towns designed by Ebenezer Howard, of which examples are Letchworth (founded in 1903) and Welwyn Garden City (founded in 1920). These designs were the forerunners of the post-war English new towns. See also **new town**.

garden suburb   A predominantly residential area or **suburb** of a town planned and built to a low density, with adequate open spaces and green areas. A term sometimes used incorrectly for a **garden city**.

garnishee   The person upon whom a **garnishment** is served and is required to hold money on behalf of a judgement debtor. The third party who, under a garnishee order, is required to withhold money.

garnishee order   See garnishment.

garnisher or garnishor   One who bring an action for, or benefits from, a **garnishment**.

garnishment   Derived from the French *garner*, 'to warn'. A legal notice given to a party to appear in a suit or legal proceeding. In particular, an order made by a court (a 'garnishee order' or 'garnishment order') that provides for the monies or personal property of a judgement debtor held by a third party, such as a bank, to be to be attached or secured for the benefit of the judgement creditor. Thus, if A owes money to B that has not repaid when due in accordance with a judgement for the debt, then the court may make a garnishee order in favour of B (the 'garnisher') on money retained in A's bank account, or money due from a debtor of A, for the amount of the debt. The order would stipulate that the bank, or A's debtor, (the 'garnishee') does not transfer the money to A, but retains it for subsequent payment to B. Similarly, a garnishee order may be granted enabling an employer to withhold part or all of an employee's wages or salary in order to pay a debt owed to a third party. Although sometimes used as synonymous with **attachment**, strictly speaking garnishment affects the property of the defendant held by a third party, rather than property held by the defendant. In the US, in some states, called a 'factoring process' or 'trusty process'.

garnishment order(US) See **garnishment**.

garanty See **guaranty**.

garth(Eng) A small enclosed area of land, a close or yard, forming part of the **curtilage** of a house and usually situated to the rear.

gas filling station(AmE) See **filling station**.

gas lease See **oil and gas lease**.

gasoline service station(AmE) See **filling station**, **service station**.

gated pasture See **cattlegate**.

gavel 1. A periodic payment made in the nature of a rent or a duty but taking the form of produce rather than money, e.g. gavel-corn, gavel-fodder, oat-gavel; especially a feudal toll or levy due to a lord or king. The word gavel may also be used to refer to any payment extracted from a tenant, interest on money due, or usury, although these meanings are virtually obsolete. See also **gale**, **gavelkind**. 2. An auctioneer's or judge's mallet or hammer.

gazump(BrE) Originally 'gazoomph' or 'gezump', a slang word that may be of Yiddish extraction meaning 'to swindle'. Commonly employed to refer to the withdrawal of a property after an informal bargain has been made, in expectation of selling it to another party at a higher price. The sale of a property to one party at a higher price, in spite of a previous verbal (and, therefore, in English law non-binding) agreement to sell to someone else at a lower price. Strictly speaking, one offer is rejected in favour of a 'better deal'. The term is also used to refer to the practice of withdrawing a property at the last minute under the threat of selling to a third party at a higher price, unless the prospective purchaser agrees to pay the same or a higher price. The term 'gazunder' may be used to refer to a similar action, but such as arises when the prospective buyer threatens to reduce his price when he considers that the market is weak and the seller will not be anxious to remarket the property. (The term 'gazunder' may be related to *guzunder* – a 'chamber pot', which is placed under the bed.) See also **gentleman's agreement**, **lock-out agreement**, **subject to contract**.

geared rent A rent that increases (or may decrease) in accordance with a change in some other income or rental value. For example, a tenant who has the ability to sub-lease premises may be obliged to pay his landlord rent that is geared to changes in the rent receivable from the subtenants, on the basis that the rent payable by the tenant is proportional to the changes in the rent receivable from the subtenants. See also **gearing**.

gearing 1. The relationship between different forms of capital, especially between owner's capital, or **equity capital** and loans or other forms of **debt capital** (e.g. debentures, loan stock, preference shares). In real estate, gearing is measured by the relationship between the equity capital invested in a property and the mortgage debt secured on that property. The principle of gearing is to borrow money, generally secured on certain fixed assets, at a rate of interest that exerts the least effect on the future profits of the business, so that business can expand beyond the restraint imposed by the amount of an owner's capital. In other words, to use 'other people's money' for one's own profit. The higher the amount of finance provided by a loan or debt capital, relative to the owner's capital, the more highly geared the venture is said to be and the higher the risk for the owner, or equity investors. On the other hand, as the interest payable on the debt capital does not vary with profits, then the greater the profit level (after meeting the cost of debt service) the greater the proportionate return to the owners or equity shareholders. **2.** A financial arrangement by which a movement in one factor has a disproportionate effect on another factor, as when an increase in the net income from an investment produces a larger increase in the income received by one investor relative to another. See also **debt-equity ratio, equity participation, leverage**.

general agent   See agent.

general and first mortgage bond(US)   See first and general mortgage bond.

general building scheme(US)   See **scheme of development**.

general conditions   Conditions in a contract that are generally found in contracts of a particular type, such as contracts that are prepared by a professional or trade organisation for use in their areas of activity.   See also **adhesion contract, conditions of sale, precedent, standard-form contract**.

general contractor (GC)   A **contractor** who is directly responsible for organizing or coordinating an entire work of construction. One who undertakes to construct or supervise the construction of an entire building, engineering or development project, rather than specific parts of a project. In particular, a contractor who accepts the entire obligations of a contract, but sub-lets parts of the work to a specialist **subcontractor** or subcontractors. The principal

contractual liability remains with the general contractor but, unless there is an express condition to the contrary (which is usually the case in a modern building contract), or the contract was entered into by reason of some special skill or quality personal to the contractor, a general contractor is entitled to assign or sub-let any part of the work to another contractor or contractors. Also called 'main contractor', 'principal contractor', 'primary contractor', or 'prime contractor' (especially when the party has contracted to do all or most of the work rather than employing a number of subcontractors); or 'original contractor' or 'ordinary contractor' (especially when used in the US to refer to the party who has contracted directly with the owner and has a right to a **mechanic's lien**). See also **management contractor**.

general damages   See **damages**.

General Depreciation System (GDS)(US) See **accelerated depreciation**.

General Development Order (GDO)(Eng) An order made by the Secretary of State for the Environment, or the Secretary of State for Wales, that permits the carrying out of certain forms of **development** without the need for **planning permission** from the local planning authority. The Town and Country Planning (General Permitted Development) Order 1995 authorises the carrying out of 84 classes of 'development', including such matters as development within the curtilage of a dwelling-house; the erection of some agricultural buildings; the carrying out of specified temporary uses; the carrying out of works by a public authority, such as road repairs; activities that are associated with another approved activity (such as tipping at a mine). However, such 'permitted development' must be confined within the scope of the Order and it does not override any condition that has been attached to a planning permission. The Secretary of State or a local planning authority has the power to withdraw any particular form of development from the order, which it uses especially in areas where such development may not be appropriate such as an area of outstanding natural beauty. See also **Special Development Order**.

general development plan (GDP)   See development plan.

General Development Procedure Order (GDPO)(Eng)   See **planning application**.

general devise   See devise.

general entail   See entailed estate/entailed interest.

general equitable charge(Eng)   A term of statutory derivation. A general equitable charge is a comprehensive expression that includes any **equitable charge** that may be registered as a **land charge** but "(a) is not secured by a deposit of title deeds relating to the legal estate affected; and (b) does not arise or affect an interest under a trust for sale or settlement; and (c) is not a charge given by way of an indemnity against rents equitably apportioned or charged exclusively on land in exoneration of other land and against the breach and non-observance of covenants or conditions; and (d) is not included in any other class of land charge", LCA 1972, s. 2(4)(iii). Thus, a general equitable charge forms a residuary class of charge that is registered as "Class C" land charge, and comprises such claims as a vendor's lien for unpaid purchase money; an **equitable mortgage** of a legal estate that has not been protected by a deposit of the title deeds; and an annuity for life (an **equitable annuity**). However, to be registrable the charge must be against land *per se* and not merely against the proceeds of sale.

general estate(US)   The entire estate left by a descendent. The term may sometimes be used to refer to the **residue** or 'residuary estate' of a descendent, i.e. the part of an estate that is not specifically devised or bequeathed.

general improvement area (GIA)(Eng)   See renewal area.

general improvement district(US)   See improvement district.

General land(NZ)   Land, other than Maori freehold land and General land owned by Maori, that has been alienated from the crown for a subsisting estate in fee simple (Te Ture Whenua Maori/Maori Land Act 1993, s. 129 (NZ)). This all the land in New Zealand, other than **Crown land**, 'Crown land reserved for Maori', and 'Maori customary land'. See also **native title**.

general legacy   See legacy.

general liability insurance   See liability insurance.

general lien   See lien.

general listing(US)   See **open listing**.

General Map(Eng)   A map, based on the Ordnance Survey maps, that is prepared and kept by the **Land Registry**, and is used as the basis for showing the position and extent of all parcels of registered land. 'General Map' may refer to a series of maps that were put together as part of the early maps used to establish compulsory land registration in England and Wales (Land Registration Rules 1925, r. 273), or it may refer to a single map that is used by the Land Registry to show every registered estate (Land Registration Rules 1925, r. 8). The General Map is then bound up in book form with a **Parcels Index**. See **Index Map**.

general mortgage   See blanket mortgage.

general offer   An **offer** to the public at large which, if accepted by any member of the public, creates a contract between the parties. A general offer may be in respect of a specified property, e.g. on a sale by open **tender**; or a more general offer, e.g. an offer to buy or sell a class of goods at a stated price. cf. **invitation to trade**(AmE)/ **invitation to treat**(BrE). See also **without reserve**.

general partner   Any member of a **limited partnership** who is empowered to act on behalf of, and thus to bind, the other partners and whose financial liability to the partnership may exceed his direct financial contribution to the partnership.

A general partner may bind the other partners in accordance with the powers granted by those partners; he is personally liable for the debts or obligations of the partnership (in the same way as any partner in a **general partnership**); and he has a fiduciary liability to the other 'limited partners'.

In the US, a general partner may be defined as "one of two or more persons who associate to carry on business for profit and who are personally liable for all the debts of partnership", Uniform Partnership Act, § 6(1), 6(15); as distinguished from a **limited partner** who is only liable to the extent of his financial contribution to the partnership. Also, any member of a 'general partnership' may also be referred to as a 'general partner'.

In English law, a general partner is defined to mean "any partner who is not a limited partner as defined by this Act", Limited Partnership Act 1907, s. 3, i.e. a general partner is anyone whose liability or obligation to the partnership is not limited to his capital contributions.

A general partner may be an individual or a corporate entity. Sometimes called an 'active partner'.

general partnership   **1.** A **partnership** where all the partners are general partners and, therefore, accept unlimited liability for the actions of the firm and are entitled to a say in the decision making and management of the partnership, except as expressly agreed to the contrary. cf. **limited partnership**. See also **general partner, joint and several liability**.   **2.** A **partnership** that has been established for a general purpose or business, such as an agency or legal practice, as distinguished from a **particular partnership** which is established for a specific transaction or purpose.

General Permitted Development Order (GPDO)(Eng)   See **General Development Order**.

general plan   **1.** See **master plan**.   **2.** See **scheme of development**.   **4.**(Eng)See **development plan**.   **3.**(US)See **comprehensive plan**.

general power   See **power of appointment**.

general property   **Ownership** of property as distinguished from 'special property' or **possession** of property.

General Register of Deeds(Aus)   A public register for interests in land that is not registered under the **Torrens title system**. This register permits a party who has an interest in land to register that interest as a protection against another party who has a similar right or to act as **notice** to a purchaser of the land. Unlike an interest in a parcel of land that is registered under the Torrens system it does not guarantee that interest; registration is not compulsory; and unregistered interests still remain valid and enforceable.

general scheme of development(US)   See **scheme of development**.

General Services Administration (GSA)(US)   A central management agency of the federal government that was first established under the Federal Property and Administrative Services Act of 1949, s. 101 with responsibility for the supply, management and general provision of services to enable federal employees to accomplish their missions. GSA is headquartered in Washington, DC and has 11 regional offices. GSA has three major divisions, the Federal Supply Service, the Federal Technology Service, and the Public Building Service (PBS). The Public Building Service of the GSA has a full range of real estate services that can be used in the management of government-owned properties, including real estate brokerage, property management, construction and repair services, security services, portfolio management, as well as services for the disposal of property that is no longer needed for federal, state or local governments. (**www.gsa.gov**).

general store   A small retail outlet that sells a wide range of unrelated merchandise, in particular goods that are for immediate consumption. See also **store**.

general tenancy(US)   **1.** A tenancy of no fixed duration.   **2.** A tenancy at will.

general vesting declaration (GVD)(Eng)   A document that may be executed by any public authority possessing compulsory purchase powers, after a compulsory purchase order has come into operation, in order to expedite the acquisition of title to land (Compulsory Purchase (Vesting Declaration) Act 1981). The use of a general vesting declaration enables the authority to acquire title to land without the need for the usual procedure of serving **notice to treat**, investigating title and then taking a conveyance.

general warranty deed(US)   See **warranty deed**.

general words(Eng)   Words that were included in a conveyance to describe easements, and other rights and privileges that are appurtenant to the subject land and are to be transferred as part of the right to the land. Since 1882, any **conveyance** is deemed to transfer "… all buildings, erections, fixture …" and such other rights as are "enjoyed with, or reputed to be enjoyed with …" the land or buildings conveyed; and if there are buildings, "all outhouses, erections, fixtures …" that form part thereof and all "… liberties, privileges, easement, rights, and advantages whatsoever, appertaining or reputed to appertain to the land, houses, or other buildings conveyed … or any part thereof …", LPA 1925, s. 62; unless a contrary intention is expressed in the conveyance (*viz.* **conveyance** for more details). Thus, the grantee acquires not only anything attached to the land, and any easements and other rights that are **appurtenant** to the land, but also any **quasi-easement** or other privileges that at the time of the conveyance were being enjoyed with the land and are not expressly excluded. (It should be noted that general words

apply to a 'conveyance', whereas a quasi-easement also passes under a will or an agreement, and quasi-easements have to be continuous and apparent.)

generalibus verba sunt generaliter intelligenda(Lat)   'General **words** are to be understood generally (or in a general sense)'.

gentleman's agreement   **1.** A **bargain** made between two persons who regard each other as honourable and who are unlikely therefore, to renege on the arrangement, even though it may not be a legally binding contract. An agreement between men of supposedly respectable and honest character. See also **estoppel**, **subject to contract**.   **2.**(US)An agreement between a number of parties who are interested in a parcel of real estate (estate agents, property owners, landlords, etc.), designed to limit the availability of that property to certain groups of people; especially an agreement to preclude dealings with minorities in a given area or district. Such an agreement, being discriminatory, is an illegal practice under the Fair Housing Act, Title VIII of the Civil Rights Act of 1968 (42 USC § 3604).

geodetic surveying   Surveying that takes account of the size and curvature of the earth and its field of gravity. Geodetic surveys are normally made by reference to a series of official benchmarks set out across the country. cf. **plane surveying**. See also **bench mark**.

geodetic survey system   **1.**(US)The United States Coast and Geodetic Survey System. A system that comprises a network of official bench marks set out across the entire country and located by latitude and longitude on the earth's surface. This system was originally established to identify government land, but may now be used for survey of any area of land. A total of 22,227 National Geodetic Survey Monuments have been set out across the United States to show control stations as a source of primary horizontal survey control. These primary control monuments are used to establish the location of federal, state, and private surveys. See also **government survey system**. **2.**(Can)A survey system established to determine the positions (and elevations) of points throughout Canada with the highest attainable accuracy. In 1909, the Geodetic Survey of Canada was created by an order-in-council and the Geodetic Survey Division of government was given a mandate to maintain, continuously improve, and facilitate efficient access to what is now known as the Canadian Spatial Reference System (CRCS). The result is a national coordinate system which serves as a reference for all mapping, charting, navigation, boundary demarcation, crustal deformation, and other geo-referencing needs. See also **cadastral map**.

geographic information system (GIS) A computer-based system that is able to capture, store, analyse and display geographically-referenced information, i.e. data that can be identified according to a location. GIS also includes the procedures, personnel, as well as the data that goes into the system. The system has the ability to relate different information in a spatial context, to analyse and update that data, display it in a computer based or other form of display and to derive conclusion about the relationships between the information.

ghetto Derived from the Italian *ghetto*, which originates from *Ægyptus* Egypt. Originally an area to which Jews were restricted to live. A word apparently used first in Venice in 1516, although Jews had been confined to areas of various cities from a much earlier date, in order to prevent their influence on other religious communities, whether Christians in Europe or Muslims in North Africa. In modern usage a ghetto may be any urban area where a racial, social or minority group, or a particular nationality, other than the indigenous population, predominates. Any area where a socially or economically deprived group has been compelled to live as a result of social or financial pressures or because of discrimination against their acquiring homes in other areas. See also **blockbusting**, **redlining**.

ghost tenant A tenant in a shopping center who rarely, if ever, trades in the leased premises thus possibly depriving the landlord of a proper level of **turnover rent**.

gift Something given or bestowed on another without a price. A transfer without price or reward. A voluntary transfer of property from one person to another without any expectation of consideration or compensation, and without any intention of regaining dominion, control or title to the property. Any irrevocable transfer of property at a price that is deliberately low with the intention of conferring a gratuitous benefit may be considered as a gift, especially for taxation purposes. On the other hand, a transfer of property in anticipation of some future economic benefit, or when there is a proposal that the donor will regain some part or special benefit therefrom, does create a gift. A gift may be made *inter vivos* (between living persons); or *causa mortis* (in anticipation of death). A gift *inter vivos* must be effected by actual delivery during the lifetime of the donor, without reference to his or her death. A gift *causa mortis is* made in expectation of death, but does not become effective until the donor dies. A voluntary conveyance or assignment is commonly called a **deed of gift**. A gift may be conditional but it must not be revocable or terminable. A valid gift requires: (i) a voluntary intention to give by the donor, although evidence may be required of the intention; (ii) an act giving effect to that intention, such as the delivery of possession, either physically in the case of a personal chattel or by a repudiation of possession in favour of the recipient; and (iii) acceptance of the gift by the recipient (acceptance is normally presumed unless there is a signified rejection thereof; and (iv) because there is no valuable consideration to support the contract, the gift must be made by **deed**, or in the case of chattels, by **delivery** or some manifestation of delivery. A gift should be made with an intention of benefaction and there should be no intention that, in return, any benefit passes to the donor; the recipient should be free to enjoy the property received; and the recipient should not be restrained in the manner in which he may dispose of the property. If a gift is made without the proper formality, it may be enforceable only in a court of equity; as might arise from the doctrine of **estoppel**. See also **capital transfer tax**(Eng), **class gift**, **endowment**, **gift tax**, **grant**, **settlement**.

gift *causa mortis* A gift in the 'cause or view' of death'. A gift from a living person, who expects to die shortly, to another living person that is intended to take effect on the death of the donor. Usually used in reference to personal property. cf. **gift *inter vivos***. See also ***donatio mortis causa***.

gift deed A deed that transfers property without or for nominal consideration. See also **deed of gift**.

gift *inter vivos* A gift made between living persons. cf. **devise**, **gift *causa mortis***.

gift over A gift that follows a preceding but limited property interest. A gift of an estate that is limited to take effect following the termination of a prior estate, such as upon the expiry of a **life estate** or a determinable interest in land.

gift tax A tax on the assessed or deemed market value of a **gift** made during the donor's lifetime without relation to the death of the donor. A gift tax is levied on the donor at the time of the gift. In particular, a 'gift tax' may be distinguished from a **succession tax** or **estate tax** which is payable on the value of a deceased's estate, which may include gifts made in contemplation of death or to take effect after death. In the US, a gift tax is imposed on the donor each calendar year on the assessed value of any property that is transferred by gift, less an annual exemption. See also **inheritance tax**.

gilt-edged security or gilt-edged stock A security or bond of the highest standing. In particular, Government securities or securities of a statutory undertaking.

Ginnie Mae(US) A popular abbreviation for the **Government National Mortgage Association**.

give To make a **gift**. 'Give' is sometimes used in a conveyance or deed of transfer to indicate an intention to make an immediate transfer of title, often in combination with, or as a synonym for, such words as '**grant**', 'transfer' or 'convey'. See also **bequest**, **devise**.

give and take fence(Aus) A fence that is constructed around geographical features rather than the legal boundaries in order to enable the adjoining landowners to make a more practical use of the land and its resources. For example, a fence that is erected to allow one of the owners to access water on an other owner's land. The right to use the other owner's land is usually granted under a **tenancy at will** or subject to termination upon reasonable notice.

glebe land 1. Land that belongs to a parish church or glebe. Land that forms part of, or provides income to, a parish church, rectory, vicarage or ecclesiastical benefice (but not land that benefits from a **tithe**). See also **ecclesiastical property**. 2. In Roman law, a plot of uncultivated land.

global insurance See **blanket insurance**.

global positioning system (GPS) A techniques that is used to establish the position of reference points on or above the Earth. GPS can be used to determine the position of any object on or above the Earth's surface by using satellites and a series of fixed stations on the ground. The results can be used for mapping, military and defence observation, environmental observation and the recording of other Earth-related activities. See also **surveying**.

go dark provision(AmE) See **continuous operation clause**.

going-concern value The value of a business as an active operating entity. The value of a business assessed on the basis of its earning capacity or potential profit rather than the value of its tangible assets. The going-concern value may include the value, if any, of intangibles such as **goodwill** and any additional value to a special purchaser. cf. **break-up value**.

going-in capitalization rate(AmE)   The capitalization rate applied to the net operating income for the first year of the holding of a property or to the **stabilized net income**. cf. **terminal capitalization rate**. See also **internal rate of return**.

going value   1. The **market value** at the time a property is offered for sale.   2. The **going-concern value**.

gold clause(US)   A provision in a contract, bond or mortgage that payment is to be made in gold. Generally, a payment in US currency is now considered an appropriate alternative. However, if parties to a lease expressly agree to such a form of payment, it may still be enforceable.

good and clear title(US)   See **clear title**, **good title**.

good and indefeasible title(US)   A title that is good and clear of all defects and cannot be defeated by the claims of another, especially an adverse possessor, mortgagee or any similar claimant. See also **good title**.

good and merchantable title(US)   A title that is free from reasonable doubt; free of palpable defects; free of litigation; and would be accepted by a prudent purchaser, or mortgagee, who has knowledge of all the facts and their legal effects. See also **good title**, **marketable title**.

good condition   See **good repair**.

good consideration   Something given as a motive for an agreement or contract, but that has no tangible value. Good consideration may include love or affection, or a strong moral obligation, and although it may be a reasonable cause for the making of a promise or a contract, in common law it will not support an **executory contract**. In particular, 'good' consideration is used in contradistinction from 'valuable' consideration, but does not connote any form of moral attribute. See also **consideration**.

good estate management(Eng)   A term used in the Agriculture Act 1947, s. 10 for a standard to which agricultural land should be cultivated and maintained "having regard to the character and situation of the land and other relevant circumstances", and a standard to which fixed equipment must be repaired, improved and maintained. See also **good husbandry**, **management scheme**.

good faith   Honesty of intention, especially honesty of fact in a transaction. An intention that is devoid of any semblance of **fraud**, dishonesty, concealment or unfair motive. A purchaser 'in good faith' accepts that the vendor will transfer what he alleges he is selling without fraud and without the purchaser having to make his own searching enquiries, other than those that are required by law, prudence or custom. In the context of a **mistaken improver** or 'good faith improver' of land, 'good faith' requires an honesty of purpose and freedom from fraudulent intent.

A duty to act in good faith is owed particularly by an **agent** or **broker** to his principal. Thus, for an agent or broker to endeavour to receive a secret profit or to obtain **commission** from, or act for, two parties without declaring his position would be a breach of good faith.

In the US, in relation to a claim to **adverse possession** under color of title, good faith has been defined as being used "in its popular sense, as the actual existing state of mind, whether so from ignorance, skepticism (sic), sophistry, delusion, or imbecility, and without regard to what it should be from given legal standards of law or reason", Wright v. Mattison, 59 US 50, 15 L Ed 280, 284 (1855) (3 Am.Jur.2d., Adverse Possession, § 133, p. 218, Necessity of good faith). cf. **bad faith**. See also *bona fide* **purchaser**, **fiduciary**, **utmost good faith**.

good faith estimate(US)   An estimate, or disclosure, of the settlement charges that a mortgagor is likely to incur at closing. See also **closing costs, settlement statement**.

good faith improver(US) See **compensation for improvements, mistaken improver**.

good-faith money   See **earnest money**.

good faith purchaser   See *bona fide* purchaser.

good husbandry(Eng)   A term used in the Agriculture Act 1986, s. 11 for a standard of management and efficiency of production required from an agricultural unit taking into account the kind of produce and the quality and quantity thereof. This standard includes, as applicable, proper grazing, mowing, cultivation, maintenance of fertility, proper tending of livestock, control of pests and disease, protection and preservation of harvested or lifted crops and general maintenance and repair, as well as **good estate management**. A tenant of an agricultural holding is under no statutory obligation to abide by the rules of good husbandry, unless expressly committed by the terms of a lease, but a failure to observe the rules may constitute grounds for the Agricultural Land Tribunal to approve a landlord's notice to quit. See also **grounds for possession, husband-like manner**.

good leasehold title(Eng)   Title to a leasehold interest that may be registered with the Land Registry when that title is satisfactory to the registrar, but does not amount to an **absolute title** because there is no assurance that the lessor has a valid right to grant the lease. "A person may be registered with good leasehold title if the registrar is of the opinion that the person's title to the estate is such that a willing buyer could properly be advised by a competent professional adviser to accept", LRA 2002, s. 10(3)). A good leasehold title is held subject to any estate, interest or right which may affect the freehold title or any superior leasehold title, but in other respects has the same effect as registration with an absolute title. See also **derogation from grant, estoppel, qualified title, possessory title**.

good marketable title   See **good title**.

good record title(US)   A title that is free of any publicly recorded encumbrance and has been recorded as having an unbroken **root of title**. In particular, a fee title that is free of any liens, encumbrances or claims. Sometimes called a 'sufficient title'. See also **good title**.

good repair   The sort of condition in which a fair minded tenant would maintain a property, but not necessarily what the landlord might like (*Cooke v Cholmondeley* (1858) 4 Drew 326, 328, 62 Eng Rep 126). In general, a term in a lease that uses the words 'good repair' or 'good and substantial repair' requires a tenant to maintain the property in as satisfactory a condition as another tenant would expect of the same property, but not better. It excludes major structural repair, alterations or any improvement required to the leased property; but does not exclude *putting* a property into a good state of repair, having regard to the age and class of building. Good repair is generally synonymous with **tenantable repair**, the latter term merely emphasizing that the standard of repair should be judged by that which would be required by an incoming tenant.

In the US, expressions such as 'good condition', 'sufficient repair' or 'first class repair' have been held not to radically change the required standard of repair. Also, the duration of the lease, the type of property and other considerations should be taken into account when interpreting such words, including the use to which the property is put (Green v. Eden, 2 Thomp & C 582 (1875); Lehmaier v. Jones, 100 App Div 495, 91 NYS 687, 689 (1905)). See also **habitable**.

good root of title   See **root of title**.

good tenantable repair   See **tenantable repair**.

good title   1.(US)A valid and marketable title. A title that is free of any litigation or palpable defect and based on the records from which it is derived, would be acceptable to a reasonable purchaser, or mortgagee as security for a loan. 'Good title' is generally considered to be synonymous with **marketable title**. Although, in several cases, the latter has been considered to be one that may or should be acceptable to a purchaser, but one that may not necessarily be acceptable to a title insurance company. See also **good record title**, **perfect title**.   2.(Eng)A **title** that may not be perfect, but enables a person to retain possession of land against any person who might present a challenge to that title; one that is free of reasonable doubt as to its legality; and can be transferred or mortgaged without fear or favour. In particular, a title that a court would accept as sufficient to grant a decree of **specific performance.** A title that would enable a purchaser to hold the property against anyone who might challenge his right to it. Also called a 'good marketable title', especially when the property can be sold without special conditions of sale that are restrictive of the purchaser's rights. See also **absolute title, beneficial owner, deposit, good leasehold title, root of title**.

goods   That which a person has at his disposal. All forms of movable property. Anything that is tangible, can be moved and has an intrinsic value, but usually excluding **money** or a 'chose in action' (company shares, debts and the like). Goods may refer to all forms of **personal property**, or it may be used in a more limited sense, such as to refer to 'household' goods, or items that may be severed from real property, e.g. crops and tenant's fixtures. 'Goods', unless the context indicates to the contrary, does not include animals, 'chattels real' (i.e. a leasehold), or a **fixture** (as that which has become part of the realty). In economics, goods may include anything of value, as where the reference is to the allocation of 'goods and services'. See also **chattels, chose, effects, movables, personal property**.

goodwill or **good will**   The favourable consideration that the proprietor of a business has won from the public. The benefits derived by a business as a consequence of an established and active trade. The value of a business over and above the value of a similar business, due to the profits that arise from the probability that customers will return to where they are accustomed to doing business or trade. Goodwill may arise from constant or habitual customers; the local position of a property; or such aspects as a reputation for skill or punctuality of service; or even from ancient partialities or prejudices. This *incremental* **profit** may be produced by the proprietor's personal abilities, or the general reputation and efficiency of the business – 'personal goodwill'; or the convenience of the location of the business to its customers – 'local or locational goodwill'; or the value brought about as a result of a monopoly position held by a business. An advantageous position that, in the short term, should be sustained by a new proprietor operating from the same premises or from new premises in close proximity. Goodwill is an intangible asset, of an indefinite life, which attaches to the name, the proprietor, the property, an employee or other more tangible parts of a business. It has no inherent value, although a property may appear to have a value in excess of its market value due to the goodwill of the occupier. Fundamentally, goodwill is a personal asset rather than something inherent in the value of a property. Goodwill is a form of **personal property**, it does not automatically pass with a transfer of land, but it may be transferred separately or with the premises from which it is generated. It cannot be sold or transferred apart from the business to which it relates and, even though it has been acquired at a considerable price, goodwill is ephemeral and must be nurtured by the new owner.

Goodwill is normally valued on the basis of the historic net profit of a business, after making adjustments for non-recurring or special items. Businesses are commonly sold on the basis of one to five times the 'adjusted net profit'. Goodwill may be assessed also by reference to the difference between the **going-concern value** of an enterprise and the replacement or **break-up value** of the entire enterprise. See also **business tenancy**[(Eng)], **compensation for disturbance**[(Eng)], **consequential damages**[(US)].

gore **1.** A small, usually triangular or roughly triangular, parcel of land. **2.**[(AmE)]A gap between two parcels of land, especially a small disputed area of land situated between and dividing two larger tracts of land.

gouging Extracting an exorbitant sum from someone; extorting an excessive price by trickery, cheating, threats, deception or an unfair advantage, e.g. obtaining a rent that grossly exceeds the market value. See also **duress**, **fine**, **premium**, **unconscionable bargain**, **undue influence**.

government lot[(US)] A quarter section of land that incorporates a lake, stream or similar feature and, therefore, comprises less than 160 acres of dry land. Such parcels are identified by lot number instead of by the conventional grid reference. See also **government survey system**, **section of land**.

Government National Mortgage Association (GNMA or Ginnie Mae)[(US)] A federal agency within the Department of Housing and Urban Development that was established in 1968 under provisions of the Housing and Urban Development Act primarily to take over "special assistance" loans of the **Federal National Mortgage Association**, i.e. loans made by FNMA at below market interest rates. In 1968 Ginnie Mae was separated from FNMA as a wholly-owned federal government association (whereas FNMA was established at the same time as a private corporation). Ginnie Mae's aim is to link the capital markets and the Federal housing market to facilitate secondary mortgage activities for federally insured or guaranteed mortgages. In particular, it specializes in purchasing loans that are difficult to sell in the private market, such as loans to those on low incomes, in distressed areas, in urban renewal projects, on Indian reservations and in Guam. It also provides guarantees to the investors who acquire mortgage-backed securities as issued by thrifts and commercial and mortgage banks provided they are federally insured or guaranteed, e.g. FHA-insured, FmHA-insured, or VA-guaranteed. The certificates that represent these guarantees are also called 'Ginnie Maes'. See also **mortgage-backed security**. (**www.ginniemae.gov**).

government survey system or **governmental survey system**[(US)] A system of land measurement and identification, established by Act of Congress in 1785, for the locating and selling of the Northwest Territory, the 'western lands' (Illinois, Indiana, Ohio, Michigan and Wisconsin). The system (now called the United States Government Survey) operates in Alabama, Florida, all states north of the Ohio river and all states west of the Mississippi, except Texas. It is based on an official survey, set out on a grid that is related to the earth's longitudinal and latitudinal lines. The grid consists of 34 'principal or primary meridian lines' (running north and south) and 32 'base lines' (running east and west). From the intersection of these lines, land tracts are marked off into squares of 24 miles called 'quadrangles'. These areas are then subdivided into 16 grids of six-mile squares (36 square miles or 23,040 acres) called a **township**. A line or column of townships running north-south is called a 'range' and ranges are numbered east and west from the principal meridian. A column of townships running east-west is called a 'tier', being numbered north and south from the base line. A tier may also be called a 'range'. Townships are also numbered north and south from the base line. Townships are further subdivided into 36 'sections', each of one square mile or 640 acres, which are technically the smallest parts of the system; although sections may be divided into 'quarter sections' of 160 acres, 'half-quarter sections' of 80 acres, or 'quarter-quarter sections' of 40 acres (which are the smallest statutory division of the system). These areas are then identified by reference to the principal meridian, the numbered range, the numbered Township, and then by compass references for the quarters and sub-divisions thereof. Further subdivision can be made by a licensed surveyor preparing a 'Plat of Subdivision' dividing the tracts into blocks, separated by streets and alleys, and then subdividing the blocks into 'lots'. Also called the 'public lands survey system (PLSS)' or the 'rectangular survey system'. See also **geodetic survey system, metes and bounds system, section of land, surveying**.

governmental act(US)   See **statute law**.

grace period   See **days of grace**.

grade   1. The lay of the land relative to adjoining land. The mean elevation of the nearest street line (usually at its center line) or of the ground adjoining a building.   2. The slope of land relative to the horizontal, usually expressed in percentage terms.   3. To cut and fill land to a given line that is usually fixed relative to a street or highway.

graded lease   A lease incorporating a **graded rent**.

graded rent   1. A rent that increases (or decreases) at specified intervals in accordance with the provisions of a lease, e.g. $1,000 in year one, $2,000 in year two, $3,000 for the remaining term of a lease. Also called a 'stepped rent', particularly in the UK. See also **graduated rent**.   2.(US)A rent, being paid for a property, that can be used as a comparable figure for valuation purposes, after adjustments to take account of size, location, age, etc. See also **comparable property**.

graduated lease(US)   See **graduated-rental lease**.

graduated-payment   adjustable mortgage loan (GPAML)   See **variable-payment mortgage**.

graduated-payment mortgage (GPM) See **variable-payment mortgage**.

graduated rent(US)   A rent that may be varied at set intervals during the term of a lease, usually starting below and then increasing at set stages until it reaches the market rental value. Also used synonymously with any form of variable rent, including a **graded rent** or a rent in a **reappraisal lease**. cf. **flat rent**. See also **step-up rent**.

graduated-rental lease(US)   A lease that contains provisions for a **graduated rent** i.e. a rent that increases at set intervals during the term of the lease. Also called a 'graduated lease', or a 'step-up lease' or 'step-down lease'.

grandfather clause(AmE)   A clause in a new statute or regulation that exempts an existing condition, business or occupation from the provisions of the new law or regulation. An **existing use** of property is said to be 'grandfathered' when it remains authorized, even though it would now be prohibited by law. In particular, a development that was authorized and has commenced under old legislation, but has not been completed and would require to be modified if started again. Sometimes called a 'saving clause'. See also **non-conforming use, vested right**.

grandfathered(US)   To have the benefit of a **grandfather clause**.

grange   1. A building where corn is stored; a granary or barn.   2. A farm house or country house with farm buildings attached. See also **curtilage**.

grant   1. To give, bestow or confer a right, power or privilege on someone.   2. To transfer an interest in land without actual physical delivery of possession, especially a right to incorporeal property, such as an **easement** or **profit à prendre**. 'Grant' is used especially to refer to a transfer of a right that is less than that held by the grantor, as with a **lease**. The word may be used in this sense as a verb or noun. The term **convey** is now more commonly used to refer to a transfer a right to real property. cf. **reservation**. See also **deed, derogation from grant, express grant, general words**(Eng)**, grant bargain**

sell and convey, implied grant, incorporeal hereditament, livery, lost modern grant, words of grant[US]. **3.** A solemn deed that transfers land from a sovereign state to an individual. In the US, a 'public grant' is a transfer of land from the government of the United States, or any particular state, to an individual. In particular, a transfer of title to land to a settler on land. See also **Crown grant, land grant**[US]. **4.**[US]In the states of California, Idaho, North Dakota and South Dakota, the use of the word 'grant' implies certain **covenants for title**. See also **bargain and sale deed**. **5.**[Aus]A transfer of a **Crown land** in fee simple or by a long-term lease (Transfer of Land Act 1893 (WA), s. 4(1)). **6.** Public monies provided for some private purpose. Financial assistance given by a public authority for a particular purpose, such as a contribution towards the cost of repairing or improving a building, improving the environment or stimulating employment. See also **mitigation work, subsidy**.

grant and demise　See **demise**.

grant bargain sell and convey　**1.** Words used in a **conveyance** to indicate that the clause thereafter forms the **operative part** of the deed, e.g. 'the vendor hereby grants unto A'. In English law since 1925 **convey** is the word more normally used in an instrument to transfer land. **2.**[US]The words 'grant, bargain, and sell' or 'grant, bargain, sell, and convey' are used in some jurisdictions in a conveyance as an indication that the grantor is giving the 'usual' **covenants of title**, but not a covenant for further assurance or a covenant to transfer an after-acquired title. Although, in a few jurisdictions, following the common law, they are only introductory words and imply no covenants of title; or, at most, that the grantor has an indefeasible estate in fee simple and has not himself impaired the title. Nonetheless, the use of such words may be considered redundant as the use of the word **grant**, or **convey**, alone is generally sufficient. See also **warranty deed**.

grant deed[US]　**1.** See **deed of grant, warranty deed**. **2.** A simple form of **deed**, used especially in California, Idaho, and North and South Dakota, to transfer a fee simple (unless stated to the contrary) and which states that the vendor has a valid title to the property he is conveying. In a grant deed the use of the word '**grant**' implies certain statutory **covenants of title**.

grant of probate　See **probate**.

grant of representation　See **probate**.

granted land[Aus]　Land in Queensland that has been granted to a group of Aboriginal people or Torres Strait Islanders. The right to such land is approved by the Commonwealth Minister after a recommendation from the Land Tribunal and the land should then be transferred as a fee simple title to trustees to be held for the benefit of the relevant Aboriginal people or the Torres Strait Islanders. However, mineral and petroleum rights are reserved to the Crown and in certain circumstances forestry and quarry materials are reserved to the State. Such land should be distinguished from land claimed by **native title** as 'granted land' is claimed in accordance with statutory provisions, whereas native title claims arise from the laws and customs of the Aboriginal peoples.

granted lands[US]　See **indemnity lands**.

grantee　The party to whom a **grant** of property is made, usually a buyer. The party in a deed to whom a conveyance is made. Although 'grantee' may be considered to be synonymous with **assigns**, a 'grantee' takes a transfer of any right to property, whereas 'assigns' take a right to property that was held by another, as with a transfer to a trustee, agent or the transfer of a lease. See also **assignee**.

granting clause[US]　The clause of a deed of **conveyance** that confirms the transfer of the subject property from the grantor to the grantee. The clause that sets out the property and rights thereover that are being transferred. See also **grant, habendum**.

grantor The person who makes a **grant** of property; one who conveys real property. See also **vendor**.

grantor trust 1.(US)See **passive trust**. 2. A form of legal trust created for the purpose of a **mortgage-backed security**, or any other form of asset-backed security, by which the investors are treated for taxation purposes as if they were the owners of a direct interest in the assets. Investors in the securitized transaction are deemed to own an undivided interest in the pool of mortgaged properties and receive a pro-rate share of the mortgage payments of interest and principal. This form of trust enables the income to be divided into tranches or 'strips' as the source of the income can be identified for taxation purposes.

grantor's lien See **lien**.

grantor-grantee index(US) A master index maintained in the public recorder's office showing alphabetically, and under the names of the grantor and grantee, all recorded instruments for the transfer of the ownership of land. The index is maintained by reference to book, or 'liber', numbers and page, or 'folio', numbers and it is normally classified by year, as well as by the names of the grantor and grantee. Sometimes called a 'names index'.

grasson or **grassum** 1.(Eng)A **fine** that was paid for the right to transfer a copyhold estate. See also **feudal system**. 2.(Scot)A premium paid in lieu of or in addition to rent.

gratis(Lat) 'Without reward'; 'without consideration'. See also **gift**.

gratuitous contract A **contract** that transfers a benefit without any legal consideration, or without any cost to the donor. See also **gift**.

grazing licence(Eng) A right to use land for pasture or mowing for part of the year. Under the Agricultural Holding Act 1986, s. 2, a tenancy of agricultural land granted for a term that is less than 'from year to year' is converted to a **tenancy from year to year** and, thereby, is given **security of tenure**. However, this provision does not apply to "an agreement for the letting of land, or the granting of a **licence** to occupy land" made (expressly or impliedly) "in contemplation of the use of land for grazing or mowing (or both) during some specified period of a year", AHA 1986, s. 2(3). In this context such a letting may be referred to as a 'seasonal grazing licence' or a 'grazing licence'. See also **agricultural tenancy**, **right of common**.

grazing right A right to graze animals on another's land. Such a right may be granted as a **licence** or may be considered as a **profit à prendre**. See also **grazing licence**(Eng), **right of common**.

green(Eng) An area of public open land situated in or near a town or village and put down to grass. At common law, a town or village green may be common land; but for registration purposes it is defined and treated separately from 'common land'. "Town or village green means [a] land which has been allotted by or under any Act for the exercise or recreation of the inhabitants of any locality or [b] on which the inhabitants of any locality have a customary right to indulge in lawful sports or pastimes or [c] on which the inhabitants of any locality have indulged in such sport or pastimes as of right for not less than twenty years", Commons Registration Act 1965, s. 22(1). Thus, the statutory definition covers lawful games, pastimes or recreational activities available to local inhabitants of a parish, manor or similar district, and land that is commonly referred to as a town or village green (*R v Oxfordshire County Council, ex parte Sunningwell* [2000] 1 AC 325, [1999] 31 EG 85, 88, [1999] 3 All ER 385 (HL)). The ownership of such land is usually obscure, but it was probably waste land of a **manor** that became vested in the local inhabitants or a local body. In England and Wales land that is used as a town or village green must be registered with a county or metropolitan council or the council of the London borough, in the 'register of town and village greens'. When such land is registered it becomes common land, preserving that right of common enjoyment in perpetuity, even if the ownership may remain uncertain.

Clayden, Paul A. *Our Common Land: the law and history of common land and village greens.* 5th ed. Henley-on-Thames, Oxon: Open Spaces Society, 2003.

Ubhi, Navjit, and Barry Denyer-Smith. *Law of Commons and of Town and Village Greens.* Bristol: Jordans, 2003.

green belt 1.(Eng)An expanse of countryside, surrounding or between towns or cities, in which development is prohibited or strictly controlled, with the intention of restraining the outward sprawl of urban development and preserving agricultural land. A term that originates from the Green Belt (London and Home Counties) Act 1938 that was passed "to make provisions for the preservation from industrial and building development of areas of land" in and around London. A green belt is intended to provide also an area of countryside for the leisure and recreation of urban residents; therefore, it is an area which, by its nature, creates a conflict between the demands of urban dwellers and the farmer. See also **access agreement**, **buffer zone**, **garden city**, **open country**. 2.(US)Landscaped or green areas that encompass a property that is held in some form of co-ownership, especially such **common areas** in a **planned unit development**.

green field site See **unimproved land**.

greenlining(US) A policy employed by organizations granting residential mortgages by which certain neighborhoods are identified for favorable consideration and in which business is actively sought. cf. **redlining**.

greenhouse A building constructed with a supporting frame, but otherwise made entirely of glass, that is used for the propagation and raising of plants, flowers and vegetables for display, sale or planting out during periods of favourable weather. See also **right of light**.

greenways Strips of landscaped land either alongside a highway or linked together in a built-up area.

grey area(Eng) See **intermediate area**.

grey property(Eng) See **clearance area**.

grid planning or **gridiron planning** A town or estate layout based on rectangular street blocks. The common form of layout of many US cities. See also **government survey system**, **lot and block system**.

gross Exclusive of any deduction; entire. A right to land **in gross** is one that is independent of anything else, i.e. it is not appurtenant, appendant or otherwise annexed to land. See also **easement in gross**.

gross adjusted income See **effective gross income**.

gross annual income The total income receivable from a property in any particular year, before any deductions. See also **gross income**.

gross area See gross building area(US), gross external area(BrE), gross internal area(BrE), gross leasable area/gross lettable area(US), gross site area(BrE).

gross building area (GBA) 1.(US)The total enclosed area of a constructed building, measured in a horizontal plan to the limit of the external structural elements, and including all floor areas, whether above or below ground. In particular, the total area of an office building "computed by measuring to the outside finished surface of permanent outer building walls, without any deductions. All enclosed floors of the building, including basements, garages, mechanical equipment floors, penthouses and the like, are calculated. Gross building area is sometimes referred to as 'construction area' in the industry", Building Owners and Managers Association

International (BOMA), *Standard Method for Measuring Floor Area in Office Buildings* (1996). If the built area bows out from an otherwise straight building line this area is included, but where a bay window bows out beyond an otherwise straight building line, that line is continued to exclude the window bay (to avoid misinterpretation see BOMA's complete *Standard Method for Measuring Floor Area in Office Buildings* ©1996; www.boma.org). Gross building area is not to be used for leasing purposes, except where an entire building is leased to a single tenant. See also **gross external area**(BrE). **2.**(Aus) "The total enclosed and unenclosed area of the building at all building floor levels measured between the normal outside face of enclosing walls, balustrades and supports", Australian Property Institute and Property Council for Australia, *Glossary of Property Terms* (2000).

gross density(US)   See **exclusionary density**.

gross earnings   See **gross income**.

gross easement(US)   See **easement in gross**.

gross effective income(US)   See **effective gross income**.

gross external area (GEA)(BrE)   "The area of a building measured externally at each floor level. INCLUDING (1) Perimeter wall thicknesses and external projections; (2) Areas occupied by internal walls and partitions; (3) Columns, piers, chimney-breasts, stairwells, lift-wells, and the like; (4) Atria with clear height above, measured at base level only; (5) Internal balconies; (6) structural, raked or stepped floors are to be treated as a level floor measured horizontally; (7) Horizontal floors, whether accessible or not, below structural, raked or stepped floors; (8) Mezzanine areas intended for use with permanent access; (9) lift rooms, plant rooms, fuel stores, tank rooms which are housed in a structure of a permanent nature whether or not above main roof level; (10) Outbuildings which share at least one wall with the main building; (11)

Loading bays; (12) Areas with a headroom of less than 1.5m; (13) Pavement vaults; (14) Garages; (15) Conservatories; [and] EXCLUDING (16) External open-sided balconies, covered ways and fire escapes; (17) Canopies; (18) Open vehicle parking areas, roof terraces and the like; (19) Voids over or under structural, raked or stepped floors; (20) Greenhouses, garden stores, fuel stores, and the like in residential property", The Royal Institution of Chartered Surveyor, *Code of Measuring Practice*. 5th ed. London: RICS Books, 2002. Certain areas such as (4), (9) to (15) and (17) to (20) may be better stated separately. Party walls in shared ownership are to be measured to their centre line (Note: this definition is accompanied in the *Code* by diagrams and detailed notes for amplification. The *Code* is intended for use in the UK only and is intended to aid understanding of area measurements.) Gross external area is used particularly in town planning, e.g. for assessing site coverage (including **plot ratio**); for council tax banding of houses and bungalows in England and Wales (when areas with a headroom of less than 1.5m are excluded); and for rating of warehouses and industrial buildings in Scotland; and for building cost estimating of residential property for insurance purposes. See also **gross internal area**(BrE), **gross building area**(US).

gross floor area   The total of all floor areas in a building, measured from the outside of the external walls, including any floor areas that project beyond the main building line. See also **gross building area**(US), **gross external area**(BrE), **gross internal area**(BrE), **gross leasable area**(US).

gross income   **1.** The total **income** receivable from a business or investment before making any deduction for expenses, management charges, taxes, etc., or any allowance for bad debts, depreciation or payment of debt.   **2.** The total income collected by a property owner before deducting any expenses or outgoings. cf. **net income**. See also **effective gross income, gross operating income**(US), **gross rent**.   **3.** The total income received by a tenant as used to determine a **percentage rent**. As a rule, this represents the income from all sales, including concessionaires, vending machines, etc., but excluding sales taxes and any deductions agreed between the landlord and tenant. Sometimes called 'gross sales'.

gross income multiplier (GIM)[US]   See **income multiplier**.

gross internal area (GIA)[BrE]   "The area of a building measured to the internal face of the perimeter walls at each floor level. INCLUDING (1) Areas occupied by internal walls, and partitions; (2) Columns, piers, chimney-breasts, stairwells, lift-wells, other internal projections, vertical ducts and the like; (3) Atria with clear height above, measured at base level only; (4) Internal open-sided balconies and the like; (5) Structural, raked or stepped floors are to be treated as a level floor measured horizontally; (6) Horizontal floors, with permanent access, low structural, raked or stepped floors; (7) Corridors of a permanent essential nature (e.g. fire corridors, smoke lobbies, etc.); (8) Mezzanine areas intended for use with permanent access; (9) Lift rooms, plant rooms, fuel stores, tank rooms, which are housed in a structure of a permanent nature, whether or not above main-roof level; (10) Service accommodation such as toilets, toilet lobbies, bathrooms, showers, changing rooms, cleaners' cupboards and the like; (11) Projection rooms; (12) Voids over stairwells and lift shafts, on upper floors (state separately); (13) Loading bays; (14) Areas with a headroom of less than 1.5m; (15) Pavement vaults; (16) Garages; (17) Conservatories. EXCLUDING (18) Perimeter wall thicknesses and external projections; (19) External open-sided balconies, covered ways and fire escapes; (20) Canopies; (21) Voids over or under structural, raked or stepped floors; (22) Greenhouses, garden stores, fuel stores, and the like in residential property", The Royal Institution of Chartered Surveyor, *Code of Measuring Practice*. 5th ed. London: RICS Books, 2002. Certain areas such as (3), (4), (5), (7), (9), (12), (13) and (20) may be better stated separately (Note: this definition is accompanied in the *Code* by diagrams and detailed notes for amplification. The *Code* is

intended for use in the UK only and is intended to aid understanding of area measurements.) A measurement used particularly in building cost estimation; estate agency and valuation of industrial buildings (including ancillary offices), warehouses, retail warehouses, department stores, variety stores and food superstores; service charge apportionment of occupier's liability; for new homes development appraisal purposes (excluding garages and conservatories); and in England and Wales, for rating assessment of industrial buildings (including ancillary offices), warehouses, retail warehouses, department stores, variety stores and food superstores and for many specialist classes of property that are valued by reference to building cost (i.e. on the 'contractor's use basis'). See also **rentable area**[US].

gross leasable area or **gross lettable area** (GLA)[AmE]   The total area of a shopping center used and occupied by tenants – excluding all common areas such as restrooms, mall corridors or pedestrian walkways, mechanical areas, car parking, and any area used for any non-retail use such as offices, apartments, etc. In particular, the 'gross leasable area' is "the measurement used to define how much space a tenant has leased in a center. GLA is determined by measuring the distance between the middle walls of space and the distance between front outside wall to back outside wall", International Council of Shopping Centers, *Keys to Shopping Center Management Series*, 1992; "the total floor area designated for tenant occupancy and exclusive use, including basements, mezzanines, and upper floors. It is measured from the center line of joint partitions and from outside wall faces. In short, GLA is that area on which tenants pay rent; it is the area that produces income", Robert J. Flynn (editor). *Carpenter's Shopping Center Management: Principles and Practices*. New York: International Council of Shopping Centers, 1984. See also **retail area**[BrE], **sales area**[US].

gross lease[US]   A lease that provides that the lessee pays only a fixed rent throughout the term of the lease, without any 'pass-through' of building expenses, i.e. the lease has no **escalation clause** and, therefore, the lessor pays all of the building operating expenses and repairs, real property taxes, insurance premiums, etc. However, the tenant is responsible for utilities and other expenses directly relating to the space he occupies. In some cases, even though some of the expenses are passed through to the tenant the lease may be called a 'gross lease'. Most apartment and some office leases are gross leases and most industrial and shop leases are net leases. Sometimes called a 'fixed lease'. cf. **net lease**. See also **straight lease**.

gross lettable area   See gross leasable area.

gross multiplier(US)   See income multiplier.

gross operating income (GOI)(AmE)   The total income generated by a real estate investment at a particular point in time, or for a particular year, before any deductions or allowances, including gross rent, operating expense contributions, license fees, etc. cf. **net operating income**. See also **effective gross income, gross income**.

gross potential(US)   See **potential gross income**.

gross population density   See **population density**.

gross profit   The profit from the sale of goods or services before the deduction of selling and administrative expenses; the profit obtained by deducting cost of goods from the actual sales price received before the deduction of expenses. cf. **net profit**.

gross redemption yield   See grossed-up redemption yield.

gross rent   The total amount payable as **rent** by all the tenants of a property, excluding any other payments, e.g. taxes, operating expenses, etc., that a tenant may be bound to pay to the landlord under the terms of a lease, and before any allowance or deduction is made for voids or defaulting tenants. In the US, gross rent and **gross income** are frequently used interchangeably, but in the UK, gross rent normally refers only to payments that are strictly rent (compensation for the use and profit to be derived from land) and does not embrace other payments made by a tenant to his landlord, such as service charge contributions. cf. **net rent**.

gross rent multiplier (GRM)(US)   See income multiplier.

gross residential density   See residential density.

gross sale price   The total consideration received by the vendor from the purchaser of a property, excluding any deduction for selling costs, fees, taxes, etc. cf. **net price**.

gross sales   See gross income.

gross site area (GSA)(BrE)   "The **site area** of a parcel of land, plus any area of adjoining roads, enclosed by extending the boundaries of the site up to the centre of the road, or 6m out from the frontage, whichever is less", The Royal Institution of Chartered Surveyor, *Code of Measuring Practice*. 5th ed. London: RICS Books, 2002. The gross site area is used as a basis for planning density control, especially for industrial and warehouse buildings. See also *ad medium filum*, **floor space index**.

gross value   1. The **capital value** of a property excluding all costs of acquiring the property, i.e. the value assuming the purchaser acquires the property free of all costs, as distinguished from the **net value** which is the value to the purchaser after deducting all costs of purchase.   2.(Eng)The value of the estate of a deceased person prior to any deduction for debts, incumberances, funeral expenses and inheritance tax (Non-Contentious Probate Rules 1954, s. 2 (SI 1954/796)).

gross yield   The return available on an

investment after deducting all costs associated with acquiring and managing the investment. cf. **net yield**.

ground floor   The floor nearest the ground level at the place of entrance or exit from a building. Where a building has two entrance levels these are commonly referred to as the upper and lower ground floors. See also **ground storey**(BrE)/ **ground story**(AmE), **first floor**.

ground landlord   The grantor of a **ground lease**; one who receives a ground rent.

ground lease   A lease of land without any building; although the lease may be 'secured' by a building or buildings erected by the lessee at a later date. A ground lease is usually granted subject to a condition that the lessee will build upon the land (in which case it may also be called a **building lease**). The lessee retains the right to the use and occupation of the building erected on the land for the term of the lease.

At common law, at the end of the lease, the land together with the improvements, reverts to the lessor. Nonetheless, in English law and in some jurisdictions in North America, there are statutory provisions that grant the ground lessee the right to acquire the landlord's interest or to extend the lease without paying for the full value of the improvements.

Ground leases are generally granted for a long term. Traditionally, ground leases were granted for 99 years, although in the UK modern ground leases are now usually granted for 125 years. In several jurisdictions in the US, the lease term is restricted to 99 years, as any lease for more than 100 years grants the right to the fee simple. The ground lessor may be a freeholder or one who is himself a lessee. See also **emphyteotic lease**, **enfranchisement**, **ground rent**, **ground rent lease**(US), **leasehold enfranchisement**(Eng), **leasehold ground rent**, **net lease**.

ground rent   A sum of money payable on an annual basis for the right to use and enjoy a parcel of land that belongs to another; **rent** payable for land that is leased for the purpose of improvement by building. 'Ground rent' may be used to refer to rent payable under a **ground lease** or a **building lease** (usually for a substantial term of years), or a rent based on the value of land excluding buildings and improvements. (In the UK, the difference between the rent of land with the improvements and the rent of a bare site before improvement may be called the 'improved ground rent'.)

In the US, in some jurisdictions, 'ground rent' may refer to a **rentcharge**, i.e. a payment reserved as an annuity by a grantor of a fee title. It may even be used to refer to rent payable under a long lease that is renewable forever, which is also called a **ground rent lease**. However, in modern practical terms, ground rent is generally used as a payment under a form of financing arrangement where the lessor has a form of secured interest in unimproved land and the lessee pays for most of what is necessary to develop the land and protect the lessor's role as a passive investor. Such a ground lease is often calculated as a percentage of income from the development or business that the ground lease is used to finance. See also **economic rent**, **leasehold ground rent**, **low rent**(Eng), **modern ground rent**(Eng), **security of ground rent**.

ground rent lease(US)   An arrangement found in Maryland (and a few other jurisdictions) by which the lessee is granted a lease of an area of land, usually for 99 years at a small rent, with the tenant having the right to renew the lease indefinitely, provided he pays a specified (usually nominal) sum of money for that right. The renewal payment is sometimes called a 'renewal fine'. The right is usually granted by the owner of the fee in return for an agreed rent, with the lessee paying all real estate taxes. If the lessee defaults in payment of the ground rent, the lessor has a right to evict the lessee; thus, the right is regarded as personal property and not a real interest in land. In most jurisdictions where such perpetual leases were created, the lessee has a statutory right to redeem the lease by paying the lessor the value of his interest. In Pennsylvania, under a similar form of arrangement, the land is conveyed, subject to the payment of a rent which thus represents a form of deferred purchase price, but the ground rent is considered more in the nature of realty and more akin to a common law **rentcharge**. See also **ground lease**.

ground storey(Eng) or **ground story**(AmE) The storey of a building to which there is an entrance from the outside on or near the ground level and, where there are two such stories, the lower of the two. The compartment of a building between the **ground floor** and **first floor**. See also **mezzanine**.

grounds for possession(Eng) The grounds available to a landlord to enable him to apply to the court in order to obtain possession of property from a tenant who has statutory **security of tenure**. English statute law provides most tenants of residential, business, and agricultural properties with a right either to the grant of a new tenancy, or to protection from **eviction**, when an existing tenancy comes to its contractual end.

A court will not grant an order for possession of a dwelling-house that is a **regulated tenancy** (or, as it was called prior to 1980, a **protected tenancy**), unless: (a) the court considers it reasonable; and either (b) the court is satisfied that **suitable alternative accommodation** is available to the tenant (or will be available to the tenant when the order takes effect); or (c) the court is satisfied that one of the statutory Cases is met (Rent Act 1977, s. 98). In certain Cases the court has a discretionary right to decide whether or not to grant an order for possession; the onus of proof being on the landlord to show reason for his being granted possession. In the other Cases the court is obliged to grant possession, without the overriding consideration of reasonableness. These Cases include a former 'owner-occupier' seeking to regain possession of a residence for his own or his family's occupation; premises that have been let on a **protected shorthold tenancy**, or an **assured shorthold tenancy**, that has now expired; and certain special types of letting, such as premises required for a retirement home; holiday homes

let out of season; students lettings out of term-time; premises required for a Minister of Religion; premises required for an agricultural employee; and lettings to members of the armed forces. In the first two instances (an 'owner-occupier' letting or a 'shorthold letting') the tenant must have been given notice, before the commencement of the tenancy, that the landlord may seek to reclaim possession at the end of the tenancy.

Neither an **assured tenancy** nor an **assured shorthold tenancy** comes to an end (but may continue indefinitely), unless the tenant voluntarily gives up possession or, following a prescribed notice by the landlord, it is terminated by a court order based on one of 16 prescribed grounds for possession. In certain cases the court has a discretionary right to grant an order for possession, but in the case of an assured shorthold tenancy the court must grant an order for possession provided the landlord has given two months' notice of termination to the tenant (which may expire on the last date of the fixed term) and provided no further assured tenancy, other than an assured shorthold tenancy (whether statutory or contractual), has come into existence (HA 1988, Sch. 2).

A landlord may not obtain possession of a dwelling let on a **secure tenancy** unless the court is satisfied that it should grant an order for possession on one of the seventeen grounds set out in the HA 1985, ss. 83-84, Sch. 2 (as substituted by the HA 1996, 174(1)). For the first eight of the grounds specified in the Act, the court must be satisfied that it is *reasonable* to make the order. For the next four specified grounds, the court must be satisfied that "suitable alternative accommodation" will be available to the tenant when the order is given. For the remaining five specified grounds, both of these conditions must be met.

In the case of a **long residential tenancy**, the tenancy is either converted into a statutory tenancy, or the landlord must obtain a court order for possession which may be granted on one of the statutorily specified grounds (L&T Act 1954, Sch. 3, as amended). If the lease is granted on or after April 1, 1990 the lease may only be terminated on grounds that correspond broadly to those applicable to an assured tenancy (Local Government and Housing Act 1989, Sch. 10, para. 4).

In the case of a **business tenancy** a landlord may be able to oppose the grant of a new tenancy on one of seven grounds and thereby persuade the court that it is not appropriate to grant a new tenancy. These grounds may be summarised as: (i) a failure of the tenant's obligation to repair such that a new tenancy "ought not to be granted"; (ii) persistent delay in paying rent; (iii) other substantial breaches of the obligations of the tenancy; (iv) the provision by the landlord of "suitable alternative accommodation" for the tenant; (v) the landlord's ability to obtain a higher rent by re-letting premises as a whole that are currently sub-let in parts; (vi) the landlord's intention to "demolish or reconstruct" the premises or a substantial part of the premises (especially when such work cannot be carried out without possession of the premises; and, provided the landlord has not acquired or created the lease within five years of termination of the tenancy); (vii) the landlord's need of the premises (combined with a fixed intention to occupy the premises) for his own business, or as his residence (in which case he must have been the landlord for five years before the termination date) (L&T Act 1954, s. 30).

An **agricultural tenancy** must be brought to an end by a duly served notice to quit. A tenant who receives such notice may serve a counter notice to the effect that it shall not take effect without the consent of the Agricultural Land Tribunal (AHA 1986, s. 26). See also **right of re-entry**.

growing crop   See **emblements, way-growing crop**.

growing-equity mortgage or **growth-equity mortgage** (GEM)   A mortgage which provides for the principal to be repaid by amounts that are increased throughout the term, or at least during the initial years, of the loan. Growth-equity mortgages are generally granted for a long term (15 to 30 years) and commonly the amounts of principal repayment are increased annually for the first three to five years of the loan term and then level off for the balance of the term. The first year payments are based usually on a 30-year **amortization mortgage** and then the payments are increased at fixed intervals (probably every year) by a specified percentage so that the net result is a repayment of the entire principal well within the 30 year term for an amortization mortgage. Also called an 'early-retirement mortgage', as the payments will repay the loan sooner than a standard amortization mortgage. Strictly speaking, any amortization mortgage is a growing-equity mortgage, because as the debt is repaid so the equity value increases; but the term generally refers to a mortgage that provides for repayments that are greater than those under a level-payment self-amortizing loan.

growth rate   The annual rate at which an income or value is assumed to grow; usually as a future prediction based on past experience.

guarantee or **guaranty**   Derived from the Old French *garantie* a variant of *warantie*, 'warranty or security'. A **collateral** agreement by which one party gives an undertaking or promise to another to be responsible for a debt or default owed by a third party. A contract by which one party (guarantor/promisor) gives a promise to another (guarantee/promisee) that if a third party (the principal debtor) does not pay a debt or meet an obligation owed to that other, then the guarantor undertakes to ensure that the debt is paid by the principal debtor. A contract of guaranty is an "accessory contract by which the promisor undertakes to be answerable to the promisee for the debt, default or miscarriage of another person, whose primary liability to the promisee must exist or be contemplated", 20 *Halsbury's Laws of England*, Guarantee and Indemnity, 4th ed. Reissue, para. 101. A guarantee is often referred to as a conditional or **collateral contract** because it is intended to lend support to, or run alongside, the primary liability of the third party, and not to act as an 'original 'agreement; in fact it cannot exist independently of the contract, the performance of which it seeks to guarantee. In that respect a guarantee may be distinguished from an **indemnity**, which is intended as a primary contract for the benefit of the party by whom a debt or obligation is owed. (An indemnity requires only two parties and does not concern itself directly with the means by which the loss arises; one who gives an indemnity is not a party to any contract or arrangement by which the liability arises.) Thus, if one party, who is uncertain as to whether he will be paid by a company for work he is about to perform, is instructed by a manager of that company to proceed with work with the words "you go on and do the work, and I will be your paymaster. I will see you paid", then the manager has provided an indemnity (even though he may anticipate that the board will pay). But if the manager had said "you go and do the work and I shall see that the board pays you", then the manager has provided a guarantee, his liability arises only if the board fails to pay. Contracts of guaranty must normally be in **writing** to be enforceable. Note: the spelling 'guarantee' is more usual in assurances as to the quality of goods, etc. and 'guaranty' in the more formal legal sense defined above, as well as in banking and financial contexts. Historically, in British English, 'guaranty' was the noun and 'guarantee' the verb, although 'guarantee' is now becoming more common in both usages. cf. **warranty**. See also **rent guarantee, surety**. **2.** A person who is entitled to the benefit of a contract guaranty. In this context, the spelling is more usually 'guarantee'.

guarantee performance agreement(US) An agreement between an original mortgagor and a party who assumes that party's mortgage by which the latter agrees to provide the original mortgagor with a guarantee against any **deficiency judgment**. Normally the guarantee is secured by a second mortgage on the property which provides the original mortgagor with the automatic right to foreclose, or exercise a power of sale, in the event that the party who has assumed the mortgage (or his successor) defaults. In some jurisdictions, guarantee performance agreements are unenforceable.

guaranteed investment contract (GIC)(US) A form of commercial fixed-rate mortgage granted by a pension fund to an insurance company.

guaranteed mortgage certificate (GMC)(US) A bond that is issued by the **Federal Home Loan Mortgage Corporation** with a guaranteed schedule of payments. Usually the certificate provides for interest to be paid semi-annually and Freddie Mac guarantees that a minimum amount of principal will be repaid at the end of every year. Also, Freddie Mac guarantees to repurchase any outstanding balance at par at the end of a specified period of time, usually 15 or 20 years.

guaranteed sale program (GSP)(US) An arrangement by which a builder or a broker agrees to purchase a property that is being offered for sale at a predetermined price if it is not sold within an agreed period of time.

guarantor A person who makes or gives a **guarantee**.

guarantor fee A **fee** paid for the provision of a **guarantee**. In particular a fee paid to a bank or financial institution that provides additional collateral or credit enhancement to the holders of **mortgage-backed securities** to be drawn on in the event that the mortgage repayments are insufficient or fail to meet the payments due to the bond holders. See also **servicer fee**.

guaranty See **guarantee**.

guaranty insurance See **fidelity guarantee insurance**.

guaranty title policy(US) See **title insurance**.

guest Someone who is invited into a home or place of lodging on a short-term basis. See also **invitee, visitor**.

H

habendum   'To have'. That which determines the size or quantum of an **estate** to be conveyed. The 'habendum' or 'habendum clause' in a **conveyance** may define, qualify or limit the extent of the estate in land that is the subject matter of the grant (i.e. it may qualify the property described in the prior **premises clause**). In practice, the habendum clause is now commonly incorporated in the premises clause.

Traditionally, a deed that granted a right of tenure contained the words *habendum et tenendum* – 'to have and to hold', the former signifying an estate of inheritance (a fee or life estate) and the latter that the land was held of a superior lord (1 *Co Litt* 6a). These words were followed by a description of the quality, i.e. the commencement date and the duration, of the estate being granted or carved out. For example, 'to hold unto the purchaser in fee simple' or 'to hold unto B for life, remainder to C in fee simple' (in the latter case B's estate may be carved out of a fee simple absolute that is held by the grantor). A habendum clause may be inserted in a lease to similar effect, e.g. 'to hold unto B for a term of twenty years from the date hereof'.

In the US, a habendum is generally considered superfluous where the estate to be conveyed is clearly set out in the **granting clause** or **operative clause**, or as part of the 'premises clause'. In any event, in the case of a conflict, the granting clause normally takes preference over the habendum; although, in the event of doubt, the courts will look at the entire instrument to ascertain the true intention of the parties.

In English law, a habendum is not essential to a conveyance of freehold land, but if there is no habendum the grantee takes the fee simple or the grantor's entire estate, unless anything is expressed to the contrary (LPA 1925, s. 60). If the duration of the estate is defined in a preceding premises clause, the grantee takes that estate. A description in the premises clause takes priority, and cannot contradict or abridge the habendum. However, the habendum may alter, vary or explain the premises clause, especially if the habendum indicates that the intention is to grant a larger estate. See also **reddendum**, **tenendum**, **words of limitation**.

habendum clause   See **habendum**.

habitable   Constructed or adapted so as to be inhabited. n particular, a landlord who is responsible for keeping a dwelling-house in **good repair**, is bound to at least make and keep it habitable. A house cannot be said to be habitable if it does not keep out the elements; or it cannot be lived in without fear of injury to person, health or safety. See also **fit for human habitation**[(Eng)], **warranty of habitability**[(US)].

habitable repair   Such repair as renders a property fit to be lived in by an intending occupier. See also **habitable**, **tenantable repair**.

habitable room   1. A room that is considered useable for living, sleeping, eating or cooking, i.e. a **living room**, study, bedroom or a kitchen used as part of the normal living space, but not a bathroom, toilet area, closet, storage area, hallway, circulation space or any similar space. Residential density restrictions or assessments that are based on 'rooms per acre' are normally based on habitable rooms. See also **habitable**. 2.[(Eng)]A room in a condition that is fit to live in, i.e. one that is **fit for human habitation**.

habitation   The state of dwelling or being inhabited. A temporary or permanent place of shelter or abode. A **dwelling-house**. See also **fit for human habitation**.

hæres[(Lat)]   'Heir'. In Roman law a person who succeeds to real or personal property, by will or by descent.

ha-ha   A sunken fence. An artificial boundary, which is designed to be hidden from view, between a formal garden or park and the surrounding countryside, in order to permit the garden to merge visually with the countryside beyond, while keeping cattle and other livestock out of the garden or park. The boundary is formed essentially by a sunken ditch and so the term is thought to be derived from the exclamation of surprise, 'ha!'. The ditch generally has a perpendicular face on the garden side, frequently made as a stone wall, and a grassed sloping face on the outer side. See also **fence**.

half a year or **half year**   In general, a period which spans one half of the number of days, weeks or months in a **year**, according to the appropriate unit of measurement. At common law, unless indicated to the contrary, 'half a year' is taken as half the number of days of the year, not 'six months', i.e. a period which spans from the end of the day upon which it commences for a further period of 182 days (fractions of a day being ignored) to include the day upon which it ends. However, when a lease provides that rent is to be payable 'half yearly' the yearly sum is payable, in two equal amounts as near as possible at equal intervals in the year, i.e. at the same date every six months.

In English law, if a tenancy commences on one of the usual **quarter days**, half a year is the period between the alternate quarter days (unless expressed to the contrary), so that notice to quit served on June 25 to expire on December 25, although covering 183 days, is not half a year's notice (the notice should have been served on or before the June 24 quarter day). On the other hand, notice served on September 28 (being before the September 29 quarter day) to expire on March 25, although only 178 days (or 179 days in a leap year), constitutes half a year's notice. See also **agricultural tenancy**(Eng), **tenancy from year to year**.

half life   The period of time before half of the principal is repaid on a pool of mortgage loans that have been included in a securitized or **collateralized mortgage obligation**.

half-quarter day   See **quarter day**.

half section(US)   See **section**.

half year   See **half a year**.

half yearly   See **half a year**.

halve back(Eng)   See **zoning**.

ham   1. A piece of land shaped like a ham or hollow of the knee.   2. An Old English word for a house; a small collection of houses; a manor or a village.

hamlet   A small village, generally comprising a shop or general store, a few houses and sometimes a church.

hammer   See **auction**, **gavel**.

hand money   See **earnest money**.

hand-over   The delivery of possession of a building site by a building contractor to the employer upon completion of the building contract. See also **practical completion**.

handsale   See **handsel**.

handsel or **hansel**   Cash or **earnest money** paid over to secure a bargain for the sale of chattels; derived from the tradition of shaking hands on a deal. Also called 'handsale'.

hangout(AmE)   A period of time by which the term of a loan exceeds the term of a lease that has been given as security. Thus, a loan granted for 25 years against the security of a 20-year lease has a 'hangout' of 5 years. As the loan 'hangs out' beyond the term of the lease, the loan will normally require a 'balloon payment' to fully pay off the outstanding principal on termination of the lease. However, if the lease is renewed, or extended, the loan may remain in effect. See also **leasehold mortgage**.

hansel   See **handsel**.

harassment   Actions, words or gestures that tend to annoy, trouble, vex or create fear in another. Frequently used to refer to acts calculated to interfere with the peace or comfort of a residential occupier, particularly in connection with an attempt to evict a tenant. Harassment includes such acts as locking out a tenant; cutting off essential services; assault (physical or verbal) or threats of assault; noise; and various forms of trickery (*R v Burke* [1990] [1990] 2 All ER 385, 389 (HL)–comparing the New York police code and the English Rent Act 1965 on aspects that are "designed to make life intolerable for occupiers"). Not to be confused with an interference with a tenant's right to **quiet enjoyment**.

In English law, it is a criminal offence to commit acts calculated to interfere with the peace or comfort of a residential occupier or a member of his household, or to persistently withdraw or withhold services reasonably required for the occupation of premises as a residence (PEA 1977, s. 1, as amended). In addition, a tenant who is a victim of unlawful harassment can sue a landlord for damages (HA 1988, s. 27).

In the US, any act of a landlord by which he seeks to recover possession of leased premises "without due process of law" and against the wishes of the tenant, is a misdemeanor. See also **constructive eviction**, **eviction**, **forcible entry and detainer**, **Rackmanism**(Eng), **right of re-entry**.

Carter, David, and Andrew Dymond. *Quiet Enjoyment: Arden and Partington's Guide to Remedies for Harassment and Illegal Eviction*. 5th ed. London: Legal Action Group, 1998.

hard cost   The direct cost of constructing a building or developing a project. A cost incurred on labour and materials that come to form part of land or building (including, if applicable, demolition and site development costs), as opposed to an associated or **soft cost** such as professional fees, loan fees and interest costs.

hard money   1. Traditionally, coins of precious metal that may be used as currency. In modern usage, coins that have been lawfully minted for circulation as **legal tender**.   **2.** Cash paid to acquire additional **equity** in an investment, especially money used to repay existing debt or based on an increase in the value of the property. See also **hard-money mortgage**.

hard-money mortgage(US)   A mortgage that provides the mortgagor with cash that he intends to use to acquire goods, or finance a business, rather than directly to finance real estate. A hard-money mortgage often takes the form of a **second mortgage**.

hardcore method(BrE)   A method of assessing the capital value of a variable income stream by which that part of the income that does not vary – the 'bottom slice' or 'hardcore rent' – is capitalised at one rate of interest (for the total investment period or, if applicable, in perpetuity) and each marginal increase (or decrease) in the income – the 'top slice' or 'incremental rent'- is capitalised separately (for the period during which it is receivable). The capital value of the investment is the total of these capitalised figures. For example, if a property is let at a rent of £10,000 per annum for 3 years and then it is estimated that the income will revert to a market rent of £15,000 per annum, the capital value may be assessed as:

'hardcore rent'		£10,000 p.a.
capitalisation rate, or years' purchase in perpetuity at 5%*		20
		£200,000
'incremental rent'		£5,000 p.a.
capitalised in perpetuity at 7%	14.29	
deferred 3 years at 7%	× 0.82	
	11.72	
		£58,600
capital value		£258,600

(*The hardcore rent is considered a more secure income than the incremental rent and, therefore, is capitalised at a lower rate of return.)

This valuation technique is called the 'split reversion method' if, after the reversion to market rent, the income is capitalised at a different rate to that used before the reversion. Thus, in the above example the hardcore rent could be capitalised at 5% for the initial three years and then capitalised in perpetuity, deferred 3 years, at 6%. Also called the 'layer method' or sometimes the 'marginal method'. cf. **term and reversion method**.

hardcore rent   See **hardcore method**.

have and hold   See **habendum**.

haybote   See **estovers**.

hazard insurance   See **liability insurance**.

hazardous waste   See **environmental audit, environmental impact assessment**(BrE), **environmental impact report**(US).

headland   A promontory. A point of land projecting into the ocean. Derived from an area of a land left at the end of a furrow where a plough turns. Where there was no other recognised boundary, this 'headland' was used to determine the limit of the land ownership.

head landlord   A landlord whose tenant has granted a sub-lease, as viewed by the subtenant. Thus, if L grants a lease to T, who sub-lets to ST, and ST then sublets to SUT, L is the head landlord of ST, and T is the head landlord of SUT. The lease from L to T is a head lease for ST, as is the lease from T to ST for SUT. The head landlord may be any lessor, who has a subtenant, up to and including the freeholder, i.e. he may be the owner of a fee simple or a leaseholder. Also called a 'head lessee' or, especially in the US, a 'superior landlord'. cf. **immediate landlord**. See also **intermediate lease**.

head lease   A lease granted to a tenant who in turn leases the demised premise to another tenant or tenants for a shorter term, i.e. to granted to a tenant who grants a **sub-lease**. If a lessee, A, creates a tenancy for a term less than his own then his subtenant, B, is likely to be expressly required to comply with most of the terms of the lease granted to A; even though there is no **privity of contract** between A's landlord and B. A head lease may be any 'superior lease', up to the freehold.

In the US, the prefix is rarely used. Alternatively called a **master lease**, especially when the lease controls or forms the basis upon which the subleases in a building are to be granted. Sometimes called an 'original lease' or 'underlying lease'. Also when the landlord is the holder of a fee interest and grants an assignment of his reversion to another so as to create a new head lease, the tenant may refer to the controlling lease as an 'over-lease'. See also **head landlord, intermediate lease, privity of estate**.

head lessee   See **head landlord**.

head rent   Rent payable under a **head lease**.

head tenant   A **tenant** who has granted a subtenancy. In the US, sometimes called the 'sublandlord' as he is a landlord in relation to the subtenant.

headline rent(BrE)   The rent payable after all inducements have expired or have been 'used up'. Sometimes called the 'target rent' as it is the level of rent that a landlord seeks to achieve. cf. **equivalent rent**(BrE).

heads of claim(Eng)   The main titles under which a claim for **compulsory purchase compensation** is submitted, e.g. compensation for land taken, compensation for disturbance, compensation for injurious affection. When a disputed claim for compensation is submitted to the Lands Tribunal for settlement, the claimant must set out "details of the compensation claimed, distinguishing the amounts under separate heads and showing how the amount claimed under each head is calculated", LCA 1961, s. 4(2). If such a claim is not made the claimant may forfeit any claim to costs that would otherwise be awarded by the Lands Tribunal.

health and safety regulations(Eng) Regulations made under statutes, e.g. the Shops Act 1950, the Factories Act 1961, the Offices, Shops and Railway Premises Act 1963, and the Health and Safety at Work Act 1974, to govern matters such as "(a) securing the health, safety and welfare of persons at work; (b) protecting persons other than persons at work against risks to health or safety arising out of or in connection with the activities of persons at work …", HSWA 1974, s. 1(1). There are numerous regulations that affect the working environment and construction activity. Workplace regulations cover such matters as opening hours for shops; cleanliness, overcrowding, temperature control, lighting, drainage and sanitary conditions of factories; safety of machinery; storage of dangerous substances; the use of hazardous substances; noxious emissions; the structural conditions and stability of premises; fire prevention and safety; as well as the temperature and ventilation of office premises, and general working condition. Regulations affecting construction activity cover such matters as safety on site; the use and storage of hazardous substances; control of noise; waste regulation and disposal; construction design and management and the operation of machinery.

In particular, regulations have been put in place to improve the overall management and coordination of health, safety and welfare throughout all stages of most construction projects by placing specific duties and obligations on clients (including clients' agents and developers), designers and contractors (Health and Safety at Work Act 1974, s. 16(1); Management of Health and Safety at Work Regulations 1992). See also **building regulations, fire certificate, overcrowding**.

Hendy J., and M. Ford. *Redgrave, Fife & Machin: Health and Safety*. 3rd ed. London: Butterworths, 1998.

Tolley's Health and Safety at Work Handbook 2004. 16th ed. Croydon, Surrey: Tolley.

Goodman, Michael J. (general editor). *Encyclopedia of Health and Safety at Work*. 4 vols. Looseleaf. London: Sweet & Maxwell, ©1962-.

hearsay Originally 'hear say'; that which one heard someone say. 'Hearsay evidence' is based on that which has been obtained or gleaned from another, usually by word of mouth, and not testimony that is derived from the witness's personal experience; nor learned, heard or seen by the witness himself. Hearsay evidence may be presented as fact, but derives its source from something that ranges from 'to the best of my knowledge' or 'what I have reason or have been given to believe', to rumour or common talk, i.e. it depends upon the veracity and competence of some person other than the bearer of the evidence. Such evidence is normally inadmissible in a court of law, although it may be permitted to support evidence that is based on first hand information. See also **comparable property**.

hebdomadal Weekly; lasting seven days. See also **week**.

hedge **1.** A boundary formed by a continuous row of low trees, shrubs or similar vegetation grown together in order to form a barrier or enclosure. See also **boundary line, fence**. **2.** A means of providing security, or reducing the risk of financial loss, in particular by acquiring rights, options or future contracts which would reduce the risk of any loss that may arise from a fall in value. See also **derivative security**.

hedge and ditch presumption A common law presumption that if a boundary is delimited by a man-made ditch, and a bank or hedge, unless there is evidence to the contrary, the bank and ditch are taken to belong to the owner of the land on the hedge-side of the ditch. The ditch is presumed to have been excavated to the limit of the land and the bank formed on the maker's own property from the excavated material and, if there is one, the hedge is planted on the bank (*Vowles v Miller* (1810) 3 Taunt 137, 138, 128 Eng Rep 54); whereas if there is only a ditch, or only a hedge, the boundary may well be taken as its center line – or other evidence may rebut the 'hedge and ditch' presumption (*Alan Wibberley Building Ltd v Insley* [1999] 1 WLR 894 (HL)).

hedgebote   See **estovers**.

height density zoning(US)   A **zoning ordinance** that sets limits to the maximum building height in a given area. Also called 'height regulations'. See also **density zoning**, **floor area ratio**.

height regulations   See **height density zoning**.

heir (f. **heiress**)   A person who succeeds by descent or succession. Historically, an heir was one who, based on statutory or blood descendancy, receives freehold land by inheritance. In modern usage, an 'heir' may be used to refer to any person who succeeds to property, whether by law or by will; although strictly speaking an heir is someone who receives property upon intestacy (the terms **devisee** or **legatee** are the formal terms used to refer to a person to whom property is given by will). An heir may include a person's **issue**, but also may be a spouse, parent, niece or nephew and such other relatives who may receive property based on the laws on intestacy.

In common law, the word 'heirs' or 'heirs of the body' (the heirs of a particular person) were considered to be **words of limitation** and not **words of purchase**, i.e. they indicated the extent of the estate to be granted and not merely who was to receive the estate. Thus, if a **freehold** estate (whether a fee simple or a fee tail) was granted by the same instrument (whether a deed or a will) "to A for life, with the remainder to his heirs", or "to A for life, with the remainder to the heirs of his body", then the freehold did not pass to A as a life estate and then to the heirs (as

might have been the intention of the grantor), but A received an unlimited freehold which he could dispose of freely during his lifetime. The rule was that such a grant passed the estate to A for life, and the remainder to A and his heirs. As a result, the life estate and the **remainder** merged together to give the recipient either the entire fee simple (if the words 'heirs' was used) or a fee tail estate (if the words 'heirs of the body' were used) ('rule in *Shelley's Case*', *Wolfe v Shelley* [1581] 1 Co Rep 93b, 76 Eng Rep 206).

In English law, the rule in *Shelley's Case* was abolished in 1925. Thus, such words as 'heir', 'heirs', 'issue', or similar words that refer to a particular class of heir or issue, are now considered to be words of purchase, i.e. they are simply part of the words that indicate who is to take the estate (LPA 1925, s. 131). The terms 'heirs' and 'heirs of the body' may be used to indicate the size of the estate to be passed. For example, 'and his heirs' or 'and his heirs and assigns' indicate that a fee simple is transferred, i.e. the interest is absolute and of unconditional inheritance. Whereas the words 'and the heirs of the body' are used to indicate that an estate of limited inheritance, an **entailed estate**, is to be granted. However, the words 'heirs' and 'heirs of the body' are no longer essential for the conveyance of a freehold, as the words 'in fee simple' or 'in fee tail' (or 'in tail male' or 'in tail female') are sufficient to pass that particular form of estate, unless a contrary intention appears in the conveyance (LPA 1925, s. 60). In a will, if there are no words of limitation (e.g. a grant "to A") a fee simple, or the testator's entire estate, now passes by the devise, unless a clear contrary intention appears in the will (Wills Act 1837, s. 28).

In the US, in most jurisdictions, the rule in *Shelley's Case* has been abolished or modified by statute, so that 'heir' or 'heirs' generally means children, without restraint as to succession, so that a grant "to A for life, and the remainder to his heirs" conveys a life estate to A and a contingent remainder in A's heirs. In particular, the rule will not normally be applied where there are other words that set out clearly the testator's intentions. Nonetheless, the Rule is still in effect in a few jurisdictions, especially in respect of the use of the words 'heirs of the body' in a deed (as opposed to a will), so that a grant "to A for life and then to the heirs of his body" will grant a fee tail and not a life estate to A.

In Canada, the rule in *Shelley's Case* is still applicable; except in Alberta and the Northwest Territories.

heirloom(Eng) Goods or personal chattels that pass by custom as an inseparable part of an inheritance, e.g. a valuable painting, an ensign of honour. A **tenant for life** may, under an order of a court, sell chattels settled together with land (inaccurately called 'heirlooms'), but the proceeds of sale become **capital money** which may be used to purchase other heirlooms or may be used in the same way as other capital money (SLA 1925, s. 67).

heirs and assigns Persons who succeed to property by inheritance and any successor to that property. If used in a deed, without further qualification, the words 'and assigns' add nothing so that the estate transferred is a fee simple. At common law, such words were essential to pass such an estate and, although no longer necessary (except in a few jurisdictions in the US), are still used in wills and deeds to indicate that an absolute and unconditional fee simple is to be transferred, as distinguished from the use of the words **heirs of the body**, which are used to transfer an estate of limited inheritance. See also **heir**, **assigns**.

heirs of the body The **heirs** of a particular person; descendents of one's bloodline. A lineal descendant of a deceased person. In common parlance, one person's 'bodily heirs', especially as distinguished from any other heir who may receive property on intestacy. If property is granted to the 'heirs of the body' and the bloodline runs out, the property will pass to the successors of the original grantor. See also **fee tail**.

herbage 1. The natural vegetation on land. Historically, the pasture and fruits that were food for cattle. 2.(Eng) A licence or liberty to pasture one's cattle on another's land. See also **grazing licence**, **right of common**.

hereditable Inheritable; that which can be inherited. See also **hereditament**, **heritable property**.

hereditament Derived from the Latin *herediare*, 'to inherit' (originally the word was 'heritage'). Any form of property, real or personal, corporeal or incorporeal, or a combination thereof, that is capable of passing by inheritance. In a specialist sense, a hereditament is **real property**, or a right to real property, as distinguished from a **personal property** which, at common law, was not considered capable of passing by way of descent to an heir. A hereditament may be 'corporeal' or 'incorporeal'. A **corporeal hereditament** is tangible and therefore traditionally capable of livery of seisin (delivery by transfer of a right of possession); it may be land, buildings or any thing that is part of or affixed to land. An **incorporeal hereditament** is intangible being annexed to or concerning a corporeal thing, but not the thing itself, and is capable of grant, i.e. a mere right that can be bestowed on someone, but not a physical object; examples being an **easement**, **profit à prendre** or a **rentcharge**.

In English law, the term is now used predominately in rating law to refer specifically to a single unit in the **rating list**; a property that is or may become liable to a rate, being a unit of such property which is or would fall to be shown as a separate item in the valuation list (General Rate Act 1967, s. 115(1); Local Government Finance Act 1988, s. 64(1)). It is used with the same meaning in planning law in the context of a 'blight notice' (TCPA 1990, s. 171(1)). See also **composite hereditament**(Eng), **tenement**.

heritable   See inheritable.

heritable bond   A **bond** secured on inheritable property, i.e. secured on land. A bond by which land is pledged as security for a loan. See also **mortgage**.

heritable property(Scot)   Originally, property that was inherited upon intestacy by the heir-in-law (usually the eldest son). Any property that is capable of being inherited. In modern Scots law, 'heritable property' (or 'heritage') refers to all real rights in land (including a lease, servitude and most forms of security over land), and a right to land that is to be acquired, such as the rights of a beneficiary and the rights under a contract for the sale of land. Heritable property may be 'corporeal', land and anything that is part of the land; or 'incorporeal', a right over land that is not tangible, such as a **servitude**.

heritage   An inheritance. An estate that may be inherited; property that could pass by descent. See also **heritable property**(Scot).

heritage building(Aus)   A building that is considered to be of architectural, historic or aesthetic significance and is considered worthy of protection. All jurisdictions have legislation that protects such properties, e.g. Australian Heritage Conservation Act 1975 (CTH); Heritage Act 1977 (NSW).

heritor(Scot)   The owner of **heritable property**, i.e. the holder of a right to land which is similar to an English freehold.

hiatus   Derived from the Latin *hiatus*, 'gap' or 'opening'. A space or break in time or continuity. In particular, a hiatus of title is a gap in a **chain of title** to adjoining parcels of land that arises as a result of a faulty legal description.

hidden defect   See **latent defect**.

hidden property   See **treasure trove**.

hide of land   As much land as could be ploughed with one plough, or sufficient land to sustain a family. Considered to be between 60 and 100 acres.

high-ratio financing   See **gearing**, **leverage**.

high-rise building   In general, a building with six or more stories above the ground level and, therefore, one for which an elevator is considered essential; the term tends to be used relative to buildings in the surrounding area, thus a 'high rise' in Manhattan would generally refer to a building of twenty stories or more, whereas in a suburban residential district it may refer to a building of five of more floors above ground level. cf. **low-rise building**. See also **skyscraper**.

high water mark   The line on a **shore** reached by water at median tides between the spring and neap. See also **foreshore**, **riparian rights**.

highest and best use   The likely **use**, selected from a number of available choices, to which an area of land may be put, in compliance with zoning and building regulations and which, at the time of an **appraisal**, produces the most profitable present value of the land. The legal use of land that, at any point in time, is likely to produce the highest return to an investor. An area of land may be considered to be at its highest and best use when it provides the optimum return to its owner or user, which may be as measured in monetary terms, or in intangible and social values, or a combination of such values. However, this value is not static. The use of land at any point in time is dependent on its 'capacity'- its ability to provide fruits and benefits. In turn this ability is a function of physical characteristics (slope, fertility, climate, load bearing capacity, etc.); the permitted or authorised use (agricultural, residential, industrial, mining commercial); intensity of use (the permitted plot or floor area ratio, planning and building height restrictions, etc.); location (accessibility, proximity to complementary uses); technological factors (building techniques, availability of plant and machinery); and the availability of other factors of production (labour, capital and management) to exploit the full potential of land. The use to which land is put is a function also of the owner's tastes and preferences and will be dependent on the demand of the end user. 'Highest and best use' thus represents a dynamic concept, a point to which land is tending. Landowners, or potential landowners, are constantly seeking to obtain a higher return from a given area of land than would be receivable by continuing the existing use. However, one use is commonly frozen at a point in time as being the use that can provide a higher or better return than any alternative. It is upon the basis of that use that an appraisal of land is generally carried out.

In the US and Canada, 'highest and best use' is an established basis for assessing **just compensation** for condemnation, i.e. account should be taken of a reasonable probability that a zoning change would be permitted; but not a special use available only to the acquiring authority, or any special purpose for which the property is being acquired (Olsen v. United States, 292 US 246, 255, 54 S Ct 704, 78 L Ed 1236 (1934); United States v. Cors, 337 US 325, 69 S Ct 1086, 93 L Ed 1392 (1949); *Krupa v Camel Resources Ltd* (1982) 40 AR 528 (Can)). Also, for the purpose of determining the **assessed value**, a property should be appraised based on its highest and best use. Sometimes called the 'optimum use'. cf. **existing use**. See also **fair market value**.

highest and best use analysis[US]   See **residual process**.

highway   A way or passage on land, made or unmade, over which the public at large has a right to pass and repass for legal purposes. A **right of way** or **road** that leads along a defined route from one town or place to another; is common to the general public; and normally may be used as a right of passage, without let or hindrance, at any time of the day or night, and any time of the year. Essentially a highway requires a right of 'common enjoyment' (i.e. not just a right for a limited class of individuals), and, as a rule, there should be a duty of public maintenance.

A highway may mean more than merely a paved roadway for vehicular passage; it may include a **footpath**, **bridleway**, **carriageway**, **driftway** or **street**. At common law, highways are of three kinds according to the degree of restriction of the public rights of passage over them. A full highway or 'cartway' is one over which the public have rights of way (a) on foot, (b) riding on or accompanied by a beast of burden, and (c) with vehicles and cattle (*Suffolk County Council v Mason* [1979] AC 705, 710, [1979] 2 All ER 369, 371 (HL)).

In the US, 'highway' may be defined as "all public roads and ways ... In its a broad or general sense, it covers every common way for travel in any ordinary mode or by any means, which the public has the right to use either conditionally or unconditionally, and thus may include turnpikes and toll roads, bridges, canals, ferries, navigable waters, lanes, pent roads, and crossroads. In a limited sense, however, the term means a way for general traffic which is wholly public", 39 Am.Jur.2d., Highways, Streets, and Bridges, § 1.

In English statute law, a highway may be understood to mean "all roads, bridges (not being county bridges), carriageways, cartways, horseways, bridleways, footways, causeways, churchways and pavements", Highways Act 1845, s. 5. There is no modern statutory definition, but 'highway' may extend to the whole or any part of a highway (other than a ferry or waterway) and where it passes over a bridge or through a tunnel, that bridge or tunnel is part of the highway (Highway Act 1980, s. 328). A **dead-end street**, **cul-de-sac**, or a public square may be, but should not be presumed to be, a highway.

As a rule a 'highway' is not limited to the area set aside for vehicular traffic, but it extends to footpaths, sidewalks and bicycle paths.

See also *ad medium filum*, **adoption**, **building line**, **cartway**, **dedication**, **easement of necessity**, **highway authority**(Eng), **highway commission**(US), **improvement line**(Eng), **nuisance**, **pedestrian precinct order**(Eng), **prescription**, **street**.

hire **1.** To permit someone to have an exclusive right to use goods, or to obtain a service, in return for an agreed sum or reward. Upon the 'hire' of goods, ownership is retained by the grantor throughout the time that the goods are hired and remains so when the contract of hire comes to an end. cf. **lease**. See also **bailment**, **hire-purchase agreement**. **2.** A payment for the use and enjoyment of movable property; sometimes called a 'hire charge'. The terms 'hire' and '**rent**' may be used interchangeably when referring to personal property or goods.

hire charge See **hire**, **hire-purchase agreement**.

hire-purchase agreement(BrE) A hybrid contract whereby an owner of goods agrees to let them on **hire** to another and grants a right for the hirer to eventually acquire full ownership of the goods. "An agreement, other than a **conditional sale agreement**, under which (a) goods are bailed or (in Scotland) hired in return for periodic payments by the person to whom they are bailed or hired, and (b) the property in the goods will pass to that person if the terms of the agreement are complied with and one or more of the following occurs – (i) the exercise of an option to purchase by that person, (ii) the doing of any other specified act by any party to the agreement, (iii) the happening of any other specified event", Consumer Credit Act 1974, s. 199(1). The price of the goods is payable by regular instalments (a 'hire charge') which are so calculated that in total they will cover the sale price of the goods, and interest on the unpaid balance. Full ownership of the goods passes to the purchaser upon the payment of the last instalment. Thus, a hire purchase is a contract that combines a form of **bailment** with an **option** to purchase the bailed goods; an option that is exercised effectively when the full price is paid. It differs from a **credit-sale agreement** which transfers ownership of the goods immediately with a purely personal obligation to pay the price in stages. It differs from a pure hiring because in the latter transaction a hirer does not contract to part with ownership.

In the US the nearest equivalent is an 'instalment-credit agreement' or a 'lease-purchase agreement' or a **finance lease**. See also **leasing**.

historic area(Eng) See **conservation area**.

historic building **1.**(Eng)A building of sufficient antiquity or historic interest as to be considered worthy of preservation. In particular, a building over 100 years old that is associated with a notable person or event in history. An historic building may be any building considered by the **English Heritage** (formerly the 'Historic Buildings and Monuments Commission for England') to be worthy of preservation or "any building which in the Commission's opinion is of historic or architectural interest", National Heritage Act 1993, ss. 33(8), 35(4). See also **ancient monument**, **conservation area**, **listed building**. **2.**(US)See **historic sites**, **landmark property**.

historic cost **1.** The actual cost paid for an asset; the original acquisition cost, which (due to subsequent expenditure or depreciation) may be more or less than the current cost. The original cost recorded in 'books of account'. The total sum of money, or its equivalent, expended in acquiring a property as established when a property first comes into a new ownership or a building comes into existence. Also called the 'historical cost'. See also **acquisition cost**. **2.**

The initial cost of constructing a building. To be distinguished from the original **purchase price**, or **book cost**, which is the cost to a particular buyer. However, these terms often are used synonymously.

historic district(US)   An area or district that has been designated by a local municipality as of special historic, architectural or aesthetic character, especially an area that contains buildings or structures that are typical of one of the significant eras of a town or city. An historic district may be designated as such by a local, state or federal government. See also **historic site**, **landmark property**.

historic place(NZ)   Any land, building or structure (including an archaeological site) that forms part of the historical or cultural heritage of New Zealand (Historic Places Act 1993, s. 2). Any such property may be protected by the issuance of a heritage order, heritage covenant or the control of archaeological sites. Historic places are listed on a register of such properties.

historic redemption yield   A yield calculated to show the total annualized return on cost from an investment since inception, taking account of the **net income** received to date and any capital profit (or loss) resulting from a deemed sale (or any increase in equity, whether resulting from a revaluation or a reduction in debt). The yield obtained by applying a discounted cash flow calculation to the total income and expenditure from the date an investment was acquired to the present, assuming the investment is sold at its present market value, i.e. the **internal rate of return** based on past performance. cf. **historic revenue yield**. See also **redemption yield**.

historic revenue yield   The **historic redemption yield** excluding any capital profit or loss (realised or unrealised), i.e. the rate of interest at which the total historic net cash flow from an investment must be discounted to equate

to the original cost of that investment.

historic sites, etc.(US)   Sites, buildings, structures or other property that are of historical, archaeological, architectural or cultural interest or of importance to the Nation and are considered worthy of retention and enhancement for present and future generations. An historic site, structure or building may be (a) listed in the National Register of Historic Places; (b) located in a registered historic district and certified by the Secretary of the Interior as being of historic significance to the district; or (c) located in an historic district which has been designated as such by a local or state law in accordance with standards laid down by the Secretary of the Interior (16 USC, Conservation, § 461 et seq.). An historic site may not be altered nor may an historic building or structure be demolished without authorization. The owner of such a structure may qualify for extended tax depreciation allowances and an investment tax credit for qualified rehabilitation expenses incurred on an historic building or structure. In addition, several states have statutes that are also designed to protect historic sites or buildings and may provide tax credits for the cost incurred on rehabilitating an historic property. See also **historic district**, **landmark property**, **transferable development right**.
Reynolds, Judith. *Historic Properties: Preservation and Valuation Process.* 2nd ed. Chicago: Appraisal Institute, 1997.

historic structure(US)   See **historic sites**.

historical cost   See **historic cost**.

historical landmark   See **landmark property**.

hoarding   1. A temporary **fence** or similar barrier put up around a site, especially a building site, to enclose and secure the site and any building works thereon.   2. A large flat vertical board or panel for the external display of advertising material. See also **advertisement, billboard**.

hold   **1.** To have a legal title, to keep or possess, or to retain **possession**, especially physical possession. 'Hold' may refer to actual possession or the right to have legal title, the right to claim possession.   **2.** In common law, to have an estate subject to the payment of rent or rendering of service, i.e. a right to **tenure**. A tenant is said to 'hold' of another; he has a right to possession although he does not need to have actual occupation. Possession signifies a right held unto oneself, whereas a person may hold something for another. A person may *hold* by force, fraud, deceit or as of right; he may keep occupation by force or as of right; but he may have possession only by exerting a right or an assumed right. See also **habendum, holding, holding over, tenancy**.

hold-over tenancy(US)   See **holding over**.

holdback(US)   **1.** A provision in a loan agreement that part of the funds will not be advanced until a certain condition (or conditions) has been fulfilled. For example, a part of the loan facility may be withheld until all, or at least a percentage, of a new building has been leased (sometimes called a 'leasing holdback'), or until a new building is completed and free of all mechanics' liens. Also, the funds so retained may be referred to as a 'holdback'. See also **floor loan, gap finance**.   **2.** See **retainage**.

holder   **1.** One who holds title to property. In particular, one who possesses or holds for collection the benefit of a **negotiable instrument**.   **2.** The owner of a **mortgage-backed obligation**. The purchaser of a security that is backed by a mortgage secured on one or more properties.

hold-harmless clause(US)   See **exculpatory clause**.

holder in due course   A person who has acquired a **negotiable instrument**, in **good faith** and for **value**, without any notice that it is overdue, has been dishonoured, or is otherwise defective. A holder in due course holds the instrument free of all third party claims. A purchaser at a judicial sale, or one who acquires the instrument under a legal process, cannot be a holder in due course; nor can a party who acquires an instrument as part of an estate, or as part of a bulk transaction that is not part of the regular course of business of the transferor.

holding   **1.** Property that is retained. Holding of land is associated with **tenure**, as distinguished from a right to occupy land. cf. **occupation**. See also **ownership, tenement**.   **2.** A right to retain property. The act of taking hold of property.   **3.** The area of land let to a tenant. Land held from a superior owner. An area of land that is held or possessed in one ownership or for one business purpose. See also **agricultural holding**(Eng), **farm, smallholding**(Eng).   **4.**(Eng)In relation to the rights to renewal of a **business tenancy**, 'the holding' means "the property comprised in the tenancy, there being excluded any part thereof which is occupied neither by the tenant nor by a person employed by the tenant and so employed for the purposes of a **business** by reason of which the tenancy is one to which [the part of the statute that provides such rights] applies", L&T Act 1954, s. 23(3). See also **business premises**.

holding agreement(US)   See **land trust**.

holding company   A company that controls one or more 'subsidiary' companies or corporations by owning or controlling a significant percentage (usually more than half) of the shares (especially the voting shares), or that is in a position to control the composition of the subsidiary company or the corporation's management or board of directors. A similar company that controls one subsidiary company is also called a 'parent company'. cf. **investment company**.

holding escrow   See **escrow**.

holding out   See **ostensible authority**.

holding over   The wilful and actual retention of control of property by a tenant following the termination or expiry of a tenancy, but without the landlord's consent (although the landlord may acquiesce in the retention of possession by the tenant, especially when negotiations are taking place to renew the tenancy).

If the landlord elects to take no action and the tenant remains in possession after the expiration of a lease without the landlord's consent, or objection, the occupier obtains a **tenancy at sufferance**. On the other hand, at common law, if the landlord acknowledges his occupation the tenant is deemed to have a **tenancy at will**. If a landlord accepts rent from a tenant who is holding over, that usually creates a **periodic tenancy**, upon terms corresponding (except as to duration) to the expired tenancy, unless there is evidence that the intention is to create some other duration of tenancy. If the expired tenancy was a tenancy for a term of years, generally the new tenancy will be a **tenancy from year to year**; in other cases the period is normally related to the periods to which the rent relates. Nonetheless, a tenancy longer than one from year to year cannot arise without the formal grant of a new term. A tenant who holds over, after being given notice to vacate by the landlord, becomes a trespasser, unless he has a statutory right to remain in possession. A tenant who remains in occupation of the demised premises after the lease has expired (whether as a tenant at sufferance or at will) is obliged to pay a 'reasonable sum' for his **use and occupation**, unless there is an express agreement to the contrary. Thus, when a landlord takes action to recover possession, he may be entitled to claim **mesne profits** for the period during which the tenant has been holding over, and, if the tenant refuses to deliver up possession when required, the landlord may be able to claim **double rent** (or, in some states in the US, triple rent) for the

relevant period. In the US, also called 'hold over'; or any tenancy created without the formal creation of a new term is a 'holdover tenancy' and the tenant a 'holdover tenant'. In Canada, also called an 'overholding tenant'. See also **business tenancy**(Eng), **waiver**.

holding period   1. The period for which it is assumed that an investment will be held. In particular, such a period as used when assessing the **internal rate of return** on an investment, or the 'holding period yield'. See also **redemption yield**. 2. The period during which a capital asset is owned, especially the period of time that determines whether a gain or loss arising from a sale of the asset is subject to 'short-term' or 'long-term' capital gains tax.

holdover tenant or **hold-over tenant**(US)   A tenant who retains possession of the demised property after a lease has expired, but usually with the tacit consent of the landlord. A tenant who is **holding over**.

holiday let(Eng)   The short-term letting of a dwelling-house for the express purpose that it be used only for accommodation during the period of a 'holiday'. A holiday letting does not qualify as a **protected tenancy**, nor as a **restricted contract** (Rent Act 1977, ss. 9, 19(7)). See also **grounds for possession**.

holographic will   A **will** drawn up entirely in the handwriting of the person in whose name it is made. In particular, a non-attested will (which in many jurisdictions is invalid).

home   A place where someone lives, either permanently or temporarily. Generally, a person's or a family's principal place of **residence**. The place where one dwells; a place where the centre of a person's domestic life is to be found. A house and grounds, or messuage, inhabited by any individual with his or her family, if any. Strictly speaking a house is the structure that contains that which we make into a home. A home is popularly said to be where you make it; an itinerant just makes a home more often. At any point in time a person normally has only one principal home, although he or she may have more than one place that is called 'home'. See also **domicile**, **dwelling house**, **matrimonial home**.

home equity conversion mortgage (HECM)(US)   See **reverse annuity mortgage**.

home equity line-of-credit (HELOC)(AmE)
A line of credit that allows the borrower to draw down a loan based on the equity value of that person's home. Such a facility is normally subordinate to any regular mortgage that is secured on the property.

home equity loan (HEL)(US)   A loan, usually in the form of a **second mortgage** or revolving line of credit, secured on the equity in a person's home. Home equity loans are commonly made to provide finance for purposes not directly related to the value of the residence, such as to acquire furniture or appliances for the home. Such loans are regulated, in particular, by the Home Equity Loan Consumer Protection Act of 1988 (HELCPA), which requires full disclosure of the terms of the loan and prevents lenders from making unilateral changes to the terms of the loan. As many HELs are provided in the form of a credit card advance, or may appear to the borrower as regular bank loans, HELCPA requires the lender to emphasize that it is taking a secured interest in the borrower's home.

home improvement grant(Eng)   See **grant**.

home-loss payment(Eng)   A payment that may be made to a residential occupier, who has been displaced from a dwelling, against his or her will, by a local or public authority (LCA 1973, ss. 29-33, as amended). For example, when displacement results from the compulsory acquisition of an interest in a dwelling. A home-loss payment is made in addition to any **compulsory purchase compensation**, being a payment made as recognition that a person is compelled to leave his home. If the strict statutory conditions required for a person to claim such a payment as of right are met, an authority possessing compulsory purchase powers has a discretionary power to make payments to any resident it displaces.

home occupation(US)   An **accessory use** of a dwelling unit for gainful employment that is incidental, subordinate and secondary to the main use of the property as a residence. Home occupation may be prescribed as a permitted use in a building that is primarily used as a dwelling.

homeowners' association or home owners' association (HOA)(US)   A non-profit organization formed by all the homeowners in a **condominium**, **planned unit development**, or similar form of subdivision, to manage and maintain the property and the owner's interests in the common areas. The association is generally an incorporated body with bylaws, and a charter that is approved by the state. The 'members' accept mutual rights and obligations as to the use and upkeep of their units, as well as the common elements, and the homeowners' association, through its elected board of directors and officers, is responsible for enforcing those rights and obligations. Accordingly, it may make such bylaws and regulations as are reasonable for the proper running of the development.

A homeowners' association is generally established upon completion of a new development (usually by the initial developer) and every unit purchaser automatically becomes a member of the association upon completion of a purchase. The control of the association passes from the developer to the unit owners, normally when between sixty and eighty per cent of all the units have been sold. The association is responsible for the control and management of the common elements and, in the case of a condominium, is in effect the overall manager of the building. In some cases the association may take over the ownership of some or all of the common elements. In addition, the association is responsible for collecting the dues or assessments that are levied on the homeowners for the upkeep of the project and has the power to impose liens on the property of any homeowner for delinquent dues. In the case of a condominium project, also called a **condominium owners' association**, a 'condominium association', or a 'condominium management association'. See also **collective ownership**, **condominium declaration**, **covenant conditions and restrictions**.

Bickel, Branden E. *Condominium Bluebook: A Handbook for Homeowner Associations*. 11th ed. Piedmont, CA: Piedmont Pub., 1999.

Freedman, Warren, and Jonathan B. Alter. *The Law of Condominia and Property Owners' Associations*. New York: Quorom Books, 1992.

Wyatt, W. S. *Condominium and Homeowner Association Practice*. 3rd ed. Philadelphia, PA: ALI-ABA Committee on Continuing Education, 2000.

homeowner's insurance policy A **comprehensive insurance** policy devised for an owner of a residential property to cover most perils, associated with the building – fire, storm, burst pipes, etc.; personal risks such as third party or public liability; liability for animals; liability to visitors and employees; and, usually, the contents of the property. Also called 'householder's comprehensive insurance'. See also **all-risks insurance**.

homestead   1.(US)A private residence, comprising a house and adjacent land, owned and occupied by a family as its **home** and to which specific statutory benefits apply. A homestead comprises the one house in which the family resides, as well as the usual appurtenances and any outbuildings that are used as a part thereof. 'Homestead' may be used to refer to the property that is occupied as the home, as well as the right to have it exempt from levy or forced sale (the **homestead right**).

homestead association(US)   See **building and loan association**.

homestead right(US)   The personal right associated with the ownership of a **homestead**. A right available to the beneficiary to maintain a **home** free from the claims of creditors against that home. The homestead right is unique to North America and originates from state constitutional or statutory provisions designed as a matter of public policy to "protect the family from dependence and pauperism", Estate of Johnson v. C. I. R., 718 F.2d 1303, 1307 (5th Cir. Tex 1983). The homestead right varies considerably from state to state. In most states it provides protection from seizure and forced sale for non payment of general debts, as long as the property is occupied as a home, subject to a statutorily prescribed limit on the area of land and the dollar amount of the home. In many states a homestead exemption applies only to real property (which can include a mobile home, a leasehold, or a beneficial interest in a land trust); although some states extend the exemption to personal property in the homestead. Generally, the homestead cannot be mortgaged or sold by a husband or wife without the written (and usually independently acknowledged) consent of both parties. In addition, the wife may enjoy certain rights to continued occupation after the death of her husband. In some states a homestead right extends to surviving family members, especially a surviving spouse and minor children (called the 'probate homestead'). The homestead right does not normally apply to protection against non-payment of real estate taxes or to a **purchase money mortgage**. In most states a homestead right does not come into existence until it is registered as such in accordance with local regulations (and in some jurisdictions it must be reregistered annually). cf. **tenancy by the entirety**. See also **business homestead**.   2.(US)A right obtained by a private citizen to acquire **public lands** after having legally entered thereon and resided on and cultivated the land for a period prescribed by statute (generally five or more years). Generally, such homestead rights (other than subsisting rights and lands in Alaska) have been repealed by the Federal Land Policy and Management Act of 1976 (43 USC § 1701 et seq.). **3.**(Can)A right of a husband or wife to a life estate in certain lands of their deceased spouse. In several provinces, the common law rights of **dower** and **curtesy** have been abolished and replaced by a statutory right of dower; a matrimonial right for the wife (or in some provinces the husband) to withhold consent to a disposition of the family residence; or other forms of homestead rights that are similar to those in the US as described in **1.** above.

homestead society(US)   See **building and loan association**.

homesteader(US)   One who has or claims a right to a **homestead**.

homologation   **1.** An action by which someone agrees or concurs. See also **estoppel**. **2.**(Scot)The act of confirming or agreeing. The act of **ratification**.

hope value   An increase in the value of land produced by a belief that there is a chance that the demand for that land will change significantly; for example, when there is a prospect that planning or zoning approval will be granted for a change to a more valuable use. 'Hope value' may be quantified as the price paid for land in excess of the **existing use value** when a purchaser considers there is a chance of obtaining consent to carry out an alternative and more valuable form of development; **development value** on a speculative basis. See also **highest and best use**.

horizontal lease   See **top-slice lease**.

horizontal ownership   See **condominium**, **flying freehold**(Eng), **strata title**.

horizontal privity(US)   The relationship that exists between the original parties to an agreement that relates to land. For example, the relationship between the original landlord and tenant, or the original parties to an easement or a covenant that affects the use of land. cf. **vertical privity**. See also **privity**.

horizontal property acts(US)   See **condominium**.

horizontal-slice participation   See **top-slice participation**.

horizontal subdivision   See **condominium**, **flying freehold**(Eng), **strata title**.

horticulture   Traditionally, the cultivation of the soil and its fruits with hand tools. In modern terms, the cultivation of a **garden**, orchard or small area of ground for the growing of trees, shrubs, flowers, fruits, and vegetables, especially for business or profit. See also **agriculture**, **allotment**(Eng).

Hoskold coefficient or **Hoskold factor**   A factor established in 1877 by Henry David Hoskold, an English mining engineer engaged in the valuation of mineral rights, which is a **dual-rate capitalization factor**, i.e. a factor that is used to capitalize income from a depreciating investment (e.g. a leasehold interest or a wasting asset) by incorporating a mathematical adjustment so that the capital value obtained is comparable to a similar, but non-depreciating, investment. The formula for this capitalization factor incorporates two rates: a 'conventional rate' (sometimes called a 'speculative rate') to apply to the income stream from the investment as for any similar investment, and a 'safe rate' that provides for a notional **sinking fund** that is set aside from the income and invested to provide a capital sum to replace the investment at the end of its economic life. The term 'Hoskold coefficient', or 'Hoskold factor', is used in the US; the equivalent term in the UK being 'dual rate years' purchase'. See also Appendix C, **Financial Formulae**, dual-rate capitalization factor[(AmE)]/**dual-rate years' purchase**[(BrE)].

hostel   1. A **lodging house**, **inn**, **public house**, or similar place that provides shelter for the public, especially the travelling public. A place where people stay in shared or modest accommodation and which provides communal facilities such as cooking, eating, recreational and washing facilities.   2. A rest house or temporary accommodation for students, nurses, the disabled, displaced, dispossessed or deprived. Generally, such accommodation is of a modest nature and is provided for a short stay, although it may be provided for a term or semester.   3. Historically, an **hotel**, but in modern usage a place that provides overnight lodging, especially in the form of a supervised shelter and particularly for young people who are hiking, bicycling or canoeing around a region or country and from one shelter to another, e.g. a 'youth hostel'. Nonetheless, in many regulatory contexts, a hostel is an hotel as it provides rooms for transient guests, even though restricted to 'members' of an association.

hostelry   An inn, lodging house, or a small hotel.

hostile possession[(US)]   Possession held adversely to the claims of the true owner; the holding of possession as one's own with the intent to dispossess the true owner. 'Hostile possession' as an element of **adverse possession** does not import ill will, but rather imports that the claimant is in possession as one who is claiming title to land. See also **forcible entry and detainer**.

hotchpot or **hotchpotch**   1. The mixing of property that belong to different persons in order to distribute the benefit of ownership of the whole equally. Any money or property that has been granted to a particular child during a lifetime which must be brought into account when determining the fair basis for the distribution of a person's estate especially on intestacy. The purpose of putting property in hotchpot is based on a common law principle that one heir should not be unreasonably favoured over another heir or heirs when following the laws of descent.

In the UK, when assessing a liability to **inheritance tax** 'hotchpot' is applied to insure that all lifetime gifts are brought fully into account. Thus, if a person makes life-time gifts of £10,000 and £30,000 (which must be brought into account if made up to seven years before death) and dies leaving £100,000, the inheritance tax is levied on the entire 'estate' of £140,000. See also **advancement**.   2.[(US)]**Community property** that is held by both parties as part of the community estate.

hotel   A place that provides transient guests or travellers with lodging and facilities for a short stay and that is open to the public as a whole and not merely to a defined private group. A building, with many rooms, which provides the public at large with paid sleeping accommodation, or board and lodging, but over which the proprietor retains the right of access to, and control of, the premises. A place where people stay (as opposed to live) for comparatively short periods while away from their ordinary home, usually on business or vacation. An hotel is generally a place where visitors are provided quality accommodation and supporting services for a short stay; as distinguished from a **hostel**, or an ordinary **lodging house**, which primarily provides refreshment and in many cases limited, cheaper accommodation. The words **inn** and 'hotel' may be considered to be synonymous; but if there is a distinction, it is that the former is smaller and may be more akin to a home, or may be regarded as more casual or informal, with fewer facilities for the business traveller, and the latter has more facilities for the business traveller and sometimes more pretension. An hotel may be a commercial hotel, essentially for businessmen or transient visitors; or a more permanent place of residence providing the occupants with a home on a 'long-stay' basis – usually on a weekly or monthly licence – or even, for some visitors (but not as a rule) a permanent place of residence. An hotel generally provides food, drink, refreshment and services such as a manned reception desk, public rooms, bellhop service, porter or concierge, phones and faxes, valet and laundry service and daily room cleaning and linen changes. In particular, these facilities are provided for the travelling public and other casual guests. In addition, an hotel may provide such facilities as meeting rooms, conference facilities, dining rooms and room service, bars, boutiques, a fitness center, and entertainment that may be available to guests and for visitors who may not be resident guests. Nonetheless, a 'hotel' need be no more than a place intended to provide good lodging. An hotel that provides a complete range of services is called a 'full-service hotel' and a 'budget hotel' provides only limited services.

In English statute law, 'hotel' is defined as "an establishment held out by the proprietor as offering food, drink and, if so required, sleeping accommodation, without special contract, to any traveller presenting himself who appears able and willing to pay a reasonable sum for the services and facilities provided and who is in a fit state to be received", The Hotel Proprietors Act 1956, s. 1(2).

In the US, most statutory definitions are fairly broad and include any building with a number of rooms that provides food and sleeping accommodation for the public. In some jurisdictions, the zoning code defines any building, or group of buildings, in which more than half of the units are used for lodging as an hotel. cf. **motel**.

Marshall, Harvey, and Hazel Williamson (editors). *Law and Valuation of Leisure Property*. 2nd ed. London: Estates Gazette, 1997.

Raleigh, Lori E., and Rachel J. Roginsky (editors). *Hotel Investments: Issues and Perspectives*. 3rd ed. Orlando, FL: Educational Institute of the American Hotel and Motel Association, 2002.

Rushmore, Stephen, and Eric Baum. *Hotels and Motels: Valuation and Market Studies*. Chicago: Appraisal Institute, 2001.

PFK Consulting. *Hotel Development*. Washington, DC: Urban Land Institute, 1996.

house A building of permanent character that has been constructed or adapted so that it may be used for living in and usually, but not necessarily, severed from another holding. A building capable of or intended for human habitation, i.e. a building that is used primarily as a **dwelling house**. This is the common meaning, but the word house (but not dwelling house) may be construed to include any building, whether it is intended for habitation, or for any one purpose. Words such as 'house of God', 'country-house', 'house of correction', 'guest-house', 'work-house' and 'roadhouse' indicate that any place where people are given shelter may be a house, and 'storehouse', 'warehouse', 'opera house', 'court house' and 'schoolhouse' indicate a place for storage or gathering of people. However, without prefix or suffix, outside of statutory qualification, in its most common usage, a house is a building for human habitation.

In English statutes, a house is generally defined by inclusion. For example, in connection with local authority loans for housing improvement a 'house' includes "(a) any yard, garden, outhouses and appurtenances belonging thereto or usually enjoyed with it, and (b) any part of a building which is occupied or intended to be occupied as a separate dwelling including, in particular, a flat", HA 1985, s. 457. In the case of a letting of a house for human habitation at a low rent and where there is an implied term that it is **fit for human habitation**, "'house' includes – (a) a part of a house, and (b) any yard, garden, outhouses and appurtenances belonging to the house or usually enjoyed with it", L&T Act 1985, s. 8(5). For the purpose of the statutory right of **leasehold enfranchisement**, or a right to an **extended lease**, a house includes "any building designated or adapted for living in and reasonably so called, notwithstanding that the building is not structurally detached, or was or is not designed or adapted solely for living in, or is divided horizontally into flats or maisonettes; and − (a) where a building is divided horizontally, the flats or other units into which it is so divided are not separate 'houses', though the building as a whole may be; and (b) where a building is divided vertically the building as a whole is not a 'house' though any of the units into which it is divided may be", Leasehold Reform Act 1967, s. 2. Thus, all houses in a terrace together are not a 'house'. Also, a building that is not structurally detached *and* where a material part lies above or below another structure is not a house for this purpose. A building of mixed use can be a house for this purpose, especially when it is "designed or adapted for living in", as with a shop with living accommodation above (*Tandon v Trustees of Spurgeons Homes* [1982] AC 755, 761 (HL)).

When used in a deed or conveyance, without qualification, 'house' includes any outbuildings, **curtilage**, orchard, or garden associated with the house (1 *Co Litt* 56b; *Bettisworth's Case* (1580) 2 Co Rep 31b, 76 Eng Rep 482; Rosencranz v. United States, 356 F.2d 313 (1st Cir. Me 1966)). A building divided horizontally into two separate maisonettes can be a 'house' in its entirety. See also **appurtenance, back-to-back house**(Eng), **boarding house, cottage, double house**(US), **duplex house, home, lodging house, maisonette, manor, mansion house, messuage, multiple occupation, public house, residence, rooming house**(US), **row house**(AmE), **semidetached house, tenement house, terrace house, town house**.

Arden, Andrew, and Caroline Hunter. *Manual of Housing Law.* 7th ed. London: Butterworths, 2003.

house agent(BrE)   See **accommodation agent, estate agent.**

housebote   See **estovers.**

householder's comprehensive insurance   See **homeowner's insurance policy.**

Housing Action Trust (HAT)(Eng)   A nondepartmental body that is set up to deal with an area of urban deprivation (generally an inner urban area). Such a body is set up when the Secretary of State considers that an area is in need of direct central government intervention to regenerate the local economy. An HAT can only be introduced into a housing area with the consent of the majority of tenants. However, once introduced the trust may benefit from substantial government aid. The intention of the trust is to use private and public funding to improve the physical condition of the 'housing action trust area' by the repair, improvement and management of the houses in the area, the living and social condition for people in the area, and the general environment of the area (Housing Act 1988, Part III).

housing action trust area(Eng)   See **Housing Action Trust.**

housing association(Eng)   A society, body or trust set up to provide housing for its members on a non-profit basis. A housing association is "a society, body of trustees or company—(a) which is established for the purpose of, or amongst whose objects or powers are included those of providing, constructing, improving or managing or facilitating or encouraging the construction or improvement of housing accommodation, and (b) which does not trade for profit or whose constitution or rules prohibit the issue of capital with interest or dividend exceeding such rate as may be prescribed by the Treasury, whether with or without differentiation as between shares or loan capital [but does not include Scottish Housing]", Housing Association Act 1985, s. 1(1). The intention of the association is to construct, improve and manage housing as economically as possible for the mutual benefit of the members of the association. See also **housing association tenancy, Housing Corporation, housing trust, Registered Social Landlord.**

Alder, Professor John, and Christopher Handy. *Housing Associations: The Law of Social Landlords*. 4th ed. London: Sweet & Maxwell, 2002.

Driscoll, James. *Housing Associations and Social Landlords – Law and Practice*. London: Butterworths, 1999.

housing association tenancy(Eng)   A tenancy of a dwelling-house created where the landlord is a registered **housing association**, a **housing trust** or the **Housing Corporation** and the tenancy would be a **protected tenancy** but for the express statutory exclusion granted for such bodies. Prior to 1980, housing association tenancies were eligible to have their rents registered as 'fair rents' in the same way as a protected tenancy (RA 1977, s. 67). After 1980, most housing association tenancies were brought within the parameters of a **secure tenancy** (HA 1980, s. 28(2)(3)). Since January 15, 1989 any new tenancy granted by such a body falls within the same regime as most other private residential lettings, i.e. it is likely to be an **assured tenancy**.

housing authority   1.(Eng)A local authority that is responsible under Acts of Parliament (the Housing Acts and Local Government Acts) for the administration of certain obligations relating to residential property, such as the provision of housing accommodation, especially for those on low income or with special needs; inspection of the condition of housing in its area; the issue of repairs notices, closing orders, demolition orders, clearance orders; and the improvement of the general standard of housing in the area under its control. See also **council housing, Housing Action Trust, secure tenancy**.   2.(US)A corporation that provides public housing or carries out urban renewal on behalf of a state or municipal authority. See also **Federal Housing Administration**(US), **public housing**.

housing cooperative   See **cooperative ownership, housing association**,

Housing Corporation(Eng)   A non-departmental public body that is responsible for the promoting and assisting of registered social landlords (RSLs) (Housing Association Act 1985, Part II (Housing Act 1996, ss. 30-38). The "Corporation" (the Housing Corporation or Housing for Wales) is required to maintain a register of "social landlords" and is responsible for the supervision and control of such organisations. It may make loans to registered social landlords and acts as agent for the Secretary of State in making grants to such entities. The Corporation may acquire land itself by agreement (or if authorised compulsorily) for resale or leasing to RSLs. It is also responsible for promoting and assisting the development of unregistered self-build societies and the publicising of their aims and principles. The Corporation may provide hostels or dwellings for letting or for sale, as well undertaking the management of such properties. See also **housing association, registered social landlord**. (**www.housing.gov.uk**).

housing estate(BrE)   A group of dwelling houses, blocks of flats or apartments, designed and built to form a single planning entity, generally with the houses having a similar design and normally designed or built by the same developer. See also **planned unit development**(US), **scheme of development**.

housing grant(Eng)   See **home improvement grant**.

housing society(Eng)   An organisation with a similar (but more limited) objective to a **housing association**. A society that (a) is registered under the Industrial Societies and Provident Act 1965; (b) does not trade for profit; and (c) is established for the purposes of constructing, improving or managing houses either for letting or, if the society's rules so require, for occupation by its members (Housing Act 1964, s. 1(7)).

housing trust   1. A private trust established to provide houses for its beneficiaries on a non-profit making basis.   2.(Eng)A corporation or body of persons established to use all or most of its funds to provide houses predominately for persons of the lower income groups (HA 1985, s. 6; Housing Associations Act 1985, s. 2). Essentially a charitable trust established to provide accommodation for families on low incomes. A housing trust is a form of **housing association**, although it must provide housing accommodation itself, it cannot carry out secondary housing activities, nor can it provide other non-housing services.

human habitation   See **dwelling house, fit for habitation, unfit for human habitation.**

hundred-percent location   See **prime location.**

hurdle rate   **1.** The minimum rate of return that is acceptable to an investor. In particular, the level of return that an investor requires to consider purchasing a property. If the hurdle rate is not achievable an alternative investment will be considered. See also **target rate of return**.   **2.** A rate of return or income that is just sufficient to cover of the cost of servicing the debt required to make an investment. See also **break-even point.**

husband-like manner(Eng)   The manner in which a tenant of an **agricultural holding** (or similar land) is, by implication, expected to maintain the property. Keeping an agricultural property in a 'husband-like manner' requires maintaining the land in "good heart and condition"; ensuring that any cultivated land is in a state for efficient production; and keeping the farm house, if any, in a **tenant-like manner**. See also **good husbandry, implied covenant.**

husbandry   The business of a farmer or rancher; the process of farming land to raise crops and livestock. In particular, farming in a domestic or well-trained manner. See also **agriculture, good husbandry, husband-like manner**(Eng).

hybrid mortgage(US)   See **equity-participation loan/equity participation mortgage.**

hybrid trust(US)   See **real estate investment trust.**

hyperamortization(AmE)   A provision in a loan agreement that after the anticipated maturity date the interest rate increases and all cash flow is first applied to amortization. The accrued interest at the 'extended term rate' is automatically added to principal.

hypermarket   A large self-service **retail** store that sells a wide range of consumer goods (food and non-food), including such items as white goods, home furnishings, garden supplies and clothing. A hypermarket is generally free standing, predominately on one level, with ample adjacent car parking space and is normally situated in an out-of-town location with good road communications. A hypermarket may be distinguished from a **supermarket** by having a gross floor area of over 5,000 square meters (50,000 square feet). A term used more in Europe than North America. cf. **department store**. See also **superstore.**

hypothec(Scot)   A form of security over movable property where possession is retained by the debtor. A right that is similar to an equitable **lien** in English law. An implied hypothec may arise when a landlord takes a 'hypothec action' for arrears of rent and thereby exercises a right to hold the tenant's movable property on the premises. A process that is similar to 'walking possession' as exercised under the English law of distress.

hypothecation   The grant of a **hypothec**. A pawn or pledge of property as security for a loan, but without the debtor parting with possession. A term of Roman Law (*hypotheca*) that is used in civil and Scots law, for any pledge of goods without a transfer of possession by the debtor (as with a ships cargo), or a letter that is granted securing all bills or documents against which advances are made under a loan agreement. If the debtor also grants a right of possession, the creditor has all the rights of a **pledge**. cf. See also **charge**.

hypothecary value or **hypothecatory value**(US)   See **collateral value**.

hypothetical   That which depends on supposition or assumption. In particular, that which is formulated as a possible law to be tested by experiment. Something taken as given for the sake of making a testable assessment or analysis, i.e. an antecedent statement made for the purpose of argument or in order to follow through its consequences, but not necessarily something presumed to be factual.

In English law, relating to rating valuation, the **rateable value** is the amount that would be paid for a property on the assumption that there is a possible tenant, a 'hypothetical tenant', prepared to take a property upon the conditions laid down in the rating legislation. This tenant is someone who might take the premises, including an existing occupier, at the estimated rent at which the premises might reasonably be expected to let from year to year. The rent is referred to as a 'hypothetical rent', as hypothetical as the tenant. Thus, the rating valuer has to determine the annual value of a property not necessarily on the basis of any existing tenancy, but on the basis of an 'assumed' or hypothetical tenancy granted in accordance with the statutory provisions. "The world of rating appears ... to be cloud-cuckoo land, a world of virtual unreality from which real cuckoos are excluded (although it seems that permission to land will be granted to a cuckoo flying in the real world if it can be demonstrated that its presence in cloud-cuckoo land is essential, not merely accidental ...). A valuation for rating purposes must be based on hypothetical not real facts", *China Light & Power Co Ltd v Comr. for Rating and Valuation* (1995) 2 HKC 42 (HK).

I

ibid or *ibidem*(Lat)   'In the same place'; 'from the same source'.

id certum est quod certum reddi potest(Lat)   'That is certain which can be rendered certain'. See **contract**, **lease**, **option**, **price**, **rent**, **term**, **tenancy for a fixed term**, **tenancy from year to year**.

id est (i.e.)(Lat)   'That is'.

idem(Lat)   'The same'; as previously mentioned.

ignorantia facti excusat, ignorantia juris non excusat(Lat)   'Ignorance of the fact excuses; ignorance of the law does not excuse'. See also **mistake**.

illegal contract   A **contract** that, by its intent rather than its form, is contrary to the established law and therefore cannot be considered in a court of law. An illegal contract may stipulate for iniquity; be contrary to the general policy of the law; be against public good or public morals – *contra bones mores*; or be created for an immoral purpose – *turpis causa*. A contract may be illegal because the subject matter, the consideration, or the purpose is illegal. A lease of premises to be used, for example, for a criminal activity or to defraud the Revenue is an illegal lease when the parties are aware of the intent to commit a crime. An illegal contract is void, i.e. it is treated in law as if it had never existed; and, unlike any other **void contract**, at law neither party can recover anything paid or transferred as a result of such a contract: the maxim being *ex turpi causa non oritur actio* – 'a right of action cannot arise from a base act'.

illegal interest   See **usury**.

illiquid asset   An **asset** that cannot readily be turned into cash; real property being one of the most illiquid of assets. See also **liquidity**.

immaterial alteration   An **alteration** to an instrument that does not materially change its intended meaning or legal effect. See also **mistake**.

immediate landlord   1. A landlord who obtains a right to physical possession upon the termination of a lease, especially as distinguished from a superior or **head landlord** whose right to physical possession depends on the termination of the lease of a person who is himself a landlord. 2. The landlord to whom a particular tenant actually pays rent.

immediate possession   In a contract for the sale of land, possession that is granted when the contract is executed, or takes effect upon the transfer of title. See also **actual possession**, **vacant possession**.

immemorial   See **appendant**, **prescription**.

immoral contract   See **illegal contract**.

immovable or **immoveable** or **immovable property**   Land, buildings, anything affixed to land, as well as an interest in land. In particular, property that can be touched, but cannot be moved physically because it is permanently fixed to land, or to a structure that itself is fixed to land, or, is directly associated with land so that it cannot exist independently of the land to which it relates. 'Immovables' may also include an estate or a charge over land (but not the proceeds of sale); it may be freehold or leasehold; a right under a mortgage (but not a debt *per se*); a right to minerals; or a rentcharge. A key factor being that the property has a fixed location and, therefore, is governed by the law of that place. cf. **movable**. See also **appurtenant**, **fixture**.

impact fee(US)   See **development fee/development impact fee**.

impeachment for waste   See waste.

imperfect mortgage(US)   A mortgage that is intended to create a legal mortgage, but is not created in the proper form and, therefore, only creates an **equitable mortgage**. In particular, a right held under an executory contract for the conveyance of land when the vendor has received promissory notes that represent the purchase monies (which are to be paid by instalments), but the title has not been transferred and is retained as security for the notes. An imperfect mortgage should be distinguished from an equitable **lien**, which may be held by a vendor who has parted with property, but has not been paid in full. cf. **installment land contract**.

implied abandonment   A failure to continue the use or enjoyment of a right or interest in property for such a period of time that it amounts to an **abandonment**.

implied acceptance   See **acceptance**.

implied accord   See **accord and satisfaction**.

implied agency   A right of **agency** that has arisen by implication. An agency that has not been created by direct or explicit words, but still represents an actual agency. A form of agency that usually arises from custom, necessity, or the nature of the relationship of the principal and the agent, and can be proven to exist from the surrounding facts or circumstances. cf. **agency by estoppel**. See also **agency of necessity**, **authority**.

implied agreement   See **agreement**.

implied assignment   An **assignment** that arises by operation of law, as compared with one that arises from the action of the parties.

implied authority   See **authority**, **ostensible authority**.

implied condition   See **implied term**.

implied contract   See contract, quasi-contract.

implied covenant   A **covenant** that, although not express, is deemed by law to form part of a deed. A covenant that may reasonably be inferred from the whole agreement and the circumstances attending its execution. At common law, a covenant may arise by implication, because either: (i) the covenant is considered implicit to the nature of the deed, or (ii) it follows from the express wording used in the deed. However, a covenant will only be implied if it is clearly consistent with the intention of the parties, or in order to give effect to the contract as a whole. As a rule, an **express covenant** upon a given subject, deliberately entered into without fraud or mutual mistake, excludes the possibility of an implied covenant of a different or contradictory nature. A covenant may be implied by code or statute law, as in the US with a **warranty of habitability**, or in English law with an obligation to provide residential premises that are **fit for habitation**.

   In common law, unless there is any express provisions to the contrary, a tenant implies that he will pay the **rent** reserved (the implication stemming especially from the use in the lease of such words as 'yielding and paying'); not commit **waste**; will rectify any dilapidation arising from his tenant's own lack of care (that which is referred to in English law as maintaining the premises in a **tenant-like manner**); not deny or disclaim (expressly or impliedly) his landlord's title; and deliver possession to his landlord at the end of the term of the lease. Unless there is an express provision to the contrary, the landlord implies that he will give **exclusive possession** to the tenant for the period of the lease; grant **quiet enjoyment**; and not cause any **derogation from grant**. The law may also insert conditions into an agreement based on the conduct of the parties; based on the facts that led to the agreement; or it may infer terms in order to give 'business efficacy' to the agreement (see **implied condition**). Nevertheless, a condition arises by implication because it can be said that the parties intended that the suggested stipulation should exist; not because it would be reasonable if it did exist. cf. **usual covenant**. See also **beneficial owner**[(Eng)], **change of use, continuous operation clause, demise, estoppel, furnished tenancy**[(Eng)], **improvement, insurance rent, landlord's access, oil and gas lease, negligence, open contract, repair, restraint on alienation, tax, tenant-like manner**.

implied dedication   Conduct by an owner of land that implies an intent to dedicate his land (or a part or right over the land) for public use. See also **dedication**.

implied easement   1. An **easement** that arises when the parties to a **conveyance** clearly intended to grant an easement, but failed to set it out in the written instrument. An easement that arises from the common intention of the parties to the transaction (*Pwllbach Colliery Co Ltd v Woodman* [1915] AC 634, 646 (HL)). Such a right may arise by **implied grant** and, in a few cases, by **implied reservation**. In general, the law does not favour implied easements as they are in conflict with the well-established principle that the terms of a real property transaction should be set down in the written instrument. 'Implied easement' may sometimes be used to refer to a **quasi-easement**, which existed before the grant, but was held over two parcels of land that were in common ownership. The term may also be used to encompass an **easement of necessity**; although the latter arises more from exigency than by an implication of grant.

In the US, some jurisdictions take the view that a purchaser of land in a subdivision acquires an easement over all the rights of way or common areas shown on the plat map. On the other hand, other jurisdictions take a narrower view of the implied right to such areas, in some cases only permitting the implied easement to apply to those rights that are necessary to the enjoyment of the acquired lot. In other cases the implied right to an easement over land that forms part of the subdivision may arise more from the principle of **estoppel**, or from **dedication**, than from any grant

or reservation of such rights. See also *jus spatiandi*. **2.** An easement or right of access that, even if not expressly set out in a lease, is implied as part of the grant, such as use of the common parts (stairways, elevators, corridors, etc.); the right to use common facilities such as laundry facilities, recreational areas; and the right to services to the property.

implied grant   A **grant** of an **easement** over land that arises by implication. An implied grant may arise: (i) as an **easement of necessity** when the circumstances are such that a property cannot be used properly without an essential means of access or a similar right; (ii) when an owner sells part of his land and a **quasi-easement** is converted into a true easement that is continuous and apparent and necessary to the reasonable enjoyment of the property granted (*Wheeldon v Burrows* (1879) 12 Ch D 31, 49 (CA); Fletcher v. Fuller, 120 US 534, 7 S Ct 667, 30 L Ed 759, 762-3 (1886); 28A C.J.S., Easements, § 3); or (iii) an easement that arises from the common intention of the parties as where the circumstances clearly indicate that the grantee of land should have the right to use the land retained by the grantor in a particular and defined manner. See also **access order, right of light**.

implied lease   See **implied tenancy**.

implied licence   A **licence** to enter onto land that may be inferred from an action or conduct of the owner or occupier and which clearly indicates that someone may enter upon and use the land for a specific purpose. Such consent can arise from the relationship between the parties, particularly as part of their normal business dealings; from **custom**; or from necessity. However, such consent does not create any interest in land and, as a rule, is terminable at will. cf. **trespass**. See also **licence by estoppel**[(Eng)].

implied listing[(US)]   A **listing** of a property that arises from the action of a property owner and a listing broker, but the terms of which are not set down in writing. In most states a listing agreement must be in writing and be signed by all the parties. See also **quasi-contract**.

implied notice   Notice that someone is presumed to have acquired from a reasonable knowledge of the facts or diligent inquiry. Notice or knowledge that a person is assumed to have because he has the means to obtain that knowledge by proper inquiry, even if he does not use it. Sometimes called 'inquiry notice' when used to refer to the type of information that one should learn about when the circumstances or surrounding facts indicate that further investigation or inquiry ought to be made. cf. **constructive notice**, **imputed notice**.

implied ratification   An acceptance, or **ratification**, of an agreement or action that arises from the conduct or action of a person rather than by an expressed approval, especially ratification that arises from **estoppel**. Implied ratification most frequently arises when someone accepts a benefit that is consistent with the act that is deemed to have been accepted, as where a principal accepts the benefit of something procured by an agent, even though it had not been expressly requested.

implied reciprocal servitude(US)   See **reciprocal negative easement**.

implied reservation   A reservation of an easement that arises from the necessity of the property that is granted, i.e. of an **easement of necessity**. In common law, an easement cannot arise by implied reservation, but must be created by an express or implied grant, or express reservation (*Wheeldon v Burrows* (1879) 12 Ch D 31, 49-50 (CA)). In the US, most jurisdictions follow the same principle, considering that a grantor cannot detract from that which he has granted, although the principle of 'implied reservation of easement' can be invoked only if there is a case of strict necessity and there is no indication that the parties intended anything to the contrary.

implied tenancy   A **tenancy** that is deemed to arise from an action of two parties in relation to land, such as may arise following entry into exclusive occupation and payment of rent. Sometimes called an 'implied lease', although as a **lease** is strictly speaking a formal instrument or 'conveyance' it cannot technically arise by implication. See also **tenancy at will**, **tenancy by estoppel**.

implied term or **implied condition**   A **term** or **condition** of a contract that, although not express, may be read into the contract if it would be reasonable so to do. A term or condition that must be read into a contract if the intention of parties is not to be defeated; usually because it is inherent in the nature of the contract, or so obvious that it 'goes without saying'. ('Terms and conditions' are commonly used together and the words have much the same meaning, although a term is a provision or proposition and a condition modifies or qualifies a contract.)

A term or condition may be implied to give 'business efficacy' to a contract, as a result of **custom** or trade **usage**, or as part of the general tenor of an agreement. "It is well settled that the parties who contract on a subject-matter concerning which known usages prevail, incorporate such usages by implication into their agreements, if nothing is said to the contrary", Hostetter v. Park, 137 US 30, 11 S Ct 1, 34 L Ed 568, 572 (1890); *The Moorcock* (1889) 14 PD 64, [1886-90] All ER Rep 530, 535). An implied term is what the parties *must* have intended, not what they *may* have intended (*Trollope and Colls v North West Metropolitan Regional Hospital Board* [1973] 1 WLR 601, 607, [1973] 2 All ER 260, 266 (HL)). In particular, a term will be inserted when, had a defect in the contract been pointed out at the outset, it would have been inserted without hesitation. The law implies conditions to give the contracting parties what they would reasonably have expected, but it will not imply a condition because one party has failed to make reasonable inquiries or make a proper examination of that which is offered as the subject of the contract.

A term or condition will not be implied if it conflicts with any **express term** of the contract (see **implied covenant**); if, within the context of the agreement, it acts to the undue detriment or burden of only one party to the contract; or when the express terms will suffice to make the contract effective in fulfilling the intention of the parties. The law will certainly not make implied promises when an express contract has been made on the same issue (Hawkins v. United States, 96 US 698, 24 L Ed 607, 610 (1877); *Lynch v Thorne* [1956] 1 All ER 744 (CA)). cf. **constructive condition**. See also **agent**, *caveat emptor*, **fit for the purpose, implied warranty, negligence, notice**.

implied trust 1. A **trust** arising from the operation of law, especially a trust that arises as a result of an equitable need to fulfil the wish or intention of a vendor or settler. For example, if A settles property, or agrees to transfer property to B to be held for the financial benefit of C, there is an implied trust between B & C; or when a property is paid for by one party but is conveyed to another. The term 'implied trust' may also be used to refer to any non-express trust, whether a **resulting trust**, which arises out of the actions and intentions of parties and to which it is closely related; or a **constructive trust**, which arises from an interpretation of the actions of the parties, especially to avoid one party being unjustly enriched to the detriment of another. 2.(US)A trust that is imposed by the courts to prevent **unjust enrichment**, especially one that is imposed to prevent fraud or a misappropriation of trust funds (Matter of Kawczynski, 442 F Supp 413, 416 (DC NY 1977)).

implied trust for sale(Eng) See **statutory trust for sale, trust for sale**.

implied warranty A **representation**, not in writing, that a given condition exists or that a property is in a particular state. In particular, a representation that a property is suitable for its intended use or purpose, or that it is in an insurable condition. In most jurisdictions in the US and in English law, there is an implied warranty that on the sale of a new residence the property is built in a good and workmanlike manner; that the house is built of suitable and proper materials; it complies with all building codes and regulations; and that the house is fit for habitation. In the US, in most jurisdictions, there is an implied **warranty of habitability**, or a statutory requirement to the same effect, upon a letting of a residential property. See also **fit for the purpose, implied term, warranty**.

impossibility of performance See **frustration**.

impound account(US) 1. An account into which a borrower is required to make regular payments to meet real estate taxes and insurance premiums in respect of the property held as security for a loan. Such accounts are generally required when the loan to value ratio exceeds 80%. See also **piti payment**. 2. A trust account into which funds are placed, or retained in **escrow**, to meet the closing costs that arise after a sale is completed, such as an expense arising from a warranty provided by the seller.

impound payments(US) See **piti payment**.

impropriation The transfer of a residence that has been in ecclesiastical ownership into lay ownership. cf. **appropriation**.

improved ground rent See **ground rent, leasehold ground rent**.

improved land 1. Land that has been partly or totally developed by the provision of roads, sewers, utilities, services, etc., especially where it has been increased in value by an **improvement**. 2. Land that has been taken into use and has been made better by cultivation and husbandry. Land put to profitable use. cf. **raw land**.

improved rent Rent payable by a tenant to reflect the value of an improvement made by his landlord, especially when the total rent then exceeds the **market rent**. cf. **virtual rent**.

improved value   **1.** The value of land or buildings taking into account any **improvement** thereto. See also **improved rent**. **2.**(US)The value of land and buildings erected thereon, as distinguished from the separate value of the land alone.

improvement   The process of making better, more desirable, or more profitable. An **enhancement** or **amelioration** in the value or quality of a property effected by the expenditure of labour or money. A permanent **alteration** or **addition** that has the effect of raising the usefulness, price, or in any way making something more advantageous; the result of an action that makes a thing more desirable. Any useful or valuable addition to land, or buildings, that becomes part of the land, or buildings. In particular, any addition that enhances the value or utility of a property and goes beyond mere **repair** or **restoration**. The provision of something new *prime facie* constitutes an improvement, but merely replacing something that is worn our or dilapidated is more likely to constitute a repair *Morcom v Campbell-Johnson* [1956] 1 QB 106, 115, [1955] 3 All ER 264, 266 (CA). On the other hand, if what is required in order to repair a property is a complete replacement by a modern equivalent, or replacement in a different form or structure, that would constitute an improvement. Repair may involve, and usually does involve, some degree of improvement, especially when something better is substituted for that which has gone before (*Wates v Rowland* [1952] 2 QB 12, 23 (CA); 41 Am.Jur.2d., Improvements, §§ 1-41). But the provision of something modern or different in kind, or something different in operation or purpose, even if it does not enhance the value, is beyond the scope of what is generally understood as 'repair'.

In the absence of any express or statutory provision to the contrary, a tenant is free, but not obliged, to make any improvement to the premises leased to him. However, such 'improvements' should be related to the authorised use of the demised premises; must not amount to a material change or alteration to the structure or fabric; and must not amount to **waste** (except, as a rule, ameliorating waste which improves the value of the property to the landlord). However, a lease may provide an absolute prohibition against improvement, especially if the improvement involves structural alteration; or the lease may provide that improvement to the premises may not be carried out without the landlord's prior licence or consent.

In English law, in all lease that contain a covenant, condition or agreement against the tenant carrying out improvements without the landlord's prior licence or consent, such a provision "shall be deemed, notwithstanding any express provision to the contrary, to be subject to a proviso that such licence or consent shall not be unreasonably withheld", L&T Act 1927, s. 19(2). In the case of a **protected tenancy** or a **statutory tenancy**, (instead of the above provisions) it is implied that the tenant will not make any improvements without the landlord's written consent; such consent is not to be unreasonably withheld, and, if unreasonably withheld, it shall be treated as given (HA 1980, ss. 81, 82). This provision does not apply in certain cases where the landlord has given notice, prior to the commencement of the tenancy, of his intention to regain possession of the premises at the end of the tenancy, nor to a **protected shorthold tenancy**. For this purpose an improvement means "any alteration in, or addition to, a dwelling-house and includes—(a) any addition to, or alteration in landlord's fixtures and fittings and any addition or alteration connected with the provision of any service to a dwelling-house; (b) the erection of any wireless or television aerial; and (c) the carrying out of any external decoration" (unless the landlord is liable for carrying out such decoration or for external repair) (HA 1980, s. 81(5). A similar provision applies to a **secure tenancy** (HA 1985, ss. 97, 98). See also **agricultural tenancy**(Eng), **betterment**, **business tenancy**(Eng), **capital expenditure**, **compensation** for improvements, **development**(Eng), **fair rent**(Eng), **fixture**, **listed building**(Eng), **market rent**, **material change in the use**(Eng), **mistaken improver**, **tenant for life**, **virtual rent**.

improvement area(Eng)　See **renewal area**.

improvement district(US)　An area or district that will benefit from local public improvements and as a result a special **assessment** is required to finance those improvements. 'Improvement district' may refer also to a separate legal entity, run by a board of directors, set up with similar powers to a local municipality to fund and carry out the local improvements. The improvement may have a right to issue its own bonds, carry out improvement works, and raise assessments from local residents to pay for the improvements. Also called a 'special assessment district' or 'special district'.

improvement grant(Eng)　See **grant**.

improvement lien　A lien that arises from improvement work carried out to another's land, especially a lien that arises by law to secure the proper payment for work carried out to land or buildings. See also **mechanic's lien**.

improvement line(Eng)　A line prescribed by a highway authority indicating the limit of an intended street-widening scheme (Highways Act 1980, s 73). See also **blight notice**, **compensation for injurious affection**.

improvement purchase(Aus)　The acquisition of **Crown land** that is occupied under a mining title, as where a person has been in occupation and has made improvements. The right is normally limited to a small area of land and the acquirer may not acquire further rights within a specified distance from the land acquired.

improvements and betterments insurance(US)　Insurance taken out by a tenant to cover the risk of loss or damage to improvements he has made to the leased premises.

imputed interest(US)　An interest rate that is imputed to a loan by law. In particular, a rate determined as appropriate by the IRS when the interest rate set in a transaction is considered to have been set artificially low; or when no interest rate is stated, as when the payment of interest has been deferred or an installment sale does not provide for interest on the unpaid amounts (26 USC, Internal Revenue Code, §§ 163, 483, 1272). Sometimes called 'legal interest'. cf. **legal rate of interest**.

imputed knowledge　See **imputed notice**.

imputed notice　Notice or information that a person is assumed to have received because it has been transmitted (expressly or constructively) to someone else who, it may be presumed, will remit the notice or information to the previously mentioned individual. For example, notice received by a legal representative or agent appointed to act for a purchaser and, therefore, assumed to be known to the purchaser. Within the law of **agency**, as a general rule, a principal may be assumed by a third party to have knowledge or notice of any matter that relates to the business for which the agent is employed and which becomes known to the agent while acting within the scope of the agent's authority (*Hiern v Mill* (1806) 13 Ves Jun 114, 33 Eng Rep 237; Mutual Life Insurance Co. v. Hilton Green, 241 US 622, 36 S Ct 676, 60 L Ed 1211 (1915)). Also called 'imputed knowledge'. cf. **constructive notice**, **implied notice**. See also **waiver**.

imputed value　A **value** attributed to a property that is not measured in monetary terms, such as the benefit of **use and occupation**. Value that is ascribed to something or arises from its **utility**, and not from its **intrinsic value** or from the worth of its components.

in advance　See **advance**, **rent in advance/rent in arrears**.

in æquali jure melior est conditio possidentis(Lat) 'In [a case of] equal right the situation of the party in possession is better'. In a case of equal claims, the rights of the party in **possession** are better.

in alieno solo(Lat) 'Against another's land'. 'On the land of another'. See **easement**.

in arrears See arrears, rent in advance/rent in arrears.

in chief See abstracted in chief.

in common See co-ownership, right of common, tenancy in common.

in futuro(Lat) 'In the future'. See **future estate, future interest**, *interesse termini*, **reversionary lease**.

in good faith See *bona fide*, good faith, utmost good faith.

in gross That which is not annexed to land. A right to land 'in gross' is not **appendant, appurtenant**, or in any other way annexed to land, but exists without benefiting land or issuing out of land. A **rentcharge** is a form of payment 'in gross' and in consequence does not give the payee any right to repossess the land for which it is payable. See also **easement in gross, gross, incorporeal hereditament, profit à prendre, right of common**.

in lieu(Lat) 'In place'; 'in stead'. See **deed-in-lieu of foreclosure, lieu lands, payment in lieu of taxes**.

in pais(Lat) Literally 'in the country'; outside of court or legal proceedings. In an informal manner, as distinguished from 'in a formal manner' or in **writing**. Outside that which is contained in documents, records, or that which is based on ascertained (rather than ascertainable) fact. See also **estoppel**.

in pari causa possessor potior haberi debet(Lat) 'In an equal cause, the party is in **possession** is to be preferred'.

in pari delicto potior est conditio possidentis [defendentis](Lat) 'In cases of equal fault, the position of the one in **possession** [or the defendant] is to be preferred'.

in personam(Lat) 'Against the person'. cf. *in rem*. See also **action** *in personam*.

in rem(Lat) 'Against the thing'. "The relation between a person and a thing is called by lawyers a *real* relation, or relation *in rem* (from the Latin *res*, 'thing') and is distinguished from a personal relation or relation *in personam*", F. H. Lawson and Bernard Rudden, *The Law of Property*. 2nd ed. Oxford University Press, 1982, p. 2. See also **action** *in rem*, **real property**.

in rem **loan** A 'real loan', i.e. a loan secured on real property. In particular, a **non-recourse mortgage**.

in situ(Lat) 'In the place'; 'in position'.

in specie(Lat) 'In actual form'. Not as a substitute or equivalent. Money *in specie* is coin and not paper money.

in tail See entailed estate, fee tail.

in terrorem(Lat) 'By way of threat'; 'by way intimidation'. In particular, a provision in a will that threatens to dispossess a beneficiary who contests the provisions of the will. See also **penalty**.

inalienable or **unalienable** Incapable of being transferred or surrendered. A right to property that cannot be, or may not be, freely transferred or alienated. Land that has been acquired as **native title** is generally inalienable, except by transfer back to the Crown or State, or to other members of the same tribe. See also **alienation, restraint on alienation, rule**

against perpetuities.

incentive fee   See **contingency fee**.

incentive zoning(US)   A provision in a **zoning ordinance** that permits a developer to take advantage of more beneficial zoning, e.g. increased density, if he provides facilities or amenities that benefit the local community or pays a 'development impact fee'. Sometimes called 'bonus zoning'. See also **contract zoning, development fee, planning gain**(Eng).

inchoate curtesy   See **inchoate interest**.

inchoate dower   See **inchoate interest, dower**.

inchoate interest   **1.** An imperfect or incomplete interest. An interest that has not fully come into effect, or is pending. For example, an interest in land or a lien that is about to be recorded.   **2.** An interest in land that is not a present interest but may become a **vested interest**, provided it is not barred, extinguished or divested by a prior event. Thus, an 'inchoate dower' is the interest that a wife may have in her husband's property that would become vested as a life interest upon his death. An 'inchoate curtesy' is the corresponding right in favour of the husband (although **curtesy** is a right that generally only takes effect upon the wife's death). See also **contingent interest, dower, future interest**.

inchoate mechanic's lien   A mechanic's **lien** that has been filed, but which relates back to the time that the affected work was commenced.

incidence   That which is **incident** or has an effect upon something else. The rate at which one cost or factor bears upon another; for example, the rate at which the cost of a parcel of land affects the total cost of a development project. See also **sensitivity analysis**.

incident   Something that follows from, appertains to or depends on another right. A privilege or burden that is accessory to an interest or estate. For example, a right of alienation is incident to an estate in fee simple (though separable in equity); a fixture becomes incident to the freehold; and a right to enter on land and take water may be incident to an easement or a profit à prendre. See also **incidence, incidents of tenure**.

incidental use   A use that is dependent on, associated with, or **incident** to the principal or main use of a property. See also **accessory use**(US), **material change in the use**(Eng), **planning unit**(Eng).

incidents of tenure(Eng)   Rights or services that formed part of the feudal rights of land **tenure**, e.g. the provision of personal services to the Crown or a Lord. Such a right when annexed to a **manor** is called a 'manorial incident'. Most feudal incidents of tenure have been abolished, but some may continue indefinitely, unless terminated by written agreement between the lord and the tenant. Those incidents that may continue are: a tenant's right of common; a right of the lord or tenant to minerals, a mine, gravel pit or a quarry; a right of the lord to hold a fair or a market; sporting rights; any liability of the lord or tenant for the upkeep of dykes, canals, ditches, sea or river walls, bridges and the like (LPA 1922, Sch. 12). Such rights have to be registered at the land registry (LRA 2002, s.88).

inclosed land   Land that is enclosed or in someway surrounded by a fence, hedge, ditch, wall, or similar obstacle in order to demarcate its privacy or limits of ownership. See also **enclosure, fence**.

inclosure   See **enclosure**.

inclusio unius est exclusio alterius(Lat) 'The inclusion of one is the exclusion of another'. See *expressio unius est exclusio alterius*.

inclusionary zoning(US)   A zoning ordinance applied to a residential development project which requires, as a condition of approval, the inclusion of a minimum amount of housing for low-income or middle-income households. cf. **exclusionary zoning**.

inclusive grant(US)   A **grant** of public land on the basis that the subject land includes an area that is the subject of a disputed title, especially when the disputed land may be obtained by an action of quiet title.

inclusive rent(BrE)   A **rent** that is paid so as to include real property taxes that are paid in turn by the landlord to the appropriate authorities. cf. **exclusive rent**.

income   'What cometh in'. In general, the increase in wealth of an individual, company or other organisation over a given period of time. Recurring periodic benefits to be derived from the application of capital or labour. Income may be 'gross' or 'net', before or after specified expenses, before or after taxes, before or after depreciation or appreciation, and may include gains from the sale of assets; but generally it is not equivalent to 'turnover' (*Yates v Yates* (1913) NZLR 281 (NZ)). In particular, money or money's worth received or earned on a recurring basis. In economic terms, pecuniary advantage earned from a 'factor of production' (land, capital or labour producing respectively rent, profit and wages as income). Gains from the sale of **capital**, but not from capital growth *per se*, may be classified as income.

Income from real property may be classified, after deduction of various expenses, as:

gross income (or, in the US, **gross operating income**) – the total receipts (gross rent, building operating expense contributions or operating cost receipts, licence fees, etc.) from all sources before any deductions or allowances.

effective gross income – the gross income, after allowing for losses due to voids and defaulting tenants.

net income – the gross income after deducting all operating or running expenses, service charges, real property taxes, insurance costs, management fees, rent losses, etc., directly related to the property. In the US, the 'effective gross income' after making these deductions is called **net operating income**, or 'net income before recapture'.

cash flow – the net income after payment of debt service (interest and principal repayment on all loans), and usually, after an allowance for depreciation – also called 'net before tax'. (Note: income may include gains from the sale of property but this is not included in cash flow.)

net cash flow (or 'net spendable income') – the cash flow after payment of income tax; this may be referred to as net income, or cash flow, after tax, or in the US, 'net after-tax cash flow' or simply 'net after-tax'.

In English statute law, 'income' from land is defined to include rents and profits (being payments received for the benefits to be derived from use, occupation or exploitation of land or buildings) (Conveyancing Act 1881, s. 2(iii); AEA 1925, s. 55(1)(v)). cf. **outgoing**. See also **profit**, **net rent**.

income analysis(AmE)   **1.** See **income approach**. **2.** An assessment of the income available from an investment or from a borrower compared to the level of debt service.

income approach or **income capitalization approach**(AmE)   One of the principal methods or 'approaches' used to determine the value of real estate. The **net income** that can be derived from a property is determined and then that income is capitalized at a rate that is considered appropriate for the risk that the income will continue to be received over the investment holding period or the remaining economic life of the property. Under this approach, the income in a particular year (generally the **stabilized net income**) may be capitalized; or the projected future cash flow (including any residual value at the end of the investment holding period) may be reduced to a capital value by the application of a **discounted cash flow** technique. See also **appraisal**, **capitalization**, **investment method of valuation**(BrE).

Appraisal Institute. *Readings in the Income Approach to Real Property Valuation.* Chicago: Appraisal Institute, 1977. Baum, Andrew, et al. *The Income Approach to Property Valuation.* 4th ed. London: Thomson, 1989.

income capitalization approach(AmE) See **income approach**.

income multiplier(AmE) A single **capitalization factor** used to convert an income stream into a present capital value. The reciprocal of the **overall capitalization rate**. An income multiplier may be a 'gross income multiplier' (GIM) or 'gross rent multiplier' (GRM); or a 'net income multiplier' (NIM) or 'net rent multiplier', depending on whether the multiplier is applied to the income or rent receivable before or after expenditure deductions. The GIM may be applied either to **gross income** or to the **effective gross income**, provided the application is consistent with the supporting analysis. An income multiplier may also be applied to the **potential gross income** ('potential gross income multiplier'). An 'income multiplier' is intended as a 'rule of thumb' method of determining capital value by the application of a single factor to a current income – a more reliable assessment of value is based on the capitalization, or ascertainment of the present value, of the projected net income. See also **capitalization factor, income, net income**.

income property A property that is held essentially for the production of income. Also called 'investment property'.

incomplete trust See **executory trust**.

incorporeal hereditament A right over **land** that is capable of inheritance, but is not tangible and does not give the owner any physical right to possession of the land. A mere right to property, as opposed to a right to the thing itself. In particular, 'incorporeal hereditament' includes an **easement, profits à prendre** and a **rentcharge**.

In English law, such diverse rights as an **advowson**, a **tithe**, a **right of common**, a **franchise** and an **annuity** are classified as 'incorporeal hereditaments' (but not necessarily the benefit of a restrictive covenant). An incorporeal hereditament cannot be seen or handled, but is a right issuing out of corporeal property (whether real or personal), a right that concerns or is annexed to, or exercisable with, a corporeal property.

Incorporeal hereditaments may be classified as: (i) **appendant**, that is of historical origin, e.g. advowson, manorial incidents; (ii) **appurtenant**, that is annexed to land, e.g. right of common, right of way; or (iii) **in gross**, that is they exist independently of land, e.g. rentcharge, rent-seck, common in gross, tithes, profit à prendre. cf. **corporeal hereditament**. See also **hereditament, incorporeal property**.

incorporeal property or **incorporeal thing** Property (or a **thing**) that is not tangible, cannot be seen, touched or otherwise sensed, but exists as a right to tangible or **corporeal property**. Property that can never be taken into physical possession and is represented only as a right or claim, e.g. a servitude, patent, debt, goodwill, copyright.

In Scots law, as in Roman law, things are classified as corporeal or incorporeal. Incorporeal property being any thing that does not have a physical presence. Incorporeal property corresponds roughly to a chose-in-action in common law. See also **incorporeal hereditament**.

increase clause(AmE) See **escalator clause**.

increment An increase in quantity, quality or value. A gradual enlargement in area, volume or character. cf. **decrement**. See also **accretion, enlargement**.

incroachment See **encroachment**.

incubator unit(AmE) A small industrial unit that is made available to meet the needs of new growing businesses. Also called a 'nursery unit', especially in the UK.

incumbrance   See **encumbrance**.

incumbrancer   See **encumbrancer**.

incurable depreciation or **incurable obsolescence**   Deterioration to a building that cannot be remedied, usually because it would be too expensive to restore or replace. Physical obsolescence is generally curable, at a cost; but economic obsolescence is normally incurable as the cost in not justifiable. 'Incurable depreciation' or 'incurable obsolescence' is used especially in appraisal terminology for a condition that is not worth making good. cf. **curable obsolescence**. See also **depreciation, obsolescence**.

indefeasible   That which cannot be defeated, forfeited, revoked or made void; especially an estate, interest or right to land that cannot be defeated by the claim of another, e.g. an easement that has been enjoyed without interruption for a period that exceeds the time needed for it to be acquired by **prescription**.

indefeasible estate or **indefeasible interest**(US)   An estate or interest in land that cannot be brought to an end as a result of a condition, restriction or limitation, i.e. an interest of indefinite duration that cannot be defeated or come to an end by the happening of a future event or the operation of a **condition subsequent**. cf. **defeasible interest**. See also **absolute estate**.

indefeasible title(US)   A title to land that cannot be defeated, set aside, or made void. cf. **defeasible title**. See also **marketable title**.

indemnity   1. Derived from the Latin *indemnitas*, 'non-detrimental'. Security or protection against loss or damage. Security against a contingent loss or injury. The making good a loss that has been suffered as a result of the act or default of another. **Compensation** or **restitution** paid by one party to another to cover a loss or injury suffered by the latter; whether arising from an agreement or otherwise. In particular,

something paid or rendered to restore the *status quo ante*. An indemnity that arises from an agreement is paid because of a separate activity that affects the agreement, unlike **damages** which are paid because of a failure to perform the agreement. See also **rectification**.   2. A **contract** by which one party agrees to accept the legal consequences of a loss that may fall on another. A provision of **security** against financial loss up to, but for no more than, an actual loss suffered. A 'contract of indemnity' is one entered into by a person who accepts a primary responsibility for a loss, even though he is not a party to any contract or act from which the loss arises. The indemnity may be provided in the form of a bond or similar form of collateral, or an agreement to provide compensation in the event of loss. Most contracts of **insurance** (except life or accident insurance) are contracts of indemnity; that is they are contracts which provide that, in the event of loss, damage or injury, an insured will be placed in the same, but no better, position than if no privation had arisen.

A contract of indemnity may be distinguished from a contract of **guarantee**, because a guarantor accepts that he will answer for the default or debt of another only as an accessory. A guarantor accepts a secondary obligation; whereas in a contract of indemnity the surety assumes a primary liability, either alone or jointly with the principal debtor. Thus, a tenant may provide a guarantee in the form of a bank deposit as security against his failure to meet his primary obligation to pay rent, but a 'tenant's default' insurance policy may be taken out by a landlord as an indemnity against the risk that the tenant cannot pay rent due to financial failure. See also **indemnity insurance, indemnity limit, reinstatement**.

indemnity insurance   1. **Insurance** that provides an **indemnity** against loss or damage directly occasioned by the insured; in contrast to **liability insurance** which provides an indemnity against a liability to another (or against damage caused to another's property). In the case of indemnity insurance, the insurer is not liable until the ultimate establishment of loss resulting from the enforcement of a liability arising against the insured; whereas with liability insurance, the insurer is responsible for the coverage as soon as the loss or damage is sustained by the insured. **2.** Insurance that is based on providing an indemnity that is assessed according to the actual loss or damage suffered; as distinguished from **contingency insurance** which provides for payment when a contingent event (e.g. death) occurs, but based on an amount specified in the policy. Under an indemnity insurance policy the insured cannot recover more than his loss. See also **reinstatement cost**.

indemnity lands(US)   **Public lands** that, by statute, may be taken from the public domain to replace land lost as a result of a previous disposition or reservation by the Land Department. Originally the term was applied to lands that were granted to replace land intended to be granted as a right of way for a new railroad, but which may inadvertently have been granted to another claimant (Weyerhaeuser v. Hoyt, 219 US 380, 31 S Ct 300, 55 L Ed 258 (1910)). Indemnity land may be distinguished from 'granted lands' or 'place lands' which are fixed once the line of the railroad has been determined. Indemnity lands must be available for acquisition under the land laws and are restricted usually by statute to land within a stipulated radius of the land that is being replaced. The term may also be applied to a land grant to a state to replace land that might otherwise have been sold or otherwise disposed of. See also **land grant**, **lieu lands**.

indemnity limit   The maximum amount of financial loss against which an **indemnity** has been provided. In particular, a limit on the level of liability accepted by an insurer. See also **valued policy**.

indented deed   See **indenture**.

indenture   **1.** A document, especially a **deed**, that establishes an agreement between two or more parties and is prepared in identical form for each party to the agreement. Traditionally, a deed between two or more parties was duplicated on the same sheet of paper or parchment and then cut, or 'indented' (cut with a jagged line like teeth), between the duplicates so that they could be verified as authentic copies when brought together. The words 'this indenture' generally are found at the start of any deed involving more than one party, even when there is no actual indenting.

In English law, a deed purporting to be an indenture need no longer be indented, or expressed to be an indenture, to have the effect of an indenture (LPA 1925, s. 56(2)).

In the US, a real estate conveyance is rarely, if ever, 'indented', but may be stated to be prepared in duplicate or as an 'indenture'. cf. **deed poll**. See also **counterpart**.   **2.**(US)A mortgage, deed of trust, or similar instrument, that acknowledges an outstanding debt of a corporation or business, or acknowledges that a corporation is bound to meet a particular obligation or obligations.

independent contractor   One who has a contractual obligation to perform certain acts on behalf of another, using his own methods; acting as his own master; only controlled as to the final product; and making decisions on any matters not specified in the contract by which he is appointed. An independent contractor is neither an employee, nor a party to a contract of service. As a rule, he performs a specific act, or series of acts, in accordance with the contract, and has no continuing responsibility to act according to the master's or employer's behest: an independent contractor is neither part nor parcel of the employing organisation. An independent contractor may or may not be an **agent**. However, he is more likely not to be an agent in the strict sense of the word, as an independent contractor makes commitments on his own behalf; in his own capacity; and is liable for any commitment made in his name. On the other hand, an agent is more likely to act in accordance with the direction of the principal. As a rule, a principal is not liable for any **negligence** of his independent contractor, but is more likely to be responsible for the acts of an agent acting in accordance with his instructions. See also **general contractor, subcontractor, vicarious liability**.

independent store   A retail store that is operated by an individual or company that is not part of a group or chain of stores and is not normally part of a **franchise** operation. As a rule, an independent store comprises no more than two or three outlets. In American English, also called 'independents'. cf. **chain store**.

independent valuer   See **expert**.

index animi sermo est(Lat)   'Words are the indication of intention'.

index lease or **indexed lease**   A lease that provides for an **index rent**. In American English, the adjectival suffix 'ed' is commonly omitted. Also called an 'escalation lease'. See also **escalator clause**.

index-linked insurance   A property insurance policy that provides for the amount of coverage to be automatically maintained in line with a specified index, usually an official cost of construction or cost of living index, to allow for variations in the cost of replacing or repairing the insured property. This form of policy reduces the need for the insured to readjust the amount of cover by making regular revaluations and, as a rule, reduces the risk that the insurer will apply the principle of **average** to any compensation paid under the policy.

index-linked mortgage   See **price-level-adjusted mortgage**.

Index Map(Eng)   A map kept by the **Land Registry** showing the position and extent of every registered title to land. As far as practicable all registered parcels are shown by reference to a **General Map** which is based on an **Ordnance Survey map** (Land Registration Rules 1925, r. 8).

See also **filed plan, Parcels Index**.

index method   1. Any method of valuation that adjusts the cost or value of a property by **indexation**.   2. A method of assessing the **reinstatement cost** of a property by adjusting the original, or some other historic cost, in line with a particular index. A subsequent adjustment may be made to take account of depreciation.   3.(US)A method of adjusting the sale price of a comparable property, when applying the **sales comparison approach**, by weighting the different factors that affect its comparative value (location, size, age, etc.) in accordance with an index or scale.

index of recorded titles or **index of registered titles**   See **grantor-grantee index**(US), **Index Map**(Eng), **land recording**(US), **land registration**(Eng), **mortgagee-mortgagor index**(US), **Parcels Index**(Eng), **tract index**(US).

index rent or **indexed rent**   A rent that is varied in accordance with a specified index. For example, a rent that is varied by annual adjustments based on an official cost of living or a construction index. In American English, the adjectival suffix 'ed' is commonly omitted. Sometimes called a 'linked rent' or 'linkage rent'. cf. **graded rent**. See also **escalation clause, indexation**.

indexation   A process of adjusting a price, income, rent, interest rate, or the consideration in a contract, in line with changes in a specified price index; especially in order to allow for the erosion of the price or the consideration due to inflation, i.e. to conserve the 'real value' of a sum of money. An initial price is related to a starting or base index figure (ordinarily taken as 100) and this price is adjusted in direct relationship to subsequent index numbers. The adjustment may be made at specified periods of time or specified movements in the index, e.g. every year or every time the index changes by, say, 5% from the base. The rent in a lease may be adjusted by relating it to movements of an official 'cost of living' index. A building contract may be adjusted in accordance with an official 'cost of construction' index; or by an agreed formula, such as :

$$p = P[0.40 \, (m/M) + 0.35 \, (l/L) + 0.25]$$

Where: p = final contract price.

P = initial or base price at start of contract.

m and M = official index of building material costs at respectively the start and end of the contract.

l and L = the official index of labour costs at respectively the start and end of the contract.

In this example the total price is indexed on the basis of a 'weighting' of 40 per cent for materials, 35 per cent for labour, and 25 per cent for fixed costs. See also **escalator**, **weighted aggregate index**.

indexed lease   See **index lease**.

indexed mortgage   See **price-level-adjusted mortgage**.

indexed rate(US)   The interest rate on an **adjustable-rate mortgage** given by the rate or 'index' used to vary the interest rate (e.g. a prime rate), plus the margin.

indexed rent   See **index rent**.

Indian lands(US)   Lands that belong to a tribe of Indians as a community, with the individual tribal member having a mere right of occupancy based on their membership of the tribe. The fee title to such land is usually vested in the United States (or in the case of the original 13 states, in the individual state) and the Indian tribe is granted a perpetual right of use and occupation – known as the 'aboriginal right of possession'. Such right is not a property right and cannot be alienated without federal authorization. Congress can take such a possessory right, although today that would be an unlikely event. Congress may also formally

grant or reserve land for Indians, or land may have been granted by treaty or executive order, and a taking of such land by the Federal Government requires the payment of **just compensation** under the Fifth Amendment. However, taking of land of unrecognized Indian title does not require the payment of such compensation (Northeast Bands of Shoshone Indians v. United States, 324 US 335, 65 S Ct 690, 89 L Ed 985 (1944)). See also **native title**.

Clinton, Robert N., et al. *American Indian Law: Native Nations and the Federal System.* 4th ed. Newark, NJ: LexisNexis, 2003.

indivisible contract   See **entire contract**, **performance**.

indorsement   See **endorsement**.

inducing cause(US)   See **procuring cause**.

industrial building   A building used for the purpose of a trade or business that involves the manufacturing, processing, fabricating, assembling or finishing of goods. A **factory**, **mill**, or similar premises, but not a building used solely for the storage and distribution of goods, i.e. not the type of building that would normally be called a **warehouse**.

In English town and country planning law, in connection with a **permitted development**, "'industrial building' means a building used for the carrying out of an industrial process and includes a building used for the carrying out of such a process on land used as a dock, harbour or quay for the purposes of an industrial undertaking but does not include a building on land in or adjacent to and occupied together with a mine", Town and Country Planning (General Permitted Development) Order 1995, Sch. 2, Part 8. See also **industrial estate**(Eng), **industrial property**, **Use Classes Order**(Eng).

industrial condominium(US)   An industrial building or estate held in **condominium ownership**.

industrial crops   See **emblements**.

industrial estate(BrE)   An area of land sub-divided and developed comprehensively for industrial use. Usually an industrial estate has a uniformity of appearance and design with common areas and services under one management. Typically it is developed by a single entrepreneur who provides the roads and main utilities for the estate and either sells or lets plots of land or builds a variety of industrial buildings for sale or lease. See also **industrial park**(AmE), **industrial property**.

industrial park(AmE)   A master planned development that is designed and laid out to incorporate predominately industrial buildings in a park-like setting with the requisite circulation, parking, landscaping, etc., required for an orderly scheme. An industrial park is generally a subdivision that is created and managed by one developer who imposes covenants on all occupiers to maintain the architectural and design integrity of the entire area for the benefit of the developer, investors, and tenants of the project. See also **industrial estate**(BrE), **planned unit development**, **scheme of development**.

industrial property   **1.** Land, improvements and machinery that are used as a functioning unit for the assembling, processing and manufacturing of finished or partially finished products from raw materials or fabricated parts. Industrial property may include factories, storage warehouses, workshops or premises used for carrying out repair or service to finished products such as laundries, dry cleaners, garages, filling stations, etc. In particular, 'industrial property' may be used in land planning or zoning to refer to property that should be located in a designated area and may be broadly subdivided into light, medium or heavy manufacturing, industrial parks and research and development facilities, and warehouse space. See also **commercial property, factory, industrial building, industrial park, light industrial building, warehouse, workshop**.   **2.** Intangible property that is related and is of value, to business or industry, e.g. copyright, patent, trademark, 'know-how', etc. This type of property, which exists only in the mind, is more usually classified as **intellectual property**.

infeftment(Scot)   The taking of possession of land by a vassal under the **feudal system**. Infeftment is the completion of the process of taking title from the superior holder of the land. See also **enfeoffment, sasine**.

infilling   That which is used to fill in a space, especially the development of an area between two existing built-up areas. Usually the development of small plots of land, between existing buildings, in such a way that the new development complements the existing.

informal contract   See **simple contract**.

informal lease   See **agreement for a lease, writing**.

infra(Lat)   'Below'; 'later'; 'underneath'.

infrastructure   The basic or underlying facilities of an urban area, especially the facilities required for a new development. In particular, transport facilities, utilities (electricity, water, sewage, etc.), as well as the associated land uses (shops, schools, etc.) that are necessary for the development of land. cf. **superstructure**.

ingress   The access, way in, or entrance to a property. cf. **egress**. See also **easement of access**(US).

ingrossment   See **engrossment**.

inhabitable   See **fit for human habitation**(Eng), **warranty of habitability**(US).

inherent defect; **inherent vice**   A constituent defect in a building. An 'inborn' fault in construction which, in due course, could make a property deteriorate into a particular condition, e.g. to settle or fall down, or could even make it unfit for use or habitation. See also **defect of title**, **implied covenant, improvement, latent defect, repair**.

inheritable   Capable of being inherited or of being granted to an heir. A preferable spelling in place of the older heritable.

inheritable fee   See **fee simple absolute**.

inheritance   **1.** Property that is received by law from the estate of a deceased person. In common law, 'inheritance' referred to an estate in land under the laws of descent in the case of intestacy (2 *Bl Comm* 201); but in general usage, it may refer to any property whether received by will or descent.   **2.** The acquisition of real property as an **heir** to another, i.e. by right of succession, rather than by devise or transfer by will. However, 'inheritance' may be used to refer to the devolution of property, or any property that devolves, on the death of its owner, whether distributed under the provisions of a will or one obtained by right of descent on intestacy. In common law, an inheritance was a right to possession of land which subsisted as long as there was someone capable of taking that land as a descendant, as distinguished from a mere right of **tenure** which reverted to the landowner upon the death of the immediate holder of that right. Thus, an inheritance was any property capable of passing to the owner's heirs. In Roman and the civil law, 'inheritance' refers to any acquisition of property, whether real or personal, by testament or by law upon the death of an owner; in common parlance the term is used in the same sense. See also **estate of inheritance, freehold, words of limitation**.

inheritance tax   **1.**(US)A state tax levied on the value of property received by an heir; to be compared with **estate tax**, or 'legacy tax' or 'succession tax', which is levied on the deceased's estate. An inheritance tax is not strictly speaking a tax on the property, but a tax payable by the beneficiary on the transmission of property from the dead to the living. However, it is necessary to look at the individual statute to determine the nature and incidence of any such tax. See also **succession duty**.   **2.**(Eng)A tax that replaced **capital transfer tax** in 1986. Inheritance tax is levied on the value of a person's total 'estate' as assessed on death. An 'estate' includes most property to which a person is beneficially entitled, less any liabilities secured thereon. Inheritance tax is payable on the 'chargeable assets' of the deceased, such as property, money and stocks and shares. See also **hotchpot**.
Tolley's Inheritance Tax, annual. Croydon, Surrey: Tolley.

inhibition(Eng)   An order or entry on the Proprietorship Register at the **Land Registry** made to prohibit, either totally or partially, any further dealing in a registered parcel of land or land affected by a registered charge, either for a specified period of time or until a specified event occurs (LRA 1925, s. 57). An inhibition may be likened to an injunction and is made, for example, in the case of fraud, bankruptcy or when the proprietor's land certificate has been lost. An inhibition is a hostile act, made in extreme cases, and is rarely encountered. Although the LRA 1925 has been repealed, an application for the entry in the register of a restriction that was pending prior to the repeal remains in effect, but no new inhibitions can be entered on the register (LRA 2002, s. 5(5)). See also **caution, minor interest, restriction**.

in-house sale(AmE)   A sale that is brought about when the broker who represents the buyer and the broker who represents the seller are both members of the same firm. In such a case the commission is retained entirely by the listing firm, rather than being split with another brokerage office; the individual broker's share being apportioned according to the rule of the listing firm. See also **dual agency**.

initial yield   **1.** The **yield** or net return from an investment at the time of its acquisition.   **2.** The net return from a new development based on the first full year's income or the **stabilized net income**, expressed as a percentage of the total development cost. cf. **running yield**. See also **cash-on-cash yield**.

injunction An order, granted at the discretion of a court of law, commanding a party to refrain from, or to take, a certain course of action, usually in order to reduce or prevent injury, or the threat of injury, whether arising from a **tort** or a **breach of contract**. An injunction is a form of equitable proceeding designed to be issued by a court to prevent damage or injury that is considered irreparable.

An injunction may be either 'mandatory' (compulsory) or 'prohibitory' (preventative or restrictive). A mandatory injunction compels someone to do something, or to undo something, i.e. it is restorative in its effect. For example, a mandatory injunction may require someone to demolish a building that has been erected illegally. A prohibitory injunction restrains a party from a course of action, e.g. from committing a **nuisance** or breaching a negative promise. Most injunctions are prohibitory. An injunction may be permanent (called 'perpetual' in English law); or interim (also called 'interlocutory' or sometimes 'temporary', 'preliminary', or 'provisional'). A permanent injunction is made after the details of a case have been heard. An interim injunction is made to preserve the status quo until the court has considered all the details of a case. An injunction is an equitable remedy, i.e. it is given at the discretion of the court. It acts *in personam* (i.e. it acts solely against the person) and, therefore, cannot 'run with the land'. In certain instances a court may award **damages** rather than grant an injunction; for example, where (i) money compensation can readily be assessed and would prove an adequate remedy; (ii) when the injunction cannot be enforced, notably in the rendition of personal services, or when it would not be reasonable to reverse a breach of a restrictive covenant; or (iii) it would be oppressive to grant an injunction. On the other hand, the courts may not grant damages when that would

still leave the offended party with a nuisance or aggravation, as with a flashing neon light. As a rule, an injunction will not be granted to prevent fairly minor acts of **waste** that have been committed to property by a tenant when pecuniary compensation is adequate for the damage to the landlord's reversion and there is no evidence that the damage will increase. cf. **specific performance**. See also **interdict**, **Mareva injunction**[(Eng)], **restraining order**[(US)], **Yellowstone injunction**[(US)].

injuria[(Lat)] 'Injury'. An infringement that gives rise to a legal right of compensation. cf. **damage**. See also *damnum sine injuria*.

injuria absque damno or *injuria sine damno*[(Lat)] 'Injury without harm'. See also **damages**.

injurious affection An action that has a harmful or deprecatory effect. In particular, a reduction in the value of a property as a result of works carried out by a public body on adjoining property. A physical interference with any right, public or private, which the owner or occupier of any property is, by law, entitled to make use of in connection with that property. The interference may be temporary, e.g. a restriction on access to, or disturbance to the use of property for a limited period of time; or it may be permanent or transitional, e.g. a change in the position of a right of way or a **severance** of the ownership of land, provided the result is to confiscate an existing right and to cause a loss in value. Sometimes called 'material detriment'. In the US, the term 'injurious affection' is generally considered to be synonymous with **damages**. See also **compensation for injurious affection**, **nuisance**.

injury The act of inflicting hurt or an invasion of a legal right, in particular when this arises from intent to do harm or commit a **tort**. "Injury is the illegal invasion of a legal right; **damage** is the loss, hurt or harm which results from the injury, and **damages** are the recompense or compensation awarded for the damage suffered",

22 Am.Jur.2d., Damages, § 2, p. 34. Injury may be a wrong or damage to someone's person, or his or her goods, and it need not be physical in nature. It can be caused by any interference with a person's legal right to enjoy something, including his or her property, a good character, or a freedom to conduct business. In particular, injury to real property, or a right or interest in real property, may arise from **trespass, waste, eviction, dispossession, ejectment, harassment,** or a disturbance of a right of **quiet enjoyment,** or from **nuisance** caused by an adjoining owner or occupier. See also **dangerous premises, injurious affection, negligence, strict liability.**

inland   See **manor.**

Inland Revenue charge(Eng)   See **land charge.**

inn   A public house or similar establishment that holds itself out as a place for receiving travellers who seek food, drink and, if so required, lodging, in return for payment. An 'inn' may be a tavern, **public house,** or **hotel,** in all of which the proprietor holds himself out ready to receive and entertain guests for compensation. It may be distinguished from a private **boarding house,** which by prior arrangement provides accommodation and usually one or more meals, at an agreed rate, for a certain period of time.

In American English, the term hotel (or motel) is generally used to encompass an establishment that historically might have been described as an inn, and the word inn is reserved for a smaller, more old-fashioned, or less well equipped establishments. See also **hostel.**

inner urban area(Eng)   An urban area of Great Britain that is considered in need of improvement due primarily to its special social needs. Loans and grants may be made available to assist with the improvement of properties in such an area (Inner Urban Areas Act 1978). See also **special area, urban development area.**

innocent conveyance   A **conveyance** that transfers only the title of the grantor, as distinguished from a conveyance that purports to convey more than the grantor's interest. In particular, a conveyance by a tenant that does not purport to grant more than the interest held and, therefore, does not create a possibility of forfeiture.

innocent improver(US)   See **mistaken improver.**

innocent misrepresentation   See **misrepresentation.**

innocent purchaser(US)   One who buys property, in **good faith,** without sufficient **knowledge,** or the means of acquiring such knowledge, as to any defect that affects the title to that property. Such a purchaser must have no reasonable basis to suspect that the person from whom he purchased the property did not have good title. See also *bona fide* **purchaser, notice.**

inquiry   Investigation to ascertain facts relating to a matter. A quest or search for information in order to ascertain truth or acquire knowledge. In British English, **enquiry** is more commonly used to refer to the raising of a question, and 'inquiry' to refer to a formal or official investigation. In American English, 'inquiry' is more common in both senses.

In English legal usage, 'inquiry' may be applied to: (i) a **requisition** made by the purchaser of a property to clarify a doubt as to the validity of any encumbrance or defect that might affect the vendor's title; (ii) **searches** made to establish any matter that might affect the use or value of the property, e.g. land registry searches, local land charge searches, inspection of the property; or (iii) a **planning inquiry** following a refusal or conditional grant of planning permission, or a delay by a local planning authority in making a decision to grant or refuse planning permission. See also **arbitration, constructive notice, implied notice, notice.**

inquiry notice   See implied notice.

inside lot   A lot situated between two other lots. cf. **corner lot**.

insolvency or **insolvent**   A condition that arises when a person is unable to meet his or her debts as they fall due for payment and cannot readily find assets to meet those debts. A situation that may be said to arise when the aggregate of a person's asset is insufficient to pay his debts. ('Insolvent' is used as a noun to refer to the inability to pay debts, or to refer to a person who has ceased to or is unable to pay debts when they are due; or as an adjective to refer to the related condition of being unable to pay debts as they fall due.) In accounting parlance, 'insolvency' or 'insolvent' is generally used to refer to a position that arises when a debtor cannot, in the normal course of business, pay debts as and when they are due; as distinguished from **bankruptcy** which arises when the debtor is subject to the provisions of a Bankruptcy Act. However, the terms are commonly used interchangeably. In particular, insolvency is used to refer to a situation that affects a company, whereas bankruptcy is applied to a person. See also **liquidation**.

inspection   See **constructive notice, due diligence, inquiry, landlord's access, patent defect, possession, searches**[Eng]**, survey**.

inspection notice[Aus]   A notice given upon completion of building work, either (as in Tasmania) by a building inspector setting out work that does not comply with the Building Regulation, or (as in Queensland) by a builder to the appropriate authority stating that work is ready for inspection.

installment[AmE]   See **instalment**[BrE].

installment contract[AmE]   See **instalment sale**.

installment credit agreement[AmE]   See **installment sale**.

installment land contract[AmE]   A contract for the sale of land that provides for the purchase price to be paid by portions or installments over an extended period of time, with the transfer of title only being effected when the last payment is made. Normally, on the execution of the contract, the purchaser is granted the right to possession of the subject property and is responsible for all operating expense (including real property taxes and insurance costs). An installment land contract may be used when the purchaser is unable, or does not wish, to obtain mortgage finance. It may also be used to permit the seller to retain the benefit of a below-market rate mortgage, or to enable the seller to postpone an effective sale when a mortgage on the property contains a **due-on-sale clause**. Also, an installment land contract may be used to finance part of the purchase price, as when the purchaser is acquiring a new home from a developer, with the majority of the purchase price secured by a first mortgage from a third party. Also called, according to the jurisdiction, a 'land contract', 'long-term land contract', a **contract for deed**, or sometimes, a 'real estate contract', 'agreement for sale and purchase', 'seller-financing contract', 'carryback financing contract' or 'seller-takeback financing'. cf. **contract for sale, rental purchase**. See also **conditional sale contract, constructive trust, equitable mortgage, escrow, executory contract, installment sale, purchase money mortgage**.

installment loan[AmE]   See **instalment loan/ instalment mortgage**.

installment note[AmE]   A **promissory note** that provides for payments to be made in two or more distinct installments.

installment sale[AmE]   1. A sale of personal property whereby the price is paid by a series of payments over a period of time and the goods are delivered in separate lots (UCC § 2-105(5); 47 Am.Jur.2d., Sales, § 681). Also called an 'installment credit agreement' or sometimes a 'time sale'. See also **credit-sale agreement**.   2. A form of sale by

installment contract where at least one payment is received after the end of the taxable year in which the disposition takes place. In the event of a sale under the 'installment sales method', the taxpayer may elect to be taxable on the gains according to the year in which payments are received, instead of the year of disposition (26 USC, Internal Revenue Code, § 453). This provision does not apply to a sale of dealer real estate or an inventory of personal property. Sometimes called a 'deferred-payment sale'.

installment sales contract(AmE) See **installment contract**.

instalment(BrE) or **installment**(AmE) An agreed sum paid as part of that which is due. A part payment of a sum of money that is owed. One of a number of regular payments made over a period of time to meet a debt or pecuniary obligation. An instalment may be distinguished from a **deposit**, as the latter is usually a single payment made to secure a contract or agreement, whereas the former is one of a series of payments due under an executed contract. See also **amortisation**, **hire-purchase agreement**, **installment land contract**(US), **interim payment**.

instalment contract(BrE) or **installment contract**(AmE) A contract that provides for the payment of the **consideration** in separate and distinct stages. Sometimes called an 'installment sales contract'. See also **conditional sale contract**, **executory contract**, **installment land contract**(US).

instalment loan or **instalment mortgage** A loan, or mortgage, that provides for the repayment of principal by instalments over a period of time, as distinguished from a loan that provides for a single 'balloon payment' at the end of the term. cf. **balloon loan**. See also **amortization loan**, **fixed-principal-payment mortgage**.

institutional investor or **institutional lender** A large organisation or society that invests or lends funds in its own right, as distinguished from a private individual, government body or public undertaking. The principal institutional investors in real estate (to a greater or lesser degree) are commercial and savings banks, insurance companies, pension funds, trust funds, investment trusts (including in the US **real estate investment trusts**) and real estate investment companies (generally called property companies in the UK). In the US, 'institutional lender' may also be defined more strictly to embrace only those institutions that invest depositor's money, under federal or state laws, as distinguished from institutions that invest funds held in their own right. Examples of the former are commercial banks, savings and loan associations and of the latter trust funds or pension funds, life insurance companies and investment trusts. See also **financial institution**, **mortgage-backed obligation**, **pension fund**.

institutional lease(BrE) A lease that is drawn up in a form that is suitable for an institutional investor, i.e. a long-term lease that is strongly in favour of the landlord and provides strict covenants on such matters as the rights of the tenant to use, alienate, alter or improve the property without the landlord's approval. In particular, the lease should be a **full repairing and insuring lease** with provisions for regular increases in rent to keep pace with market values or inflation. See also **rent review clause**, **standard-form contract**.

institutional property 1. Property owned by or used for the purposes of a public authority or a government department, e.g. a hospital, school, library, etc. A property used by a non-profit establishment for public use. 2. Property held by an **institutional investor**. In particular, investment property or property that might be considered suitable for an institutional investor. See also **prime property**.

instroke The right to work a leased **mine** from an adjoining mine. If a lessee of a mine can access it from an adjoining mine, instead of sinking a shaft from the surface, he is entitled to work the mine by instroke, unless expressly deprived of that right under his lease. cf. **outstroke**.

instrument   1. A formal document that is set down in **writing** and is normally authenticated by the signature of the author. A document that formally records or confirms a legal act or agreement, such as a **bond**, **deed**, **lease**, **conveyance**, **mortgage**, or **bill of exchange**. An instrument is evidence of the existence of an agreement, especially one that creates rights and obligations between two or more parties; conveys or creates a charge over land; or brings a business relation into effect. In the US, an instrument (primarily in relation to personal property) may be defined to include "a **negotiable instrument**, or a **security** or any other writing which evidences a right to the payment of money and is not itself a security agreement or lease and is of a type which in the ordinary course of business transferred by delivery with any necessary indorsement or assignment", UCC § 9-105(1). See also **specialty**, **statutory instrument**(Eng), **trust instrument**(Eng), **vesting deed**(Eng).   2.(NZ)See **Land Transfer land**.

insurable interest   An interest in property that is sufficient for the holder to be able to sustain a pecuniary loss or detriment as a result of damage to, or destruction of, the property (*Lucena v Craufurd* (1806) 2 Bos & PNR 269, 322-3, 127 Eng Rep 630, 643 (HL); *Kosmopoulos v Constitution Insurance Co of Canada* [1987] 1 SCR 2, 34 DLR (4th) 208, 216, 226 (Can); Crabb v. Calvert Fire Ins. Co., 255 SW.2d 990, 991 (Ky Ct App 1953)). A lessee has an insurable interest; unlike a licensee or a tenant at will who have transitory rights and cannot claim to suffer detriment as a direct result of the destruction of the property occupied by them. A mortgagee has an insurable interest in the property charged to him, as does the sole shareholder of a company that owns the insured property. See also **mortgagee clause**.

insurable title   A title to property that is sufficiently definite that a reputable insurance company would approve and provide insurance against any potential defect. In particular, a title upon which an insurance company would grant cover, subject to any minor defect that is noted on the policy. cf. **marketable title**. See also **title insurance**.

insurable value   See insured value.

insurance   A contract by which one party (the insurer) agrees, in return for the payment of a **premium**, to indemnify another (the insured) against pecuniary loss, damage or prejudice, arising as a result of a fortuitous events or particular perils; especially when the insured has a material interest in something that will be destroyed or damaged if the event or peril occurs (*Lucena v Craufurd* (1806) 2 Bos & PNR 269, 301, 127 Eng Rep 630, 642 (HL); State v. Blue Crest Plans, 72 AD.2d 713, 421 NYS.2d 580 (1979)). The insurer receives as consideration for this agreement, a premium (whether as a single payment or more usually a series of payments) that is assessed by the insurer as adequate for the **risk** assumed. A contract of insurance, called an **insurance policy**, provides protection or cover against the occurrence of an uncertain event, either uncertainty as to whether the event will happen at all or uncertainty as to when the event will happen.

An insurance contract is one that requires **utmost good faith** (*uberrimae fidei*) between the parties. In particular, an insurance contract requires full disclosure by the insured of any facts that might affect the insurer's assessment of the assumed risk. Thus, the retention of information that would lead one of the parties not to accept the bargain amounts to a fraud – a form of misrepresentation – and is sufficient to make an insurance policy void.

Insurance may be classified broadly as: (i) life insurance (or life **assurance**) – insurance on the life of the policyholder or another person; (ii) **fire insurance** and marine insurance – insurance against damage or destruction of property, vehicles, or marine resulting from external factors such as fire, flood, storm, riot, aircraft, etc.; and (iii) **casualty insurance** – insurance against damage or destruction to property arising from the actions of the insured or any third party.

Unless there is an express agreement to the contrary, neither the landlord nor the tenant has an obligation to insure the demised premises. However, most well drawn leases set out the respective obligations of the parties for the insurance of the demised premises. As a rule, the landlord insures the property; and, in most cases (except for short-term residential tenancies), the premium is recharged to the tenant as an 'insurance rent'. In some case, the tenant may agree with the lessor to insure the premises in his own name, with the landlord named as a party to the policy. Insurance monies paid under such policies must generally be applied to reinstate the demised premises. See also **all-risks insurance, builder's risk insurance, comprehensive insurance, co-insurance, consequential loss insurance, contingency insurance, contractor's all-risks insurance, double insurance, first-loss insurance, indemnity insurance, insurance value, liability insurance, mortgage insurance, mortgagee clause, property insurance, reinstatement basis, subrogation, title insurance, valued policy**.

Birds, Sir John. *Modern Insurance Law*. 4th ed. London: Sweet & Maxwell, 1997.

Dobbyn, John F. *Insurance Law in a Nutshell*. 3rd ed. St. Paul, MN: West, 1996.

Hardy Ivamy. E.R. *General Principles of Insurance Law*. 6th ed. London: Butterworths, 1993.

Huebner, Solomon S., et al. *Property and Liability Insurance*. 4th ed. Upper Saddle River, NJ: Prentice-Hall, 1995.

Keeton, Robert E., and Alan I. Widiss. *Insurance Law: A Guide to Fundamental Principles, Legal Doctrines, and Commercial Practices*. St. Paul, MN: West, 1988.

insurance certificate   A certificate issued by an insurer confirming that an **insurance policy** is in force. The certificate usually states the parties, the amount of cover provided, the period of the policy and summarises the risks covered. See also **binder, cover note**.

insurance clause   A clause in a lease that sets out the respective obligations of the landlord and the tenant for **insurance** of the demised premises. Each party to a lease may insure for such loss as may arise to that party in the event of damage or destruction of the leased premises. It is common practice for an insurance policy to be taken out in the name of the landlord, with the tenant being responsible for reimbursing the premium for that policy. An insurance clause frequently provides for an abatement of rent if the insured premises are rendered unusable and provides that the insurance monies will be used to reinstate the leased premises at the earliest opportunity. If leased premises are destroyed by fire, unless there is an express condition to the contrary, a landlord is not under any **obligation** to reinstate, but if the tenant pays the insurance premium he has the ability to require reinstatement and, in certain cases, an insurer may direct that money paid out is used to reinstate the premises. The tenant usually covenants not to carry out any activity on the leased premises that will vitiate the policy or increase the premium payable. See also **frustration, full repairing and insuring lease, rent-loss insurance, subrogation, triple net lease**.

insurance cover   See **cover**.

insurance policy   A document that sets down the terms and conditions of an **insurance** agreement. A contract whereby one party (the insurer), in consideration of a premium, undertakes to indemnify another (the insured) against loss or prejudice arising from a particular, but uncertain event. The event may be uncertain as to whether it will occur, or when it will occur. See also **blanket insurance, index-linked insurance, long-term insurance agreement, title insurance**.

insurance premium   The amount payable, at one time or from time to time, by an insured party under a contract of insurance for the maintenance of the policy; the sum of money that is set down in an **insurance policy** as the price the insured pays for the undertaking by the insurer to pay for a loss sustained by the insured as a result of an event against which the insurance is provided. See also **premium, service charge**[BrE].

insurance rent   A payment made by a tenant to his landlord to meet the cost of the premium for an insurance policy taken out in respect of the demised premises. See also **rent**.

insurance value   See **insured value**.

insured   A person who under the terms of an **insurance policy** is provided with an indemnity against pecuniary loss or damage. The 'insured' is not only the person named in the policy, but may be anyone who is insured under the policy. Also called an 'assured', especially when the policy is referred to as one of 'assurance'. See also **mortgagee clause**.

insured closing agreement[US]   An agreement by which a title company employs an agent to carry out the formalities required for a **closing** and provides insurance for the acts of the agent.

insured mortgage   See **mortgage guarantee insurance, mortgage insurance**.

insured value   The value of a property as ascertained for the purpose of an insurance policy; being a limit to the amount of indemnity provided by the policy in the event of loss. This value is normally ascertained as the **reinstatement cost**, i.e. the cost of rebuilding the insured property at the time when such replacement may be required. Thus, it is not a 'value' in the sense of an opinion of value as with the estimate of the open market value of a property. Also called the 'insurable value' or 'insurance value'. See also **actual cash value, cover, insurable interest, reinstatement basis, valued policy**.

insurer   The party to an insurance policy who undertakes to accept the specified risks or underwrites the policy. The party that agrees to provide an **indemnity** in the event of loss.

intangible asset   An **asset** that has no physical substance, such as a trademark, patent, franchise or copyright. In particular, an asset shown in a company's balance sheet that would have little or no value independent of the business as a whole, for example, preliminary setting up expenses and **goodwill**. See also **going-concern value, intangible property, intellectual property**.

intangible property   Property that cannot be physically detained, touched or handled, e.g. a debt or an easement, as distinguished from **tangible property**. Property that has no intrinsic and marketable value, but is merely a representation or evidence of value, such as a stock certificate, bond or promissory note. Normally the only evidence as to the ownership of intangible property is a written or oral agreement, supported by tangible evidence that reinforces the agreement. See also **bond, certificate of deposit, chose, incorporeal property, intellectual property, promissory note, stock**.

integration clause[US]   See **merger clause**.

intellectual property   Property that is represented by the physical manifestation of original thought, e.g. copyright, patents, trademarks, registered designs. Sometimes subdivided into industrial property (patents, trademarks, design, etc.) and copyright.

intended easement   See **implied easement**.

intensification of use   See **change of use, material change in the use**[Eng], **non-conforming use, planning unit**[Eng].

inter alia[Lat]   'Amongst other things'.

inter esse termini[Lat]   See *interesse termini*.

inter vivos(Lat) 'Between living persons'. See **gift**, **living trust**.

interdict A prohibitory decree of a court. A term in Scottish or the civil law for a remedy that is similar to an **injunction**.
Scott Robinson, S. *The Law of Interdict*. 2nd ed. London: Butterworths, 1994.

interesse termini(Lat) **1.** 'An interest in a term'. The right to property that a tenant acquires before actual entry onto the property. In English law, the doctrine of *interesse termini*, which required that a tenant actually enter onto land before a valid lease came into effect, has been abolished (LPA 1925, s. 149(1)(2)). Similarly, in the US, it is generally not necessary for a tenant to enter into possession before a lease comes into effect. **2.** A right to a lease that will take effect in the future, generally after the termination of another lease. The term *interesse termini* may be used to refer both to the tenant's rights before the leasehold begins if the leasehold is to begin in the future, and also to the tenant's rights after the leasehold has begun, but before he takes possession. In the former sense, the time before commencement is not a part of the term of the lease that will come into effect.

interest **1.** A legal right, title or share. A right or title to property. An advantage or detriment affecting property. A claim against land, especially against the land of another. In relation to land, an interest, in the broadest sense, means any **estate**, **title**, **lien** or **right** in or over land; but not a claim, such as a debenture or a floating charge. An interest in land may be a right to hold and enjoy land itself, e.g. as a **fee** interest, a **life interest** or a **leasehold interest**; or it may be a right to use or to restrict the use of land, e.g. an **easement**, **profit à prendre** or a **restrictive covenant**. It may be a **legal interest** or an **equitable interest**, depending on how it is created and against whom it can be enforced. Although an 'interest' in land may include an **estate**, it may be distinguished from an estate which is a specific or quantitative right over the land itself. In a restricted sense an interest may be any right to land that is less than an estate, but greater than a mere personal right to land.

In the US, an 'interest' in land, as used in the **Statute of Frauds**, may be said to mean "some portion of the title or right of possession, and does not include agreements which affect land but which do not contemplate the transfer of any title, ownership, or possession", 72 Am.Jur.2d., Statute of Frauds, § 47. In that context, an interest in land includes any legal or equitable interest. In particular, it includes a contract for the sale of land; a right to the possession of land; a lease; an agreement for a lease; an easement, a profit à prendre; a mortgage; the right of a landlord to the receipt of rent and, in most situations, a lien as well as an agreement for the sale of mineral and mining rights. In some jurisdictions an **option**, especially where it clearly creates a contract for the sale of land, is considered an interest in land. In The American Law Institute, *Restatement of Property* (1936), the word 'interest' is used "both generically to include varying aggregates of rights, privileges, powers and immunities and distributively to mean any one of them", § 5. In The American Law Institute, *Restatement of Contracts* (1932), an 'interest in land' is defined as "Any right, privilege, power or immunity, or combination thereof, relating to realty which under the rules of law governing that subject (a) is property in realty, and (b) does not fall within the definition of goods in Section 200", § 195. In the Internal Revenue Code for the taxation of Real Estate Investment Trusts, which deals with income derived from an "interest in real property", that term is defined to include "fee ownership and co-ownership of land or improvements thereon, leaseholds of land or improvements thereon, and options to acquire leaseholds of land or improvements thereon, but does not include mineral, oil, or gas royalty interests", 26 USC, Internal Revenue Code, § 856(c)(6)(C).

In English law, an option to purchase a lease is an "interest" within the meaning of the LPA 1925, s. 56(1) (which refers to the right of a person to take an 'interest' in land even though he is not named as a party to a conveyance or other instrument by which the subject land is transferred). In determining whether a contract for the disposition of an "interest in land" should be in **writing**, such an interest means "any estate, interest or charge in or over land", LP(MP)A 1989, s. 2(6). See also **beneficial interest, common interest, concurrent estate, conditional interest, contingent estate, conversion, defeasible interest, determinable interest, entailed estate, executory interest, future interest, inchoate interest, insurable interest, minor interest**[Eng], **overreachable interest**[Eng], **overriding interest**[Eng], **partial interest, right of pre-emption, several estate, shifting interest, vested interest.** **2.** A price for using someone else's **money**. A sum paid or accrued, over time, as compensation for being deprived of the use of money, especially when there is no right to share in the profit obtained by the person using that money. Interest is a payment received for lending a sum of money, or parting with capital. The reward for parting with liquidity or for not hoarding money for a period of time; "for the importance of money essentially flows from its being a link between the present and the future", J.M. Keynes, *The General Theory of Employment, Interest and Money* (1936) p. 293.

The cost of borrowing money, the 'rate of interest', is a function of: (a) the use to which a borrower can profitably put that money; (b) the loss which the lender sustains for parting with the money; and (c) the period of time for which the money changes hands – that is, the 'marginal productivity of capital' (the **internal rate of return** available to the user); the 'liquidity preference' of the lender; and the 'time preference'. This cost may be expressed by the formula, $i = Prt$, so that if a sum of money, or principal P, is parted with for a period of time t, and the charge made for parting with that money, expressed as a decimal, is r, then the total interest paid is i. Interest is generally expressed as a percentage of the principal or capital employed, i.e. as a rate of return or rate of interest, for a period of time. See also **accrued interest, apportionment, compound interest, customary interest**[US], **discount rate,**

effective annual interest rate, interest table, nominal interest, simple interest, usury, yield.

interest factor   The reciprocal of a **rate of interest**. A factor used to find the present or future value of a unit of money. See also **interest table**.

interest in expectancy   See future interest.

interest in land   See conversion[Eng], interest, land.

interest on condition subsequent   See conditional interest.

interest on interest   See compound interest.

interest-only loan   See standing loan.

interest-only (IO) **bond** or **interest-only security**   A security or bond that provides for the beneficiary to receive only interest payments. In particular, a security backed by a pool of mortgage loans by which the interest payments are made to the holder and the principal payments are made to another party. cf. **principal-only bond**. See also **real estate mortgage investment conduit**.

interest rate   See interest.

interest rate buy-down   See buy-down.

interest rate cap   A limit or ceiling placed on the increase or decrease in the interest rate charged on a loan. The limit may be fixed from one period of time to another, e.g. annually – a 'periodic cap'; or for the entire period of the loan – an 'overall cap'. When the upper limit of the rate is fixed, the level is called a 'cap' for short. When the lower limit is fixed, it is called a 'floor'. When there is a limit to the range within which the rate can fluctuate the arrangement, it is called a 'collar'. In the case of a residential loan, the rate may be capped by fixing the total amount of the monthly payments so that they will not increase above a stipulated upper limit. The limit may be set as part of the basic loan agreement, or may be fixed by a separate agreement. In either event, a premium is payable by the borrower for the benefit of the reduction of the risk of interest rate fluctuations. Sometimes called an 'adjustment cap'.

interest rate ceiling   See **adjustable-rate mortgage, interest rate cap**.

interest rate swap   An agreement by which the holders of two different loans exchange the interest rates that they receive on their respective principal amounts, i.e. the parties swap their respective interest rate exposure. For example, the holder of a floating rate loan may swap the interest receivable for the interest receivable from a fixed rate loan in order to reduce the risk of interest rate fluctuations. In that case, the seller of the floating rate loan or 'note' would pay a premium to the holder of the fixed rate note.

interest reipublicæ ut quilibet re sua bene utatur(Lat)   'It is in the interest of the state that each person should make good use of his own property'.

interest subject to a condition   See **conditional interest, fee simple conditional**.

interest table   A mathematical table that sets out the value of one unit of money, after allowing for **compound interest**, either as a **future value** or a discounted or **present value**. Also referred to as an 'annuity table'. See also Appendix C, **Financial Formulae**.

interest upon condition precedent   See **contingent interest**.

interest upon condition subsequent   See **conditional interest**.

interest upon interest   See **compound interest**.

interference with goods   See **conversion, trespass**.

interior   See **internal**.

interim award   An award made by an arbitrator prior to his final decision. An interim award may be of two kinds. It may be an award of a sum pending final determination of the total amount due, or it may be an interim decision on a particular issue or issues between the parties. In the US, usually called an 'interlocutory award' or an 'interlocutory decree'. See also **arbitration, interim payment, interim rent**.

interim certificate   See **certificate of valuation**.

interim injunction   See **injunction**.

interim finance or **interim loan**   A loan obtained for a short period of time (generally one to three years) until permanent or long-term finance is obtained. In particular, **construction finance**. cf. **permanent loan**. See also **bridge loan**.

interim payment   A payment made as part of the consideration due under a contract, usually for performance of an agreed part of the work, service, or obligation required under the contract. In particular, payment made under the terms of a building contract for work completed. The most common basis of payment under a building contract is for the contractor to be paid the value of the estimated quantities of work done and materials supplied (usually as stipulated in an architect's certificate), less any retention sum held as security against satisfactory completion of the entire contract. As an alternative, the interim payment may be based on an agreed sum, or a percentage of the total contract price, that is paid at predetermined stages of the building work – such payments being commonly referred to as 'stage payments'. If there is no express provision for interim payments, it may be considered an **implied term** of the contract that payment should be made for work at stages prior to completion of the entire contract, especially when the contract work is spread over a long period of time or when it can be shown that it is to be carried out in a number of stages and a contractor may be permitted to discontinue further work until an interim payment is made. See also **instalment, interim award,** *quantum meruit,* **substantial performance**.

interim rent(Eng)   A rent that the court may determine as reasonable for a tenant to pay when a **business tenancy** continues after the end of its contractual term, pending the establishment of the terms for a new tenancy (L&T Act 1954, s. 24A, as added by LPA 1969, s. 3). The purpose of this provision is to ensure that the tenant does not benefit unduly from a delay in agreeing to the terms of a new tenancy (either because of protracted negotiations or because of the time taken to refer the matter to the courts for determination). The 'interim rent' is fixed on the basis of **market rent**, but on the assumption that the premises are let on an annual tenancy, and having regard to the rent and terms of the expired tenancy. Thus, an interim rent is likely to be fixed at a level between the rent payable under the expired lease and the rent that is determined for the new tenancy.   **2.** A rent that may be agreed in respect of a **long residential tenancy** that has come to its contractual end and the landlord has offered to grant the tenant an assured tenancy. Such a rent may be proposed by the landlord to take effect when the long tenancy ends. If the tenant disputes the proposed rent he may apply to the rent assessment committee to fix an appropriate rent (Local Government and Housing Act 1989, Sch. 10).

interlineation   Writing between the lines of a document, which has the effect of an **alteration** thereto.

interlocutory award(US)   See **interim award**.

interlocutory decree(US)   See **interim award**.

interlocutory injunction   See **injunction**.

intermediary   See **broker, commission merchant, middleman**.

intermediate area(Eng)   See **development area**.

intermediate estate   An **estate** in land situated in time between two other estates; an estate situated between a 'greater' and a 'lesser' estate. For example, if A, the holder of the fee simple, grants a life estate to B and thereafter to C, B has an intermediate estate (at least while A is alive). Also called an 'intervening estate'. See also **contingent estate, intermediate lease, merger**.

intermediate grant(Eng)   See **grant**.

intermediate lease   The interest held by a tenant who himself has granted a lease; the 'intermediate party', being both a lessor and a lessee, but neither a freeholder nor occupier. If the owner A of a freehold (or a fee estate) leases his property to B, who in turn leases it to C, A has a freehold subject to a lease (in the US called a leased fee estate), B has an intermediate lease and C holds a sub-lease. Also called a 'mesne tenancy' or sometimes a 'sandwich lease', i.e. a lease held by someone who is sandwiched between the holders of leasehold interests in the same property. See also **head lease, lease-and-leaseback financing**.

intermediate-term loan   See **medium-term loan**.

intermediate theory(US)   See **mortgage**.

intermediation   The process whereby money is placed with banks or savings institutions, thus enabling them to make loans. In particular, the placement of funds with the bank or institution that offers the highest rate of interest. cf. **disintermediation**.

intermingled fund(US)   See **commingled trust fund**.

intermittent easement(US) An **easement** that is only used occasionally, such as a right to flood a neighbours land when the water level in a lake or pond significantly exceeds the normal levels.

internal Relating to the inside or interior of a property. Within the limits of a building structure. As a rule a covenant in a lease to carry out internal repair is interpreted by the exception of that which forms an **external** part of a building, i.e. is exposed to, or forms part of, the outside. See also **tenantable repair**.

internal area See **gross internal floor area, net internal area**.

internal rate of return (IRR) The rate of interest that discounts a series of future cash flows or income returns to make them equal to the total cost or outlay on the investment that generates those cash flows or income returns. An internal rate of return considers the time at which the cash flow is received as well as the total sum of the cash flows. It was called the 'rate of return over cost' by Irving Fisher, and 'the marginal efficiency of capital' by J. M. Keynes "that rate of discount which should discount the value of a series of annuities, given by the return from the capital asset during its life, just equal to its supply price", *The General Theory of Employment, Interest and Money* (1936), p. 135. The internal rate of return is used to make comparisons between alternative investments; to decide if the return is sufficient to warrant parting with money; or to decide if it is worth borrowing money at a given rate of interest in order to make an investment. It is a measure of the inducement to invest because it measures the return of capital, i.e. it is a 'derived return'. It may be contrasted with the rate of interest incorporated in a **capitalisation factor** (years' purchase or Inwood factor) which is an 'applied return', i.e. one used to ascertain the capital value of an investment, given the interest rate or the cost of parting with or borrowing money.

The IRR may be 'modified' by discounting any negative cash flows (expenses) at a specified safe rate (a lower rate) and the positive income is discounted at the normal investment rate. This 'modified internal rate of return' is sometimes called an 'adjusted rate of return'. If the calculation uses different rates of return for reinvestment of income at different stages of the holding period (as when part of the income is held in a deposit account and not assumed to be reinvested in the primary investment) the result is called the 'financial management rate of return'. The internal rate of return may be calculated at a given point in time, but assuming the investment is sold at a series of future dates such as at the end of year 1, year 2, year 3, etc. Called a 'rolling IRR'.

Also called the 'discounted (or discounted cash flow) rate of return'; the 'actuarial investment return', the 'overall rate of return'; the 'investment rate of return', or sometimes the 'investor's rate of return' or 'true rate of return'. See also **discounted cash flow, redemption yield**, Appendix C, **Financial Formulae**.

Akerson, Charles B. *The Internal Rate of Return in Real Estate Investments*. Chicago: Appraisal Institute, 1988 rev. ed.

internal repair See **internal, repair**.

interpleader An equitable proceeding that is instigated by a third party who is innocently situated between two other parties and who may become a litigant in a dispute. For example, an action brought by a stakeholder or escrow holder, or a party who is holding proceeds of sale, when the rights to those monies is disputed, in order to decide on the distribution of the funds and avoid being prejudiced personally by the claimants to those funds. The third party is said to require the other parties to interplead their claims and thereby to apply for relief by way of interpleader.

interpretation clause or **interpretation section** 1. A clause in a contract which specifies that, for the purpose of that contract, words or phrases shall have the meaning specified in that clause. 2. A clause or section of a statute or code which specifies that the words and phrases used in the statute, or in a related statute, shall have a given meaning when used in the specified statute. For example, in English law, the entirety of the Interpretation Act 1978 and, in land law, the LPA 1925, s. 205; or, in the US, the 'definitions section' of the Fair Housing Act of 1968, § 3602 or the Uniform Commercial Code § 8-102. See also **words**.

interruption   The breaking of a continuous right of enjoyment. In relation to **adverse possession** or **prescription** an interruption must be some act or occurrence that breaks the continuity of use, enjoyment or possession and is clearly acknowledged as such. As a rule, interruption does not occur if the person claiming a right is under a disability, or there is fraud, deliberate concealment or a mistake. cf. **abandonment**. See also **disturbance**.

interruption insurance   See **consequential loss insurance**.

Interstate Land Sales Full Disclosure Act of 1968 (ILSFDA)[US]   See **statement of record**.

interval ownership   See **timeshare**.

intestacy   Without making a **will**. Intestacy arises when a person, who may be called an 'intestate', dies without making a will for the disposition of his or her property, or makes a will that proves to be null and void. See also *bona vacantia*, **hotchpot**, **succession**.

intra vires[Lat]   'Within the power'. An act is *intra vires* when it is within the authority or powers of the person or company performing that act. cf. *ultra vires*.

intrinsic value   The essential and inherent **value** of a tangible asset. The value of a property based on its constituent parts, i.e. the materials of which it is built, or the cost of reproducing it, rather than its value as influenced by 'market conditions'. A value based more on fact than opinion, as with a value that is more related to surrounding conditions (communications, neighbouring property, physical surroundings, etc.) than personal preferences. A value that is essentially devoid of influence from such factors as individual partiality, future expectations and speculative influences. The intrinsic value of a thing may be contrasted with its 'real' value, i.e. that which it will actually fetch or the benefit it will truly give. In the case of the value of a company, the intrinsic value may be considered analogous to the **break-up value** arrived at from an orderly sale of the company's assets. cf. **market value**.

introduction clause or **introductory clause**   The opening words or a clause at the beginning of a **deed**. The introduction may form part of, or may be followed by, a **recital**. See also **preamble**.

introduction of purchaser   See **commission**, **ready willing and able**, **procuring cause**.

introductory clause   See **introduction**.

inure or **enure**   To operate or take effect. To devolve on to someone. An interest in land may be said to inure to the benefit of someone when it passes by operation of law or the quantum of that interest is fixed. For example, when an 'after-acquired title' passes under a **covenant for further assurance**. See also **vest**.

inutility   See **obsolescence**.

invalid   Not binding; of no legal force or effect; void. See also **illegal contract**, **void contract**, **voidable contract**.

inventory   1. An itemised list, or **schedule**, that describes a number of items of personal property with reasonable particularity. For example, items that are to be included in a sale by auction; chattels that are to be included in a lease of real property; or a list of the personal assets of a deceased person as prepared by a legal representative. See also **fixture**. **2.** A **stock** of goods held by a firm for the purpose of trade or production. A stock of property available for sale or lease. In particular, the total amount of 'space' available in a particular market, or the total amount of property held by one company. See also **land bank**.

inventory value   The value of an **inventory**. See also **book value**.

inverse compulsory purchase(Eng)   See **blight notice, purchase notice**.

inverse condemnation(US)   The process by which a property owner may require the payment of **just compensation** when his property is adversely affected by the activities of a government authority, even though there has been no exercise of the power of **eminent domain**. 'Inverse condemnation' may be instigated when the actions of a public authority amount to a 'taking' of property, as with the taking of physical possession; a significant interference with the reasonable enjoyment of the property; or a deprivation of its beneficial use.

A landowner may require a government body to pay damages for the loss in the value of his land when he has been deprived of all economically beneficial use of the land as a result of government regulation, ordinance or code (Lucas v. South Carolina Coastal Council, 112 S Ct 2886, 2899-2902, 120 L Ed.2d 798 (1992)). Inverse condemnation does not occur merely because a public agency is exercising its reasonable powers to control and regulate the use of land – its **police power** (Pennsylvania Coal Co. v. Mahon, 260 US 393, 416, 43 S Ct 158, 67 L Ed 322, 28 ALR 1321 (1922)). Instances in which compensation may be payable for inverse condemnation include such matters as a permanent restriction or limitation on the economic use to which the property can be put, a temporary prohibition of development, as when the restriction denies the owner all use of the property for a considerable period of time. However, there is no inverse condemnation or

'regulatory taking' of property where the value of land is diminished during the process of "governmental decision making", Agins v. City of Tiburon, 447 US 255, 100 S Ct 2138, 65 L Ed.2d 106, 113 n. (1980). Nor is there inverse condemnation if the authority is seeking to control an activity that amounts to a public nuisance; it is "the right of society ... to be exempt from the proximity of dangerous and noxious trades" and "the duty of the owner of real estate, in the midst of many habitations, to abstain from ... using it [in a manner] dangerous to the lives, health, or comfort of the inhabitants of such dwellings", Commonwealth v. Alger, 7 Cush 53 (Mass 1851) (Lucas v. South Carolina Coastal Council, *supra* (1992)). Compensation may be payable in the event of a temporary prohibition of development, as when the restriction denies the owner "all use of his property" for a considerable period of time (First English Evangelical Lutheran Church of Glendale v. County of Los Angeles, 482 US 304, 107 S Ct 2378, 96 L Ed 250 (1987); 210 Cal App.3d 1353, 258 Cal Rptr 893 (1989)). Sometimes called 'reverse condemnation' or 'constructive condemnation'. See also **condemnation, taken for public use**.

Eagle, Steven J. *Regulatory Taking.* 2nd ed. Newark, NJ: LexisNexis, 2001.

Eaton, James D. *Real Estate Valuation in Litigation.* 2nd ed. Chicago: Appraisal Institute, 1995.

inverse order of alienation   The doctrine of inverse order of alienation applies to the satisfaction of a debt secured by a mortgage or lien on a property which has been sold or encumbered in parts or parcels at different times. Provided the debtor is not expressly entitled to satisfy his claim from the entire property at the outset, then any claim must be satisfied in the reverse order in which the land was sold or alienated, starting with any land still held by the debtor; and then only resorting to the next parcel if there then is insufficient collateral. An analogous, but diverse, doctrine to the equitable doctrine of **marshalling**.

invest   **1.** To give possession. To endow with a privilege, power or authority. See also **vest**.

2. To make an **investment**. To put out money in anticipation of income or profits.

investment   **1.** The employment of **capital** or labour for the purpose of income or financial gain. Expenditure of money to acquire property in anticipation of future **income, interest** or **profit**. Ceding of an immediate right to money, or any pecuniary benefit, in exchange for a hope that the sum laid out will accumulate to a higher sum, or produce an incremental benefit, either as income or capital appreciation, at a future date. An addition to a stock of capital arising over time, either by an increase in the worth of the capital or by the retention of income generated by that capital. 'Investment' may include the laying out of money as capital by a business; the purchase of securities, stocks, shares or any other form of property; as well as money lent against security, or deposited in order to produce interest. See also **risk**.   **2.** The **equity** value or a share of the value of a business. See also **investment value**.

investment analysis   An analysis or study made to decide if the return to be derived from an **investment** is sufficient to warrant the risk inherent in making that investment. A study of the relationship between acquisition price or cost and the anticipated future cash flow to be derived from a real estate investment. A process by which the relative merits of alternative forms of investment are examined. Such analysis may be broadly classified as 'fundamental analysis' and 'technical analysis'. The former analyses the intrinsic factors – income, projected earnings, comparable investment yields, etc. The latter analyses extrinsic factors – trends, general price levels, investors' attitudes, market conditions, etc. See also **feasibility analysis, internal rate of return, net present value, pay-back period, portfolio analysis, sensitivity analysis**.

Baum, Andrew. *Commercial Real Estate Investment*. London: Estates Gazette, 2002.

investment bank   An enterprise or institution that provides investment management and advisory services to companies, institutional and selected private customers. Investment banks advise on corporate financial activities, including arranging and advising on mergers and acquisitions; arranging and underwriting long-term share capital issues, private placement, and block trading of stocks and shares; and the financing of business both domestically and internationally in the form of principal transactions and brokerage transactions for private and institutional clients. In addition, investment banks may undertake wholesale foreign exchange and commodity transactions. Unlike a commercial bank, an investment bank does not undertake the normal services of banking, such as taking deposits and lending money to private individuals nor the retail exchange of currencies.

investment company   **1.** A company that is owned by a number of stockholders and uses its own capital to invest in the securities of other companies, or makes investments in other enterprises; generally without being directly involved in the management of those companies or enterprises.

In the US, defined as "any issuer which—(A) is or holds itself out as being engaged primarily, or proposes to engage primarily, in the business of investing, reinvesting, or trading in securities; (B) is engaged or proposes to engage in the business of issuing face amount certificates of the installment type; … or (C) is engaged or proposes to engage in the business of investing, reinvesting, owning, holding, or trading in securities, and owns or proposes to acquire investment securities having a value exceeding 40 per cent of the value of such issuer's total assets (exclusive of government securities and cash items) on an unconsolidated basis", Investment Company Act of 1940, as amended (15 USC § 80a-3) – such companies now being regulated by the Investment Company Amendments Act of 1970.

An investment company may be 'closed-end' or 'open-end'. A **closed-end investment company** trades its shares like the shares of any other company, its business being investing in stocks, real estate or other investments. An **open-end investment company** buys and sells its own shares as investors seek to increase or reduce their holdings. The price of the shares in a closed-end investment company, as for any other company, is dependent on the market assessment of the performance of the company, as contrasted with an open-end investment company (called a **mutual fund** in the US or a **unit trust** in the UK) the price of which is entirely dependent on the underlying value of its investments. Frequently an investment company, either by statute or under its articles of association, is prohibited from holding more than a small percentage of the shares of any one company (except another investment company) and may not distribute capital profits. Sometimes an investment company is referred to as an 'investment trust', although strictly speaking it is a **company** and not a **trust**. An investment company may be distinguished from a **holding company**, as the primary objective of the former is the investment of funds under its management, whereas the latter aims for control of the owned companies, usually for production, operating, marketing, or similar purposes. See also **closed-end fund**, **real estate investment trust**.   2. A financial institution that pools the resources of a number of investors in order to make diversified investments under common management. In the US, also called a 'mutual company', especially when the profits are distributed entirely to the investors.

investment interest   Interest paid, or accrued, for a loan that is used to acquire or hold **investment property**.

investment method of valuation(BrE)   A method of assessing the value of a property on the principle that its capital value is a function of: (a) the **income** that a property produces, or is capable of producing; and (b) the **rate of return** that a property investor requires in order to be induced to accept the risk of investing in that property. The process of valuation may be summarised as follows:

(i) estimate the total income that will be received from the investment, based on the current income receivable, or the highest income that could be obtained; (ii) estimate the projected net income by making deductions for vacancies; defaulting tenants; and expenses that the landlord is obliged to pay and will not be able to recover from the occupiers, i.e. non-recoverable service charges, management fees, etc.; (iii) decide on an appropriate life expectancy for the projected net income – this may be taken as perpetual for a freehold modern building, but may be limited by the termination of a leasehold interest or the economic life of a building; (iv) capitalise the total projected net income at an appropriate rate (**years' purchase** or **capitalisation rate**) to reflect the rate of return considered appropriate for the investment.

The capitalisation of income may be a **straight capitalisation** (applying an 'overall capitalisation rate' or 'years' purchase in perpetuity') if the income represents a level sum receivable for an unlimited period or in perpetuity; or **annuity capitalization** (applying a factor that takes account of variations in the projected income, such as the 'present value of one per period' or 'years' purchase for a term of years') if the income represents a variable sum or is receivable for a limited period. A variable income may be capitalised also by the **term and reversion method**, or by the **hardcore method**.

The investment method is used primarily to value property that is held for investment, but it may be used to value an owner-occupied property, especially when there is no direct comparable sale values, or when the property is more suitable for investment. See also **discounted cash flow**, **income approach**(AmE).

investment property   Property acquired for retention as an investment, especially property acquired in order to provide income, as distinguished from property acquired for use and occupation. Sometimes called 'income property'. cf. **occupation property**. See also **commercial property**, **development property**.

investment rate   See **investment yield, remunerative rate**.

investment rate of return   See **internal rate of return**.

investment risk   See **risk**.

investment tax credit(US)   A tax incentive granted to encourage investment in plant, equipment and buildings. In particular, a tax reduction granted to encourage investment in a particular fiscal year.

investment trust   A misnomer for an **investment company**. Strictly speaking the investment vehicle is a company with shareholders and not a trust with beneficiaries. However, the company makes investments as if it were acting in the capacity of a trustee. Although an 'investment trust' is strictly a **closed-end trust**, that buys and sells its own shares according to the demands of its investors, the term is commonly (but erroneously) used to refer to an **open-end trust** or **mutual fund**. cf. **unit trust**(BrE). See also **business trust, real estate investment trust**(US).

investment value   **1.** The value of a property that has been acquired, or is held, purely for investment, i.e. for the benefit of the income or profit to be derived therefrom, rather than for use and occupation. The term 'investment value' is frequently used to refer to the value of a property to a particular investor, as distinguished from the more objective **market value** or **intrinsic value**. See also **income approach**(AmE), **investment method of valuation**(BrE).   **2.** The value of a company based on the value of its shares or stock, i.e. its value as an investment as distinguished from its **book value**. See also **going-concern value**.

investment yield   A single rate of return or yield that an investor expects to receive from a particular form of investment; an **all-risks rate** considered appropriate for a given investment, based on a comparison with similar investments.

See also **internal rate of return, remunerative rate**.

investment yield rate(US)   See **equity yield rate**.

investor   One who makes an **investment**. A person or body that parts with money to acquire a right to receive a future income or benefit, either in the form of a cash flow or the benefit from holding a tangible asset that can be resold later at an increased value.   An investor is considered to be a person who makes a prudent decision to lay out money for a medium to short term in search of a reasonable return for the risk entailed. He may be contrasted with a **speculator** who makes hazardous ventures with a view to short-term profit or gain.

investor's rate of return   See **internal rate of return**.

invitation to bid or **invitation to tender**   A request to one or more persons, or to the public at large, to submit an **offer** to supply goods, provide services, or the carrying out of work, especially construction work for the person making the invitation. In common law, an invitation to tender is generally considered equivalent to an **invitation to trade**(AmE)/**invitation to treat**(BrE) and, therefore, is not intended to form any part of a contract; the 'invitation' requires the submission of an *offer* as a prerequisite to a contract. However, sometimes the invitation may require that the response constitute an 'offer' that is capable of immediate **acceptance**. See also **quotation, tender**.

invitation to trade(AmE) or **invitation to treat**(BrE)   An invitation or inducement to submit an **offer** with a view to entering into a contract. A declaration of a willingness to enter into negotiation; especially setting forth the terms on which an offer for sale would be considered. An invitation to treat is a precursor to an offer, but does not constitute an offer. It is an offer to negotiate – to receive offers – an offer to chaffer. The most common instance of an invitation to treat arises when goods are displayed in a shop window with a price tag. These goods may be withdrawn by the shopkeeper at his own free will, without fear or favour, unless the goods are marked in a definitive way and indicate to the customer that they can be bought provided the price is tendered, as may be the case with special offers. Whether a statement constitutes an offer capable of acceptance, or merely an invitation to treat or trade, is judged from the intention of the declarant, taking account of matters such as business practices, express wording and consequent actions (*Pharmaceutical Society of Great Britain v Boots Cash Chemists (Southern) Ltd* [1953] 1 QB 401, [1953] 1 All ER 482 (CA); *Gibson v Manchester City Council* [1979] 1 WLR 294, [1979] 1 All ER 972 (HL); S.S.I. Investors, Ltd v. Korea Tungsten Mining Co. 80 AD.2d 155, 438 NYS.2d 96 (1981); 17A Am.Jur.2d., Contracts, § 44).

An advertisement that an auction will be held, or an auctioneer's request for bids, constitute an invitation for bids and not an offer, giving the auctioneer the right to withdraw the property until he indicates acceptance. However, the same rule may not necessarily be considered to apply if the property is submitted for sale **without reserve**.

In American English, the term 'invitation to treat' is rarely used, instead such expressions as 'invitation to bargain', 'invitation to make an offer', 'invitation to deal', 'invitation to negotiate', 'request for offer', 'solicitation for offers' or 'entertainment of bids' may be used to similar effect. See also **asking price, quotation**.

invitee A person who goes onto land at the express or implied invitation of the person who has control thereover Generally, an invitee goes onto land for a short period of time, for the purpose of business, or for some other manifest or mutually agreed reason, e.g. as a customer in a shop, a visitor to an office, a passenger at a railway station, a postal or courier delivery person, or a guest in a home. An invitee may be distinguished from a **licensee** as the latter is not strictly invited, but his presence is merely tolerated (Bennett v. L. & N. R.R. Co., 102 US 585, 26 L Ed 235, 238 (1880) (*Fairman v Perpetual Investment Building Society* [1923] AC 74, 80 (HL)).

At common law, an occupier of property has a **duty of care** to an invitee for the safety and condition of the property, especially to prevent injury to that person from an unusual danger. In particular, an owner of land has a duty to inspect his premises and to discover any dangerous condition and rectify it, or adequately warn the invitee.

In the US, some jurisdictions follow the common law view that the liability to an invitee is stricter than that owed to a licensee. On the other hand, other jurisdictions do not accept this distinction and impose the same or a higher duty in respect of either party.

In English law, since the Occupiers Liability Act 1957, s. 2, a "common duty of care" is owed to all "visitors", whether invitees or licensees. Moreover, the 'occupier' of premises to which a person is invited, or is permitted to be there, "must be prepared for children to be less careful than adults" OLA 1957, s. 2(3)(a), and "may expect that a person, in the exercise of his calling, will appreciate and guard against any special risks ordinarily incident to it, so far as the occupier leaves him free to do so", OLA 1957, s. 2(3)(b). A warning may absolve an occupier from being held to have failed in his duty of care, provided it is established that the visitor clearly ignored the occupier's warning or accepted the risk of entering the premises in spite of the warning (OLA 1957, s. 2(4), 2(5)). See also **negligence, trespass, visitor**.

involuntary alienation(US) See alienation.

involuntary conversion 1. The **conversion** of property into cash against the wishes of its owner, which may arise from condemnation, theft, loss or a similar act. 2.(US)The loss of property by destruction, theft, seizure, requisition, condemnation or threat of requisition or condemnation. In such circumstances a liability to tax on any gain may be deferred by the acquisition of a replacement property (26 USC, Internal Revenue Code, § 1033).

involuntary conveyance   See **involuntary transfer**.

involuntary lien   See **lien**.

involuntary transfer(US)   The transfer of property, or a right to property, to another against the owner's will; as in condemnation, or foreclosure. Sometimes called an 'involuntary conveyance'. cf. **voluntary transfer**.

involuntary trust   A trust that arises from operation of law. A term sometimes used for a **constructive trust**. See also **resulting trust**.

Inwood factor(AmE)   A term for the **present value of one per period** derived from tables showing such factors, first published in 1811 by William Inwood. An Inwood factor can be used to assess the value of an income property by applying the factor to a fixed income stream for a given period of time, or summating the capital values obtained by applying the factor to a series of fixed incomes generated by the investment over different periods of time. Also called an 'ordinary annuity coefficient'. See also **annuity capitalization**, **single rate capitalization factor**.

ipso facto(Lat)   'By the deed itself'.

irredeemable ground lease(US)   A **ground lease** that does not contain any provision for the tenant to purchase the land or extend the term at the end of the lease, i.e. there is no right to pay a capital sum to acquire the fee interest. See also **redemption**.

irrevocable license(US)   See **license**.

irrevocable trust(US)   A **trust** created to hold property which, once it has been established, cannot be terminated by the settlor or creator of the trust. This form of trust is used primarily when the intention is to transfer property as a gift prior to the death of the grantor. Usually the property is transferred to a trustee to be held for the benefit of a third party, with the clear intention that the grantor cedes any right to regain the property. If properly planned the creator of an irrevocable trust is not liable to federal income tax, because the trust property is treated as having been transferred to the ultimate beneficiaries when the trust is created and not on the death of the creator of the trust. cf. **bare trust**. See also **trust property**.

irrigation farm lease(Aus)   A lease of Crown land granted in perpetuity upon condition that the land is improved by irrigation and erection of a residence. Upon fulfilling the conditions the lessee has a right to acquire the land (Crown Lands (Continued Tenures) Act 1989, s. 3, Sch. 1 (NSW)).

irritancy(Scot)   The **forfeiture** of a right as a result of the contravention of a condition of a contract or a neglect to perform an obligation. In particular, an irritancy clause permits the landlord to terminate the lease for the breach of a condition that goes to the route of the lease, such as non-payment of rent or an assignment without a required consent from the landlord.

Islamic mortgage   A mortgage that is granted in a way that complies with the requirements of Shariah or Islamic law, that is a mortgage upon which no interest (*riba*) is charged. Such a 'mortgage' may be effected by a transfer of the subject property to the lender who then grants the borrower a right to occupy the property subject to the repayment of the cost of the property, plus a payment for the right of occupation (an arrangement that is based on trade financing – *murabaha*). At the end of the term the borrower owns the property outright. Alternatively, the financier may receive regular payments to cover the cost of the property and then receives a premium before the title is granted to the occupier. Another method permits the borrower to take title to the property and pay part of the cost himself, with the balance being advanced by an Islamic institution who in turn retains a lien on the property until the amount due is repaid in full, with the payment for occupation or an agreed premium. Also, the arrangement may take the form of a joint venture (*musharaka*) whereby the financier and the occupier have a share of the equity value of the property that is realised when the property is sold. See also **usury**.

isoval A line on a map drawn to link points at which land has the same value. An isoval is similar to a contour line linking points of the same elevation.

issue A person's descendant. Strictly speaking a person's children, but in most contexts any person who is descended from a common ancestor. In particular, those who are left as surviving children, and the descendents of children who predeceased someone who has died. Prima facie 'issue' includes descendants of every degree, in the absence of any explanatory context to the contrary.

When used in a will as a **word of limitation**, 'issue' may be considered equivalent to **heirs of the body** or lineal descendants. However, it is an ambiguous word and, if the context so admits, it may be used as a 'word of limitation', especially in a will. Nonetheless, in a deed it is generally a **word of purchase**, i.e. it is not intended to limit or cut down the estate granted, but to pass the estate to descendants, lineal descendants, or offspring. See also **heir**.

issuer An organization that issues securities to the public. In particular, an organization that provides a guarantee for securities backed by a pool of mortgages. See also **mortgage-backed obligation**, **special purpose corporation**.

issues and profits That which comes from land, whether on, above or below the surface. The revenue produced by real property. The term is generally used in the context of 'rents, issues and profits' to refer to any **rent**, income, substance, incremental revenue or **profits** that can be derived from the use or ownership of land, especially as may be attached by a mortgagee who takes possession or appoints a receiver in the event of default by the mortgagor. 'Rents, issues and profits' covers anything derived from the realty, but not personalty or a business placed thereon, i.e. it does not cover revenue derived from a business conducted on the property. Thus, income to be derived from subleasing office space or charges for the use of spaces in a parking lot represent 'issues and profits' from real property, but generally income from a business per se, such as hotel room charges, is considered as income from personal property.

ius accrescendi(Lat) See *jus accrescendi*.

J

janitor   A person hired to assist in the general day-to-day running of a building, especially general maintenance, and such functions as cleaning, making minor repairs and sometimes responsibility for the security of the building; but not property management or leasing. See also **caretaker**, **concierge**.

JCT contract^(BrE)   See **Joint Contracts Tribunal**.

jerry-built   Built insubstantially. Not built to last, or built cheaply and with flimsy material. A term of uncertain origin; it may derive from: (i) Jeremiah who prophesied that nothing was substantial unless built by the heart and that even Jerusalem would fall to the Babylonians; (ii) the walls of Jericho which fell to the Israelites under Joshua; (iii) a 'jury' mast: a temporary mast put up after a storm to enable a ship to continue its passage; or (iv) a firm of builders (the Jerry Brothers) who operated in Liverpool at the end of the 19th century and built shoddy houses. A jerry-builder puts up houses using cheap and substandard materials, usually on speculation, in order to sell them at a quick profit to unsuspecting or ill-advised purchasers. See also *caveat emptor*, **inherent defect**, **negligence**.

jetsam   Parts of a ship or goods that are thrown overboard to lighten a ship in a time of peril and sink and remain under water (*Constable's Case* (1601) 5 Co Rep 106a, 77 Eng Rep 218). Jetsam may subsequently be washed ashore but, if there is no owner, they become the property of the sovereign State. cf. **flotsam**.

joinder   A joining or putting together, as of two or more parties or documents. In order to satisfy a requirement that an agreement be properly evidenced in **writing** (especially in order to satisfy the **Statute of Frauds**) it may be permissible to accept the 'joinder of documents', i.e. the reading together of related documents so as to form, in effect, a single document. For this purpose, in order to construe two documents as if they were one, it is necessary (a) for one of the documents to be in writing and to contain an authorised signature; (b) that there is a reference, express or implied, in that document to the second document; and (c) that the two documents when read together provide a sufficient and complete note or memorandum of the terms of the agreement. Similarly, someone may agree to be a party to an agreement or action, i.e. to be joined, or a 'joinder', thereto, even though he is not an active party to the agreement or action. Although in English law, on or after September 27, 1989 a contract for the sale or other disposition of an interest in land must incorporate all the agreed terms in one document (LP(MP)A 1989, s. 2(1)).

joint adventure   See **joint venture**.

joint agency   An **agency** arrangement by which two or more agents cooperate together so that from the principal's point of view they are one agent. Commonly, a joint agency takes the form of an **exclusive agency**, and **commission** is shared between joint agents if either one of them successfully concludes his duties. However, if nothing is agreed in advance the agent who is the 'effective' or **procuring cause** of the transaction receives the fee to the exclusion of the other agent or broker. cf. **dual agency**. See also **cooperating broker**^(US), **joint agent**.

joint agent or **joint broker**   An **agent** or **broker** who undertakes to act together with, and in the same capacity as, another agent. The same authority given to two or more persons in the same way is presumed to be given to them jointly, unless there is something express or implied to indicate a contrary intention. Agents or brokers appointed jointly are required to undertake a specific task in cooperation with one another, but usually have a several liability to the principal.

In the US, also called a 'co-agent' or 'co-broker'

or, when the broker is not directly appointed by the principal, but acts in cooperation with the appointed broker to endeavor to bring about a transaction, a **cooperating broker** or a 'participation broker'. In the latter instance the participating broker contracts directly with the appointed broker and generally the principal has no obligation to the participating broker, unless he expressly agrees or acknowledges that the brokers are acting in a joint capacity. cf. **multiple agency**. See also **joint and several liability**.

joint and several covenant   A covenant that is accepted by two or more parties as binding on them not only in their individual capacity (severally), but jointly. When two or more parties execute a deed the covenants are binding on them jointly and severally, unless there is an express provision to the contrary. See also **joint and several liability**.

joint and several liability or **joint and several obligation**   The liability of two or more parties in both their individual capacities (severally) and all together (jointly). A party who has a joint and several liability may be required to discharge an entire obligation, notwithstanding any right of recourse to any other party or parties. As a rule, unless there is an express agreement or words of severance, two or more parties who accept a joint obligation are jointly *and* severally liable for the fulfilment of that obligation (although a claimant may not recover more than his singular claim from joint and several parties). In the civil law, called 'solidary liability' and in Scots law, 'conjunct and several liability'. See also **partnership**.

Joint Contracts Tribunal (JCT)^(BrE)   A committee, comprising representatives of most of the major bodies involved in building construction in the UK, whose primary function is to establish standard forms of **building contract**. The Royal Institute of British Architects and the National Federation of Building Trades Employers first established a standard form of contract for general

building work in 1909. Since then many additional bodies, including The Royal Institution of Chartered Surveyors, local authorities, the Association of Consulting Engineers, and the Federation of Associations of Specialists and Sub-Contractors, have formed the constituent bodies of the Tribunal. In addition to standard contracts, the Tribunal produces notes on building practice and various standard forms such as completion certificates and insurance contracts.
Chappell, David. *Understanding JCT Standard Building Contracts*. 6th ed. London: E. & F. N. Spon, 2000.

joint development company   See **joint venture**.

joint estate   See **joint tenancy**.

joint interest   A right to joint ownership of a property. See also **common interest, joint tenancy**.

joint mortgage   1. A **mortgage** granted to two or more mortgagors who are jointly liable for the entire obligation.   2. A mortgage granted by two or more mortgagees who have a mortgage on the same property but advance separate sums. The mortgagees may have equal rights over the mortgaged property; although frequently one mortgagee has a prior charge, even though the mortgages are granted in one mortgage deed. Also called a 'contributory mortgage'. See also **participation mortgage, priority**.

joint ownership   Ownership by two or more parties, regardless of their relationship to each other. See also **co-ownership, collective ownership, community property, joint tenancy, partnership, tenancy in common**.

joint planning board^(Eng)   A body established by the Secretary of State for the Environment, with representatives of two or more local planning authorities (which may be county planning authorities or district planning authorities), to administer development proposals that affect more than one of the authorities (TCPA 1990, s.

2). Such Boards are established mainly for major areas of planning control such as a national park. See also **planning authority**.

joint possession See **unity of possession**.

joint property(Scot) A right to the ownership of property held by two or more inter-related persons, either by virtue of a trust, or a contractual or quasi-contractual bond such as a partnership or unincorporated association. The property is held as if the owners were a single entity, i.e. as co-proprietors, and none of the owners has an independent right to dispose of his right to the property, except by a disposition of the whole. In the event of the death of any one of the proprietors, the property is held by those who remain. cf. **common property**.

joint purchaser A person who acquires property together with one or more other persons, either as a **joint tenancy**, a **tenancy in common** or any other form of **co-ownership**. See also **resulting trust**.

joint tenancy or **joint estate** 1. A form of **co-ownership** or 'concurrent interest' by which two or more owners (joint tenants) are entitled at the same time to the same **estate**, without any distinct or separate interest in the land. (In this context, the word tenancy denotes **tenure** or 'holding' of an estate in land as a form of ownership and not a tenancy in the sense of a relationship of landlord and tenant.) A joint tenancy is an estate in land that creates a 'right of survivorship', i.e. on the death of any one owner the interest passes to the survivor. A joint tenancy vests in each owner a right *in solido*, i.e. a right to joint possession of, and equal shares in, every part of the property and of the whole. In addition, there is the essential 'right of survivorship' or *jus accrescendi* – 'right of accrual'. The right of accrual means that the entire estate eventually passes to the last survivor as his sole property, at which stage the joint tenancy comes to an end. The joint owners take equal shares in any rents and profits to be derived from the

property; are equally responsible for the costs of repairs, taxes, etc.; and have the same, concurrent, rights of use and occupation – they are to the outside world as one.

A joint tenancy must have 'four unities': (i) unity of title: it must be created by the same act or instrument, without 'words of severance' – words that express any intention that the owners are to take distinct and separate shares; (ii) unity of time: the joint interests must be created simultaneously; (iii) unity of interest: all the owners must have the same nature and duration of estate – for example one owner cannot have a third interest and the other two-thirds; and (iv) **unity of possession**: each party holds a right to possession of the entire property so that no action for trespass can be brought by one owner against another. All these four elements must exist and persist, otherwise the co-ownership will be considered as a **tenancy in common**. In the eyes of the law and to any third party, an estate held as a joint tenancy is a single estate and can be devised or conveyed only by all the joint tenants acting together, or by the last survivor. Thus, one joint tenant's interest cannot be passed by a will, as the right of survivorship of the other joint tenant(s) would override it. Among themselves, the joint tenants have rights and claims similar to those between any other property owners, provided they act consistently with the interest held. Joint tenancies arise most frequently between family members where the intention is to pass one part of the interest to a survivor. However, although historically, unless there was an indication to the contrary, a conveyance to two or more persons was presumed to create a joint tenancy, the law is now strict on the creation of a joint tenancy and prefers to construe co-ownership as taking the form of a tenancy in common.

A joint tenancy may come to an end in a number of ways that are essentially means to destroy one or more of the four unities (time, title, interest, and possession) essential to the maintenance of a joint tenancy (although unity of possession may remain if the joint tenancy is converted into a tenancy in common). The joint tenancy will come to an end if: (i) One of the joint tenants alienates his interest, either by sale or mortgage, so that the parties hold the land as tenants in common, which includes an involuntary alienation, as when one party's interest is vested in a trustee in bankruptcy. (ii) One of the joint tenants acquires a larger share than the other co-tenants. (iii) There is a voluntary **partition** so that the owners agree to hold separate shares in a specific portion of the property and thereby break the unity of possession. In English law, a joint tenant has a statutory right to partition the ownership by giving the appropriate notice and effectively forcing a sale of the property (LPA 1925, s. 36(2)). Similarly, in the US, a joint tenant may file a suit to partition the interest and thereby obtain a court order to provide each owner with separate and equitable shares in the property or to arrange for the sale of the property. If there are three or more joint tenants and one of the owners disposes of his interest, the new owner may acquire a tenancy in common, but the remaining owners can continue to hold as joint tenants *inter se*. (iv) There is a sale to a new owner. (v) The joint tenancy is converted into a tenancy in common as when there is an act of **severance**, which arises from any act that is inconsistent with the continued existence of such form of ownership. In particular, a "course of dealing" which intimates that one of the parties is seeking to create a tenancy in common may have the effect of severing the joint tenancy. For example, entering into a contract of sale without the consent of the other co-tenants. Such a course of dealing must make it clear that the one joint tenant no longer desires his shares to be held in joint tenancy and that intent must be made clear to the other party. (vi) One joint tenant criminally kills the other. Severance may also arise by mutual agreement.

In the US, in most jurisdictions, a tenancy in common is considered to arise when two or more parties acquire a property together; unless the parties expressly and clearly state that a joint tenancy, or 'estate in joint tenancy', is to be created. Also, many jurisdictions have abolished the automatic right of survivorship, so that the individual owner's interest can pass to an heir or a person named in that owner's will; unless the deed that transfers the interest to the joint tenants expressly states that upon the death of one owner his share will go to the survivor(s).

In English law, a joint tenancy must be held subject to a **trust for sale**, with the joint owners holding the **legal estate** in the land as trustees for themselves (LPA 1925, s. 36(1)). cf. **joint tenure**. See also **marital property**[(US)], **matrimonial home**[(Eng)], **tenancy by the entirety**. **2.** A tenancy held concurrently by two or more parties; a tenancy held by 'joint lessees'. In legal usage the term 'joint tenancy' refers to the form of ownership in **1.** above, although such a right may be held under a lease as well as by direct title to land, provided the four 'unities' are present. Sometimes called a **cotenancy**, although that term is generally used in a more generic sense, especially to cover a joint tenancy or a tenancy in common.

joint tenant   The holder of a **joint tenancy**. Sometimes used to refer to the holder of any form of **cotenancy**. Sometimes called a 'co-lessee'.

joint tenure   An arrangement whereby a **partnership** is established for a short and fixed period of time. A joint tenure is usually an informal arrangement and is not a commonly used form of partnership. cf. **joint tenancy**.

joint undertaking   See **joint venture**.

joint venture   A business venture between two or more parties who combine their money, skill and expertise for a single enterprise, usually for profit. The joint venture partners share in the risks and rewards of the venture in an agreed manner and have a joint voice in its management. A joint venture is usually more limited in scope than a **partnership** because with a joint venture only a single enterprise, transaction, or business purpose, is intended and the venture terminates when that purpose has been fulfilled. For most legal purposes, and especially for taxation, a joint venture is normally treated as a partnership, unless it has been incorporated in another form, e.g. as a corporation. Sometimes called a 'joint adventure' or a 'joint undertaking'. See also **equity participation, syndicate**.

46 *Am.Jur.2d.*, Joint Venture, §§ 1–79.

48A *Cor.Jur.Sec.*, Joint Ventures, §§ 1–73.

Magnus, Alan P., and Robert Kidby. *Property Joint Ventures: Structures and Precedents*. London: Sweet & Maxwell, 2001.

joint wall   See **party wall**.

judgement creditor(BrE) or **judgment creditor**(AmE)   A creditor who has received the benefit of a direction from a court, requiring a debtor to pay him an outstanding debt, but one who has not yet been paid. See also **caution**(Eng), **garnishment**.

judgement debtor(BrE) or **judgment debtor**(AmE)   A debtor against whom a direction has been made by a court to pay an outstanding debt.

judgment lien(US)   A statutory **lien** against real or personal property granted by a court order as security for the payment of a debt. A lien granted by a court to a **judgment creditor** upon a property or properties of the judgment debtor. A judgment lien is granted against the property of the debtor, but unlike a mortgage does not relate to any specific property. Unlike a common law lien, a judgment lien can only come into existence in accordance with the local state statute (although the origin of the right to exercise such a lien is considered to be derived from the English Statute of Westminster 1285 (13 Edw. I) c. 18; Snead v. M'Coull, 12 Howard 407, 53 US 407, 13 L Ed 1043, 1046 (1852)). A **writ of execution** may subsequently be issued which enables the sheriff to seize and sell as much of the debtor's property as is necessary to pay the debt. See also **attachment**.

judicial dictum   See *obiter dictum*.

judicial foreclosure(US)   Foreclosure carried out under the auspices of a court of law as opposed to 'non-judicial foreclosure' whereby the lender has a **power of sale** as set down in the mortgage document and need not revert to a court of law. (Non-judicial foreclosure is rare and is only permitted in a few jurisdictions.) In the event of default, proper notice must be given to the mortgagor and any other interested party of the intention to offer the property for sale; the sale must be carried out strictly in accordance with the terms of the mortgage and the law; the sale must be advertised and conducted in good faith; and is normally subject to an **upset price** that has been determined by the court, after it has obtained an independent appraisal. Also called 'foreclosure by action or suit'. In some jurisdictions, a **deficiency judgment** is not permitted after a 'power of sale' foreclosure, accordingly a judicial foreclosure may be sought to protect the lender's right in this respect. A judicial foreclosure is also used when there is a dispute as to the priority of the claimants, in order to ensure that the 'correct' price is obtained. Nonetheless, a judicial foreclosure is complicated, time consuming and costly. cf. **strict foreclosure**. See also **foreclosure sale**, **statutory foreclosure**.

judicial partition(US)   See **partition sale**.

judicial precedent   See **precedent**.

judicial sale(US)   A sale of property made as a result of a judicial proceeding. A sale made under a judgment, order, or degree of a court of competent authority; the court being the effective vendor. A judicial sale may take place to partition the co-ownership of property (a **partition sale**); as part of the process of foreclosure (a **foreclosure sale**); or as part of bankruptcy proceedings. The sale is usually conducted under the direction of a sheriff or other legally appointed representative of the court and is normally made by public auction. Upon completion of the sale, the sheriff or other officer conducting the sale may issue a **certificate of sale** confirming that title to the property will pass to the designated purchaser, after any statutory period allowable for redemption by the former mortgagor. No sale takes place until the court has approved it. A judicial sale may be distinguished from an 'execution sale' whereby the property is sold by a sheriff or other officer in accordance with a statutory provision under a writ of execution to satisfy a debt. An execution sale is made to satisfy a particular sum of money; normally takes place by public auction; the sheriff or officer is the vendor; and usually the sale is effected as soon as the property is 'knocked down' to the highest bidder. See also **forced sale**, **power of sale**, **statutory right of redemption**.

jumbo mortgage(US)   A mortgage that is for a larger principal amount would be eligible for purchase by Fannie Mae or Freddie Mac.

junior department store(US)   See **department store**.

junior finance(US)   A loan secured by means of a second or **junior mortgage**.

junior mortgage(US)   Any **mortgage** that is subordinate in terms of interest, principal or right of redemption to a first mortgage, whether as a second or a subsequent mortgage. See also **priority**, **second mortgage**.

junk bond   A debt security that is rated as speculative-grade or below 'investment grade', i.e. rated by Standard & Poor's below BBB- or by Moody's Investor's Service below Baa. In particular, a bond that is considered a high risk, carries a commensurately high rate of interest, and has no conversion rights.

junk fee   A fee that is charged at a rate that is well above that which would be applied in normal market conditions or to a creditworthy and well-advised borrower. A fee that is charged for a service that is not truly provided, as when an 'underwriting fee' is charged but the underwriter does not accept any risk.

jurat   A certificate, usually issued by a government official or notary public, confirming that a writing or **affidavit** was sworn to by the person who signed it. The certificate states when, where and before whom it was sworn. cf. **acknowledgment**.

jus abutendi, jus fruendi, jus utendi(Lat)   In the civil law, the rights to 'dispose' (or even destroy), to 'enjoy the fruits' and to 'use' property. See also *abusus*, **ownership**, *usus*.

jus accrescendi or ***ius accrescendi***(Lat)   'A right of accrual'; 'a right of survivorship'. Under a **joint tenancy**, the accession of property from a number of the joint tenants to a smaller number of those tenants by dint of survivorship, "till it passes to a single hand, and the joint tenancy ceases", *Wharton's Law Lexicon*, 14th ed., 1938.

jus disponendi(Lat)   'The right of disposition or alienation'. In the civil law, a right to goods retained after the owner has parted with possession. In common law, *jus disponendi* may be used to refer to a right vested in a beneficiary to require a trustee to convey the legal estate that is held in trust. See also **bare trust**.

jus habendi et retinendi(Lat)   'A right to have and retain'. See **habendum**.

jus in personam(Lat)   'Right *in personam*'; 'right against the person'. A right that can be exercised against a person as distinguished against a right *in rem* which can be exercised against property. cf. *jus in rem*.

jus in rem(Lat)   'Right *in rem*'; 'right to a thing'. A right that implies a dominion over property independently of any personal rights between parties. cf. *jus in personam*. See also **action *in rem***.

jus in re(Civ)   'Right against a thing'. See **real right**.

jus possessionis(Lat)   'A right of **possession**'.

jus spatiandi^(Lat)　A term essentially of Roman law. A right to wander at will over an undefined area of land that belongs to another, especially for the purpose of recreation and instruction. A right that is not considered in Roman, or in common law, to be capable of forming the subject matter of a **servitude** or **easement**, as the right or area is too vague or indefinite. Thus, it is generally created as a personal **licence**. However, the right may form the subject matter of an easement if the area of land is sufficiently confined or defined, as with an enclosed park or a communal garden enjoyed by several houses. See also **customary right, implied easement**.

jus tertii^(Lat)　'The right of a third party', as where a tenant claims his landlord's title belongs to someone else. See also **estoppel**.

just compensation^(US)　Compensation payable on the exercise of the power of **eminent domain**, i.e. on **condemnation** by a public authority. The Fifth Amendment to the Constitution requires that private property shall not be "taken for public use, without just compensation". In addition, under the Fourteenth Amendment no State may deprive a person of property "without due process of law", which includes an obligation to pay just compensation (Chicago, Burlington, and Quincy R.R. Co. v. Chicago, 166 US 226, 17 S Ct 581, 41 L Ed 979 (1867)). In nearly half the states, this principal has been broadened to cover cases not only where private property is taken, but also if it is 'damaged' by a public authority. However, any increase in value of the subject land attributable solely to actions of the expropriating authority must be disregarded (Kerr v. South Park Commissioners, 117 US 379, 29 L Ed 924, 927 (1886); United States v. Reynolds, 397 US 14, 90 S Ct 803, 25 L Ed.2d 12 (1970)). Also, there may be an 'offset' for any increase in the value of any land retained by the expropriated landowner which is a result of the activities of the expropriating authority.

The amount of just compensation is normally based on the **fair market value** of the land taken (United States v. 50 Acres of Land, 469 US 24, 33, 105 S Ct 451, 83 L Ed.2d 376, 385 (1984)); or strictly speaking the "market value fairly determined", United States ex rel. T.V.A. v. Powelson, 319 US 266, 63 S Ct 1047, 87 L Ed 1390, 1397 (1943). The property is valued in its **highest and best use**, so that if the land that is to be condemned is likely to be re-zoned in a way that will increase its value, then the owner can base his claim for compensation on the higher value, provided the re-zoning is probable, and there is definite demand for the re-zoned land (Miss. and Rum River Boom Co. v. Patterson, 98 US 403, 25 L Ed 206, 209 (1878); United States v. 50.8 Acres of Land, 149 F Supp 749, 752 (DC NY 1957); United States v. Meadow Brook Club, 259 F.2d 41, 45 (2d Cir. NY 1958)). As a corollary, "if existing zoning restrictions preclude a more profitable use, ordinarily such use should not be considered in the evaluation", United States v. Meadow Brook Club, *supra* at 45 (United States v. 27.93 Acres of Land, 924 F.2d 506, 513, 514 (3d Cir. Pa 1991)). In a federal acquisition, compensation is not normally payable for disturbance to the use or business, as that is not a 'taking'; but **severance damages** may be payable for a loss or reduction in the value of a parcel of land resulting from a 'partial taking' of land.

Sometimes called 'due compensation' or 'full compensation' being the compensation that will make an owner of property pecuniarily whole for the loss or reduction in market value as a result of the public taking. See also **before-and-after method, consequential damages, valuation date, inverse condemnation, unit rule**.

just terms^(Aus)　The basis on which the Commonwealth has a right to acquire land or private property. 'Just terms' requires the payment of reasonable **compensation** (Commonwealth of Australia Constitution Act 1900, s. 51(xxxi)). The payment should aim "to place in the hands of the owner expropriated the full money equivalent of the thing of which he has been deprived. Compensation prima facie means recompense for loss, and when an owner is to receive compensation for being deprived of real or personal property his pecuniary loss must be ascertained by determining the value to him of the property taken from him", *Nelungaloo Pty. Ltd v Commonwealth* (1948) 75 CLR 495, 571, [1948] 1 ALR 145 (Aus). The amount of compensation is based on the **market value** of the property taking into account all the circumstances, such as ignoring the value attributable to the effect any scheme for which the Commonwealth is acquiring the property and considering the competing interests of both parties.

just title(US)   **1.** A term of the civil or French law, for a title that arises from a presumption of a valid grant. See also **color of title**. **2.** An imperfect title, but one that has all the appearance of being valid. See also **good title**.

justus titulus(Lat)   'just title'.

k-factor   See **mortgage constant**.

keep in repair   An obligation that requires the landlord or tenant to keep the demised premises in the same state of **repair** as when the tenant was granted possession of the property. The term is commonly used in a lease in such phrases as "to maintain and keep in good repair" where it conveys a similar meaning to **maintenance**, i.e. to at least maintain the status quo (fair or natural **wear and tear** excluded). This obligation does not require the tenant to make the property better than it originally was (*Southwark L.B.C. v Mills* [1999] 4 All ER 449, 455 (HL)). See also **tenantable repair**.

keep-open clause   See **continuous operation clause**.

key lot or key plot   1. A lot that has special value either because of its strategic location or its value to an adjoining landowner. See also **corner lot**, **plottage value**.   2. A lot that faces onto more than one rear yard. A lot that abuts the rear boundary of a corner lot and the secondary street.

key money   1. A single payment that is paid to secure a leasehold interest, either as a new lease or the assignment of an existing lease. A **fine** or **premium** paid for a right to acquire a property; especially a non-returnable sum paid by a tenant before he is granted possession of a property, either at the start of a new tenancy or on the assignment of an existing tenancy. Key money commonly refers to a payment made to acquire a right that has no marketable value, i.e. it is paid over and above the value of any **profit rent** or the value of any improvement made by an outgoing tenant.
In English law, the demanding of key money for a right to occupy residential property is, as a rule, illegal (*viz.* **premium**).
In the US, a payment given by a tenant to a landlord in consideration for the grant of a lease may be referred to as a 'bonus deposit'. See also **deposit**, **fair rent**(Eng).   2. A **commission** paid to an agent, broker or accommodation agent for the privilege of being put forward as a potentially suitable tenant for a property.   3. A sum paid by an incoming tenant for an advantage to be derived from acquiring a lease of a property. In particular, a sum of money paid by a retail tenant for the right to take over fixtures, goodwill, or merely for the privilege of being represented in a shopping center.

key plot   See **key lot**.

key tenant   A tenant of a high financial standing who occupies a major or significant amount of space in a property. A tenant who is a major occupier of a commercial property. In particular, a tenant who takes a major part of an office building or a shopping center under a pre-leasing agreement. See **anchor tenant**.

kickback   1. A percentage payment exacted for the privilege of being permitted to take a share in a business venture. A portion of the purchase price for a property paid to one of the parties to the transaction, or his agent or representative, as an inducement to the consummation of the deal; especially when the deal is favourable to the party paying the kickback. See also **broker**.   2. Payment of money or property made to a public official, company employee, client, or customer, as an inducement to give favour to the person making the payment, i.e. a secret rebate or bribe. For example, a payment made by a building contractor or a seller of property to an individual to induce him or her to persuade their employer to enter into a contract with the payee. If a real estate broker receives a commission on the sale of a property, it is generally illegal for that broker also to receive a referral fee from a lender who grants a loan secured on that property, unless the buyer is aware of such a 'kick back' to the lender. In addition, it is illegal for a broker to pay a share of his commission to a non-licensed broker.

kicker equity   See **equity participation**.

kicker mortgage loan   See **equity-participation loan**.

kickout clause[US]   See **recapture clause**.

kiting[AmE]   **1.** A practice of writing a check against funds that are not available in the hope that funds will become available before the check is presented for payment. Issuing a check on one bank and depositing it in another bank to endeavour to convey the impression that funds are available, especially to cover an unapproved overdraft; the payee then hopes for a windfall before the check is presented to the first bank. The term may refer also to fraudulently changing the amount written on a check, as from $600 to $6000.   **2.** The illegal practice of preparing a duplicate contract, but with terms that differ from the original or true contract, in order to obtain an extra benefit, such as a higher loan. See also **dual contract**.

knock down   The acceptance of the final bid in an **auction**, usually signified by the fall of the auctioneer's hammer. In the US, also referred to as 'struck off'.

knock-out agreement   See **bidding agreement**.

knowledge   Awareness as to a fact or condition; the act of knowing or understanding. Knowledge may be actual, or it may be presumed to have been acquired if it can be obtained by reasonable and diligent inquiry. Knowledge does not have to mean to "know for certain and beyond possibility of contradiction", but it generally means to know with sufficient confidence to justify taking some form of action, such as taking legal and other advice Knowledge is sufficient to put a person on guard and call for inquiry. Mere suspicion or a vague and unsupported belief does not normally mean that someone has knowledge of some fact or event; but reasonable belief, especially if it could be supported upon inquiry, will normally suffice to say that someone knew about the fact or the occurrence of the event. In law, knowledge and **notice** are generally considered to be synonymous, so that one is deemed to have knowledge of that which is imported by **constructive notice**. See also **implied notice**, **notice**.

L

laches Derived from the Old French *laschesse*, 'slackness', 'carelessness', or 'negligence'. The neglect, omission or unreasonable delay in asserting or enforcing one's rights, or in performing a duty. Laches embraces the maxim *vigilantibus, non dormientibus, jura subveniunt*, 'law aids those who are vigilant, and not those who sleep on their rights' or 'law aids the vigilant, not the indolent' (2 *Co Inst* 690; Wing. 692). Laches provides in **equity**, an end to litigation similar to that supplied in law by a statutory **limitation** on a right of action, although laches is not based on any specific period of time, but the reasonable determination of the court. The doctrine of laches may bar an equitable remedy such as a claim for **rescission, rectification, specific performance** or an **injunction**, or may be used against a beneficiary who seeks to recover trust property from a trustee after the former has unduly and indubitably acquiesced in accepting the trustee's retention of his property. Laches may be distinguished from **abandonment**, in that the latter is dependent upon intention and is voluntary, whereas laches defeats intention and acts against the will. In the US, sometimes called the 'doctrine of stale demands'. cf. **estoppel**.

Lady day See **quarter day**.

laesæ fidei(Lat) 'Breach of faith'. See **good faith**.

lake See **littoral land, shore, water rights**.

Lammas day See **quarter day**.

land A dry part of the earth's surface; any part of the earth's surface that can be owned and exploited, whether mountain or valley, pasture or desert, town or country, dry land or land covered with water (or ice). 'Land' may be considered as any part of the earth's crust and that which is a part thereof – although generally 'land' excludes the oceans. The meaning of 'land' may be extended to all that is annexed to it, whether by man or nature, including buildings and fixtures. Land may also include any **estate, interest,** or **right** in or over land, i.e. that which is classed as **real property**.

In economics, land is more than the surface of the earth; it is a natural resource, a commodity, and a primary source of wealth; it is one of the factors of production (the others being labour and **capital**) without which there can be no economic activity. It is regarded as the one economic resource that is provided by nature, as distinguished from the other resources, which are provided by man. "The term 'land' often means different things depending upon the context in which it is used and the circumstances under which it is considered. Like a cut diamond it has many facets. Most important among these are the views of land as (1) space, (2) nature, (3) a factor of production, (4) a consumption good, (5) situation, (6) **property** and (7) capital (three other facets of land – concept of land as a deity, as a community, and as a store of wealth may also be noted)", Raleigh Barlowe, *Land Resource Economics; The Economics of Real Estate*. 4th ed. Prentice-Hall, 1985, p. 10.

In the legal sense, land is any ground, soil or earth; growing trees or bushes; growing crops (except **emblements**); water in the form of a spring, well, lake or pond (at least while it is on the land); anything permanently or intentionally fixed thereon; any **mine** or any **mineral** (including coal, metallic ores, oil and gas) while beneath the land; and reasonable use of the air space above. A right to the ownership of land includes the **natural rights** appertaining thereto, and anything affixed or growing on the land that has become part of the land, e.g. any **fixture**, building, and *fructus naturales* (crops that grow naturally) but, as a rule, not the produce of land that is the result of one year's labour and can therefore readily be harvested and removed – *fructus industriales* or emblements. 'Land' comprehends "all things of a permanent, substantial nature, being a word of very extensive significance … For land, says Sir

Edward Coke [1 *Co Inst* 4], comprehendeth in its legal signification any ground, soil, or earth whatsoever; as arable, meadows, pastures, woods, moors, marshes, furzes, and heath. It legally includeth all castles, houses, and other buildings: for they consist, it is said, of two things; land, which is the foundation; and structure thereon: so that if I convey the land or ground, the structure or building passeth with it", 2 *Bl Comm* 16, 17. Land may be divided horizontally, vertically or otherwise, and either below or above ground. Thus, separate ownership may exist in strata of minerals, in the space occupied by tunnels, or in different storeys of a building", 39(2) *Halsbury's Laws of England,* Real Property, 4th ed. Reissue, para. 76.

In theory, land is defined by law as a right that extends as far above and below the surface as is physically possible. A principle expressed by the maxim *cujus est solum, ejus est usque ad coelum et ad inferos,* 'he who possesses land, possesses to the sky above and to the depths below'. However, this historical view has been restrained by common law and statute; hence, aircraft, above a reasonable height, may fly over land (*Bernstein v Skyviews,* [1978] QB 479, [1977] 2 All ER 902; Hinman v. Pacific Air Transport, 84 F.2d 755 (9th Cir. 1936), cert. den. 300 US 654). Also, **mineral rights** may be severed from the surface right; or, as in the United Kingdom, oil, gas and coal may be limited to the State.

Land includes 'tenements' and 'hereditaments'. However, **tenement** is a word of greater scope than land and includes any thing that may be held and **hereditament** includes not only lands and tenements, but also whatever may be *inherited,* be it corporeal or incorporeal, real, personal or a combination thereof.

In English law, "when used in a lease or other assurance, 'land' includes, if there is nothing to restrict its technical meaning, all kinds of land, whether arable, meadow or otherwise, and also everything on or under the soil, all buildings erected on it, and all mines and minerals beneath it and the air space above it to such height as may be necessary for the ordinary use and enjoyment of it and the structures on it. A lease of woods includes not only the trees, but also the land whereon they grow. Words which are appropriate for granting part of the profits of land do not carry land itself ... (but) Where the soil under the water is intended to pass the expression 'land covered with water' should be used. A grant of all profits of land is, however, equivalent to a grant of land itself", 27(1) *Halsbury's Laws of England,* Landlord and Tenant, 4th ed. Reissue, para. 130.

In English statutes, 'land' is defined in a number of different ways. The Interpretation Act 1978, ss. 5, 22(1), Sch. 1 (which applies to any Act of Parliament passed after January 1, 1979) defines land to include "buildings and other structures, land covered with water, and any estate, interest, **easement**, **servitude** or right in or over land". In the Land Clauses Consolidation Act 1845, s. 3 (which is applicable to compulsory purchase) land includes "messuages, lands, tenements, and hereditaments of any tenure". The LPA 1925, s. 205(1)(ix) (as amended by the Trusts of Land and Appointment of Trustees Act 1996, Sch. 4) defines land to include "land of any tenure, and mines and minerals whether or not held apart from the surface, buildings or parts of buildings (whether the division is horizontal, vertical or made in any other way) and other corporeal hereditaments; also a manor, an advowson, and a rent and other incorporeal hereditament, and an easement, right, privilege, or benefit in, over, or derived from land". The SLA 1925, s. 117; the LRA 1925, s. 3; the LCA 1925, s. 20; and the Trustee Act 1925, s. 68 contain definitions similar to (but slightly varied from) the LPA 1925. The Limitation Act 1990, s. 38(1) (which relates to limitations on the time for actions to recover land) defines land to include "corporeal hereditaments, tithes and rentcharges and any legal or equitable estate or interest therein, including an interest in the proceeds of the sale of land held upon **trust for sale**, but except as provided above in this definition does not include any incorporeal hereditament". The LRA 2002, s. 132(1) defines land to include "(a) buildings and other structures, (b) land covered with water, and (c) mines and minerals, whether or not held with the surface". The TCPA 1990, s. 336(1) defines land to mean "any corporeal hereditament, including a building" (and for the purposes of Part IX of the Act which deals with the acquisition or appropriation of land for planning purposes) it "includes any interest in or right over land". The Land Compensation Act 1961, s. 39 (which deals with the assessment of compensation for the compulsory acquisition of land) defines land to mean "any corporeal **hereditament**, including a building as defined by this section, and includes any interest or right in or over land and any right to water" ('building' being defined as "any structure or erection or any part of a building as so defined, but does not include plant or machinery comprised in a building"). In the Acquisition of Land Act 1981, s. 7(1) (which deals with the powers of compulsory purchase) land includes "(a) any messuage, tenements and hereditaments, and (b) in relation to compulsory purchase under any enactment includes anything falling within any definition of the expression in that enactment".

The Ontario Act, s. 1(c) defines land to include "messuages and all other hereditaments, corporeal or incorporeal, money to be laid out in the purchase of land, any share of such hereditaments, any estate of inheritance, any estate for life or lives or other estate transmissible to heirs, any possibility, right or title of entry or action, and any other interest capable of being inherited, whether any of the foregoing are in possession, reversion, remainder, or contingency". In the Uniform Act, which relates to Limitation of Action and is applicable in several Canadian Provinces, land includes all corporeal hereditaments, and any share or any freehold or leasehold estate or any interest in any of such hereditament or estate.

In New Zealand, land is statutorily defined to include "messuages, tenements, and hereditaments, corporeal and incorporeal, of every kind and description, and every estate or interest therein, together with all paths, passages, ways, waters, watercourses, liberties, easements, and privileges thereunto appertaining, plantations, gardens, mines, minerals, and quarries, and all

trees and timber thereon or thereunder lying or being, unless specially excepted", Land Transfer Act, s. 2 (NZ) (Property Land Act 1952, s. 2 (NZ); Interpretation Act 1999, s. 2 (NZ)). See also **accession, accretion, accommodation land, agricultural land, air rights, building land, common land, estate, fixture, immovable, land economics, littoral rights, public lands, *res nullius*, real property, riparian rights, settled land**(Eng)**, strict liability, trespass, treasure trove, waste land, water rights**.

land agent   1. An agent who is responsible for the management of an agricultural or country estate and whose responsibilities extend from supervising the physical upkeep and improvement of the land to the maintenance of good landlord and tenant relations. Also called a 'land steward'. See also **estate management**.   2.(US)A **broker** who specializes in raw land or agricultural property. In the western states and Canada, a 'land agent' was someone charged with the sale of large tracts of land.   3.(Aus)A person licensed to act for a fee, gain, or reward in matters or proceedings relating to **Crown land** or land under the control of the Minister (Land Agents Act 1927, s. 3 (NSW)). A person who is registered and permitted to carry out the business of selling, purchasing, or dealing with land, or businesses on behalf of others or on his own behalf, or conducting negotiations for those purposes. A legal practitioner and a person who engages in mortgage financing (Land Agents Act 1994 s. 4 (SA)). See also **real estate agent**.

land assemblage(US)   See **assemblage**.

Land Authority for Wales   See **Welsh Development Agency**.

land bank   1. A stock of land held for future development. In particular, land held by a real estate development company or a homebuilder to ensure a steady program of future development. 2. A financial institution that specialises in making loans, usually mortgage loans, for the purchase of land, especially farmland. 'Land banks' were first established in England in 1695 to issue notes based on the security of land, but such institutions died out by the start of the 18th century.

In the US, land banks were first established in the 18th century to make loans secured on farm property, usually at favorable rates of interest. Land banks now take the form of the Federal Land Banks and joint stock land banks that specialize in long-term agricultural loans.

land capitalization rate(AmE) A **capitalization rate** that may be used to convert income from land into a capital value for the land. Land capitalization rate may be expressed by the symbol R_L. See also **land residual technique**.

land certificate 1.(Eng)A certificate issued by the **Land Registry**, under seal, to the **registered proprietor** of a parcel of land as evidence of title to registered land (LRA 1925, s. 63(1)). A land certificate should be distinguished from an **official certificate of search**, which provides details of entries on the Land Charges Register, and may be issued to an intending purchaser of unregistered land as evidence of charges that affect the land, but it is not evidence of title.

With the advent of electronic conveyancing, a land certificate will no longer issued by the Land Registry. Proof of ownership of land is provided by the register itself and, when a title is registered, a certificate of registration, or 'title information document', will be provided to the registered proprietor (Land Registration Act 2002). See also **caution, charge certificate**. 2.(US)A certificate or written order that was formerly issued by a municipal authority to a party that had acquired a right to public lands confirming the right to the designated area of land, subject to the completion of any outstanding legal formalities. Such a document was also called a 'land warrant' when issued by the local office of the United States Land Office. See also **headright certificate, public lands**.

land charge(Eng) An encumbrance that may be entered on the Register of Land Charges, which forms part of the **Land Charges Register**, in order to protect the beneficiary from the possibility that a purchaser of unregistered land may claim that he was not aware of the encumbrance and, therefore, is not bound by it. The registration of any matter in the Land Charges Register is deemed to constitute "actual **notice** of ... the fact of such registration, to all persons and for all purposes connected with the land affected ... so long as the registration continues in force", LPA 1925, s. 198(1). In other words, any instrument or matter entered on the register is 'deemed' to be known to a purchaser, whether or not he makes enquiry. A land charge is registered in the name of the **estate owner** of the land to be affected.

The various encumbrances that may be entered on the register of land charges are set out in the LCA 1972, s. 2 (as amended) and denominated as classes A to F. They include such matters as a **rentcharge**; a charge on land that is imposed by statute; any of the following (not being a local land charge): (i) a **puisne mortgage**, (ii) a **limited owner's charge**, (iii) a **general equitable charge**, (iv) an **estate contract**; (v) an Inland Revenue charge (as for unpaid inheritance tax); (vi) a **restrictive covenant** (created after 1925), but not one between landlord and tenant; (vii) an **equitable easement** (created after 1925); (viii) a spouse's statutory 'rights of occupation' of a **matrimonial home**. It is important that, before taking a conveyance of unregistered land, the prospective purchaser should make a search of the Land Charges Register, either personally or by obtaining an **official certificate of search** from the Land Registrar. A purchaser of registered land is not required to make a land charges search (LRA 2002, 86(7)). cf. **local land charge**. See also **constructive notice, overreached interest, priority notice, searches**.

Land Charges Register(Eng) A register, maintained by the Land Registrar at the Land Charges Department of the **Land Registry**, that sets out details of encumbrances against unregistered land that may be registered in order to give actual **notice** to an intending purchaser of the existence of the encumbrance

(LCA 1972, s. 1(1)). The entire register is divided into five separate registers: (i) register of pending actions; (ii) register of annuities (which applied only to annuities created before 1925); (iii) register of writs and orders affecting land; (iv) register of deeds of arrangement affecting land; and (v) register of land charges (being the most significant of the five registers). The register is augmented by an index, maintained by the Land Registrar, where all entries can readily be traced. (The Land Charges Register applies to unregistered land and should be distinguished from the 'Charges Register' at the Land Registry which contains details of encumbrances against registered land.) cf. **local land charges register**. See also **Companies Charges Register, land charge, official certificate of search**.

land contract[US]   1. See **installment land contract**.   2. A **contract** for the sale of real property. Any contract by which one party agrees to sell and the other to purchase real property in consideration of a money price, or other payment, from the buyer to the seller. cf. **option**. See also **contract for sale** (of land).

land damages[US]   See **just compensation**.

Land Department of the United States[US]   A term that covers the federal land authorities, which consist of the Secretary of the Interior, the **Bureau of Land Management** and their subordinate officers. This department is entrusted with the acquisition, disposition and control of public lands (excluding land that is part of a national forest or a national park) and for determining claims to **public lands** that the government is empowered to dispose of.

land development   The improvement of land by the process of **development**. In particular, the opening up, laying out, or changing and improving the potential of land by the provision of utilities, new roads or street improvements and the subdivision of land for resale.

land development loan   A loan made to enable a developer to make land improvements, such as grading and provision of roads and utilities, usually as part of the process of **subdivision**. See also **construction finance, land loan**.

land economics   An art or social science that deals with the use and allocation of land as a scarce resource, including all permanent buildings, improvements or any other additions that are made to land. Land economics is concerned with the marketing, distribution and allocation of land and its products, its efficiency in the production process and its role in the welfare of the community. "It is concerned with man's economic use of the surface resources of the earth and the physical and biological, economic and institutional factors that affect, condition, and control his use of these resources", Raleigh Barlowe, *Land Resource Economics; The Economics of Real Estate*. 4th ed. Prentice-Hall, 1985, p. 4. It involves the study of the characteristics of land; the classification and patterns of land uses; the planning and development of land; the ownership and legal control of land; land as a commodity or as a source of wealth; the taxation of land; and economic theories of land, in terms of its price or value and the concept of **highest and best use**. See also **economic rent, land-use planning, location theory**.

Balchin, Paul N., and Jeffrey L. Kieve. *Urban Land Economics and Public Policy*. 5th ed. London: Macmillan, 1995.

DiPasquale, Denise, and William C. Wheaton. *Urban Economics and Real Estate Markets*. Upper Saddle River, NJ: Prentice-Hall, 1996.

Harvey, Jack. *Urban Land Economics*. 4th ed. London: Macmillan, 1996.

O'Sullivan, Arthur. *Urban Economics*. 5th ed. New York: McGraw-Hill, 2004.

land gavel   See **gavelkind**.

land grant[US]   1. A transfer of title to real property. See also **grant**.   2. A grant of **public lands** by the United States government or a state government. A grant of land in the public domain made by Congress for a particular purpose, e.g. a grant of land to a corporation for industrial development, to a railroad company to aid the construction of a new railroad, or to a university for a new educational building or college.

land improvement   See **development, improvement, land reclamation**.

land jobber(US)   A person who makes a business of buying and selling land for profit.

Lands Improvement Company(Eng)   A British government sponsored institution, first established in 1853, that makes long-term loans for the improvement of agricultural property and certain recreational and amenity land. The Company is now governed by Special Acts of Parliament passed between 1920 and 1969.

land lease   See **ground lease**.

land leaseback   See **land sale-and-leaseback**.

land loan(US)   A loan secured against land, especially land held for future development. See also **mortgage**.

land locked   See **landlocked, easement of necessity**.

land option   See **option**.

land owner   See **landowner**.

land patent(US)   See **patent**.

land planning   See **land-use planning**.

land purchase-and-leaseback   See **sale-and-leaseback**.

land reclamation   The winning back of land for a useful purpose. The recovery of **wasteland** for productive use. The conversion or restoration of **derelict land** so that it may be cultivated or developed for occupation or profit, including filling, levelling, draining, irrigating and any other form of land (but not building) improvement.

land recording or **land recordation**(US)   The delivery of deeds or other title-related documents to an official government office in order to record a right or claim to land. The basis of land recording is that the entry of the title at an official court or registry acts as a **constructive notice** to anyone interested in a particular parcel of land. The system sets out the identity of the owner and any mortgages, charges, liens or encumbrances affecting the land and enables a prospective purchaser, mortgagee, private title insurance company, or other interested party to verify the status of the title to every parcel of land. A recorded deed takes priority over any unrecorded deed, even though the recorded deed may have been issued later.

Every state and the District of Columbia has a recording law, although the system of land recording varies considerably from state to state. Broadly, the system may be classified as: (a) a notice system; (b) a race-notice system; or (c) a pure race system. Under the notice system, which applies in nearly half the states, an instrument is not binding on any party who acquires land (or places a mortgage on land) in good faith (a *bona fide* purchaser); for **value**; and does not have **notice** (actual or constructive) of that instrument. Under this system, recording is constructive notice. Under the race-notice, which applies in twenty four states and the District of Columbia, basically the first party to record the instrument has priority, subject to the rule that, until recording has been executed, priority is determined by notice. Under the race system, which applies in Louisiana and North Carolina (and for some instruments in Arkansas, Ohio and Pennsylvania), an instrument is only binding when it is recorded, regardless of notice, and priority is determined by the date of recording. Under any of these recording systems certain interests, such as short-term leases and certain spousal rights, are binding on a purchaser regardless of notice or recording, thus requiring the purchaser to make enquiry of the seller and inspect the property. See also **abstract of title**, **acknowledgment**, **grantor-grantee index**, **land registration**(Eng), **mechanic's lien**, **mortgagee-mortgagor index priority**, **title insurance**, **tract index**, **Torrens title system**.

land register   See Land Registry(Eng).

land registration   1.(US)See **land recording**, **Torrens title system**.   2.(Eng)The recording of title to land on a formal register, so that an owner may deal with land by reference to that register rather than by reference to title documents held by the existing landowner. The purpose of land registration is (a) to record all rights and interests affecting the registered land; (b) to provide that specific rights over land, in particular trusts, are excluded from the register and, therefore, on a sale of land these rights are transferred from the land to the proceeds of sale; and (c) to provide a guarantee by the State as to the validity of a registered title so that, if the title as registered proves defective, compensation is paid from a public fund to an owner who is consequently deprived of his land. In England and Wales, land registration is effected by the recording of details of titles to land and certain rights thereover at the **Land Registry**, and evidence of the registration was provided in the form of a **land certificate**. Any such registered title is then guaranteed and may be transferred without further investigation of, or concern with, any former rights to the land. Land registration is intended not only to affirm title to land, but also to record rights that affect, and are transferred with, a title. However, it is not intended to, nor will it, validate an otherwise invalid claim to land. Although, with effect from October 13 2002, no new land certificates will be issued, as registration itself is proof of ownership, and only a certificate confirming the registration of title to the legal estate will be issued (LRA 2002, Sch. 10, para. 4).

A title registered at the Land Registry may be accepted by the Land Registrar as an **absolute title** (either an absolute freehold title, or an absolute leasehold title); as a **possessory title** (either a possessory freehold title or, rarely, a possessory leasehold title) when the title is based on a claim of adverse possession; or as a **qualified title** when the Registrar is not entirely satisfied that he can register an absolute title. In addition, a lessee may register a **good leasehold title** when there is uncertainty as to the title of the lessor.

Land registration also provides a means to protect certain interests in land that do not themselves represent a title to land, but are capable of binding a purchaser of land when they are registered. Such an interest is referred to as a **minor interest**. Other interests in registered land are assumed to be ascertainable by inspection of the land and by making diligent enquiry and, thereby, are binding on the purchaser of the land. Such interests are called **overriding interests**. See also **Companies Charges Register**, **land charge**, **Land Charges Register**, **local land charges register**.

Harpum, Charles, and Janet Bignell. *Registered Land: Law and Practice under the Land Registration Act 2002.* Bristol: Jordans, 2002.

Land Registry(Eng)   A government department that is responsible to the Lord Chancellor for keeping and maintaining the Land Register of England and Wales. Its main purpose is to register title to land in England and Wales and to record dealings once land is registered. Any unregistered land in England and Wales is registrable within two months of a conveyance of the **legal estate** or many other major forms of dealing in land (LRA 2002, ss. 4-8). In addition to registering the legal estate, the Register is used as a means to enter a **minor interest** against the registered estate in order to grant protection for such interests against a purchaser of a 'legal estate for valuable consideration'. In addition, the Registry accommodates the **Land Charges Register**, which sets out details of various encumbrances affecting unregistered land. The administrative headquarters of the Land Registry is situated at Lincoln's Inn Fields, London, and actual registration is made through one of nineteen District Registries. The Register at each District

Registry is divided into three parts: (1) a 'Property Register', which identifies and describes the registered land and the estate held therein and any incidental interests or benefits affecting the land (including any exemption from an **overriding interest** and details of easements, restrictive covenants, or other rights, privileges and conditions affecting the land); and, for leasehold land, details of the lease (leases for 21 years or more), together with exceptions and reservations to the lease. In addition, the Property Register indicates the boundaries of the registered parcels of land by reference to a **filed plan** of the land, with each title being allocated a title number. (2) A 'Proprietorship Register', which contains the name, address and a description of the proprietor of the land, describes the form of title that is registered (absolute, good leasehold, qualified or possessory), and details of any restrictions on the proprietor's right of sale (e.g. a trust for sale or a strict settlement), together with any **restriction, caution** or **inhibition** affecting the proprietor's right to deal with the land. (3) A 'Charges Register', which details rights *adverse* to the land, such as mortgages, charges and restrictive covenants and, in general, any **notice** entered to protect lesser interests (including any lease) affecting the registered land, as well as all such dealings with registered charges or encumbrances as are capable of registration (Land Registration Rules 1925, rr. 2-7). An **Index Map** and a **Parcels Index** is available for inspection, together with a list of pending applications, to enable an interested party to ascertain whether or not a particular parcel of land is, or is about to be, registered. See also **charge certificate, General Map, land certificate, land registration**. (www.landreg.gov.uk).
Timothy, Patrick. *Wontner's Guide to Land Registry Practice.* 19th ed. London: Pearson, 1995.

land rent Rent derived from land. In particular, rent from an area of unimproved land as represented by the excess of income and profits from that land over the cost of maintaining the land in its productive use. See also **economic rent, ground rent, rental value**.

land residual approach or **land residual technique**[AmE] A method of appraising land, separately from the buildings or improvements standing thereon. A notional income that is considered to represent a fair return on the building or improvements alone (usually a percentage of the replacement cost), based on the highest and best use, is deducted from the actual or potential income receivable from the entire property and the balance, a deemed **ground rent**, is capitalized at a rate considered appropriate to the land alone. cf. **building residual technique**. See also **abstraction approach, residual method of valuation**[Eng], **residual process**.

land sale-and-leaseback A sale-and-leaseback of land that is intended to be developed. Unimproved land is sold by a real estate developer to a financial institution and is then leased back to the developer with a concurrent loan from the institution, secured by a mortgage on the developer's leasehold interest. The loan is intended to provide finance for the development of the site. Usually the lender provides all the financing and acquires a share of the equity to be derived from the completed development; the developer provides the design and building expertise. Sometimes called a 'land-leaseback' or 'land purchase-and-leaseback'. cf. **project sale-and-leaseback**. See also **equity participation, lease-and-leaseback financing**.

land sales contract[US] See **installment sale**.

land scrip[US] See **land certificate**.

land settlement 1.[US] The settlement of public lands by homesteaders. See also **homestead**. 2.[Eng] See **settlement**.

land speculator See **speculator**.

land steward See **land agent**.

land surveying See **surveying**.

land surveyor   See **surveyor**.

land tax   A tax levied on the beneficial owner of land; that is, on the rights and benefits to be derived from the ownership of real property. In Australia, a land tax is levied in the Australian Capital territories and all States on the unimproved value of taxable land, generally on the owner of the land. See also **property tax, real estate tax**.

land-tenant   A person in actual **possession** or occupation of land. A lessee in possession. See also **terre-tenant**.

land tenure   The rights to hold, use and dispose of land. See also **estate, feudal system, tenure**.

Land Titles Office (LTO)(Aus)   A body established in each State or Territory to register interests in land, whether **native title** rights or interests under the **Torrens title system**. See also **register of titles**.

Land Transfer land(NZ)   Land that has been registered in accordance with the Land Transfer Act 1952 (NZ). Most land in New Zealand that has been alienated from the Crown in fee simple, and certain lands that have been alienated by lease or statutory licence, is now registered. When land is registered the Registrar issues a **certificate of title** setting out the name of the registered proprietor, a legal description of the land, the nature of the estate held, details of encumbrances, restrictions, and other interests (such as mortgages, leases and easements) and a plan is annexed to the certificate. Transfers of land, mortgages, and leases are effected by registration of documents in the form required by the Land Transfer Act 1952. Such documents are called 'instruments' and an instrument is registered by entering a 'memorial' on the certificate of title, or any other document of title such as a mortgage or lease. See also **Torrens system of title**.

Land Tribunal(Aus)   A tribunal established in the State of Queensland to hear claims made to **native title** by Aboriginal people or by Torres Strait Islanders. See also **claimable Crown land, National Native Title Tribunal**.

land trust(US)   A form of trust that is created under statutory provisions whereby land is placed in trust in order to conceal the identity of the true owner or owners. Title to the land is transferred to the trustee (usually a bank or title company) by means of a **deed of trust**, and a 'trust agreement' is drawn up so that the creator of the trust effectively retains the management and control of the trust property. Generally, the trustee or 'land trustee' is only required to execute deeds and take such actions as directed by the beneficiary (called the beneficiary's 'power of direction'). The beneficiary, in turn, is entitled to receive the income from the trust property and is responsible for decisions on such matters as collection of rents, insurance, repairs and payment of taxes and, generally, has the power to mortgage or sell the trust property. As a rule, the beneficiary is free to assign or pledge his interest, but he cannot partition his interest if there are other beneficiaries. A land trust may be created to enable land to be held for the benefit of a number of co-owners, or owners of a partial interest in land, so that the owners as a whole are protected in the event of a bankruptcy or judgment against one of the owners. A land trust may also be used to hide the identity of an owner who is seeking to assemble a number of separate parcels of land. A Trust Number is commonly used to identify a land trust and a 'land trust certificate' may evidence the beneficiary's entitlement under the trust. The trust is usually created for a specific purpose and for a defined period of time.

'Land trust' is sometimes used synonymously with 'deed of trust' (or a 'trust deed mortgage'), which is used to create a form of mortgage. However, strictly speaking a 'land trust' is the form of device described above, being used primarily to conceal the true identity of the landowner. These forms of land trust are only acknowledged in certain states that adopt a liberal interpretation of the English **Statute of Uses**. That Statute, which was passed in 1535, provided that the creation of a trust that left the trustees without any discretionary powers effectively vested the land in the trustees. Accordingly, a strict adaptation of that statute would not allow for 'land trusts'.

In California and Nevada, a similar arrangement is also called a 'holding agreement'. See also **bare trust, estate company, property trust, trust for sale**.

land trust certificate(US)   See **land trust**.

land use   See **land economics, highest and best use, use**.

land-use intensity system (LUI)(US)   A form of land-use planning that is based on a system of comprehensive interrelated building ratios, such as building coverage, living unit, floor area, open space, recreation area and parking ratios. The system is based on a land-use intensity scale instead of the more conventional system of height, setback, and density controls. The LUI system is used especially in planned unit developments. See also **density zoning, planned unit development**.

land-use planning   A system, usually supported by force of law, designed to control and plan the future use of land. Land-use planning is effected by regulations that are intended to order and regulate the use and development of land. In particular, land-use planning includes or encompasses: **zoning**, which primarily defines or restricts the type of land use; controls on **density**, which limit the intensity of land use, in terms either of building units or population; and **plot ratio** or **floor area ratio** controls, which restrict the volume and height of new buildings. See also **development plan, land economics, town and country planning**(Eng).
Kaiser, Edward J., et al. *Urban Land Use Planning*. 4th ed. Urbana, IL: University of Illinois Press, 1995.

land value   1. See **economic rent, land rent,**

residual method of valuation(Eng), **residual process**(US), **value**.   2.(NZ)The value that an owner's estate or interest in land might be expected to realise (assuming it is unencumbered by any mortgage or charge) assuming at the time of valuation the land is "(a) Offered for sale on such reasonable terms and conditions as a bona fide seller might be expected to impose; and (b) No improvements have been made on the land", Rating Valuations Act 1998, s. 2(1) (NZ). 'Capital value' is the land value as defined, including improvements made to the land.

land warrant(US)   See **land certificate**.

landed estate   1. A large estate, especially one with a substantial residence or **manor house**. 2. An **estate** or interest in land.

landed property   A popular term for **real property**. Also used to refer to rural as distinguished from urban property. See also **land**.

landlady   1. A woman who owns real property that she leases to others. A female **landlord**.   2. A woman who owns or manages an inn, a boarding house or a rooming house.

landlocked   An area of land, surrounded by property owned by other parties, to which there is no legal right of access. In particular, a parcel of land that has no access to a public road. See also **easement of necessity**.

landlord   One who permits another (a **tenant**) to have **exclusive occupation** of land, for a certain duration, under a contract of **tenancy** termed a **lease**, in return for a right to a payment called **rent**. A landlord may be considered as the person who, but for the tenant, would be entitled to possession of the land, i.e. someone who is entitled to the immediate **reversion** under the lease by which his tenant was granted possession. A landlord may be the freeholder of the land; but any holder of an interest in land (including a person who is himself a tenant, or a mortgagee) who grants a lease (or tenancy) is a landlord. A landlord has the right to: (i) demand any rent that is due; (ii) levy **distress** (although this is no longer an easily used remedy); (iii) bring an action for **breach of covenant**; (iv) if available, exercise his **right of entry**; and (v) regain the land at the end of the determined period (unless prevented by statute) – generally known as his **right of re-entry**.

In English statute law, for the purpose of an **agricultural tenancy**, landlord "means any person for the time being entitled to receive the rents and profits of land", Agricultural Holdings Act 1986, s. 96(1). For the purpose of a **business tenancy**, the landlord, called the "competent landlord", is either the owner for the time being of the fee simple or, if there is an intermediate landlord and a subtenant, the immediate landlord, provided that landlord's interest will not expire within 14 months, otherwise the next immediate landlord (L&T Act 1954, s. 44(1), as extended by the LPA 1969, s. 14). In the case of a **protected tenancy**, a landlord includes any person deriving title under the original landlord (i.e. a person who is himself a tenant and has in turn created a tenancy – an 'intermediate tenant') and any person who, other than the tenant, would be entitled to possession if the existing tenant did not have statutory security of tenure (Rent Act 1977, s. 152(1)). See also **head landlord, negligence, determination, repair**.

landlord's access   The right reserved by a landlord to enter onto the property that he has leased to another, in order to inspect the property, carry out repairs, or for any other purpose, without disturbing the tenant's possession. A lease grants a tenant a right to **exclusive possession** of the demised premises, which includes the right to exclude the landlord for the duration of the tenancy. Thus, a landlord has no right of access to the demised premises, unless there is an express agreement or provision in the lease, a right is given by statute, or a right can be implied, as when a landlord has a statutory obligation to carry out repairs. However, a provision is inserted in most leases giving the landlord a right of access, at reasonable times and subject to reasonable notice, to inspect the state of the premises and to ensure that the tenant has complied with the terms of the lease. cf. **right of re-entry**. See also **distress, entry, implied covenant, quiet enjoyment, schedule of dilapidations**.

landlord's consent   See **change of use, improvement, landlord's access, restraint on alienation**.

landlord's fixture   See **fixture**.

landlord's improvement   An **improvement** carried out to leased premises by the landlord or at the landlord's expense. See also **fixture**.

landlord's lien   A **lien** placed on the property of a tenant, situated on the demised property, for unpaid rent. Such a lien can only be imposed by statute law. See also **distress**.

landlord's warrant   See **distress**.

landmark   1. A mark or structure that is used to designate a boundary of land, especially a fixed object placed conspicuously to identify an important limit.   2. A notable building or feature on the land. A building or structure of architectural, historical, archaeological or cultural significance. An improvement that has a special character or is of special historic, cultural or aesthetic interest. See also **historic sites**.

landmark property(US)   1. A building, structure or monument that has been designated of architectural, cultural or historical significance and, therefore, worthy of preservation.

The designation of a 'landmark property' (or any similar designation) is an exercising of **police power** and, therefore, does not normally entitle the landowner to compensation for the limitation on future development, provided the property owner is left with what has been described as a "reasonable beneficial use of the landmark site", Penn Central Transp. Co. v. City of New York, 438 US 104, 98 S

Ct 2646, 136, 57 L Ed.2d 631, 657 (1978). Also called an 'historical landmark' (if that is the reason for the restriction). See **historic sites**.   **2.** A property that has a special appeal to an investor (especially a foreign investor) because of its location, design, historic association, or quality of construction and for which he would pay a premium above market value. See also **trophy property**.

landowner or **land owner**   **1.** Any party that may be considered the **owner** of land. In common usage, the 'landowner' is the person who has the superior title to the land, which generally means the holder of the fee interest. However, one who exerts dominant control over land or has the right to the rents and profits may be considered the landowner. The term landowner should be judged by the context, the holder of a long-term ground lease is almost invariably a 'landowner', but one in possession under a short-term tenancy is not a 'landowner' unless so designated. See also **estate owner**(Eng), **landlord**.   **2.** A holder of a substantial area of land.

Lands Tribunal(Eng)   A quasi-judicial body, established by the Lands Tribunal Act 1949 (as amended), whose purpose is to deal with disputes arising from statutory issues involving the valuation of land. The tribunal deals with such matters as **compulsory purchase compensation** (including apportionment of rent where only part of the land acquired is subject to a lease); **compensation for planning restrictions**; appeals from a **valuation tribunal** against rating assessments; applications for modification or discharge of a **restrictive covenant**; disputes over a **right of light**; and a disputed **blight notice** or similar disputes relating to land, as well as applications to act as an arbitrator in disputes relating to land under a reference by consent. See also **arbitration, Leasehold Valuation Tribunal, sealed offer**.

landsman   **1.** A person who works on the land. **2.**(US)A person who seeks out and negotiates areas that may be suitable for oil and gas leases. See also

oil and gas lease.   **3.** An old term for a **land-tenant** or **terre-tenant**.

lane   A narrow way or passage, whether in public or private ownership. In particular, a **street** or path generally running between a constraint on both sides such as a hedge, bank, wall or row of houses. cf. **highway**.

lappage(US)   The overlapping of the title deeds in respect of the same area of land, especially when there is a claim arising by adverse possession and the possession of one part of the land is being used as a claim to the entirety of the land within the same bounds of the title deed. See also **color of title**.

lapse   A fall from an agreed or accepted standard. The termination of a right or privilege as a result of a passage of time. Termination, or failure, of a right or privilege due to an omission to exercise that right or privilege; especially the loss of an interest in land due to the failure to renew the interest. A lapse arises, for example, from the failure to perform a condition of a contract, such as a failure to pay rent or a failure to give notice of an intention to exercise an option. An **offer** is considered to have lapsed (a) with the passage of time, either because a prescribed period of time has passed for acceptance or, if there is no period prescribed for acceptance, after a reasonable time; (b) upon the failure to fulfil a condition attached to the offer; or (c) as a rule, on the death of the offeror or offeree before acceptance. An insurance policy will lapse if it is not renewed and the premiums paid before its expiry or within the **grace period**. cf. **abandonment, expiration**. See also **laches, rejection of an offer, revocation, time is of the essence**.

lapsed land(US)   Public land that has been entered under a grant of **patent**, but has been lost by a failure to comply with the conditions of the patent, as when specified payments have not been made to the government or the land has not been cultivated or built on as required by the grant of patent (Hawkins v. Barney's Lessee, 5 Pet 468, 30 US 467, 8 L Ed 194 (1831)). See also **abandonment, limitation**.

lapsed patent(US)   See **lapsed land**.

large-lot zoning(US)   See **exclusionary zoning**.

lasting improvement(Can)   See **mistaken improver**.

latent damage   See **latent defect**.

latent defect   A defect that is not discoverable from careful inspection; is not obvious on examination; and may not be discovered until some further, consequent, damage or defect has become observable (*Victoria University of Manchester v Hugh Wilson* (1984) 2 Con LR 430; Reliance Insurance Co. v. Brickenkamp, 147 So.2d 200, 91 ALR2d 1290 (Fla App 1962)). A 'latent defect' in leased premises is a defect that could not be discovered by the exercise of ordinary and reasonable care and is not manifest. It is a defect that is hidden or concealed, not only from sight but also from being discovered upon reasonable enquiry.

'Latent defect' may refer to: (a) a defect in the structure or condition of real property; or (b) a **defect of title** that is not apparent or ascertainable from a search of public records. In either case, a vendor of property is liable for any defect of which he is fully aware, is not a matter of public record, and which he fails to draw to the purchaser's attention. On the other hand, he is liable for a clearly apparent or **patent defect**, unless he has granted some form of warranty to the contrary: the maxim being *caveat emptor*, 'let the buyer beware'. A mortgage, charge, or lien on a property may be considered a latent defect if not disclosed by a vendor of the property, as such encumbrances are not normally apparent to the purchaser. A building contractor is liable for a latent defect that arises as a result of his workmanship, including any substantial defect that affects the stability, usability or value of the building work, unless there is an express contractual provision to the contrary, until such time as any right of action is barred by statute. In English law, in cases of negligent workmanship (but not personal injury or breach of contract) the statutory period is limited to three years from the earliest date on which the plaintiff had the knowledge in order to bring an action, with a long stop of 15 years. In this context such a defect is referred to as 'latent damage'. A latent defect is sometimes called a 'hidden defect'. See also **apparent easement, constructive notice, misrepresentation, negligence, repair, warranty of habitability**.

lateral support   The support for land given in a vertical plane by adjoining ground. The lateral support of land is considered a natural right; it is an incident to the ownership of land. The right of lateral support from adjoining land consists in having the soil in its natural position remain in its natural position without being caused to fall away by excavations or improvements made on adjacent land (*Dalton v Angus* (1881) 6 App Cas 740 (HL)). Generally, this right does not extend to providing support to accommodate additional weight imposed on the land, as by raising the level of the land, or by the erection of buildings or other improvements (although undermining support without due care and attention may amount to **negligence**). In the US, in some jurisdictions, this common law right has been modified or extended by statute. cf. **subjacent support**. See also **natural rights, right of support, subsidence**.

law   See **bylaw, code, common law, custom, equity, ordinance, statute law**.

law day   The date on which an obligation falls due. In particular, the exact day specified in a contract upon which money is to be paid. For example, a day set down in a mortgage deed for the repayment of the principal. See also **defeasance clause, maturity date, tender**.

Law Society Conditions of Sale(Eng)   See **conditions of sale**.

lawful entry   Entry on land in accordance with the due process of law. cf. **trespass**. See also **eviction, landlord's access, right of entry, right of re-entry, recovery**.

lawful interest or **lawful rate of interest** See **legal rate of interest**.

lawful money   Money, in any form, that is legally acceptable as a medium of exchange in a particular country. Unless there is a custom or agreement to the contrary, lawful money normally means **legal tender**. See also **cash, hard money**.

lawyer-title policy(US)   See **title insurance**.

layer method(Eng)   See **hardcore method**.

lay-land   See **lea-land**

lea-land   Land that is left fallow, or uncultivated for a year; land that is 'laid-down' to grass. See also **fallow land**.

lease   1. A contract that creates the relationship of **landlord** and **tenant**. A contractually binding agreement that grants a right to **exclusive possession** of land or buildings for a fixed or renewable period of time, usually in return for a periodic payment called **rent**. The term of a lease may be for a life, a term of years, a succession of periods, or even at will, provided the period is certain or capable of being made certain and is less than that held by the grantor. The rent (provided one is required) is usually a periodic payment, but it may be a single premium. A lease may commence immediately, or may be made to commence at a future date. 'Lease' normally refers to a written document, although it is possible to have a **parol lease** (i.e. one made by word of mouth, which is sometimes erroneously called an 'oral lease').

A lease of land may be considered a dual transaction. A **conveyance** of a right to exclusive possession of land (thereby creating an interest in land), and a **contract** requiring payment for the use and enjoyment of the land. Thus, a lease is said to create **privity of estate** and **privity of contract**. The contract (which itself is called a lease when made in writing) may be express or implied. Nonetheless, by that contract a **landlord** (or, strictly speaking, a **lessor**) cedes or makes a **demise** of a right to property to a **tenant** (or, strictly speaking, a **lessee**); a right that may be freely alienated or transferred, unless there is an express stipulation to the contrary. The word **tenancy** is usually reserved for short-term agreements, especially a periodic tenancy, a tenancy at will or a tenancy at sufferance; a 'lease' being a formal grant of a right to possession of a property for a period of time, especially when made by deed. However, the words lease and tenancy may be used interchangeably.

A lease may be distinguished from an **easement** which grants, or restrains, only a right of user and does not grant a proprietary right; whereas a lease is normally a proprietary right over land for a duration. An easement does not confer any right to possession, but is merely a right to derive a benefit from, or impose a restriction on, land.

A lease may be distinguished from a **licence** as the latter merely grants a personal right of use and occupation, with no intent to grant an interest in land, whereas a lease grants an estate in land. A licence merely authorises something that would otherwise be illegal. However, whether a right to occupy land grants a lease or a licence depends on: (a) the intention of the parties; (b) the exclusivity of the occupation; (c) the terms of the agreement and its mode of creation; and (d) such matters as a payment in the nature of rent, any provision for re-entry reserved by the landlord, and obligations placed on the occupier such as to **repair**, insure or pay property taxes.

A good and valid lease (i) may be made only between parties who are legally competent to grant and to accept the property demised; (ii) should relate only to property that can be identified with certainty; (iii) must relate to property that is capable of being the subject-matter of such a demise; (iv) must be made for a defined or definable period of time; (v) must deliver a right to possession (at present or in the future); and (vi) in most cases (other than leases for a year or less) must be in **writing** and signed by the parties to the lease. The lessor must retain an interest in the property that is the subject of the demise – a **reversionary interest** – otherwise he will have no further right to regain the property and will have made an outright transfer of his interest in the land. A lease may be granted by a freeholder or a person who also holds a lease (a leaseholder); in the latter case, the lease is more commonly called a **sub-lease** or 'under lease', but nonetheless it is a lease. A lease may be granted for any period of time, provided it is certain or can be rendered certain (2 *Bl Comm* 143; *Prudential Assurance Co Ltd v London Residuary Body* [1992] 2 AC 386, [1992] 3 All ER 504 (HL); 51C C.J.S., L & T, § 215).

A lease must effectively transfer an interest in land; a mere intent so to do, or a simple contract to grant a lease (an **agreement for a lease**), requires further evidence to create a formal lease. Consequently, the term 'lease' is frequently reserved for a document made by **deed**, and a less formal document is merely an 'agreement', 'tenancy agreement' or a 'contract of tenancy'. However, an instrument may be construed as a lease if the essential terms are fixed, especially if possession is taken under it and if the covenants that would be inserted in the lease are to be binding at once.

A lease may come to an end or be determined by **expiration** of the term ('effluxion of time'); by **disclaimer**; by **forfeiture**; by **surrender**; by **merger**; by **enlargement**; by **notice to quit**; by notice exercised in accordance with an express covenant (in particular an option to break a lease granted for a term of years, as in the event of a rent revision); by becoming a **satisfied term**; or, sometimes, by **abandonment** or **frustration**.

In addition to the grant of the right to property and the contract itself, 'lease' may be used as a verb for the act itself or, in North America and Australia, to refer to the property held under such a contract, and the word is increasingly used with reference to a similar right to personal property, especially major items of equipment.

In English statute law, in relation to a right to **relief** from a landlord's right of re-entry or forfeiture of a lease, 'lease' is defined to include "an original or derivative under-lease; also an agreement for a lease where the lessee has become entitled to have his lease granted; also a grant at a fee farm rent, or securing a rent by condition", LPA 1925, s. 146(5)(a). In relation to a claim for **compensation for improvements**, by a business tenant, a 'lease' means "a lease, under-lease or other tenancy, assignment operating as a lease or under-lease, or an agreement for such a lease, under-lease, tenancy or assignment", L&T Act 1927, s. 25(1). cf. **bailment, leasing, usufruct**. See also **assignment, building lease, condition, counterpart, determination, equitable lease**(Eng), **exception, fixture, flat lease, graded lease, graduated-rental lease, gross lease, ground lease, habendum, implied covenants, index lease, intermediate lease, leasehold, legal lease**(Eng), **master lease**(US)**, mining lease, net lease, occupation lease, oil and gas lease**(US)**, percentage lease, periodic tenancy, perpetually renewable lease, proviso, reddendum, security deposit, term of years, usual covenant, use and occupation, use clause, waste**.

Butterworths/Ross: Commercial Leases. 5th ed. Looseleaf. London: Butterworths, ©1998.

Friedman, Milton R. *Friedman on Leases.* 2 vols. 4th ed. New York: Practicing Law Institute, 1997.

Luxton, Peter, and Margaret Wilkie. *Commercial Leases.* Welwyn Garden City: EMIS Professional Publishing, 1998.

2. The legal act by which an owner of land, or landlord, transfers a lesser estate to another, a tenant, for an ascertainable duration subject to various terms and conditions, or covenants, especially subject to the payment of rent. **3.**(Aus)An area of land leased for mining purposes, i.e. the subject matter of a **mining lease**.

lease and release(Eng)   See **release**.

lease at will(US)   See **tenancy at will**.

lease by estoppel   See **tenancy by estoppel**.

lease concession   See **rent concession**.

lease extension   See **extension**, **option to renew**, **renewal**.

lease for a term of years or **lease for years**   A **lease** that grants a right to possession of land for a **term of years**. 'Lease for a term of years' may be used also to refer to a lease for a definite period of time that has reference to a period of a year or any number of years, especially if the rent is determined by reference to an annual payment. See also **tenancy for years**.

lease for life(Eng)   See **tenancy for life**.

lease *in futuro*   See **reversionary lease**.

lease in possession   A lease that has already granted a right to **possession**, as distinguished from a **reversionary lease** which is restricted so as not to commence until a future date.

lease in reversion   See **reversionary lease**.

lease-and-leaseback financing   A form of **sale-and-leaseback** transaction, used to finance a real estate development project, by which the developer retains the freehold and acts as landlord to the occupational tenants, but provides a financial institution or lender with a long-term **intermediate lease** of the completed development as security for the funds advanced. The lease/leaseback financing is contained in three documents: (1) A finance agreement, entered into before the development work commences, which provides that: (a) the freeholder/developer will carry out a specified form of development of a site; (b) the lender will agree to provide funds for the development – this may exclude the cost of the site, which is acquired and paid for normally by the developer; (c) the developer will lease the completed development to the lender and will accept a simultaneous sub-lease back from the institution, for the same period (less a few days); and (d) the developer will agree to grant sub-underleases (occupational leases) of the completed development at open market rents. (2) A long-term (generally 99 or 125 years) head-lease of the completed development granted to the lender at a nominal rent. (3) A sub-lease back to the developer for the same term as the head-lease (less a few days) at a **finance rent**. (The finance rent is calculated to provide the lender with a satisfactory return on the total funds advanced and commonly **equity participation** in the net income received from the completed development.) As an alternative, the developer may carry out the development using interim finance provided by the lender. When the development is fully let, the developer leases it to the lender at a nominal rent, and then takes a lease back at a finance rent geared to the full occupational rent. The parties' share of the occupational rent is geared so as to provide a return to each party commensurate with their respective risk/return expectancies.

A further alternative is that employed by a landowner, such as a public authority, who does not wish to be directly involved in the development process, but wishes to grant the occupational lease and retain control of the completed development. The landowner grants a lease of the site to the developer. The developer carries out an agreed scheme and leases it back to the landowner. The developer receives an agreed return or fee for his involvement (which may be a single premium or a rent geared to the rents received from the occupational tenants), but the landowner grants the occupational leases. This form of transaction may also be used when the landowner does not wish to part with the fee title. Also called a 'reverse leaseback' or 'sandwich leaseback'. See also **side-by-side participation**.

lease in reversion   See **reversionary lease**.

lease insurance   See **tenant's default insurance**.

lease option   See **finance lease, option to purchase**.

lease renewable forever   See **perpetually renewable lease**.

lease-mortgage(US)   An arrangement whereby a landowner grants a renewable lease, with an option to purchase, and also executes a mortgage in favor of the lessee for the agreed purchase price. The lease rent and the mortgage interest payments are the same and are thus set off one against the other. A lease-mortgage may be entered into when a formal approval to an outright sale of property is required, but has not yet been granted. Also called a 'lease-purchase mortgage loan'.

lease-purchase   1. See **rental purchase**.   2. See **hire-purchase agreement**(Eng).

lease-purchase mortgage loan(US)   See **lease-mortgage**.

leaseback   See **sale-and-leaseback, lease-and-leaseback financing**.

leased department(US)   An area in a **department store** that has been leased to an outside operator. 'Leased department' may refer to such an area, whether it has been granted by **lease**, or merely on **license**, and the agreement that grants this right may be called a 'department lease', although it may not in strict legal terms be a lease. The lessee (or licensee) is responsible for the provision of his own merchandise and for the selling activities in the leased area, but generally shares some facilities with the department store operator, such as credit control, delivery and marketing. The operator of the leased area normally pays a fixed rent or fee, and may well agree to pay a **percentage rent** if sales exceed a pre-agreed level.

leased fee estate or **leased fee interest**(US)   A **fee estate** that has been granted to another on lease, i.e. the interest of a lessor or landlord who holds a fee interest that has been granted under a lease. A leased fee estate represents a right to receive rent for the term of a lease together with the reversionary right to the leased land (i.e. together with the right to legal possession of the fee at the end of the lease). cf. **leasehold estate**. See also **intermediate lease, lease-holder's interest**.

leased premises   Premises that form the subject matter of a lease. Also called **demised premises**. See also **demise**.

leasehold or **leasehold interest**   An interest in land held from another for a defined duration (or a duration that is capable of being defined), subject to the payment of a consideration called **rent**. A right to **exclusive possession** of land for a term of years as granted by a **lease** or an **agreement for a lease**. A leasehold may be held for a **term of years**, or any other fixed duration; as a **periodic tenancy**; or it may be held as a **tenancy at will** or a **tenancy at sufferance**; although the latter two interests are more in the nature of rights of occupation than rights under a lease.

In common law, a leasehold interest is referred to as a 'chattel real', because strictly it is a personal right to real property and is considered as coming within the laws relating to **personal property**; although this distinction is less prevalent in many modern contexts. Thus, the devise of 'real estate' does not include a leasehold (1 *Co Litt* 46a). However, an intention to the contrary may be construed from surrounding words. In English law, a general devise of 'land' or 'land and tenements', or the like, will pass the testator's leasehold estates, unless there is an expression to the contrary (Wills Act 1837, s. 26). However, in the US, some jurisdictions still follow the common law rule, so that the reference to 'real estate' does not include a leasehold, unless the intention or surrounding words indicate to the contrary.

A leasehold interest may be created by contract; by statute (e.g. a **statutory tenancy**); or may arise by estoppel (as a **tenancy by estoppel**). It may be bought or sold, mortgaged or charged, held for the purpose of use and occupation of the leased property, or in turn made the subject of a lease for the purpose of investment – subject only to the conditions set out in the lease by which it is created. cf. **freehold**. See also **absolute leasehold**(Eng), **good leasehold**(Eng), **legal estate**, **possessory leasehold**(Eng), **real estate**, **term of years**.

leasehold condominium See condominium.

leasehold enfranchisement(Eng) The purchase of the freehold interest in a property by the holder of a long-term lease of that property (especially by the holder of a long-term **ground lease**), subject to the payment by the leaseholder of recompense for the loss by the freeholder of his right to rent from the property.

In English law, a number of statutes have been enacted to permit the holder of a long-term lease to extend its term or to acquire the freehold reversion. For example, a lease originally created for a term of not less than 300 years, with an unexpired residue of not less than 200 years, where no rent or money value is payable and which is not liable to be determined by re-entry for a breach of condition, may be enlarged into a fee simple (LPA 1925, s. 153).

The most common (or at least the most commonly used) form of 'leasehold enfranchisement' is the right of a tenant of a leasehold **house** to acquire the freehold on "fair terms" (Leasehold Reform Act, 1967, as amended). Basically, the house must have been (a) originally let as a **long tenancy**, i.e. for "a term of years certain exceeding twenty-one years", even though it may subsequently have been extended by the parties; and (b) granted at a **low rent**; or (c) the house was originally let for 35 years, even if not at a low rent (Leasehold Reform Act 1967, as amended). The term is still considered to be one of 21 years, or more, notwithstanding that (i) it is, or may become, terminable before the end of that term by notice given by the tenant; or (ii) the landlord has a right of termination by re-entry or forfeiture for breach of a condition of the lease. These provisions do not apply merely because a tenant

has been in occupation for 21 years; the lease must have been granted originally for a term in excess of 21 years. In addition, at the date of the tenant's claim of his right to enfranchise (which must be made in a prescribed form), the tenant must have occupied the whole or part of the house as his only or main **residence** for the previous three years, or periods amounting to three years in the previous ten years. The price payable to acquire the freehold is based on the value of the house subject to the existing lease, if sold in the open market by a willing seller, but subject to a number of statutory assumptions, which includes a split of any **marriage value** that exists between the value of the leaseholder's interest before and after the sale, as well as a payment for any development value that the freeholder may lose (Leasehold Reform Act 1967, s. 9 as amended). The price may be as agreed between the parties, or failing agreement by the **Leasehold Valuation Tribunal**, with a right of appeal to the **Lands Tribunal**. Certain landlords (notably most public bodies) are exempt from these provisions, and the Act does not apply to certain types of tenancy (such as a **business tenancy**).

In addition, there are complex provisions for other tenants to acquire, or have a right of pre-emption, over the landlord's freehold. For example, "qualifying tenants" who occupy flats in a "self-contained" building (or a part of a building that is capable of being considered as a self-contained building) have the right to a "collective enfranchisement" in the event that the landlord intends to dispose of the freehold (Leasehold Reform, Housing and Urban Development Act 1993, Part I, Ch. I, as amended). See also **enfranchisement**, **enlargement**, **extended lease**, **management scheme**, **redemption**(US), **right of pre-emption**, **secure tenancy**.

Aldridge, Trevor M. *Residential Lettings: Statutory Rights of Leaseholders and Tenants.* 11th ed. London: Sweet & Maxwell, 1998. Part II "Enfranchisement and New Leases".

Clarke, D. N., and Andrew Wells. *Leasehold Enfranchisement and Right to Manage.* 2nd ed. Bristol: Jordans, 2003.

Kenny, Phillip. *The Tenant's Right of Pre-emption: the right of first refusal under the Landlord and Tenant Act 1987 Part I.* London: Blackstone Press, 1999.

Radevsky, Anthony, and Damian Greenish. *Hague on Leasehold Enfranchisement.* 3rd ed. London: Sweet & Maxwell, 1999.

leasehold estate(US)   An **estate** held by a lessee or tenant. The right to use and occupy real estate for the term of a lease, subject to the terms and conditions of that lease and usually subject to the payment of rent. cf. **leased fee estate**. See also **legal estate, leasehold**.

leasehold financing   A loan that is secured against a **leasehold interest**. A loan may be secured on any leasehold interest, but loans are rarely secured on leasehold terms of under five years. Leasehold financing is more commonly granted against the security of a long-term ground lease for terms in excess of 50 years, where the lender is less concerned about the depreciating nature of the asset he holds as security. See also **leasehold mortgage**.

leasehold ground rent   A **ground rent** receivable by a person who holds a leasehold interest, as distinguished from a ground rent receivable by a freeholder. Anyone who is granted a ground lease may, in turn, sub-let the demised land to another and, as a rule, the sub-lease is granted at a higher rent than is payable to the superior landlord. Thus, a leasehold ground rent that is higher than the rent payable to the superior landlord is sometimes called an 'improved ground rent' (although the latter term is more commonly used to refer to the difference between the rent of bare land and land with improvements thereon).

leasehold improvement   An **improvement** made to leasehold property by the lessee, especially an improvement that increases the value of the landlord's reversion. See also **compensation for improvements, fixture**.

leasehold insurance   Insurance provided to cover a leaseholder against a loss of the use of the demised premises, e.g. the loss of rent receivable from a subtenant in the event that the premises are destroyed by fire. See also **improvements and betterments insurance, rent-loss insurance**.

leasehold interest   See **leasehold**.

leasehold mortgage   A mortgage secured on a **leasehold**. Generally, the mortgagee's position is subordinate to the lessor; i.e. if the mortgagee exercises a power of sale or forecloses, he sells or takes only the lessee's interest. See also **leasehold financing, subordination**.

leasehold reform(Eng)   See **leasehold enfranchisement**.

leasehold title(Eng)   See **absolute title, good leasehold title, possessory title**.

Leasehold Valuation Tribunal (LVT)(Eng)   One of a number of local tribunals established to determine values on **leasehold enfranchisement**; the rent on the grant of an **extended lease**; and other related matters under the Leasehold Reform Act 1967 (Leasehold Reform Act 1967, s. 21, as amended). Since 1996, a local leasehold valuation tribunal has authority to deal with disputed service charges as between a landlord and tenant of residential property (L&T Act 1985, s. 19B, as inserted by HA 1996). The Leasehold Valuation Tribunal is made up of members drawn from the same panel as members of the **Rent Assessment Committee** (Leasehold Reform, Housing and Urban Development Act 1993, s. 88(1)). There is a right of appeal from a decision of the Leasehold Valuation Tribunal to the **Lands Tribunal**.

leasehold value   The value of a **leasehold interest**. The capital value of the difference between (a) the rent contractually payable by the lessee and (b) either the rent being received by the lessee under his existing sublease(s) or the market rent obtainable; "the difference between the value of the use and occupancy of the leasehold for the remainder of the tenant's term, … less the agreed rent that the tenant would pay for such use and occupancy", United States v. Petty Motor Co., 327 US 372, 66 S Ct 813, 90 L Ed 729, 736 (1946). (This may be negative if the lessee is paying in excess of the market rent; then, as a rule, the leasehold interest may be sold only at a 'reverse premium', i.e. the lessee pays the purchaser to accept an assignment of his lease.) A leasehold interest is a wasting asset and should be valued by using a **dual-rate years' purchase**(BrE)/ **Hoskold factor**(AmE); i.e. a factor that provides for a 'sinking fund rate' to cover the cost of replacing the lease at the end of its term, in addition to a 'remunerative rate' to provide a return on the capital value. See also **positive leasehold**(US), **profit rent**(Eng).

leaseholder   A **lessee**. One who is entitled to an interest in land in accordance with the terms of a lease. One who has the benefit of a **leasehold interest**. A term used more generally in British English.

lease-holder's interest(AmE)   The interest of a person who has leased his property to another, i.e. the interest of a **lessor** (who may be a freeholder, or a person who has a leasehold interest and, in turn, grants a lease). A lease-holder's interest is basically a right to receive a contractual rent, as specified in a lease, together with a reversionary interest at the end of that lease. 'Lease-holder's interest' is not a legally recognized term, but it may be used to distinguish it from a **leasehold interest** which is the interest held by a person who has been granted a lease, a 'lessee'. Also called a **leased fee estate** when the grantor of the interest holds a fee interest.

leasing   1. The grant of a **lease** of property, i.e. the creation of a right of tenancy.   2. The act of taking a property on lease.   3. The hiring of an asset, usually for its economic life and with a right for the hirer to acquire the asset at the end of the leasing period. "A lease is a contract between a lessor and lessee for the hire of a specific asset selected from a manufacturer or vendor of such assets by the lessee. The lessor retains ownership of the asset. The lessee has possession and use of the asset on payment of specified rentals over a period", Equipment Leasing Association. Such a contract is a form of **bailment**, as distinguished from a **lease** which creates an interest in property for an ascertainable period of time; although a 'leasing' does not create an express debtor/creditor relationship. Leasing is commonly used by companies to finance the cost of major assets – the asset is acquired by a finance company and leased to the user, generally at a **finance rent**. Sometimes called a 'bailment lease'. cf. **conditional sale contract**. See also **finance lease**, **operating lease**. PricewaterouseCoopers. *Tolley's Leasing in the UK*, 2000. Soper, Derek R., and Robert M. Munro (editors). *The Leasing Handbook*. New York: McGraw-Hill, 1993. Wainman, David. *Leasing*. 2nd ed. London: Sweet & Maxwell, 1995.

leasing costs   The costs incurred by a landlord in leasing vacant space, including agent's or broker's fees, marketing and advertising expenses and legal fees. Leasing costs may include concessions granted to a tenant, especially any **tenant improvement allowance**(AmE)/**fitting-out allowance**(BrE). See also **rent concession**.

leasing holdback(US)   See **holdback**.

legacy   **Personal property** left as a gift under a **will**. In its strict legal sense, 'legacy' is applied to money, a monetary annuity, goods, or any other personal estate and the term **devise** applies to real property. However, the terms are commonly used interchangeably so that 'legacy' may be used to refer to any kind of estate, real or personal, left to someone under a will. A 'specific legacy' is a gift of a designated property, and a 'general legacy' is intended to be given from the general assets or a group of assets of the estate, as with 'one of my oil paintings to A'. A 'residuary legacy' is a gift that is to be made after all other claims on the estate have been satisfied, including any specific or general legacies. See also **bequest**.

legal assignment   1. An assignment made without the need for any resort to a court of equity. 2.(Eng)An **assignment** of a legal estate made by **deed** (LPA 1925, s. 52(1)). cf. **equitable assignment**. See also **legal lease**.   3.(Eng)A legal assignment of any debt or other legal choses-in-action made in **writing**; as an **absolute assignment** (not purporting to be by way of charge only); and coupled with an express notice to the debtor, trustee, or any other person against whom the assignor might have had a right of action (LPA 1925, s. 136). Also called a 'statutory assignment'. See also **novation**.   4.(US)An assignment that transfers the entire interest of the assignor.

legal charge(Eng) An interest in land that creates a **charge** that can subsist, or be conveyed or created, "at law", i.e. a charge that is capable of being referred to as a **legal estate** (LPA 1925, s. 1(4)). A legal charge may be created either: (i) as "a **rentcharge** in possession issuing out of or charged on land being either perpetual or for a term of years absolute", LPA 1925, s. 1(2)(b); or (ii) as "a **charge by way of a legal mortgage**", LPA 1925, s. 1(2)(c). A legal charge must be entered on the register of titles at the Land Registry by the chargee to be enforceable (LRA 2002, Sch. 2, s. 8). cf. **equitable charge**. See also **legal interest, legal mortgage**.

legal chose-in-action   See **chose**.

legal closing(US)   See **closing**.

legal consideration   **Consideration** that is legally sufficient to support a contract. Legal consideration need not be a pecuniary sum, as long as it provides an advantage to the recipient, or creates a detriment for the donor.

legal description(US)   A **description** of a parcel of land by reference to a formal survey, the **metes and bounds system**, a formal map (e.g. Tract 18, Block 2, Lot 1), or any other such method of describing land. The term 'legal description' is used in contradistinction to a 'popular description'

such as a street address. Sometimes referred to by lawyers as 'the legal'. See also **plan**.

legal easement(Eng) An **easement** that is a **legal interest**. The term 'legal easement' does not appear in English statute law, but may be used to describe an easement "which is capable of subsisting or of being conveyed or created at law", i.e. one that is (a) held "in or over land for an interest equivalent to an estate in fee simple absolute in possession or a term of years absolute", LPA 1925, s. 1(2)(a) – that is, the servient tenement must be held as a **legal estate**; and (b) created by statute, **deed** or **prescription**, in any of which three instances the easement is created by a formalised agreement that is either visibly expressed or is presumed by law to have been so expressed. An easement that fails to satisfy either of these requirements is not a 'legal easement', but may be an **equitable easement**. A legal easement, unlike an equitable easement, is enforceable against any party who acquires a right to the servient land, in fact against the 'whole world', irrespective of whether that party had **notice** of the easement. See also **overriding interest**.

legal estate   1. An **estate** that is capable of subsisting or being conveyed or created 'at law', as distinguished from an estate that is recognised only 'in equity'. A legal estate is recognised in common law as a right to retain possession and ownership of land and is said to be actionable *in rem*. In contrast, an **equitable estate** is only enforceable in equity and, therefore, is considered capable of being converted to monetary consideration without detriment to the holder. 'Legal estate' may refer also to an estate that is created by operation of law, as distinguished from one that is created by agreement, devise or conveyance.   2.(Eng)An **estate** that is capable of subsisting, being conveyed, or being created, "at law", as distinguished from an **equitable estate** which can only be recognised as an equitable right to land, i.e. can be recognised only in a court of equity. Since 1925, the *only* estates in land which are capable of subsisting or being conveyed as legal estates are "an estate in **fee simple absolute in possession**" and "a **term of years absolute**", LPA 1925, s. 1(1) (LRA 2002, s. 132(1). Any other estate is by exclusion an **equitable interest**. A legal estate is one protected by law as 'good against the whole world'; unlike an equitable interest which may not be binding against a *bona fide* **purchaser** for valuable **consideration** and, therefore, may be converted compulsorily into a monetary consideration. The holder of a fee simple absolute in possession who grants a lease remains the holder of a legal estate because the right to receive rent and profits, if any, is considered to be a right to **possession** (LPA 1925, s. 205(1)(xix)). Similarly, if the holder of a term of years absolute grants a sub-lease he remains the owner of a legal estate. Accordingly, a number of legal estates may exist concurrently in the same piece of land. For example, if A is the holder of a fee simple absolute in possession of Blackacre and he grants a lease for a term of years absolute to B, who in turn grants a sub-lease for a term of years to C, and A grants a 'charge by way of a legal mortgage' to D, then A, B and C have legal estates in Blackacre, and D has a **legal interest**. (Note: for the purpose of the LPA 1925 any interest or charge that is "authorised to subsist or to be conveyed or created at law" – and frequently referred to as 'legal interest' – is referred to as "legal estate" in the Act (LPA, s. 1(4).) In the case of registered land, although the only estates that are capable of registration are those that can subsist 'at law' under the LPA 1925, s. 1 – the equivalent to legal estates for unregistered land – the important division is "between estates and interests which appear on the register and those which do not, rather than between legal estates and equitable interests", E. H. Burns, *Maudsley & Burn's Land Law. Cases and Materials.* 7th ed. London: Butterworths, 1998, p. 27. A legal estate cannot be created or subsist as an undivided share in land, i.e. as a tenancy in common, nor can it be held by an infant (LPA 1925, s. 1(6)); in both instances the right to the land is held in trust, the trustee holding the legal estate and the tenant in common, or infant, a beneficial equitable interest. With

certain exceptions (notably assents by personal representatives and leases for not more than three years, which need not be in writing) a legal estate cannot be conveyed unless made by **deed** (LPA 1925, s. 52). See also **legal lease**.

legal estoppel   See **estoppel**.

legal interest   1. An **interest** in land that is enforceable 'at law', as contrasted with an **equitable interest** which is only enforceable in equity. A legal interest binds anyone who acquires the land that is the subject of the legal interest; it is said to be "good against the whole world". 2.(Eng)An interest in land that is enforceable against any purchaser of the land (although, if it is a registrable interest that has not been registered, it does not bind a purchaser of the land who pays valuable consideration). In English law, since 1925, the *only* legal interests or legal charges in or over land that are capable of subsisting, or of being conveyed or created, at law are: "(a) An **easement**, right, or privilege in or over land for an interest equivalent to an estate in **fee simple absolute in possession** or a **term of years absolute**; (b) A **rentcharge** in possession issuing out of or charged on land being either perpetual or for a term of years absolute; (c) A **charge by way of a legal mortgage**; (d) Any other similar charge on land which is not created by an instrument; (e) Rights of entry exercisable over or in respect of a legal term of years absolute, or annexed, for any purpose, to a legal rentcharge", LPA 1925, s. 1(2).

The interests under (a) include rights of way and rights to take natural produce from land (**profit à prendre**), provided the interest is created for a period equivalent to a "fee simple absolute in possession" or a "term of years absolute". The interests under subsection (e) do not include a **right of re-entry** reserved by an assignor of a lease (such a right being an equitable right), unlike the same right if it is reserved on the grant of a legal lease (*Shiloh Spinners Ltd v Harding* [1973] AC 691, 719, [1973] 1 All ER 90, 97 (HL)). In this context, a right of entry is considered to be the same as a right of re-entry, i.e. it is not merely a right to enter onto land to do something (such as carry out repairs), but a right to retake possession of the land (*Shiloh Spinners, supra* at 720, at 98). In the LPA 1925, any **legal estate**, legal interest, or **legal charge** is called a "legal estate" and the owner of any such interest is an **estate owner** (LPA 1925, s. 1(4)). However, it is not uncommon to refer to the interests in the LPA 1925, s. 1(2) as 'legal interests', and to reserve the term 'legal estate' for those interests referred to in the LPA 1925, s. 1(1). Note: These interests *can* be legal interest, but they must be created by the proper formalities (usually by **deed**) to be enforceable 'at law'. cf. **equitable interest**. See also **doctrine of estates, legal easement, legal mortgage**. **3.** The maximum rate of interest permitted by law for the use of money. See also **legal rate of interest, usury**. **4.** The rate of interest fixed by law when no express rate is fixed in an agreement or loan.

legal lease(Eng) A lease that creates an estate in land for a **term of years absolute** (which may be a lease for a month or even 1,000 years) and is made using proper formalities. (Such a lease is referred to as a **legal estate**: LPA 1925, s. 1.) A legal lease normally must be made by **deed** (LPA 1925, s. 52(1); except in the case of a lease "taking effect in **possession** [i.e. not in the future] for a term not exceeding three years (whether or not the lessee is given power to extend the term) at the **best rent** which can be reasonably obtained without taking a **fine**", LPA 1925 s. 54(2). In the later case, the lease will be a legal lease, whether created in writing or by parol. A legal lease may be distinguished from an **equitable lease**, which is deficient in one or more of the statutory requirements, and, therefore, is enforceable only in equity. See also **agreement for a lease**.

legal lien See **lien**.

legal life estate(US) A **life estate** that arises by operation of law, e.g. a right of **dower** or **curtesy**, as distinguished from a conventional life estate that is created by will or grant.

legal memory See **lost modern grant, prescription**.

legal mortgage(Eng) A **mortgage** that is "capable of being effected at law" because it is granted over a **legal estate** and is made in accordance with statute. A legal mortgage may be created in two ways: (i) by a lease (or sub-lease) for a **term of years absolute**, with a provision that the term ceases if the loan is repaid in full on a fixed date (called a "provision for cesser on **redemption**"); or (ii) by a "charge by **deed** expressed to be by way of a legal mortgage" (*viz.* **charge by way of a legal mortgage**) (LPA 1925, s. 85; LRA 2002, s. 132(1)). A legal mortgage of a leasehold is made similarly by a sub-lease or a legal charge (LPA 1925, s. 86). A mortgage made in any other form only creates an **equitable mortgage** (or an **equitable charge**). See also **charge**.

legal mortgagee(Eng) A **mortgagee** who holds a **legal mortgage** (LPA 1925, s. 205(1)(xvi)).

legal notice **1.** A **notice** prescribed by law, as distinguished from one prescribed by contract. See also **notice to quit**. **2.** See **constructive notice**.

legal owner One who has a **legal estate**, as distinguished from the holder of an equitable estate. (As either the holder of a legal estate or the holder of an equitable estate can be referred to as a 'legal owner' of land, it is preferable to refer to these parties as the 'holder of the legal estate' or the 'holder of the equitable estate'.) cf. **beneficial owner**. See also **estate owner**(Eng).

legal possession **Possession** that has been acquired in accordance with a legal right. Possession that has been taken in good faith, free from any form of deceit or fraud, and without violation of any contractual relation. See also **constructive possession**.

legal rate of interest The highest rate of interest that may be charged by law. Also called 'lawful interest'. cf. **imputed interest**. See also **annual percentage rate**, **usury**.

legal representative   Someone who has authority to represent another in the conduct of their legal affairs. A term of no fixed legal meaning, but generally used to refer to an executor or administrator of a will. In particular, a **personal representative**, or someone who succeeds to the rights of another such as a trustee or receiver. A legal representative may also be an heir or devisee who has authority to deal with a deceased's property. See also **agent**.

legal right of redemption   See **equity of redemption**, **statutory right of redemption**[US].

legal servitude   A **servitude** that can be enforced at law, as distinguished from one that can only be enforced by equity. A misleading term, as 'servitude' is a term more in use in the civil law where there is no such distinction as legal and equitable right to land. See also **legal easement**[Eng], **legal interest**[Eng].

legal tender   Any form of **money** that a debtor may tender to a creditor and must be accepted in settlement of a debt, provided it is offered in the correct amount and in accordance with the terms of the obligation owed.

In the US, Treasury notes of the United States and United States coins are legal tender for all debts, public charges, taxes, duties and dues (31 USC § 392).

In England and Wales, legal tender includes coins of the Realm up to amounts specified by statute (Coinage Act 1971, s. 2; Currency Act 1983, s. 1) and notes of the Bank of England up to any amount – provided such currency has not been called in (Bank Notes Act 1954, s. 1). Scottish bank notes are not legal tender in England and Bank of England notes over £5 are not legal tender in Scotland.

Strictly, cheques and bills of exchange are not legal tender. Sometimes called 'lawful money'. See also **cash**, **tender**.

legal title   1. A title that can be enforced as of right, as distinguished from an **equitable title** which may only be enforced in equity and, therefore, at the discretion of the court.   2.[US]A title that can be enforced as of right, as distinguished from a claim or a mere paper title that cannot be substantiated. A title that does not carry any beneficial rights. A claim to property based on **possession** of the title deeds and a claim established by **adverse possession** may be described as a 'legal title'. See also **marketable title**, **lien**.   3.[Eng]A title held by way of a **legal estate** and, therefore, one that is capable of registration as such at the Land Registry; any other interest in registered land can only be a **minor interest** or be protected by registration as an **overriding interest**. See also **absolute title**.

legal waste   Waste that is permitted, as distinguished from 'equitable waste', which consists of wanton or malicious damage to a property.

legatee   A person in whose favour a **legacy** is made, i.e. one who receives property (in particular, personal property) under a will. See also **heir**.

legator   A person who grants or bequeaths property (in particular, personal property) by will. The word **testator**, which has much the same meaning in modern usage, is to be preferred whenever possible. See also **legacy**.

lender participation   See **convertible mortgage**, **equity participation**, **equity participation loan**.

lender's policy[US]   See **title insurance**.

lessee   1. One who holds an interest in land as created by a **lease**. Strictly, a lessee is a person who holds such an interest directly from the freeholder (to whom the term applies if nothing is expressed to the contrary). However, in general usage, and especially in the UK, **tenant** is used when the right to hold the land is for a short term.

Also, a party to a lease of personal property is more usually called a lessee.

In English statute law, a 'lessee' may be defined to include "an underlessee and a person deriving title under a lessee or under-lessee", LPA 1925, s. 205(1)(xxiii). In the case of a **restricted contract**, the person who is granted the right to occupy a dwelling as a residence by virtue of such a contract, or anyone deriving title from that occupier, may be referred to as a 'lessee' (RA 1977, s. 85(1)). cf. **licensee**. See also **leaseholder**.   **2.** A word that is sometimes used to refer to a **bailee**, although strictly speaking a lessee holds under a lease and a bailee under a contract of bailment.

lessor   **1.** An owner of real property who grants a **lease** to another. Strictly, in common law, the possessor of a freehold interest who creates a lease, although 'lessor' may refer a party that hold an interest under a lease and grants a sub-lease or underlease. In English statute law, a 'lessor' may be an "underlessor and a person deriving title under a lessor or underlessor", LPA 1925, s. 205(xxiii).   **2.** A word that is sometimes used to refer to a **bailor**, although strictly a lessor holds under a lease and a bailor under a contract of bailment.

lessor's access   See **landlord's access**.

let   **1.** To permit another to use and enjoy property. To **demise** or grant a lease of property to another for a period of time. See also **leasing**. **2.** A grant of any interest in land, including the grant of a lease, sub-lease, licence or easement. Normally 'let' connotes the relationship of landlord and tenant – one who is granted a mere licence to occupy property is not strictly *let into possession* of the premises. The word 'let' is generally considered to have the same meaning as **demise**, although the latter has a more formal import denoting the grant of an interest in land for a term. Nonetheless, the use of the word 'let' in a lease implies a covenant of **quiet enjoyment** (*Spencer's Case* (1583) 5 Co Rep 16a, 77 Eng Rep 72; *Jones v Lavington* [1903] 1 KB 253, 257-258 (CA);

Bulmer v R (1894) 3 Ex CR 182, 224 (Can); Trimble v. Seattle, 231 US 683, 34 S Ct 218, 58 L Ed 435 (1914)); as well as a **covenant for title** (*Jones v Lavington, supra* at 258).   **3.** To award a construction or building contract, especially following the receipt of two or more bids for a job.

lettable area   The area of a building that is the subject of a lease. This may the 'gross' or 'net' area, but it is essentially the area for which a tenant pays rent. In particular, it is the area that is allocated to each tenant in a multi-let building and that is used in the calculation of the apportionment charges for the repair and maintenance of the common areas. See **demised premises**, **gross leasable area**(AmE), **rentable area**(AmE), **net internal area**(BrE), **retail area**, **sales area**.

letter of attorney   See **power of attorney**.

letter of comfort   **1.** A written instrument issued by one party to another whereby the former undertakes to use his best endeavours to ensure that a third party fulfils his obligations to the latter, but without there being any contractual or other form of legal commitment. Commonly issued by a parent company to assist a subsidiary in obtaining a loan.   **2.**(Eng)An informal **valuation** made to support a proposed purchase of the subject property. The level of research undertaken prior to issuing a letter of comfort is less than that entailed with a formal valuation, as it is merely intended to indicate that the price that the prospective purchaser plans to pay is not exorbitant. Also, the provider of the letter may be required to submit his opinion in a limited time frame and may not have carried out extensive market research.

letter of credit (LC)   **1.** A formal instrument, or letter, issued by a bank, or other lender, confirming its willingness to allow the party to whom the letter is addressed to draw on the credit of the bank, or lender, up to a specified limit and subject to such other condition as may be set out in the letter. A letter of credit may be classified as

a 'commercial letter of credit', or a 'traveller's letter of credit' (see **2.** below). A commercial letter of credit is addressed by a bank to a third party, to whom credit is to be extended, confirming that the issuing bank will, as required under the terms of the letter, meet the financial obligations owed to that third party. Generally, a letter of credit allows the funds to be drawn in the event of a failure of the principal to make due and prompt payment to the party to whom it is addressed. Any advance or payment made against the letter of credit is met by the bank which, in turn, debits the customer's account or otherwise seeks redress against the customer. A letter of credit may also be a 'standby' letter, which permits the beneficiary to draw directly on the issuing bank in the event of a failure of the principal or account party to meet his obligations. The bank provides its credit in place of the account party, who in turn has provided the bank with collateral during the term that the letter of credit is outstanding. In particular, a standby letter of credit may be issued to provide a mortgagee with additional security for the principal/mortgagor's obligations. See also **performance bond**.   **2.** A letter, issued at a customer's request, by which one bank requests a correspondent bank to honour drafts, or extend credit, to that customer up to a specified limit. Such letters of credit are referred to as a 'traveller's letter of credit' as they are issued to enable a trader to obtain credit from a foreign bank. The letter of credit is valid for a specified period of time, during which the recipient is able to obtain credit from another bank (an associate or correspondent bank in a foreign country) and then to acquire goods that are to be delivered to the customer.
Sarna, Lazar. *Letters of Credit: The Law and Current Practice*. Looseleaf. Toronto: Carswell; London: Sweet & Maxwell, 1984.

letter of exchange   See **bill of exchange**.

letter of intent (LOI)   A letter, note or **memorandum** setting out a clear intention to take a certain course of action or to enter into a formal agreement. In particular, a letter or other form of writing confirming an intention to enter into a **bargain**, without intending to create any legally binding contract. After a letter of intent is submitted in acceptable terms, both parties usually negotiate in good faith upon the details of the final contract and carry out any requisite **due diligence**. In order to ensure that the LOI does not create a binding **contract**, the sender should make that 'intent' known and preferably have the recipient acknowledge that fact. See also **conditional contract, subject to contract, tender**.
Michael P. Carbone, and Stephen G. Stwora-Hail, *Using Letters of Intent in Real Estate Transactions*. Probate & Property, 42-49 (Jan/Feb 1997).

letter of transmittal   A letter that accompanies a formal report, such as an appraisal or valuation report. A letter of transmittal should contain the date, the details of the party to whom it is addressed and a summary of the purpose and salient features of the report, including such matters as the basis of valuation, the value and any major constraints or restrictions that apply to the report. The party who is the signatory to the report should also sign the letter. See also **appraisal report**[(AmE)], **valuation report**[(BrE)].

letters of administration   See **probate**.

letting scheme   A scheme of development incorporated into a long-term lease.

letting value   **1.** See **rental value**.   **2.**[(Eng)]The maximum rent that may legally be demanded under the Rent Acts. The best annual return obtainable in the open market, either as determined by reference to the highest rent achievable, or by adding the decapitalised value of any premium payable to a lower rent (Leasehold Reform Act 1967, s. 4(1); *Johnston v Duke of Westminster* [1986] AC 839, 845 (HL)). See also **registered rent**.

levee   An artificial embankment or mound of earth constructed along the margins of a stream or river to contain the stream or river to its natural boundaries, or to constrain the flood waters.

level rental(US)   See flat rent.

level-payment lease   See flat rent.

level-payment mortgage   See **amortization loan, fixed-principal-payment mortgage**.

leverage   Literally 'the action of levering or raising up'. The use of borrowed money, **debt capital**, in order to increase the total amount invested in a property. The purpose of leverage is to use debt capital (in addition to the **equity capital** provided by the owner), in order to produce a 'gearing effect' on the equity invested. Thus, leverage is referred to sometimes as 'trading on the equity' or, colloquially, using 'other people's money' (OPM). The higher the ratio of debt to equity, the higher the leverage on the investment.

When the annual cost of servicing the debt (repaying interest and principal) is less than the **free and clear return** from a real estate investment, the result is called 'upside leverage' or 'positive leverage'. The reverse, which may effectively increase the amount of debt secured against the investment, is called 'downside leverage', 'negative leverage' or 'reverse leverage'. See also **financial leverage, finance, gearing, negative cash flow, operating leverage**.

leverage ratio   See **debt-equity ratio**.

leveraged buyout   The purchase of a business mainly with borrowed money secured on the assets of the business. A type of acquisition that makes the business highly leveraged, so that the purchaser hopes to make an above average return on his equity holding. A leveraged buyout is commonly carried out by the management of the business – it is then called a 'management buyout'. See also **convertible mortgage, leverage**.

leveraged investment   A property investment acquired with the use of borrowed money. See also **leverage**.

leveraged refinancing(US)   See **wraparound mortgage**.

leviable value(Can)   The fair market value of the property of a deceased that passes to any person, after the authorised statutory deductions have been made.

levy   **1.** The imposition of a fine or tax on property, or the fine or tax so imposed. In most jurisdictions, a levy on land may only be carried out in accordance with a statutory regulation and must be by an unequivocal act of an authorised officer indicating his intention to single out certain real property for the satisfaction of a debt. See also **distress**.   **2.** To raise or exact a sum of money by legal process or authority. Money collected as a **tax, assessment** or **duty**.   **3.** To seize in satisfaction of a legal claim; to place an attachment on real or personal property. In particular, the taking of physical possession of property by an authorised officer. A levy on goods may be enforced by physically removing the goods (after an inventory has been made for submission to the levee), or the levying officer may leave an assistant in charge of them. See also **attachment, distress, seizure**.

lex loci(Lat)   'The law of the place'. As a rule, real property is subject to the law of the area or country in which it is situated – *lex loci rei situs* – but personal property is subject to the law of the place where a transaction is made; unless the parties expressly elect for a different system of law or, taking into account all the circumstances, the courts can infer their intention to adopt a different system.

lex loci actus(Lat)   'The law of the place where the act is performed'. See *lex loci*.

lex loci contractus(Lat)   'The law of the place of the contract'. See *lex loci*.

lex loci rei sitae or **lex loci situs**(Lat)   'The law of the place where the property is situated'. See *lex loci*.

lex non cogit ad impossibilia(Lat)   'The law does not compel the impossible'.

lex non scripta(Lat)   'The unwritten law', i.e. **common law**. cf. *lex scripta*. See also **custom**.

lex rei situs or ***lex situs***(Lat)   'The law of the place where the property is situated'; 'the law of the locality'. Generally, the law of real property is applied according to where the property is situated, unless there is an agreement to the contrary. See also *lex loci*.

lex scripta(Lat)   'The written law', especially **statute law**. cf. *lex non scripta*.

lex terrae(Lat)   'The law of the land'.

liability   1. An amount or sum of money that is owed. A legal or pecuniary **obligation**. Any form of **debt** or obligation, whether absolute or contingent. In particular, something owed by one person to another; a duty to pay money or provide a service. An express or implied obligation to pay for work done or services provided. See also **contingent liability**, **joint and several liability**, **surety**.   2. An obligation of a business to transfer assets or pay for goods or services rendered. A claim against a corporation, whether present of future, due in the short or long term. cf. **asset**. See also **current liability**.   3. An obligation to do, or refrain from doing, something for which one would be answerable in law. An obligation that may be enforced by an action in a court, i.e. arising out of a **contract**. A person who enters into a contract is liable to fulfil the obligation undertaken or promise given, or to pay a sum due, or to otherwise complete his part of the contract. See also **duty of care**, **encumbrance**, **strict liability**, **vicarious liability**.

liability insurance   **Insurance** protection taken out to indemnify someone against claims for damage or injury that the insured may cause by an act or omission to the person or property of a third party, whether arising from a breach of contract or tort. Insurance against a liability to pay compensation, to make restitution, or to reimburse money or money's worth to a third party, e.g. to protect an employer against injury sustained by an employee, or against injury or damage caused to another's property. Liability insurance does not arise as an obligation for the insurer until the insured is held to be liable for a loss suffered and is normally granted up to a specified limit. Sometimes called 'hazard insurance', although such a term may be tautological as a hazard is a risk, or probability of loss, and therefore, to the insurer, all insurance (except life) may be considered a form of hazard insurance. cf. **indemnity insurance**.

liber number   See **grantor-grantee index**.

licence(BrE) or **license**(AmE)   1. In British English the noun is spelt 'licence' and the verb 'license' (and the adjective is spelt 'licensed'); in American English 'license' is generally used in both instances. A personal and non-assignable consent, given by an owner or occupier of land, or granted by law, authorising or permitting another to be or to do some act on land that would otherwise be prohibited or unlawful. Authorisation to enter on land and carry out an activity thereon that would otherwise be unlawful or constitute a **trespass** (*Thomas v Sorrell* (1673) Vaugh 330, 351, 124 Eng Rep 1098, 1109; *Street v Mountford* [1985] AC 809, 818, [1985] 2 All ER 289 (HL); Bateman v. Ursich, 36 Wash.2d 314, 220 P.2d 314, 316, 18 ALR2d 1440 (1950)). In particular, a dispensation or permission given in such a form that it passes no estate, nor alters or transfers any interest in property (although the recipient may well be interested in the subject land); but authorises one party (a **licensee**) to enter lawfully and stay on another's property (that of the **licensor**) for an agreed purpose, until the permission is revoked.

A licence may be given as: (i) a 'bare ('gratuitous', 'mere' or 'simple') licence' – without seal or valuable consideration, i.e. the person's presence on land is merely tolerated and, because there is no contractual obligation established thereby, it may be revoked at any time at the will of the grantor, although the licensee must be given a reasonable period to vacate the land based on the nature of the right originally granted; (ii) a 'contractual licence' – which is granted in writing or for consideration (as with a theatre ticket or a right to use a commercial parking lot), and which may be revoked in accordance with the terms, express or implied, of the agreement or contract; or (iii) a 'licence coupled with an interest' in land – such as consent given to a person with an interest in land (e.g. a tenant) to cut and remove timber or to extract minerals, which is normally revocable only when the interest has been terminated. In the US, the latter form of license is sometimes called an 'irrevocable license' as it cannot be revoked at the will of the licensor (although that term is self contradictory as a license cannot truly be irrevocable).

A licence may be distinguished from an **easement** because the latter creates an interest or right to land, and requires that the interest it creates benefits another parcel of land; whereas a licence is merely a personal right or privilege to use another's land. Normally a licence can be readily revoked, whereas an easement can only be terminated or extinguished in accordance with the terms of its grant; it cannot be revoked. Also, a licence may be created informally (either by parol or an act which shows the assent of the licensor). An easement can only be created by grant, whether actual, presumed or implied. Merely calling an agreement a licence does not prevent it from creating an easement if an interest in land is created that has all the attributes of an easement.

Whether an agreement is a **lease** or a licence is dependent on the intention of the parties. The use of words such as 'let', 'lessor', etc. do not create a lease if the clear intention is to create a licence. Factors that mitigate in favour of a lease include the use of the word **rent** (or a payment that resembles rent); an arrangement that cannot readily be revoked; obligations on the occupier to carry out repairs; express prohibitions against sub-letting or altering the premises; and a covenant for quiet enjoyment. Factors mitigating in favour of a licence include

payment of a daily charge; a grant of consent for a very short duration; absence of any express provision as to notice to vacate the premises; an arrangement that is made for an undefined period of time; and sharing premises with the landlord. The occupation of a room in an hotel, guest house or lodging house is usually a mere licence, but when the occupant is permitted to use his room as he wishes for a set period of time and to exclude the proprietor's 'dominion', as with a serviced apartment, it is more likely that a tenancy has been created.

In English law, considerable importance is given to the distinction between a lease and a licence because the laws that provide **security of tenure** to a lessee do not apply to a licensee and, in many cases, **rent control** legislation does not apply to a licensee. In this context, when deciding whether an agreement for the occupation of property is a lease or a licence, the courts will look at: (i) the intention of both the parties and not just the form of wording used in the agreement (*Street v Mountford, supra*); and (ii) the mode of creation and the terms of the agreement. A mere stipulation in a document that it does not create a lease or tenancy, or that it does not grant exclusive possession, is not sufficient to ensure the creation of a licence. It is necessary to look at the whole document to decide whether obligations are being imposed that are more in keeping with those of landlord and tenant (*Elmdene Estates Ltd v White* [1960] AC 528, 538, [1960] 1 All ER 306, 309 (HL)). See also **eviction, grazing licence**[Eng], **implied condition, licence by estoppel**[Eng], **lodger, mining lease, protected occupier**[Eng], **service tenancy**. **2.** Permission to do something that, if not properly authorised, would be a nuisance, tort, or would otherwise be illegal. A right or dispensation granted to one party (the licensee) permitting an activity to be engaged in that otherwise would be a breach of the law; or would infringe a monopoly position that has been established by another (in particular, as established by the State – although, in that case, it is usually referred to as a **privilege** or **franchise**). For example, a licence may be granted to permit a person, and that person alone, to sell alcohol, to operate a 'market', or to exercise a particular business or profession. It is a right that dies with the person to whom it is given. A licence may be required to carry out an activity, or perform a duty, that otherwise is prohibited by statute law, for example to carry out building work that is controlled by an ordinance or building regulation. See also **building permit**(US), **permit, planning permission**(Eng), **real estate license**(US), **site licence**(Eng). **3.** Written consent granted by a lessor permitting a lessee to vary a **covenant** or **condition** of a **lease**, e.g. to assign, sub-let, change user, carry out alterations, etc. See also **change of use, improvement, restraint on alienation**. **4.**(US)See **broker, real estate license**.

licence by estoppel(Eng) A licence or, strictly speaking a form of proprietary **estoppel** that comes into existence when a licensee has taken action, especially one involving the expenditure of money on land, with the consent, encouragement or acquiescence of the landowner and, as a result, has been lead to believe that he may continue to exercise a privilege he has so gained (*Ramsden v Dyson* (1866) LR 1 HL 129, 170 (HL)). This situation may arise when a person is allowed to build on land with the understanding that he will be permitted to reside in the premises he constructs; or when a person builds and encroaches on his neighbour's land, but is given to understand by the neighbour that a wall of the building had been correctly placed on the boundary line. In such cases, the licensor may be considered to acquire more than a mere licence and it could be said that "some licences are indeed interests in land. The law on this point is still in the process of development, but it seems that a new right *in alieno solo* [against another's land] has emerged ...", E. H. Burn, *Cheshire and Burn's Modern Law of Real Property*. 16th ed. London: Butterworths, 2000, p. 662. Nonetheless, a licence by estoppel cannot be recorded against unregistered land, but is only protected by the doctrine of notice. On the other hand, in the case of registered land, it may be considered as a form of **overriding interest** and,

as such, can be protected by registering a caution or notice. Also called a 'licence coupled with an equity'. See also **constructive trust**.

licence coupled with an interest See **licence**(BrE)/**license**(AmE).

licence coupled with an equity(Eng) See **licence by estoppel**.

licence to assign See **fine, restraint on alienation**.

license See **licence**.

licensed premises(AmE) Premises that are authorised to be used for the sale and consumption of intoxicating liquor – which may be a **public house, hotel**, restaurant, or an 'off-license' (which sells intoxicating liquor for consumption off the premises). See also **bottle shop**(Aus).
Marshall, Harvey, and Hazel Williamson, eds. *Law and Valuation of Leisure Property.* 2nd ed. London: Estates Gazette, 1997.
Westbrook, R. W. *The Valuation of Licenced Premises.* London: Estates Gazette, 1983 rev. ed.

licensee **1.** One who holds a right granted under a **licence**. A person who is allowed to enter onto the land of another for his own convenience, profit, or benefit, but whose presence thereon is merely tolerated. In particular, one who has been granted a right to be on land when his presence would otherwise be unlawful (*Thomas v Sorrell* (1673) Vaugh 330, 351, 124 Eng Rep 1098, 1109). A licensee has an express or implied right to enter on another's land, but unlike a **tenant** does not have a right to exclude others (especially the owner of the land) from possession. A licensee enters on land for his own purpose and not the purpose of doing business with the licensor. Thus, he or she is not a customer, a servant or a trespasser, but has merely a right to be on the land in a manner that without the consent of the owner would amount to a **trespass**. cf. **invitee**. See also **lodger, negligence, visitor**. **2.** A person given a privilege or franchise to engage in a business or trade. Commonly used to refer to a person who has a right to sell intoxicating liquor from licensed premises. **3.**(US)A person who holds a valid **real estate license**. See also **broker**.

licensor or **licenser**   One who grants a right under a **licence**.

lie in grant   A right to property that may be transferred by **grant** (a solemn deed or charter). Property that is capable of being transferred only by deed. Interests in land, including advowsons, commons, rents, reversions and other intangible rights, 'lie in grant' as they can only be passed by deed (2 *Bl Comm* 317); as distinguished from goods which 'lie in livery', i.e. are transferred by physical delivery.

lie in livery   See **livery**.

lien   A legal right or claim held by one person (lienor) against property, real or personal, belonging to another (lienee) as security for the payment of a debt or the performance of an obligation. A lien is a means by which a creditor secures a lawful right over property – reinforcing his position against general creditors – in order to coerce another to meet his obligations, even though **title** to the property (but not necessarily possession) remains with the debtor.

A lien may be classified as a 'common-law lien' (also called a 'legal', 'retentive' or 'possessory' lien) being a right against property that has been transferred tacitly as security for an obligation; "a right in one man to retain that which is in his possession belonging to another, till certain demands of him, the person in possession are satisfied" (*Hammonds v Barclay* (1802) 2 East 227, 235, 102 Eng Rep 356)", Whiteside v. Rocky Mountain Fuel Co., 101 F.2d 765, 769 (10th Cir. Colo 1939)). A common-law lien arises by implication, as distinguished from a lien created by express agreement or by statute. A common-law lien usually arises when personal property is handed over for a specified purpose, e.g. for repair,

and cannot exist without possession. A person may not claim a lien over goods that are merely on his premises if another party, a tenant or licensee, has effective control.

A possessory lien may be a 'general' lien; or a 'particular', 'specific' or 'special' lien. A 'general lien' is a right to retain any personal property belonging to the debtor that comes into the possession of the creditor and relates to the same line of business, until all the debts arising from that line of business have been cleared; especially a lien by which certain agents (e.g. a lawyer, factor, banker or stockbroker) hold goods or documents belonging to their principal until their account has been settled in full. A 'particular lien' is a right to retain possession of property that is the subject of a particular debt. For example, an architect or surveyor may retain plans until the expenses or fees due for producing those plans, or executing works related thereto, are paid in full. However, a possessory lien is merely a right to hold the property until the debt is paid and does not confer any right for the possessor to sell or otherwise deal in the property, unless there is an agreement between the parties to that effect.

A lien may be 'equitable', that is a right which, unlike a common-law lien, is not dependent on possession of property and, therefore, is enforced only in equity (Walker v. Brown, 165 US 654, 17 S Ct 453, 41 L Ed 865-866 n. 1 (1896)). An equitable lien arises most frequently out of a contract when one party has not fulfilled his obligation and the law considers it fair to enforce payment by not objecting to an attachment of the debtor's property. For example, an equitable lien may arise (i) when land is conveyed to a purchaser before the purchase money is paid in full – a 'vendor's lien' or 'grantor's lien'; or (ii) when a purchaser has paid the purchase price but has not been granted possession or received title – a 'purchaser's lien' or 'grantee's lien'. In such cases, if the obligation is not met when due, the party entitled to enforce that obligation may apply to the court either, in the former case, for a direction that the property be sold to meet the outstanding debt or, in the latter case, for an order for possession. (A vendor is not entitled to a lien if he has obtained a mortgage on the property he has sold.) Similarly, a purchaser who pays a deposit upon the execution of a contract of sale may obtain a lien on that sum until the conditions of the contract have been satisfied. An equitable lien may be considered as a 'voluntary' lien in that it arises initially out of a voluntary act of the parties, as opposed to an 'involuntary' or 'statutory lien', which arises from a statutory provision. cf. **charge**. See also **bailment, contract for sale, encumbrance, general equitable charge, mechanic's lien, purchase money mortgage**(US)**, seizure, substantial performance, tax certificate**(US)**, tax deed**(US)**.

lien holder   See **lienor**.

lien statement(US)   See **reduction certificate**.

lien theory(US)   See **mortgage**.

lienee   A person whose property is subject to a **lien**. However, in Australia, 'lienee' may be used to refer to the beneficiary of a lien.

lienor   A person who has a **lien** over another's property; the holder of a lien.

lieu lands(US)   **Public lands** that may be granted to a settler in place of land that had previously been granted, but where title thereto has not been perfected. The alternative lands are selected by the claimant from lands designated by the Department of the Interior in *lieu* of the original or 'base' lands, claims to which are then relinquished. See also **indemnity lands**.

life annuity   An annuity that is payable for a person's lifetime. Sometimes called a 'rental annuity'. See also **reverse mortgage**.

life estate   A right to an **estate** in land that is limited for the duration of a person's life. A life estate is equivalent to a **freehold**, but as it is limited for the life of a person, it carries no right of inheritance. A life estate may subsist for the life of the holder of the estate in land, or for the life of another person. If the estate is held for the life of someone other than the beneficiary, it is called an estate *pur autre vie*. In the latter instance the other person, the *cestui que vie*, determines the length of the life, even if he outlives the holder of the interest – a grant 'to A for the life of B' lasts as long as B lives, regardless of A's life span.

A life estate is the shortest form of freehold and, although it can be transferred to another (unless constrained by the express or implied terms upon which it was granted), the right to hold the estate ends with the death of the person for whose life the estate was created. It is not a fee estate (although a life estate and a fee estate are the only forms of estate that can exist as 'freeholds') and a life estate cannot pass to the heirs of the life tenant. On the other hand, during the subsistence of the estate, the holder has the legal and beneficial rights to the land, subject to the restraint that he must not commit **waste**. Upon the termination of the life estate, by operation of law the estate may return to the original grantor – called the grantor's right of **reversion**. Alternatively, it may be created so that it goes to another person – called a **remainder**. Also, a life estate may be created subject to a contingency, i.e. it may end upon the occurrence of a specified event, such as if the land is no longer used for a particular purpose or if the holder achieves a specified status (e.g. gets married). See also **curtesy, dower, estate for life**(US)**, estate in tail after possibility of issue extinct, tenant for life, usufruct, words of limitation**.

life interest   **1.** An interest in property (real or personal) that is held for the life of an individual, whether for the life of the holder of that interest or the life of another. See also **conditional interest, determinable interest, life estate, tenancy for life**. **2.**(Eng)An interest granted by the holder of a fee simple to another (**tenant for life**) for a life – either the life of the grantee or the life of another (*cestui que vie*, 'he for whom the life subsists'). Such a right is created by a grant of land under a **settlement**. The holder of a life interest is called the 'tenant for life', i.e. a person who has tenure for life; but is not a tenant in the sense of one of the parties to any relationship of landlord and tenant. The essence of a life interest is to grant for a lifetime a right for a person or persons to enjoy the benefits or fruits of land and then to direct the right to those benefits to a third party. A modern life interest is similar to a feudal **life estate**, except that the estate need not revert to the grantor on the death of the tenant for life, but may then pass to another person nominated by the grantor (i.e. there need not be a **reversion** to the grantor, instead there may be a **remainder** to another party). A life interest may be created by deed, or by will, and may or may not be made subject to the payment of rent.   **3.** A right to the income from a property for life. Such a right does not amount to an ownership interest in the property.

life of a building   See **depreciation**, **economic life**, **wasting asset**.

life tenant   A person who has an estate in land for a life, either his or her own life, or the life of another. The holder of a **life estate**, i.e. one who holds the equivalent interest to a freehold, but only for a lifetime. See also **tenant for life**.

liferent(Scot)   A right to use another's property (movable or immovable) for the grantee's life in the same way as if one were the owner. A form of personal servitude for life over another's property. Similar, in respect of land, to a life estate in English law, although liferent is not a tenure but a form of usufruct.

lifting clause   A provision in a junior mortgage that permits the senior mortgagee to refinance, provided the amount of the new loan does not exceed the amount outstanding at the time the junior mortgage was granted. See also **subordination**.

light   **1.** A single window pane. See also **pavement light**.   **2.** See **ancient lights**, **right of light/right to light**.

light industrial building   A building used for an industrial purpose that generally would not be detrimental to a residential area, i.e. it would not cause excessive environmental disturbance such as noise, vibration, smell or air pollution. See also **industrial building**, **Use Classes Order**(Eng), **warehouse**.

like-kind exchange(US)   See **tax-free exchange**.

limit   A point or line where something stops or is intended to stop. A terminal point. A restriction or restraint. See also **boundary**, **bounds**, **call**, **limitation**, **term**.

limit of credit   See **line of credit**.

limit of indemnity   See **indemnity limit**.

limitation   **1.** The act of defining the extent of something. A certain time allowed for an action to take place or to be brought. A 'limitation of action' means a period of time, specified by statute law, within which proceedings to enforce a right must be brought to a court of law before that right is 'barred'. cf. **laches**, **prescription**.   **2.** The specification, or the maximum period specified, for which a particular **estate** in land can exist. A limitation is built into the primary formula that fixes the period for which an estate or interest may last; thus it is generally preceded by such words as 'until'. It may be distinguished from a **condition**, which grants a right for a specified period, but includes a provision making it terminable on the happening of a specified event, i.e. the interest is granted 'on condition that'. A 'limitation' of an estate in land may be distinguished from an estate 'subject to a **condition subsequent**', in that with the former it is the contingency or event that automatically brings the estate to an end, whereas with the latter some action must be taken to defeat the estate, usually the exercise of a right of re-entry by the grantor (or his heirs) of the original estate. An event that defines when the estate may come to an end is sometimes called a 'collateral limitation'. See also **conditional limitation, determinable interest, estate on limitation**[(US)], **special limitation, words of limitation**. **2.** The marking out of a limit or **boundary line** of a property. **3.** A restriction placed on the use to which a property may be put. See also **change of use, restrictive covenant**.

limited appraisal[(US)] An appraisal that is carried out in a restricted manner, as to either its content or conditions, or the purpose for which it is to be used. cf. **complete appraisal**. See also **Departure Rule, summary appraisal report, restricted appraisal report**.

limited certificate of title[(NZ)] A **certificate of title** issued to a registered proprietor of land when the District Land Registrar is not satisfied as to the exact area, position or the boundaries of the land to be registered, or when the Registrar is not satisfied as to the owner's title.

limited common elements[(US)] See **common elements**.

limited company See **limited liability company**.

limited estate Any estate in land that is less than a **fee**. cf. **absolute estate**.

limited fee A fee interest in land that is less than a **fee simple**. A fee simple interest that may be defeated or come to an end for any one of a number of reasons. A term that has no strict legal meaning, but may be used to refer to a **qualified fee, base fee**, or **fee tail**. See also **conditional fee, determinable fee**.

limited liability company or **limited liability corporation** A business organisation in which the liability of the shareholders is limited to the amount of their paid-up shares and up to, but not beyond, any shares not paid up. See also **company, corporation, limited partnership**.

limited liability partnership (LLP) **1.**[(US)] See **limited partnership**. **2.**[(Eng)]A body that is incorporated (with a separate personality from its members) by two or more persons for "any lawful business with a view to a profit" (Limited Partnership Act 2000, ss. 1, 2). An LLP has members and not shareholders, directors or partners. It does not have a memorandum and articles of association, and its constitution is set out in a document that is private to its members. A limited partnership is a corporate body that may sue and be sued and contract in its own name, but it is managed in a similar way to a partnership (although it is governed by company and not partnership law). As a rule, unlike a **partnership**, the members of an LLP are not liable for the acts or defaults of fellow members. Such an entity is treated as a partnership for tax purposes so that each member is assessed for tax on his or her share of the LLP's income and gain, and the partnership itself has no separate liability for tax.

limited owner **1.** In general, an **owner** of property who has an estate or interest less than absolute ownership, i.e. the holder of a **qualified fee**. **2.**[(Eng)]Any owner of an estate in land, other than the owner of a **fee simple absolute**, including the possessor of a life estate (**tenant for life**), or an entailed interest (**tenant in tail**). cf. **estate owner**. See also **statutory owner**.

limited owner's charge[(Eng)] An **equitable charge** that is acquired by a **tenant for life** or a **statutory owner** who has discharged his liability to inheritance tax or other liabilities for which special priority is given by statute.

limited partner A **partner** whose liability is limited to the amount of capital contributed to the partnership. A member of a **limited partnership** who provides the capital, but who takes no active part in the management and cannot bind the partnership by his own acts or conduct. English statute law provides that a limited partner "shall at the time of entering into such partnership [a limited partnership] contribute thereto a sum or sums as capital or property valued at a stated amount, and … shall not be liable for the debts or obligations of the firm beyond the amount so contributed". Also, "A limited partner shall not during the continuance of the partnership, either directly or indirectly, draw out or receive back any part of his contribution, and if he does so draw out or receive back any such part shall be liable for the debts and obligations of the firm up to the amount so drawn out or received back", Limited Partnership Act 1907, s. 4(2)(3). A body corporate may be a limited partner. Also called a 'special partner', a 'sleeping partner', or a 'dormant partner'. cf. **general partner**. See also **passive investor**.

limited partnership A **partnership** in which one or more partners, **general partner**(s), are appointed to manage the partnership business and to accept full responsibility for the conduct of the firm and the partnership's debts, and one or more partners, **limited partner**(s), contribute capital to the partnership but take no active part in its management and incur no liability beyond their capital contributions. The general partners are remunerated normally as salaried employees and the limited partners receive the profits (or share in the losses) of the enterprise, although the general partners may also be limited partners.

All states in the US and the District of Columbia have statutes that regulate limited partnerships and, with the exception of Louisiana, these are based on the Uniform Limited Partnership Act of 1916 (ULPA) or the Revised Uniform Limited Partnership Act of 1976 (RULPA). The RULPA defines a limited partnership as "a partnership formed by two or more persons under the provisions of the Uniform Limited Partnership Act, having as members one or more general partners and one or more limited partners", § 101(7). In the US, also called a 'limited liability partnership'. See also **joint venture**, **limited liability partnership**.

limited period permission(Eng)   See **General Development Order**, **planning condition**.

limited security(Eng)   See **security of tenure**.

limited title(Aus)   A title that has been registered but where the boundaries have not been accurately surveyed. Such title is granted in some states when land title is being converted from the 'old system' to a registered Torrens title.

limited title guarantee(Eng)   A form of title to land that, when expressed as such, contains implied 'covenants for title'. The grant of land "with limited title guarantee" implies that the person making the disposition of the property (a) has the right to dispose of the property as he purports to, with the concurrence of any other person conveying the property (a 'covenant for right to convey'); (b) will at his own cost do all that is possible to give the title he purports to (a 'covenant for further assurance'); and (c) has not, since the last disposition for value, (i) charged or encumbered the property or granted any third party rights that remain in existence at the time of the disposition, or (ii) allowed any such charge, encumbrance or rights to affect the property and is not aware that any other person has done so (except for matters to which the disposition is made subject) (LP(MP)A 1994, ss. 1(1)(2), 3(3)). This provision does not apply to any matter that is within the actual knowledge of the person to whom the disposition is made (LP(MP)A 1994, s. 1(3), 6(2)). In the case of a disposition of a leasehold interest (whether or not made for valuable consideration) the grant of a 'limited title guarantee' implies that (a) the lease is subsisting at the time of the disposition; and (b) there is no subsisting breach of the lease or anything that would render the lease liable to forfeiture (LP(MP)A 1994, ss. 1(1)(2), 4(1)). cf. **full title guarantee**.

limited warranty deed(US)   See **warranty deed**.

line   A demarcation, **boundary line**, or limit, especially of a plot of land. See also **building line**, **improvement line**.

line of credit   An amount of credit or a loan made available by a bank to an established customer to cover the day-to-day business needs or **working capital** of the customer, up to an agreed maximum. This facility is intended to supplement, but not replace, interim finance; it commonly takes the form of an overdraft; and is subject to regular review by the lender. For example, a developer may be granted a line of credit to cover unexpected variations of expenditure for a building project. A line of credit may also be granted by a business supplier to an established customer. Also called a 'credit line' and the agreed maximum facility the 'limit of credit' or, where the credit is constantly varying but subject to a specified limit, a 'rolling credit'. See also **facility**.

line-of-sight easement(US)   See **visibility clearance**.

lines and corners system(US)   See **metes and bounds system**.

linear city   A form of city design where development has been planned along one principal axis or thoroughfare. cf. **ribbon development**.

linkage rent or **linked rent**   See **indexed rent**.

liquid asset   Cash, or an asset that is readily convertible into cash. Sometimes called a 'quick asset'. cf. **fixed asset**. See also **current asset**.

liquidated damages   A particular sum of money, set out in a contract or agreed between the parties, that is intended as a genuine pre-estimate of the amount of **damages** to be paid in the event of default by one of the parties. The specified sum, no more and usually no less, is payable as the agreed and pre-determined ('liquidated') damages in the event of a **breach of contract**. If there is no such specified sum in a contract, the injured party may claim such damages as are occasioned. For example, a building contract may specify a fixed sum, as liquidated damages, to be paid by the contractor, for each day that building work remains outstanding after the agreed completion date (J.E. Hathaway and Co. v. United States, 249 US 460, 39 S Ct 63, 63 L Ed 707 (1918); *Percy Bilton Ltd v Greater London Council* [1980] 2 All ER 623 (HL)). Liquidated damages are a genuine pre-estimate of the loss that may result from a breach of contract and as such are recoverable in a court of law; as contrasted with a **penalty** which is intended to be a burden or punishment imposed to ensure completion of a contract, or is designed to make the result of a default more profitable to the party against whom it runs, and is likely to be set aside by a court. See also **deposit**, **unliquidated damages**.

Eggleston, B. *Liquidated Damages and Extensions of Time.* 2nd ed. Oxford: Blackwell Science, 1998.

liquidation   1. The 'winding-up' of the affairs of a business or a company. The sale of a company's assets for cash and the repayment, as far as possible, of all its debts, especially when a company has ceased trading as a result of **insolvency**. Liquidation may arise compulsorily, usually at the instigation of the creditors, as when a bankrupt person seeks to obtain as much cash as possible to repay his debts. It may arise voluntarily when the owners have achieved the purpose for which the company was established, or when they agree that they wish to discontinue trading. In either case, a liquidator is appointed to assume control of the company, arrange for the orderly sale of its assets and discharge its liabilities. Liquidation is the process required prior to the winding-up of a company. cf. **bankruptcy**.   2. The process of converting an asset into cash. See also **conversion**, **liquidity**.   3. The extinguishment of a debt by payment.

liquidation value   1. The value of property when it is sold as a result of the **liquidation** of a business. Generally, such value is restricted by the time available for sale and the knowledge by the buyers that the property has to be sold. See **forced-sale value**.   2. The amount per share that is paid to shareholders, in particular preferred shareholders, on the **liquidation** of a corporation.

liquidity   1. The state of holding liquid assets. 2. The ease with which assets may be converted into cash. In the case of a property investment, the ease with which an investor anticipates being able to convert that investment back into cash – the degree of liquidity – is one of the factors that affects the capital value of the investment. Thus, a sizeable investment in one property is likely to demand a higher return for an investor than an investment in a smaller, more liquid, but otherwise comparable property. In the case of a business, liquidity refers to the ability of that business to raise cash to pay its debts as they arise, without unduly affecting the operation or purpose of the business. See also **current asset**, **risk**.

liquidity ratio   A ratio that measures an organisation's ability to meet its current obligations; e.g. the ratio of current assets (cash, trade receivables and marketable securities) to current liabilities. Also called the 'acid-test ratio' or 'quick ratio'. See also **liquidity**.

lis pendens or ***lis pendente***(Lat)   A 'pending action; a 'pending lawsuit'. The common law doctrine of *lis pendens* provides that, if a person acquires land subject to a pending action, the land may be subjected to any claims arising from the final outcome of the action and the acquirer remains bound to the judgement. In the US, many states have codified the procedure for filing a notice of *lis pendens* or a 'notice of pendency'. See also **constructive notice**, **pending land action**(Eng).

list-back agreement(AmE)   An agreement by which a purchaser of a property agrees that in the event of a resale he will list the property with the broker who introduced the property, or with a **multiple-listing service** of which the broker is a member. If such an arrangement is made a condition of accepting a listing, it may be a violation of state anti-trust laws. See also **tying agreement**.

listed building(Eng)   A building considered to be of "special architectural or historic interest" and, therefore, included in a list of such buildings prepared by the Secretary of State; or included in a list prepared by **English Heritage**, or other person or body, and approved by the Secretary of State (Planning (Listed Building and Conservation Areas) Act 1990, s. 1). A building (which may include any object or structure fixed or within the curtilage of a building) is included in the list because it, or part of it, may be worthy of preservation on its own merits; because it forms part of a group of buildings that may be worthy of preservation as a whole; or because it contains a particular feature that may be worthy of preservation. The buildings included in the list are classified as Grade I or Grade II. The appropriate grade depends on whether the building is considered of exceptional interest, or merely worthy of consideration so as to warrant further examination if alteration or demolition is likely (*DOE Circular 8/87*, "Historic Buildings and Conservation Areas—Policy and Procedure"; PPG 15 "Planning and the Historic Environment").

No person may demolish, alter or extend a listed building "so as to affect its character as a building of special architectural or historic interest" without a **listed building consent** (P(LBCA)A 1990, ss. 7, 8)). Similarly, it is an offence to carry out any work that affects the character of a listed building without consent (P(LBCA)A 1990, s. 9). It is also a criminal offence to cause damage to a listed building (P(LBCA)A 1990, ss. 59, 60; Criminal Justice Act 1982, s. 37). See also **ancient monument**, **building preservation notice**, **conservation area**, **local land charges register**, **repairs notice**.

Campbell, Gordon. *Heritage Law & Policy: Listed Buildings and Conservation Areas*. Isle of Wight: Palladian Law Publishing, 2001.

Mynors, Charles. *Listed Buildings and Conservation Areas*. 3rd ed. London: Sweet & Maxwell, 1999.

Suddards, Roger and June Hargreaves. *Listed Buildings*. 3rd ed. London: Sweet & Maxwell, 1995.

listed building consent(Eng)   Approval

obtained from a local planning authority (or, in the event of an appeal, from the Secretary of State) to alter, extend, or demolish a **listed building** (P(LBCA)A 1990, s. 8). If considered appropriate, a listed building consent may be given unconditionally; or it may be granted subject to conditions, such as the approval by the local planning authority of details of the proposed work. See also **compensation for planning restrictions, conservation area, purchase notice.**

listed building enforcement notice(Eng)
See **listed building.**

listed price(US)   See **listing price.**

lister(US)   See **listing broker.**

listing(US)   The placing of a property by a seller, or renter, with a real estate agent or **broker**, under the terms of an agreement which provides that the broker will endeavor to secure a purchaser, or tenant, for that property in return for which the agent will receive a **commission**. The agreement may take the form of an **open listing** (or 'general listing'); an **exclusive listing** (either as an 'exclusive agency' or an 'exclusive right to sell'); or a **multiple listing**. In any event, merely listing a property with a real estate agent does not entitle that party to any compensation, until a sale or other transaction has resulted from the actions of the agent. Sometimes called an 'authorization to sell'. The term 'listing' may also be used to refer to the property that the broker has for sale or rent. See also **agency, list-back agreement, net listing, procuring cause.**

listing agent or **listing broker**(US)   An **agent** or **broker** retained by a property owner to offer a property for sale, or rent, and to endeavor to find a suitable buyer, or tenant. The broker may be retained to act on an exclusive basis, or may work with other agents in seeking prospective parties. Sometimes called the 'listor', or as it is occasionally spelt 'lister'. See also **dual agency, listing, real estate agent.**

listing agreement(US)   An agreement by which an owner or landlord retains a **broker** to procure a buyer or tenant for a specified property or properties. Such an agreement may take the form of an **open listing**; an 'exclusive listing' (as an **exclusive agency** or an **exclusive right to sell**); or a **multiple listing**. A listing agreement is usually in **writing** and, in many jurisdictions, it may be unenforceable if it is not made in writing, either because a state law requires a written agreement, or because a court will not enforce a right in equity that relates to a transaction that must be in writing to comply with the **Statute of Frauds**. See also **agency agreement, commission, contract, extender clause.**

listing broker(US)   See **listing agent.**

listing contract(US)   See **contract, listing agreement.**

listing officer(Eng)   See **valuation officer.**

listing price(US)   The price at which a seller of property lists his property for sale with a real estate broker. Also called the 'listed price'. See also **asking price, listing.**

listor(US)   See **listing agent.**

literal construction or **literal meaning** The construction or meaning given to a word in its ordinary, commonly understood sense. In interpreting a contract based on the literal construction "the grammatical and ordinary sense of the word is to be adhered to, unless that would lead to some absurdity, or some repugnance or inconsistency with the rest of the instrument, in which case the ordinary or grammatical sense of the word may be modified, so as to avoid that absurdity and inconsistency, but no further", *Grey v Pearson* (1857) 6 HL Cas 61, 106, 10 Eng Rep 1216, 26 LJ Ch 472, 481 (HL). However, the courts may depart from the literal construction of a word or words when such an interpretation clearly does not have regard to the intent of the parties as gathered from the entire contract.

In interpreting statutes, it must be assumed that words are used precisely and exactly, not loosely or inexactly; if a word has one probable meaning, it is given that meaning – its primary or literal meaning – unless that creates an absurdity or a manifest hardship; it is for the judges to find the judicial meaning of the language used in the statute, but not to legislate for parliament's or the administrator's meaning. If there is only one meaning for a word, the 'literal rule' provides for it to be given that meaning notwithstanding the result. See also **word of art**, **words**.

littoral land   Land that borders the sea, especially land washed by waves and coastal currents ('littoral' being derived from the Latin *litus* meaning 'seashore'). 'Littoral lands' may sometimes be taken to include the shore of a lake, especially a navigable lake. Littoral land may be distinguished from **riparian land**, as the latter relates to the bank of a river, although the terms are often used interchangeably as the rules relating to both are similar. See also **foreshore**, **littoral rights**.

littoral owner   See **littoral rights**.

littoral proprietor(US)   See **littoral rights**.

littoral rights   The rights concerning land abutting the **shore** of an ocean, sea or lake. In English common law the seashore belongs to the Crown, and in most jurisdictions in the US it is vested in the state. The adjoining 'littoral owner' or 'littoral proprietor' has a right of access to the shore, but may not remove any sand as of right. cf. **riparian rights**. See also **accretion**, **foreshore**, **water rights**.

livery   Literally '**delivery**'. The transfer of title to land by giving physical **possession**. Historically, a transfer of land was said to be made or 'lie in livery' and rights over the land (such as advowson, common rents, reversions, etc.) were said to **lie in grant**, i.e. land was transferred by a giving of possession. Incorporeal rights over land (such as easements) had to be made by deed, as they could not be transferred by the giving of physical possession. See also **corporeal hereditament**.

living room   A room that is used for the principal activities in a residence. A room in a residence that is used for habitation, especially as part of the more permanent process of living, as contrasted with a room available for ancillary uses. A living room may be a room used for social activities during a considerable part of the day, including a sitting room, kitchen or bedroom, but not a bathroom, toilet, storage area, hall or garage. What constitutes a 'living room' should not be too narrowly constrained but based on the type of property. Thus, a kitchen may be considered a sitting room in some properties, but may not be so considered in a large mansion house, especially if it is only used for food preparation and cooking. See also **habitable room**.

live trust(US)   1. See **special trust**.   2. See **living trust**.

living trust   A **trust** that is executed by a property owner ('trustor') during his or her lifetime, as distinguished from a 'testamentary' trust which arises upon death. As soon as the property is placed into a living trust, the trustees have responsibility for its management and control in accordance with the terms of the trust instrument. Sometimes called an '*inter vivos* trust' or, in the US, a 'live trust'. See also **land trust**(US), **special trust**, **voluntary trust**.

load factor(US)   See **loss factor**.

loan   The grant of a sum of money to someone for a period of time on the basis that it will be repaid with or without **interest**. The act of transferring personal property to another on the understanding that it, or its equivalent, will be returned, or repaid, after a specified time, with or without recompense for its use. A transaction by which one person (a creditor or lender) delivers something of value – goods, money or anything of pecuniary worth – to another (debtor or borrower) on the basis that it will be returned after a period of use. When a loan takes the form of money (the **principal**) usually it is repayable, whether by instalments or as lump sum, with a reward for its use, called interest. A loan of money may be secured by a **lien**, **charge**, or **mortgage** on property owned by the borrower, in order to give the lender some form of security against non-payment of the debt owed to him. The process of entering into this form of agreement is called **financing**, funding, or obtaining an advance. An **instalment sale** is not a loan because the money paid over is not intended to be paid back, although it may create a debt. cf. **conditional sale contract, investment, sale**. See also **bailment**.

loan capital   See **debt capital**.

loan closer(US)   See **closer**.

loan commitment   See **commitment**.

loan constant   See **mortgage constant**.

loan cover or **loan coverage**   See **cover**, **debt-coverage ratio**.

loan fee   A charge made by a lender for making a loan, over and above payment of interest. See also **commitment fee, front-end loading**.

loan origination fee   See **origination fee**.

loan participation   See **convertible mortgage, participation loan**.

loan points   See **discount points**.

loan policy(US)   See **title insurance**.

loan ratio   See **loan-to-value ratio**.

loan service   See **debt service**.

loan servicer   See **servicer**.

loan servicing   The administration of mortgage loan, as with the collection of payments due from the borrowers. See also **servicer**.

loan-to-value ratio (LTV)   The ratio of the amount granted as a **loan** to the appraised or **market value** of a property held as security for that loan. The ratio of the amount of a loan to the value of the property available as security for the loan is normally expressed as a percentage. This ratio generally falls within the range of 60 to 80% of the value of the property, at the time the loan is granted. Factors that are taken into account when deciding on the appropriate ratio include: (i) the type of property; (ii) the ease with which the property can potentially be sold; (iii) the risk of default by the borrower; and (d) the availability of additional collateral. Also called a 'loan ratio'. cf. **debt-equity ratio**. See also **discount points**, **mortgage insurance**.

loan value   See **collateral value**, mortgage value.

local assessment(US)   See **assessment**.

local authority search(Eng)   See **local land charge**.

local customary right(Eng)   See **customary right**.

local improvement assessment(US)   See **assessment**.

local improvement district(US)   See **improvement district**.

local land charge(Eng)   A charge, order or notice that is secured against land in order to ensure the recovery of money owed to a local authority, a Minister of the Crown, or a government department. A local land charge binds successive owners of the land for as long as the charge remains in force (LLCA 1975, s. 1). Such matters are not apparent from the title deeds or from an inspection of the property, but arise as a result of a statutory right. Local land charges include such matters as a financial charge for work done by a local authority under a statute which the authority seeks to recover, e.g. repair works to a private street; a planning charge (such as an enforcement notice, a compensation notice, a building preservation notice, or a tree preservation order); a positive covenant affecting land enforceable by a public authority, such as a **planning obligation** entered into by a land owner with a local authority; and a proposal to acquire land, e.g. a compulsory purchase order. A local land charge should be recorded in the **local land charges register** maintained by the local authority, and details of such a charge may be obtained by a personal search of the register, or by obtaining an **official search certificate** from the local authority (called generally a 'local authority search'). The registration of a local land charge constitutes actual **notice** of the charge to all persons and for all persons connected with the land affected (LPA 1925, s. 198(1), as amended). A local land charge that is not registered does not affect the enforceability of the charge, but if a purchaser for valuable consideration obtains an official search certificate that does not reveal the charge, then he may be entitled to compensation from the authority that should have registered the charge (LLCA, s. 10). A local land charge is registered against the land, unlike a **land charge** which is registered in the name of the proprietor. A local land charge can be registered against a registered or an unregistered title to land. See also **overriding interest**.

Boothroyd, Jan E. *Garner's Local Land Charges*. 12th ed. London: Shaw & Sons, 1998.

local land charges register(Eng)   A register of local land charges maintained by a District Council in England and Wales, a London Borough Council or the Common Council of the City of London. A register of local land charges is maintained by each local authority containing details of various charges, burdens or other restrictions against land (whether registered or unregistered land) arising from the authority's own actions or the action of a Ministry of the Crown or a government department. The register is divided into twelve parts and entries are made against the land itself (as opposed to entries at the Land Registry where charges are registered against the estate owner). Details of items on a register may be obtained by a prospective purchaser of land either by a personal search or by a request to the Registrar of the local land charges register for an **official search certificate** (LLCA 1975, s. 9). cf. **Land Charges Register**. See also **local land charge**.

local law   A law that applies only to a particular district, area of local government, municipality, or state, as distinguished from a general law that applies to all things or to a particular group or class of persons. See also **bylaw, custom, ordinance**.

local ordinance(US)   See **ordinance**.

local plan(Eng)   See **development plan**.

local planning authority(Eng)   See **planning authority**.

local rates(Eng)   See **rates**.

local search(Eng)   An enquiry made to ascertain details of any **local land charge** registered against a parcel of land. Any person may search, or requisition a search of a local land charges register. The search may be made in person, or by requesting an **official search certificate** (LCA 1975, ss. 8, 9). See also **searches**.

local tax   See **assessment**(US), **rates**(Eng).

local valuation courts(Eng)   See **valuation tribunals**.

location   1. The situation of a property in relation to other properties and to the facilities that serve the property such as roads, public transport, complementary uses, etc. In real estate, 'location' is commonly used to refer to the economic rather than geographical position, i.e. it reflects the relative importance and hence the value attached to the property. Synonymous with **situs**. See also **location theory, prime location**. **2.** A site or building occupied or available for occupation. **3.** A parcel or tract of land, particularly an area marked out for official purposes. Also, the act of staking out an area of land, especially an area that forms the domain of a new settlement. In the US, 'location' may be used to refer to the selection of a property for entry under a right of **homestead**. **4.**(US)In mining law, the act by which the boundaries of a claim are marked out by the 'locator' of the vein or body of mineral-bearing rock in order to appropriate the rights thereto. The 'location' gives public notice of the extent of the claim. See also **mining claim**. **5.** A contract for the letting or hiring of personal property. Also, the act of letting or hiring personal property.

location plan   A plan showing the location of a site or building and drawn to a sufficiently large scale to show a site in relation to the surrounding area, normally to a scale of 1/2500 or larger. cf. **site plan**.

location theory   An economic theory devised to explain the factors that account for the **location** of a particular economic user and the associated hierarchy of land values. Location theory seeks to explain where consumers and producers will settle and establish economic activity; to explain the preference for one site or location compared with another; to produce an explanation of relative land values; and to explain movements in land values over time. The basis of most location theories is the principle of 'comparative advantage' – land is fixed in space and limited in quantity (at least in the short term) and in a free economy each area of land tends to produce those products, or to be used for the purpose, for which it has the greatest ratio of advantage or the least ratio of

disadvantage compared with any other area of land. See also **highest and best use, land economics**.

locational obsolescence   See **obsolescence**.

lockbox agreement(US)   An agreement by which a borrower agrees that funds will be paid into a bank account and only paid out under the strict conditions of the agreement. A lockbox agreement may be entered into whereby all income from a property that is granted as security for a loan is first paid into a Deposit Account, and then on a regular basis (usually weekly) transferred to a designated 'Lockbox Account'. Non of the funds in these accounts is available to the borrower, but is used first to pay the loan obligations, and only then are remitted to the borrower. The lockbox account is generally set up at an independent bank and that bank only makes transfers in accordance with the instructions of the lender. See also **assignment of rents**.

lock-in provision   1. A provision in a loan agreement or mortgage note that the loan may not be repaid before maturity or within a prescribed period of time. Sometimes called 'lock-out protection' as the provision of the loan agreement protects the lender against having to take back the funds before he has planned to reinvest them. See also **clog, equity of redemption, prepayment privilege**.   2. A provision in a loan agreement that permits the borrower to fix the interest rate, or the margin, for the term of the loan. A provision in a loan commitment by which the lender agrees to fix the interest rate for a specified period of time. Also called a 'rate lock', especially when the lender fixes the interest rate for a period of time during the term of the loan.

lock-out agreement   An agreement by which a vendor of property, who is already in negotiation with a prospective purchaser, undertakes not to negotiate with any third party for a specified period of time. A lock-out agreement gives the prospective purchaser an opportunity to endeavour to reach a formal agreement with the vendor during the term of the agreement. Such an agreement must comply with the formalities required of any other **contract**. cf. **option**. See also **conditional contract, subject to contract, writing**.

lock-out protection   See lock-in provision.

locus contractus(Lat)   See *lex loci contractus*.

locus in quo(Lat)   'The place in which' something is claimed to have been done; as in **trespass**. The premises described in a writ.

locus regit actum(Lat)   'The place governs the act'.

locus sigilli (LS)(Lat)   'The place of the **seal**'. The words or initials that are sometimes inserted in a circle at the end of a document to indicate the place for fixing a seal.

lodger   One who lives or dwells in a place for a short time, especially somewhere that is owned or controlled by another. A person who passes the night or a short period of time in a given place. One who occupies hired rooms in a **lodging house**. In particular, a temporary resident, or licensee, who resides in and in some way shares and has permissive occupation of a property that is also the place of residence of the owner, and may or may not be provided with **board**. A lodger is a person who pays to live in another's house, may have **exclusive occupation** of part of the house for a short time, but is subordinate to the owner in terms of mastery of the house; it matters not whether any payment for the use of the property covers board and lodging, or board alone. A lodger generally only occupies part of the property, such as a spare room in a house, and the owner essentially retains direct control, supervision or care of the entire house. The person who has exclusive control over the outside door of a house is not a lodger, but typically the householder. A lodger is not normally a **tenant**, but a **licensee** of the premises he occupies. See also **licence, resident landlord**(Eng)**, restricted contract**(Eng)**.

lodging   A place to stay; sleeping accommodation. See also **board and lodging, inn, hotel, lodging house**.

lodging house   A house where rooms are let as temporary lodgings; especially a place where living accommodation is provided as furnished accommodation with limited or no **board**. A lodging house is intended only as a place where the residents stay for a short period of time, generally for a few nights, or maybe a few weeks, but there is no intention to create a long-term relation as with a tenancy. As a rule, a lodging house only has a small number of rooms (between 3 and 15) and the rooms in lodging houses are not intended to be occupied as separate dwellings. A lodging house may be distinguished from an **inn** or **hotel**, as essentially the latter are available to all who seek accommodation, whereas a lodging house is generally more restrictive and the residents of an inn or hotel are transient, whereas a lodger has a greater degree of permanency. Also, an inn or hotel normally provides a broad range of facilities (although the distinction between an inn and a lodging house may be gauged primarily by the average length or the permanency of the guests' stay). In the US, also called a 'rooming house', especially if it is very rudimentary. cf. **apartment house**(AmE)**, apartment hotel**. See also **common lodging-house, lodger**.

loft   An upper room or storey, especially of a warehouse or factory. An attic space. The term is now commonly used to refer to a work space in a converted warehouse or similar building that is used as office or workshop space predominately for small businesses or professions. In particular, a loft building is a former multi-storey industrial building that has been converted principally for small business users or for combined living and work space. A loft is commonly completed only to a shell condition. See also **studio**.

lollipop condominium(AmE) A **condominium** unit that is situated on top of another condominium, with the benefit of a common entrance area at ground level, the shared use of the elevator shaft and other common areas. The stem of the lollipop is the elevator shaft and any other form of access from the ground level entrance to the individual unit.

long lease 1. See **long-term lease**. 2.(Eng)For the purposes of a 'collective right of leasehold enfranchisement' of a number of flats in a building, a long lease is primarily "a lease for more than 21 years, whether or not it is (or may become) terminable before the end of that term by notice given by or to the tenant or by re-entry, forfeiture or otherwise", Leasehold Reform, Housing and Urban Development Act 1993, s. 7(1). This definition is extended by the rest of section 7 (as inserted by the HA 1996, Sch. 9, para 3) to include various similar forms of lease, such as a perpetually renewable lease, and to exclude certain other leases, such as certain forms of life tenancy. See also **extended lease**, **leasehold enfranchisement**, **long tenancy**. 3. See **right of first refusal**.

long residential tenancy(Eng) A **tenancy** of a **dwelling-house** that is let as a separate dwelling on a "long tenancy", which is defined as a tenancy granted "for a term of years certain exceeding 21 years", even though it may subsequently have been extended by the parties. The lease must not be terminable by the landlord during the term, although the tenant can have an option to break the lease, provided he can demonstrate that he has the right to remain as lessee for the initial period of 21 years. A 'long tenancy' granted at a **low rent** does not come to an end on the expiration of the contractual term, provided the tenant still occupies the dwelling-house as his residence, but continues automatically until the landlord takes steps to end it, unless the tenant gives notice to terminate the tenancy. If the landlord wishes to obtain possession he must serve a prescribed notice on one or more of the statutorily permitted **grounds for possession** and then seek a court order (L&T Act 1954, Part I, Sch. 3; LGHA 1989, s. 186, Sch. 10). Alternatively, the landlord can convert the continuing tenancy into an **assured tenancy**. These provisions do not apply to the types of tenancies (agricultural, business, on-licensed premises, exempt landlords, etc.) that could not be a **protected tenancy**, or if granted on or after April 1, 1990 could not be an assured tenancy. See also **leasehold enfranchisement**, **long tenancy**.

long tenancy(Eng) 1. "A tenancy granted for a term of years certain exceeding twenty-one years, whether or not the tenancy is (or may become) terminable before the end of that term by notice given by or to the tenant or by re-entry, forfeiture or otherwise", Leasehold Reform Act 1967, s. 3(1); as well as a tenancy that may be perpetually renewable (unless it is a sub-lease and the superior tenancy is not a long tenancy), which may be a legal or equitable tenancy, but not a tenancy granted as a form of security. In certain cases, a tenancy that is terminable by notice after death or marriage of the tenant is not a long tenancy (LRA 1967, s. 3(1), as amended). A tenancy that has subsequently been extended by the parties so that the total term exceeds 21 years may be a long tenancy (LRA 1967, s. 3(4)). The holder of a long tenancy of a **house** that was granted at a **low rent** may have a right of **leasehold enfranchisement** or a right to an **extended lease**. 2. See **secure tenancy**. 3. See **long residential tenancy**.

long-term insurance agreement An insurance policy for a fixed number of years, commonly 3 to 5 years. In return for the commitment to one insurer for that term, the insured generally receives a reduction in the annual premium. Also called a 'term policy'.

long-term land contract(US) See **installment land contract**.

long-term lease In general, a lease granted for a fixed initial term (not being a **periodic tenancy**). In the US, a lease for 10 years or more may be considered as a long-term lease, whereas in the UK, a long-term lease generally refers to a lease for 20 years or more. cf. **short-term lease**. See also **ground lease, emphyteotic lease, long residential tenancy**[(Eng)], **tenancy for a term of years**.

long-term finance or **long-term loan** A loan granted for a fixed term, generally in excess of ten years, as contrasted with **interim finance**. Such a loan may take the form of a mortgage, debenture or sale-and-leaseback financing. Also called a 'permanent loan (or financing)'. cf. **short-term finance**.

long-term policy See **long-term insurance agreement**.

lord of the manor A proprietor or owner of a **manor**.

loss **1.** An amount by which the proceeds from the sale of an asset fall short of the cost of acquiring that asset. An amount by which the aggregate expenditure incurred in running a business exceeds the aggregate income generated by that business, over a given period of time – generally one financial year. cf. **profit**. See also **damage, damages, indemnity**. **2.** The act of losing something, or something that cannot be recovered. A failure to find or regain possession of something. cf. **gain**. See also **ademption, consequential loss insurance**.

loss factor[(AmE)] The difference between the **usable area** and the **rentable area** of an office building expressed as a percentage of the rentable area. For example, if the usable area of an office floor is 8,000 sq. ft. and the rentable area is 10,000 sq. ft. the loss factor is 20%. This factor expresses the percentage of floor space for which a tenant pays rent but cannot derive benefit therefrom due to corridors, elevator shafts, utility ducts, stairwells, etc. within the area leased to him. Also called a 'load factor' or 'partial floor factor' or, when expressed as a percentage of the usable area, an 'add-on factor', thus the add-on factor = (loss factor × rentable area)/usable area. In the above example the add-on factor is 25%. See also **efficiency ratio**.

loss of profit See **compensation for disturbance**[(Eng)], **damages**.

loss-of-profits insurance See **consequential loss insurance**.

loss-of-rent insurance See **rent-loss insurance**.

loss of the bargain See **damages**.

loss-payable clause or **loss payable clause** A clause in an insurance policy that sets out the order in which payments are to be made in the event of a loss. The loss-payable clause may well provide that, in the event of a payment for property damage, the proceeds will be paid to the mortgagee, or beneficiary under a deed of trust, or any other party who is specified as having a valuable interest in the property, to the extent of their interest in the property, and before any payment is made to the owner of the property. Under such a provision the mortgagee is considered merely as the party appointed to receive money in the event of a loss, but if the mortgagor is unable to recover under the policy (as in the event of his act of arson), the mortgagee has no entitlement to payment either. Sometimes called a 'mortgage loss-payable clause', 'simple loss-payable clause' or an 'open-mortgage clause'. cf. **union mortgage clause**. See also **insurable interest, mortgagee clause**.

loss payee The party named in an **insurance policy** as the beneficiary in the event of a payment under the policy. See also **mortgagee clause**.

loss rent An amount by which the market rental value of a property exceeds the contractual rent due from the tenant. See also **negative leasehold, reverse premium**.

lost grant See **lost modern grant**.

lost modern grant   A common law doctrine that may be applied when establishing a right to an **easement** or **profit à prendre** by **prescription**. Under the doctrine of lost modern grant, it is assumed that when a right has been enjoyed for an extensive period of time, then that right must have been granted at some point, and thus the existing state of affairs can be explained only by the loss of the records of the grant.

The doctrine was introduced as a fiction to circumvent a situation that arose when a right to land had been established by common law prescription, based on the rule that it had been enjoyed for as long as anyone could remember, i.e. since the start of 'legal memory' (originally taken to be 1189 – the start of the reign of King Richard I), but the person who had been deprived of that right was able to demonstrate that the user must have commenced at some time after 1189 (for example, because a building that benefited from the easement or profit à prendre must have been erected after 1189) and, therefore, was able to defeat the claimant's right. The doctrine seeks to demonstrate that, nonetheless, the extensive period of user is sufficient to support the view that the right must have been granted, but only the evidence of the original grant is missing. A claim to a 'lost modern grant' is available only when common law prescription cannot be applied and it must be based on stronger evidence than common law prescription. It is rebutted if it can be shown that the right is of a type that is not capable of being acquired by **grant**; that the user has not been enjoying it 'as of right' (i.e. because it was taken by force, secretly, or without permission); or that at some stage during the period of enjoyment the right could not have existed, as when the person who would have made the grant was not at that time capable of making it. In essence, such a right can only be claimed (a) if a right over land has been enjoyed as of right, and without interruption, for an extensive period (usually more than 20 years); (b) during the period of user there was someone capable of making the grant; (c) it is reasonable to assume that a deed of grant was made after 1189 (a 'modern grant') but it must subsequently have been lost (an assumption that is not rebutted by circumstantial evidence to the contrary); and (d) as a result, the user can be shown to have a lawful right to continue to enjoy the easement or profit (*Dalton v Angus* (1881) 6 App Cas 740, 773 (HL)). A prescriptive right cannot arise by 'lost modern grant' if it is a right that is in contravention of a statute.

In the US, the 'fiction of the lost grant' has been rejected in most jurisdictions and the acquisition of rights over land is dictated by the Statute of Limitations. However, the same principle exists in the doctrine of 'presumption of grant' that may be applied in establishing the right to land after an extended period of time. In those jurisdictions that accept such a doctrine, the required 'memory' is generally no more than 30 years, and may be as short as 20 years.

lot   **1.** A small area of land, especially one of several parcels into which a larger area of land has been subdivided. A defined or measured parcel of land with fixed or determinable boundaries. A tract of land indicated on a plan or map of an area set aside for future development. Although generally a 'lot' is a relatively small area of land, especially an area allocated to a particular use or held in a single ownership, it may be used to refer to any area of land.

In the US, a 'city lot' generally means any plot of land within the city limits, especially a parcel that forms part of an area that has been formally laid out for development or an area of undeveloped land that is bounded by other properties. Also, when used without qualification, a 'lot' is part of a '**Township**'; especially a defined subsection of a **section of land** or a part of a block, that has been measured and given an allocated number on a formal survey and plat, e.g. Lot 1, Block 2. See also **allotment**, **lot and block system**, **parcel of land**, **parceling**, **plat**, **plottage**. **2.** (Aus)An individual **unit** of property as held under **strata ownership**. Also called a 'flat unit' or a 'home unit'. A lot corresponds to the privately held 'unit' in a **condominium**.   **3.** That which fortuitously determines what we are to acquire.

lot and block system(US)   A system of land identification used in towns laid out on a grid system. Under this system each street block, and each lot within that block, is allocated a number – thus Lot 7, Block 10, identifies a specific parcel of land. The system may be used for land recording and land transfer. cf. **metes and bounds system**. See also **plot map**.

lot coverage   See **building coverage**.

lot entitlement(Aus)   The extent of the rights held by an individual owner of land in a subdivision. The lot entitlement includes the ownership of the lot and is stated as a number on a plan of the subdivision. The lot entitlement also entails a 'lot liability', which is the owner's proportion of the responsibility for the general expenses of the body corporate that holds the common areas (Subdivision Act 1988, s. 3(1) (VIC)).

lot line(US)   A line used to mark the boundary of a tract of land, especially to set the limit of contiguous land. See also **boundary line**.

lot number   A number given to a particular parcel of land to identify it as part of a survey. See **lot**, **lot and block system**(US).

love and affection   See **consideration**.

low-cost housing   Housing provided to people of limited income or whose income is considered in need of supplementation by the state.

low rent(Eng)   In the case of a **long residential tenancy**, a "low rent" is, in simplified terms, a yearly **rent** that (a) if the lease was granted or contracted for before April 1, 1990 is not more than two-thirds of the **rateable value** of the premises; or (b) if granted on or after April 1, 1990, is not more than £1,000 in Greater London, or not more than £250 elsewhere (RA 1977, s. 5; HA 1988, Sch. 1, para. 3A; Rating (Housing) Regulations 1990). This rent is assessed by leaving out of account any payments for maintenance, repairs, insurance, rates and services; although the rent can take the form of a payment in the form of services. A long tenancy of a dwelling-house at a low rent (which includes no rent) is not capable of being a **protected tenancy** or an **assured tenancy**; but it is given similar security of tenure when it comes to a contractual end, but under different statutory provisions.

In the case of a right to **leasehold enfranchisement**, the definition of a low rent is broadly the same, except that if the lease started before April 1, 1963, the rent must not be more than two-thirds of the "letting value" on the date of the commencement of the lease (Leasehold Reform Act 1967, s. 4(1); Leasehold Reform, Housing and Urban Development Act 1993, s. 8). In the case of a progressive or graded rent, as a rule the question of whether there is a low rent is determined by reference to the highest rent payable under the lease (*Woozley v Woodall Smith* [1950] 1 KB 325).

low-rent tenancy(Eng)   See **low rent**.

low-rise building   A building of four stories or less, i.e. one generally not requiring an elevator. cf. **high-rise building**.

low-start mortgage   See **deferred-payment mortgage**, **variable-rate mortgage**, **variable-payment mortgage**.

lower owner(US)   A **riparian owner** whose land is down stream of another landowner.

lucrative title(US)   See **community property**.

lump-sum adjustment   A single sum added to, or deducted from, the value of a property to make it a suitable **comparable** for assessing the value of another property. See also **quantity allowance**.

lump-sum contract   1. A form of **building contract** in which the contractor submits a single (all-inclusive) price for building works. Normally this form of contract is entered into only after competitive prices have been obtained by tender; or, at least, when the employer has been able to satisfy himself that the sum is reasonable and that the work can be properly completed by the contractor at that price. Under a lump-sum contract, the contractor is not obliged to disclose the actual costs incurred. On the other hand, he accepts the risk of material and labour cost increases.

In common law, failure to complete a lump-sum contract usually prevents the contractors from recovering the agreed price, or any part thereof, unless the contractor can show that there has been **substantial performance** of the work required under the contract (*Cutter v Powell* (1795) 6 Term Rep 320, 101 Eng Rep 573; Dermott v. Jones, 23 Howard 220, 64 US 220, 16 L Ed 442 (1859)). However, this rule must be treated with caution where the employer has benefited by the work done by the contractor, especially when the employer may be partially culpable for the non-performance of the entirety. Also called a 'stipulated-sum contract'. See also **entire contract**, *quantum meruit*, **substantial performance**. **2.** A contract that provides for the consideration to be paid in one sum (usually on completion) rather than by instalments. cf. **instalment contract**.

lump-sum-plus-fixed-fee contract A **lump-sum contract** that provides for the payment of a fixed fee on completion of the work, in addition to the agreed lump sum price. Usually used to refer to a contract where the method used to arrive at the total contract price is based upon the cost of labour and materials, plus an agreed percentage for overhead and profit. See also **cost-plus contract**.

M

made land   Land that is reclaimed from the sea or a lake by filling or tipping, especially when the land is an extension from the shore. See also **polder**.

made-up land   Land that is brought up to the level of the surrounding area by artificial means. In particular, an area of land the level of which is raised by tipping waste material. See also **land reclamation**.

magnet store   See **anchor store**.

mail   See **acceptance, offer, service**.

main contractor   See **general contractor**.

main residence   See **domicile, home, principal private residence**(Eng), **principal residence**(US).

maintenance   The act or process of keeping or preserving something in an existing state or condition. In particular, keeping a property in good working order. Maintenance is a continuous process that may involve **repair**, but requires a greater degree of attention to the general upkeep of the property than repair. Maintenance is primarily protective, whereas repair is restorative. Maintenance of a building requires actions that will, at least, prevent a decline from the existing condition and generally requires an element of anticipation. Maintenance is not intended to extend the useful life, or improve the efficiency, of a building; that would constitute an **improvement**. It does not include significant works of rebuilding; nor does it include making material alterations; but it may include repair works that result in an element of improvement. In a lease 'to maintain' the premises primarily means to keep in the same condition as when the lease was granted (normally excluding deterioration due to normal **wear and tear**). See also **deferred maintenance, keep in repair, preventative maintenance**.

maintenance bond   A **bond**, or contract of insurance, which provides an **indemnity** against poor or defective workmanship in a building.

maintenance expense   Any cost or expense incurred on the **maintenance** of a building. See also **operating expense**(US), **service charge**(Eng).

maintenance fee(US)   A charge payable by a property owner for the cost or expense of maintaining that property. In particular, a charge levied against the owner of a condominium property for the upkeep of the property. See also **management fee**.

maintenance period   See **defects liability period**.

maisonette   1. A self-contained dwelling, normally on two floor levels, forming part of a house or apartment building. See also **duplex, flat**. 2. A small **house**. A dwelling unit in a two-storey house that has the appearance of a single house, but is divided internally into independent dwellings or apartments with separate means of access at ground floor level. Each of the floors may be referred to as a 'maisonette'.

major retail center (MRC)(US)   A concentration of retail stores, in an urban or suburban location, that draws custom not only from the immediate neighborhood, but also from an area that extends well beyond. The stores may be located in a planned **shopping center**, or in a main street or neighborhood development. The United States Bureau of Census (1966, pt. V) uses the term 'major retail center' to refer to a major commercial center or grouping of retail stores, provided it does not form part of the **central business district**.

major tenant   See **anchor tenant, key tenant, prime tenant**.

make good To **repair** so as to make as good as new, or the best approximation thereto. In particular, to restore a damaged property to the condition it was in before damage was occasioned, not merely to pay compensation or to provide something similar. See also **restore**.

mala fide(Lat) 'In **bad faith**'. The adverb or adjective is *mala fide* and the noun is *mala fides*. cf. ***bona fide***. See also **misrepresentation**.

mall 1. A covered or shaded area set aside for pedestrian use. A term commonly used to refer to a public walkway in a shopping center, i.e. a 'shopping mall' that is enclosed and is generally air-conditioned. 2.(US)A large or regional **shopping center**.

man-land ratio(US) See **population density**.

management agreement A contract between an owner of property and a **managing agent** which sets out the duties to be performed by the agent, the terms and conditions of appointment, arrangements for the payment of expenses, accounting and reporting requirements, as well as the agent's remuneration. See also **power of attorney**.

management contract A term that is used to cover a wide variety of construction contracts. In particular, it refers to a contract whereby a **general contractor** is selected with whom the employer negotiates at an early stage of the planned work and one where the contractor is remunerated by a fee based on the cost of the construction price. See **construction management**.

management fee The **fee** charged by a **managing agent** for his services. Usually a fee based on a percentage of the total income collected by the managing agent from the property under his management. In the US, sometimes called a 'maintenance fee'. See also **management agreement**.

management scheme(Eng) A scheme by which a single landlord of a large leasehold estate of dwelling houses was able to restrict the tenant's statutory right of **leasehold enfranchisement** under the provisions of the Leasehold Reform Act 1967. If the landlord had a 'management scheme' approved within two years of the 1967 Act, he was exempt from its provisions (Leasehold Reform Act 1967, s. 19). This exemption was permitted where it was considered that "in order to maintain adequate standards of appearance and amenity and regulate development" it was "in the general interest that the landlord should retain power of management in respect of the houses". Generally, schemes were approved only for landlords of large well-established housing estates, e.g. estates owned by Housing Trusts, Housing Associations, New Town Corporations, or the Church Commissioners. A similar scheme may be approved under the provisions of the Leasehold Reform, Housing and Urban Development Act 1993, to enable a landlord to obtain an exemption from his tenants' rights to 'collective enfranchisement' under that Act (LRHUDA 1993, Ch. IV, Part I).

managing agent An **agent** appointed by an owner of real estate to control and direct the day-to-day running of a property. His duties include, *inter alia*, collecting rents, operating expenses and other charges due from the tenants; payment of outgoings and running expenses; keeping proper accounts for the properties under his control; supervising problems that arise between landlord and tenant; and arranging for routine property repairs and maintenance. A managing agent is vested with general powers; that is, he is to exercise his duties with judgement and discretion, using his own expertise and acting with limited direction from his principal on matters within the nature of his appointment. However, his duties remain those of an agent, not an **independent contractor**, and he must not decide on matters of policy without reference to his principal. See also **estate manager**, **management fee**, **property management**.

mandant(Lat)   See **mandator**.

mandatary   One to whom a **mandate**, command or charge is given.

mandate   **1.** Derived from the Latin *mandatum*, 'to enjoin' or 'to commit'. An **authority** given by one person (the mandator) to another (the mandatory) to act on the grantor's behalf. A contract by which authority is given to another to conduct business on the grantor's behalf. See also **power of attorney**.   **2.**(US)An order from a superior court to an inferior court directing that action be taken subsequent to an appeal. An order or decree given by a court or judicial officer (an 'order of mandate') that authorises the enforcement of a judgement or decree.   **3.**(Civ)Authority given to an agent, or employee, to perform specified duties on behalf of a principal, or employer.   **4.** A signed document used to grant a special authority to an agent, or employee, by a principal, or employer.   **5.** The gratuitous transfer of goods to another under a contract which provides that certain actions will be performed with the goods, i.e. a form of **bailment** without reward for the bailee. cf. **deposit**.

mandator   One who gives a **mandate** to another. Also called a 'mandant'.

mandatory   Obligatory. Required to be done or performed, especially something that needs to be done in an affirmatory manner. Compulsory, not a matter allowing for discretion or equivocation. See also **injunction**, **specific performance**.

mandatory injunction   See **injunction**.

manor   Derived from the Old French *manier* or *manoir*, 'dwelling' or 'habitation'. A large house or hall that forms part of an estate. In particular, a large estate that formed an economic unit of rural society in medieval England. After the Norman conquest, manors were established by those who owed direct fealty to the King (knights, the Church, etc.) and by the 11th century a manor was any unit owned by a lord, subject to an ultimate fealty to his Sovereign. Generally, a manor comprised a principal residence (manor house) and the surrounding land was retained by the lord of the manor for his personal use and the use of his household and his servants – the 'demesne land' or 'inland'. In addition, some of the land around the manor may have been held by free tenants as 'socage' or 'knight service', i.e. subject to the rendering of fixed or predetermined services to the lord of the manor. Beyond was 'tenemental land' or 'outland', occupied by those who were termed 'villeins' because they rendered various services, variable at the will of the lord, in return for their continued right (termed 'villeinage') to hold or 'tenant' the land. The remainder of the land was **waste land** (woods and scrubland), which was normally the greater part of the manor and generally could be used as common pasture.

The manorial system was a fulcrum for a steady evolution of land tenure from one based on labour service, or serfdom, with a dependency that denied any true right to private property, to a modern system of ownership, whereby land can be held freely (whether in perpetuity, as with a fee simple absolute, or for a more limited duration, as with a periodic tenancy). During the period for which the land was held, the holder's right could not be impeded by a superior lord (whether the Crown or a private landlord) without due process of law.

A Lordship of the Manor can still exist, being a right between the Crown and the freeholder. Such a right entitles the owner to be called 'Lord of the Manor' and to retain the manorial records that may date back to before the Norman Conquest (1066). See also **enclosure, feudal system, incidents of tenure**.

Barnsley, A. W., and C. *Manorial Law*. London: A.W. & C. Barnsley Legal Research and Publishing, 1996.

Jessell, Christopher. *The Law of the Manor*. Chichester: Barry Rose Publishers, 1998.

manor house   See **manor**.

manufactured housing(US)   See **mobile home**.

manse   **1.** The residence of a clergyman, especially

one that is assigned to and occupied by a Presbyterian clergyman. **2.** A large imposing residence. **3.**(Eng)A hide (120 acres) of land, being a measurement used in particular in the Doomsday Book.

mansion house **1.** A large dwelling-house, especially one that forms part of an estate. Generally, the term 'mansion house' includes not only the dwelling-house, but also the buildings within its **curtilage**. In the US, the term 'mansion house' is sometimes used interchangeably with 'dwelling house' and 'homestead', especially in connection with a surviving spouses statutory right of **dower** or **curtesy**. See also **messuage**. **2.**(Eng)An important residence on a **manor**; the chief residence of the lord of the manor being the 'principal mansion house'. In the case of a settlement of land, the main house, if any, and the land occupied therewith (provided it is not a farmhouse nor a house with 25 acres or less of accompanying land) is deemed to be the 'principal mansion house' or 'capital messuage'. If a **tenant for life** wishes to dispose of a 'principal mansion house' he must obtain the consent of the trustees of the settlement or an order of the court, if (i) the settlement was made before 1926, unless there is a provision expressly dispensing with this requirement, or (ii) the settlement is made after 1925, and there is an express provision requiring such consent or order to be obtained (SLA 1925, s. 65). See also **settled land**.

manus mortua(Lat) 'A dead hand'. See **mortmain**.

Maori customary land(NZ) Se **native title**.

Maori freehold land(NZ) Se **native title**.

map A graphic representation, or a picture, usually on a flat surface, of certain features of a given area of land, prepared in order to show their relative positions; especially a representation that shows lines of communication (roads, watercourses, railroads, bridges, etc.), administrative boundaries, cities, towns, landmarks, mountains, lakes, key locations, etc. A map shows, usually to scale, such details of an area as have been established by a survey. The survey may have been made in one of a number of different ways, the details of which are transposed onto the map. For example, the map may show the relief or the topography of the land; the economic or demographic conditions of the area; or such details as boundaries, monuments, buildings or lines of communication. See also **plan**, **plat map**(US), **surveying**.

march (pl. **marches**) A property limit or **boundary line**. Territory of official jurisdiction; 'to march' with another country or state means to have a common border, as Scotland borders England or Canada the United States. In Scotland, boundaries or 'marches' were originally set out with March stones, especially in order to 'mark' the limits of an estate.

margin **1.** A sum of money that exceeds what is absolutely necessary. An amount by which the **market value** of an asset, offered as security or collateral for a loan, exceeds the amount of the loan. This excess is the borrower's **equity capital** and represents the lender's margin of safety. If the value of an asset falls below the amount of the loan, the margin is said to 'run-off'. The amount of margin required by a lender depends on: (i) the credit rating of the borrower; (ii) the type and liquidity of the **collateral**; and (iii) the degree of risk in realizing the market value of the asset. See also **debt-equity ratio**, **gearing**, **mortgage value**. **2.** An area of land left undeveloped between a property boundary and a new building. A zone *non aedificandi* or 'set-back' area. See also **building line**. **3.** The outside edge of an area of land, especially the edge of a body of water. Strictly, the center of a stream or river is the 'margin' or boundary between two areas of land that border a watercourse. However, 'margin' may refer also to the outside edge of an area of land that fronts a body of water, especially a lake or pond. See also *ad medium filum aquæ*. **4.** The spread between the base interest rate (such as a major bank's Prime Rate or inter-bank rate) on which a loan is made and the rate charged to the borrower. The amount added to the interest rate charged on a loan to represent the lender's profit, i.e. the difference between the lender's cost of funds and the rate charged to borrowers. **5.** The gross profit from a transaction. In particular, an amount below which a business or enterprise becomes unprofitable. **6.** A sum of money, or other property, deposited with a stockbroker to provide security against trading losses incurred on behalf of his principal. The down payment required prior to obtaining a loan to acquire stocks or shares. **7.** A loan made by a stockbroker or commodity broker to enable a customer to acquire securities or commodities for a higher amount than the capital available to the customer, with the securities or the commodities being held as security for the loan. **8.** A payment on account of a purchase. In particular, in futures trading, the amount that a buyer or a seller is required to deposit to ensure a commitment to take delivery during the designated period of time for the contract. This amount is normally set by a futures exchange. **9.** An obsolete term for a **boundary line**.

marginal efficiency of capital   The increased return that may be obtained by investing one unit of capital; the return engendered by a marginal increase in investment. The marginal efficiency of capital reflects the propensity to invest. Thus, if the discounted income generated by an investment is greater than its cost, the investment will be profitable and, other things being equal, it is worth undertaking. See also **internal rate of return**.

marginal income   **1.** Income received, or capable of being received, from an investment above a given base level. For example, the amount by which the market rent of a property exceeds the amount payable contractually by an existing tenant. See also **hardcore method**(Eng), **top-slice income**.   **2.** An income that is just sufficient to cover the cost of maintaining an investment.

marginal land   Land that, at any point in time, (given a particular level of supply and demand) is just worth cultivating. Land that yields an income marginally higher than the cost of producing that income. Land that is not worth exploiting or bringing into production. See also **economic rent**.

marginal method(Eng)   See **hardcore method**.

marginal note   A heading or brief description set out in the margin of a statute or legal document. Such a note is not intended to form any part of the document and does not have any legal effect. A marginal note is intended for guidance or reference and is applied to the main text only in cases of complete ambiguity or contradiction.

maritagium(Eng)   A **portion** given to a daughter at her marriage. A gift of land made to a woman and the heirs of her body. See also **entailed estate**.

marital property(US)   Property held by a husband and wife during marriage. In 'common law states', matrimonial property, or 'marital property', may be held as a **joint tenancy**, a **tenancy in common**, or (in a few states) as a **tenancy by the entirety**. In a few 'common law' jurisdictions, **dower** and **curtesy** are still recognized. In 'civil law states' (which means states that at one time were under civil law jurisdiction), and a few other states that have adopted the same system, marital property is held as **community property**. In most jurisdictions, matrimonial property (whether held as a common law tenancy in common or the civil law community property) cannot be disposed of without the written consent of both parties. In the case of co-habitees, none of the marital property rights apply, although co-habitees may own property in any form of co-ownership. Also, one of the co-habitees may be able to establish a right to property in the form of a **resulting trust** or **constructive trust**. cf. **separate property**. See also **homestead**, **matrimonial home**(Eng).

mark   See **signature**, **witness**.

marked corners(US)   See **marked lines**.

marked line(US)   A line between monuments or 'marked or established corners' as used in a description of the boundaries of real estate, as distinguished from a line that designates the courses and distances between adjoining boundaries or a line based on a surveyor's field notes. Marked lines are considered more certain of ascertainment on the ground than lines based on other data.

market 1. A public place where people meet, at an appointed time, in order to conduct business either in one or a variety of goods. "A market is a place to which sellers who have not found buyers take their goods in the hope of finding buyers, and to which buyers resort in the hope of finding the goods they want", *Scottish CWS Ltd v Ulster Farmers' Mart Co Ltd* [1959] 2 All ER 486, 495 (HL). Any **retail store**, **shop** or **shopping center** may constitute a market. However, in common usage, a market refers to a public area or square where a number of stalls are set up, normally on certain days of the week by public licence, for the sale by the stallholders of goods or provisions, at the most competitive price. It may also be a place in a town where particular goods are brought for sale, especially for sale to trade buyers, such as a 'cattle market', 'cotton market', 'farmer's market', 'furniture market' or a 'computer market'. 2. A public place where buyers and sellers are permitted to gather without let or hindrance to trade in goods. 3. Any aggregation of potential buyers and sellers, or any network that brings together potential buyers and sellers, so that a **price** is established at which goods or commodities are traded. In this sense, a market does not require a fixed place. When buyers and sellers come together, or are brought together (for example, by a **broker**), with the intention of making a bargain so that the ownership of goods may be transferred at a price fixed by consensus, there is a market.

A 'perfect' market may be said to exist when complete information is available regarding the properties offered for sale in a particular market; when buyers have no special preference between those properties; when sellers are quite indifferent to whom they sell; and both buyers and sellers have full knowledge of prices and availability of properties in other parts of the market. Most markets are considered to be 'imperfect' because, for the same goods, transactions take place in diverse places; restraint may be placed on certain buyers or sellers; and the goods may not be readily divisible, so that a unit price cannot be created. The market for land is highly imperfect. It is distorted by the heterogeneous nature of land; the imbalance of knowledge and negotiating skills of buyers and sellers; the lack of reliable or detailed information on real estate transactions; the illiquidity of land as an asset; and the differences in extraneous factors that affect buyers and sellers of real estate, e.g. taxation, government rent controls, availability of finance. The free exchange and availability of information in a perfect market makes the price of goods – the **market price** – readily ascertainable; the more imperfect the market the more unpredictable and speculative the price. See also **market value**.

market analysis An assessment of level of supply and demand for a particular property or type of property in a given market area, including a study of the factors that may impact the level of supply and demand for such property. A market analysis may include an assessment of the quantity and quality of competing property and planned additions to the existing stock, determination of current rent levels and rental trends and other factors that may affect the market such as demographics, employment trends, household income and expenditure and an assessment of the preferences for different types of property. "A study of the real estate market conditions for a specified type of property", Appraisal Standards Board, *Uniform Standards for Professional Appraisal Practice (USPAP)*. Washington, DC: The Appraisal Foundation, 2004 edn. See also **feasibility analysis**, **market survey**.
Schmitz, Adrienne, and Deborah L. Brett. *Real Estate Market Analysis*. Washington, DC: Urban Land Institute, 2001.

market approach to value(US) See **sales comparison approach**.

market area See **catchment area**.

market comparison approach(US) See **sales comparison approach**.

market-data approach(US) See **sales comparison approach**.

market garden(Eng) An area of land, together with buildings thereon (greenhouses, potting sheds, etc.), used as a **garden** or nursery for the growing, cultivation and production of fruit, hops, seeds and vegetables, on a modest scale, for the purpose of trade or business. A market garden may be a domestic garden or it may be larger than a domestic garden, but it is more intensively cultivated, and is operated on a smaller scale, than an **agricultural holding** or **farm**. See also **allotment**, **compensation for improvements**.

market method See **comparison method of valuation**.

market overt or **market ouvert**(Eng) A public and open **market**. A market that is authorised and regulated by law, so that anyone who buys goods, according to the usage of the market, acquires a good title to the goods, provided he buys them in good faith and without notice of any defect or want of title on the part of the seller (Sale of Goods Act 1979, s. 22). A market overt can only be held at particular times and places as fixed by law.

market price The **price**, or consideration, actually paid in a particular **market**. The price that is paid in an open, unrestricted and free market. Market price is sometimes used synonymously with **market value**, although the market price is the sum actually paid (or as set by the seller) and market value the real or estimated worth, the price at which, in a given market, it is considered that supply and demand are equal and goods will readily change hands for money. In economics, the cost of producing a commodity is referred to as the 'cost price' or 'natural price' and "the actual price at which any commodity is commonly sold is called its market price. It may be above, or below, or exactly the same with its natural price", Adam Smith, *Wealth of Nations* (1776), Book One, Ch. VII.

market rent or **market rental** 1. The market value for renting purposes. The **best rent** at which a property might reasonably be expected to let with vacant possession in the open market when offered by a willing lessor to a willing lessee, after allowing for a reasonable period for marketing, taking full account of the lease terms that are imposed on the use and enjoyment of the demised property, and assuming that there is no premium or fine payable by the lessee. The market rent is generally the value of the premises on the above basis, excluding any special incentives or concessions offered to prospective tenants. Also called the 'market rental value' or 'open market rent'. Such expressions as 'current market rent', 'fair and reasonable market rent' and 'best rent' convey the same meaning and only serve to emphasise that the rent should not be constrained by special factors, or to confuse. See also **economic rent, equivalent rent**(Eng), **fair rent**(Eng), **open market rental value**(Eng), **rack rent**.
Royal Institution of Chartered Surveyors. *Appraisal & Valuation Standards*. 5th ed. London: RICS Books, 2003, PS 3.4.
2.(Eng)See **agricultural tenancy, assured tenancy, business tenancy**.

market survey A survey of an area to ascertain the demand and competition for a property and to determine the general market conditions as they may affect that property. cf. **feasibility analysis**. See also **market analysis**.

market value (MV) The most probable price that a specified property might reasonably be expected to realise if sold in the normal course of business for cash, after allowing a reasonable time for exposure to potential buyers and assuming the seller is willing to sell without any element of compulsion. The amount that a property might be expected to realise, usually expressed in money terms, when it is offered for sale in an open market, for a reasonable period of time, by a **willing seller**, in order to enable the property to be brought to the attention of all or most potential and willing buyers and when the transaction is not affected by any special circumstances that might affect the buyer, the seller or the property.

"The most probable price which a property should bring in a competitive and open market under all conditions requisite to a fair sale, the buyer and seller each acting prudently and knowledgeably, and assuming the price is not affected by undue stimulus. Implicit in this definition is the consummation of a sale as of a specified date and the passing of title from seller to buyer under conditions whereby: 1. Buyer and seller are typically motivated; 2. Both parties are well informed or well advised, and acting in what they consider their best interests; 3. A reasonable time is allowed for exposure to the market; 4. Payment is made in terms of cash in U.S. dollars or in terms of financial arrangements comparable thereto; and 5. The price represents the normal consideration for the property sold unaffected by special or creative financing or sales concessions granted by anyone associated with the sale", Appraisal Standards Board, *Uniform Standards for Professional Appraisal Practice (USPAP)*. Washington, DC: The Appraisal Foundation, 2004 edn. as applicable to federally-related transactions (which is "any **real estate-related financial transaction** which—(A) a federal institutions regulatory agency or the Resolution Trust Corporation engages in, or contracts for, or regulates; and (B) requires the services of an appraiser"). The Uniform Standards of Professional Appraisal Practice points out that persons performing appraisal services that may be subject to litigation are cautioned to seek the exact legal definition of market value in the jurisdiction in which the services are being performed.

"The estimated amount for which an asset should exchange on the date of valuation between a **willing buyer** and a willing seller in an **arm's-length transaction** after proper marketing, wherein the parties had each acted knowledgeably, prudently and without compulsion. ... *Market Value* is understood as the value of an asset estimated without regard to costs of sale or purchase, and without offset of any associated taxes", The Royal Institution of Chartered Surveyors, *Appraisal & Valuation Standards*. 5th ed. London: RICS Books,

2003, PS 3.2., 3.3.2. This definition is settled by the International Valuation Standards Committee (IVSC), Toronto, Canada. A detailed Commentary on the definition is set out in the *Appraisal & Valuation Standards*. When applying this definition the valuer may also be required to add a statement of what is being valued and any assumptions that are inherent in the valuation.

The Australian Property Institute and the Property Council of Australia have also adopted this definition (*Glossary of Property Terms*, 2000). A similar definition has been adopted by the Basel Committee on Banking Supervision in the *Criteria in defining commercial real estate lending: Supplement to the New Basle Capital Accord* (Jan 2001).

'Market value' is the amount that a property might be expected to bring, as distinguished from **market price**, which is the amount for which a property is sold at a given date; although the terms are sometimes used interchangeably. Market value is established by reference to the transactions in the normal and regular course of business; it is based on evidence from private treaty sales of similar properties. It is an estimate of worth based on certain implicit assumptions, namely: (i) neither the buyer nor the seller is under any undue influence or duress to consummate the bargain and both are motivated to conclude a transaction; (ii) a reasonable time is allowed to negotiate a bargain, given the type of property and the state of the market; (iii) the bargain is concluded subsequent to an arm's-length negotiation; (iv) both parties are well informed or well advised as to the terms of the transaction and are acting in their own best interest; (v) the sale is concluded as a simple cash (or equivalent) transaction; (vi) no account is to be taken of any special circumstances, such as special or creative financing, any concession or 'kick back', or an additional bid from any **special purchaser**.

In English statute law, market value is defined as "the price which [an asset] might reasonably be expected to fetch on a sale in the open market". No reduction being made for the fact that the whole of the asset (to which a gain under the Act may be charged) are being placed on the market at the same time (Taxation of Chargeable Gains Act 1992, s. 272-274; Finance Act 2003, s. 118). See also **actual cash value, fair market value, highest and best use, open market value**(BrE), **value**.

market value approach(US)   See **sales comparison approach**.

marketability study   See **feasibility analysis**.

marketable record title(US)   A right to land that has been established by an unbroken **chain of title**, without defects thereon, and therefore, by virtue of a state statute, is free of all defects that predate the statutory time period required to prove the validity or 'marketability' of such a title. In some states, 'marketable record title' statutes, or Marketable Title Acts, have been enacted to provide a limit as to the period of time after which a right or claim can be made against land. In most states, this time period is 30 years. The purpose of such statutes is to limit the need for lengthy title searches for every new transaction and to simplify the enforceability and recording of encumbrances. See also **marketable title**.

marketable title   1.(US)A **title** that is free from reasonable doubt as to its validity and that an intelligent and prudent person, competently advised, should accept without requiring any reduction from the fair market value. A title that is sufficiently free from defect that a reasonable informed person would acquire it, or accept it as security for a mortgage or lien, without fear of litigation or a decrease in market value. In particular, a title that would be supported in equity if the vendor seeks a decree of **specific performance** requiring the purchaser to accept it. Marketable title may be used to refer to a title that is not free of any suspicion, but is good enough to be accepted without detriment as to the value of the property being acquired. In the context of title insurance, the use of the word 'marketable' refers to legal issues that may impair the owner's right to use or transfer the property and not purely to economic value; although the possibility of obtaining title insurance does not of itself make for a marketable title, as the premium for such insurance may be too high for a reasonable purchaser. cf. **unmarketable title**. See also **cloud on title, free and clear title, good title, good and merchantable title, marketable record title, perfect title, warranty deed.   2.**(Eng)See **good title**.

marriage value (MV)(Eng)   An increase in value, or a release of latent value, brought about either by the merging of two interests in the same property or the merging of two adjoining or contiguous properties into common ownership. The most common instances of marriage value arise when a property is let at less than its market rental value and the respective interest of the landlord and tenant are merged, or when a site that may be undevelopable in its own right is added to a larger developable site.

For the purposes of a right of 'collective' **leasehold enfranchisement** under the Leasehold Reform, Housing and Urban Development Act 1993, the participating tenants must pay the aggregate of the value of the landlord's existing interest in the property being acquired and at least 50% of the 'marriage value'. This marriage value is defined as the difference between the total value of the participating tenants' interest after enfranchisement, and the sum of (i) the freeholders' interest subject to the existing leases, and (ii) the value of the tenant's interests prior to enfranchisement (ignoring the right to enfranchisement) (LRHUDA 1993, Sch. 6, as amended). See also **compulsory purchase compensation**(Eng), **extended lease, plottage value**(US).

marshalling   Arranging or disposing in order, especially of assets according to their **priority** for creditors. The equitable doctrine of marshalling permits a creditor, or mortgagee, to claim simultaneously against all properties held as security, provided that he does not unreasonably deprive any other party, who may have a claim against only one of the properties, of his right to security. The doctrine is intended to permit all creditors of a single debtor to be satisfied in the most equitable way possible. Thus, if A mortgages Stone

House and Timber Cottage to B (as a first charge) and subsequently mortgages Stone House (as a second charge) to C, then B must satisfy his charge from Timber Cottage first; only then, if his debt is still not satisfied can B claim against Stone House. After that, C has a right to claim against Stone House. In the US, sometimes called the 'two funds' doctrine. See also **inverse order of alienation**.

Martinmas   See **quarter day**.

Maryland ground lease(US)   See **ground rent lease**.

Massachusetts trust(US)   See **business trust**.

master deed(US)   **1.** The standard form of deed used for the sale of a **condominium**. This document is submitted along with the **condominium declaration** when a condominium building is submitted for recording with the state. In the case of a leasehold condominium, also called a 'master lease'.   **2.** See **declaration of restrictions**.

master lease(US)   **1.** A lease that controls any sublease or subleases that is granted in a property. In particular, a lease that is granted to a lessee who takes a lease of an entire project or building, but intends to sublease all or most of the space. See also **head lease**.   **2.** A lease that is in a standard form and is intended to act as a guide when granting new leases in a particular building or development scheme. See also **standard-form contract**.   **3.** See **master deed**.

master limited partnership (MLP)(US)   A legal entity that takes the form of an ordinary **limited partnership**, but the ownership interest is held as tradable securities. Unlike a conventional partnership, an MLP has a limited life and generally is created for a particular form of asset investment (especially for oil and gas exploration). MLPs may be structured to provide the investors with a tax-deferred income return. However, since the Tax Reform Act of 1986, such entities are normally taxed as regular corporations.

master mortgage(US)   A standard form of mortgage contract that is recorded at a public records office by a mortgagee and sets out the basic terms upon which a number of individual mortgages are to be granted. A master mortgage is recorded to save the expense of duplicating most of the mortgage terms every time a mortgage is granted on similar terms. When a new mortgage is granted, only the basic terms are recorded (term, property secured, interest rate, etc.) and the remaining conditions are indicated by reference to the recorded master mortgage. Nonetheless, the actual document executed by the mortgagor sets out all the mortgage terms. See also **standard-form contract**.

master plan   An overall plan, usually accompanied by a detailed written text, prepared as a guide to proposals for the future long-term growth and planning of an area. The plan sets out such matters as demographic growth projections, infrastructure proposals, community facilities, land use zoning, etc. More detailed plans are intended to be fitted into the framework set down in the master plan. Also called a 'general plan'. cf. **comprehensive plan**(US). See also **development plan**, **regional plan**.

master planned community (MPC)(US) See **planned unit development**.

master servicer   See **servicer**.

material breach   See **breach of contract**, **condition**.

material change in the use(Eng)   An activity that is considered to be a form of **development**, and therefore, to be subject to planning control (TCPA 1990, s. 55(1)). The term is not defined further in the TCPA 1990, although the change of a single dwelling-house to two or more separate dwellings, as well as an increase in the superficial area or height of a refuse or waste dump, is specified as a material change of use. A material change of use primarily covers a change in the character of land or a building; a substantial or considerable change of use; or a significant intensification of the use of land or a building (*Palser v Grinling* [1948] AC 291 (HL)). Whether an intensification of use is a 'material change' is a matter of fact and degree that is ultimately a matter for the Secretary of State to decide on appeal. "A change of *kind* will always be material – e.g. from house to shop or from shop to factory. A change in the *degree* of an existing use may be 'material', but only if it is very marked. For example, the fact that lodgers are taken privately in a family dwelling-house would not in the Minister's [now the Secretary of State's] view constitute a material change of use in itself so long as the use of the house remains substantially that of a private residence. On the other hand, the change from a private residence with lodgers to a declared guest house, boarding house or private hotel would be 'material'", *Ministry of Town and Country Planning Circular No. 67* (1949). This circular does not have force of law, and is of no further effect, but it reflects the original intention when this phrase was first inserted in the TCPA 1947. The effect of a change of use on the general planning requirements of an area may be relevant when determining whether a change is material, as this may increase the burden on the services that a local authority has to supply. An intensification of an existing use is unlikely to be material unless there is a change that is substantial (especially when it significantly affects the appearance of the property or increases such matters as traffic generation); but a change in the *nature* of the use as from a dwelling to a shop is material. In particular, the change in the 'planning unit' (an area considered as a whole for planning purposes) must be looked at, i.e. it is necessary to consider the entirety; not just a part of the whole, or a part of a building within the unit. A mere cessation of user *per se* cannot be construed as a material change (that would mean that a landowner would require planning permission to cease an activity); but if one of a number of uses of a parcel of land ceases and a remaining use is intensified there may well be a 'material change of use'. See also **permitted development**, **Use Classes Order**.

material considerations(Eng) See **planning application**.

material detriment See **injurious affection**, **severance**.

materialman(US) A supplier of goods or materials under a building contract. In particular, someone who has supplied material that has been used in the construction, improvement or repair of a building and may thereby be entitled to the benefit of a **mechanic's lien**.

matrimonial home(Eng) Property owned and lived in by the parties to a contract of matrimony. A place where a man and woman have established a **home** together as husband and wife. In modern English law, husband and wife, like any individuals, have separate rights to any property held in their sole name. On the other hand, the matrimonial home may be held in accordance with an express agreement for the benefit of both parties as a **joint tenancy** or, more usually, as a **tenancy in common**. When the property is held in the sole name of one party, then the other party may still have an equitable interest in the home: in the words of Lord Denning, M.R. "it is entirely appropriate to describe [husband and wife] as equitable tenants in common of the land – that is of the land [and buildings] itself – until sale: and then after sale, in the proceeds of sale", *Williams & Glyn's Bank Ltd v Boland* [1979] Ch 312, 331, [1979] 2 All ER 697, 703 (CA). The entitlement of each party to the proceeds of sale depends upon (a) their respective contributions to the cost of acquiring the property, whether as a direct payment of the initial price, a contribution to repayment of a mortgage, or in exceptional cases, by indirect contributions (*Gissing v Gissing* [1971] AC 886 (HL); *Lloyds Bank plc v Rosset* [1991] 1 AC 107, [1990] 1 All ER 1111 (HL)); and (b) any contribution in money or money's worth to the improvement of the property, provided that the contribution is of a "substantial nature" and provided there is no agreement to the contrary, express or implied (Matrimonial Proceedings and Property Act 1970, s. 37). In the case of (a), a **resulting trust**, or sometimes a **constructive trust**, is said to arise, with the husband and wife (as with unmarried couples) as beneficiaries according to the amount of their respective contributions; in the case of (b), statute imposes a trust to the same effect, but only for married couples. See also **co-ownership, marital property**(US)**, overriding interest**.

Duckworth, Peter. *Matrimonial Property and Finance.* 5th ed. London: Pearson, 1996.

maturity date   The date on which an obligation, such as a bill of exchange, bond, mortgage, etc., becomes due to be paid in full. See also **law day, redemption date, yield to maturity**.

McCarthy rules(Eng)   See **compensation for injurious affection**.

meadow land   Land that is used as meadow, i.e. land upon which grass is grown for hay or pasture. A meadow may also be "an upland area covered with grass and herbs and commonly surrounded by woodland", *Webster's Third New International Dictionary*®, *Unabridged*, ©1993. In the North America, 'meadow land' may be used also to refer to a swampy or marshy area, or to a flat area of land near a river, but above the high water mark, as distinguished from the **bottom land** that lies along the river and is regularly flooded by the river waters. See also **agricultural land, grazing licence**(Eng).

meander line(US)   A line established by a land survey to represent the edge of a waterway or the border of the sea or lake. A meander line does not always correspond with the shoreline or water's edge, it is commonly measured to the top of any bank along a waterway and is intended to show the contour of the land around the water's edge.

However, a meander line is an irregular line that courses the banks of navigable streams or other navigable waters. A meander line is set primarily as a means of ascertaining an area of land that is to be sold (especially public lands) and not to determine the boundary line for title purposes. The actual boundary is the "water line" which is the high water mark of the **foreshore**, or the center point of a river or steam. See also *ad medium filum aquæ*.

means of access   See **access, easement of necessity**.

measured contract   A form of contract where the cost is based on the measured value of the work performed. Such contracts may take a variety of forms, but are essentially applied when the extent of the work cannot readily be ascertained at the outset. For example, the contract price may be: (a) left entirely open and be determined based on actual costs incurred, plus an agreed fee for profit and overhead; (b) based on a schedule of rates, all or some of which are agreed at the outset; or (c) partly agreed, with a provision for determining variations or cost incurred for unforeseen work. See also **cost-plus contract**.

measurement and value contract   See **fixed-price contract**.

measurement contract   See **fixed-price contract**.

mechanical core   See **service core**.

mechanic's lien   A statutory **lien** placed on land or a building erected thereon (including anything permanently attached to the building) to secure a debt that has arisen as a result of work carried out by a contractor who has provided labor or materials used in construction work to land or buildings. A mechanic's lien is found in the civil law and is recognised in French law, but it is not recognised as such in the common law (the nearest common law equivalent is the 'equitable lien'). A mechanic's lien arises entirely from the provisions of the applicable statute and is recognised in all jurisdictions in the US (except Louisiana) and all provinces in Canada (except Quebec). Such a lien arises by statute to secure priority for the payment of work carried out by the contractor and not as a result of any express term of the contract.

A mechanic's lien covers value added to the building, but does not cover such items as overheads or offsite equipment, and does not normally cover items that have not been installed on the site. The right to levy a mechanic's lien arises as a result of state statutes and is intended to provide a greater protection to the debtor, than a common-law lien. The means for levying of a mechanic's lien varies considerably from state to state.

A contractor, subcontractor, a supplier of materials ('materialman') or a laborer may obtain a mechanic's lien. If such a supplier is not paid when due, a mechanic or materialman can obtain a lien on the land or building upon which the work has been carried out, subject to complying with the requisite statutory formalities. A mechanic's or materialman's lien may take priority over most other mortgages, except one recorded before any work commenced. Prior to being able to assert a right to a mechanic's lien, the contractor must be able to demonstrate that there has been **substantial performance** of the work for which the payment is being claimed and frequently this requires the production of the architect's certificate that the work has been carried out in accordance with the contract. Also, the claimant must notify the owner of the property (and in some jurisdictions fellow mechanics or materialmen) or file notice of his claim at the appropriate public office (or in some jurisdictions all of the former), within a specified time after completing the work, or supplying the labor or materials. The specified time varies from thirty days to six months, depending on the jurisdiction and the type of contractor or supplier. Sometimes called a 'contractor's lien'. See also **architect's certificate, foreclosure**.

mediation   A voluntary and informal process by which two or more parties to a dispute appoint an independent third party to assist them in reaching a negotiated settlement of their differences. The process is normally non-binding and does not affect any rights that the parties may have to an alternative form of dispute resolution in the event that a satisfactory settlement is not reached as a result of the mediation. cf. **adjudication, arbitration**. See also **without prejudice**.

medium filum(Lat)   'The middle thread or line'. See *ad medium filum*.

medium filum aquæ(Lat)   'The middle thread or line of the water or stream'. See *ad medium filum aquæ*.

meeting of the minds   See **agreement**.

megalopolis   Derived from the Greek *megalo*, 'great', and *polis*, 'city'. A very expansive city; a densely populated area that is larger than a conurbation, usually comprising more than one city; or a city and a major urban area around that city. 'Megalopolis' was used by Epaminondas of Thebes in 371 BC to describe the joining together of many small cities into a large city for administrative purposes and also by Jean-Iona Gottman in 'Megalopolis: the Urbanized Seaboard of the United States' (1961) to describe the multitude of cities on the east coast of the US. cf. **metropolis**.

meliorating waste   See **waste**.

melioration(US)   See **compensation for improvements**.

memorandum   Derived from the Latin *memorare*, 'to bring to mind' or 'to remember'. A written summary or brief note of the terms of an agreement. In order to satisfy the requirements of the **Statute of Frauds**, a 'memorandum' need not be in any particular form nor contain every term, provided it contains the essential elements that would support a valid contract. Specifically: the parties, an adequate description of the property, the consideration, the date and details of any other matter that may be material to, or form a condition of, the contract that the memorandum is intended to support. The memorandum may be contained in a letter, bill of sale, minutes of a meeting, telegram, fax, etc., and may even be contained in more than one document. See also **agreement for a lease**, **binder**, **endorsement**, **joinder**, **part performance**, **rider**, **subject to contract**, **writing**.

memorandum of insurance   See **binder**, **cover note**.

memorial   1. See **monument**.   2.(NZ) See **Land Transfer land**.

merchandise   Any item that a merchant normally buys or sells, whether by wholesale or retail. **Goods** or chattels that are normally bought and sold, but generally not real property. **Personal property** that is the subject matter of trade.

merchantable title(US)   See **good and merchantable title**, **marketable title**.

merchants' association   An association of tenants and merchants in a **shopping center**, organized to advertise, promote and improve the attraction and management of the center. "[A] not-for-profit corporation organized to conduct merchandizing programs, community events, shopping center decoration programs, advertising programs and publicity programs, and to coordinate joint member cooperative advertising and marketing functions, events, and endeavors for the general benefit of the shopping center. The association acts as a clearing house for suggestions, ideas, and programming of merchandising events, and it serves as a quasi-court for handling complaints and differences of opinion", International Council of Shopping Centers, *Fundamentals of Shopping Center Marketing*, 1983. Also called a 'tenants' association'.

mercantile agent   See **commission merchant**, **factor**.

mere equity(Eng)   A right that may be enforced between two parties in equity, and concerns land, but does not create any interest in land. A 'mere equity' defies precise definition, but includes such rights as **specific performance**; **rectification** or **rescission** of a contract; or an **injunction**. Thus, it should be distinguished from an **equitable interest**, which is an interest in land that can be enforced as such, but only in equity. See also **estoppel**.

mere licence   See **licence**.

merger   1. The absorption of one estate in land by another. The combining of two or more interests in the same property into the hands of the same person, at the same time, with there being no intermediate estate, so as to extinguish all but the larger interest. A situation that most commonly arises when a landlord acquires the interest of his direct tenant, the tenant's interest then being extinguished by operation of law. Also, if the same person acquires a legal and an equitable interest in the same land with the clear intention that the interests should merge, the equitable interest will lose all effect. For two estates to merge they must be held by one and the same person, at one and the same time, and in one and the same right. Thus, a merger cannot take place if there is an intermediate estate, for example, if there is a mortgage on a leasehold interest; nor if the lease and the reversion are held in different capacities, as by a trustee and a beneficiary respectively; nor if one estate is acquired by purchase and the other by right of a spouse.   2. The absorption of a less formal agreement or bargain by a more formal arrangement or document. For example, a merger takes place between a contract for the sale of land and a deed of **conveyance** so that the latter extinguishes the former. As a rule, the contract is extinguished to the extent that the conveyance is intended to cover the same ground. However, the contract may remain as a **collateral** agreement to the conveyance if it covers a separate matter, or if there is a clear warranty that is intended to survive the closing. cf. **surrender**. See also **merger clause**, **satisfied term**, **termination**, **unity of possession**. **3.** The combination of two or more parcels of land into a single ownership, or common use and control. See also **assemblage**.

merger clause(US)   A clause in a written agreement which specifies that the writing shall constitute the entirety of a contract and that there is no **warranty**, representation or agreement that can have any effect on the agreement, other than that which is expressed in the written agreement. Sometimes called an 'integration clause'. See also **express term**, **merger**.

meridian   One of a series of imaginary lines that run north and south on the surface of the earth and is numbered according to the degrees of latitude.

In the US, the **government survey system** is based on 'principal meridian lines' of which there are 36 marked out across the United States at 24 mile intervals. Base lines running east and west, also at 24-mile intervals, form squares called 'quadrangles'. The principal meridians are subdivided at six-mile intervals to form the east-west boundaries of 36 square mile blocks or 'townships'.

mesne   Intermediate. That part in between a beginning and end in time. Occurring between two dates. See also **intermediate lease**, **mesne assignment**, **mesne profits**.

mesne assignment   **1.** An assignment of a lease that takes place between the time of the grant of the original lease and a more recent assignment. For example, if A grants a lease to B, B assigns to C, and C assigns to D, then the assignment by B is a mesne assignment in that it arises between the original grant and assignment to the current lessee D. A conveyance that makes such a transfer is called a 'mesne conveyance'.   **2.** The creation, or assignment, of an **intermediate lease**.

mesne charge or **mesne encumbrance**   A charge, or encumbrance, that is situated in time or **priority** ahead of one charge, or encumbrance, but behind another. See also **redeem up foreclose down**.

mesne conveyance   An intermediate conveyance. Any **conveyance** in the chain of title between the first and last conveyance of the property. See also **mesne assignment**.

mesne encumbrance   See **mesne charge**.

mesne mortgage   See **mesne charge**.

mesne profit   Profit arising during an intervening period. 'Mesne profits' are represented by the value of use and occupation of land during the time it is held by someone who has wrongfully retained possession. For example, profits lost as a result of being wrongfully dispossessed from land; or profits obtained when a party has wrongfully retained possession, as by a trespasser or a tenant who retains a property, or 'holds over', after the termination of his lease. A claim for mesne profits can be joined with an action for the recovery of the land, i.e. it is a form of damages for **trespass**, damages that arise from the relationship of landlord and tenant. The claim is brought to remedy a tort and not for a breach of contract (as any contract has been satisfied) and is joined with an action for **ejectment** (or, as it is called in English law, **recovery**).

In English law, the right to mesne profits between a landlord and tenant is derived from the Common Law Procedure Act 1852, s. 214. A payment of mesne profits is a form of damages and is based on the equivalent of "fair value of the premises" for the period of wrongful occupation. In the case of a tenant who retains possession after the end of his lease, the amount is usually based on the former rent, but it may be higher (or lower) if justifiable.

In the US, an action for mesne profits must be joined with an action for ejectment of the wrongful possessor. Although a common law remedy, in

some states the entitlement to mesne profits is regulated by statute. The measure of the amount of mesne profits is generally based on the rental value of the demised property. See also **compensation for improvements, forfeiture, mistake, mistaken improver, penalty rent**[US], **tenancy at sufferance, use and occupation**.
Pawlowski, Mark. '*Claim for Mesne Profits–A Restitutionary Remedy?*' [1994] Lit. vol. 13/7, 278-287.

mesne tenancy   See **intermediate lease**.

messuage   A **house** together with any outbuildings, yard, garden, field or orchard, used therewith. In particular, a dwelling-house, together with the **curtilage** and land and building **appurtenant** thereto. A property that is lived in, together with the premises used at the same time and as an essential part of the occupancy.

metayage system   A form of land **tenure** by which a landowner permitted his land to be occupied and cultivated in exchange for a share (usually one half) of the produce of the soil. The farmer had no right to the land itself, but only to the produce. See also **sharecropping lease**.

mete   1. To distribute by subdivision; to assign by measurement.   2. A **boundary** or meeting point of boundary lines. See also **metes and bounds system**.

metes and bounds system   A method of describing a plot of land by specifying the dimensions of its boundaries (its *metes* or measurements) and identifying the limits of those boundaries (*bounds*). "*Metes* means to measure or to assign measurement, and *bounds* means the boundaries of the land and extent of the property", Walter G. Robillard et al., *Brown's Boundary Control and Legal Principles*. 4th ed. New York: Wiley, 1993, p. 48. 'Metes' are the lineal measurement of the boundary and 'bounds' the points used to reference those boundaries or changes of direction. Bounds are referenced by points of the compass or angular references. A description of a parcel of land under this system starts at one point (the 'tie' or 'point of beginning') and sets out the boundary lines and their changes in direction, sometimes by reference to landmarks, until the description returns to, or 'closes' at, the starting point. For example, starting at point A (as described); thence N 42° W for 300 yards; thence S 10° E for 600 yards to a (specified monument); and so on, until returning to the tie point. Also called the 'butts and bounds system' (*butts* being the 'corners' or 'ends') or sometimes the 'lines and corners system'. cf. **lot and block system**. See also **monument**.

methods of depreciation   See **depreciation**.

methods of valuation   See **valuation**.

metropolis   Derived from the Greek *metropolites*, 'mother city'. The chief town or city of a country. A capital or major city. In Great Britain, the London area is sometimes referred to as 'the metropolis', as is New York in North America. See also **metropolitan area**.

metropolitan area (MA)   The area of a city and the dependent area around it. A densely populated area around a dominant commercial center, in particular the area from which the **central business district** draws its primary business and trade. "A large population nucleus, together with adjacent communities having a high degree of social and economic integration with that core", U.S. Census Bureau. A 'metropolitan area' may take in any immediately dependent urban area, but generally it does not extent to the entirety of a **conurbation**. A metropolitan area may also be defined on the basis of a political or administrative area.

The US Census Bureau defines metropolitan areas as Metropolitan Statistical Areas (MSAs) (originally called 'standard metropolitan statistical areas' (SMSAs)) that are relatively freestanding metropolitan areas, and may be measured on the basis of: (i) a county or group of contiguous counties with a population of 50,000 or more; or

(ii) an urbanized area (one with a population density of 1,000 per square mile) with a population of at least 50,000, together with a dependant area of at least 100,000 inhabitants (in New England SMSAs are made up of towns or cities, not counties, and the dependent area is included if it has a population of at least 75,000). A metropolitan area that has more that one million persons and consists of a large urbanized county, or a cluster of counties that have very strong internal economic and social links, may be referred to as a 'primary metropolitan statistical area' (PMSA). Two or more dependent PMSAs may be referred to as a 'consolidated metropolitan statistical area'. For example, Cincinnati-Hamilton; New York-Northern New Jersey-Long Island; San Francisco-Oakland-San Jose; and Chicago-Lake County.

In the UK, the 'Metropolitan Area' is the whole of Greater London, in contradistinction to the City of London. See also **metropolis**.

mews(Eng) Historically, a cobbled alleyway or yard, originally leading to stables or accommodation for carriages, commonly with workers' residences above. In modern parlance, a mews retains the same sort of street scene, but is more likely to be converted to a predominately residential use with small town houses and professional offices, or an area of garages, storage units and workshops.

mezzanine   Derived from the Italian *mezzanino*, 'middle'. A storey inserted between two others. A storey between two principal stories of a building, usually immediately above ground level. A floor level inserted within an established envelope in order to provide additional floor space, but one that usually covers a smaller area than the floors above and below and has a reduced floor to ceiling height.

mezzanine finance   A loan that ranks after senior debt, but before equity capital. Normally mezzanine finance is unsecured, carries a risk that is similar to equity, and earns interest at a rate that is several percentage points above the secured debt, but still ranks for payment of interest before any dividends are paid to owners of the equity capital. Mezzanine finance may also take the form of a convertible loan or may carry the right to 'equity kicker', i.e. a loan with a right to a share of the profits.

Michaelmas   See **quarter day**.

middleman   A person who introduces deals, but takes no part in the consummation of the transaction. A person who is employed solely to introduce new listings or to seek out prospective purchasers for another agent or **broker** to negotiate with, or merely seeks to bring two parties together but leaves them to negotiate between themselves. A middleman is employed merely to bring the parties together but does not act as the **agent** of either party, whereas a broker is an agent of one of the parties. Thus, a middleman does not have the strict **fiduciary** liability to the parties to a transaction that are accorded to an agent. Colloquially called a 'bird dog', especially when one who merely points out a prospective purchaser. See also **dual agency**.

Midsummer day   **quarter day**.

military clause(US)   A provision in a lease granted to a member of the military that permits the tenant to terminate the lease in the event of his or her discharge, transfer, or any other military circumstances that require a change of permanent residence by the tenant.

mill   1. A mechanical apparatus that is used to grind corn, grain, flour or anything similar. Also, a building in which machinery is installed for the same purpose. A building in which machinery is installed in order to carry out a particular form of manufacture, especially one where material is pressed, ground, cut, woven or spun. The word mill primarily means a machine, particularly one designed for grinding. It is also commonly used to refer to a building or collection of buildings with machinery where a process of manufacturing is carried on. Traditionally, a mill was an establishment that required a significant supply of water to provide the power to drive the machinery or for use in the processing.

The use of the word 'mill' in a conveyance of real property transfers all rights or easements that are **appurtenant** thereto, such as a head of water or mill pond, as well as flood gates and the like that are in existence at the time of the conveyance and are necessary to the proper use of the facility, unless such appurtenances are expressly excluded (*Liford's Case* (1614) 11 Co Rep 46b, 77 Eng Rep 1206, 1215).

In the US, a mill may be used to refer to an area of land that is acquired from the public domain; is close to a **mining claim**; is not part of the mineral bearing land; is used for processing the ore, or other processes associated with the mine; but is not held by the owner of the mining land and does not exceed five acres in extent (30 USC § 32). See also **appurtenance**, **factory**, **fixture**. **2.** One tenth of one per cent; one part per thousand. In the US, a mill is commonly used to compute real estate taxes, e.g. tax is levied at the rate of $x mill of tax per $1,000 of assessed value.

mine An underground working made, as a pit or other form of excavation with shafts, tunnels, etc., for the purpose of extracting ore, precious stones, or any other **mineral**. In its primary signification, a mine is an underground operation, although generally it is taken to include structures, machinery, minerals, etc., placed on the surface and associated with the mine. A mine is an excavation in the earth from which ores, coal, or other mineral substances are removed by digging or other mining methods, and in its broader sense 'mine' may be used to denote the stratum, vein, seam, lode, or deposit of minerals, as well as the space left when the mine has been worked. The essence of what constitutes a mine is the mode in which the extraction is made, and not the geological or chemical nature of the extracted material. Thus, neither an oil nor a gas well is a mine.

In English statute law, "mines and minerals" are defined to include "any strata or seam of minerals or substances in or under any land, and powers of working and getting any such minerals or substances", LRA 2002, s. 132(1). cf. **quarry**. See also **mining lease**, **mining operations**(Eng), **right of support**, **waste**.

mineral(s) A naturally occurring inorganic substance, normally in solid crystalline form, which may be a single element, but is usually a compound or co-mixture of compounds. Any substance that is obtained by mining, especially the ore of a metal. Whether a particular substance is a mineral depends on the context in which the term is used and may depend on a local custom adopted, as in a particular industry or trade. 'Mineral' is "[a] widely used general term referring to the nonliving constituents of the earth's crust that includes naturally occurring elements, compounds and mixtures that have a definite range of chemical composition and properties. Usually inorganic, but sometimes including fossil fuels (e.g. coal), minerals are the raw materials for a wide variety of elements (chiefly metal) and chemical compounds. Minerals can be and many are synthesized to achieve purity greater than that found in natural products", Richard J. Lewis, *Hawley's Condensed Chemical Dictionary*. 13th ed. rev. New York & Chichester: Wiley, 1997. In real property law, 'minerals' generally includes coal, oil, gas, diamonds and most other natural carbon derivatives, unless expressly excluded. In its ordinary and common meaning mineral may be used to include every description of stone and rock deposit, whether containing metallic or non-metallic substances. However, in many cases sand, gravel, sandstone, brick-earth, clay soil and the like have been held not to be classified as 'minerals', and a reservation out of a grant of land of 'minerals' generally refers to a substance of special value and not the soil itself. Also, minerals may be interpreted to include only substances that naturally occur in a solid state; or, in the strictly scientific sense, so as to excluded organic compounds. On the other hand, slat water may be considered as a mineral, especially as it is a source of other minerals, such as bromine.

In English law, in a conveyance when minerals

were made a **reservation** from the grant of land, 'minerals' have been held to mean "everything except the mere surface, which is used for agricultural purposes; anything beyond that which is useful for any purpose whatever, whether it is gravel, marble, fireclay, or the like comes within the word 'mineral' when there is a reservation of the mines and minerals from a grant of land; every species of stone, whether marble, limestone, or ironstone, comes, in my [Lord Romilly M.R.] opinion, within the same category", *Midland Railway Co v Checkley* (1867) LR 4 Eq 19, 25.

In English planning law, 'minerals' includes "all substances of a kind ordinarily worked for removal by underground or surface working, except that it does not include peat cut for purposes other than sale", TCPA 1990, s. 336(1). Minerals are broadly defined in respect of **settled land** as "All substances in, on or under the land, obtainable by underground or surface working", SLA 1925, s 117(1)(xiv). See also **mine, mineral rights, oil and gas lease**(US).

mineral lands(US)   Land that contains known deposits of a valuable or precious **mineral** or minerals and where the expense of extraction would be justified. In this context, mineral is used in a broad context so as to cover marble, slate, petroleum products as well as more conventional ores or precious metals (Northern Pac. Rly. Co. v. Soderberg, 188 US 526, 23 S Ct 365, 47 L Ed 575, 584 (1902)).

mineral lease   See **mining lease, oil and gas lease**(US).

mineral rights   The right to extract any **mineral** found under the surface of **land**. Normally these are owned and conveyed with land, unless specifically excluded, or reserved by law. cf. **surface right**. See also **mineral lands, mining lease, oil and gas lease**(US), **profit à prendre**.

mineral royalty   See **royalty**.

minimum price   1. See **reserve price/ reserved price, upset price**(US).   2. See **asking price**.

minimum rent   See **base rent, dead rent**.

mining by outstroke   See **outstroke**.

mining claim   An identified parcel of land, containing precious metal in its soil or rock, to which a miner has title to the soil (St. Louis Smelting & Refining Co. v. Kemp, 104 US 636, 26 L Ed 875, 879 (1882); 30 USC § 23). Once a mining claim has been made its boundaries are marked out – the **location** established; the process that gives public notice of the claim. Once the claim has been 'located', it must normally be worked within a statutorily specified period of time or it is lost. "The interest in a mining claim, prior to the payment of any money for the granting of a **patent** for the land, is nothing more than a right to the exclusive possession of land based upon condition subsequent, a failure to fulfill which forfeits the locator's interest in the claim", Black v. Elkhorn Min. Co., 163 US 445, 16 S Ct 1101, 41 L Ed 221, 223 (1896).

mining lease   An agreement by which a lessor grants or permits another a right to explore for, extract and remove minerals from a designated area of land (which may include any form of mineral and coal, but strictly not oil or gas). The right granted might be a true **lease**, or a mere **licence**. The right may also be granted as a **profit à prendre**, to which may be annexed an **easement** for access. However, if there is a grant of an exclusive right of occupation of a defined area or strata of land for a period of time at a fixed charge, the right will be construed as a lease; especially if words of **demise** are used, or there is a reservation of rent. A mining lease differs from an ordinary lease in that it grants the lessee a right to extract and retain material taken from the land together with a limited right of access, usually until the **mine** is exhausted. Generally, the landowner receives a fixed sum, or **dead rent**, from the licensee or tenant, together with a **royalty** based on the quantity of mineral extracted. A mining lease may be granted for a specified or determinable period of time; or sometimes it may be limited until the mine is exhausted, i.e. until the purpose for which the lease was granted is 'satisfied'.

In the US, also called a 'mineral lease', especially when it takes the form of an agreement permitting the exploration of land for minerals, and then, if minerals are discovered, it grants the right to take the minerals, either for a definite term or as long as they can be produced in paying quantities with a reserved royalty.

In English statute law, a mining lease is defined as "a lease for mining purposes, that is, the searching for, winning, working, getting, making merchantable, carrying away, or disposing of mines or minerals, or purposes connected therewith, and includes a grant or licence for mining purposes", LPA 1925, s. 205(1)(xiv). In connection with a tenant's statutory right to compensation for improvements, a 'mining lease' (which is expressly excluded from provisions of the L&T Act 1927, s. 17(1)) means "a lease for any mining purposes or purposes connected therewith", and 'mining purposes' include "the sinking and searching for, winning, working, getting, making merchantable, smelting or otherwise converting or working for the purposes of any manufacture, carrying away, and disposing of mines or minerals, in or under land, and the erection of buildings, and the execution of engineering and other works suitable for those purposes", L&T Act 1927, s. 25(1). In the case of the rights of a **tenant for life** of settled land a mining lease is similarly defined in the Settled Land Act 1925, but expressly includes "a grant or licence for any mining purposes", SLA 1925, s. 117(1)(xv). See also **instroke, mineral, oil and gas lease, outstroke, satisfied term.**

mining license   A **license** granted to extract coal or minerals from land without granting any estate or interest in the land. cf. **mining lease.**

mining operations(Eng)   Work in connection with the operation of a **mine.** In English town planning law, 'mining operations', which are included with the definition of the term **'development'** (and therefore requires planning permission), include "(a) the removal of materials of any description—(i) from mineral-working deposits; (ii) from deposits of pulverised fuel ash or other furnace ash or clinker; or (iii) from a deposit of iron, steel or other metallic slag; and b) the extraction of minerals from a disused railway embankment", TCPA 1990, s. 55(4). In connection with 'permitted development' under a **General Development Order**, mining operations "means the winning and working of minerals, in on or under land, whether by surface or underground working", Town and Country Planning (General Permitted Development) Order 1995, art. 1(1) ('Development Ancillary to Mining Operations' is defined in the Town and Country Planning (General Permitted Development) Order 1995, Part 19). See also **mineral.**

mining rent   Rent payable under a **mining lease.** Rent, or a payment in the nature of rent including a **rentcharge, royalty** or licence fee paid for a right to extract and remove material from a mine.

mini-permanent loan (miniperm or mini-perm)   A loan granted for a medium term (3 to 7 years) but on the basis that it will be amortised over a long term (25 to 30 years). See also **balloon loan.**

mini-warehouse(US)   A warehouse building, usually on one level, that is subdivided into small compartments for storage purposes. Also called a 'mini-storage facility'. See also **nursery unit.**

minor interest(Eng)   An interest in registered land that prior to October 13 2002 was required to be registered for its protection. Minor interest did not include: (a) the registered title *per se* (a registered freehold or registered leasehold title); (b) an **overriding interest**; and (c) any interest entered on the register prior to 1926 and still subsisting (LRA 1925, s. 3(xv)). Unless a minor interest is entered on the register of the land, a **purchaser** who pays 'valuable **consideration**' for a **legal estate** takes that estate free of the interest. Minor interests are a residual group of rights over registered land that are neither created nor transferred by registered dispositions; and are unlikely to be discovered (at least in theory) by a thorough examination of the land itself, or by reasonable enquiry or by searches of the local land charges register. A minor interest is considered, therefore, to require protection by registration – actual **notice** of their existence being irrelevant. Minor interests include such rights as restrictive covenants, rentcharges, short leases, and rights of a spouse in possession. With effect from October 13 2003, many of the interests in land that would have been minor interests (in particular, most lease with over 7 years to run, easements and profits à prendre) are required to be registered, and a land owner is required to disclose to the Land Registry details of such interest of which he or she has knowledge (Land Registration Act 2002). Thus, minor interests are effectively abolished. See also **caution**, **notice**, **restriction**.

minor tenancy[Eng]   A tenancy for a term of one year or less. In connection with the service of notice effecting a **general vesting declaration**, a 'minor tenancy' means "a tenancy for a year or from year to year or any lesser interest", Compulsory Purchase (Vesting Declarations) Act 1981, s. 2(1). See also **short-term tenancy**.

misdescription   A description of property that does not give a clear and precise statement of fact and, therefore, does not represent the truth. 'Misdescription' has no particular legal meaning and in that respect may be considered as synonymous with **misrepresentation**. However, the term 'misdescription' may be applied to a statement that comes to form part of a contract, rather than a statement that induces someone to enter into a contract. In particular, 'misdescription' may be used to refer to an error in an agent's **particulars of sale** (a broker's **property brief**[US]) that is not intended to form an inherent part of a contract of sale, but if it induces someone to enter into a contract, will amount to a 'misrepresentation'. A misdescription may make a contract void if it amounts to **fraud** or if it produces a substantially different contract to that which would have been intended by the parties had a true description been made. Non-disclosure of facts, known to a vendor or his agent, may in certain circumstances constitute an implied misdescription.

A misdescription in a deed does not invalidate the document if it is clear from the rest of the text what is intended. The maxim of law is *falsa demonstratio non nocet cum de corpore constat*, 'a false description does not vitiate a document when the thing is described with certainty'.

In the US, the term 'misdescription' is generally only used in a legal sense to refer to an erroneous description of the subject-matter of a deed, and then it usually falls within the ambit of a **mistake**, or it is used synonymously with misrepresentation.

In English law, it is a criminal offence to make a "false or misleading statement" about property matters in the course of estate agency business or property development business, unless the person making the statement can show that he took all reasonable steps and exercised all due diligence to avoid the offence (Property Misdescription Act 1991, ss. 1, 2). cf. **puffing**. See also *caveat emptor*, **cy-près doctrine**, **deceit**, **exclusion clause**, **good faith**, **latent defect**, **professional negligence**, **voidable contract**.

Murdoch, John. *The Estate Agents and Property Misdescriptions Acts*. 3rd ed. London: Estates Gazette, 1993.

Rowell, Roland. *Regulating the Sale of Property*. Birmingham: CLT Professional Publishing, 1993.

mismatching   The use of short-term finance for a long-term investment, most notably the use of an overdraft or demand loan for the purchase of a real property investment. Also, the use of a loan in one currency to finance an investment acquired with another currency.

misrepresentation   A presentation of false or misleading information, especially when made recklessly or with intention to deceive. A false or misleading statement made by one party to a contract (or his agent) which, although not forming part of the contract, induces another to enter into the contract upon terms or conditions that are different from those actually in existence. "In my [Denning L.J.] opinion any behaviour, by words or conduct, is sufficient to be a misrepresentation if it is such as to mislead the other party. If it conveys a false impression, that is enough", *Curtis v Chemical Cleaning and Dyeing Co Ltd* [1951] 1 KB 805, [1951] 1 All ER 631 (CA). A misrepresentation must relate to matters of fact and not law, intention or opinion; thus using such statements as 'desirable location', 'excellent view', is not a representation of fact but only the salesperson's opinion – usually referred to as **puffing**. In general, if the person making a representation knows, or ought to know, that the statement is false and likely to mislead there is a misrepresentation. Misrepresentation must induce someone to enter into a contract to constitute an actionable wrong. A statement does not constitute misrepresentation if the person accepting it is aware that it is untrue; does not take any account of it when deciding to enter into a contract; or clearly uses his own judgement or expertise when assessing the representation (*Attwood v Small* (1838) 6 Cl & F 232, 7 Eng Rep 684 (HL); 37 C.J.S., Fraud, § 34, 37). Furthermore, no one can plead misrepresentation if he never hears the claims being made. On the other hand, a person who makes a false representation cannot claim that he thought the other party would know better. "No one is entitled to make a statement which on the face of it conveys a false impression and then excuse himself on the ground that the person to whom he made it had available the means of correction", *Nocton v Lord Ashburton* [1914] AC 932, 962 (HL) (17 C.J.S., Contracts, § 163 n. 15).

At common law, in order that a party to a contract may claim misrepresentation and rescind the contract or claim damages, the representation should be fraudulent, i.e. there must be an intention to deceive. If the person making the representation believed the statement to be true, he may be culpable of 'innocent misrepresentation' but, as a rule, the contract remains binding. However, "if a man, who has or professes to have special knowledge or skill, makes a representation by virtue thereof to another – be it advice, information or opinion – with the intention of inducing him to enter into a contract with him, he is under a duty to use reasonable care to see that the representation is correct, and that the advice, information or opinion is reliable. If he negligently gives unsound advice or misleading information or expresses an erroneous opinion, and thereby induces the other side to enter into a contract with him, he is liable in damages", *Esso Petroleum Co Ltd v Mardon* [1976] QB 801, 820, [1976] 2 All ER 5, 16 (CA). Further, under English statute law, a person may still be liable for damages "notwithstanding that the representation was not made fraudulently, unless he proves that he had reasonable ground to believe, and did believe, up to the time the contract was made that the facts represented were true", Misrepresentation Act 1967, s. 2(1)). The latter provision does not apply to an **auctioneer** who is liable only for common law 'fraudulent misrepresentation'; although an auctioneer may be liable for **negligence**, if his representation is clearly of that nature.

Silence or non-disclosure may constitute misrepresentation when it might reasonably be expected that a party to a contract would make a declaration on a substantive matter affecting the contract. In particular, when silence distorts a positive representation; when there is a **fiduciary** relationship between the parties; when the silence arises from a professional person with specialist knowledge who might reasonably be expected to draw an innocent party's attention to a known defect; or when there is a contract (such as an insurance contract) entered into *uberrima fides*, in 'utmost good faith'.

In the US, the common law distinction between innocent misrepresentation and fraudulent or 'known' misrepresentation is no longer considered of particular significance. If damage is suffered and there was a factual misrepresentation the loser has a prima facie right to recompense, either to damages or a right to rescind the contract. As in modern English law, a party who has the greater knowledge or experience has the higher duty to take care in his or her representations. Thus, a vendor of land is presumed to know the extent and boundaries of his own land, and if the purchaser suffers damage by reason of such representations, he has good cause of action against the vendor. This latter principle is increasingly being extended to real estate brokers, especially in home sales, where the purchaser is inexperienced and relies on the representations of an experienced, knowledgeable and qualified broker. cf. **estoppel**. See also **misdescription, professional negligence, rescission, voidable contract, warranty**.

Rowell, Roland. *Regulating the Sale of Property*. Birmingham: CLT Professional Publishing, 1993.

Handley, The Hon. Mr. Justice K. R. *Spencer-Bower, Turner & Handley: Actionable Misrepresentation*. 4th ed. London: Butterworths, 1999.

missives of sale(Scot)   Letters that are exchanged between parties to an agreement for the sale of **heritable property**. Such letters contain the fundamental term of the agreement and generally confirm the position on such matters as servitudes, planning permission, confirmation that proper title will be provided on completion and the condition of the property.

Cusine, Douglas, and Robert Rennie. *Missives*. 2nd ed. London & Edinburgh: Butterworths, 1999.

mistake   Something that is taken amiss. An erroneous or misconceived notion of a fact at the time it is acted on. A belief that does not accord with the facts. "An unintentional act, or **omission**, or **error** arising from ignorance, surprise, imposition, or misplaced confidence. 1 Story Eq. Jur. (14 Ed.) § 155", Burgess v. Byrd, 69 SW.2d 529, 531 (Tex Civ App 1934). In relation to a contract, a mistake is generally considered to have arisen when there has been no *consensus ad idem* on an important aspect of the agreement, i.e. no precise 'meeting of the minds'; when there is a different perception of the existence, nature, identity of the subject matter; or even when there is

misunderstanding as to identity of the parties to the contract. In order to nullify a contract, a mistake must be of such a nature that it may be said that no contract would have resulted had the parties realised the true situation. It is not sufficient that the parties merely took a different view from each other as to the respective benefit or burden arising from the contract. A mistake operates so as "to negative or in some cases to nullify **consent**", *Bell v Lever Brothers, Limited* [1932] AC 161, 217 (HL).

When, as the result of a mistake, a contract is fundamentally different from that intended by the parties it is voidable at the instigation of the aggrieved party, i.e. the contract may be treated as if it had never come into existence. However, in law, mistake is narrowly defined and generally the courts will seek to enforce a contract, especially when the parties can achieve substantially what they contracted for, and award damages for any loss suffered by an aggrieved party. If there is a mutual or common mistake, but the parties act in such a way as to infer the existence of an agreement or licence, or one of the parties were to treat property as his own even though obtained as a result of a mistake, the parties are, by the doctrine of **estoppel**, unable to claim that there is no contract. A serious mistake, one that is so serious that it cannot be rectified, renders a contract **void**; but, if the mistake is insufficiently serious to render the contract void the contract may be voidable, for example, if there is a common or mutual mistake so that both parties are labouring under the same misconception. Thus, a mistake as to the actual property to be conveyed is likely to make a contract void (or 'voidable' at the election of the purchaser); whereas a mistake as to the area of land to be conveyed may be redressed by **rectification**, or **reformation** (as it is more generally referred to in the US).

A clear distinction should be drawn (although the distinction may be a fine one) between a mistake, **misrepresentation, misdescription**, misunderstanding (see *caveat emptor*), and ignorance of the law (*ignorantia juris neminem excusat* – 'ignorance of the law does not excuse'). Thus, if A sells a parcel of land to B, and a boundary dispute subsequently arises, this may be due to (i) a mistake, if a previous owner had moved the evidence of the true boundary, a fact of which A and B are both ignorant; (ii) a false representation or a misdescription (depending on whether it induces the contract or subsequently comes to form part of the contract) made by A to B that certain landmarks represented the boundary (possibly in order to increase the price) knowing that, on further investigation, this would prove false; (iii) a misunderstanding as to the true position of the boundary fence even though this may be clearly shown on the title deeds (although this may constitute a mutual mistake); or (iv) a purchaser may not have realised that an interest in the land was binding on him because it was recorded and, therefore, he is deemed to have **constructive notice** thereof. See also **rescission, voidable contract**.

mistaken improver A party who carries out improvements to another's property under the mistaken belief that he has a right or title to that property. For example, a person who builds on land that is believed to be included within the boundaries of land that has been acquired. In common law, based on the principle of **estoppel**, a land owner who acquiesces in the improvement of his land by another has an obligation to recognise the value of those improvements and to pay compensation before asserting his title to the land (*Ramsden v Dyson* (1866) LR 1 HL 129, 170 (HL); 31 C.J.S., Estoppel and Waiver, § 106).

In the US, most jurisdictions have enacted statutes (called 'good faith improver acts', 'occupying claimants' acts' or 'betterment acts') which provide that if a person has occupied land and carried out improvement in a good faith belief of a right to possession (usually under color of title), if that party is subsequently dispossessed, he is entitled to compensation for the improvement or to have the value of improvements offset against a claim by the landowner for mesne profits

In Canada, several provinces have statutes that provide for compensation to be payable to a person who has made a "lasting improvement" to another's land. See also **compensation for improvements, restitution, unjust enrichment**.

mitigation of damages or **mitigation of loss** A doctrine that requires an injured party to exercise reasonable diligence to minimise their **damages** after they have suffered injury, or to take reasonable steps to reduce a loss as a result of a **breach of contract**. A claimant for damages cannot seek redress for a loss that arises from their own inactivity or conduct, especially when that increases the loss. See **abandonment, compensation for disturbance**(Eng)**, contributory negligence, insurance, subrogation**.

mitigation work(Eng) Work carried out by a public authority to reduce or abate the **injurious affection** caused by its activities, e.g. insulation work carried out to a house adjoining a highway or an airport in order to reduce the effect of noise on the occupiers of the house. Various statutes impose a duty on or give power to authorities to carry out mitigation work to reduce the effect of their actions on adjoining landowners, especially subsequent to a compulsory acquisition of part of an owner's land (The Land Compensation Act 1973, Part II; Highways Act 1980, s. 282; Civil Aviation Act 1982, s. 79).

mixed action An action that involves both a real and a personal action. For example, an action to recover possession of real estate and for waste committed to the property. See also **action *in personam*, action *in rem***.

mixed estate(US) An estate in land that has the characteristics of being **personal property**, in the sense of a lease, and **real property**, in the sense of a right to the freehold. For example, a ground lease for 99 years, with continuous rights of renewal. Sometimes called 'mixed property'.

mixed fund A trust or company that invests in both real property and personal property. See also **hybrid real estate investment trust**.

mixed insurance policy An **insurance policy** that covers various groups or classes of property. For example, a policy that covers 'valued' and 'unvalued' risks. See also **unvalued policy**, **valued policy**.

mixed property A right to property that has a status compounded of real and personal property, e.g. a right to a lease of a building and a right to the plant and machinery in the building. See also **mixed estate**(US).

mixed tenancy(Eng) A **tenancy** of a property that is used for two or more purposes. For example, a shop with living accommodation in the same building and let to the same tenant. In English law, a determination as to which is the dominant user may have important ramifications when considering the statutory provisions that apply to the tenancy. If the property that is the subject of the tenancy comprises **business premises**, it may be governed by the Landlord and Tenant Acts; if it is essentially a **dwelling-house**, it may be governed by the Rents Acts, or if it is an **agricultural holding**, it may be governed by the Agricultural Holdings Acts. cf. **multiple tenancy**.

mixed-use development (MUD) A development that includes two or more different uses, such as offices and retail, or office, hotel and retail buildings.

Schwanke, Dean. *Mixed-Use Development Handbook*. 2nd ed. Washington, DC: Urban Land Institute, 2003.

mixed use property A single property that is used for two or more different purposes. Used especially in the context of a real property tax assessment or in a planning or zoning determination. See also **planning unit**(Eng), **use**.

mobile home A structure that is designed or adapted as a dwelling but is capable of being transported from one place to another; whether because it is mounted on its own wheels and can be towed, or it is capable of being mounted on a vehicle and transported from one location to another location. In many cases, mobile homes have all or most of the facilities of a regular **home**.

In the US, the Mobilehome Dealers Association defines a 'mobile home' as "a movable or portable dwelling built on a chassis, designed without a permanent foundation, suitable for connection to utilities, and intended for year-round living". In federal law relating to construction and safety standards, a 'mobile home' is called a 'manufactured home', a term that also covers structures of a specific size that are intended for use as a dwelling and that can be transported in one or more sections (National Manufactured Housing Construction and Safety Standards Act of 1974, 42 USC § 5401).

A mobile home (or anything similar), so long as it remains as such, i.e. 'mobile' or 'moveable', is not real property, but a **chattel**. However, it may become a **fixture** if it is so affixed to land that the intention is that it forms part of the land and the owner is not intending to move it elsewhere (George v. Commercial Credit Corp., 440 F.2d 551 (7th Cir. Wis 1971); cf. Sigrol Realty Corp. v. Valcich, 212 NYS.2d 224 (1961), aff'd 11 NY.2d 668, 180 NE.2d 904 (1962); *Elitestone Ltd v Morris* [1997] 2 All ER 513 (HL) drawing on cases from New York, Illinois and Queensland, cf. *Canadian Imperial Bank of Commerce v Nault* (1985) 66 AR 313 (Can)).

mock auction A sale by **auction** at which a genuine effort to sell a property at the highest price bid is thwarted or made a sham. For example, holding an auction of cheap goods and making the purchase of such items a condition of entry to bid for more expensive items, or inducing bids from parties who have been deliberately introduced to bid up the price, but have no intention of making the final bid. Any fraudulent or unreasonable act, e.g. the introduction of sham bidders, who pretend to be real bidders, used to prevent the proper price being realised at a sale by auction, may amount to a conspiracy or be against public policy and enable the sale to be set aside or will prevent its enforcement.

English statute law makes it an offence to

promote or conduct, or to assist in the conduct, of a mock auction for the sale of certain chattels. For this purpose, a mock auction takes place if: (a) goods are sold to the final bidder at less than the final bid, or a discount or credit on part of the purchase price is paid to the purchaser; (b) the right to bid at an auction is restricted to persons who previously have bought or agreed to buy one or more articles; or (c) articles are given away or offered as gifts at the auction (Mock Auctions Act 1961, s. 1(3)). See also **bidding agreement**, **puffer**.

mode or category of occupation(Eng) See *rebus sic stantibus*, **tone of the list**.

model home or **model house**(AmE) A dwelling-house, usually on an estate or complex of similar homes, that has been completed, is ready for occupation and made available to be inspected by persons who may be interested in acquiring a property of similar design and build. A new home that is a model for another which is to be built to a similar design and specification, but on a different site on a planned unit development or a different part of a condominium or apartment complex. See also **show house**.

modern grant See **lost modern grant**.

modern ground rent(Eng) **1.** The ground rent of a site, based on the current market rental value of that site, assuming that it is cleared of buildings and is to be let on a long-term ground lease (usually for 50 years or more). **2.** The amount that is payable, under the provisions of the Leasehold Reform Act 1967, either when a **long residential tenancy** that is subject to the provisions of the Act is made into an **extended lease**; or when it is assumed that the lease will be extended and the capital value of a site is being assessed for the purpose of **leasehold enfranchisement**. In this respect, a modern ground rent is equivalent to the rent that is considered to represent the letting value of the site of a house, excluding the value of any buildings thereon, but

assuming that the site can be used for any purposes for which it had been, or could lawfully have been, used during the period of an existing tenancy (LRA 1967, s. 15(2)).

modernisation(Eng) or **modernization**(US) The act of bringing a property up to current standards of usage, design, layout and facilities. Modernisation includes putting property into a good state of **repair** and decoration, providing modern finishings and replacing outdated mechanical equipment with modern equipment. See also **improvement**, **refurbishment**, **renovation**.

Modified Accelerated Cost Recovery System (MACRS)(US) See **accelerated depreciation**.

modification and assumption agreement An agreement between a mortgagee and mortgagor by which the terms of a mortgage are varied, generally as an increase in the interest rate, when the mortgage is assumed by another party. The agreement usually releases the mortgagor from any future personal liability. See also **assumption**.

modification order See **change order**(US), **revocation order**(Eng).

modified fee See **qualified fee**.

modified internal rate of return See **internal rate of return**.

modified pass-through See **fully-modified mortgage-backed security**, **mortgage-backed security**.

moiety A half interest, e.g. a half interest held under a **joint tenancy**, a **tenancy in common**, or as a right to a **party wall**. When a person bids successfully at auction for a 'moiety' of a piece of ground, he will purchase that half of the ground, and if his bid is based on a price per unit of measure, the purchase price will be that price multiplied by the number of units – not half that amount. 'Moiety' is sometimes used to refer to any fractional part of a property, e.g. a third or quarter, especially when a party only holds such a part. See also **undivided interest**.

money   Believed to be derived from *Moneta*, the temple of the Roman goddess Juno, which housed the mint in ancient Rome. Anything that passes from hand to hand as a readily acceptable medium for the exchange of articles of value, or is kept as a store of value. An item or commodity used to express debts or liabilities, or that is acceptable as a means to discharge debts or liabilities. "The natural and primary meaning of money is **cash** or coin of the realm … Still, in the common acceptation of the word there is a more extensive meaning given to it", *Barrett v White* (1855) 24 LJ Ch 724, 726 (53A Am.Jur.2d., Money, § 1). Money has been defined in a literal sense "by Mr. Walker in *Money, Trade, and Industry* as that which passes freely from hand to hand through the community in final discharge of debts and full payment for commodities, being acceptable equally without reference to the character or credit of the person who offers it and without the intention of the person who receives it to consume it or apply it to any other use than in turn to **tender** it to others in discharge of debts or payments for commodities", *Moss v Hancock* [1899] 2 QB 111, 116.

In economics, money is reputed to serve four basic functions: (i) as a unit or medium of **exchange** – "it is a machine for doing quickly and commodiously, what would be done, though less quickly and commodiously, without it", John Stewart Mill, *Principles of Political Economy* (1848), Book III, Ch. VII, para. 3; (ii) as a denominator or measure of **value** or **wealth** – "in the first place money appears in the function of a mere instrument for measuring the value of individual parts of wealth … But money also appears in a second or higher function, that is, it embraces the value itself that is measured by it … Therefore money gives its owner a general power of wealth … and … appears as an independent bearer of

such power", Fredrich Karl von Savigny, *Das Obligationenrecht* ["Law of Contracts"] (1851), vol. i. p. 405; (iii) as a store of value or purchasing power – "It is not for its own sake that men desire money, but for the sake of what they can purchase with it", Adam Smith, *The Wealth of Nations* (1776), Book Four, Ch. I. Although it may be asked, "why should anyone outside a lunatic asylum wish to use money as a store of wealth? Because … our desire to hold money as a store of wealth is a barometer of the degree of our distrust of our own calculations and conventions concerning the future … The possession of actual money lulls our disquietude", J. M. Keynes, *The General Theory of Employment* (1937) Quart. J. Econ. p. 216; (iv) as a standard or means for deferred payment, a link between the present and the future – money "acts as a guarantee that we may have what we want in the future: though it is not needed at the moment, it insures the possibility of satisfying a need when it arises", Aristotle, *Ethics*, Book 5. Money may take the form of coins, bank notes or similar currency; negotiable paper money, promissory notes (e.g. cheques, postal orders, money orders); precious metals; or any goods that are accepted by society as readily exchangeable, without question and without being used up in the process. In some contexts or uses, it may be more limited, but money may also be used to refer to any capital, property and anything else that is transferred in commerce.

In law, money must be acceptable as a medium of exchange and must be capable of being expressed authoritatively as a recognised unit of account; in particular, it means **legal tender**. This quality may be attributed to "all chattels which, issued by the authority of the law and denominated with reference to a unit of account, are meant to serve as a universal medium of exchange in the State of issue", F. A. Mann. *Legal Aspects of Money*. 5th ed. Oxford: Clarendon Press, 1997, p. 8. "'Money' means a medium of exchange authorized or adopted by a domestic or foreign government as a part of its currency", United States Uniform Commercial Code § 1-201(24). The Uniform Commercial Code does not require that "money" be 'legal tender', although it should be something that is "given credence or honor by the authority of a government", UCC § 1-201:362. The Code expressly includes federal reserve notes and excludes checks and coin collections from the definition of money (UCC § 1-201:363, 1-201:362; American Law Reports, *Annotations and Cases*, Anno: 40 ALR4th 346: UCC—"Money"). "[M]oney as commonly understood is not necessarily legal tender. Any medium which by practice fulfils the function of money and which every one will accept in payment of a debt is money in the ordinary sense of the word", *Reference re Alberta Legislation* [1938] SCR 100, [1939] 2 DLR 81, 92 (Can).

In its contemporary usage money, or 'money supply', refers to the sum total of cash and credit available in the economy, including cash, legal tender, demand deposits at the bank (or similar guardians of such liquid assets), accountable credit extended to facilitate the acquisition of goods, and, sometimes, time deposits. Money supply may be broadly classified as i) Currency, cash in the hands of the public and demand deposits at commercial banks (M_1); ii) Currency, plus demand and time deposits at commercial banks (M_2); Currency, plus demand and time deposits and liabilities of non-bank financial intermediaries (M_3). See also **capital money**, **interest**, **money's worth**.

money or money's worth(Eng)   A term that is used in several English statutes (e.g. LPA 1925, s. 203(xxi)(xvi)(xxiii); LCA 1925, s. 13(2)) and encompasses **money** and **money's worth**, and is intended to cover all forms of monetary, as well as non-monetary consideration, such as land or chattels or stocks and shares (even if the amount is not adequate or merely nominal (*Midland Bank Trust Co Ltd v Green* [1981] AC 513, [1981] 1 All ER 153 (HL)); but not merely an emotional consideration, such as love and affection. Unlike **value** or 'valuable consideration', the term used alone excludes the consideration of a future marriage.

money weighted rate of return   See **internal rate of return**.

money's worth(Eng)   Anything that can achieve or procure the same purpose as **money**. That which is capable of producing money; something that "can be turned into money", *Tennant v Smith* [1892] AC 150, 156 (HL), i.e. land, chattels, goods, shares that can be converted into cash, coin of the realm, bank notes or bank demand deposits.

'Money's worth' is a term used in English land law to refer to some present **consideration**, as referred to a contract; "the price or consideration given for property where property is acquired in return for something other than money, such as services or other property, where the price or consideration which the acquirer gives for the property has got to be turned into money before it can be expressed in terms of money", *Secretan v Hart* [1969] 3 All ER 1196, 1199 (although it need not equate to the value of the property acquired (*Midland Bank Trust Co Ltd v Green* [1981] AC 513, [1981] 1 All ER 153 (HL)). 'Money's worth' may mean also that which is given in satisfaction of an existing debt. See also **money or money's worth**.

month   Commonly a 'calendar month' based on the Gregorian calendar. However, in some places or contexts, a month can be any period of 30 days; 1/12th of a year, a calendar month; or a period that is a measure of the moon's time of revolution or the cycle of its phase changes – a lunar month. At common law, a month traditionally was "a lunar month, or 28 days, unless otherwise expressed", 2 *Bl Comm* 141 (1 *Co Litt* 135b). However, in all English statutes since 1978, a 'month' means a calendar month, unless otherwise qualified (Interpretation Act 1978, Sch. 1); and "in all deeds, contracts, wills, orders and other instruments" executed, made or coming into operation after 1926 it means a "calendar month", unless the context otherwise requires (LPA 1925, s. 61).

In the US, "'month' is now universally computed by the calendar, unless a contrary meaning is indicated by the statute or contract under construction", 74 Am.Jur.2d., Time, § 9 (Guaranty Trust & S.D. Co. v. Green Cove Springs & M.R.

Co., 139 US 137, 11 S Ct 512, 35 L Ed 116 (1891)); and many states have enacted legislation that 'month' when used without qualification, means a calendar month. (Although some states have enacted that a month-to-month tenancy of residential premises requires not less than 30 days written notice of termination, excluding the day of service.)

In mercantile or commercial contracts, it is a calendar month, unless there is evidence to the contrary and in a mortgage, unless there is evidence to the contrary, a month is a calendar month. However, in the US, in many contracts effecting loans, a month may be a 'business month' of 30 days (so that annual interest is apportioned on the basis of a 360 day year) – although the documentation should clearly state such a period if that is intended.

A 'calendar month' is strictly one of the twelve spans on the calendar, e.g. all of June or all of September. However, when a period of time is required to cover a given number of months, that period begins at the start of the numbered day and ends immediately before the day of the calendar month that bears the same number; so that, 'four months commencing *on* September 30' ends at midnight on January 29, not on January 30. Rent payable 'every three months, *commencing on* November 30' is due on February 28, May 30, August 30 and November 30; but rent payable 'every three months hereafter' under a lease '*from* November 30' is due on March 1, June 1, September 1, December 1, as the **day** of the date is excluded in law. However, the time span does not extend into a subsequent month, so that 'three months commencing on November 30' ends on February 28, and 'three months commencing on November 30' ends on February 28 in a non leap year and February 29 in a leap year; but strictly speaking an action taken on January 31 is later than 'four months *from* September 30' (*Migotti v Colvill* (1879) 4 CPD 233 (CA); *Dodds v Walker* [1981] 1 WLR 1027, [1981] 2 All ER 609, 611 (HL); Jablon v. City of New York, 177 Misc 838, 21 NYS.2d 764, 766 (1941)). A month without further designation is taken to be the month of the current year, unless there is evidence of a contrary intention. See also **six months**.

month-to-month tenancy[US] or **monthly tenancy**[Eng]   A tenancy that continues for one month and thereafter from **month** to month, for an indefinite duration, until determined by proper notice of termination. A **periodic tenancy** that continues until determined by one month's notice, normally to expire on the anniversary of the commencement date, or the date on which rent is normally due. cf. **tenancy from year to year**. See also **notice to quit**.

monthly tenancy   See **month-to-month tenancy**.

monument   1. A visible landmark, structure or building, especially a structure erected to mark a notable event or person. A memorial stone or building; an object erected to commemorate a person or event. See also **historic sites**[US]. 2.[US] A permanent, tangible object on the land, such as a stone, a post, mature tree, a mound, spring. etc., that is used to define a **boundary line** or a point that is the limit of such a line. A monument may be 'physical' (stone, tree, river); 'natural' (tree, river, lake); artificial (**bench mark**, stake, fence post); 'legal' (as used in a legal document); or 'record' (as set out in a deed by adjoining landowners). See also **geodetic survey system**, **metes and bounds system**, **permanent monument**[US]. 3.[Eng] In the context of an **ancient monument** "'monument' means: (1) any building, structure or work, whether above or below the surface of the land, and any cave or excavation; (2) any site comprising the remains of any such building, structure or work or of any cave or excavation; and (3) any site comprising, or comprising the remains of, any vehicle, vessel, aircraft or other movable structure or part of it which neither constitutes nor forms part of any work which is a monument within (1) above", Ancient Monuments and Archaeological Areas Act 1979, s. 61(1).   4. See **muniment**.

moral obligation   A duty or obligation that a person ought rightly to perform, but is not legally bound to fulfil. See also *assumpsit*, **consideration**, **gentleman's agreement**.

mortgage   The grant of an interest in real or personal property as security for a debt, with a provision for the release of that property upon the repayment of the debt in full. A transaction by which one party (**mortgagee**) accepts a claim or title to property from another (**mortgagor**) as security for the payment of a debt (or the discharge of some other obligation), for which the property is given, subject to a proviso that when the loan is repaid, or the obligation discharged, the property is released or returned to the mortgagor free of the mortgagee's claim. A "**conveyance** of land or an **assignment** of chattels as a security for the payment of a debt or the discharge of some other obligation for which it is given", *Santley v Wilde* [1899] 2 Ch 474 (CA) (UPC, § 1-201(25)). The debt or obligation may be referred to as the 'mortgage debt'.

Historically, a mortgage was created by a transfer of title to a property as security for the payment of a debt and the property was only transferred back when the debt was paid in full. However, this concept has been radically changed in most jurisdictions. In particular, the mortgagor has an inviolable right to recover his property by repaying the debt – called his **equity of redemption**. In addition, there are statutory restrictions on the mortgagee's right of **foreclosure** (i.e. the right to retain the mortgaged property); and, in some jurisdictions in the US, there is a **statutory right of redemption** after foreclosure. Thus, a mortgage of land may no longer be considered as a **conveyance**, but more as a form of **lien** or **charge** or, in a few jurisdictions in the US, a 'defeasible conveyance'.

In the US, those states that accept the common law view that property is conveyed to the mortgagee, together with a strict right to possession, with a **reconveyance** upon satisfaction of the debt, are referred to as 'title theory' (or 'common law theory') states. Other jurisdictions, which consider that neither title nor possession is granted to the mortgagee, but only a right to satisfy the debt from the proceeds of sale of the property, a right that is akin to a lien, are called 'lien theory' states (United States v. Commonwealth Title Ins. and T. Co., 193 US 656, 48 L Ed 831 (1904)). In a few 'intermediate states' a 'hybrid', or 'intermediate', form of mortgage is adopted. The 'hybrid' mortgagee is considered to hold a conditional title, which 'vests' in the mortgagee only in the event of default by the mortgagor. With a 'hybrid mortgage, the mortgagor is allowed to retain possession and act as the owner in all respects, unless there is an event of default. The lien theory states tend to be west of the Mississippi river, and the title theory states, except for Florida, New York, Illinois, Indiana, Kentucky, Michigan, Wisconsin, and South Carolina, to the east. (Louisiana does not adopt any of these theories as it follows the civil law.)

A mortgage may be distinguished from a **pledge**, or pawn of personal property, as the pledgee, or pawnbroker, gains possession of the property but ownership remains with the pledgor. It may be distinguished from a 'charge', which conveys no interest in property, but merely gives a right to take certain steps involving the charged property; usually, in the event of default by the borrower, either to appoint a receiver to collect rent from the property, or to apply to a court to enforce a sale of the property and claim settlement of the debt from the proceeds. However, the word 'charge' is often used to indicate a mortgage transaction that lacks certain formalities, but in all other respects is exactly like a mortgage. A mortgage may be distinguished from a 'lien' as a lien is strictly not an interest in land, but a claim to be satisfied from the proceeds of land; a lien arises by operation of law, rather than directly by contract (except in 'lien-theory states' in the US, where the transaction resembles a mortgage, but is said to grant only the rights of a lien as the lender is entitled to have his debt satisfied only by exercising his power of sale against the property).

In modern English law, a mortgagee is usually

granted a form of 'legal charge', or is granted a lease, with a right of termination upon repayment of the debt. The first mortgagee will usually retain the title deeds until the mortgage debt is discharged in full. The mortgagor's equity of redemption, especially as enshrined in the doctrine that **once a mortgage, always a mortgage**, remains a central feature of the mortgage, and in addition, there are the stringent statutory regulations that govern a mortgagee's right to **possession** and strict limits on the right of **foreclosure**.

A mortgage may come to an end or be discharged by **redemption**; by the mortgagee exercising his **power of sale**; by foreclosure; by **merger**; or by operation of law, i.e. a **receipt** endorsed on, or annexed to, the mortgage, signed by the mortgagee, acknowledging that the debt has been paid in full. A mere prepayment of the mortgage debt before the maturity date does not automatically discharge the mortgage, unless there is a **prepayment privilege** in the mortgage deed.

In the US, a mortgage may also be classified as: (a) a **regular mortgage**, when an interest in land is conveyed to the mortgagee, subject to an equity of redemption held by the mortgagor; (b) a mortgage made by way of a **deed of trust**, whereby the secured property is held by a third party unless and until the debt is repaid; or (c) an **equitable mortgage**, which arises when it can be shown that it was intended that property should be held as security for a debt, but no formal deed to that effect was prepared.

A mortgage comprises two simultaneous transactions: (i) a written transfer of an interest in land (or a demise or charge of land), as security for that debt (the **mortgage deed**); and (ii) a personal contract for the payment of a debt (a **promissory note** or in the US sometimes called the 'mortgage note'). In English legal practice, these agreements are normally incorporated in one document – the 'mortgage deed', whereas in the US, they are commonly set out in separate instruments. See also **adjustable-rate mortgage, amortization loan, assignment of rents**[US]**, assumption, balloon mortgage, blanket**

mortgage, bulk mortgage, chattel mortgage, close-ended mortgage, consolidation, debenture, due-on-sale clause, equitable charge, equitable mortgage, first mortgage, leasehold mortgage, legal mortgage, puisne mortgage, purchase money mortgage, sub-mortgage, tacking, Welsh mortgage.

Clarke, Wayne, et al. *Fisher & Lightwood's Law of Mortgages*. 11th ed. London: Butterworths, 2002.

Cousins, Edward F. *The Law of Mortgages*. 2nd ed. London: Sweet & Maxwell, 2001.

mortgage assumption[US]   See **assumption**.

mortgage-backed bond (MBB)   See **mortgage-backed obligation**.

mortgage-backed obligation (MBO) or **mortgage-backed security** (MBS)   An investment instrument that represents an undivided ownership interest in a group of mortgages. A **security** or similar form of obligation that is backed by a pool of loans secured by mortgages. The security granted to the investor may provide that the loan is repaid by principal payments received from the underlying mortgages – 'pass-through' securities, i.e. the security or obligation represents an undivided interest in the loans secured by the mortgages. Alternatively, the 'issuer' of the security may undertake to make payments to the investor without direct regard to the cash flow received from the borrowers – 'non-pass-through' securities. Alternatively, the security may be a 'modified-pass-through' so that the holder of the security is guaranteed monthly payments of interest, regardless of whether the payments of interest and principal are adequate to meet such payments. Pass-through, unlike non-pass-through, securities are not retained on the balance sheet of the originator or issuer of the securities. Non-pass-through securities normally take the form of bonds, called 'mortgage-backed bonds'.

The investor in non-pass-through securities may be provided with additional collateral or 'credit enhancement' in the form of a letter of

credit, additional equity capital or guarantees, or insurance as provided by a **mortgage-security insurer**, to be drawn on in the event that the mortgage repayments are insufficient or fail to meet the payments due to the bond holders. The offering of the securities, bonds or obligations backed by a pool of mortgages is referred to generally as a 'securitized-mortgage offering'. Called a 'commercial mortgage-backed security' (CMBS) when the mortgages are secured on commercial properties only. Similar securities or bonds backed by other forms of collateral or assets, such as credit-card receivables, car loans or mobile home loans, are called 'asset-backed securities or bonds', as distinguished from the various forms of 'mortgage-related securities'. See also **collateralized mortgage obligation, Federal Home Loan Mortgage Corporation, Federal National Mortgage Association, fully-modified mortgage-backed security, Government National Mortgage Association, participation certificate, real estate mortgage investment conduit, securitization.**
Davidson, Andrew S., and Michael D Herskovitz. *Mortgage-Backed Securities: Investment Analysis & Advanced Valuation Techniques.* Chicago: Probus Press, 1994.
Fabozzi, Frank J. (editor). *The Handbook of Mortgage Backed Securities.* 5th ed. New York,: McGraw Hill, 2001.
Ferran, Ellis. *Mortgage Securitisation—Legal Aspects.* London: Butterworths, 1992.
Kuhn, Robert L. (editor). *Mortgage and Asset Securitization. Volume V of the Library of Investment Banking.* Homewood, IL: Dow-Jones Irwin, 1990.

mortgage banker 1. A person, corporation or firm that specialises in originating, selling and servicing mortgage loans. A mortgage bank uses its own or borrower funds (as opposed to depositors fund) to originate mortgage loans and then sells these loans to other institutions. A mortgage bank will generally seek to retain the right to service these loans, i.e. to collect monthly payments, pay taxes and insurance, pursue delinquent payments, and generally provide information on the status of the loans. Generally,

loans made by mortgage banks only take the form of interim finance, i.e. loans for a maximum period of five years. cf. **mortgage broker**. See also **secondary mortgage market**. 2. A firm or company that specialises in acquiring packages or pools of mortgage loans and selling them to investors as mortgage-backed securities. See also **mortgage-backed obligation**.

mortgage bond See bond.

mortgage broker One who, for gain or reward, acts as an intermediary between a party seeking a mortgage loan and a supplier of mortgage money. A party who acts as an agent and seeks out funds that will be used to make a loan that is to be secured by a lien or mortgage on real property. Unlike a **mortgage banker**, a mortgage broker does not normally take any part in the servicing of the loan. Many mortgage brokers are also licensed as real estate brokers.

mortgage buy-down[US] See **buy-down**.

mortgage capitalization rate[AmE] See **mortgage constant**.

mortgage certificate[US] 1. An instrument that evidences the existence of a mortgage and states the principal terms of the mortgage. See also **estoppel certificate**. 2. See **participation certificate**. 3. See **mortgage insurance certificate**[US].

mortgage clause See mortgagee clause.

mortgage coefficient[AmE] See **Ellwood capitalization rate, mortgage constant**.

mortgage commitment See **commitment**.

mortgage company A company that specialises in raising capital in order to make mortgage loans. Mortgage companies may use their own capital to make the loans (although they then normally only make short-term loans) or they may act as middlemen raising the capital from life insurance companies, pension funds or other financial institutions. A mortgage company may also undertake related activities, such as purchasing mortgages, mortgage servicing and title insurance. See also **mortgage banker**.

mortgage constant 1. The amount (expressed as a percentage) required to repay the entire principal, together with interest thereon, over the period for which a loan is made. This constant may be calculated from the formula for the **annuity one will purchase**, which produces a single percentage that is sufficient to pay interest at the rate stated for the loan and to repay principal. This single amount or 'constant', when multiplied by the initial loan amount, produces the annual cost of debt service. Given that the debt service is a fixed sum, the initial payments are mostly payments of interest, the amount of principal being repaid increasing gradually (and consequently the interest reducing gradually) throughout the term of the loan. Also called a 'debt-service constant', an 'annual loan constant' or 'loan constant', 'k-factor', 'partial payment factor', 'mortgage capitalization rate' (especially when derived by dividing the amount of the initial principal by the annual cost of debt service), or 'constant' (c.) for short. In the US, when this factor is used in the **Ellwood capitalization rate** it is called the 'mortgage coefficient' (R_M) and is calculated at the **equity yield rate**. See also Appendix C, **Financial Formulae**. 2. The percentage ratio of the annual debt service on a mortgage and the average principal outstanding on the loan during the loan. This percentage may be expressed also as the relationship between the regular amount required to pay capital and interest under an **amortization loan** and the initial loan amount.

Mortgage Corporation(US) See **Federal Home Loan Mortgage Corporation**.

mortgage debenture See **debenture**.

mortgage debt The total **debt** owed by a party who has mortgaged property as security for that debt. See also **mortgage money, recourse**.

mortgage debt service See **debt service**.

mortgage deed A written instrument that records the terms of a **mortgage** loan. A **deed** that specifies the property granted as security, the obligations and duties of the mortgagor and mortgagee and the terms for redemption. A mortgage deed conveys or grants an interest in the property, to be held as security for a debt, and creates a binding personal contract between the parties, i.e. if made in respect of real property it is both a **conveyance** or **demise**, and a **loan** document. (In the US, there may be separate documents with the loan terms being contained in a 'promissory note' that is personal between the parties.) See also **charge by way of a legal mortgage**(Eng), **deed of trust**(US).

mortgage discount Discount points payable by a mortgagor.

mortgage duty or **mortgage tax** A tax payable on the registration or recording of a mortgage deed, usually on the amount of the mortgage loan. See also **recording tax, stamp duty**(Eng), **stamp tax**(US).

mortgage endowment insurance See **endowment mortgage**.

mortgage-equity capitalization technique(AmE) A method of assessing the value of an income-producing property by taking into account not only the capitalized value of the income available from the property, but also any existing or available mortgage finance appropriate for the property. This form of appraisal is based on the principle that the price that will be paid for an income-producing property is equal to the sum of the amount of **equity capital** available to purchase the property and the amount of **debt capital** that can be raised using the property as security, i.e. unlike the conventional 'income approach', it brings into account the effect of 'leverage'.

The projected net operating income from the property to be appraised is capitalized by a single factor (an 'overall rate') derived from a formula that takes account of some or all of the following: (i) the return on equity required by a purchaser (**equity yield rate**); (ii) the mortgage interest and amortization rate; (iii) the loan period; (iv) the ratio of debt to equity (loan ratio); (v) capital appreciation (or depreciation); (vi) the holding period. This technique may also be used as a method of investment analysis to ascertain any one of these variables, in particular the equity yield rate, given the other variables. See also **band-of-investment rate**, **Ellwood capitalization rate**.

Gibbons, James E. *Mortgage-Equity Capitalization: Ellwood Method*. Chicago: Appraisal Institute, 1980.

mortgage guarantee bond   See **mortgage insurance**.

mortgage guarantee insurance   See **mortgage insurance**.

Mortgage Guaranty Insurance Corporation (MGIC)(US)   An independent insurance corporation that is owned by Northwestern Mutual and provides insurance cover to enable lenders to grant larger loans to qualified borrowers than is otherwise permitted due to the regulation of the lender. MGIC covers the risk of granting loans for more than conventional loan-to-value ratios, e.g. loans that exceed 80% of the appraised value. This insurance is needed to protect the provider of the mortgage if the mortgage applicant cannot provide the required percentage down payment. If MGIC decides to underwrite the insurance, then the mortgage includes this insurance with the cost (premiums) added to the monthly mortgage payment. MGIC is licensed to operate in all 50 states and Puerto Rico and has 20 field offices throughout the US. See also **mortgage insurance**. (**www.mgic.com**).

mortgage-holder(US)   See **mortgagee**.

mortgage instrument   Any **instrument**, including a mortgage deed, promissory note, or deed of trust that forms part of the documentation used to secure a mortgage loan.

mortgage insurance   **1. Insurance** taken out by a mortgagee to provide protection against the mortgagor defaulting on his obligations. Insurance that protects the lender in the event of a need to foreclose or take any similar action. Usually cover is provided in the event of the mortgagor's death or disability, or sometimes against the risk that the mortgagor might become bankrupt or lose his employment. More strictly called 'mortgage guarantee insurance'. Many lenders are restricted, by government regulation or their own rules, in making mortgage loans for an amount that exceeds more than 75-80% of the appraised value of the mortgaged property. In order to make larger loans, lenders take out mortgage insurance to cover the extra risk. The cost of such insurance is generally recharged to the borrower as a 'mortgage insurance premium', either payable annually or more usually as an amount added to the regular monthly mortgage payments. In the US, called 'private mortgage insurance' (PMI) when such insurance is provided by a private (non-governmental) corporation (one of the largest of such insurers being PMI Group, Inc.). See also **Farmers Home Administration**(US), **Federal Housing Administration**(US), **Mortgage Guaranty Insurance Corporation**(US), **mortgage-security insurance**, **Veterans Administration loan**(US).   **2.** An insurance policy taken out to cover the risk that in the event of the mortgagee having to exercise his **power of sale** to realise the debt, the property held as security will provide insufficient capital to repay the outstanding principal. Also called a 'mortgage guarantee bond'.   **3.** Insurance taken out to repay the outstanding balance of a mortgage loan in the event of the death of the mortgagor prior to the final date for redemption of the mortgage. Also called 'mortgage redemption insurance' or 'mortgage protection insurance', 'mortgage life insurance' or 'credit life insurance' (although the latter term may apply to similar insurance provided against any form of loan). See also **endowment mortgage**.

mortgage insurance certificate (MIC)[US] A certificate issued by the Department of Housing and Urban Development as evidence that the **Federal Housing Administration** has insured a mortgage or mortgages.

mortgage insurance premium (MIP)[US] See **mortgage insurance**.

mortgage investment company An **investment company** that specialises in mortgage business, either by direct mortgage lending or arranging, purchasing or selling mortgages.

mortgage lender See **mortgagee**.

mortgage lender's policy A title **insurance** policy taken out by the mortgagee to provide an indemnity in the event that the title to the property held as security proves to be defective. A mortgage lender's policy covers not only the title to the mortgaged property, but also insures the validity of the mortgage placed on the property and its priority. See also **mortgage insurance**.

mortgage lending value See **mortgage value**.

mortgage lien[US] A lien secured against a property that is held as security for a **mortgage**. A term that is used especially in a 'non-title theory' state to refer to the right of the lender to have priority over other lenders, usually by having a power of sale over the mortgaged property.

mortgage life insurance See **mortgage insurance**.

mortgage loan A loan secured by a mortgage. A term used to emphasise that a loan is secured by a mortgage on property. If the property is real estate, also called a 'real estate loan'. See also **debt capital**.

mortgage loan insurance See **mortgage insurance**.

mortgage loss-payable clause See **loss-payable clause**.

mortgage money[Eng] "Money or **money's worth** secured by a **mortgage**", LPA 1925, s. 205(1)(xvi)).

mortgage note A promissory **note** that sets out the terms of a loan that is secured by a **mortgage**. In the US, a mortgage is generally set out in two documents; the 'mortgage note, which sets out the financial terms and usually makes the borrower personally liable for the loan, and the **mortgage deed**, which secures the property that is the subject of the mortgage. In English legal practice, these stipulations are normally incorporated in one document.

mortgage out[US] See **equity out**.

mortgage participation See **equity-participation mortgage, participation mortgage**.

mortgage participation certificate See **participation certificate**.

mortgage-pass-through bond (MPTB) See **mortgage-backed obligation**.

mortgage-pass-through security See **mortgage-backed obligation**.

mortgage placement fee See **placement fee**.

mortgage pool See **collateralized mortgage obligation, mortgage-backed obligation**.

mortgage protection insurance   See mortgage insurance.

mortgage REIT(US)   See **real estate investment trust**.

mortgage redemption insurance   See mortgage guarantee insurance.

mortgage-related security (MRS)   See mortgage-backed obligation.

mortgage sale   A sale of a property when a mortgagor has defaulted on his obligation and either the mortgagee has exercised his **power of sale** or a court order has been granted, subsequent to a request for an order of **foreclosure**, requiring that the property be sold. See also **foreclosure sale**.

mortgage-security insurance   Insurance provided to the issuer of a **mortgage-backed obligation** to reduce the risk to the holders of the security. The insurer covers the difference in the risk associated with the income from the underlying mortgages and that associated with a particular level of 'investment-grade rating' as provided to the holders of the securities. Such insurance may be provided by a government insurance agency, such as the **Federal Housing Administration**, the **Farmers Home Administration**, the **Veterans Administration**, or by a private insurer such as a **Mortgage Guaranty Insurance Corporation** or other private mortgage insurance companies. cf. **mortgage insurance**.

mortgage servicer   See **servicer**.

mortgage tax   See **mortgage duty**.

mortgage trust(US)   See **real estate investment trust**.

mortgage value   The value of a property for the purpose of accepting it as security for a loan. Strictly, this is equivalent to the **market value** and an advance by way of a mortgage is restricted usually to a percentage (generally no more than 80 per cent) of that value, unless there is additional collateral or insurance. However, a valuer commonly adopts a conservative approach to a valuation prepared for mortgage purposes. Furthermore, in a bullish property market the English courts have said that the valuer "can reasonably be required to be aware of the fact that the market is 'high' or unusually buoyant, when such are the circumstances, and to guard against overconfidence in such market conditions. He can reasonably be required to consider what the position of the property may well be in circumstances of forced-sale within six to twelve months of his valuation", *Corisand Investments Ltd v Druce and Co* (1978) 248 EG 315, 322.

The European Parliament and Council has defined the term 'mortgage lending value' as "The value of the property as determined by a valuer taking a prudent assessment of the future marketability of the property by taking into account long-term sustainable aspects of the property, the normal and local market conditions, the current use and alternative appropriate uses of the property. Speculative elements may not be taken into account in the assessment of the Mortgage Lending Value. The mortgage lending value shall be documented in a transparent and clear manner. At least every three years or if the market falls by more than 10% the mortgage lending value and in particular the underlying assumptions concerning the development of the relevant market shall be assessed", Directive 2000/12/EC. This directive was issued in connection with bank solvency ratios and is intended to ensure that valuations prepared for a banks on this basis takes account of the long-term sustainability of the value as used for risk assessment. This directive is based on the *Criteria in defining commercial real estate lending: Supplement to the New Basle Capital Accord* (Basel Committee on Banking Supervision, Jan 2001). cf. **forced-sale value**. See also **collateral value**.

mortgagee   A mortgage lender. One who receives or holds the benefit of a **mortgage**. A lender who accepts an interest in, or a claim over property as security for a debt or obligation owed to him, whether obtained by means of a mortgage deed, lien or charge. In the US, a mortgagee is sometimes called a 'mortgage-holder'.

A mortgagee has a right to take **possession** of the mortgaged property, either as actual possession or a right to grant leases (although he normally foregoes this in favour of the mortgagor); to foreclose or sell the property (according to the law) in the event of default by the mortgagor; to hold the title deeds; to appoint a receiver; and usually a right to sue the mortgagor for the debt.

In English law, a mortgagee is defined to include a person who receives a 'charge by way of a legal mortgage', or anyone who derives title from the original mortgagee (LPA 1925, s. 205(1)(xvi)). See also **consolidation, foreclosure, legal mortgagee**(Eng), **mortgagee clause, power of sale, receiver, recourse, tacking**.

mortgagee clause or **mortgagee insurance clause**   A clause in a fire insurance policy, as taken out by a mortgagor, that refers to the interest of the **mortgagee** in the mortgaged property. The clause may require only that the mortgagee is informed if any claim is made under the policy; or, more usually, it requires that any money paid under the policy goes direct to the mortgagee to the extent of the amount of the mortgage, in which case it is usually called a '**loss-payable clause**' or an 'open-mortgage clause'. A mortgagee has no claim upon money paid under an insurance policy taken out solely in the name of the mortgagor, but under a 'loss-payable clause' any payment that would be due to the mortgagor is paid to reduce the mortgage debt.

In English law, if a mortgage is made by deed, the mortgagee has the power to insure the mortgaged property against loss or damage by fire, and to add the premium to the mortgagor's debt with equal priority (LPA 1925, s. 101(1)); unless there is a declaration in the mortgage deed that no insurance is required or the mortgagor has accepted an express obligation, or has agreed with the mortgagee, to maintain the insurance (LPA 1925, s. 108(2)).

In the US, if the mortgage documents require the mortgagor to insure the property for the benefit of the mortgagee, in the event of a payment under the insurance policy, the mortgagee is entitled to have the proceeds paid to reduce the mortgage debt (Sureck v. U.S. Fidelity & Guaranty Co., 353 F Supp 807 (DC Ark 1973)). However, if there is no provision for the mortgagee to be covered by the mortgagor's policy, the mortgagee is not entitled to make any claim on that policy (Columbia Ins. Co. v. Lawrence, 10 Pet 507, 35 US 507, 9 L Ed 512 (1836)). Sometimes called a 'mortgage clause'. See also **reinstatement basis, union mortgage clause**.

mortgagee loss clause(US)   See **union mortgage clause**.

mortgagee-mortgagor index(US)   An index maintained at the public recorder's office to show details of all mortgages that affect a recorded property under the name of the mortgagee and mortgagor. See also **land recording**.

mortgager   See **mortgagor**.

mortgaging out(US)   Payment of the entire purchase price for a property with funds borrowed by way of a mortgage secured on the property. In particular, obtaining a mortgage for an amount that equals the total cost or market value of a property, thereby enabling an owner to avoid providing any equity or to release his own **equity**.

mortgagor   One who offers an interest in, or claim over, a property to a lender (**mortgagee**) as security for a debt, i.e. one who grants a **mortgage** of property. A mortgagor has a right to the income and profits from the mortgaged property and is normally granted a right to possession by the mortgagee. A mortgagor retains a beneficial interest in the mortgaged property and is entitled to reclaim his interest on repayment of the debt – called his **equity of redemption**.

In English statute law, a mortgagor is defined to include "any person from time to time deriving title under the original mortgagor or entitled to redeem a mortgage according to his estate, interest or right in the mortgaged property", LPA 1925, s. 205(1)(xvi)).

In the US, occasionally spelt 'mortgager'. See also **once a mortgage always a mortgage**.

mortis causa(Lat)   'On account of death'. See gift *causa mortis*.

mortmain   Literally a 'dead hand'. Land, or an interest in land, held by any body that has an indefinite life, i.e. a corporation aggregate, ecclesiastical, or temporal. Since such a possessor of the land cannot die, in that sense the land is inalienable (Perin v. Carey, 24 Howard 465, 65 US 465, 16 L Ed 708 (1860)).

In the US, in some jurisdictions, mortmain statutes have been passed to protect next of kin from sizeable charitable gifts that have been made shortly before death, to the detriment of the family (American Law Reports, *Annotations and Cases*, Anno: 6 ALR4th 603: Mortmain Statutes—Validity and Effect). These statutes are not derived from the English Mortmain and Charitable Uses Acts of 1888, 1891 and 1925 (which are now all repealed) but provided that land could only be given to charities if certain conditions were met. Raban, Sandra. *Mortmain Legislation and the English Church 1279-1500*, Cambridge University Press, 1982.

most-favored tenant clause(US)   A clause in a lease which provides that the tenant will be given the same concessions that are given to other tenants in the same building or complex.

motel   An abbreviation of 'motor hotel'. An **hotel** primarily intended to cater for visitors who arrive by automobile. An hotel, located along or near a major highway and with ample car parking, that caters particularly for the motorist. Generally, a motel provides medium to low price facilities for one-night residents and tourists, and in some instances provides meals or even caters for small conferences and meetings. However, some modern motels provide facilities similar to full-scale hotels, with restaurants, meeting and assembly rooms, swimming pools, telephones and internet services, and full room service. The essential difference from a hotel is that a motel has ready access to a major highway, is normally situated on the outskirts of a major urban area, and is provided with ample car parking that is generally situated close to the guest rooms.

Mother Hubbard clause(US)   **1.** See **anaconda mortgage**, **dragnet clause**.   **2.** A clause in an **oil and gas lease** that provides that all the lessor's owned land is included in the area for exploration, even though not part of the metes and bounds survey description of the leased land. Also called a 'cover-all clause'.   **3.** A clause in a deed of grant that describes the mineral rights over land being transferred by reference to the grantor's entire ownership in a particular area, including all contiguous or adjacent land. The intention is to avoid excluding any small area of land that is not known to be held in the same ownership by virtue of an incorrect survey or a mistake. Such a clause does not operate to transfer a large separate parcel.

movable or **moveable**   **1.** In Roman, civil or Scots law, any property that is not affixed to the soil, and therefore can readily be transported from one place to another without thereby changing its nature. Property, or a '**thing**', may be categorised as moveable property or **heritable property** (or heritage). Moveable property comprises any 'thing' other than land, as well as anything that has been affixed and has become part of the land (including buildings). Traditionally, moveable property was that which was inherited upon intestacy by anyone other than the heir-at-law (usually the eldest son). This distinction no longer exists and the primary residual difference is the means by which these different categories of property may be legally recovered. cf. **immovable**.   **2.** Any property that can be transferred from place to place. cf. **fixture**. See also **chattel**, **goods**.

movable fee or **movable freehold**   **1.** A **fee** estate in land that, although a continuing estate, may from time to time change its position. In particular, land that may be acquired or lost as the sea or a river advances or recedes; land that is gained or lost by **accretion** or **reliction**.   2.(Eng)A fee simple interest in **lot meadows**, where two or more persons hold an interest in a measured area of meadow land, but the precise part owned is determined by the grant of lots at a specified time.

moveable   See **movable**.

mowing licence(Eng)   See **grazing licence**.

multiple agency   1.(Eng)The placing of property for sale with more than one **agent** at any one time, on a non-exclusive basis. The agents act independently of each other and only the one who is the 'effective cause' or procuring cause' of a transaction, i.e. one who introduces a purchaser **ready, able and willing** to purchase the property, receives a commission. Sometimes called a 'mixed agency'. cf. **exclusive agency**. See also **joint agency, multiple listing, open listing**(US). 2.(US)See **dual agency**.

multi-family dwelling or **multiple-family dwelling**(US)   A residential property that contains accommodation for two or more families or households. See also **apartment house, tenement house**.

multi-family housing(US)   Residential property designed to accommodate three or more families, whether in a single building or on a housing project that contains a number of houses.

multiple listing(AmE)   A listing agreement entered into with a member of a multiple listing organization in a particular area. In effect, an **exclusive right to sell** granted to the organization, but with the provision that the details will be circulated to other members of the organization. Instructions to sell a property are submitted by the seller to a broker who, as a member of the listing organization, is obliged to make details available to other members, although the seller

remains contracted directly to the original listing broker. The listing broker then submits a list of properties on which he is retained either to a central bureau (a **multiple listing service**) or circulates the details to the other members of the organization who generally act as subagents. In the event of a successful sale, the commission is divided either (a) between the broker who introduced the purchaser (selling broker) and the broker to whom the listing was given (listing broker); or (b) between all the members of the organization on an agreed basis. Multiple listing is sometimes used (incorrectly) as synonymous with **multiple agency**. Referred to sometimes as a 'compulsory listing', especially when the brokerage fraternity in a particular area are predominantly members of an organization that has a virtual monopoly on conducting property sales. cf. **exclusive listing, open listing**. See also **cooperating broker, franchise**.

multiple-listing service (MLS)(AmE)   An arrangement by which real estate brokers place their listings together so that all members of the multiple-listing service have an opportunity to sell properties listed by other members of the service. The original or 'listing' broker obtains an **exclusive right to sell** and then agrees to supply details of the listed property to all members of the service, usually through a central office operated by a local real estate board or association. When any member of the service, other than the listing broker, makes a sale the commission is divided between the listing broker and the selling broker who effects the sale. A fee may also be payable to the central office. Multiple-listing services are used especially for residential properties. Such an arrangement should not preclude any licensed broker from joining the listing service as that may violate antitrust statutes, especially when such a prohibition severely limits a broker's ability to compete with member brokers. The arrangement may also constitute an illegal restraint of trade. The fixing of commission rates by the members of the service, or 'blacklisting' low commission listings, may be contrary to the provisions of state anti-trust laws or constitute illegal 'price fixing' under the Sherman Anti-Trust Act of 1890, § 1 (United States v. Nat'l Association of Real Estate Boards, 339 US 485, 70 S Ct 711, 94 L Ed 1007 (1950); McLain v. Greater Minneapolis Area Board of Realtors, 444 US 232, 100 S Ct 502, 62 L Ed.2d 441 (1980)). Also, a multiple listing agreement may contravene state legislation designed to maintain business and professional codes and prevent price fixing. See also **list-back agreement, multiple listing, office exclusive**.

multiple occupation(Eng)   A "house in multiple occupation" (HMO) is one that is "occupied by persons who do not form a single household", Housing Act 1985, s. 345, as amended. Local authorities have powers to control the registration and management of HMOs, as well as the regulation of **overcrowding** (HA 1985, Part XI). See **common lodging-house, control order, demolition order, repairs notice**.

multiple-perils insurance   See comprehensive insurance.

multiple regression analysis (MRA)   See **regression analysis**.

multiple tenancy   A **tenancy** of premises that would normally form the subject of two or more lettings. For example, a tenancy of two separate apartments; of a retail store and adjacent office premises; or of a dwelling-house and an adjoining workshop. cf. **mixed tenancy**.

multiplier   A factor that is used to capitalise income, i.e. a **capitalization factor**. See also **income multiplier, years' purchase**(BrE).

multi-storey building   A building comprising two or more stories, especially one that exceeds four stories. See also **high-rise building, storey**(BrE)/**story**(AmE).

municipality   1. A predominately urban area (a city, town or other form of urban district) that has a corporate or statutory right of self-government.   **2.** An urban local authority that has political responsibility over a defined area.

muniment   A written document that evidences, fortifies, or otherwise relates to an owner's title to property. A **title deed**. Generally, referred to as 'muniments of title'. See also **abstract of title, land certificate, official certificate of search**.

mutation   A change. The transfer or conveyance of a right to property from one person to another.

mutatis mutandis(Lat)   'With the necessary changes having been made', i. e. things are to remain the same except for what is essential. For example, a lease may be renewed at a different rent *mutatis mutandis*, that is, the other terms and conditions of the expired lease remain unaltered.

mutual company(US)   See investment company.

mutual consent   See agreement, contract.

mutual covenant   A covenant that is binding on both parties to the extent that the performance by the one party is a condition precedent to the performance by the other. Under mutual covenants, either party may recover damages from the other for injury resulting from a breach of the covenant in his favour. Also called a 'reciprocal covenant'. See also **covenant, positive covenant**.

mutual equitable servitude(US)   See reciprocal negative easement.

mutual easement(US)   See **reciprocal easement**.

mutual fund(US)   1. A fund that is managed by an investment company and which invests in a diversified portfolio of stocks, bonds or other investments; an investment company that sells its stock and invests the proceeds in the stock of other securities with the value of its stock being directly determined by the value of the underlying securities. The company buys back its stock if the investors wish to redeem their capital. A mutual fund is generally 'open-ended' with the capital raised and managed varying according to investor demand; although the fund may be 'close-ended' with the size of the fund being fixed at the outset and is closed to new investment once the stipulated amount of capital has been raised. The company or 'fund' has a Board of Directors that is responsible for overall fund strategy and policy, with active management carried out by a management company that is usually the entity that has set up the mutual fund. The management company is generally responsible investment advice and for the buying and selling of investments. See also **investment company**, **unit trust**[(Eng)]. **2.** The equity capital held by an **investment company**.

mutual investment company[(US)]   An **investment company** that raises its share capital by buying and selling its own shares according to the demand of its investors. Also called a 'mutual investment trust', although the owning vehicle is generally incorporated and not strictly a trust.

mutual investment trust   See **mutual investment company**.

mutual loan association[(US)]   See **savings and loan associations**.

mutual mistake   See **mistake**.

mutual option   See **option**.

mutual trust[(US)]   See **open-ended trust**.

mutual savings bank[(US)]   See **savings bank**.

N

naked contract 1. A contract that is lacking in some essential element, especially **consideration** and, therefore, is void. See also **void contract**. 2. A bare promise; a **bargain** that has not been consummated in proper legal form. See also **agreement for a lease**, **agreement for sale**.

naked debenture A **debenture** that contains only an acknowledgment of a debt and does not provide any specific right of recourse to an asset or assets of the debtor company. Also called an 'unsecured note'. cf. **mortgage debenture**. See also **floating charge**.

naked possession(US) Possession of property without any apparent right or pretence to ownership. In particular, actual possession without **color of title**. cf. **seisin**. See also **adverse possession**.

naked title(US) 1. The title granted to a trustee when a mortgage is created by means of a **deed of trust**. See also **equitable title**. 2. A title granted when the transferor neither makes a representation, nor gives any guaranty as to the validity of that title. Also called a 'bare title'. See also **quitclaim deed**.

naked trust See **bare trust**.

names index(US) See **grantor-grantee index**.

named insured A party specified in an **insurance contract** as a person entitled to protection under the policy. In a fire insurance policy, this may be the property owner or, if applicable, a mortgagee or a purchaser under a contract for sale. See also **fire insurance**, **insurable interest**, **loss-payable clause**, **mortgagee insurance clause**.

named-perils insurance See **comprehensive insurance**.

named sub-contractor See **nominated subcontractor**.

National Conditions of Sale(Eng) See **conditions of sale**.

National Conveyancing Protocol(Eng) A Protocol (the Law Society Council Statement and National Conveyancing Protocol, Third Edition) that was introduced by the Law Society in 1990 for use in domestic conveyancing. The Protocol sets out a 'preferred practice' and is intended to streamline conveyancing by the use of standard documentation (in particular the Law Society's Standard Conditions of Sale (Second Edition) 1992). The Protocol sets out the steps to be followed by the respective solicitors acting for the buyer and seller during the contract and conveyancing stages. In particular, it sets out steps to be taken by the solicitors to obtain information relating to the transaction from the buyer and the seller; requirements to keep the other party's solicitor informed of progress; and requirements to keep the buyer and seller informed of relevant steps required of them. The Protocol also sets out steps to be taken to ensure coordination with the seller's estate agent. See also **conditions of sale**.

national domain Land owned by a national government. See also **domain**.

National Native Title Tribunal(Aus) A tribunal established to consider **native title** applications (Native Title Act 1993, s. 107). See also **Land Tribunal**.

national park An area of countryside considered to be of special importance because of its outstanding natural beauty, or historic or scientific interest and set aside by a national government for the preservation of the natural environment. The first 'national park' was formally established in 1872 as Yellowstone Park, in Montana and Wyoming. Today more than 100 nations contain some 1,200 national parks or equivalent natural reserves.

In the United States of America, National Park Service, a federal bureau in the Department of the Interior, administers the National Park System. The Service promotes the national parks, as well as national preserves, national monuments, national recreation areas, national seashores, lakeshores, historic parks and sites. The System now comprises more than 350 areas in 49 States, the District of Columbia, American Samoa, Guam, Puerto Rico, Saipan, and the Virgin Islands.

In England and Wales, there are now 11 national parks: the Lake District, the Peak District, Dartmoor, Exmoor, the Norfolk Broads, the Yorkshire Dales, North York Moors, Snowdonia, Northumberland, Pembrokeshire Coast and Brecon Beacons. Generally, such areas are in private ownership with arrangements made to facilitate public access and ensure preservation of the landscape. Since 1995, 'National Park authorities' have been established with the object of taking over the management and fostering of national parks and to be the sole planning authority for the parks (Environment Act 1995, s. 63, Sch. 7, 8, 9). See also **access agreement**(Eng), **area of outstanding natural beauty**(Eng), **area of special control**(Eng), **Countryside Agency**, **joint planning board**(Eng).

National Register of Historic Places(US)
See **historic sites**.

National Trust(Eng)   The 'National Trust for Places of Historic Interest or Natural Beauty'. A charitable trust established in 1895 by Octavia Hill, Sir Robert Hunter, and Canon Hardwicke Rawnsley, who were concerned about the impact of uncontrolled development and industrialisation. The trust was set up to act as a guardian for the nation by acquiring and protecting threatened countryside and buildings. It was subsequently incorporated with perpetual succession with power to "purchase take hold deal with and dispose of lands or other property without

licence in mortmain", National Trust Act 1907, s. 3; as well as to promote "the permanent preservation for the benefit of the nation of lands and tenements (including buildings) of beauty or historic interest and, as regards lands, for the preservation (so far as practicable) of their natural aspect features and animals and plant life", National Trust Act 1907, s. 4. Its powers were extended by the National Trust Acts of 1919, 1937 and 1939, so that it may now acquire alone, or jointly with other bodies or person, land, buildings or any other property. The National Trust has particular responsibility for the promotion and preservation of land or buildings of national interest or architectural, historic or artistic interest or importance, as well as similar furniture, pictures and chattels, and make these available for public viewing and enjoyment. The National Trust is a private registered charity that raises finance from the public. The trust is headquartered in London and serves England, Wales, and Northern Ireland. A parallel organisation, the National Trust for Scotland, was founded in 1931 and is headquartered in Edinburgh. Property owned by the Trust may be declared 'inalienable' so that such property may never be sold or given away without express Parliamentary authorisation. The National Trust (together with the National Trust for Scotland) is now the third largest landowner (by area) in Britain behind the State and the Crown, owning around 700,000 acres of land and some 350 homes, gardens, buildings or other places such as battlefields. (**www.nationaltrust.org.uk**).

nationalisation   See **expropriation**.

native title   The right of an indigenous people to the possession, enjoyment and use of **land** and waters, as recognised by common law. A right that is not an absolute form of private property, but is a qualified dominion based on prior possession of the land. A right that is dependent on the natives' right to continue to enjoy the land "in their own way or for their own purpose", Mitchell v. United States, 9 Pet 711, 34 US 711, 746, 9 L Ed 283 (1835). Native title comprises a right to the usufruct and habitation of the land, but it is not a right that can be alienated, except to other members or trustees of the same peoples. Also, such rights cannot be taken by the government without compensation, although it may be considered subservient to the right of the State (or Crown). Native title survives a Crown or State's acquisition of sovereignty and is not lost without a clear and unambiguous declaration of such an intention (*In re Southern Rhodesia* (1991) AC 211, 233 (PC)).

The European system of land law is derived from the principle that land is held or 'owned' by a succession of rights (freehold or leasehold, easements or servitudes, life interests or entailed interests) and in essence is a commodity to be used and traded. This right may be considered to be at variance with the rights as held by many nations where land is held by the community, the village or the family, and not by an individual or single entity. All members of the community have equal rights to the land, although in many cases the Chief or Head of the tribe or society has charge over the use of the land and in some cases is loosely referred to as the 'owner' or 'trustee' of the land. An individual may have rights to cultivate part of the land, but has no right to transfer that right, which always remains vested in the community.

During the colonial period of settlement, some of the 'discovered' land was considered *terra nullius* (land belonging to no-one). Under the principles of the common law of England, if such land was 'deserted and uncultivated', it could be peopled from a "mother country", 1 *Bl Comm* 106. On the other hand, a claim of sovereignty over a land does not unequivocally carry an absolute right of ownership; and "a mere change in sovereignty is not to be presumed to disturb rights of private owners", *Amodu Tijani v The Secretary, Southern Nigeria* [1921] 2 AC 399, 407 (PC) (United States v. Percheman, 7 Pet 51, 32 US 51, 87, 8 L Ed 604 (1833)). However, there arose a conflict between those who claimed sovereignty and considered that any land that was empty was theirs as of right, and those who were living on the 'discovered' land and did not acknowledge any such claims to their lands.

In the United States, the original inhabitants were admitted to be the rightful occupants of the soil, "with legal as well as just claim to retain possession of it", Johnson v. M'Intosh, 8 Wheat 543, 21 US 543, 574, 5 L Ed 681, 688 (1823); but this right was "necessarily, to considerable extent, impaired", *supra* at 591, 693. This impairment was a recognition of the right of the conqueror "to appropriate to themselves so much of [North America] as they could respectively acquire", *supra* at 572, 688. The right of occupation of the Native American tribes (the 'aboriginal right of possession') was recognised in specific lands and is considered good against all but the Sovereign and can only be terminated by Sovereign act. Such a right is now generally referred to as a right to **Indian lands** or 'Indian Title'.

In Canada, the First Nations have a relationship with the land; a connection to 'Mother Earth'. Their right to be on the land is not held as any form of ownership, nor as a personal or exclusive right to land. The law of Canada recognises three features of Aboriginal title: (i) Aboriginal title arises from the people's prior occupation of Canada; (ii) Aboriginal land can only be alienated to the Crown in the right of Canada; (iii) Aboriginal title is held communally by the "aboriginal nation" and each First Nation makes decisions about the use and holding of land in their respective Traditional Territory. Thus, to establish Aboriginal title the land must have been occupied prior to the assertion of British sovereignty; there must be a continuous possession from before that time to the present; and the occupation must have been exclusive (*Calder v British Columbia (Attorney General)* [1973] SCR 313, 4 DLR (3d) 145 (SCC Can); *Delgamuuku v British Columbia* [1998] 1 CNLR 14 (SCC Can)). Aboriginal title provides exclusive use of the land and the use must be consistent with the group's attachment to the land.

In Australia, the term 'native title' has been said to "conveniently describe the interests and rights of indigenous inhabitants in land, whether communal, group or individual, possessed under the traditional laws acknowledged by and the traditional customs observed by the indigenous inhabitants", *Mabo v Queensland (No 2)* (1992) 175 CLR 1, 57, 107 ALR 1. Subsequently this definition has formed the basis for the statutory definition: "the communal, group or individual rights and interests of Aboriginal peoples or Torres Strait Islanders in relation to land or waters, where: (a) the rights and interests are possessed under the traditional laws acknowledged, and the additional customs observed, by the Aboriginal peoples or Torres Strait Islanders; and (b) the Aboriginal peoples or Torres Strait Islanders, by those laws and customs, have a connection with the land or waters; and rights and interests are recognised by the common law of Australia", Native Title Act 1993, s. 223(1). "Rights and interests" in this context includes "hunting, gathering or fishing rights and interests", Native Title Act 1993, s. 223(2). This right requires that the indigenous people have maintained their "connection" with the land and that their title has not been extinguished by acts of Colonial, State, or Commonwealth governments. The right may extend from the right to use land for a specific purpose (for fishing or a right to visit a sacred site) to a permanent right to possession of land (as with the right recognised in *Mabo* of the Meriam people to possess most of the island of Mer). Native title cannot be extinguished unless there is a clear and plain intention to do so. Native title may be surrendered to the Crown voluntarily or extinguished by the Crown, but it cannot be alienated to anyone who is not a member of the relevant clan, group of Aboriginal people or Torres Strait Islanders.

In New Zealand, 'Aboriginal title' was a right over land and water enjoyed by indigenous people up to the time of colonisation. The Crown acquired an underlying or **radical title** that was considered to go with the sovereignty, but that title was subject to rights to exclusive and undisturbed possession of the lands enjoyed by the indigenous people (*Re Lundon & Whitakers Claims Act 1871* (1871) 2 NZCA 41, 49). These rights are usually, although not invariably, communal or collective. These rights

cannot be given up, except by the free consent of the indigenous occupiers, and then only to the Crown strictly in accordance with the provisions of any applicable statute (*Te Runanmanganui o Te Ika Whenua Inc Society v Attorney-General* [1994] 2 NZLR 20, 23-24). Land in New Zealand in now held as **Crown land**; **General land**; Maori customary land (which overlies the Crown's radical title, but cannot be alienated except to the Crown – few such areas now subsist); Maori freehold land (where the customary interest has been converted to fee simple – many of such lands are held in multiple ownership as tenancies in common); General land owned by Maori (freehold land with more than four owners the majority of whom are Maori); and Crown land reserved for Maori (Te Ture Whenua Maori/Maori Land Act 1993, s. 129). Customary land and Maori freehold land are legally termed 'Maori land'.

Bartlett, Richard H. *Native Title in Australia.* North Ryde, NSW: Butterworths, 2000.

Boast, Richard, et al. *Maori Land Law.* Wellington: Butterworths, 1999.

Clark, B. *Indian Title in Canada.* Toronto: Carswell, 1987.

McNeil, Kent. *Common Law Aboriginal Title.* Oxford: Clarendon Press, 1989.

Melville, Robert. *An Overview of Aboriginal and Treaty Rights and Compensation for their Breach.* Saskatoon, Sask.: Purich Publishing Ltd., 2001.

natural rights   Such rights as may be considered an ordinary incident to the ownership of **land** in its natural state, unless curtailed by agreement or statute or lost to another by prescription. The term is essentially one of the common law and includes in particular: (a) a right to receive air that comes through a defined passage, in an unpolluted state (but not the free passage of air itself; (b) a right not to have the support of land itself undermined by an owner of adjacent or subjacent land as by mining or excavation activity; or (c) a right of a riparian owner to the free flow of water in its natural state, in flow, quantity and quality (subject to the common law rights of extraction by an upper riparian owner), and for surface water to be discharged onto the lower land of his neighbour. In common law, there is no natural **right to light**, such a right must be acquired as an easement or preserved by a restrictive or negative covenant. A natural right cannot be acquired by grant (whether express, implied or presumed). In that respect it may be distinguishable from an **easement**, which must be acquired by grant, either actual, implied or presumed. A natural right cannot be derived from any artificial addition to land. Thus, there is no natural right of support for a building on land, unless there is an express easement or right to that effect.

In the US, the term 'natural rights' generally refers to the rights of lateral and subjacent support of the land in its natural condition and the right to the free flow of water in a natural watercourse and the discharge of surface water from a higher to a lower plane. These rights are inherent in the land – *ex jure naturæ* – rights without which an owner cannot properly enjoy the use of land. See also **lateral support, public rights, right of air, right to fish, right of support, riparian rights, water rights**.

natural servitude   See **natural rights, servitude**.

natural wear and tear   See **fair wear and tear**(BrE), **wear and tear**(AmE).

Nature Conservancy Council (NCC)(Eng) See **English Nature**.

navigable waters   See **highway, riparian rights, road**.

nec vi, nec clam, nec precario(Lat)   'Not by violence, not by stealth, not by entreaty'. A term derived from Roman law to describe essential elements for establishing a right over land by **prescription**; to acquire such a right it must have been *longus usus nec per vim, nec clam, nec precario* (1 *Co Litt* 113b). A prescriptive right must not be claimed as a result of force, secret

user, nor must the right have been obtained with permission. See also **adverse possession**.

necessity, **agency of**   See **agency of necessity, quasi-contract**.

necessary easement   See **easement of necessity**.

necessary repair(US)   Such repair as is necessary for the use of a property for the purpose for which it is leased. A covenant in a lease to carry out "necessary repairs" includes such repairs as would be require to maintain the property for its intended use, but does not require the tenant to put the premises in better condition than they were at the commencement of the term. It does not extend to making such repairs as would improve the property or make it suitable for another use after the lease expires. cf. **good repair**. See also **implied covenant, tenant-like manner, tenantable repair**.

negative amortization(AmE)   A situation that arises when a loan balance is increasing rather than decreasing, i.e. when the payments being made on a loan are less than the interest that is accruing thereon. Negative amortization most commonly arises when a mortgage loan provides for level monthly payments to cover interest and principal (an **amortization mortgage**) and the actual payments made are below the scheduled payments. Negative amortization may also arise under a **variable-rate mortgage** when a lower payment on account of interest is allowed than the face rate on the mortgage and the difference is accrued and added to the outstanding principal.

negative cash flow   A situation where the gross income from an investment is insufficient to meet operating expenses, taxes and the annual cost of debt service, i.e. the **cash flow** is insufficient to meet all outgoings associated with holding the investment. See also **alligator, deficit financing, leverage**.

negative covenant   A **covenant** that limits an action. A covenant that restricts the use or development of land in some way, especially so as to benefit another parcel of land. cf. **positive covenant**. See also **restrictive covenant**.

negative declaration(US)   See **environmental impact report**.

negative easement   An **easement** by which the owner of land (the 'dominant tenement') limits a right or benefit over adjoining land (the 'servient tenement'), such as a right not to have an adjoining landowner obstruct the flow of light or air or not to remove a right of support. However, the right granted is not truly an 'easement' as it creates a restriction or servitude and not a right or privilege to enjoy a benefit from the use of another's land. Thus, the terminology is confusing and the term **equitable servitude** or 'equitable restriction' is preferred in many cases where the right limits the use of land.

As a rule, English law does not recognise a negative easement, because such a privilege is merely a right to insist that a person use his land in a certain, but limited, way (*Moore v Rawson* (1824) 3 B & C 332, 107 Eng Rep 756); a true right or privilege to prevent the use of land, for the benefit of other land, being a **restrictive covenant**. At common law, negative easements are limited to light, air (in a defined channel), view (in rare cases), lateral support, and the taking of water from an artificial stream. Negative easements are generally regarded with disfavour, the common law preferring to consider such a right as a 'positive easement', as with a right to receive light across a given area of land, or to regard the right as an imposition of a **restrictive covenant** (*Phipps v Pears* [1965] 1 QB 76, [1964] 2 All ER 35 (CA)). Sometimes called a 'subservient easement' or an 'equitable restriction'. See also **natural rights, real covenant**.

negative equity   A situation that arises when the amount of a mortgage loan exceeds the value of the mortgaged property. Negative equity may arise when the value of the property declines, but the amount of outstanding principal remains constant (or does not decline by the same amount). It may also arise when the amount of outstanding loan principal is increasing, as when the total amount of monthly payments (of interest and principal) are fixed, but the interest rate on the mortgage loan is increasing, i.e. a form of **negative amortization**.

negative gearing   A position that arises when the cost of **debt service** exceeds the **cash flow** from an investment. In the US, more commonly called 'negative leverage'. See also **deficit financing**, **gearing**.

negative leasehold(US)   The situation where the rent payable under a lease (**contract rent**) exceeds the **market rent**. See also **profit rent**(BrE).

negative leverage   See **leverage**.

negative profit rent   See **profit rent**.

negative servitude   See **servitude**.

negligence   An omission, failure, or statement that a *reasonable* person, guided by the standards expected during normal human acts or conduct, would not perpetrate because it is likely to result in loss or injury by a person to whom a standard or **duty of care** is owed. A failure to exercise the degree of care in a given situation that a reasonable man under similar circumstances would exercise to protect others from harm. "Negligence is the omitting to do something that a reasonable man, guided upon those considerations which ordinarily regulate the conduct of human affairs, would do or the doing of something which a reasonable man would not do", *Blyth v Birmingham Waterworks Co* (1856) 11 Exch 781, 784, 156 Eng Rep 1047 (*British Railways Board v Herrington* [1972] AC 877, 907, [1972] 1 All ER 749, 765 (HL); Baltimore & P. R. Co. v. Jones, 5 Otto 439, 95 US 439, 24 L Ed 506, 507 (1877)). Negligence covers both acts that a man or woman would not commit and statements that would not be made, for fear that they might cause hardship to another. A failure, whether knowingly, wilfully or intentionally to exercise the kind of ordinary care or attention which, in all the circumstances of the case, might foreseeably cause harm, damage or injury is negligent behaviour and is a breach of that duty which any person owes to another. In order to be able to claim negligence, an offended party must demonstrate that he was owed a duty of care, or reasonable standard of care, by another person; that there was a breach of that duty; that he has suffered damage as a result of the negligent act and that damage is not too remote from the negligent act (i.e. there is a 'proximate cause' between the act or statement and the damage suffered); and that the party suffering the damage was not acting in an unreasonable manner so as to cause or add to the damage or injury suffered (i.e. there has not been an element of **contributory negligence**).

Negligence may arise from an omission, miscarriage or a false statement but, unlike **misrepresentation**, does not arise directly from a contractual relationship (although it may flow from a breach of an express or implied obligation arising out of a contract that requires reasonable care or skill). It is a separate tort from, but may arise together with, a **nuisance**. For example, when a property owner fails to repair and maintain premises his neighbour may suffer injury from falling material, and also be obstructed in the proper use and enjoyment of his property.

Negligence may arise in a number of instances that specifically relate to real estate. For example: (i) A landowner permitting something to escape from land when he knows, or should know, that danger is likely to arise therefrom – a **strict liability** owed by a landowner to the public at large. (ii) A liability owed by an occupier of premises to exercise a proper duty of care towards any **visitor** (which includes a licensee and an invitee). (iii) A landowner's liability for a failure to take steps to prevent injury to children who are likely to **trespass** on his land, especially by protecting items that may attract and be dangerous

to children (in the US called the 'attractive nuisance doctrine'); the landowner is expected to provide an obstacle to any child who might approach something dangerous on the land, an obstacle that clearly indicates that going any further is entering into dangerous or forbidden territory (*British Railways Board v Herrington* [1972] AC 877, 940, [1972] 1 All ER 749, 794 (HL) (Union Pacific R. Co. v. McDonald, 152 US 262, 38 L Ed 434 (1893). (iv) A failure of a person who takes on work for, or in connection with, the erection, conversion or enlargement of a dwelling-house (which may include a contractor, subcontractor, architect, engineer, surveyor or any other professional person) to ensure that the work is carried out in a workmanlike or professional manner; that proper materials are used; and that the house is fit for habitation when completed. (v) The failure of a landlord, who is under an obligation to his tenant for **repair** or **maintenance** of all or part of the demised premises, whether an express obligation or an obligation that is implied (for example from his right of entry to carry out repairs or maintenance), to properly carry out his obligations, and thereby risk harm being occasioned to a user of the premises – a duty that arises when the landlord knew, or might reasonably have known, of the defect (although, in the US, some jurisdictions do not accept that the landlord is liable for negligence resulting from his failure to repair the demised premises, as they are under the control of the tenant as far as any third party is concerned.

The above list of areas where negligence may arise is by no means exhaustive, it serves to illustrates the need for any person having control of land, buildings or anything attached thereto, to take reasonable care that the property is safe for any intending or likely user; a liability that extends to owners and occupiers, their agent and managers, and their professional advisers. In this branch of the law, which has evolved rapidly in the past 25 years, the courts are trenchant when seeking to protect the weak from the strong; especially the ordinary man against a possessor of real estate who fails to maintain his asset in a safe and secure condition, but still expects or invites others to enter thereon.

A person cannot escape a liability for negligence merely by giving notice that he is not liable to anyone for a negligent act or omission, unless that is reasonable in all the circumstances and with due deference to the visitor or trespasser. A licensee (as well as an invitee) must be warned of any dangers of which the occupier or owner is aware and in the absence of such warning the licensee cannot be expected to "take the premises as he finds them", Public Service Co. of New Hampshire v. Elliot, 123 F.2d 2, 6 (1st Cir. NH 1941) In English law, this principle is encompassed in the statutory provision that "a person cannot by reference to any contract term or to a notice given to persons generally or to particular persons exclude or restrict his liability for death or personal injury resulting from negligence", Unfair Contract Terms Act 1977, s. 2(1). See also **laches**, **professional negligence**, **trespass**, *volenti non fit injuria*.

negligent waste(US)   See **waste**.

negotiable instrument   A written document that may be assigned or transferred in the normal course of business. A written instrument that constitutes an obligation to pay money (or, sometimes, to deliver a security for money) and passes a good title merely by **delivery**, or by **endorsement** and delivery. In particular, an unconditional order or promise to pay a definite sum of money (but not a mere **receipt**) signed by the maker of the **instrument**. "A written and signed unconditional promise or order to pay a specified sum of money on demand or at a definite time payable to order or bearer", United States Uniform Commercial Code, § 3-104(1). A person who accepts a negotiable instrument in **good faith** and for **value** (the '*bona fide* holder'), without **notice** of any defect (a 'holder in due course'), obtains an indefeasible title and a right of action in his own name, even if the transferor's title was defective. Thus, unlike most other contracts, a negotiable instrument does not necessarily rely on **privity**

of contract, nor is it entirely ruled by the maxim *nemo dat qui non habet*, 'no one can give what he does not possess'. A negotiable instrument may take the form of a bank note, **check**(AmE)/**cheque**(BrE), a **bill of exchange**, **certificate of deposit**, **promissory note** or a bearer bond or bearer share, provided it is transferable by delivery and payable to order or to the bearer. See also **commercial paper**, **negotiation**.

James, Jennifer. *Richardson's Guide to Negotiable Instruments*. 8th ed. London: Butterworths, 1991.

Seidel, Richard W., et al. *Negotiable Instruments and Check Collection: The New Law in a Nutshell*. 4th ed. St. Paul, MN: West, 1993.

negotiation   1. A discussion or bargaining process between two parties conducted with a view to concluding an **agreement** or settling a dispute on a matter of mutual concern. The process whereby parties treat with another in order to bring about a result or reach a settlement. The process of bargaining and haggling with another party with a view to arranging a sale or other form of business transaction.

The process of negotiation may be conducted directly between the parties, or through an intermediary or negotiator. In the latter case the 'negotiator' should act as a mediator and adopt an impartial stance from both parties to the potential transaction, otherwise he may be considered a **subcontractor** or a mere **middleman**.

In English law, in the context of finding a purchaser and "conducting negotiations with any prospective purchaser" in order to effect a sale and thereby earning a commission, negotiation has been held to mean "conferring with the prospective purchaser, or his representative, with a view to agreeing a sale", and not simply giving advice to the agent's own principal, the seller (*Hoddell v Smith* (1976) 240 EG 295, 301). When an intermediary or agent has been appointed to negotiate and 'arrange' a sale of property, then negotiation may be described as that process "which passes between parties or their agents in the course of or incident to the making of a contract; and if the negotiation is brought to such a close as leaves the principal at liberty to say, 'I accept the offer'—then the agent has done all that a negotiating agent can do, and within the meaning of the rule he has arranged the sale, the sale afterwards being effected", *Re Macgowan, Macgowan v Murray* [1891] 1 Ch 105, 116 (CA).

In the US, when a license is required for a **broker** or salesman to "negotiate" a sale or purchase of real estate, the term may be defined as "'to hold intercourse or treat with a view to coming to terms upon some matter, as a purchase or sale, a treaty, etc.; to conduct communications or conferences as a basis of agreement; as to *negotiate* a purchase of a house' [Webster's New International Dictionary (2d Ed.)]", Massie v. Dudley, 173 Va 42, 3 SE.2d 176, 179 (1939). See also **bargain, commission, estate agent**(Eng), **invitation to trade**(AmE)/ **invitation to treat**(BrE), **procuring cause, real estate license**(US), **subject to contract, without prejudice, writing.** **2.** The transfer of a **bill of exchange** or **negotiable instrument** from one person (whether the first or subsequent holder) to another, by delivery or endorsement and delivery, in such a manner that the transferee becomes the possessor of the document.

negotiator   See **negotiation.** cf. **middleman.**

neighbor(AmE) or **neighbour**(BrE)   **1.** One who lives in an adjoining house or in close proximity; "one who lives near or next to another; one who occupies a near or adjoining house, one of a number of persons living close to each other, especially in the same street or village", *The Oxford English Dictionary*, 2nd ed., 1989. In relation to a liability for a **tort**, 'neighbours' have been defined as "persons who are so closely and directly affected by my act that I ought to reasonably have them in contemplation as being so affected when I am directing my mind to the acts or omissions which are called in question", *M'Alister (Donoghue) v Stevenson* [1932] AC 562, 580 (HL) (although a liability in tort may extend beyond neighbours to invitees, licensees or even trespassers, depending on the circumstances. See also **negligence.** **2.** Any **adjacent** or **adjoining** owner or occupier of

land. In relation to a **right of support** for land, a 'neighbouring landowner' may be described as "the owner of that portion of land, whether a wider or narrower strip of land, the existence of which in its natural state is necessary for the support of [the] land", *Birmingham Corporation v Allen* (1877) 6 Ch D 284, 289 (CA). See also **access order**(Eng), *ad medium filum*, **boundary line, derogation from grant.**

neighborhood(US) or **neighbourhood**(BrE) **1.** The immediate vicinity; an area in close proximity. The immediate environs of a property; the area nearby. A term of relative measure given the area of application. In the context of a zoning ordinance or regulation, a neighborhood is the area in the vicinity; the area that has common geographical, physical and social characteristics. See also **adjacent, neighbor**(AmE)/**neighbour**(BrE). **2.** An area of a town or city that makes up a distinct community. **3.** A number of people who form a cohesive unit usually within a larger area or district. See also **neighboring unit**(AmE)/ **neighbouring unit**(BrE), **shopping center.**

neighborhood shopping center   See **shopping center.**

neighborhood unit(AmE)
or **neighbourhood unit**(BrE)   A homogeneous urban or suburban area of predominately residential property that has grown up or, more usually, has been created to facilitate ease of access to essential services and to provide a balanced and identifiable community. A neighborhood unit is a distinct and territorial grouping of people established as a self-contained entity, i.e. with retail stores, schools, meeting halls, service industries, recreation areas, etc. The 'neighborhood unit' grew in popularity in North America during the 1920's and 30's as a form for new housing development. In the UK, the 'neighbourhood unit' was adopted after World War II as the model for many of the new town housing developments, as well as being the norm for numerous new housing schemes. Such units of

development have been termed 'neighbourhoods', 'districts', 'residential communities' or even 'villages'. The ideal size for such communities is a subject of contention, but is commonly considered to fall within the range of 1,000 to 10,000 persons so that the area is large enough to support local facilities, but not so large as to lose the sense of neighbourliness.

neighboring property(AmE)
or **neighbouring property**(BrE)   Property adjoining, in close proximity, or in the same vicinity, as the subject property. See also **adjacent**, **neighbor**(AmE)/**neighbour**(BrE).

nemo contra factum suum [proprium] venire potest(Lat)   'No one can go against his own act or deed.' See **derogation from grant**, **estoppel**.

nemo dare potest quod non habet(Lat)   'No one can give that which he has not'. See **covenant for title**, **estoppel**, **sub-lease**.

nemo dat qui [quod] non habet(Lat)   'No one can give who possesses not'; 'no one can give what he does not hold'. In particular, no one can be given a better **title** than he has himself.   See also **negotiable instrument**.

nemo est haeres viventis(Lat)   'No one is the heir of one who is living'. No one can be an **heir** during the life time of his ancestor.

nemo plus juris ad alium [alienum] tranferre potest, quam ipse habet(Lat)   'No one can transfer a greater right to another than he himself has'. Thus, the title of an assignee can be no better than that of his assignor. See also **assignment**.

net after-tax cash flow(US)   Cash flow available from an investment after payment of income tax. Generally, the cash available for distribution to the owner or investor(s) in the property. See also **income**.

net asset value (NAV)   The **net worth** (value of all assets less liabilities) of the ordinary stockholder's funds. The net asset value of a company is generally stated as a price per share outstanding. Not to be confused with the **asset value** per share which is based on the current market value of all assets assuming a break-up of the company. See also **break-up value**.

net assets   See net worth.

net before recapture(US)   See **net income before recapture**.

net before tax(US)   See income, net income.

net book value   See book value.

net capital   The present or **net worth** of a business; the difference between the total assets and the total liabilities of a corporation.

net cash flow   **Cash flow** after deducting any liabilities for tax, loan interest and principal payments and allowing for depreciation. **Income** that may be distributed free of all liability. Also called 'net operating cash flow' or 'net spendable income'. cf. **net income**. See also **net after-tax cash flow**(US).

net commission or **net fee**(US)   A commission or fee payable to a broker based on the 'net' price received by the seller, i.e. the price received after all charges and expenses directly related to the transaction. Thus, if a broker is to receive a commission in the event that the sale price exceeds a 'net price', no commission is payable until the 'net' to the seller exceeds the stipulated price. See also **net listing**.

net cost   The actual amount paid for, or the cost of, a property after taking account of any benefit or income received in return. cf. **gross cost**. See also **acquisition cost**, **equity**.

net current assets   See **working capital**.

net discounted revenue   See **net present value**.

net discounted value   See **net present value**.

net effective rent   See **effective lease rate**.

net equity   The amount of **equity** actually invested in a property, excluding debt service and any fees, charges or expenses paid to third parties.

net earnings   See **earnings**, **net operating income**(US).

net estate   The amount of a deceased's estate after payment of all debts, funeral expenses and administration expenses, but before deducting any estate taxes.

net floor area   See **net internal area**(Eng), **rentable area**(US), **usable area**.

net income   The difference between total revenue and total expenditure from an investment. The annual **income** received, or likely to be received, from an investment in a property, after deducting all operating costs and expenses directly related to that property. Net income may be expressed as 'before tax' (or 'net before tax') or 'after tax' (or 'net after tax'); or 'before debt service' or 'after debt service'. Net income is calculated before any allowance for depreciation. cf. **gross income, net cash flow**.

net income before recapture(US)   The **net operating income** before any allowance for depreciation.

net income multiplier (NIM)(US)   See **income multiplier**.

net income ratio (NIR)(US)   The ratio of **net operating income** to **effective gross income** – the complement of the **operating expense ratio**.

net internal area(BrE)   "The usable area within a building measured to the internal face of the perimeter walls at each floor level. INCLUDING (1) Atria with clear height above, measured at base level only [but see 11]; (2) Entrance halls (but see 13); (3) Notional lift lobbies; (4) Kitchens; (5) Built-in units, cupboards, and the like occupying usable areas; (6) Ramps of lightweight construction to false floors; (7) Area occupied by ventilation/ heating grilles; (8) Area occupied by skirting and perimeter trunking; (9) Areas severed by internal non-structural walls, demountable partitions, whether or not permanent, and the like, where the purpose of the division is partition of use, not support, provided the area beyond is not used in common; (10) Pavement vaults. EXCLUDING (11) Those parts of the entrance halls, atria, landing and balconies used in common (see (1) and (2)); (12) Toilets, toilet lobbies, bathrooms, and the like; (13) Lift rooms, plant rooms, tank rooms, other than those of a trade process nature, fuel stores and the like (14) Stairwells, lift-wells, and permanent lift lobbies; (15) Corridors and other circulation areas where used in common with other occupiers or of a permanent essential nature (e.g. fire corridors, smoke lobbies, etc.) (16) Areas under the control of service or other external authorities including meter cupboards and statutory service supply points; (17) Internal structural walls, walls enclosing excluded areas, columns, piers, chimney breasts, other projections, vertical ducts and the like; (18) The space occupied by permanent and continuous air-conditioning heating or cooling apparatus, and ducting in so far as the space it occupies is rendered substantially unusable (where such apparatus is present its area may be stated separately for valuation purposes) (19) Areas with headroom of less than 1.5m; (20) areas rendered substantially unusable by virtue of having a dimension between opposite faces of less than 0.25m (See diagram E [in the *Code*]) (21) Vehicle parking areas (the number and type of spaces noted)", The Royal Institution of Chartered Surveyor, *Code of Measuring Practice*. 5th ed. London: RICS Books, 2002. Certain areas such as (1), (2), (6), (10) and (19) may be better stated separately (Note: this definition is accompanied in the *Code* by diagrams and detailed notes for amplification.) A measurement used for estate agency and valuation of shops and supermarkets, offices, and some business use properties; rating of shops (including supermarkets, and most business use), and composite hereditaments; and service charge apportionment for occupiers. cf. **gross internal area**. See also **rentable area**[US].

net leasable area[US]   See **rentable area**.

net lease or **net-net-lease**[US]   A lease that requires the lessee to pay the **operating expenses** resulting from his occupation of the premises and other expenses such as real estate taxes and assessments and insurance premiums. Under a 'net lease' (or 'single net lease') the lessee generally pays the real estate taxes and expenses resulting directly from his occupation such as janitorial expenses; under a 'net-net lease' (or 'double net lease') he also pays the cost of insurance; and with a 'net-net-net' (**triple net lease** or 'absolute net lease') he pays all repair and maintenance costs. However, the term net lease is sometimes used in a generic sense for any lease that provides that the lessee is to pay all or most of the property outgoings and the landlord receives his income 'net' of expenses (or the expenses are a minor part of the income) – except, as a rule, his own management fees and debt service costs. A net-net lease is sometimes called a 'partial net lease'. Also, the term 'net-net lease' is used sometimes to refer to a 'triple net lease' (although the latter imposes a stricter liability on the lessee).

net lease financing   See **sale-and-leaseback**.

net lettable area (NLA)[US]   See **rentable area**.

net listing[US]   A form of agency **listing** that provides for the principal to receive an agreed price for a property and for the broker to retain as commission any sum received above that price. In some jurisdictions, net listing agreements are prohibited as they are considered to place the broker in a position that is potentially in conflict with his duty to procure the best deal for the principal. Where such an agreement is legal, the agreed price should be realistically achievable. Also called a 'net sale contract'. See also **contingency fee**, **net commission**.

net-net lease[US]   See **net lease**.

net-net-net lease   See **net lease**, **triple net lease**.

net occupiable area (NOA)   See **net internal area**[BrE], **rentable area**[US], **usable area**.

net operating cash flow   See **net cash flow**.

net operating income (NOI)[US]   **Net income** receivable from a property after all operating expenses have been paid and an allowance has been made for bad debts and defaulting tenants, but before payment of capital or interest on any loans (i.e. before 'debt service') and before income taxes. Also called 'operating income'. NOI may be expressed by the symbol I_0. cf. **cash flow**. See also **income**, **net income before recapture**.

net operating profit   See **net profit**.

net option   An **option** that grants the option holder a right to acquire a property at a specified net price to the seller, i.e. the option holder agrees to bear all transaction costs.

net population density   See **population density**.

net present value (NPV)   The difference, at a given discount rate, between the **present value** of (a) the total net income to be derived from an investment and (b) the total expenditure and outgoings incurred in making and maintaining that investment, taken over the projected life of the investment. Net present value is used especially to compare or to assess the viability of alternative investments. The income and expenditure from each alternative is reduced or discounted to a common base, i.e. a single value is determined by discounting to the present day (or the date of the initial investment) the amounts receivable over and above the amounts payable for each investment. A positive NPV indicates that an investment is profitable and the higher the NPV, the better the profitability of that investment. Also called the 'net discounted value' or the 'net discounted revenue'. See also **capitalisation**, **discounted cash flow**, Appendix C, **Financial Formulae**.

net price   The **price** paid for a property excluding any fees, commissions, discounts, taxes, i.e. the true consideration paid for the property. See also **acquisition cost**.

net profit   Profit after deducting selling and administrative expenses and depreciation, which may be measured either before or after tax. Net profit may be classified before the cost of debt finance – 'net operating profit', or after all costs - 'clear, or net, profit for distribution'. cf. **gross profit**. See also **net income**.

net realisable value[(BrE)] or **net realizable value**[(AmE)](NRV)   The **market value** of a property after allowing for all the cost of sale, i.e. the net amount that a seller can expect to receive in cash.

net redemption yield   A redemption yield after tax. cf. **grossed-up redemption yield**.

net rent or **net rental**   1. An amount of rent stipulated in a lease as payable without the tenant having any right to make deductions from that rent. Thus, a net rent is payable clear of any deductions. A tenant who pay a 'net rent' cannot withhold monies to pay for such matters as insurance or property taxes.   2. The total amount payable by the tenant(s) of a property as specified under the lease(s) as **rent**; excluding any other payments the tenant may make to his landlord, such as operating expense or property tax charge contributions, insurance premium reimbursements, interest on late payments, etc. See also **net income**.   3.[(US)]The rent receivable from the tenant or tenants of a building after an appropriate deduction or allowance for voids or defaulting tenants. See also **effective gross income**, **income**.   4. The rent receivable by a landlord after deducting all expenses of operating the property, including the cost of all repairs and taxes relating to the building for which the landlord is liable.

net rent multiplier   See **income multiplier**.

net rentable area[(US)]   See **rentable area**.

net residential density   See **residential density**.

net retail floor space   See **retail area**[(Eng)].

net return   See **net yield**.

net sale contract[(US)]   See **net listing**.

net site area   See **site area**.

net spendable income   See **net cash flow**.

net usable area   See **net internal area**[(BrE)], **rentable area**[(US)], **usable area**.

net value   The **capital value** of a property after taking into account all costs of purchase, as distinguished from the **gross value** which assumes that the property is acquired free of all costs.

net worth   The value of the total assets (excluding fictitious assets) of an organisation, less the total liabilities (excluding the owner's capital), i.e. the total value of the owner's share of a business. In accounting, the 'net worth' of a corporation is commonly taken as equivalent to the **book value** of the equity and preference stockholders' interest, including retained reserves, although this basis of valuation may not fully take account of the current market value of all the assets of the corporation. Also called the 'net assets' or 'total equity' of a corporation; or an 'owner's equity'. cf. **asset value**, **break-up value**. See also **equity capital**, **net asset value**.

net yield   The yield represented by expressing the **net income** (after deducting all operating expenses) receivable from an investment as a percentage of the total **acquisition cost** of that investment. The return on an investment after taking into account the cost of managing that investment and any losses incurred during the holding period. Net yield may be expressed as 'before tax' or 'after tax'; or 'before **debt service**' or 'after debt service'. Also called the 'net return'. See also **cash-on-cash yield**, **free and clear return**, **net redemption yield**.

network analysis   A generic term for several techniques used in the planning and control of a project by which the stages in the project are set out in sequence and inter-related by means of a diagrammatic representation, in order to determine the sequence of work that produces the optimum use of time at the minimum cost. See also **critical path analysis**, **project evaluation and review technique**.

new assessment   See **reassessment**.

new development(Eng)   See **compensation for planning restrictions**.

new-for-old insurance   See **reinstatement cost**.

new money   1. Additional capital, usually in the form of equity capital, that is provided to fund a project.   2. The loan proceeds that are obtained from a **wraparound mortgage** over and above the amount of the existing loan.

new tenancy(Eng)   See **business tenancy**, **extended lease**.

new town   A town that is developed as an entity over a relatively short time span (10-20 years) usually to meet an urgent housing need, as compared with a town that develops by natural growth, over several generations. The objective of most new town development is to relocate population from a large city or conurbation and establish an autonomous community with a comprehensive range of services including housing, shopping centers, hospitals, schools, industrial facilities, social facilities, etc.

In Great Britain, the post-war new towns are commonly regarded as a direct descendant of the **garden city** movement. The term 'New Town' specifically refers to an area designated for development under the provision of the New Towns Acts of 1946, 1965 or 1981. Since 1977, no further New Towns have been created in Great Britain and, as the development of the existing New Towns has been completed, the administration and ultimate disposal of their assets has been transferred to the **Commission for the New Towns** or the local authority for the area. See also **development corporation**(Eng), **garden city**.

new town development corporation(Eng) See **development corporation**.

New Towns Commission(Eng)   See **Commission for the New Towns**.

new valuation   See **revaluation**.

no bid(US)   A situation that is said to arise if the Veterans Administration (VA) (or since 1989 the Department of Veterans Affairs) elects not to pay off a loan in the event of foreclosure and take control of the foreclosed property, but merely pays the amount that the VA guaranteed and leave the property with the lender. In the event that a lender who has a VA guaranteed loan seeks to foreclose on a property, the VA can elect to authorize the lender to bid at the foreclosure sale for an amount up to the lesser of the 'net value' (which is the appraised value less selling and administrative expenses) and the loan balance. If the lender acquires the property, he conveys it to the VA in return for the VA's payment of the lender's debt (including foreclosure expenses). The VA will then seek to recover all or part of the amount paid out from the subsequent sale of the property. Alternatively, if a third party outbids the lender, the lender receives the proceeds of the sale and the VA pays the difference up to the amount of its guarantee. However, if the VA determines that it is not financially beneficial to acquire the property, it declares a 'no bid' and only pays the lender the amount of its guarantee. In such a case, the lender retains the property, which he can then resell, probably at an overall loss. See also **Veterans Administration loan**.

no set-off certificate(US)   See **estoppel certificate**.

no-buy pledge(US)   An agreement entered when it is proposed to convert a tenanted building to condominium or cooperative ownership, by which the tenants promise not to proceed with the purchase of their units until the majority of those who signed the agreement have accepted that the best deal has been reached by the promoters (usually a tenants' association) of the proposed change in the form of ownership.

no-compete clause(US)   See **non-competition clause**.

no-deal, no-commission clause(AmE) or **no-deal, no-fee clause**(BrE)   A clause inserted in an agency or brokerage agreement that no **commission** or **fee** will be paid by the principal unless a particular result is achieved, usually the completion of the transaction and the payment of the purchase price in full. As a rule, such a provision requires absolute performance, unless the principal acts capriciously or in bad faith to avoid the final transaction. cf. **ready able and willing**(BrE)/**ready willing and able**(AmE). See also **procuring clause**.

no-scheme world(Eng)   See **compulsory purchase compensation**.

noise   See **derogation from grant**, **mitigation work**, **non-conforming use**, **nuisance**.

nominal company   See **nominee company**.

nominal consideration   **1.** Consideration that has no significant value (e.g. $1 or £1) but is included in a contract that is not made by deed to preserve its apparent validity under common law. See also **peppercorn rent**.   **2.** A nominal amount included in a contract to indicate that an outright gift is not intended.

nominal damages   See **damages**.

nominal interest rate   **1.** The interest rate payable for a period of one year assuming the entire principal remains outstanding during the year and interest is accrued only once a year, as compared with the **effective annual interest rate** which is the true rate payable when interest is compounded at intervals of less than a year.   **2.** The basic annual interest rate quoted on a promissory note or on a loan agreement and levied throughout the term of the loan on the initial amount of principal, notwithstanding that the interest is compounded other than annually or repayments of principal are made by installments during the term of the loan. Thus, if a sum of $10,000 is borrowed for one year at a 'nominal interest rate' of 10% per annum, and the principal is repayable monthly by equal instalments, then $1,000 is payable as interest even though the total amount of principal is not available for the full year. Sometimes called an 'add-on interest rate' 'face rate', 'face interest rate' or 'nominal loan rate'. See also **annual percentage rate**, **coupon rate**, **face value**.

nominal loan rate   See **nominal interest rate**.

nominal rate of return or **nominal yield**   **1.** The **dividend yield** when related to the **nominal value** of a share, as contrasted with the same yield when related to the market value of the share.   **2.** The rate of return on an investment based on the ratio of the current annual income to the current capital value. In particular, the rate of return specified on a share, or similar financial instrument, as a percentage of the nominal or **par value**. The nominal yield, or 'nominal dividend yield', is the basis normally used by a corporation for expressing its rate of dividend return. Also called the 'nominal return'. cf. **effective rate of return, equivalent yield**. See also **coupon rate**.

nominal return   See **nominal rate of return**.

nominal share capital   The capital that a company is authorised to raise rather than the amount actually paid-up by the shareholders. The total **face value** of the share capital of a company. See also **nominal value**.

nominal trust(US)   See **passive trust**.

nominal value   1. A value stated as a matter of form, which bears no relationship to **market value**. 2. The face value as indicated on a stock of a corporation, i.e. the **par value**.

nominal yield   See **nominal rate of return**.

nominated subcontractor   A **subcontractor** or supplier selected by the employer as distinguished from one appointed at the sole discretion of the main or principal contractor. Generally, a nominated subcontractor is appointed or selected to carry out specialist work, or work that the employer requires be carried out by a particular firm. As a rule, at the time that the main contractor is invited to tender for work, the employer will specify that a specialist subcontractor of the employer's choice undertake certain work. However, in spite of the intervention of the employer, there is no **privity of contract** between the employer and the subcontractor, and the contractor is totally responsible for the work of the nominated subcontractor, unless the employer makes an express stipulation to the contrary. The employer usually remains responsible for renomination if the subcontractor

fails to fulfil his obligations or repudiates the subcontract. Some building contracts provide the main contractor with a right of objection to a nominated subcontractor if that will substantially impair his ability to perform the conditions of the main contract. A subcontractor may be nominated on the basis that the main contractor is required to use that firm or supplier. He may also be 'named' as one of a group of subcontractors from whom the main contractor can select one of his own preference; although the architect may reserve the right to make the final selection, usually after verifying that the subcontractor can deliver the standard of workmanship, etc. required by the client.

nominee   One who is appointed or nominated to act on behalf of another party. Sometimes used to refer to an **agent** or **trustee**.

nominee company or **nominee trust**   A **company**, or **trust**, formed to hold property or an investment in name only, i.e. as a **fiduciary**, or trustee, for another party, such as an overseas resident who wishes to conceal his identity. A company that is effective in name only as the benefit or obligation accrues to the other party or **beneficiary**. Sometimes called a 'nominal company'. See also **passive trust**.

non aedificandi(Lat)   'No building'. An area of land where all building is prohibited, such as alongside a highway or between buildings. A **servitude** *non aedificandi* provides the owner of one parcel of land with the right to prevent the owner of adjoining land from building and thereby interfering with an existing right of light, prospect, or air. This restriction may extend above (to restrict balconies, etc.) or below the land (to restrict basement construction, etc.). It may arise as a restriction between adjoining land owners, or it may be imposed as a condition to the grant of a planning or building authorisation. See also *altius non tollendi*, **setback**.

non-alienation clause(US)   See **restraint on alienation**.

non altius toliendi(Lat)   See *altius non tollendi*.

non-ancestral estate   An **estate** that is acquired other than by descent or devise. Sometimes used to refer to an estate acquired by purchase or agreement, as distinguished from an estate acquired by operation of law. cf. **ancestral estate**.

non-apparent easement   An **easement** the existence of which cannot readily be ascertained from a cursory inspection of the property. In particular, an easement that is enjoyed at certain intervals or times and leaves no sign of its existence at other times, such as a right of way over an unmarked or unmade path. cf. **apparent easement**. See also **discontinuous servitude**, **notice**.

non-assumption clause(US)   See **assumption clause**.

non-competition clause   A clause in a contract by which one party undertakes not to carry on competitive business during the term of the contract or for a specified period after the contract ends. For example, a clause in a lease, especially a lease of retail premises, by which the lessee agrees not to carry on a competing use within a specified radius of the subject property, either during the period of the lease or for a reasonable period after the expiration of the lease; or the lessor undertakes not to use other property retained by him for a competitive purpose. Such a clause may not be enforceable if it is an unreasonable restraint on trade (*McEllistrim v Ballymacelligott Co-operative Agricultural and Dairy Society* [1919] AC 548, 562 (HL); Sherman Anti-Trust Act of 1890, § 1; Goldberg v. Tri-States Theatre Corp., 126 F.2d 26 (8th Cir. Neb 1942)). However, in some jurisdictions in the US, it has been held to be an acceptable provision in a lease of a unit in a shopping center, when it is inserted in all the leases to ensure that there is a reasonable balance between the competing trades and to maintain the economic diversity of the center. Also

called an 'exclusive clause' when the lessee is granted an exclusive right to trade in certain goods in or around a particular retail center; and a 'radius restriction clause', or sometimes a 'radius clause' or a 'reverse radius clause', when the lessor undertakes not to permit property to be used for a competing use within a certain distance from the leased premises. Also referred to as a 'covenant not to compete' or a 'no-compete' clause. cf. **user clause**. See also **restrictive covenant**.

non-conforming use or **non-conforming user**   A use of land or a building that, although started legitimately, is now in conflict with the current zoning or land use regulations for the area in which the land or building is situated. A user that is no longer considered to be compatible with the surrounding area, especially a user that would not be permitted if the use were reintroduced into the area. For example, an industrial building situated in a residential area. In most planning or zoning systems, a non-conforming use may continue unabated and the prohibition of its continuance would constitute a form of expropriation or condemnation of the property. However, any expansion or intensification of such use is normally prohibited or severely limited. Also, in the event of an **abandonment** of such a use, it may not normally be resumed because approval will not be forthcoming for the 'new' use. In addition, such uses may be constrained where it is considered to create a public **nuisance** or the local municipality may offer inducements or an alternative property to remove such uses.

In the US, zoning provisions may be enacted to 'amortize' legal non-conforming uses (especially signs or billboards) so that the use is to terminate after a specified period of time. Such regulations may be a valid exercise of the municipality's **police power** where there is considered to be a reasonable balance between the public gain or benefit and the private limitation on the use of the property, especially taking into account the period of amortization permitted. However, if the regulations are too restrictive they may amount to a 'taking' of the property, entitling the landowner to **just compensation**. Whether an alteration, extension, reconstruction or change to a non-conforming use is permissible is dependent on the particular provision of the zoning ordinance. However, a permanent intensification of the use; a change in location, area or volume; a new activity; or a change that significantly impacts the neighborhood will normally be considered to be violation of the applicable zoning ordinance.

In English planning law, an expansion or intensification of a non-conforming use is likely to be considered a **material change in the use** for which planning permission would be required, but is unlikely to be granted. On the other hand, a requirement to discontinue a non-conforming use following the service of a **discontinuance order** may entitle the owner to compensation. See also **existing use**, **vested right**(US), **grandfather clause**(US).

non-conventional mortgage(US)   See conventional mortgage.

non-derogation from grant   See derogation from grant.

non-disturbance agreement(US)   See **non-disturbance and attornment agreement, subordination**.

non-disturbance clause(US)   **1.** A clause, inserted in a mortgage agreement (or made as a separate agreement), which specifies that in the event of **foreclosure**, the mortgagee undertakes not to terminate a lease of the subject property. In the case of leases granted after the mortgage, as the mortgagor normally has no right to lease the mortgaged property (without the approval or agreement of the mortgagee), a mortgagee who has power to oust the mortgagor has the same right against the lessee. Accordingly, a lessee may execute an 'attornment agreement' by which he acknowledges the mortgagee's right to the rent in the event of foreclosure and the mortgagee agrees not to disturb the lease so long as the lessee complies with its terms. Sometimes called a 'recognition clause'. See also **attornment**.   **2.** A provision in a conveyance of a property which reserves the **mineral rights** to the seller provided that their exploitation does not conflict in any way with the surface use of the property.

non-disclosure   A failure to reveal facts or important information that has a direct bearing on a transaction. See also **latent defect, misdescription, misrepresentation, utmost good faith**.

non-exclusive listing(US)   See **open listing**.

non est factum(Lat)   'It is not (his) deed'. A plea, made by someone in whose name a deed is executed, that the document is not his. For example, a deed that someone disclaims because he was totally misled as to the effect of the contents, or a deed that results from **fraud, forgery** or other falsehood.

nonfeasance   The neglect or failure of a person to do that which he ought to do. For example, the total failure of an agent to carry out the duties entrusted to him. See also **laches, negligence**.

non-free tenure(Eng)   See **villeinage**.

non-freehold estate(US)   An estate that is not a **freehold**. A term that may be applied to a leasehold estate, which is a right of possession but not of ownership.

non-judicial foreclosure(US)   See **judicial foreclosure**.

non-merchantable title(US)   See **unmarketable title**.

non-negotiable instrument   An instrument that is not transferable merely by **delivery** but must be transferred by **assignment**. An instrument that is not payable to the order of the bearer. cf. **negotiable instrument**.

non-recourse mortgage   A mortgage granted on the basis that the lender's right of action in the event of default by the mortgagor is limited only to property held as security for the loan; there being no right of recourse against the borrower personally. See also **deficiency judgment**(US), **dry mortgage, exculpatory clause, mortgagee, recourse**.

non sequitur(Lat)   'It does not follow'.

non-specified property offering(US)   See **blind-pool offering**.

non-tenure   A form of common law plea in response to a **real action** that the defendant did not hold the land on the day the writ was issued (a 'special denial'), or that he never held a right to the land in question (a 'general denial').

non-use   See **abandonment, adverse possession, discontinuance**.

non user   See **abandonment, discontinuance**.

non-valued policy(US)   See **unvalued policy**.

non-waiver clause   A clause in a lease which provides that an action such as the acceptance of rent by the landlord does not act as a **waiver** of his right to pursue his claim for possession subsequent to any notice or proceedings that have already been instigated. In English law, such a provision is not normally of any effect; "there is a logical inconsistency in the landlord claiming that the lease is at an end while at the same time relying on a provision in the same lease in order to prevent a waiver", 1 *Woodfall's Law of Landlord and Tenant*, para. 17.096. However, it has been accepted in Australia, New Zealand and some jurisdictions in the US, as providing the landlord with protection from an 'accidental' waiver; but such a provision must be set out in writing, as there can be no implied waiver following the acceptance of rent. Nevertheless, under the principles of **election** and **estoppel**, it may be unadvisable to rely on such a provision, at least without a written confirmation that the rent is accepted 'without prejudice' to the landlord's right of action.

nook of land   An obscure parcel of land; an area of land of uncertain dimensions. A purchaser of a 'nook of land' is unsure of the exact area he has acquired.

normal wear and tear   See **fair wear and tear**(BrE), **wear and tear**(AmE).

noscitur a sociis(Lat)   'Know it from its associates'. The meaning or interpretation of a word can be gathered from the context or by reference to the meaning of the words associated with it. This rule of interpretation propounds that "a word is known from the company it keeps", Jarecki v. G.D. Searle & Co., 367 US 303, 81 S Ct 1579, 307, 6 L Ed.2d 859, 863 (1961); or that "English words derive colour from those that surround them", *Bourne v Norwich Crematorium Ltd* [1967] 1 WLR 691, 696, [1967] 2 All ER 576, 578. cf. *ejusdem generis*. See also **implied term, words**.

notarize(US)   To certify the authenticity of a document by or in the presence of a **notary public**. See also **deed**.

notary or **notary public**   An officer authorised to administer oaths; to attest and certify copies of documents (in particular those of public record); and to acknowledge contracts, deeds and other written documents; particularly when these are or may be produced in legal proceedings. See also **acknowledgment, affidavit**.

notation on title(Aus)   The method by which easements are recorded on a **Torrens certificate of title**.

note   1. A notation; a brief written record. A short account of an event, action, information or something similar, especially when made to assist the memory or as a summary to be used later in a more detailed report. A note may create or form part of an agreement, although it is generally used to precede a formal agreement. See also **memorandum, Statute of Frauds, writing**. **2.** An unconditional **promise**, evidenced in writing, to pay a sum of money at a specified time to a particular person or the bearer of the written evidence. "A promise other than a certificate of deposit", UCC § 3-104. Commonly called a **promissory note**, or when secured by a mortgage, a **mortgage note**. cf. **debenture**. See also **bond**.

note financing   See **secured loan**.

note mortgage   See **secured loan**.

note rate   The rate of interest that is accrued on a promissory note or mortgage; the 'true' or **effective annual interest rate**.

notice   **1.** Information, advice or a warning brought to a person's knowledge or attention. A formal intimation or warning of something. In law, a person has 'notice' of a fact when: (a) he has actual **knowledge** of it; (b) he has received notification of it; or (c) based on all the facts and circumstances known to him at the time in question he has reason to know that the fact exists. One may have knowledge but not proper *legal* notice, and one may have legal notice (as through an agent) without having personal knowledge. As a rule, to have legal notice it must be communicated in the right way.

Notice may be actual, constructive, implied, and presumptive notice. **Actual notice** (sometimes called 'express notice') is that which is given directly or brought to a person's attention, usually in writing. **Constructive notice** is deemed by law to have been acquired, as with a fact that a person would discover by making reasonable inquiry, such as examining a public record or inspecting a property. (Sometimes called 'statutory notice' when statute law imparts that information has been brought to a person's notice, or 'record notice' when the information can be ascertained from a public record.) **Implied notice** is that which a person is assumed to have because he has the means to obtain that knowledge by reasonable

inquiry. **Imputed notice** is notice (actual or constructive) received by an agent or attorney and thereby assumed, for the purpose of the business or transaction in hand, to be known to the principal or client; "notice by construction of law, as, where notice to an agent is notice to a principal", *Hiern v Mill* (1806) 13 Ves Jun 120, 33 Eng Rep 237, 239.

In English law, the *equitable doctrine of notice* forms the basis for determining whether an equitable interest is binding on a third party who acquires an interest in land. The principle being that equitable rights to land are binding on all persons who acquire an interest in that land, except for a *bona fide* purchaser of a **legal estate** for **value** who does not have 'notice' of those equitable rights. Thus, if such a purchaser does not have actual, constructive or imputed notice of an unregistered interest, he takes the land free of those rights; although the onus of proof that such notice has not been received rests primarily on the purchaser. Notice of an equitable interest that is registered as a **land charge** is given by registration; if such an interest should be, but is not, registered it is not binding regardless of notice. This principle only applies to unregistered land; in the case of registered land, notice is substituted by the requirement of registration. See also **abatement notice**(Eng), **completion notice**(Eng), **counter notice**, **enforcement notice**(Eng), **notice to quit**, **overreachable interest**(Eng), **repairs notice**(Eng), **service, stop notice**(Eng).   **2.**(Eng)An entry on the Charges Register at the **Land Registry** of an interest, right or claim to registered land; especially a **minor interest**, or a registrable lease or charge created by a registered proprietor of land. Such an entry may be made to protect certain lesser interests or rights affecting registered land (or claims to such rights) that might otherwise not be binding on a purchaser of registered land. cf. **caution**.   **3.** An entry on the charges register at the Land Registry of the **burden** of an interest affecting a registered estate or registered charge. A notice does not make the interest that is entered on the registry valid, but if it is valid it will have priority over any subsequently registered interest. Such a notice may be 'agreed', if it is made by, or with the consent of, the registered owner of the estate or charge and the registrar is satisfied as to the applicant's claim. A notice may be 'unilateral' when the registered owner does not consent, and the registrar does not approve the validity of the claim. (LRA 2002, s. 32). See also **priority notice**.

notice of assessment(US) A notice given, by a state or local tax agency, to an owner of real property of the **assessed value** placed on his property.

notice of claim(Eng) See **notice to treat**.

notice of completion 1.(US)A notice that must be filed in some states at the public records office, following completion of construction work, in order to secure the contractor's **mechanic's lien** rights. A notice of completion starts the running of the time for the lien to remain valid based on the state statute. 2.(Eng)See **completion notice**.

notice of default A **notice** given to a party to a contract, in particular a tenant or a borrower, stating that there has been a **default** or failure to perform a substantial term or the terms of the contract. The notice usually provides that, if the default is not rectified within a specified period of time, action will be taken to terminate the contract or to seek damages.

notice of entry(Eng) Notice given by an authority possessing compulsory purchase powers, served with or subsequent to a **notice to treat**, stating that the authority intends to exercise its right to enter and take possession of land (Compulsory Purchase Act 1965, s. 11(1)(2), Sch. 3). See also **general vesting declaration**, **right of entry**, **valuation date**.

notice of objection to severance(Eng) See **severance**.

notice of pendency(US) See *lis pendens*.

notice of practical completion(Aus) See **certificate of practical completion**.

notice to quit or **notice to vacate** Express notice given by an existing landlord to his existing tenant stating that a tenancy is brought to an end and that the landlord intends or will seek to regain **possession**. A term that may be applied also to notice from a tenant to his landlord, stating that the tenant intends to deliver up possession of the premises when permitted by the lease. Notice that, on its expiry, is intended to bring to an end the relationship of landlord and tenant. (The more usual legal term is 'notice to quit', although in American English the term 'notice to vacate' is increasingly used.)

A valid notice to quit must be given strictly in accordance with the terms of the agreement by which the tenancy is created, or in accordance with any statutory provision that affects the tenancy. It must be plain, unconditional and unequivocal and must: (i) state the premises to which it relates (and relate to the whole of the premises, unless the lease, or a statute, permits partial termination); (ii) specify, in accordance with the terms of the letting, the correct **date** or **day** for the termination of the tenancy, or the correct date must be ascertainable with certainty; (iii) be unconditional, so that it is clear that possession is demanded of the tenant, and when that possession is to take effect; (iv) must show that it has come from the landlord or his authorised agent; and (v) be properly delivered.

At common law, notice to quit need not be in any particular form; provided it is expressed so that a person of ordinary capacity receiving the notice cannot mistake its nature and intent. It need not necessarily be in **writing** – unless the tenancy is created in writing, or written notice is required by statute; but, to avoid uncertainty, it is preferable for the notice to be in writing and properly served. Notice to quit is necessary to terminate any **periodic tenancy**. However, strictly notice to quit is not required to terminate a tenancy for a term of a year, or one granted for any other definitive period, unless expressly stipulated for in the lease, or required by statute.

In the US, in most states, notice to terminate a periodic tenancy must be given for the term prescribed by statute and, in many jurisdictions, must be in writing and, as a rule, must be served in person, by certified or registered mail with a returned receipt as acknowledgment; or by posting clear notice on the premises if the tenant cannot be located (the fundamental requirement is that, in order to ensure "due process", there is an "opportunity to be heard" and, therefore that the tenant is "informed that the matter is pending", Greene v. Lindsay, 456 US 444, 102 S Ct 1874, 72 L Ed.2d 249, 255 (1982); Cal CC, §§ 1162, 1946). After the proper service of notice, if the tenant does not vacate freely, the landlord must continue to follow the "due process", as by an action through the courts for recovery of possession of the property; usually by a statutory form of **ejectment**, or a similar summary 'landlord and tenant proceeding' for possession. Thus, 'notice to quit' is not the equivalent of a court process that requires the tenant to vacate.

In English law, various statutes require that notice to quit be given for a particular period of time, be in a prescribed form, or that the notice conveys certain information to a tenant such as his right to continued occupation or to a new tenancy. In any event, service of notice to quit should be prepared with care and preferably with professional advice; ; "It cannot be denied that the law upon notices to quit is highly technical; but technicalities are too deeply rooted in our law to be now got rid of," *Sidebotham v Holland* [1895] 1 QB 383 (CA) (Harry's Village, Inc. v. Egg Harbor Tp., 89 NJ 576, 446 A.2d 862, 867(1982)). See also **break clause**, **protected tenancy**, **security of tenure**, **service**, **time**.

notice to repair(Eng)   See **repairs notice**, **schedule of dilapidations**.

notice to treat(Eng)   A formal notice served, pursuant to a **compulsory purchase order**, upon a person who is believed to have an interest in land stating the intention of an authority possessing the compulsory purchase powers to acquire that interest. Notice to treat is given to "all the persons interested in, or having power to sell and convey or release, the land, so far as known to the acquiring authority after making diligent inquiry", CPA 1965, s. 5(1). Any tenant, no matter how short his interest, is entitled to notice to treat (although, in the case of a periodic tenancy for a year or less, the authority may acquire the landlord's interest and, if it does not require immediate possession, terminate the tenancy by service of notice to quit). Notice to treat does not need to be served on the beneficiary of an easement, a restrictive covenant, or a licence affecting the land; although the beneficiary of such a right may be entitled to compensation if that right is extinguished by the acquiring authority. The notice need not be in any particular form but must describe the land to which it relates; request details of the owner's precise interest in the property and the amount of his claim for **compensation**; and stipulate that the acquiring authority is willing to treat and pay compensation for the purchase of the interest to which the notice relates (CPA 1965, s. 5(2)).

When coupled with an agreement of the proper compensation to be paid, a notice to treat constitutes a binding **contract**; however, "it is not until compensation is agreed or assessed that the equitable title in the land [i.e. the right to acquire the interest in land] passes to the party who has served the notice to treat", *West Midland Baptist (Trust) Association (Inc.) v Birmingham Corporation* [1968] 1 All ER 205, 216 (CA), aff'd [1970] AC 874, [1969] 3 All ER 172, 184 (HL). Following receipt of a notice to treat the recipient must submit a claim ('notice of claim') for compensation to the acquiring authority within 21 days. See also **blight notice, compensation for disturbance, general vesting declaration, purchase notice**.

notice to vacate(US)   See **notice to quit**.

notorious possession(US)   Possession that is so conspicuous and open that a diligent owner would be presumed to be aware of it – a requisite of **adverse possession**. Also called 'open and notorious possession'. Within the rule that to constitute adverse possession it is necessary that the possession be 'actual, continuous, notorious, and hostile', 'Notorious' in this context means open, undisguised, generally known. 'Notorious possession' is sometimes used synonymously with 'adverse possession'. See also **hostile possession**.

novation   A term originating in Roman law. An act by which, with the consent of all the parties to a **contract**, a new contract is substituted in place of an existing contract, and the existing contract is discharged in full. Usually, but not necessarily, a third party is substituted for one of the parties to the old contract, either a new obligor or a new obligee, or both. Also, a new obligation may be substituted for the old obligation, but all or some of the parties remain the same. Novation means "that there being a contract in existence, some new contract is substituted for it, either between the same parties (for that might be) or between different parties; the consideration mutually being the discharge of the old contract", *Scarf v Jardine* (1882) 7 App Cas 345, 351 (HL). The essential requirements of novation are: (i) a previous valid contract; (ii) an agreement by all the parities concerned to create a new contract; (iii) the extinguishment of the old contract; and (iv) the creation of a valid new contract. Novation may create a contract that is similar in many respects to the old contract, but there must be a fundamental change from the old contract. For example, the old party is released from all obligations and is replaced by the new party; or the old contract is completely replaced, in form or content, by the new one. cf. **accord and satisfaction**, **subrogation**. See also **privity of contract**.

novus actus interveniens(Lat)   'A new act intervening'. See **damages**.

nude contract   See **naked contract**.

nudum pactum(Lat)   A **naked contract**.

nuisance   A cause or source of annoyance, vexation or inconvenience to another. An unreasonable use of property, usually in a continuing way, so as to cause considerable inconvenience, annoyance or harm to another. An action or conduct, or lack of action or conduct, that results in an interference with another's reasonable enjoyment of, or legal right to enjoy, the use of a property or a right thereover, or an interference with the legal rights of a person.

Nuisance at law is an action that is not capable of precise definition, but it may be categorised as 'public nuisance' and 'private nuisance'. Public nuisance (in the US also called 'common nuisance') basically comprises acts that cause **damage**, **injury**, inconvenience or annoyance to the public generally, or has a deleterious effect on the rights to which every citizen is entitled. The doing or failure to do something that injuriously affects the life, health, safety or welfare of the public; the carrying out of work or a form of behaviour that unreasonably interferes with the comfort or peaceful enjoyment of the environment by the community at large. A public nuisance may be considered [per Lord Justice Denning] as "a nuisance which is so widespread in its range or so indiscriminate in its effect that it would not be reasonable to expect one person to take proceedings on his own responsibility to put a stop to it, but it should be taken on the responsibility of the community at large", *A-G v P. Y. A. Quarries* [1957] 2 QB 169, 191 (CA). Public nuisance must affect a substantial sector of the public, not just a few people; it must affect an entire community or neighborhood (Spur Industries, Inc. v. Del E. Webb Development Co., 108 Ariz 178, 494 P.2d 700, 705 (1972)).

'Private nuisance' comprises acts that affect an individual or group of individuals; "the unreasonable use by a man of his land to the detriment of his **neighbour**", per Lord Denning M.R. in *Miller v Jackson* [1977] QB 966, 980, [1977] 3 All ER 338, 344 (CA). Or, the "unreasonable interference with the use or enjoyment of a property interest [held by] an owner or possessor of land", William Prosser et al., *Cases and Materials on Torts*. 9th ed. New York: Foundation Press, 1994, p. 811; or, "a nontrespassory invasion of another's interest in the private use and enjoyment of land", The American Law Institute, *Restatement Second, Torts* § 821D (1979). Nuisance may be considered a common law wrong. However, a public nuisance may also arise from legislative enactments – sometimes called a 'statutory nuisance'. For example, acts in contravention of a local ordinance, code or statute such as emitting smoke, fumes, gas, dust, steam, smell or effluvia; transmitting vibrations or noise from premises; or accumulating or depositing toxic matter.

In case of real property, nuisance normally arises from the use of one property in such a way that it causes an interfere with another person use and enjoyment of their property. In particular, an action that diminishes the value of a property – for example, the obstruction of a right of way, or allowing something to escape and encroach onto another's land such as water, smoke, fumes, smell, effluvia, noise, animals, trees, etc. Nuisance is not finite; it depends on surrounding circumstances. Thus, something that may be a nuisance in one area may not be a nuisance in another and a nuisance in a residential district may not be one in an industrial area. "A nuisance may be merely a right thing in a wrong place,—like a pig in a parlor instead of the barnyard", Village of Euclid v. Amber Realty Co., 272 US 365, 47 S Ct 114, 71 L Ed 303, 310 (1926).

The word 'nuisance' is commonly found in a lease and, in combination with the words 'annoyance', 'grievance' or 'inconvenience', extends beyond normal nuisance and imparts a particular obligation to act in a more restrained manner between landlord and tenant and between neighbours.

If a tenant causes a nuisance from the premises he occupies, normally he is liable. However, the landlord may be liable for the nuisance if he is himself responsible for creating the nuisance, as by failing to meet his repairing obligation or letting or re-letting premises knowing that they are likely to be used so as to cause a nuisance. cf. **trespass**. See also **abatement**, **damages**, derogation from grant, disturbance, encroachment, injunction, negligence, public rights, quiet enjoyment, spite fence, strict liability.

nuisance order(Eng) An order issued by a court ordering a person to comply with an **abatement notice** or **prohibition notice** (PHA 1936, s. 94). The order may be issued when a person has failed to abate a statutory nuisance.

nuisance value The price of tolerating the continuation of a **nuisance**, or the reduction in the value of a property due to the existence of a nuisance.

null and void Of no legal effect; unenforceable. That which binds nobody. See also **void contract**.

nullity An act that has no legal effect whatsoever. See also **void contract**.

nuncupative will A **will** that is made orally before witnesses just prior to death and subsequently reduced to writing. Such wills are generally invalid, except in special cases such as for military personnel on active service or mariners at sea. In some jurisdictions, nuncupative wills are not recognized in any circumstances, and in a few jurisdictions, they are only applicable to bequests of personal property with a low value.

nursery finance Finance granted to assist the start up of a new business, especially when the lender takes an equity or profit-sharing position in the business. See also **equity participation**.

nursery unit See incubator unit.

nut(US) A slang term for overheads or the total expense involved in undertaking a project.

O

obiter dictum(Lat) 'A saying by the way'. An observation made by a judge, when expressing his decision on a case, that is not intended as a binding statement of law because it does not relate directly to the facts before him. cf. ***ratio decidendi***.

obligant(Scot) An **obligor**.

obligation 1. A tie or **bond** that commits one person to another. Something that one is bound to do, or one agrees to forebear, whether entered into freely or imposed by law. A personal promise given by one party (an obligor) to another (an obligee) to perform a particular duty or to pay a sum of money such as a debt. 'Obligation' is a generic term that refers to any duty, whether arising from contract, law, a bare promise, a gentleman's agreement, or a moral commitment. Specifically, it is "a bond with a condition annexed and a penalty for non fulfillment ...", *Webster's Third New International Dictionary®, Unabridged*, ©1993. An obligation may be 'personal', where it binds an individual; or 'real' where it binds real property, as when it arises from an easement or mortgage. See also **debt**, **liability**, **quasi-contract**. 2. An **instrument**, or any other form of written agreement, that sets out the terms of a promise or agreement that is enforceable by law. In particular, an agreement to pay money or carry out a specific action. See also **contract**, **planning obligation**(Eng).

obligation bond(US) A **bond** by which a mortgagor provides a personal surety to the mortgagee separate from the mortgage obligation, especially for non-payment of real estate taxes and insurance premiums and sometimes interest.

obligatory advance clause(US) See **future advance**.

obligee A promisee or **creditor**. The person to whom a duty is owed; the beneficiary of an obligation. The person to whom a bond is made payable. See also **mortgagee**.

obligor A promisor or **debtor**. A person who is the subject of a duty or liability to another (the 'obligee'); one who gives a bond or **obligation**, or enters into a contractual commitment to another. See also **guarantor**, **mortgagor**.

obsolescence Derived from the Latin *obsolescere*, 'to grow old' or 'to fall into disuse'. A process whereby something falls into disuse, or becomes worn-out or unproductive, due to changes in design, style, economic activity or public need. A decline in the market value of a property due to extrinsic and not inherent factors, i.e. due to causes that go beyond physical **deterioration** or **wear and tear**. Obsolescence may be classified as 'economic' or 'functional'. Economic obsolescence (sometimes called 'environmental' or 'locational' obsolescence) is caused by changes arising outside the property's immediate parameters, e.g. changes in local planning or zoning, changes in the nature of the neighbourhood, or a shift in demand to substitutes. Functional obsolescence (sometimes called 'physical obsolescence') arises from changes in consumer demand or in the suitability of property for its existing use; especially when there is a more cost-effective alternative available, or there is a deficiency in the property itself so that it no longer meets modern requirements, e.g. a lack of central heating or of an automatic elevator in an office building. Obsolescence may be referred to sometimes as 'inutility' – as something is obsolete when it is 'no longer of use'. See also **depreciation**, **economic life**.

obsolete Incapable of providing any economic or material benefit. Of no further use, or no longer used. Worn out. Out of date. See also **obsolescence**.

obstructive building(Eng) A building that, due to its contact with or proximity to other buildings, is dangerous or injurious to health

(Housing Act 1985, s. 283(1)). The Housing Act 1985, ss. 283-288 gives a local authority power to order the owner of an obstructive building to demolish the whole or part of that building. The owner has a right to make representations to the authority; to request the authority to purchase the property; or to be paid compensation for any loss resulting directly from the order. If the owner does not comply with the order (or the authority does not agree to acquire the property) the local authority has powers to enter and demolish the property and recharge the cost (less any salvage value) back to the owner.

An obstruction or projection from a building that prevents the proper use or passage along a **street** may be removed by order of a highway authority or local authority, subject to a right of appeal to a magistrates court (Highways Act 1980, s. 152). A building may not be erected over a public **highway** without a licence granted by a highway authority (Highways Act 1980, s. 177). See also **dangerous structure**, **demolition order**, **purchase notice**.

occupancy   1. The taking or holding of physical **possession** of a property; the type and character of the use of property. Occupancy and **occupation** derive their meaning from the verb 'occupy'; "the former being used to express the state of holding or possessing any object, the latter to express the act of taking possession. He who has the occupancy of land enjoys the fruits of it", George Crabb, *Crabb's English Synonyms.* 1816. Reprint, London: Routledge, 1982. Occupancy may also be used to refer to the taking of possession, especially of a property that has no apparent owner; in that respect it is synonymous with 'actual' possession, as distinguished from 'constructive' possession. See also **constructive notice**, **entry**.   2. The taking and holding of property under a lease or **tenancy**. See also **occupancy agreement**.   3. The act of becoming an **occupant** of property.   4. The condition or degree to which a building is occupied. See also **occupancy rate**.

occupancy agreement   An agreement that permits a person to enter into **occupation** of a property prior to completion of the proper legal formalities for the transfer of that property. An occupancy agreement normally creates a mere **licence** to use land, rather than any form of tenancy. See also **agreement for a lease**, **tenancy at will**.

occupancy certificate(US)   See **certificate of occupancy**.

occupancy cost   The total cost to a tenant of occupying a property, including rent, real estate taxes, repairs, operating expenses and any other **outgoings** directly resulting from the tenant's use and enjoyment of the property. See also **cost-in-use**, **equation of rents theory**.

occupancy cost ratio   The ratio of a tenant's total **occupancy cost** to his gross turnover. A ratio that is generally only applicable to retail tenants. Sometimes referred to as the 'rent-to-turnover ratio' (although that would generally be a lower amount).

occupancy lease   See **proprietary lease**.

occupancy permit   See **certificate of occupancy**.

occupancy rate   1. The percentage of a property that is rented or occupied. See also **absorption rate**, **vacancy allowance**.   2. The ratio of the income actually received from a building to the income that would be receivable if the building was fully occupied.   3. The ratio of population to an amount of occupiable accommodation, e.g. persons per habitable rooms or persons per dwelling. See also **density**, **population density**.

occupant   1. One who enjoys the right to the **possession** of property. One who occupies or resides in a property, especially a residential property. An **occupier** of a property. In particular, one who has a right to 'actual' possession, as distinguished from someone who has 'constructive' possession or a future right to possession. Thus, a tenant may be an occupant of a property, but a landlord has no more than a future right to possession, or a right to possession of the rents and profits. In the US, 'occupant' is used more commonly than 'occupier'. **2.** "1. a: One who takes the first possession of something that has no owner and thereby acquires title by **occupancy**. b: One who takes possession under title, lease, or tenancy at will", *Webster's Third New International Dictionary®, Unabridged*, ©1993. Thus, an 'occupant' has a present and legal claim to enter onto property and exclude others, as does a tenant. See also **adverse possession**.

occupation   1. The act or process of taking **possession** of real property for the purpose of use or enjoyment. The ability to hold property in order to enjoy the fruits therefrom; to have uninterrupted user; or to exercise control thereover. A person in occupation has control, or a degree of control, over a property and essentially actual possession; but unlike a 'possessor' he does not necessarily exert any claim to ownership, which arises as a wholly independent right. Occupation includes possession as its primary element (and the terms may be used synonymously); although 'occupation' also includes a physical presence or an intention to maintain control, whether with or without the consent of the owner or legal possessor. Thus, occupation is a question of fact, unlike **title** which is a question of law. On the other hand, 'possession' may be actual and constitute occupation, or it may be 'constructive', which is a right that will be enforced by law, but does not necessarily include or constitute occupation. 'Occupation' may suggest that there is a legal right to possession, but it may denote "nothing more than physical presence in a place for a substantial period of time ... Its precise meaning [in any particular statute] ... must depend on the purpose for which, and the context in which, it is used", *Madrassa Anjuman Islamia of Kholwad v Municipal Council of Johannesburg* [1922] 1 AC 500, 504 (PC).

In a lease, occupation does not necessarily mean personal use and occupation, but the right to occupation of all that passes under the lease. Occupation may even be enjoyed 'vicariously' as when a person has merely installed furniture in a property, or 'constructively' when someone exercises control over a property. Thus, a person can remain in occupation through a wife or family member when away on business, at sea or in prison. On the other hand, a person who shows a clear intention to part with the use and enjoyment of premises is considered, *prima facie*, to have parted with occupation.

In the US, in connection with the use and enjoyment of property, the term **occupancy** is more commonly used for occupation. See also **constructive notice**, **exclusive occupation**, **matrimonial home**(Eng), **occupier**, **rateable occupation**(Eng), **security of tenure**, **unoccupied**. **2.** In common usage, the employment, **business** or **profession** in which someone is involved. See also **occupation lease**.

occupation lease   A 'lease' granted to a person for use in conjunction with his employment or trade. In particular, a lease granted to a tenant whose employment is related directly to the subject matter of the lease, e.g. a lease of a cottage to a farm worker or a lease of a property to be used during a period of hunting or fishing. In many cases, an 'occupation lease' may really be no more than a **licence** to occupy a property, tied to the conditions of employment, and not a true **lease**. cf. **occupational lease**. See also **service tenancy**, **tied accommodation**(Eng), **tied house**(Eng).

occupation property   Property acquired or leased for use or occupation by the holder, as distinguished from **investment property**, which is held to generate income and profit. See also **occupational lease**, **owner-occupier**.

occupation trust(Eng)   See **trust for sale**.

occupational lease   A lease granted for the purpose of personal occupation and enjoyment. In particular, a lease granted to a tenant who intends to use a property for his own purposes, as compared with a building lease, or a lease granted to a person who intends to grant a sub-lease and derive income therefrom. 'Occupational lease' and **occupation lease** may be used interchangeably, although the latter term more usually refers to a lease granted to a tenant who intends to use the property in conjunction with his or her employment or trade. Also called a 'space lease'. See also **business tenancy, occupation, proprietary lease**.

occupied   See occupation, occupier.

occupier   1. A person who has a right to take or maintain possession of property without necessarily having an estate interest or claim to the property. One who takes and retains **possession** of property. One who has **occupation** or occupies land or buildings, which generally includes one who has a right to occupy land or buildings. 'Occupier' is a term of imprecise meaning. In common usage, an occupier is someone who is living in a property or has use of it for a business or similar purpose, especially someone who uses a property on a more than transient basis. In law, it may mean any person who has a right to exercise control over a property, even if he does not physically exercise that right.

In English law, in connection with a **duty of care** owed to a **visitor** to a property, it was said by Lord Denning that "wherever a person has a sufficient degree of control over premises that he ought to realise that any failure on his part to use care may result in injury to a person coming lawfully there, then he is an 'occupier'", *Wheat v E. Lacon and Co Ltd* [1966] AC 552, 578 (HL). Thus, in certain cases a managing agent may be considered as the 'occupier' of a property.

In the US, the occupier of a property is more commonly called an **occupant**, especially in the context of one who takes possession under some right or claim. cf. **trespasser**. See also **rateable occupation, residential occupier**(Eng), **squatter**.   2. One who follows or carries on a particular **occupation**; a trader or dealer.

occupier's liability   See negligence, visitor.

occupy   See occupancy.

occupying claimant's acts(US)   See mistaken improver.

off-balance-sheet lease   See synthetic lease.

off-going crop   See way-going crops.

off-license(BrE)   See licensed premises.

off-shore company (**bank** or **trust**)   A company (bank or trust) that has established its place of registration in a country that is not where it conducts its principal business or derives most of its income. In particular, an 'off-shore' country, that has low rates of taxation and, in some cases, limited legal regulation. Normally an off-shore company (bank or trust) conducts business in different parts of the world to its place of registration, but aims to be subject to the taxes, if any, and regulation by the 'off-shore' country only. If the principal activity of the company (or trust) is in a particular 'on-shore' country, or the shareholders (or beneficiaries) are resident in an 'on-shore' country, then that country will claim, especially for taxation purposes, that the company (or trust) is not 'off-shore' but should be liable to the appropriate fiscal and legislative policy of the 'on-shore' country. See also **tax haven**.

off-site cost   A cost incurred in developing land that is not directly related to the site itself, such as the cost of providing access across an adjoining site or a contribution to the cost of utilities (water, electricity, gas or sewage) that serve several sites.**off-plan**   See sale off-plan.

off the plan(Aus)   See sale off-plan.

offer   1. To declare a willingness to enter into a **bargain**.   2. A proposal to do something. A proposal put forward voluntarily by one party for **acceptance** or **rejection** by another. A proposition by one party (offeror) that, if unconditionally accepted by another (offeree), constitutes an agreement. An offer, to be capable of forming the subject matter of a **contract**, must be certain in all its terms; it must amount to more than an indication that something is available for sale or a mere indication of a price at which an item can be acquired; and there must be a clear intention on the part of the offeror to be bound by an acceptance of that offer. A request for an offer to be made or for someone to make a bid (as made by an auctioneer or when soliciting prices for work to be carried out) is not an offer (*Payne v Cave* (1789) 3 Term Rep 148, 100 Eng Rep 502; United States v. Daniels, 231 US 218, 34 S Ct 84, 58 L Ed 191 (1913)).

An offer may be withdrawn at any time until it is accepted unconditionally, but an offer remains capable of acceptance until the offeree is made aware of its withdrawal. If no period is stipulated within which an offer may be accepted, and it is not expressly withdrawn, a 'reasonable' time is allowed within which acceptance may be effected. An offer sent by mail (unlike an acceptance sent by mail) is not effective until it reaches the other party. A conditional offer is not accepted unless all of the conditions attaching to the offer are accepted. An acceptance that is subject to a variation in a condition of the offer constitutes a **counter offer**; that is, it creates a new offer that, in turn, must be accepted to create an agreement. cf. **invitation to trade**(AmE)/ **invitation to treat**(BrE), **promise**. See also **bid**, **general offer**, **lapse**, **quotation**, **repudiation**, **revocation**, **specific performance**, **subject to contract**, **tender**.

offer and acceptance   See **contract**.

offer price   See **asking price**.

offer to sell   See **invitation to trade**(AmE)/ **invitation to treat**(BrE).

offeree   A person who receives an **offer**. See also **optionee**.

offering sheet   A one-page summary of the principal terms of a mortgage that is offered to investors in the secondary mortgage market.

offeror   A person who makes an **offer**. See also **optionor**.

office   Derived from the Latin *officium*, 'perform a task' or *opus*, 'work'. A place where people work or are employed to work, but not for the purpose of manufacture, retail or similar activities. A place where a person or groups of people place desks, tables, computers, filing, storage cabinets and similar items in order to carry out predominately management, administrative or clerical work. Premises used primarily for administering the affairs of a business, profession, government, industry, service entity or any similar organisation, whether conducted by a commercial or non-profit enterprise.

Under English planning law, 'office' refers to a building where people work in management, administration, etc. but does not include premises that are more in the nature of retail premises, such as a building society or estate agents office where the general public are regular visitors. For the purpose of English statutory provisions relating to the health, safety and welfare of persons employed to work in "office premises", 'office' means a building or part of a building, used for office purposes, and office purposes include "the purposes of administration, clerical work, handling money and telephone and telegraph operating", Offices, Shops and Railway Premises Act 1963, s. 1(2)(a)(b). This statute (as amended by the Health and Safety at Work, etc., Act 1974 and ministerial orders made thereunder) provides that office premises, where persons are employed, are, *inter alia*, to be kept clean, ventilated and properly lit, maintained at a reasonable temperature during working hours, and provided with proper washing and sanitary facilities, as well as first-aid facilities. See also **commercial property, fire certificate, overcrowding, shop**.

Gause, Jo Allen, et al. *Office Development Handbook*. 2nd ed. Washington, DC: Urban Land Institute, 1998.

White, John R. (editor). *The Office Building from Concept to Investment Reality*. Chicago: Appraisal Institute, 1993.

office copy   An exact copy of an official document certified as such by the holder of the original. In particular, a copy of a judicial document made by a court official and sealed by the court. In England and Wales, a copy of subsisting entries recorded at the **Land Registry** as issued to an intending purchaser by the Land Registrar and attached to the **land certificate** or **charge certificate**. See also **certified copy**.

office exclusive(US)   A **listing** that is granted to one real estate firm or broker to the exclusion of all others. In particular, a listing agreement under which the listing broker, although a member of a **multiple listing service**, agrees that he will be the only broker that will show the property, even though the listing broker may continue to cooperate with other members of the service (a requirement of the **National Association of REALTORS®**).

office-hotel(AmE)   An office building that is designed for use as a **timeshare**. Generally, such a building has similar facilities to those found in an hotel, such as concierge services, business services (a central telephone, message center, fax, internet and E-mail facilities, photocopiers, etc.), conference and meeting rooms, as well as secretarial services and other support facilities. See also **serviced office**.

Office of Equal Opportunity (OEO)(US)   A federal agency that is part of the Department of Housing and Urban Development and has responsibility for administering the provisions of the Fair Housing Act. See also **fair housing laws**.

Office of Thrift Supervision (OTS)(US)   A branch of the Department of the Treasury that is the primary regulator of the 'Thrift Industry'. The OTS was established in 1989 to regulate federal and state chartered savings and loan associations and mutual savings banks that have federal deposit insurance. The OTS also issues federal charters for federal savings and loan associations. See also **Federal Housing Finance Board, mutual savings bank, savings and loan associations**. (**www.ots.treas.gov**).

office park   See **business park**.

official certificate of search(Eng)   A certificate issued by an officer of the **Land Registry** pursuant to an application from a person who is seeking to ascertain whether there is an encumbrance that has been registered in the name of an **estate owner** of unregistered land. With the advent of electronic conveyancing, official certificates of search will no longer be issued. Instead a 'title information document' will be provided as a copy of the register to the **registered proprietor**, and any person may inspect and make copies of the register of title, subject to conditions that may be imposed by the Land Registry (Land Registration Act 2002, ss. 66, 67). cf. **land certificate, official certificate of search**. See also **Index Map, minor interest, search**.

official plan(Eng)   See **filed plan**.

official search certificate(Eng)   A certificate issued by a Registrar of a local land charges register pursuant to an application for details of any **local land charge** registered against a parcel of land (LLCA, 1975, s. 9). Such a certificate is valid only at the date of issue. cf. **official certificate of search**.

offset   1. A land marker or stake placed by a surveyor when he is unable to place the marker where an actual survey point or line is to be established. The surveyor makes field notes as to the true position of the marker or the line that is being run.   2. See **set-off**.

offset statement(US) See **estoppel certificate**.

oil In a real estate context, 'oil' normally refers to mineral or crude petroleum oil, i.e. deposits of hydrocarbons found in subsurface reservoir rock formations that is extracted for refinement primarily into gasoline (petroleum), kerosene and diesel or light fuel oil. This liquid oil may be extracted under natural pressure or by pumping, sometimes in conjunction with gaseous hydrocarbons. In some instances, the term oil is defined to include natural gas, although such an inclusion should be clearly expressed. See also **mineral**, **mineral rights**, **oil and gas lease**, **waste**.

oil and gas lease(US) A **lease**, or similar right, by which a party is permitted to explore and extract naturally occurring oil and gaseous hydrocarbons, on an exclusive basis, from beneath the surface of the land. An oil and gas lease differs from a normal lease of real estate in the following ways: (i) although the lessee is granted a right to explore and extract oil over or under a particular surface area, the oil or gas percolates from one area to another under the surface until drawn or expelled; (ii) once the oil or gas is extracted it becomes personal property; (iii) the payment for the right usually takes the form of a **royalty** based on the quantity, or the value, of oil or gas extracted (although a **bonus** is commonly payable as an initial consideration for the grant of the lease, or a **delay rental** may be payable until the lessee starts drilling); and (iv) because the lessee has control over exploration and extraction, various covenants are implied into the lease, unless expressly varied to the contrary; for example, to drill exploratory wells (and usually other wells if the initial wells are dry); to diligently and properly operate the wells; to drill offset wells to protect against drainage of the oil; to diligently market the extracted produce until the resource is exhausted (Merrill, Covenants implied in Oil and Gas Leases, 1940; E. Kuntz. A Treatise on Oil and Gas, §§ 54.1-56.5); and (v) if the lessee discontinues exploration work, as when there is no more oil or gas, the lease usually comes to an end, whether by abandonment, surrender or forfeiture.

In some jurisdictions, oil and gas are considered to be owned as part of the land, i.e. ownership only extends directly below the surface within the boundaries of the designated area of land and on this premise an oil and gas lease "is an **incorporeal hereditament** or a **profit à prendre**. It is an interest in real property", United States v. Stanolind Crude Oil Purchasing Co., 113 F.2d 194, 198 (10th Cir. Okla 1940). The oil remains the property of the owner of the land, even though a prospector may have a lease of the land and the oil does not become personal property until it is brought to the surface (Black v. Solano Co., 114 Cal App 170, 299 P 843, 845 (1931)). In other jurisdictions, oil and gas are not considered to be owned until extracted or 'captured' so that the right granted is not a lease, nor an interest or right to land, but more in the nature of a **usufruct** or a **servitude**; an incorporeal right to take possession of land (in the form of a license or an easement, or a combination of such rights) in order to extract oil and gas (Nunez v. Wainoco Oil and Gas Co., 606 So.2d 1320, 1325-6 (La App 1992); 58 C.J.S., Mines and Minerals, § 195). However, the right that is granted over land by an 'oil or gas lease' depends not only upon the jurisdiction, but the nature of the rights that are granted. In particular, it depends on whether there can be considered to be a grant of an exclusive right to possession over an area or strata of land for a period of time, which would thereby provide the criteria that would create a true 'lease'. See also **ancillary easement**, **cessation clause**, **continuous operation clause**, **economic interest**, **entirety clause**, **Mother Hubbard clause**, **primary term**, **rule of capture**.

Hemingway, Richard W. *Hornbook on the Law of Oil and Gas*. 3rd ed. St Paul, MN: West, 1991.

Kuntz, Eugene. *A Treatise on the Law of Oil and Gas*. St Paul, MN: West, 1977-91 with annual supplements.

old-for-old insurance See **reinstatement cost**.

old system title(Aus) A **title** to land that is based on the traditional title deeds or **chain of title**, as distinguished from title held under the **Torrens title system**. Also called 'common law title'.

olographic will   See **holographic will**.

omission   **1.** The failure to fulfil or complete a required action; neglect of a duty. See also **laches**, **mistake**, **negligence**.   **2.** Something left out by accident. A part of a document left blank. See also **misrepresentation**, **mistake**, **slip rule**(Eng), **utmost good faith**.

omne quod [solo] inædificatur solo cedit(Lat)   'That which is built upon the soil becomes a part of the soil'. See **fixture**.

omnes licentiam habere his quæ pro se indulta sunt, renunciare(Lat)   'Everyone has the right to renounce those things that have been conferred for their benefit'.

omnes res suas liberas et quietas haberet(Lat)   'That he should retain all his property free and undisturbed' (I *Bl Comm* 291).

omnibus clause(US)   **1.** See **dragnet clause**. **2.** A provision in a judgement for the distribution of property under a will that "all other property" is to go to a beneficiary or beneficiaries named in a will. See also **residuary estate**.

on   In relation to real property, 'on' usually means actually at the property or on the surface, being more definitive than 'at'; although in relation to a building it may mean 'in' the building and not merely affixed to the outside. See also **time**.

on or before   See **time**.

once a mortgage, always a mortgage   A maxim which stresses the principle that in equity a **mortgage** is intended solely as security for a loan and not as a means to secure a collateral advantage for the mortgagee. In other words, once the mortgagor has paid back his debt to the mortgagee, the purpose of the mortgage has come to an end

and the property should be released unencumbered. "The principle is this – that a mortgage must not be converted into something else; and when once you have come to the conclusion that a stipulation for the benefit of the mortgagee is part of the mortgage transaction, it is but part of his security, and necessarily comes to an end on the payment off of the loan", *Noakes & Co Ltd v Rice* [1902] AC 24, 33-34, [1900-3] All ER Rep 34 (HL). Thus, if a company lends money on condition, for example, that the mortgaged property is used only for the sale of the mortgagee's products, he cannot insist on this tie continuing when the mortgage is redeemed; or prevent redemption for fear of losing that tie. However, the mortgagee may be able to sustain a collateral agreement if it is part of a separate and later agreement; if it can be demonstrated that the advantage is not unfair and unconscionable; it does not create a penalty preventing the redemption of the mortgage; and it is not inconsistent or repugnant to the right to redeem (*Reeve v Lisle* [1902] AC 461 (HL); *Kreglinger v New Patagonia Meat and Cold Storage Co Ltd* [1914] AC 25, 53, 61 (HL); Peugh v. Davis, 6 Otto 333, 96 US 332, 24 L Ed 775 (1877)).

In the US, some jurisdictions take the view that a collateral advantage should be enforceable when the transaction is entered into by experienced business people who are legally represented. See also **equity of redemption**, **option**, **solus agreement**.

one action rule(US)   See **deficiency judgment**, **recourse**.

one hundred percent location   See **prime location**.

one transaction rule(US)   A rule applied in some states (e.g. Florida, Kansas, Texas, Wyoming) which stipulates that if a person or firm performs a single action, of a form defined by statute, then that person or firm is deemed to be acting as a broker and requires a broker's or **real estate licence**. The state statutes list the work of a broker or a salesperson (e.g. Tex Occ C, § 1101.002) and limits any such work to a person who has a state licence. This rule may be contrasted with other statutes that do not consider a person or firm is involved in the practice of real estate brokerage unless there are a number of 'transactions' sufficient to establish a course of conduct. On the other hand, in states that do not have a statutory 'one transaction' rule, a single action may constitute acting as a broker, especially if done by a person engaged in selling property 'as a whole or partial vocation'.

onerous contract   **1.** A **contract** where the costs outweigh the benefits. See also **adhesion contract**.   **2.** A contract supported by valid consideration, i.e. one where a benefit is conferred in exchange for a burden that is imposed. cf. **gratuitous contract**.

onerous covenant   **1.** A **covenant** requiring the performance of an obligation that is more onerous to perform than the benefit or advantage to be derived therefrom, e.g. a covenant in a lease which, if performed, would add far less to the value of the lessee's interest than the cost of undertaking the obligation. A covenant that is unduly one-sided. See also **adhesion contract**, **frustration**, **undue influence**.   **2.** A covenant that imposes on a tenant an obligation that is greater than that which would be 'usual' for the type of tenancy. cf. **usual tenancy**.

onerous title(US)   **1.** A title acquired for valuable consideration, whether the payment of money, the rendition of services, or the discharge of an obligation, as distinguished from a title acquired by gift.   **2.** A term derived from the civil law in relation to **community property**, for property acquired by the husband and wife during marriage from their own industry or savings (Civ Code La 1900, art. 3556).

opus citatum [op. cit.](Lat)   'The work cited before'; 'as previously mentioned', e.g. a book or article referred to earlier in a text.

open and notorious possession   See **notorious possession**.

open contract   **1.** A **contract** left open for interpretation by implication of law. In particular, a valid contract that contains only the minimum requirements for validity – the names of the parties, the subject matter (e.g. a description of the subject property) and a statement of the price or **consideration**. An open contract rests on the principle *id est certum est quod certum reddi potest* – 'that is certain which can be rendered certain'; it does not rest on the need to spell out every detail of the parties' requirements. A contract may be entirely open, or it may be partly open to the implications of the law, with some details contained in a **formal contract**.   **2.**(Eng)A contract for the sale of land that is not made by correspondence, but is left open as to the covenants that the vendor is providing. In such a contract the vendor implies, in particular, that: (a) he will abstract and produce documents, at his own expense, to show evidence of his **title** to the land for at least 15 years; (b) if he owns such an estate, he is selling a **fee simple**, with **vacant possession**, free of any **encumbrance**; (c) upon completion he will convey a **good title** to the property, he will convey the identical property to that which he has contracted to sell, and will deliver the title deeds to the purchaser (*White v Foljambe* (1805) 11 Ves 337, 345-6, 32 Eng Rep 1121); (d) all matters reasonably required for, or enjoyed with, the estate are to be conveyed to the purchaser; (e) **completion** of the conveyance of the property will take place within a reasonable time, subject to receipt of the purchase monies; and (f) he requires no payment, as a deposit or otherwise, prior to completion (LPA 1925, ss. 42-45, as amended by the LPA 1969, part III). An open contract made 'by correspondence' (which means any contract contained in a letter or letters that have passed between the parties) is governed by the Statutory Conditions of Sale 1925, subject to any contradictory conditions set out in the correspondence (LPA 1925, s. 46). See also **conditions of sale**, **contract for sale**, **memorandum**, **note**, **writing**.

open country(Eng)   In relation to the provision of public access to the countryside by means of an **access agreement** or **access order**, 'open country' is any land that is considered by the authority with whom the agreement or order is made to consist wholly or predominately of mountain, moor, heath, down, cliff or foreshore, including any bank, flat or other land adjacent to the foreshore, and (if in the countryside) includes woodlands, any river or canal, any expanse of water through which a river or part of it runs, and certain other lands associated therewith (National Parks and Access to the Countryside Act 1949, s. 59(2); Countryside Act 1968, s. 16, as amended). In relation to a right of access on foot to **access land**, "open country is moor, meadow or down, but excluding improved or semi-improved grassland", Countryside and Rights of Way Act 2002, s. 1(2). See also **national park**.

open easement(US)   See **apparent easement**.

open-end clause   1. See **future advance**.   2. See **dragnet clause**.

open-end commitment   A **commitment** by which a lender agrees to increase the amount advanced, up to a specified limit, without the need for any immediate assurance regarding the repayment of the loan. An open-end commitment is commonly made as part of a construction or project loan whereby the lender agrees to fund the total cost of the project as it progresses, subject to certain controls or guidelines. See also **open-end mortgage**.

open-end deed of trust   See **open-end mortgage**.

open-end fund(US)   See **open-end investment company**.

open-end investment company or **open-ended investment company** (OEIC)   An **investment company** that is not limited as to the amount of its share capital and may issue and redeem shares on a regular basis, usually by reference to its net asset value. Generally, the shares of an open-end investment company are not traded on the open market; instead, the company sells and buys back its own shares as the investors increase or reduce their holding in the company. The company makes investments or acquires new assets as and when it sells new shares to investors and funds the purchase by using reserves or selling investment or assets. Thus, it is 'open ended' in that its share capital is not fixed. In the US, also called a **mutual fund** or sometimes an 'open-end fund'. cf. **closed-end investment company**. See also **unit trust**(BrE).

open-end mortgage or **open-ended mortgage**   A **mortgage** that provides the mortgagor with the facility to increase his borrowing up to a specified limit without providing additional security, as in the case of a mortgage that provides funding for improvement to the mortgaged property. Such a mortgage has the advantage that interest is not paid on the funds until they are advanced. Normally all advances under an open-ended mortgage are made by agreement between the parties in accordance with stipulated guidelines. In most cases, as the obligation of the mortgagee is 'mandatory', the additional advances rank with the same **priority** as if the advances had been made at the outset. Sometimes called an 'open mortgage'. A **deed of trust** that contains a similar provision is called an 'open-end deed of trust'. cf. **closed-end mortgage**. See also **dragnet clause**(US), **future advance**, **subordination**, **tacking**.

open-end trust or **open-ended trust**   A **trust** that enables the trustees to make or vary investments, or the size of the trust, at their discretion. An open-ended real estate trust may invest in any type of real estate, unless specifically restricted by the trust deed, and may acquire and dispose of assets without direct reference to the beneficiaries. See also **protective trust**, **special trust**, **syndicate**.

open entry(US)   An entry onto land in an open and non-clandestine manner as a precursor to a claim by **adverse possession**. See also **notorious possession**.

open for prepayment   A loan that has passed the time at which repayment of the principal is permitted. See also **prepayment privilege**.

open house(US)   A practice by which other brokers or prospective purchasers make a property available for viewing on certain days of the week and between certain hours. Normally the property is left open and manned by the listing broker for the benefit of the other brokers. Open listings are used principally for residential properties and the primary purpose is for the listing broker to make the property or 'listing' available for viewing by other brokers to ensure that the property is fully exposed to the market.

open land   1. An area of land that is not totally enclosed and is generally not used for any intensive purpose. Vacant land that is not built on and upon which no business is regularly carried out.   2. An area of land that is open to the air and unbuilt on, but is used for a business such as a car breakers' yard or a builder's yard may not be considered as strictly 'open land'. See also **common land**(Eng), **open space**, **wasteland**.

open listing(US)   An arrangement by which a property owner places his property with one or more brokers on a non-exclusive basis. Under an open listing, the seller normally reserves the right, at any time, to introduce the property to a new broker in addition to any appointed broker, unless there is an agreement to the contrary with one or more of the brokers. With an open listing, the broker who is considered the **procuring cause** of a transaction, usually the one who introduces a buyer or tenant **ready, willing and able** to consummate a transaction, is the only one entitled to a **commission**. Also, with an open listing, if the seller finds a purchaser through his own efforts, he is under no obligation to pay a commission to any broker. An open listing is usually revocable at any time, unless there is an agreement to the contrary; although some state licensing laws require all listing agreements to have a specified expiration date. Open listings are common with new housing projects where the house builder or developer employs his own on-site staff and lists the property with all brokers in the area. When there is no indication as to the basis of appointment, a listing is usually presumed to be an open listing. Sometimes called a 'general listing, or a 'multiple agency' or 'multiple brokerage' when the property is placed with two or more brokers. In Australia, also called a 'common listing'. cf. **exclusive listing**, **multiple listing**. See also **unilateral contract**.

open market   A **market** in which business is conducted without limitation as to the participants. A market that enables every person desirous of purchasing to come in and make an offer, and no one is excluded. In particular, it is not a market that is limited to a small circle of people or members of a particular group or organisation (*Inland Revenue Commissioners v Clay and Buchanan* [1914] 3 KB 466, 475 (CA); *Lynall v IRC* (1972) AC 680 (HL)). See also **market overt**.

open market value (OMV)(BrE)   The price that a property might be expected to realise if sold in a free, uncontrolled and open market. The term 'open market value' may be used to emphasise that the market is to be overt and available to every person who might constitute a buyer in the market in which the property might normally be sold, and is not limited or restricted to any selected group of purchasers. An 'open market' requires that the property is brought to the attention of any person who might (a) wish to know that the property is being offered for sale; (b) be willing or desirous of purchasing the property; and (c) be prepared to submit an offer for the property.

The Royal Institution of Chartered Surveyors used this term with a definition that is similar to market value. However, the RICS now considers that there is no material difference between the two bases and that open market value should not be used in reporting, although if appropriate a valuer may add that 'market value' produces the same figure (The Royal Institution of Chartered Surveyors. *Appraisal & Valuation Standards*. 5th ed. London: RICS Books, 2003, PS 1.1.8.)

When assessing **compulsory purchase compensation**, the amount of compensation is based essentially on the 'open market value' (subject to the statutory regulations). In this respect, the value is to be "ascertained by reference to the amount obtainable in the open market [which shows an intention to include every possible purchaser]. The market is to be the open market, as distinguished from a limited class only, such as members of a family. The market is not necessarily an auction sale. ... [The value] is such amount as the land might be expected to realise if offered under conditions enabling every person desirous of purchasing to come in and make an offer, and if proper steps were taken to advertise the property and let all likely purchasers know that land is in the market for sale", *Inland Revenue Commissioners v Clay and Buchanan* [1914] 3 KB 466, 475 (CA). cf. **forced sale value**. See also **market value, valuation date**.

open mine rule   See **waste**.

open mortgage(US)   **1.** A **mortgage** that permits the mortgagor to repay the principal in full at any time, without a **prepayment penalty**. See also **equity of redemption**.   **2.** A mortgage that has passed its date of maturity, but has been neither terminated by the mortgagee requesting payment of the outstanding balance in full, nor formally extended.   **3.** See **open-end mortgage**.

open-mortgage clause(US)   See **loss-payable clause, mortgagee clause**.

open offer   See **general offer**.

open planning   Arranging the interior of an office or residence with the minimum use of walls or partitions between the main areas of activity.

open policy   See **unvalued policy**.

open possession   See **adverse possession, notorious possession**(US).

open space   An area of land that is unbuilt on. Land that is left undeveloped and is reserved for public or recreational use. Unimproved land that is set aside for public or private use, especially by residents in the same neighbourhood. For example, a public park, square, common, heath, garden or a burial ground.

In English statute law, in connection with a right of a local authority to acquire land compulsorily, or the appropriation of land that it has acquired, 'open space' is defined in a number of similar ways, e.g. "any land laid out as a public garden, or used for the purposes of public recreation, or land which is a disused burial ground", Acquisition of Land Act 1981, s. 19(4); TCPA 1990, s. 336(1). See also **common land**(Eng), **green belt, national park, open country**(Eng), **open land, park, planned unit development**(US), **preservation district**(US).

open space zoning(US)   See **density zoning**.

operating budget   See **budget**.

operating cost   See **operating expense**.

operating expense(AmE)   An **expense** or **outgoing** that arises from running and maintaining a property. Periodic expenditure (fixed or variable) that is necessary in the long term to maintain a given level of income from a building and to ensure the proper upkeep and operation of that building. Operating expenses may include the costs of non-structural repair and maintenance, supplies for general maintenance, decoration, utilities (gas, water, steam, electricity), cleaning, heating or air-conditioning, security, refuse collection, road or ground maintenance, salaries, wages and other payroll costs, management fees and administrative expenses, usually insurance premiums (both for the property and associated risks), and frequently, a reserve or sinking fund to provide for the replacement of obsolete equipment. Operating expenses do not include capital expenditure, mortgage payments or debt service, real estate taxes, depreciation, or any other expense or outgoing that is not a result or function of the operation of the property. Sometimes called 'operating costs'. See also **escalation clause**, **net operating income**, **service charge**[(BrE)].

Building Owners and Managers Association International, *Downtown and Suburban Office Building: Experience Exchange*, Annual Report, Washington, DC: Building Owners and Managers Association International.

Urban Land Institute. *Dollars and Cents of Shopping Centers Triennial Report*. Washington, DC: Urban Land Institute, 2004.

operating expense ratio (OER)[(US)]   The ratio of **operating expense** to **effective gross income** expressed as a percentage – the complement of **net income ratio**. Also called the 'operating ratio' when the same ratio is based on the financial income and expenses of a corporation or an investment.

operating income[(US)]   See **net operating income**.

operating lease   A lease that merely requires periodic payments for the use of an asset and where there is no intention that the lessee will acquire ownership on or before the end of the lease term. 'Operating lease' originally referred to a lease of personal property, but may now be used to refer to a lease of any form of property where the intention is primarily that the lessee will have a use of the property, but unlike a **finance lease**, the lessor is intended to remain as the owner of the property.

Under the US Statement of Financial Accounting Standards, any lease that is not a finance lease (a "capital lease"), is an operating lease. A lease is considered as an operating lease if any one of the following criteria is met: (i) the net present value of the lease payments is less than 90% of fair value of the property; (ii) the lease term is granted for less than 75% of estimated economic life; (ii) the lessee does not have an option to purchase the property at a 'bargain' price; or (iv) the lease does not contain a provision that ownership of the property is to pass to the lessee at the end of the term. Upon the grant of an operating lease, unlike a finance lease, the property remains a balance sheet asset of the lessor. Thus, the transaction does not create any new asset or liability to the lessor or lessee.

In the UK, most leases of real property (even long-term full repairing and insuring leases) are treated as operating leases and are not shown in the tenant's accounts as assets or liabilities but only as annual obligations. See also **leasing**, **synthetic lease**.

operating leverage[(US)]   A means of increasing the return from an income-producing property by arranging for as many operating expenses as possible to be fixed (e.g. by entering into long-term service contracts) so that as the income from the property increases, the net income to the investor increases in a greater proportion. cf. **financial leverage**. See also **leverage**.

operating profit or **operating loss**   The profit (or loss) that a company or enterprise makes in the normal course of business, or from its principal trading activities, excluding any profits that arise from extraordinary operations, such as the sale of real property assets. See also **net operating income**.

operating ratio   See **operating expense ratio**.

operating statement   A statement of the income and expenditure of a business, or a property investment, over a period of time. Generally, an operating statement shows the actual income and expenses with a comparison to the planned **budget**. See also **effective gross income**[(US)], **financial statement**, **operating expense**[(US)].

operational land[(Eng)]   Land, or an interest in land, held by a statutory undertaker [such as a gas or electricity undertaking] for "the purpose of their undertaking", TCPA 1990, ss. 263-264, 336.

operations(Eng)   Activity on land that is considered by the Town Planning Acts to change the physical characteristics of the land and therefore to constitute **development**, for which planning permission is required. In particular, an activity that results in "some physical alteration to the land, which has some degree of permanence to the land itself", *Parkes v Secretary of State for the Environment* [1978] 1 WLR 1308, 1311 (CA). Such activity may comprise **building operations**, **engineering operations**, or **mining operations**.

operations and maintenance (O&M)(AmE) An ongoing program to contain or remediate environmental contamination in a building. See also **environmental audit**.

operative clause   1. See **operative part/ operative words**.   2. The clause in an **insurance policy** that sets out the obligations of the insurer.

operative part or **operative words**   The part, or words, of an instrument that give effect to the object of that document. The clause in a **conveyance** that effects the transfer of the property, e.g. "the vendor (A) hereby conveys Blackacre unto the purchaser (B) in fee simple". The words that give effect to the form of agreement intended, or that set out the principal object effected; as distinguished from introductory matter or a **recital** that are essentially supporting statements. The operative part of a deed is introduced commonly by such words as "this instrument hereby conveys" or "by this deed". The part or words of a deed that create its particular character, e.g. as a mortgage, lease, etc. See also **convey, demise, grant, granting clause**(US), **habendum, let, parcels clause, premises clause, testatum, words of grant**(US).

opinion of title(US)   See **abstract of title, certificate of title**.

opportunity cost   The cost foregone in following one course of action instead of another. The expenditure that would be incurred in producing or acquiring alternative goods or services. The advantage or benefit surrendered in order to acquire something else. "If the choice lies between the production or purchase of two commodities, the value of one is measured by the sacrifice of going without the other", J. P. Davenport, *The Formula for Sacrifice*, (1893) Econ. pp. 567-8. Thus, the true cost of an office building may be the number of houses that could be constructed for the same price. The opportunity cost of capital to an investor is the rate of return that is foregone when one form of investment is made in place of another. See also **cost-benefit analysis**.

opportunity-cost rate of return   See **target rate of return**.

optimum use   See **highest and best use**.

option   A choice. A right to do or not to do something, such as a right to accept or reject an offer within a specified or reasonable period of time. An agreement by which one party ('optionor') binds himself to transfer property to another ('optionee'), within a fixed, or reasonable, period of time, at a stipulated price. An option to sell property is a continuing offer whereby the owner agrees with another that the latter shall have the privilege of buying the property, upon certain terms, within a specified time. Thus, an option is a form of **unilateral contract**, at least until the holder of the option gives notice of his intention to exercise the right. An essential feature of an option is that the optionee has sole control over the choice that he is permitted to make and may withdraw therefrom at will. An option may be considered as a continuing, irrevocable offer to sell made by the grantor; an ordinary offer coupled with a **promise** not to withdraw the offer during the period of the option (Warner Bros. Pictures v. Brodel, 31 Cal.2d 766, 192 P.2d 949, 952 (1948); *Mountford v Scott* [1974] 1 All ER 248, 254, aff'd [1975] Ch 258 (CA)).

An option may be considered as a **conditional contract**, i.e. a contract subject to a condition that permits the grantee to convert the agreement into a contract of purchase. However, strictly an option depends upon the wishes of one of the parties, whereas a conditional contract is dependant on some outside event. Furthermore, an option allows some period of time for it to take effect (which may be construed by the courts as a 'reasonable' time if no absolute limit is expressed); whereas a conditional contract does not have to be subject to such a constraint, as the condition may not be time based.

An option may be 'mutual' or 'unilateral'. It is 'mutual' when either party has the right to exercise the option upon the happening of a specified event or at a particular time. For example, when a lease continues automatically because neither party exercises their right to terminate the lease at the end a fixed term. An option is 'unilateral' when it may be exercised by only one party. The most common forms of unilateral option are the **option to purchase** and the **option to sell**, also called, respectively, a **call option** and a **put option**. An option to purchase is a promise to sell given by an owner of property which is kept open for a defined or definable period of time. An option to sell is a right available to an owner of property to require another party to purchase that property within a defined or definable period of time.

An option, to be enforceable, must contain the requirements of any valid **contract** (details of the parties, consideration, duration, date, principal terms). In particular, the price to be paid must be ascertained, or be capable of being ascertained, with certainty, on or before the time fixed for exercising the option. A price that is to be determined based on a method that a court can use without the parties having to express their views, such as by independent appraisal or arbitration, is generally acceptable; but an option to purchase or lease a property merely at an "agreed rent" or an "appraised value" is unlikely to be enforceable, and the time within which the option is to be exercised must be ascertained, or ascertainable, with certainty.

An option may be distinguished from a **right of first refusal** or a **right of pre-emption**, either of which provides the beneficiary with a right to buy *if and when* the owner chooses to sell; whereas an option is available as a continuing right that essentially may be exercised at a specified time or on specified conditions, but at the optionee's choice. However, the exact wording and intent of the agreement needs to be considered when distinguishing such rights. In the US, some courts have taken the view that the use of words such as 'first privilege' or 'first refusal' have little effect and are only indicative of when an option may be exercised. However, as a rule, a right of first refusal (or a similar right) does require to be initiated by the action of the property owner and may be considered little more than a 'mere hope' that the option holder can acquire the property.

The completion of an option agreement does not give an agent a right to a **commission** for 'effecting a sale' of the subject property (unless there is an express provision in the agency agreement to that effect), because the sale of the property is contingent upon the decision of the option holder to exercise, or not, his right to purchase.

Also called a 'time bargain' when the agreement is limited within a specified period of time. cf. **agreement for sale and purchase**[US], **contract for sale**. See also **clog**, **covenant running with the land**, **equitable interest**[Eng], **equity of redemption**, **estate contract**[Eng], **fetter**, **hire-purchase agreement**[BrE], **overriding interest**[Eng], **ready able and willing**, **renewal**, **time**, **time is of the essence**, **unilateral contract**, **writing**.

Castle, Richard. *Barnsley's Land Options*. 3rd ed. London: Pearson, 1998.

option listing[US]   An arrangement by which the owner of a property lists that property with a broker and grants the same broker an **option to purchase** on specified terms. A broker who obtains an option listing is expected to market the property actively and is normally entitled to exercise his option only after the principal is satisfied that a reasonable effort has been made to find an independent purchaser. In any event, the broker has a fiduciary responsibility to his principal and should act in the **utmost good faith** to ensure that he is not taking advantage of his privileged position. Such forms of listing are discouraged or are illegal in many states. See also **listing**.

option money   Money paid to secure an **option**. Normally this sum is lost if the option is not exercised, but sometimes it may be set-off against the total consideration for any property acquired. See also **earnest money**.

option period   The period of time for which an **option** remains exercisable. As a rule, the longer the period during which the holder of an option may exercise his right, to buy or sell, the more valuable the option.

option to cancel   See **termination**.

option to purchase   A right or privilege that gives the holder of an **option** a right to purchase a property. A contract that gives one party a right to acquire a property at a price that is agreed in advance, or can be ascertained within a given period of time or at a future date. An option to purchase grants the privilege of buying at a later date and on certain terms, but it is not in itself a concluded agreement of sale or purchase. Also called a **call option**. See also **estate contract**[(Eng)], **finance lease, hire-purchase agreement**[(BrE)], **option**.

option to renew   A right given to a tenant to obtain a new lease upon the expiration of the current term, provided the tenant is not in default. An **option** to **renew** a lease grants the tenant a right to a new lease on the same terms as the old lease, except where expressly modified (usually at an increased rent, but for the same term). Unless expressly stated an option to renew does not grant a further automatic right of renewal. See also **extension, renewal**.

option to sell   A right or privilege available to a property owner whereby he can require another party to purchase that property within a defined or definable period of time, usually at a pre-

agreed price. Also called a **put option**. See also **option, option to purchase**.

option to terminate   A right or **option** available to the landlord or the tenant, or to both, to terminate a lease at will or upon the happening of a specified event. For example, a landlord's right to terminate the lease in the event that the demised property is to be rebuilt or sold; or a tenant's right to terminate if the premises are destroyed entirely or are unusable. See also **frustration, termination**.

optionee   The party to whom an **option** has been granted; the option holder. Sometimes called the 'offeree'.

optionor or **optioner**   One who has granted an **option** to another; the option giver. Sometimes called the 'offeror'.

oral contract   A verbal and unwritten **contract**. A contract made 'of many words' could be verbal, but unless done by word of mouth, or conveyed by speech, it is not oral. Most contracts relating to real property must be in **writing**, and therefore, an oral real property contract is generally unenforceable. cf. **implied contract, verbal contract**. See also **open contract, simple contract, Statute of Frauds**.

oral lease   See **agreement for a lease, parol lease**.

ordinance   An authoritative direction. A local law. A legislative decree or order made by a body that is a properly established arm of government. In particular, an order made by a municipal authority that is subordinate to the State. For example, a regulation, code or bylaw made by a town or city that affects the use of property in the area under its control, e.g. a **zoning ordinance, building code**, safety code, etc. cf. **bylaw**. See also **building regulations**[(Eng)], **police power**[(US)].

ordinary annuity capitalization[(AmE)]   The

capitalization of a series of future regular incomes by the application of a **single-rate capitalization factor** (in the US called an 'Inwood factor' and in the UK, a 'single-rate years' purchase'); to be distinguished from the application of a **dual-rate capitalization factor** (in the US called a 'Hoskold factor' and in the UK, a 'dual rate years' purchase'). See also **annuity capitalization**.

ordinary contractor   See **general contractor**.

ordinary conveyance[US]   A conveyance used to transfer an interest in property voluntarily between two parties, as distinguished from a transfer of property by virtue of a court order.

ordinary interest[US]   Interest calculated or charged based on 360 days to a **year** (12 months of 30 days each), unpaid interest being compounded every 30 days. See also **month**.

ordinary meaning rule   A rule for the construction of contracts, especially contracts of insurance, when the meaning of a word or term is in doubt. If there is no other rule for interpretation, words are to be understood "in their plain, ordinary and popular sense", *Robertson v French* (1803) 4 East 130, 135, 102 Eng Rep 779. When in doubt interpretation should be based on the context, and the most commonly accepted meaning as understood by men or women of the world of reasonable intelligence; although technical words must be given their strict technical meaning. See also **literal rule**, **term** (or **word**) **of art**, **words**.

ordinary repair   Such **repair** as is required to keep a property in good condition and order, but not such repair as requires renewal or replacement. See also **good repair**, **tenantable repair**.

ordinary use   The use of land or buildings to the extent that arises during the normal course of occupation for the purpose intended. A use based on the ordinary or common notions of mankind, as distinguished from a use that is outside reasonable limits, or beyond customary or habitual levels. See also **air rights**, **custom**, **dilapidation**, **fair wear and tear**[BrE], **right of light**, **usual covenant**, **water rights**, **wear and tear**[AmE].

ordinary wear and tear   See **fair wear and tear**[BrE], **wear and tear**[AmE].

Ordnance Survey® (O.S.)   A body founded in 1791 to be responsible for surveying and mapping Great Britain and for the publication of official topographical maps of the country. Today Ordnance Survey is Great Britain's national mapping agency. It is an independent government department and Executive Agency to the Secretary of the Environment. See also **Ordnance Survey map**. Owen, Tim, and Elaine Pilbeam. *Ordnance Survey. Ordnance Survey: Map Makers to Britain Since 1791*, Southampton: Ordnance Survey, 1992.

Ordnance Survey map   A map of a part of Great Britain produced by the **Ordnance Survey**. Such maps are currently published at scales ranging from 1:25,000 (4 cm to 1 km or approx. 2½ in to 1 mile) to 1:625,000 (1 cm to 6.25 km or approx. 1 in to 10 miles). An important feature of many of the Ordnance Survey maps is the representation of relief in the form of contours, bench marks, spot heights, and derived from all of these, hill-shading and tints. The Ordnance Survey also produces large scale plans at three scales, 1:500 (80 m by 80 m of ground detail); 1:1250 (200 by 200 m of ground detail); and 1:2500 (400 m by 400 m of ground area). These plans are suggested for use in conveyancing, insurance claims, home referencing, property location plans and property presentations and reports. It also produces plans that can be viewed on screen at scales from 1:200 to 1:10,000, and printed as required. These plans have a wide range of uses, including site development, planning applications, construction, conveyancing, land and estate management, environment and conservation, including area measurement reports.

The Ordnance Survey maps are continuously updated and are Crown Copyright. Permission to produce Ordnance Survey maps must be obtained on each occasion a copy is required, or, by means of a standard licence in the case of public bodies, various professional and business firms, educational institutions and printers. Applications for a specific consent or a licence are made to Copyright Branch, Ordnance Survey, Romsey Road, Maybush, Southampton, UK, S016 4GU. Ordnance maps are distributed by retailers and authorised agents, or can be ordered online (**www.ordnancesurvey.co.uk**).

original contractor or **originating contractor**   See **general contractor**.

original cost   The actual amount spent on the construction of a building, as distinguished from the present cost of replacing or reproducing the property. See also **acquisition cost**, **book cost**.

original face amount(US)   The original amount of principal as stated on a **mortgage-backed security**. See also **face amount**.

original lease(US)   See **head lease**.

origination fee   A fee charged by a lender for making a loan and usually payable when the loan agreement is entered into. An origination fee is intended to defray the lender's costs of granting a loan, including credit checks, appraisal of the collateral, preparation of loan documentation and the lender's closing costs. This fee does not necessarily cover the lender's legal costs, which may be charged separately. Such a fee is generally between 0.5% and 3% of the amount of the loan, depending on the risk entailed in accepting the loan. Also called a 'loan origination fee' or 'service fee'. cf. **finance fee**. See also **commitment fee, discount points**.

ostensible authority   Authority that someone holds out as having, but has not been truly granted. Authority that has a pretence of being real. In particular, authority that a principal has not expressly granted, but intentionally or through want of care allows a third person to believe the agent possesses. Ostensible authority may arise when: (a) a principal allows his agent to act in such a way that a third party would believe that the agent had the required authority to perform the act he is performing, and if appropriate, to bind the principal; (b) a principal allows his agent to act as if he still had authority after an agency relationship has been terminated; (c) a principal knowingly permits his agent to give the impression of having more authority than he has actually been given; or (d) the principal fails to inform a third party, with whom he knows the agent is treating, that the agent's authority has been strictly limited.

Ostensible authority may act as a form of **estoppel** so as to bind the principal to the agent's acts in the same way as if actual authority had been given, because the agent, with his principal's concurrence, may permit the third party to alter its position relying on the agent's representations or actions. Thus, in English law, ostensible or apparent authority has been termed 'agency by estoppel' or, in the US, 'authority by estoppel'. (**Agency by estoppel** may also arise when the doctrine of estoppel creates a contract of agency; as distinguished from the true application of the doctrine of ostensible authority, by which the agent is permitted to bind his principal.) Ostensible authority may also be called 'apparent authority'; although the latter term refers particularly to the authority that a principal has not actually given, but which the principal knowingly or negligently permits the agent to exercise, the authority that the principal in some way holds out that the agent possesses, or the authority that a third party may reasonably believe that an agent has been given. See also **agency of necessity**.

other real estate owned (OREO)(US)   See **real estate owned**.

ouster   The wrongful **dispossession**, or intentional exclusion, of someone from real property; in particular, from freehold property or a right of inheritance. Ouster of a freehold may include **abatement**, **disseisin**, **discontinuance**, or **deforcement** (3 *Bl Comm* 167). Ouster arises most commonly when a **tenant in common** wrongfully excludes, or endeavours to deny the title of, another tenant in common of the same property. Ouster may be 'actual' when the claimant is precluded from possession, or 'constructive' when a sufficient act is carried out to indicate the intention to claim possession. cf. **eviction**. See also **adverse possession**, **ejectment**.

out-of-the-money option An **option** with no intrinsic value because the price for exercising the option is higher than the cost of the option.

outbuildings Buildings used in connection with a main building; buildings that form part of a property, especially a dwelling-house, but which are not physically attached thereto. In particular, buildings that are accessed from the outside and not by a direct link to the main building. See also **accessory building**, **curtilage**, **outhouse**.

outflow An amount that goes out. A term used especially in the **cash-flow** analysis of a project or investment. See also **discounted cash flow**, **outgoing**.

outgoing tenant's valuation(Eng) See **tenant right**.

outgoing A **charge** or **expenditure** arising from the use and maintenance of property. A term frequently used as a 'catch-all' for any disbursement or payment made by an owner or occupier of real property. To an owner or landlord, 'outgoings' include all costs arising as a result of ownership. In particular, if a property is let, the expenditure that is not recoverable from a tenant, as well as management expenses and income lost due to voids and defaulting tenants. To an occupier or tenant, 'outgoings' include any expenditure arising as a result of use and occupation, including repair and maintenance

costs, rent or other expenses payable to a superior landlord, taxes (or other similar dues or levies) and insurance costs (including any premium payable by the tenant for insurance effected by the landlord). cf. **income**. See also **operating expense**(AmE), **rates**, **service charge**(BrE).

outhouse A building adjoining, or that is part of, a dwelling-house. An outhouse belongs to a dwelling-house or comes within the **curtilage** of a dwelling-house. See also **ancillary building**, **appurtenance**.

outland(Eng) See **tenemental land**.

outlet center or **outlet store** A retail store that is operated by a manufacturer or producer primarily to sell its own products at a discount to regular retail prices. In particular, a store that is run by a large retailer or a department store, in order to sell goods that have not sold in its regular stores usually due to fashion changes or overstocking. An outlet store may also sell goods bought in from other manufacturers, but at a discount to the regular retail store prices. See also **retail warehouse**(BrE).

outline planning permission(Eng) See **planning permission**.

outsourcing The transfer of responsibility for the performance of a service to an independent professional service or advisor. For example, the transfer of responsibility for the management of a corporation's real estate management to an independent manager

outstanding balance The current amount of a loan or mortgage that remains to be paid. See also **estoppel certificate**.

outstanding natural beauty(Eng) See **area of outstanding natural beauty**; **national park**.

outstanding term 1. The period remaining until the expiration of a lease that has been granted for a term of years.   **2.** A period of time remaining when the purpose for which a lease was granted has been achieved. See also **satisfied term**.

outstanding title(US)   A title held by someone who is not a party to an action between two other parties and may defeat the rights of either party. In particular, in an action for **ejectment**, a title held by a third party the successive right to which is being asserted in order to defeat the claim of the person seeking ejectment. In order to defeat a recovery in an action for ejectment, the defendant must show that the 'outstanding title' was beyond dispute and not the mere possibility of title.

outstroke   A right to convey minerals to the surface from one **mine** through another (as accepted by the owner or lessor of the mine through which the minerals are brought). If such a right of outstroke is granted, a royalty may be payable, which is called a 'wayleave rent' or 'way lease rent'. cf. **instroke**. See also **wayleave**.

over-and-above money(US)   See **end money**.

over-insurance   Insurance of a property for more than its 'actual cash value' or **reinstatement cost**; insurance for a sum that exceeds the maximum loss that might be sustained in the event of a claim (even after taking full account of projected inflation). Over-insurance has no advantage for the insured, as the insurer is not normally obliged to pay more than the true loss suffered by the insured, i.e. the insurer has only contracted to provide an **indemnity**. Over-insurance merely results in the payment of an excessive premium by the insured. On the other hand, grossly over insuring a property, especially when intentional, may be contrary to the provisions of an insurance policy or may constitute a fraud as it reduces the insured's incentive to preserve or protect the property. cf. **under-insurance**. See also **double insurance, valued policy**.

over-lease(US)   See **head lease**.

over the mortgage(US)   An expression used to indicate the price or **equity** that a purchaser must pay for a property over and above the amount of a mortgage loan that is to be transferred with the property. See also **assumption**.

overage   **1.** An amount that exceeds a specified or recorded level. For example, the profit from a development above the total cost. The sale of a property may be made on the basis that the sale price will be based in part on an 'overage' payment that is equal to a percentage of the gross receipts from the sale of the developed property. Similarly, an overage payment may be based on an increase in the value of the property as a result of an improvement in the amount of permitted development. See also **equity participation**.   **2.** A rent paid in addition to a fixed or **base rent**. In particular, that part of the rent that exceeds the base rent or guaranteed minimum rent in a turnover or percentage lease. In the US, also called an 'override'. See also **percentage rent**.   **3.** Discount points that exceed the cost of selling a mortgage in a secondary property without incurring a loss.

overall capitalization rate or **overall cap rate** (OCR)(AmE)   A single **capitalization rate** used in the income approach to appraisal. A capitalization rate that is used to convert the net operating income in a particular year into an estimate of the capital value. This rate is selected, or calculated, to provide a rate of return that is sufficient to recapture the capital cost of an investment and provide a satisfactory return to the investor (i.e. it includes a **sinking fund rate** and a **remunerative rate**). However, unlike a **dual-rate capitalization factor**, the overall rate is not determined purely by a mathematical calculation, but by reference to 'overall' returns on comparable investment sales, or by application of a **band-of-investment rate**. Overall capitalization rate may be expressed by the symbol R_0. See also **all-risks rate, straight capitalization, years' purchase**(BrE)

overall rate (OR) or **overall rate of**

return (ORR)[AmE]   **1.** The rate of return on an investment obtained by dividing the **net operating income** by the **purchase price**.   **2.** See **internal rate of return**.

overall yield rate[AmE]   The rate of return on the total amount of debt and equity invested. The ratio of **net operating income** (before debt service) to the total capital invested. Overall yield rate may be expressed by the symbol Y_O. cf. **cash-on-cash return**. See also **free and clear return**.

overbid   An amount paid over and above the **market value** of a property to reflect the special value to a particular purchaser or tenant. See also **special purchaser**.

overbuild   To build more properties than are normally demanded in a particular market. See also **boom**.

overburdening[US]   The use of an **easement** for an improper or more intense purpose to that for which it was intended or granted. An extreme case of 'overburdening' may result in the loss or termination of the easement if the unauthorized use cannot be severed from that which was originally granted.

overcrowding   A condition where more people occupy property than is considered healthy.
   In English law, a dwelling-house (being "premises used or suitable for use as a separate dwelling") may be overcrowded if it exceeds either (a) the "room standard"; or (b) the "space standard". The room standard is exceeded if the number of rooms is such that any two, aged 10 or over, of the opposite sex, not being husband and wife, have to sleep in the same room. The space standard is exceeded if the number of persons occupying the house exceeds a statutorily permitted ratio of persons per room and per floor area of living accommodation (HA 1985, ss. 325, 326). In the case of a house in **multiple occupation** (HMO) (i.e. a house or flat where the occupiers do not form a single household, including a hostel), the standard is determined by the local housing authority, based essentially on the number of rooms available for sleeping purposes, subject to a right of appeal by the person having control of the property (HA 1985, ss. 358-364). A factory must not be so overcrowded while work is being carried out "as to cause risk of injury to the health of the persons employed in it (Factories Act 1961, s. 2(1)). A similar standard is applied to most offices, shops and railway premises (Offices, Shops and Railway Premises Act 1963, s. 5(1)). These statutes also stipulate the minimum amount of space to be allocated for each person employed, or working in the premises. See also **common lodging-house**, **rent book**.

overflow right   See **flowage easement**.

overhead or **overhead cost**   The indirect costs of running an organisation. An expense that is incurred independently of the level of activity, e.g. rent, real estate taxes, property insurance premiums.

overhead rights   See **air rights**.

overholding tenant[Can]   See **holding over**.

over-improvement   An **improvement**, or work of improvement, to a property that costs more than the amount it adds to the market value of the property.

overlapping mortgage[US]   See **wraparound mortgage**.

overreachable interest[Eng]   An interest in property that, in the event of a sale of the property, is considered readily transferable from the property to an interest in the proceeds of sale. A form of interest, or power, affecting land that is held in trust which does not bind a **purchaser** of a **legal estate**, whether or not he has notice thereof (LPA 1925, s. 2(1)). In particular, an interest (which may be legal or equitable) in **settled land** that is considered capable of being detached from the property and converted into a claim against the proceeds of sale (the **capital money**), if and when the property is sold (in this context 'settled land' may include personal property that is part of the settlement). Such interests are statutorily defined being principally the interests of the beneficiaries of the trust and certain financial charges. The principle of having 'overreachable interests' in land is to enable the purchaser of a legal estate to acquire that estate free of such interests without adversely affecting the financial benefit enjoyed by the holder of the interest (even though the purchaser may know of the existence of the interest). Such interests should be (or in most cases must be) registered for their protection (either for unregistered land as a **land charge**, or for registered land by an entry of a **notice, caution** or **restriction** on the register). cf. **overriding interest**. See also **capital money, conversion, minor interest, strict settlement, trust for sale**.

override　1.(US)See **extender clause**.　2.(US)See **overage**.　3. A share of a **commission** received by a subordinate or salesperson that is paid to the managerial personnel.　4.(Eng)To render an interest in land void. An interest is said to be overridden when a **legal estate** is acquired by a *bona fide* **purchaser** for **value** without **notice**, i.e. by a purchaser who, acting in good faith, is not informed, and is unable reasonably to ascertain, that the interest exists and he has paid valuable consideration for the legal estate. In that event, the new owner of the legal estate takes that estate free of the 'overridden interest' and the original holder merely retains a right over the proceeds of sale. See also **overriding interest**.

overriding interest　An interest or encumbrance that affects **registered land** and has priority over other interest in the same land, even though it has not been registered or the owner of the land does not have knowledge of the existence of the interest. In English law, an interest or encumbrance that affects **registered land**, but is "not entered on the register", LRA 1925, s. 3(xvi).

This is the kind of right that affects registered land and is binding on the proprietor of registered land, even though he may have no actual knowledge of the interest and irrespective of whether the interest is entered on the land register. Overriding interests are a group of rights over land that a purchaser of registered land is assumed by law to be able to find by making proper enquiries and searches. For example, by physically inspecting the property, making enquiries of any occupier, making appropriate requisitions to the vendor (especially on such relatively minor rights as short leases and easements), and examining the local land charges register. Most overriding interests are legal rights, but many are equitable. Overriding interests include such interests as a **legal easement**; an **equitable easement**, rights acquired or being acquired under the Limitation Acts (such as rights claimed by **adverse possession**, or a contract for the purchase of land); the rights of every person in actual **occupation** of the land; a **local land charge** (unless protected by an entry on the register); and leases *granted* for a term not exceeding twenty-one years (but not an **equitable lease**, such as an agreement to grant a lease) (LRA 1925, s. 70(1), as amended). An overriding interest may be entered on the register for convenience (or may be entered by the Registrar at his discretion), but need not be so for protection. However, if entered on the register it ceases to be an overriding interest and is protected by that entry, i.e. it becomes a **minor interest**. With effect from October 13 2003, many of the interests in land that would have been overriding interests (in particular, most lease with over 7 years to run, easements and profits à prendre) are required to be registered, and a land owner is required to disclose to the Land Registry details of any overriding interest of which he is aware (Land Registration Act 2002). cf. **overreachable interest**. See also **notice**.

overriding lease　See **concurrent lease**.

overriding mortgage(US)　See **wraparound mortgage**.

overriding royalty(US) A right to a share of the working interest or production payable under an oil or gas lease held free of the expense of production. An overriding royalty is held by someone other than the lessor and does not require the recipient to contribute to the cost of exploration, development or maintenance. It may be an entitlement to a royalty retained by the lessee when a sublease is created, or a royalty receivable when a fractional or partial interest in the benefits of the oil or gas lease is granted to a third party. An overriding royalty only continues as long as the original lease and does not entitle the holder to any continuing payment if the sublessee or owner of the other fractional interest obtains a further right to exploitation of the oil or gas rights. 'Overriding royalty' may sometimes refer to a share of the royalty that is receivable by the lessee, but is not part of a royalty payable to the lessor or someone claiming through him. See also **oil and gas lease**, **royalty**.

overspill Population, originating from a crowded conurbation, that spills out into the surrounding countryside or is relocated to an area away from the main center, such as to a **new town**. People who, due to a shortage of living accommodation, or a lack of employment, move out of an urban area into the surrounding countryside to establish new communities. Overspill emanates especially from a population that is considered surplus to the normal capacity of a town or city to maintain, except by unduly stretching its available facilities. See also **decentralization**.

overt Open to public view, not disguised or secret. See also **market overt**.

owelty See **partition**.

owned real estate (ORE)(US) See **real estate owned**.

owner 1. One who has **ownership** of property. One who has **dominion** over a property, to use as he pleases, except as restricted by law or by agreement. A person in whom a property is beneficially vested and who has the occupation or control of it. An owner of real property may be any person who has an estate or interest in land, whether legal or equitable; provided he has a right to exclusive enjoyment, and not a mere licence. However, in common parlance and as a primary meaning in law the owner of land is the holder of a fee simple, or the freeholder. A mortgagee not in possession and a tenant holding under a periodic tenancy, or any short-term lease, are not normally considered to be owners. *Prima facie*, an owner has a right to possession, a right of alienation, and has a right to recover a property from all others; but any one, or all of these rights, may be restrained or fettered. An owner may part with possession to a bailee, pledgee, thief or squatter; his right of alienation may be restrained under a deed of settlement; and his right to recover the property may be shackled by law. Nevertheless, he remains the owner until the power of control is transferred, voluntarily or involuntarily, to another. "A person who has the totality of the rights, powers, privileges and immunities which constitute complete property in a thing is the 'owner' of the 'thing', or 'owns' the 'thing' … The owner may part with many of the rights, powers, privileges and immunities that constitute complete property and his relationship to the thing is still termed ownership both in this Restatement and as a matter of popular usage", American Law Institute, *Restatement of Property* § 10, Comments *b* and *c* (1936). The term 'owner' generally refers to one who has dominion over the property, which clearly means the owner of the fee and the holder of a long-term ground lease in possession. Whereas it does not normally include the holder of a short-term or periodic lease. However, the term must be construed according to a statute in which it is used. It generally refers to one who has dominion over the property, which clearly means the owner of the fee and the holder of a long-term ground lease in possession. Whereas it does not normally include the holder of a short-term or periodic lease. In a mechanic's lien statute, an owner usually includes the holder of a fee simple, a life estate, a leasehold, or a purchaser in possession under an executory contract.

In English planning law, an "owner, in relation to any land means a person, other than a mortgagee not in possession, who, whether in his own right or as trustee for any other person, is entitled to receive the **rack rent** of the land, or, where the land is not let at a rack rent, would be entitled if it were so let", TCPA 1990, s. 336(1) (This section does not apply to the requirement to notify an owner about a planning application nor a representation to a local planning authority that may be made by an owner following a planning application – in those cases, the owner is the estate owner of the fee simple or the holder of a tenancy with not less than seven years unexpired: TCPA 1990, s. 65(8)). A similar definition is contained in the Clean Air Act 1993, s. 64(1) and the Environmental Protection Act 1990, s. 81A(9), which expressly include a person receiving the **rack rent** as "agent or trustee for another person". For the purpose of compulsory purchase an owner is "any person having power to sell and convey the land to the authority", CPA 1965, s. 1(b). In English rating law, an owner of a property is the "person entitled to possession ...", Local Government Finance Rate Act 1988, s. 65(1), Sch. 4A, para. 1(1). In connection with the right to enforce an **estate rentcharge**, an owner of land is "a person, other than a mortgagee in possession, who is for the time being entitled to dispose of the fee simple of the land, whether in possession or reversion, and includes a person holding or entitled to the rents and profits of the land under a lease or agreement", Rentcharges Act 1977, s. 13(1). See also **absentee owner**, **beneficial owner**, **bundle of rights theory**, **estate owner**, **landowner**, **reputed owner**. **2.** In connection with a building contract, the owner may be: (i) the party who owns the land upon which the building work is carried out; (ii) the principal party to the contract, who pays the **contractor** for the building work; or (iii) the client of a professional advisor employed in connection with the building work.

owner finance(US)   See **installment land contract**.

owner-occupier(BrE)   or   **owner-occupant**(AmE)   A person who is both the **owner** and the **occupier** or **occupant** of a property.

In English statute law, for the purpose of the right to serve a **blight notice** or **purchase notice**, 'owner-occupier' is defined as a freeholder or a tenant having a tenancy granted (or extended) for a term of years certain of which at least three years remain unexpired; provided he has been in **occupation** of the whole or a substantial part of the 'owner's interest' for six months prior to the service of the notice, or at least six of the twelve months prior to the service of the notice, or in the case of an agricultural unit the *whole* of the unit has been occupied either for a period of six months prior to the service of the notice or for a period of at least six months of the twelve months prior to the service of the notice (TCPA 1990, s. 168). In the case of a right to **compensation for injurious affection** (as payable when an interest in land is depreciated by 'physical factors' caused by the use of public works), ' owner-occupier' means a person who occupies the whole or a substantial part of the land with an owner's interest in that land or, if the land is an agricultural unit, occupies the whole of the land (LCA 1973, s. 2(5)). In the case of an advance made by a local authority to assist a displaced residential occupier to acquire or construct a dwelling in substitution for one taken by an authority by compulsory purchase, an 'owner-occupier' is a person who owns the freehold or a tenancy for a term of not less than three years and is the occupier of the dwelling (LCA 1973, s. 41(9)(a)). See also **grounds for possession**(Eng), **leasehold enfranchisement**(Eng), **resident landlord**(Eng).

owner of record(US)   **1.** One who has acquired and holds title to land by a valid conveyance that has been recorded in the office of the register of deeds. In particular, the person upon whom notice is served of an intent to transfer title under a tax deed.   **2.** The 'true' owner of land, whether recorded as such or ascertainable by other means. See also **record owner**.

owner trust   A trust established to issue a **collateralized mortgage obligation**. See also **issuer**.

owner's equity   See **net worth**.

owner's, landlord's and tenant's public liability insurance (O.L.&T. insurance) See **public liability policy**.

owner's liability insurance   Insurance that provides a property owner with protection from liabilities that arise from the ownership of property, especially liability to the general public. See also **contractor's all-risk insurance, public liability policy**.

owner's policy(US)   See **title insurance**.

ownership   The right of one person to exercise power and control over property to the exclusion of others; the right of an **owner**. Ownership has been described as "the greatest possible interest which a mature system of law recognises. ... Ownership comprises the right to possess, the right to use, the right to manage, the right to the income of the thing, the right to the capital, the right to security, the right or incidents of transmissibility and absence of term, the prohibition of harmful use, liability to execution, and the incident of residuarity", Tony Honoré, *"Ownership", Oxford Essays in Jurisprudence*, 1961, pp. 105, 109 . A right to the exclusive use, possession and enjoyment of a thing for a period of time, together with a right to transfer that thing to others; subject to any rights or duties owed to others and limitations imposed for the public good. The maintaining of a rightful **title** to property, with or without **possession**, especially a title that is protected by law.

Ownership includes a right of physical user, a right of possession, a right to derive financial benefit therefrom, a right to dispose in whole or in part, and, in theory, a right to waste or destroy. In its most absolute form, ownership is made up of the rights described in Roman legal terms as *utendi, fruendi* and *abutendi* – use, enjoyment, and abuse or destruction, i.e. to do as one likes (within the confines of the law). Put another way, ownership may comprise all or most of the rights attaching to property; namely occupation, possession, use, transfer, alienation, gift, management, charge, or even destruction and absolute ownership (*dominium*) is the combination of all these rights.

In common law, ownership of land was removed from the substance of land, and considered as an abstract right called an **estate** – a right to maintain a better title than another. "While it is usual to speak of the 'ownership of land', what one owns is properly not the land, but rather the rights of possession and approximately unlimited user, present or future. In other words, one owns not the land but rather an estate in the land", 1 *Tiffany on Real Property*. 3rd ed., 1939, § 2, p. 4. This concept, which is founded on the feudal system of **tenure**, makes an owner no more than a holder of land from another; ultimately from a tenant of the Crown or some other Lord. "Quite apart from this practical difficulty, however, the truth is that English law has never applied the conception of ownership to land. 'Ownership' is a word of many meanings, but in the present context [that of defining the **doctrine of estates**] we can take it to signify a title to a subject-matter, whether movable or immovable, that is good against the whole world. The holder of the title, such as the holder of a motor car, has real right as opposed to a personal right—he is the absolute owner", E. H. Burn, *Cheshire and Burn's Modern Law of Real Property*. 16th ed. London: Butterworths, 2000, p. 26. However, in modern law, when a person holds land as an estate of **fee simple absolute** there is no significant difference from the form of ownership recognised by the Romans (although in Roman Law, which recognises no real distinction between real and personal property, ownership could more truthfully be described as 'absolute' in law: someone either had ownership or no ownership at all; as distinguished from possession which is a right that can only be protected by a personal action, not a real action for the land). Thus, it has been said (in application to English law) that "by slow degrees, the statement that there is no absolute ownership of land has been deprived of most of its important consequences", F. W. Maitland, *Collected Papers* (1911), vol. i. p. 196.

Ownership, as well as being absolute, may be limited in quantity or quality; may be corporeal or incorporeal; may be present or future; may be exercised in respect of real property or personal property; and may be a real right or a personal right. Nevertheless, whatever form it takes, ownership is subject to the powers of government and the laws of the land (especially taxation, building, zoning or planning restrictions, 'police powers', expropriation, and escheat or *bona vacantia*); any obligations or duties owed to the public at large; any constraint imposed by a person who has a greater or more absolute form of ownership; and any limitation imposed by the grant of a lesser right or interest. See also **co-ownership**, **collective ownership**, **cooperative ownership**, **perfect ownership**[US], **seisin**, **several estate**.

P

package-deal contract   See **design-and-build contract**.

package insurance policy   An insurance policy that covers a number of different risks of loss, especially those associated with a particular status or activity, e.g. a **homeowner's insurance policy**. Also called a 'combined insurance policy'. See also **blanket insurance**.

package loan   A loan granted to a builder to provide financing for a number of properties on a housing project or planned unit development. cf. **spot loan**.

package mortgage(US)   A mortgage secured on real and personal property. In particular, a mortgage secured on a residence and major items of equipment that are permanently situated in the residence. See also **fixture**.

packing   Filling a building with tenants upon terms that are inferior to those obtainable in open market conditions, usually in order to present a 'fully-leased' building to a prospective purchaser or lender.

pacta sunt servanda or ***pactum est servandum***(Lat)   'Agreements [and stipulations of a contact] are to be observed'. 'An **agreement** is to be kept'. A maxim that embodies the principle that a promisor to a contract should expect to abide by his obligations or commitments. See also **gentleman's agreement**.

pad(AmE)   **1.** An area in a mobile home park that is allocated for the placement of a **mobile home**. Such an area is generally paved and supplied with utilities.   **2.** An area of land underlying an individual unit in a **condominium**. See also **planned unit development**.   **3.** An area of land in a shopping center that is used or allocated for use by a major retailer, especially a freestanding commercial user such as a major department store or a fast-food outlet. See also **pad sale**.

pad sale(AmE)   A sale, or a long-term ground lease, of a site in a shopping center to a major retailer. The purchaser or tenant is responsible for building the retail store on the site, which although an independent building, forms an integral part of the shopping center. See also **anchor tenant**, **reciprocal easement**.

pais   See **estoppel**.

panic peddling(US)   See **blockbusting**.

paper   Written evidence of a debt, especially evidence of a short-term debt that is not made under seal. A **bill of exchange**, **promissory note**, **mortgage**, or similar contract for the payment of a sum of money, usually on or by a specified date. 'Paper' may be sold, usually at a discount, to a lender or factor, or may be pledged as security for a loan. See also **commercial paper**, **instrument**, **negotiable instrument**, **writing**.

paper title(US)   **1.** A title that is demonstrated by a chain of documents or conveyances. A term that is commonly used to refer to a title that appears valid, or has the **color of title**, but is not indisputable. cf. **good title**.   **2.** See **record title**.

par value   **1.** The nominal or **face value** of a bond, share of stock or a security. In the case of a bond, the par value is the amount at which the obligor undertakes to redeem the bond at maturity. cf. **market value**. See also **redemption value**.   **2.** The **principal** outstanding on a mortgage loan at a given point in time. The price at which a mortgage can be sold without any discount.

paramount lease(US)   A lease that is above or superior to another; a lease held by a lessor whose lessee has granted a sublease. See also **head lease**.

paramount possession   Possession as held

571

by someone in their own right and not derived or held by virtue of another's right to possession, especially possession held by an owner as distinguished from possession as held by a tenant. cf. **derivative possession**.

paramount title   A **title** that is superior to another. A stronger or better title to that claimed in opposition thereto. **Eviction** can arise 'by title paramount' when a landlord who has a superior title to the immediate landlord takes action to dispossess the under-tenant. The term is sometimes used merely to refer to a title that is better or stronger than another. cf. **derivative title**.

parcel of land   1. A specified area, or **plot** of land, usually in single ownership. A **contiguous** area of land held in the possession of one party, especially a claimant to compensation for the expropriation of such land (United States v. Easements and Rights over Certain Land, 259 F Supp 377, 382 (1966)). A continuous tract or plot of land held in the same ownership and not separated by any intervening land in another ownership. See also **hereditament, lot.**   2. An area of land that has been subdivided as a part of a larger estate or tract of land.   3. A **section of land**, or a half, or a quarter section (*Ost v Turnbull* (1977) 81 DLR (3d) 161 (Can)). Any contiguous sections or parts thereof, as distinguished from a **tract** which is an area of land of indefinite extent.

parcel identification   See grantor-grantee index[US], index map[Eng], lot and block system[US], plat book, plot plan, tract index[US].

parceling[AmE] or **parcelling**[BrE]   The act of dividing land into separate plots for sale or development. cf. **assemblage, plottage**. See also **plat**.

parcella terrae[Lat]   A 'parcel of land'.

parcels clause   The section of a **deed** or **conveyance** that describes the subject property. The parcels clause generally starts with the words "All that …" and then describes the property by reference to an address or by reference to a **plan**.

A description of a property by reference to a precise verbal description of the boundaries and appropriate land marks (i.e. metes and bounds) is satisfactory if based on a formal survey of the land; but a description solely by name, address, or by a mere statement of a land area tends to be too vague or uncertain. A description of a parcel of land by reference to a plan is good, provided the plan is to an adequate scale, and has been prepared and clearly marked for the purpose. However, a mixed form of description may be disastrous: "as long as only one species of description is resorted to in describing parcels, no harm is done … If, however, several species of description are adopted, risk of uncertainty at once arises, for if one is full, accurate, and adequate, any others are otiose if right, and misleading if wrong", *Eastwood v Ashton* [1915] AC 900, 915-916 (HL) (*Scarfe v Adams* [1981] 1 All ER 843 (CA)). See also **exceptions and reservations, description, general words, premises clause**.

Parcels Index[Eng]   An index of every parcel of land as registered at the **Land Registry** (Land Registration Rules 1925, r. 8). This index shows the number by which various parcels of registered land are referenced on the **General Map**, the title number for each registered parcel, and the number of any registered caution or priority notice that affects a parcel of land (Land Registration Rules 1925, r. 274).

parcenary   See **coparcenary**.

pari passu[Lat]   'With equal step'; 'without preference'; 'at the same rate'; 'equally'.

parish   1. An area that falls within an administrative boundary of the established church; "the ecclesiastical unit of area committed to one pastor …", *Webster's Third New International Dictionary*®, *Unabridged*, ©1993.   2.[Eng] The smallest area of local government, having been originally an ecclesiastical parish.   3.[US] In Louisiana, the smallest civil division of the state, corresponding to a county in other states.

parity clause(US) A clause in a mortgage which provides that when more than one note is secured by the same mortgage, all the notes have equal priority, i.e. there is parity between all the loans.

park **1.** An area of land set aside for public recreation, pleasure, rest, amusement or ornament. A place to which the public resort for open-air leisure and recreation. See also **dedication**. **2.** An area of forest or land preserved in its natural state for public enjoyment. See also **national park**. **3.**(Eng)Historically, an enclosed area of ground that is stocked with beasts for hunting and is held by royal grant or prescription. cf. **chase**, **common land**, **forest**. See also **enclosure**. **4.** A privately owned and enclosed area of countryside, especially gardens, woodlands or pasture attached to a country house or manor house.

parking area or **parking lot** An open area of land used for the stationing of motor vehicles, generally for an appreciable period of time in a day. In particular, an area where members of the public are charged for parking their vehicles for a short period of time. See also **garage**.

parking ratio or **parking index** The ratio of the number of parking spaces provided for a building to the gross lettable or rentable area of that building. The number of parking spaces per building units, e.g. spaces per dwelling or spaces per hotel room.

parol Oral; executed by word of mouth only, not in **writing**, by **deed** or under **seal**. See also **parol lease**.

parol contract Strictly, a contract made by word of mouth. In particular, a contract that is not in **writing**. In law, a 'parol contract' may refer also to a contract that is in writing, but not under seal, i.e. a **simple contract**. For the purpose of the **Statute of Frauds**, a contract that is partly in writing but leaves an essential part to be agreed by word of mouth is a parol contract, and therefore is unlikely to satisfy the requirement of that statute that certain contracts for the transfer of land must be in 'writing' to be enforceable. See also **oral contract**.

parol lease A **lease** that is made verbally; one that is not made in **writing**. (Strictly speaking a parol lease is one made by word of mouth – an 'oral lease'; but 'parol lease' may be used to refer to any lease that has come into effect, as by taking of possession and payment of rent, but has not been put in writing.)

In the US, in most jurisdictions, a lease for three years or less (or in some states, one year or less) is enforceable, provided there is evidence of the agreement, as by the payment of rent or the taking of possession of the property. Longer leases are required to be in writing.

In English law, a parol lease may be enforceable in the same way as one made in writing and properly signed, provided: (a) it takes effect "in possession", i.e. immediately; (b) it is made "for a term not exceeding three years" (i.e. it is not for a definite term that exceeds that period); and (c) the tenant pays "the best rent which can be reasonably obtained", without the tenant being obliged to pay a **fine** or premium (LPA 1925, s. 54(2)). Otherwise, the interest created is only a **tenancy at will**, even though there is a payment of consideration (LPA 1925, s. 54(1)). See also **agreement for a lease**, **legal lease**, **parol contract**.

parsonage A house for a parson, minister of the church, or incumbent of a **parish**. At common law, a certain portion of land, and the tithe, established for the maintenance of a minister of the church, usually being the entire **benefice**. The house, land, parish church, tithes, etc., that are set aside to provide fruits and benefits for a parish priest. See also **glebe land**.

part owner **1.** A person who holds an interest in property in **co-ownership**, whether held by a **coparcener**, **joint tenant**, or **tenant in common**. **2.** One who has a **partial interest** in land.

part payment or **partial payment**   1. **Payment** of a sum of money that is less than the total amount due to discharge a debt or liability. In general, part payment does not constitute **satisfaction** of the whole of a debt (*Pinnel's Case* (1602) 5 Co Rep 117a, 77 Eng Rep 237; *Foakes v Beer* (1884) 9 App Cas 605, 616 (HL); Occidental Life Ins. Co. v. Eiler, 125 F.2d 229 (8th Cir. Mo 1942)). However, a payment of part of a debt or obligation may amount to satisfaction, provided there is clear evidence (usually in writing or some demonstrable form) that the part payment has been accepted by both parties as a discharge of the full amount, or it is accompanied by some substituted consideration. See also **accord and satisfaction**, **deposit**, **lien**.   2. A payment, being one of a number of such payments made, generally at fixed intervals, under an **instalment sale**. In the US, more commonly called a 'partial payment'.   3. A payment made to reduce a part of the principal owed under mortgage loan. Unless there is an express agreement to the contrary, any payment, or part payment, under a mortgage agreement is first applied to pay interest while the balance, if any, is used to reduce the principal debt. See also **amortization loan**, **instalment**.

part performance   1. See **doctrine of part performance**.   2. The performance by a party to a contract of less than is required under the terms of the agreement. Under an **entire contract**, part performance of the contract does not entitle the performing party to recover a partial payment. However, a contract has to be clearly intended by both parties to be 'entire' and indivisible; otherwise, in equity, the courts will usually accede to payment upon part performance when the work has clearly conferred a benefit on one of the parties. In American English sometimes referred to as a 'partial performance'. See also **substantial performance**, *quantum meruit*.

partial condemnation(US)   See **partial taking**.

partial eviction   The actual or constructive eviction of a tenant from part of the demised premises. 'Partial eviction' usually requires eviction from a substantial part of the premises, or for a substantial period of time, in order to relieve the tenant of any obligation to pay rent. See also **constructive eviction**, **quiet enjoyment**.

partial floor factor(US)   See **loss factor**.

partial interest   An interest in land that is less than a fee simple absolute. A partial interest in land may be created as a result of a physical subdivision of land (horizontally or vertically); the grant of a limited right of user, whether in terms of time, type or person, or the grant of a financial charge or mortgage over land. Partial interests include also the benefit of land held in trust; a right to land held in co-ownership or collective ownership; the right to an easement or any other form of servitude; a leasehold interest, and a life interest. The term 'partial interest' derives its origin from the **bundle of rights theory** propounded in the US by which land is considered as a collection of rights to land, the fee owner having a complete bundle of rights and any other owner has a partial interest. See also **doctrine of estates**, **fractional interest**.
Keating, David M. *Appraising Partial Interests*. Chicago: Appraisal Institute, 1998.

partial net lease(US)   A lease where, in addition to rent, the lessee pays operating expenses, taxes, insurance and maintenance, but not the cost of repairs. cf. **triple net lease**. See **net lease**.

partial payment(US)   See **part payment**.

partial payment factor(US)   See **mortgage constant**; Appendix C, **Financial Formulae**, **annuity one will purchase**.

partial performance   See **doctrine of part performance**.

partial reconveyance deed(US)   See **partial release clause**.

partial redemption(US) See **partial release clause**.

partial release A partial **release** of a condition attached to the grant of an estate or interest in land. In most cases, a partial release of a condition does not amount to a total release of that condition and the release of a condition does not mean that the condition must be complied with in the future. In particular, a **waiver** of a time restraint does not normally waive in its entirety the performance of the condition to which the restraint is attached. See also **partial release clause**(US).

partial release clause(US) A provision in a mortgage that allows for the release of part of the property that is held as collateral. In particular, the release of certain properties from a **blanket mortgage**, generally upon repayment of a specified part of the principal. A mortgage secured on a number of building lots, or on units in a condominium, will normally provide for the release of individual properties as they are sold, free and clear of the blanket mortgage, subject to the proceeds of sale being used to reduce the outstanding principal (sometimes in greater proportion than the amount secured by individual property). Partial release is not normally permitted if the mortgagor is in default under any of the terms of the mortgage agreement. A deed that gives effect to a release of part of the property held under a mortgage is called a 'partial release deed' or a 'partial reconveyance deed'. Alternatively, the blanket mortgage may contain a 'special recognition clause' that has a similar effect, i.e. the mortgagee undertakes to recognize the rights of the individual owners even if the mortgagee forecloses on the entire project. The individual units may have an 'allocated loan amount' by which the total mortgage debt is reduced as each property is released from the blanket mortgage. Sometimes called a 'takeout provision' – individual purchasers being able to 'take out' their properties from the blanket security. See also **release clause**.

partial release deed See **partial release clause**.

partial sale The sale of part of the interest held in a property. For example, the sale of a **partial interest**; the sale of a building separately from the land (or vice-versa); or the sale of a share of a joint venture. See also **partial taking**, **severance**.

partial taking(US) The taking of part of an owner's land, or a partial interest in land, by an exercise of the power of **eminent domain**, i.e. the compulsory **severance** of some part of a right of ownership. See also **before-and-after method**, **severance damages**, **taken for public use**.

partial zoning(US) A zoning ordinance that is made to apply to only part of an area within a particular municipality. Partial or 'piecemeal zoning' may be considered as unenforceable if it contravenes the requirement for comprehensive land use planning of a municipality, especially when it applies to a single block or street. See also **spot zoning**.

partially disclosed principal(US) See **undisclosed agency**.

partible Capable of being divided. 'Partible lands' or a 'partible inheritance' refers to real property that could be divided among children. See also **coparcenary**, **gavelkind**.

participating broker or **participating agent**(US) See **cooperating broker**.

participating mortgage(US) See **participation mortgage**.

participation See **equity participation**, **public participation**, **slice**.

participation certificate (PC) A certificate provided to a purchaser of a **mortgage-backed security** which states that the holder is entitled to an ownership interest in the underlying mortgages and sets down the percentage share of the securities that the holder is entitled to receive. A participation certificate is a negotiable instrument and may be sold to other investors. See also **Federal Home Loan Mortgage Corporation**.

participation clause(US)   See **escalation clause**.

participation lease   See **equity participation, slice**.

participation loan or **participation mortgage**   1. See **equity-participation loan**. 2. A mortgage provided by two or more lenders who act together in order to spread their risk. The mortgage loan may be granted initially by one mortgagee who then, as the 'lead lender', sells part of the loan to other lenders. Usually the mortgaged property is held in trust for the participating mortgagees. Also called a 'participating mortgage' or a 'fractionalized mortgage'. See also **participation certificate**.

particula   A small piece of land. See also **particular estate**.

particular agency   See **agency**.

particular estate   An estate for life or for years that is carved out of another estate and precedes a future estate or interest. A particular estate may be a **remainder** or **reversion**, although the term is more generally applied to the former. Thus, if A grants a life estate to B with the property passing thereafter to C, B has a particular estate and C has the remainder. In the US, 'particular estate' may be used to refer to any estate that is less than a **fee simple**. See also **rentservice**.

particular lien   See **lien**.

particular partnership   A partnership established for a specific purpose, enterprise or transaction. cf. **general partnership**. See also **joint venture**.

particular purchaser   See **special purchaser**.

particular tenant   The holder of a **particular estate**.

particulars of sale   1. Particulars of a property that is to be offered for sale or to let, normally setting out a brief description of the property and the terms upon which it could be acquired. The particulars of a property that is to be offered for sale by private treaty may be submitted by a vendor, or his agent, to prospective purchasers. However, as a rule, such particulars do not constitute a formal **offer**, but merely an **invitation to trade**(AmE)/**invitation to treat**(BrE). See also **exclusion clause**, **misdescription**, **misrepresentation**, **property brief**(US), **puffing**. 2. Details of a property that is to be offered for sale by **auction**. In particular, a document that sets out the terms and conditions of the sale. Such a document is deemed to form part of the contractual terms upon which the property is to be offered for sale.   3. The part of a contract for the sale of land that describes the subject matter of the contract, i.e. it sets down a physical description of the property and the interest to be sold. cf. **conditions of sale**. See also **plan**, **premises**.

parties   1. Those who are involved in a transaction or agreement. "They that make a deed and they to whom it is made are called parties to the deed", *Terms de la Ley*.   2. The opposing litigants in judicial proceedings. See **party**.

parting wall   See **party wall**.

partition   The division, into separate shares, of an interest in property that is held in co-ownership, i.e. a division into several ownership. In particular, the division of an interest in land held as a **joint tenancy**, **tenancy in common**, or tenancy by **coparcenary**, into separate, or sole, ownership interests. The splitting of a right to joint possession of land so that the respective parties have separate rights of ownership: a means by which co-ownership is destroyed. Partition of an interest in real property can be enforced only with the consent of all the co-owners (voluntary), or by order of a court (compulsory or judicial). Partition does not transfer or create a new interest in land, but merely severs the **unity of possession** so that each party may enjoy his separate estate at his own pleasure. See also **apportionment**, **participation sale**, **partition wall**, **severance**.

partition fence See **fence**, **party fence**.

partition sale A sale made to **partition** joint rights of ownership, especially a sale of real property that is held in joint or common ownership subsequent to a court order. A partition sale is generally made when the owners are unable to agree to an equitable subdivision of their interests in the property. Thus, it is not a sale in the sense of a voluntary disposition, but is a form of action between the owners. Upon completion of the sale, the proceeds are divided between the parties in proportion to their original shares in the jointly owned property. Also called 'judicial partition'.

partition wall A wall used to divide areas of a building internally. Generally, a 'partition' is not part of the structure or carcass of a building, it is non-loadbearing, and it extends vertically between floor and ceiling only at one level. See also **party wall**.

partner A member of a **partnership**. One who joins with another, or others, in an unincorporated business with a view to sharing in the profit and accepting a liability for the losses. A person or entity that contributes property or money, in conjunction with one or more other persons or entities, in order to carry on a joint business for common benefit, and share in the profits (or losses) of the business in agreed proportions. See also **active partner**, **general partner**, **limited partner**, **sleeping partner**.

partnership A voluntary, but unincorporated, business relationship established by two or more persons (partners) who act together in order to carry on a trade, profession or occupation, with a view to making and sharing profits arising from their endeavours. The partners contribute their property, money, skill, experience, toil and energy (or some or all of those) towards the joint aim of profit, while accepting the common risk and possibility of loss. A partnership may be distinguished from a **company**, which carries on its business separately and distinctly from the interests of the individual shareholders who are normally free to transfer their shares without the approval of the other shareholders.

A partnership may take the form of a **general partnership** in which each and every partner shares in the profits and losses of the partnership; is involved in the management and conduct of the partnership; and is liable for the debts of the partnership to the full extent of his property ownership, as if he were a sole proprietor. It may also take the form of a **limited partnership** in which one or more partners (general partners) are responsible for the debts of the partnership in their entirety, and one or more partners (limited partners) contribute capital, in accordance with the terms of the partnership agreement; but, as a rule, the limited partners are not liable for debts beyond the amount of their contributions (paid or unpaid). cf. **agency**. See also **joint venture**.

I'Anson, Roderick C. Banks. *Lindley and Banks on Partnership*. 17th ed. London: Sweet & Maxwell, 1995.

partnership property Property owned by a **partnership**, whether obtained by contribution of the partners, or from profits, less losses, arising from the business of the partnership.

party **1.** One who has made an agreement or entered into a transaction, either as a sole party or with others. **2.** A person, company or association of persons that is involved in a real action or transaction, e.g. a landlord, tenant, vendor, purchaser, mortgagor, mortgagee, agent, principal, trustee, etc.

party fence A **fence** that is erected on the boundary of adjoining parcels of land and which belongs to two persons as part owners, but does not form part of a building. A fence that is held in the same ownership structure as a **party wall**. A fence erected on or near the boundary and owned by one party is not strictly a party fence. Also called a partition fence. See **party fence wall**[(Eng)].

party fence wall[(Eng)]   "[A] wall (not being part of a building) which stands on lands of different owners and is used or constructed to be used for separating such adjoining lands, but does not include a wall constructed on the land of one owner the artificially formed part of which projects into the land of another", Party Wall etc. Act 1996, s. 20. See also **party wall**.

party structure   A **structure** that separates buildings, stories, or rooms and belongs to two persons as part owners. The structure may be a partition, floor, or any other form of structure and may be vertical or horizontal.

In English statute law, 'party structure' means "a **party wall** and also a partition or other structure separating buildings or parts of buildings approached solely by separate staircases or separate entrances", Party Wall etc. Act 1996, s. 20.

party wall   A wall, or similar structure, that has been erected on the boundary of adjoining parcels of land that are held in separate ownership. In particular, a wall that acts as a support for buildings on both sides of a common boundary.

A party wall may be held in one of four different ways: (i) as a **tenancy in common**, i.e. the adjoining owners have equal shares and obligations in respect of the wall; (ii) by being owned as two longitudinal strips, with each contiguous party having entire rights over the strip on his side; (iii) by being held solely by one landowner, but subject to the right of the other party to have it maintained as a dividing wall between the two properties; or (iv) by being divided longitudinally, with cross-easements in favour of each of the parties. In common law, a party wall is presumed to be held in the first way, unless there is evidence or an agreement to the contrary. However, in most situations, a party wall is held in the fourth way, with each party being considered as an owner in severalty of half the wall (or the part that stands on his land if the dividing line has not

been drawn evenly) and subject to an agreement that sets out the rights and obligations of the parties; especially the rights of support and maintenance. In English law, a party wall can no longer be held as a tenancy in common and any wall that was held as such is now held in separate longitudinal ownership, with cross-easements in favour of each of the parties (LPA 1925, s. 38).

In England and Wales, any party wishing to carry out most forms of building work that affect a party wall must serve a statutory notice on the adjoining owners prior to carrying out such work. In most cases there must be an agreement as to such work and, failing agreement, there are statutory provisions for resolution by obtaining an 'award' from a surveyor (or surveyors) appointed by the parties (Party Wall Act 1996). For this purpose, 'party wall' means "a wall which forms part of a building and stands on lands of different owners to a greater extent than the projection of any artificially formed support on which the wall rests" but not so much of such a wall as separates buildings belonging to different owners (Party Wall etc. Act 1996, s. 20). These provisions apply to a **party fence wall** (but not a simple garden fence) and a **party structure**.

In the US, in most jurisdictions, there are statutes regulating the rights and obligations of owners of party walls. In the event of a dispute, the municipal body responsible for zoning and housing regulation may resolve the issue. Alternatively, the party wall agreement may provide for submission to arbitration. Otherwise, the matter is resolved by seeking a declaratory judgement from a court of law.

Also called a 'dividing wall', 'common wall', 'shared wall' or sometimes a 'division wall', 'joint wall', 'partition wall', 'parting wall' or 'wall in common'. See also **common elements**, **right of support**.

Anstey, John. *Party Walls and What to do With Them.* 5th ed. London: RICS Books, 1998.

Bickford-Smith, Stephen, and Colin Sydenham. *Party Walls: Law and Practice.* Bristol: Jordans, 2003.

The Royal Institution of Chartered Surveyors. *Party Wall Legislation and Procedure Guidance Note.* 5th ed. London: RICS Books, 2002.

pass To change hands, especially on death. To **transfer** or be transferred, especially to an heir or devisee on the death of an owner of property. See also **devise, revert, vest**.

passage See **right of passage**.

passageway A way for passage between one point and another, whether inside a building as with an aisle or corridor; between buildings as with an **alley** or **lane**; or over land as with a **footpath, sidewalk, street, road**, or **highway**. See also **bridleway, driftway, right of way**.

passim(Lat) 'In various places'; 'here and there'. Also used to indicate a general reference to a book or legal authority.

passing rent The **rent** actually being paid at a point in time. See also **contractual rent**.

passing yield See **current yield**.

passive income(US) Income that a taxpayer receives from an investment or business in which he or she does not take an active or material part. Income from real estate is generally passive income. cf. **active income**.

passive investor An investor who does not take any active part in the management of his investments, but merely invests his funds in order to receive an income or make a capital gain. See also **absentee owner, limited partnership, sleeping partner**.

passive trust A **trust** that gives the trustees no active duties to perform, but merely an obligation to hold property for the beneficiary. In particular, a trust that arises when the entire management of the trust property is in the hands of the beneficiary; the beneficiaries are usually permitted to take control or possession of the trust property; and the retention of legal title is not essential to the performance of any of the duties that are the responsibility of the trustee.

Sometimes called a 'dry trust', 'nominal trust', or a 'grantor trust', especially when the grantor retains control over the income or the subject of the trust (or both) and for taxation purposes the grantor is considered to be the owner thereof. Occasionally called a 'fixed trust' when the trustees' role is limited or fixed at the time the trust is created. cf. **active trust, discretionary trust**. See also **bare trust**(Eng).

passive waste(US) See **waste**.

pass-through or **passthrough**(US) 1. A provision made by the Internal Revenue Service whereby income, profits, depreciation, etc. may be passed through a partnership or S corporation (a small corporation formed in a similar way to a partnership) to individual partners or shareholders free of tax (26 USC, Internal Revenue Code, § 1366). Sometimes called a 'flow-through'. See also **real estate investment trust**. 2. See **escalation clause**.

pass-through certificate A certificate that represents the holder's right to a pool of mortgages under a **mortgage-backed security** and represents the right to an income stream from that security. A pass-through certificate may represent a right to stock in a corporation, or a beneficial interest in a trust, to which the ownership of the mortgages have been transferred. See also **participation certificate**.

pass-through clause(US) See **escalation clause**.

pass-through security(US) See **mortgage-backed security**.

past consideration See **consideration**.

pastoral land(NZ) Land that is owned by the Crown and is set aside or leased for pastoral use (Land Act 1948, s. 51).

pastoral lease(Aus) A lease of **Crown land** that is granted for pastoral purposes. Pastoral leases were granted to settlers under statutory provision and, therefore, are not governed by common law. This is not a lease in the modern sense of the word, as in most cases the occupier does not have a right to **exclusive possession**, but a statutory right to use for the land for pastoral purposes for a period of time (which may be an annual right, a term of years or even a perpetual right), with the Crown holding a right of reversion. The occupier may also have a right to acquire the land during, or at the end of, the lease term. However, the form the lease took varied considerably both from State to State, as well as within a State. Pastoral purposes in this context may include the keeping and breeding of sheep, cattle or other animals, as well as the use of land for purposes that are incidental to a pastoral enterprise. Where a pastoral lease does not confer exclusive possession, it does not necessarily override or extinguish a **native title** (*Wik Peoples v Queensland* (1996) 187 CLR 1, 122 (Aus)) and, at the end of the lease, the land reverts to the Crown. On the other hand, where there is a conflict between the statutory right and native title, the pastoral lease prevails (*Wik Peoples v Queensland, supra* at 190). The Crown retains all rights to minerals, petroleum and timber on such land.

pasturage 1. Grazing land. The keeping of stock on land for grazing or pasturing. See also **agistment, pasture**. 2.(Scot)The right to graze sheep or cattle on common land or another person's land.

pasture An area of **land** that is normally covered with grass or herbage and set aside for the grazing of cattle or other livestock. To keep stock on land for feeding from the grass or herbage thereon. See also **agistment, agricultural land, farm, grazing licence**(Eng), **lay-land, profit à prendre, right of common, right of pasture, stinted pasture, tenant-right**(Eng), **waste**.

patent 1. Obvious; open to view on public inspection. See also **patent defect**. 2.(US)An instrument that grants or transfers title to **public lands** from the government or state to a private individual. Any instrument that ratifies, confirms or provides evidence of a previous grant or conveyance of public lands. "A patent is the highest evidence of title, and is conclusive as against the government, and all claiming under junior patents or titles, *until set aside* or annulled by some judicial tribunal (U. S. v. Wall, 2 Wall 525)", United States v. Mullan, 10 F 785, 792 (9th Cir. Cal 1882). Also called a 'land patent' or sometimes 'letters patent'. 3. A conveyance or grant of land to someone who has made a **homestead** entry and has complied with all the statutory conditions thereof. See also **alienation**. 4.(US)A grant of a right to extract minerals from public lands.

patent defect A defect that is clearly visible or obvious. A defect that can be discovered by prudent and ordinary care, as distinguished from a **latent defect** that is hidden and would not be discovered by a careful inspection. The English courts have held that a defect is not patent if it can only be discovered by minute inspection, such as a purchaser cannot reasonably be expected to make. A purchaser of property is not generally liable for latent defects, but is nearly always required to accept patent defects, unless there is an agreement to the contrary. See also *caveat emptor*, **defect of title, inherent defect**.

path A track or way over land, especially one that is well trodden or habitually and constantly used. See also **footpath, highway**.

patio house(US) A single-family residence on a separate lot that is placed on the lot line on one side but is set back on the other three sides to provide for a patio or garden court. The house is usually L-shaped and has no basement.

patrimony 1. An inherited estate. An estate or property held by ancient right. In particular, property inherited from a father's estate or that of his paternal ancestors. 2. The ancient estate of an institution, corporation or church.

pavement A paved surface. In British English, the hard surfaced area at the side of a public highway that is set aside for pedestrians. In

American English, called the 'sidewalk'.

pavement light(BrE)   A form of window or light set into a pavement in order to let daylight into a basement or cellar. Usually it is made of solid glass blocks set in a cast-iron frame. See also **ancient lights**.

pavilion   Derived from the Old French *pavillon*, 'butterfly-like'. Originally a large tent rising to a peak. A light or semi-permanent structure, usually with a high-peaked roof, especially one used for the purpose of ornament. A shelter erected for those engaged in a sport or recreation. A summer-house, bandstand or similar structure erected for pleasure in a garden or park. Also, a pavilion may be put up for the purpose of an exhibition, either as a separate building or as an attachment to a larger building, and, although intended to be of a temporary nature, may be left in place after the original purpose has been fulfilled. In many cases, such buildings are of elaborate design and were exhibits in their own right or become exhibits, as with the Brighton Pavilion in England and many national pavilions erected for world fairs or Expos in, for example, Paris, New York, Montreal, Osaka and Seville.

pawn   **1.** The actual or constructive delivery of personal goods to another as security for a loan, debt or engagement, i.e. a form of **bailment**. The person who delivers the goods (pawnor) retains title thereto, and the holder of the goods (pawnee) is obliged to take good care of the goods while they are in his possession. If the debt is not paid when due the pawnee has a right to dispose of the goods, but must account to the pawnor for the net proceeds of sale, if any, that exceed the amount of the outstanding debt. If the debt is duly paid, the goods must normally be returned to the pawnee in the same condition as when first pawned. See also **pledge**.   **2.** Personal property given as security for a debt or other form of engagement. **3.**(US)In Louisiana, a form of pledge or lien on the produce of real property by which the pledgee is entitled to enter into legal possession in order to receive the rents and profits (**fruits**) to use towards repayment of interest and principal due on the loan (La CC, § 3101).

pawnee   One to whom goods are delivered in **pawn**.

pawnor or **pawner**   One who delivers goods to another to be held in **pawn**.

pay-back analysis or **pay-back method**   A method of **investment analysis** that measures the time required for the total net income or cash flow, generated by an investment, to equal the initial capital cost of that investment. A simple method of comparing investments that takes no account of the stage at which income is received over the pay-back period; nor the discounted value of money or the interest that could be earned on the income received over the life of the investment. The period of time taken for the income to equate to the initial cost is called the 'pay-back period'. For example, if an investment of $1,000 produces a net income of $200, $300 and $500 in the first, second and third years respectively, the pay-back period is three years. See also **discounted rate of return**.

pay-back period   See **pay-back analysis**.

pay rate   The rate at which interest on a loan must be paid to keep it current or to ensure that it is not in default. A loan agreement may provide for interest to be payable at a rate less than the actual interest rate charged, with the balance being accrued and added to the principal. Under such an arrangement, the actual interest rate may be slightly higher than would normally be the case in order to compensate the lender for accepting a slower repayment of the loan. cf. **actual rate**. See also **bow-tie loan**.

payment   Something given or delivered as remuneration for property, goods or services, or to discharge a debt or obligation. The discharge of a debt or obligation by any method that has been agreed upon whether by **money**, or any other form of pecuniary benefit. Nonetheless, in order to constitute a 'payment', in its broadest sense, the debtor must have given something in a form that is agreed as appropriate. In order to discharge a debt or obligation, a payment in whatever form must represent **satisfaction** of that claim. Thus, payment of **rent** should be made to the landlord, or his appointed agent, in **cash**, unless the lease specifies otherwise. A cheque does not represent payment until it is accepted, or certified, by the paying bank and the funds transferred to the payee. cf. **set-off, tender**. See also **accord and satisfaction, bank draft, cashier's check**(AmE)/**cashier's cheque**(BrE)**, deposit, part payment**.

payment bond   A **bond** given by one party, usually an insurance company, to another as a surety for the payment of the obligations to a third party. For example, a bond that provides a public authority with a guarantee that if a general contractor fails the subcontractors will be paid. The term is frequently used synonymously with **performance bond**, although strictly the latter requires the grantor of the bond to ensure that the contract is completed, whereas the former is intended to ensure that all third parties to the contract, such as subcontractors, are duly paid for the work they have performed. See also **completion bond**.

payment-capped   adjustable-rate mortgage   An **adjustable-rate mortgage** that provides for the payments due from the borrower to increase by no more than a stipulated amount. Usually the increase is set so that the total payments of interest and principal will not exceed a given percentage increase, either in any one year or over the term of the loan.

payment in advance   See **advance payment, rent in advance/rent in arrears**.

payment in lieu of taxes (PILOT)   A form of municipal funding used to pay for the financing needed to carry out improvements to a blighted, conservation or economic development area. An estimate is made by the municipality of the increase in the assessed values of the properties in the district that would result from the planned improvement to the area. For each year that the post-plan assessed value exceeds the pre-plan assessed value of the taxable property in the district, tax on the increase in the assessed value is abated. In place of the amount of tax that is abated, an amount is paid into a special fund to act as security for bonds that the municipality has pledged as security to pay for the cost of the improvements. This is not strictly a tax, but an **assessment** against the properties (Tax Increment Financing Com'n v. J.E. Dunn Const. Co., 781 SW.2d 70, 77 (Mo banc. 1989)). See also **tax increment financing**.

payment to amortise one ($, £, ¥, etc.)   See Appendix C, **Financial Formulae**.

peaceable possession(US)   See **peaceful possession**.

peaceably and quietly   A term used in a lease to describe the tenant's right to **quiet enjoyment** of property, i.e. without interruption of possession, and not, as it may seem, a right to be undisturbed by noise.

peaceful enjoyment(US)   See **quiet enjoyment**.

peaceful possession   Possession obtained, or exercised, without threats, force or resistance. Peaceful possession of land is such as is acquiesced in by any rival claimant and must be continuous and not interrupted by any adverse suit or action to recover the land. Also called 'peaceable possession'. cf. **adverse possession, hostile possession**.

peak pitch   The best retail location in a shopping center and, therefore, the position that generates the highest rental value. Also called the 'prime trading location' or 'prime pitch'. See also **highest and best use, prime location**.

pecunia(Lat)   In the civil law and old English

law, any form of property; **things** in general. (In the Domesday Book, *pecunia* is used to refer to cattle or beasts, which were a primary source of wealth or property; hence the derivations 'cattle' – 'chattel' – '**capital**'.) See also **pecuniary consideration**.

pecuniary consideration   Consideration that takes the form of **money**. Strictly, consideration as paid in cash or a readily acceptable medium of exchange, i.e. 'money' in its primary sense. However, a payment by means of an exchange, or some form of gain in monetary value, may be taken as pecuniary consideration; especially as distinguished from 'good consideration' which has no tangible value and may take the form of love, affection or a strong moral obligation. See also **money's worth**, **premium**, **valuable consideration**.

pedestrian precinct   See **precinct**.

pedestrian precinct order(Eng)   An order made by a local planning authority by which the authority limits the public vehicular use of a highway, other than a trunk road or principal road (TCPA 1990, s. 249). The intention of such an order is to improve the "amenity of part of their [the local planning authority's] area". Such an order may restrict the type of vehicles that may use the highway, the persons by whom vehicles may be used on the highway, or in what circumstances, or at which times the highway may be used. The effect of such an order is to improve the use of the area for pedestrians, especially shoppers, and thus it is commonly called a 'pedestrian precinct order'. A party who suffers damage, or a loss in the value of an interest in land, as a result of a loss of lawful access to a highway is entitled to compensation for any damage or loss or depreciation in value of the interest that is directly attributable to the order. See also **compensation for planning restrictions**.

pedestrianisation(BrE)
or **pedestrianization**(AmE)   The conversion of a public highway or street into an area with limited or no vehicular access. See also **mall**, **pedestrian precinct order**(Eng), **precinct**.

pedis possessio(Lat)   'Possession by a foothold'. The doctrine of *pedis possessio* may be a basis of a claim for **adverse possession**. However, it is normally only applied to a claim to a mine; a prospector for valuable minerals who is in actual possession (*pedis possessio*) and actively searching for minerals may thereby defeat the rights of another prospector.

penal rent   1. A rent that substantially exceeds the **market rent** of a property. See also **rack rent**. 2. A charge for late payment of rent that exceeds the loss suffered by the landlord to whom the payment is due and, therefore, may be construed as a **penalty** and as such will not be recoverable. However, an increased payment, such as a reasonable rate of interest on arrears, may be considered as a payment for the loss actually suffered by the landlord and may be recoverable as for any other rental payment. cf. **penalty rent**(US). See also **additional rent**, **double rent**. 3. An increased rent that is payable in the event of a breach of covenant by the tenant. See also **liquidated damages**, **penalty**.

penalty   A sum of money payable as a redress for a fault, error or injury. Something inflicted, for example, to secure the due performance of a contract. A sum of money, or a **fine**, specified in a contract as payable in the event of a breach of a condition of that contract. A sum that is intended, as a rule, to exceed the loss or damage suffered, or likely to be suffered, as a result of a breach of a contract and, therefore, to act as an incentive to performance. A penalty may be contrasted with **liquidated damages** which is a sum that is intended to equal the actual loss suffered and may be made payable in lieu of performance. If the sums stipulated for are extravagant and unconscionable in amount in comparison with the greatest loss that could conceivably be proved to have resulted from the breach of contract, then the amount will be construed as a penalty. "The essence of a penalty is a payment of money stipulated as *in terrorem* of the offending party to act as an inducement [to the performance of a contract]; the essence of liquidated damages is a genuine pre-estimate of damage", *Dunlop Pneumatic Tyre Co Ltd v New Garage and Motor Co Ltd* [1915] AC 79, 86 (HL). A penalty is designed to punish, whereas liquidated damages are intended as a fair compensation for the breach.

There is no one rule as to whether a payment will be construed as a penalty, rather than liquidated damages. The courts will give weight to the nature of the contract, the intention of the parties, the result of the payment, and not just to the literal language of the agreement. The securing of a larger sum to pay a smaller sum mitigates against the expression of liquidated damages. A sum is more likely to be construed as a penalty when it is made payable for a number of different breaches, especially when they may be both major and minor; when there is an obligation to pay a larger sum in the event of one act rather than another; or when the payment is due merely for a delay in performance. A payment that is out of proportion to the actual loss may be accepted as liquidated damages if that is the clear intent of the parties. Interest is generally considered to be a liquidated damage for the wrongful withholding of money, provided the debtor knows what he is to pay, when he is to pay it, and he has freely undertaken to make such a payment. The intention should be to cover the creditor's loss without unreasonably penalizing the debtor – "a penalty covers but does not assess the damages". Any sum, or provision in a contract, which permits one party to recover more than the true loss, or to retain more than a reasonable entitlement, in the event of default on that contract, is likely to be construed as a penalty. See also **deposit**, **penal rent**, **forfeiture**, **pre-payment penalty**, **security deposit**, **usury**.

penalty interest   See **penalty**.

penalty rent(US)   A payment that may be due from a lessee who holds over at the end of his lease, after having been requested to vacate. Some states provide that a landlord may recover double, or in some states triple, the rental value from a tenant who, without the landlord's consent, intentionally retains possession of the demised premises after the expiry of the lease. Such a payment is not true rent, but strictly speaking a form of damages for wrongly retaining possession of the leased premises. cf. **mesne profits**, **penal rent**. See also **double rent**, **holding over**.

pendens(Lat)   See *lis pendens*.

pendente lite(Lat)   'During the pendency of a suit'. While an action is pending.

pending action   A legal action or proceeding that has been filed with a court, or an action for which a summons has been served. See also *lis pendens*, **pending land action**(Eng).

pending land action(Eng)   "Any action or proceeding in court relating to land or any interest in or charge on land", LCA 1972, s. 17(1). A pending land action may be registered against unregistered land as a **land charge** and, if not so registered, it does not bind a purchaser of the land to which it relates, unless the purchaser has express (and not merely constructive) **notice** of the action (LCA 1972, s. 5(7)). See also **Land Charges Register**, *lis pendens*.

pennage   A payment for the right to erect pens at a **market** or **fair**. See also **stallage**.

pension fund   An institution that holds and invests funds that it has received from individuals on trust with the intention that those individuals will receive an income or lump-sum payment on their retirement in later years. Pension funds are generally established by corporations, unions or government bodies and receive income from the employer and employee that is invested to provide for the payment of a pension upon the retirement of the employee. See also **institutional investor**.

penthouse   1. Derived from Old French *pentis*,

'attached on'. A self-contained apartment, or flat, or any other enclosed area located on the top floor of a building. In particular, a separate floor added to, or constructed above, the main structure, commonly with a recess, walkway, or terrace around the perimeter. A penthouse unit is generally considered to be the most prestigious and, therefore, most valuable unit in a building. **2.** An annex, or structure joined onto another building with a lean-to roof; especially a form of shelter over a passage or arcade.

peppercorn rent   A form of **nominal consideration** payable for the right to take a lease of a property. In particular, a term used in English law to refer to a token **rent**, made payable under a lease as an acknowledgement of a higher estate in land, i.e. of the relationship of landlord and tenant. (The term is derived from the payment of rent by means of what was the highly valued commodity of pepper.) A lease, being a document that at common law must be made by **deed**, strictly does not require consideration and, therefore, stipulating for such a rent is intended merely to indicate that the landlord is retaining a right to regain the property at the end of the lease term. In practice, the peppercorn rent is never demanded or paid.

per(Lat)   'By'; 'by means of'; 'as stated by'.

per annum(Lat)   'By the **year**'; 'yearly'; on an annual basis; every **year**. *Per annum* may mean by the year, every year, through the year, yearly, or even during the year, with separate authorities for these various meanings. However, the suffix 'per annum' is normally intended to denote that the amount is for a complete year – payable 'yearly' – and not that it is to be apportioned during the year.

per autre vie(Lat)   'For the life of another'. See **life estate**.

per capita(Lat)   'By heads'; 'according to the number of individuals'. A term used in the law of succession to denote that the descendants take

property in equal shares, i.e. as so much 'per head'. cf. *per stirpes*.

per cent or percent   By parts of a hundred; in every hundred. A percentage, or a proportion based on hundredths. In English law, it has been decided that if a rate is stated as a 'per cent', without any further qualification, either expressly or as can be implied from the context, "that rate means 'per cent per annum' as if the words 'per annum' were written in", *London and Harrogate Securities Ltd v Pitts* [1976] 3 All ER 809, 814-815.

per centum(Lat)   'By parts of a hundred'; 'as a percentage'. See **per cent**.

per curiam [per cur](Lat)   'By the court'. A decision of a court, as distinguished from a decision delivered by one judge; or a decision given but not written.

per diem(Lat)   'By the **day**'; 'daily'.

per mensum(Lat)   'Per **month**'; 'by the month'; 'monthly'.

per my et per tout   Law French for 'by the half and by all'. One of two joint tenants is said to hold a half and an entire interest in land, but no right separate from the other party (2 *Bl Comm* 182). See also **joint tenancy**.

per pais(Lat)   'By the country'. See **estoppel**.

per pro or per procurationem(Lat)   'By proxy'; 'by procuration'; 'as an agent'. 'Per pro' or 'p.p.' express that an authority is made by procuration or **power of attorney**.

per quod(Lat)   'By reason of which'.

per se(Lat)   'By itself'; 'in its own right'.

per stirpes(Lat)   'By stock'; 'by roots'; 'by right of representation'. A term derived from the civil law and used in the law of succession to denote that the property is distributed according to the 'right of representation'. Accordingly, the children of any one descendant receive their shares in accordance with their parent's entitlement, as if that parent had been living, and not equally with all other members of the same generation. Taking property *per stirpes* is known also as taking by right of representation. cf. *per capita*.

per tout and not per my   Law French for 'by the whole and not by the moiety'; "by all, and not by half", 2 *Bl Comm* 182. See **tenancy by the entirety**.

per year   Annually. See **per annum, year**.

per centum(Lat)   'By a hundred'; 'by parts of a hundred'; a percentage.

percent   See **per cent**.

percentage   A rate **per cent**; part of a whole expressed as the unit fraction of a hundred.

percentage lease   A lease of retail premises that provides for the payment of a **percentage rent**, i.e. a rent based, in whole or in part, on the value of the tenant's gross revenue or income from defined sales or, in some cases, a percentage of the net profit. In the UK, more commonly called a **turnover lease**. See also **'continuous operation' clause, recapture clause**.

percentage rent   A **rent** that is payable in respect of retail premises and which is based on an agreed percentage of the sales, turnover, receipts or profit achieved by the tenant as a result of the business or operations conducted by the tenant in the demised premises. Normally a minimum or **base rent** is payable throughout the term of the lease and additional rent or **overage** is payable when the agreed percentage of the gross sales (or other defined level of income) exceeds the base figure. Alternatively, the rent may be based on a percentage of the tenant's net profit,

but that is less common because of the difficulty of defining 'net profit'. In some cases the percentage rent may not be payable until the tenant has achieved an agreed threshold of sales, or the percentage may vary according to the level of sales (or profit). In some cases, the rent may be based entirely on a percentage of the tenant's sales. The percentage rates for retail premises vary for different types of trade and may range, for example, from one to two per cent of gross sales for a trade with a low profit margin, e.g. a food supermarket, to over ten per cent for a trade with a high margin, such as a jeweller. In the UK, also called a 'turnover rent' (although percentage or turnover rents are not common in the UK). See also **continuous operation clause, gross income, percentage lease, recapture clause**(US).

Halper, Emanuel B. *Shopping Center and Store Leases*. 2 vols. rev. ed. Looseleaf. New York: Law Journal Seminars-Press. McAllister, Patrick. *Turnover Rents*, Reading, Berks.: College of Estate Management, 1994.

perfect ownership(US)   A term derived from the civil law concept of **ownership** for the absolute right recognised originally in Roman law (*dominium*). "Perfect ownership gives the right to use, to enjoy, and to dispose of one's property in the most unlimited manner; this is called *usus*, *fructus*, and *abusus* [Civ. Code, art. 491]. These rights must be united in the same person to constitute perfect ownership", Wilson v. Ætna Ins. Co., 161 So 650, 652 (La Ct App 1935).

perfect title(US)   A title that is good and valid beyond reasonable doubt. A title that is free, in law and in fact, of any doubt as to its validity. A title that includes the legal and equitable rights to a property and is free from litigation, palpable defect, and grave doubts, and can readily be recorded. 'Perfect title' may be considered to be synonymous with **marketable title**, 'merchantable title' or similar terms, as well as 'good title'; although strictly 'perfect title' requires a higher standard. See also **absolute title, good title**.

perfecting lien(US)   The recording, or filing

of notice, of a **mechanic's lien** to ensure its enforceability.

perfecting title(US)   See **cloud on title**.

performance   The carrying through of something to **completion**. The discharge of a **promise**, **obligation** or duty *in toto*. Completion of all the requirements, or fulfilment of all the terms, of a contract – the effect being to **discharge** the contract. Strictly, a contract is discharged by performance only when the performance is entirely complete according to the terms of the contract. A court is more likely to accept that performance has taken place if what has been done fulfils substantially the intentions of the parties. Accordingly, if only minor aspects of the contract remain incomplete, it is more likely to award **damages** for the loss suffered than to grant an **injunction** and thereby insist on completion down to the last detail. Thus, if a builder substantially completes a building, but leaves some minor work unfinished, the contract may be treated as performed and the builder would be entitled to recover the contract price, less an appropriate deduction for the defective work – but not if the work done is substantially different from the work contracted for.

The performance of the obligations of a contract may be 'divisible', or 'indivisible' ('entire'). A divisible obligation permits the one party to insist upon performance without necessarily permitting the other party also to require performance. For example, paying rent in full, when due, even though the tenant has no prior right to insist on the landlord carrying out a repairing obligation. An indivisible obligation means that one party cannot insist upon performance unless he has fulfilled, or is clearly willing, to fulfil his side of the bargain. See also **accord and satisfaction, commission, divisible contract, entire contract, part performance, set-off, specific performance, substantial performance, tender**.

performance bond   A **bond** given by one party, usually an insurance company or surety company, to another as a surety for the proper performance of a contract by a third party. The bond takes the form of a **guarantee** so that, if the third party fails to meet his obligation or contractual duty, the guarantor undertakes to complete the obligation or duty without extra cost to the holder of the bond and, if necessary, pay all suppliers or subcontractors. Usually the surety has the option of taking over the contract directly, or employing another contractor to perform the work. Also called a 'surety bond', or sometimes a **completion bond**, although the latter term also has another meaning. cf. **payment bond**. See also **bid bond**.

performance mortgage(US)   A mortgage that provides for the cost of **debt service** to be met by income from the mortgaged property. See also **equity participation, participation mortgage**.

period contract(Aus)   See **term contract**.

periodic estate(US)   See **estate from period to period, periodic tenancy**.

periodic repayment(AmE)   See **amortization loan, part payment**.

periodic tenancy   A **tenancy** that continues for a succession of fixed and regular periods, until the landlord or tenant gives due notice of **termination**. The periods may cover any time span – day to day, week to week, month to month, quarter to quarter, year to year – but the tenancy remains as one continuous tenancy running on from one period to another until terminated; it is not a series of renewable contracts (except in a few jurisdictions in the US that consider a tenancy from month to month as a tenancy that recommences each month). A periodic tenancy may be created expressly; may arise by implication, as when a person takes, or retains, exclusive possession of land and pays a regular rent; or may be created by statute. A periodic tenancy can only be terminated by a notice that covers not less than an entire period and the notice must unequivocally expire at the end of that period; the obligation to pay rent continuing until the tenancy has been determined. If the period is not formally agreed, it is implied from the manner in which the rent is calculated and not (except in a few states in the US) from the regularity with which the rent is paid. Thus, a rent that is stipulated as so much *per year* creates a **tenancy from year to year**, even if the rent is payable monthly or quarterly. In the US, also called a periodic estate. cf. **tenancy for a fixed period**. See also **estate from period to period**[US], **month-to-month tenancy, tenancy at will, week-to-week tenancy**.

permanent commitment   A commitment by a financial institution, or any other potential lender of money, that it will provide a permanent or **long-term loan** at a future date. Commonly applied to a commitment granted to a property developer that funds will be available to replace an **interim loan** when a development is completed and/or fully let.

permanent financing   See **permanent loan**.

permanent improvement   An **improvement** to real estate that is so made that it cannot be removed and becomes part of the property. See also **fixture, mechanic's lien**.

permanent injunction[US]   See **injunction**.

permanent loan   A long-term loan used to finance a completed development or an investment, as distinguished from **interim loan** or a similar form of short-term or temporary financing. See also **takeout commitment**.

permanent leasehold[US]   A perpetual leasehold interest, i.e. a lease that has been granted so that it can last forever. See also **perpetual lease**.

permanent monument[US]   A monument or landmark that takes the form of a natural or artificial boundary or limit and will, or is intended to, endure as such. A permanent monument may be, for example, "a mountain, ridge, hogback, canyon, gulch, river, stream, waterfall, cascade, lake, inlet, bay, arm of the sea, monuments of stone or boulders, drifts, tunnels, or open cuts", 30 USC § 28 note 162. In particular, a monument that is used to determine the location or limit of a mining claim.

permanent reference mark (PRM)   See **bench mark**.

permission   An act of permitting or formally consenting to an act or deed, especially one that would otherwise be unlawful. cf. **acquiescence**. See also **authority, consent, permit, planning permission**[Eng], **licence**[BrE]/**license**[AmE].

permissive possession[US]   Occupation of real property by one person with the consent of the owner or a person who would otherwise be entitled to possession. The term is loosely used for someone who has permission to occupy land without any understanding as to its term of duration, including a tenant at will. Sometimes called 'subservient possession'. cf. **adverse possession, hostile possession**. See also **license, tenancy at will**.

permissive use   1.[US]The **use** of property with the express or implied permission of the owner or any other person who has the right to use the property. In particular, a use that is not hostile or adverse to the owner. See also **license, permissive possession, tenancy at will**.   2.[Eng]An interest in land that arose under the feudal system of landownership by which the legal title to land was passed to one person, but the **use** or benefit was granted to a third party (the *cestui que use* or beneficiary) who effectively had a 'permissive use' of the land.

permissive waste   See **waste**.

permit   To give leave to an action. A written order or **licence** granted by a person or organisation, especially a government body, formally approving an activity by another. See also **authority, building**

permit(Eng), certificate of occupancy(US), franchise, permission, planning permission(Eng).

permitted development(Eng)   Development that may be undertaken without a need for planning permission because it is included in one of the classes of permitted development set out in a **General Development Order** – this order has the effect of granting planning permission for a specified class or type of development (TCPA 1990, ss. 58(1)(a), 59; Town and Country Planning (General Permitted Development) Order 1995 (SI 1995/418)). This 'permitted development' should be distinguished from certain forms of development that are specifically excluded from being classified as "development" by virtue of the TCPA 1990, s. 55(2). See also **article 4 direction, certificate of lawfulness, planning permission, Use Classes Order**.

permitted development order(Eng)   See **General Development Order**.

permitted use(US)   See **special-use permit**.

permitted zoning use(US)   A use of property that is permitted as of right under an existing **zoning ordinance**. Also called 'as of right' zoning.

perpetual lease   **1.** A lease that is granted to last 'in perpetuity', i.e. indefinitely. A perpetual lease has no fixed or ascertainable duration and, therefore, at common law is void. In the US, in some jurisdictions, a perpetual lease may be construed as a conveyance of a fee, subject to the reservation of a rent (or strictly a **rentcharge**). In the US, sometimes called a 'permanent leasehold'. A lease that merely continues from period to period (month to month, year to year, etc.), until terminated by notice to quit, is a **periodic tenancy**, not a perpetual lease. cf. **perpetually renewable lease**. See also **term**.   **2.**(Aus)A lease of **Crown land** granted in perpetuity, subject to certain conditions such as the payment of rent and the cultivation and improvement of the land. The lease was frequently granted at a premium with a low rent for the term of occupation and the lessee had a right to purchase the land during the term of the lease. Such leases take a wide variety of forms and may include a 'closer settlement lease', a 'conditional lease', a 'homestead selection lease' or a 'settlement purchase lease' depending on the terms and conditions of use and the rights to purchase the freehold.

perpetually renewable lease   A lease for a fixed term that provides the tenant with a right to renew his tenancy for as long, or for as many fixed terms, as he requires. A lease that provides for one or more specific right of renewal is not a perpetually renewable lease, but if the renewed lease clearly carries over the covenant for renewal to every successive term, then there is a perpetually renewable lease. The creation of a perpetually renewable lease generally requires a clear expression of such intent.

In English law, a perpetually renewable lease is automatically converted into a lease for a term of 2,000 years from the date at which the term commenced, or if an underlease for 2,000 years less one day (LPA 1922, s. 145, Sch. 15, para. 5).

In the US, the courts are loath to construe a covenant to renew as applying more than once and will rarely recognize a perpetually renewable lease. Also, several jurisdictions limit the maximum duration for which a lease of land can be granted, usually to not more than 99 years, or even less for agricultural land. Some jurisdictions take the view that a perpetually renewable lease is equivalent to the grant of a fee interest. cf. **perpetual lease**. See also **ground rent lease**(US), **rule against perpetuities.**

perpetuity   **1.** The quality of continuing forever, or for an indefinite period. An interest in land may be said to be created 'in perpetuity' if the interest is so created that it will continue for an unlimited period of time, e.g. a **freehold**. See also **rule against perpetuities**.   **2.** See **years' purchase**.

perquisitor(Eng)   One who acquires property other than by inheritance; "one who acquires an estate by sale, gift, or by any other method, except only that of descent", 2 *Bl Comm* 220. See also **purchaser**.

person An individual (a natural person), whether male or female. In law (especially statute law), a 'person' may be any legal entity, including a corporation, firm, society, legal representative, trustee, association, partnership, and any members of any such entity; although in most contexts the term does not include a sovereign body, state or municipal corporation.

personal accident insurance See **accident insurance**.

personal action An action that is brought against an individual, including a claim to recover a debt, enforcement of a personal obligation, breach of contract and a claim for damages from an action. cf. **real action**. See also **action** *in personam*.

personal chattel See **chattel**.

personal covenant A **covenant** that is enforceable only between the two parties to a contract. A covenant of which neither the benefit nor the burden may be assigned, i.e. a covenant that does not 'run with the land'. A term that has increasingly limited application to real property transactions, as in the US several jurisdictions enforce covenants that in some way relate to land (even though they may appear personal in nature). In English law, for leases created as from January 1, 1996, all lease covenants are enforceable between the parties to the lease, whether or not they 'touch or concern the land' (Landlord and Tenant (Covenants) Act 1995, s. 3(1)). cf. **covenant running with the land**, **real covenant**. See also **privity**, **restrictive covenant**, **recourse**.

personal effects A term of no precise legal definition, but generally used to refer to any **goods** or **effects** that are special to the owner. In particular, tangible **personal property** of a testator, such as would be taken when a person moves home, including money, jewellery, clothes, household furniture and effects, ornaments, books, records, silverware, china, cars, televisions, radios, personal computers, etc. 'Personal effects' does not normally include money or a claim to money. See also **personal estate**.

personal estate The **personal property** of an individual, including money (but not monetary value when represented by **real property**), goods, debts, choses-in-action, stocks, shares and loans. 'Personal estate' may be considered as any property other than a freehold; or as synonymous with a personal chattel if the context so admits, i.e. it may include a leasehold. If a person devises, for example, his "personal estate", "personal property, estate and effects" or "personal estate whatsoever and wheresoever", unless the context clearly indicates to the contrary, it may be taken that he intends to pass all personal property, but not real property. In English statute law, 'personal estate' may be extended to "leasehold estates and other chattels real, and also to monies, shares of government and other funds. securities for money (not being real estates), debts, choses-in-action, rights, credits, goods, and all other property whatsoever which by law devolves upon the executor or administrator, and to any share or interest therein", Wills Act 1837, s. 1. cf. **real estate**. See also **bequest**, **chattel**, **estate**, **movable**.

personal liability 1. The **liability** of an individual for a debt or obligation either apart from, or in addition to, security given for that debt. If necessary, a personal liability may necessitate the realisation of a person's entire assets to satisfy the debt. See also **exculpatory clause**, **limited liability company**, **subject to mortgage**. 2. A claim or liability against a person, as distinguished from a claim against property. See also **deficiency decree**[US], **recourse**.

personal liability insurance See **accident insurance**.

personal property Property that is not classified as **real property**, i.e. any form of property that is not land, any property attached to land (as a **fixture**), or any interest in land. Personal property includes money, goods, moveable chattels, debts, accrued rents, shares, etc. (sometimes called 'pure personalty' or 'chattels personal'); as well as a **leasehold** (sometimes called 'chattels real'). Personal property may be **corporeal property**, i.e. tangible or movable – furniture, clothing, etc.; or incorporeal, i.e. intangible – debts, goodwill, patents, a partnership interest, etc. It may be divided into 'choses-in-possession' – property that can be recovered by physical possession; and 'choses-in-action' – property that can be recovered only by an action at law.

A **leasehold** may be referred to as personal property because historically it was enforced as a right between the parties to the lease, and not as an action to recover land itself (although the hiring of land is normally treated as a branch of real property, and the hiring of pure personalty as a branch of **bailment**, contract or tort). However, in English and American law, leaseholds are now regarded more a part of the law relating to real property than personal property.

In a will, 'personal property' does not strictly include land or any interests therein, but if the context so admits, it may include a fee interest or any other property that is owned by the testator personally. See also **chose**.

personal representative Any legally appointed representative. A person appointed to administer the affairs of another, especially to deal with the estate of a deceased person, either in accordance with the terms of a will (as an **executor**) or in accordance with the rules on intestacy (as an **administrator**).

In the US, the personal representative usually means 'administrator' or 'executor'. In English statute law, a 'personal representative' is defined as "the executor, original or by representation, or administrator for the time being of a deceased person", AEA 1925, s. 55(1); LPA 1925, s. 205(xviii).

The estate of a deceased person devolves to the personal representative until it is wound up. 'Personal representative' is also used synonymously with **legal representative**. See also **estate owner**(Eng).

personal residence An individual's **home** or place of **abode**. See also **homestead**, **principal private residence**(Eng), **principal residence**(US), **residence**.

personal restriction or **personal servitude** A **restriction** or **servitude** 'in gross', i.e. one that exists between two parties to a transaction, but that is not **appurtenant** to any land; a covenant that is intended to bind the parties to the transaction, but is not intended to encumber property in the event that it is transferred to a third party. cf. **real servitude**. See also **easement in gross**, **profit à prendre**.

personalty See **personal property**.

personam(Lat) See *in personam*, action *in personam*.

phase I, II & III audit(US) See **environmental audit**.

phony sale(AmE) The sale of a property at a price that is artificially inflated, or one where the price in the sale contract is significantly below the amount actually paid. See also **fraud**, **fraudulent conveyance**, **simulation**.

physical deterioration Deterioration of property due to decay of the materials of which it is made. Deterioration that arises primarily from age and use. See also **depreciation**, **obsolescence**, **fair wear and tear**(BrE), **wear and tear**(AmE).

physical depreciation See **depreciation**.

physical life The period for which a building may be used before **physical deterioration** or **obsolescence** end its viable existence. The period of time for which a building is expected to remain in a sound condition, as distinguished from the **economic life** at the end of which the building has no viable economic value.

physical possession   See **possession**.

physical occupancy   See **occupancy**.

physical value   The value of a building as determined by assessing its reproduction or **reinstatement cost**, after allowing for depreciation. See also **inherent value**.

piccage or **pickage**   A toll or levy imposed for the privilege of breaking ground to install a booth or stall at a market or fair. See also **pennage**, **stallage**.

pick of land   A narrow parcel of land that runs into a corner.

picle   From the Latin *piccolo*, 'small'; a small **close** or enclosure.

piecemeal zoning(US)   See **partial zoning**.

piece of land   See **parcel of land**, **tract**.

piecemeal development   The development of an area in a gradual, sporadic or *laissez-faire* manner. Development carried out in an area where there is no overall planning or development control. cf. **comprehensive development**. See also **ribbon development**.

pied-a-terre   A small home or flat, especially when used as a place of short-term resort. Commonly refers to a second place of residence, such as an apartment maintained in a city by a country dweller. See also **apartment**.

piggyback loan(US)   A loan made by two lenders as one party to a mortgage agreement. Normally one lender provides the largest part of the funding and has priority over the other; although, unlike a standard first and second mortgage arrangement, the 'piggyback' lenders join in a single mortgage agreement. The party providing the 'top up' or 'piggy back' part of the loan is generally repaid first from the borrower's repayments of capital. See also **joint mortgage**, **participation mortgage**.

pin money   An allowance made by a husband to his wife for her personal and private expenses (originally money for such costs as dressmaking, etc.). In particular, in English law, a provision made in a **settlement** as a yearly charge on the husband's real property.

pipe   See **drain**, **pipeline**, **sewer**.

pipeline or **pipe-line**   **1.** A conduit that runs over or under the ground and is used for the transportation of oil, gas, water or other liquids. Generally, a tube or system of tubes used for the transportation of a liquid or gaseous substance from a store or source of supply to a place of consumption or further storage. A pipeline may be distinguished from a **drain** as the latter conveys waste materials away to a point of disposal. 'Pipeline' may also be different from a 'pipe', as a 'pipeline' conveys the idea of a line of pipe running over or under the earth, carrying with it the right to an **easement**.

In English statute law, a pipe-line has been defined as "a pipe (together with any apparatus and works associated therewith), or system of pipes (together with any apparatus and works associated therewith), for the conveyance of anything other than air, water, water vapour or steam", but excluding "a drain or sewer" and most pipes within a building or used for agricultural purposes (Pipe-lines Act 1962, s. 65). See also **culvert**, **easement**, **wayleave**.   **2.** The means by which loans are processed from the initial application to closing of the loans and, if appropriate, the placement of the loans in a secondary market.   **3.**(US)A term used by a lender to refer to the total inventory of loans that are in process from application to closing. The 'pipeline' may also include closed loans that are held pending resale in the secondary mortgage market.

piscary See **right to fish**.

piti payment(US) A payment under a loan agreement which includes 'principal', 'interest', 'taxes', and 'insurance'. A mortgagor is required sometimes, especially under home loans, to pay not only interest and principal, but also to pay monthly into an escrow account a pro-rated part of the real estate taxes and insurance premiums that are likely to fall due in respect of the mortgaged property. Several states have enacted laws to regulate such escrow payments. Also, the Real Estate Settlement Procedure Act of 1974 (12 USC § 2609) limits such escrow payments to an amount that is sufficient to cover the taxes and insurance premiums that next fall due, plus a two-month cushion and, once the regular payments have started under the loan, the tax payments are limited to one-twelfth of the annual taxes and other charges. Also called an 'impound payment', 'escrow payment' or 'reserve payment'. See also **budget mortgage**.

place 1. A particular locality or building; a **location**; a **site** or situation. A place may be any locality, from a small area of land or a room in a building to a town, city, county, state or country. See also **situs**, *lex loci*. 2. A short street, especially a dead-end street or cul-de-sac. A public square. 3. To arrange or allocate something, as with placing a loan or investment with someone. See also **placement**, **placement fee**.

place lands(US) See **indemnity lands**.

place of abode See **abode**.

placement 1. The granting of a loan or mortgage. The making of an investment. See also **financing**, **funding**. 2. The offering of new shares in a company to a number of selected investors rather than to the public at large.

placement fee A fee paid to a broker for introducing a borrower. Normally the term 'placement fee' is used to refer to a fee paid by the lender to a mortgage broker for assisting with 'placing' funds with a borrower, as opposed to a **finance fee** which is paid by the borrower for finding the lender or source of funds. Called, if appropriate, a 'mortgage placement fee'.

placer claim(US) A claim to a mining right where the minerals are not found in a vein, lode or ledge, but lie in a loose condition in softer material that lies under the land, i.e. the minerals do not lie fixed in the rock, but are in a loose state over which the claim has been placed within defined boundaries (Clipper Min. Co. v. Eli Min. & L. Co., 194 US 220, 24 S Ct 632, 48 L Ed 944 (1904)). See also **mining claim**.

plan 1. A drawing or sketch of an area of land laid out on a flat surface. A means of indicating the boundaries of a parcel of land, especially to show the limits of a plot of land that is to be the subject of a transfer or that has been allocated for a project of development. A plan is normally a representation of a horizontal plan, although in the context of a set of building or architectural drawings, 'plans' may well include sections and elevations. A plan is commonly drawn or marked on paper, with markers to indicate vertical points. It may also be set out in computer graphics, with a three-dimensional representation of the surface of the land.

A plan merely annexed to a document has little significance and a plan expressed to be "for identification only" does not prevail over a clear written description. However, a plan may be used for clarification of the boundaries of the land to be conveyed when the description is insufficient (*Wigginton & Milner Ltd v Winster Engineering Ltd* [1978] 1 WLR 1462, [1978] 3 All ER 436 (CA); 26 C.J.S., Deeds, p. 875). If land is expressed to be "more particularly described" or "delineated" on an attached plan, then that plan prevails over the written description in a conveyance (*Eastwood v Ashton* [1915] AC 900 (HL)). In particular, if a description is incomplete a plan drawn to scale will be taken as determining evidence of the boundaries of the parcel of land. A plan should be intended to form or substantiate a **description** in a deed only when it has been professionally prepared and is not in any way at odds with the description; otherwise, it will be otiose or misleading. See also **filed plan**[(Eng)], **location plan**, **parcels**, **plat**[(US)], **site plan**, **plot plan**, **survey**. **2.** A large-scale **map** of a small area. See also **cadastral map**. **3.** A line drawing, diagram or sketch of a building, or a proposed **building**, taken as a horizontal section and shown on a flat surface. The term 'plans' commonly refers to a set of drawings of a new or proposed building, especially those that form part of a building contract. cf. **elevation**. See also **specification**, **working drawing**. **4.** An overall scheme or layout for the future development of an area. A proposed means of achieving a development objective as set out in a written report, incorporating maps and diagrams. See also **development plan**, **master plan**, **planning**.

plane surveying Surveying in order to define an area on the earth's surface, disregarding the curvature of the earth. cf. **geodetic surveying**.

planned amortization class (PAC)[(US)] See **real estate mortgage investment conduit**.

planned community zoning[(US)] See **density zoning**.

planned development project[(US)] See **planned unit development**.

planned unit development (PUD)[(US)] A large area of land that is developed, operated and maintained as a single entity in accordance with an approved outline development plan. Such a development may consist of individual family homes; garden apartments or high-rise apartments; industrial, commercial, or mixed use projects; or a condominium project. A PUD is generally intended to provide for an above average density of development by creating building clusters, shared areas of open space and shared recreational facilities for the use of individual property owners. The owners are free to use the interior of their properties as they wish, but accept mutual restrictions on the use and management of the common areas and constraints on the maintenance and appearance of the exterior based on a unified scheme of development.

A planned unit development is generally instigated by a single developer who obtains the zoning and, if necessary, subdivision approvals and usually develops the streets, utilities, lighting, water supply, sewer lines, etc. Individual lots are then sold to individual homeowners or 'unit holders'. In some cases, the developer may construct homes or other buildings on some or all of the lots before disposing of the lots. The unit holders may be shareholders in a corporation that holds title to and is responsible for the common areas, or the ownership of the common areas may be transferred to a **homeowners' association**. Also called a 'planned development project' or simply a 'planned development'; or, if a residential development, a 'master planned community', 'community unit plan' or 'unitary development'. See also **cluster development**, **de minimis PUD**, **floating zone**, **scheme of development**, **statement of record**[(US)], **subdivision**.

planning **1.** The preparation of a plan, diagram or scheme. The organisation of details for the design and implementation of a development or building project. **2.** A system, normally backed by the force of law, for the control and regulation of the use and development of land within a given municipality. A means by which the development of an area, district or region is systematically controlled in order to ensure an economic use of resources, the **aesthetic** appearance of the area, the regulation of physical growth and the improvement of the social fabric of the area. **Zoning** may be considered as a means of land planning, although planning is a term that is broader in scope. Broadly speaking 'planning' connotes the systematic development of an area with particular reference to the location, character and extent of streets, squares, parks and to kindred mapping and charting. 'Zoning' relates to the regulation of the *use* of property. See also **land-**

use planning, town and country planning(Eng). 3. The positive process by which the use and improvement of land is set forth from the standpoint of **amenity** and convenience, but not necessarily profit. 4. The process by which a government authority controls and directly intervenes in the normal economic forces rather than relying on a free market mechanism; normally referred to as 'economic planning'. A process whereby the State coordinates and channels the actions of individuals in the interest of the common good. See also **police power**.

planning advantage(Eng)   See **planning gain**.

planning agreement(Eng)   See **planning obligation**.

planning appeal(Eng)   An application to the Secretary of State made by a party who: (a) has been refused **planning permission**, or granted it subject to conditions; (b) refused consent to matters reserved by an outline planning permission; or (c) refused an application for any approval required under a **General Development Order**, or granted such approval subject to conditions (TCPA 1990, s. 78(1)). There is a similar right of appeal if an applicant for planning permission has not received a decision from the local planning authority within the prescribed statutory time limit (TCPA 1990, s. 78(2)). See also **called-in planning application**, **certificate of lawfulness**.

planning application(Eng)   A formal request to a local **planning authority** for **planning permission** (TCPA 1990, s. 62). An application for planning permission may be submitted by any person but, if the applicant is not the **owner** of the subject land (a freeholder or holder of a lease with not less than seven years unexpired), the owner *must* be informed (or reasonable steps must be taken to inform him) of the application. In addition, if the land constitutes or forms part of an **agricultural holding**, any agricultural tenant *must* be informed of the application. In addition, a

General Development Order or a Special Development Order may provide that notice is given of any application for planning permission and a certificate to that effect issued by the applicant (TCPA 1990, s. 65; Town and Country Planning (General Development Procedure) Order 1995, art. 6(1)(6), Sch. 2, Part 1, Part 2).

When dealing with the application, the authority shall have regard to the provisions of the **development plan** in force, "so far as material to the application, and to any other material considerations", TCPA 1990, s. 70(2); including any representations relating to the application (TCPA 1990, s. 71(2); Town and Country Planning (General Development Procedure) Order 1995, arts. 19, 20). When the planning authority has fully considered the application, it may: (a) grant permission, either unconditionally or subject to such conditions "as they think fit"; or (b) refuse planning permission (TCPA 1990, s. 70(1)). The decision must be in writing and if permission is refused, or granted subject to conditions, the reasons for such decisions must be stated. A local planning authority is required to maintain at its offices a register of all planning applications and decisions, and to make the register available for public inspection (TCPA 1990, s. 69).

Planning permission may be granted also by: (i) a 'General Development Order' or a 'Special Development Order'; (ii) the existence of a **simplified planning zone**; (iii) an order designating an **enterprise zone** or the grant of permission by the enterprise zone authority; or (iv) the deemed grant of permission by a government department under the provisions of section 90 of the 1990 Act (TCPA 1990, s. 58). See also **called-in planning application**, **certificate of lawfulness**, **planning appeal**, **planning certificate**.

Brown, Henry, and Adrian Salt. *Planning Applications*. 3rd ed. Oxford: Blackwell, 1998.

White, Sasha. *Planning Appeals*. Welwyn Garden City: EMIS Professional Publishing, 1997.

planning assumptions(Eng)   The statutory assumptions that may be made when assessing

compulsory purchase compensation as to the type of planning permission that could be granted for the development of the area of land in question. These assumptions are set out in the Land Compensation Act 1961, ss. 15-16, and "any planning permission which is to be assessed in accordance with any of the provisions of those sections is in addition to any planning permission which may be in force at the date of the **notice to treat**", LCompA 1961, s. 14(2). Basically, this provision enables the landowner, when the **open market value** of his land is being assessed, to bring into account (in addition to any subsisting planning permission or any **permitted development**) certain 'prospect' of obtaining planning permission. However, factors such as the likelihood that planning permission might reasonably be granted for a use shown on the development plan; the availability of sewage facilities; the time at which the permission would be granted; and any **planning condition** that the planning authority would be likely to impose must be taken fully into account in deciding on the factors that may be brought into account. These provisions are made to assist a landowner in determining the planning permission that would be granted if no compulsory purchase was proposed, but they do not preclude any other reasonable assumption as to the likely form of planning permission that a prospective purchaser might anticipate (LCompA 1971, s. 14(2)). Thus, it may be assumed that planning permission for certain alternative forms of development would be available, but this does not mean that there will be a demand for that development. See also **certificate of appropriate alternative development, hope value, special suitability or adaptability**.

planning authority(Eng)   A public body responsible for considering, formulating and implementing local or central government policies and proposals for the use and development of land. The local planning authority may be: (a) the county council; (b) the district council (metropolitan or non-metropolitan); (c) the London borough council; or (d) the Common Council of the City of London (TCPA 1990, s. 1, Sch. 1). See also **development corporation, development plan, joint planning board, planning commission**(US), **urban development corporation, Urban Regeneration Agency**.

planning blight(Eng)   See **blight, blight notice**.

planning board or **planning commission**(US)   A board established by a city, county or other municipal authority to control the use and development of land. Generally, a planning commission is responsible for preparing a **comprehensive plan** for consideration by the state legislature; reviewing development and rezoning proposals; and generally advising and administering changes in land use within a community area or county. The formal approval of zoning or planning proposals is normally made by the city council or other municipal authority, based on recommendations from the planning commission. The constitution, power and role of the 'planning board', or 'planning commission', varies considerably from one area to another. Sometimes called a 'planning agency' or 'plan commission'.

planning certificate(Eng)   A term that is not used specifically in English planning law, but could be applied to various certificates issued in connection with planning and development, including: (i) a **certificate of lawfulness**; (ii) a **certificate of appropriate alternative development**; (iii) a certificate accompanying a **planning application**, as required by the TCPA 1990, s. 65, specifying that the applicant has complied with the provisions of any development order regarding the giving of notice or publication of the application and, in particular, that if the applicant is not the owner of the subject land, he has notified the **owner** that the application has been made or, if the owner is not known, has taken appropriate steps to trace the owner by advertising locally or placing a notice on the land, and (if appropriate) has notified any tenant of an **agricultural holding** of the application.

planning charge(Eng)   See **local land charge**.

planning commission(US)   See **planning board**.

planning condition(Eng)   A restriction or restraint imposed by a planning authority when it approves an application to carry out development, i.e. a condition that is made a prerequisite to the carrying out of development pursuant to a grant of **planning permission**. When determining a planning application, a local planning authority "may grant permission, either unconditionally or subject to such conditions as they think fit … [and] In dealing with such an application the authority shall have regard to the provisions of the **development plan**, so far as material to the application, and to any other material considerations", TCPA 1990, ss. 70(1)(a), 70(2). A local planning authority may also impose conditions "(a) for regulating the development or use of any land … or requiring the carrying out of works on such land, so far as appears to the local planning authority to be expedient for the purposes of or in connection with the development authorised by the permission; (b) for requiring the removal of any building or works authorised by the permission, or the discontinuance of any use of land so authorised, at the end of a specified period, and the carrying out of works required for the reinstatement of land at the end of that period", TCPA 1990, s. 72(1). Permission granted subject to the latter conditions may be referred to as 'planning permission granted for a limited period' (TCPA 1990, s. 72(2)). Such conditions, which must be reasonable, may also take the form of: (a) regulations to control the appearance, layout, design, etc. of the development; or (b) a stipulation as to the time within which the building or other operations must be commenced (TCPA 1990, s. 72(3)). Such conditions must be limited so that: (i) they do not fundamentally change the general law; (ii) they relate to Planning Acts (or are imposed for a proper **planning purpose**); (iii) they are reasonable; and (iv) they are sufficiently certain and unambiguous. Certain conditions are expressly permitted by statute, e.g. the preservation of trees; control of the use of other land of the applicant; and, in certain cases, that the permission is personal to the applicant. See also **planning appeal, planning obligation, planning gain**, *ultra vires*.

Langham, Richard. *Conditions and Planning Obligations*. Welwyn Garden City: EMIS Professional Publishing, 1996.

planning consent(Eng)   See **planning permission**.

planning control   1.(Eng)See **enforcement notice, planning permission**.   2.(US)See **zoning, zoning ordinance**.

planning decision(Eng)   See **planning permission**.

planning enforcement(Eng)   See **discontinuance order, enforcement notice, revocation order**.

planning enquiry(Eng)   See **planning inquiry**.

planning fee(Eng)   A payment to cover the cost of processing a **planning application**.

planning gain(Eng)   A benefit secured for the 'community as a whole' at the expense of a recipient of planning permission. A 'planning gain' is extracted from the recipient of planning permission, by the local planning authority, as a *quid pro quo* for the right to carry out a particular form of development – especially when such development would not otherwise be readily approved. A planning gain may take any form (a concession, surrender of an existing right, or even expenditure) provided there is a true benefit for the community; it is directly relevant to the development for which planning permission is being sought; and it is fairly and reasonably related to the permitted development. 'Planning gain' is a means by which the local authority endeavours to recoup, for the public in general, some of the

betterment that is presumed to accrue to a landowner when he is granted planning permission. The gain is secured either by the imposition of a **planning condition**, or more usually by means of a **planning obligation** that is accepted by the recipient of the permission. Sometimes called 'planning advantage'. See also **incentive zoning**(US).

Wenban-Smith, A., and B. Pearce. *Planning Gains: negotiating with planning authorities.* London: Estates Gazette, 1999.

planning inquiry(Eng) **1.** A quasi-judicial hearing of a case for the grant or refusal of **planning permission** held by an inspector appointed by the Secretary of State for the Environment, following an appeal against a local planning authority's decision on a planning application. See also **planning appeal**. **2.** A search or inquiry made to obtain details of any planning consent, and conditions attached thereto, which relate to a particular parcel of land. A local planning authority is required to maintain at its offices a register of all planning applications and decisions, and to make the register available for public inspection (TCPA 1990, s. 69). See also **local land charge**.

planning obligation(Eng) An obligation accepted by a person who is seeking to develop land by which some form of restriction or limitation is imposed on the development or use of that land, or a sum is made payable to the local planning authority, in order to facilitate the grant of **planning permission**. The 'obligation' takes the form of an agreement (or sometimes a unilateral acknowledgement) by which a prospective applicant for planning permission voluntarily accepts a particular commitment, or commitments, in order to obtain an approval that might otherwise not be granted, or may be granted subject to more onerous conditions. The agreement may: (a) restrict the development or use of the land in some specific way; (b) require particular operations or activities to be carried out on the land; (c) require the land to be used in a specific way; or (d) require a sum or sums to be paid to the authority (TCPA

1990, s. 106(1) as amended). A planning obligation may achieve a **planning gain**, such as the provision of additional services or a mix of planning uses, that may be difficult to achieve by the imposition of numerous planning conditions. However, the 'planning obligation' should not fundamentally impose a greater level of restriction on the use or development than might be imposed by the use of planning conditions. A planning obligation is registrable as a **local land charge**. See also **contract zoning**(US), **planning condition**.

Department of the Environment, *Circular 1/97* 'Planning Obligations'.

Langham, Richard. *Conditions and Planning Obligations.* Welwyn Garden City: EMIS Professional Publishing, 1996.

planning permission(Eng) The formal written consent given by a **planning authority** (whether a local planning authority or the Secretary of State) to a proposal for the **development** (or a **material change in the use**) of land. Planning permission is required for any activity that is included within the statutory definition of "development", excluding: (i) the resumption of a prior use of land upon expiration of planning permission that has been granted for a limited time; and (ii) a use that may lawfully be carried out when another use has been prohibited by an **enforcement notice**. Planning permission may also be 'granted': (a) by being considered a 'permitted development' by virtue of a **General Development order**; (b) by virtue of a **Special Development Order**; (c) where a **simplified planning zone** is in force, or an **enterprise zone** has been designated; (d) by "government authorisation" for certain forms of development that are 'deemed' to have planning permission; or (e) for the display of an **advertisement** in accordance with the Town and Country Planning (Control of Advertisement) Regulations 1992 (TCPA 1990, ss. 57-58, 220-222).

Consent may be given as 'detailed' or full planning permission, or in 'outline'. Detailed planning permission approves all matters relating to the development and no further consent is required, although the permission may be granted subject to a **planning condition**. Usually 'outline' planning permission is sought so that a landowner may have an indication of the category of development that will be permitted and of basic aspects that are relevant to that development, such as the plot ratio or density. See also **abandonment, certificate of lawfulness, completion notice, planning appeal, planning application, planning certificate, planning condition, planning obligation, revocation order.**

Denyer-Green, Barry, and Navjit Ubhi. 3rd ed. *Development & Planning Law*. London: Estates Gazette, 1999.

Duxbury, Robert M. C. *Telling and Duxbury: Planning Law and Procedure*. 12th ed. London: Butterworths, 2002.

Forbes, David. *Planning Law: A Handbook for Conveyancers and Property Professionals*. 2nd ed. Welwyn Garden City: EMIS Professional Publishing, 1999.

Heap, Sir Desmond. *An Outline of Planning Law*. 11th ed. London: Sweet & Maxwell, 1996.

Tromans, Stephen, and Robert Turrall-Clarke. *Planning Law Practice and Precedents*. Looseleaf. London: Sweet & Maxwell, ©1991.

Grant, Professor Malcolm (editor). *Encyclopaedia of Planning Law and Practice*. 6 vols. Looseleaf. London: Sweet & Maxwell.

planning purpose(Eng)   1. A term used in the Town and Country Planning Acts to signify one reason that may be used by a local authority to justify the **compulsory purchase** of land. A term that is not defined precisely, but includes the acquisition of land for such purposes as comprehensive redevelopment; the proper planning of an area; the relocation of population or industry; improvement of environmental facilities, etc.   2. A reason for the imposition of a **planning condition**. A planning authority can grant or refuse planning permission, or impose conditions, having regard to the development plan in force for the area and "any other material consideration", TCPA 1990, s. 70(2). However, such conditions must be reasonable.

planning register(Eng)   See **planning application**.

planning restrictions(Eng)   See **compensation for planning restrictions**.

planning scheme(Aus)   A document and plans that set out the land use policies or zoning for a municipality.

planning title(Eng)   See **planning inquiry**.

planning unit(Eng)   A physical area of a building, or a piece of land, that is to be considered as a single unit when determining whether there has been a **material change in the use** of a property and, therefore, a breach of planning control. When seeking to establish whether a property has undergone a material change of use, it is necessary to look at an area used for a particular purpose as a whole, i.e. to consider the entire 'planning unit'. The planning authority should exclude from its deliberations any area used for a different or unrelated purpose, but must include as part of the planning unit those areas whose user is ancillary or incidental to the primary purpose. The essential criterion in deciding whether the planning unit has materially changed its use is whether there has been a significant change in the use of the entirety – a change in the total character of the property and not merely a change in one section of the unit.

plant   1. A **factory**, **workshop** or similar building where industry is carried on, including machinery and equipment therein.   2. The equipment and machinery that is installed for the running of a building or buildings, including heating or air-conditioning units, elevators, electric sub-stations, water tanks, etc. See also **facilities management**.   3. The buildings, equipment, machinery or apparatus used in the running of a trade or business, especially a manufacturing business. See also **fixed asset, fixture, trade fixture**.   4. A young **tree**, sapling, shrub, vine or herb, especially one that is capable of being planted out in its permanent habitat. See also **emblements, fixture**.   5. See **title plant**.

plat(US)   1. A small parcel of land; an area of level

land. See also **plot**.　**2.** A representation on a flat surface of a tract of land showing the boundaries by natural or artificial markers and lines. A **plan** or map, especially one that shows in detail the actual or proposed subdivision or uses of a larger area of land. A plat may also show the boundaries of property in a vertical plane, as with a condominium. See also **plat map**.

plat book(US)　A public record in which is maintained records of a subdivision, including details of the lot or parcel numbers and the dimensions of individual lots. See also **plat map**.

plat map(US)　A map of a specific area or district, usually drawn to scale, showing the location and detailing the boundaries of individual lots or parcels of land together with streets, alleyways, etc. Plat maps are prepared for most urban areas and are usually the means of indicating the legal boundaries of land, especially the legal boundaries of land when a large area of land is sold off in lots. Individual lots are usually identified by reference to a **lot and block system**, e.g. Lot 6, Block 2. Thus, land is said to be 'platted' when it is laid out in lots, blocks and streets that are designated on a map or **plat**. A plat map may be prepared by a local tax assessor's office to show the boundaries of land ownership for taxation purposes – a 'tax plat'. A plat map may be prepared primarily for identification purposes following a detailed survey of an area – a 'plat of survey' or 'identification plat'; or to show an area of land that is to be subject to a subdivision – a 'plat of subdivision'. cf. **plot plan**.

plat of subdivision(US)　See **subdivision**.

pledge　A transaction by which goods, or documents of title to goods, are transferred to a creditor as security for a debt or obligation owed to him. On the grant of a pledge, ownership remains with the borrower (pledgor), but in the event of default the property may be sold by the lender (pledgee). A pledge is a form of **bailment** or delivery of goods and chattels as a security for the payment of a debt or performance of an engagement upon the express or implied understanding that the thing deposited is to be restored to the owner, as soon as the debt is discharged, or the engagement has been fulfilled. The thing deposited as security is called a **pawn** or pledge; the party making the deposit, the pawnor or pledgor; and the person who receives it in his possession, the pawnee or pledgee. A pledge may be considered as a form of **lien**. However, a lien grants only a charge on the subject matter, whereas a pledge grants a right for the pledgee to take possession and control of the subject matter, usually with a power of sale in the event of default. Also, a pledge arises from the agreement of the parties; unlike a lien which generally arises by operation of law as a means of coercing one party into meeting an obligation. An essential element of a pledge is that there must be delivery (actual or constructive) of possession of the property to the pledgee, together with a right for the pledgee to assign the property, as necessary, to satisfy the debt. In that respect, it may be distinguished from a **mortgage** by the absence of a transfer of possession of the property to the lender. However, as with a mortgage, the payment of the debt entitles the pledgor to redeem the property before it is capable of being assigned by the pledgee. The deposit of title deeds to land creates an equitable mortgage or an equitable charge and not a pledge, because the subject-matter is a right to real property. cf. **assignment**, **warranty**. See also **promise**, **security**.

pledged-account mortgage (PAM)(US)　A mortgage arrangement by which the mortgagor places funds into an account that is pledged to the lender and is used to supplement the mortgage payments. Used particularly when the borrower is granted a reduced interest rate in the early years (as with a 'graduated' or **variable-payment mortgage**) and the pledged funds are available to be drawn on to avoid **negative amortization**. See also **flexible loan insurance plan**.

pledgee　One who obtains a **pledge** over personal property; the party with whom property is in pledge or on **pawn**.

pledgor or **pledger**   One who makes or gives a **pledge** of personal property.

plot   A small area or parcel of land, especially an area demarcated for a particular use or purpose. A parcel of land delineated for a particular purpose on a plan, normally representing land held in single ownership; especially one of a number of similar parcels, each of which is intended for separate development. In the US, generally called a **lot**. See also **plat**(US).

plot plan   **1.** A plan that shows the precise boundaries of a parcel of land and, if applicable, the limits of any buildings that have been placed on the site. See also **site plan**.   **2.** A plan showing the subdivision of an area of land into separate plots or lots. Normally the plan also shows estate roads, parking areas, areas of landscaping, and areas for building and may show other details such as services or utilities. A plot plan is usually prepared prior to **parceling**. See also **plat map**.

plot ratio(BrE/Aus)   The relationship between the total **gross external area** of a building and the **site area** of the land (excluding the surrounding roads, if any) on which that building stands. A plot ratio is defined in order to restrict the volume and thereby the height of buildings that can be placed on land. In Australia, sometimes called a 'building density ratio'. cf. **floor space index**. See also **density**, **floor area ratio**(US), **site coverage**.

plottage(US)   **1.** The bringing of two or more parcels of land into common ownership or control. 'Plottage' may refer also to the added value that may accrue when two or more lots are brought into one ownership so that the entire plot can be used to better advantage. cf. **parceling**. See also **assemblage, plottage increment**.   **2.** The area of a **plot of land**.

plottage increment or **plottage value**(AmE)
The increase in value resulting from **plottage**, i.e. from the bringing of two or more areas of land

into the same ownership, especially when the entire area can be used to better advantage than as individual lots. Also called 'assemblage value' or simply 'plottage'. See also **marriage value**(BrE).

ploughbote   See **estovers**.

pocket listing(US)   A **listing** that is kept for the sole use of a broker or salesperson and not shared with other members of a brokerage office or **multiple listing service**. Pocket listings are generally discouraged as they are contrary to the rules of the brokerage house listing service.

***Pointe Gourde* rule**(Eng)   See **compulsory purchase compensation**.

point   **1.** A particular place, especially one with no particular dimension. A point on a boundary line is one or other of the extremities of the line; the spot where two boundaries join or cross (a point of intersection).   **2.** The smallest unit by which a variation in a price is measured – a point may be one unit of value, e.g. $1 or £1; 1/32nd of a unit; 1/100th of a unit; or even 1/1000th of a unit, e.g. the exchange rate of a currency may change by 25 points from 1.725 to 1.750. See also **basis point**.   **3.** In financing, one per cent of the amount of a loan. In particular, 'points' refers to **discount points** added on the principal, or a single payment made at the start of the loan period, as distinguished from the interest rate charged during the term of the loan – the latter being referred to sometimes as 'percentage points'. Discount points are usually a one-time charge added to a loan in order to increase the return to the borrower. See also **annual percentage rate, loan fee, origination fee**.   **4.** A unit of measurement used to indicate variations in a price or stock, especially one unit of measurement that is related to a base or index number. An increase of an index from 105 to 110 is 5 points, and a fall from 50 to 45 is also 5 points (but a true fall of 10%); hence a point is sometimes called an 'absolute percentage'.

point of beginning (POB)(AmE)   See **metes and bounds system**.

polder   Low lying land that is reclaimed from the sea or a lake by the construction of dykes or dams.

police power   The power of promoting the interests of society as a whole by limiting the freedom of an individual to act or use his property at will. In particular, the constitutional power available to a sovereign authority to legislate in such a way as to impair the use or value of private property for the benefit of the public at large. The right of a government, especially of a state, to restrict, regulate and control the individual's free use of land and buildings by law and precept – as by taxation, public health and building regulations, zoning ordinances, and pollution or environmental controls and, in some jurisdictions, rent control. Police power involves the regulation of property to prevent its use in a manner that is detrimental to the public interest, as distinguished from **eminent domain**, which involves the 'taking' of property for public use. However, if the exercise of police power goes so far as to totally impede the proper or beneficial use of land, or if it amounts to a restriction not truly related to the regulation of the development, then it may amount to a 'taking' and, therefore, require the payment of **just compensation** to the landowner (Pennsylvania Coal Co. v. Mahon, 260 US 393, 416, 43 S Ct 158, 67 L Ed 322, 28 ALR 1321 (1922); Dolan v. City of Tigard, 512 US 374, 114 S Ct 2309, 129 L Ed.2d 304, 323 (1994)).

Police power may be exercised, without compensation, provided it is intended for the public good; is not unduly oppressive on one individual or group of individuals; is intended to affect only one parcel of land; is not clearly arbitrary and unreasonable; and has a reasonable relation to the public health, safety, morals, peace and quiet or "general welfare" of the community (Village of Euclid v. Amber Realty Co., 272 US 365, 47 S Ct 114, 71 L Ed 303, 314 (1926); Berman v. Parker, 348 US 26, 75 S Ct 98, 99 L Ed 27, 37—Anno: Federal Police Power (1954)). 'Police power' is based on the maxim *sic utere tuo et alienum non lædas*, 'so use your own property as not to injure another's', and has developed into the power of the state to limit the unhindered use of land—"the powers of government inherent in every sovereignty to the extent of its dominions. ... the power to govern men and things within the limits of its dominion", License Cases, 5 Howard 504, 46 US 504, 581, 12 L Ed 256, 291 (1847). cf. **inverse condemnation**. See also **aesthetic**, **building controls**, **bundle of rights theory**, **condemnation**, **escheat**, **ordinance**.

policy of insurance   See **insurance policy**.

poll   See **deed poll**.

pond   An open body of water that is confined either by a natural or artificial barrier, but one that is normally without an outlet. A pond is relatively stagnant, and is larger than a puddle but smaller than a lake. See **land**, **water rights**.

pooled fund   An arrangement whereby a number of investors place funds collectively into a common form of investment; a vehicle for investment used especially when a number of investors combine their resources to acquire a larger investment than could be acquired by any one investor. See also **blind-pool offering**, **investment company**, **securitization**.

pooling clause(AmE)   A clause in an **oil and gas lease** in which two or more tracts of land may be brought together in one lease, for the purpose of drilling and usually with the intention of forming a joint venture to share in the benefits of any resultant exploitation.

pooling agreement(AmE)   An agreement that permits separately owned interests held under an oil or gas lease to be brought together for the purpose of obtaining a well permit when the separate permits would not be considered under regulations designed to limit the number of wells in a given area ('well spacing' regulations).

poor man's mortgage(AmE)   See **installment land contract**.

population density The ratio that expresses the relationship between a unit of land area (acre, square meter) and the average number of people occupying that area. Population density may be considered a function of accommodation or **residential density**, i.e. the number of residential units on a given area of land, and **occupancy rate**, i.e. the number of persons per residential unit of accommodation. See also **density**.

portfolio 1. Derived from the Italian *porto-folio* or *portofogli*, papers carried together or, in commerce, securities held together. All the investments or securities held by a person or institution. 2. Investments held indirectly, e.g. through a **mutual fund** or **investment trust**, rather than directly.

portfolio investment Investment in the shares of a company or a range of investments, as distinguished from a direct investment made by the purchase of assets or real property. The investment of funds into a number of diversified areas or diversified properties.

portfolio loan A loan that is originated and retained by a lending institution and not sold in the **secondary mortgage market**.

portfolio management The overall management, control and supervision of a number of investments (a **portfolio**), with the aim of maximising the **return** and minimising the **risk**. Portfolio management involves a continuous and active process of review to determine areas where action can be taken to improve the return and reduce the risk, both on the individual investments and on the entire portfolio. Portfolio management is carried out within given risk-return parameters. In particular, within the objective criteria of the investor in terms of liquidity, finance, diversification, preferences for income or capital growth, etc. The art of portfolio management is to optimise the return on the entire range of investments while recognising the level of risk that the investor is prepared to accept. Portfolio management of real estate includes such matters as supervision of **property management**; analyzing the composition of the portfolio (the **portfolio mix**); examining the performance of individual investments relative to one another, to objective targets, as well as to alternative forms of investment; and reviewing the entire portfolio relative to such targets or to other investment returns. See also **asset management, facilities management**.

portfolio mix The composition of an investor's **portfolio** of investments. The portfolio mix of a number of investments may be expressed as, for example, the percentage invested in different geographical areas; different sectors (bonds, equity shares, property, cash); different dates of maturity; different degrees of liquidity; or different sizes of investment.

Hudson-Wilson, Susan., and Charles H. Wurtzebach (editors), *Managing Real Estate Portfolios*, Burr Ridge, IL: Irwin, 1994.

Pagliari, Joseph L., Jr. (editor). *The Handbook of Real Estate Portfolio Management*. Burr Ridge, IL: Irwin, 1995.

Dubben, Nigel and Sarah Sayce. *Property Portfolio Management: An Introduction*. London & New York: Routledge, 1991.

portfolio turnover The ratio of the value of all sales and purchases in a given period of time to the total value of a **portfolio**. Thus, a portfolio turnover of 10% in one year means that the value of all property traded is equivalent to one tenth of the value of the portfolio (generally as valued at the start of the period).

portion 1. An allotted part. A part or share of an estate received by gift, will or inheritance. In particular, in English law, a share left under a **strict settlement** to the settlor's children to be received by them when they attain their majority, or if left to a female, when she achieves majority or when she marries. See also **dower, endowment,** *per capita, per stirpes*. 2.[Aus]That part of a parish into which it is divided for land title purposes.

positive covenant A promise or agreement whereby two or more parties undertake to carry

603

out a particular action, i.e. a **covenant** that requires some positive action rather than placing a limit on an action. A positive covenant does not need to be worded in a positive fashion, provided the intention is to call for a positive action. A positive covenant affecting land may arise in a lease (a 'landlord and tenant covenant'); or between the owners of adjacent parcels of land (commonly called a 'vendor and purchaser covenant' as it generally arises when a vendor of land imposes a covenant in the deed of conveyance).

In common law, a 'landlord and tenant covenant', whether positive or negative, is enforceable between any person who takes an estate in the land (whether by acquiring the landlord's reversion or an assignment of the tenant's interest) provided the covenant affects the subject matter of the lease, i.e. it 'touches and concerns' the land (a **covenant running with the land**), and there is **privity of estate** between the parties taking action on the covenant. Although, in English law, for leases entered into after January 1, 1996 all covenants are enforceable by or against any party who takes an assignment of the landlord's or tenant's interest – whether the covenant affects the subject matter of a lease or not, i.e. the covenant does not need to 'touch and concern the land' (Landlord and Tenant (Covenants) Act 1985, s. 3(1)).

A 'vendor and purchaser covenant' is enforceable as a contractual obligation between the original parties to the agreement. However, if one of the parcels of land is disposed of, the covenant may not be so readily enforced by, or against, the new owner of the land. At common law, the *benefit* of the covenant (the covenantee's right to have the duty performed), whether positive or negative, passes to the new landowner; essentially so long as the covenant 'touches and concerns' the land and is intended to run with the land. On the other hand, the *burden* of a positive covenant (such as an obligation to repair a building on the land) does not pass to the purchaser of the land. While this apparent anomaly is generally not applicable to negative or restrictive covenants, in common law it remains applicable to positive covenants. However, English law now recognises a number of techniques and devices by which that burden may be enforced against a subsequent owner of the affected land, especially in the case of a **scheme of development**.

In the US, several jurisdictions follow the common law principle, so that positive covenants that are clearly personal in nature (other than those between landlord and tenant) are not enforceable against a subsequent acquirer of the land who does not have notice of the agreement. However, covenants that involve the expenditure of money on land, or involve its use in a direct and not a collateral way (covenants that 'touch and concern the land'), are generally enforceable against the acquirer of the servient land, provided the covenant is one that the courts can reasonably enforce. In particular, covenants that form part of a scheme of development are normally enforceable, whether they are positive or negative. In the US, also called an 'affirmative covenant'. cf. **negative covenant**, **restrictive covenant**. See also **real covenant**.

positive easement   See **easement**.

positive leasehold[US]   A **leasehold interest** that has a marketable value, i.e. one where the rent payable under the lease (the **contract rent**) is less than the current **market rent**. See also **leasehold value**.

positive leverage[US]   See **leverage**.

positive servitude   See **servitude**.

positive spread investment (PSI)   An investment that provides a return that exceeds the cost of the capital (debt and equity) required for its acquisition. See also **cash-on-cash return**, **weighted average cost of capital**, **yield gap**.

possession   The detention and control of property, together with the continuous and express intention to retain that property to the exclusion of others. Possession of real property generally means being on the property. Possession may be held irrespective of ownership or title; it consists primarily of "actual **occupancy** as distinct from **ownership**", *The Oxford English Dictionary*, 2nd ed., 1989. Possession is generally a matter of fact, but may not be lawful; whereas ownership is a right recognised and protected by law. Ownership is a right to enjoy the use and benefit thereof and usually includes the right to destroy and, especially, includes the right to dispose of the subject to another. Possession may include some of these rights but not all. 'Possession' may be considered in four senses: firstly, physical or 'actual possession'; secondly, possession as attributed to someone by law; thirdly, a right to possession, with the authorisation of another; and fourthly, 'constructive possession', an inferred right or intention to hold possession. In its most common usage, possession implies *de facto* or 'actual possession'. This normally means that there is some physical presence, and not merely some entitlement in law. 'Actual' possession is considered to be the most basic form of possession, being the physical detention of property; or in the case of land, actual entry and occupancy. Possession as attributed to someone by law (sometimes called 'possession at law' or 'legal possession') is that right to retain control which is protected when there is title. Possession with the authorisation of another is a right that arises, for example, from a licence or a lease permitting the use of land; it creates a form of title, but one that endures only for a certain period of time. Constructive possession (sometimes called 'legal possession' or 'possession in law') is a right to possession of land as attributed by law, without the necessity of actual possession.

'Possession' upon purchasing real property does not mean necessarily personal or physical entry into possession but, if a property is tenanted, a right to receive the rents and profits.

In the English statutory use of the phrase "interest in possession", 'possession' indicates that there is a "present right of present enjoyment", *Pearson v IRC* [1981] AC 753, 772 (HL). In that respect, it may be distinguished from a right in **reversion** or in **remainder**. However, an owner who has granted a lease has a right to possession, as possession in this context is defined to include "receipt of rent and profits or the right to receive the same, if any", LPA 1925, s. 205(1)(xix) (SLA 1925, s. 117(1)(xix)). cf. *dominium*, occupation. See also **adverse possession, bailment, constructive notice, constructive possession, custody, double rent, eviction, exclusive possession, grounds for possession**(Eng), **holding over, implied notice, mortgagee, possessory interest**(US), **seisin, taking possession, unity of possession, vacant possession**.

possession claim(Eng) A claim for the recovery of possession of land or buildings (Civil Procedure Rules 1998, r. 55.1(a)). Such a claim may be brought by a landlord; a mortgagee; as a claim against trespassers; or as a claim by a tenant seeking relief from forfeiture. The claim is normally started in the county court for the district where the land is situated, although in certain cases it may be started in the High Court. See also **claim form**.

possession order(Eng) An order granted by a court of law consenting to the grant of possession of premises to a landlord. In particular, an order granted by a county court consenting to the termination of a **statutory tenancy** of a dwelling-house that would otherwise continue to benefit from security of tenure. See also **ejectment, eviction, writ of possession**.

possession recovery See **ejectment**(US), **forcible entry and detainer**(US), **grounds for possession**(Eng), **possession order**(Eng).

possessions **Things** that are owned or capable of being owned. The aggregate of a person's tangible wealth. **Goods** and **chattels**. Possessions may include real and personal property, although in common usage the term is used to refer to 'goods and chattels'. See also **chose**.

possessory interest 1. An interest in land that gives the holder a right to current **possession** of the land. See also **vested interest**. 2. An interest in property held by a person who has the use and occupation of property combined with an intention to exclude others. In particular, a right as held by an owner-occupier, a right held under a lease, or the right held by any other grant of a right to **possession** of property. The holder of a licence, easement, or a profit à prendre does not normally have a possessory interest, although a licensee may be granted that right for a short duration. cf. **reversionary interest.   3.**(Eng) See **possessory title.**

possessory interest in land(US)   See possessory interest.

possessory leasehold(Eng)   See **possessory title.**

possessory lien   See **lien.**

possessory title(Eng)   **1.** A title to land that may be registered at the Land Registry by a person in **adverse possession** when the registrar is satisfied that the person is "in actual possession of the land, or in receipt of the rents and profits of the land", and "that there is no other class of title with which he may be registered" LRA 2002, ss. 9(5), 10(6). The applicant may be registered as proprietor, with either a freehold estate or a leasehold estate. The registration with possessory title has the same effect as registration with **absolute title**, except that it does not affect the enforcement of any estate, right or interest subsisting at the time of registration, or then capable of arising (LRA 2002, s. 11(7)). A possessory title may be converted to an absolute title (or, if appropriate, a good leasehold title), without qualification, if the registrar is satisfied as to the proprietor's title, and there is normally an entitlement to conversion after the proprietor has been in possession for 12 years (LRA 2002, s. 62).   **2.** A **title** to property based on a period of actual possession rather than on a deed, will or similar document. Title claimed after a lengthy, uninterrupted, period of **adverse possession.**

possibility   A future event that may, or may not, happen. An event that is contingent on another event or action. An interest in land that is dependent on an event the occurrence of which is uncertain, e.g. the death before a given date of a tenant for life. See also **contingent estate, fee tail after possibility of issue extinct, possibility of reverter.**

possibility of issue extinct   See estate in tail after possibility of issue extinct.

possibility of reverter   A form of **future interest** in land that arises when a person grants a fee simple interest in land to another subject to a contingent event that, if it occurs, would automatically return the fee to the grantor or his heirs. The creation of a **determinable fee** effectively grants the entire fee estate, subject only to the possibility that it may return to the grantor without further action if the given event occurs – the 'possibility' of a reverter (2 *Bl Comm* 109; Helvering v. Hallock, 309 US 106, 60 S Ct 444, 84 L Ed 604, 612 n. 6 (1939)). See also **conditional fee, fee simple defeasible**(US)**, rule against perpetuity.**

post   See **acceptance, offer, service.**

post-occupancy evaluation (POE)(AmE)   The assessment of the strengths and weaknesses of a facility after it has been occupied. The purpose of the evaluation is to review user satisfaction and suitability, efficiency technical performance, and to assess value for money.

post office   See **office, shop.**

potential gross income (PGI)(US)   The maximum **gross income** that can be derived from an investment in property assuming it is 100% leased at market rents and there are no defaulting tenants. cf. **effective gross income.**

potential gross income multiplier (PGIM)(AmE)   See **income multiplier.**

potior est conditio possidentis(Lat)   'Better is the condition of the possessor'. The position of the person in possession is to be preferred.

power **1.** Ability to do, or control, something; especially an ability that arises out of a position of ascendancy. An ability, usually derived from one person and given to another, to exert an influence over a third party; especially a legal authority or capacity to act for another. **2.** An **authority** given by one person (donor) to another (donee) whereby the donee is permitted to deal with or dispose of real or personal property, either for the benefit of the donee or others, where the property is not owned, or not owned solely, by the donee. An authority given to a person to dispose of property which is not his own. A power may be absolute or limited by the donor; nonetheless, it is a discretionary right, unlike a **trust** which generally provides the trustee with particular obligations to perform. A power leaves the act to be done at the will or discretion of the holder of that power, whereas the duties of a trustee are generally mandatory. A power is a right to deal with property in a special way and is distinct from a right of **use** or **ownership**, i.e. it is not a form of property *per se*. cf. **dominion, duty**. See also **power of alienation, power of appointment, power of attorney, power of sale**. **3.** A document that grants legal authority. Thomas, Geraint. *Thomas on Powers*. London: Sweet & Maxwell, 1998.

power appendant or **power appurtenant** An ability to deal with property based entirely on the nature of the estate over which a **power** exists, e.g. the power held by a life tenant to dispose, or grant leases, of the interest that he holds for his (or another's) life.

power center(US) A **shopping center** that comprises predominately discount or 'off-price stores' and, due to its size and price competition, is able to act as a major or powerful draw for consumers. "A type of super community shopping center that contains at least one super anchor store (perhaps a discount department store or warehouse club), multiple off-price category-specific anchors, and only a minimal number of small, side-space tenants that together constitute no more than 10 to 15 percent of the total gross leasable area (GLA)", O'Mara, W. Paul et al., *Developing Power Centers*. Washington D.C.: Urban Land Institute, 1996, p. 1. A power center does not normally have one dominant anchor store, but comprises a number of medium-size stores, which together provide significant pulling power. A power center generally has more than 250,000 square feet of space.

power coupled with an interest A power over property that is accompanied by an interest in that property, or where the holder of the power has a right to deal with the property, as distinguished from a 'naked power' whereby the holder has no interest or right over the subject property. See **agency coupled with an interest**.

power of a mortgagee See **mortgagee**.

power of advancement(Eng) See **advancement**.

power of alienation An authority given to someone which permits that person to grant, sell, assign, or otherwise transfer an interest in property. See also **alienation, restraint on alienation**.

power of appointment An authority given, by deed or will, to enable a person to select or choose who is to receive property, or a benefit from property that is the subject of the power, whether it be the enjoyment of an estate or the income therefrom. The person granting the authority, who usually owns the property, is called the 'donor'; the person to whom that authority is given is the 'donee' or 'appointor'; and the person who will receive the benefit, or in whose favour the appointment is made, is the 'appointee' or 'object of the power'. The donee does not have a direct or beneficial interest in the subject property. A power of appointment may be distinguished from a **trust**, because the former gives a discretion to the appointor (who may not be compelled to make any appointment); whereas if a trust directs the trustees to do something, it is imperative that they do it, otherwise that duty may be effected by a court of law. A power of appointment may be: 'general', when the donee has an unrestricted ability to select the beneficiaries, which may include the donee; 'particular', 'limited' or 'special', when he must choose from a limited class of beneficiaries (e.g. the children of the donor); or 'hybrid', when he may grant the power to anyone, except a specified class or group of persons. A power of appointment may be: 'collateral', when the appointor has no present or future interest in the subject property; 'in gross', when he has some interest in the property, but one that cannot be affected by the exercise of the power (as where the holder of a fee simple settles land on others and reserves to himself a special power); or 'appendant' or 'appurtenant', when the power is affected by the nature of the estate that has been granted, as with a life estate where leases will be limited by the life in question. In the US, sometimes called a 'dispositive power'. See also **power, rule against perpetuities**.

power of attorney   A written instrument by which one person or persons (**principal**, appointor, or constituent) authorises another (**attorney** or agent) to act on his behalf, or represent him or her, in a general or specified manner. A power of attorney may be 'general' or 'special'. 'Power of attorney' may refer also to the authority granted by the principal to the attorney or to the instrument by which the power is granted (which may also be called, if appropriate, a 'letter of attorney'). See also **authority**.

power of leasing   The power of a **mortgagor** in possession to grant leases of the mortgaged property.

power of sale   1. The right of a mortgagee to sell property, secured by a **mortgage**, upon default of the mortgagor. The power of a person who has a right to the proceeds of sale of property held as security for a debt to substitute money for property sold. In particular, the means by which a mortgagee exercises his power as contained in mortgage deed to sell the property pledged as security for the mortgage loan, without recourse to a court of law.

In the US, 'power of sale', or 'power of sale foreclosure' generally refers to the procedure by which property is sold upon a default by the mortgagor. In many jurisdictions, this is the only means for recovering the value of the property held as security for a mortgage. In some jurisdictions, the power of sale cannot be exercised directly by the mortgagee, but must be exercised either by a sheriff or, in some states, by a public trustee or similarly authorized party. This power must be exercised strictly in accordance with the loan documentation, as well as any power of sale statute, in particular as to the notice requirements that must be given to the mortgagor or any other affected party. However, the procedure is generally less formal than a **judicial foreclosure**.

In English law, provided the mortgage is made by **deed**, a mortgagee has a power, when the mortgage money becomes due and is not paid by the mortgagor, to sell the mortgaged property (LPA 1925, s. 101(1)(i)). A power of sale may be exercised without recourse to a court of law, but there are detailed statutory conditions that must be met before that power can be exercised (LPA 1925, ss. 101-107). The power of sale is the most common remedy available to a mortgagee in the event of default by the mortgagor. It may also be made the appropriate remedy by a court of law, instead of the grant of consent to **foreclosure**. If the mortgage is not made by deed, the mortgagee may not sell the mortgaged property without the mortgagor's consent, or without recourse to a court to ask for a sale in order to discharge the mortgage debt. Also, under English law, once a power of sale has accrued, the mortgagee may exercise that power as he chooses. He need not wait for the market to improve, nor need he give the mortgagor's interest greater importance than his own, provided he does not seek to cheat the mortgagor. On the other hand, he must take reasonable precautions to obtain the true **market value** of the mortgaged property at the date on which he decides to sell, and the sale must be a genuine sale by the mortgagee to an independent purchaser at a price honestly arrived at. However, a building society is under a statutory obligation to obtain the best price that can reasonably be obtained (Building Societies Act 1986, Sch. 4).

In the US, 'power of sale' may refer also to a clause in a mortgage deed, or **deed of trust**, whereby the mortgagee, or trustee, is given the power, in the event of default by the mortgagor, to sell the property by public auction, without the intervention of a court of law or appropriate authority. Thus, a deed of trust may be described as "a mortgage with power of sale", Bank of Italy Nat'l T. & S. Ass'n v. Bentley, 217 Cal 644, 20 P.2d 940 (1933). cf. **strict foreclosure**(US). See also **foreclosure sale**(US), **once a mortgage, always a mortgage, receiver**. **2.**(Eng)The right of a **tenant for life** to sell settled land, or any part thereof, or any easement, right or privilege over the land, at the best price obtainable (SLA 1925, s. 38). See also **capital money, overreachable interest**.

power of termination   See **right of re-entry, termination**.

practical completion   The completion of building construction work to a point at which a building or structure can be used for the purpose for which it is intended. Completion of all the work that has to be constructed, other than *de minimis* items and items that amount to latent defects under the terms of the contract. Also called 'substantial completion'. See also **certificate of completion**(US), **certificate of practical completion**(Eng), **substantial performance**.

praedial   Things or rights that relate to **land**. In the civil law, 'praedial' denotes the virtual equivalent of 'real', meaning that something has become part of the land or building; "solid movables [which] seem to be fixed to the houses by the will of the ancestor", 2 *Bl Comm* 428.

praedial servitude or **predial servitude**   In Roman, civil law, or Scots law, a **servitude** or easement over the land of another. (In Louisiana, spelt 'predial' (La CC, 650).) See also **real servitude**.

prairie value   The value of an area of land in its natural and unimproved state. See also **raw land, waste land**.

preamble   **1.** The introductory part of a contract, statute or ordinance. For example, the opening words of the Constitution of the United States or a general explanation of the purpose and effect of an Act of Parliament, an Act of Congress or a municipal ordinance. The preamble follows the title, precedes the enacting clauses, and sets out the spirit or intent of the document. As a rule, it is not intended to have any legal effect but merely to explain the objective of the document. See also **recital**.   **2.**(Eng)A description of the general requirements of each trade in a **bill of quantities**.

precarious possession   Possession at the will of another. See also **tenancy at will**.

precario(Lat)   'Entreaty'; 'permission'. See also *nec vi nec clam nec precario*, **prescription**.

precatory words   Words of entreaty or suggestion – precatory being derived from *precari*, 'to pray'. In particular, words in a will or trust deed requesting (but not directing) that something be done; for example, 'desiring that', 'in the full confidence that', or 'being my dying wish that'. Words used in a will or to create a trust should be imperative and not precatory. Thus precatory words do not normally form part of the enforceable provisions of the will.

precedent   **1.** A judgement or decision of a court that acts as a basis for determining future legal decisions in similar cases. A precedent may be 'original' and create new rules, or be 'declaratory' and apply existing rules. In **common law**, as a rule, a single precedent, in particular one that is reasoned by a court of superior jurisdiction, is binding on a court when considering a similar case. cf. **custom**. See also **condition precedent**, *ratio decidendi*. **2.**(Eng)A draft document that is used as a guide for others, e.g. a **standard-form document**. See also **conditions of sale, form document**(US).
Butterworths Encyclopaedia of Forms and Precedents. 50 vols. 4th ed. Looseleaf. London: Butterworths.

precedent estate(US) See **preceding estate**.

preceding estate An **estate** that comes before a limited **future estate**. Sometimes called the 'prior estate' or, in the US, a 'precedent estate'. See also **particular estate**, **qualified fee**, **remainder**.

precinct 1. A part of a town or city set aside for political or administrative purposes. In particular, in the US, a geographical and legal subdivision of a county, a voting district, or as a police district. See also **civic center**. 2. An area or part of a territory (e.g. a town) that has definite bounds or functions, especially one demarcated by an imaginary line or by a physical limit such as a wall. In land-use planning, the term is often used to refer to an area set aside for shopping and associated pedestrian areas; especially an area that is traffic free, i.e. a 'pedestrian precinct'. See also **pedestrian precinct order**(Eng).

precinct scheme(Aus) A scheme that is established for the **subdivision** of an area of land into separate community developments where there are two or more uses. A precinct plan shows the areas for the different uses and is used as the basis for further subdivisions into neighbourhood plans or strata plans. A precinct scheme is drawn up mainly to deal with a large mixed-use development. See also **community scheme**, **strata scheme**.

preclosing(US) An arrangement prior to a **closing** by which the parties to a real estate transaction agree to the principal issues that might arise at the closing, such as the form of documents, proration of costs, etc. Also called a 'dry closing', especially when all the documents are agreed in their final form and only the final signature and disbursement of funds remains. See also **escrow**.

predatory lending(AmE) Any one of a number of ways of lending that is made using deception or fraudulent practices, such as charging high loan fees, equity skimming, or charging excessive insurance premiums. See also **disclosure**

statement, fraud, settlement statement, unconscionable bargain, undue influence, usury.

predecessor in title One who previously held title to a property and through whom another has established his **root of title** to that property.

predial servitude(US) See **praedial servitude**.

pre-emption See **leasehold enfranchisement**, **pre-emption entry**, **right of pre-emption**.

pre-emption entry(US) Open and peaceful entry onto **public lands** to establish a pre-emptive title. In particular, an entry made onto an area of unappropriated public lands, under the provisions of an Act of Congress of 1841 (or subsequent provisions), in order to claim a right to purchase that area of land. Pre-emption entry takes effect from the time of actual entry, unlike entry onto land that is to form part of a **homestead** which does not take effect until the right is recorded at the land office. See also **open lands**, **patent**.

pre-emptor One who has a **right of pre-emption**.

preentry(Eng) A customary right of a tenant, who is to take over a farm in the spring, to enter onto land before his tenancy begins in order to prepare the land and sow crops. cf. **entry**.

preferred creditor A creditor with a claim that takes precedence over one or more other creditors. See also **priority**.

preferred return or **preferred yield** The percentage return or yield that one investor, or a lender, receives from an investment before any income is paid to any other investor or lender. Thus, if an investor in a joint venture is to receive a 'preferred' return of 7%, he will receive all the income as long as the investment yields 7% or less. As and when the investment return exceeds 7%, the parties divide the income over and above the preferred return according to the terms of their agreement. A preferred yield should be distinguished from a 'guaranteed yield' because, with the latter, one party guarantees to make up the difference between the income received from the investment and the yield level stipulated in the agreement between the parties. Also called a 'priority return' or 'priority yield'.

prefunding commitment   See **forward commitment**.

prejudice   **1. Injury** or **damage** to a person's rights. See also **without prejudice**.   **2.** A tendency to favour one side, or one point of view, over another.

prelease(AmE)   An agreement to grant a lease that is entered into before the subject property is ready for occupation. In particular, an agreement for a lease entered into before, or while, a building is under construction. In Britain, generally called a 'pre-let' and in Australia, a 'pre-lease agreement'. See also **agreement for a lease**, **license**.

pre-lease agreement(Aus)   See **prelease**.

pre-let(BrE)   An agreement for a lease entered into before, or while, a building is under construction. See also **prelease**(AmE).

preliminaries(BrE)   An introduction to a **specification** or **bill of quantities**. The preliminaries, or strictly the 'preliminary clause', sets out items that are not a direct part of the physical work of a building contract, but are essential to the execution of that work. In particular, a section of a building contract that sets out matters that do not affect any particular trade. For example, the names of parties to a building contract; a description of the site; the respective liabilities of the employer and contractor; an outline of the work involved; work to be undertaken by nominated subcontractors; general conditions of the contract; and contingencies. cf. **preamble**. See also **provisional sum**.

preliminary enquiries(Eng)   See **title search**.

preliminary injunction   See **injunction**.

preliminary report(US)   See **title report**.

premises   **1.** A proposition or statements made as a preface to something else.   **2.** A description of a definite property, especially a house or building. A distinct part of a property; or that which is closely associated with, or is appurtenant to, a property, e.g. the **curtilage** or land surrounding a property, and used in connection with that property. "The word 'premises' is of broader meaning than the word '**building**'. It may mean land alone or land with buildings and appurtenances", Township of Maplewood v. Tannenhaus, 64 NJ Super 80, 165 A.2d 300, 303 (1960).

In English statute law, in the context of **business premises** (L&T Act 1954, s. 23(1)), 'premises' has a broad meaning equivalent to property in the common usage; it has a meaning that is not confined only to buildings, "'it means also at least the land on which the buildings are erected and the land immediately surrounding the buildings ... [as well as] some incorporeal hereditament such as, for instance, easements.' [*Whitley v Stumbles* [1930] AC 544 (HL)]", *Bracey v Read* [1963] Ch 88, 94, [1962] 3 All ER 472, 476-477. Similarly, in the context of a liability for 'defect premises' (Defective Premises Act 1972), 'premises' encompasses the entire property. See also **appurtenance, demised premises, hereditament, premises liability, tenement**.   **3.** That part of a deed that actually effects the transfer. Strictly speaking, the part of the deed that precedes the **habendum** and describes the subject matter of the deed.   **4.** The subject matter of a **lease** or **conveyance**. "In strict conveyancing language the word 'premises' is used as meaning the subject matter of the **habendum** in a lease", *Whitley v Stumbles* [1930] AC 544, 546 (HL). See also **premises clause, recital**.

premises clause   The clause in a formal deed that describes the property to be conveyed. That part of a conveyance that precedes the **habendum**

which, in turn, describes the duration of the interest to be granted. The premises clause or merely the 'premises' may also include those sections or paragraphs that contain any introduction, a statement or recital of the facts and reasons for the grant, names of the parties, the consideration, as well as the subject-matter, i.e. it is the part that 'goes before' the detailed provisions of the conveyance. In the US, sometimes called the 'caption' as it forms part of the introductory part of a deed. See also **parcels clause**.

premises liability　The liability of an owner or occupier for the condition of a property, especially for the risk of injury to any person who may enter onto the property. See also **duty of care**, **fit for habitation**[(Eng)], **fit for the purpose**, **invitee**, **negligence**, **strict liability**, **trespass**, **visitor**, **warranty of habitability**[(US)].

premium　**1.** A bonus or bounty. A payment made as an inducement to action or as a reward for loss. An amount that exceeds the proper or reasonable **consideration** for an agreement; especially a payment made to encourage a loan or induce a bargain. In particular, a sum of money paid merely for the privilege of obtaining a right to property, e.g. a capital sum paid at the start for the right to take the lease. A premium may represent a form of **fine** required for a right to property; it may be a capitalised prepayment of **rent**; or it may be a deposit as **security** for unpaid rent or damage to the demised premises. A premium usually takes the form of cash, but it may take any other form that represents money's worth, e.g. goods, services or acceptance of a loan.

In English valuation practice, the term 'premium' is commonly used as a payment for the right to acquire a lease, i.e. it is the single payment made for the purchase of the **leasehold value**. In English law, 'premium' generally refers to a payment for a right to enter into a property, i.e. a penalty or **key money** paid by the tenant for a right to possession. In the case of many forms of residential tenancy, it is illegal to demand a premium in addition to rent, for the grant, renewal, or continuance of the tenancy.

In the US, a single upfront payment of rent is referred to simply as 'advance rent', 'advance rental' or 'rent in advance' and, if the payment is for the right to acquire or take an assignment of a lease, it may be referred to as a 'bonus deposit'. cf. **discount**. See also **deposit**, **security deposit**.　**2.** Consideration paid for a chance to receive a reward or bonus; e.g. an amount paid above the par or face value of a share, or the price paid for an option. An amount charged by the lender for the grant of a loan.　**3.** Consideration to be paid, at one time or from time to time, by an insured party under a contract of insurance; the sum of money that is set down in an **insurance policy** as the price the insured pays for the undertaking by the insurer to pay for a loss sustained by the insured as a result of an event against which the insurance is provided – the price of an **indemnity**.　**4.** The consideration paid for the assignment of a lease, normally as represented by the capitalised value of the difference between the rent payable under the lease, i.e. the contract rent, and the market rental value of the demised premises. 'Premium' may also be used to refer to any payment that is made by a tenant that amounts to: (i) the value over and above the market value of the leasehold interest, as paid for the purchase of a lease; (ii) the price paid over and above the value of the tenant's fixtures and fittings; or (iii) consideration paid for the purchase of **goodwill**. See also **reverse premium**.

premium rent　A rent that is above the market value. In particular, a rent that is paid by a retailer for a store in a prestigious or special location.

prepaid expense　**1.** An **expense** paid before it is due, or paid for a benefit not yet received. In particular, an expense that covers a future period such as a new fiscal year or the period after the transfer of a property. For example, an insurance premium paid for a forthcoming year or rent paid in advance. See also **deferred charge**, **rent in advance/rent in arrears**.　**2.**[(US)]An expense paid in advance of a real estate closing, such as an insurance premium, or mortgage interest paid when there is a mortgage in place that is to be assumed by the purchaser.

prepared to purchase 'Prepare' is derived from the Latin *præparare*, 'to make ready' or 'to procure'. A person who has been procured as being a ready purchaser beforehand. One who is **ready, willing and able** to complete the purchase of a property. See also **prospective purchaser**.

prepayment **1.** A **payment** in advance. In particular, in real estate, the payment of rent before the due date or a partial or total payment of the outstanding balance on a mortgage before the due date. See also **prepaid expense, prepayment fee, rent in advance/rent in arrears**. **2.** The payment of a note or mortgage debt before its date of maturity. See also **prepayment privilege**.

prepayment clause A clause in a mortgage deed that makes a provision for the mortgagor to repay the outstanding debt before the due date. cf. **acceleration clause**. See also **equity of redemption, prepayment penalty**.

prepayment fee or **prepayment penalty** A special charge or **penalty** demanded of a mortgagor when a mortgage is repaid before it becomes due. Although a prepayment penalty may be valid 'per se', an extortionate amount will be considered a **clog** or **fetter** on the **equity of redemption**.

In the US, courts will generally uphold the validity of prepayment fees, especially when both parties are knowledgeable and had reasonably equal bargaining positions. However, many states regulate the amount of prepayment fees that may be demanded, especially for residential real estate loans. In a few jurisdictions, any prepayment fee is prohibited and in many other jurisdictions, the amount is limited or the period during which the fee may be demanded is restricted.

Also called a 'pay-off penalty' or 'early redemption charge', or a 'prepayment premium', especially when the amount is a fixed as a percentage of the balance amount outstanding and that percentage declines during the early years of the loan. See also **lock-in provision**.

prepayment premium See **prepayment fee, prepayment privilege**.

prepayment privilege **1.** The right of a mortgagor to repay the outstanding principal, in full or in part before the normal maturity date, without paying a **penalty** or any other form of fee. Also called an 'anticipation privilege'. See also **acceleration clause, equity of redemption, lock-in provision, prepayment clause, prepayment fee**. **2.** (US)The right under an **installment land contract** to be permitted to prepay the entire balance of the purchase before the date set for payment in the contract.

pre-sale The sale of a new property before construction is completed, in particular before construction has commenced. See also **forward commitment, sale off plan**.

prescription The acquisition, or extinguishment, of a right over another's land (such as an **easement, profit à prendre**, or other **incorporeal hereditament**) by the uninterrupted use and enjoyment of that right for an extensive period of time. Prescription, like **custom**, results from established user and reaches a point at which the law says that the user is sufficient evidence that it was properly obtained and should continue unabated: "prescription and custom are brothers, and ought to have the same age, and reason ought to be the father, and congruence the mother, and use the nurse, and time out of memory to fortify them both", *Rowles v Mason* (1612) 2 Brownl & G 192, 198, 123 Eng Rep 892. However, prescription (unlike custom) is claimed as a personal right and cannot be claimed by the public at large.

Prescription may be distinguished from **adverse possession** or 'limitation' in that prescription applies only to incorporeal hereditaments (intangible rights to land such as easement or profits à prendre), whereas adverse possession applies to land itself and other corporeal hereditaments (tangible property). Prescription creates a new or substituted right to an intangible claim over land (or technically recognises that the right should be allowed to continue to exist); whereas limitation destroys one person's right to claim that the law should protect his right to hold land. Limitation is essentially governed by the period fixed by law; whereas prescription rests on a presumption of some previous grant and is based upon principles established by the common law. Prescription is based on **user**, whereas adverse possession is based on occupation and possession that are the necessary rights inherent in the ownership of land.

The acquisition of a right by prescription is not readily accepted by the courts, and requires: (i) a period of actual and continuous user, although minor interruptions are permissible provided the right has been enjoyed as and when required; (ii) that the use was acquiesced in by the party against whom it is claimed and enjoyed as of right, the right cannot arise from the grant of a mere privilege or 'permissive use'; (iii) that it is enjoyed *nec vi, nec clam, nec precario* – 'not by force, not by stealth, not with permission'; (iv) that it is claimed as an incorporeal right against a corporeal hereditament and, normally, against a fee simple estate; and (v) that it can be said to **lie in grant**, i.e. it is the form of right to property that can be transferred by deed and it is not merely a personal right or a right in the nature of personal property (which in this context includes a leasehold).

A prescriptive right may be claimed: (i) by common law; (ii) under the doctrine of **lost modern grant**; or (iii) based on statute law. At common law, it is necessary to show that the use had existed since 1189 or as far back as any witness can recall; unless there is absolute proof that the right could not have existed in 1189 or must have come into existence at some time after 1189, as when a building that forms an essential object of the right has been erected after 1189. 'Lost modern

grant', or 'presumed grant', circumvents the later restraint imposed by common law by assuming that there was a grant of the right before 1189, but the deed of grant has been mislaid. In practice, the courts recognise that if it can be shown that the right has been enjoyed for living memory (usually taken as over 20 years) it is likely to support a prescriptive claim, unless there is evidence that at some point during the 20 years there was no person capable of making or receiving the grant or such grant would contravene a statute.

The more usual means of establishing a prescriptive right is based on statute law. Thus, in English law, an easement (other than a right of light) can generally be established by 20 years of uninterrupted use 'as of right', and a profit à prendre and a right of common require 30 years. A right of light must have been enjoyed for 20 years, but the use need not have been exercised as of right (Prescription Act 1832, ss. 1-3). A claim to any such prescriptive rights will be defeated if it can be shown to have been enjoyed by *vi* (force), *clam* (secrecy), or *precario* (permission).

In the US, the basic principles of *nec vi, nec clam, nec precario* and the need for actual, adverse, open, continuous and uninterrupted user are essential to the establishment of a prescriptive right. The prescriptive right can never be acquired merely by the "consent, permission, or indulgence of the owner" of the property affected; there must be a distinct and positive assertion of a hostile right brought home to the owner by words or acts. However, the doctrine of lost modern grant and many of the common law rules have been largely superseded by statute law. The periods of time required to acquire a right by prescription correspond in most jurisdictions to those required to acquire title by adverse possession. In most jurisdictions, an easement for light and air or lateral support cannot be acquired by prescription, nor can a right to a view be established as a prescriptive easement. Other easements and profits à prendre require 5, 10 or 20 years, according to the jurisdiction.

Once acquired, a prescriptive right cannot be

enlarged beyond the user that was enjoyed during its period of acquisition; at least it must not fundamentally change the character or identity of the right or significantly increase the burden on the servient land.

In Australia and Canada, most jurisdictions have passed legislation to remove the right to acquire negative easements (air, light and support) by prescription.

In the US, although the terms 'prescription' and 'adverse possession' may be used to refer to a right over land and the rights to the ownership of land respectively, in most jurisdictions the process for the acquisition of such rights has virtually merged. Some courts use the terms 'prescription' and 'prescriptive period' in relation to the adverse possession of real property; and in some jurisdictions the acquisition of title to property by adverse possession is termed 'prescription'. cf. **dedication**. See also **tacking**.

prescriptive easement(US)   An easement acquired by **prescription**, as distinguished by one obtained by **grant**. Also called an 'easement by prescription'.

prescriptive title(US)   A title to land acquired by 'prescription' (or, more strictly speaking, by **adverse possession**).

present   1. To **offer**, **tender** or deliver; for example, a document or instrument for payment. See also **delivery**.   2. A **gift**.

present estate or **present interest**   An estate, or interest, in **possession**; an estate in land vested-in-possession. cf. **future estate, future interest**. See also **vested interest**.

present value (PV)   1. The value of a right to a future sum of money after allowing for a **discount**, or reduction in value, due to the effluxion of time. Also called 'present worth'. See also **net present value**; Appendix C, **Financial Formulae**.   2. The current value of something after taking full account of depreciation, or

appreciation, and any improvement or wear and tear. See also **market value**.   3. The value of something at the present time, as distinguished from the original cost.

present value of one   See Appendix C, **Financial Formulae**.

present value ratio   The ratio of the **present value** of the cash flow receivable from an investment to the present value of the expenditure incurred in making the investment. The ratio of 'cash inflows' to 'cash outflows'. See also **net present value**.

present worth   See Appendix C, **Financial Formulae**.

present worth factor(US)   See Appendix C, **Financial Formulae**.

presents   A word used in a **deed** to refer to the deed itself, e.g. "and now by these presents it is agreed that …".

preservation area(Eng)   See **area of outstanding natural beauty, conservation area, preservation district**.

preservation district(US)   An area of land or a district that is designated to be maintained in substantially its present condition. A preservation district may be an urban area, or it may be an open space, scenic area, beach, forest, etc. See also **historic sites**.

preservation order(Eng)   See **building preservation notice, tree preservation order**.

presumed grant   See **easement, prescription**.

presumption   1. An inference, or taking something for granted, based on other established facts. A presumption continues until rebutted by other evidence. See also **constructive notice, hearsay, lost modern grant, prescription**,

resulting trust. **2.** The taking of **possession** or **occupation** of something without due right. A 'presumptive title' is one based solely on actual occupation, without any apparent legal right to possession. See also **presumptive title, seizure**.

presumption of grant(US) See **lost modern grant**.

presumptive title Title that is acquired in good faith based on **possession**, but without any actual legally established right. See also **adverse possession, color of title**(US).

presumptive trust(US) See **resulting trust**.

preventative injunction See **injunction**.

preventative maintenance Maintenance or repair carried out to a building, plant or equipment in order to prevent, or in anticipation of, excessive deterioration or need of repair at a later date. See also **deferred maintenance**.

price That which is given for something bought. The **cost** at which something is obtained, expressed in terms of **money** or its equivalent. The actual amount paid for something in the open market. The amount or worth (generally in the form of money) paid or demanded for, or placed on, something. A measure, in terms of money, of the exchange **value** of property, goods or services. "Price, to an economist, is what is given in exchange for a good or service. Price, in this sense, is determined by the forces of supply and demand, Adam Smith ... called our notion of price 'value in exchange', contrasted to 'value in use' ... Economists take care to distinguish the words 'price' and 'value', they also distinguish the *price* of an object (what it sells for) from its *cost* (the expense of making the object)", Joseph E. Stiglitz, *Economics* (2nd ed. 1993), pp. 91, 92. Wages are the price of labour; **interest** the price for the use of money; **profit** the price of capital; and **rent** the price for use and occupation of land. Price, cost and value are given a similar meaning when converted to a pecuniary unit, but clear distinction should be drawn between these terms because a property may cost one amount, then be priced at another, but be valued at a third figure – it is important to know the value of property and not just the price, for therein lies a profit (or loss). See also **asking price, custom, fair price, market price, market value, purchase price, reserve price**(BrE)/**reserved price**(AmE). **2.** The amount set out in a contract for the sale of property; called in law the **consideration**. The price or consideration under a contract should be certain or capable of being made certain. A price that is to be determined based on a method that a court can use, without the parties having to express their views, such as by independent appraisal or arbitration, is an acceptable consideration to support a contract; but an option to purchase or lease a property merely at an "agreed rent" or an "appraised value" is unlikely to be enforceable. See also **conditional contract, rent**.

price-earnings multiplier See **price-earnings ratio**.

price-earnings ratio The ratio of the market value of an ordinary share in a company to the net annual earnings after tax available for distribution to the holder of one ordinary (equity) share in the company. Effectively, a price earnings (P/E) ratio represents the number of years required for the earnings of a company, which are available for distribution to the ordinary shareholder (i.e. after the payment of any dividends due to preference or minority interest shareholders), to 'pay back' the cost of acquiring a share in the company. When applied in reverse, to the earnings of a company, in order to assess the capital value of a share, the ratio is called a 'price earnings multiplier', or 'earnings multiplier' (in effect this multiplier is equivalent to the **capitalization factor**(AmE) or **years' purchase**(BrE) that is used to capitalise the income from a property). The P/E ratio is the reciprocal of the **earnings yield**. See also **yield**.

price-level-adjusted mortgage (PLAM) A

mortgage loan in which repayment rate is linked to a measure of changes in prices, usually retail prices as based on a cost-of-living or consumer price index. If the interest is fixed (or varies with market conditions) and the outstanding principal is adjusted, the mortgage is usually called a 'price-level-adjusted mortgage' or an 'inflation-adjusted mortgage'. If the interest rate is adjusted in line with a specific index, it is called an 'index-linked mortgage' or 'indexed mortgage'. In the latter case, part of the interest rate may be fixed and part may be adjusted in line with inflation. See also **adjustable-rate mortgage, equity of redemption**.

price take-off method(US)   See **quantity survey method**.

prima facie(Lat)   'On first appearances'; 'on the face of it'. Based on appearance, without better evidence or explanation. *Prima facie* evidence is that which is accepted in law as fact, unless or until rebutted by evidence to the contrary.

primary and secondary rental(US)   A payment in the nature of **rent** that includes both a fixed figure for the property – a true or 'primary rent', and a figure that is determined periodically to cover **operating expenses** – a 'secondary rent'. See also **advance service charge**(BrE).

primary contractor   See **general contractor**.

primary easement(US)   An **easement** that has another easement appendant thereto. For example, a right of way that includes the additional right to enter onto the servient premises for the purpose of repair and maintenance. cf. **secondary easement**.

primary finance(US)   A loan that has the **first priority** in the event of a default, e.g. a first mortgage.

primary term(US)   The period of time under an **oil and gas lease** during which the lease may be kept in existence by the lessee, even though there is no production in paying quantities. This term is usually for 5 or 10 years; after that period

the lease will be extended only if there is 'production in paying quantities' thereby enabling the operator to have an opportunity to make a profit. See also **continuous operations clause**.

primary trade area (PTA)(US)   The **catchment area** from which the majority of trade is drawn to a shopping center or retail store; normally taken as the area from which 60% to 70% of shoppers are drawn.

primary use(US)   The principal use to which a property is put' as distinguished from an **accessory use**, which is merely incidental thereto and, for zoning ordinance purposes, does not affect the primary authorized use. See also **exclusive use, planning unit**(Eng).

prime contractor(US)   See **general contractor**.

prime cost   **1.** The direct cost or expense of a commodity, excluding general overheads and profit.   **2.** The actual cost incurred by a contractor on labour and materials on a particular project. Specifically, the sum paid to a contractor, subcontractor or supplier based on the actual wages or salaries incurred (excluding off-site staff) and the supply of materials or equipment at cost, plus an agreed percentage for overhead and profit. See also **day work, provisional sum**.

prime-cost contract   See **cost-plus contract**.

prime-cost sum   See **provisional sum**.

prime covenant   See **covenant**.

prime lease   See **head lease**.

prime location   The most sought after location for a particular purpose. As a rule, a 'prime location' is that part of an urban area at which land values are at their highest; the location where a business might expect to achieve the highest profit relative to any other location (also called a 'one hundred percent location' or a 'hundred-percent location').

A property may be considered to be in a prime location if it is in the very best position by virtue of demand from prospective occupiers, availability of communications, and proximity to associated uses. Strictly, for any one use, 'prime location' should be applied to only one position, but it tends to be used to describe any good, well established, location—thus making strict definition irksome. cf. **secondary location**. See also **highest and best use, peak pitch, prime property**.

prime parcel(US)   See **prime property**.

prime pitch   See **peak pitch**.

prime property   The choicest or most sought after property. A property considered by an investor to be of the best quality due to such factors as location, age, condition, and security of income. Strictly speaking, a 'prime property' is one that is situated in a **prime location**; suitable for the most discerning occupier; constructed to the highest standard of design and finish, with the most modern facilities; in a first class state of repair; and, if applicable, let to prime tenants (e.g. a credit-rated corporation, major institution or government body) at the current market rent, with the tenant paying all the cost of maintaining and repairing the building. Owing to the dearth of such properties, the term 'prime property' is sometimes used to embrace a property that lacks one or more of these qualities or characteristics, but in most respects is close to this definition. A prime investment property is one that would be valued by adopting the highest capitalisation rate (or the lowest yield) applicable to the category of investment. An area of land or lot upon which a prime property is located is sometimes called a 'prime parcel'. See also **Class A office building, investment property, trophy building**.

prime tenant   **1.** The largest single occupier of a property, or a tenant of good financial standing and reputation who occupies a substantial part of a building. It may be an essential requirement to the financing of a new development project that a prime tenant has been secured. In a shopping center, a prime tenant may be a departmental store and, in an office building, a corporation with a first class or 'investment grade' credit rating. See also **anchor tenant, key tenant**.   **2.** See **head lessor**.

prime trading location   See **peak pitch**.

primogeniture   The condition of being the first born among several children of the same parents; the right to succeed to property as the first born, especially as the eldest son (2 *Bl Comm* 214). The feudal rule of primogeniture provided that the eldest son took all the real estate of intestate parents to the total exclusion of all others; if there is no male heir, females take equally as coparceners. This rule was abolished in English law in 1925. It has also been abolished in the US. See also **coparcenary, entailed estate, intestacy**.

principal   **1.** One who appoints another to act on his behalf; one who appoints another to act as his **agent**. A principal, although he has authority to act on his own behalf, uses the services of another to arrange a transaction for which he will ultimately become liable. See also **agency, undisclosed principal**.   **2.** One of the main parties to a transaction; a person who accepts a primary liability to provide an indemnity for an undertaking or burden accepted by another.   **3.** The capital sum of a debt, as distinguished from the **interest** charged or earned thereon. A capital sum invested with interest.

principal contractor   The contractor who has a direct relationship with the employer or owner, as distinguished from a **subcontractor**. See also **general contractor**.

principal home(Eng)   The place that is a persons main or only **home**. See also **principle private residence**.

principal mansion house   See **mansion house**.

principal meridian line(US)   See **meridian**.

principal moneys   The amount advanced under a loan, as distinct from the interest or any other sum arising out of the agreement. In particular, the **principal** advanced as distinguished from accrued interest that may have been added to the principal amount outstanding.

principal of substitution   See **cost approach**(US), **opportunity cost**.

principal-only (PO) **bond** or **principal-only security**   A security or bond that provides for the beneficiary to receive only repayment of principal. In particular, a security backed by a pool of mortgage loans that provides for the holders to receive payments based on repayments of principal as made by the underlying mortgages. The interest payments are made to other bond holders. cf. **interest–only bond**.

principal private residence(Eng)   The place of residence in the UK accepted by the Inland Revenue as being a person's 'main' home and thus generally eligible for exemption from capital gains tax. An individual may claim such exemption upon disposal of an interest in "(a) a dwelling house or part of a dwelling house which is, or has at any time in his period of ownership been, his only residence, or (b) land which he has for his own occupation and enjoyment with that residence as its garden or grounds up to the permitted area", Tax on Chargeable Gains Act 1992, s. 222(1). The 'permitted area', as a rule, is one acre (including the site of the dwelling house). Where someone owns two or more private houses, he may elect that one be treated as his 'principal private residence' or failing an election the Inland Revenue will judge which house falls within that definition. Capital gains tax will be payable on the sale of any other residence which belongs to that person. See also **principle residence**(US).

principal residence(US)   The place of **residence** accepted as being a person's 'main' home, which may be a single-family home, an apartment, condominium, trailer or houseboat so long as it represents a place of residence. A liability for capital gains tax on a person's 'principal residence' may be deferred in certain circumstance. To qualify as a 'principal residence', the taxpayer must have owned and used the property as his or her principal residence for a period aggregating three years during the last five-year period prior to the date of the sale or exchange of the residence (26 USC, Internal Revenue Code, § 121). See also **principle private residence**(Eng).

principal vesting deed(Eng)   See **vesting document**.

prior appropriation(US)   See **water rights**.

prior charge or **prior mortgage**   A charge, or mortgage, that has **priority** over another (subordinate) obligation and, therefore, may claim satisfaction of its secured debt before the subordinate obligation. See also **first mortgage**.

prior estate   See **preceding estate**.

priority   Something that comes before or precedes, especially that which comes before in time. A superiority of one security over another as recognised by law. In particular, a payment that is made in preference to another, as with distributions to debtors. See also **preferred return**, **priority of a mortgage**.

priority notice(Eng)   A notice lodged at the Land Charges Department of the Land Registry against a parcel of unregistered land by a person who intends to register a **land charge**. The notice must be lodged on form K.6 not later than 14 clear days before the charge is intended to take effect and has the effect that if the charge is made, and provided it is registered within 30 days of the priority notice, it takes effect as if it had been registered at the time the priority notice was lodged (LP(MP)A 1926, s. 4(1); now the LCA 1972, s. 11(1) and the Land Charges Rules 1974, r. 4). Such a notice is used when a rapid succession of transactions takes place, as when a restrictive covenant is placed on land and the land is then immediately mortgaged before the covenant is duly registered.

priority of a mortgage The order in which competing claims of mortgagees are met out of monies realised from the sale of the mortgaged property; especially when the net proceeds from the sale of the property prove insufficient to satisfy all the competing claims. (This right of 'prior' claim is against the property and is independent of any right that a mortgagee may have to sue the borrower on any personal covenant.)

In English law, prima facie, a mortgage ranks according to its time of creation; although priority is governed also by the rule that 'where the equities are equal, the law prevails', so the holder of a **legal mortgage** who does not have **notice** of an **equitable mortgage** will take priority. The complex rules for determining the priority of mortgages may be summarised as: (i) a mortgage protected by a deposit of the title deeds relating to the legal estate depends for its priority on the date on which the mortgagee obtained a deposit of the deeds; (ii) a mortgage that does not take the form of a deposit of the title deeds relating to the legal estate should be registered as a land charge (either as a **puisne mortgage**, if a legal mortgage, or a **general equitable charge**, if an equitable mortgage), and priority is determined by the date of registration (LPA 1925, s. 97); (iii) a mortgage of an **equitable interest** is governed by the date upon which the holder of the legal estate (e.g. the trustee of a settlement of a trust for sale, or the estate owner) is given 'notice' of the mortgage; except that a mortgagee who has actual or constructive notice of a prior mortgage cannot alter his later priority merely by giving notice to the holder of the legal estate; (iv) the priority of a mortgage protected by the deposit of title deeds, and of a mortgage of an equitable interest, may be upset by fraud, gross negligence (especially in seeking the title deeds), misrepresentation, or by estoppel; (v) if the land is registered, the priority of a legal mortgage depends on the date upon which a **registered charge** is created (unless the register otherwise states) or, if the mortgage has not been registered, the date of entry of a **caution** or a **notice**, and not according to the date of creation of the mortgage (LRA 1925, ss. 26, 29, 106 (3)(a)(c)) – the priority of competing equitable mortgages in registered land, as with unregistered land, is dependent upon the date upon which notice is given to the holder of the legal estate; and (vii) in the case of a registrable company charge, since 1985, priority is dependent on the date of registration of the charge (Companies Act 1985, s. 404(1) as inserted by Companies Act 1989, s. 99). Thus, a prospective mortgagee should: (i) seek out the **title deeds** relating to the legal estate, if the land is unregistered, or obtain a copy of the **land certificate**, if the land is registered; (ii) enquire of any existing mortgagee whether he has agreed or undertaken to tack on a further advance to his existing mortgage loan; (iii) search the Land Charges Register, if the land is unregistered, or the Charges Register of the Land Registry, if the land is registered; (iv) notify the holder of the legal estate that he has taken a charge on that interest, if the property offered as security is an equitable interest only; (v) make reasonable enquiries and inspect the property to ascertain whether there are any rights or interests that patently might affect his security, e.g. a person in possession; and (vi) search the **Companies Charges Register** at Companies House if the mortgagee is a company.

In the US, most jurisdictions require a mortgage to be recorded to be enforceable. In such cases, priority is determined by the date of recording and not by the date of execution of the instrument, provided that, at the time of the recording, the party recording the instrument acquired the right for valuable consideration, acted in good faith and does not have **notice** (actual or constructive) of any prior claim. Where recording is not applicable, priority depends primarily on the common law rule of *prior in tempore, potior in jure* – 'first in time, superior in right', i.e. the date of creation of the mortgage; unless there is an agreement or a statutory provision to the contrary. However, a legal mortgage may take priority over any equitable mortgage, even if there is no notice to the legal mortgagee of the grant of the equitable mortgage. As between equitable mortgages, where an equitable mortgagee has notice of a prior equitable mortgage, the prior mortgagee normally takes priority (barring negligence, misrepresentation or fraud). In several jurisdictions, a **purchase money mortgage** executed at the same time as a deed for the purchase of land (but not necessarily money advanced for the construction of a building on the property) has priority over a previously recorded lien. Thus, a mortgagee who executes a mortgage agreement should ensure that the property has been acquired for cash, or risk loosing his priority. A real property tax lien takes priority over all mortgages or liens. In the majority of states, a **mechanic's lien** takes priority over any mortgage or encumbrance entered into after the construction work has commenced. See also **after-acquired clause**(US), **charging order**(Eng), **fixture**, **marshalling**, **minor interest**(Eng), **priority notice**(Eng), **subordination**, **tacking**.

priority return or **priority yield**   See **preferred return**.

private dwelling-house   A dwelling-house occupied by a private person, a family, or closely connected or related persons, but not one divided into separate dwellings or apartments, nor one occupied for business purposes. The use of premises as a 'private dwelling-house' may include sharing with friends or with a paying guest, but does not encompass the conversion to a multiple dwelling without, as a rule, infringing zoning or planning regulations. A property used, or converted, to a **lodging house** or a **boarding house** is unlikely to be classified as a 'private dwelling-house', because then there may not be privacy of entry and exit, or the principal use can no longer be considered as a dwelling for a private family. See also **principal private residence**, **Use Classes Order**(Eng).

private easement   See **private right of way**.

private land(Aus)   Land that the Crown has contracted to sell, or that is no longer owned by the Crown. See also **Crown land**.

private mortgage insurance (PMI)(US)   See **mortgage insurance**.

private nuisance   See **nuisance**.

private offering or **private placement**   The offering or placement of an investment with a limited number of investors, as distinguished from an offering to the public at large. A private offering may be subject to less stringent regulation than an investment that is offered to the public at large as it may not have to comply with the regulations that pertain to public offerings. See also **blue-sky laws**, **blind-pool offering**.

private property   Property held in private ownership, whether held by an individual (or individuals) or a corporation, as distinct from property held by a government or state body. Property held by one individual or a number of individuals to the exclusion of all others, as distinguished from **common property**.

The right of an individual or a group of individuals to acquire and hold private property without restriction or confiscation, except by due process of law, is one of the basic civil rights recognised in democratic liberal states. Once acquired, the right to retain private property is normally protected by government; it is a right that is dependent for its existence on Sovereign or Government power, "without the protection whereof, every man would have equal Right to the same", Thomas Hobbes, *Leviathan* (1651), Ch. XXIX. The right to hold private property is recognised in the Bible (*Kings* 1, xxi); in *Magna Carta* 1215, c. 39; in the French Declaration of the Rights of Man and the Citizen 1789 (art. 17); in the Fifth Amendment to the Constitution of the United States ("no person shall … be deprived of … property, without due process of law; nor shall private property be taken for public use, without just **compensation**"); and the Fourteenth Amendment ("nor shall any State deprive any person of ... property, without due process of law"); as well as in the United Nations Universal Declaration of Human Rights 1948, art. 17: "1. Every one has the right to own property alone as well as in association with others. 2. No one shall be arbitrarily deprived of his [or her] property".

In the US, the term "private property" as used in the Fifth Amendment to the Constitution applies to such property as belongs absolutely to the individual and of which he has the exclusive control and dominion (i.e. it does not include a right that is also a public right as with a right of navigation on a tidal river). Property of a specific, fixed, and tangible nature, capable of being held in possession and transmitted to another, as well as most rights of user and enjoyment of such property (Scranton v. Wheeler, 179 US 141, 21 S Ct 48, 45 L Ed 126 (1899); Corn v. City of Lauderdale Lakes, 95 F.3d 1066, 1074-6 (11th Cir. Fla 1966)). The term property in this context has a broad meaning, encompassing real and personal property, as well as an interest in the property. cf. **communal property**, **public property**. See also **community property**(US), **compulsory purchase**(Eng), **eminent domain**, **expropriation**, **ownership**, **police power**(US), **possession**.

Harris. J. W. *Property and Justice.* Oxford: Oxford University Press, 1996.

Waldron, Jeremy. *The Right to Private Property.* Oxford: Clarendon Press, 1988.

private residence   See **principal private residence**(Eng), **principal residence**(US).

private right of way   A right of way that is limited to one person or a number of persons, but not to the public at large. cf. **highway**. See also **easement**.

private sale   A sale of property carried out other than by **auction**. A sale made as a private act between two parties without any public advertisement or third party intervention.

private zoning(US)   See **restrictive covenant**.

privilege   A right to do or restrain another from doing a specific act or carrying on a particular business. A benefit, exemption, or advantage enjoyed by one person, as distinct from that which is enjoyed as a common advantage or could be enjoyed by the world at large. See also **easement, franchise, option, priority, power, profit à prendre**.

privileged will(Eng)   A will made by a soldier, sailor or airman in actual military service, or a seaman being at sea, regarding their "movables, wages and personal estate" which need not be made in accordance with the usual statutory formalities (Wills Act 1837, s. 11, as amended by Wills (Soldiers and Sailors) Act 1918).

privity   Derived from the Latin *privitas*, 'private'. A tie between two parties that is recognised by law, e.g. that of **contract, tenure, covenant**, blood, etc. A mutual or successive relationship to the same right, interest or property. The mutual relationship that exists between two parties, either as parties to a contract – **privity of contract**; or as parties having a tie to the same estate in land – **privity of estate**. Also, a relationship between any parties where there is a succession of interest in the same property, including a lessor and lessee, assignor and assignee, donor and donee, executor and testate, grantor and grantee. See also **horizontal privity**(US), **vertical privity**(US).

privity of contract   The relationship that exists and extends between the parties to a **contract**. Privity of contract represents the notion of the right of the parties to the contract to sue or be sued; a right, or burden, that persists even though one of the parties has assigned the benefit or obligation of the contract to another. A contract once entered into must be performed, or discharged by subsequent agreement. For example, with a lease (which is a form of contract), a lessee remains liable upon his express covenants, notwithstanding an assignment.

In common law, only the parties to a contract, or

those in 'privity' with it, can take an action for a breach of its provisions. Strictly, a third party cannot take a legal action in respect of a contract to which he is a 'stranger', even though he may have suffered a loss because the contract has not been performed. However, this doctrine is tainted by a number of qualifications. For example: (i) the enforcement of an implied promise or **quasi-contract** in order to prevent an unjust enrichment; (ii) a person may be an implied party to the contract, especially where there is a lien or collateral obligation that affects the third party or there is an intention to create a trust for a third party; (iii) a person may take action under the contract if he can demonstrate that the contract was intended to be for their benefit; (iv) a person may take another's place as party to a contract if he can demonstrate that the other was contracting on his behalf, even though the intervening party was unknown to the other original party to the contract at the time the bargain was struck – the doctrine of **undisclosed principal**; (v) in the law of real property, if two parties have a mutual interest in the same land, e.g. a lessor and an assignee, there is said to be **privity of estate** and each of those parties may have a right to sue or be sued by the other on matters that 'touch and concern the land'; (vi) in certain circumstances, if a right under a contract is assigned to a third party, that party may enforce his right against the remaining original party to the contract; (vii) statute law has intervened to make rights of action available for third parties to a contract. In English law, the LPA 1925, s. 56(1) stipulates that a person may acquire the benefit of a right to land or other property, although he is not named as a party to a conveyance or other instrument, provided that the deed purports to confer that benefit on him. Also, as from January 1, 1996 virtually all covenants in leases are enforceable by or against any party who acquires a right to the lease (including a mortgagee in possession) – whether or not the covenant 'touches or concerns' the land (Landlord and Tenant (Covenants) Act 1995, ss. 1, 2, as amended). In addition, since 1999, any third party to a contract may enforce a condition if: (i) the contract expressly so provides; or (ii) the contract purports to confer a benefit on the third party, unless upon a proper construction of the terms of the contract it appears that the parties did not intend that the condition be enforceable by the third party (Contracts (Rights of Third Parties) Act 1999, s. 1).

In English law, for any tenancy entered into on or after January 1, 1996 the original tenant (and any party to whom he assigns the lease) is liable to perform the covenants of the lease only during the period that he holds the tenancy and he cannot derive any benefit from the landlord's covenants once he has assigned his interest. On the other hand, prior to an assignment, as a condition of granting consent to an assignment of the lease, the landlord can always obtain a guarantee that the assigning tenant will remain liable under the terms of the lease (L&T (Covenants) Act 1995, ss. 5, 16). A landlord who assigns his reversion remains liable for the covenants in the lease throughout its term, unless he obtains an express release from the tenant (L&T (Covenants) Act 1995, s. 7). In addition, where the assignee remains liable under the lease, the landlord must serve notice on the former tenant within six months of any rent or service charge arrears in order to be able to claim for such payments. This latter provision also applies to tenancies created before January 1, 1996 (L&T (Covenants) Act 1995, s. 17).

In the US, a few jurisdictions have adopted the 'English rule' that no one can sue or be sued on a contract to which he is not a party, whilst accepting many similar exceptions to those noted above. However, most jurisdictions (either by precedent or by statute) accept the 'American rule' which may be broadly stated to the effect that a third party may sue to enforce a contract or promise made for his benefit, even though he is a stranger to the contract. However, even though there is no right of action on a contract between two parties, there may be another course of action available, such as an action for a **tort**, breach of **warranty**, or one arising from a **strict liability**. See also **implied contract**, **novation**, **sub-lessee**, **subrogation**, **trust**.

privity of estate A mutual relationship that

is considered present between two parties who have an interest in the same estate in land at the same time. The **privity** that exists between successors in title to the same land. For example, privity of estate exists between a lessor and lessee; between tenants in common; and between a tenant for life and a remainderman. There is said to be **privity of contract** *and* privity of estate between the original parties to a **lease** – the former relationship arising as an incidence of the contract and the latter as an incidence of the lease creating a tie to an estate in land. (It should be noted that there is privity of contract between the parties to an **agreement for a lease**, but strictly no privity of estate until the lease is formally executed.)

Privity of contract and privity of estate persist simultaneously between a lessor and lessee as long as a lease continues. Thus, the existence of privity of estate has no practical significance, at least until either party assigns its interest to a third party. If either the lessor or lessee makes an **assignment** of his interest to a third party, the privity of estate between the original parties no longer exists, but the privity of estate exists between the lessor, or the lessee (whichever remains as party to the lease), and the new party to the lease. In other words, if there is a right to the same property between a direct landlord and a direct tenant there is privity of estate. On the other hand, a tenant who sublets land does not transfer his estate to the subtenant, but merely carves a shorter estate out of his interest and, therefore, there is no privity of estate between a head lessor and a sub-lessee. Also, if a tenant sublets the demised premises and subsequently that tenant's interest expires, even though the subtenant remains in possession of the premises, there is no longer privity of estate because the original tenant no longer has an interest in the land.

The effect of privity of estate is that most lease covenants are enforceable between those parties who are linked by privity of estate; even though there is no privity of contract to enable an action on the contract to be enforced. A lessor can enforce a covenant *in* a lease against an assignee; but not, as a rule, against a **sub-lessee** (unless the sub-

lessee has directly covenanted with the lessor to observe the terms of the lease). Nonetheless, at common law, a covenant may be enforced as a result of the relationship of privity of estate only if it is a 'real' covenant, i.e. it is a **covenant running with the land** (also referred to as a covenant that 'touches and concerns the land' or 'has reference to the subject matter of the lease'). A covenant that is purely 'personal', for example an undertaking by the tenant to pay money to a third party, or that the landlord will not operate a competitive business at another property that is situated near the demised premises, does not 'touch and concern the land' and cannot be the subject of privity of estate.

In the US, some jurisdictions take a less strict view on the requirement for the covenant to 'touch and concern' the land and will enforce most covenants where there is a relationship of privity of estate, provided the acquirer has **notice** of the existence of the covenant.

In English law, for tenancies beginning on or after January 1, 1996 and for most covenants in other leases, the benefits and burdens of landlord and tenant covenants are enforceable by and against any party who acquires a right to the lease (including a mortgagee in possession), whether or not the covenant 'touches or concerns' the land (L&T (Covenants) Act 1995, s. 2(1)); the principle being that all lease covenants are part of the whole transaction. In the US, sometimes called 'privity of title'. See also **horizontal privity**[US], **restrictive covenant, sub-lease, vertical privity**[US].

privity of possession[US] A relationship that exists between two parties that have successive rights to possession of property, as with two claimants to **adverse possession** of a property. See also **privity, tacking**.

privity of title[US] See **privity of estate**.

pro emptore[Lat] 'As the buyer'; 'by the title of a purchaser'.

pro forma statement A statement 'according

to form', i.e. one that shows how a situation might develop. For example, a schedule of the projected income and expenses for a real estate investment over a given period of time. See also **feasibility study**, **operating statement**.

pro rata(Lat) 'In proportion'; 'at the rate of'. See also **apportionment**.

pro tanto(Lat) 'For so much'; 'to that extent'; 'as far as it goes'. A payment made *pro tanto* is a part payment or a payment on account. A purchaser *pro tanto* acquires a **partial interest** (something less than a complete interest) e.g. a lease. A *pro tanto* **assignment** means an assignment of part of the demised premises, but not a sub-lease.

probate The formal procedure by which a court of competent jurisdiction (such as a probate court) signifies that a **will** has been proved as valid, thus enabling the will to be recorded and the **executor** to administer the effects. 'Probate' may also be used to refer to the entire process of administering the estate of a deceased person, or the documents issued by the court to grant the executor authority to deal with the estate of a deceased.

In the England and Wales, probate is administered by the Probate Office. In order to get a grant of probate it is necessary to apply for a 'Grant of Representation'. This may take the form of a 'Probate' issued to one or more of the executors named in the deceased's will; or 'Letters of Administration' issued when there is a will but no executors are named, the executors are unwilling or unable to grant probate, or there is no will or no valid will. See also **administration of an estate**.

probate homestead(US) See **homestead**.

proceed order(US) See **change order**.

proceeds The price or consideration received from the sale of property. Value received for something when converted into money or an equivalent; the total revenue received from something as a result of a sale, disposition, investment or business venture. In particular, the **income** or **revenue** from a property investment. See also **yield**.

procreation See **words of procreation**.

procuration fee See **finance fee**, **finder's fee**.

procuring cause The act or process by which an **agent** or **broker** finds a party who carries a transaction through to the stage required by the principal. In order to be the procuring or 'effective cause' of a transaction, the agent's efforts should be such that they adequately relate to the service for which the principle expected to pay. The 'procuring cause' is the cause that, through a series of events, without break in their continuity, results in the prime objective of the employment of the broker. A broker is deemed to be the procuring cause if he brings together the parties who then consummate the transaction, or he is instrumental in the ultimate consummation of the deal. A broker may be the procuring cause even if others participated in the negotiations, or the principal concluded the negotiations, provided his origination could be traced as an active contribution to the final outcome.

Generally, an agent or broker is considered to be the procuring cause of a transaction when he has procured, introduced, or 'caused to be introduced', a buyer who is **ready**, **willing and able** to acquire the subject property on the terms specified in the agency agreement, unless the agreement specifies that the **commission** is payable only on the **closing** of the transaction. As a rule, a mere 'dry' introduction is not sufficient to amount to being the 'procuring cause', especially if the agent takes no further part or interest in the subsequent negotiations. Where there is more than one broker claiming to have achieved the result, the procuring cause is the one who brings about the required transaction, not the one who made an introduction that resulted in an abandoned agreement; "it is the broker who shakes the tree not the one who runs up and picks the apples who is entitled to the commission", Brennan v. Roach, 47 Mo App 290 (1891). If the broker is the procuring cause, but the owner chooses to take over the final negotiations, or use another agent for the same purpose, and concludes the transaction, the broker is normally entitled to a commission. Sometimes called the 'inducing cause'. See also **extender clause, no-deal, no-commission clause**.

profession A vocation or occupation by which a person earns his or her living and that requires the application of educational knowledge and specialised skills, especially when that skill is of a mental or intellectual nature, rather than purely of a physical or manual nature. Profession is impossible to define precisely. Carrying on a **trade**, or acting as a property agent or broker is not strictly a profession, as it does not fundamentally require extensive educational training; but the work of a valuer, appraiser, or a property investment analyst may be said to be carrying on a profession, as it requires a special level of skill. cf. **business**. See also **professional negligence**.

professional expert A person who is skilled in a **profession**, especially one qualified by education and with a broad depth of experience in a particular area of expertise. See also **expert witness**.

professional indemnity insurance See professional liability insurance.

professional liability insurance A form of insurance that provides an **indemnity** against claims for financial loss arising from **professional negligence**, or other forms of wrong, neglect or misleading advice or treatment given by a skilled professional. Also called 'professional indemnity insurance', or 'malpractice insurance', when issued to members of the medical or allied professions. Such insurance is normally issued on a 'claims-made basis', i.e. any payment under the policy is dependent on when the claim is made, regardless of when the event giving rise to the claim occurred. See also **errors and omissions insurance**.

Enright, W. Ian B. *Professional Indemnity Insurance Law.* London: Sweet & Maxwell, 1996.

professional negligence Negligence that occurs when a person, using his professional skill and judgement, fails to perform his duties according to the standards expected of him. A person who enters into a learned profession undertakes to bring to the exercise of it a reasonable degree of care and skill. This is a level of skill that is required because a person is holding out that he has an expertise that is not available to a lay practitioner. This level of skill is normally dictated by standards laid down as a minimum by a professional association of which the practitioner is a member, or a level of skill that the public might reasonably expect from an experience of the services provided by other members of that profession.

In the US, generally called 'malpractice', especially as applied to the legal, medical or accounting profession. See also **duty of care, misrepresentation, valuer**.

Jackson, Rupert, and John Powell. *Jackson & Powell on Professional Negligence.* 5th ed. London: Sweet & Maxwell, 2002 with cumulative supplements.

Joyce, Lindsay, and Keith Norris. *Valuer's Liability*, 2nd ed. Sydney: The Australian Institute of Valuers and Land Economics, Inc., 1994.

Virgo, John, and Ralph Wynne-Griffiths. *Surveyors' Liability: Law and Practice.* Bristol: Jordans, 1998.

proffer A sum of money that has been agreed as payable for a planning or zoning benefit that has been granted to a landowner. See also **development fee**[US], **planning obligation**[Eng].

profit Pecuniary gain. A benefit, advantage, or gain that can be measured in monetary terms. An amount by which **income** exceeds the **expenditure** committed in order to earn that income, measured over a period of time, commonly a year. The amount by which the proceeds of sale of an asset exceeds the cost of that asset; the excess of return over outlay. In economics, profit is considered as the reward for **risk**, the financial benefit or remuneration for enterprise. It arises from uncertainty, unlike **interest** which arises from a contractual obligation, or **rent** which is derived from the ownership of property. See also **beneficial occupation**, **economic rent**, **mesne profits**, **price**, **profit à prendre**, **profit rent**[BrE], **profits**.

profit à prendre   A right to enter onto the **land** of another in order to take something therefrom that is a produce of the soil and is capable of separate ownership, such as minerals, timber, crops, fruits, pasture, turf, stones, sand, gravel, or even the soil itself; as well as game and fish on land that when killed are capable of ownership. A profit à prendre is not a possessory interest in land, but the subject matter must emanate from the land and be capable of ownership. Water from an open running stream, from a spring or a well, or a right to water cattle at a pond, cannot form the subject of a profit à prendre because the water when taken is not deemed to be part of the soil *per se* and, unless stored in a reservoir or an enclosed pond, is not considered capable of private ownership (although the right to take water may form the subject of an **easement**). A profit à prendre may be distinguished from an easement in that an easement is enjoyed without taking anything from the land itself, and a profit is a right **in gross**, i.e. it does not need to (although it can) benefit another parcel of land (2 *Bl Comm* 34). (In some jurisdictions in the US, an easement is considered also capable of existing 'in gross', but at common law an easement unlike a profit must always be **appurtenant** to land.) A profit à prendre differs from a **licence** in that (like an easement) it creates an interest in land and is not revocable at will (although a licence may not be revocable at will if it is coupled with an interest in land). A profit à prendre may be enjoyed by one person alone, a 'several profit'; or, in most cases, in common with others, a 'profit in common' or **right of common** (although, unlike an easement,

it cannot be enjoyed by a fluctuating class of persons such as the inhabitants of a village). A profit à prendre may be appurtenant, i.e. attached to the land (the 'dominant land') that is benefited by the right and only be enjoyed by the owner of the dominant land; or it may be **appendant**, i.e. annexed to land by operation of law as having been enjoyed from time immemorial.

A profit à prendre may be created by express **grant**, or by express **reservation**, or by **prescription** (or 'presumed grant'); but not by custom. A profit à prendre may be extinguished by: express **release**; by implied release, e.g. by **abandonment**; by the product being exhausted or otherwise ceasing to exist; by unity of the beneficiary and the owner or possessor of the land from which the produce arises (**unity of seisin**); or, in rare instances, by statute.

In the US, a profit à prendre is frequently referred to as a 'right of common' (25 Am.Jur.2d., Easements and Licenses, § 4; Black's Law Dictionary (6th ed. 1990), 'profit, *profit à prendre*'). See also **issues and profits**, **oil and gas lease**[US], **overriding interest**[Eng], **right of common**, **servitude**, **usufruct**, **vicinage**.

Gaunt, Jonathan, and Paul Morgan. *Gale on the Law of Easements*. 17th ed. London: Sweet & Maxwell, 2002.

profit and loss statement (P&L)   See **financial statement**.

profit in common   See **right of common**.

profit rent[BrE]   The difference between the rent reserved under a lease, i.e. the contractual rent, and the rack rent or **market rent** of the demised property, especially the amount by which the lease rent exceeds the market rent. In the US, usually called 'positive leasehold', if the market rent exceeds the contractual rent; or 'negative leasehold', if the market rent is less than the contractual rent. See also **excess rent**, **leasehold value**, **top-slice income**.

profit sharing   See **equity participation**.

profitability ratio (PR) or **profitability index** (PI)   The ratio of the present value of the future anticipated income from a property to its cost. Ideally, this should be 1 when the property is first acquired and increase over time. Although, if the property is held as a leasehold interest, any anticipated increases in income may be outweighed by the depreciation in value as the lease shortens.

profits   The benefits or gains that arise from the actual use or ability to use **land**. 'Profits' denote produce or part of the soil, whether as trees, crops, mines, herbage, etc. (1 *Co Litt* 4b). 'Profits' generally means the right to take something from the soil, being 'profits à prendre' and is used in the term 'rents, issues and profits' to refer to anything that may be derived from land, including the taking of the substance of the land itself. See **issues and profits, mesne profits, profit à prendre**.

profits basis of assessment(BrE)   See **profits method of valuation**.

profits insurance   See **consequential loss insurance**.

profits method of valuation(BrE)   A method of valuing property based on the tenant's ability to pay for the benefit to be derived from the use of that property, i.e. the ability to pay a portion of the commercial profits or receipts that can be derived from the use of the property. Generally, this method of valuation is applied only to premises that are used for a trading purpose, such as a petrol filling station, a retail shop, public house, hotel or restaurant. The simplest way of applying this method is to assume that a tenant can pay as rent a certain percentage of the profits of the business. If a capital value is required, it is assessed by capitalising the assumed rent.

This method of valuation is used in particular to assess the **rateable value** of a property for which there is little comparable evidence of similar premises let on the open market, but for which there is comparable evidence of turnover and trading profits. Although the statute is now repealed, the 'profits basis' may still be described as "the ascertainment of the value of [a] hereditament by reference to the accounts, receipts or profits of an undertaking carried on therein", General Rate Act 1967, s. 115(1). However, the rateable value is based on what a hypothetical tenant could reasonably afford to pay and does not have regard to whether an actual tenant is a flourishing trader or is carrying out business at a loss. Also called the 'accounts method of valuation', and in rating valuation, the 'profits test' or 'profits basis of assessment'. See also **percentage rent**.

profits test(BrE)   See **profits method of valuation**.

program evaluation and review technique   See **project evaluation and review technique**.

progress certificate(AmE/Aus)   A certificate, issued by an architect, engineer or other professional during the course of a building or other improvement, confirming for the benefit of the owner the value of work carried out and normally authorizing **progress payments**.

progress payments   Periodic payments made, in accordance with the terms of a construction contract, for the cost of work carried out by the contractor. Usually such payments are paid in relation to the value of the work carried out under the contract. A **retention sum** is normally deducted from such payments to safeguard against inadequacies in the work. See also **certificate of valuation, instalment, progress certificate**(US).

progression of value theory   A theory that the value of a property is increased by the quality or value of surrounding properties. cf. **regression of value theory**.

progressive rent   A rent that increases automatically during the term of a lease, whether by reference to a particular time or by reference to a particular contingency, e.g. a **graduated rent** or an **indexed rent**.

prohibition   **1.** A **prerogative order** issued to prevent a lower court from exceeding its authority. Such an order is anticipatory so that, unlike an order of *certiorari*, it is intended to prevent an action rather than to remedy an existing deficiency. cf. *mandamus*.   **2.**[Aus]A provision in a planning instrument stipulating that a particular form of development or use is absolutely prohibited.

prohibition notice[Eng]   **1.** A notice served by a local authority on a person who is causing a statutory **nuisance** that is likely to recur, especially a nuisance arising from a building defect of a structural nature. The notice requires the owner or occupier of the premises to take steps to prevent a reoccurrence of the nuisance (Public Health (Recurring Nuisances) Act 1969, s. 1).   **2.** A notice served by an authorised inspector stating that a particular activity may risk causing personal injury and that it should cease until the specified issue has been remedied. cf. **abatement notice**.

prohibitory injunction   See **injunction**.

project   Derived from the Latin *projectus*, 'thrown forward'. A planned undertaking. A specific **plan** or design, especially one prepared for a new land improvement, construction or building scheme. See also **development**, **planned unit development**.

project analysis or **project appraisal** A comprehensive analysis of the financial viability of a development project. An assessment that takes account of economic demand, cost, design, finance, marketing, cash flow, and any other factors likely to indicate whether or not a project would be profitable. The analysis includes establishing criteria against which the project may be assessed and the means for judging the results as the development progresses. See also **discounted cash flow**, **feasibility analysis**.

project evaluation and review technique (PERT)   A form of **network analysis** used to ascertain, and control, the most efficient way of allocating resources to a project. PERT aims to plan and schedule events, but not necessarily to monitor the activities or actual work to be done. It does not relate cost to time, but aims to set down alternatives in order to show at any point in time the optimistic, pessimistic, or the most likely, course that the project will take. This technique of evaluation depends on feedback more extensively than **critical path analysis** for the control of variations in the project. Also called a 'project network analysis' or 'program evaluation and review technique'. See also **Gantt chart**, **project management**.

project management   The systematic planning, coordination and control of a project from inception to completion. The organisation of the resources required for a project, in terms of materials, equipment and skills, so that the requisite items are available at the right time and in the right place, and so that the project is carried through with the maximum efficiency and at the minimum cost. The aim of effective project management is to focus the decision making process on one person, the project manager, in order to facilitate communication and reduce misunderstanding, and to enable the project manager to report succinctly to the employer or principal so that he in turn can report back and instruct those who are responsible for carrying through the project. In particular, the project manager needs to foresee and predict as many problems and dangers as possible, and to plan and organise the project to ensure the most timely and cost effective completion of the project. See also **management contract**, **project evaluation and review technique**.

Cleland, David I. *Project Management: Strategic Design and Implementation*. 3rd ed. New York: McGraw-Hill, 1999.

Herzner, Harold. *Project Management*. 6th ed. New York: Van Nostrand Reinhold, London: International Thomson Business Press, 1997.

Reiss, G. *Project Management Demystified*. London: E. & F. N. Spon, 1996.

Walker, Anthony. *Project Management in Construction*. 3rd ed. Oxford: Blackwell, 1996.

project sale-and-leaseback   A **sale-and-leaseback** of developed property, both land and buildings; especially of a newly completed development. cf. **land sale-and-leaseback**.

project valuation(BrE)   A simplified form of the **residual method of valuation** that uses only unit costs. A rough method of valuation used especially to value a development site. The valuation is made on the basis of the permitted **plot ratio** for the site. The rent per unit of permitted development is assessed and then capitalised, and the unit cost of the building work is then deducted, leaving a balance available which represents the estimated unit price for the purchase of the site.

projection period   See **holding period**.

promise   1. A declared intention or undertaking given by one person (promisor) to another (promisee) that one will do or not do something. An undertaking that something shall happen, or shall not happen, in the future. An undertaking to bestow something on another, or an assurance that something will be brought about. Usually an assurance which, when acted upon, will bestow a benefit on the person receiving the promise. A promise may be considered to fall between a mere declaration of intent, which is not expected to have any legal effect, and an **agreement**, which amounts to consent by two or more parties. cf. **representation**. See also **bargain, estoppel, offer, oral contract, warrant**.   2. A **pledge**, or **earnest**, given or received.   3. The mutual undertakings given and received by the parties to a **bilateral contract**. A promise in a contract may be a **condition** thereof, but a condition is not necessarily a promise. See also **covenant**.

promisee   One who receives a **promise**.

promisor   A person who gives a **promise**.

promissory estoppel   See **estoppel**.

promissory note   A promise in writing that secures a debt. Defined in English statute law as "an unconditional promise in writing made by one person to another, signed by the maker [or promisee], engaging to pay, on demand or at a fixed or determinable future time, a certain sum of money, to, or to the order of, a specified person or bearer", Bill of Exchange Act 1882, s. 83. The written document may be referred to as a 'promissory note', a 'bond' or simply a **note**. "A note is an irrevocable promise to pay made by the maker ... A writing may be a promissory note although it is not negotiable. A promissory note is evidence of the underlying debt but is not itself a loan or a debt", United States Uniform Commercial Code, § 3-104:11. A bank note is a promissory note with the bank as promisor. A mere acknowledgment of a debt, e.g. an IOU, is not a promissory note, nor is an offer of employment that promises payment. A promissory note, to take effect, must be delivered to the promisee. A promissory note may be payable by instalments, but it is invalid if made payable on the occurrence of a contingent event. The promisee may retain it until payment is due or he may transfer it to another. The recipient must act in **good faith** when he acquires the note, without knowledge of any defect, if he in turn is to claim the payment when due. cf. **bill of exchange**. See also **mortgage note, negotiable instrument**.

promoter   1. A person or body that initiates a business venture, such as a scheme for the development of property. One who conceives and brings about new business and provides or obtains the requisite finance. In particular, a person who takes an active part in forming and raising finance for a new corporation. A person or body that provides finance for a new venture, in anticipation of deriving a profit therefrom, may also be referred to as a promoter. Professional advisors, lawyers, accountants, real estate consultants, etc. are not regarded as promoters when acting in their professional capacity. See also **developer, property developer**. 2.[US]The party that sets up a condominium owners' association or an association formed to manage the ownership of a cooperative apartment property. 'Promoter' is not a term of law, but a business term for the party who initiates the project and is usually the founding member of the association. Usually referred to as the 'developer' when the party is responsible for the original development, or the **declarant** when responsible for the condominium declaration.

property   Derived from the Latin *proprius*, 'one's own' or 'belonging to one'. Anything that by its nature is capable of **ownership**, i.e. that which belongs or could belong to some person or persons. A right that a person has to withhold something from others, and is so protected by law. A thing or right that has a monetary value and is capable of transfer. Property is everything that may belong to a man or woman, and includes any thing that is capable of ownership and is protected as such by law and all rights that are of such a nature.

In common parlance, property is considered to be any object *per se*, i.e. a tangible thing; or the right to use, possess, enjoy and dispose of a thing. However, in jurisprudence and ethics it is referred to frequently as a benefit, or burden, that one person receives, or bears, against another.

—"that sole and despotic **dominion** which one man claims and exercises over the external things of the world, in total exclusion of the right of any other individual in the universe", 2 *Bl Comm* 2 (1765).

—"the right to use and abuse. It is the absolute, irresponsible domain of man over his person and his goods. If it ceases to be the right to abuse, it would cease to be property", Pierre-Joseph Proudhon, *Système des contradictions economiques, ou Philosophie de la misère* (1846).

—"The term property may be defined to be the interest which can be acquired in external objects or **things**. The things themselves are not, in a true sense, property, but may constitute its foundation and material, and the idea of property springs out of the connection and control or interest which, according to law may be acquired in them or over them", C. R. Noyes, *The Institution of Property*, 1936, p. 357.

Property may be classified as **real property**, that is land or any right appertaining to land; or **personal property**, any property that does not relate to land. Property, as a right of ownership, may mean **corporeal property** (e.g. land, chattels or goods) or **incorporeal property** (e.g. a right of way, profit a prendre or a choses-in-action). See also **bundle of rights theory, hereditament, possession, private property, real estate, trespass, trust property**.

Harris. J. W. *Property and Justice*. Oxford: Oxford University Press, 1996.

F. H. Lawson, F. H., and Bernard Rudden, *The Law of Property*. 3rd ed. Oxford: Oxford University Press, 2002

Munzer, Stephen R. *A Theory of Property*. Cambridge University Press, 1990.

Penner, J. E. *The Idea of Property in Law*. Oxford: Clarendon Press, 1997.

property bond[BrE]   A form of property 'unit trust' that is administered by an insurance company. The purchaser of the bond acquires a single premium life assurance policy with profits linked to investment in real property. The premium may be payable as one lump sum or by regular instalments over the life of the policy. In practice, this investment is treated as if it were a purchase of units in a trust, the price of the units being related to the value of the underlying assets. cf. **property unit trust**.

property brief[AmE]   A written summary setting out details of a property that is being offered for sale, generally as prepared by the listing broker. This summary usually sets out a brief description of the property and indicates the price, and any other basic terms, at which the property may be acquired. A property brief is not intended as a legal document and normally will contain a **disclaimer clause** to that effect. Also called a 'fact sheet'. See also **particulars of sale**[Eng].

property company   A company that invests primarily in land and buildings. cf. **property unit trust**. See also **property investment trust**.

property details   See **particulars of sale**(Eng), **property brief**(US).

property developer   A person, or body, with an interest in real property who undertakes development or redevelopment, including the overall control of the building, financing and letting process. Commonly 'property developer' refers to any organisation that acquires land with the intention of building and reselling at a profit, as compared with an **institutional investor** who may undertake property development but with the intention of retaining the completed investment. In the US, generally called a 'real estate developer'. See also **developer, speculator**.

property development   See **development, development analysis, residual method of valuation**(BrE).

property index certificate (PIC)(Eng)   A certificate that represents a right to an investment that is based on the performance of an index, such as the performance of an index that is based on the value of a number of properties. In practice the investment is a form of bond with a variable coupon that pays a return, on redemption or maturity, based on the underlying index.

Property Information Form(Eng)   A form that is submitted by a solicitor to a seller, upon receiving instructions to act for the sale of a domestic property, requesting information about the property. Such a form is used when the solicitor is acting in accordance with the Law Society's recommended **National Conveyancing Protocol**. This form is also called a 'Seller's Property Information Form'. In addition, the seller is provided with a 'Fixtures, Fittings and Contents Form' which is to be completed to set out details of items that are to be included, or excluded, from the sale.

property insurance   Insurance against a **risk** associated with the ownership, use and occupation of property. Insurance of real estate is obtained to provide an **indemnity** against loss or damage arising from such matters as: (i) fire (whether occasioned by explosion or otherwise), but usually excluding spontaneous combustion, and fire resulting from earthquake, subterranean fire, riot, civil commotion, war, rebellion, revolution, and similar risks; (ii) lightning and thunderbolts; (iii) explosion (with similar exclusions to fire cover), unless caused by boilers; (iv) vehicular impact, aircraft and articles falling therefrom; and (v) storm, tempest, flood and burst pipes. The exceptions mentioned, as well as damage resulting from subsidence, landslide and structural defect, may be covered by obtaining **extended-perils insurance**. (However, damage caused by radioactivity and nuclear explosion is not normally insurable.) In addition, insurance may be taken out to cover loss of rental income, as well as operating expenses that may be incurred while the building is undergoing repair. Injury to the public is usually covered by a separate **public liability insurance**. See also **all-risks insurance, comprehensive insurance, consequential loss insurance, engineering insurance, rent-loss insurance, special perils**. Huebner, Solomon S., et al. *Property and Liability Insurance*. 4th ed. Upper Saddle River, NJ: Prentice-Hall, 1996.

property investment trust   An **investment company** that raises money by the sale of shares and invests the proceeds either indirectly in the stocks or shares of real estate companies or directly in real property. Generally, investment is made on a discretionary basis so that, although the investment vehicle is a company, it performs its functions in the same manner as a trust. cf. **property unit trust**(BrE). See also **business trust**(US), **investment trust, property bond**(BrE), **real estate investment trust**(US).

property line   See **boundary line**.

property management The specialised function of ensuring the profitable operation and management of owned, leased, or sub-leased real property, including land, buildings and building equipment. This function includes, as directed by the owner, developer or landlord, the collection of rents and other income; verification and payment of expenses; if applicable, the apportionment and collection of operating expenses or service charges; supervision of repairs, maintenance and cleaning of the property; liaison with tenants and occupiers; notification of rent escalations and lease renewals; the keeping and rendering of accounts; if necessary, the appointment of caretaking staff; regular inspection of the property; liaison with local and public authorities; and any other matters that affect the efficient running of the property. These responsibilities may be carried out directly by the owner, or by a **managing agent**. A managing agent or 'property manager' may be responsible for all aspects of management (or may be appointed to perform only specific functions, e.g. collecting rent), but normally he is not responsible for major building works, property appraisals or tax assessment, tax returns, negotiating rent revisions, releasing of vacant space, or zoning or planning matters, unless specifically appointed to perform such duties. Although generally a separate function, property management may be considered to fall within the ambit of **facility management**. See also **asset management**, **estate management**, **portfolio management**.

property manager A party appointed to carry out the responsibilities and exercise the function of **property management**. See also **managing agent**.

property owner An **owner** of a property; a person who has ownership of property. See also **estate owner**(Eng), **landlord**, **landowner**.

property owner's liability insurance See **public liability insurance**.

property register See **cadastre**, **land registration**, **terrier**.

Property Register(Eng) See **Land Registry**.

property report(US) 1. See **appraisal report**. 2. See **condominium declaration**, **statement of record**.

property residual technique(AmE) 1. The valuation of land and the buildings thereon as a single entity, rather than as separate elements as in the **land residual technique** or the **building residual technique**. 2. A method of valuing an income-producing property that may be carried out in two different ways: (1) Capitalizing the **net income** attributable to the land. An income is assessed that will accumulate, at compound interest, to replace or recapture the cost of buildings. This income is deducted from the total income to arrive at the income applicable to the land, and the resultant income is capitalized. An amount is then added for the cost of replacing the buildings. This method is applied only when the buildings or improvements that are to be recaptured represent a fairly insignificant part of the total value, e.g. a farm building. (2) Capitalizing the net income, before recapture, for a fixed term (e.g. the remaining term of a lease) and adding the **reversionary value** as a capital sum based on an assessment of comparable properties. The property residual technique is not a separate method of appraisal; it is a combination of two approaches adapted so that, in the first instance, the residual value of the land, and in the second instance, the reversionary value, is the more significant factor.

property syndicate See **syndicate**.

property tax A tax levied against the deemed value or against the income arising from property, rather than against an individual or a legal entity. In the US, a tax on real property is also called a 'real estate tax' or 'realty tax'. See also **assessment**, **capital gains tax**, **estate tax**, **inheritance tax**, **rates**(Eng), **land tax**,

recording tax, stamp duty(Eng)**, stamp tax**(US)**, transfer tax.**

Tolley's Property Taxes annual. Croydon, Surrey: Tolley, 2004.

property trust A generic term for an investment vehicle by which a portfolio of properties is held in **trust**. See also **investment trust, property unit trust**(Eng)**, real estate investment trust**(US)**.**

property unit trust (PUT)(Eng) **1. A unit trust** that invests in real property. A 'unit trust scheme' must be authorised by the Secretary of State (FSA 1986, s. 75). Such schemes do not normally permit a direct investment in real property. However, regulations may be made to exempt a single property scheme to allow for such trusts to be created and quoted on a 'recognized exchange' (FSA 1986, s. 86; SI 1989/28). Generally, such trusts are authorised only to accept funds from organisations whose business is to invest in securities, e.g. pension funds, insurance companies, etc. **2. A unit trust** that specialises in the purchase of shares in property companies. Such PUTs may also hold other liquid investments and may invest a small percentage of their total capital directly in commercial or industrial property. However, if a significant part of the capital is invested directly in property it will require to be 'authorised' as in **1.** above. cf. **property investment trust**. See also **property bond**.

proposal **1.** Something put forward for acceptance or rejection. An expression of a desire or willingness to perform an undertaking or to enter into a contract. A proposal may be in the form of an **offer**; or merely an **invitation to trade**(AmE)**/invitation to treat**(BrE) or a solicitation for offers. **2.**(Eng)A written proposal that an alteration should be made to the non-domestic **rating list** (Local Government Finance Act 1988, s. 55). Effectively, a proposal is a challenge to the rating assessment placed on a property. A proposal to alter the rateable value of a **hereditament** in the rating list may be submitted by any person who is aggrieved by the inclusion of a property in the list or by its value.

proposal bond *See* **bid bond**.

propositus(Lat) 'The person proposed'. The person immediately concerned; the person from whom descent is traced. A **testator**.

proprietary **1.** Belonging to; in the nature of **ownership**. The characteristic of being in the nature of **property**; of or pertaining to property. **2.**(US)An owner; one who possesses or holds property in his own right. A word mainly of historical use.

proprietary estoppel See **estoppel**.

proprietary interest A right to the ownership of property; an interest that is actionable *in rem*, 'against the thing', and not merely *in personam*, 'against the person'. A right to property that represents an **estate** or **interest** in land, as distinguished from a personal right granted by a **licence** which is not an 'interest in land'. See also **proprietary rights**.

proprietary lease A lease between the owner/corporation that holds a property in **cooperative ownership** and the tenant/stockholder who is granted a right to occupation of a particular unit. Such a 'lease' is more in the nature of a personal contract which is tied to the ownership of stock in the owning corporation and there is no rent as such, although the tenant is responsible for the payment of expenses incurred by the corporation. Also called an 'occupancy lease'.

proprietary rights The rights that arise from the **ownership** of a property. In particular, the **natural rights** to land, as distinguished from acquired rights, such as easements or leases. See also **bundle of rights theory**(US)**, proprietary interest**.

proprietas(Lat)   'Property'; 'ownership'; that which is peculiarly one own.

proprietor   **1.** An owner of property. One who has title to a property; one who exerts control over something. In particular, a legal **owner** of property. A proprietor has a full right to dispose of the thing he possesses, but that right might be deferred in time.   **2.** A person who derives **profit** from an enterprise, including a landlord. See also **landowner**, **registered proprietor**.   **3.** The person who engages a building contractor. In this context, also called the employer, client or **principal**; the 'proprietor' is normally the owner of or controls the property on which the building is being constructed.

proprietorship   **1. Ownership**, in particular the right to hold property, or a right to property, against the claims of others.   **2.** The legal right to use property (corporeal or incorporeal) for a defined or undefined period of time, usually upon exclusive terms.

Proprietorship Register   See **Land Registry**.

prorate   To assess proportionately; to divide or distribute proportionately.   See also **apportionment**, *pro rata*, **quarterly**.

prorations(AmE)   A part of the **closing costs** or other payments that has been apportioned, as at the date of closing, between the buyer and seller when the ownership of a property is transferred from one party to another. For example, if at the date of closing $1,000 has been paid by the seller in respect of an insurance policy and 50% of that amount relates to the period after closing, a proration of $500 is due from the buyer to the seller. See also **apportionment**.

prospect   See **prospective purchaser**.

prospective purchaser   A potential or interested purchaser of real property (*Drewery v Ware-Lane* [1960] 3 All ER 529, 532 (CA)). A prospective purchaser must have a good prospect of acquiring the property, but need not be as well qualified as one who is **ready**, **willing and able** to purchase. See also **prepared to purchase**.

prospectus   A document that sets out the terms and conditions under which investors are offered an opportunity to make an investment, especially in shares, debentures or securities of a corporation. "[A]ny prospectus, notice, circular, advertisement, letter, or communication, written or by radio or television, which offers any security for sale or confirms the sale of a security ...", 15 USC § 77b(10). See also **private offering**.

protected furnished tenancy(Eng)   See **furnished tenancy**.

protected interest(Eng)   An interest in registered land that is entered on the Land Registry and thereby protected in the event of a dealing in that land. 'Protected interests' are the kind of interests (which may be legal or equitable) that would be entered on the Land Charges Register in the case of unregistered land. For example, a lease for over 21 years, a restrictive covenant, or a contract for sale. See also **caution**, **minor interest**, **notice**, **inhibition**, **restriction**.

protected long tenancy(Eng)   See **long residential tenancy**.

protected occupier(Eng)   An occupier of **tied accommodation** who is employed as a forestry or agricultural worker and is granted a statutory right to remain in occupation when his or her employment is terminated. Such a worker has a right to continue in occupation as a statutory tenant "if and so long as he occupies the dwelling-house as his **residence**". The worker must be a "qualifying worker", which requires that he has been employed full-time in **agriculture** for not less than 91 out of the last 104 weeks prior to the termination of his or her employment. Also, the worker must have a "relevant licence or tenancy" of a dwelling-house or part of a dwelling-house, which means essentially an exclusive right of occupation that would have been a **protected tenancy** but for the fact that the licence or tenancy may have been at a low rent (Rent (Agriculture) Act 1976, as amended). Since January 15, 1989 no new 'protected agricultural occupancies' can be created; instead the occupier of tied agricultural accommodation (whether a licensee or a tenant) becomes entitled to an "assured agricultural occupancy", i.e. he may acquire a right to an **assured tenancy** even if a low rent or no rent is payable, but with protection from eviction similar to that of a protected agricultural occupier in the event of termination of the occupier's employment (HA 1988, ss. 24, 25, Sch. 3). These rights are available only if the occupier's immediate landlord is the occupier's employer, or the employer has made some arrangement with the immediate landlord for the housing of the person employed by him in agriculture. See also **eviction**, **service tenancy**.

protected shorthold tenancy(Eng)   A form of tenancy of a dwelling-house that could be granted after November 28, 1980 and before January 15, 1989 and, provided it fulfilled certain conditions, could be brought to an end without any security of tenure when the term for which it was granted expired. As a rule, any new tenancy granted on or after January 15, 1989 on similar conditions takes the form of an **assured shorthold tenancy** (HA 1988 s. 34(2)).

protected tenancy(Eng)   A tenancy of a **dwelling-house** (either an entire house or part of a house provided it is "let as a separate dwelling"), granted before January 15, 1989 (or in a few cases after that date, as where a new tenancy is granted by the same landlord to a former protected tenant, or a former protected tenant has been granted "suitable alternative accommodation"), that has security of tenure and statutory protection as to the level of rent that can be charged (RA 1977, s. 1). A number of forms of tenancy cannot be a protected tenancy, including an **agricultural tenancy**, a **secure tenancy**, a **protected shorthold tenancy**, an **assured tenancy**, and

premises let by a **resident landlord** or let at a **low rent** (RA 1977, ss. 6-26, as amended). Generally, no new protected tenancies can be created after January 15, 1989 (other than as a renewal of an existing protected tenancy); any such letting is now likely to be an assured tenancy or an **assured shorthold tenancy** (HA 1988, Part I). See also **company letting**.

protection from eviction   See **eviction**, **security of tenure**.

protective covenant(US)   *See* **restrictive covenant**.

protective trust   A **trust** that contains a provision by which it may be terminated on the occurrence of a specified event because that is considered to be in the best interest of the beneficiary, e.g. if the beneficiary tries to sell his interest or becomes bankrupt, at that stage the trust income is applied for a better purpose, such as the support of the beneficiary's family. A protective trust is generally made when property is to be held for the lifetime of the beneficiary. Also called a 'spendthrift trust' when the provisions are primarily aimed against improvidence or incapacity, or an 'alimentary trust' when it is intended to provide income and support to a particular beneficiary. cf. **bare trust**, **discretionary trust**. See also **active trust**, **determinable interest**.

protector of the estate(Eng)   A person or persons appointed under a settlement, or if necessary a court, to prevent the holder of an **entailed estate**, who only has a right in remainder, from effecting a complete disentailment of the interest, i.e. one who has to consent to **barring the entail** by the tenant in tail who is not in possession. If a special protector is not appointed, the tenant for life in possession of the settled land is usually the protector (Fines and Recoveries Act 1833, ss. 22, 33). See also **base fee**.

provision for cesser on redemption(Eng)   See **mortgage**.

provisional agreement   An agreement reached between two or more parties which, although normally creating a binding contract, requires that certain details or formalities are still to be arranged. See also **conditional contract, gentleman's agreement**.

provisional sum   A sum of money included in a building cost estimate, or set down in a **bill of quantities**, for work that cannot be determined precisely (due, for example, to unknown site conditions), or for an item that has not yet been decided on, e.g. items of hardware, light fittings, floor coverings. In particular, a sum set down as an estimate to cover work or services to be provided by a nominated subcontractor or goods to be obtained from a nominated supplier. Also called a 'prime-cost sum' as the contractor is not paid a stated sum but only the actual cost or **prime cost** (a 'pc sum'), as determined when the applicable work is completed. 'Provisional sum' refers sometimes to an allowance for an item that is known about, but the selection of the item has been left as the owner's option. In the US, also called a 'cash allowance'. See also **contingency sum**.

proviso   A clause in a written contract or deed, usually beginning with words such as 'provided always that ...', that imposes a **condition, limitation** or qualification on the performance or operation of the agreement, e.g. a clause in a lease giving the landlord a right of re-entry in the event of a breach of covenant. In particular, a proviso is a qualification to a previous stipulation, covenant or condition. cf. **exception**. See also **right of re-entry, terms and conditions, usual covenant, warranty**.

proviso for redemption   See equity of redemption.

proviso for re-entry   See forfeiture clause, right of re-entry.

proximate procuring cause(US)   See procuring cause.

proxy   1. A contraction of 'procuracy' – management or direction of the affairs of another. A person appointed to act, or the document appointing a person to act, on behalf of another. In particular, an authority to vote at a meeting. See also **mandate**.   2. A letter or **power of attorney**.

public auction   The sale of a property by **auction** following extensive advertising to attract public attention. A public auction is used most commonly in uncertain market conditions; for the sale of unusual property; for the sale of small investment properties or farms where the potential purchasers may be widespread geographically; or following the exercise by a mortgagee of his **power of sale**. In the US, also called a 'public sale', especially when carried out under a judicial authority. See also **tax sale**(US).

public dedication.   See dedication.

public domain   1. Land owned or controlled by a government. See also **domain**.   2.(US)All the lands and waters in the possession or ownership of the United States, including land owned by the several states, as distinguished from land owned by private individuals or corporations (Winters v. United States, 143 F 740, 748 (9th Cir. Mont 1908), aff'd 207 US 564). See also **public lands**.

public easement(US)   A **right of way** or a restriction on building created or imposed over land for the benefit of the public at large. See also **dedication, easement in gross, footpath, highway, scenic easement**.

public grant(US)   See grant.

public highway   See highway.

public house   1.(BrE)A place licensed to sell intoxicating liquor to the public at large for consumption on the premises. Unlike an **hotel**, a public house does not essentially offer sleeping accommodation. See also **inn**, **licensed premises**, **tied house**.   2.^(US)A place of public accommodation; an inn or hostelry.

public housing   Housing provided by central or local government, especially housing provided at affordable cost by a local municipality for low-income individuals and families. See also **council house**^(BrE).

Public Housing Administration (PHA)^(US) A federal agency that was established to assist local housing authorities with the building of low-income housing by making or supporting loans or making contributions with which to finance such housing. The functions of the PHA have now been transferred to the **Department of Housing and Urban Development** (5 USC § 624).

public index map^(Eng)   See **Index Map**.

public land^(US)   **1.** Land owned by a public authority or government. In particular, land held in the general **public domain** (Wallis v. Pan American Petroleum Corp., 384 US 63, 86 S Ct 1301, 16 L Ed.2d 369 (1966)).   **2.** Federal land that is open to public use or land that is held by the government for conservation purposes. See also **public property**, **public lands**.

public lands^(US)   Lands of the government of the United States that are not held or reserved for any special government or public purposes, but are open for public sale or other disposition under general laws. Lands that are not held back for any particular purpose, but "such as are subject to sale or other disposition under general laws", Newhall v. Sanger, 92 US 761, 763, 23 L Ed 769 (1876).
In modern usage, the term 'public lands' is defined by the **Bureau of Land Management** as "The Federally-owned public lands [which] include National Parks and National Forests, lands managed by the Bureau of Land Management, and U.S. Fish and Wildlife Service Refuges. These

lands are owned by all Americans" (Federal Land Policy and Management Act of 1976, 43 USC §§ 1701-1784). See also **public land**.

public lands survey system (PLSS)^(US) See **government survey system**.

public liability insurance   Insurance against the risk of injury to members of the public (other than employees) or to another's property from matters that arise from the ownership of property or from the conduct of a business. Also called 'property owner's liability insurance', 'third-party liability (TPL) insurance', or merely 'liability insurance'. Such insurance may also be called 'owner's, landlord's and tenant's (O. L. & T.) insurance' when the policy covers all the parties who have an interest in the property. cf. **property insurance**. See also **professional liability insurance**.

public market   See **market overt**.

public notary   See **notary**.

public nuisance   See **nuisance**.

public offering document^(US)   A document or **prospectus** that sets out all material facts relating to an investment that is to be offered to the general public. Such a document must be made in accordance with the regulations that relate to the particular form of investment. If the investment is offered only in a particular state, generally the document need comply only with the state regulations, but most public offerings must also comply with federal regulations, such as those set out by the Securities and Exchange Commission (SEC). See **condominium declaration**, **declaration of restrictions**.

public open space   See **open space**.

public park   An area of open space that is usually improved by landscaping, and is set aside and maintained for public pleasure, exercise, amusement or ornament. See also **national park, open space, park**.

public participation(BrE)   A process whereby new development proposals, especially for areas of comprehensive development, new highways, and major public works, are presented to the public for their comment and to give them the chance to sharing in the formulation of planning policies and proposals. Such participation is increasingly used to obtain public reaction to a development or planning proposal outside the requirement for a public hearing. See also **planning inquiry**.

public path(BrE)   See also **bridleway, footpath**.

public property   Property owned by a State or government body. Property that may be enjoyed by the public at large, or a large sector of the public. Property that belongs to the state or a political subdivision thereof – such as a county, city, town or similar entity – and that is used exclusively for public purposes. cf. **private property**. See also **public domain, public lands, highway, open space**.

public recorder's office(US)   An office where details are recorded of documents that relate to the transfer of interests in land. Also called a County Recorder's office, a Registrar's office or a Bureau of Conveyances. See also **land registration**.

public reserve(Aus)   Land that is set aside by the Crown, or a local council or municipality, for use by the public for recreation or public enjoyment. A public park.

public rights   Rights that may be exercised by any member of the public; for example, a public right of way or a **highway**. Public rights generally arise by statute (as with a public highway); or may arise by **dedication** of the right, either by express dedication, or by continuous, open, and unobstructed user by the public for an extended period of time. cf. **natural rights**. See also

foreshore, right of common.

public road or **public roadway**   See **highway**.

public sale   A sale in which members of the public are invited to participate and where any such member may make an open bid; a sale of property conducted with due notice that any member of the public may attend and may buy. See also **auction, foreclosure, foreclosure sale**(US), **power of sale, public auction, public lands**.

public sector housing   See **council house**(BrE), **public housing**.

public sector tenancy(Eng)   See **secure tenancy**.

public sewer   See **sewer**.

public trustee(Eng)   A government office, originally established under the Public Trustee Act 1906, to take on the role of **trustee** when a trust exists but no person has been appointed to administer that trust, as when there is no will made by a deceased or no trustee is nominated under a settlement. See also **trust corporation**.

public utilities   Services that are provided to all members of the public, such as electricity, gas, water, drainage and sewage disposal. Although such services or utilities may be provided by a privately-owned corporation, the services are provided to all members of the public who are prepared to subscribe for them; the tariffs levied for such services are subject to regulatory review; and the provision of the services can be modified or discontinued only in accordance with the rules of the regulatory authorities. See also **easement in gross**(US), **wayleave**(Eng).

public utility   An organisation or corporation that provides services, such as water, electricity, gas, telephone, transportation or telecommunications to the public at large. A public utility generally has an oligopoly in view of the special nature of the service it provides and, therefore, may be subject to more stringent government regulation than other entities. See also **public utilities**.

public utility company(US)   A private company that provides **public utilities** for the public at large. See also **public utility**.

public utility easement   See **easement in gross**(US), **wayleave**(Eng).

public way   See **highway**, **street**.

publici juris(Lat)   'Of public right'. Used to describe property that may be used by any member of the public, e.g. a highway or public footpath, or a right to light or air. See also **natural rights**, *res nullius*.

puffer   One appointed to bid, usually on behalf of an owner or auctioneer, at a sale by auction in order to excite interest and force up the bidding, but without any real intention to purchase the property offered for sale. Fictitious bidding, or the secret employment of a person to bid up the price of property, in order to make others think that someone is prepared to purchase, when he has no such intention, is a **fraud**. In English law, at an auction for the sale of land, provided that it is made known in the particulars or conditions of sale available to all potential bidders that the vendor, or a person acting on his behalf, is bidding there is no such fraud (Sale of Land at Auctions Act 1867, s. 6). In this context, a puffer is anyone appointed to bid on behalf of the owner (1867 Act, s. 3). However, there should be only one puffer. Also called, especially in the US, a 'sham bidder', 'capper', decoy duck', or in Scots law a 'white bonnet'. See also **mock auction**, **reserve price**(BrE)/**reserved price**(AmE).

puffing   1. Making an exaggerated statement about a property that is being offered for sale, in order to endeavour to enhance its attributes and thereby its price, e.g. "superior residence", "much sought after location". "[U]ndue or inflated commendation uttered or written in order to influence public estimation; an extravagantly laudatory advertisement or review of a book, a performer or performance, a tradesman's goods, or the like", *The Oxford English Dictionary*, 2nd ed., 1989. Puffing can be seen as highly subjective and is generally not a **misrepresentation**. It is a form of exaggeration that is so obvious to any interested party that he will take no account of it. However, it may be a misrepresentation if the statement assigns a benefit to a property that it clearly does not possess. Puffing can rarely be a defence to 'misrepresentation' when a third party relies on it and there is an increasing (and perhaps unfortunate) legislative trend to restrain descriptive embellishment. See also *caveat emptor*, **representation**.   2. The act of employing a **puffer** to bid up prices at an auction. Also called 'by-bidding'. cf. **buy-in**.

Pugh clause(US)   A clause in an **oil and gas lease** which provides that only land within a pooled unit for drilling or production purposes forms part of an indivisible obligation and that the lessor may terminate the lease in respect of other lands.

puisne mortgage   1. Any mortgage that is subordinate to a first mortgage. In English law, prior to 1926, a puisne mortgage was any such mortgage, and the term is used in the US with the same meaning. See also **junior mortgage**(US). 2.(Eng)A **legal mortgage** of unregistered land that is not protected, in terms of **priority**, by the mortgagee holding the title deeds to the legal estate of the mortgaged land (LCA 1972, s. 2(4)). Usually the first legal mortgagee holds the title deeds and any other legal mortgages are puisne mortgages. The priority of a puisne mortgage depends on its date of registration as a **land charge**, not on the date of its creation. If a puisne mortgage against unregistered land is not registered, it loses its priority (LPA 1925, s. 97). cf. **equitable mortgage**, **general equitable charge**. See also **overreachable interest**, **tacking**.

puller tenant(US)   See **anchor tenant**.

punch list(US)   A list of minor defects of construction that is prepared, usually by the architect for the project, when the building work is practically complete. The owner may accept that the contract has been 'substantially performed', subject to completion of the items set out in the punch list. See also **defects list, practical completion, substantial performance**.

punitive damages   Damages that exceed the actual loss suffered and are intended to have the effect of a penalty because of the reckless or wanton act of the defendant. Also called 'exemplary damages' or 'vindictive damages', or in the US sometimes 'smart money'. cf. **liquidated damages**.

pur autre vie(Lat)   Pronounced 'per ohter vee'. 'For the life of another'. See **life interest, tenant for life**.

purchase   Derived from the Old French *pourchacier*, 'seek to obtain'. To buy. To procure or acquire ownership of something voluntarily and in exchange for valuable consideration; to buy or acquire for money or an equivalent. The consummated action of a **purchaser**. "The word purchase (*perquisitio*) is applied in law to any lawful mode of acquiring property by the person's own act or agreement, as distinguished from acquisition by acts of law, as descent, escheat and the like. A purchase in the above sense includes **acquisition**, not only under contract of sale for a valuable consideration, but also by gift or without consideration, and by devise [1 *Co Litt* 18b; 2 *Bl Comm* 241]", S. M. Leake, *Digest of the Law of Property in Land*, 1874, p. 153.
"'Purchase' includes taking for sale, discount, negotiation, mortgage, pledge, lien, issue or reissue, gift or any other voluntary transaction creating an interest in property", United States Uniform Commercial Code § 1201(32).
In English statute law, 'purchase' may be defined to have a meaning that corresponds to 'purchaser' (LCA 1972, s. 17(1); LPA 1925, s. 205(xxi)). cf. **descent**. See also **estate contract**(Eng), **option, sale, words of purchase**.

purchase agreement   See **agreement for sale**.

purchase and leaseback   See **sale-and-leaseback**.

purchase and assumption transaction(US)   An arrangement by which the **Federal Deposit Insurance Corporation** takes over an insolvent bank or savings and loan association by setting up a new institution (a 'bridge bank'), or using an existing institution, to purchase the assets of the insolvent entity and assumes control and takes over responsibility for the management of the entity.

purchase contract   See **contract of sale, contract for sale**.

purchase cost   See **acquisition cost**.

purchase money   The **money**, or equivalent value, required as **consideration** to acquire a particular property or a particular interest in property. See also **completion**.

purchase money deed of trust (PMDT)(US)   See **purchase money mortgage**.

purchase money mortgage (PMM)(US)   A mortgage obtained by a vendor of land from the purchaser as security for all or part of the unpaid purchase monies and entered into at the time of the sale or as a sequel to the same transaction. Since the mortgage deed is entered into concurrently with the conveyance of the property, it usually takes priority over all other mortgages. A mortgage granted to a third party lender that is entered into contemporaneously with a sale might also be considered a purchase money mortgage, provided the loan proceeds are for the purchase. A similar arrangement secured by means of a deed of trust is called a 'purchase money deed of trust'. Sometimes called a 'take-back mortgage' or 'take-back deed of trust'. See also **deficiency decree**(US), equitable mortgage, lien, priority of a mortgage.

purchase money resulting trust(US)   See resulting trust.

purchase money security agreement(US) See **conditional sale contract**.

purchase notice(Eng)   A notice served by an **owner** of land on a local authority requiring the authority to acquire his property when, following an action of the authority (such as a refusal of planning permission), the server of the purchase notice is able to demonstrate that, as a result of the action, his land is "incapable of **reasonably beneficial use** in its existing state" and cannot be rendered capable of reasonable beneficial use after taking full account of any form of existing planning permission or any **permitted development** (TCPA 1990, s. 137). If a local authority accepts a purchase notice, it is deemed to be authorised to acquire the interest of the owner compulsorily and to have served **notice to treat** (TCPA 1990, s. 139). The situations that may provide a land owner with a right to serve a purchase notice include: (i) a refusal of planning permission, or a grant of permission subject to conditions; (ii) a revocation or modification of planning permission; or (iii) an order requiring the discontinuance of an existing use of land or the removal of an existing building or works from land (TCPA 1990, s. 137(1)). In addition, a purchase notice may be served following: (i) a refusal of any consent under a tree preservation order (TCPA 1990, s. 198(4)); (ii) a notice requiring the demolition of an obstructive building (Housing Act 1985, s. 284); (iii) a notice that had been served requiring the improvement of a dwelling in a general improvement area or a housing action area (Housing Act 1985, s. 227); or (iv) a notice refusing (or conditionally approving) listed building consent (Planning (Listing Buildings and Conservation Areas) Act 1990, s. 32-36; Planning (Listed Buildings and Conservation Areas)

Regulations 1990). See also **blight notice, inverse condemnation**.

purchase offer   See offer.

purchase option   See option to purchase.

purchase price   The cash, or monetary equivalent, actually paid by a purchaser to acquire a property. **Consideration** paid consequent upon a contract for the sale of property. See also **acquisition cost, price**.

purchase tenure land(Aus)   A form of tenure granted by the Crown by which the holder had the right to purchase the fee simple subject to the performance of certain conditions such as the payment of the full price of making improvements to the land. No new purchase tenure lands can be granted after 1989. See also **conditional purchase tenure**.

purchaser   A person who acquires property for money or its equivalent. One who acquires property from another for valuable consideration and not by gift, bequest or descent. Thus, 'purchaser' is a term of broad meaning and should be interpreted from its context, or, in many cases, strictly in accordance with an applicable statute law or regulation. A person who acquires a property for valuable consideration, by exchange, or in consideration of marriage may be a purchaser; but a person who acquires property by adverse possession, by testament, as a result of intestacy, or by gift, is not normally a purchaser.

In English statute law, a purchaser may be defined as one who acquires property "in good faith for valuable **consideration** and includes a lessee, mortgagee or other person who for valuable consideration acquires an interest in property … ", except in certain parts of the Act 'purchaser' only means "a person who acquires an interest in or charge on property for **money or money's worth**"; and in reference to a **legal estate** a purchaser includes "a chargee by way of a legal mortgage"; and "where the context so requires 'purchaser' includes an intending purchaser", LPA 1925, s. 205(1)(xxi). (For this section 'valuable consideration' includes a covenant in consideration of a future marriage, but does not include "nominal consideration in money", and 'money's worth' excludes the consideration of a future marriage.) The definition in the LPA 1925 also applies to 'trusts for land' (Trusts of Land and Appointment of Trustees Act 1996, s. 23(1)). For the registration of a **land charge**, "'purchaser' means any person (including a mortgagee or lessee) who, for valuable consideration, takes any interest in land or in a charge on land", LCA 1972, s. 17(1). In connection with the rights of a purchaser to compensation where he does not have notice of registration of a **local land charge**, "a person purchases land where for valuable consideration, he acquires any interest in land or the proceeds of sale of land; and this includes cases where he acquires as lessee or mortgagee, and shall be treated as including cases where an interest is conveyed or assigned at the purchaser's direction", LLCA 1975, s. 10(3)(a). In connection with **settled land** "'purchaser' means a purchaser in good faith for value, and includes a lessee, mortgagee or other person who in good faith acquires an interest in settled land for value; and in reference to a legal estate includes a chargee by way of legal mortgage", SLA 1925, s. 117(1)(xxi). In the Administration of Estates Act 1925, 'purchaser' is defined to mean "a lessee, mortgagee or other person who in good faith acquires an interest in property for valuable consideration, also an intending purchaser and 'valuable consideration' means marriage, but does not include a nominal consideration in money", AEA 1925, s. 55(1)(xviii).

In many US state statutes, 'purchaser' is broadly defined, so that it may include a mortgagee (especially in title theory states and in relation to fraudulent conveyances and land recordation), but generally the term does not include a lienee. See also *bona fide* **purchaser**.

purchaser for value A **purchaser** who acquires title or an interest in property upon the payment of valuable **consideration**. A term that is used in the context of a *'bona fide* **purchaser** for value without **notice'** being a person who acquires property in good faith, for reasonable consideration, without being aware of a claim or encumbrance against the property and, therefore, acquires that property free of that claim or encumbrance.

purchaser in good faith See *bona fide* **purchaser**.

purchaser without notice See *bona fide* **purchaser, notice**.

purchaser's lien See lien.

purchaser's policy(US) See **title insurance**.

pure easement(US) See **easement appurtenant**.

purpose of valuation See **valuation**.

put or **put option** An **option** available to a holder of property, stock, or a commodity to sell to another at a previously agreed price and at a future date. Normally the party who has agreed to purchase the subject matter has paid a certain sum of money (a premium) for the benefit of being able to buy at the agreed price; usually because the buyer expects to make a profit when the subject matter is acquired. cf. **call option**.

pyramid zoning(US) A **zoning** classification that permits any use within a zoned area that is compatible with or below the most restricted use. Thus, a zone for 'heavy industry' (the base of the pyramid) is virtually unrestricted and allows for all use above in the hierarchy, whereas, an area designated for 'single-family dwellings' (usually the peak of the pyramid) is limited to that use only. Uses may also be limited to those in the same strata of the pyramid, e.g. other use of the same group of classification. Also called 'cumulative zoning' as each zoning classification allows for the accumulation of less restrictive uses, i.e. uses higher up the pyramid. cf. **exclusive use zoning**.

Q

qua(Lat) 'In the capacity of'; 'considered as', e.g. *qua* trustee – 'as a trustee'.

quælibet concessio fortissime contra donatorem interpretanda est(Lat) 'Every grant is to be interpreted [or construed] most strictly against the grantor'. See also *contra proferentem*.

quadrangle   1. A square or rectangular courtyard, especially such an area that is surrounded by large buildings.   2.(US)An area of land comprising a square of 24 miles on each side as set out under the **government survey system**. 'Quadrangle' may refer also to an atlas sheet published by the U.S. Geological Survey Office that covers such an area.

quadrant   1. A quarter of a circle. Any one of four more or less equal parts into which an area or district is divided.   2. An instrument used in surveying to measure altitude.

quadruplex(US)   A residential building comprising four separate units contained on two levels with each unit having separate entrances. Four attached dwellings that form one structure with each unit having two party or common walls and two separate walls. cf. **duplex**.

qualified acceptance   1. **Acceptance** made subject to a reservation or condition. A qualified acceptance is generally not intended to constitute an acceptance of an **offer** upon the terms upon which it was made and, therefore, is effectively rejection of the offer, i.e. it amounts to a **counter offer**. See also **conditional acceptance, conditional contract, subject to contract**.   2. The acceptance of a **bill of exchange** subject to a condition, such as a postponement of the date for acceptance.

qualified constructive trustee   See **constructive trust**.

qualified covenant   1. A **covenant** that is qualified either by a **condition precedent**, by a **condition subsequent**, or by a **limitation**.   2. A covenant that is qualified by words that limit the liability of the covenantor.

qualified estate(US)   An **estate** in land that is limited in some way, such as with a **fee tail**, **conditional fee** or an **estate on condition** (Carpenter v. City of New Brunswick, 135 NJ Eq 397, 39 A.2d 40, 43 (1944)). An estate that may last forever, but one that has a qualification attached that provides for the possibility of a premature termination of the estate. cf. **absolute estate**. See also **qualified fee**.

qualified fee   A **fee** interest in land that is limited or modified in some way so that the beneficiary may not hold it forever. A qualified fee or **determinable fee** is a fee interest like any other in that it may last forever, but it has a limitation that was attached when the estate was granted, which if it occurs, will bring the estate to an end and transfer the right to possession of the land to another. For example, a fee granted as long as the land is used for school purposes. Although the terms 'qualified' and 'determinable' are synonymous when applied to a fee interest, the latter is preferred in English law. Similarly, **base fee** and qualified fee were used historically to denote the same form of interest; although 'base fee' in English law is now used to refer to a particular form of estate that can arise when a holder of an entailed estate seeks to bar or 'disentail' the rights of succession. Furthermore, the term 'qualified fee' may be used to refer to a **conditional fee**, but such confused usage (or even the use of the term 'qualified fee') is best avoided in English law.

In the US, the terms 'base fee', 'determinable fee', 'qualified fee', 'fee subject to an **executory interest**' and 'fee subject to a **conditional limitation**' (all of which automatically come to an

644

end *if* a specified event occurs and vest the fee in another) are used interchangeably. The American Law Institute's *Restatement of Property* considers that the use of the terms 'conditional fee', 'conditional limitation', and 'qualified fee' undesirable, preferring the term 'estate in **fee simple defeasible**' (p. 120, special note (1936)). The Restatement also considers the use of the term 'base fee' (*q.v.*) undesirable. A qualified fee may also be called a 'modified fee' or 'qualified fee estate'. cf. **absolute estate**. See also **estate on condition, fee simple conditional, fee simple determinable, fee tail, qualified title**(Eng).

qualified fee estate(US)   See **qualified fee**.

qualified interest   See **conditional interest, qualified property**.

qualified property   1. A limited right to property, e.g. personal property against which a bailee has a right to possession. A precarious form of ownership that lasts only as long as it is enjoyed, as with a right of light.   2. Property that has no owner, e.g. wild game, fish, water, but which may be reduced to private ownership in certain circumstances (2 *Bl Comm* 391). See also *res nullius*.

qualified purchaser   A prospective purchaser who has a demonstrated financial ability to complete a purchase; a purchaser who is 'able' to consummate a transaction. See also **ready willing and able**.

qualified title   1.(Eng)A registered title to property granted when an **absolute title** has been applied for, but the Land Registrar is unable to accept the application due to a defect in the title. When an owner of land applies to register an absolute title, but can only prove a limited right due to some defect or prior claim, the registrar may accept the title subject to a specified prior claim or subject to an excepted estate, right or interest that is placed on the register (LRA 1925, ss. 7, 12; LRA 2002, ss. 9, 10). A qualified title may arise when a document or evidence of title has been mislaid, or when the title

can be established only for a limited period, but the registrar considers that a title should still be registered. Registration with qualified title has the same effect as registration with absolute title, except that it does not affect the enforcement of any estate, right or interest which appears from the register to be excepted from the effect of registration (LRA 2002, s. 11(6)). See also **adverse possession, caution, possessory title.   2.**(Aus)A title to land that has been registered under the **Torrens title system**, but one that has not been verified by the Registrar-General and therefore is provided with a limited guarantee.

qualified trustee   See **constructive trust**.

quality of estate   The nature of an **estate** in land according to its certainty, e.g. freehold or leasehold, present or future, or according to its manner of enjoyment, e.g. solely or in common. cf. **quantity of estate**. See also **habendum**.

quantities   The part of a **bill of quantities** that sets out a description of the individual items to be costed and provides a place to insert the quantity of each item required.

quantity allowance(BrE)   An allowance or deduction made, when assessing the value of one property in order to apply it to value another, in order to take account of a significant difference in size between the respective properties. As a rule, a larger property has a lower value per unit area compared with a smaller one. Thus, a deduction (usually as a percentage) may be made from the unit value of a **comparable property** before applying that unit value to estimate the value of another property. It is a means of giving account to the view that there is greater competition for smaller properties, or less competition for larger properties. A quantity allowance should be made only when there is evidence that demand for large properties is likely to be more limited than for smaller ones, and not when supply and demand are reasonably in balance or when there is a shortage of larger properties. A term that is used especially in rating valuation. See also **zoning**.

quantity of estate   The nature of an **estate** in land according to its term or duration, e.g. a life interest or lease for 99 years. Also called the 'quantum' of an estate. cf. **quality of estate**.

quantity survey   See **quantity surveying**, **quantity survey method**.

quantity survey method   A method of estimating the replacement cost of a building by adding together the cost of every component required to construct that building – materials, labour, overheads, profit, etc. Also called the 'price take-off method'. See also **cost approach**, **quantity surveying**, **unit-in-place method**(US).

quantity surveying   The economic and financial measurement, analysis and control of building or construction work. In particular, the process by which the cost of building work is estimated by breaking down the building into its component parts – materials, labour, time, overheads, profit, etc. – and ascertaining a price for each of these parts in order to arrive at a cost for the whole. This process may be divided into three basic stages: (i) measuring the dimensions of the proposed building or construction work from the architect's drawings (**taking-off**); (ii) working out the volumes, areas, etc. of the building (**squaring the dimensions**); and (iii) **working-up** the totals (including **abstracting**, i.e. grouping similar items together) and pricing the work by applying appropriate cost rates. These detailed workings generally are set down in a **bill of quantities** that may then be used by a building contractor to establish a contract price.

Quantity surveying may also include related work, such as considering the most economical form of layout, materials and methods of construction; estimating the time for building work, cost planning in conjunction with all members of the construction team; advising on alternative forms of building contract and building contractor; preparing tender documents; project control; valuation of completed construction work; preparing and agreeing accounts with contractors; settling cost disputes; and any similar work. In the US, usually referred to as the preparation of the 'quantity survey'. See also **estimate, quantity surveyor**.

Seeley, Ivor H. *Quantity Surveying Practice*. 2nd ed. London: Macmillan, 1997.

Willis, Andrew, and William Trench. *Willis's Elements of Quantity Surveying*. 9th ed. Oxford: Blackwell, 1998.

quantity surveyor(BrE)   A professional who advises on the measurement and valuation of building and engineering works. A quantity surveyor advises on construction costs; estimates the cost of building work; advises, analyses and supervises the cost aspects of a building contract; and carries out other work associated with the process of **quantity surveying**. A quantity surveyor is employed by a building owner or architect and has no direct or contractual relationship with the builder, unless there is a clear intention to create such a relationship. His primary duty is to prepare detailed quantities, based on plans prepared by the architect, to enable the builder to estimate the amount for which building work can be executed. In the UK, a quantity surveyor is a separate professional advisor from an architect or engineer (which is not normally the case in the US and most European countries). In the US, a person who performs a similar function is generally employed by an architect or a building contractor and is called an 'estimator'. A person may not describe himself as a 'chartered quantity surveyor' unless he is a member of the Royal Institution of Chartered Surveyors (*Royal Institution of Chartered Surveyors v Shepherd* (1947) 149 EG 370). See also Appendix A, **Real Estate Associations**, **The Royal Institution of Chartered Surveyors**.

quantum(Lat)   'Amount'. See **quantity of estate**, *quantum meruit*.

quantum damnificatus(Lat)   'The amount of damage suffered'. See also **damages**.

quantum meruit(Lat)   'As much as is earned'; as much as he deserved. A payment on the principle of *quantum meruit* owes its origin to the doctrine of *assumpsit*, 'he promised', i.e. that a person undertook work on the understanding that he would be paid for the effort. An action for *quantum meruit* may arise (a) from a **quasi-contract**, i.e. a contract that is not made expressly, but arises when the actions of the parties demonstrate that there is an intention to accept the mutual benefits and burdens that are in the nature of a contract; or (b) when it can be shown clearly that a person is to be paid for work done, or services rendered, but the appropriate amount of that payment has not been expressly set out in a contract, cannot readily be ascertained by reference to any agreement, or negotiations as to the appropriate amount cannot be concluded. There is an established equitable principle that one party to a contract (express or implied) should be reimbursed for the benefit rendered to the other party to that contract, even if the contract has not been fulfilled in its entirety (*Planché v Colburn* (1831) 8 Bing 14, 131 Eng Rep 305; Chicago v. Thomas Tilley, 103 US 146, 26 L Ed 371 (1881)). *Planché v Colburn* set out three sets of circumstances that may give rise to a *quantum meruit* payment: (i) when there is an agreement that a 'reasonable', but unspecified, payment should be rendered; (ii) when it is intended that work should be paid for, but no sum of money is specified; and (iii) when a contract has been cut short due to unforeseen circumstances (as when it has been recognised as void), but it is reasonable that a payment should be made for work done up to that stage.

A principal whose liability to pay a **commission** to an agent is expressed to be contingent upon success, promises to pay only if the agent's objective is achieved, especially if the principal has not obtained any benefit. There can be no implied liability to pay an agent for services when there is an express liability to pay only for success. However, where the principal decides not to proceed with a transaction for which he has received valuable services from an agent, he may be obliged to make a *quantum meruit* payment for the labour and materials of the agent.

A person who is induced to provide a service in anticipation of receiving a contract (for example, a builder who makes estimates and provides advice or obtains quotations beyond what would normally be expected of him, or someone who provides a beneficial service that has been used, such as photocopying) may be entitled to a payment for the benefit he has rendered; or a payment may be due where work is not done strictly in accordance with the terms of the contract but a clear benefit is derived from the work done (Dermott v. Jones, 23 Howard 220, 64 US 220, 16 L Ed 442 (1859); *British Movietonenews Ltd v London and District Cinemas Ltd* [1952] AC 166, [1952] 1 All ER 208 (HL)). However, as the right to such payment is based on equity, it is recoverable at the discretion of the courts and, generally, an award will not be made when the claimant has deliberately abandoned or refused to complete the contracted work. See also **implied contract**, **part performance**, **unjust enrichment**, **void contract**.

quantum valebant(Lat) 'As much as it is worth'. A basis used to assess a price for goods or materials when no price is agreed on.

quare clausum fregit(Lat) See **trespass** *quare clausum fregit*.

quarry Derived from the Old French *quarriere*, a place where a person cuts stones into 'quarters'. A place where mineral (especially rock, marble, gravel, lime, clay, stone and the like) is extracted but, unlike a **mine**, one that is not underground. A quarry is usually open at the top and the front, and the materials extracted are generally different from those extracted from a mine (which is predominately a source of precious or semi-precious minerals, coal or fossil fuels).

In English statue law, a quarry is defined as "an excavation or system of excavations made for the purpose of, or in connection with, the getting of minerals (whether in their natural state or in solution or suspension) or products of minerals, being neither a mine nor merely a well or borehole or a well and a borehole combined", Mine and Quarries Act 1954, s. 180.

quarter day   A day that is accepted by legal custom as being appropriate when a payment is due 'quarterly' or on each of the 'quarter days' (or on the 'usual quarter days'). In the US, and in Continental European countries, the commonly accepted 'quarter days' are January 1, April 1, July 1, and October 1 (although corporate stock dividends are sometimes paid on February 1, May 1, August 1, and November 1). In England, Wales and Northern Ireland, the quarter days for the payment of rent are referred to as the 'usual quarter days' being March 25 (Lady day); June 24 (Midsummer day); September 29 (Michaelmas); December 25 (Christmas day). In Scotland, the 'quarter days' are Whitsunday, Martinmas, Candlemas and Lammas. Each of these days was a moveable feast, but they have now been fixed by law as May 28 (Whitsunday); August 28 (Lammas day); November 28 (Martinmas); February 28 (Candlemas) (Term and Quarter Days (Scotland) Act 1990). May 28 and November 28 are the 'term days' upon which most agricultural tenants take entry or move out. See also **apportionment**, **month**, **quarterly**.

quarter section   A square piece of land that is one quarter of a **section of land**, i.e. ¼ of a square mile (160 acres). Strictly, the area is of regular dimension, but if the lay or form of the land so dictates (as by a lake or river), it may be of irregular shape and comprise more or less than 160 acres. A quarter section was the area of land that could be claimed as a homestead. See **government lot**.

quarterly   Four times a year; every quarter (of the year); every three months. This may be every 91 days, every quarter day, or at three-month intervals. If nothing is expressed to the contrary, an annual sum payable 'quarterly' is due every quarter of a year from the commencement date, taking the most probable quarterly interval. As a rule that means on the same date every three months; although, unless there is clear evidence of an intention to the contrary a **month** does not run into the next month, so that quarterly from May 31 would fall on August 31, November 30 and February 28 (or February 29 in a leap year).

In English law, in relation to rent payments, if a lease starts, or rent is payable, on a 'usual' **quarter day**, then the rent is payable on the next subsequent quarter day (unless there is an agreement to the contrary) (*Vanaston v Mackarly* (1796) 2 Lev 99, 83 Eng Rep 468).

quasi(Lat)   'As if it were'; 'similar to'.

quasi-contract   A contract that is imposed by law to ensure reason and justice between two or more parties in their business dealing. An agreement that parties purport to enter into by their actions, resulting in one party being enriched at the expense of the other, so that the former is under an obligation to make **restitution** to the other as if a contract had been established between them. A quasi-contract is an obligation that the law creates in the absence of an agreement; especially in situations involving **unjust enrichment**. An arrangement that manifestly is not a **contract**, and does not arise from a tort, but one that the law is prepared to enforce; it is not based on the apparent intention of the parties. Thus, it may be referred to as a "contract implied in law", as distinguished from a "contact implied in fact". Quasi-contracts arise most frequently when a person has received a pecuniary benefit by a mistake of fact; as a result of an ineffective or incomplete contract, arising from a necessity; when money is paid for something, but another should have made the payment, as where a surety pays in place of the principal debtor; or where an unfair advantage or duress has been used to secure a pecuniary benefit. Sometimes called a 'constructive contract'. cf. **implied contract**. See also **agency of necessity**, **compensation for improvements**(US), **constructive trust**, **estoppel**, **mistaken improver**, *quantum meruit*.

quasi-easement   A right over one parcel of land in favour of another parcel of land which has all the elements for a valid **easement**, except that both parcels of land are in the same ownership. This right comes to life when one of the parcels of land is transferred to a new owner who would expect to continue to enjoy the separated land in the same manner, and with the same benefits, as his predecessor. A quasi-easement is one that can be seen to belong, or to be detectable as belonging, to the property granted. For example, a drain or watercourse that is in existence; a right over a made track, path or driveway; or a well that is used to provide water to a house. A quasi-easement must be necessary and have been enjoyed as a continuous and apparent right between the jointly owned parcels of land. A quasi-easement is not expressly granted and, although it may include an **easement of necessity** that is not apparent, or an easement that would be clearly within the intention of the grantor and grantee of the land as one that was technically enjoyed during the unity of ownership, it does not include a right that is not obvious or has to be established anew. "On the grant by the owner of a tenement of part of that tenement as it is then used and enjoyed, there will pass to the grantee all those continuous and apparent easements (by which, of course, I mean *quasi* easements), or, in other words all those easements which are necessary to the reasonable enjoyment of the property granted, and which have been and are at the time of the grant used by the owners of the entirety for the benefit of the part granted", *Wheeldon v Burrows* (1879) 12 Ch D 31, 49 (CA) (United States v. O'Connell, 496 F.2d 1329, 1332-3 (2d Cir. NY 1974).

In the US, "it is a general rule that a conveyance of property carries with it by implication all incidents rightfully belonging to, and essential to the full enjoyment of, such property, at the time of the conveyance", 26 C.J.S., Deeds, § 106.

In English law, such a right is now reinforced by statute as any **conveyance** is deemed to transfer "all ... ways, waters, watercourses, liberties, privileges, easements, rights and advantages whatsoever, appertaining or reputed to appertain to the land, or any part thereof, or, at the time of conveyance, demised, occupied or enjoyed with, or reputed or known as part or parcel of or appurtenant to the land or any part thereof"; as well as "all ... sewers, gutters, drains, ways, passages, lights, watercourses, liberties, privileges, easements, rights, and advantages whatsoever, appertaining or reputed to appertain to the land, houses, or other buildings, conveyed" and anything **appurtenant** thereto, unless any of these things are expressly excluded (LPA 1925, s. 62(1)(2)). cf. **equitable easement**. See also **general words**, **implied grant**.

quasi-entail   An **entailed estate** (or 'entail') granted for the life of someone other than the holder of the interest. An estate in land that arises when an interest in land is granted to a person and the heirs of his body to be held *pur autre vie* (for the life of another), i.e. it is granted to that person and his descendant only for as long as the other person, the *cestui que vie*, lives. For example, if A who only holds a life estate settles his interest in land on "B and the heirs of his body and thereafter on C", B has a quasi-entail which comes to an end on the death of A; in effect, A did not have a sufficient interest at the outset to grant a true entailed estate.

quasi-estoppel   See **estoppel**.

quasi-possession   **Possession** of a right, as compared with possession of a thing. In effect, the **enjoyment** of the right, as with an easement.

quasi-realty[US]   Movable property that has the appearance of realty and passes to an heir, such as title deeds, court rolls, or heirlooms.

quasi-rent   **1.** A payment for the use of personal property, e.g. a payment made under a leasing agreement. (Strictly, **rent** is a payment for the use of real property, but 'rent' is commonly employed to refer to a payment under a contract for the hire of personal property.)   **2.** See **economic rent**.

quasi-tenant at sufferance   A subtenant who continues to occupy land after his own and his landlord's lease has come to an end, without the head-landlord consenting or dissenting. See also **tenancy at sufferance**.

que estate   Norman French for 'whose estate'.

Land in which an interest, in the nature of an easement or profit à prendre, has been acquired by **prescription**.

qui approbat non reprobat(Lat) 'He who accepts cannot reject'. See **election**.

qui facit per alium facit per se(Lat) 'He who acts through another is deemed to act for himself', i.e. the authorised acts of an agent are the acts of a principal. A fundamental principle of **agency**. See also **vicarious liability**.

qui prior est tempore, potior est jure or ***qui prior est in tempore, prior est in jure***(Lat) 'He who is first in time, is the strongest in law'; 'he who is the first in time, is the first in right'. A maxim that may be upheld, in equity, where the merits of a claim for **priority** are equal.

qui sentit commodum sentire debet et onus(Lat) 'He who enjoys the benefit ought also to bear the burden'. See **equitable servitude**(US), **positive covenant**.

quick asset See **liquid asset**.

quick ratio See **liquidity ratio**.

quick take(US) A procedure in the event of **condemnation** by which the condemning authority is authorized by the court to take immediate title and possession of land in advance of the final determination of the **just compensation** that will be payable to the landowner.

quidquid plantatur solo, solo credit(Lat) 'That which is fixed to the soil, becomes a part of the soil'. See **fixture, leasehold, enfranchisement**.

quid pro quo(Lat) 'Something in return for something'. See **consideration, contract**.

quiet enjoyment The right of a purchaser, or lessee, not to have his proper use and enjoyment fettered or substantially interrupted by any act of the vendor, or lessor, or any lawful act of someone rightfully claiming under or in trust for the vendor, or lessor. A landlord who covenants to give quiet enjoyment undertakes that during the tenancy he will not interfere in a substantial or serious manner with the tenant's lawful **possession** and **enjoyment** of the demised premises. The right of quiet enjoyment refers in the main to such matters as denial of a right of possession or reasonable enjoyment, rather than to noise or physical disturbance as implied by the phrase. Such interference may arise even if there is no direct interference with the tenant's physical possession or enjoyment. A landlord must not, for example, subject a tenant to persistent intimidation or threats of physical eviction, continually obstruct access to the premises, cut off or persistently interrupt the utility supply, or otherwise prevent a tenant from peacefully using the premises for the purpose for which they were let. A breach of the covenant for quiet enjoyment does not arise merely from a temporary inconvenience that does not interfere with the estate, title or possession of the demised property, as for example when the landlord has to carry out essential repairs or alterations. Examples of a breach of the covenant of quiet enjoyment include severely impeding a tenant's ability to conduct his business; impeding access to a leased property; or impairing the safety of those entering the premises. A covenant for quiet enjoyment is normally contained in any well-drawn lease. However, there is an **implied covenant** for quiet enjoyment in every grant of a tenancy of land, unless (in rare cases) there is an express condition to the contrary or there is a statutory provision that may override such a provision. In the US, also called 'peaceful enjoyment' and the covenant is sometimes referred to as a 'covenant for possession'. cf. **derogation from grant, harassment**. See also **constructive eviction, covenant of title**(US), **demise, eviction, peaceably and quietly, re-entry, usual covenant**. **2.**(Eng)One of the covenants that by statutory implication a vendor undertakes to provide if he sells land as **beneficial owner** and for valuable consideration, i.e. he undertakes that "the subject matter shall remain to and be quietly entered upon ... and enjoyed ... without any lawful interruption or disturbance ...", LPA 1925, s. 76, Sch. II, Part I. See also **covenant of quiet enjoyment**.

Carter, David, and Andrew Dymond. *Quiet Enjoyment: Arden and Partington's Guide to Remedies for Harassment and Illegal Eviction.* 5th ed. London: Legal Action Group, 1998.

quiet title action(US) An action or suit brought in a court of law to establish a **good title** to real property, especially an action taken to remove a **cloud on title**. The action is brought against any person who maintains a claim to the subject property in order to establish the validity, or otherwise, of that claim. Also called an 'action for quiet title'. See also **deraignment of title**, **quitclaim deed**.

quieting title(US) See **quiet title action**.

quiete clamare(Lat) 'To give up all claims'. See also **quitclaim deed**.

quit **1.** To set free or release; to leave or give up possession permanently. In particular, to vacate leased premises. See also **notice to quit**. **2.** Free and clear. To give up or renounce. See also **renunciation**.

quitclaim(US) To proclaim free; to release or renounce a claim. See **quitclaim deed**, **renunciation**.

quitclaim deed(US) A deed of conveyance that transfers such right, title or interest in a property as the grantor has, without giving any warranty as to the grantor's title to the property. The grantor cedes or 'quits' any claim, right or title that he has, or claims to have, to a property, i.e. it is a release of a present interest or right to land (United States v. California & Oregon Land Co., 148 US 31, 13 S Ct 458, 45 L Ed 354 (1889), note—Quitclaim deeds, their construction and effect). A modern quitclaim deed does not contain any **covenants of title**, but uses such words as "remise, release and quitclaim" (such words being synonymous in this context) to demonstrate a manifest intention to convey such interest as the grantor has to the grantee (but no more). A quitclaim is used especially when the grantor purports to have certain rights to land and thereby may be lifting a **cloud on title**; when a property has been acquired at a judicial sale and the grantor can give no warranty as to title; or when the grantor knows that there is likely to be a lack or defect of title. Sometimes called a 'release deed'. cf. **bargain and sale deed**, **warranty deed**. See also **title insurance**.

quittance **1.** An abbreviation of 'acquittance'; a **release**. The discharge of an obligation or debt. See also **accord and satisfaction**. **2.** A document that acknowledges the discharge or payment of a debt.

quod aedificatur in area legate cedit legato(Lat) 'That which is built on ground that is granted by will passes to the devisee'. See **fixture**.

quod certum reddi potest(Lat) See *id certum est quod certum reddi potest*.

quod meum est sine me auferri non potest(Lat) 'What is mine cannot be taken away without my consent' (but see **compulsory purchase**(Eng) and **eminent domain**(US)).

quod vide [q.v.](Lat) 'Which see'.

quotation A document by which a person gives a prospective customer or employer an indication of the terms upon which the former is prepared to undertake specific business. A statement of the price at which a contract may be entered into; commonly used in relation to building work. A quotation is generally not intended to constitute an **offer**, but is intended as an invitation to be permitted to submit a formal offer that would then be capable of acceptance so as to form a **contract**. An offer is intended to form a basis for a contract; a quotation is intended to be used for comparison, further analysis, or negotiation – but not for acceptance as the basis of a contract. See also **bid**, **estimate**, **invitation to trade**(AmE)/**invitation to treat**(BrE).

R

rachmanism(Eng)   The exploitation of a tenant of residential property by taking advantage of a position of weakness due to his or her income, age, race, etc. The term is derived from Perec Rachman who, in London between 1954 and 1960, intimidated statutorily protected tenants into giving vacant possession. A term now used to refer to any form of **harassment** or exploitation of residential tenants, which seeks to extract exorbitant rents or to evict the occupants in order to realise a higher price for a property by selling it with vacant possession. See also **eviction**.

rack rate   The published room rate in an hotel. Generally the full rate that is charged to a casual traveller. See also **average daily room rate**.

rack rent   The highest annual rent at which a property can be let; the full yearly value of a property. In modern English usage, rack rent merely signifies the best **market rent** obtainable for a property, especially as distinguished from a lower rent payable under an existing contract of tenancy. As a rule, the payment of a **premium** indicates that the rent payable is not a rack rent. Rack rent is generally based on the assumption that the tenant pays his own occupancy costs (taxes, utilities and maintenance expenses) and the landlord pays for repairs.

In English statute law, 'rack rent' is defined in certain statutes as a rent that is "not less than two-thirds of the rent at which the premises might reasonably be expected to let from year to year" excluding all tenant's rates and taxes and costs of repair, insurance and other expenses; a definition that is aimed at excluding premises that are let on a **ground rent** (Public Health Act 1936, s. 343; Highways Act 1980, s. 329(1), as amended).

Radburn   A form of layout for a residential estate, originally designed for the town of Radburn, New Jersey, USA, in which pedestrian access is segregated almost entirely from vehicular access by means of bridges and underpasses, and by means of a network of footpaths that lead to the front of each house, but do not abut onto the road as on a conventional estate. Vehicular access is provided by feeder roads from which a series of cul-de-sacs give access to the rear of each the house where parking areas and garages are located. An adaptation of this type of layout was commonly used for the design of many of the housing estates developed in the post-war English new towns.

radical title(Aus/NZ)   The title as held by the Crown. A term that is based on the principle that all land is ultimately held from the Crown, although a more modern view is that upon assuming sovereignty the English Crown did not acquire title to all land in Australia or New Zealand. Also called 'ultimate title' or 'final title'. See also **Crown land, native title**.

radius clause or **radius restriction clause**   See **non-competition clause, restrictive covenant**.

range   1.(US)See **government survey system**. 2.(US)See **range land**.   3. The difference between the upper and lower limits of a scale, as with a price in the range of $1-3 million. The difference between the smallest and largest values in a frequency distribution. The group of values in a permissible group of variables. 4. A row of buildings or sections of a building. 5.(Aus/NZ)A tract of hilly or mountainous country. 6. A direction line.

range land(US)   An open area of land used for grazing. In particular, a large tract of open government-owned land that is used for grazing cattle, sheep or other livestock. Over the Great Plains, an area over which domestic animals are allowed to roam is also called a 'range'. See also **public lands**.

range line(US)   See **base line, government survey system**.

ransom strip A strip of land that fronts a public highway and, because it is in separate ownership, prevents an owner of another parcel of land from obtaining access to the highway, i.e. a piece of land that prevents a landlocked owner from fully exploiting his land, thus placing him in a position of being held to 'ransom' by the owner of the strip of land. See also **compulsory purchase compensation**(Eng), **easement of necessity, marriage value**(BrE).

ratable estate(US) A taxable estate; property that is designated as subject to taxation.

ratable property(US) Property that is capable of being assessed, rated or appraised for taxation. See also **assessed value, rateable property**(Eng).

ratable value(US) The value of a property as assessed for the purpose of taxation. See also **assessed value**.

ratchet clause(Aus/NZ) A clause in a lease which provides that upon a rent review, or the application of an indexation variation, the rent will not fall below the amount payable prior to the variation. Alternatively, the clause may provide that the rent will never fall below a lower limit, such as the rent at the start of the lease, the rent established at a previous rent review, or any other agreed amount. Also called an 'underpinning clause'. See also **rent review clause**(BrE).

rate 1. In proportion. A direct relationship between amounts, e.g. a **ratio** of income to capital value, or interest to principal, expressed as a percentage. cf. **factor**. See also **discount rate, interest rate, rate of return**. 2. According to **value**; a charge, payment or estimate made according to an assessed quality or value, especially when measured against some other unit. For example, a charge made by a contractor for an amount of work done. 3. To estimate the worth or value of something; to place a value on, or fix a price for, an item or commodity. See also **assessment**. 4.(Eng)A local tax to which the occupier of a property is subjected. In particular, a tax based on the **rateable value** of a property and levied by an authority that has jurisdiction over a district in which the property is situated in order to pay for services provided by that authority. See also **rates**.

rate cap See **interest rate cap**.

rate lock See **lock-in provision**.

rate of interest The rate at which a sum of money earns **interest**, i.e. the rate, usually on an annual basis, at which a price is paid for borrowed money. See also **compound interest, discount rate, effective annual interest rate**.

rate of return The relationship, expressed as a percentage, between the net income or profit derived from an investment and the capital value or cost of that investment, usually calculated at an annual rate. See also **amortisation rate, average annual return, capitalisation rate, discounted rate of return, cash-on-cash return, internal rate of return, overall rate of return, sinking fund rate, true rate of return, yield**.

rateable hereditament(Eng) See **hereditament**.

rateable occupation(Eng) Occupation of property that is of such a nature that it is deemed sufficient to create a liability for the occupier to pay **rates**. This term is not defined by statute, but English case law has established that it requires four elements or 'tenets of rating': (i) 'actual occupation', i.e. physical possession by which the occupier derives some benefit from the tangible use thereof – a mere intention to occupy a property is not sufficient to constitute rateable occupation, nor does a legal right to possession alone; (ii) **exclusive occupation**, or sufficiently exclusive for the purpose of the person having that right, i.e. a right to exclude others from the property in the same way as the occupier; and (iii) occupation that is of value to the occupier, i.e. 'beneficial occupation'; (iv) occupation of a reasonably permanent nature. See also **completion notice**.

rateable occupier(Eng)   A person who is in **rateable occupation** of a property.

rateable property(Eng)   Property that is capable of being the subject of a liability for **rates**; "lands [which includes everything on, under or above the surface of the **land**, as well as buildings], mines, ... and a right to use any land for the subject of advertising", Local Government Finance Act 1988, s. 64(2)(4). In particular, property that is the subject of a rating assessment, including unoccupied property, as distinguished from property that is exempt by statute (such as agricultural land) or is exempt because it is incomplete or under reconstruction and, therefore, not capable of beneficial occupation. See also **hereditament**, **ratable property**(US), **rateable occupation**, **rating list**.

rateable value (RV)(Eng)   The net annual rental value of property (a **hereditament**) as determined for the purpose of rates. In the case of a non-domestic hereditament the rateable value "shall be taken to be an amount equal to the rent at which it is estimated the hereditament might reasonably be expected to let on three assumptions: (a) ... that the tenancy begins on the day by reference to which the determination is to be made. (b) ... that immediately before the tenancy begins the hereditament is in a reasonable state of repair, but excluding from this assumption any repair which a reasonable landlord would consider uneconomic. (c) ... that the tenant undertakes to pay all the usual tenant's rates and taxes and other expenses necessary to maintain the hereditament in a state to command the rent mentioned above", Local Government Finance Act 1988, s. 2(1), Sch. 6, as amended. Also called an 'assessed value'. See also **rating valuation**, **Uniform Business Rate**.

rates(Eng)   A tax paid to a local authority by an occupier of property on the basis of the assessed annual value (the **rateable value**) of that property.

The amount of this tax is expressed as uniform amount per pound of rateable value as determined for each property. The tax is paid by the occupiers of most properties in the local authority's area of jurisdiction and the revenue is used to finance the needs of the authority levying the charge, or the needs of any authority that has levied a precept on that authority. Similarly, a levy made by a statutory body to pay for local utilities also may be called rates, e.g. water rates, drainage rates. A rate represents a charge for the benefit of occupying a property to which the authority provides a service and it is payable by anyone who is deemed to be in **rateable occupation** of a property. Rates are an imposition spread over a district to cover expenses in that district, as distinguished from a levy or assessment imposed on a particular property to pay for an expense directly related to that property. See also **Council Tax**, **duty**, **rate**, **tax**, **Uniform Business Rate**, **usual covenant**.

ratification   The approval, confirmation or sanctioning of an act or agreement, especially an act or agreement made by another, that did not have prior authorisation. For example, a person may ratify a prior action, which has been performed on his account, in order to give effect to that action as if it had been authorised originally. In particular, a principal may ratify the act of his agent after the event, even though, at the time the act was carried out, it was outside the agent's normal duties or was not expressly incorporated in the terms by which the agent was appointed. As a rule, in order for ratification to be effective: (i) the principal must be fully aware at the time of the ratification of all the circumstances and facts surrounding the agent's action; (ii) the agent whose act is sought to be ratified must have purported to act as an agent; (iii) at the time the act was done the principal must have been in existence, be capable of being ascertained, and have been competent to act as principal; (iv) at the time of the ratification the principal must be capable legally of doing the act himself or authorising it to be done; and (v) at the time of the ratification the act must still be capable of ratification, i.e. there must be something to ratify. cf. **estoppel**. See also **agency, authority, estoppel, homologation**.

rating   1. The process of assessing the value of a property for local property taxation purposes. See also **rates, rating valuation**.   2. The evaluation of the risk involved in making a loan or investment. See **credit rating**.

rating lists(Eng)   Lists that show details of property that are subject to rates. The list may be a 'local' or a 'central' non-domestic rating list. The local list is compiled and maintained by the **valuation officer** who has responsibility for a particular area. It provides details of each non-domestic **hereditament** in its area of application and the **rateable value** of those hereditaments. The inclusion of a property on the list establishes the liability to non-domestic rating (Local Government Finance Act 1988, s. 52(1)). A completely new valuation list should be prepared every five years and submitted to the appropriate local authority for implementation. The rating list is available for inspection by members of the public at the offices of the local authority. See also **tone of the list**.

rating valuation(Eng)   The **valuation** of a property for the purpose of levying rates thereon; the assessment of the **rateable value** for property. The value of a property (**hereditament**) for rating valuation purposes represents the deemed annual value of the property at the appropriate **valuation date**, assuming: (i) the 'hereditament' is vacant and available for letting; and (ii) the premises are as they stand at that date – *rebus sic stantibus* – but are basically in good repair. In addition, when determining the rateable value of a hereditament, regard should be had to the general level of assessed values for other properties on the rating list – the **tone of the list**. This process is based more on statutory rules than the more accepted process of

determining the value of a property.

The principal methods used for this form of valuation are: (i) the **comparable method of valuation** based on the rental value of similar properties; (ii) the **contractor's basis**; (iii) the **profits test**; or (iv) the **formula method** (for certain properties owned by statutory bodies). The valuation is carried out by the **valuation officer** for the area in which the property is situated. It is submitted to the person who has the benefit of **rateable occupation** of the property, who may accept the assessment or appeal by way of the **valuation tribunal**. Each hereditament is separately assessed; although a property that is sub-divided or has a mixture of uses, but is occupied as a whole, is generally valued as a whole. See also **proposal**.

Bond, Patrick, and Peter Bond. *Rating Valuation Principles and Practice*. London: Estates Gazette, 2003.

Plimmer, Frances. *Rating Law & Valuation*. London: Pearson, 1998.

Roots, Guy (general editor). *Ryde on Rating and the Council Tax*. 14th ed. 2 vols. Looseleaf. London: Butterworths.

Smith, Ken R. *Valuation for Rating*, 2nd ed. Reading, Berks.: College of Estate Management, 1991.

ratio(Lat)   'Reason'; 'cause'. See also ***ratio decidendi***.

ratio   A rate or proportion. The relationship of one number to another; the result of dividing one number by another. Ratios are frequently used as management tools – for example, ratios may be calculated to indicate the financial standing of a company, including: (i) a financial ratio, e.g. **current ratio, debt-equity ratio, liquidity ratio**; (ii) an investment ratio, e.g. **price-earnings ratio, dividend yield** (a ratio expressed as a percentage); and (iii) an operating ratio, e.g. **debt ratio, debt-coverage ratio, default ratio**, or profit/turnover, profit/capital employed, debtors/sales ratios. cf. **factor**. See also **efficiency ratio, expense ratio, floor area ratio**(US)**, loan-to-value ratio, net income ratio, operating expense ratio, plot ratio**(BrE)**.

Fisher, Clifford E. *Rates and Ratios Used in the Income Approach*. Chicago: Appraisal Institute, 1995.

ratio decidendi[(Lat)] 'The reason for deciding'; 'the reason for a [judicial] decision'; the ground on which a decision proceeds. The *ratio decidendi* of a case is the legal ruling that may act as a **precedent**, especially for an inferior court. cf. ***obiter dictum***. See also ***stare decisis***.

ratione soli[(Lat)] 'By reason of the soil'. A person who has a right to hunt or shoot wild animals has a *ratione soli* to those animals while they are on the land. See **land**.

ratione tenuræ[(Lat)] 'By reason of **tenure**', i.e. because a person holds land.

ratione tenuræ suæ[(Lat)] 'By reason of his own **tenure**'.

raw land Land in its natural state; land that has never been cultivated, built on or improved. See also **agricultural land**, **unimproved land**, **wasteland**.

raze To tear down a building; to lay level with the ground; to carry out **demolition**. Raze, like erase, signifies complete removal, or making even with the ground.

re[(Lat)] 'In the matter of'; 'in the case of'.

ready, able and willing[(BrE)] or **ready, willing and able**[(AmE)] An expression used to describe a prospective purchaser who is in a position to sign a *binding* contract; one who is prepared, legally capable and financially able to purchase a property. An agent or broker's **commission** may be made payable upon condition that he procures a purchaser who is 'ready, willing and able' to execute an unconditional contract on terms specified by the seller. In such an instance, as a rule, if the agent fulfils that condition then, even if the seller refuses to conclude the sale or withdraws the property, he has earned his commission. The expression 'ready, able and willing' or 'ready, willing and able' has been adopted and thoroughly reviewed in English and American case law leading to almost identical interpretations (*Christie Owen & Davies Ltd v Rapacioli* [1974] QB 781, [1974] 2 All ER 311 (CA); McGavock v. Woodlief, 20 Howard 221, 61 US 221, 15 L Ed 884 (1858), Note: "When a broker, to sell real estate, is entitled to commissions"; Dotson v. Milliken, 209 US 237, 28 S Ct 489, 52 L Ed 768 (1908) (Ellsworth Dobbs, Inc. v. Johnson, 50 NJ 528, 236 A.2d 843 (1967)). Although, in the US, in a few jurisdictions, the view has been taken that a person cannot be considered 'ready, willing and able' to complete until a binding and enforceable contract is signed, or even until the transaction is closed (a view shared under English law by the provisions of the Estate Agents (Provision of Information) Regulations 1991, SI 1991/895).

'Ready and willing' means that the purchaser must be prepared to enter into the contract on the terms offered and such a position should not be impeded by an outside factor, such as the fact that a prospective purchaser of a lease was not a suitable assignee for the existing landlord. A purchaser cannot be said to be 'ready' if the essential terms are not agreed upon (Gabrielli v. Fabian, 167 AD.2d 684, 563 NYS.2d 266 (1990)). In particular, 'willing' means that the purchaser should be prepared to put his signature to a binding contract on the terms offered and be bound thereby. As a rule, a person is not 'willing' to purchase if all he has done is sign a conditional contract, such as a contract 'subject to finance', at least until the condition is fulfilled (*Graham & Scott (Southgate) Ltd v Oxlade* [1950] 2 KB 257 (CA); Woodland Realty, Inc. v. Winzenreid, 82 Wis.2d 218, 262 NW.2d 106 (1978)). A purchaser cannot be said to be 'willing to purchase' if he is unable to complete the purchase or, at least, prove a willingness to execute an unconditional and binding contract (and the seller is able to do so). The execution of an **option to purchase** does not normally make the purchaser willing to *purchase*; at least until the option is exercised and there is a binding and unconditional 'contract to purchase'.

'Ability' to purchase depends primarily on financial ability. This does not necessarily mean that the funds must be immediately to hand in the bank. If the purchaser has sufficient and demonstrable financial means, or if the required funds can be realised from the sale of another property in time to consummate the proposed transaction, the purchaser may be considered 'able to purchase' the property.

In summary, in English law, it has been said that for a person to be 'ready, able and willing' to buy a property on terms deemed acceptable to the seller, the purchaser "must be a person who is 'able' at the proper time to complete; that is, he must have the necessary financial resources. He must also be 'ready'; that is, he must have made all necessary preparations by having the cash or a banker's draft ready to hand over. He must also be 'willing'; that is, he must be willing to hand over the money in return for the conveyance ... I [Lord Denning] can see no sensible distinction between instructions to 'find a purchaser', 'find a party prepared to purchase', 'find a purchaser able and willing to complete the transaction' and 'find a person ready, willing and able to purchase'. The rights and liabilities of house owners in these cases should not depend on fine verbal differences. If an estate agent [or broker] desires to get full commission not only on sales, but also on offers, they must use 'clear and unequivocal language': See *Luxor (Eastbourne) Ltd v Cooper* [1941] AC 108, 129 (HL) per Lord Russell", *Dennis Reed Ltd v Goody* [1950] 2 KB 277, 287, 288 (CA) (*Savills Land & Property Ltd v Kibble* [1998] EGCS 170 (CA); Tristram's Landing v. Waite, 367 Mass 622, 327 NE.2d 727, 731 (1975) – which suggests that there is a need for a closing of the transaction as a prerequisite to demonstrating the purchaser's 'financial ability').

The words **prepared to purchase** may be considered to incorporate all three of the requirements of 'ready, willing and able'. See also **exclusive agency, extender clause, no-deal, no-commission clause.**

real action   An action that is taken to recover a thing, as distinguished for a **personal action** that is taken against an individual. See **action** *in rem*,

ejectment, **forcible entry and detainer, writ of right, real property, recovery, writ of entry**.

real asset   See **fixed asset, real estate**.

real burden[(Scot)]   An obligation that affects land and is not solely personal to the parties. A real burden may be a right to restrict another in his use of land, or it may be a right to a sum of money that is secured by land. In the latter case, it may also be called a 'pecuniary' real burden and both rights may be called 'real conditions'. 'Real burden' is similar to a **restrictive covenant** as used in the common law. See also **servitude**.

real chattel   See **chattel**.

real covenant[(US)]   A **covenant** by which the holder of one parcel of land undertakes to do or refrain from doing something on that land usually for the benefit of the holder of another parcel of land. A covenant that is so related to an estate in land that the benefit passes to a purchaser or assignee of the land and may be enforced at law. A real covenant is one that can be said to 'touch and concern' the land (a **covenant running with the land**) and, therefore, may be enforced by a successor to the promisee's estate, or enforceable against a successor to the promisor's estate, provided the successor has **notice** of the covenant and it is intended to bind the successor.

A real covenant may arise between a landlord and tenant (a 'landlord and tenant covenant'); or between fee owners or neighbours (sometimes called a 'vendor and purchaser covenant' as it usually arises upon a sale of land). A positive covenant may be enforced at law and hence the remedy is one for damages, as distinguished from an 'equitable restriction' or **equitable servitude** that is only enforceable in equity and for which the remedy may be an injunction to prevent a breach of the covenant, or specific performance to require compliance with the covenant.

A real covenant is enforceable, as with any covenant, between parties to the agreement. However, the extent to which a real covenant is enforceable by or against a new owner of the land varies between jurisdictions. Some jurisdictions follow the common law principles that depend to a large degree on whether it is the *benefit* or *burden* that is being enforced (*viz*. **restrictive covenant**). Other jurisdictions take a more liberal view that a covenant should be enforced as long as it 'touches and concerns' the land, i.e. it is not purely personal. Whereas other jurisdictions take the view that any covenant that impedes the free use of land should be enforced only when it is for the benefit of several landowners. All jurisdictions accept this latter principle when a real covenant is part of a **scheme of development**. A real covenant may be an 'affirmative' or **positive covenant**, or a 'restrictive' or **negative covenant**.

A real covenant may be distinguished from an **easement**, as a covenant is a promise respecting the use (or 'non-use') of land, whereas an easement is a grant or reservation of an interest in land that permits someone to go onto land and do something. A real covenant must be created expressly; it cannot arise by implication or prescription. Sometimes called a 'running covenant'. cf. **personal covenant**. See also **privity of contract, privity of estate, restrictive covenant**.

real effects   See **real property**.

real estate   Land and anything permanently fixed thereto, as well as any rights or interests in land, including estates of fee simple, fee tail, estates for life and other similar rights to hold land. A right or claim that attaches to the very substance of land, as distinguished from **personal estate** which belongs to a person and, as such, is temporary and movable. Historically, 'real estate' meant property that was capable of being recovered by a *real* action (i.e. an action which sought to recover true possession of the property and not merely a bare claim supported by recompense). Thus, in a strict legal sense, real estate does not include a **leasehold**, which is regarded in the common law as personal estate (a 'chattel real') and is capable of recovery only by a

personal action between the parties. However, this common law anachronistic interpretation of 'real estate' has been superseded generally by the more modern view that a leasehold (especially a lease for a fixed term of more than one year) is real estate.

In English statute law, 'real estate' may be defined to extend to "manors, advowsons, messuages, lands, tithes, rents, and hereditaments, whether corporeal, incorporeal, or personal, and to any undivided share, thereof, and to any estate, right, or interest (other than a chattel interest) therein", Wills Act 1837, s. 1, as amended. Thus, it does not include a leasehold interest, which is a 'chattel'. However, it would normally include a **rentcharge** that is limited in the same way as a freehold. In connection with the devolution of property on a personal representative on a person's death, "'real estate' includes—(i) Chattels real [a leasehold interest] and land in possession, remainder or reversion, and every interest in or over land to which a deceased person was entitled at the time of his death; and (ii) Real estate held on trust (including settled land) or by way of mortgage or security, but not money to arise under a trust for sale of land, nor money secured or charged on land", AEA 1925, s. 3(1). See also **chattel, freehold, fixture, real property**.

real estate agent or **real estate broker**[(US/Aus)]   An agent who specializes in the business of real estate, especially the buying, selling and leasing of such property. A real estate agent is generally a licensed real estate **broker**, but the term is frequently used to refer to a licensed **salesperson** employed by a real estate broker. The term 'real estate agent' is used in preference to 'estate agent' in Queensland and New South Wales. See also **estate agent**[(BrE)].

real estate appraisal   See **appraisal, valuation**.

real estate appraiser[(AmE)]   See **appraiser**.

real estate assessment[(AmE)]   See **assessment**.

real estate broker   See **broker, middleman, real estate license**.

real estate commission (REC)[US]   A board established at state level to make and enforce regulations to protect the public in their dealings with those involved in real estate transactions; in particular, to control the licensing of persons engaged as real estate brokers or salespersons. See also **real estate license**.

real estate corporation[AmE]   A corporation that invests in **real estate**. See also **real estate investment trust, real estate operating company**. See also **property company**[BrE].

real estate contract[US]   See **contract for deed, contract for sale, instalment contract, land contract**.

real estate credit   A loan granted against the security of **real estate**. See also **finance**.

real estate development   See **development, development analysis**.

real estate investment trust (REIT)[US]   A corporation, business trust, or association that is (a) managed by one or more trustees or directors and pools the funds of a large number of investors in order to place money exclusively in real estate, whether by direct investment, by financing, by leasing arrangements, or by a combination of such methods; and (b) has a tax status that enables the beneficial owners to be subject to only one level of taxation. Real estate investment trusts originated in the United States under the Real Estate Investment Act of 1960, which was enacted to enable a group of investors to participate in real estate without the income derived from the underlying investments being subjected to taxation both at a corporate and at an individual level. A REIT is much like a mutual fund, being essentially a passive investment vehicle. Control is vested in the trustees or directors, and a REIT's income must accrue from such sources as rent and mortgage interest, and not from property trading and development, with at least 75% of the trust's income being derived from real estate. A REIT may be 'self-administered', i.e. it is managed by the employees of the trust, or it may be 'externally advised'. The beneficial ownership of a REIT is evidenced by transferable shares, or by transferable certificates of beneficial interest, and its special tax status distinguishes it from a domestic corporation.

A REIT is not taxed as a separate entity (except on its retained earnings), provided that the trust follows the statutorily prescribed rules, including: (1) it has not less than 100 shareholders or beneficiaries; (2) it is not more than 50% owned by five or fewer individuals; (3) at the end of its fiscal year at least 75% of its assets are held as real estate (including real estate loans and securities), cash or government securities; (4) the real estate is not held primarily for sale; (5) at least 75% of its income is derived from rents, mortgage interest and gains from the sale of real estate; and (6) it distributes 95% or more of its income to its investors (26 USC, Internal Revenue Code, §§ 856-860). The investors are taxed only in their individual capacities. Most insurance companies and other financial institutions cannot elect to be REITs (26 USC, Internal Revenue Code, § 856(4)), although they may invest in REITs.

A REIT may specialize in direct property investment (especially income-producing property) – an 'equity trust' or 'equity REIT'; in mortgage lending – a 'real estate mortgage trust' (REMT) or 'mortgage REIT; or it may invest in equity and mortgage interests – a 'hybrid trust', combination trust' or 'hybrid REIT'. A REIT may have an indefinite life, as with any other corporate entity, or it may be established with the objective that it will sell off its investment within a specified period of time – a 'finite life real estate investment trust' (FREIT). See also **real estate mortgage investment conduit**.

Fass, Peter M., et al. *Real Estate Investment Trusts Handbook*. St. Paul, MN: West, 2000 ed.

Garrigan, Richard, and John Parsons (editors). *Real Estate Investment Trusts*. New York, McGraw Hill, 1997.

Mullaney, John A. *REITs: Building Profits with Real Estate Investment Trusts.* New York: Wiley, 1998.

Magor, David L. *Distress for Local Taxation and Rent.* London: Institute of Revenues, Rating and Valuation, 1999.

real estate license(US) A license required by a person who wishes to act in real estate transactions as an **agent** or **broker** (including a **salesperson**). All states and the District of Columbia require that any person who wishes to act as a real-estate broker or real-estate salesperson must have a real estate license from the state in which they are doing business. Also, in many jurisdictions, there is no entitlement to a **commission** unless the broker (or the salesperson he employs) has a license at the time he is hired for the transaction for which the commission is being claimed. A real estate broker must be qualified by examination, and a broker or salesperson must have and maintain the state's specified amount of real estate experience. Several states also require that any person who carries on business relating to real estate (including a leasing agent, property manager, mortgage broker, and trust deed servicer) must have a current real estate license. Certain parties, such as attorneys, trustees in bankruptcy, and in some states, auctioneers, are exempt from this requirement – although they may be subject to separate regulation. See also **one transaction rule**.

real estate listing See **listing**.

real estate mortgage investment conduit (REMIC)(US) A form of **mortgage-backed security** that allows the income to be taxed only when received by the bond holder and not by the entity that holds the right to the mortgages. Under the provisions of the Tax Reform Act of 1986, any corporation, partnership, trust company or similar organization may elect for REMIC status. In order to maintain this status, the entity must abide by strict rules; for example, it must invest only in 'qualifying mortgages' (generally only first mortgages) and permitted investments (generally short-term interest-bearing investments), and it must pass the income from the mortgages through to the holders of the securities (26 USC, Internal Revenue Code, §§ 860A-860G). As with a **collateralized mortgage obligation**, REMICs may be separated into different maturity classes so that the different groups of investors receive their income at different stages, based on the income received from the underlying mortgages, or different interest rate classes. For example, a REMIC class may have an interest rate that changes periodically over the life of the security (an 'average rate class'); a rate that changes at a floating rate (a 'floating rate class' or 'floater'); or a rate that is adjusted in inverse proportion to a given index or interest rate (an 'inverse floating-rate class' or 'inverse floater'). A class may also be created that enables the investors to receive a constant rate of pre-payments of principal ('planned amortization class'), or that provides for certain investors not to receive any cash payments until all other investors have been paid off ('Z class'). Foreign investors in REMICs are exempt from withholding tax.

real estate mortgage trust (REMT)(US) See **real estate investment trust**.

real estate operating company (REOC)(US) A publicly-traded company that directly invests in and operates real estate. Usually this is a corporate entity with the equity stock traded on the capital markets. A REOC should have at least 50% of its assets invested in real estate and be substantially involved in the development and management of the real estate. The term is generally used to refer to any real estate company that has nor elected to operate as a **real estate investment trust**.

real estate owned (REO)(US) Real estate that has been acquired involuntarily by a bank or institution through foreclosure, or a deed-in-lieu of foreclosure, as distinguished from property that is the subject of a non-performing loan ('non-performing real estate') but title has not been taken back by the lender. Also called 'owned real estate' (ORE), or 'other real estate owned' (OREO) especially to draw a distinction between such property and other property held by the bank as operating assets.

real estate partnership(US)   A **partnership** established to invest or trade in real estate.

real estate-related financial transaction(US)   In connection with the preparation of a written appraisal for a federal financial institution, this term means "any transaction involving—(A) the sale, lease, purchase, investment in or exchange of real property, including interests in property, or the financing thereof; (B) the refinancing of real property or interest in real property; and (C) the use of real property as security for a loan or investment, including mortgage-backed securities", Financial Institutions Reform, Recovery and Enforcement Act of 1989, Sec. 1121 (12 USC § 3350(5)). Any such transaction that requires a Federal Financial Institutions Regulatory Agency (FFIRA) to engage the services of an appraiser is referred to as a 'financially related transaction' (FRT), and only licensed or certified appraisers can perform an appraisal to be used in an FRT. Also, such an appraisal must comply with the **Uniform Standards of Professional Appraisal Practice** (USPAP) (12 USC §§ 3331-3351). See also **market value**.

real estate security(US)   An investment contract made in connection with the sale of a promissory note that is secured, directly or indirectly, by a charge or lien on real property. All real estate securities (unless expressly exempt) must be registered with the Securities and Exchange Commission (SEC) and usually with the state securities commission for any state in which the securities are offered for sale. The principal SEC exemptions apply to certain 'private offerings' and 'intrastate offerings' (those offered only to residents of one state). The sale of a condominium is generally not treated as a real estate security,

except for the sale of units that are offered as investment opportunities by way of rental. See also **blue-sky laws**, **red herring**, **securitization**.

real estate syndicate   A **syndicate** or group of investors who combine together as an association, joint venture or partnership for the purpose of real estate investment. In particular, a syndicate that is formed when the purchase of a single property or a portfolio of properties would be too costly for the individual members. See also **syndication**.

real estate tax(US)   A tax levied on the assessed value of real estate without direct reference to the use to which the property is put or the business conducted on the property. See also **assessment**, **land tax**, **property tax**.

real interest rate or **real rate of return** The interest rate, or rate of return, after taking inflation into account. Thus, if the annual interest rate is 8% and inflation 3%, the 'real' rate of interest is 5%. cf. **effective annual interest rate**.

real owner   See **beneficial owner**, **true owner**.

real property   A right to **land** or to anything that 'touches and concerns' land. Real property is **property** that can specifically be recovered, i.e. it can be recovered by a **real action**. Real property includes land, any interest in land, and any thing that has been attached to land in such a way that it has become a part thereof. A right to a **leasehold** is not strictly 'real' property because it was regarded as no more than a personal right between parties to a contract that, if infringed upon, could be replaced by damages. However, in modern English legal practice, real property is generally considered to embrace land, as well as all interests or rights that extend to land itself – including a leasehold. On the other hand, the following essential differences exist between real and personal property: (i) an **easement** or a **profit à prendre** can only exist in respect of real property; (ii) the means for the transfer of **ownership** are different (in particular most contracts or agreements relating to real property must be in **writing** and in many cases must be recorded, whereas personal property may be transferred merely by delivery or by oral agreement); (iii) time limits under Statutes of Limitation are different; (iv) real property requires more thorough and complex investigations of title, with **possession** carrying less importance in the law of real property than personal property; (v) the tax treatment of real property is significantly different (primarily because land is immovable and is taxed in its situs); and (vi) real and personal property are governed by different rules as to descent and probate. **Emblements** or industrial growing crops are generally not real property.

In several states in the US, there are many state definitions of real property and these definitions usually include land, **tenements, hereditaments** (corporeal or incorporeal), that which is immovable from land by law, that which is incidental or appurtenant to land, and all rights thereto and interests in land. Most jurisdictions follow the common law rule that leaseholds are 'chattels real' and, therefore, personal property; although several jurisdictions assimilate leaseholds into real property. Also called 'realty'. See also **appurtenance, chattel, corporeal property, fixture, incorporeal property, mortgage, things**.

Burn, E. H. *Cheshire and Burn's Modern Law of Real Property.* 16th ed. London: Butterworths, 2000.

Burns, E. H. *Maudsley & Burn's Land Law: Cases and Materials.* 7th ed. London: Butterworths, 1998.

Goo, S. H. *Sourcebook on Land Law.* 2nd ed. London: Cavendish Publishing Ltd., 1997.

Harpum, Charles. *Megarry & Wade: The Law of Real Property.* 6th ed. London: Sweet & Maxwell, 1999.

Sparkes, Peter. *A New Land Law.* 2nd ed. Oxford & Portland, OR: Hart Publishing, 2003.

real representative See **personal representative**.

real right 1. A right to property that entitles the person vested with that right to take possession of the property and hold it against the whole world, as contrasted with a personal right which entitles a person only to exert a claim against another in order to compel performance of an obligation. **2.**(Scot) A right that may be exercised against the whole world, as with a right to property itself. Real rights include: (i) ownership (*dominium*); (ii) rights in security (including a pledge, security over **heritable property** and a floating charge); (iii) a proper **liferent**; (iv) **servitude**; (v) lease; (vi) **possession**; (vii) rights held by the public (such as a public right of way); and (viii) exclusive privilege (such as the traditional right of the merchant guilds in a royal burgh and intellectual property). See also **action in rem**, **real action**.

real security A **mortgage** or **charge** secured on property (real or personal) as contrasted with a personal obligation or guaranty which grants only contractual rights against a third party to a debt or obligation. See also **lien, pledge, rentcharge, security**.

real servitude A **servitude** that restricts or limits the use of land, as distinguished from a personal servitude which is enforceable only between particular persons. See also **easement, restrictive covenant**.

real value Value excluding changes in the purchasing power of money. The real value of a property may alter due to physical changes, e.g. improvements to the property, changes in the neighbourhood, or changes in the supply and demand for the property, rather than changes in the purchasing power of money. See also **intrinsic value**.

realisation(BrE) or **realization**(AmE) The process of disposing of an asset, business or property, especially by converting it into money. See also **liquidation, sale**.

Realtist(US) See Appendix A, **Real Estate Organizations and Professional Association, National Association of Real Estate Brokers**.

REALTOR®   The registered trade mark used by a member of a local or state board that is affiliated with the National Association of REALTORS (NAR). Associates of the NAR use the term REALTOR-ASSOCIATE. The term REALTOR® and REALTOR-ASSOCIATE may only be used by members and the use of the term is governed strictly by the rules and regulations of the association, including the requirement that members abide by the NAR **code of ethics**. See also Appendix A, **Real Estate Associations, National Association of REALTORS**.

realty   See **emblements, fixture, real property**.

realty reappraisal(US)   The periodic revaluation of a property. See also **revaluation lease**.

realty tax(US)   A tax on real property. See also **assessment, property tax, rate**.

reappraisal   1. The determination of a revised or updated **appraised value** of a property.   2. The **reassessment** of the value of a property, or a group of properties, as when the properties in an assessment district are revalued. See also **revaluation**.

reappraisal lease(US)   A lease that provides for the rent to be adjusted at specified intervals to a level that will be based on a percentage of the appraised capital value of the property. See also **revaluation lease**.

reasonable care   See **duty of care**.

reasonable compensation   See **just compensation**.

reasonable market value   See **fair market value, market value**.

reasonable rent   The rent at which a property might reasonably be expected to let. See also **fair rent, market rent, restricted contract**.

reasonable repair   See **tenantable repair**.

reasonable restraint on alienation   See **restraint on alienation**.

reasonable time   See **time is of the essence**.

reasonable use doctrine   1. A doctrine of common law that one should use one's property in such a way that it does not cause injury to others, nor unreasonably fetter another's lawful use and enjoyment of their property. See also **negligence, nuisance**.   2. See **water rights**.

reasonable wear and tear   See **fair wear and tear**(BrE), **wear and tear**(AmE).

reasonably beneficial use(Eng)   A use that, in all the circumstances, is of some particular benefit to the landowner. A term that is used in relation to a **purchase notice**. In this context, there must be no reasonable prospect of deriving a benefit from the land, even after taking full account of any form of development that may be permitted, either because it is authorised by a general development order or use classes order, or because it does not require planning permission. Thus, an agricultural use, which does not require planning permission, may be beneficial; therefore, in this context it may take the land outside the application of a purchase notice. However, in the final analysis, what constitutes reasonably beneficial use is primarily a matter of fact and degree. See also **revocation order**.

reassessment   The process of fixing a new or a revised **assessment**. A **reappraisal** of a property for local taxation purposes. A reassessment may be made when it is considered that a particular property is out of line with the value of comparable properties, or when all the properties that are liable to a particular tax are considered to need revaluation in order to bring them up to their current value. Sometimes called 'reappraisal'. See also **proposal**(Eng), **revaluation**.

reassessment clause(US)   See **revaluation clause**.

rebate   A repayment or refund; a retroactive **abatement**. For example, a return of part of the interest due on a loan because of early repayment of the loan. cf. **discount**. See also **kickback**, **rent concession**.

rebuild   To replace or restore a building or structure to its original, or near original, state or condition. In particular, to demolish and reconstruct the whole, or a substantial part of a building in a similar, but not necessarily identical, form. It is possible to rebuild without producing a replacement in the same style or shape; it is not necessary that the replacement is used for the same purpose; and it may be possible as part of the process of rebuilding to make minor alterations or additions that were not part of the original building or structure. However, the process must go beyond mere alteration or **repair**; there must be a 'building anew'. Structural alteration and repair, while retaining substantially the same building, cannot amount to rebuilding. See also **reconstruction**, **reinstatement**.

rebus sic stantibus(Lat)   'The thing as it stands'.

In the UK, when making a **rating valuation**, the assessment is made *rebus sic stantibus*. The property is valued in its existing state, and according to the circumstances, as at the date of the valuation, and not as it might be or could be made to be. Thus, the valuer must ignore benefits that would arise if the property were altered, and any benefit that would arise from another mode or category of occupation. When assessing **compulsory purchase compensation**, the interest being acquired is to be valued *rebus sic stantibus*, just as it occurred at the date of **notice to treat**; thus the claimant may not seek recompense for changes he may bring about at a later date, – for example, by granting a new lease at an enhanced rent. See also **tone of the list**.

recaption   The act of peacefully retaking goods or chattels that have been wrongfully retained by another, especially after wrongful distraint.

recapture   **1.** The recovery of invested capital in the form of **net income**, as a result of mortgage amortisation, or by equity appreciation. In particular the return *of* capital, as distinguished from the return *on* capital. See also **net operating income**, **recapture clause**.   **2.** The recovery of a tax benefit such as a deduction or credit that has previously applied. In the US, when the rate of income tax was higher than the capital gains tax rate, and a gain on the sale of a real property was treated as ordinary income and not as a capital gain, any depreciation above the straight-line rate 'recaptured' on a sale of the property. However, this provision is no longer applicable.

recapture clause(US)   **1.** A clause in a lease that permits the lessor to terminate the lease and regain possession upon a stipulated condition; for example, if the lessee seeks to assign the lease or sub-let or, in a percentage lease, if the lessee fails to maintain a stipulated level of turnover or profit. The latter instance (which is also called a 'kickout clause') normally applies only to a lease that provides for no minimum or base-rent. See also **continuous operation clause**(US), **right of re-entry**.   **2.** A clause in a lease which provides that the lessor can take back space if it is not occupied by the lessee within an agreed period from the start of the lease.   **3.** A clause in a **ground lease** that provides the tenant with a right to purchase the landlord's interest at a specified time during the lease.

recapture rate(AmE)   **1.** The annual rate at which the capital invested in a property is recovered from the net income the investment generates, after payment of interest on any loans secured on the property. Also called the 'capital recovery rate' or sometimes a 'capitalization rate'.   **2.** The rate at which the cost of a wasting asset is recovered. The annual rate that is allowed for the replacement of the asset. See also **overall capitalization rate**, **sinking-fund rate**.

recasting(US) Rescheduling or rearranging the term, or **priority**, of an existing loan, especially when a loan has fallen into default. See also **workout agreement**.

receipt A written acknowledgement, submitted by a recipient to a payer, that a payment has been made or goods delivered. In a contract for the sale of land, receipt is used to refer only to the acknowledgement of the consideration given for the property, not the acknowledgement of a grant of property *per se*. A receipt is not necessarily required in a cash or ready-money transaction because, in effect, there is no debt. cf. **release**. See also **deposit**.

receipt clause See **receipt**.

receiver 1. A person appointed by a court to administer and deal with property when it is considered that an independent party should take control in place of the person currently holding or managing the property. A receiver may be appointed in the event of bankruptcy; in the event of receivership; on the dissolution of a partnership; or when a property is the subject of litigation. A receiver, as a rule, is not appointed to manage a business, but to realise the assets and pay the debtors, although he may be permitted to manage a business in order to obtain the best return for the debtors. 2. An independent party appointed by a court to hold and conserve property that is the subject of litigation, or when the property is owned by someone who is mentally incapable, and to administer that property as an agent of the court. 3. A person appointed by a **mortgagee** to collect income and manage property; usually in lieu of foreclosure or as an alternative or prior to the mortgagee arranging to take possession and sell the property.

reciprocal contract See **bilateral contract**.

reciprocal conveyance See **exchange**.

reciprocal covenants See **mutual covenants**.

reciprocal easement(US) An **easement** that is binding upon the grantor and grantee so that the rights available to one party are dependent on the rights available to another. Reciprocal easements are common in complex real estate projects. They are used especially in major shopping center projects where the operation of the center depends upon the mutual cooperation of a number of owners and tenants, and the common or reciprocal use of some areas of the center. An agreement that gives effect to such an arrangement is called a 'reciprocal easement agreement' (REA) or, as it normally forms part of a more comprehensive agreement that governs the development and running of a shopping center, a 'construction operation and reciprocal easement agreement' (COREA), 'reciprocal easement and operating agreement' or a 'declaration and reciprocal easement agreement' which, as the name implies, covers matters other than pure easement rights. For example, a department store operator may have access to a car parking lot owned by the shopping center developer, as well as rights with other tenants over the common areas. The agreement may also provide for such matters as restrictions on the use of a retail store; control over opening hours; provisions for the maintenance of the common areas; restrictions on the mortgaging of a retail store; an option for the shopping center owner to acquire a store that is resold or released, as well as the type of operator who is permitted to run an individual store. See also **continuous operation clause, covenants conditions and restrictions, reciprocal negative easement**.

reciprocal easement agreement (REA)(US) See **reciprocal easement**.

reciprocal negative easement(US) A restriction or **negative easement** that arises where a common owner of two or more parcels of land sells one of the parcels, as part of a **scheme of development**, and sets up restrictions in favour of the retained parcel(s) so that the restrictions will mutually affect the retained parcels. Such restrictions are intended to have common benefit and burden for all the lots, as where each lot is restricted to private residential use in order to prevent the construction of other non-complementary uses. In many jurisdictions, provided the basic principles are applicable, such restrictions may arise by implication; but in some jurisdictions the restrictions must be imposed by deed, and in many jurisdictions they must be recorded in order to provide notice to each purchaser of the existence of the restriction. Sometimes called the doctrine of 'mutual equitable servitudes' or 'implied reciprocal servitudes'. See also **equitable servitude, negative easement**.

recission(US)   See **rescission**.

recital 1. A formal statement, normally forming the introduction to a **deed** or other formal **instrument**, that sets out its purpose and matter. A recital may be 'narrative' or 'introductory'. A narrative recital is a statement of facts, such as a statement of the history that led up to the making of a deed, or an exposition of the subject matter of a deed or a previous related deed. An introductory recital is a statement of the motive or necessity for the rest of the document. A recital usually starts with the word 'whereas'; for example, a statement at the start of a conveyance—"Whereas W is the owner of the fee simple absolute in Whiteacre …". A recital is not essential to a contract or conveyance, but it is common (although arguably unnecessary) practice to explain the reason or object for entering into an agreement. A recital is not a substantive part of that which is agreed, and the **operative words** of a deed when expressed in clear and unambiguous language are not to be controlled, cut down or qualified by a recital. However, a recital may clarify an ambiguity in the substantive part of a deed and, in the absence of any contrary statement or fact, a recital may have the effect of an **estoppel** to any thing or action that clearly conflicts with it. cf. **preamble**. See also **premises**.   2. A statement in an insurance policy that a premium has been paid or that the insurer has received a proposal to insure a certain risk.

reclamation of land   See **land reclamation**.

recognition clause(AmE)   A clause in a mortgage deed that provides that the mortgagee will recognize the rights of other parties. For example, a clause in a blanket mortgage which provides that, in the event of a partial release of one or more properties from the mortgage, the mortgagee will recognize the rights of a purchasers of a released property. See **non-disturbance clause**.

recompense   See **compensation, damages,** *quantum meruit*, **unjust enrichment**.

reconciliation(AmE)   1. The process in an **appraisal** of giving weight to the different factors that affect the value of a property, as when the value of a comparable property is adjusted for its size relative to the value of the subject property. 2. When different approaches to an appraisal have been applied, arriving at a final figure by balancing the importance of the result obtained from each approach. Also called 'correlation' or the 'correlation process'. See also **approaches to value**.

recondition   To restore to a good condition; to give a new lease of life. Reconditioning generally does not include replacement of structural materials, plant or equipment, or making improvements and, therefore, does not go as far as **renovation** or **refurbishment**. Reconditioning of a building is intended to extend the economic life of a building and includes carrying out neglected or deferred maintenance, but it does not include providing anything new or substantially different.

reconstruction   The act of rebuilding, or of reforming a structure, in a similar manner. In particular, the rebuilding of all or a substantial part of something that existed but has lost its entity. Reconstruction is carried out after demolition or destruction (in part or in total) of a building, or group of buildings, and essentially requires a substantial replacement or recreation of that which has been demolished or destroyed. cf. **repair**. See also **construction, rebuild, rehabilitation, renewal**.

reconversion   **Conversion** back; the reverse of the process of **conversion**. In particular, the changing of money into real property, especially when the law has presumed that a property has been converted into money. Thus, if land is held on trust under the provision of a will that it is to be sold and the proceeds distributed to the beneficiary, the law presumes that the beneficiary's interest is no more than an entitlement to the proceeds of sale; reconversion arises if the beneficiary is able to regain a right to claim the land itself. See also **trust for sale**(Eng).

reconveyance   **1.** A transfer of a title to property back to the original grantor. See also **redemption, sale and buy-back**.   **2.**(US) The transfer of property held under a **deed of trust** back from the trustee to the borrower or trustor when the debt secured by the deed of trust has been paid in full. See also **absolute conveyance, partial release clause**.   **3.**(Eng) A deed that transfers an interest in property back from the mortgagee to the mortgagor upon discharge of a mortgage debt. At common law, a mortgage was considered as a conveyance of an interest in property and a reconveyance was required to redeem the property. However, a **receipt** or **memorandum**, annexed to the deed that transferred a right to property as security for a debt, normally provides sufficient evidence that the debt has been discharged and the property reconveyed to the mortgagor (LPA 1925, s. 115). See also **discharge, redemption**.   **4.**(Scot) See **renunciation**.

record notice(US)   See **constructive notice, notice**.

record owner(US)   One who is recorded as the holder of a registered title to land, as distinguished from one who holds title under a system of unrecorded deeds. The holder of a **record title**. Sometimes called the 'registered owner'. cf. **owner of record**.

record title(US)   **1.** A title that is duly recorded and is considered to represent a complete right to the ownership of land, without defect. See also **good record title, perfect title**.   **2.** A title that is created by deed or other written instrument, as distinguished from a title that is recognized by law, as with a title acquired by adverse possession. In this context sometimes called a 'paper title'.   **3.** A legal title, as distinguished from an equitable title.

recordation(AmE)   The act of recording a document at a public recorder's office. See also **constructive notice, land recording**.

recorded map(AmE)   A **map** that has been recorded at the office of the county recorder.

recorded plat or **recorded survey**(AmE) See **plat**.

recorder(US)   An officer who is responsible for documents that are deposited at a **public recorder's office**. An officer appointed to record or enroll deeds, mortgages, liens, and other legal documents that are required to be recorded as a matter of public record. In addition, the recorder is required to maintain an index and to assist those who seek to obtain details of the recorded documents. Also known as a 'recorder of deeds', a 'registrar of deeds', a 'commissioner of deeds', or sometimes a 'register'. See also **registrar**.

recording   See **land recordation/land recording**(AmE), **land registration**(Eng).

recording tax   A tax levied upon the recording of a contract, deed, mortgage or other instrument relating to real estate, usually based on the value set out in the document. See also **stamp duty**(Eng), **stamp tax**(US).

recoupment   **1.** The recovery of that which has been expended. The recovery of a loss by a subsequent gain. For example, a public authority may seek to recoup part of the cost of a development project by acquiring more land than it requires for the project and, when it has completed the development, selling the surplus land at a price that has been enhanced by the development. cf. **recapture**. See also **abatement, betterment**. 2. A cross claim under a contract for damages. Thus, when one party claims damages for breach of contract, the other party may seek to recoup part of the amount claimed by making his own claim. A term used more in the US than in English law. cf. **set-off**.

recourse note A note or memorandum that provides a lender with a personal right of **recourse** against a borrower or a guarantor, in addition to any right of recourse to property held as security for the loan.

recourse A right to demand payment from someone. In particular, the right of a lender, or **mortgagee**, to take a personal action against the borrower, or mortgagor, if the proceeds from the sale of a property offered as security are inadequate.

In English law, because a mortgage is both a conveyance of an interest in land and a contract for a debt, the mortgagee may pursue his rights against the secured property and, unless there is an express agreement to the contrary, he has the concurrent right to sue under the contract for the personal debt owed by the mortgagor.

In the US, some states specify that unless there is an express provision in the mortgage deed, or some other instrument, the mortgagee's remedy is confined to the property mentioned in the mortgage. In several 'one action' states an action against the secured property and against the borrower must be prosecuted as a single claim, and in some states a personal judgment cannot be obtained until all claims against the security have been satisfied. See also **non-recourse mortgage, deficiency judgment**(US).

recoverable amount In accounting, the amount of the capital invested in an asset, or the outstanding capital cost, that can be recovered from cash flow and disposal of the asset at the end of an assumed holding period. See also **recapture rate**.

recovery 1. The act of regaining that which has been lost or is missing. See also **restoration, subrogation**. 2.(Eng)A form of action that replaces **ejectment** and is brought by a party who has been wrongfully dispossessed to enable him to regain possession of land. cf. **right of re-entry**. See also **adverse possession, disentailing assurance, eviction, mesne profits**.

recovery rate The rate at which the capital invested is returned from cash flow. Also used synonymously with **recapture rate**. See also **amortisation rate, pay-back analysis**.

rectangular survey system(US) See **government survey system**.

rectification 1. The act of putting something right that was made faulty by accident or inadvertence. The correction of something, as a matter of discretion, that is erroneous or doubtful. For example, the correction of a document when the parties to an agreement realise that it does not state what they had intended, usually due to a **mistake** or a clerical error.

Rectification of a document does not create a new agreement or vary the bargain reached; it merely records that which had been agreed previously. Rectification does not create two agreements, an agreement and a rectifying agreement, nor an agreement with a rider effecting a correction, but one agreement to be read as if it had been originally drawn in its rectified form. In effect, the court first rectifies or reforms the contract and then decrees **specific performance** of the contract as rectified.

Rectification is essentially an equitable remedy and is granted only at the discretion of the court. Before a court will order rectification of a document, it is necessary to establish, beyond reasonable doubt, what had originally been agreed and that it is proper to substitute that which was really agreed in place of that set down in the documentation. In the US, the more usual term for this process is **reformation**. cf. **rescission**. See also **deed of rectification**(Eng)/**deed of reformation**(US), **mere equity**, *non est factum*, **restitution**.   **2.**(Eng)An alteration to an entry at the **Land Registry**, pursuant to an order of a court or at the instigation of the registrar. Such a rectification may be made, for example, when the court decides that a person should be registered as having an estate, right or interest in registered land or a right to or over a registered charge; when the entry has been made by error or omission; where two or more persons have been registered as proprietors of the same registered estate or of the same charge; when an entry on the register has been obtained by fraud; when a **legal estate** has been registered in the name of a person who, if the land had not been registered, would not have been the **estate owner**; where a mortgagee is registered as the proprietor instead of as the holder of a charge (and the proprietor still has a right of redemption); or when all the interested parties consent (LRA 1925, s. 82). With effect from October 13 2003, a rectification of the register to correct a mistake, bring the register up to date, or to give effect to any estate, right or interest that prejudicially affects the title of a registered proprietor is called an **alteration** (LRA 2002, s. 21, Sch. 4, para. 1). See also **slip rule**.

rectory   The residence of a rector; a **parsonage**. See also **glebe land**.

red herring(AmE)   A preliminary prospectus for the sale of a security that has been filed with the Securities and Exchange Commission (SEC). Derived from the red printing along the left margin or on the front cover that is required to indicate that the securities referred to may not be sold until the prospectus has been approved by the SEC and the securities authorized for sale.

reddendum   That which is to be paid or rendered. The reddendum clause in a contract takes back something from that which is granted, either as a form of a payment or as a limit to the estate that is granted. In particular, the clause in a lease which specifies the **rent** payable (or the basis for calculating the rent payable) and its due date. Such a clause normally starts with such words as "yielding and paying". In the event of a conflict between the reddendum and the **habendum** (which specifies the commencement date and term of a lease), the habendum prevails. See also **additional rent**.

reddendum clause   See **reddendum**.

redditus or *reditus*(Lat)   'A return'; 'that which is rendered'. A return or compensation paid for the possession of land, i.e. **rent**.

redditus assisus(Lat)   'A fixed **rent**'.

redeem up, foreclose down   A maxim that applies when there are several mortgages on the same property and one of the mortgagees seeks to redeem a superior mortgage. A mortgagee who wishes to redeem a prior mortgage (i.e. pay off the debt owed to a prior mortgagee and step into his shoes) must redeem any mortgage situated in terms of priority between his own mortgage and the prior mortgage – 'redeem up' and also he must foreclose on all subsequent or junior mortgages and on the mortgagor's interest – 'foreclose down'. Thus, if a property is mortgaged by M_0 to M_1, M_2, M_3, M_4 and M_5 (in that order of priority) and M_4 wishes to redeem M_2's mortgage, he must redeem the mortgage of M_3 and foreclose on M_4 and M_0. Only M_1's mortgage can subsequently remain in force. The maxim applies only to court proceedings and is based on the principle that, before a court will permit redemption, the entitlement of any prior mortgagee, whose claim would be affected by the redemption, must be ascertained and any subsequent mortgagee, and the mortgagor, must be foreclosed upon – i.e. given the opportunity of redeeming the debt of their respective prior mortgages – or, if they fail to take that opportunity, lose their claim against the property. The maxim does not apply in reverse; a mortgagee who forecloses does not need to concern himself with prior, but only with subsequent, mortgages. See also **redemption**.

redemption   1. Derived from the Latin *redimere*, 'to repurchase' or 'to buy back'. The recovery of one's unfettered rights. In particular, redemption is the process by which a **mortgage** on land is cancelled, by repaying the total debt (including principal and interest), and title to the property is restored free and clear of the mortgage. Redemption is more than 'repayment' of the debt; it is the complete satisfaction of an obligation and reclaiming of the property held as security. A **mortgagor** has a contractual right to have his property reconveyed or released to him when the debt is paid in full. In addition, equity recognises that a mortgage should be no more than security for a debt and that a mortgagor must have the right (called his **equity of redemption**) to have his property released to him, without hindrance, after he has repaid all sums due (including principal, interest and any proper costs) to the mortgagee. This right is inviolable and cannot be precluded by the mortgagee, nor may the mortgagee seek an unfair or unconscionable collateral advantage prior to allowing redemption. On the other hand, the mortgagee may postpone the mortgagor's right of redemption for a reasonable time. A right of redemption is not confined to the mortgagor (or anyone else to whom he has transferred his equity of redemption), it may be exercised by any other person who has an interest in the mortgaged property, or who is liable to pay the mortgage debt. Such a person does not necessarily acquire the property unencumbered, but he 'steps into the shoes' of the mortgagee who has been redeemed and becomes a mortgagee himself. Redemption may take place on the date set down in the mortgage deed—'legal redemption' or, in certain circumstances, at a later date—'equitable redemption'. A mortgagor who transfers to another his right to redeem – his equity of redemption – loses that right unless he is sued subsequently on a personal covenant or there remains privity of contract with the mortgagee.

In English law, a mortgaged property may be reclaimed when the debt is repaid, as appropriate, by: (i) the mortgagor physically retaking **possession** (although a more formal process is usually required); (ii) the return of the title deeds or an annulment of a registered charge; (iii) a **reconveyance** of the title to the mortgagor (although such a formality is generally not necessary); (iv) a **receipt** for the monies paid endorsed on the mortgage deed; or, rarely, (v) forcing a sale of the property and claiming the proceeds. English statute law provides that any person entitled to redeem mortgaged property may have a judgement or order of sale in place of his right of redemption (LPA 1925, s. 91(1)). Alternatively, subject to complying with the terms of the mortgage that permit a reconveyance or surrender, the mortgagor may require the mortgage debt to be assigned to a third party (LPA 1925, s. 95).

In the US, the process of redemption depends on whether the property is in a 'title-theory' or 'lien-theory' state, and whether the redemption takes place before or after the initial right of redemption. Redemption may refer to the exercise of the contractual right of redemption; the exercise of the equitable right of redemption; the performance of the conditions necessary to remove the mortgagee's lien; or the exercise of the **statutory right of redemption**. See also **foreclosure**, **once a mortgage always a mortgage**, **option**, **redeem up foreclose down**, **unconscionable bargain**, **undue influence**, **usury**. 2.[US]The purchase by a lessee who holds a **ground lease** of the landlord's reversionary interest. See also **leasehold enfranchisement**[Eng].   3. The **repurchase** of a property at the same or an enhanced price.   4. The repayment of a loan at the end of a specified period of time. The discharge of the principal as well as the interest in full, as distinct from the mere payment of periodic sums as they become due. The repurchase of a note, bond, debenture or other instrument of debt by paying its full value to the holder. See also **release**, **redemption yield**.   5. The repurchase of shares by the issuing corporation in order to redeem or pay off the value of the shares.

redemption certificate(US)   See **certificate of redemption**.

redemption date   1. The date on which a fixed-term loan is repaid at 'par value'; or an investment is sold after a specified or assumed holding period. In the former case, the date is also called the 'maturity date'. A term most commonly applied to the repayment date on government stock or bonds. See also **redemption yield**.   2. The date on which a mortgage debt is repayable in full, or the date on which the final repayment of capital is due. See also **acceleration clause**, **equity of redemption, redemption**.

redemption fund   See **sinking fund**.

redemption period(US)   The period of time within which a mortgaged property may be redeemed after an event of default. In particular, the statutory period of time allowed for the recovery of a property by the former owner after it has been sold at a **foreclosure sale**. See also **statutory right of redemption**.

redemption value   The value of an investment when it is sold, especially at the end of its planned holding period. The value of a stock or bond at the date fixed for maturity or at a specified date in the future. When assessing the **internal rate of return** on an investment that is to be held for a number of years, the income receivable at the end of the investment period is usually capitalised at a lower rate (or higher yield rate) than that applied to the initial income, either to take account of the higher risk of receiving the final income, or to take account of deterioration of the investment.

redemption yield   The average annual rate of return from an investment or loan, over its assumed life or holding period (up to the **redemption date**), taking account of the total projected net income and any capital profit (or loss) on resale of the investment or redemption of the loan. A redemption yield on an investment is the same as the **internal rate of return**; but 'redemption yield' is used in particular when referring to bonds or government securities, or when the profit on resale of the investment represents a significant factor in determining the average annual return over the life of the investment. In the case of a real estate investment, a redemption yield may be calculated to take account of projected income and capital gain (or loss), assuming future inflationary growth, over a number of years (commonly 10 or 15 years), in order to make a comparison of the return obtainable from long-term government securities.

redemptioner   One who pays off a mortgage or charge by **redemption**. In the US, 'redemptioner' generally refers to a party who has a right to redeem a property from a mortgage; in particular, one who has a subsequent lien and thereby a right to redeem after a property has been sold upon foreclosure of a prior mortgage.

redevelopment   The act or process of rebuilding an area; especially an area that has reached the end of its economic life, or a blighted area that requires complete renovation and renewal. The **development** of an area of land as an entity by replacing buildings or groups of buildings, usually with entirely new buildings that are constructed on a new layout and using a different design. Although redevelopment generally entails building anew, the clearance of an area of land and its preparation for resale may also be considered redevelopment, as the result is a process of new development. See also **comprehensive development, urban renewal**.

reditus(Lat)   'rent'.

redlining or **red-lining**(US)   A practice by which an investor or lender demarcates an area that he considers to be unsuitable for property investment or lending, usually on the basis of the ethnic or racial nature of the neighborhood surrounding a property. It is unlawful under the federal Fair Housing Act of 1968, ss. 804, 805 (42

USC §§ 3604, 3605) to discriminate in the making of real estate loans, or the granting of insurance, in connection with a dwelling on the grounds of race, color, religion, sex, handicap, familial status, or national origin (73 ALR Fed 899: Fair Housing Act—Redlining). Other federal legislation also prohibits similar practices, such as the Consumer Credit Protection Act of 1968, Title VII (Equal Credit Opportunity Act) (15 USC § 1691 et seq., and the Home Mortgage Disclosure Act of 1975 (12 USC §§ 2801 to 2811). In addition, the Office of Thrift Supervision issues regulations that prohibit redlining by lenders under its control. cf. **greenlining**.

reducing-balance depreciation   See declining-balance depreciation.

reduction certificate(US)   A certificate prepared by a mortgagee, usually prior to the transfer of a mortgage loan, setting out details of the rate of interest, the outstanding balance, the maturity date and any claims that may be asserted. Also called a 'statement of condition of lender' or, if it relates to the position under a deed of trust, a 'beneficiary statement', or, in the case of a lien, a 'lien statement'. See also **estoppel certificate**.

re-entry   See **forfeiture**, **right of re-entry**.

re-entry for condition broken(US)   **1.** The taking back of a right to possession of land by the grantor, or his successor, when there has been a breach of a condition that was imposed on the grant of an estate. See also **estate on condition**.   **2.** See **right of re-entry**.

re-evaluation lease(US)   See **reappraisal lease**.

reference schedule(Aus)   A schedule to a lease that sets out the variables in the lease, such as the rent, operating expenses and the lease term. The schedule is usually set out at the start of the lease in order to provide a useful source of reference to the principle points that may require attention at particular times during the term of the lease.

referential settlement   A **settlement** that incorporates a reference to an earlier settlement.

referral fee   See **finder's fee**.

refinancing   **1.** Taking out a new loan to replace an existing loan; especially the replacing of an interim loan with a long-term or permanent loan. Also referred to as 'refunding'. In the US, if a new mortgage is taken out and the proceeds utilised to repay an existing mortgage before it is due, this is referred to as 'advance refinancing'. See also **financing**, **wraparound mortgage**.   **2.** The sale of a loan or debt by the original lender, in advance of its due date for repayment, as a means of recovering the amount outstanding. See also **discounting**.

reformation(AmE)   **1.** Derived from the Latin *reformatio*, 'the act of reforming' or 'changing for the better'. The act of putting right that which is faulty due to an accident, **mistake** or inadvertence. In particular, the correction of something, as a matter of discretion, that is erroneous or doubtful. For example, the correction of a document by a court at the request of one of the parties who has realized that the agreement does not state that which was intended, usually because of a **mistake** or a clerical error.

Reformation does not create a new agreement, or vary the bargain reached; it merely records that which had been agreed previously. The court merely creates one agreement to be read as if it had been originally drawn in its rectified form. In effect, the court first rectifies or reforms the contract and will then decree **specific performance** of the contract as rectified. Reformation is an equitable remedy and, therefore, is granted only at the discretion of the court. Before a court will order rectification of a document it is necessary to establish, beyond reasonable doubt, what had originally been agreed and that it is proper to substitute that which was really agreed in place of that set down in the documentation. In English law, the process is more usually called **rectification**. cf. **rescission**. See also **deed of rectification**(Eng)/**deed of reformation**(US), **mere equity**, *non est factum*, **restitution**.

reformation deed(US)   See **deed of rectification**(Eng)/**deed of reformation**(US).

refunding   See **refinancing**.

refurbishment   The process of making as good as new, including essential modernisation and **renovation**. The restoration of a building in order to give it a new lease of life; in particular, so as to restore a former usefulness and style. Refurbishment does not aim to alter the essential fabric and design of a building, but to modernise and repair it, in order to preserve the building, while replacing worn or outmoded components. Refurbishment generally goes further than reconditioning, but does not extend to **reconstruction**. See also **rehabilitation**.

regional plan(Eng)   A non-statutory form of **development plan** prepared for a large area of a country or region. The primary intention of a regional plan is to link together plans prepared by local planning authorities (e.g. structure plans) with plans prepared on a national level. Sometimes called a 'strategic plan'.

Glasson, John. *An Introduction to Regional Planning: Concepts, Theory and Practice.* 2nd ed. London: UCL Press, 1992.

regional shopping center   See **shopping center**.

register   1. A book, written record, or other permanent volume in which important information is systematically recorded and indexed for future reference. In particular, an official public record of land ownership, together with associated interests and encumbrances. See also **Companies Charges Register**(Eng), **Land Charges Register**(Eng), **land registration**(Eng), **Land Registry**(Eng), **land recording**(US), **local land charges register**(Eng), **planning inquiry**(Eng),

registered land.   2.(US)See **recorder**, **registrar**, **Torrens title system**.

register of planning applications(Eng)   See **planning application**.

register of sasines(Scot)   The General Register of Sasines is an official register of the most recent valid conveyance of land ownership (*dominium*). Upon a transfer or 'substitution' of ownership of feudal land, the disposition is registered in the register of sasines. This may be distinguished from the conveyance of non-feudal land, which is registered in the Land Registry. The Register of Sasines records deeds relating to individual pieces of **heritable property**, rather than details of the owner. See also **sasine**.

register of titles(Aus/NZ)   A record of titles to land. A register under the **Torrens title system** that sets out a description of the registered land, the registered proprietor, details of any estate or interest in the land that is capable of registration and any registered dealing that affects the land, and any other information that relates to the land and can be recorded under the applicable legislation. See also **Land Transfer land**(NZ).

register of town and village greens(Eng)   See **green**.

register of writs and orders(Eng)   See **Land Charges Register**.

registered charge(Eng)   1. A legal mortgage or charge over registered land that has been created by **deed** and has been entered on the Charges Register of the **Land Registry** in the name of the proprietor of the charge (LRA 1925, s. 3(xxiii), ss. 25, 26). A registered charge is the usual means by which a mortgage of registered land is effected and may be created by a **charge by way of a legal mortgage**; or by an express lease of freehold land, or (if appropriate) a sub-lease of leasehold land, in favour of the mortgagee. Once registered, a 'registered charge' comes into effect and the Registrar issues a **charge certificate** in favour of the mortgagee. Thus, a registered charge is a legal interest that can be created or disposed of by means of a 'registered disposition'.   **2.** "A **charge** the title to which is entered in the register [the register of titles at the **Land Registry**]", LRA 2002, s. 132(1). cf. **land charge**. See also **charge certificate, legal interest**.

registered disposition(Eng)   A **disposition** that is made by a proprietor of registered land "by way of transfer, charge, lease or otherwise and to which (when required to be registered) special effect or priority is given … on registration", LRA 1925, s. 3(xxii). See also **registered charge, registrable disposition**.

registered estate(Eng)   **1.** The **legal estate**, or any other registered interest, of which the owner is registered as the proprietor (LRA 1925, s. 3(xxiii)).   **2.** "A **legal estate** the title to which is entered in the register [the register of titles at the **Land Registry**], other than a registered charge", LRA 2002, s. 132(1).

registered encumbrance(Eng)   A general term for any **encumbrance** on land that is registered or recorded so that it will remain binding on a purchaser of the land or any interest therein. Such an encumbrance is registered for its own protection. If not registered, it is not normally binding on third parties, so that any person who subsequently acquires the land is freed of the encumbrance. See also **equitable interest, land charge, Land Charges Register, local land charge, minor interest, registered charge**.

registered land   **1.** Land that is registered under the **Torrens title system**, or a system of land registration based thereon. See also **land recordation**(US).   **2.**(Eng)An area of land that forms the subject matter of **land registration**. In particular, any estate or interest in land registered at the Land Registry (LRA 1925, s. 3(xxiv)).   **3.**(Eng)"A **registered estate** or **registered charge**", LRA 2002, s. 132(1).

registered land certificate(Eng)   See **land certificate**.

registered owner   **1.**(US)See **record owner**.   **2.**(Eng)See **registered proprietor**.

registered proprietor   **1.**(Eng)The party entered on the Proprietorship Register at the **Land Registry** as the holder of a registered title to land (LRA 1925, s. 3(xx)). A registered proprietor who has acquired an area of land in good faith is guaranteed a good title to the land, subject only to any **entry** on the register (which may be a caution, notice, inhibition or restriction) and any **overriding interest**. In the case of settled land, the registered proprietor is the **tenant for life**. With effect from October 13 2003, the 'registered proprietor' is the owner of the **registered estate** as named in the 'proprietorship register'. The registered proprietor may be: (i) a proprietor who is in physical possession of the land; or (ii) a proprietor who is physically in possession and is entitled to be registered as the proprietor, and possession of another person is attributed to the registered proprietor (for example, where a tenant is in possession, and the registered proprietor is the landlord) (LRA 2002, s. 131). See also **absolute title, proprietor in possession**.   **2.**(Aus/NZ)The registered holder of the estate in land as held in **fee simple** under the **Torrens title system**. See also **Land Transfer land**(NZ).

registered rent(Eng)   **1.** A **fair rent** established by a rent officer, or a Rent Assessment Committee, for a residential property that is subject to a **regulated tenancy** and registered at the local town hall. On or after January 15, 1989 no new regulated tenancies can be created and a newly created tenancy of a dwelling-house is likely to be either an **assured tenancy** or an **assured shorthold tenancy** (HA 1988, s. 34).   **2.** A rent payable under a **restricted contract**, as determined by a **rent tribunal**, and registered by a local authority, which has a duty to keep an up-to-date register of such rents. The register must contain details of the rent, the contract, and the dwelling to which the contract applies (RA 1977, ss. 79-81).

registered social landlord (RSL)(Eng)   A landlord that is a registered charity and is registered with the **Housing Corporation**. Broadly, an RSL may be a registered charity that is a **housing association**, a registered industrial or provident society, or a registered company. The body must be non-profit and have as its objects or powers the provision, construction, improvement or management of: (a) houses to let; (b) houses for members of the body (where membership is limited to those who are entitled or prospectively entitled to occupy a house managed by that body); or (c) hostels (HA 1996, s. 2).

registered title(Eng)   See **land registration**.

registered valuer(Aus/NZ)   A **valuer** who is accredited or registered with a professional organisation as suitably qualified by education and experience. In Australia, a 'registered valuer' is accredited and registered with an appropriate State chapter of the Institute of Valuers and Land Economists or a State licensing body. In New Zealand, the valuer is registered with the Valuers Registration Board under the Valuers Act 1948. See also Appendix A, **Real Estate Associations, Australia and New Zealand**.

registrable disposition(Eng)   Any **disposition** of a registered estate or registered charge that is required to be completed by **registration**, i.e. a disposition of an estate in land that does not operate at law until the relevant requirements are met for the its registration at the **Land Registry** (LRA 2002, ss. 27, 132(1)).

registrable interest(Eng)   An interest in land that can be registered. Since 1925, the only estate in land that can be registered in the name of a proprietor is a **legal estate** (and an **overriding interest** that was registered before 1925), any other interest in registered land takes effect in equity as **minor interest** (LRA 1925, s. 2(1)). A legal estate is the only interest in land that can be registered; any other interest in registered land, i.e. a minor interest, is *entered* on the register against the registered estate. On or after December 1, 1990 all land in England and Wales is compulsorily registrable when there is a conveyance of a 'legal estate' (i.e. a *sale* of the freehold, the *grant* of a lease for more than 21 years, or an assignment on *sale* of a lease with more than 21 years still to run). If the registration is not applied for within two months of the sale or grant, the legal estate vests in the transferor, who then holds it upon trust for the transferee (LRA 1925, s. 123). See also **absolute title**, **good leasehold title**, **land registration**, **qualified title**, **possessory title**, **registrable estate**, **registrable disposition**.

registrar   1.(Eng)In England and Wales, an official appointed to maintain records at the **Land Registry**.   2.(US)One who is appointed to compile and maintain a public register of deeds, mortgages, liens and other instruments affecting the title to, or creating an encumbrance over, land. A term used especially in counties that have adopted the **Torrens title system**, where such an official is called the 'Registrar of Titles' or 'Registrar of Deeds'. In some counties called a 'register'. See also **recorder**.

registration   See **land recording**(US), **land registration**, **Torrens title system**.

registration duty or **registration tax**   A tax payable on the registration of a formal document or right, especially an *ad valorem* tax payable on the registration of title following the transfer of an interest in property. cf. **stamp duty**. See also **conveyance tax**(US), **recording tax**(US).

regress   Going back; the act of retaking **possession**, especially by a person who has been wrongfully dispossessed. See also **right of re-entry**.

regression analysis   A statistical model that is used to show the average relationship between dependent variables. In particular, to show the degree to which the change in one factor is more or less affected by other factors. Simple linear regression shows the relationship between a single dependent variable and an independent variable. Multiple regression analysis shows the relationship between the dependent variable and two or more independent variables. Regression analysis may be used to show the relationship between such variables as value and population, income, distance or time. Regression analysis differs from **correlation** as it is used to predict the possible effect of one or more changes on a given factor, whereas correlation only shows the strength of the relationship between two factors. See also **sensitivity analysis**.

regression of value theory   An appraisal theory that the value of any one property tends to be drawn to the lowest level of property values in the neighbourhood. (A theory that may be considered akin to Gresham's law: "bad money drives out good".) cf. **progression of value theory**.

regular mortgage(US)   A **mortgage** that conveys an interest in land to the mortgagee, with a provision that the mortgage will be void on repayment of the entire debt; as distinguished from a mortgage that grants a mere right over property as security for a debt such as an **equitable mortgage**, the creation of a **deed of trust**, or a mere deposit of title documents with the lender. A term that is used only in those states that recognize a mortgage as a transfer of property (title theory states) and has no application in lien theory states. Sometimes called a 'technical mortgage'.

regulated tenancy(Eng)   A tenancy of a dwelling-house that is either a **protected tenancy** (i.e. a contractual tenancy that is afforded statutory security of tenure and rent regulation) or is a **statutory tenancy** (i.e. a tenancy that comes into existence when a protected tenancy comes to an end contractually), unless excluded from the statutory provisions that affect such tenancies (Rent Act 1977, ss. 18, 24(3), 143). On or after January 15 1989, no new regulated tenancies can be created and a newly created tenancy of a dwelling-house is likely to be either an **assured tenancy** or an **assured shorthold tenancy**. See also **fair rent**.

regulatory taking(US)   See **inverse condemnation**.

rehabilitation   The process of restoring to a habitable condition, especially restoring a property to its original condition without changing the design or style. Rehabilitation is carried out generally as part of a program for the improvement and restoration of buildings in a specific area. The rehabilitated buildings are returned, as far as possible, to their original condition, but with the provision of modern conveniences, both for the buildings and for the area as a whole, together with an upgraded standard of accommodation. In particular, rehabilitation refers to the process of improving the living conditions in a residential area that has fallen into a state of urban decay, especially when government assistance is provided. Rehabilitation may include partial reconstruction and redevelopment, in order to improve the environment in which the buildings are situated, but does not extend to changing the basic character of the area, its form, or the structure of the buildings. See also **refurbishment**, **rehabilitation order**(Eng), **renewal area**(Eng), **renovation**, **urban renewal**.

Reilly's law   See **catchment area**.

reinstate   See **reinstatement**.

reinstatement   1. The replacement or restoration of a property to its original condition; the act or process of returning something to its former state. The act of rebuilding a property that has been demolished or destroyed, has collapsed, or has fallen into a state of ruin or dilapidation.

In an insurance policy, the meaning of 'reinstate' depends on whether the property in question is a building or a chattel. A building is reinstated *in situ*, whereas a chattel is reinstated *in statu*. Thus, reinstatement of a building requires, as far as is possible, that the damage is made good where the building stands; but with chattels, reinstatement requires that the chattel *per se* is put back as it was, but not necessarily where it was. However, under most insurance policies, an insurer has no greater obligation when reinstating a building after a fire than to put the building in substantially the same state as it was before it was damaged; nor is the insurer bound to pull down the old walls and replace them entirely on account, for example, of defects in the foundations. See also **rebuild**, **repair**, **reinstatement basis**. **2.** The act of restoring a loan to its agreed contractual status, i.e. paying arrears up to date.

reinstatement basis A basis on which an insurance policy is accepted so that, in the event of a total loss, the insurer agrees to meet the **reinstatement cost** for an equivalent property. As a rule, the insurer undertakes to pay the cost of replacing or reinstating the property with the nearest equivalent, but no better, and limits his total liability to the insured value stated in the policy. In some cases, the insurer's liability may be limited to the **actual cash value** of the loss suffered by the insured (in effect taking account of the depreciated cost of the property)—at least unless or until the property's true cost of reinstatement is ascertained.

In English law, in certain circumstances an insurer may be obliged to reinstate, rather than pay monetary compensation: (a) when the policy expressly so requires; (b) when the property is held in trust or by a mortgagee in possession, or is an ecclesiastical property; or (c) if the insurer suspects arson or fraud, or when requested by the person interested in the property (Fire Prevention (Metropolis) Act 1774, s. 83: this Act, in spite of the title, applies to the whole of England, but not to Lloyd's underwriters). In addition, a mortgagee may be able to insist that any monies received under a policy effected on the property that is the subject matter of his security be applied in or towards the discharge of the mortgage debt (LPA 1925, s. 108(4)). An insured cannot, without giving prior notice, reinstate of his own accord and then ask to be reimbursed by the insurer with the cost he has incurred. See also **average**, **indemnity**, **insurance rent**, **new-for-old insurance**.

reinstatement clause **1.** A covenant in a lease that provides for the premises to be reinstated by one or other party to the lease, in the event that the demised premises are destroyed by fire or any other accident.

At common law, the destruction of the demised premises by fire or an act of God does not terminate the lease and strictly the tenant's obligation to pay rent continues unless there is an express agreement to the contrary. As a rule, a covenant by the lessor to repair or keep the premises in repair requires that the lessor reinstate the premises in the event of partial or total destruction by fire or other casualties. However, many leases of commercial or industrial premises provide the lessor with an option to terminate the lease in such instances, especially if the damage is substantial. As regards the continuing liability to pay rent, if the lease can be said to be frustrated, as where the demised premises are only part of a building and the tenant has no interest in the land, the lease may be said to have come to an end. Similarly, the lease would be frustrated if the property is washed away by the sea.

In the US, in some states the obligation to pay rent does not come to an end unless there has been a destruction of the entire subject matter of the lease, so that nothing remains capable of being held or enjoyed. However, many states have enacted statutes that relieve the tenant of an obligation to pay rent if the premises are destroyed to the point of being untenantable, especially in the case of residential property; or, at least, the rent is suspended for a reasonable time to allow the lessor to reinstate the premises. See also **frustration**, **set-off**. **2.** A clause in a lease that provides that the tenant is to reinstate the premises to the same condition that they were in at the start of the lease. This includes removing any fixtures and fittings that the tenant is permitted to remove (notably trade fixtures) and carrying out repairs and decoration in accordance with the provisions of the lease. See also **fixture**, **repair**, **schedule of dilapidation**, **trade fixture**.

reinstatement cost   **1.** In valuation terms, the total **cost** of a property obtained by assessing the cost of acquiring an equivalent area of land (or the value of the land on which any building stands) and adding the estimated cost of replacing the building, after allowing for depreciation. See also **cost approach**(US), **equivalent reinstatement**(BrE), **reinstatement method of valuation**(BrE).   **2.** In insurance, the cost of replacing a building that has been destroyed in order to provide, as far as possible, a suitable replacement in terms of design and efficiency. The cost of rebuilding a property in its present form at current prices. Such cost should allow for any modifications to meet statutory requirements that apply to the new building works and any physical conditions that have to be complied with to permit the rebuilding, as well as the cost of complying with environmental conditions and costs required to protect adjoining property. The cost also includes site clearance, fees, planning application costs, and any taxes applicable to the construction work. Such cost may be based on the assumed provision of an equivalent modern building, either without any allowance for depreciation of the original building at the time of destruction – 'new-for-old' – or after an appropriate allowance for depreciation – 'old-for-old' (old-for-old insurance is also called **indemnity insurance** because it provides a true indemnity for the actual loss suffered). However, if there is no provision as to which basis to adopt, the insurer need pay for no more than an equivalent property 'as was', i.e. the policy is said to be on a **reinstatement basis**. cf. **reproduction cost**. See also **reinstatement**.

reinstatement cost approach(US)   See **cost approach**.

reinstatement method of valuation(BrE)   A **valuation** of a property based on an assessment of its **reinstatement cost**, i.e. the cost of acquiring an alternative site and the cost of rebuilding a similar, but not necessarily identical, building.

This method of valuation is used in particular to value a property for which there is no ready market, e.g. a school, hospital or church, and although strictly the assessed amount is not a **market value**, it is taken as the best approximation thereto. Sometimes called the 'cost of replacement method', the 'contractor's method' or the 'contractor's test'. See also **contractor's basis**, **cost approach**(US), **depreciated replacement cost**, **equivalent reinstatement**.

reinstatement value   See **equivalent reinstatement**, **reinstatement cost**.

reinvestment rate   The rate at which income received from an investment is assumed to be reinvested during the holding period of the investment. In a conventional income appraisal, this is assumed to be the same as the rate of return on the investment. However, this rate need not be the same as the rate of return on that investment and the 'income capitalization rate' can be adjusted to allow for a different reinvestment rate.

rejection of an offer   Declining to accept an offer. Rejection of an offer occurs if and when: (a) the notification of rejection is received by the offeror; (b) an offer is made subject to conditions; or (c) a counter offer is submitted to the offeror. cf. acceptance. See also **lapse**, **revocation**.

relation back   The rule or doctrine of 'relation back' provides that a document may relate back to a date that is earlier than the one upon which it is executed, if that gives effect to the intention of the parties. Thus, a deed placed in escrow, and subsequently delivered, may 'relate back' or take effect from the date on which it was originally escrowed. In such a case, the death of the grantor does not prevent title passing in accordance with the escrow instructions. A similar principle may not apply to an option agreement. See also **escrow**, **further advance**.

re-lease   To grant a new **lease** of property that previously has been let, either to a tenant whose period of occupation has come to an end or to a new tenant. Synonymous with 're-let'. cf. **release**. See also **renewal**.

release   1. The act of giving up or relinquishing a right, claim or privilege, especially one arising from a contract. The extinguishment of a debt or claim by payment. A release may be distinguished from a **receipt** because a release extinguishes the claim, and when given in itself terminates the debt; whereas a receipt is only evidence of payment. A receipt will not extinguish the debt if there is clear evidence that payment has not been made (in part or in whole). The release of a mortgage debt means that the total debt, including interest and principal, has been paid and the property that was held as security has been returned to the mortgagor unencumbered. A document that acknowledges the discharging of a debt or the extinguishment of a right may also be called a release, or a 'deed of release'. See also **accord and satisfaction, extinguishment, surrender, writing**.   2. The giving up of a legal right of action, whether expressly, by implication or by operation of law. cf. **estoppel**. See also **renunciation**.   3. The conveying back of an estate. The **relinquishment** of an interest in land to one who currently has possession; especially the surrender of a right to a larger estate, which may be either a **remainder** or a **reversion**, to the holder of an inferior estate in the same land. For example, the ceding of a remainderman's right to a tenant for life so as to give the latter a fee interest, or the granting of one co-owner's rights to the other. cf. **re-lease**. See also **abandonment, quitclaim deed, lease and release, release deed**.   4.(Scot)See **renunciation**.

release clause   1. A clause in a mortgage that permits the release of all or some of the properties held as security for a loan. See **partial release clause**.   2. A provision in a contract that enables one of the parties to escape from its provisions in the event that a specified event does or does not occur, as with a provision in a **conditional contract**. In particular, a provision in a contract for sale which enables the seller to terminate the contract in the event that he receives a higher offer within a specified period of time, or after the prospective buyer has been given the opportunity to equal any bona fide higher offer.

release deed(US)   1. A deed that frees a debtor's claim over a property that has been charged or granted as security for a deed, especially a deed that terminates a **deed of trust** so as to free the property to the debtor (trustor). As a rule, when a mortgage loan is repaid in full the mortgagee's security interest in the mortgaged property is extinguished and the full legal ownership restored to the mortgagor, without the need for any deed of reconveyance or release. However, it is common practice to execute some form of release deed; in particular, to record the fact at the public records office and thereby discharge the recorded mortgage. Also called a 'deed of reconveyance', 'deed of release', 'discharge deed' or sometimes a 'deed of satisfaction'. See also **release, reconveyance, satisfaction certificate**.   2. See **quitclaim deed**.

release of mechanic's lien   See **mechanic's lien**.

release, remise and forever quitclaim(US) See **quitclaim deed**.

releasee   A person who is released from a contract, debt or obligation.

releasor or **releaser**   A person who grants a release; one releases another party from an obligation.

relessee   A person who is granted a new lease.

relessor   A person who grants a new lease or re-leases a property.

re-let   See **re-lease**.

reliction   Derived from the Latin *relictus*, 'leaving behind'. The gradual process by which land may be left permanently exposed as the sea, a lake or a river recedes. Also, the land so left. This land comes into the ownership of the abutting owner, provided the land has been exposed by a gradual, but permanent process. See also **accretion**, **dereliction**.

relief   1. A legal remedy or redress. In particular, a remedy obtained from a court of equity against a grievance, wrong, or injustice. A remedy granted at the discretion of a court to redress an injustice when a claim to a **penalty** or a right of **forfeiture** has arisen. Relief may take the form of an **injunction**, a decree of **specific performance**, relief against **forfeiture** of a lease, or **rescission** of a contract.   2.(Eng)An equitable remedy sought by a tenant from a court against a landlord's right of re-entry or **forfeiture** under a lease. When a landlord takes proceedings to enforce a right of re-entry or forfeiture under a lease as a result of the tenant's default, the tenant may apply to the court for relief from the effect of that an action. In that case, the court may grant or refuse relief as it thinks fit, having regard to the circumstances and the conduct of the parties (LPA 1925, s. 146(2)). Whether such relief is granted depends, *inter alia*, on: (a) the nature of the breach; (b) whether the tenant is able and willing to remedy the breach; (c) whether the tenant's default was wilful; (d) whether the breach involves an illegal or immoral user; (e) the gravity of the breach; (f) the conduct of the landlord; (g) the personal and financial position of the tenant; and (h) the disparity between the value of the property of which forfeiture is claimed and the damage caused by the breach.

  Relief against forfeiture of a lease has the effect of extinguishing any effect that the forfeiture might have had, so that a **subtenant**, who might have lost his right to the demised premises because the head-lease was to have been forfeited, is reinstated as if the forfeiture was deemed not to have taken place at all. Strictly, any sub-lease comes to an end if the head lease is forfeited. However, the subtenant also has a right to apply for relief and, if granted, he may take over the whole or any part of the head-leased property "for the whole of the lease or any less term … [upon such terms as the court] may think fit", LPA 1925, s. 146(4).

  'Relief' may also be granted against a requirement that a tenant carry out internal decorative repairs to a house or other building, after the court has had regard to "all the circumstances of the case", LPA 1925, s. 147(1). This provision does not apply if the decoration is necessary for the maintenance or preservation of the structure; to keep the premises in a habitable or sanitary condition, to comply with a statutory requirement; or when the tenant is expressly required to decorate at the start of the lease or yield up the premises in a specified state of repair at the end of the term (LPA 1925, s. 147(2)). See also **grounds for possession**.   3. A reduction or removal of a liability or obligation, e.g. a reduction in a liability to pay a tax or levy.   4. A payment made under the **feudal system** of land tenure by a tenant to the lord of the manor upon succeeding to land by descent.   5. The topography of a land surface.

relinquishment   The act of giving up, surrendering, or abandoning a right or thing. See also **abandonment**, **release**, **surrender**, **waiver**.

relocation   1. The removal to a new location. See also **suitable alternative accommodation**. 2.(Scot)The tacit renewal of a lease on similar terms when a tenant holds over after the original lease has expired.

relocation clause   A clause in a lease that enables the landlord to require a tenant to move to alternative accommodation. A relocation clause may be inserted when the lessor anticipates that he will require the demised premises for redevelopment, or when he wishes to be able to relocate a tenant in order to rationalise the space occupied by the tenants in an office building or shopping center. Such a clause normally requires the landlord to offer reasonably comparable space. If there is no such express provision it may still be considered that there is an implied condition to that effect, as to insist that a tenant move to space that is patently less suitable (in either size or cost) could be construed as a breach of the tenant's covenant for **quiet enjoyment.**

rem(Lat)   'Thing'. See **action** *in rem.*

remainder   1. A residual interest or **estate** in land. An estate in land that comes into effect, as a right to possession, upon the natural determination of an immediately preceding estate; was created at the same time and by the same instrument as the preceding estate; but does not revert to the original grantor of the estate that has come to an end. Thus, if a person creates two or more estates in land that follow in time, e.g. a grant "to A for life, then to B for life, then to C in fee simple", the estate preceding the remainder (B's interest) is called a **particular estate** (from the Latin *particula*, 'small part') and the interest thereafter (C's interest) is the remainder (from the Latin *remanere*, 'left over' or 'remaining'). If the estate were to pass back to A, after B, then A's interest would be a **reversion** (A being the original grantor) and not a remainder. A remainder may be described as a **future interest**; the element of futurity is the time at which it becomes an interest in possession after the natural termination of a prior particular estate. A future interest that arises or springs up upon the occurrence of a designated event, such as if a person attains a certain age or at a specified date in the future, is not a remainder. A remainder may be 'vested' or 'executed'; or 'contingent' or 'executory'. A vested remainder takes effect after another estate is 'spent', i.e. as soon as the particular estate ends, which is usually on the death of the holder of the particular estate. However, a vested remainder requires that the person who will hold the remainder be ascertained at the outset. A contingent remainder represents a possibility or prospect of an estate. In particular, an estate that is granted to someone as yet unborn; one whose right is dependent on the life of another; or one whose right is dependent on surviving to a given age or surviving the life of another. For example, an estate granted "to A for life, remainder to the children of A" (when A has no children as yet); "to A for life, and then to B if B survives A"; and "to A for life, and then to those children of A who reach 21" (assuming that none of the children has yet reached 21) all create contingent remainders in favour of the potential successors. A contingent remainder is not strictly an estate in land at all, but merely represents the possibility of acquiring an estate after some dubious or uncertain event, so that, in the US, it may be called an 'executory remainder'; or a 'remainder subject to a condition precedent'. A contingent remainder may become a vested remainder when the contingent event occurs or when the person who will obtain the future estate is ascertained.

In the US, an estate in remainder is sometimes called an 'ulterior estate', as distinguished from the particular estate that has determined. Also, in some jurisdictions, a contingent remainder in fee is said to be 'in abeyance' when it is limited to take effect in possession upon the termination of the particular estate, but the holder of the particular estate has not yet been ascertained. The person who holds the interest in the remainder is termed the 'remainderman', but his interest is called a 'reversionary interest'. See also **contingent interest, future estate, waste.** 2. An estate or interest in real property, or an entitlement to the proceeds of sale thereof, left after the expenses of administering a will and the express wishes of the testator have been satisfied. cf. **residue.** 3. The ultimate **beneficiary** under a trust. See also *cestui que trust.*

remainder interest   An interest in land that comes into existence as a **remainder.** Such an interest may also be called a 'reversionary interest', although that is generally used to refer to an interest that will arise in **reversion.**

remainder person   See remainderman.

remainder subject to a condition subsequent(US)   See remainder.

remainderman   One whose interest in land

comes into effect, as a right to possession, after another interest has expired, but who was not the grantor of the interest that has come to an end, i.e. one who holds or is entitled to an interest in **remainder**. cf. **reversioner**. See also **waste**.

remaining economic life The period of time before a property reaches the end of its **economic life**. The time left for an investor to recover (or recapture) the capital he has invested in a property.

remeasurement contract A form of **building contract** in which the price is based initially on approximate quantities (of material and labour) and an agreed schedule of rates for the work. Work is carried out and paid for during the contract period on a basis of 'best estimate' and the final price is established when all the work is completed. However, unlike a **cost-plus contract**, many of the elements that make up the price are fixed, or capable of being fixed, at the commencement of the contract. This contract is used when the exact work and, therefore, the quantities cannot be determined precisely; for example, when, at the commencement of a contract, the extent of the building work is concealed. cf. **lump-sum contract**. See also **fixed-price contract**.

remedies See **accord and satisfaction**, **damages, distress, equity, injunction, liquidated damages, rectification, relief, rescission, specific performance**.

remise To give up, **surrender**, or **release** a claim. The terms 'remise' and 'remit' are used in a deed of surrender of an estate in land to signify that the grantee gives up all rights or claims to the land. In the US, 'remise, release and quitclaim' are operative words used in a **quitclaim deed**. cf. **demise**.

remit **1.** To send back; putting back. To send money, especially to pay for goods or services. To annul a debt or fine by payment. See also **remise**, **tender**. **2.** To refrain from exacting something; to desist from extracting a penalty. To give up. See also **release, surrender, waiver**.

remittance **1.** Money sent by one person to another, especially as payment or settlement (in whole or in part) of a debt. **2.** An instrument by which money is remitted from one person to another.

remote vesting See **rule against perpetuities**.

remoteness of damage See **damages**.

remoteness rule See **rule against perpetuities**.

remuneration See **commission, compensation, fee**, *quantum meruit*, **unjust enrichment**.

remunerative rate **1.** A rate of interest that provides an investor with an acceptable return on his investment taking account of the risk, but makes no allowance for recovery of the invested capital. Also called the **investment rate**. cf. **accumulative rate**. See also **dual-rate capitalization factor**[AmE]/**dual-rate years' purchase**[BrE] **2.** The rate at which profit is generated from an investment.

render **1.** To yield, return or pay. A statement of the **rent** to be paid under a lease is frequently preceded by the words 'rendering and paying'. See also **reddendum**. **2.** A **royalty** paid in kind.

renegotiable-rate mortgage (RRM) A loan, or mortgage, granted subject to a condition that permits the lender to vary the rate of interest at stipulated times or on specified conditions, such as after an agreed number of years. A renegotiable-rate loan is effectively a long-term loan, where the interest rate is reviewed at the end of each set period, i.e. the rate is revised by agreement from one period to another. A renegotiable-rate loan may be distinguished from an **adjustable-rate**

mortgage, which provides for the rate of interest to be varied in line with an autonomous interest rate or index. Also called a 'rollover mortgage' (ROM), especially when the loan is effectively renewed or 'rolls over' at the end of a set term. See also **Canadian rollover mortgage**.

renew **1.** To restore to a new condition; to put something as far as possible into the same state or condition as it was before any damage, destruction, deterioration or dilapidation occurred. See also **rebuild, repair.** **2.** To grant something anew; to begin again. See also **option to renew, renewal. 3.** To replace an existing loan, that was granted for a fixed period of time and has now come to an end, with a new loan. cf. **refinancing**. See also **rollover loan**.

renewal **1.** The act or process of making anew. The **restoration** or revival of something. Renewal requires that the substituted item or property is new, as distinguished from **reinstatement** which may entail putting back an old item or property but in serviceable or useable condition. Renewal may involve the replacement of all or a substantial part of a property, but replacement of a small part of the whole cannot amount to a renewal of that whole. See also **reconstruction, renovation, urban renewal.** **2.** The making of a new agreement or contract. The carrying forward of the terms of a contract for a new period of time. The renewal of a contract may mean to continue with the agreement on the same terms, but for an extended period of time, or to enter into a new agreement between the parties. However, 'renewal' generally means to create a new agreement upon the expiration of the existing agreement, as distinguished from an **extension** that prolongs the duration, but otherwise leaves all the terms unchanged. cf. **re-lease**. See also **business tenancy**[(Eng)]**, novation, option to renew, perpetually renewable lease, renew, reversionary lease**.

renewal area (RA)[(Eng)] An area that primarily contains housing accommodation and where the local housing authority is satisfied that the living conditions are unsatisfactory and can most effectively be dealt with by declaring it a 'renewal area' in order that the authority can use its powers in such an area to improve or repair the premises in the area; to ensure the proper and effective management and use of the housing accommodation; and to improve the well-being of the residents of the area. A renewal area is generally intended to be improved within 10 years (LGHA 1989, ss. 89-100). A renewal area is intended to be more extensive than a **general improvement area** or a **housing action area**, both of which it replaced as a means of dealing with a run-down housing area (LGHA 1989, s. 98).

renewal fine[(US)] See **ground rent lease**.

renewal option See **option to renew**.

renovation Derived from the Latin *renovare*, 'to make new'. The process of restoring or putting back to a former state, especially something that has been substantially impaired by time and neglect. A process that may include **repair** and **improvement**; but not complete reconstruction, nor a substantial modification or alteration to the structure. See also **refurbishment, rehabilitation, renew**.

renovation grant[(Eng)] See **grant**.

rent **1.** A periodic payment or return that a tenant makes to an owner of land, as recompense for a right to use and profit from the **exclusive occupation** of that land, or any other corporeal property, for a determinable period of time. A contractual payment (whether in a monetary form or otherwise) for the use of land; remuneration that a tenant is bound to make for the exclusive right to receive the fruits and benefits of land. Rent is a payment that stems from the relationship of **landlord** and **tenant** and is an acknowledgement of that relationship, and if there is no express covenant in the **lease**, or an agreement for a lease, there is an implied covenant to pay a reasonable rent for the use and occupation of the occupied premises. Rent arising from the relationship of landlord and tenant is strictly called **rentservice**; as distinguished from a **rentcharge**, which is a burden due by an owner of land to another party with whom there is no relationship of landlord and tenant. However, the term 'rent' may be used sometimes to cover either form of payment, and in common usage it is used to refer to a payment from a tenant to a landlord.

Rent must be certain in its character, or must be expressed in such a way as to be capable of being made certain, in respect of both the amount due and the time when it is due. In this respect, the maxim adopted is *id certum est quod certum reddi potest*, 'that is certain which can be rendered certain'. A rent that is "to be agreed" is uncertain and therefore unenforceable. However, as a rule, a rent that is to be determined "having regard to the market valuation of the property" or "to be fixed by arbitration" at the time it is to be fixed is a valid rent; it is capable of being made certain and, therefore, may be enforced as such. Normally rent is a pecuniary payment, but it may be made payable in goods or services, although if the payment is to take the form of part of the produce of the land it is not strictly rent. A payment outside the terms of a lease, or made after a lease has expired, e.g. **mesne profits**, is not strictly rent.

Rent should be paid to the landlord, or his agent, not to a third party and, in common law, it is payable on the demised premises, on the day that it is due, in **cash** (although if a landlord indicates that he will accept a cheque the landlord cannot refuse such a form of payment at a later date, as long as the cheque is honoured. However, a lease may specify, or it may be agreed, that rent is to be payable at any named interval, in any form, and at any place agreed between the parties or in any manner that is practical to the parties. Commonly rent is made payable at weekly, monthly, or (especially in commercial leases in the UK) quarterly intervals, in advance, but if no date is fixed, it is payable at the end of the period by reference to which the rent has been assessed. When a **day** is fixed for payment, the rent is in arrears if not paid by midnight of that day.

The obligation to pay rent terminates when the relationship of landlord and tenant comes to an end, which can be: (i) when a lease for a fixed term comes to an end; (ii) when the tenant is evicted (actually or constructively); (iii) if a lease is surrendered or frustrated; or (iv) if the tenant abandons the premises and the landlord re-enters and re-lets the premises.

In English statute law, rent is defined to include "a rent service or a rentcharge, or other rent, toll, duty, **royalty**, or annual or periodic payment in money or money's worth, reserved or issuing out of or charged upon land, but does not include mortgage interest", LPA 1925, s. 205 (xxiii). (The AEA 1925, s. 55(1) and the LRA 1925, s. 3(xxv) contain similar definitions, although the former statute excludes a royalty.) See also **abandonment, apportionment, assignment of rents**[US]**, assize rent, base rent, best rent, contractual rent, dead rent, distress, double rent, dry rent, equity rent, eviction, excess rent, exclusive rent**[BrE]**, fair rent, fee farm rent, forfeiture, gale rent, gold clause, graded rent, graduated rent, gross rent, ground rent, head rent, improved rent, inclusive rent**[BrE]**, insurance rent, interim rent, issues and profits, leasehold ground rent, market rent, net rent, penal rent, percentage rent, peppercorn rent, primary and secondary rental, profit rent**[BrE]**, quit rent, rack rent, reddendum, registered rent, rent control, rent in advance/rent in arrears, rent review clause, rent roll, rental, tonnage royalty, turnover rent, virtual rent.** **2.** In economics, rent is the excess of income over and above the minimum required to keep a factor of production in its present use, i.e. it means **economic rent**; "the economic return that accrues or should accrue to land from its use in production", Raleigh Barlowe, *Land Resource Economics; The Economics of Real Estate.* 4th ed. Prentice-Hall, 1985, p. 162. See also **quasi-rent**.

rent abatement   See **set-off**.

rent acceleration clause   See acceleration clause.

rent achievement(US)   See **holdback**.

Rent Assessment Committee(Eng)   A body that hears appeals against the decisions of a **rent officer** on the determination of the **fair rent** for a regulated tenancy of a dwelling-house. A Rent Assessment Committee normally comprises three members drawn from a rent assessment panel (appointed for a particular area by the Lord Chancellor and the Secretary for the Environment) – usually a surveyor, a layperson and a legally qualified chairperson (RA 1977, Sch. 10). It is a tribunal and not a court and is concerned only with determining the rental value of dwellings that come within its jurisdiction. A Rent Assessment Committee does not need to take account of the decision of the rent officer, but acts as an independent **expert** for the purpose of determining a fair rent. An appeal against a decision of a Rent Assessment Committee can be made to the High Court, but only on a point of law. Since 1988, if the holder of an **assured tenancy** disagrees with the rent proposed upon the renewal of the tenancy, he can apply to a Rent Assessment Committee to determine the appropriate level of rent, assuming that the landlord is willing to let the premises and ignoring the fact that there is a sitting tenant (HA 1988, s. 6). See also **Leasehold Valuation Tribunal**, **rent tribunal**.

rent book(Eng)   A book, or similar document, that must be provided to any person who is granted a right to occupy premises as a **residence** "in consideration of a rent payable weekly", L&T Act 1985, s. 4(1). The book must set out details of the landlord's name and address; the amount of rent payable; and various details of the other letting terms as prescribed by regulations made by the Secretary of State (L& T Act 1985, s. 5; Rent Book (Forms of Notice) Regulations 1982, as amended). It is a criminal offence for a landlord not to provide the requisite rent book, or similar document, with the prescribed information.

rent charge or **rent-charge**   See rentcharge.

rent concession   A discount from an established or market rent granted as an inducement for a particular tenant to enter into a lease. Such a discount may take the form of a direct reduction in the rent for all or part of the term of the lease; or some other concession granted by the landlord to a prospective tenant, such as the provision of assistance towards the cost of fitting out the tenant's space, or an agreement to maintain certain operating expenses or service charges at a fixed level. A 'rent concession' is intended to be a temporary provision; it is not a mere 'rent reduction' for the term of the lease. The aim of a rent concession is to maintain the general rent level in a building, or to create that illusion, in order to maintain the apparent value of the property – especially when negotiating with other tenants. Also called a 'lease concession'. See also **cash back**, **tenant improvement allowance**, **virtual rent**.

rent control   The regulation by law of the maximum level of rent that a landlord is permitted to charge a tenant for a particular property. Rent control may take the form of a temporary restriction on rent increases (usually as an anti-inflationary measure); linking rent levels or rent increases to an artificial statutory formula; or establishing a procedure for determining the maximum level of rent that may be charged based on a statutorily defined rental level, a **fair rent**(Eng), or some other defined level of 'rental value'. Alternatively, the control regulation may give the tenant a right to apply to an independent tribunal or a court to determine the appropriate **market rent** for the property and may then state that the landlord may not increase that rent for a fixed period of time. See also **registered rent**(Eng).

rent convergence   The bringing of rents into line with market value, especially when rents have been controlled or regulated and are gradually increased to their market level.

rent day   A day appointed or agreed for the payment of **rent**. Rent does not accumulate on a daily basis, but falls due for payment on an appointed or agreed day, such as a day of the week, month or year. See also **apportionment, quarter day, rent in advance/rent in arrears.**

rent deposit   See **deposit, security deposit.**

rent escalation   See **escalation clause.**

rent free period   A period during which a tenant is exempt from the obligation to pay rent. Normally granted at the start of the lease to act an incentive to a new tenant. The duration of the concession depends on market conditions and may vary from a few months to permit the tenant to fit out the premises, to several years when the landlord's aim is to attract major tenants during a period of oversupply of similar accommodation. See **effective lease rate, equivalent rent**(BrE)**, rent concession.**

rent gradient   A graphical representation of the relationship between the rent paid for a unit of property and its distance from a given point – usually from the central business district or the area of highest rent. As a broad rule, the rent for a parcel of land may be considered to decline in inverse proportion to the square of the distance from the place of highest value. See also **catchment area.**

rent guarantee   A **guarantee** or **surety** given to a landlord for the payment of rent by the tenant. Such a commitment may arise as part of the lease, in which case it is a surety, or it may be a collateral contract, in which case it arises only after the tenant has wholly failed in his obligations. The extent of the guarantee depends on the language used. If it is part of the lease, without qualification, the guarantor may be liable for all financial failings of the tenant, but usually a guarantee only applies to a failure to pay rent during the subsistence of the existing lease.

rent holdback(US)   See **holdback.**

rent in advance or **rent in arrears**   Rent is not due until the tenant has enjoyed the use of the property for the period that the payment is intended to cover; thus, it is payable in **arrears**, unless there is a clear agreement to the contrary. In modern leases it is more commonly made payable in arrears, "whether or not demanded", and the first amount is payable before possession of the leased premises is given. Rent is due on the date specified in the lease (or the appropriate anniversary of the commencement date), unless that day is a legal or public holiday in which case the liability for payment is postponed to the next day. See also **apportionment, distress.**

rent inclusion(US)   A rent that is charged to incorporate an operating expense, e.g. a rent that is billed to include the **base rent** and utility charges. See also **net lease.**

rent insurance   1. See **rent-loss insurance.** 2. See **use and occupation insurance.**

rent limit   See **registered rent.**

rent-loss insurance   Insurance obtained by a landlord to cover the loss of rental income from an investment, following damage caused by fire or special perils, until the building is restored and the tenant(s) can retake possession. Also called 'loss-of-rent insurance' or simply 'rent insurance'. The term 'rent-loss insurance' is more commonly used in the above sense, although it is sometimes used to refer to insurance that guarantees a landlord a fixed rental income from his property; or insurance that provides cover for the rent that a tenant may have to pay during the period that his leased premises cannot be occupied due to damage by fire or other such perils. cf. **tenant's default insurance, use and occupation insurance.**

rent multiplier(US)   See **income multiplier.**

rent officer(Eng)   A person appointed by, but

independent of, a local authority to determine the **fair rent** for a dwelling-house, in accordance with the provisions of the Rent Acts (Rent Act 1977, s. 63, as amended). An appeal against the decision of a rent officer may be made to a **Rent Assessment Committee** by either party to the tenancy. See also **certificate of fair rent, registered rent**.

rent policy   See **rent-loss insurance**.

rent reduction   A reduction in the amount of rent contractually due to a landlord under a tenancy. A rent reduction is a permanent facility granted to a tenant. cf. **rent concession**. See also **accord and satisfaction, set-off**.

rent register(Eng)   See **certificate of fair rent**.

rent registration(Eng)   See **registered rent**.

rent regulation   See **rent control**.

rent review clause(Eng)   A clause in a lease that permits the lessor or lessee to seek a reassessment of the rent of the demised premises at a specified interval or intervals, without any corresponding right for the lease to be determined at that stage. A rent review clause provides for the rental value of the demised premises to be reassessed, usually by reference to the then current **market rent**; as distinguished from a 'rent variation' or escalation clause by which the amount of rent is varied by reference to an index or price variation or is simply varied by a stated amount at specified intervals. A rent review clause is intended to keep the landlord's return in line with market conditions prevailing at the time of the review, while enabling the tenant to have secure possession for the term of the lease. It provides the tenant with a certainty as to his level of rent during the intervals between the rent review dates and still enables the landlord to combat the eroding value of the income he receives.

The operation of a rent review clause is a matter of law and valuation. It is a question of valuation and negotiation, supported if necessary by reference to an **expert** or **arbitrator** to determine the rent in cases when the landlord and tenant are unable to agree, and a reference to a court when there is a dispute over the interpretation of the provisions of the lease. See also **escalation clause**(US), **graduated rent, indexed rent, ratchet clause**(Aus/NZ), **revaluation lease, time is of the essence**.

Bernstein, Ronald, and Kirk Reynolds. *Essentials of Rent Review*. London: Sweet & Maxwell, 1995.

Barnes, Michael (editor), *Hill & Redman's Guide to Rent Review*. London: Butterworths, 2001.

Kemp, Margaret. *Drafting and Negotiating Rent Review Clauses*. London: Pearson, 1996.

rent roll   A schedule of the tenants and total **rent** received or receivable from a particular property, or the total rent received or receivable by a particular investor from his real estate portfolio, over a stipulated period of time.

rent service   See **rentservice**.

rent skimming(AmE)   See **equity skimming**.

rent stabilization(US)   See **rent control**.

rent-to-turnover ratio   See **occupancy cost ratio**.

rent tribunal(Eng)   A tribunal that was responsible for fixing reasonable rents in respect of a **restricted contract** (Housing Act 1980, s. 72). See also **Rent Assessment Committee**.

rent up   To fill up a new building with tenants. In the US, 'rent up' is also used to refer to the period of time taken to lease up a new building. See also **takeout commitment**.

rent variation clause(US)   See **escalation clause**.

rentable area(AmE)   The area let, or available for letting, in a commercial building. The area for which a tenant is deemed to pay rent. A term most commonly applied to such an area in an office building when the rent payable by a tenant is determined by applying an amount per unit area. 'Rentable area' is defined by the Building Owners and Managers Association International (BOMA) as the area of an office building "computed by measuring from the inside surface of the outer masonry building wall (but where the outer building wall is 50 per cent or more of glass, the rentable area shall be measured from the inside of glass area) to the finished surface of corridor side of partitions, or to the opposite outer masonry wall or glass surface whichever is applicable to the letting, including columns or projections necessary to the building". It is the "result of subtracting from the 'gross measured area' of a floor the 'major vertical penetrations'". No deduction is made for columns and projections necessary to the building and spaces outside the exterior walls, such a balconies, terraces, or corridors, are excluded. Ancillary areas, e.g. bathrooms, closets, etc., are generally included for single tenant floors or where a tenant has exclusive use thereof. Exclusions are made for certain shared areas; in particular, stairways, elevator shafts, ventilation stacks, air or service ducts, flues, etc., together with their enclosing walls. Thus, it is equivalent to the 'usable area', with its associated share of the floor common areas and the building common areas (those areas that provide services to the tenants of the building). To avoid misinterpretation of this definition see the BOMA's complete *Standard Method for Measuring Floor Area in Office Buildings* (1996) (**www.boma.org**). The American National Standards Institute defines rentable area in a similar way. It refers to the rentable area of a single tenancy floor as the 'full floor rentable area', and the rentable area of a multiple tenancy floor as the 'net rentable area', being the sum of all rentable areas on that floor, excluding areas not exclusively let to one tenant. The rentable area of a building is generally fixed for the life of a building and is rarely affected by changes in corridor size or configuration. Sometimes called the 'lettable area'. See also **net internal area**[BrE].

rentable-to-usable ratio[US]   See **loss factor**.

rentage[US]   **1.** The **base rent** in a lease, excluding any payment of a turnover rent; that is, the fixed minimum rent payable under a turnover or percentage lease. cf. **overage**.   **2.** A true or primary **rent** for land as paid under a lease, excluding any other payment made by a tenant to his landlord, such as operating cost contributions. See also **primary and secondary rental**.

rental   **1.** An amount paid as **rent**. A payment received periodically for the use of property. In particular, an annual payment for the hire of goods. See also **rental value**.   **2.** A corruption of rent roll – the sum total of rent receivable from a particular property for a defined period of time, usually a year.   **3.**[US]A property that is granted in return for rent, especially a residential property.

rental agent[US]   An **agent** or **broker** who acts as an intermediary in bringing together parties seeking property owners and those who are seeking to rent property. 'Rental agent' may refer also to a party who provides information on available properties in return for a fee that is payable by the prospective tenant. See also **accommodation agent**[Eng].

rental agreement   A **lease**. An express form of tenancy agreement. A term that is applied mainly to a short-term tenancy agreement, particularly when granted for residential property.

rental annuity   See **life annuity**.

rental area   See **gross leasable area**, **rentable area**.

rental equivalent   See **effective lease rate/ effective rental rate**.

rental escalation charge[US]   A payment made by a tenant, as required under an **escalation clause**, to cover an increase in **operating costs**.

rental method(BrE)   A method of valuation used to determine the annual rental value of a building by reference to rent paid for comparable properties. In particular, the valuation of a property for rating purposes using the **comparison method of valuation**. See also **investment method of valuation**, **rating valuation**.

rental multiplier(US)   See **income multiplier**.

rental period   The period of time or intervals covered by a payment of **rent**. The period in respect of which a payment of rent falls due. See also **apportionment**, **gale**, **rent in advance/rent in arrears**.

rental pool(US)   An arrangement by which a number of apartment owners pool their properties for renting and agree to share the proceeds and expenses of all the properties on an agreed basis – usually in proportion to the rental value or the area of the properties.

rental property(US)   Property that is subject to a lease (or leases), i.e. an income-producing or **investment property**. Property for which rent is paid or received.

rental purchase   A means of purchasing a property by which the whole or part of the purchase price is paid in three or more instalments, but the vendor retains the deeds to the property until all, or a specified part, of the purchase price is paid. The vendor enters into a contract for the sale of the property conditional upon payment of the purchase price by instalments. Until the final instalment is paid, the purchaser is permitted to occupy the property under a form of lease or licence, and title to the property is not transferred until the conditions of the contract are met in full. A rental purchase differs from a lease with an option to purchase, as the latter does not have any effect unless the option is exercised, i.e. it is a unilateral contract. In the US, also called a 'lease-purchase'. See also **conditional contract**, **installment land contract**(AmE), **installment sale**(AmE).

rental shortfall   1. The amount by which the rent from a property falls short of debt service. See also **default ratio**.   2. The amount by which the rent payable by a tenant is less than the market rent.   3. The amount by which the rent actually received in a given period is less than the rent payable under a lease, due to a defaulting tenant or a late payment. See also **effective gross income**.

rental value   1. The annual amount at which a property might reasonably be expected to let in the open market, assuming that the terms upon which it is let are similar to those upon which properties of a similar nature are normally let. See also **market value**.   2. See **use and occupation**.

rental value insurance   See **use and occupation insurance**.

rentcharge(Eng) or **rent charge** or **rent-charge**(AmE)   An annual or other periodic payment made for land when an owner has transferred land to another, but has not created a relationship of landlord and tenant. A payment made in the nature of rent but where the owner has no future interest in, or **reversion** to, the land. A rentcharge arises most frequently when the price for the purchase of land is made payable in whole or in part as an annual equivalent. It is a form of charge on land that, if it falls into arrears, enables the payee to take a personal action for the money; may entitle him to levy **distress**, or take possession of the land until the payment is made; but does not entitle him, as with **rentservice**, to regain the land.

In English law, no new rentcharges can be created after August 22, 1977, except: (a) one that relates to a **scheme of development** (one that is created to enforce a restrictive covenant or a payment for the maintenance of property) – an **estate rentcharge**; (b) one that has the effect of making the land upon which it is charged **settled land**; (c) certain forms of statutory rentcharge made in order to enforce a payment for improvements to land; or (d) a rentcharge created under an order of the court. All existing rentcharges are to be redeemed by not later than July 22, 2037 (Rentcharges Act 1977, ss. 2, 3). In this context, a rentcharge is defined as "any annual or other periodic sum out of land, charged on or issuing out of land, except – (a) rent reserved by a lease or tenancy, or (b) any sum payable by way of interest", Rentcharges Act 1977, s. 1.

In the US, rent charges were created only in a few Eastern states (notably Maryland, Pennsylvania and New York) and are now virtually obsolete. In such jurisdictions, they were usually created by means of a **ground rent lease**, which was in the nature of a long-term or perpetual lease. See also **fee farm rent**, **general equitable charge**, **legal interest**[Eng], **quit rent**, **right of re-entry**.

renter   One who holds land subject to the payment of rent, i.e. a **tenant** or **lessee**.

rentier   Originally a person whose income was derived solely from interest earned on government securities; the word being derived from the French *rente*, a particular form of interest-bearing government bond. In modern terms, rentier is applied to any person whose income is unearned, i.e. is derived solely from the ownership of capital, rather than one whose income is derived from his own labour. A rentier may be a person who inherits wealth; a retired person; or an institution that specialises in fixed interest investments. See also **economic rent**.

rents and profits   Income to be derived from land. The total of 'rent' and 'profits' accruing from a property on an annual basis. See also **issues and profits**.

rents insurance[US]   See **rent-loss insurance**.

rentservice or **rent service**   A payment made to an owner of land for the right to use and occupy his land. Rentservice is a payment for a right to a tenancy, i.e. a relationship created between a landlord and a tenant, as distinguished from a **rentcharge** which is a periodic payment for land, but one that is not paid as a consequence of a landlord and tenant relationship so that the recipient has no interest or **reversion** in the land because he has sold his interest to the payee of the rentcharge. Thus, rentservice is the payment that is more commonly called **rent**, and in common law it carries an automatic right to levy of **distress** for non payment.

renunciation   1. The giving up of an available right or privilege. Renunciation of a contract must go beyond refusal or omission to perform some part of the contract; it must amount to an absolute refusal on the part of an individual to perform the contract; it amounts to a refusal to perform the outstanding obligations of the contract in their entirety. An agent renounces his authority to perform the duties entrusted to him when he indicates, expressly or impliedly, that he does not intend to continue to act for his principal. cf. **abandonment**. See also **repudiation**, **termination**. 2. The act of giving up, surrendering or abandoning a right, interest or title; especially when nothing of value is received in exchange. In English law, the term 'renunciation' is not generally used to refer to the surrender of a right to land; it is replaced by **surrender** or **release**.   3.[Scot]The giving up of a right to property, either expressly or by implication. Thus, a tenant may give up or renounce his lease in favour of the landlord; or an owner of a corporeal moveable may renounce the right to hold the property by abandonment.

repair   Derived from the Latin *reparare*, or the Old French *reparer*, 'to make ready' or 'to put in order'. Restoring a property to a good or sound condition, especially following deterioration through use, misuse, damage, injury, decay or dilapidation. The process of making good, fixing or mending defects, especially in order to restore damage so that a property appears substantially as if the damage had never occurred. Repair includes **maintenance** and, when necessary, may involve the **renewal** of some *parts* or elements of a property; although renewal as such is more than repair. Repair generally requires some element of anticipation to prevent future deterioration. However, repair does not include **reconstruction, alteration, improvement, renewal** *in toto*, or any other such work that would improve the value or change the character of a property, although such activities may well involve or encompass an element of repair.

The exact extent of a tenant's obligation under a lease is dependent on the type of building, its condition, as well as the exact wording of the repairing covenant in the lease. For example, a covenant "to put into repair" may include reinstating or putting dilapidated property into a good state of repair where that can be implied from the lease; but it does not require making changes of a permanent substantial or unusual character. It does not involve carrying out work that constitutes an improvement; it requires only the replacement of something that is already there, as and when it has become dilapidated or worn out. However, it may entail the provision of something new if that is the best way to carry out the repair. Whether what is required of a tenant is repair or reconstruction is a question of fact and the degree of work involved.

A tenant's covenant to repair is commonly preceded by such words as 'good', 'proper' 'sufficient', 'necessary', 'substantial' or 'habitable' and such words convey much the same meaning as **tenantable repair**, i.e. to keep and leave a property in such condition as a new tenant might expect to find it having regard to the type of property. However, such words do not extend the requirement to making good deterioration arising from **fair wear and tear**[(BrE)]/**wear and tear**[(AmE)]. When interpreting a repairing covenant in a lease it is necessary to look at the particular building, its state at the date of the lease, and the precise terms of the lease. The obligation must not be looked at *in vacuo*.

Unless there is an express obligation under a lease, at common law, a tenant has no obligation to repair, although he must make good damage caused by his own fault or negligence, i.e. he must

not commit permissive or wilful **waste**, nor must he let the premises deteriorate further by not carrying out ordinary or 'tenantable' repairs. In addition, in the absence of any statutory requirement or an express provision in the lease, there is no implied covenant by a landlord to **repair** (*Gott v Gandy* (1853) El & Bl 845, 118 Eng Rep 984, 985; Edwards v. N. Y. & H. R.R. Co., 98 NY 245, 247, 50 Am Rep 659 (1885)). On the other hand, in English law and in most jurisdictions in the US, a landlord who retains control over the common parts (lifts, staircases, refuse chutes, etc.) is expected to maintain those areas in order to ensure that the building can be utilised adequately and safely (*Liverpool City Council v Irwin* [1977] AC 239, [1976] 2 All ER 39 (HL); American Law Reports, *Annotations and Cases*, Anno: 67 ALR3d 490: Exterior Stairs Used in Common by Tenants; Anno: 67 ALR3d 587: Interior Stairs Used in Common by Tenants). The landlord may be obliged to carry out certain repairs in order to insure that the leased premises comply with building, safety, and public health regulations, unless such an obligation is placed expressly as an onus on the tenant. Also, a landlord may have an implied obligation to carry out repair if that impacts the tenant's obligations, as when the failure to repair the exterior prevents the proper repair and maintenance of the interior. However, the landlord is only liable for complying with an implied repairing covenant if he has **knowledge** of the defect or after he has **notice** of the defect (*O'Brien v Robinson* (1984) 13 HLR 7 (HL)). Also, under English law, the landlord may have a statutory obligation to repair, as with certain short-term residential tenancies and an obligation to ensure that any **premises** he permits to be used by anyone are not dangerous or defective due to a want of repair on his part (Defective Premises Act 1974, ss. 1(1), (4).

In the US, many states have passed laws or ordinances that affect the repair rights and obligations of both the landlord and tenant of residential property. In particular, some jurisdictions require the landlord to keep the premises in a proper condition for occupation and, in some states, the tenant has the right to withhold rent or vacate if the landlord fails to make essential repairs. In addition, several jurisdictions consider that the landlord is committed to a **warranty of habitability** in respect of residential property.

In English statute law, in connection with the exclusion of certain rights to compensation for disturbance for a business tenancy, 'repairs' is defined to include "any work of **maintenance**, decoration, or restoration, and references to repairing, to keeping or yielding up in repair and to state of repair shall be construed accordingly", L&T Act 1954, s. 69(1). See also **clear lease, constructive eviction, damages, external, forfeiture, full repairing and insuring lease**(BrE), **good repair, inherent defect, keep in repair, relief, repairs notice**(Eng), **right of entry, set-off, triple net lease**(AmE), **tenant-like manner**(Eng).

repairing lease   See **full repairing and insuring lease**(BrE), **net lease**(AmE), **repair, triple net lease**(AmE).

repairs grant(Eng)   See **grant**.

repairs notice(Eng)   **1.** A notice served by a local authority on a person "having control" of a dwelling-house, or a house in multiple occupation, that is considered **unfit for human habitation**, requiring that person to render it fit (Housing Act 1985, s. 189, as amended). See also **charging order, closing order**.   **2.** A notice served by a landlord on his tenant indicating that repairs, which are the tenant's express responsibility under a lease, have not been carried out and that the landlord intends to enter into the demised premises, carry out the repairs himself, and reclaim the cost from the tenant; or a notice served by the landlord after the work has been carried out in order to recover the cost of the repairs from the tenant. Such a notice may be enforced only if provided for in the lease, either as an express right, or a right that is implied because the landlord has covenanted to **repair** the demised premises. See also **right of entry, schedule of dilapidations, specific performance**. **3.** Notice served on the owner of a **listed building**

by a local planning authority, or the Secretary of State, specifying works that are considered necessary for the proper preservation of the building (Planning (Listed Building and Conservation Areas) Act 1990, s. 48).

replacement cost or **replacement value** The estimated cost, at current prices, of replacing a building with a similar structure. Generally, 'replacement cost' refers to the cost that would be incurred in providing a similar building using currently available materials and modern building standards of design and layout. In the case of an insurance valuation, the replacement value does not allow for obsolescence as, in the event of loss, the insured requires to be able to meet the total cost of replacing the damaged building. See **depreciated replacement cost, reinstatement cost, reproduction cost**.

replacement cost approach(US)   See **cost approach**.

replacement value   See **reinstatement cost**.

report   See **appraisal report**(US), **credit report, environmental impact report**(US), **title report**(US), **valuation report**(BrE).

repossession   **1.** The retaking of **possession**. See also **mortgagee**.   **2.**(AmE) The reclaiming of a right to possession of property when the possessor has ceased to pay for the right to continue in possession; for example, when a purchaser fails to keep up his payments under an installment contract or any other form of **conditional sale contract** (UCC § 9:503). See also **dispossession, recovery, right of re-entry**.

representation   **1.** An oral or written statement being an assertion of fact, as compared with an expression of an opinion. A statement on a matter of law or an expression of an intention. In particular, an account that is made with the clear intention of influencing an action, especially a statement that is relied upon when a party enters into a contract. A representation may form part of a contract, i.e. it may be a **term** or **condition**, or it may be a 'mere representation'. A 'mere representation' is intended as a statement of opinion and is clearly not intended to entice the recipient into a contract or legal obligation without further investigation. A distinction between a representation of fact that is intended, or should be known will be relied on, as part of a contract and a 'mere representation', or **puffing**, is a question of degree dependent on the surrounding facts and the relative positions of the parties. Strictly, silence is not a representation, but silence or concealment, under circumstances where one ought to speak and to reveal the truth, is regarded as being in effect a representation. Also, in such circumstances, silence may act as a form of **estoppel**. A representation falls short of a **warranty**; it may amount to a clear expression of fact but, of itself, it is not intended to form a promise as to the validity of the fact. See also **agency**, *caveat emptor*, **misrepresentation**, **utmost good faith**.   **2.** The act of representing another, as by an **agent** or **attorney**.

reprobate   To refuse to accept; to reject. In particular, to refuse to accept an instrument or deed because it is faulty due to forgery or fraud. See also **approbate and reprobate, estoppel**.

reproduction cost   The cost, at current prices, of making a copy or replica of a building. In particular, the cost of an identical building or structure, irrespective of the economic benefit of such a process, i.e. the cost of providing a facsimile with all the inherent benefits and deficiencies. The cost of a building that is as close as possible to an original in respect of its design, appearance, style, layout and materials. A cost that may be expended, for example, to replace an ancient monument or an historic building. The term may be used to refer to the cost of producing a building using similar materials, but the essential element is to produce a building that, as far as practical, is the same as that being replaced. cf. **reinstatement cost.**

repudiation   The act of disclaiming or refusing to accept. The **renunciation** or **disclaimer** of a right or privilege. In particular, the action of refusing to discharge a duty or obligation, or accept a debt. An intimation, by words or conduct, of an intention not to perform the obligations of a **contract** *in toto*. The denial of the existence of a contract, in the form of saying that 'there never was a contract'. In particular, a claim that a contract is not binding due to some fact such as **fraud**, **mistake**, **duress**, **undue influence**, or that an essential **condition** has been breached by the other party. A party to a contract may repudiate it in express terms, or it may be repudiated by implication, as when a course of action is embarked on which prevents the party from proceeding with the promise or obligation contained in the contract. If repudiation occurs before any breach of a contract has occurred, it may be called an 'anticipatory repudiation' or 'anticipatory breach'. The words 'breach' and 'repudiation' are sometimes used interchangeably. However, a 'breach of contract' is the failure, without legal excuse, to perform any promise which forms the whole or any part of a contract; whereas 'repudiation' means the rejection, **disclaimer**, **renunciation** of a duty, promise or relation. Thus, by an 'anticipatory breach' the party to the contract indicates simply, by some action, that he does not intend to perform as the contract requires; whereas by repudiation there is a renunciation of the 'contract' because an essential element is missing, the contract is incapable of performance, or the other party has taken an action that changes the essential nature of the agreement. cf. **abandonment, frustration**. See also **breach of contract, rescission, time is of the essence.**

repurchase   The **purchase** of a property that has previously been owned by the purchaser. The word 'repurchase' is sometimes used as synonymous with **redemption** in the sense of reclaiming of title to property that has been secured by way of a mortgage; the traditional view of a mortgage being that the property was conveyed to the mortgagee and is reconveyed when the mortgage obligation is satisfied in full. See also **repurchase agreement**.

repurchase agreement   1. A contract that gives a vendor a right to repurchase a property on specified terms at a fixed date; especially an agreement between a vendor and purchaser of property to the effect that, if the purchaser desires to resell within a specified period of time, the vendor may reacquire, or have an **option** to reacquire, the property. Also called a 'buy-back agreement' or 'sale and buy-back agreement'. See also **right of pre-emption**.   2. An agreement between the purchaser and seller of a **mortgage-backed security** by which the seller or issuer agrees to purchase back the securities at a specified price and on a specified date.   3. A form of short-term financing by which the holder of a portfolio of properties sells an interest in the portfolio, subject to a right of the borrower to repurchase the interest at a specified future date.

reputed owner   1. A person who appears to be, may be inferred to be, or claims to be the **owner** of a property. A term generally used in connection with the ownership of goods. The reputed owner is the person who has physical possession, even after he may have sold them or lost his rights to another. In particular, a person who conveys to the minds of the world at large a reputation of ownership.

In the US, in the case of **mechanic's lien** the 'reputed owner' is the person who from all appearances has the title to, and possession of, the property; one who from all appearances or supposition is the owner. cf. **true owner**.   2.(Eng)A person who might reasonably be assumed to be the **owner** of a property, especially as based on previous dealings. In the case of a requirement to serve notice on the 'reputed owner' of land, such person may be taken to be anyone who, after diligent enquiry, is believed to be the owner of the land in question. See also **notice to treat**.

request for bid (RFB) or **request for proposal** (RFP)   An invitation to submit a bid or **offer** to acquire a property, or to supply goods or services. Generally, such a request is not an offer and the submission of bids alone does not create a binding **contract**. See also **quotation**.

required rate of return   See **target rate of return**.

requisition   1. The taking of property or a right to property, especially possession of property, as a temporary measure by a government authority. Commonly used to refer to the temporary taking of goods, or the occupation of housing, to meet the needs of a military authority. Requisition should be distinguished from **expropriation**, or **compulsory purchase**, which are permanent means of taking property.   2.(Eng)An **inquiry** made to elucidate a matter affecting a property that is to be transferred or charged. In particular, an inquiry regarding an **abstract of title** as made by a prospective purchaser's or mortgagee's solicitor of a vendor's or mortgagor's solicitor. A requisition may require the vendor or mortgagor to demonstrate that a particular matter that appears to be a **defect of title**, is not, or to explain how he intends to rectify a doubt or defect of title. A requisition is strictly speaking an inquiry relating to a matter of title, especially a matter arising from a perusal of the abstract of title. cf. **searches, time is of the essence**. See also **official certificate of search, title**.   3.(Eng)A request made to the Registrar of the Land Registry or to a local authority for an official certificate setting out details of any encumbrances registered against a particular parcel of land. See also **official certificate of search, official search certificate**.   4. In the civil law or Scots law, a formal request to perform an obligation, usually as made by a notary public.

res(Lat)   A 'thing'. Any thing that may be the subject matter of **ownership**, whether corporeal or incorporeal; personal or real; movable or immovable. A term used especially to refer to a particular thing as object *qua* object, rather than a right or interest in that object. See also **action** *in rem*, **chattel**, *res communes*, *res derelictæ*, *res nullius*.

res derelictæ(Lat)   Property that has been abandoned and has no apparent owner, e.g. **flotsam**, **jetsam**, and **treasure trove**. cf. *res nullius*. See also **abandonment**, **possession**.

res extincta(Lat)   A thing that has ceased to exist. In particular, the subject matter of a contract that has ceased to exist as a result of a **mistake**.

res gestae(Lat)   'Things done'. A matter that is ancillary to a main or principal fact, but so closely connected with that fact as either to form one continuous transaction with it or to be necessary to give meaning to it. See also **part performance**.

res ipsa loquitor(Lat)   'The thing speaks for itself'. In a claim for **negligence** the onus of proof is placed on the plaintiff, but the facts of a particular accident may provide *prima facie* evidence of a negligent act on the part of the defendant.

res nullius(Lat)   A term of Roman law used to refer to property that has no owner. A thing that does not belong to anyone. Property that does not have an owner, either because it never had an owner, such as wild animals or fish in the ocean; or because it has been abandoned by its owner (*res derelictæ*) or has been left on intestacy without a successor. In particular, property that is not considered capable of ownership, e.g. air and waters of the ocean. See also **possession**, *res communes*, **treasure trove**.

res perit domino or **res perit suo domino**(Lat)   'The loss falls on the owner'; 'the destruction of a property falls to the owner'.

res sua nemini servit(Lat)   'No one can have a **servitude** over his own property'. See also **quasi-easement**.

resale   1. The sale of property that has been acquired from another, generally within a short period of time. cf. **sub-sale**.   2. The sale of property to a third party after it has been sold to another, such as when a person sells goods because the purchaser is in default in paying the full purchase price. See also **power of sale**.   3.(US)A sale of a property after a **judicial sale** by the same procedure in the event that the purchaser fails to comply with his bid or the sale is annulled.

rescheduling agreement   See **workout agreement**.

rescind   Derived from the Latin *rescindere*, 'to cut apart' or 'to tear asunder'. To cut off, take away or remove. To cancel, annul or abrogate a contract by **rescission**. The act of withdrawing an **offer** or contract by operation of law or by mutual consent. cf. **breach of contract**.

rescission   The act of abrogating, cancelling, vacating or annulling. The annulling or the unmaking of a contract. In particular, the 'undoing' of a contract *ab initio*, as if it had never existed. The termination of a contract by mutual consent of the parties; by a court order pursuant to a condition in the contract; or as a consequence of a fraud, failure of consideration (e.g. non-payment of rent), or a material breach or default. Rescission may be distinguished from **repudiation** as the latter is a refusal to accept the contract – an indication of an intention not to perform the contract; whereas rescission is the act or process of terminating, annulling, or abrogating the contract as if it had never existed and restoring the parties to their respective positions before any agreement was entered into. Rescission refers to the state of things as they were when the contract was made, whereas repudiation refers to the state of things at the time of the refusal to be bound by the contract.

A contract may be rescinded where there has been a **mistake**, **fraud**, **undue influence**, a **misrepresentation**, or one of the parties is physically or mentally incapable of effecting the contract. A contract may be rescinded also if there is an express provision entitling one party to terminate the agreement when the other party cannot, or will not, fulfil the terms of the agreement. Rescission of a contract *ab initio* is an equitable remedy; that is, it is given at the discretion of the court, and it is granted only when **restitution** can be effected as if the contract had never existed. *Restitutio in integrum*, 'rescission in full', must be possible.

Rescission should not be confused with the **termination** of a contract by one party when an essential condition of the contract has not been performed. With termination, there is no element of restoring the *status quo ante*, because part of the contract has been performed or come into existence as a binding agreement between the parties – a terminated contract had an existence that has been brought to an end, usually prematurely. By comparison, a rescinded contract is treated as if it never existed. See also **deposit, election, revocation, voidable contract**.

reservation   1. A right or interest withheld or retracted from the subject-matter of a grant. For example, the taking back by a landlord of something that would otherwise be a right granted under a lease, as with a right to enter onto the demised premises in order to carry out repairs. A reservation is something new taken back or 'reserved' from that which has been granted; something regranted to the grantor, such as an easement. On the grant of a lease, the principal item reserved by a landlord is rent.

A reservation may be distinguished from an **exception**, which is something that exists but is not granted. An exception is always some thing or right that is not granted at all. A reservation is always of some thing taken back out of that which is clearly granted. A reservation arises out of the right or interest regranted and not from the words used. Thus, a statement such as "reserving unto the vendor" does not necessarily create a reservation. A reservation normally arises only by an express re-grant; although it may sometimes arise by implication, as with an **easement of necessity**. A reservation may be permanent, as with

an easement, or it may have a limited duration, as with a life estate. cf. **grant**. See also **condition**.   2. An area of publicly owned land set aside for a particular purpose, e.g. for a school or for future development.   3.(US)An area of public land that has been held back or appropriated for a particular purpose, such as a public park or military base. In particular, an area of land (administered by the Bureau of Indian Affairs) that has remained in the ownership of an American Indian tribe or that has been set aside for their perpetual use and enjoyment. See also **Indian lands, reserved lands**.

reservation price   See **reserve price, upset price**(US).

reserve   1. To set aside. To exclude or retain. To keep in store for a future use or special purpose.   2. A sum of money set aside for a particular purpose. An amount of money set aside to meet a future liability, such as the cost of future repair or maintenance. Money set aside or invested to accumulate with the additions of interest or dividends to meet a future contingent claim. See also **sinking fund**.   3. An area of land set aside for a particular purpose, as with land reserved for scientific or recreational purposes or because of its historic interest. An area of land that is especially worthy of conservation because of its ecological, archaeological, geological or physiological attributes. See also **public reserve**(Aus), **reservation, reserved land**.   4.(Aus/ Can)An area of land that is available for the exclusive use of Aboriginal peoples, or Bands of First Nations. See also **native title**.

reserve land(NZ)   Land, commonly **Crown land**, that is set aside for public purpose.

reserve payment   See **piti payment**.

reserve price(BrE) or **reserved price**(AmE) The minimum price that must be bid at a sale by **auction** before the vendor will sell; if this reserve price is not reached the property is 'bought in' by the vendor. During an auction, when a bid has been made that is equal to or exceeds the reserve price, the auctioneer will state, usually, that the property is 'on sale', i.e. is put on **offer**. If a principal submits a property to an auctioneer for sale "subject to a reserve price", the auctioneer is given no authority, either expressly or impliedly, to accept a lesser price. As a rule, until the reserve price is reached every price suggested by the auctioneer, and every bid or offer, including the final one (acceptance of which is signified by the fall of the hammer) is conditional on the final sale price being equal to or higher than the reserve price. In the US, sometimes called a 'reservation price'. See also **upset price**(US), **without reserve**.

reserve title(US)   To hold back title or ownership of a property until the price has been paid in full.

reserved land   1.(US)Land that has been appropriated for the use of the federal government, or one of the states, and is no longer part of the public domain. For example, land that has been reserved for military use, or land that has been made available as an Indian **reservation**. 2.(US)**Public lands** that have been set aside for sale or disposition. See also **appropriation**. 3.(Aus)Land that is retained by the Crown as not available for sale or lease. Land set aside for public recreation or conservation. See also **Crown land**, **reserve**.

reserved matters(Eng)   See **planning permission**.

reserved price(AmE)   1. See **upset price**.   2. See **reserve price**.

reserved way   A right of way created by means of a **reservation** set out in a conveyance or deed of grant. See also **easement of necessity**.

resettlement   See **barring the entail**.

residence   1. A place of **abode** or place of habitation, whether temporary or permanent. The place to which a person most frequently resorts for living purposes, i.e. a place where a person more usually sleeps on successive or regular days or weeks. A person has his residence wherever he normally lives. It is more than a place where a person has a physical presence from time to time, such as an hotel. A residence may be distinguished from a **domicile**, which is the place that someone considers, or is deemed to consider, as a fixed and permanent home (although a person's main residence is a primary factor in deciding a domicile). A person may have only one domicile, but he or she may have more than one place of residence at the same time. A person may be 'ordinarily resident' where he or she resides in the normal course of life, as opposed to a temporary place of residence. A person may be 'habitually resident' where there is a regular physical presence for a significant period of time. See also **principal private residence**(Eng), **principal residence**(US).   2. A place used as a **home**. In particular, a dwelling-house of some standing or pretension.   3. A building used to house students. Usually called a 'hall of residence'.

resident freeholder(US)   The owner of a freehold interest in land who is also resident of the city, town or district where the land is situated. In particular, a term that is used to refer to a property owner who is considered resident in an area in order to enable him to obtain a licence or permit, or to be able to object to public work such as the construction of a highway.

resident landlord(Eng)   A landlord of a dwelling-house (that is not part of a "purpose built block of flats") who, at the time he grants a tenancy, occupies as his residence another dwelling within the same building. A tenancy of a dwelling-house let by a 'resident landlord' cannot be a **protected tenancy** or an **assured tenancy** (although it may be a **restricted contract**). A 'resident landlord' must have occupied the dwelling at the time he granted the tenancy as his or her only or principal home (Rent Act 1977, s. 12; Housing Act 1988, Sch. 1, paras. 10, 17, 20). These provisions are intended to exclude a tenant, who rents part of a person's home, from having the security of tenure that would be afforded to a similar tenant if the landlord were not resident in the same building. See also **grounds for possession**.

residential density   A ratio that expresses the average relationship between a unit area of land and the number of residential or household units occupying that unit area, e.g. houses per acre, dwellings per hectare, bed spaces per acre. Residential density may be expressed as: (i) 'overall residential density' – the average number of units per unit of land contained within a total area, in particular the entire area of a town; (ii) 'gross residential density' – the average number of units per unit of land contained within a given residential area (e.g. within a neighbourhood or a particular development area), including all residential land, and land used for parking, playgrounds, primary schools, retail stores and common open space, but excluding land that is used for secondary schools, for institutional property (hospitals, central libraries, etc.) and for any other purpose that is considered to serve other residential areas; or (iii) 'net residential density' – the average number of units per unit of land contained within a given residential area, including land used for ancillary open space, yards, gardens, etc., but excluding land used for any non-residential purpose (e.g. local retail stores and schools). The net residential density excludes common open spaces and may exclude the streets and public rights-of-way, or may include the local streets up to the centre line. Residential density is also called 'accommodation density'. cf. **population density**. See also **density**.

residential district ordinance(US)   A **zoning ordinance** that relates to a particular residential block or district, but is not made applicable to the entire municipality in which the property is situated. See also **spot zoning**.

residential occupier(Eng)   A person who occupies premises "as a residence, whether under a contract or by virtue of any enactment or rule of law giving him the right to remain in occupation or restricting the right of any other person to recover possession of the premises", PEA 1977, s. 1(1). See also **eviction**, **harassment**.

residential tenancy(Eng)   A tenancy of a dwelling-house (which may include a flat). See also **assured tenancy**, **assured shorthold tenancy**, **controlled tenancy**, **protected tenancy**, **protected shorthold tenancy**, **secure tenancy**, **shorthold tenancy**, **statutory tenancy**.

residual approach(US)   See **abstraction approach**, **land residual technique**, **residual process**.

residual capitalization rate(AmE)   See **terminal capitalization rate**.

residual commission   See **deferred commission**.

residual estate   See **residuary estate**.

residual method of valuation(BrE)   A method of **valuation** that is used to estimate the amount that it is worth paying for land or buildings that are to be developed or redeveloped. The application of the residual method is based on the principle that the price to be paid for a property that is suitable for development is equal to the difference between the completed value of the highest and best form of permitted development and the total cost of carrying out that development. Thus, the net capital value of the completed development is assessed (after deducting any costs of sale) on the assumption that it has been developed for the most valuable form of development, and from that value is deducted the cost of all construction and building work required to carry out the development (including all ancillary costs, e.g. purchase costs, letting fees, finance, etc.), as well as an appropriate allowance for profit on the development.

The residual method may be used to estimate

the value of a property that is being held for development, or is to be offered for sale; as well as being adopted to estimate the anticipated profit from a development project. In practice, it is the principal means of development analysis and is widely adapted as the basis for setting up the **budget** for most development projects. The residual method of valuation, by its nature, is based on a considerable number of variables (rent, investment yield, construction costs, building period, letting or sales period, finance costs, fees, property taxes and all other ancillary costs) and these must be assessed based on the valuer's expectations of the future. Thus, it is a highly subjective method of valuation and should be used with caution. See also **abstraction approach**[US], **building residual technique**[US], **development property**, **land residual technique**[US], **project valuation**, **residual process**[US].

residual process or **residual technique**[AmE]   A method of appraisal, based on the **income approach**, used to estimate the value of a plot of land excluding any buildings thereon, or to estimate the value of a building separate from the land. An income is assessed that is considered appropriate to the plot of land, or the building – usually by deducting from the income receivable from the land and buildings together an income estimated as appropriate for the land, or buildings, alone. This income is then capitalized at a rate that is appropriate to the element being valued, i.e. the land excluding the buildings thereon, or the buildings excluding the land. Also called 'highest and best use analysis', especially when used to determine the value of the land for its **highest and best use**. See also **building residual technique, land residual technique, residual method of valuation**[BrE].

residual valuation   See **residual method of valuation**[BrE], **residual process**[US].

residual value   1. The value of an interest in property for the remaining, or residual, term of a lease. The **present value** of the right to receive the rent and profits reserved under a lease for the rest of its term. cf. **reversionary value**.   2. The value of a property at the end of its useful or **economic life**. See also **scrap value**.   3.[Eng] The value of land as determined by the **residual method of valuation**.   4. The value of land used for mining or as a quarry, after all extraction work has been completed.

residuary clause   A clause in a will that set out the provisions for the disposal of any remaining property, after all prior express conditions, devises or bequests have been made, and all legal obligations discharged. See also **residue**.

residuary estate   1. An **estate** that remains after another estate has been terminated.   2. That part of a person's estate that has not been expressly devised. See also **devise**.   3. The value of the estate of a testator left for the purpose of a general **devise**, after all other legacies have been satisfied and all charges, debts, legacies and costs have been paid. See also **residuary clause, residue**.

residuary legacy   See **legacy**.

residue   That which remains after something is withdrawn or deducted. In a 'residuary clause' in a will, such as "all the remainder and residue of my property", the term 'remainder' usually refers to real property and 'residue' to personal property. See also **remainder, residual value, residuary estate**.

Resolution Trust Corporation (RTC)[US]   A federal agency established by Congress in 1989 to manage and dispose of failed savings and loan associations and banks. The RTC is managed by Thrift Depositor Protection Oversight Board (formerly the Oversight Board) which is responsible for reporting to Congress on the activities of the RTC and, in particular, its achievements in disposing of real estate that has come under its control. Most of the functions of the RTC have now been fulfilled.

resoluto jure concedentis resolvitur [jus] concessum(Lat) 'The grant of a right comes to an end on the termination of the right of the grantor'.

resort property A property that primarily caters to vacation, recreation or leisure activities. See also **hotel, timeshare**.
Urban Land Institute, *Resort Development Handbook*. Washington DC: Urban Land Institute, 1997.

respondeat superior(Lat) 'Let the **principal** answer'. A maxim that arises from the principle that a master is liable for the actions of a servant who is acting within the proper terms or scope of his employment. Similarly, a principal is liable for the acts of his agent, provided they are carried out within the powers granted and arise from a relationship that is in the nature of an employer and employee. The maxim '*respondeat superior*' arises from the rule that a principal is supposed to know and control the way in which an employee works; whereas he is not required to answer for the acts of an **independent contractor** who has a greater discretion in the way in which he carries out his duties. See also **vicarious liability**.

rest A specified interval. One of a series of similar stages at which a payment is due, as with the times for the payment of interest or principal under a mortgage.

rest residue and remainder See **remainder, residue**.

restaurant A place where meals and refreshments are served to the public generally, or sometimes to select members of the public, for consumption on the premises. See also **hotel, inn, public house**.

restitutio in integrum(Lat) 'Restitution in its entirety'; 'restoration to the original position'. A common law principle adopted when assessing **damages** in actions for breach of contract or tort. See also **rescission**.

restitution 1. Derived from the Latin *restitutio*, 'to reset up' or 'to re-establish'. In its common usage, the act of restoring something, either to its owner, or to its former physical state. See also **reinstatement, restoration**. 2. An equitable remedy that enables someone to recover property when it has been obtained dishonestly, officiously, unconscionably, or under duress. Restitution is founded on the principle of payment for **unjust enrichment**, as when a person unjustly or unfairly obtains money or property for which he should expect to pay. The principle of restitution maybe applied also when someone has carried out work to property that has benefit for the owner, but for which no recompense has been paid. Restitution is intended to restore to the person who has carried out work the value parted with in carrying out the work. Restitution may be distinguished from **damages** as the former is intended to restore the *status quo ante*, whereas damages are intended to restore the *status quo post*. 'Restitution' may also be used to refer to the returning of stolen goods, or sometimes in English law to the recovery of land when a person has been illegally dispossessed. cf. **recovery**. See also **constructive trust, quasi-contract**, *quantum meruit*, **rescission**. **3.** Compensation or reparation paid for loss or damage caused to another.
Birks, Peter. *An Introduction to the Law of Restitution*. Oxford: Clarendon, 1985, Reprinted 1996.
Fridman, Gerald H. L. *Restitution*. 2nd ed. Scarborough, Ont.: Carswell, 1992.
Goff, R., and Jones, G. *The Law of Restitution*. 6th ed. London: Sweet & Maxwell, 2002.
Palmer, George E. *The Law of Restitution*, 4 vols. New York, NY: Aspen Publishers, ©1990, with cumulative supplements.
Virgo, Graham. *The Principles of the Law of Restitution* (1999), Oxford: Oxford University Press, 1999.

restoration The act of returning something, either to a person, or to its former and, as far as possible, to an identical state or condition. Putting all or part of a property back into its original state, whether by **renewal** or **reconstruction**. See also **reinstatement, renovation, restitution**.

restraining order(US)   An order that requires a party to desist from a course of action or to maintain the status quo until a hearing of a disputed issue can be held. An **injunction** that restrains but does not compel an action. Although the terms 'interlocutory injunction' and 'restraining order' are sometimes used interchangeably, the latter refers to a requirement for a temporary suspension of action at least until a case can be heard, whereas the former usually persists throughout the pendency of the action.

restraint of trade   See **equity of redemption, non-competition clause, restrictive covenant, solus agreement**(Eng).

restraint of alienation   See **restraint on alienation**.

restraint on alienation   A restriction placed on the right of a person to transfer property to another. Generally, any condition that permanently restricts a person's right to transfer an absolute right to property or a fee interest is void, because it is repugnant to the interest held by that person; in effect it prevents the free use and transfer of property. However, an absolute prohibition on a tenant's right to assign or sub-let will normally be enforced by a court (although it will construe such a provision strictly and, if there is doubtful language, in favour of the tenant).

At common law, any tenant (except, as a rule, a tenant at will or the holder of a personal right of occupation) is free to assign or sub-let, the whole or any part of the demised premises, unless expressly prevented under the terms of the lease. However, most leases contain an express covenant restricting, entirely, or to some degree, the assignment, sub-letting, charging or otherwise parting with the demised property, either absolutely or without the landlord's prior consent. Such an express covenant frequently provides that the landlord's consent to an alienation of the property is not to be 'unreasonably or arbitrarily withheld'.

In the US, where the landlord's consent is required to an assignment or sub-letting (and there is no requirement that such consent can only be withheld 'reasonably'), in some jurisdictions, the landlord may arbitrarily refuse such consent; he may be able to demand some reasonable form of financial recompense; or he may impose such conditions as he sees fit, prior to granting his consent to the alienation. On the other hand, some jurisdictions consider that consent to alienation should be refused only if the landlord has a good faith reason to object, based on reasonable commercial standards. In the US, instances in which consent has been considered to have been withheld *reasonably* include: (i) failure to furnish sufficient financial information as to the prospective lessee; (ii) a failure of the prospective tenant to reveal the intended use to be made of the property; (iii) a threat that the tenant will vacate other premises owned by the same landlord. Instances where consent has been considered to have been withheld *unreasonably* include: (i) any violation of an anti-discrimination law; (ii) arbitrary considerations of personal taste, sensibility, or convenience; and (iii) a withholding of consent "which fails the tests of good faith and commercial reasonableness".

In English law, in any lease (except a lease of an agricultural holding or an assured tenancy) containing a covenant or condition against assignment, sub-letting, charging, or parting with possession of a demised premises or any part thereof *without* consent or licence, is deemed to be "subject to a proviso to the effect that such licence or consent is not to be unreasonably withheld", L&T Act 1927, s. 19(1), although this provision does not absolve the tenant from an obligation to seek consent from the landlord. In the case of a lease granted for more than 40 years, made on condition that the leased land is to be used for the erection or substantial improvement, alteration or addition of buildings, the tenant may, notwithstanding a prohibition on assignment, assign the premises (or sub-let, charge or otherwise part with possession) without consent, provided the assignment is made more than seven years before the end of the term, and the lessee notifies the lessor of the assignment within six months (L&T Act 1927, s 19(1)(b) – a provision that does not apply to government or public authorities, nor statutory or public utility companies). Also, a landlord may not demand a **fine** or **premium** for granting such consent, although he may require a reasonable sum for any legal or other expenses incurred in this respect (LPA 1925, s. 144; L&T 1927, s. 19(1)(a)). In Great Britain, it is generally unlawful to discriminate against an intended assignee or sub-lessee on the grounds of sex, race or religion (Sex Discrimination Act 1975, s. 30, 31; Race Relations Act 1976, s. 24). When a tenant submits a written application to his landlord for consent to assign, sub-let, etc., and the provision in the lease is that the consent is not to be unreasonably withheld, the landlord is obliged to make a decision on the application within a reasonable time. The landlord must then reply in writing, giving his consent, stating any conditions that apply to the consent or, if the consent is withheld, give the reasons for that decision (L&T Act 1988, s. 1).

In English law, what constitutes 'withholding consent *unreasonably*' depends on the nature of the property; the type of tenant; the other terms of the lease; any effect on the landlord's existing rights; and any effect on the landlord's reversionary interest, provided such effect is likely to arise. As a rule, it is necessary for the tenant to prove that the consent was unreasonably withheld, and not for the landlord to prove that he was justified in withholding his consent. The reason for refusal of consent should be directly related to the letting; it should not be wholly independent of the relationship of landlord and tenant as created by the subject lease; and account should not be taken of some other matter that might be of collateral benefit to the landlord. A landlord should not seek to prevent a tenant from parting with his tenancy merely because the change might have an adverse affect on neighbouring premises owned by the same landlord.

Instances in which English courts have held that consent to an assignment has been withheld

reasonably include: (i) the complete inadequacy of the financial standing of the assignee, when related to the level of rent under the lease; (ii) a significant adverse effect on the landlord's own trading interests; and (iii) a significant effect on the value of the landlord's interest or the letting value of the rest of the same property, but not solely on the ground that it might create management problems. Instances in which consent has been held to have been withheld *unreasonably* include: (i) a refusal when a parent company of a minor subsidiary was not prepared to act as surety; (ii) a refusal for fear that the proposed assignee would vacate other property owned by the landlord and that those premises would be difficult to relet; (iii) the refusal of the consent of a superior landlord; (iv) a refusal by the landlord in an attempt to regain possession before the end of the lease; and (v) a requirement that the tenant must first offer to surrender his lease back to the landlord.

In the US, a restraint on alienation may sometimes be referred to in two ways: a 'disabling restraint', which prohibit a transfer; and a 'forfeiture restraint', which provide for a forfeiture of the right to the property in the event of a transfer. See also **due-on-sale clause**(US), **partial release**, **rule against perpetuities**.

restraint on use   See **use clause/user clause**.

restricted appraisal report(US)   An appraisal report that is similar to a **self-contained appraisal report** except that it is limited so that it may only be used by the client and only for limited purposes. In particular, a report that "contains a prominent use restriction that limits reliance on the report to the client and warns that the report cannot be understood properly without additional information in the workfile of the appraiser". The report must also identify and explain any departures from the required standard (See **Uniform Standards of Professional Appraisal Practice**, Standard Rule 2-2(a), which contains a detailed explanation of these standards). cf. **summary appraisal report**. See also **limited appraisal**.

restricted contract(Eng) A contract, entered into before January 15, 1989, by which "one person grants to another in consideration of a rent that includes payment for the use of furniture or for services, the right to occupy a dwelling as a **residence**", RA 1977, s. 19(2). A holder of a restricted contract has no security of tenure as such, but the tenant has the right to postpone a notice to quit by up to six months (RA 1977, ss. 103-106A). See also **eviction, furnished tenancy, tied accommodation**.

restricted land(US) A term that referred to land that was granted to Native Indians, but the alienation of which was restricted by conditions imposed by Congress which were said to be intended "to protect the Indians from their own incompetence", Kenny v. Mills, 250 US 61, 39 S Ct 417, 418, 63 L Ed 845 (1918).

restricted use appraisal(US) See **limited appraisal, restricted appraisal report**.

restricted tenancy(Eng) See **restricted contract**.

restriction **1.** A **limitation** or prohibition placed on the actions of someone. In particular, a limitation placed on the use of property, including an **encumbrance**; a **restrictive covenant**; a **planning condition**(Eng) or **zoning ordinance**(US); a **restraint on alienation**; or a **user clause**. See also **building code, building controls, building regulations, covenant, qualification**. **2.**(Eng)A means by which any transfer, charge, disposition or other form of **dealing** in registered land is prevented until certain conditions or requirements, that are specified on the land register, have been dealt with (LRA 1925, s. 58). A restriction is used most commonly to protect a **minor interest**. **3.** An entry on the register of land titles at the Land Registry that is made to regulate the circumstances in which a disposition of a **registered estate** or a **registered charge** may be made. A restriction prevents any entry being made on the register the disposition conforms to the terms of the restriction (LRA 2002, s. 40). cf. **caution, inhibition**. See also **overreachable interest**. **4.**(US)See **covenant, conditions and restrictions**.

restrictive covenant **1.** A **covenant** in a contract that restricts or regulates a course of action. In particular, a covenant in a lease that restricts the lessee's use of, or ability to transfer, the demised premises. See also **restraint on alienation**. **2.** A private agreement by which a holder of a parcel of land (the covenantor) undertakes to accept a restriction, or **covenant**, placed on the use to which he may put his land, or the type of development that may be carried out on the land, for the benefit of the holder of another parcel of land (the covenantee). A restrictive covenant between the owners of two parcels of land may be referred to as a 'vendor and purchaser covenant', because it is the form of covenant that is created when a landowner sells part of his land and wishes to prevent the new landowner from carrying out an activity or developing the land in a way that would be detrimental to the value or amenity of the land he has retained; as distinguished from a leasehold covenant which is entered into between a landlord and tenant. The land sold with the burden of the covenant is called the 'servient tenement' (or sometimes the 'burdened tenement') and the land that is held to benefit from the covenant is called the 'dominant tenement' (or sometimes the 'benefited tenement'). A restrictive covenant is passive in nature; it restricts the owner of the servient tenement in his freedom to use his land; but it is negative in that it does not require the expenditure of time, labour or money; thus a restrictive covenant is described, especially in North America, as a **negative easement**. However, unlike a true **easement**, at common law, a restrictive covenant may be entered into only by express agreement and may not be acquired by implied grant or prescription, and it does not require the same strict certainty as to the subject matter as an easement.

In the same way as a covenant in a lease, a vendor and purchaser covenant is clearly enforceable between the original parties to the agreement because there is **privity of contract** between the parties. Furthermore, in English law, and in most jurisdictions in the US, a restrictive covenant may be enforced by any person who is identified when the covenant is entered into as a beneficiary of the covenant (such as a successor to the owner of the land or the owner of adjoining land), provided the covenant is one that 'touches and concerns' the land itself, even if that person is not specifically named as a party to the original conveyance by which the covenant was created.

Once either party has parted with their interest in the land, there is neither privity of contract (unless a new agreement is made), nor **privity of estate** (as with a leasehold covenant), between the owners of the affected lands to enable the covenant to be enforced directly. Nonetheless, the covenant may be enforceable provided it conforms to the complex rules that have been developed from English common law. As a rule, the *benefit*, or right to enforce a covenant, whether positive or negative, passes to a successor in title to the land. On the other hand, the *burden*, or the restraint imposed on land, is not considered capable of running with the land (although there are a number of ways in which the burden may be made enforceable against a person who acquires the land). Nonetheless, being an equitable right, this right of enforcement is dependent on the discretion of the courts.

Under English statute law, any person claiming under the covenant (a lessee, **successor in title** or anyone deriving title from a successor) may enforce the *benefit* of the covenant, as if he were expressed as such in the original covenant, provided the covenant was made for the benefit of the land owned by the covenantee (LPA 1925, s. 78) and, unless a contrary intention is expressed, the successors of the original covenantor (which includes all owners and occupiers of the land) are deemed to be parties to the covenant (LPA 1925, s. 79; *Tophams Ltd v Earl of Seton* [1967] 1 AC 50, [1966] 1 All ER 1039 (HL)).

In the US, a restrictive covenant, as well as being considered as a 'negative easement', may be called a **real covenant**, being a right that affects real property and which passes or 'runs with the land', i.e. a covenant that is enforceable as a real action and not merely a personal right. It may also be called a 'private zoning' or a 'restrictive zoning', as distinguished from public zoning, or sometimes a covenant contained in a 'deed of restriction'. See also **contract zoning**(US), **equitable interest**(Eng), **equitable servitude**(US), **land charge**(Eng), **minor interest**(Eng), **planning obligation**(Eng), **servitude**.
Francis, Andrew. *Restrictive Covenants and Freehold Land: A Practitioner's Guide.* London: Sweet & Maxwell, 1999.
Newson, G. L. *Preston & Newsom's Restrictive Covenants Affecting Freehold Land.* 9th ed. London: Sweet & Maxwell, 1998.
3. A condition contained in a contract that restricts the right of one of the parties, for the benefit of the other party, to act freely after the contract has come to an end. For example, a clause in a lease which provides that after the expiration of that lease, the tenant is not to trade for a specified period of time within a defined radius of the premises that were leased to him; or a similar provision that restricts the type of items that a retailer may sell. Such a restriction may be invalid as an unreasonable restraint of trade, unless it is considered reasonable as between the parties and is consistent with the public interest. See also **non-competition clause.** **4.**(US)A restriction on the use and development of land that is accepted by the grantor and grantee in order to maintain or enhance the lands in a particular area, i.e. a restriction that forms part of a general plan for the development of an area or tract of land, especially when it is being subdivided for sale to a number of different buyers who intend to share in a common scheme of development, use and management. A covenant that forms part of a **scheme of development.** **5.** A covenant in a contract of employment or service which limits or restricts the employment or business of one of the parties in favour of the other when the contact comes to an end; usually by providing that the activity may not be carried on within a stipulated area or radius or for an agreed period of time.

restrictive injunction See **injunction**.

restrictive zoning[(US)] **Zoning** rules imposed by a local government body that limit the use of land, or a building, to one particular user, such as for warehouse storage. See also **restrictive covenant**.

resulting trust A **trust** that is not created expressly, but arises from the construction of the acts of two parties or by implication of law. In particular, a trust that arises when money is paid for property by one person, but the property is conveyed to another under circumstances which give rise to an implication that the property is to be held, partly or wholly, for the benefit of the payee. A resulting trust may arise: (i) when a purchase is made by one person but the money is provided (in whole or part) by another on the understanding that the other will receive an interest in the property; or (ii) when the owner of a property omits to transfer some **equitable interest** to the purchaser, or transfers an equitable interest that is not intended to pass with the legal estate. In the US, the first form of resulting trust may be called a 'purchase money resulting trust' and, in some states, that form of resulting trust is recognised as a statutory right. In either case, an interest in the property is held on trust for the benefit of the party who should have received, or will ultimately receive, that interest. A resulting trust may be considered as similar to, or as a form of, an **implied trust**; however, it must arise from the intent of the parties at the time of the transfer. A resulting trust terminates if an express trust is created or declared to the same effect. In the US, sometimes called a 'presumptive trust'.

Under English statute law, a resulting trust is not implied in the case of a voluntary conveyance merely because the property "is not expressed to be conveyed for the use or benefit of the grantee", LPA 1925, s. 60(c). cf. **constructive trust**.
Chambers, Robert. *Resulting Trusts.* Oxford: Clarendon Press, 1997.

resumption The taking back of premises that had been granted under a lease. See also **right of re-entry, repossession**.

retail Derived from the Middle French *retaillier*, 'to cut up' or 'to divide into pieces'. The sale of goods in small quantities, especially to an ultimate consumer. The sale may be transacted in a **retail store, chain store, department store**, retail **market** or any similar outlet, or by mail order; as well as by **auction**. To be contrasted with 'wholesale', which consists of the sale of goods to a retailer, wholesaler, or an industrial consumer who intends to resell them or use them for business needs as supplies or equipment.

retail area[(BrE)] The floor area of a shop, which is assessed as "the **net internal area (NIA)**. INCLUDING (1) Storerooms and ancillary accommodation formed by non-structural partitions, the existence of which should be noted; (2) Recessed and arcaded areas of shops created by the location and design of the window display frontage; EXCLUDING (3) Storerooms and ancillary accommodation formed by structural partitions; (4) Display cabinets which should be identified separately", The Royal Institution of Chartered Surveyor, *Code of Measuring Practice.* 5th ed. London: RICS Books, 2002. (Note: this definition is accompanied in the *Code* by diagrams and detailed notes for amplification.) This definition is used primarily for estate agency and valuation work in respect of shops and supermarkets. See also **sales area**[(US)].

retail buyer A person who purchases property for use and occupation, as contrasted with a purchaser who buys purely for the income or profit to be derived from property. See also **investment property**.

retail center See **major retail center, shopping center**.

retail lot sale[(US)] The sale of a land lot to the ultimate customer, e.g. to a person who intends to build a house thereon for his or her occupation. In particular, a sale of a number of lots to the same party.

retail store   A store in which goods are sold by **retail**. A store that sells goods to the ultimate consumer in small quantities and, usually, in the final wrapping or packaging. See also **chain store, department store, shop, shopping center, supermarket, variety store**.

retail store mix(US)   See **tenant mix**.

retail trade area   See **catchment area**.

retail warehouse(BrE)   A building that is constructed like a **warehouse**, but is used for the sale of goods directly to the general public. The goods are generally stored in a similar way to a distribution warehouse and are sold in larger quantities, but at lower prices than conventional retail stores. See also **outlet center**.

retainage(US)   A sum of money that is held back under a building or construction contract until the contractual obligations are complete. In particular, a retainage is withheld from the contractor until the architect (or sometimes an engineer) has certified that the work is satisfactory and until the building is free of all mechanic's liens. A retainage is intended to provide a reserve from which the employer will be able to pay for any defects or omissions that may arise under the contract if the contractor (or subcontractor) is unwilling to rectify them. Usually the sum held back is based on a percentage (commonly 10%, or 5% for large contracts) of each progress payment that is due during the course of the contract. In British English, more commonly called a **retention sum**. Also called a 'holdback'. See also **liquidated damages**.

retained agent   See **agent, sole agency**.

retained life interest(US)   A term used in relation to **estate tax** for the interest in land retained by the grantor of a **life interest** (26 USC § 2036).

retained percentage(US)   See **retention sum**.

retainer   1. A fee paid to a professional advisor, consultant, or lawyer to retain that person's services.   2. See **retention sum**.   3.(Eng) A document that expresses the terms upon which a lawyer has been engaged. In particular, a document given to a barrister by a solicitor engaging the barrister to act and appear for a party in litigation.

retaking   See **repossession, right of re-entry**.

retention   The withholding of possession of property that has been sold to another, until payment of the sale price has been made in full. See also **lien, retention sum**.

retention rate   A percentage allowance made to the cash flow estimated as receivable from an investment property to provide for the possibility of tenants renewing their leases, or exercising renewal options, upon expiry of the current leases. An allowance for the possibility of the landlord retaining the existing tenants in the building. Applied especially in **discounted cash-flow** analysis.

retention period   See **maintenance period, retention sum**.

retention sum   Part of the total money due to a building contractor for work done, but held back by the employer from the contractor (or by a contractor from a subcontractor) to provide a reserve from which the employer (or contractor) will be able to pay for any defects or omissions that the contractor (or subcontractor) is unwilling to rectify. Usually the sum held back is based on a percentage (commonly 10%, or 5% for large contracts) of each progress payment that is due during the course of the contract. These accumulated retentions are held generally until the employer's supervising architect certifies that the building works have been completed satisfactorily. Sometimes called a 'retainer' or 'contingency reserve' or, in the US, a 'retainage', 'retained percentage' or 'holdback'. See also **certificate of completion**(US), **certificate of practical completion**(BrE), **defects liability period**.

retentive lien　See lien.

return of capital　See internal rate of return, recapture.

return on capital　See rate of return, recapture, yield.

return on equity　See cash-on-cash return, earnings yield.

return on investment (ROI)　See rate of return.

revaluation　**1.** The making of a new assessment of the value of a property by the same valuer or appraisal organization. A revaluation connotes an existing **valuation**, and a revaluation means a new estimation of the same property, usually at a later date to the original valuation. The updated value may be obtained, for example, for incorporation in a company's balance sheet; for taxation purposes (especially for local property taxation); or to induce a lender to provide additional finance by using the new value as security for a higher, or new, loan. Also called, especially in the US, **reappraisal**. See also **reassessment**.　**2.**(Eng)The reassessment of the **rateable value** of all properties for the purpose of the levying of the **Uniform Business Rate**, which is to be carried out every five years.

revaluation clause(US)　A clause in a lease that provides for a reassessment of the rent to market value at specified intervals. Also called a 'reassessment clause'. See also **escalation clause**, **rent review clause**(BrE).

revaluation equity　An increase in the **equity** of a property that arises as a result of a revaluation.

revaluation lease　A lease that provides for the rent to be revised during the term by means of a revaluation carried out by an independent appraiser or valuer. 'Revaluation lease' may refer to a lease that contains a provision for the rent to be revised by reference to the **market rent** of the leased premises, or by reference to an agreed percentage of the reassessed capital value of the premises. See also **reappraisal lease**(US), **rent review clause**(BrE), **percentage lease**.

revaluation reserve　An amount, set out in the financial statement or balance sheet of a company, that represents an increase in the value of a property following a **revaluation**.

revenue　That which comes back. The gross receipts of a business or enterprise. Income that is received back as a result of an investment. The total return from any form of property. The annual rents, profits, interest or other issues from property. In particular, investment income as distinguished from wages or salaries. See also **gross income**, **profit**, **yield**.

revenue stamp　A stamp that is affixed to a document as evidence that a tax has been paid. In the US, prior to 1968, a federal revenue tax was payable on transfers of real property. This tax has now been abolished, but several states now levy a **stamp tax** on similar transactions. See also **stamp duty**(Eng).

reverse annuity mortgage (RAM)　An arrangement by which a capital sum is advanced based on a mortgage secured on the equity value of a person's home and the proceeds are used to purchase an **annuity** to pay interest (and possibly some amortisation of capital) on the loan and to provide an income for the home owner for a specified period of time or, more usually, for the life of the borrower. The mortgage debt may be repaid during or at the end of its term, as with any other loan, by a sale of the property or a refinancing, or on the death of the borrower, by a sale of the property, or from the proceeds of a life insurance policy. Such mortgages are generally granted to provide a retirement income based on the capital value held in a person's home. Also called an 'annuity mortgage', an 'equity-conversion mortgage' or a 'home equity conversion mortgage'. See also **Federal Housing Administration**[US], **reverse mortgage**.

reverse condemnation[US]   See **inverse condemnation**.

reverse leaseback   See **lease-and-leaseback financing**.

reverse leverage   See **leverage**.

reverse mortgage   An arrangement by which an owner grants a mortgage on his property in return for an annual income. The mortgagor receives an annual income for a specified period of time, or for life, and the mortgagee obtains repayment of the capital as a lump sum, either at a specified future date (generally from an insurance policy that is payable on the death of the borrower) or by the sale of the mortgaged property. After the mortgage is put into place, the payments made to the property owner, together with accrued interest thereon, effectively reduce the equity value of the mortgaged property. Alternatively, the interest may be foregone or reduced in exchange for a share in any increases in the capital value of the property, called a 'split-equity mortgage'.

   In the US, for the purposes of the Truth-in Lending Act, a reverse mortgage, or 'home equity plan', is a non-recourse loan; secured on the borrower's principal dwelling; securing one or more advances; and repayment of principal, interest and any shared appreciation or equity is due only after the dwelling ceases to be the borrower's principal dwelling (15 USC §§ 1647-8). See also **reverse annuity mortgage**.

Nauts, Charles, and David A. Bridewell. *Reverse Mortgages—A Lawyers Guide to Housing and Income Alternatives*. Chicago: ABA, 1997.

Scholen, Ken. *Your New Retirement Nest Egg: A Financial Guide to Reverse Mortgages*, 2nd rev. ed., Apple Valley, MN: NCHEC Press, 1996.

reverse premium   **1.** A sum of money paid by an assignor of a lease to a prospective assignee as an inducement to take over the liabilities under the lease. In particular, a sum paid when the contract rent exceeds the market rent, i.e. when there is a **negative leasehold** or a negative **profit rent**.   **2.** See **tenant improvement allowance**[US].

reverse yield gap   See **yield gap**.

reverser   **1.** See **reversioner**.   **2.**[Scot]One who has granted a **wadset** (a form of mortgage) of his land. Also spelt 'reversor'.

reversion   **1.** Derived from the Latin *revertor*, 'returning again'. The part of an **estate** in property that remains when a person grants an estate (a **particular estate**) to another for a shorter duration to that which he holds. For example, the interest retained by an owner of a fee simple who grants a life interest to another, or by a freeholder who grants a tenancy for a term of years. Reversion may also be used to refer to the process by which an estate in land returns to a person who has granted a shorter estate to another – the return of land to the grantor, and his heirs, after the grant is over. Reversion may refer to that which is left continuing during the particular estate, which is the most common sense; or the returning of land after the particular estate has ended. A reversion is not created by the grant of an estate or interest in land, but comes into existence when another estate or interest is carved out of the same land and, thereby, the grantor defers his right to actual or physical possession of the land. A reversion may be distinguished from a **remainder**, which is an estate that is granted but comes into effect, as a right to possession, after another estate has come to an end; a remainder is an estate that cannot return to the grantor. A reversion arises by act of the law being the part of the interest that will return to the grantor after the duration of the grant, whereas a remainder arises by act of the parties. There can be only one reversion of an estate (i.e. the estate returns only to the original grantor), but there can be any number of remainders (i.e. a succession of estates can be made to pass to different persons in respect of the same land). Sometimes called a 'reverter' or a 'right of reverter'. See also **escheat, possibility of reverter, rent, reversionary interest, reversionary value.** **2.** The rights of a beneficiary under a trust who obtains the absolute right to the trust property on the death of a **tenant for life.**

reversion factor(US)   See Appendix C, **Financial Formulae.**

reversionary income   See **reversionary investment.**

reversionary interest   The right to the future use and enjoyment of real property upon the termination or expiration of an existing right to possession, as upon the expiration of a current lease or a life interest. An interest in land that represents the right to a **reversion.** A 'reversionary interest' may be distinguished from a 'remainder interest' as the former returns to the original grantor, whereas the latter passes to some other party; although 'reversionary interest' may sometimes be used to refer to either form of interest. See also **reversionary lease, tenancy, vested estate.**

reversionary investment   An investment that enjoys the prospect of a substantial increase in value as a result of the expiration of a lease or the termination of a life interest. In particular, property that is currently let at less than its market rent, but has a foreseeable prospect of being let at the full annual value. For example, a property leased at a rent that is fixed for a number of years, but which can be let at the full annual value at the end of that period of time (the 'reversionary period'), either because there is a provision in the lease for a rent review or

the landlord then will be free to grant a new lease. The income that arises at the end of the reversionary period is called the 'reversionary income'. cf. **reversionary interest.** See also **equated yield**(BrE), **hardcore method**(BrE), **term and reversion method**(BrE).

reversionary lease   A lease that is restricted so as not to commence until a future date. A future lease or lease '*in futuro*'. In particular, a lease that commences after the expiration of an existing lease. A lease that will come into effect with the benefit of actual **possession** upon the occurrence of a future event (such as the determination of a prior lease), as compared with a 'lease in possession' which started at some past date or, strictly, on the prior commencement date of the lease. As a rule, a lease that does not commence within the period dictated by the **rule against perpetuities** (generally a life in being plus 21 years) is void. Also, in English law, a lease that does not take effect for more than 21 years is generally void (LPA 1925, s. 149).

In the US, also called a 'lease in reversion'. cf. **concurrent lease.** See also **legal estate, renewal, reversion, rule against perpetuities.**

reversionary value   The value of a property assuming that it is resold after a set period of time' The amount an owner receives on resale of an interest in property after a period of ownership. The **present value** of a property at the end of a specified period of time, especially upon the expiration of a lease. The value of a **reversionary interest.** See also **redemption yield.**

reversioner   One who holds an interest in **reversion.** A person who has a right to an interest in land, such as a right to physical possession, after the interest that he has granted in the land has come to an end. Sometimes called a 'reverser', especially in Scots law. cf. **remainderman.**

reversor(Scot)   See **reverser.**

reverter   See **possibility of reverter, reversion.**

reverter clause(US)   A provision in a contract or deed for the sale of land that provides for the land to revert to the grantor in the event of a violation of a covenant or restriction on ownership. For example, a provision that the land will return to the grantor if it is no longer used for the purpose for which it was granted. See also **possibility of reverter**, **scheme of development**.

revest(US)   1. The act of returning property to its owner; the vesting of property again. To return an estate to the grantor after the termination of a **particular estate** that he had granted. See also **reconveyance**, **vest**.   2. To reinvest income or capital received from a property.

review appraiser(US)   An independent **appraiser** who is commissioned to review an appraisal or appraisals carried out by other appraisers, especially an appraiser who is employed by a bank, insurance company or government department to perform such a function. See also **fee appraiser**.
Sorenson, Richard C. *Appraising the Appraisal: The Art of Appraisal Review*. Chicago: Appraisal Institute, 1998.

revocable trust   See **bare trust**.

revocation   The recalling of an act or deed that has been made; which may be the revocation of an order, an **offer**, a **will**, an agent's **authority**, a **power of attorney** or any similar withdrawal of that which has been granted. An **offer** (unless forming an option) may be revoked, as a rule, at any stage before it is accepted; but it remains in effect until a clear notice of revocation has reached the offeree. Thus, if revocation is made by mail it takes effect when the letter is received, not when it is mailed (unlike the common law rule that acceptance of an offer may be communicated when it is posted). Revocation may not be effected during any period for which the party seeking to withdraw has previously indicated, expressly or impliedly, an intention to be bound by the original offer or commitment.
   An agent's authority may be revoked expressly or by implication. Revoked by implication may

arise, for example, when a principal appoints another party to perform the same act and, thereby, prevents the original agent from continuing to perform his duties. An agent is not entitled to a **commission** for a service performed, such as introducing a purchaser, after his authority has been revoked, unless the service clearly was performed during the period of the authority. However, an agent cannot be deprived of his existing rights, and an agency agreement for the sale of land usually provides that a commission is payable upon the introduction of a purchaser during the term of the agreement, even if a resultant sale to that purchaser does not occur until a later date. See also **extender clause**(US), **subject to contract**.

revocation order(Eng)   An order made by a local authority, or sometimes by the Secretary of State, by which **planning permission** that has already been granted is revoked (TCPA 1990, ss. 97, 100). Such an order may be made at any stage before the development that had been authorised is completed or before any authorised change of use has been carried out, but it cannot affect building or other operations already carried out, or a change of use that has already taken place. A similar order – a 'modification order' – may be served modifying (or, in effect, partly revoking) any planning permission that has already been granted. Compensation is payable to an affected landowner for financial loss suffered as a direct result of a revocation order (TCPA 1990, s. 107). See also **compensation for planning restrictions**, **discontinuance order**, **purchase notice**.

revolving credit or **revolving loan**   Credit, or a loan, that is renewable on a cyclical basis up to a set maximum limit, i.e. a loan that may be paid back or drawn down as the borrower wishes within the specified or agreed limit. See also **commitment**, **rollover loan**.

rezoning   To change the **zoning** allocated to an area of land. An amendment to a zoning code to reclassify a specific parcel of land. See also special-use, permit, spot zoning, zoning variance.

ribbon development or **ribbon building**
The development of a succession of predominately residential buildings along the frontage of a major highway leading to a town or city, with individual properties having direct access to the highway. This form of development is restricted almost entirely to the highway frontage, with land to the rear of the buildings left undeveloped. In the US, where such development is also called 'roadside development' or 'string development', many urban areas demonstrate this form of uncontrolled growth.

rider   An addition or amendment attached to a legal document, often taking the form of a separate sheet of paper, which is intended to form an integral part of the document. See also **codicil**, **endorsement**.

right   1. A proper, open, and just claim to something, especially when protected by law. An **interest** in property; a **privilege** or other claim to property. 'Right' may be employed broadly to denote either: (i) that which is just and equitable; or (ii) a claim or privilege enjoyed by a person or persons, especially when given the protection of the law. For example, "no one shall be subjected to arbitrary interference with his privacy, family, home or correspondence, nor to attacks upon his honour or reputation. Everyone has the right to the protection of the law against such interference or attacks ... (1) Everyone has the right to own property alone as well as in association with others. (2) No one shall be arbitrarily deprived of his property", Universal Declaration of Human Rights, arts 12, 17: adopted by the General Assembly of the United Nations on December 10, 1948. A right, in its abstract sense, is independent of man-made law and regulation; it is that which benefits man (as with a right to freedom of speech or expression), unlike a **title**, privilege or similar claim which is dependent on the support of the law. See also **authority**, **ownership, private property, seisin, writ of right**.   2. A legal claim of **title** to a thing, i.e. a claim that can be sustained against others. An 'enjoyment as of right' (as related to a prescriptive claim to property) means an enjoyment that is had openly and notoriously, without leave, and without danger of being treated as a trespasser. Something enjoyed 'as of right' is freely held; held *nec vi, nec clam, nec precario* – 'not by violence, not by stealth, not by entreaty'. See also **prescription**.

right by prescription   See prescription.

right in common   See right of common.

right in gross   A right that is personal to the holder and is not attached to land. A right *in personam*. See also **in gross**.

right *in rem*   See *in rem*.

right of access   1. A legal right to enter upon particular premises. See also **access, landlord's access, easement of access, neighbor**[(AmE)]/**neighbour**[(BrE)], **right of entry**.   2. A right to obtain access to a property from a street or highway. See also **easement of necessity, right of way**.   3. The right that a tenant has over premises that are not included in the demise, either in order to gain access to the demised premises or to have reasonable use of the premises (as with a right to common parking areas). See also **appurtenance, easement**.   4. The right that the public has to enter onto property, as with a right to enter into a building as a **licensee** in order to conduct business with the owner or in accordance with an express or implied invitation from the owner or legal occupier. See also **invitee, private property**.

right of action   A right to bring an **action**.

right of alienation   See **alienation, restraint on alienation**.

right of buy-back   See right of pre-emption.

right of common   One of a number of rights that one or more persons may have, to take or use something that is produced by another's land. A right of common is a form of **profit à prendre** enjoyed by one or more persons as a customary right, in common with others. The right may be: (i) 'common of **pasture**' or 'common of pasturage' – a right to graze cattle; (ii) 'common of **pannage**' – a right for swine to forage in a wood; (iii) 'common of **piscary**' or 'common of fishery' – a right to fish; (iv) 'common of **turbary**' – a right to cut peat; (v) 'common of **estovers**' – a right to take timber for agricultural building or repair; or (vi) 'common in the soil' – a right to take sand, gravel, stone or minerals for use on the commoner's holding. In general usage, a 'right of common' is a right to use land that has been left open for the use and enjoyment of the inhabitants of a local district.

A right of common may be: (i) **appendant**, i.e. limited to certain ancient rights to plough the land with horses and oxen and to manure the land with a restricted number of cows and sheep; or (ii) **appurtenant**, i.e. a right that is acquired by grant or by prescription and is attached to one area of land to use another piece of land, generally to graze such animals as are agreed or accepted by custom (*Tyrringham's Case* (1584) 4 Co Rep 36b, 37a, 76 Eng Rep 973, 975). A right of common may be held 'in gross', when it is not held to benefit another parcel of land. Also, it may have arisen *pur cause de vicinage* – 'by reason of vicinage' – being a customary right for cattle to stray onto adjacent unfenced common land. In England, statutes have been passed to limit the rights of common in woodlands in order to encourage the growth of timber (e.g. New Forest Act 1949, s. 12). Sometimes called a 'right in common' or a 'profit in common'. See also **cattlegate, common land**.

right of contribution   The right of one who has discharged part of a common liability on behalf of another to recover that amount from the other. In particular, the right of one co-owner to recover essential expenditure (such as the cost of urgent repairs or taxes) that he has incurred in respect of the jointly owned property. See also **tenancy in common**.

right of entry   1. The right, peacefully, to take or resume **possession** of land; especially a right to enter onto land for the first time, whether as a purchaser of an interest in that land or at the start of a tenancy. cf. **right of re-entry**. See also **taking possession**.   2. A right to enter onto land as a **licensee, visitor** or **invitee**. cf. **trespass**.   3. A right that a landlord might reserve to himself to enable him to go onto land granted under a tenancy. In particular, a right to enter onto a property to carry out repairs or improvements. A right of entry may involve entering onto land, but it need not exclude the tenant's continued right of possession; unlike a **right of re-entry**, which is adverse to the tenant's continued possession. A landlord has no implied right of entry onto leased property during the subsistence of the tenancy, although if he covenants to repair he has an implied right of entry for that purpose. He may also have a right of entry under a statutory provision. In some English statutes, 'right of entry' and 'right of re-entry' are treated synonymously (Law of Property (Amendment) Act 1926, Schedule, amending LPA 1925, s. 7(1)). See also **forfeiture, landlord's access, reservation**.   4.(Eng)The right of an authority that has powers of **compulsory purchase** to enter and take possession of land, without the consent of the owner, in pursuance of those powers. See also **notice of entry**.   5.(Eng)The statutory right of a local or public authority to enter onto private land that may be subject to compulsory purchase in order to carry out survey work, including the carrying out of soil tests (CPA 1965, s. 11(3); TCPA 1990, s. 324). Compensation is payable for any damage caused by the local authority in the exercise of these powers (CPA 1965, s. 11). Some statutes provide similar powers even though the land is not subject to compulsory purchase (e.g. Local Government (Miscellaneous Provisions) Act 1976, s. 15, as amended; HA 1985, s. 260).

right of entry for condition broken(US) See **right of re-entry**.

right of first refusal   **1.** A right to be permitted an opportunity to acquire a particular property before it may be sold to another, but on similar terms. A right that can be exercised only when the owner has received a bona fide offer for the property from a third party. The term is colloquial and connotes that the owner of a property, prior to proceeding with a sale, will intimate the bona fide selling price, and other relevant terms, to the person holding the right of first refusal. If the holder of the right agrees to that price and the other terms, the property is sold to him on that basis. The term 'right of first refusal' is generally considered to be synonymous with a **right of pre-emption** (thus it is sometimes called a 'pre-emptive right of first refusal'). However, a right of pre-emption may be considered to come into existence before the property is offered for sale, or even upon the occurrence of some other condition; whereas a right of *first* refusal requires the obtaining of a third party's proposal as a precondition to the offer to the beneficiary or as a basis for determining the price. cf. **option**. See also **restraint on alienation**, **void contract**.   **2.**(Eng)See **leasehold enfranchisement**.

Radevsky, Anthony, and Wayne Clark. *Tenant's Right of First Refusal*, London: Butterworths, 2001.

right of fishery   See **piscary**, **right of common**.

right of light(BrE) or **right to light**(AmE) The reasonable right to the continuous passage of light to land without obstruction by adjoining buildings or structures, in particular through an opening or window. At common law, a landowner has no automatic right to a free flow of light (or air, or an unobstructed view) from adjoining land, although he may obtain such a right in the form of an **easement** when the light comes through a defined aperture. (In practice, a right of light is more usually *safeguarded* by a **restrictive covenant** or **negative easement** over adjoining land, thereby giving the building owner the right to prevent the owner of adjoining land from building or placing anything that obstructs the passage of light to his land.)

A right of light may be obtained by express **grant** or express **reservation**, or sometimes by implied grant or implied reservation; by **prescription** (although only in exceptional cases); or by **estoppel**. The right may be terminated by express or implied **release**; by **waiver** or by **abandonment**; or by a **merger** of the ownership of the lands benefited and burdened by the right.

In English law, when a prescriptive right of light is established, the beneficiary is entitled to an uninterrupted flow of sufficient light, according to ordinary notion, for the comfortable or beneficial use of the building in question, based on the use to which the building is normally put (*Colls v Home and Colonial Stores Ltd* [1904] AC 179, 204 (HL)). Thus, the right may vary according to the user and the surrounding circumstances. In the case of a greenhouse, sufficient light is required for its ordinary use as a greenhouse, i.e. for growing plants, and not merely sufficient illumination to work in it. Also, once obtained, the beneficiary cannot impose an increased burden by altering his user or repositioning or enlarging a window.

In the US, in most jurisdictions, a right of light may only be acquired by an express grant or reservation. A prescriptive or implied right is generally considered to be an impediment to land development. In those jurisdictions that do recognize the possibility of an implied grant of a right to air, such a right is only accepted in cases of real and obvious necessity.

In Australia, all jurisdictions have enacted legislation to the effect that a right of light cannot arise by prescription after a given date, which was stipulated as being between 1901 and 1907 (according to the commencement date for the State legislation). See also **ancient lights**, **daylight factor**.

Anstey, John. *Rights of Light and How to Deal with Them.* 3rd ed. London: RICS Books, 1997.

Ellis, Patrick. *Rights to Light.* London: Estates Gazette, 1989.

Bickford-Smith, Stephen, and Andrew Francis. *Rights of Light: The Modern Law.* Bristol: Jordans, 2000.

right of necessity   See **easement of necessity.**

right of occupation   See **matrimonial property**(Eng), **protected occupier**(Eng), **security of tenure, statutory tenancy**(Eng).

right of passage   Specifically, a right to be ferried across a stretch of water, but also a right to pass or repass along a **highway**, street, or any similar **right of way**. See also **easement, easement of necessity.**

right of pasture or **right of pasturage**   A right, usually granted by licence, to graze cattle or sheep on another's land that is laid down permanently to grass or wild herbage. The ploughing up of any land laid down as meadow or pasture may be a form of agricultural **waste**. See also **agistment, grazing licence**(Eng), **right of common.**

right of possession   See **possession.**

right of pre-emption   1. The right to acquire a property before it is offered to others; pre-emption being derived from the Latin *præemptio,* 'buy before'. A right of pre-emption, unlike an **option**, cannot be exercised unless and until the vendor decides to offer the property for sale. An option gives the holder a right to compel the sale of the subject property according to the terms of the agreement, whereas a pre-emption merely requires the owner, when and if he decides to sell, to offer the property first to the person entitled to the pre-emption, at the stipulated price. Upon receiving such an offer, the pre-emptioner may elect whether he will buy. If he decides not to buy, then the owner of the property may sell to anyone. A right of pre-emption may be looked on as a two-step process: (i) the decision of the seller to offer the property for sale; and (ii) the decision of the holder of the right of pre-emption to exercise or forego his right. At the second stage, the pre-emption may be converted into a form of option. A 'right of pre-emption' and a **right of first refusal** may be considered as synonymous. However, they may be distinguished in that the former does not necessarily predicate an offer from a third party, but enables the beneficiary to make an offer to buy upon specified terms, at a time to be determined by the vendor or offeror (usually before offering the property for sale to any third party), and a right at that stage for the offeror to accept or reject the offer, whereas the term 'right of first refusal' implies that there will be another interested party. A right of pre-emption may be considered a personal right and not an interest in property, at least until the property is offered for sale.

A right of pre-emption reserved by a vendor who sells land that is intended for development, but which is not developed within a specified period of time, may also be called a vendor's 'right of buy-back'. Also called a 'first option to buy'. See also **leasehold enfranchisement, restraint on alienation.**   2.(US)A right of a settler to acquire such **public lands**, up to a designated acreage, at a given price, subject to complying with the requisite statutory requirements, usually by establishing a residence or cultivating the land, or both (Nix v. Allen, 112 US 129, 5 S Ct 70, 28 L Ed 675 (1884)). See also **pre-emption entry.**   3. The right to acquire or use property before another, as with the right of an upper riparian landowner to take water before the lower riparian owner. See also **water rights.**

right of property   The free right to use, enjoy and dispose of **property**, without control or diminution, except as limited by the law of the land (1 *Bl Comm* 138). See also **private property.**

right of prospect   See **right of view.**

right of recourse   See **recourse.**

right of redemption   See **equity of redemption**, **redemption**.

right of re-entry   **1.** The legal right of a person to regain **possession** of land that has been granted to another, either after that right has come to an end by expiration of its term, or when the right has been terminated as a result of a breach of a condition. In particular, the right of a landlord to regain possession from his tenant, whether following notice to quit or otherwise. A right of re-entry may be exercised 'peacefully' or 'by process of law'. Peaceful re-entry arises when a landowner physically retakes possession of the land without legal proceedings, as when a tenancy has been brought to an end and the tenant voluntarily quits the leased premises. The process of law is exercised against the wishes of the possessor, as when a landlord takes an action to recover possession from his tenant pursuant to a claim for **forfeiture** of the lease. A proviso for re-entry is inserted into any well drawn lease, empowering the lessor to seek to re-enter the demised premises when rent is in arrears for a stipulated period of time (commonly 14 or 21 days), or when the lessee is otherwise in **breach of a condition** of the lease Such a right does not give the landlord an automatic right to re-enter the property, but if there is no such proviso, the landlord has no right of re-entry during the course of the lease, unless the tenant is in breach of a **condition** (and not merely a subsidiary **covenant**) of the lease (called in the US 'right of re-entry for condition broken'). The terms 'right of re-entry' and **right of entry** are frequently used interchangeably; however, the former clearly implies a right to regain possession of that which was enjoyed before, whereas the latter more particularly implies entry anew. See also **equitable interest**, **eviction**, **legal interest**(Eng), **relief**, **security of tenure**, **usual covenant**, **waiver**. **2.** An interest in land held by a person who has transferred an **estate** in the land on 'condition subsequent', i.e. a future right to the land that may be converted into an immediate right if the transferor exercises a right he has reserved (the 'right of entry or re-entry') to regain the estate.

In English law, a fee simple conveyed subject to covenants and restrictions for which there is a "legal or equitable right of entry or re-entry" in the event of a breach, is still considered to be a 'fee simple absolute' (LP(A)A 1926, Schedule, amending LPA 1925, s. 7(1)) and, therefore, to be a **legal estate**. (This amendment was intended to apply to land held subject to the payment of a rentcharge but appears to apply to any **conditional fee simple**.) cf. **possibility of reverter**. See also **fee simple absolute in possession**(Eng), **estate on condition**(US).   **3.**(Eng)A right of a vendor of land, or his successor, who has retained a **rentcharge** over the land, to enter the land at any time in the future if the annual payment falls into arrears and to levy distress; lease the land to a trustee to raise income until all the arrears are paid; or to bring proceedings for the recovery of the land (LPA 1925, s. 121) or, if provided for by the instrument that created the rentcharge, to simply re-enter and take back the land. cf. **right of entry**.

right of reverter   See **reversion**.

right of support or **right to support**   **1.** A right by which an owner of land is entitled to lateral and subjacent support from adjoining land, either for the soil or subsoil. A common law right that is a natural incident to the ownership of land (*Dalton v Angus* (1881) 6 App Cas 740 (HL)). This common law right only applies to land in its natural state, it does not impose an obligation to provide extra support to combat the load imposed by a new building on adjacent land (*Wyatt v Harrison* (1823) 2 B & Ad 871, 110 Eng Rep 320; *New Westminster (City) v Brighouse* (1892) 20 SCR 520, 538 (Can); The American Law Institute, *Restatement Second, Torts* § 817c (1979)); although a landowner can acquire an **easement** for that purpose (or may be **negligence** if he mindfully excavates without taking reasonable precautions to prevent the collapse of his neighbour's property). This right of support does not apply to natural erosion, unless a landowner is negligent in the prevention of future erosion on his land and thereby undermines his neighbour's land, or he fails to inform his neighbour of a defect of which he is patently aware and that could affect the stability of his neighbour's land. A landowner may not dig up or mine his land so as to cause his neighbour's land to collapse. Also, a landowner may be liable for **negligence** if he mindfully excavates without taking reasonable precautions to prevent the collapse of his neighbour's property.

In English law, it has been held that a landowner can divert water flowing in an undefined channel without being liable for a consequent land slippage, but he may not divert water with wet sand, silt, or brine, as that is equivalent to removing land (*Lotus Ltd v British Soda Co Ltd* [1972] Ch 123).

In the US, the 'English Rule' that provides for the unrestricted right to divert water in an undefined channel has been superseded in most jurisdictions by the 'American Rule' that limits the drawing of underground water to that which is reasonably necessary for the use on the adjacent land. The American rule provides remedies for subsidence caused by negligent or excessive extraction; also, as in English law, the removal of water and silt requires reasonable care so that it does not to undermine the lateral support to the adjoining land.

With regard to the right of support of a building by an adjoining building, unless there is an **easement** (express or implied) requiring the maintenance of support, the common law does not grant any natural right to such support. However, as a rule, if a property owner removes a common wall, he owes a duty to support adequately, or weatherproof, the remaining part of the wall between his property and his neighbour's. See also **lateral support, natural rights, quasi-easement**. **2.** An **easement** for the support of land received from neighbouring land. An easement of support may be obtained in respect of an extra load imposed on the land itself as a result of a building or structure, or it may be obtained in respect of a right to the support of one building by another. See also **party wall**.

right of survivorship　　See **joint tenancy, tenancy by the entirety**.

right of view or **right to view**　　A right for the owner of one property to an unobstructed view over an adjoining property. In common law, such a right is generally considered to be too vague to constitute the subject of an **easement**: "there is no such right known to law as a right to a prospect or view", *Phipps v Pears* [1965] 1 QB 76, 83, [1964] 2 All ER 35, 37 (CA).

In the US, several jurisdictions accept that a right to a view cannot be acquired by **prescription**, but can only be acquired by express grant. However, some jurisdictions may acknowledge a right to view as acquired by prescription, although it would generally have to be acquired by a long, continuous and manifest user. A right to a view may be effectively created by a **restrictive covenant** (or **negative easement**) imposed on the use or development of adjoining land in order to protect a view. Also, planning or zoning laws may prohibit the construction of building, fences or other structures beyond a certain height and thereby protect a right to a view.

The civil law of Louisiana recognizes a 'servitude of view'. Such a right takes the form of a right to prevent the erection of buildings on the servient land when that would obstruct the view from the dominant land. It is a "continuous, apparent **servitude** which can be established only by title, destination of the owner or acquisitive prescription", La CC, art. 765. See also **right of light**.

Greed, John A. *View Point: a Point of View on Rights of View.* Bristol: University of West of England, 2000.

right of way　　The right of one or more people, or the community at large, to pass and repass over the land of another without interference. A right of way may be granted as a private right, usually in the form of an **easement**, or it may be granted as a **lease** or **licence**. A right of way may also be granted as a public right, i.e. a **highway** – a right for the public at large to pass over a set route without having a set origin or destination. A right of way generally confers ancillary rights, such as a right to stop for loading and unloading at and for a reasonable period of time. Once granted, a right of way cannot be unduly enlarged as a result of a radical change in the nature of the use of the dominant tenement (unless there is an additional grant). A right of way may take several forms, e.g. a right on foot, on horseback, in a vehicle or to drive cattle, and the extent of that right is determined by the terms of the express **grant** by which it was created, or by the means of the implied use over a period of time. See also **custom, dedication, easement of necessity, easement in gross, right of passage, wayleave**.

Blackford, Simon. *Rights of Way*. 2nd ed. Welwyn Garden City: EMIS Professional Publishing, 1999.

right of way by necessity(US) See **easement of necessity**.

right of way *ex via termini* A right of way over the land of another 'confined to a particular path or road'.

right of way in gross(US) See **easement in gross**.

right *pur cause de vicinage*(Eng) See **vicinage**.

right, title and interest 1.(US)Operative words used in a conveyance to confirm that the grantor or assignor is transferring his entire interest (Spreckels v. Brown, 212 US 208, 29 S Ct 256, 53 L Ed 476, 479 (1909)). In particular, the words are used in a **quitclaim deed** to confirm the estate or interest being transferred, without providing any representation as to the extent of that estate or interest. The use of all three words may be considered excessive because, in most cases, **interest** would encompass the entirety of the transferor's rights or title. However, the tendency is to use all three words just to be sure. See also **release**. 2. Words used in a writ executed against land that is granted as security for a debt which indicate that the creditor is securing whatever interest in the land is held by the debtor.

right to air A right to the passage of air over land or through a defined aperture to or from adjacent property. A right to air through a defined aperture or channel can be acquired as an **easement**, but in the common law a landowner has no general or natural right to the flow of air to, or from, his land (*Hunter v Canary Wharf Ltd* [1997] AC 655, [1997] 2 All ER 426 (HL)). However, if a landowner enjoys a right to the flow of air over his land, the polluting of that air (except when authorised by statute, by express or implied grant, or by prescription) may create a **nuisance**. In the US, most jurisdictions do not consider that a **negative easement** (such as air, light and support) can arise by prescription. In Australia, all jurisdictions have enacted legislation to the effect that a right to air or light cannot arise by prescription after a given date, which was stipulated as being between 1901 and 1907 (according to the commencement date for the State legislation). In Canada, most provinces have enacted legislation to a similar effect. See also **derogation from grant, natural rights, right of light, strict liability**.

right to buy See **leasehold enfranchisement**(Eng), **right of pre-emption, secure tenancy**(Eng).

right to fish A right to take fish from waters belonging to another for personal consumption. An owner of land has an absolute right to take any fish in water entirely on his **land**, unless limited by statute law. A riparian owner (one who owns land adjoining a watercourse) owns the bed of a stream, or the non-tidal parts of a river, to the middle of the watercourse – *usque ad medium filum aquæ*; has a right to fish up to that boundary; and is the absolute owner of any fish when they are caught and killed in that part of the river (even if caught by an unauthorised person). A right to fish may be granted to another as a **profit à prendre**, either as a several or sole right; or as a **right of common** (a 'common of fishery' or a 'common of piscary') with the grantor or with any third party. See also *ad medium filum aquæ*, **piscary**.

right to let down the surface   A right to excavate land in order to lower the surface of the land. Such a right is granted usually as an easement that permits the excavation of land in connection with mining operations, even though this may undermine the adjoining land. See also **right of support**.

right to light   See **right of light**.

right to support   See **right of support**.

right to view   See **right of view**.

right to water   See **littoral rights, riparian rights, water rights**.

rights   See **natural rights**.

rights of occupation(Eng)   See **matrimonial property**.

ring fencing   An arrangement by which an agent limits the exposure of a property to the market in order to sell it to a known or friendly purchaser who usually pays a 'bribe' for the advantage of a favourable purchase price. An arrangement that is normally illegal and fraudulent.

ring, auction   See **bidding agreement**.

riparian land   Land, or strictly the bank, that abuts a **watercourse** ('riparian' being derived from the Latin *ripa* meaning 'bank'). In particular, land that abuts a river or stream, as distinguished from **littoral land** which abuts the sea or inland waves, including those of a lake. Riparian land is that parcel that abuts the watercourse; is held as part of land title; as well as land within the watershed of the watercourse. The ownership of riparian land

entitles the holder to particular benefits with regard to the water flowing in the watercourse. In some contexts, riparian land and littoral land may be used interchangeably, as several of the rights appertaining thereto are virtually identical (especially between rivers and lakes). See also **batture, natural rights, riparian rights**.

riparian owner   See **riparian rights**.

riparian rights   The rights appertaining to the ownership of land that is situated on or forms the bank of a river or natural **watercourse**; in particular, the bank of a non-tidal watercourse. In particular, 'riparian rights' are those common law rights recognised in Great Britain and the eastern United States. An owner of land that abuts a stream or river – a 'riparian owner' – has **natural rights** to the water therein, as long as the land is in contact with the flow of the stream (*Lyon v Fishmongers' Co* (1876) App Cas 662 (HL); *Merritt v Toronto (City)* (1912) 6 DLR 152, 163 (Can); United States v. 1,629.6 Acres of Land, 335 F Supp 255, 268-272 (D Del 1971)). This right arises as a result of the ownership of the land abutting the watercourse and not from the ownership of the bed of the stream. (The soil itself may be owned separately and, if the river is permanently diverted, the dry land may be used by the owner of the land to which it is annexed as he so wishes.)

A riparian owner has various rights in connection with the water that runs along the bank that he owns, either as 'non-consumptive', which entail uses associated with the existence of the water running along the land; or 'consumptive' rights, which entail the taking of the water for his use. These riparian rights, which are applicable to the non-tidal watercourse, include: (i) a right of access to the water, including a right to navigation, up to the point where the tide ebbs and flows (the public having the right to navigate the tidal part of the river up to the same point, unless limited by statute); (ii) a right to draw water for 'ordinary' use connected with the land adjoining the watercourse; (iii) a right to receive a free flow of water in its natural course and state, unaltered in quality and quantity by an upper riparian owner, except for the 'ordinary' use of that land owner; and (iv) an exclusive **right to fish** (except as limited by statute). A riparian owner may also own the subsoil of a non-navigable watercourse (which he usually does up to the thread of the stream – *ad medium filum aquæ*), and he has the right to acquire land by the gradual and virtually imperceptible process of **accretion**. In addition, in the US, most jurisdictions recognize a right to build a wharf or pier into the water – called 'wharfing out' (subject to appropriate state zoning and building regulations).

Under the common law, after the point where the tide ebbs and flows, the watercourse is vested in the Crown, unless it has been expressly granted to a subject or that right has been precluded by some binding authority (*Malcomson v O'Dea* (1863) 10 HL Cas 593, 11 Eng Rep 1155 (HL); *A-G of Straits Settlement v Wemyss* (1888) 13 App Cas 192 (PC)). In the United States, navigable waters (those up to the tidal reaches) are the public property of the individual state, being held in its sovereign capacity in trust for the public (In re Opinion of the Justices, 365 Mass 681, 313 NE.2d 561 (1974). cf. **littoral rights**. See also **injury to land, reliction, water rights**.

risk   Derived from the French *risque*, or the Italian *risicare*, 'to run into danger'. The possibility or peril of loss, destruction, or injury; the relative uncertainty of an event occurring. Risk is a function of lack of knowledge; the less that is known about the probable turn of events, the greater the risk: "risk varies inversely with knowledge", Irvine Fisher, *The Theory of Interest*, 1930, p. 221. In general usage, risk denotes a chance of loss, either loss arising from chance or the wind of fortune, or loss as distinguished from gain or **profit**. In investment, risk is equated with the sacrifice of something at the present, especially money, in the hope of a better outturn or profit in the future; it implies a choice of alternatives.

Real estate development and investment is concerned with speculative risks, such as the possibility of an increase or decrease in income or capital value; the possibility of a change in the cost or availability of finance; the possibility of a change in taxation; the possibility of a change in the value of money; and the possibility of adverse government intervention, e.g. condemnation/compulsory purchase, or rent control, and risks that are associated with the **environment**, such as pollution and the existence of hazardous waste or deleterious materials.

In **insurance**, risks may be 'speculative' or 'pure'. A speculative risk is one that arises from a business activity and, therefore, may result in a loss (or profit). A pure risk can only lead to a loss, in particular a loss that arises from an **act of God**, theft, fire, etc. An insurer will normally provide an **indemnity** only against a pure risk, as insurance concerns itself with factors that are entirely beyond the insured's control. In an insurance policy, 'risk' may be used to refer to the peril insured against; the subject matter that is at risk; or the circumstances in which a claim would be met. See also **all-risks insurance, contractor's all-risks insurance, credit rating, downside risk, due diligence, excepted risk, risk capital, risk rate, sensitivity analysis, speculator**.

risk capital   Capital invested in a project that is likely to be lost in its entirety in the event of failure of the project. Capital invested on a speculative basis. Generally, **equity capital** is the risk capital, as distinguished from debt capital which has a higher priority or is secured on the assets of the borrower, thereby minimising the risk of total loss. See also **risk, seed money, venture capital**.

risk premium   An increase in a price or rate of interest made in order to take account of a particular risk, especially when determining a **capitalisation rate**. See also **component capitalization rate, risk rate**.

risk rate   The rate of return that an investor considers appropriate for an accepted **risk**. A **rate of return** on an investment that is sufficient to induce someone to part with money in order to make that investment. The price of accepting a risk expressed as an annual percentage of the total amount of money that might be lost. See also **all-risks rate, component capitalization rate, investment analysis, remunerative rate.**

river A substantial and natural course of water that flows in a more or less defined channel to another river, a lake or the sea. The water may run continuously, or it may flow along the same, or approximately the same, course during a season of rain or snowmelt. See *ad medium filum aquæ*, **highway, riparian rights, right to fish, stream, water rights.**

river boundary See accretion, *ad medium filum aquæ.*

road A route or way over which vehicles, people and animals have a means of passage from one place to another. A line of communication, thoroughfare, or way over land that is accessible to individuals or the public in general. A route set aside for the free passage of the public or for individuals by licence or permission of the owners. A road is generally a hard surfaced or paved route that leads from one built area to another. In that respect, it may be distinguished from a **street**, which is a paved way that runs through, or is contained within, an urban area. A road may be a **highway**, although a highway is generally a made-up road that is designed to carry traffic from one town or city to another and is usually limited as to its points of entry and exit and is restricted from pedestrian use. A road may include a bridge, lane, footpath or other forms of passage over land.

roadhouse(US) An **inn** or tavern situated on a road. A place that provides food and drink and is usually licensed for dancing and, sometimes, for gaming.

roadside development(US) See **ribbon** development.

roll(US) See tax roll.

rollover expenses(US) Expenses associated with re-letting a property, such as a leasing commission or the costs of refitting the property.

rollover mortgage (ROM) See renegotiable-rate mortgage.

roll-over relief(Eng) A provision which enables a **capital gains tax** liability on an asset (which includes land and buildings) to be deferred when the proceeds of sale are used to acquire a similar replacement asset in order to continue a business. The replacement asset must be acquired one year before the sale, or three years thereafter (Taxation of Capital Gains Act 1992, ss. 152-164, 247-248).

rolled-under loan(US) A loan that is renewed at an interest rate that is lower than the one that has matured.

rolled-up interest See accrued interest.

rolling credit See line of credit.

rolling internal rate of return See internal rate of return.

room An interior part of a house or building given aside for a particular purpose, especially as part of a dwelling. An enclosed area or space in a building bounded by walls or partitioning. See also **bedsitting room, living room.**

room yield In an **hotel**, the average effective income derived for the rooms that are occupied, obtained by multiplying the average daily room rate by the occupancy rate. Thus, if the average daily room rate in a given month is $100 and the occupancy rate is 75%, the room yield is $75.

rooming house(AmE) A house where bedrooms are made available for paying guests, usually over an extended period of time. See also **boarding house, lodging house.**

root of title A document or instrument that

starts a claim of **title** to unregistered land; the documents that start an **abstract of title**. A *good* root of title should show clearly the extent of the estate to be transferred (in terms of both its quality and quantity); must have no 'cloud over it'; and must not be dependent on extrinsic evidence. It should include reference to all legal and equitable interests.

In English law, as a rule, a purchaser of land may require a root of title to be traced back at least 15 years in order to be satisfied that the seller has a 'good' root of title (LPA 1925, s. 44(1); LPA 1969, s. 23).

In the US, in most jurisdictions, a root of title should extend back to a government grant or over 30 years. See also **chain of title**, **good title**, **marketable title**.

row house(AmE)   A **house** annexed to another house on one or both sides and forming part of a row of similar houses. One in a row or series of houses of similar design or size that are attached to one another on each side by common walls, or in the case of the end house, by one common wall, and which usually has its own frontage to a public road or public place. See also **party wall**, **terrace house**(BrE).

royalty   A share of the profits or produce paid for the privilege of using another's property, whether in the form of a right to extract a natural resource from land, or for the privilege of using a right to intellectual property, i.e. a payment for a patent, trade mark or copyright. A payment made for the use of property (real, personal or intellectual) that is paid normally as a percentage of the revenue or profit to be derived therefrom, free of the obligation to meet the costs of production, marketing, distribution or similar business costs.

A royalty may be payable in money or in kind. A royalty payable as money may not be considered as a corporeal or real property interest, but merely a debtor-creditor relationship. Whereas a royalty that is related to the produce of land is more likely to be a property interest. Where a royalty is paid under the provisions of a lease, it is normally a part of the **reddendum** under the lease; it is true **rent**, even though it is paid by reference to the produce, rather than the value of the land itself. However, it may be distinguished from 'rent' by being a payment that is related to the quantity of material extracted from land; whereas rent is a fixed amount that is not dependent on the amount of material extracted. See also **dead rent**, **delay rental**(US), **escheat**, **overriding royalty**(US), **royalty interest**(US).

royalty apportionment clause(US)   See **entirety clause**.

royalty interest(US)   The interest held by the party to an agreement for the exploration and production of oil and gas whose only involvement is to be paid a royalty. A right to receive a share in the income from an oil or gas well (whether as the landlord's **royalty** or an **overriding royalty**), but without the obligation to pay for any costs of drilling, production, or operating the well. cf. **working interest**. See also **oil and gas lease**.

rubberizing(AmE)   Stretching the loan criteria by which a bank agrees to make loans in order to increase the amount of business generated. For example, increasing the **loan-to-value ratio** or reducing the **debt-coverage ratio**.

rule against perpetuities (RAP)   A basic rule of property law that an interest in land is void if it is granted so that it will not take effect, or **vest** (i.e. 'vest-in-interest'), until a date that is considered to be too far into the future. The rule restricts the creation of any interest in land that is made subject to a contingent event that prevents someone from having an absolute right to possession until a point in time considered to be too remote. The principle underlying the rule is that a 'perpetual' postponement of a right to possession of land is considered contrary to public policy because it 'ties up' the use of land and prevents its free alienation. Accordingly, most legal systems have sought to define a 'perpetuity period' within which an interest in land must vest, and according to the rule a **contingent interest** or an **executory interest** is considered void if it is created so that it might not come into possession until after the end of the 'perpetuity period' (*Duke of Norfolk's Case, Howard v Duke of Norfolk* (1681) 3 Ch Cas 1, 22 Eng Rep 931). In common law, the 'perpetuity period' is basically an existing (human) life or lives in being (whether they have an interest in the land or not), plus 21 years, including an allowance for gestation (*en ventre sa mère*), from the date when the interest is granted (in the case of a grant *inter vivos*) or the date of a testator's death (in the case of a devise). "No interest is good unless it must vest, if at all, not later than twenty-one years after some life in being at the creation of that interest", John Chapman Gray, *The Rule against Perpetuities*. 4th ed. Boston, Mass.: Little Brown, 1942, § 201.

Normally, "the estate *must* vest, if at all, within a life or lives in being and twenty-one years after; it is not sufficient that it *may* vest within that period, it must be good in its creation; and unless it is created in such terms that it cannot vest after the expiration of a life or lives in being, and twenty-one years, and the period allowed for gestation, it is not valid, and subsequent events cannot make it so", *Dungannon (Lord) v Smith* (1846) 12 Cl & F 546, 563, 8 Eng Rep 1523 (HL). Thus, if at the time the interest is created it is capable of vesting within the specified life in being, it is valid; but if that is not possible, it is void. So a gift "to the first child of A to marry" is void because that child may as yet be unborn and may marry more than 21 years after the death of A.

In English law, the rules for determining whether the 'perpetuity period' has been exceeded are complex and now depend on whether the instrument creating the interest is made before or after July 1, 1964. Since the Perpetuities and Accumulations Act 1964, the rules have been reformed and, to a degree clarified, in particular by the introduction of a period for which it is permitted to 'wait and see'

whether the land will vest within the required period. In addition, a testator may specify that the interest will vest within not more than 80 years (PAA 1984, s. 1).

In the US, in some jurisdictions, the rule against perpetuities is still based essentially on the common law rules. However, in several states (as well as in many jurisdictions in Australia, Canada, New Zealand and in Northern Ireland), the rule is governed by statute, which allows for a period of 'wait and see' (generally of up to 90 years) in order to ascertain if the interest actually does vest before the end of the common law period. In a few states, the 'perpetuity period' is limited to 99 years. Also called the 'doctrine of remoteness' or the 'rule against remote vesting'.

Maudsley. R. H. *The Modern Law of Perpetuities*. London: Butterworths, 1979.

Morris, J. H. C., and M. B. Leach, *The Rule against Perpetuities*. 2nd ed. London: Stevens & Sons, 1962, Reprint ed. with 1964 supplement, Sweet & Maxwell, 1986.

rule against remote vesting   See **rule against perpetuities**.

rule in *Dumpor's Case* (Eng)   See **partial release**.

rule in *Rylands v Fletcher* (Eng)   See **strict liability**.

rule in *Shelley's Case* (Eng)   See **heir**.

rule in *Spencer's Case* (Eng)   See **covenant, covenant running with the land**.

rule in *Wheeldon v Burrows* (Eng)   See **quasi-easement**.

rule of 72   A rule of thumb that the number of years required for an investment to double in value can be found by dividing the annual compound interest rate into 72. For example, if an investment provides a 12% annual compound return, it will double in value in 6 years. A similar 'rule of 115' may be applied to ascertain the period in which an investment will triple, i.e. an investment returning 8% will triple in just under 15 years.

rule of 78 A rule of thumb for calculating the outstanding portion of an annual payment due under a prepayment contract, especially an **amortization loan** that is repayable monthly. The sum of the number of months outstanding is divided by 78 (being the sum of the digits 1 to 12) to express the proportion of the annual payments outstanding. For example, at the end of month 7, 50/78ths of the total annual payment is outstanding $(8 + 9 + 10 + 11 + 12 = 50)$. See also **sum-of-the-years-digits depreciation**.

rule of 115 See **rule of 72**.

rule of capture[US] A principle of an **oil and gas lease** by which the landowner, or lessee, is permitted to take oil or gas that is extracted from drilling on his land, even though the oil or gas migrates from adjoining land through the substrata (Railroad Comm'n of Texas v. Rowan & Nichols Oil Co., 310 US 573, 60 S Ct 1021, 1023, 84 L Ed 1368, 1372 (1939)).

rules of conduct[BrE] Rules laid down by the governing body of a professional organisation by which a member of that organisation is required to conduct his professional duties, e.g. the rules or bye-laws laid down by the Royal Institution of Chartered Surveyors, the Royal Institution of British Architects, or the Law Society. These rules are published by the appropriate organisation and incorporate details of disciplinary powers and procedures to be adopted to enforce such rules. See also **code of ethics**[AmE], **duty of care**.

rules of good husbandry See **good husbandry**.

run off See **margin**.

running costs or **running expenses** See **operating expense**[US], **service charge**[BrE].

running covenant See **real covenant**.

running foot[US] See **frontage**.

running line See **call**.

running repair Repair that arises during the day-to-day use of a property, such as mending fuses, replacing tap washers or replacing a broken window pane. See also **repair**, **tenantable repair**.

running with the land See **covenant running with the land**, **easement**, **privity of estate**, **restrictive covenant**.

running yield The yield from an investment at a particular point in time, i.e. the relationship of the income at that time to the original cost, or the then market value, expressed as a percentage. Also called the 'flat yield', 'straight yield' or, if taken at the present point in time, the 'actual yield' or 'current yield'. cf. **initial yield**. See also **cash-on-cash yield**.

rural property Agricultural, farming or non-urban property, i.e. property in the country or outside a built-up area. 'Rural property' may include a small settlement such as a village or isolated community. See also **agricultural land**. Appraisal Institute. *The Appraisal of Rural Property.* 2nd ed. Chicago: Appraisal Institute, 2000.

rurban property Property, situated outside the limits of a town or city, that is in the process of transition from being **rural** to becoming urban in character. Generally, an area situated just beyond the suburbs.

Rylands v Fletcher[Eng] See **strict liability**.

S corporation(US) A small business corporation formed in a similar way to a partnership that has elected to pass all its taxable income and losses through to its shareholders and, thereby, it does not generally pay tax in its own right (26 USC, Internal Revenue Code, §§ 1361, 1366).

safe rate The **rate of return** from an investment that is considered to have the lowest level of risk. Generally taken as the rate of interest receivable from a bond or security issued by a government with a hard currency (e.g. US treasury bills, UK gilt-edged securities, German Bunds, etc.). In the case of real estate, a safe rate is generally represented by the return receivable from land that has been leased on a long-term ground lease and upon which a building has been erected and leased to a tenant or tenants of the highest financial standing. See also **risk rate**.

safety clause(US) See **extender clause**.

sale The **transfer** of property, or a title to property, from one party to another for a financial consideration, called the price. In connection with real property, 'sale' may be used to refer to any means by which title is transferred for consideration. Although strictly speaking a 'sale' is not complete until actual **delivery** of title to the property; in some contexts (especially for taxation purposes), a sale may be deemed to have taken place when a binding and unconditional contract has been executed. A transaction such as an assignment for the benefit of creditors, or a transfer of title in consideration for an extinguishment of a debt, is not normally a 'sale', but merely the means by which the financial transaction (the reduction or extinguishment of a debt) is effected.

When an agent or broker is to be paid a **commission** upon the 'sale' of a property, unless there is an agreement to the contrary, a sale generally means a completed transaction. On the other hand, the execution of an unconditional and binding contract may be considered equivalent to a sale, because at that stage the purchaser is the equitable owner of the property. However, to avoid disputes in this context, it is better to use more comprehensive terminology if the intention of the principal is that commission is only to be payable upon the **completion** of a transfer of a valid title.

A sale may be distinguished from an **exchange** by a lack of separate consideration; especially when the properties are considered to have equal value. 'Sale' is used principally to refer to a transfer of corporeal property or tangible property. A transfer of incorporeal or intangible property (e.g. easements and profits), as well as a transfer of the right to a lease is generally referred to as an **assignment** or **cession**. However, the grant or transfer of a long-term ground lease, or a lease combined with an option for the lessee to purchase the lessor's interest, may be regarded as akin to, or a simulation of, a sale; especially when considering the treatment of a transaction for tax purposes.

In the US, in connection with assessing a tax liability, the criterion in determining whether a transaction is a sale or an exchange is whether there is a determination of value of things exchanged; if no price is set for either property it is an "exchange", but if each property is valued and money paid, it is a sale (Gruver v. C. I. R., 142 F.2d 363, 366 (4th Cir. 1944). cf. **bailment**, **gift**, **mortgage**, **option**. See also **auction**, **bargain**, **bill of sale**, **conditional sale**, **conditions of sale**, **contract for sale**, **contract of sale**, **conveyance**, **grant**, **installment sale**(AmE), **power of sale**, **public sale**, **purchase**, **sell**, **subject to contract**, **trust for sale**, **writing**.

sale and buy-back(US) A sale of property with a concurrent contract between the parties in which the vendor agrees to repurchase the property under an **installment contract**. The purpose of such an arrangement is that the purchaser is treated as being the owner of the property for the purpose of depreciation deductions and the seller is entitled to the interest deductions for the interest portion of the installment payments. cf. **sale-and-leaseback**. See also **repurchase agreement**.

sale-and-leaseback   A form of real estate financing whereby an owner sells his property and simultaneously takes a long-term lease of the property from the purchaser. The purpose of the transaction is to enable the vendor to realise the immediate capital value of his property and at the same time to retain possession. He may retain physical possession, as with a retailer or an industrial company; or the right to receive rent and profits, as with a developer. A sale-and-leaseback may be used when a property owner considers that the annual cost (in the form of rent) will be lower than for an alternative form of finance, such as a conventional mortgage (although in the long run, increasing rental payments, and the foregoing of possible capital appreciation may make the arrangement more expensive than a mortgage loan). The alternative between ownership and leasing may be analyzed by means of a **discounted cash flow** appraisal, especially after giving full weight to the tax implications. A sale-and-leaseback may be used when mortgage financing is in short supply; when the seller is unlikely to be able to qualify for a mortgage loan on suitable terms; or to enable the seller to realise 100% of the value of the property when a mortgage loan is unlikely to exceed 70-80% of the market value of the property. It is also used where a company seek to raise finance on a portfolio of its operational properties. Sometimes called a 'purchase and leaseback', although the later term looks at the transaction from the purchaser's viewpoint. Also called 'net lease financing' as the lease back generally takes the form of a **net lease**. cf. **sale and buy-back, purchase money mortgage**. See also **land sale-and-leaseback, lease-and-leaseback financing, project sale-and-leaseback, slice**.

sale-buyback(US)   See **sale and buy-back**.

sale by acre(US)   The sale of land on the basis that the price is based upon an agreed price per acre. cf. **sale in gross**.

sale by tract   See **sale in gross**.

sale by aversionem(Civ)   See **sale** *per aversionem*.

sale in gross(US)   A sale of a tract of land by reference to a name and description, as opposed to a sale by reference to a map, plat or a detailed boundary **description**. A sale of land by description but without any indication as to its acreage, especially when the buyer is familiar with the boundaries of a tract of land. For example, the sale of "Lone Star Ranch in Hill County, Texas" or the sale of "the enclosed paddock". A purchaser of land 'in gross' cannot expect to obtain an abatement of price if he familiarizes himself with the land and later finds it is smaller than he had thought. Also called 'sale by tract'. cf. **sale by acre**(US). See also **Mother Hubbard clause, sale** *per aversionem*.

sale-leaseback(US)   See **sale-and-leaseback**.

sale off-plan   The sale of a building or part of a building before it is complete, especially the sale of flats in a block before the entire complex is finished. In Australia, also called a sale 'off the plan'. See also **self-financing development**.

sale per aversionem(Civ)   Literally a sale by 'turning away'. A term of Roman or civil law that refers to a sale of land based on a gross price, without a stipulation of the exact area of the land. Under such an arrangement the purchaser is presumed to be accepting the land purely by reference to the boundaries and cannot expect to receive any abatement of the price if the area is less than he might have expected. cf. **sale by acre**. See also **sale in gross**.

sale price   1. The total **price**, in money or money's worth, paid over on the transfer of property. In a contract the 'price' is usually the same as the **consideration**, although the proceeds of sale received by a vendor, after deducting all costs directly associated with the sale, e.g. lawyer's fees, agent's commission, etc., may be referred to as the 'net sale price' or **net price**. **2.** The price at which a property is expected to sell in the open market. See also **market value**.

sales area(US) The area of a retail store that can be used for selling, excluding storage space. See also **gross leasable area**, **retail area**(BrE).

sales comparison approach(AmE) A method of appraising or estimating the value of a property by reference to the actual price obtained for similar or **comparable property**. The prices achieved from the recent sales of comparable properties are analyzed and adjusted for differences in location, size, age, condition, date of sale, 'special suitability' or any other appropriate factor, and then the 'adjusted price' is applied to arrive at a 'value' for the property under consideration. This method is limited by the availability of data on recent and directly comparable property, but it is the most reliable and accepted method of appraising real estate. However, in the final analysis, the opinion of value arrived at is dependent on the appraiser's skill and experience rather, than any scientific formulation. Also called the 'market-data approach', 'market approach to value', 'direct sales comparison approach', 'comparison approach', 'comparative market analysis', or 'comparative sales method'. See also **appraisal**, **comparison method of valuation**(BrE).

sales contract See **contract for sale**.

sales mix See **tenant mix**.

salesperson(US) A person retained in a brokerage office (either as an employee or an independent contractor) to assist with showing property and the preliminary work in finding prospective clients and putting deals together. A salesperson is less experienced or qualified than a **broker** and is not responsible for executing the listing agreement or finalizing the particular brokerage transaction. A salesperson is an employee of the broker and has no right to sue for the brokerage commission. However, a salesperson must possess a **real estate license** issued by the state in which he is practicing and a broker may be denied the right to a commission in the event that a transaction is effected through an unlicensed salesperson. Also called an 'associate broker', 'broker-associate', 'affiliate broker' (especially when an independent contractor) or sometimes an 'associate licensee'.

salvage value An amount realised, or estimated to be realised, upon the sale of a property that has reached the end of its **economic life**. A sum of money that is received for a property that would otherwise be destroyed, given away, or written-off, because it is considered to have no further value.

salvo jure(Lat) 'Without prejudice'.

sandwich house(US) See **terrace house**.

sandwich lease See **intermediate lease**.

sandwich leaseback See **lease-and-leaseback financing**.

sasine(Scot) Pronounced 'say-zeen'. The possession of land. The act of giving and taking possession of land. See also **register of sasines**, **seisin**.

satellite tenant(US) A small trader in a shopping center who is dependent on a larger **anchor tenant** for the generation of customer traffic.

satellite town A town that is dominated by, or is dependent on, another town or city. For example, a town separated from a major city or metropolis, usually by a green belt or any other form of protected countryside, but to a large extent economically and socially dependent on that city. See also **garden city**, **new town**.

satisfaction   1. The execution or performance of an agreement. The termination of a contract or obligation by **performance**, i.e. by the discharge in full of what is due, such as by repayment of a loan, mortgage, lien or note. See also **accord and satisfaction**, **satisfaction certificate**[US], **satisfactory completion**.   2. Recompense for an injury done or a debt owing. See also **compensation**.   3. Something given in part or entire **settlement** of a prior claim by the donee. In particular, as part of a settlement by **accord and satisfaction**, satisfaction being the delivery of the substituted consideration.

The equitable 'doctrine of satisfaction' provides that if a person makes a payment or performs an act that has an unclear intention, but is aimed apparently at satisfying a debt or performing an obligation, the court may accept that the payer has discharged the debt or obligation, provided the payment or act is a sufficient substitute.

satisfaction certificate[US]   A formal written acknowledgment from a debtor or mortgagee, his personal representative or assigns, confirming that a loan has been repaid in full (including any arrears of interest); that all the terms and conditions of a mortgage agreement have been complied with; and that the property charged has been or will be released to the creditor or mortgagor. Any document that has a similar effect may also be called a 'document of satisfaction', a 'satisfaction piece', or sometimes merely a 'satisfaction'. See also **release deed**.

satisfaction piece[US]   See **satisfaction certificate**.

satisfactory completion   Completion of work to a standard deemed satisfactory to a reasonable person. When building work is required to be done to the "satisfaction of the owner", the work should be completed to the satisfaction of a reasonable person. See also **substantial performance**.

satisfactory title   See **marketable title**.

satisfied term   1. A tenancy for a term of years that, because of the fulfilment of the purpose for which it was granted, has come to an end before its stipulated expiration date. For example, a lease of a mine that has terminated under a provision that it will end when the minerals being extracted are exhausted. A tenancy for a term of years that has become a satisfied term merges with the interest held by the landlord and ceases accordingly. See also **merger**, **mining lease**, **oil and gas lease**, **outstanding term**.   2.[Eng]The discharge of a **mortgage** by repayment of the monies owed (LPA 1925, s. 116).

saving clause[US]   1. See **severability clause**. 2. See **grandfather clause**.

savings and loan association (S&L)[US] An association, formed under federal or state law, that accepts interest-bearing deposits or savings from the public, in return for which it issues shares in the association to its members. A savings and loan association is quasi-public in nature, but is managed by its members for their mutual benefit and financial interest. Saving and loan associations offer a broad range of loans primarily for home-financing purposes and such loans are predominately for a fixed term and in many cases at a fixed rate. In addition, many S&Ls make consumer loans, usually secured on the assets of the lender. Although S&Ls are essentially local in their operations, they are regulated at a national level by the **Office of Thrift Supervision**. Sometimes called a 'thrift association' or 'thrifts', as along with the savings banks they were founded to encourage saving among the poorer members of society. See also **building and loan association**, **thrift association**.

savings bank   1.[US]A state chartered bank that accepts deposits from third parties and pays interest on those deposits, but the profits of the bank are paid to the stockholders or retained as reserves by the corporation. Savings banks were founded to accept deposits from the poor and many of the earlier banks were 'mutual' and as such they were owned by the investors and distributed all there profits as dividends. The management of a mutual savings bank is headed by a board of trustees or managers. Most of the mutual savings banks are found in the northeast. Savings banks may also be incorporated. See also **savings and loan associations**.   2.(Eng)A society that is formed for the purpose of accepting deposits from savers. Such associations were formed to hold deposits for safekeeping and return them when requested by the depositor. Unlike a commercial bank, a savings bank, or as they are now called a 'trustee savings bank', only lends its funds to those who have deposits with the bank (Trustee Savings Bank Act 1985).

scale   1. A graduated table.   2. An indication of the relationship of distances on a map or plan; a representative fraction, e.g. 1/500. An equally divided line on a plan, map, or chart that is used to convert map measurements to actual measurements.   3. A series of graduated marks set out on a strip of wood, plastic or card that is used for measuring distance.

scale fee   A fee paid in accordance with an authorised or recommended scale. In particular, a **fee**, or **commission**, based on a level of charges recommended by a trade or professional body. Generally, a scale fee is based on a percentage of the value of the property to which the fee relates. The publication of a scale fee by a body whose members provide specialised professional services may be considered to be taking advantage of a monopolistic position. Accordingly, the law generally restricts organisations from insisting that its members base their charges only on a published scale fee. See also **multiple-listing service**(US).

scarcity value   The extra **value** attached to something due to an exceptional shortage in its supply relative to needs or demands. Although scarcity is a primary determinant of value, 'scarcity value' may be considered as the extra premium attached to something on account of a short-term dearth or deficiency in its availability. It represents an increase in value that arises because, in the short term, the demand for something substantially exceeds the available supply – a value that theoretically cannot be sustained in the long run. In economic theory, scarcity value cannot be sustained because a high price will induce extra production, increased supply, and drive prices down or alternatively, a substitute will be forthcoming. However, an insatiable propensity to consume – 'the more we have, the more we want – combined with the inflexibility of many production processes (especially due to the time required to establish new facilities), can sustain an element of scarcity almost indefinitely. See also **economic rent**, **fair rent**(Eng), **market value**.

schedule   Derived from the Latin *schedula* 'a small slip of paper'. Although historically a short appendix to a document, a schedule is now frequently a fairly significant addition or statement that contains explanatory parts of the main text. A detailed list, inventory or table set down in writing. A formal list added or appended to a document, especially a legal or financial document or statute. A 'schedule' is usually a sheet or sheets of paper annexed to a contract, deed, statute, deposition, or other instrument, extending the terms that are mentioned in a principal document; especially those terms that are at variance with the general or standard terms of a document. A schedule is often attached to a lease setting out details of such items as fixtures or fittings, rules and regulations, or services to be provided by one of the parties. A schedule may be added to an insurance policy (especially to a **blanket insurance** policy) to enumerate the risks covered by, or excluded from, the policy, or to specify the properties covered by the policy. See also **rent roll**, **schedule of dilapidations**(BrE), **schedule of quantities**(AmE), **schedule of rates**.

schedule of condition(BrE)   A written survey

that sets down a description of the physical condition and state of repair of a property which is to be altered in some way, for example by renovation, or is to be the subject of a lease. cf. **schedule of dilapidations**.

schedule of dilapidations(BrE)   A list of items of **repair** or **maintenance** that a landlord requires a tenant to make good in order to comply with the terms of a lease. An interim schedule of dilapidations may be submitted to a tenant at any time during the term of a lease, when the landlord determines that a tenant has not fulfilled his repairing obligations, providing there is a covenant in the lease permitting the landlord (or his agent or surveyor) to enter the demised premises in order to view their state of repair. A final schedule of dilapidations may be submitted on expiry of the lease, setting out repairs and decorations that should have been carried out by the tenant during the term of the lease. cf. **schedule of condition**. See also **dilapidation**, **landlord's access**, **repair**, **right of entry**.
Royal Institution of Chartered Surveyors. *Dilapidations: A Guidance Note*, 4th ed. London: RICS Books, 2003.

schedule of quantities(AmE)   A schedule that describes the work or duties to be performed by a building contractor and against which the cost of the work can be marked, particularly when submitting a tender for building work. cf. **schedule of rates**. See also **bill of quantities**(BrE), **fixed-price contract**.

schedule of rates   A schedule to a building contract that sets out the agreed rates to be charged for work done and against which the quantity of materials and labour can be marked. cf. **schedule of quantities**. See also **bill of quantities**(BrE).

scheduled gross   The projected **gross income** that can be expected from a property investment. cf. **effective gross income**.

scheduled monument(Eng)   See **ancient monument**.

scheduled property   1. In insurance, an individual property described in an insurance policy schedule that covers a number of other properties. Normally the insured value is set down alongside the description or address of the property. See also **blanket insurance policy**.   2. See **ancient monument**(Eng), **listed building**(Eng).

scheme of development   A scheme by which an owner of a defined area of land divides it up into a number of separate lots for sale (or lease) and imposes on the purchasers (or lessors) restrictions as to the use and development of the land by means of uniform covenants restricting the use to which the grantees may put the lots, with the express intention that the area as a whole, and each and every lot, will benefit thereby. The essential aim of the scheme is that each purchaser will have the benefit of the same restrictions as those to which he has been subjected (Besch v. Hyman, 221 App Div 455, 223 NYS 233 (1927); *Re Dolphin's Conveyance* [1970] Ch 654, 662, [1970] 2 All ER 664; *Texaco Antilles Ltd v Kernochan* [1973] AC 609, [1973] 2 All ER 118 (PC)).
In order to be able to enforce the provisions of a scheme of development each purchaser of an area of land (or his successor), as well as the common vendor, must have a right to enforce the restrictions for his own benefit (technically by suing for breach of a negative or **restrictive covenant**), and by the same token, must accept the burdens imposed on his use of the land. Thus "reciprocity is the foundation of the idea of a scheme … [and a purchaser] must know both the extent of his burden and the extent of his benefit", *Reid v Bickerstaff* [1909] 2 Ch 305, 319, [1908-10] All ER Rep 298 (CA) (*Re Palmer v Reesor* (1914) 6 OWN 622, 624 (Can)) (in the US called the 'doctrine of **reciprocal negative easement**'). The reciprocal benefits and burdens are referred to as 'equitable servitudes' (as they are rights originating from the English Court of Equity – *Tulk v Moxhay* (1848) 2 Ph 774, 41 Eng Rep 1143).
In the US, a scheme of development is usually called a 'general scheme of development', or it may be referred to as a 'common plan of

development' (5 Powell on Real Property, § 672), a 'common scheme of development', a 'general building scheme', 'general plan' or 'uniform plan of development', a 'neighborhood scheme', and the restrictions may be referred to as 'general plan restrictions', 'reciprocal negative easements', 'implied reciprocal servitudes' or, sometimes, 'mutual equitable servitudes'. (In English and Canadian law, it has been said that strictly a 'scheme of development' is a genus, and a particular instance of such a scheme is referred to as a 'building scheme' for the area (*Brunner v Greenslade* [1971] Ch 993, [1970] 3 All ER 836; *Scharf v Mac's Milk Ltd* [1965] 51 DLR (2d) 565 (CA Can).) In British English, a similar scheme applied to a block of flats may be referred also as a 'flat scheme'. See also **declaration of covenants and restrictions**(US), **planned unit development**(US).

scheme of management See **management scheme**.

scheme world(Eng) See **compulsory purchase compensation**.

science park A mixed industrial and office development that is intended for use by firms involved primarily in advanced scientific research, development and production of scientific instruments. The 'park' is a form of campus, usually sited near a university or college, which aims to provide modern premises in a pleasant environment with readily accessible support facilities for the users and to provide a link between the academic institutions and the building users. Also called a 'research park, 'innovation center' or 'technical center' See also **business park**.

Carter. N. *Science Parks.* Cambridge: The UK Science Park Association, 1989.

scienti non fit injuria(Lat) 'No injury is done to one who knows of the facts'. See also *volenti non fit injuria.*

scintilla temporis(Lat) 'A brief moment of time'. In particular, the time between the execution of two coincident documents or instruments. For example, the period of time between the completion of the purchase of a property and the execution of a mortgage.

scrambling possession(US) A condition where two or more persons are struggling for possession of land, especially when there may be no legitimate claim to the land and the possession of one of the parties may well amount to a trespass. See also **adverse possession**.

scrap value The **value** of something when it is only suitable as waste or for recycling. The value of a property when it has reached the end of its **economic life**. The value when something can no longer profitably be put to the purpose for which it was originally intended. See also **residual value**.

seal A mark or impression used to ratify, confirm or authenticate a document or signature. In particular, a mark affixed in order to effect a **deed**. Originally, a seal was embossed in wax or imprinted onto a glued wafer of paper, but today it may take any form that can be considered as sufficient authenticity of the maker's mark. Even a signature over words such as 'sealed with my seal 'or a witnessed signature in a circle on a document marked *locus sigilli* (or L.S.), 'place of the seal', will suffice (*First National Securities v Jones* [1978] Ch 109; Jacksonville, M. P. R. & N. Co. v. Hooper, 160 US 514, 16 S Ct 379, 40 L Ed 515, 521 (1896)).

In English law, a seal is no longer essential to create a deed, provided the instrument "makes it is clear on its face" that it is intended to be a deed ("whether by describing itself as a deed or expressing itself to be executed or signed as a deed or otherwise") and it is duly executed by being signed, properly witnessed in the presence of the signatory, and there is **delivery** (LP(MP)A 1989, s. 1).

In the US, in most jurisdictions, except in some eastern states, the common law need for a seal has been abolished (or, in some jurisdictions, there is a need only for a parenthetical reference or a mark that shows the intent to create a deed). However, a seal may be required to authenticate a contract executed by a corporation, and a few jurisdictions still require a lease to be made under seal. See also **acknowledgment**.

sealed and delivered   See **signed sealed and delivered**.

sealed bid   A **bid** made under seal, i.e. placed in an envelope and sealed until the time set for its consideration. A sealed bid is a common requirement when competitive offers are made in response to an **invitation to tender** for building work or for the provision of services. The sealed offers are submitted before a specified time and then opened for consideration at that time. Also, sealed bids may be requested when a property is offered for sale, especially when there are a number of interested parties prepared to purchase the property at a price in excess of the asking price.

sealed contract   A contract made under **seal**, i.e. a **deed**. See also **specialty**.

sealed offer   1. An unconditional **offer**, submitted by one party to a dispute to the other, that is placed in a sealed envelope to be opened by an independent expert or an arbitrator after the dispute has been settled. The offer is not intended to take precedence over the independent determination of the dispute. It is indicative of the final offer made prior to the submission of the dispute for independent determination and it may be taken into account prior to deciding on a fair allocation between the parties of responsibility for payment of the expert's or arbitrator's costs. Sometimes called an 'unconditional offer'. 2.(Eng)An offer submitted by an authority, that is compulsorily acquiring land, prior to a reference to the **Lands Tribunal**, indicating the amount of compensation that it is prepared to pay for the land being acquired. The offer is submitted to the Lands Tribunal, in a sealed envelope to be opened after the Tribunal's award. As a rule, if the Tribunal's award exceeds the authority's sealed offer, the costs

of the proceedings are paid by the authority and, in the reverse case, the claimant pay them. This rule only applies to costs incurred after the sealed offer is submitted to the Tribunal. In order to take advantage of this provision, the claimant must have previously submitted a detailed claim to the acquiring authority for compensation (Land Compensation Act 1961, s. 4; Lands Tribunal Rules 1975, r. 50). In any event, the award of costs remains a matter of discretion for the Lands Tribunal.

search certificate(Eng)   See **official certificate of search, official search certificate**.

search(Eng)   1. See **title search**.   2. See **official certificate of search, official search certificate**.

searches(Eng)   Enquiries made by a purchaser of land, or an interest in land, to determine the existence of any **encumbrance** that affects the vendor's title to the land. In particular, searches of the **local land charges register,** enquiries of the local authority (e.g. as to planning or highway proposals), and, where appropriate, company register searches, of a register of **common land,** an Area Coal Board Office, or any statutory body that may have a right that affects the land such as the authority that is responsible for a railway or canal that runs near the property. cf. **requisition**. See also **Companies Charges Register, constructive notice, Index Map, Land Charges Register, overriding interest, planning inquiry, priority notice, title search**.

Pugsley, K. *Enquiries of Local Authorities and Water Companies: A Practical Guide.* London: Callow Publishing, 2002.
Silverman, Frances, et al. *Conveyancing Searches and Enquiries.* Bristol: Jordans, 2003.

seashore   See **foreshore, littoral land, shore**.

seasonal grazing licence(Eng)   See **grazing licence**.

seasoned loan   A loan that has been outstanding for a number of years and the lender has substantially complied with the terms thereof throughout that period of time. Such a loan is considered a low risk to a purchaser.

second-hand evidence See **hearsay**.

second mortgage A mortgage granted against the security of a property that already has been charged with a **first mortgage** and, therefore, a mortgage that ranks as a lower **priority** in the event of any claim against the secured property. A mortgage may be ranked as first, second, third, etc., according to its priority. In practice, any mortgage that is subordinate to a first mortgage may be termed a second mortgage or, especially in the US, a **junior mortgage**. See also **general equitable charge**[Eng], **puisne mortgage, subordination, tacking**.

secondary approach to value[US] Any method or approach to an **appraisal** that is used as a check on the principal or 'primary' method of valuation. A secondary approach may be used either to lend support to the primary valuation or to verify the **highest and best use** for a property.

secondary easement[US] An **easement** that is required, or is available, to accomplish the intended purpose of a primary or existing easement. An easement that is **appurtenant** to an existing easement. For example, a right to enter onto land in order to clean a ditch that runs across the servient land and forms the subject matter of an existing easement; or, a right to use an existing right of way to enter land in order to test for the presence of minerals. cf. **ancillary easement, primary easement**.

secondary finance or **secondary loan** Finance, or a loan, secured by means of a **second mortgage**. A loan that is ranked behind another in order of **priority**.

secondary liability See **contingent liability**.

secondary location A relative term, although generally it is used to describe any position that is inferior to a **prime location**. A location, within a given town or neighbourhood, that does not secure the highest value, or one that is located on the fringe of the **central business district**.

secondary mortgage market A market in which existing mortgage loans or mortgage-backed securities are bought and sold. This market provides liquidity to the originators of mortgage loans and enables institutions to invest in the mortgage market without the need to be directly involved with making direct mortgage loans. See also **Federal Home Loan Mortgage Corporation, Federal National Mortgage Association, finance house, Government National Mortgage Association, mortgage-backed obligation**.

Lederman, Jess (editor). *The Secondary Mortgage Market.* Burr Ridge, IL: Irwin, 1992 rev ed.

secondary use See **shifting use**.

secret commission or **secret profit** See **agent**.

secret trust A **trust** in which the creator or settlor does not identify the true beneficiary. In particular, a trust that arises when property is stated in a will to be left to a particular person, but in a separate document that person is stated to be holding the property on trust for another, such as an illegitimate child or mistress whose identity is not known to other members of the family. Such an arrangement would normally become known upon admission of the will to probate. See also **land trust**[US].

section of land[US] An area of land, being one mile square (640 acres) into which a **Township** is divided. A Township is divided into thirty six sections, which are numbered from 1 to 36 starting in the north-east corner, then running east to west and then back west to east in six rows to finish in the south east corner. Each section is in turn subdivided into quarter sections of 160 acres and then into halves of 80 acres or quarter-quarters of

40 acres. These divisions are then designated by reference to the points of the compass. Thus, 'NW¼ SE¼ sec. 5' refers to the north-west quarter of the south-east quarter of section no. 5. Although not officially part of the township sub-division, a quarter section can be further subdivided, so that N½ SE¼ SW¼, sec. 3 is the northern half of the south-east quarter of the south-west quarter of section   3. See also **fractional section**, **government survey system**; Appendix C, **Table of Measurements**.

section number(US)   The number given to a **section of land** under the government survey system.

section 106 agreement(Eng)   See **planning obligation**.

section 146 notice(Eng)   See **forfeiture**.

secure tenancy(Eng)   A tenancy of a **dwelling-house** "let as a separate dwelling" by a 'public sector' authority to an individual (or individuals) for occupation as his or her "only or principal home" Housing Act 1985, ss. 79-80. A 'secure tenancy' may be one granted for any period of time (and may even be a licence, if the occupier is granted exclusive possession), provided a separate dwelling is let to an individual (or a number of individuals as a joint tenancy) for use as that person's (or one of the person's) only or principal home. The landlord of a secure tenancy must be one of a number of statutorily prescribed public sector bodies (HA 1985, s. 80, as amended). A secure tenancy cannot be terminated until a court order for possession has been given on one of the statutorily prescribed **grounds for possession** (HA 1985, ss. 83-84, Sch. 2). A number of tenancies are expressly precluded by statute from being secure tenancies. These include a tenancy granted for a fixed term exceeding 21 years; a tenancy granted to certain employees of the landlord; a tenancy granted to a student attending a designated course at a university or a college of further education; and certain short-tem tenancies. In addition, the following cannot be secure tenancies: a **business tenancy**; a tenancy of a dwelling that forms part of an **agricultural holding** and is occupied by a person who is responsible for control of farming; a licence to occupy an almshouse; and a tenancy of licensed premises (a public house or the like) (HA 1985, s. 79(2), Sch. 1). A person who has held a secure tenancy for at least two years may have a 'right to buy' the property that has been leased to him at a discounted price, either a right to buy the freehold, if the property is a **house**, or a right to a long-leasehold interest, if the property is a **flat** (HA 1985, ss. 118-131).

secured creditor   A creditor who holds a loan that is secured by a charge, lien or mortgage on property, or any part thereof, owned by the debtor. cf. **unsecured creditor**. See also **recourse**, **secured loan**.

secured ground rent(Eng)   A **ground rent** paid for land upon which a building or buildings have been erected. The ground rent is said to be 'secured' because, in the event of the ground rent not being paid the landlord has the benefit of a right to the extra value provided by the additions to the land. If the buildings are let, the security of a ground rent may be measured by the ratio of the ground rent to the market rental value, or the contractual rent receivable for the property. Thus, if the market rent is £50,000 and the ground rent £10,000 the ground rent is five times secured – the higher the security the lower the risk of the ground rent not being paid and, therefore, the higher the capital value of the ground rent. The ratio may also be termed 'cover', i.e. in the above example the ground rent is five times covered. cf. **unsecured ground rent**. See also **security of ground rent**.

secured loan   A loan against which property has been pledged or mortgaged as **security**. See also **recourse**.

securities Instruments that represents security for a debt, including stocks, bonds, notes, debentures, or any certificate that signifies that the holder has a right to repayment of a debt. Written instruments that are used for the financing of an enterprise or business and signify that the holder has made an investment in the business or enterprise. A generic term for stocks, debentures, shares or funding certificates of a similar nature; an instrument or certificate that confirms that a debt is owed to the holder or that the holder has an ownership interest in a corporation, partnership or any similar entity. The term 'securities' is used in its primary sense to refer to a debt or claim that is in some way secured. However, it may also be used to refer to any form of investment in an enterprise, whether secured or not.

In English statute law, 'securities' are defined to include "stocks, funds and shares", Conveyancing Act 1881, s. 2(xiv); LPA 1925, s. 205(1)(xxv); SLA 1925, s. 117(1)(xxiii). A more extensive definition of securities is given in statutes that concern taxation and financial regulation, e.g. the Income and Corporation Taxes Act 1988, s. 710(1)-(3); Companies Act 1989, s. 207. See also **security**.

securitisation(BrE) or **securitization**(AmE) The packaging of a number of asset-backed loans or mortgages into tradable securities. The conversion of a pool of investments or a number of loans into the right to a bond or security that is partially or wholly dependent on the income from the underlying investments or loans. The process of transferring certain receivables, such as consumer loans, mortgage loans, corporate bonds or trade receivables from their owner or beneficiary to a separate entity which in turn issues and sells such securities as a representation of an interest in such receivables. Also called 'structured finance', or in the US sometimes 'equitization' as the equity interests in property are converted to publicly-traded securities. See also **collateralized mortgage obligation, mortgage-backed security, real estate investment trust, real estate mortgage investment conduit, real estate security, syndication**.

Baums, Theodor, and Eddy Wymeersch, eds. *Asset Backed Securitization in Europe*. The Hague, London & Boston: Kluwer, 1996.

Campbell, Gordon. *Environmental Liability*. Welwyn Garden City: EMIS Professional Publishing, 1998.

Burrows, Jane (general editor). *Current Issues in Securitisation*. London: Sweet & Maxwell, 2002.

Ferran, Ellis. *Mortgage Securitisation—Legal Aspects*. London: Butterworths, 1992.

Glennie, D. G., et al. (editors). *Securitization*. The Hague, London & Boston: Kluwer, 1998.

securitized mortgage offering(AmE) See **mortgage-backed security**.

security 1. Something given, deposited, or pledged as an assurance that an obligation will be met, or as a safeguard against a loss. Property (real or personal) pledged, mortgaged or hypothecated to underwrite the repayment or recovery of a debt. In the event that the obligation is not met the holder (grantee) of the security resorts to the property for the amount of the debt. In general, in the event of a sale of the security, the balance of the proceeds remaining after the debt has been repaid in full belongs to the grantor or debtor. A personal guaranty to answer for the debt or debts of another may be referred to as a 'personal security', as distinguished from a **collateral security** which may be given in addition to the borrower's personal liability. Security may also be classified as 'active' or 'passive'. Active security means that the debtor has a right to sell the property to meet his claim. Passive security means that the debtor holds the property until the claim is met in full, as with a possessory **lien** or **pawn**. See also **charge, debenture, deposit, lien, mortgage, pledge, security deposit, warranty**. 2. The expectation or degree of confidence that something will happen, e.g. of an income being received at a future date. A factor that may be considered to be inversely related to **risk**; thus, the greater certainty of something happening the lower the risk of it not happening. Security is an important factor when determining the value of a property. **3.** Written evidence, or an **instrument**, that shows that assets have been given as a guaranty or warranty for a debt. A written confirmation that the holder has a right to property or assets not in his possession. Such an instrument is negotiable and in most cases is marketable. See also **bond, negotiable instrument, securities, stock. 4.** See **security of tenure**.

security capital Capital that is secured by means of a pledge, lien or mortgage. See also **debt capital, fixed charge, security**.

security deed(US) A term that is used in a few states (in particular, Georgia and Wyoming) for a deed that conveys a legal title to land as security for the payment of a debt; as distinguished from a grant to the lender of a 'power of sale' in the event of default (Scott v. Paisley, 271 US 633, 46 S Ct 591, 70 L Ed 1124 (1926)).

security deposit A **deposit** paid as good faith for the proper performance of the terms of a contract. In particular, money deposited by a tenant with his landlord, or the landlord's agent, as security for the proper performance of the terms of the lease, especially the due payment of rent and the repair and maintenance of the leased premises. A security deposit may be wholly or partially retained by the landlord on the termination of the lease, if it constitutes a genuine representation of the loss or damage suffered by the landlord as a result of the tenant's action (or lack thereof), but not if the amount held can be considered as a **penalty** against the tenant.

In the US, several jurisdictions have enacted statutes that: restrict the amount of security deposit that can be demanded by a landlord; regulate the landlord's rights to retain security deposits; and, in some jurisdictions, require the landlord to pay interest on the tenant's security deposit at a prescribed statutory rate. See also **collateral, liquidated damages, premium, security**.

security of tenure The right of a tenant to retain possession of a property at the end of a contractual period of tenure, notwithstanding the **expiration** of a lease or the service of a proper **notice to quit** by the landlord. In particular, a statutory right of a tenant to the grant of a new or continuing tenancy, or to protection from **eviction**.

In English law, most effective security now available to residential tenants is the prohibition against a landlord evicting a 'residential occupier' without recourse to a court of law (Protection from Eviction Act 1977, s. 1). Such an action is a criminal offence; as is the use or threat of violence for the purpose of securing entry into any premises where there is known to be someone opposed to the entry (Criminal Law Act 1977, s. 6). In addition, a residential tenant is provided with differing forms of security, or protection from eviction, depending on whether the occupation is classified as an **assured tenancy**; **assured shorthold tenancy**; **protected tenancy**; **restricted contract**; **secure tenancy**; **shorthold tenancy**; or a **long residential tenancy**. The degree of security may be referred to as 'full security' if the tenant has a right to retain possession for life (or even to pass that right to a successor) as with a 'protected tenancy' or an 'assured tenancy' (unless the landlord is able to regain possession in accordance with strict statutory rules); or 'limited security' if the right may be retained for less than the tenant's life time.

In the US, provided the landlord follows the "due process of law", a tenant can be evicted at the end of the lease term or following the service of a legal notice to vacate. However, in many jurisdictions there are strict statutory rules as to the process to be followed, especially for residential properties, before a court will grant the landlord a right to enforce possession of the premises. In the case of a federally-assisted low-rent housing project, the tenant must be advised of the reasons for the eviction and given the opportunity to reply and explain any default that represents the reason for the proposed eviction (Thorpe v. Housing Authority, 393 US 268, 89 S Ct 518, 21 L Ed.2d 518 (1968)). See also **agricultural tenancy, business tenancy**(Eng), **ejectment, extended lease**(Eng), **farm business tenancy**(Eng), **grounds for** possession(Eng), matrimonial home(Eng), protected occupier(Eng), rent control, statutory tenancy(Eng).

see-through building   A vacant building, especially a building that is devoid of tenants.

seed money   Funds provided for the start-up of a new business or venture. See also **front money**.

seigniorage or **seignorage**   1. Lordship or *dominium* over land. See also **seignory**.   2. Traditionally, a duty levied by the crown on the right to mint coins. The profit made by a government on issuing gold or silver coinage. 3.(US)The difference between the rate of interest on a securitized mortgage and the rate of interest payable on the underlying mortgage loans.

seignory or **seigniory**   1. The right or authority of a feudal lord, especially one who held directly from the Crown.   2. The land that comprises a **manor**.

seisin or **seizin**   1. Pronounced 'see-zin'. Derived from the Latin *saisin*, or Old French *seisir*, 'to take **possession**' or 'to seize land'. A word associated with feudal possession, in the sense of an enjoyment of land to the exclusion of others; as contrasted with a right to actual possession or **occupation**. There is said to be 'unity of seisin' or **unity of possession** when an owner of land that is burdened by an easement or restrictive covenant acquires the land benefiting from the easement or restrictive covenant and thereby extinguishes that encumbrance (or vice versa), i.e. when the dominant tenement and servient tenement come into common control.

In the US, a general **warranty deed** is said to contain a '**covenant of seizin**' by which the grantor is deemed to own and to convey the estate or interest that he undertakes to convey or in some jurisdictions that the grantor is transferring an indefeasible fee simple. See also **disseisin**. 2.(Eng)The act by which a new freeholder was invested with a right to land subject to the right of fealty to a lord or sovereign.

seisinee   One who holds a right of **seisin** over land.

seizure   The act of taking **possession**, especially by legal authority, execution or warrant. The act of taking hold or capturing property by force. The forcible taking of possession, in particular by a civil authority or an individual in order to enforce an action or judgement. Taking possession of goods as punishment for a hostile or wrongful act. See also **sequestration**.

self-amortizing mortgage(AmE)   See **amortization loan**.

self-build housing association or **self-build housing society**(Eng)   A form of **housing association** in which the members join together in a cooperative to acquire land and build houses for purchase or occupation by its members. The labour is provided chiefly by the members of the association, rather than any firm of building contractors. "[A] housing association whose object is to provide, for sale to, or occupation by, its members, dwellings built or improved principally with the use of its members' own labour", Housing Act 1985, s. 1(3).

self-contained appraisal report(US)   A written **appraisal report** that identifies and describes the real estate being appraised; states the real property interest being appraised; states the purpose and intended use of the appraisal; defines the value to be estimated; and states the effective date of the appraisal and the date of the report. In addition, the report sets downs the extent of the process of collecting, confirming, and reporting the data used for the preparation of the report, together with the assumptions and limiting conditions, opinions, and conclusions that supports the analysis. The report should describe the information considered, the appraisal procedures followed, and the reasoning that support the analyses, opinions, and conclusions. It should also describe the appraiser's opinion of the **highest and best use**, when such an opinion is necessary and appropriate; explain and support the exclusion of any of the usual valuation approaches; describe any additional information that may be appropriate to show compliance with, or clearly identify and explain permitted departures from, the specific guidelines of the standard form of valuation; and include a signed appraisal certificate in accordance with the required standard (**Uniform Standards of Professional Appraisal Practice**, Standard Rule 2-2(a), which contains a detailed explanation of these requirements). cf. **restricted appraisal report**; **summary appraisal report**. See also **appraisal date**.

self-financing development   A development that is financed before completion by the proceeds from its sale or by the income generated over a short period of time, so that it does not require permanent or long-term financing. For example, a residential project where individual units are sold before or during construction to provide funds for the cost of the building work. Also called a 'self-liquidating investment'.

self-help   Action taken by an individual to redress a wrong committed against that person. In particular, an action taken to prevent a **nuisance**, **trespass** or similar inconvenience, or to recover goods that have been wrongfully taken or withheld, without recourse to a court of law. Although, at common law, certain forms of action, notably **distress**, may be legal if carried out under certain rules, self-help is generally illegal.

In the US, any form of self-help that involves the taking of property may well contravene the Fifth Amendment of the Constitution as being "without due process of law". It may also infringe the Fourth Amendment right to be free of unreasonable searches and seizures; "physical entry of the home is the chief evil against which the wording of the Fourth Amendment is directed", Payton v. New York, 445 US 573, 100 S Ct 1371, 63 L Ed.2d 639, 650. See also **abatement**, **eviction**, **recaption**, **relief**, **squatting**.

self-insurance   Insurance provided, in whole or in part, by the insured himself. The insured may set up a special fund in respect of the possibility of financial loss, or may simply accept the risk entailed. See also **average**, **co-insurance**.

self-liquidating investment   See self-financing development.

self-liquidating loan   A loan that is planned to be paid off from the sale of the property on which it is secured. See also **amortization loan**, self-financing development.

sell   To transfer property to another for **money** or valuable **consideration**. To dispose of property by **sale**. 'Sell' does not normally encompass an **exchange** or **barter**, but if the context so admits, especially when it is intended to be all embracing, it may do so.

In the US, when a broker is instructed to "sell" a property, that normally means no more than to negotiate a sale on satisfactory terms. See also **dispose**.

sell and convey   Words that may be used in a **conveyance** to indicate that the seller is conveying a property for valuable consideration, but otherwise carrying the same meaning as 'convey' alone. cf. **grant bargain sell and convey**.

seller   One who offers goods or property for sale. In particular, a person who transfers property for money. 'Seller' is used especially to refer to someone who trades in goods or personal property. Thus, in English statute law, a seller is defined as a person who "agrees to sell goods", Sale of Goods Act 1979, s. 61(1)); and in the US a 'seller' may be defined as "a person who sells or contracts to sell goods", UCC § 2-103(1)(d). See also **sell**, **vendor**.

seller-financing contract(US)   See installment land contract.

seller-takeback financing(US)   See installment land contract.

seller's lien   See **lien, purchase money mortgage**.

seller's option   See **purchase option**.

semi-annually   Half yearly; twice a year; every six months. An amount payable 'semi-annually' is due twice a year at the same intervals and, therefore, if there is no alternative means of computation, would be due on the same date every six months (months being computed as calendar months). However, a period of **half a year** may be taken as 182 days (fractions of a day being ignored). See also **time**.

semi-detached dwelling or **semi-detached house**   A dwelling that is attached to another building or dwelling by one common wall, but in other respects is designed as an independent dwelling. One of a pair of dwelling-houses, linked together by one common or party wall, with separate entrances and usually separate approaches and driveways. In the US, also called a **double house**. See also **duplex house**, **party wall**.

senior mortgage   A mortgage, especially a **first mortgage**, that has **priority** over one or more other mortgages. cf. **junior mortgage**.

sensitivity analysis   A method of evaluating risk by which an analysis is made of the effect, on a fixed factor, of changes in one of a number of variables, e.g. an analysis of the sensitivity of changes in profit to changes in any one factor that might affect that profit. Thus, each of the variables in a development project (rent, construction costs, financing costs, the leasing period, or sale price) is assumed, in turn, to change by a given percentage and the percentage change in the total profit of the project is then calculated in order to establish which variable has the greatest impact on the overall profitability. Alternatively, as each variable changes so the **internal rate of return** is measured for the project. Sensitivity analysis may also be used to assess changes in each variable where differing fixed amounts are given for each of the other factors; or to show the interdependence of any one variable on any other, given a fixed amount for the remaining functions. For example, to show the percentage profit against changes in the rent levels and the leasing periods, or the effect of different interest rates and selling prices on the internal rate of return for the project. Sensitivity analysis aims to identify the critical variable, but it does not take account of the probability of a change in any one of the variables.

separate estate   An estate or interest in property the ownership of which is enjoyed by a person in his or her own right, without any right or part thereof being shared with another. See also **several ownership**, **separate property**.

separate hereditament   A single unit or **hereditament** that is treated as a separate unit for rating purposes. See also **composite hereditament**.

separate property   1. Property that is held by one person independently of any other, as distinguished from **common property** in which one or more other parties share a joint interest. 2.(US)In a jurisdiction that recognizes **community property**, separate property is that property which is owned by either spouse for their exclusive benefit. Separate property may be property owned before a marriage or property acquired during marriage (whether by inheritance, will or as a gift), or any property acquired from income or proceeds derived from other separate property. Separate property may be divided sometimes into 'dotal property' which is brought to the husband, as a **dowry**, to assist with the expenses of the marriage establishment, and 'extradotal property' or 'paraphernal property' which is no part of the dowry. 'Separate property' can only exist during the existence of the marriage relation. As a rule, any property acquired during the marriage ('marital property') is not separate property, unless one spouse can be shown to have been acquired it independently of the other, or with independent resources.   3. A separately owned area or unit in a **condominium**.

sequestration 1. Derived from the Old French *sequestrer*, or the late Latin *sequestrare*, 'one standing apart'; depositing a thing in dispute. A legal process by which a person is temporarily deprived of possession of his property, or right to property, until he has performed an action required by a court of law, e.g. the repayment of a debt. In the case of real property a court of law or other competent authority, such as a sheriff or commissioner, may sequester the right to rents and profits until a debt is paid. cf. **attachment**, **garnishment**. 2.(Scot)The act of taking control of the property of a bankrupt in order to arrange for its disposal for the benefit of the creditors. 'Sequestration for rent' is the court process by which movable property on the leased premises is taken to satisfy a claim for arrears of rent. See also **hypothec**. 3. In international law, the **seizure** of private property for use by the state.

service The act of bringing something to a person's attention, especially in a fashion prescribed by law, whether actively or constructively. The act of formally delivering a **notice**, **writ**, summons, or any other form of document relating to court proceedings. The service of a notice may be said to have been effected when the contents of the notice are communicated, in the manner prescribed by law, to the person required to receive it. Service may be made by personal delivery, by mail, or by any other acceptable means of communication. Service may be 'personal', i.e. showing the original or leaving a copy with someone; or 'substituted', i.e. brought to a person's knowledge by advertising, sending, leaving, or affixing a notice to a person's place (or last known place) of residence. If notice is to be 'given' or 'received' it may be submitted either in writing or orally, but if it is to be 'left' or 'served' then, as a rule, it should be in writing. In the US, unless there is a statutory requirement or express agreement to the contrary, service must be personal. Where a non-personal or 'substituted' notice is permitted, the notice must be calculated to provide actual notice in order to make certain that it ensures "due process of law", which includes reasonable efforts to seek out and find the whereabouts of the person affected (Mullane v. Central Bank & Trust Co., 339 US 305, 70 S Ct 652, 94 L Ed 865, 873 (1950)). In the absence of any stipulation in the contract to the contrary, proper service implies receipt thereof.

In English law, a notice in respect of real property is normally sufficiently served if it is left at the last-known place of abode or business in the United Kingdom. In most cases, it may be validly served if sent by registered post, provided it is not returned undelivered or there is evidence that the notice was not properly sent (*viz.*: e.g. LPA 1925, s. 196; L&T Act 1927, s. 23(1)). See also **debt service**, **reputed owner**.

service apartment(AmE) or **service flat**(BrE) An apartment or flat let at a rent that includes a payment for services, such as internal cleaning, linen, cooking facilities, etc., but not for **board** (although prepared meals may be provided on request). cf. **boarding house**, **restricted contract**(Eng), **service tenancy**(Eng).

service business or **service trade** A business, or trade, that provides a service to the general public. An establishment that is involved primarily in selling services, especially one located in retail premises rather than in an office, e.g. a bank, real estate agent, insurance broker, travel agent. See also **service industry**.

service charge A fee or charge levied for the cost of processing a transaction, e.g. the cost of arranging to record a transfer of ownership. See also **commitment fee**, **service charge**(BrE), **servicer fee**.

service charge(BrE) A periodic charge or expense incurred in running a building, especially a cost or expense that benefits more than one party (whether a tenant or owner-occupier) in a multi-occupied building. In particular, such costs as are regularly recharged by a landlord to a tenant in accordance with the terms of a lease and which vary from time to time according to the actual expenditure incurred on running the building, but not **rent** payable for the demised premises *per se*. A service charge may include expenditure on repair, maintenance, cleaning, refuse collection, lighting, heating or air-conditioning, security, staff costs, property management expenses or fees, contributions to a sinking fund for replacement of plant and machinery, including those charges incurred in the upkeep of the common areas of a property. An insurance premium is not normally a service charge, unless expressly stated as such, and is normally dealt with in most leases as a separate matter and, if there is no provision in the lease, it cannot automatically be recharged to the tenant.

A tenant of a **flat** or other dwelling (which means a building or part of a building intended to be occupied as a separate dwelling) is entitled to receive a properly audited statement of the service charges to be made by the landlord and the tenant may insist on the landlord only charging for the "reasonable cost" of such services, in respect of works carried out to a "reasonable standard" (L&T Act 1985, ss. 18-30, as amended). See also **advance service charge, apportionment, operating expense**[US].

Freeman, Philip, et al. *Service Charges: Law and Practice.* 3rd ed. Bristol: Jordans, 2002.

The Royal Institution of Chartered Surveyors. *An Elemental Analysis of Service Charges.* London: RICS Book, 1995.

Sheriff, G. *Service Charges for Leasehold, Freehold and Commonhold.* London: Butterworths, 2002.

Young, Michael. *Service Charges in Commercial Property.* London: Estates Gazette, 1992.

service core   A part of an office building, frequently in the center, or on one side of the carcass of the building, in which the principal mechanical services are grouped together, e.g. elevators/lifts, fan rooms, utility ducts, etc. The 'service core' of a building may also include the area containing common toilets or washrooms, janitor closets, stairwells, and lobbies around the elevator core. In the US, also called simply the 'core' or 'core space'. Sometimes called the 'mechanical core'. See also **common areas, loss factor, net internal area**[BrE], **rentable area**[US].

service flat[BrE]   See **service apartment**.

service industry   An organisation or enterprise involved in work, or in carrying on an operation, that is aimed primarily at providing a service to the public. In particular, a business that receives goods for the purposes of repair, treatment or maintenance; or a business that carries on a similar activity by visiting the owners of such goods. For example, motor vehicle repair, laundry, dry cleaning, photographic processing, fuel delivery, window cleaning, repairing and servicing of domestic appliances, hiring of goods. Such an enterprise can operate from a location that acts as a receiving house for the goods to be serviced, repaired, etc., or a location that acts as a base for those providing the service. See also **service business, industrial building**.

service licence   See **service tenancy**.

service life   See **economic life**.

service occupancy   See **service tenancy**.

service property[US]   A property that is used for the operational purpose of a business, trade or occupation and has little use for any other purpose, e.g. a clubhouse, restaurant, school. See also **special use property**.

service station or **service facility**   Premises used predominately for the repair and servicing of motor vehicles, although a part of the premises may be set aside for the sale of vehicles or component parts. The premises may also include facilities for the sale of gasoline, auto parts and may have an area for the sale of other items for travellers. See also **filling station, garage**.

service tenancy[Eng]   **1.** A **tenancy** granted to a person who is an employee of the landlord, usually to enable that person to better perform his or her employment. 'Service tenancy' is commonly used to refer to a form of occupation that is not a tenancy at all, but merely a licence granted to an employee – also called a 'service occupancy'. However, the term 'service tenancy', is ambiguous as it may also be used to describe a tenancy (or licence) under which the landlord provides services to the tenant or occupier, as in the phrase 'service apartments'. See also **occupation lease, protected occupier, restricted contract, tied accommodation**. **2.** A tenancy of a **service apartment**.

service tenant(Eng) A person who is granted a **service tenancy**. See also **grounds for possession**.

service trade See **service business**.

serviced apartment or **serviced flat** See **service apartment**.

serviced office An **office** where the occupier is provided with services over and above those available to normal office tenants, such as the use of telephones, fax, computers, internet services, photocopiers, mail services and secretarial facilities. Such premises are usually let on short-term tenancies or licenses. See also **licence**.

servicer A party that is responsible for collecting mortgage and other related payments and then dispersing the proceeds to the holders of a **mortgage-backed security**. The servicer's responsibilities may include collecting all monthly payments and forwarding the proceeds to the owners of the loans, after making any permitted deductions for fees and expenses; reminding mortgagors when payments are due; collecting overdue payments; administering any escrow balances that have been set up to pay for real estate taxes and insurance premiums; providing tax information to mortgagors, where applicable; and, if necessary, initiating foreclosure proceedings. The servicer may be a bank-related entity, a mortgage banker or a similar institution. The servicer is remunerated by a servicing fee, and may

also benefit from interest earned on the escrow funds, as well as any float retained during the period between the receipt and payment of funds. When there are several servicers of a structured financing the party that is responsible for collecting the income from all the servicers is called a 'master servicer'.

servicer fee A fee paid to the **servicer** of a mortgage-backed or asset-backed security.

services **1.** Facilities provided by a landlord or management company for the benefit of the occupier of a building; such as the maintenance and repair of common areas, central heating or air-conditioning, electricity, cable facilities, water, window cleaning, etc. See also **board, operating expense**(AmE), **service charge**(BrE). **2.** Piped or ducted facilities provided to a building, e.g. water, electricity, gas, telephones, drainage. Services may be classified as 'private' when situated within a site boundary and 'public' when situated off-site. Also called, especially in the US, 'utilities', especially when provided by a public or semi-public undertaking. See also **easement in gross, public utilities, wayleave**.

services easement See **easement in gross, wayleave**.

servicing fee See **servicer fee**.

servicing income The income received by a servicer in the form of fees. In particular, the fees paid to a mortgage bank or similar financial institution for collecting payments due on a loan and paying the proceeds to an investor(s) who has acquired the benefit of the loan. See also **servicer**.

servient estate or **servient tenement** The land or tenement that is burdened with an encumbrance. The parcel of land over which an **easement** runs, or the land that is constrained by a **restrictive covenant** created for the benefit of another parcel of land. In the US, also called the 'servient premises' or sometimes the 'burdened tenement'. cf. **dominant estate**. See also **right of way, tenement**.

servient premises(US)   See **servient estate**.

servient tenement   See **servient estate**.

servitude   **1.** Subjection or subservience of property. Any liberty, privilege, right or advantage annexed to, and adversely affecting, land. In particular, a right *in rem*, annexed to a piece of land, which entitles the owner of that land to do something or prevent the doing of something on another's land. A term that is not strictly one of common law, although it may sometimes be used to refer to any burden over land, including an **easement, profit à prendre** or **restrictive covenant** (*Dalton v Angus* (1881) 6 App Cas 740, 821 (HL)). cf. **positive easement**. See also **encumbrance**.   **2.** A right in Roman, civil or Scots law annexed to a defined piece of land (the *praedium dominans*-dominant land) which entitles the owner of that land to do or prevent someone from doing something on another piece of land (the *praedium serviens*-servient land). The right may be a 'positive servitude', which is the right of the owner of one parcel of land, by reason of his ownership, to use the land of another for a special purpose. It may also be a 'negative servitude' by which the proprietor of the servient land is obliged to suffer something to be done upon his property by another. A right that may be considered analogous to an **easement** in common law (Moyle, *Institutes of Justinian* (5th ed. 1912), p. 214). The primary distinction being that an easement is a right that is enjoyed and a servitude is suffered. A servitude may also be classified as a 'real servitude' or a 'personal servitude'. A real servitudes (also called a 'landed servitude', 'praedial servitude' or sometimes a 'service real') is one that is attached to land (Frost-Johnson Lumber Co. v. Salling's Heirs, 150 La 756, 91 So 207, 245 (1920)). A personal servitude is a right that is personal to the beneficiary and ends on his death, including the right of **usufruct**, use, or habitation. A servitude may arise by grant, or may arise as a natural consequence of the ownership of land ('natural servitude'), as with a right of support for the land or a riparian right.

In the US, 'servitude' is increasingly used as a generic term for rights that are created between land owners, including easements, profits, and covenants that run with the land. "A servitude is a legal device that creates a right or an obligation that runs with the land or an interest in land. ... The servitudes covered by this Restatement are easements, profits and covenants. ...", The American Law Institute, *Restatement Third, Property (Servitudes)*, § 1.1 (2000). The term does not normally apply to covenants in leases, mortgages, other security devices, and profits from the removal of timber, oil, gas and minerals. See also **real covenant**(US).

servitude of drip(US)   See **easement of drip**.

servitude of view(Civ)   See **right to view**.

set   An old word for 'let' or **lease**.

set aside   Land that is reserved for a particular purpose. Agricultural land that is used for a different purpose to that of the primary use of the surrounding land. Agricultural land that is not used for crop production, especially land that is left fallow or only used for grazing usually to conform to a subsidy requirement.

set-aside letter   A letter by which a lender agrees to provide funds for payment to a party other than the borrower, as with a provision that the lender will set aside funds to pay a contractor who is supplying work for the completion of secured property.

setback or **set-back**   **1.** A limitation on how close to a property line (or some other designated line) an owner can build. The minimum horizontal distance between the lot or **boundary line** of a property and a **building line** that has been prescribed for that property space A setback is usually required by planning, zoning or highway regulations, i.e. an area along or around a property that must be left free of all buildings. A requirement or **ordinance** to 'set-back' buildings may be prescribed to keep new buildings a set distance from a highway in order to maintain a uniform frontage; or to keep a standard distance between the boundary of a plot of land and any building work that may be erected on that land, essentially to maintain adequate light and air around the building. In some cases, a set-back may be established as a precursor to a street widening and, therefore, constitute a taking of land for which **just compensation** is payable. This area may also be called a 'yard' when it is an area that is to be maintained as open space (or a 'side yard' or 'front yard' depending on where it is located). **2.** The placing of an upper storey of a building further back, in the horizontal plan, from the floor below. Zoning or planning regulations commonly require the upper stories of a high-rise building to be set back a distance that is equal to, or exceeds, the height between stories in order to improve the appearance of the building from ground level and to provide adequate light to the lower levels of adjoining buildings.

set-back line   See **building line**.

setback ordinance[US]   See **setback**.

set-off or **setoff**   **1.** An act by which one party to a contract sets all or part of the cost of performing his obligations under the contract against the cost of an obligation or duty owed to him by the other party to the contract, either as a result of the same or a closely related contract. In particular, the discharge or reduction (in whole or in part) of a monetary sum owed to a creditor by an amount due to the debtor. In effect, the one party acknowledges the justice of the demands of the other party, but sets up a demand of his own to counterbalance or discharge the other's demand, in whole or in part. Set-off, although distinguishable in practice from a reduction in the consideration payable under a contract due to a failure of **performance**, may be considered akin

to the latter; the financial effect being similar. Set-off may be applied only as a result of a direct relationship between two parties and not by the involvement of a third party who happens to have a debt with both parties.

In common law, as a rule, a tenant may not refuse to pay rent due on the premise that he is withholding payment in order to set-off an obligation that the landlord has not met, such as the landlord's failure to carry out repairs or pay property taxes. However, a tenant may have a right of set-off if he has given prior and proper notice and then discharged a repairing obligation that it is reasonable to consider is the landlord's obligation – especially when this results from a defect in a new building, or an obligation that the landlord cannot deny, in which case the tenant has not received that which he has contracted for (*Taylor v Beal* (1591) Cro Eliz 222, 78 Eng Rep 478; *British Anzani (Felixstowe) Ltd v International Marine Management (UK) Ltd* [1980] QB 137, [1979] 2 All ER 1063, 1070; *Muscat v Smith* [2003] 1 WLR 2853, 40 EG 148 (CA)). However, such a right may be excluded (and often is) under an express provision of the lease.

In the US, some jurisdictions accept the common law principle that the tenant's obligation to pay rent is independent of the landlord's obligation to repair. However, many jurisdictions accept, or have enacted statutes to the effect that, for residential property, the landlord has a **warranty of habitability** in respect of the leased premises. Accordingly, a tenant may make essential repairs and deduct the cost against rent that has become due; or, in some cases, withhold rent in the event of the landlord's failure to fulfil this obligation (although such rent may have to be paid into court or a separate escrow account). In addition, in an action by the landlord for unpaid rent, in some jurisdictions a tenant may be able to set-off damages for a breach by the landlord of his obligations under the lease; including an obligation to repair or improve the leased premises. See also **compensation for improvements**. **2.**[Eng]A reduction in the compensation payable upon the compulsory purchase of land as a result of an increase in the value of adjoining land retained in the same ownership. Most statutes that provide for the payment of compensation for the compulsory purchase of land, or the payment of compensation for injurious affection, provide that this compensation is to be reduced by any increase in the value the land attributable to the activities of the acquiring authority. cf. **recoupment**. **3.** A reduction of the amount of **just compensation** payable on the expropriation of land as a result of an increase in the value of adjoining land retained in the same ownership (Bauman v. Ross, 167 US 548, 17 S Ct 966, 42 L Ed 270 (1897)). In federal takings, the set off is applied against the combined value of the land acquired and the land retained. In some states any set off is applied only against the value of the land retained. See also **benefits, betterment, compulsory purchase compensation**.

Jones, Neil F. (solicitors). *Set-Off in the Construction Industry*. 2nd ed. Oxford: Blackwell Science, 1999.

Derham, S. Rory. *Set-off*. 2nd ed. Oxford: Clarendon Press, 1996.

settled estate(Eng)   An estate in land that passes in accordance with the provisions of a **settlement**. See also **settled land**.

settled land   **1.**(Eng)Land conveyed to several persons in succession. Land, or any estate or interest in land, that is the subject of a **settlement** (SLA 1925, s. 2). Settled land may be held: (a) in trust for any person by way of **succession**; (b) as an **entailed estate**; (c) as a **determinable interest**; (d) as a **conditional interest**; (e) on behalf of a minor until he attains majority; or (f) as part of a marriage or family settlement. Each party entitled to land under the settlement may use the land only on condition that he does not limit the other party's future rights of enjoyment. As a rule, a purchaser of a **legal estate** in settled land does not need to concern himself with the terms of the settlement, provided he deals with the **tenant for life** (or the **statutory owner**), acts in **good faith**, and the document that transferred the land to tenant for life (or the statutory owner) – the "principal vesting instrument" – is seen to contain the requisite statutory information (SLA 1925, s. 110). See also **rentcharge, settled estate, strict settlement, trust instrument, vesting document, waste**.   **2.** Land or a colony that has been acquired by settlement and not by conquest or cession (*Mabo v Queensland (No 2)* (1992) 175 CLR 1, 107 ALR 1). In Australia, used especially to refer to land granted by the Crown to a settlor or a person who uses the land for agricultural purposes. See also **Crown land, native title**.

settlement   **1.** The act or process of resolving a dispute between parties, especially a civil dispute, without recourse to a determination by a court of law. An agreement by which parties to a dispute ascertain what is due from one to the other.   **2.** The **determination** of a contract by agreement. In particular, termination of an agreement by the payment of a debt or account in full. The fulfilment of an obligation to another by means of monetary recompense. See also **accord and satisfaction, satisfaction**.   **3.** The payment of the balance due on the transfer of real property. See also **closing, completion statement**(Eng), **settlement statement**(US).   **4.** A formal **grant** or **conveyance** of property, or something that is granted or bestowed on another.   **5.** A **disposition** of real or personal property, made by agreement, deed, will or other instrument, or any number of instruments (or, in rare cases, by statute), with the intention that the property is to be enjoyed by a number of persons or classes of persons in succession. As a rule, the creator of the settlement, the 'settlor', places the property in trust and designates the beneficiaries and the terms on which they may take the property. In English law, until 1996, there were two ways of tying up property, i.e. of creating a settlement: (i) the **strict settlement** and (ii) the **trust for sale**. A strict settlement could arise where the intention was that the land itself should pass to the successors, i.e. to create an entailed estate, a base fee or determinable fee, or a similar form of interest that is limited to a form of succession, especially when it was intended that no one person can deprive the others of their future rights of enjoyment as stated in the instrument (SLA 1925, ss. 1, 117(xxiv)). A trust for sale arose if the land was intended to pass only as a form of investment and could just as well be converted into money, immediately or at a future date. Any instrument by which property was made to pass to persons consecutively may be called a 'settlement', but when the word 'settlement' is used alone it is taken, by common usage, to mean a 'strict settlement'. In the SLA, s. 1, the predominate feature of a strict settlement was that land was limited in trust for persons "by way of succession". Since 1996, any settlement of land to be held in trust must be created as a **trust of land**. See also **derivative settlement, doctrine of estates, referential settlement, settled land, trust.** 6.(US)The occupation of public lands by placing improvements or establishing a residence thereon, especially with the intent, in good faith, of obtaining title thereto from the government under the pre-emption law of the United States. The actions on the land must be more than blazing a trail around a parcel of land, placing notices and erecting posts at the four corners (Great Northern Rly. Co. v. Reed, 270 US 539, 46 S Ct 380, 70 L Ed 721 (1926)).

settlement costs(AmE)   See **closing costs**.

settlement purchase(Aus)   A grant of **Crown land** on a lease to a settlor or a person who will improve the land, together with a right to purchase the freehold. The price is usually based on the value of the unimproved land and may be payable by instalments or at the time the land is acquired. See also **conditional purchase tenure, Crown lease**.

settlement statement or **settlement sheet**(US)   A detailed statement of all the costs and expenses to be incurred at a real estate closing (whether a sale, lease, mortgage or any other transaction), showing the net amount payable by the purchaser, lessee or borrower. A settlement statement is intended to set out full details of the costs to be paid at closing, including all fees and expenses. The statement sets out details of all **closing costs**, including any amounts previously paid as earnest money. The statement may be prepared, usually on a standard pro-forma, by the seller's attorney (or sometimes by his broker) or by the title insurance company.

In the case of a mortgage loan secured on a residential property that comprises between one and four units, made by any lender whose deposits are insured, or regulated, by any agency of the federal government, the settlement statement is required to be set out in a uniform manner (usually by the use of the uniform settlement statement prepared by the Department of Housing and Urban Development (HUD-1 form)) to provide the home buyer advance notice and a good faith estimate of all closing costs (Real Estate Settlement Procedure Act [RESPA] of 1974 (RESPA), 12 USC § 2601 et seq.). The intention of RESPA is to protect home buyers from surprises at closing and to regulate the amount of any escrow payment required to cover advance payments of real estate taxes and insurance premiums; although the actually amounts payable may varying when the final costs are ascertained. Also called a 'closing statement' or sometimes an 'adjustment sheet'; or, when the closing is made through an escrow account, an 'escrow statement'. See also **completion statement**(BrE).

settler   1.(US)One who has made a **settlement** on **public lands**. A **homesteader**.   2.(Aus)A person who settles on land granted or leased from the Crown. See also **Crown land**.   3. See **squatting**.

settlor   1. One who creates a **settlement**, either by will or by a disposition of property, during his or her lifetime. One who settles property or an income on another called a **beneficiary**. See also **testator**.   2. One who creates a **trust**. A person who has transferred property to another to hold as trustee for the benefit of a third party. One who has created a **voluntary trust**. See also **trustor**.

severability clause(US)   A provision in a

contract that if one part of the contract is deemed to be unenforceable the rest of the contract will still remain binding on the parties. Also called a 'saving clause'.

severable contract   A **contract** that may be divided into separate or apportionable obligations that can be separately enforced without destroying the unity of the entire contract. A contract that has two or more parts, or promises, and is intended to permit those parts, or promises, to be treated independently. Under a severable contract, a breach of one part, or one condition, of the contract does not create a breach of the entire contract. On the other hand, a failure to pay for part of the work or services provided under a severable contract may permit the suspension of the obligation to complete any further work or supply any further services, at least until payment is made in full or in accordance with the terms of the contract. Also called a 'divisible contract'. cf. **entire contract**.

several   Relating to one individual; having a separate and distinct existence. 'Several' is opposed usually to 'joint' or '**common**'. See also **joint and several liability, several estate**.

several estate or **several interest**   An estate or interest in land owned separately, i.e. entirely by one party without any other party joined therein. Ownership held by a person as a sole right. A several interest may be an absolute right or a successive right to land. It may be distinguished from a **concurrent estate**; the ownership of **common land**; and any form of **co-ownership**, where an interest in land is shared with another at one and the same time. Also called an 'estate in severalty', a 'several tenancy', a 'tenancy in severalty', an 'entire tenancy', or 'individual ownership' or 'sole ownership' (the word tenancy is used in this context to indicate a right of '**tenure**' or ownership and not a right to hold land for a limited duration from a landlord). See also **estate in severalty**.

several pasture   See **sole common of pasture**.

several tenancy   See **several estate**.

severalty   See also **estate in severalty, several estate**.

severance   1. Division into parts. For example, the division of an area of land held in one ownership into areas of separate ownership especially when the original owner retains part of the land. See also **partition, severance of a reversion**.   2. The conversion of a **joint tenancy** into a **tenancy in common**, or the destruction of such an estate in land. A joint tenancy may be converted into a tenancy in common by destroying one of the four unities that is essential to the maintenance of such an estate or it may be destroyed altogether and converted into separate estate in one or more persons. A joint tenancy may be severed or destroyed "by destroying any of its constituent unities", 2 *Bl Comm* 185. Severance of an existing joint tenancy may arise from any act that is inconsistent with the continued existence of such form of ownership, i.e. destruction of one or more of the four unities (time, title, interest, and possession) that are essential to the maintenance of a joint tenancy. In particular: (i) by one of the joint tenants transferring his interest during his lifetime to another party (who, because he did not acquire his interest at the same time, or as part of the same title deeds, becomes a tenant in common); (ii) by one of the parties acquiring a greater interest, or selling a lesser interest, than the others; (iii) by mutual agreement between the joint tenants; or (iv) when it is clear to the other tenant(s) that, from the nature of the dealings of one of the joint tenants, the intention is to destroy the essential 'unity' of a joint tenancy, e.g. bankruptcy of one of the parties or when one party is negotiating to rearrange the interests without any intention to involve the other party, or by homicide of one party by another. See also **partition**.   3. The acquisition of part of an area of land in order to separate it from other land, especially when the acquisition is made by an authority possessing condemnation or compulsory purchase powers. See also **compensation for**

severance[Eng], **injurious affection**, **severance damages**[US]. **4.** "The rejection from a contract of objectionable promises or the objectionable elements of a particular promise, and the retention of those promises or those parts of a particular promise that are valid", M. P. Furmston, *Cheshire, Fifoot & Furmston's Law of Contract.* 14th ed. London: Butterworths, 2001, p. 470. Severance of a contract may arise when the contract is **void** because it is contrary to statute law, but the court considers that a part of the contract nonetheless should be performed as envisaged by the parties. **5.** The act of removing something attached to land. In particular, the removal of a **fixture** from land. **6.** The conveyance of land whereby the mineral rights and the use of the land are separated, either the mineral rights are reserved or excepted from the grant, or the mineral rights are granted but the surface use is reserved, or only the surface right is granted but the mineral rights are retained. See also **mining lease**, **oil and gas lease**.

severance compensation See **compensation for severance**[Eng], **severance damages**[US].

severance damages[US] Compensation paid for the loss or reduction in the value of a parcel of land resulting from the **partial taking** of land from an owner by the exercise of the power of **eminent domain**. In the event of a partial taking of land, compensation is payable not only for the value of the land taken, but also for the loss in value of the land retained by the same owner (United States v. Grizzard, 219 US 180, 55 L Ed 165 (1911)). Severance damages may arise from the taking and the resultant severance, or from the works carried out on the land taken by the expropriating authority. On the other hand, no increase in value of the retained land can be brought to account as a result of the project to be undertaken by the condemning authority on the severed land (United States v. Miller, 317 US 369, 376-377, 63 S Ct 281, 87 L Ed 336, 345, 147 ALR 55 (1942)). "It should be noted that the term 'severance damages' is a misnomer. While many state constitutions differ by guaranteeing compensation when property is 'damaged' as well as when it is 'taken', the pertinent Federal Constitution provision is '… nor shall private property be taken for public use, without **just compensation**'. Under the Federal rule, compensation is paid for 'takings' not damages'. Thus in some of the states the compensation may include items the federal rules exclude as being **consequential damages**", Interagency Land Acquisition Conference, *Uniform Appraisal Standards for Federal Land Acquisitions, 2002 edition,* p. 28.

In federal land acquisitions, wherever possible the compensation should be assessed as one amount, based on the **before-and-after method** of appraisal. "In partial taking cases, the proper measure of compensation is the difference between the fair and reasonable market value of the entire ownership immediately before the taking and the fair and reasonable market value of what is left immediately after the taking", United States v. 9.20 Acres of Land, More or Less, 638 F.2d 1123, 1127 (8th Cir. 1981). However, this may not always be practical (as with a minor easement acquisition). Also, in state cases, where appropriate, the 'damages' may be assessed by determining the value of the land taken and then adding the loss resulting from any reduction in value of the land retained. When applying the latter method allowance must be made for any benefit accruing to the retained land as a result of the use of the acquired land, as well as taking into account any reasonable action that the landowner can take to 'cure' the damage occasioned. See also **benefits**.

severance of a reversion A transfer of part of a **reversionary interest** to another party, as when a landlord sells part of the land that is the subject of a lease to another. When such a severance has taken place every condition of the tenancy is apportioned and becomes annexed to the severed part (including the right to determine the lease by notice to quit or otherwise), so that every landlord may enforce those conditions that relate to the severed part (LPA 1925, s. 140).

However, the tenancy continues as one agreement, i.e. there are not a number of separate tenancies brought into existence.

severance tax(US)   A tax charged on the value of a natural resource levied at the time it is extracted or severed from the land, e.g. on forest products, coal, oil or minerals.

sewer   An artificial conduit, usually underground, constructed for the discharge of rain or storm water, waste water, waste matter, effluent or similar noxious matter. It may take waste or effluent from houses, or other buildings, to a place of discharge, usually to a treatment plant. A sewer may also be a conduit for waste water from land or streets, generally on a large scale, to a river or to the sea.

In English statue law, a sewer is defined as a conduit that is intended to serve more than one building, or yards appurtenant to buildings, as distinct from a **drain** which runs from a single building (Public Health Act 1936, s. 343(1)) and a 'public sewer' which is a sewer constructed or adopted by a local authority for the drainage of a number of properties (PHA 1936, s. 20).
Wilkinson, H. W. *Pipes, Mains, Cables and Sewers*. 6th ed. London: Pearson, 1995.

shadow line   The line that joins the highest point of a building and the furthest point of the shadow caste by that building. This line may be used to impose a limit on the height of new construction.

sham bidder(US)   See **puffer**.

share   **1.** A partial use or enjoyment of something in conjunction with another. Any one of the parts into which a property, or invested capital, is divided. **2.** A joint right to a part of the equity **capital** of a corporation. See also **stock**.   **3.** The monetary interest of a shareholder in a limited company or partner in a partnership.   **4.** The ownership units into which a company is divided.   **5.** Those parts of a person's estate given to a particular beneficiary.

The parts of an estate to which one or more beneficiaries are entitled. See also **portion**.

share capital   The amount of shares issued, or authorised to be issued, by a company. See also **capital, equity capital, stock**.

share lease(US)   **1.** A lease that provides for the rent to be payable in the form of a share of the crops to be derived from the land that is the subject of the lease. See also **sharecropping lease**.   **2.** See **percentage lease**.

share rent   A rent calculated to provide the landlord with a share of the benefit received by the tenant from his use of the leased land. In particular, rent payable under a **sharecropping lease**. See also **metayage system, percentage rent, royalty, slice**.

share-tenant   See **sharecropping lease**.

sharecropping lease   A form of agricultural tenancy, derived from the European **metayage system**, found especially in Middle Western and Southern states, by which the landowner leases land, machinery, tools, seeds and stock and the tenant ('sharecropper', 'share-tenant' or 'cropper') undertakes to provide a percentage of the crop, or proceeds from the sale of livestock, as a form of rent (a 'crop rent'). The arrangement may take the form of a **lease**, but in many cases is no more than a **licence** whereby the cropper is permitted to cultivate the land and raise crops and to receive a share of the crops that he produces in exchange for his labour. Whether the sharecropper is a tenant, or is merely a 'cropper' who has no interest or estate in the land, depends on the intent of the parties and the words of the agreement. However, unless there is a clear agreement to the contrary, the cultivator of the land is more likely to have no more than a right to the land (as an employee or licensee), which terminates when the annual crop is collected. In some states, the rights of a sharecropper are governed by statute and in at least one state (Kansas), if each of the parties provides half the seeds and shares half the crops, the arrangement is considered to be equivalent to that of landlord and tenant. In Australia, such an arrangement may also be called a 'sharefarming agreement'.

sharefarming agreement(Aus)   See **sharecropping lease**.

shared-appreciation mortgage (SAM)(US) See **equity-participation mortgage**.

shared-equity mortgage (SEM)(US) A form of mortgage in which there are two or more parties liable for the mortgage debt, with one party having the right to use and occupy the mortgaged property and the other is investor who agrees to assist with the mortgage payments, normally as a tenant in common and co-mortgagor. In return for the financial assistance, the latter receives a share in the equity value of the mortgaged property, usually in direct proportion to his percentage contribution to the mortgage payments.

shared-ownership lease(Eng)   An arrangement by which two parties acquire an interest in a property, as joint owners or 'tenants-in-common', and one of the parties simultaneously grants a lease of his interest to the other. In addition, the party who is granted the lease is generally granted an option to acquire the other party's interest at a future date, usually at market value. Typically, a shared-ownership lease is entered into between an investor or developer and a homeowner in order to reduce the homeowner's initial capital outlay. During the term of the lease the tenant pays only for his share in the ownership of the property, but he is able to occupy the entire property. At a later stage, the homeowner generally has the opportunity to acquire the entire property. Alternatively, the tenant may have options to acquire additional shares in the property, usually in tranches, until he has acquired a 100% interest. This latter process is called **staircasing**. See also **equity-participation mortgage**.
Allen, Patrick. *Shared Ownership - a stepping stone to home ownership*. London: Her Majesty's Stationery Office, 1982.

shell lease   A lease that is granted of a property in an unfinished or 'shell' condition. A lease of a **shell property**. cf. **turnkey lease**.

shell property   An unfinished or 'shell' unit in a new development. The vendor or landlord of the shell unit provides the main structure, with utilities supplied to a base point and the purchaser or tenant is responsible for all other fit-out work, including the installation of partitioning, flooring, ceiling work, plumbing, heating, internal lighting and electrical outlets, as well as bathroom and kitchen fitting if required. See also **fixture**.

Shelley's Case(Eng)   See **heir**.

shelter   See **tax shelter**.

sheriff's deed(US)   A deed given to the purchaser after a property has been sold by a **judicial sale**, or sale pursuant to a mortgage foreclosure sale, which has been conducted by the sheriff under powers conferred on him by a court order. Such a deed only warrants title as was held by the debtor.

sheriff's sale(US)   See **judicial sale**.

shifting clause(Eng)   A clause in a deed of **settlement** which provides that, in certain stipulated circumstances, the settled property will devolve in a different way to that primarily prescribed; for example, to "A for life unless B becomes a Doctor of Medicine". See also **conditional interest**, **defeasance**.

shifting interest   See **shifting use**.

shifting use   An interest in land that is transferred from one **beneficiary** of a settlement to another if a stipulated event arises, as when the interest is given to a wife and her child for life before the child is born, or to a widow unless she remarries. The interest is referred to as a 'shifting use' because the beneficial right to enjoy land was at one time referred to as a **use** (being an equitable right recognised only by the English Courts of Chancery) and, upon the occurrence of the event stipulated for at the time the use was granted, the 'use' is cut short or 'shifts' to the new beneficiary. A similar interest, called a 'springing use', arises when there is no preceding limitation in the instrument that granted the use, but the use arises in the future in order to extinguish the grantor's estate. For example, when a fee was granted to B for the 'use' of X (an infant) when she attains 21 (or is called to the Bar), then X's estate 'springs up' or takes effect at the stipulated future time or event. If X dies before attaining 21, the estate is vested absolutely in B. Also called an 'executory use', or a 'secondary use' (2 *Bl Comm* 335). In the US, in some statutes, a 'shifting use', 'springing use' and an **executory devise** may all be classified simply as 'future estates'; and in most jurisdictions the terms shifting and springing use are virtually obsolete. The American Law of Real Property, § 4.53 takes the view that such interests, whether created by will or *inter vivos*, are now called **executory interests**. See also **conditional limitation**(US), **executory interest, future interest**.

shop   Derived from the Middle English *shoppe* or *sceoppa* 'booth'; the Old French *eschoppe* 'lean-to booth'; or the Old High German *scopf* 'porch or vestibule'. A place where goods are displayed, usually in small quantities, for sale to the ultimate consumers. A place, comprising a building or part of a building, normally but not necessarily of a permanent character, where the public are invited and resort for the purpose of trade or business of a **retail** nature. A center of activity for the reception, storage and distribution of goods, merchandise or even ideas. (The term 'retail' is derived from the French *retainer*, 'to cut off'; divide into small pieces, hence a shop is a place where goods are sold predominately in small quantities.) The word 'shop' may be used also for a commercial establishment where goods are made, repaired and stored, and in that sense is synonymous with **store** and **workshop**. "In England the word 'shop' is understood to be a structure or room in which goods are kept and sold at retail. ... In this country

[America], however, such a building is usually called a 'store'. And universally so in the Western and Pacific coast states, where shop is understood to be a building in which an artisan carries on business, or laborers, workmen, or mechanics, by use of tools or machinery, manufacture, alter, or repair articles of trade. ... In conversation we speak of a store as a place where goods are exposed for sale, thus giving it the same meaning as 'shop'. Still we recognize a difference between the meaning of these two words. Thus, we do not call the place where any mechanic art is carried on a store, but we give it the name shop, as a tailor's shop, a blacksmith's shop, a shoemaker's shop", State v. Hanlon, 32 Or 95, 48 P 353, 354 (1897).

In English planning law, the term 'shop' is considered to cover premises where any business in the nature of retail, or what is related or appropriate thereto, is carried on. However, under the **Use Classes Order**, a 'shop' is deemed to be confined to uses within a building and the term is not applicable to a similar use of open land (*Crawley v Secretary of State for the Environment* [1990] JPL 742). See also **market, market overt, office, shopping center**.

shopping center(AmE) or **shopping centre**(BrE)   "[A] concentration of **retail** stores and service establishments in a suburban area usually with generous parking spaces and usu. planned to serve a community or neighborhood", *Webster's Third New International Dictionary*®, *Unabridged*, ©1993. A group of retail stores built to an integrated design, together with associated facilities such as banks, restaurants, filling stations, etc., as well as ample off-street parking and delivery facilities. A shopping center is constructed usually to a uniform architectural or building plan and is intended to serve a particular community, neighborhood, district or region. In many cases, such a center is maintained under the control of a single owner or manager. "A group of retail and other commercial establishments that is planned, developed, owned, and managed as a single property. On-site parking is provided. The center's size and orientation are generally determined by the market characteristics of the trade area served by the center. The two main configurations of shopping centers are malls and open-air strip centers", International Council of Shopping Centers, *Research Quarterly*, 'Shopping Center Definitions'.

Shopping centers may broadly be classified as:

'Local' centers—comprising a small group or parade of stores, predominately independently run, primarily serving a local population (generally under 2,000 people), with a **gross leasable area** (GLA) of under 25,000 square feet (or under 2,500 square meters).

'Neighborhood' or 'convenience' centers—comprising a supermarket, a small variety of general stores, and a number (about 10 to 20) of specialist stores principally selling convenience goods and personal services, serving a neighborhood of around 10,000 people situated within a radius of under five miles. These centers have a gross leasable area from around 25,000 to 50,000 square feet (2,500 to 5,000 square meters). Neighborhood centers are "[d]esigned to provide convenience shopping for the day-to-day needs of the immediate neighborhood, these centers are usually anchored by a supermarket supported by stores offering drugs, sundries, snacks, and personal services. The majority of neighborhood centers range from 30,000 to 100,000 square feet of GLA and are sited on 3 to 10 acres", Robert J. Flynn (editor). *Carpenter's Shopping Center Management: Principles and Practices*. New York: International Council of Shopping Centers, 1984.

'District', 'community', 'secondary' or 'sub-regional' centers—similar to a neighborhood center, but larger and containing additional facilities such as a junior department store, a large supermarket or a large variety store; around 25 to 75 retail stores; and serving a larger trade area – around 50,000 to 200,000 people. These centers are intended to serve a district, part of a major region, or a small town and have a gross leasable area of around 100,000 to 250,000 square feet (10,000 to 25,000 square meters).

'Regional' centers—generally characterized by providing 'one-stop' shopping, i.e. providing a similar range of goods to that found in a **central business district**, incorporating an enclosed mall, two or more major department stores, a complete range of small stores (generally 100 or more), as well as ancillary facilities, such as banks, movie theatres, restaurants, etc. A center that is intended to serve a population of over 250,000 people and ranging in size from a gross leasable area of 250,000 to well over one million square feet (25,000 to over 100,000 square meters). A center with around one million square feet of gross leasable area, or larger, and at least three anchor stores is also referred to as a 'super-regional shopping center'. A regional center that is at the lower end of the size range, especially where there are other larger centers in the same trade or catchment area, may be called a 'sub-regional center'.

A shopping center may also be a number of retail units in the central area of a town or city; for example, one developed at random over a period of time – the traditional 'high street' or 'main street' center; or a center that has the same facilities as a regional center and is part of the central business district. In the lay sense, a shopping center is any group of shops that provide most forms of convenience shopping and a degree of comparison shopping; in the professional sense it is normally a planned development. See also **anchor tenant, catchment area, continuous operation clause, non-competition clause, shop, specialty shopping center, store, strip center, tenant mix**.

Alexander, Alan A., and Richard F. Muhlebach. *Shopping Center Management*. Chicago: Institute of Real Estate Management, 1992.

Beddington, Nadine. *Shopping Centres: Retail Development, Design and Management*. 2nd rev. ed. London: Butterworth Architecture, 1991.

Beyard, Michael D., and W. Paul O'Mara. *Shopping Center Development Handbook*. 3rd ed. Washington, DC: Urban Land Institute, 1999.

Robert J. Flynn (editor). *Carpenter's Shopping Center Management: Principles and Practices*. New York: International Council of Shopping Centers, 1984.

Urban Land Institute. *Dollars and Cents of Shopping Centers*. Washington, DC: Urban Land Institute, 2004.

Vernor, J. D., and J. Rabianski. *Shopping Center Appraisal and Analysis*. Chicago: Appraisal Institute, 1993.

White, John Robert, and Kevin D. Gray (editors) in assoc. with the Urban Land Institute. *Shopping Centers and Other Retail Properties: their investment, development, financing and management*. New York: Wiley, 1996.

William Reed Publishing. *Shopping Centre and Retail Directory 2004*. Crawley, Sussex: William Reed Publishing Ltd., 2004.

shopping mall   See **shopping center, mall**.

shore   Land bordering a large body of tidal water, especially bordering the ocean, a sea or a lake, that is alternately wet and dry between the mean high and low water marks. The seashore is such land that is ordinarily washed by the sea, i.e. up to the ordinary high tide. Thus, for land that is bounded by the sea, the 'shoreline' is the boundary line between private and public property.

In English law, the 'shore' *prima facie* belongs to the Crown, unless custom indicates that the public have a right thereover; and in the US after the American Revolution, the title to the 'shore' below high water mark became "vested in the individual states as sovereigns, subject only to the restricted constitutional powers of control of the Federal Government", 78 Am.Jur.2d., Waters, p. 827. In some states, such land has been ceded to private ownership and in others it is retained by the state for public enjoyment. In the case of a large body of inland water, such as a lake or river, the 'shore' is the land that is contiguous with such water and is washed by natural movements of the water, but unlike the land bordering the sea, its limit is incapable of exact definition and the use of a more definable limit, such as the top of a bank, is more appropriate.

In the US, in those states that followed the common law, the shoreline is set by the mean high water mark; the 'shore' being the land between the ordinary high and low water mark (Borax Consolidated v. Los Angeles, 296 US 10, 56 S Ct 23, 80 L Ed 9 (1935)). In other states that have adopted the civil law view, it is taken as the highest point washed by the sea in winter (*Just. Inst.* II, 1, 3; Humble Oil & Refining Co. v. Sun Oil Co., 190 F.2d 191, 194 (5th Cir. Tex 1951)). In some contexts, the term 'shore' may be used synonymously with **beach**. See also **accretion, foreshore**.

short-form document(US)   A written document that sets out the basic terms and conditions of an agreement and refers to a **form document**, or related documents, for the other terms and conditions. A short-form document is intended primarily as a summary of the principal document and may be used so that only the parties to the agreement are aware of all the terms. See also **open contract**.

short-term finance or **short-term loan** A loan that may be recalled within a period of one year or less. cf. **long-term finance**. See also **current liability, interim finance, rollover loan**.

short-term lease   A term that depends on the country of application. A lease for one year or less is clearly a short-term lease. In the United Kingdom, and other countries where commercial leases are generally granted for 15-25 years, a lease for five years is a short-term lease. In the US, and especially in continental Europe, where commercial leases are generally granted for 3, 5 or 10 years, a short-term lease is one granted for less than 5 years. In particular, a short-term lease, or 'short-term tenancy, is one granted for a year or less. cf. **long-term lease**. See also **periodic tenancy, writing**.

shorthold tenancy(Eng)   See **assured shorthold tenancy, protected shorthold tenancy**.

show house(BrE)   A house presented for viewing and inspection, especially a dwelling-house that has been completed, is ready for occupation and made available to be inspected by persons who may be interested in acquiring a property of similar design and build. A house that prospective purchasers can visit in order to view a property that is representative of what they may buy. Generally, a new house that is a model for another that is to be built to a similar design and specification, but on a different site. See also **model home**(AmE).

shut-in royalty(US)   See **delay rental**.

sic utere tuo ut alienum non lædas(Lat) 'So use your property as not to interfere with that of others'. A desirable but misleading maxim, as a landowner may be permitted to use his land and cause interference with another. What is essential is that he does not cause damage that will be restrained or penalised by the law; "a useful test is perhaps what is reasonable according to the ordinary usages of mankind living in society, or more correctly in a particular society", *Sedleigh-Denfield v O'Callaghan* [1940] AC 880, 903 (HL). See **encroachment**, **nuisance**, **strict liability**.

sick-building syndrome (SBS)   A health risk that arises from poor indoor air quality. Generally, SBS arises in an air-conditioned office building where the occupiers suffer from illness (fatigue, ear nose and throat irritations and headaches). The problem normally arises because of an inadequate rate of air circulation, poor filtration and lack of humidification. In particular, a failure to clean the air ducts and regularly service the equipment.

side-by-side lease   See **side-by-side participation**.

side-by-side participation A form of **equity participation** whereby the partners in an investment project, or joint venture, share in the total cash flow received from that investment in an agreed proportion. For example, a property that is leased to a tenant on a long-lease and the tenant, in turn, sub-lets to other tenants upon terms which provide that the head landlord will receive a proportionate share of the rents payable by the subtenants. This arrangement may also be referred to as a 'side-by-side', 'income-sharing', 'vertical', or 'back-to-back' lease. Also called 'vertical-slice participation', or in the US, 'straight-up participation'. cf. **top-slice participation**. See also **lease-and-leaseback financing**.

side lines(US)   1. The lines of a highway that are laid out on either side and at equal distance from the center line, and define the territory covered by the highway. See also **building line**. 2. Lines defined by municipal ordinance, or by restrictive covenants, to mark the limit of construction within the boundaries of a building lot. cf. **lot line**.   3. The limits of a mining claim each side of the middle of the vein as measured at the surface.

sidewalk(US)   A portion of a highway that has been set aside for pedestrians. A walkway generally running alongside a street or road and used by pedestrians to the exclusion of vehicles. See also **footpath**, **pavement**.

sight triangle(US)   See **visibility clearance**.

sign   See **advertisement**, **billboard**.

signature   A person's name or mark written with his own hand as evidence that he intends to be bound by or accepts that which goes before. A signature is the accustomed mode in which a person places his name. A signature is usually executed with one's own handwriting, although any mark that is the customary form used by a person for that purpose would normally constitute an acceptable signature.

A signature need not be, but usually is, placed at the end of a document; unless the instrument must be '*sub*scribed', i.e. signed at the 'end'. Normally, what is essential is that the signature clearly signifies the intention of an individual to authenticate a document *in toto* and to be bound thereby.

A **will** should be signed at the end. In English law, a will must be signed at the end and witnessed by two parties (Wills Act 1837, s. 9, as substituted by Administration of Justice Act 1982, s. 17). In the US, many jurisdictions require a will to be 'subscribed', i.e. signed at the end, and witnessed by two independent parties, and in some jurisdictions it must be witnessed by three parties.

In English statute law, a signature on a **deed** includes "making one's mark on the instrument", LP(MP)A 1989, s. 1(4). See also **execution**, *non est factum*, **signed, sealed and delivered**, **subscribe**.

signed, sealed and delivered   A phrase which indicates that a **deed** (a 'contract under seal') has been entered into; that is, that these three actions have been completed. Traditionally, signing, sealing and delivery were the most complete form of evidence that a person had expressly agreed to be bound by an agreement. See also **acknowledgement**, **delivery**, **seal**, **signature**.

silence   See **estoppel**, **representation**.

silent partner   A partner who supplies capital for a business and shares in the distributed profits, but takes no active part in the general management or affairs of the business. A silent partner does not appear as such without special enquiry. Also called a 'dormant partner' or 'sleeping partner'. cf. **general partner**. See also **limited partnership**, **passive investor**.

simple contract   A contract made orally or in writing; but not by **deed**, special instrument or by a court record. A contract other than a **specialty** (one under seal) or a contract of record (one recorded under a statutory provision). A simple contract may be express or implied, or partly express and partly implied. Liability under a simple contract is founded on the objective appearance of the agreement, rather than the formalities employed. Also called an 'informal contract', although such an agreement would not normally be in writing (or at least may only be partly in writing). cf. **specialty contract**. See also **agreement**, **consideration**, **equitable lease**[(Eng)], **parol contract**, **parol lease**.

simple interest   Interest paid or computed only on the original principal of a loan and not on the aggregate of the principal and any accrued interest. Interest computed only on the principal sum, from the start of a loan to repayment of the debt. 'Simple interest' may refer sometimes to interest computed on the basis that each day is 1/360th of a year. In the absence of any provision to the contrary, 'interest' means simple interest. On the other hand, if a mortgage deed provides for interest to be compounded and added to the principal the **compound interest** will generally rank with the same priority as the outstanding principal.

simple licence   See **licence**.

simple trust   1. A **trust** by which property is transferred by one person to be held by another as trustee, but without any further direction. The trustee has no active duties to perform, and therefore the law governs such duties. As a rule, the beneficiary has a right to possession of the property and may require the trustee to execute any transfer of the trust property as he directs. See **bare trust**.   2. A trust not created by any formal instrument, but brought into effect in a manner prescribed by law. cf. **special trust**. See also **constructive trust**, **implied trust**, **statutory trust for sale**[(Eng)].

simplified planning zone (SPZ)[(Eng)]   An area where a local authority has established a 'simplified planning zone scheme' which specifies certain forms of **development** that are permitted without the need for **planning permission** (TCPA 1990, ss. 82-87, Sch. 7 as modified). The establishment of an SPZ takes the form of a map defining the zone, together with a written statement with diagrams, plans, etc. setting out the authority's views on the appropriate development for the area. The scheme may take the form of a 'specific scheme' that lists certain permitted uses; or a 'general scheme' that permits a broad range of developments, with certain exclusions. The scheme may impose conditions or limitations on the permitted development, or may expressly reserve certain matters for detailed consideration by the local planning authority. SPZs have been designated primarily to encourage the development of old industrial areas; they are localised schemes; and as such have a 10-year life span. An SPZ cannot be adopted in a national park, the Broads, an area of outstanding natural beauty, an approved green belt, a conservation area, a site of special scientific interest, or any other such protected area.

simulation   A fictitious sale, especially one made to give a false or deceptive appearance to a transaction. "A simulation is a feigned, pretended act; one which assumes the appearance without the reality. Being entirely without effect, it is held not to have existed, and, for that reason, it may be disregarded or attacked collaterally by any interested person", Houghton v. Houghton, 165 La 1019, 116 So 493, 495 (1928) (Fritscher v. Justice, 472 So.2d 105, 107 (La Ct App 1985)). The law may look at the true nature of a transaction, especially tax laws, and any secret contract, or 'back-letter' or **counter-letter** takes effect only as between the contracting parties and does not affect any third party.

single-family detached (SFD)(AmE)   See **detached house**.

single purpose vehicle (SPV)   See **special purpose corporation**.

single-rate capitalization factor(AmE) or **single-rate years' purchase**(BrE)   A **capitalization factor**, or **years' purchase**, used to capitalise a level annual income that is assumed to continue indefinitely. In effect, this factor is the same as the **present value of one per period**. A single-rate capitalisation factor or single rate years' purchase is used to convert an income into a capital value, so that the income represents a return on the capital value, but, unlike a **dual-rate capitalization factor**(AmE)/**dual-rate years' purchase**(BrE)), it does not provide for any part of income to be set aside to provide for replacement of the capital value at the end of a given duration, i.e. it does not provide that a **sinking fund** is set

aside to replace the capital value. In the US, also called the '**Inwood factor**' (or 'Inwood coefficient'). See also **annuity capitalization**.

sinking fund (s.f.) A fund created by setting aside regular sums of money, over a given period of time, to accumulate to a predetermined amount (generally with interest accrued thereon), usually to meet a fixed cost or liability. A sinking fund is a means of amortising the cost of a specific obligation (e.g. the cost of replacing capital equipment), or providing for the repayment of a known debt, at a future date. A charge or allowance made against the revenue or profits of an organisation in order to provide for the cost of replacing an asset at the end of its useful or economic life. In American English also called an 'amortization fund'.

sinking fund accumulation factor(US) See Appendix C, **Financial Formulae**.

sinking-fund factor   See Appendix C, **Financial Formulae**.

sinking-fund method of depreciation   A means of allowing for depreciation by deducting or writing-off from the capital cost or value of an asset an amount equivalent to a **sinking fund**. Also called the 'reinvestment method of depreciation'.

sinking-fund rate   The rate of compound interest applied when assessing a **sinking-fund factor**. Generally, the rate will be one that is considered 'safe', as the intention is to accumulate capital at the minimum risk. Also called the 'accumulative rate', 'amortization rate' or 'recapture rate'. cf. **remunerative rate**. See also **dual-rate capitalization factor**(AmE)/**dual rate years' purchase**(BrE), **safe rate**.

sit-in   Occupation of a property for the purpose of protest or obstruction to its use. In law, a sit-in may amount to **trespass**. See also **squatting**.

site   1. The place or situation marked out for a particular purpose. An area of land that has been improved and is ready for use. The place on which something is situated or a particular use is carried on, especially in a local sense. "The *site* is the *spot* on which anything stands or is situated; it is more commonly applied to a building or any *place* marked out for a specific purpose; as the *site* on which a camp has been formed", George Crabb, *Crabb's English Synonyms*. 1816. Reprint, London: Routledge, 1982. A site represents a designated area, as distinguished from a **location** which represents where something is to be found. A location indicates the position of a site relative to other uses of land. Thus, a site can be surveyed, but a location is merely assessed or analyzed. See also **situs**. **2.** The place or situation of a particular building, user, development project, town, etc. **3.** An area of land delineated for improvement, development or redevelopment. See also **lot, plot**.

site analysis   An assessment of the potential of unimproved land, or land that is being considered for development or redevelopment. The examination of the suitability of a site for a particular scheme of development. See also **feasibility analysis, highest and best use, residual method of valuation**(BrE), **residual process**(US).

site area (SA)   The total area of a given parcel of land measured in a horizontal plane. In particular, the total area within an owner's title boundary; or the total area of land within the boundaries of a site intended for development or redevelopment. The site area is generally measured to the ownership boundaries and excludes the roads, streets or alleyways that abut the site (the 'net site area'). See also *ad medium filum*, **gross site area**(BrE).

site cover or **site coverage**   The proportion of a site that is covered by buildings or structures, usually expressed as a percentage of the total **site area**. Also called the 'building coverage'. See also **floor area ratio**(US), **plot ratio**(BrE).

site development   The provision of infrastructure to an area of land before buildings are erected on it. Site development generally includes clearing and levelling the site and the provision of roads and utilities (electricity, water, gas, drainage, sewers, lighting).

site licence(Eng)   A licence granted by a local authority authorising the use of an area of land for the siting of touring caravans (that is, for caravans that are capable of being moved from one place to another) (Caravan Sites and Control of Development Act 1960, Part I, as amended). Before a site licence may be granted, **planning permission** must be obtained for the siting of a **caravan** or caravans. Once planning permission has been obtained a local authority may not refuse a site licence, but it may impose conditions relating to the siting of the caravans (1960 Act, s. 5). A site licence is not required in certain cases, e.g. stationing a caravan within the curtilage and associated with a private dwelling-house, provided the caravan is used as incidental to the enjoyment of the house; specific short-term stays; stationing a limited number of caravans for part of the year; building site caravans; seasonal accommodation of agricultural and forestry workers on agricultural and forestry land; caravans used by certain 'exempt bodies' or travelling showmen (1960 Act, s. 2, Sch. 1).

site of special scientific interest (SSSI)(Eng)   An area of land considered to be of value for scientific purposes by reason of its flora, fauna, or unusual geological or physiological features. An SSSI is proposed as such by the government financed **Nature Conservancy Council**. The Council must notify its proposals to the local authority for the area in which the site is situated, as well as to the Secretary of State for the Environment and every owner and occupier of any area deemed to have special scientific interest. Any person notified of such a proposal may make representations or objections to the Council and such representations or objections must be considered before an area is designated formally as a site of special scientific interest.

Public access is severely limited to any SSSI and

neither development nor any potentially harmful operation may be carried out in such an area without the Nature Conservancy Council being formally notified and giving its consent, or until a period of three months elapses from the date the owner or occupier gave notice of its intention to carry out work (Wildlife and Countryside Act 1981, ss. 28-33, as amended).

site plan   A **plan**, prepared to scale, showing the existing boundaries and the position of any buildings, structures or other permanent features thereon. A site plan may be prepared for any of a number of different purposes. It may merely show the details of the existing condition or land uses, or it may show the principal features of a proposed development, including proposed streets, building lines, lot boundaries, landscaped and parking areas, etc. See also **filed plan**(Eng), **location plan**, **plot plan**.

site value   The value of an unimproved area of land taking into account the benefit of any permission to build in accordance with planning or zoning regulations. The site value is normally based on the market value of a parcel of land that is held as a fee simple title, free of all leases or mortgages. Sometimes referred to as the **residual value** of a plot of land. See also **cleared site value**(Eng), **land residual technique**(US), **residual method of valuation**(BrE).

site value tax   A tax that is levied based solely on the value of a parcel of land, excluding any buildings erected thereon. See also **land tax**, **property tax**.

sitting rent   See **virtual rent**.

sitting tenant   1. A tenant who is in physical possession of a property. In particular, a tenant who is protected from **eviction**, or one who remains in possession upon the expiration of a lease. In the US, in the latter instance, also called a 'holdover tenant'. See also **holding over**, **tenancy at will**. 2. A tenant who has an immediate right to possession of property, as distinguished from a tenant who has a **reversionary interest**.

situs   1. A word of Latin origin for a 'local position'. The **location** or situation of a property (real or personal). The place to which personal or intangible property is deemed to belong for legal or tax jurisdiction purposes, which in many contexts is the place of residence of the owner. Real estate always has a fixed situs, i.e. a particular property cannot change its legal or fiscal jurisdiction. A personal contract has no situs, but is governed by the place where it is to be performed. See also *lex loci*.   2. The preferred location for the establishment of a business or a new building, especially from an economic point of view.

six months   A period of time equivalent to six successive periods of a **month**, which generally means six calendar months. However, if the context so admits, it may be a period of 180 days (as when interest is calculated on the basis of a 360 day year) or even six lunar months. Six months may be, but need not be, equivalent to **half a year**. In the case of a **tenancy from year to year** (a 'yearly tenancy'), unless there is an express agreement to the contrary, notice of termination is, at common law, **half a year** (to expire on the anniversary of the date on which the tenancy commenced), but if the tenancy started on a **quarter day**, notice must coincide with the second succeeding quarter day.

sky factor   See **daylight factor**.

sky lease(US)   See **air lease**.

sky sign   See **advertisement**, **air space**.

skyscraper   A building that appears to touch the sky, or at least one that from street level obliterates a large part of the view of sky. A skyscraper is generally one that is at least 20 floors high. In New York in 1902 the Flat Iron building at 23 floors was considered a skyscraper, but by the 1990's a building would need to exceed 40 or even floors to warrant the same accolade. See also **high-rise building**.

slander of title   A false and malicious statement, made orally or in writing, that brings or tends to bring into question a person's right or title to real or personal property and thereby causes loss or injury.

sleeping partner   See **silent partner**.

sleeping rent   See **dead rent**.

slice   A portion of a sum of money or income received by one of a number of investors, especially a part of the total income received by the investors under an **equity participation** agreement. By way of illustration, the net income, or cash flow, from a property investment may be divided so that an institutional or passive investor receives all the income up to an agreed percentage return on cost – a **priority return**; an agreed percentage over and above the 'priority return' is received by a developer or managing partner; and any residue or **top-slice income** is divided between the investors in an agreed proportion based on the relative sums invested and the risks entailed by the respective investors. See also **side-by-side participation**, **top-slice participation**.

slice method(BrE)   See **hardcore method**.

sliding-scale rent   See **graded rent**, **graduated rent**, **indexed rent**.

slip rule(Eng)   A rule that gives the registrar of the Land Registry a discretionary right to correct "any clerical error or error of a like nature" on the register or on any plan or document referred to therein, provided the correction can be made without detriment to any registered interest (Land Registration Rules 1925, r. 13). See also **rectification**.

slum   An urban area, neighbourhood, district, a group of properties, or even a single residential property that is characterised by a squalid or excessively dilapidated condition and, therefore, is dangerous to the health of the resident population. Property characterised by overcrowding, decay, decrepitude, poor arrangement or layout, and a lack of proper sanitary conditions, frequently occupied by very poor, socially deprived, destitute or underprivileged families. See also **back-to-back house**(BrE), **clearance area**(Eng), **ghetto**, **housing action area**(Eng), **improvement area**(Eng), **unfit for human habitation**(Eng).

slum clearance   A process of clearing decrepit or **slum** property, especially residential property that is **unfit for human habitation**, usually combined with the building of modern property as a replacement. The improvement of an area of substandard housing by tearing down dilapidated and inferior buildings and, in most cases, replacing them with new buildings, particularly apartment houses or other multiple dwellings.

In the US, the **Department of Housing and Urban Development** (HUD) is the principal public body responsible for slum clearance. See also **blighted area**, **clearance area**(Eng), **housing action area**(Eng), **urban renewal**.

slump   A sustained and, frequently, sudden and substantial decline in prices or economic activity. The period in a trade or business **cycle** when economic activity declines at its fastest rate. A sudden fall in prices and activity, especially as consequence of a depression, or a milder depression. cf. **boom**.

smallholding(BrE)   A piece of land, not being or forming part of a **farm**, generally detached from a residence, that is used for agricultural production usually in order to supplement the income of a private individual or family. A smallholding is usually greater than one acre and not more than fifty acres. cf. **allotment**. See also **agricultural holding**(Eng), **cottage holding**.

smart building   A building that has a high level of automated facilities, such as computer controlled HVAC, fire safety, and security access systems and advanced telecommunication services. In particular, a smart building provides the tenant with a secure environment, has state-of-the-art telecommunications and is designed for efficient use of energy and water resources.

smart damages or **smart money**(US)   See **punitive damages**.

smoke   See **nuisance**.

snob zoning(US)   See **exclusionary zoning**.

social housing(Eng)   Housing that is provided for people whose personal circumstances make it difficult to meet their housing needs in the open market. Such housing may be provided by a landlord who is able to provide accommodation at a subsidised rent, as with a local authority or a **registered social landlord**, or by the provision of a form of low-cost home ownership, as with a **shared-ownership lease**. See also **council house**, **housing association**.

social landlord(Eng)   See **registered social landlord**.

society   A group or association of individuals formed together voluntarily for common interest or purpose. A commercial society is one formed for a business purpose but generally, unlike a **company** or **partnership**, not for the prime object of making a profit; it has no legal status *per se*, but is created to outlast the life of any individual member. A society may be constituted as a club, institution, corporation or any other organisation or association of persons, especially when those persons accept a common rule, share a common belief, or are involved in a common trade or profession. See also **building society**, **partnership**, **syndicate**.

Society for the Protection of Ancient Buildings(Eng)   A private organisation first established in 1887 by William Morris to fulfil the purpose explicit in its name. The society maintains records of historic and important buildings in England and Wales and makes efforts to find uses for any such building that is under threat of demolition. The Scottish Society for the Protection of Ancient Buildings has a similar function is Scotland. See also **ancient monument**, **English Heritage**.

soft cost   A cost associated with a development project that is not directly attributable to physical construction or improvement of the property, i.e. a cost that is not a **hard cost**. In particular, architectural, engineering, cost consultancy, project management and similar professional fees, legal and accountancy fees, planning or zoning approval expenses, real estate taxes (if incurred during the development period), interest and loan arrangements fees.

soft dollars(AmE)   Investment in real estate that qualifies for tax deduction in the year the money is spent.

soft loan   A loan on which interest is charged at a rate that is well below the market rate.

soft money   1. Money paid that does not augment the amount of **equity** invested in a property, e.g. interest payments on a mortgage loan.   2. Money paid as **carrying charges** while holding property pending development.   3.(US)Money paid for a property under a **purchase money mortgage** as part of the purchase price.   4. An undependable source of finance.

soil   The surface of the earth, especially dry **land** that may be ploughed or dug. See also **alluvion**, **fixture**, **mineral**, **profit à prendre**, **right of support**.

sole agency   An agency agreement whereby a specified **agent** is appointed to sell (or otherwise dispose) of a property on the understanding that the principal will not enter into an agreement with any other agent or broker in respect of the subject property (usually for a given period of time and/or in a given district). However, the agency may be exclusive or sole to that agent, but it does not preclude the principal from acting of his own accord. If a transaction results directly from a contact and the efforts of the principal, the agent or broker is normally precluded from receiving any payment. Also called, especially in the US, an **exclusive agency**. cf. **sole selling rights**.

sole agent   See **sole agency**.

sole common of pasture   A right of pasture available to commoners alone, rather than the owner of the land. Also called 'several pasture'. See also **right of common**.

sole corporation   See **corporation**.

sole owner   See **sole tenant**.

sole ownership(US)   See **several estate**.

sole possession(US)   See **exclusive possession**.

sole right to sell   See **exclusive right to sell**.

sole selling right(BrE)   An arrangement by which an estate agent is given sole responsibility for negotiating the sale of a property and the principal agrees to pay a commission to the agent even if a sale is made to a purchaser who is introduced by another party or a purchaser who is found by the principal. If an unconditional contract is executed with a purchaser during the period of the appointment (or, as a rule, after the expiration of the agreement, with a purchaser introduced by the agent during that period) the principal is liable to pay a fee, and any agreed expenses, to the estate agent (Estate Agents (Provision of Information) Regulations 1991; *Dowling Kerr Ltd v Scott* [1996] EGCS 177; *Christie Owen & Davies plc v King* (1998) SCLR 786 (Scot)). Such an agreement depends on the terms of the appointment and not necessarily because the agreement uses the words 'sole selling rights (or

any similar phrase). Under the provisions of the Estate Agents (Provision of Information) Regulations 1991, which were made under the Estate Agents Act 1979, s. 18, any agent entering into such an agreement is required to explain in writing the significance of the terms used, using the form of explanation contained in the regulations. cf. **sole agency**. See also **exclusive right to sell**(AmE).

sole tenant   One who holds property in his own right, as distinguished from one who holds an interest in property in conjunction with others. 'Sole tenant' normally refers to a person who is an owner in the more common use of the word (i.e. a 'sole owner'), as distinguished from someone who holds an interest as a result of the relationship of landlord and tenant. The term may sometimes be used to refer to a tenant who holds from a landlord, but not in common with any other tenant. cf. **joint tenant**. See also **several estate**.

solo cedit quod solo implantatur(Lat)   'What is planted in the soil belongs to the soil'. See **fixture**.

solo cedit quod solo inædificatur(Lat)   'That which is fixed to the soil becomes part of the soil'. See **fixture**, **tree**.

solus agreement(BrE)   An agreement by which a retailer or distributor of merchandise ties himself to buy goods from a particular supplier. A form of agreement that is entered into frequently in conjunction with a loan or mortgage agreement between a retailer and a supplier; especially for the retail supply of petroleum products. A solus agreement may be void if it unreasonably restrains the trading activity of a retailer or is considered to be prejudicial to the public interest (*Esso Petroleum Co Ltd v Harper's Garage (Stourport) Ltd* [1968] AC 269, [1967] 1 All ER 699 (HL); *Amoco Australia Pty. Ltd v Rocca Bros* [1975] AC 561 (PC)). A solus agreement in a lease is a **covenant running with land** and, therefore, is binding upon an assignment of the lease (*Regent Oil Co v J.A. Gregory*

(Hatch End) Ltd [1966] Ch 402, 432-3, [1965] 3 All ER 673, 680). A solus agreement in a mortgage may be an unreasonable restriction on the mortgagor's **equity of redemption** if it is required to remain in force after the mortgage has been repaid in full; or it may be void if it is an unreasonable restraint on the mortgagor's trade (*Esso Petroleum v Harper's Garage, supra*). Also called an 'exclusive dealing agreement'. See also **once a mortgage always a mortgage, redemption, void contract**.

sovereign land   Land over which a sovereign entity has claimed **dominion**. Land that is owned by a state or federal government. See also **allodial system, Crown land, Crown lands, domain, eminent domain, native title, police powers**.

space lease(US)   See **occupational lease**.

space plan   A preliminary plan of an area of office building, prepared in accordance with the requirements of a prospective occupier, to show the partition walls, internal office layout, and the position of desks, service or utility outlets, etc.

spec property   See **speculative property**.

special adaptability(Eng)   See **special suitability or adaptability**.

special agent   See **agent**.

special area(Eng)   1. An **inner urban area** of Great Britain where it is considered by central government that special social needs exist and where the appropriate local authority is authorised: (a) to make loans for site preparation and site development work; (b) to make grants to assist a person taking a lease of premises intended for industrial or commercial purposes; and (c) to make grants to assist a small firm (one employing no more than fifty employees) to pay interest charges on loans taken out to finance the purchase and development of land (Inner Urban Areas Act 1978, ss. 8-11). See also **urban development area**. 2. See **area of special control**.

special assessment(US)   See **assessment**.

special assessment district(US)   See **improvement district**.

special benefit(US)   See **before and after method, benefits**.

special charge or **special lien**   A charge, or **lien**, secured on specified property, as distinguished from a **floating charge** which is secured on all the assets of a corporation. A charge or lien that can only be enforced as security for the performance of a particular obligation. See also **fixed charge**.

special condition(AmE)   A condition set out in a contract for the sale of land, that must be satisfied before the contract becomes binding. For example, a condition that the sale will not proceed unless the purchaser obtains suitable finance, or satisfies himself of certain facts provided to him by the vendor. See also **conditional contract, subject to**.

special conditions of sale(Eng)   See **conditions of sale**.

special contract   1. A contract under seal; a **specialty contract**.   2. A contract that contains provisions that are not typical for the type of agreement being made.   3. A contract that is not one used in every-day business transactions. 4.(US)A contract whose terms are set out expressly and that is not in any way dependent on implication.   5. See **entire contract**.

special damages   See **damages**.

special development area(Eng)   See **development area**.

Special Development Order (SDO)(Eng) An order made by the Secretary of State by which **planning permission** is granted for development that is carried out in accordance with a general plan for a particular area, such as a new town or an urban development area, or for a special project, such as a nuclear waste reprocessing unit (TCPA 1990, ss. 58, 59). cf. **General Development Order**.

special district(US) 1. See **improvement district**. 2. A district that is zoned for a special use, such as an area of open space, an historic preservation district, or an area for planned development. See also **historic district, planned unit development**.

special entail or **special tail** A entailed estate or **fee tail** that is limited to the children of specified parents or a particular spouse of the testator (2 *Bl Comm* 113). Also called a 'special estate tail'.

special estate tail See **special entail**.

special exception or **special exception use**(US) See special-use permit.

special grant(BrE) See **grant**.

special legacy See **legacy**.

special liability insurance or **specific liability insurance** 1. Insurance against a specific risk of a claim from a third party, such as a claim made by a client as a result of professional negligence; as contrasted with insurance against a claim from the public at large. See also **liability insurance**. 2. **Contingency insurance** against a specified risk.

special lien See **lien, special charge**.

special limitation A **limitation** placed upon the grant of an **estate** in land which amounts to a contingent event that, if it arises, returns the estate to the grantor, without the need for any further action such as the exercise of a right of re-entry. "The term 'special limitation' denotes that part of the language of a conveyance which causes the created interest automatically to expire upon the occurrence of a stated event, and this provides a terminability in addition to that normally

characteristic of such interest", The American Law Institute, *Restatement of Property* § 23 (1936). cf. **conditional limitation, executory limitation**.

special partner See **limited partner**.

special perils Any risk associated with the ownership or control of property that may be insured against, other than fire. "Those perils which are not covered by, or which are excluded from, the normal fire policies issued by insurers", M.G. Eagle, *Special Perils Insurance*, 1963, p. 2. Property insurance policies are frequently provided against fire and against 'special perils', which covers such matters as explosion, storm, flood, riot and civil commotion, impact (vehicular or aircraft), malicious damage, subsidence and accidental breakage. See also **all-risks insurance, comprehensive insurance**.

special permit(US) See **special-use permit**.

special power See **power of appointment**.

special property 1. A right to the ownership of property that is subordinate to an absolute or unconditional right of ownership. Also called 'qualified property'. See also **special use property**. 2.(US)An interest in property that is less than a right of ownership, such as a right held by a mortgagee or bailee. Special property includes the right of a bailee to hold goods as security until the outstanding debt is paid or the obligation is performed.

special purchaser A purchaser, or prospective purchaser, who pays or is prepared to pay a higher price for a property because of his particular position; such as a person who has an interest in an adjoining property; another interest in the same property, e.g. a lessee who is seeking to acquire his lessor's interest; or a person with a vested interest in a property. See also **arm's length transaction, marriage value**(BrE)**, vested interest**.

special purpose See **special suitability or adaptability**.

762

special purpose corporation (SPC) or **special-purpose entity** (SPE)   A corporation, or other entity, that is set up for a special or single purpose. For example, a corporation that is set up to hold a single asset or one that is set up in order to be financially independent from the activities of other associated entities. A special-purpose entity may be used to hold real estate so that the stock can be transferred without liability for taxes that may otherwise be levied on the direct transfer of the underlying asset. Special-purpose vehicles are also used in mortgage securitization to isolate the ownership of the separate assets or mortgages from the entity that holds the securitized bonds (the **issuer** of the bonds). Also called (depending on its purpose or objective) a 'single-purpose vehicle' (SPV) or a 'bankruptcy remote corporation' (BRC) (when it is incorporated so that it will not be affected by the insolvency of other associated corporations). Where the entity has more several assets it may be called a 'substantive lessor entity'. See also **real estate investment trust, simulation, synthetic lease**.

special purpose property or **special-use property**(US)   Property that is designated, equipped and used for a particular purpose A property that may readily be used only for a single purpose, e.g. an oil refinery, power station, church, school, hospital and the like, or a limited number purposes. A property that, by reason of its construction, specification or arrangement, may be considered as having no ready alternative use as it currently stands. Such property is not generally bought and sold in the open market (except as part of a business that occupies the property) and cannot be said to have a market value in the ordinary sense of the term due to the limited purposes to which the property may be put.

In the US, in condemnation proceedings, the measure of **just compensation** for 'special use property' or 'special purpose property' is normally based on the **cost approach**, i.e. an estimate of the cost of a suitable alternative site and reproducing a similar building, after allowing for depreciation or obsolescence. It may also be possible to determine the value based on a potential income approach, although this may only be a useful check on the level of value. See also **depreciated replacement cost**(BrE), **equivalent reinstatement**(Eng), **replacement cost, specialty**.

special recognition clause(US)   See **partial release clause**.

special scientific interest(Eng)   See **site of special scientific interest**.

special suitability or adaptability(Eng)   An attribute that arises as a direct consequence of a proposal by a public authority to acquire land for a purpose for which it has obtained statutory compulsory purchase powers. When assessing **compulsory purchase compensation** "the special suitability or adaptability of the land for any purpose shall not be taken into account if that purpose is a purpose to which it could be applied only in pursuance of statutory powers, or for which there is no market apart from the special needs of a particular purchaser or the requirements of any authority possessing compulsory purchase powers" LCompA 1961, s. 5(3). Clearly, any area of land may be specially suitable for the purpose to which it is put, or may be specially suitable or adaptable for a use to which it could be put – special suitability or adaptability being a factor that contributes to determining its **market value** – but if that special attribute arises solely as a result of the acquiring authority's underlying reason for purchase, it must be ignored when determining the appropriate amount of compensation.

special tax assessment(US)   See **assessment**.

special trust   A **trust** created for a specific purpose and which requires the trustee to exercise particular duties as defined in the trust deed. A special trust may be distinguished from a **simple trust** whereby the trustee merely acts as a repository for the trust property. cf. **passive trust**(US). See also **active trust**.

special-use permit or **special permit**(US) A permit that authorizes a change of use from that specified in an existing **zoning ordinance**, to a use that is considered compatible with the existing classification. A special-use permit may be granted when the use is not considered to have an adverse effect on the neighboring property or is considered to be in harmony with the general purpose or intent of the comprehensive plan for the municipality. For example, a nursery school or church in an area zoned for residential use. A special-use permit may be granted for a use that is specified in the zoning ordinance (a 'permitted use'); or, in some jurisdictions, it may refer to a use that is permitted subject to compliance with certain conditions (a 'special exception use' or a 'conditional use'). In other jurisdictions, the terms 'special-use permit' and 'special exception' may be used interchangeably, having the same legal import. The term 'conditional use permit' may also be used when a permit is granted for a use that the regulations expressly permit, but when the permit is granted subject to a determination by an administrative officer or zoning board that the use is proper and desirable for the designated zoning and not detrimental to the general welfare of the neighborhood. cf. **zoning variance**. See also **conditional zoning**, **non-conforming use**.

special-use property See **special-purpose property**.

special value The value of a property that is due to special circumstances, such as the value to a **special purchaser** or the value that would be attributable to unusual economic circumstances. In particular, a value that exceeds the **market value** due to exceptional circumstances. See also **fair market value**(US), **special suitability or adaptability**(Eng).

special warranty deed(US) See **warranty deed**.

specialized property See **special-purpose property**.

specialty See **specialty contract**.

specialty or **specialty property**(US) A property that is uniquely adapted for use by a particular business and cannot readily be used for any other purpose. A building that is specially built or is intended for a particular purpose and for which, therefore, there is no ready market or no sales are made of such properties. In condemnation proceedings, such properties are generally assessed on the basis of the **cost approach**. See also **special-purpose property**.

specialty contract A **contract** under **seal**. In particular, an obligation to pay a debt accepted under seal, or arising under statute or as an obligation of record. The mere fixing of a seal to a document does not necessarily make it a 'specialty' (to which a longer statutory limitation period applies); the contract should use language to indicate that it is intended as such. Sometimes called a 'formal specialty'. cf. **simple contract**. See also **deed**.

specialty shopping center A shopping center that has no major anchor tenant and comprises a group of specialty stores that are generally not part of any major group or chain. Normally the center is on one level with an open pedestrian mall. A particular form of specialty center is the 'festival mall' (first termed by the Faneuil Hall Marketplace in Boston) which is based on a theme such as a food market with a large number of stalls or stores aimed to attract tourist traffic, combined with an entertainment theme. Other forms of such centers may be termed 'fashion centers' when the center is concentrated on apparel shops, boutiques and similar high-end stores, usually aimed at the higher price point.

specialty store A retail store that sells only a restricted type of merchandise, such as men's wear, women's wear, confectionery, used books or jewellery. In particular, a store that sells high quality or unusual goods, or goods that can be sold at a premium. cf. **variety store**.

specie See *in specie*, **money**.

specific agent See **agent**.

specific charge A **fixed charge**, i.e. a charge upon one or more designated properties. cf. **floating charge**.

specific implement(Scot) See **specific performance**.

specific insurance policy **1.** Insurance against specific perils or specific risks as stipulated in the insurance policy. **2.** An insurance policy that covers a number of properties and specifies a limit for each property. See also **blanket insurance**.

specific lien See **lien**.

specific performance A remedy by which a court of law compels a party to perform a contract in accordance with, or substantially in accordance with, its agreed terms, especially when the court considers it equitable that the contract should be carried through to a conclusion, instead of awarding **damages** against the defaulting party. "The specific performance of a contract is its actual execution according to its stipulations and terms; and is contrasted with damages or compensation for the non-execution of the contract", Sir Charles Fry. *A Treatise on the Specific Performance of Contracts*. 6th ed. London: Sweet & Maxwell, 1921, Reprint ed. 1985, p. 2. In particular, specific performance is an equitable remedy granted when a contract would not otherwise be enforceable in law due to a lack of proper formality. This form of order is awarded based on the maxim 'equity looks on that as done which ought to be done' or 'equity imputes an intention to fulfil an obligation' (*Walsh v Lonsdale* (1882) 21 Ch D 9 (CA); 27A Am.Jur.2d., Equity, § 116).
A decree or order of specific performance is an equitable remedy and, therefore, is granted at the discretion of the court. In particular, a specific performance is only decreed, where the party wants the thing *in specie*; and cannot have it any other way. Thus, it is normally used only in cases when the subject matter of the contract is unique or has a special character and, therefore, damages would be inappropriate or would provide inadequate compensation. Specific performance will not be granted to enforce a contract purely for personal services or a contract where there is no consideration. Similarly, specific performance will not normally be granted to enforce an agency or partnership contract. Nor will it be granted when it would require a continuing intervention by the court. Specific performance is generally available as a remedy for a failure to perform a contract for the sale of land, as the subject matter is unique. Although the courts will not grant such a decree in cases of misrepresentation; duress, fraud, unreasonable delay or, in certain cases, a mistake; when to do so would cause hardship; or if the contract is illegal. Where **time is of the essence** the party seeking completion can apply for a decree when the time has expired. If time is not of the essence, the offended party can still obtain a decree if the other party fails to perform when given reasonable notice, and the court will normally grant such a decree, provided it will not cause injustice to either party (*Raineri v Miles* [1981] AC 1050, [1980] 2 All ER 145 (CA); 77 Am.Jur.2d., Vendor and Purchaser, § 83). Specific performance is rarely granted to enforce a lessor's obligation to repair; the courts are more likely to grant damages, or allow the tenant to terminate the lease.
Also called 'specific relief' or, in the US, the order may be called a 'bill of specific performance'. In Scots law, a similar remedy is called a 'specific implement'. cf. **rescission**. See also **deposit**, **part performance**.

specific relief See **specific performance**.

specification **1.** An exact or detailed description of the subject matter of a contract. **2.** A detailed written or printed description of the work required to be undertaken as part of a building contract. A specification of the work includes such matters as dimensions, the quantity and type of materials, mode of construction, and describes the quality and standard of workmanship, finishing, etc. that are required of the builder or contractor. A specification is normally prepared by an architect, estimator, quantity surveyor or consulting engineer for the guidance of a building contractor and generally forms part of the **building contract** documents and is related to the drawings or plans of the project. See also **bill of quantities**(BrE), **schedule of quantities**(AmE).

specified-property offering(US)   An offering of property to a group or syndicate of investors on the basis that the investors are provided at the time of their initial investment with details of the particular property or properties in which they will be investing, as distinguished from a **blind-pool offering** where selection of the property is left entirely to the discretion of the investment managers.

speculation   The taking of risk, especially by the purchase of goods, stocks, bonds, etc. with a view to short-term gain. See also **speculator**.

speculative property   Property that is developed without any known end user, i.e. a property that is built on the speculation or hope that there will be a tenant or buyer when, or shortly after, it is completed. Called 'spec property' for short. See also **property developer**, **speculator**.

speculator   Derived from the Latin *speculari*, 'spy out' or 'to watch'. A person who ponders on the future course of events; engages in reasoning *a priori*; or ventures into matters that are fanciful or unreal. In business, a person who participates in hazardous ventures, or exceptional risk-taking, with the hope of realizing extraordinary profit; especially someone who buys and sells in anticipation of short-term profit. One who is "largely concerned, not with making superior long-term forecasts of the probable yield of an investment over its whole life, but with foreseeing changes in the conventional basis of valuation a

short time ahead of the general public", J. M. Keynes, *The General Theory of Employment, Interest and Money* (1936), p. 154. Commonly used in a deprecatory sense to describe anyone who indulges in highly risky or rash trading as contrasted with ordinary trade or business. A speculator is someone whose activity falls between that of a gambler and a merchant adventurer; his actions are normally 'hazardous', but with a fair prospect of financial gain if the results of those actions are successful.

Land speculation has been defined as "the holding of land resources, usually in something less than their **highest and best use**, with the primary managerial emphasis on resale at a capital gain rather than on profitable use in current production. Traditionally, the land speculator has shown little interest in the returns he could secure from the operation of his real estate resources. He tends instead to regard property as a commodity that he can buy and sell at a profit", Raleigh Barlowe. *Land Resource Economics; The Economics of Real Estate*. 4th ed. Prentice-Hall, 1985, pp. 201-202. See also **bear**, **bull**, **property developer**, **risk**.

Spencer's Case(Eng)   See **covenant**, **covenant running with the land**.

spendable income   The income available to an investor, either after taking account of all outgoings and taxes, or after making a provision for a **sinking fund** to replace the cost of a wasting asset. See also **net cash flow**.

spendthrift trust(US)   See **protective trust**.

spes successionis(Lat)   'A hope of succeeding to property'.

spite fence(AmE)   A fence or similar structure erected on the boundary of land with no particular purpose other than to aggravate or restrict the rights of an adjoining owner. As a private matter, there is nothing to prevent someone from erecting a fence or wall as high as he pleases on his own land, although the height of any fence or structure is generally limited by local building or zoning regulations and, in some circumstances, the erection of a high or dangerous form of fence may be deemed to create a private **nuisance**. In the US, several jurisdictions have passed statutes that control the height or appearance of neighboring fences, thereby preventing the erection of *spite fences*. See also **right of light, right to view, scheme of development**.

split-equity mortgage   See **reverse mortgage**.

split financing   Financing that has been obtained for two or more separate but related purposes. For example, financing that is obtained from the same source, but is provided under separate agreements to cover (a) the cost of land acquisition, and (b) for the construction of buildings, or improvements to buildings, on that land; or financing that is provided for the purchase of different interests (a fee and a lease) in the same property. Also called 'component financing'.

split-level house   1. A house with stories at different levels but designed for occupation by one family. In particular, one where the living areas are on different levels; or where the upper and lower living areas only partially overlap as where the lower level is left void or is used as a garage. See also **duplex house**.   2. A house that is built partly on one storey and partly on two stories. In American English also called a 'bi-level house'. See also **maisonette**.

split rate   1. A separate **capitalization rate** applied to land and buildings, or applied to different parts of an income. See also **hardcore method**(BrE).   2. The rate of interest on a **wraparound mortgage**.

split reversion method(BrE)   See **hardcore method**.

split trust   An investment trust that provides the investors with different forms of return. For example, a trust that invests in short- and long-term bonds, or invests for income growth and for capital growth, and permits the investor to switch between the alternative investments.

splitting fees   An arrangement by which an agent or broker divides his fee or commission with another agent or broker. This may arise, for example, where an agent who is retained by a principal to find a suitable buyer pays part of his fee to a third party for introducing such a prospect; or where the fee is divided with the agent representing the other party to the transaction, either by both agents dividing their pooled fees or by the seller's agent receiving a share of the buyer's agent's fees. The former, which represents a form of **joint agency** is common practice. The latter, which is a form of **dual agency**, is normally unacceptable and may entitle the principal to consider the appointment of the agent void, unless he has clearly agreed to the arrangement. See also **cooperating broker**(US).

spot loan(US)   A loan granted directly to an individual house purchaser, as opposed to a **package loan** granted to a builder to cover a number of properties on planned development or in a building complex.

spot zoning   1.(US)The **zoning** of a small area of land, or one or more properties, for a use that is not in harmony with the normal zoning plan for the area, especially if a small area is rezoned in a way that does not conform to the surrounding neighborhood. Spot zoning is normally invalid if the permitted use is very different from the surrounding area; the area involved is small; or it can be shown that the municipality has favored one landowner to the unreasonable detriment of the surrounding area, or in order to prejudice the intention of a comprehensive plan. For example, it may be considered illegal where an area of land is designated for industrial use in an area zoned residential use, even when the intention is to retain a business in a particular municipal district. On the other hand, it may be valid if it is made for the benefit of the community at large, as with the rezoning corner properties for commercial use to provide services in a residential district. 'Spot zoning' is site specific and does not include a use that is compatible or necessary to the overall zoning, such as a neighborhood shopping center that serves the local residents. cf. **floating zone**. See also **contract zoning, exclusionary zoning, special-use permit, zoning variance**. 2.(Can) The zoning or rezoning of a particular site for a use that is not in conformity with the general planning for the area.

spread The difference between the purchase and sale price of a commodity or share. The difference between the cost of funds and the rate at which a loan is made. The difference between the bid and asked price of a commodity. The 'yield spread' is the percentage difference between the return on two different investments. A 'positive spread investment' by an institution is one that exceeds its average cost of capital. See also **arbitrage, margin, point**.

springing use See **shifting use**.

spuilzie(Scot) An action that may be taken to recover property that has been taken by **vitious dispossession**, i.e. without consent or judicial warrant. A remedy that is similar to the common law remedy of ejectment.

spurious easement See **easement in gross**.

square(US) Under the **government survey system** an area of 24 miles by 24 miles. Sometimes called a 'quadrangle'. See also **block, section of land**.

squaring the dimensions(BrE) See **working-up**.

squatter 1. One who, without any right or semblance of title, enters on an unoccupied house or land, intending to stay there as long as he can.

A person who enters onto land, legally or illegally, and refuses to leave when he has no right to stay and has been requested to leave may be referred to as a squatter; although generally a squatter is someone who enters on land or into a building without any bona fide claim and without the consent of the owner. A squatter is considered incapable of acquiring title to land by **adverse possession** as his occupation is generally not considered 'adverse' to the true owner, although an 'adverse possessor' is commonly referred to as a squatter and a claim by adverse possession as 'squatter's rights'.

In English statute law, it is an offence if any person(s) fails to leave premises when requested to do so by a "displaced residential occupier", or a "protected intending occupier" (i.e. the holder of a freehold interest, or a leasehold interest with not less than 21 years to run, who acquired that interest, for money or money's worth, for his own occupation as a residence) (Criminal Law Act 1977, s. 7). See also **dispossession, possessory title, trespass**. 2.(US) Historically, one who entered onto **public lands** of the government of the United States in order to claim title. See also **homestead, squatting**.

squatter's rights(US) See **adverse possession, squatter**.

stabilized net income(US) The average **net operating income** that is generated by a property excluding extraneous or non-recurring income and expenditure. The stabilized net income shows the revenue excluding distortions, such as the costs of substantial capital improvements or a high level of vacant accommodation during the initial renting period. The stabilized net income of a new building is generally taken as the income for the first year after the building is fully leased.

staff appraiser(US) An **appraiser** who is a member of the staff of a lending institute. cf. **fee appraiser**.

stage payment See **interim payment**.

staircasing The gradual increase in the equity interest held in a property. For example, an increase in percentage of the ownership held by a person who has a lease of the property and a partial ownership interest in the property. See also **equity sharing**.

stake 1. A wooden or metal post that is designed to be driven into the land to mark the **boundary** or limit of land. See also **fence, monument, offset**. 2. A share in an investment or joint venture. See also **equity sharing**.

stakeholder One who holds money or property on behalf of rival claimants until a dispute over that item has been resolved. A third party appointed by two or more other parties to hold money pending the resolution of a dispute between those parties. A stakeholder is a mere depository for the parties to a contract, is not a party to the contract, and unlike an **agent**, may not be enjoined for the return of the money.

In common law, as followed by several jurisdictions in the US, a payment made to a third party as a form of **deposit**, or **earnest money**, prior to the execution of a formal contract for the sale of land is generally considered to be held by that party acting as a 'stakeholder', unless there is an agreement or stipulation to the contrary, and as such the payment must be returned to the prospective purchaser if no contract results; the proposed vendor having no responsibility for the stakeholder's failure to repay the deposit (*Sorrell v Fitch* [1977] AC 728 (HL); 30A C.J.S., Escrow, § 10). On the other hand, when a formal contract is executed, if there is no evidence to the contrary, the money is generally treated as being held by that party as agent for the vendor, and the purchaser must take action against the vendor when seeking a return of the deposit, although he may enjoin the agent in the action (*Edgell v Day* (1865) LR 1 CP 80; 30A C.J.S., Escrows, §§ 9-10).

In the US, most jurisdictions take the view that a broker who receives a deposit or earnest money from a prospective purchaser of real estate holds the money as a stakeholder and, if a sale cannot be completed, because of the vendor's failure to complete (as when he cannot provide good title), the broker is obliged to return the money to the purchaser. The broker cannot simply retain any commission due to him from the deposit as he is liable to the purchaser as trustee or stakeholder.

In American English, in common usage, a 'stakeholder' refers to someone who holds money as part of a gaming contract. cf. **escrow agent**. See also **conditions of sale**.

stallage(Eng) The right to place a stall in a **fair** or **market**, or a payment made for the privilege or convenience of placing a stall on the soil, or using standing room for cattle or goods, in a market or fair. See also **pennage, piccage**.

stamp duty(Eng) A duty raised by requiring stamps, acquired from the government, to be affixed to most legal or official documents. Stamp duty may be a fixed amount, or *ad valorem*, that is, in proportion to the value of the property that forms the subject matter of the document. As a rule, the amount of the duty is assessed based on a percentage of the consideration stated in the **instrument**, subject to exemptions for small transactions. Stamp duty has been abolished for all instruments except stock and marketable securities (Finance Act 2003, s. 125). In the case of land and buildings, it has been replaced by **stamp duty land tax**. See also **certificate of value, conveyance tax, registration duty, stamp tax**(US).
Nock, Reg. *Understanding Stamp Duty on Property*. London: Law Society Publishing, 2003.

stamp duty land tax (SDLT)(Eng) A tax that replaces **stamp duty** on land and property. The tax is levied on most transfers of an interest in land or buildings, including leases. The tax is levied on the **market value** of the property transferred. In the case of a lease, the tax is levied on the total rent payable during the term of the lease, with a statutorily prescribed discount (Finance Act 2003, Part IV).
Nock, Reg. *Stamp Duty Land Tax: The New Law*. Bristol: Jordans, 2004.

stamp tax(US) A tax or duty levied as an *ad valorem* tax on the execution of a written instrument, such as a stock transfer, a deed for the transfer of real estate or on the grant of a mortgage. The payer of stamp tax is required to purchase official stamps ('tax stamps') from the tax or revenue office and fix them to the appropriate instrument for its authentication. See also **stamp duty**(Eng).

Standard Conditions of Sale(Eng) See **conditions of sale**.

standard contract See standard-form document.

standard depth(Eng) See **standard unit**.

standard deviation A statistical measure of a frequency distribution or dispersion. A measure of the divergence of one set of measurements from the mean. Measured by the square root of the average of the squares of the deviations from the mean. Also called the 'root-mean-square deviation'.

standard fixed-payment mortgage (SFPM) See **amortization loan**.

standard-form contract or **standard-form document**(Eng) A printed document in which the general terms and conditions are set out in a standard form so that it may be used for any number of transactions relating to similar business or a similar type of transfer. For example, a 'standard-form lease' would set out the general conditions and covenants, but leave such details as the names of the parties, the subject property, the duration, and the amount of rent to be inserted by the parties or their advisors. Standard-form documents, or 'standard documents' are usually produced by authoritative bodies to assist those that use such documents by being time saving, consistent and, theoretically, less liable to misinterpretation. A standard-form contract may be one that is commonly accepted in a particular business as conducted between experienced parties, e.g. bills of lading or insurance policies. It may also be a form of contract that is offered on a 'take it or leave it basis', i.e. an **adhesion contract**. See also **conditions of sale**, **form document**(US), **precedent**, **usual covenant**.

standard lease(Eng) See standard-form contract.

standard metropolitan statistical area (SMSA)(US) See metropolitan area.

standard mortgage clause or **standard mortgagee clause** See union mortgage clause.

standard unit(BrE) A unit of property of given dimensions, especially one taken as a standard for units in a new development or as a standard when applying the **comparison method of valuation**. In particular, a term used to refer to a shop unit that is considered to be of standard dimensions for valuation purposes: commonly a unit with a frontage of 20 or 25 feet (6.10 or 7.62 meters) and a standard depth of 60 or 100 feet (18.29 meters or 30.48 meters). See also **unit cost**, **zoning method**.

standby commitment or **standby loan** See **commitment**, **forward commitment**.

standby contract An agreement by which it is agreed that, on a specified date, an agreed number of mortgages will be sold in the form of a **mortgage-backed security** at a specified price.

standby fee A fee paid by an applicant for a loan as an act of earnest intent. 'Standby fee' may be used synonymously with **commitment fee**, but it may refer also to a fee payable at the time of a loan application, unlike a 'commitment fee' that is payable when the lender agrees to make a loan available. As a rule, a standby fee is intended to be retained by the lender if a loan facility is offered but not taken up or closes within a specified time limit. If a standby fee is paid at the time of the application it is normally set against any fee due to the lender at a later stage.

standing loan or **standing mortgage**
1. A loan requiring the payment of interest only during its term. The total amount of the principal is repayable at the end of the term. Usually a short-term or medium-term loan granted at a fixed rate of interest. Also called a 'straight loan', a 'term loan', a 'flat loan' or simply 'an interest-only loan'. cf. **amortization loan**. See also **balloon loan**.   **2.** A short-term loan made available as a temporary measure until an alternative and more permanent loan can be obtained. In particular, a loan granted to cover a period from completion of a development project until long-term financing is available or the project is sold. See also **gap finance**.

standstill agreement   An agreement by which the parties agree to postpone legal or precipitous action for a given period of time or until an alternative agreement is reached. For example, an agreement whereby a mortgagee agrees not to commence foreclosure proceedings while a mortgage loan is being restructured. See also **workout agreement**.

stare decisis(Lat) 'To abide by a decided case'. A principle that if a similar point comes forward for judicial consideration a previous decision on the same issue should be applied, unless a good cause can be shown to the contrary. A principle that is an inherent part of the **common law**. See also **precedent**.

start rate   The interest payable for the first year of an **adjustable-rate mortgage**, or payable for an initial term when the interest rate is lower than for the rest of the term.

start-up money   See **front money**.

state board of equalization(US)   See **board of equalization**.

state rule(US)   See **before-and-after method**.

statement of condition(US)   **1.** See **reduction certificate**.   **2.** See **balance sheet**.

statement of record(US)   A written statement prepared, in accordance with the provisions of the Interstate Land Sales Full Disclosure Act of 1969, by a **developer** of land that is to be sold as subdivision lots, setting out details of the owner of the land, the conditions of sale and, in particular, the availability (or non-availability) of roads, water, utilities or other amenities. The statement must also set out any specific problems relating to the land to be sold, such as soil conditions, liens and encumbrances. The statement must be filed with the Office of Interstate Land Sales Regulation (OILSR) (which is part of the Department of Housing and Urban Development) before contracts are entered into for the sale of lots in a **subdivision**. Once the statement is filed, the OILSR issues a 'property report', which contains details of the property and must be supplied to any prospective purchaser or lessee, at least 48 hours before a contract of sale or lease is signed. In addition, the landowner must give the purchaser or lessee the option to revoke the contract or the lease within seven days of its execution. A number of exceptions are made as to the types of property to which this filing requirement applies, including: (i) subdivisions containing less than twenty-five lots; (ii) subdivisions in which all lots are 20 acres or larger; (iii) condominium in which each unit has been completed before sale; (iv) land on which there is an existing residential, commercial, condominium, or industrial building or the buyer or lessor is obliged to build within two years; (v) land zoned or restricted to commercial or industrial development where the purchaser is involved in commercial or industrial business; (vi) sales or leases of lots to builders who are engaged in the business of constructing and reselling residential, commercial or industrial properties; and (vii) leases that are granted for a term of less than five years (without any provision for renewal) (15 USC § 1702).

statement of title(Aus)   See **abstract of title**.

status quo(Lat) 'The state in which things are'. See *rebus sic stantibus*.

status quo ante[(Lat)] 'The same state as before'. See **restitution**.

statute law or **statutory law** Written law as established by legislative authority, especially as distinguished from unwritten **common law**. Law which derives its origin from rules made by a legislative branch of government – in the UK, Parliament with Royal Assent; in the US, for federal laws, the Senate and House of Representatives with Presidential Assent, and for state laws the State Senate and Assembly, with the assent of the Governor. In the US, 'statutory law' refers particularly to a state law or enactment, as distinguished from a federal law or a municipal ordinance. See also **bylaw, ordinance, police power**[(US)].

Statute of Frauds "An Act for the Prevention of Frauds and Perjuries", 29 Car. II (1676), c. 3. An English statute that became effective from 1677 to prevent the use of **fraud** and perjury as a means of enforcing supposed agreements. The statute provided that certain types of contracts or engagements could not be brought before a court of law, unless evidenced by some **note** or **memorandum** in **writing** which was duly signed. In particular the statute provided that all "Lease, estates, interests of freehold, or terms of years, or of any uncertain interest of, in to or out of any messuage, manor, lands, tenements or heritages, made or created by livery of seisin only, or by parol, and not put in writing, and signed by the parties so making or creating the same, or by their agents thereto lawfully authorised by writing, shall have the force and effect of leases and estates at will only", sec. 1. The statute excluded leases for three years or less made at a rent of more than two-thirds of the market rental value. However, any assignment or surrender of a lease had to be made by deed or put in writing. The purpose of the Statute of Frauds was not to overturn contracts between parties merely on the ground of a lack of proper formality, but to prevent a claim to the benefit of a contract that has been brought about by perjury, fraud or similar action. Thus, contracts could still be enforced in equity if there was a sufficient act of **part performance** to support the agreement. In English law, this statute has been largely repealed or replaced by other enactments, notably for lease *not exceeding three years* by the LPA 1925, s. 54(2); and for contracts made on or after that date by LP(MP)A Act 1989, s. 2.

The English statute became effective in the American colonies and in some states has been accepted as part of the common law. All the states, except Louisiana and New Mexico, have adopted a similar statute, with some variations in language to extend or limit the provisions. In most jurisdictions, leases for a term of one year or less are excluded from the provisions of the statute (but not a lease that has a right to be extended for more than one year). Most rights, restrictions or covenants relating to land are affected by the Statute of Frauds and, therefore, must be in writing to be enforceable; although in some jurisdictions an equitable restriction may be enforced even though it is not in writing, and some jurisdictions do not apply the statute to covenants or restrictions as they are not considered 'interests in land'. See also **estoppel, interest, part performance, signature, will.**

American Law Reports, *Annotations and Cases*, Anno: 110 ALR5th 277: Statute of Frauds—E-mail.

Statutes of Limitation 1.[(US)]Federal or state statutes that limit the time during which an action can be started or a right enforced. After the specified period of time, no action can be started to enforce a right or recover a property, even if there was originally a valid course of action. In most states, the time limit within which an action can be brought on a contract is between 4 and 10 years. Claims to title to land by **adverse possession** require from 10 to 20 years uninterrupted possession in most jurisdictions before a counter claim can be defeated. Most other real estate contracts cannot be enforced after 6 years, with a few states requiring as long as 8, 10, 15 or even 20 years. cf. **laches**. See also **adverse possession, limitation.** 2.[(Eng)]Statutes passed to fix a period of time within which proceedings must be taken in order to enforce a legal right of action. If proceedings are not taken within the specified statutory time limits, a right of action is barred. Limitations Acts are negative in that they bar an action; as compared with **prescription**, which creates a new or substituted right to an intangible claim (e.g. an easement) over land.

In English law the principal time limits for actions to be taken in connection with real property, from the "date on which the action accrued", are now consolidated in the Limitation Act 1980 and may be summarised basically as: (a) an action on a simple contract, for arrears of rent, to recover interest on a mortgage (except when there is a previous incumbrancer in possession), and in tort – six years (LA, ss. 2, 5, 19); (b) an action on a contract under seal – twelve years (LA, s. 8); (c) an action to recover any principal sum of money secured by a mortgage or charge, or to recover the proceeds of the sale of land – twelve years (LA, s. 20); (d) an action to redeem land from a mortgagee in possession – twelve years (LA, s. 16); and (e) an action to recover any interest in land (including a foreclosure action) – twelve years (LA, ss. 15, 20(4). It should be noted that "where in the case of any action for which a period of limitation is prescribed by this Act either – (a) the action is based on **fraud** of the defendant, or (b) any fact relevant to the plaintiff's right of action has been deliberately concealed from him by the defendant, or (c) the action is for relief from the consequences of a **mistake**, the period of limitation shall not begin to run until the plaintiff has discovered the fraud, concealment or mistake (as the case may be) or could with reasonable diligence have discovered it", LA 1980, s. 32(1). This postponement of the running of time in cases of fraud, concealment or mistake does not apply to an "innocent third party" who purchases the property for valuable consideration (LA 1980, s. 32(3)). Also, if a party is under a disability (e.g. an infant or of unsound mind) the period may not be deemed to commence until that person ceased to be under the disability or died, whichever occurs first, subject to a long stop of 30 years (LA 1980, s. 28). In the case of a future interest (which includes an interest in **reversion** or **remainder**), the person entitled to the interest may have six years from the date that the interest falls into his possession to bring an action, if that is longer than 12 years from the date the adverse possession is taken (LA 1980, s. 15(2), Sch 1, para 4). See also **adverse possession**.

statutorily protected tenant(Eng) One of a group of 'tenancies' that are referred to as 'statutorily protected tenancies' in the Protection from Eviction Act 1977, s. 8 (as amended) and which are not affected by that statute, but are provided with their own particular form of statutory protection. These tenancies (or rights of occupation) are: (i) a **protected tenancy** (Rent Act 1977); (ii) a **long residential tenancy** (as defined by the L&T Act 1954, Part I); (iii) a right held by a **protected occupier** (Rent (Agriculture) Act 1976); (iv) a **business tenancy** (L&T Act 1954, Part II); (v) an **agricultural tenancy** (AHA 1986); (vi) an **assured tenancy** (including an 'assured agricultural occupancy') (HA 1988, Part I); (g) a tenancy that comes to an end at the end of a **long residential tenancy** (LGHA 1989, Sch. 10); and (vii) a **farm business tenancy** (Agricultural Tenancies Act 1995). See also **assured shorthold tenancy**, **eviction**, **grounds for possession**, **protected shorthold** tenancy, **restricted contract**, **statutory tenancy**.

statutory assignment See **legal assignment**.

statutory charge(Eng) See **statutory mortgage**.

statutory conditions of sale(Eng) See **conditions of sale**.

statutory declaration(Eng) A written statement of facts signed by the person making the declaration and attested by a notary public, Justice of the Peace, or Commissioner for Oaths. The Interpretation Act 1978, Sch. I states that such a declaration is one made in accordance with the Statutory Declarations Act 1835, which has the effect of making a false declaration akin to perjury.

A statutory declaration may be used in extra-judicial proceedings to much the same effect as a declaration made in court under oath. A statutory declaration is generally made when it is not possible to find the true owner of an interest in land; when it is necessary to establish a fact relating to any claim that might affect that interest, e.g. the period of time for which a person has been in possession of land; or when title deeds have been lost. See also **affidavit**, **affirmation**.

statutory dedication　See **dedication**.

statutory estate(US)　An estate or interest in land created by statute law, e.g. a homestead right, dower, curtesy, or community property, as distinguished from an estate created under common law, such as a life estate of a fee tail.

statutory eviction(US)　See **constructive eviction**.

statutory foreclosure(US)　**Foreclosure** that is carried out by an execution of the **power of sale** as contained in a mortgage deed (or lien document) in direct satisfaction of the debt, without recourse to the courts, but strictly in accordance with a state law that regulates such sales (Mowry v. Sanborn, NY, 11 Hun 545, 548). cf. **strict foreclosure**. See also **foreclosure sale**.

Statutory Form of Conditions of Sale(Eng) See **conditions of sale**.

statutory formula(Eng)　See **formula method**.

statutory land use plan(Eng)　See **development plan**.

statutory law　See **statute law**.

statutory lien　See **lien**, **mechanic's lien**.

statutory mortgage(Eng)　A **mortgage** made by deed in one of the forms set out in the LPA 1925, Sch. IV. A 'statutory mortgage' may be made,

or transferred, merely by reference to the schedule to the statute, thereby reducing the length of the mortgage document (LPA 1925, ss. 117, 118). Also called a 'statutory charge'. See also **charge by way of a legal mortgage**.

statutory notice(Eng)　**Notice** given or served in accordance with a statute, e.g. notice given by a landlord, under the L&T Act 1954, s. 25 stating his intention to terminate a **business tenancy**. See also **forfeiture**, **notice to quit**.

statutory nuisance　A **nuisance** that is laid down as such by statute, especially statutes passed to reduce environmental pollution or prevent damage to health, safety or welfare. See also **abatement**.

statutory order(Eng)　See **statutory instrument**.

statutory owner　1. A person who is deemed by statute to be the **owner** of a property.　2.(Eng)A person who is vested with the powers of a **tenant for life** when a life interest has been created by a **strict settlement**, but there is no tenant for life, or when there is no one qualified to act as the tenant for life as when the land has been left to a minor. The statutory owner may be a person of full age designated by the settlement; or the trustees of the settlement (except where they have power to convey the settled land, by order of a court or otherwise, in the name of the tenant for life); or, when the beneficiary of a will is under 18, the personal representative of the testator if no **vesting instrument** has yet been made or otherwise the trustees of the settlement, until the property is independently vested in the beneficiary (SLA 1925, ss. 23, 26, 117(1)(xxvi)).

statutory redemption period(US)　See **statutory right of redemption**.

statutory right of redemption(US)　A statutory right that is available in some states by which the mortgagor (or anyone claiming through or under him and in some cases a junior mortgagor) may redeem the property, within a specified period *after* a **foreclosure sale**, usually by paying the amount tendered at the sale, plus a statutorily prescribed rate of interest and certain other expenses. The statutory period for redemption generally ranges between six months and a year. Such a right is distinct from the common law **equity of redemption** that arises *before* foreclosure or a foreclosure sale.

statutory tenancy(Eng)   **1.** A generic term for a right of occupation that is brought into effect by statute law after a tenancy comes to the end of its contractual term. Strictly, the right is not a tenancy at all but a "status of irremovability", *Keaves v Dean* [1924] 1 KB 685, 686 (CA). The term 'statutory tenancy' may be used to refer to any form of residential tenancy that is given statutory protection, or to the "statutory tenancy" referred to in **2.** below. cf. **contractual tenancy**. See also **statutorily protected tenancy**.   **2.** A right to remain in occupation of a **dwelling-house** (whether a house or part of a house) when a **protected tenancy** comes to an end, or is brought to an end, in accordance with the terms by which it was created (which may be by forfeiture or any other common law method of terminating a contract of tenancy) (RA 1977, s. 2(1)(a)). It is a personal right available to the person, who immediately before the termination of a protected tenancy, was in occupation of a dwelling-house as a protected tenant. A statutory tenancy cannot be assigned or sold and does not pass to the personal representatives of a deceased statutory tenant, nor to a trustee in bankruptcy; and it continues only as long as the tenant "occupies the dwelling-house as his **residence**". On the death of a statutory tenant (or the protected tenant) the right of irremovability may be transmitted either to the surviving spouse (if any) of the original tenant or, otherwise, a "member of the tenant's family", providing the successor was residing with the tenant immediately before his or her death (and for six months prior thereto if the successor was not a spouse). The spouse continues as a statutory tenant, but any other successor is entitled to an

assured tenancy (RA 1977, s. 2(1)(b), Sch. 1, as amended). See also **regulated tenancy**.

statutory tenancy at sufferance(US)   See **tenancy at sufferance**.

statutory trust(Eng)   A trust that arises as a result of a statutory provision. In particular, a trust that arises in cases of co-ownership (whether as a **joint tenancy** or a **tenancy in common**) (LPA 1925, s. 34-36); intestacy (AEA 1925, ss. 33, 47); or a conveyance of a legal estate to an infant (LPA 1925, s. 19). See also **implied trust**, **statutory trust for sale**.

statutory trust for sale(Eng)   A **trust for sale** that expressly or impliedly comes into existence by virtue of statute. A statutory trust for sale may arise when: (i) land is transferred (by devise or conveyance) to two or more persons as tenants in common, i.e. when there is a **tenancy in common** (LPA 1925, s. 34(2)); (ii) land is transferred (by devise or conveyance) for the benefit of two or more persons as joint tenants, i.e. when there is a **joint tenancy** (LPA 1925, s. 36(1)); (iii) a legal estate is conveyed to two or more persons jointly – not as mortgagees or trustees – of whom at least one is an infant (LPA 1925, s. 19(2)); (iv) trustees have taken property that has been freed of a mortgagor's right to repay the debt, as by **foreclosure** (LPA 1925, s. 31); (v) in certain cases, when trustees of a settlement have invested the proceeds of sale of personal property in land (LPA 1925, s. 32(1)); or (vi) a person dies **intestate** and personal representatives are appointed to administer that person's estate (AEA 1925, s. 33(1)). In cases (i)-(v), where the trust arises under the LPA 1925, the land is held under a 'statutory trust' "upon trust to sell the same and to stand possessed of the net proceeds of sale, after payment of costs … and subject to such powers and provisions, as may be required to give effect to the rights of the persons … interested in the land …", LPA 1925, s. 35. Unlike an express trust created to deal with **settled land**, a statutory trust for sale requires the trustees, as far as possible, to respect the wishes of the beneficiaries. The trustees are required to give effect to the rights of those who are interested in the land, i.e. the current beneficiaries, as opposed to those who were interested in the land, i.e. the original settlor. Sometimes called an 'implied trust for sale'.

stay-open clause   A clause in a lease of retail property that requires the tenant to stay open for business during certain stipulated hours. See **continuous operation clause**.

steering(US)   A process by which racial and ethnic groups are encouraged to acquire homes in areas occupied by other members of the same group and discouraged from areas occupied predominately by other racial or ethnic groups. Such a process is illegal under the Fair Housing Act of 1968.

step mortgage   See **step-rate mortgage**.

step-down lease(US)   See **graduated-rental lease**.

step-down rent   See **step-up rent**.

step-rate mortgage   A mortgage loan granted for a long term (usually 20 or 25 years) at an interest rate that increases at predetermined stages during the period of the loan. Such a mortgage, although rare, may be granted to ease the mortgagor's costs in the early years. Sometimes called a 'step mortgage'. See also **adjustable-rate mortgage**.

step-up clause(US)   See **escalator clause**.

step-up in basis(US)   An increase in the **basis** of a property. In particular, the establishment of a new basis when a property is acquired by decedent, which generally is based on the fair market value of the property at death or the alternative valuation as provided in the Code (26 USC, Internal Revenue Code, § 1014).

step-up lease   1. A lease that contains a **step-up rent**.   2.(US)A **graduated-rental lease**, i.e. a lease that contains a rental that increases in stages,

either by specified amounts or by being based on periodic reappraisals.

step-up rent or **step-down rent**   A form of **graduated rent** that starts at a low (or high) level, especially a level that is well below (or above) market value, and increases (or decreases) automatically at stages during the term of the lease, normally until it reaches the market rent current at the time at which the lease was entered into.

stepped rent   See **graded rent**.

stet(Lat)   'Let it stand'.

stinted pasture   The right to turn out as many, but no more, cattle onto **common land** as is sufficient to manure and stock the land. A common of pasture 'without stint' means that the number of cattle is 'unmeasured', i.e. not properly ascertained (3 *Bl Comm* 239). The right of pasture may also be 'stinted', i.e. limited, in respect of time. See also **cattlegate**.

stipulated damages   See **liquidated damages**.

stipulatio(Civ)   'Stipulation'. An undertaking or security for the performance of a contract. In Roman law, the most formal type of contract.

stipulation   A formal requirement or express demand that forms part of an agreement. A statement that may be a mere admission of a fact or may form an article or constituent clause of a contract. An item specified in a contract. In particular, a **condition** that restricts the action of one or more of the parties to a contract. See also **proviso**, **restrictive covenant**.

stock   1. Property held for sale, leasing, development or similar future use or occupation. See also **inventory**, **land bank**.   2. Capital invested in or lent to a business or enterprise. An ownership or **equity** interest in a corporation. The aggregate of the shares (ordinary or preferential) of a corporation or joint-stock company; but not the unsecured loans. Stock may be distinguished from a **share** by being fully paid up, whereas a share may be part paid. Also, 'share' may be used to refer to one or a number of ownership interests, as in 3,000 shares, and stock as a more generic term, as in a 20% 'stock holder'.

In the US, stock refers particularly to 'capital stock' or 'common stock', which provides an ownership interest in a corporation, with a right to a dividend payment out of profits, but with no priority over other stockholders. In the UK, and many other countries, 'stock' is used particularly to refer to debentures or the preferred stock of a company, which do not provide the holder with any ownership interest, or to bonds issued by a government or a municipal authority. cf. **bond**, **debenture**. See also **security**. **3.** A fixed-interest security granted by a government authority. **4.** An estate or property that produces income. **5.** A family, or a line of descent. An ancestor from whom others are descended. The first person to hold property that is to be transmitted by **succession**.

stop list   See **blacklist**.

stop notice   1.(US)A notice served upon a construction lender (or sometimes the owner of a property) by a subcontractor or supplier who has not been paid for work or services provided in connection with the construction project for which the lender is providing funding. The notice requires a portion of the undisbursed construction loan proceeds to be set aside for the payment of an amount due to the subcontractor or supplier. The right to serve a stop notice, which is only available in a few states, is derived entirely from state statutes. It is intended to provide extra protection for unpaid subcontractors and suppliers, especially when a **mechanic's lien** might be of limited effect due to the priority of the construction lender in respect of all future advances. The lender may remove the notice by paying the amount due to the appropriate debtor or he may dispute the amount and the parties

would then have to resort to an alternative course of action.   **2.**(Eng)A notice served by a local authority (or, in some cases, the Secretary of State) upon any person who has an interest in land, or any person who is carrying on an activity on land, that is the subject of an **enforcement notice**, stipulating that a "relevant activity" being carried out on the land must be stopped within a specified period (in most cases being not less than three days nor more than twenty eight days) (TCPA 1990, s. 184). A stop notice may be served after an enforcement notice has been served in order to prevent further activity until the outcome of the enforcement notice has been decided, but the stop notice must be served before the enforcement notice takes effect. The effect of a stop notice is to bring an enforcement notice into immediate effect and thus require the suspension of all further activity on the land. A stop notice is a temporary expedient against which there is no appeal.

store   A building where goods are kept, as well as being displayed for sale to the general public. In particular, a place where a large variety of goods are made available for sale whether wholesale or retail. In the US, 'store' is commonly used to refer to a business establishment where goods are kept for retail sale and in that respect corresponds to the term **shop** as used in British English. Whereas in British English 'store' is commonly used to refer to a place where goods are kept, which may be part of a retail establishment or other commercial premises, or a separate **warehouse**, **garage**, or similar building. In the latter respect, the term corresponds generally to 'storehouse' as used in American English. Also, in American English, 'store' is used to refer to a building in which goods are stored by the government, as with a military store or a building in which imported goods are kept under bond. See also **chain store**, **department store**, **retail store**, **warehouse**.

storehouse   A building for the storing of goods of any kind; a repository. See also **store**, **warehouse**.

storey(BrE) or **story**(AmE)   All those parts of a building on the same floor level, especially at a level above the ground. The space in a building between consecutive floor levels, or between the highest floor level and the roof. "Each of a number of tiers or rows (of orders, columns, window mullions or lights, etc.) disposed horizontally one above another", *The Oxford English Dictionary*, 2nd ed., 1989. Probably derived from a practice in medieval times of painting a series of pictures on mullions or horizontal bands set out between windows to depict a tale or story. When describing the height of a building the number of 'stories' (or 'storeys') does not normally include the basement, although a basement is *in esse* a storey. See also **basement**.

straight capitalization(AmE)   The **capitalization** of an income by the application of a single factor, or multiplier, which assumes that the income is receivable in perpetuity; as compared with **annuity capitalization** which applies a factor, based on the present value of one unit, for a given period of time. Also called 'direct capitalization'. In the UK, the application of a **years' purchase** (YP) in perpetuity is equivalent to straight capitalization and the application of a YP for a period of time is equivalent to annuity capitalization. See also **overall capitalization rate**.

straight lease(US)   A lease with a rent that is fixed throughout its term, i.e. with a **flat rent**.

straight-line depreciation   A method of allowing for **depreciation** by which the cost of an asset, or the total amount to be written off, is divided by the number of years over which the asset is to be depreciated, and the resulting quotient deducted each year from the initial amount. In accounting, an allowance is made each year of an equal amount, or a fixed percentage, which is set against the profits of a company to provide for the replacement cost of the asset at the end of its economic life. This method of deprecation assumes that the asset being depreciated declines in value at a constant rate over its estimated life. The depreciation may be applied over the estimated **physical life** of the building, or the **economic life** which takes account of the functional and economic attributes of the building. For example, a building may have an estimated physical life of 30 years, but due to good maintenance it may have an economic life of 50 years. Accordingly the depreciation is applied over the longer period. In assessing the 'value' of a property under the cost basis(AmE), or based on the depreciated replacement cost(BrE), the economic life is generally more appropriate. Depreciation based on the economic life is sometimes called the 'economic age-life method of depreciation' or the 'age-life method'. cf. **accelerated depreciation**.

straight-line recapture   The **recapture** of the cost of an investment by equal periodic amounts.

straight lining or **straightlining**(AmE)   Averaging the rents payable by the tenant over the remaining life of the lease. Rent receivable under many commercial lease increases over the term of the lease, as a result of straight lining the total rent is divided by the unexpired term, as a result the revenue is overestimated in the early years and underestimated in the later years.

straight loan   See standing loan, unsecured loan.

straight pass-through   A mortgage-backed security that provides for the purchaser of the securities to receive payments based entirely on the amounts collected from the mortgagors without any form of collateral insurance or income guarantee.

straight rent(US)   See flat rent.

straight-term loan   See standing loan.

straight-up participation(US)   See side-by-side participation.

straight yield   See **running yield**.

strata office(Aus)   An office that is owned by **strata title**. Generally used in agency to refer to an office floor or floors that are being offered for sale in the form of strata ownership.

strata plan(Aus)   A plan that sets out the physical details of all the elements of a property that is held under **strata ownership**. A strata plan includes a location plan, details of each individual 'lot' or unit and the common property, shows easements that affect the property, and sets out the distribution of rights and liabilities between the units. When this plan is registered at the Land Titles Office it brings into existence a **strata scheme**.

strata scheme(Aus)   The **subdivision** of land into separate lots that are to be sold as **strata title**. The land is subdivided into lots for sale and common property that is to be held by a corporate body for the benefit of the unit holders. The strata scheme sets out the regulations for the use and development of the individual lots, the management of the common areas and the relationship between the individual owners. See also **strata plan**.

strata title   A form of **co-ownership** of property, established for example in Australia and New Zealand, by which land is subdivided into two or more 'stratas' or cubic spaces of thin air, with individual owners acquiring title to individual spaces or lots- in substance, a space within the confines of a wall, floor and ceiling, with undivided rights over the common areas. A corporate body holds the common areas, with the individual unit holders having a share in that body. A strata title is effected by the recording of a division of a building into different layers and the issuance of certificates of title that recognises the separate units of ownership, as well as the ownership of the common property. The body corporate is responsible for the management of the building and the upkeep of the common areas, including the enforcement of the by-laws that are imposed on the individual owners and for raising the levies from the individual owners to pay for repairs and insurance. Similar to a **condominium** as found in North America or a **commonhold** as now found in the UK. See also **strata plan**.

Bugden, Gary F. *Strata Title Management Practice in New South Wales*. 6th ed. Sydney: CCH Australia, 1993.
Ilkin, Alex. *Strata Title and Community Title Management and the Law*. 3rd ed. North Ryde, NSW: LBC Information Services, 1998.

strategic plan   See **regional plan**.

stratum estate   1.(Aus)A fee simple interest in a part of a building that is subdivided so that individual owners may hold different stratas of the building. See also **flying freehold**.   2.(NZ)A right to a **unit** of land, or a unit in a building, where such property is subdivided into similar units, together with a right over the common parts. An estate that comprises "(a) the fee simple (or, as the case may be, the estate as lessee or licensee) in the unit … ; and (b) the undivided share in the fee simple estate (or, as the case may be, the estate as lessee or licensee) in the common property to which the proprietor of the unit is entitled; and (c) the undivided share in the fee simple estate (or, as the case may be, the estate as lessee or licensee) in all the units to which the proprietor of the unit is entitled if the unit plan should be cancelled", Unit Titles Act 1972, s. 4. See also **strata title**.

stream   A course or body of water that runs under gravity in a narrow defined channel on or under the surface of the ground. A narrow, natural course of water forming a small **river**, rivulet or brook. A seepage or percolation of water that does not run in a defined course is not a stream, but water running in a course underground, or under a glacier, can be a stream. In common usage, any flowing body of water may be referred to as a 'stream' of water. See also *ad medium filum aquæ*, **riparian rights**, **water rights**, **watercourse**.

street A thoroughfare or roadway, especially in an urban community, that is generally paved and provides a public right of access for vehicles and pedestrians (although either or both may be restricted to some degree). In particular, a way that has houses or other buildings running in a more or less continuous row along one or both sides. 'Street' includes the gutters, curbs, sidewalks or footpath that run alongside, and in common parlance the word may be used to refer to the houses or buildings on either side.

A street may be distinguished from a **road** where the emphasis is on the coming and going, whereas in a street the primary concern is with access to and from houses or buildings. Thus, a **cul-de-sac** or **dead-end street** is a street, although it may also be called a 'road'. Generally, a street is wider than an **alley**; narrower than a boulevard; separates blocks of buildings; acts primarily as a means of local passage; and may be contrasted with a 'road' which runs right through a city, town or village. A street is more usually defined as a public way, but can also be a 'private street' as where it serves a privately gated residential area.

In English statute law, 'street' may be given an extended meaning so as to encompass a way or area that would, not necessarily be covered in the ordinary meaning of the word; for example, a street "includes any **highway** and any road, lane, footpath, square, court, alley, or passage, whether a thoroughfare or not, and includes part of a street", Highways Act 1980, s. 329(1)). A similar definition is contained in the Public Health Act 1936, s. 343(1) and in various statutes dealing with public utilities and road traffic.

street works(Eng) Works carried out, normally by a highway authority, in order to provide or maintain a **street**, including drainage work, surfacing or resurfacing, paving, making good a street and the provision or repair of lighting (Highways Act 1980, s. 203 (3)).

strict foreclosure(US) The judicial process by which a mortgagee is able to **foreclosure** on mortgaged property so that, after the mortgagor has been given a fixed time (usually six months to a year) to repay his outstanding debt and the debt remains unpaid, the property is vested absolutely in the mortgagee. Strict foreclosure is started by a 'foreclosure suit' by which the mortgagee seeks to have title to the property vested in him, without resorting to a sale of the property. The courts may accede to that request after the mortgagor is given time to remedy any defect, but in some cases the courts may insist on a sale of the property, especially if it has a value in excess of the outstanding debt. Once the court has issued an order or decree of foreclosure the mortgagor has no subsequent right of **redemption** or the right, as in some jurisdictions, to insist on a **foreclosure sale**. The effect of strict foreclosure is to vest title to the property in the mortgagee and bar the mortgagor's **equity of redemption**. Strict foreclosure is rarely used and is now only recognized in a few states.

strict liability Liability without fault. In a real property context, a term primarily of English law that refers to a liability for damage or injury for which a person is culpable, irrespective of any intentional, inadvertent or meditated neglect. A liability that arises because a person is involved with an exceptional or hazardous activity, or because someone exerts control over dangerous property. Strict liability is a form of **tort** for which the law allows little scope for an evasion of blame because there is an unnatural element of danger attached to the activity that is carried out on the land.

Strict liability may arise in English law from: (i) the bringing or keeping of something on land that is likely to cause damage or injury if it escapes; (ii) the keeping of animals that belong to a dangerous species or are known to have dangerous characteristics, or keeping animals in terrifying circumstances; or (iii) the ownership or use of dangerous or defective property, or the conducting of hazardous operations on land. In respect of (i), it was said by Blackburn J., when establishing the 'rule in *Rylands v Fletcher*', that "the person who for his own purposes brings on his lands and collects and keeps there anything likely to do mischief if it escapes, must keep it in at his peril, and if he does not do so, is *prima facie* answerable for all the damage which is a natural consequence of its escape", *Rylands v Fletcher* (1868) LR 1 Ex 265, 279, aff'd LR 3 HL 330, 339 (HL) (*Cambridge Water Co v Eastern Leather Plc* [1994] 2 WLR 53 (HL)). This liability extends for example, to the escape of water from a reservoir (as in *Rylands v Fletcher*); the escape of noxious waste, gas, vibration or even noxious persons; and the escape of fire (except when a fire starts accidentally, and without gross negligence: Fire Prevention (Metropolis) Act 1774, s. 86). In respect of (iii) a person is strictly liable for injury if he (a) keeps explosives, poisons, etc.; (b) is responsible for dangerous premises; or (c) carries on any dangerous activity on land.

In the US, although the term 'strict liability' is used in the above context, it is more generally used to refer to the liability of manufacturers for their products or the liability of an employer to an employee during the performance of his or her duties. Nonetheless, whatever the context, an owner of land is liable for abnormally dangerous or "extrahazardous" occupation or use of his land. Injury or damage resulting from 'strict liability' may include such events as an accident while drilling for oil; damage from the storage of high explosives; concussion caused by blasting; and the escape of sprayed pesticides. Also, in a few jurisdictions, a landlord may have a strict liability for injury to a tenant caused by a defect in the premises that existed at the time the premises were let. Also called 'liability without fault' or 'absolute liability'.

Leigh, L. H. *Strict and Vicarious Liability.* London: Sweet & Maxwell, 1982.

strict settlement(Eng)   A **settlement** of land that is created when a person is seeking to ensure that his or her estate will be preserved intact for future generations, i.e. so that land itself may be 'kept in the family'. A strict settlement of land (called the **settled land**) may be made by deed, will, an agreement for a settlement or other instrument (or occasionally by Act of Parliament), when a landowner wishes to ensure that a succession of persons will enjoy the benefits of using, owning and controlling land; and not, as with a **trust for sale**, the enjoyment of the land primarily as an investment or as a source of income, or merely a claim over the proceeds of sale. The Settled Land Act 1925, which governs the creation and disposition of settled land, provides that a number of similar interests in land, however created, are to be treated as strict settlements (referred to in the Act merely as a "settlement" (SLA 1925, ss. 1, 117(xxiv))). On or after January 1, 1997 no new strict settlement can be created and any grant of land to be held in succession is held as a **trust of land** (Trusts of Land and Appointment of Trustees Act 1996, s. 2). See also **base fee**, **entailed interest**, **estate owner**, **rule against perpetuities**.

strip center(AmE)   An open-air **shopping center** that is made up of a row of stores served by a readily accessible common parking lot, and usually designed to serve a small district or neighborhood area. A strip center may have a canopied walkway along the store frontage, but it does not have a fully enclosed walkway or mall. A strip center generally has a dedicated service yard to the rear. Sometimes called an 'open center'.

strip development(US)   See **ribbon development**.

stripped mortgage-backed security (SMBS)   A **mortgage-backed security** that provides for the payment of separate amounts of interest and principal from the underlying securities. See also **split trust**.

structural alteration or **structural change**   An **alteration** or change that affects the **structure** of a building. An alteration that affects the vital nature or characteristic appearance of a building. In a lease that prohibits structural alterations, this normally extends to any alterations, modifications or works that affect the main structural elements of the building, especially any work that may affect the structural integrity of the building. Similarly, a structural change is one that affects the vital or essential structural elements of a building, especially a change to the structural appearance.

structural defect Any defect in the **structure** of a building. A defect that affects an integral part of the structure or something that immediately supports it. In particular, a defect that renders a building unsafe for use or occupation. See also **latent defect**.

structural repair **Repair** to the **structure** or main fabric of a building. Structural repair includes repair to the foundations, main walls, floors, the roof and any associated elements, but not the windows doors and the services such as a generator of elevator. The main water supply and the drains may be considered part of the structure as they are usually an integral part thereof, but items such as a downspout or cables are not.

In English law, a covenant in a lease that the landlord will carry out structural repairs has been held to be limited to that effect; it does not require the carrying out of repair to the finishes or decorative work (*Granada Theatres v Freehold Investments (Leytonstone) Ltd* [1959] Ch 592, [1959] 1 All ER 176 (CA)). See also **external**, **implied covenant**, **latent defect**.

structural survey A **survey** of the **structure** of a building primarily to ascertain its functional integrity. The inspection and investigation of the structural elements of the property in sufficient detail to advise the client on any aspects that might impact on the future structural integrity of the property. In particular, the survey should report on any aspects that fall short of the minimum legal requirements for the use of the property and advise on any work that will be required to maintain the property in its current use. A structural survey is normally only limited to an inspection of the visible, exposed and accessible parts of the fabric of the building. However, the survey report should

refer to any noticeable problems that may require further testing or investigation and any defects (such as the use of deleterious materials or wood boring insects) that are common to the particular property given its age, general condition or mode of construction.

structure Derived from the Latin *stuere*, 'to heap together' or 'to build'. An object that is made of component parts, especially one that comprises different things that are held together in some way. Something that is built or constructed, whether on, above or below the ground (or the sea) and that is of substantial size. Any **edifice**, **building** or **construction**, or something that is built or constructed in the nature of a building. Although every building is a structure, not every structure is a building. Thus, a bridge is a structure, but not a building. 'Structure' may be used to refer to components that are put together in a particular way, as for the creation of a building, a stadium or a monument.

Commonly 'structure' is used to refer to the main frame or load-bearing parts of a building; as well as to the walls, panels, floors, windows, doorways, the roof, and any other erections that are an integral and interdependent part thereof, especially when an adjunct of or an ancillary to a building. In particular, a structure is something of a substantial nature; built as a whole, usually from a number of different parts or components; and, generally, erected as a permanent edifice. The structure comprises the primary parts of a building, which may include the water supply, drainage, etc., but not the internal fixtures, fittings, finishings and decorations. A structure is something of a substantial size that is built up from component parts and intended to remain permanently on a permanent foundation. Anything permanently attached to a building may become part of the structure; but anything that can be moved from place to place, although in the nature of a structure, in general is not regarded as a structure. When a building is completed the primary components are essentially a structure, but anything added subsequently, which does not alter the building, is not normally a structural element; although it may be a **fixture** and thus become part of the structure. See also **infrastructure**.

structure plan(Eng)   See **development plan**.

structured finance   See **securitization**.

studio   1. Derived from the Latin *studere*, 'to study'. A room or space comprised predominately of one open area that is used for study or artistic activities. A place used for work that has some artistic endeavour, such as a workplace for a painter, sculptor, photographer, architect or designer. See also **efficiency apartment**, **loft**, **studio apartment**.   2. A room or building used for the production of motion pictures or for radio or television broadcasting.

studio apartment   An apartment that is contained primarily in one open area, which comprises the living and sleeping space and sometimes the kitchen area, but generally with a separate bathroom and toilet area. A small compact apartment, especially one that has been created by the conversion of an older building that has high ceilings and large windows. Commonly called a **studio** for short.

subagent or **sub-agent**   A subordinate **agent**. A person, or organisation, appointed by one who is himself an agent in order to carry out the duties or responsibilities, or a part thereof, entrusted to that agent, or to assist the principal agent in performing the duties entrusted to him. An agent, the main or principal agent, may not appoint another, as subagent, to perform duties or act in a capacity beyond the powers conferred on the main agent. An agent is entrusted with particular power and authority by the principal, which normally requires elements of acumen, skill, discretion or judgement, and that power or authority is not intended to be passed to another. The maxim is *delegatus non potest delegare* 'a delegated party cannot be delegate' and this maxim that an agent cannot,

without authority from his principal, devolve upon others obligations to the principal that the agent has undertaken to personally fulfil (*De Busche v Alt* (1878) 8 Ch D 286, 310 (CA); 3 Am.Jur.2d., Agency, § 7, 154). However, there may be instances where delegation is an acceptable part of the nature or custom of a particular business, or it may be necessary in an emergency.

An agent may be authorised (expressly or by implication) to appoint a subagent and, in that event, the subagent may be considered as the agent of the principal if he has effective control of the business and the principal is aware of his appointment. Unless there is an express or implied agreement to the contrary, or the agent was authorised to employ a subagent, there is no **privity of contract** between a principal and a subagent. Thus, the principal cannot sue the subagent for **negligence** (unless the subagent was employed in a special capacity for which he may owe a **duty of care** to the principal or the principal accepted the liability of the subagent for the work being performed). For the same reason, a subagent cannot claim a **commission** from the principal; he must claim from the agent who employed him, unless the principal agrees to remunerate the subagent or impliedly recognises that obligation. See also **subcontractor**, **power of attorney**, **ratification**.

sub-agreement   See **sub-sale**.

sub-basement   A storey, or one of several such stories, situated below the first basement of a building.

sub-charge   A **charge** issued against the security of an existing charge or mortgage debt.

subcontract   A **contract** entered into by a party who has executed a contract with third party. In particular, a contract entered into by a general building contractor with a **subcontractor** who in turn undertakes to perform part of the work or supply materials needed in the performance of the main contract.

subcontractor   **1.** One who has entered into a contract, express or implied, to carry out all or part of the duties or obligation that have been contracted for by another party. A person or firm that undertakes to perform a duty or obligation, in whole or in part, for which another has accepted a direct contractual obligation. In particular, a firm that is employed by a main or **general contractor** to carry out work that forms part of the contractual obligations of that general contractor, especially work of a specialised nature, e.g. mechanical, electrical, plumbing or finishing work under a building contract, or the supply of specialist materials required under the main contract. A subcontractor has an obligation, or **privity of contract**, with his principal, master or employer (the main contractor); but, as a rule, has no contractual relationship with the party (the main employer) for whom the work or duty ultimately is being performed. A contracting party is free to transfer work to another, i.e. to enter into a new contract (a subcontract), unless expressly prohibited or unless it is clearly contrary to the basis for the foundation of the contract; but in so doing, he cannot assign his duties. See also **nominated subcontractor, subagent**.   **2.** See **sub-purchaser**.

subdivision   **1.** The division of a lot, tract or parcel of **land**, either vertically or horizontally, into two or more lots, parcels or sites for the purpose of sale, lease or development either immediately or at a future date. See also **parceling**(AmE)/**parcelling**(BrE), **partition**.   **2.** An area of undeveloped land that has been divided into separate lots, especially for sale to individual purchasers who intend to build on the lots. In the US, in most jurisdictions, land cannot be subdivided for sale without prior approval by the local municipality. This usually requires the registration of a map – 'subdivision plat' or 'plat of subdivision' – showing the dimensions of the individual lots and associated developments such as streets, utilities, lighting, sewer lines, etc. (American Law Reports, *Annotations and Cases*, Anno: 11 ALR2d 524: Subdivision Maps or Plats).

See also **planned unit development, reciprocal negative easement, statement of record**.
Lovell, Douglas D., and R. S. Martin. *Subdivision Analysis*. Chicago: Appraisal Institute, 1993.

subdivision plat(US)   See **subdivision**.

subinfeudation or **subfeudation**(Eng)   See **feudal system**.

subjacent support   **1.** The support that land receives from the underlying strata of the earth. cf. **lateral support**. See also **natural rights, right of support**.   **2.** The support that the upper part of a building receives from the lower part.

subject plan(Eng)   See **development plan**.

subject to   **1.** Words that limit or qualify a contract, especially words that create a **conditional contract**. The words 'subject to' (and similar connotations) are regularly used in English contract law; whereas in American practice more pedantic language is required, such as 'conditional upon the lessor's approval' for 'subject to the landlord's consent'). Words that usually indicate that the contract is not to take effect until a specified **condition** has been fulfilled or a specified event has occurred. Words such as 'conditional upon' and 'depending on' have a similar meaning. See also **contingent sale contract, letter of intent, subject to contract, subject to finance, subject to survey, words of limitation**.   **2.** Words used to introduce items to which the subject matter of a contract is limited, or upon which the contract is made conditional, such as defects of title, encumbrances, liens, restrictions, prohibitions, etc. See also **exception**.

subject to average   See **average**.

subject to contract   Words used, primarily in English law, especially in connection with contracts relating to real property, to indicate that something set down in writing is not intended to commit the writer until a **formal contract** is exchanged (*Law v Jones* [1974] Ch 112, [1973] 2 All ER 437 (CA)). In English law, since 1989, there is a strict requirement that contracts for the sale of land are made in **writing** (LP(MP)A 1989, s. 2). Accordingly, the use of the words 'subject to contract' may be considered to be less effective in mitigating the possibility of creating a binding contract, whether orally, by correspondence or any other form of memoranda (or a combination thereof). However, the use of the words 'subject to contract' helps to ensure that no binding contract is created, through notes or correspondence, until a formal document is completed and signed. On the other hand, a binding contract may still come into effect if a court would be able to decide from the signed documentation that the statutory requirements have been met. Furthermore, the use of the words 'subject to contract' continues to be applicable to contracts that are expressly excluded from the statutory provision (LP(MP)A 1989, s. 2(5)).

The use of the words 'subject to contract' may have a negating effect on the intention of the parties. For example, if a notice served by a landlord to increase the rent payable by a tenant is made 'subject to contract', the tenant could take it that the landlord's intention is that the rent the landlord is seeking is not necessarily to be based on the figure in the notice, but on a figure ascertained after negotiation; thus, the notice amount would have no legal effect. The use of such words to indicate an intention not to be contractually bound is recognised primarily in English law and may be of little effect elsewhere. See also **agreement for a lease, conditional contract, estoppel, gazump, gentleman's agreement, negotiation, oral contract, subject to, subject to finance, subject to survey, waiver**.

subject to finance or subject to financing

An agreement between two parties for the transfer of an interest in property, subject to a condition that the purchaser can obtain satisfactory financing. A form of conditional (or even contingent) contract that is likely to be considered void for uncertainty, unless the terms

and basis upon which the financing is to be arranged can be readily established.

In English law, the courts will generally not enforce a contract 'subject to finance', or 'subject to a satisfactory mortgage', as it is considered similar to an agreement **subject to contract**; the parties by the use of such words indicating an intention not to be bound until the finance is obtained and a formal contract is entered into (*Lee-Parker v Izzet (No. 2)* [1972] 1 WLR 775, [1972] 2 All ER 800).

In the US (where such a contract may be called a 'contingent finance offer'), and in many Commonwealth countries, the courts are more likely to enforce a contract 'subject to finance' when: (i) the type and terms of the loan being sought are specified (usually within set criteria); (ii) a time limit is set in which the finance must be sought and obtained; (iii) the purchaser undertakes to act in good faith and to use his best endeavours to secure a reasonable loan on the terms specified; and (iv) a provision is made whereby the seller has the ability to procure a loan on behalf of a purchaser if the purchaser has not taken steps to do so. See also **conditional contract, ready willing and able**.

subject to mortgage

1.(US)An arrangement by which the purchaser, or grantee, of a property acquires the property with an existing mortgage left in place, but does not accept any personal liability for the mortgage debt. In effect, the vendor remains personally liable to the mortgagee for the mortgage debt and, as between the vendor and purchaser, it is agreed that in the event the debt is to be satisfied out of the property, or by the vendor. The transfer of a property to another party 'subject to mortgage' does not relieve the mortgagor of his personal responsibility for the debt, unless the mortgagee expressly agrees. In any event, a sale subject to mortgage may only be made if there is no **due-on-sale clause** in the mortgage deed, or if the prior consent of the mortgagee has been obtained.

A purchaser 'subject to mortgage' does not automatically, but normally does agree to pay the interest or principal repayments under the mortgage agreement. The vendor accepts that, if the purchaser defaults in meeting his obligations, the property can be lost to the mortgagee or disposed of by foreclosure sale and the grantor may then be personally liable for any deficiency. On the other hand, the vendor retains the right to repay the loan in full and in that case he has a right of **subrogation** of the mortgagee's rights and may foreclose on the property as against the purchaser. cf. **assumption**. See also **acceleration clause, due-on-sale clause, reduction certificate**. **2.** See **conditional contract, subject to finance**.

subject to prior sale A term used, especially by real estate agents, to signify that a property may be withdrawn from the market or from a proposed **auction** sale, at any stage if a contract for sale is entered into with another party, i.e. the vendor is not bound to accept an offer or submit the property for sale by auction if he chooses to dispose of the property to another party, or he decides to retain the property. See also **gazump, subject to contract**.

subject to survey A phrase that may be added to an offer, or incorporated in an agreement, to indicate that a prospective purchaser does not intend to proceed with a purchase, unless he is able to obtain a physical or structural survey report that he deems to be satisfactory. See also **conditional contract, ready willing and able, subject to contract**.

sublandlord(US) See **head tenant**.

sub-lease or **sublease** A **lease** granted by an existing lessee to a third party of the same demised property, but for a term that is shorter than that held by the grantor. A grant of part of the interest held under a lease, but with the retention by the grantor of some part of the unexpired term of that lease. The portion held by the grantor is termed the **reversion**. A sub-lease of all or part of the demised premises may be granted for any period that is shorter than the term

held, provided the sub-lessor retains some interest in the land granted (even for as short as one day), otherwise the grant constitutes an **assignment** of the lessor interest. The authorities on the distinction between a sub-lease and an assignment are "to be found dealt with at length in all the textbooks, and perhaps the most authoritative reference that I can give with regard to them is in Platt on Lease (vol. I, pp. 9-19). There are ten pages of discussion of the authorities. ... I [Lord Greene] think it is sufficient to say that, in accordance with a very ancient and established rule, where a lessee, by a document in the form of a sub-lease, divests himself of everything he has got ... he from that moment is a stranger to the land, in the sense that the relationship of landlord and tenant, in respect of tenure, cannot any longer exist between him and the so called sub-lessee. That relationship must depend on **privity of estate**", *Milmo v Carreras* [1946] KB 306, 311-312 [1946] 1 All ER 288, 290 (CA) (49 Am. Jur.2d., L & T, § 1077).

Note: sub-lease is generally hyphenated in British English (as in the *Oxford English Dictionary*), but not in American English (as in *Webster's Third New International Dictionary, Unabridged*). cf. **concurrent lease**. See also **head lease, intermediate lease, relief, restraint on alienation, sub-lessee, surrender**.

sub-lessee or **sublessee** A lessee or tenant who holds an interest in property by virtue of a **sub-lease**, i.e. one who holds a right under a lease from a lessor who himself holds an interest by virtue of a lease. At common law, there is no **privity of contract** between the original lessor and a subtenant, so that no right of action exists between those parties; any action must be taken directly between the head lessor (L) and his tenant (T), or between (T) and his subtenant (ST). Similarly, if T has an option to renew the lease this does not entitle the ST to the same rights. Also, at common law, ST's interest comes to an end if T's interest is brought to an end by forfeiture; but not if it is a voluntary surrendered, as the surrender transfers T's interest subject to ST's rights. This latter principle is reinforced by English statute law, so that on a surrender or a merger of L and T's interests, ST effectively steps into T's shoes (LPA 1925, ss. 139, 150)). On the other hand, a unilateral termination of the head lease (as by the service of a valid notice to quit by L) will terminate the sub-lease, unless the sub-lessee has a statutory right to retain possession. Also called, especially in English law, a 'subtenant' or sometimes an 'underlessee'. See also **attornment**.

sub-lessor or **sub-lessor**   A lessee or tenant who grants a **sub-lease** to another, one who holds a lease and grants a lease of the same property to another, retaining to himself a **reversionary interest**. Also called, especially in English law, an 'underlessor'.

sub-let or **sublet**   1. To grant a **sub-lease**. Synonymous with under-let. cf. **assign**.   2. To enter into a contract with a **subcontractor**.

sub-mortgage or **submortgage**   A **mortgage** granted upon the security of an existing mortgage, i.e. a mortgage of an existing mortgagee's interest in a property. Sometimes called a 'derivative mortgage' or a 'mortgage of a mortgage'.

subordination   The arranging of rights or things in order of rank or **priority**. In particular, the act of moving a mortgage (or lien) to a lower priority. The process by which a debtor agrees to reduce his right to make a claim behind that of another party. In particular, an agreement by which a mortgagee accepts that in the event of a default by his mortgagor he will permit a party who has a lower priority to take precedence in making his claim against the mortgaged property or the proceeds of sale. For example, a seller of land who has been granted a purchase money mortgage against land that is to be subdivided and resold may agree to defer or subordinate his claim in favour of a lender who agrees to provide finance for the development of the subdivided lots in return for a higher interest rate or a share of the proceeds of sale of the subdivided lots. See also **second mortgage**.

subordination agreement   1. An agreement by which the holder of a mortgage or lien agrees to defer his **priority** in favour of another lender or lien holder. Such an agreement may be entered into to establish the priority of two or more mortgages executed on the same property at the same time. Such an agreement may also be entered into to change the priority of an existing mortgage in favour of a new mortgagee, as when a purchaser of development land has granted an purchase money mortgage to the vendor but now needs to grant a first mortgage to a new lender to finance construction, but wishes to retain the purchase money loan as a second charge on the property. See also **subordination**, **subordination non-disturbance and attornment agreement**.   2. An agreement by which an owner of leased property agrees to defer his rights to the collection of rents, or take possession, in favour of a mortgagee in the event of a default under a loan secured on the leased property.

subordination clause   A clause in a mortgage by which a junior mortgagee agrees that the senior mortgagee will maintain his **priority** in the event of a renewal or refinancing of the senior mortgage.

subordination, non-disturbance and attornment agreement (SNDAA)[US]   An agreement between a lender and a tenant that provides for: (a) **subordination** of the tenant's interest, i.e. that interest is to remain subordinate to the rights of the lender's mortgage or deed of trust; (b) non-disturbance of the tenant's rights under the lease, provided the tenant complies with the terms of the lease; and (c) **attornment** by the tenant, i.e. the tenant agrees he will continue to fulfil all his obligations under the lease in the event of a foreclosure sale, deed-in-lieu of foreclosure or a similar transfer of the lender's interest.

sub-purchaser   A person who acquires property from another immediately after that other acquires the property, especially when one party contracts to buy a property then, simultaneously, undertakes to resell it to another, a 'sub-purchaser'; thus the first purchaser acts purely as a conduit for the sub-purchaser. See also **lien, sub-sale**.

sub-regional center   See **shopping center**.

subrogation   Literally 'to ask in another's place'. The substitution of a third party for an existing party to a contract so that the third party may enforce a claim arising from that contract, in the same way as the existing party. The principle of subrogation (sometimes called the 'substitution doctrine') provides that if one person discharges the debt or liability of another then the former may take the place of the latter for any resultant claim against a third party. Thus, if A owes money to B, and C discharges that debt, then C has a right to recover money from any third party who owes money to A, as if he were in A's place for that purpose. C must have been under some obligation regarding the debt (for example if he has acted as a **surety**), or have some interest to be protected when paying the debt, and must discharge the debt in its entirety. In such cases by paying the debt equity acknowledges C's right to be reimbursed by taking over rights, remedies or claims available to A; even though those rights and claims have not been expressly assigned or ceded to C. The substituted party takes over all the rights and duties of the original party, even though effectively the contract may not have been formally assigned to him. In **insurance**, the insurer has a right of subrogation, that is a right to pursue the insured's claims against a third party in respect of the insured property in order to reduce or mitigate the amount of loss or residual liability of the insurer. In particular, the insurer may take over property for which he has paid an **indemnity** to cover its loss. The insurer is entitled to step into the insured's shoes and benefit from any right or claim that would be available to the insured in respect of the subject matter of the insurance, provided that any sum so recovered is limited to the loss for which the insurer has provided an indemnity, i.e. he may recover only what he has

actually paid by way of indemnity to the insured. cf. **abandonment, novation**. See also **guarantee**.

subrogee   One who is entitled to collect the debts due to a third party; one who is entitled to assume a right of **subrogation**.

subrogor   One whose rights have been taken over by another (the 'subrogee') under an act of **subrogation**.

sub-sale   The **sale** of a property immediately after it has been acquired, usually as a result of an agreement entered into simultaneously with the original purchase contract (a 'sub-sale contract' or 'sub-agreement'). Sometimes called a 'flip-sale'. The sale of the rights under a purchase contract is known also as **trading on the equity**. See also **privity of contract, sub-purchaser**.

subscribe   **1.** Literally 'to write under', as one's name. To place one's **signature** at the end of a document. Subscribe may sometimes be used to refer to the giving of assent to or attesting a document, especially a will. In the US, in some jurisdictions, an estate in real property (other than an estate at will or for a term not exceeding one year) must not only be transferred in **writing**, but must be 'subscribed' by the party disposing of the same, or his authorised agent. See also **attest**.   **2.** To agree to purchase shares in an undertaking; especially a newly formed company. To agree to make an investment.

subsequent condition   See **condition subsequent**.

subservient possession   See **permissive possession**.

subsidence   The shifting, slipping or sinking of land, especially when the soil sinks under the weight of a building. Subsidence may arise when the soil is unsuitable for the building erected on it; when the foundations are inadequate for the purpose; as a result of a substantial change in the water content of the soil; or as a result of the removal of the subsoil, as in mining or as a result of building work. See also **right of support**, **subsurface right**.

subsidiary vesting deed(Eng)   See **vesting document**.

subsidised rent(BrE) or **subsidized rent**(AmE)   **1.** A rent that is reduced by a payment made to the tenant, generally by a party other than the landlord. For example, a grant by a government agency to a local municipality enabling the authority to charge a lower rent for a home than would normally be considered economic, or to charge a rent that is below the market value. cf. **rent concession**.   **2.** A rent that is below the level that would normally be charged by a landlord, either as charged directly or by some form of concession by the landlord, such as by a reduction in operating expenses charged to the tenant. In the US, also called a 'subsidy rent'.

subsidy   A grant of financial assistance which may take the form of a gift of money or pecuniary benefits such as a price reduction or tax concession. In particular, aid given by central or local government to a private individual, enterprise or corporation, especially when such aid is given to assist that party in achieving a government's economic objectives or to benefit the public in general. See also **buy-down**(US), **capital allowance**(Eng), **subsidized rent**, **tenant improvement allowance**(US).

subsidy rent(US)   See **subsidized rent**.

subsoil   See **subsurface right**.

substantial completion   See **substantial performance**.

substantial performance   Completion or **performance** of a contract in good faith to a point when it may be said that the beneficiary has substantially received or obtained that for which

he had contracted. The completion of the duties or obligations under a contract to a point where it may be said that any further breach would be considered immaterial. The legal 'doctrine of substantial performance' may discharge a promisee from an obligation to carry out further work under the contract, as literally interpreted, when such performance detail would be inequitable. The principle of the doctrine is that if a party to a contract has completed his obligations, but has failed in a minor or relatively unimportant way, the promisor may not repudiate the contract and refuse all payment as if the contract had not been properly performed. This is based on the maxim *de minimis non curat lex* – 'the law does not concern itself with trifles'. However, the doctrine may not necessarily relieve the promisor of his right to claim damages for any actual loss suffered as a result of the non-completion of that for which he clearly contracted for. There is no hard and fast rule as to what constitutes substantial performance. Thus, if a builder completes a house but has used different, though adequate, materials to those specified, the owner of the house may be obliged to accept that the house is completed – subject to a right of **set-off** for any loss in value he has suffered, especially when the owner has taken possession of the building. This doctrine is one of equity and, therefore, is a matter for the discretion of the courts. See also **lump-sum contract**, *quantum meruit*.

substantial repair   See **repair**, **tenantable repair**.

substantive lessor entity (SLE)(US)   See **special-purpose corporation/special-purpose entity**.

substituted basis(US)   The **basis** of a property acquired in a **tax-free exchange**. The basis of a property acquired in a tax-free exchange (a § 1031 exchange) is the same as the adjusted basis of the property given up (the 'relinquished property'), increased by any additional consideration paid for the property acquired (the 'replacement property'), and reduced by any consideration received from the purchaser (26 USCA, Internal Revenue Code, § 1016(b)). See also **boot**.

substitution doctrine   See **subrogation**.

substitution of liability   See **novation**.

substitution value   The value of a property based on the cost of a suitable alternative. A basis for the objective valuation of any property, especially when applying the **sales comparison approach**[US], or the **comparison method of valuation**[BrE]; or when assessing the reinstatement cost of a building. See also **cost approach**, **opportunity cost**.

subsurface right   The right of a landowner to the stratas or subsoil underneath his **land**. Strictly, an owner of land owns the subsoil *ad centrum*, 'to the center of the earth' and, therefore, he may grant a right for another party to use the subsoil or substrata of his land. This right may take the form of (i) a right to remove material (in the form of a **profit à prendre**); (ii) a right of passage under the land in order to gain access to or from adjoining land (in the form of an **easement**); or (iii) a right to enter and use space under the land (as with a **lease** of a space under the land). See also **mineral rights**, **mining lease**, **oil and gas lease**, **right of support**.

subtenancy   See **sub-lease**.

subtenant   A **sub-lessee**; a tenant who holds by virtue of a sub-lease. One who holds a right to all or part of a property from another who is himself tenant, provided the interest of the former is for a shorter term than that held by the latter.

subtopia   A word compounded by the architect Ian Nairn (in 'Outrage', Architectural Press, 1955) from 'suburbia' and 'utopia' to denote "the world of universal low density mass ... an even spread of abandoned aerodromes and fake rusticity, wire fences, traffic roundabouts, gratuitous notice boards, car parks, and 'Things-in-Fields'"; i.e. uncontrolled suburban sprawl, or any form of urban development that is ill-conceived, ill-designed and unsightly. cf. **urbanity**. See also **ribbon development**.

suburb   Derived from the Latin *sub*, 'close to' and *urbs*, 'town'. An area on the outskirts of a town or city, especially an area that has developed into a separate community but still relies for much of its support, in terms of employment, shopping and other services on the main town or city. Commonly used to refer to a predominately residential area, that has developed on the fringe of a town or city adjacent to the countryside, especially an area from where many of the residents commute to work in the town or city. See also **bedroom community**.

suburbia   A word used, commonly in a derogatory sense, for a **suburb** of a town or city.

succession   The process by which an interest in property passes to another on the death of the owner. The receipt of property from the estate of a decedent, either by **inheritance** or by **will**, but not by grant, life-time gift, purchase or contract. Succession more particularly refers to the passing of property by will, but it may refer to the acquisition by any means upon the death of another, but not as a result of a bona fide contract of purchase or loan. See also **devise**, **intestacy**, **settlement**.

succession duty or **succession tax**[US]   A tax levied against the value of property received from a deceased person. A tax on the benefit of acquiring property by inheritance, will or succession upon the death of the owner. cf. **estate tax**. See also **inheritance tax**.

succession words[US]   See **words of limitation**.

successor   One who follows in place of another. Any person, other than a creditor, who acquires land by **succession**. In particular, one who receives property by statutory succession, as on intestacy, as distinguished from a **devisee** who receives property by will. See also **assignee**, **heir**.

successor in interest or **successor-in-interest** **1.** One who takes property in the place of another. One who takes ownership or control of the property of another. In particular, one who takes the interest of a judgement creditor; or one who takes property by law, rather than purchase. **2.** A corporation that takes the control of property following merger, amalgamation, or a change of name.

successor in title One who takes over the title to property from another. In particular, one who takes over the benefit or burden of an easement or restriction affecting land. In English law, in relation to the right to enforce the benefit or burden of a covenant relating to land, a "successor in title" is defined to include "the owners and occupiers for the time being of the [such] land", LPA 1925, ss. 78(1), 79(2). See also **restrictive covenant**, **successor**.

successors and assigns Words used in a deed to indicate any party (in particular another corporation or subsidiary corporation) that succeeds through acquisition, amalgamation, consolidation or merger to the ownership or burdens of a corporation. See also **heirs and assigns**.

sufferance Consent to, or acceptance of, an action that has not been expressly authorised, but is implied by the failure to condemn or interfere with that action. cf. **estoppel**. See also **tenancy at sufferance**.

sufficient consideration Consideration that is considered adequate to bind a contract or support a bargain. 'Sufficient consideration' need not be equivalent to the value of the property acquired and may even be nominal if that is acceptable to the parties. cf. **valuable consideration**.

sufficient repair Such **repair** as will keep a property in a safe and reasonable condition for the purpose intended. See also **tenantable repair**.

sufficient title See **good and merchantable title**, **good record title**.

suggestio falsi(Lat) 'A statement of a falsehood'; an active **misrepresentation**. cf. ***suggestio veri***.

sui generis(Lat) 'Of its own kind', i.e. the only one of its kind. cf. ***ejusdem generis***.

sui juris(Lat) 'Of his own right', i.e. subject to no legal incapacity; capable of entering into a contract.

suitable alternative accommodation(Eng) Premises to which it might reasonably be expected that an occupier would move in order that an existing property can be vacated and used for another purpose.

In the case of a **protected tenancy** or **secure tenancy**, "suitable alternative accommodation" is a dwelling-house to which a tenant might reasonably be expected to move in order that he can vacate an existing dwelling and, as a result, the landlord can obtain a court order for possession (Rent Act 1977, s. 98(1), Sch. 15, Part IV).

A landlord of premises that are subject to a **business tenancy** where the tenant has a statutory right to a new tenancy, may oppose the tenant's application for a new tenancy when "the landlord has offered and is willing to provide and secure the provision of alternative accommodation". The accommodation must be "suitable for the tenant's requirements (including the requirements to preserve goodwill) having regard to the nature and class of business and to the situation and extent of, and the facilities afforded by, the holding". Regard must be had also to the "terms of the current tenancy and all other relevant circumstances", L&T Act 1954, s. 30(1)(d). See also **grounds for possession**.

suitable for the purpose See **fit for the purpose**.

sum-of-the-years-digits depreciation (SYD depreciation) A method of allowing for **depreciation** that provides for a greater rate of depreciation in the earlier years. The total amount to be depreciated is divided by the summation of the number of years over which the asset is to be depreciated (the sum-of-the-years-digits) and the result is multiplied each year by the number of years outstanding. For example, if depreciation is to be allowed over 6 years, in year 1 the depreciation would be 6/(6 + 5 + 4 + 3 + 2 + 1) or 6/21 × the total to be depreciated; in year 2, 5/21 × the total, and so on. The sum-of-the-years-digits, D, may be obtained by the formula:

$$D = \frac{n(n+1)}{2}$$

Where: n = the number of years.

summary appraisal report(US) An **appraisal report** that provides a summary of the salient features of an **appraisal**. A summary appraisal report should identify and provide a summary description of the real estate being appraised and state the property interest held. The report should state its purpose and intent; define the value to be estimated; state the effective date and the date of the report. In addition, it should summarize the process used to collect, confirm and report the data used in the report; state all assumptions and limiting conditions, opinions, and conclusions that support the analyses; summarize the appraiser's opinion of the **highest and best use**, when such an opinion is necessary and appropriate; explain and support the exclusion of any of the usual valuation approaches. It should also summarize any additional information that may be appropriate to show compliance with, or clearly identify and explain permitted departures from, the specific guidelines of the standard form of valuation, and include a signed valuation certificate (**Uniform Standards of Professional Appraisal Practice**, Standard Rule 2-2(b),

which contains a detailed explanation of these requirements). cf. **restricted appraisal report, self-contained appraisal report**. See also **appraisal date**.

summary possession proceedings(US) Legal proceedings by which a landlord seeks to regain possession of property from a tenant, either in the event of a material breach of a condition of the lease (such as non-payment of rent), or after the lease has expired and the tenant is holding over without consent or legal right. Every state, as well as the District of Columbia, Guam, Puerto Rico and the Virgin Islands, has a statute governing the procedure for the eviction of a tenant for a material breach of his lease. In some jurisdictions, such procedure may only be applied in the event of a non-payment of rent. Summary possession proceedings is a statutory remedy and is separate from any common law right available to the landlord. See also **eviction**.

summation approach or **summation method**(AmE) An approach to an appraisal of a property based on the addition of the value of all components utilized to create the whole. The summation approach may be used synonymously with the **cost approach** by which the value of a property is based on the cost of acquiring a suitable alternative site and adding the depreciated cost of replacing the building. Such a method is used primarily when there is no ready comparable information on the market value of the property. It may refer also to the approach to assessing the amount of **just compensation** payable in condemnation proceedings by which the value of a leased property is based on the value of the fee interest subject to the benefit of a leasehold interest, plus the value of the leasehold interest. See also **depreciated replacement cost**(BrE).

summation rate(AmE) See **component capitalization rate**.

super-regional shopping center See **shopping center**.

superette   See **supermarket**.

superficies solo cedit(Lat)   'Anything attached to the land becomes part of it'. See **fixture**.

superfluous land(Eng)   Land acquired by compulsory powers but not required for the purpose of the undertaking envisaged See also **recoupment**.

Superfund(US)   The popular name for the Comprehensive Environmental Response, Compensation, and Liability Act of 1980 (CERCLA). A federal law enacted in 1980, and amended by the Superfund Amendments and Reauthorization Act of 1986 (SARA), that created a tax on chemical and petroleum industries and imposed obligations on owners, occupiers, users or operators and lenders involved with hazardous materials and environmental remediation of land. CERCLA established prohibitions and requirements concerning closed and abandoned hazardous waste sites; provided for liability for releases of hazardous waste at these sites; and established a trust fund to provide for cleanup when no responsible party could be identified. The Act also revised the National Contingency Plan (NCP), which provided guidelines and procedures needed in respond to releases and threatened releases of hazardous substances, pollutants, or contaminants. The Act, and its related regulations, provides powers for the **Environmental Protection Agency** to limit the spread of hazardous waste from an area of land or to clean up a contaminated site and recover the cost from the owner or operator of a contaminated site, or any party who generated the contamination. All parties are jointly and severally liable for the cost of complying with the EPA's requirements and have a strict and retrospective liability for any contamination.

superior landlord   See **head landlord**.

superior lease   See **head lease**.

superior lien   A **lien** that has priority over another lien.

superior title   A title that may supersede another. In particular, title held by a vendor of property who has not received all the purchase monies and has retained a vendor's lien for the balance of the amount owed. See also **paramount title**.

supermarket   A large self-service retail establishment, usually on one level, predominately selling food, convenience goods, and household supplies, and in many cases a limited range of items of clothing and domestic hardware. Normally these goods are arranged in open display, with goods of a similar type being grouped together in the same area, and purchases are paid for at a number of checkout counters near the exit. A small store of this type may be called a 'superette'. See also **hypermarket**, **superstore**.

superstore(BrE)   A retail store that predominately sells food, convenience goods and household supplies and has a net internal floor area in excess of 2,500 square metres. See also **hypermarket**.

supplemental deed or **supplementary instrument**   1. A **deed**, or **instrument**, that is added to and becomes part of an existing deed (or instrument). For example, a deed that provides for an existing lease to be extended to cover an additional parcel of land. A supplemental deed does not affect the main deed, except for such modifications as those set out in the supplement, i.e. it acts as if it were endorsed onto the original deed. Sometimes called an 'accessory instrument'. See also **codicil**.   2.(US)A deed provided to a purchaser at a **tax sale** when a previous deed was defective or invalid.

supplemental mortgage(US)   A mortgage deed that is used to consolidate the terms of an existing mortgage, but does not create any new principal debt or obligation. In particular, to a mortgage deed that does not create new mortgage indebtedness and, therefore, is not subject to recording tax (City of New York v. Procaccino, 46 AD.2d 594, 364 NYS.2d 582 (1975)).

support   See **lateral support**, **natural rights**, **right of support**.

suppresio veri(Lat)   'Suppression of the truth'. A suggestion of falsehood; a form of passive **misrepresentation**. See also **utmost good faith**.

supra(Lat)   'Above'; 'upon'; 'prior to'.

surcharge   An additional payment or **premium** for the supply of goods or services. In particular, a payment that is intended to offset an extra cost incurred by a supplier. See also **penalty**.

surety   1. An undertaking given to a third party to answer for the debt, default or omission of a creditor as if the person giving the undertaking had pledged his or her own credit. A surety is a form of insurance for the debt or obligation but, unlike a **guaranty**, it is a direct and primary undertaking binding the grantor alongside the principal or original debtor. The person who grants a surety (who may himself be called a 'surety') is primarily liable for the payment of the debt or performance of the obligation of another; whereas a guarantor promises to answer for the payment of a debt, or the performance of some duty, only in the event of the failure of another person. In the US, in some jurisdictions, the distinction between a surety and a guaranty has been abolished by statute or judicial construction. As a rule, a contract of surety must be in **writing** to be enforceable. In American English, 'suretyship' is frequently used to refer to the relationship, as distinguished from a 'surety' who is the person that grants the undertaking'. cf. **warranty**. See also **letter of credit**.   2. One who underwrites the performance of another. A person who gives a commitment to meet another's obligations, liabilities or debts in the event that the other person fails to meet his obligations direct. A surety gives a commitment or indemnity at the same time and, usually, within the same document as the primary obligation, unlike a **guarantor** or **insurer**. A surety gives an undertaking that the debt will be paid, a guarantor undertakes to see that the debtor will pay that which is due. Thus, a surety is liable, at the same time as, and not after, the party being assisted. See also **collateral warranty**, **subrogation**.

surety bond   See **fidelity insurance**, **performance bond**.

surety insurance   See **fidelity insurance**.

suretyship   See **surety**.

surface right   The right to use the surface of land. Land may be divided into stratas of ownership. Thus, a landowner may retain, or grant to another, the right to use the surface of the land (at surface level or to a given height above or depth below the ground). He may also retain the surface rights (including the area above) and grant the right to exploit the subsurface to a third party, as with the right to extract **minerals**. cf. **air rights**, **subsurface right**. See also **right of support**, **soil**.

surface water   Water that comes onto land from rain or melting snow but does not run in a defined **watercourse** or **channel**. Water that is not in a natural stream, river, pond or lake or does not form into a defined body of water, other than a bog or marsh. In common law, a landowner can collect such water or channel it as he wishes. In the US, some jurisdictions adopt the 'common enemy doctrine', based on the common law, which permits a landowner unrestricted right to channel water away from his land; whereas other jurisdictions limit such right to 'reasonable use', which takes account of potential damage to a neighbour's property. See also **nuisance**, **strict liability**, **water rights**.

surrender   The act of yielding or giving up a right, or claim to possession of something, to another. In particular, a voluntary act by which the holder of a particular estate in land gives up or restores that estate to the holder of the immediate **remainder** or **reversion** so that the particular estate merges with the remainder or reversion. The giving up of the interest held by a tenant to his landlord, with the landlord's consent, so that the tenant's interest is lost in favour of the landlord prior to the termination of the tenancy by effluxion of time.

Upon surrender of an interest in land, that interest becomes absorbed or swallowed up by the greater estate (the remainder or reversion), as distinguished from a **release** by which the greater estate descends, or is given up, to the holder of the lesser estate. The estate given up must not be greater than that held by the party accepting the surrender, otherwise it cannot merge therein. Thus, a tenant for life cannot surrender his estate to a tenant holding for a term of years. Also, there must be no intervening estate, so that a subtenant cannot surrender his lease to the holder of the fee interest while the lease to the head tenant remains in effect. A surrender arises from the agreement of the parties, express or implied. In that respect, it may be distinguished from **abandonment** by which the tenant illicits an intention not to continue with his right of possession and on that understanding the landlord reclaims the premises. A surrender does not relieve the tenant of his past obligations, unless it is brought into effect by **accord and satisfaction**; however, it does relieve him of future obligations to the landlord. A surrender must be of the tenant's entire estate or term, although only part of the demised premises may be surrendered. A surrender is a means by which the lease is terminated and in that respect may be distinguished from an **assignment**. However, the transfer of a lease to a superior (but not the immediate) landlord is not a surrender, but operates as an assignment of the lease.

Surrender may be express or by operation of law. Surrender by operation of law arises when it can be implied from the circumstances that the parties have put an end to their relationship. For instance, a surrender may be implied when the tenant gives up possession with the consent of the landlord, or if the landlord re-lets the premises, provided there is a manifest intent by the landlord to take back the premises. A surrender may also arise, based on the principle of **estoppel**, when there has been a verbal agreement that has been acted on by one party to the detriment of the other. cf. **merger**. See also **apportionment, remise, renunciation, sub-lessee, writing**.

surrender-back clause A clause in a lease that requires a tenant to offer to surrender his interest back to the landlord before he is free to transfer it to a third party. Only if the landlord refuses to accept a surrender of the lease can the application to assign be considered in the manner prescribed in the lease. Such a clause may be considered an unfair **restraint on alienation** by the tenant. See also **assignment**.

surrender clause(US) A clause in an **oil and gas lease** which provides that the lessee can give up his lease and all further liabilities, usually upon giving a specified period of notice and paying an agreed sum of money.

surrender value 1. The consideration that may be realised by a tenant surrendering his rights under a lease. A tenant who holds a property at a contract rent that is below the current market value, may be able to obtain a capital payment for surrendering that lease and giving the landlord the benefit of releasing the property (to the original or a new tenant) at a higher rent. See also **leasehold value, marriage value**(BrE)**, surrender**. 2. In insurance, a cash sum paid by an insurance company to the insured when he decides to surrender his rights under an insurance policy; in particular when the policy is cancelled before its maturity date. Generally, the surrender value is equivalent to the loan value, but is less than the present value of the policy if it was held until maturity.

surrogate 1. A person appointed to act in another's place, e.g. a deputy. One who stands in for another. A substitute. cf. **agent**. See also novation. 2.(US)In some jurisdictions, a judge in a probate court.

survey **1.** The process by which the boundaries of a designated area of land, or all or part of a building, are determined and the area contained therein is measured. The measurement and recording of the dimensions of land and any buildings or other features on the land, whether in a horizontal or vertical plane, or both. See also **cadastral survey, government survey system**(US), **Ordnance Survey**(BrE), **surveying**.
Williams, Mitchell G. (editor). *Land Surveys: A Guide for Lawyers and Other Professionals*. 2nd ed. Chicago: ABA Publications, 1999.
2. A map, plat, or other form of recording that shows the boundary to land as prepared by a **surveyor**. A description in words and figures that clearly identifies the location of land or a specific parcel or area of land. **3.** A formal and critical examination of a site, building, structure, or other tangible property. A detailed inspection of tangible property in order to ascertain its present condition, situation, use, value, tenure, etc.; or to determine the precise position of the boundaries or the dimensions of a property. See also **appraisal report**(AmE), **right of entry, structural survey, subject to survey, valuation report**(BrE). **4.** The collection, recording, compilation and interpretation of information; especially when this information is required prior to preparing or proceeding with a plan or project of development. See also **feasibility analysis, project appraisal**.

surveying **1.** The action of preparing a **survey**. **2.** The science of making large scale, accurate, geometrical measurement in order to produce, in graphical or numerical form, a representation of an area of the earth's surface, in both horizontal and vertical form, together with a representation of the natural and man-made features of that area. The principal forms of surveying real property are cadastral surveying, to show property boundaries; **topographical surveying**, to produce maps or plans; **geodetic surveying**, to take account of the curvature of the earth's surface; as well as more specialised fields such as engineering and mine surveying. See also **cadastral survey**.
Bannister, Arthur, et al. *Surveying*. 7th ed. London: Longman, 1998.
Brinker, Russell C., and Roy Minnick (editors). *The Surveying Handbook*. 2nd ed. New York: Chapman & Hall, 1995.
Robillard, Walter G., et al. *Clark on Surveying and Boundaries*. 7th ed. Charlottesville, VA: Lexis Publishing, 1997 with annual supplements.

surveyor A person who prepares a **survey**. A person who undertakes the science (or art) of surveying including a land, building, mining, or hydrographic surveyor. In the UK, the role of a 'surveyor' may encompass the disciplines of a **quantity surveyor**; a **valuer**; **estate manager**; a town planner, land economist or an **estate agent**, being anyone involved in measuring or assessing the value or use of property. In the US, the word is usually limited to a land surveyor, one who is engaged in the occupation of measuring land surfaces and establishing land boundaries and such related work.
Virgo, John, and Ralph Wynne-Griffiths. *Surveyors' Liability: Law and Practice*. Bristol: Jordans, 1998.

survival clause(US) A clause in a lease which provides that if the landlord terminates a lease because of the tenant's default and evicts the tenant, the tenant's liability for any unpaid rent survives such eviction.

survivorship The fact of living longer than another person or persons. See also **joint tenancy**, *jus accrescendi*, **tenancy by the entirety**.

suspensive condition(Civ) A **condition** that must be fulfilled before a contract comes into effect. "That which depends on a future and uncertain event, or on an event that has actually taken place, without it yet being known to the parties", La CC, art. 2043. A term used in the civil law that is broadly equivalent to **condition precedent** in the common law. In the US, outside Louisiana, normally called a 'suspensory condition'.

suspensory condition(US)   See **suspensive condition**.

swap   A financial transaction where two parties or investors agree to exchange their respective rights to different income streams. A swap is usually made to enable the parties to adjust their overall risk or cash flow exposure. For example, under an 'interest-rate swap' the holder a long-term fixed-rate note swaps that income stream with the right to the income steam from a floating-rate note over the same term as the fixed-rate note. The loan instruments do not actually change hands, but the parties agree to swap the debt-service obligations. A payment is made by one party to the other, or counter party, to compensate for the difference in the present values of the cash flows over the term of the instrument agreement (including an allowance for fees and any new-issue costs of the shorter term loans). In a foreign exchange swap a spot sale may be exchanged for a forward purchase or a spot purchase may be traded for a forward sale.

sweat equity   **1.** The equity value in a property that is earned by a developer who increases its worth through his intangible efforts, such as obtaining zoning or planning consent, negotiating option rights, producing schematic drawings for a potential form of development, negotiating terms for a pre-letting. The developer usually converts his sweat equity into a share in the future value of the completed development.   **2.** Work carried out by a borrower to improve a property, at his own cost in terms of labour and materials, which is credited as part of the down payment required by a lender.

sweetener   An inducement to someone to enter into a contract or to make a financial commitment. A gift, reward or bribe given to mollify someone. See also **equity kicker**, **kickback**.

sweetheart lease   A lease that is granted at a rent that is significantly below the market value. Such a lease generally arises in a retail project when a landlord grants a lease on concessionary terms to attract a particular tenant who will act as a magnet for other tenants.

swing loan(US)   **1.** See **bridge loan**.   **2.** A loan made on the basis of the security of a property owner's assets, without being secured by a charge or mortgage on any of those assets.

synallagmatic contract   A contract that imposes reciprocal obligations. A contract by which the parties exchange promises thereby creating mutual obligations, as compared with a **unilateral contract** in which a promise is exchanged for an act. A term more commonly used in the civil law. In Anglo-American law, **bilateral contract** is a more usual term for such a contract; unless there are more than two parties to the agreement.

syndicate   An association or body of persons established for the purpose of a business venture or undertaking that is essentially too large for the individuals; or by individuals who wish to subject a venture to common management. A group of investors or financiers who combine together for the purpose of a particular transaction or in order to promote a new business, especially when such persons combine together for a limited or specific duration. The association may take the form in law of a **society**, **partnership**, or **company**. A 'property syndicate' may be established in any one of these forms, or even as a **tenancy in common**, to hold one or more properties on behalf of a number of investors. As rule, such an investment vehicle is a closed fund; as distinguished from a **property unit trust** or a 'real estate mutual fund' which are open-ended forms of investment vehicle. See also **joint ownership**, **joint venture**, **syndication**.

syndication   **1.** A means by which an investment is made available to a wide range of investors. A syndication brings together a larger number of investors or financiers than would otherwise make a particular investment. Usually a professional investment manager undertakes to provide the services that are not available to the individual investors and offers the investors the opportunity to acquire a share in an investment that would otherwise be too large for their own more limited resources. For example, the sponsor of the syndication provides the corporate, legal and tax advice and the extensive managerial resources that it would not be practical or economic for the individuals to provide. The sponsor forms a **syndicate**, to acquire and manage the investment, and invites a group of private investors, or the public as a whole, to acquire shares, or any other appropriate participating interest, in that syndicate. Also called 'securitization' or in the UK, especially when used as a means of investing in one or a limited number of properties, 'unitisation' – the investor acquiring a 'unit' share in the investment. See also **blind-pool offering**, **limited partnership**, **mutual fund**.

Jarchow, Stephen R. *Real Estate Syndication: Securitization after Tax Reform*. 2nd ed. New York: Wiley, 1988.

McMahon, Greg. *Property Syndication: Exploding the myth surrounding illegal property syndication*. Brisbane, Qld: Teys McMahon, 1999.

2.(US)A word sometimes used for a **syndicate**.

synthetic lease(US) A lease that is entered into as part of a financing arrangement, primarily to enable the parties to derive particular accounting and tax benefits, i.e. a lease that is classified as a lease for accounting purposes, but as a loan for tax purposes. Such leases are entered into frequently between related entities. For example, a lease between an owning and operating company, both of which are part of the same holding corporation, in order to remove an asset from the balance sheet of the operating company. The lease is structured as an **operating lease** so that the subject property meets those attributes that permit the asset and associated liabilities to be recorded in the accounts of the lessor and not on the balance sheet of the operating lessee. A synthetic lease may also be entered into as part of a financing arrangement for the acquisition or construction of commercial property. The owner/developer grants an operating lease to a tenant who wishes to be a corporate end user and obtains non-recourse finance from a third party long-term creditor, usually a bank or financial institution. The lessor has the benefit of depreciation allowances and any investment tax credits, as well as interest expenses on the debt, while the lessee is able to record the rent as a tax-deductible expense. "[A] lease financing structure that qualifies as an operating lease for accounting purposes, but as a leveraged asset purchase for tax purposes", E & Y Kenneth Leventhal Real Estate Group/Pennsylvania Bar Institute, *Synthetic Leases—Bond Leases* (1997). Sometimes called an 'off-balance-sheet lease', a 'tax ownership/operating lease', or a 'tax retention operating lease'. See also **special purpose corporation**.

Nancy R. Little, *Unraveling the Synthetic Lease*, Property & Probate, 23-25 (Jan/Feb 1997).

synthetic real estate(US) A right to property that does not include actual right of ownership, such as a right to a **mortgage-backed security** or **derivative security**.

T

T mark(BrE)   A mark in the form of a T, placed on a plan to indicate who owns a boundary fence, hedge, wall or any other form of **boundary line**. The mark is placed along the boundary line on the side of the owner of the form of demarcation. A 'T' mark is used for identification purposes only and has no legal significance.

T & I custodial account   A 'taxes and interest' account. An account set up prior to the issue of a mortgage-backed security into which payments are made to ensure the prompt payment of real estate taxes and insurance premiums in respect of the securitized properties.

tacit approval   Approval to a course of action by implication, especially as a result of silence on the part of the person affected by the result. See also **implied term, estoppel**.

tacit relocation   A term derived from Roman law and used in the civil law and Scots law, for the renewal of a lease by operation of law when the landlord and tenant have failed to take steps to end the lease after it has reached the end of its term. Such a renewal is made on the same terms as the expired lease, although it is generally limited to a maximum duration of one year. See also **hold over, tenancy at will**.

tack   1. See **tacking**.   2.(Scot)A contract for the hire of goods. A lease. See also **hire**.

tack duty or **tack rent**(Scot)   A payment for a right of tenure. Rent under a lease.

tacking   1. 'Adding on'. The joining of a subsequent, but subsisting, **mortgage** to an existing mortgage in order to defer the **priority** of an intervening or second mortgage. For example, the acquisition of a first mortgage by a third mortgagee in order to postpone the priority of the second mortgagee. In English law, the common law right for a later mortgagee to acquire a superior mortgage and thereby defer the priority of an intermediate mortgage has been abolished, except in certain cases where a **further advance** is made by the junior mortgagee (LPA 1925, s. 94).

In the US, the common-law doctrine of tacking is generally not recognized because a mortgage given as security for a particular debt, whether present or prospective, is not considered enforceable for another and different debt. In any event, in many jurisdictions, the priority of any mortgage is generally determined by the date of recording and a subsequent mortgagee cannot alter his priority without the consent of a prior mortgagee. cf. **consolidation of mortgages**. 2.(US)The adding or combining of successive periods of possession in order to establish a title to land by **adverse possession** or periods of use to establish a right by **prescription**. As a rule, to establish a title to property by adverse possession, the possession must be continuous (unless interrupted by periods of recognized disability, fraud, etc.) and there must be a 'transfer' of possession. But, because adverse possession is a means of barring an existing title, successive periods of adverse possession by successors in title may be added together. Thus, tacking of periods of adverse possession by parties between whom there is **privity** of possession (e.g. vendor and purchaser, decedent and heir, husband and wife, and co-tenants) may be brought into account when barring a title to property, provided that the periods are not interrupted by one party giving up possession before the other takes over. 3. The adding of terms or conditions, to a contract, e.g. as a **rider**. See also **supplementary deed**.

tacking of further advance   See **further advance**(Eng)/**future advance**(US).

tail   See **entailed estate, fee tail**.

tail after possibility   See **estate in tail after possibility of issue extinct**.

tail male or **tail female**   See **fee tail**.

taille   An estate in tail, i.e. a **fee tail**.

tailzie or **tailye**(Scot)   The grant of a perpetual right of succession to land. Such rights are now obsolete.

take it or **leave it contract**   See **adhesion contract**.

take off   See **taking-off**.

take possession   See **taking possession**.

take property(US)   See **eminent domain, just compensation, taking for public use**.

take-back mortgage or **take-back deed of trust**(US)   See **purchase money mortgage**.

take-down   See **draw-down**.

take-down search(US)   See **bring-down search**.

taken for public use(US)   A term derived from the Fifth Amendment to the Constitution, which states that no private property shall be "taken for public use, without **just compensation**". In this context, the word 'taken' has been held to mean the deprivation of the rights of a former owner, rather than the accretion of a right or interest to the sovereign. 'Taking' may be the actual removal of the right to property, or a significant removal, destruction or limitation of the right to use private property, as with the requirement that a private lagoon be made available to the general public (Kaiser v. United States, 444 US 164 (1979)). "Government action short of acquisition of title or occupancy has been held, if its effects are so complete as to deprive the owner of all or most of his interest in the subject matter, to amount to a taking", United States v. General Motors Corp., 323 US 373, 65 S Ct 357, 89 L Ed 311, 318, 156 ALR 390 (1945). A permanent physical occupation of private property, that is authorized by a government or municipal authority, may also constitute a taking for which just compensation is payable (Loretto v. Teleprompter Manhattan CATV Corp., 458 US 419, 102 S Ct 3164, 73 L Ed.2d 868 (1982)). However, the normal exercise of **police power** does not amount to a 'taking'; but is merely an acceptable form of government 'regulation'. See also **eminent domain, exaction, inverse condemnation**.
Eagle, Steven J. *Regulatory Taking*. 2nd ed. Newark, NJ: LexisNexis, 2001.

takeout commitment   An agreement or **commitment** to make a loan, or to purchase a property, at a future date, usually subject to certain conditions, such as that a building is completed and let. A takeout commitment may take the form of a binding agreement by which (a) a lender agrees to provide a long-term loan to replace an interim loan or a construction loan; or (b) a financial institution agrees with a real estate developer that, when a particular building is completed to agreed plans and specification and leased to provide an agreed income, the institution will purchase the building at a price calculated by reference to an agreed capitalisation rate that will be applied to a determinable income level (also called a 'forward sale' or 'buy-out'). For the arrangement to be a true 'commitment', it should be a binding agreement and not merely a **letter of intent**. It should be in **writing** and should contain the essential terms for a binding contract; although it may well be hedged with various conditions to protect the lender. Also referred to as a 'forward or pre-funding commitment' or, when the commitment is converted to a loan, a 'takeout loan', 'takeout finance', or an 'end loan'. See also **finance**.

takeout finance or **takeout loan**   See **takeout commitment**.

takeout provision(US)   See **partial release clause**.

take-up rate(BrE)   See **absorption rate**.

taking(US)   See **taken for public use**.

taking possession   Obtaining a right to **possession** of property. The vesting of property, or a title to real property, in someone. Upon the completion of the purchase of real property, 'possession' does not, of itself, mean personal occupation. If a property is tenanted and a purchaser is placed in a position to receive rents and profits he will be given a right to 'possession'. Mere **entry** onto land is not *per se* equivalent to taking possession. Although the terms 'entry' and 'taking possession' are frequently used synonymously, entry is the going onto land as a privilege or right, whereas taking possession may be subsequent to a consent or approval, but may also be adverse or against the wishes of the owner or rightful claimant. cf. **access**. See also **acquisition, adverse possession, seisin, vacant possession**.

taking-off   A process in **quantity surveying** by which the quantity of materials required for a building contract is assessed: Detailed measurements are taken from the architect's prepared drawings and plans and these measurements are used for the purpose of determining the particular quantities of materials required to construct the buildings. The measurements 'taken off' the plans are usually set out in the **bill of quantities** as the basis for assessing the cost of the building works. In the US, also called 'figuring'. See also **abstracting, billing**.

tangible property   Property that has a physical or sensory existence and is necessarily corporeal, i.e. land, buildings, goods, merchandise and chattels; but not any form of property that is represented by a right of action (choses-in-action) nor an **incorporeal hereditament**. cf. **intangible property**. See also **corporeal property**.

target-cost contract(BrE)   See **cost-plus contract**.

target rate of return   A rate of return that an investor sets out to achieve from a particular investment. Normally this is represented by the annualized return projected for the life of the investment, i.e. the expected **redemption yield** or **internal rate of return**. A target rate of return may be based on the return required (a) to provide the investor with a return that exceeds the cost of his capital by a margin that is sufficient to provide a reward commensurate with the risk involved in parting with that capital; or (b) to equal, or exceed, the anticipated return from a comparable investment. Also called a 'criterion rate of return', or an 'opportunity-cost rate of return' as it represents the rate of return that could be achieved from an alternative investment. See also **hurdle rate**.

target rent   See **headline rent**.

tax   **1.** A compulsory, but authorised, contribution, usually of a pecuniary kind, made by the general body of subjects or citizens to a sovereign, governmental or municipal authority. A tax must be authorised for a public purpose; be enforceable at law; and the obligation to pay it must be imposed compulsorily on a group of persons or organisations. However, it need bear little relation to the benefit received by any payer of the tax. A tax is levied against persons or property in general, as distinguished from any **assessment, charge** or **levy** which is imposed on one or a small group of individuals, or against one or a group of properties. See also **capital gains tax, escalation clause, inheritance tax, land tax, outgoing, property tax, rates, value added tax**.   **2.** To assess the value of a property, particularly for official purposes.   **3.** To make the subject of a **levy**.

tax abatement   A reduction, in part or in total, in a local tax for a specific period of time; such as an **abatement** granted when access to a property is severely restricted by a government body. See also **rebate**.

tax base(US)   **1.** The value of a property used to apply a rate of taxation. The **assessed value** of a property to which a tax rate is applied to determine the actual tax payable. See also **basis**. **2.** The assessed value of all properties in a particular tax district.

tax basis(US) See basis.

tax book(US) See **tax roll**.

tax certificate(US) 1. See **certificate of sale**. **2.** A certificate issued by a county treasurer or other local tax official confirming that all real estate taxes have been paid in respect of a particular property or indicating the amount of any unpaid tax in respect of that property.

tax credit A credit that may be offset against a future tax liability; generally a credit that arises from a previously overtaxed income. Unlike a **tax deduction**, a tax credit may be deducted from a tax liability in full, not merely from taxable income. See also **historic sites**.

tax deduction An amount that may be deducted from income or from a capital gain prior to calculating the tax to be charged thereon. cf. **tax credit**. See also **capital allowance**, **depreciation, tax shelter**.

tax deed(US) An instrument issued after a **tax sale** by which the taxation authority effects the transfer of title from the owner to the purchaser. In some jurisdictions, the tax deed takes effect immediately after the sale, subject to being annulled or defeased if the tax is paid within a period allowed for redemption by the defaulting taxpayer. In other jurisdictions, the deed does not take effect until after the redemption period. In the latter case, a **certificate of sale** is issued as evidence that the purchaser has a right to the property. In either case, a tax deed is a creature of statute and only vests unencumbered title when the statutory conditions that govern tax sales have been complied with. Sometimes called a 'treasurer's deed'. See also **redemption period**.

tax delinquency(US) A failure to pay a tax when due, especially when this results in a **tax sale** of the delinquent tax payer's property.

tax-deferred exchange(US) See **tax-free exchange**.

tax escalation clause(US) See **escalation clause**.

tax foreclosure(US) Seizure and sale of property to meet a liability for unpaid tax. See also **sequestration, tax sale**.

tax-free exchange(US) The exchange of one real property for another in order to defer a potential tax liability. Property held for use in a trade or business, investment, or to produce income may be exchanged for a "like-kind" of property without creating an immediate liability for capital gains tax. 'Like-kind' essentially refers to real property as such, rather than to the quality or quantity of property. The transaction must be an **exchange** and not a sale of property followed by the reinvestment of the proceeds in another property and the property must not be in an excluded category (such as stock-in-trade or other property held primarily for sale). If the exchange of properties does not take place simultaneously, then the property acquired in exchange must be identified as such not later than 45 days from the sale and must be acquired within 180 days (or by the due date in which the transferor's tax return is due in respect of the transferred property). Any gain realized by the transfer of either property by way of exchange is not recognized, but is deferred until the newly acquired property is disposed of by way of a future taxable disposition (26 USC, Internal Revenue Code, §§ 1031-1034). Any money paid to balance the difference in values of the properties (called boot) is taxable. See also **tax shelter**.
Fainsbert, S. B., et al. *Real Property Exchanges*. 2nd ed. Looseleaf. Berkeley, CA: Continuing Education at the Bar, 1994.

tax haven A country or state that levies no taxation, or very low levels of taxation, usually to attract foreign investors. A country that accepts, and normally encourages, foreign investment by charging far lower tax rates than would be payable by the investors in their own country. See also **off-shore trust**.

tax increment financing (TIF)(US)   Bonds that are issued to finance the improvements to the infrastructure in designated inner city areas without the need to increase the city's tax base. The amount of finance raised is based on the difference between the assessment base before and after the improvements, and is repaid from the increased revenues that will be generated. The finance may also be used to fund the construction of low-income housing and to acquire land for redevelopment.

tax lien   See lien.

tax list(US)   See **assessment roll**.

tax map   See cadastral map.

tax participation clause(US)   See escalation clause.

tax plat(US)   See plat map.

Tax Retention Operating Lease (TROL)(US)   See **synthetic lease**.

tax roll(US)   See **assessment roll**.

tax sale(US)   A sale of a property at the instigation of the taxing authorities, when the owner of the property has failed to meet a tax liability. A sale of property for the non-payment of taxes under a special statutory power exercised to divest the owner of his property without his consent. The sale is usually by public auction, but it may be arranged by tender or sealed bids. In some jurisdictions, the purchaser acquires an immediate title (**tax title**) and possession of the property offered for sale. In other jurisdictions, the purchaser's rights to title are postponed in order to enable the delinquent tax payer a specified period of time in which to repay the tax and redeem the property, and the purchaser is granted a **certificate of sale** or 'tax certificate' pro tem. Thus, depending on the jurisdiction, the contract for the purchase of the property may be deemed to be directly between the owner and the purchaser, or between the taxing authority and the purchaser. cf. **judicial sale**. See also **tax deed**.

tax shelter   An investment that is used to reduce or defer a liability for tax; or, in broad terms, a **tax credit** or **tax deduction** that is available only to a particular group of taxpayers, e.g. those who pay mortgage interest. Real estate is one of the principal forms of tax shelter because depreciation, loan interest and tax losses from previous tax years may be deducted from income in order to reduce the owner's total tax liability. The 'sheltered' income is the amount that is free of tax. See also **tax-free exchange**(US).

tax stamp(US)   See **stamp tax**.

tax title(US)   The title granted to a person who has acquired a property at a **tax sale**. The title may grant a right to possession of the property and a right to accede to the owner's title; but usually it is subject to a condition that the delinquent tax payer has a right to recover the property provided he pays the tax due within a specified time. In the latter case, the purchaser's claim is represented by a **certificate of purchase** or 'tax certificate' issued by the taxation authority, which is converted into a title if the tax payer fails to meet his liability in full. In a few jurisdictions, a **tax deed** may be granted after the sale and that is considered as an immediate conveyance of a good title.

tax-stop clause(US)   A clause in a lease which provides that the lessee will pay any taxes above a given level, usually above that payable at the start of the lease. See also **escalation clause**.

taxable gain   See capital gain.

taxable value   See **assessed value**[US], **rateable value**[Eng].

taxation of costs   The means by which a court determines the amount of costs that are to be awarded in a court action; in particular that the lawyer's bills of costs are fair and reasonable in relation to the work done – 'taxation' in this context being used to refer to the process of determining a charge or duty.

tear   See **fair wear and tear**[BrE], **wear and tear**[AmE].

technical estoppel[US]   Estoppel by record or by deed.

technical mortgage[US]   See **regular mortgage**.

telehotel   A building that is used to house telecom carriers, internet service providers (ISPs), IT companies or similar companies. These buildings, or parts of buildings, are usually leased with basis services and the occupiers install their own hardware in suites or racks. The operators of these buildings may provide additional services such as IT maintenance, web hosting, disaster recovery and serviced office suites. Network operators and internet service providers often sublet or licence space to their own customers.

temporary injunction   See **injunction**, **restraining order**[US].

temporary planning permission[Eng]   See **General Development Order**, **planning condition**.

temporary restraining order (TRO)[US]   See **injunction**, **restraining order**.

tenancy   1. A right to hold land from another, subject to an acknowledgment of the eventual right of that other to regain the land. A relationship, created by means of a contract (express or implied) termed a **lease**, by which one party (**landlord**) grants another (**tenant**) a right to possession of land for a defined or definable period of time, usually in exchange for a payment called **rent**. An essential element of a tenancy is that the landlord retains an interest in the land (called his **reversionary interest**); otherwise he will have made a grant or conveyance of his entire right to the land. A tenancy creates more than a contractual right; it is a right to land that, for the duration of the contract, is enforceable against anyone, including the landlord.

A tenancy requires three other essential elements: (i) an identifiable landlord and tenant, i.e. a person cannot be a tenant of himself nor of land that has no known owner; (ii) the property demised must be clearly identifiable and the tenant must have a degree of **exclusive possession** of that property; and (iii) the right to the property must be granted for a period of time or **term** that is certain, or capable of being made certain. Normally, the tenant is required to pay rent as an acknowledgment of a fealty or obligation to another, and to observe certain conditions, either as expressed in the lease or as implied by law. A tenancy may be created by a lease; a sub-lease or underlease; an **agreement for a lease**; or merely by implication as when a person enters into possession of another's land and pays rent.

In English statute law, in relation to a **business tenancy**, tenancy is defined to mean "a tenancy created either immediately or derivatively out of the freehold, whether by a lease or underlease, by an agreement for a lease or underlease or in pursuance of any enactment (including this Act), but does not include a mortgage term or any interest arising in favour of a mortgagor by his attorning tenant to his mortgagee", L&T 1954, s. 69(1). A tenancy created for the purpose of granting security by means of a mortgage, as well as a tenancy created by way of a trust under a settlement, is excluded from the term 'tenancy' when used without further qualification.

In common usage, the word 'tenancy' generally refers to a short-term or periodic tenancy and the word 'lease', especially one created by deed, refers to a tenancy for a fixed period. cf. **licence**(BrE)/ **license**(AmE). See also **agricultural tenancy**(Eng), **assured shorthold tenancy**(Eng), **assured tenancy**(Eng), **controlled tenancy**(Eng), **long residential tenancy**(Eng), **minor tenancy**(Eng), **periodic tenancy**, **protected shorthold tenancy**(Eng), **protected tenancy**(Eng), **regulated tenancy**(Eng), **secure tenancy**(Eng), **statutory tenancy**(Eng), **tenancy at sufferance, tenancy at will, tenancy by estoppel, tenancy by the entirety, tenancy for a fixed term.** **2.** The duration of the right to retain possession of property that is owned by another. The period for which a person has a right to hold a property as granted under a lease. **3.** The holding of any form of title to land. In particular, a joint holding of land, as in **joint tenancy** or **tenancy in common**. This usage of the term 'tenancy' is derived from **tenure**, i.e. a holding of land (it does not denote the modern relationship of landlord and tenant referred to in **1.** above).

tenancy agreement An agreement to create a **tenancy**. See also **agreement for a lease, parol lease, periodic tenancy**.

tenancy at a low rent(Eng) See **low rent**.

tenancy at sufferance or **tenancy by sufferance** A tenancy that comes into existence when a person, who had legally entered into possession of a property, remains there without the consent, or dissent, of the person entitled to possession, and without statutory authority. A tenant at sufferance has only a right of naked possession; stands in no **privity** to the landlord; and consequently, may normally be removed without formal notice to quit (unless entitled to a statutory notice). In particular, a tenancy at sufferance arises when a person wrongfully holds over at the end of a lease, or when a person remains in possession after the termination of periodic tenancy or a life estate. A tenancy at sufferance may follow on from any form of tenancy (including a tenancy at will or a life tenancy); but it cannot be created as a sub-letting by one who is himself a tenant at sufferance. In any event, such a 'tenancy' can only exist while there is possession. Unlike a **tenancy at will**, a tenancy at sufferance is neither consented to, nor objected to, and may be considered to constitute a wrongful act. A tenant at sufferance differs from a trespasser only to the extent that he originally entered into possession with the landlord's consent, and if a tenant at sufferance is requested to leave the demised premises, and fails to do so, he becomes a trespasser. On the other hand, if the landlord consents to his continued occupation, or effectively waives the tenant's wrong, then the tenant becomes a tenant at will or, if the acknowledgment is sufficient (as by the acceptance of rent) a **periodic tenancy** is created.

A tenant at sufferance has no obligation to pay rent and the landlord cannot distrain for payment (it is not a true tenancy), but the tenant may be liable to pay **mesne profits**, or in the US, in some jurisdictions, a **penalty rent**. In English law and in some jurisdictions in the US, a tenant at sufferance who has been requested to give up possession to his landlord and who wilfully holds over (and has no statutory right to retain possession) may, be charged double the 'annual value' of the premises during his period of continuing possession (unless he is a weekly or quarterly tenant). Alternatively, the landlord may bring an action for **trespass** and claim damages for any loss suffered as a result.

In the US, a person who is granted a statutory right to remain in possession when a contractual tenancy comes to an end may be said to hold a 'statutory tenancy at sufferance'.

Also called a 'tenancy on sufferance' or, in the US, an 'estate by sufferance' or '**estate at sufferance**'. cf. **disseizin**. See also **double rent, holdover tenant, security of tenure**.

tenancy at will An arrangement whereby a person occupies land, with the consent of the owner, as if he were a tenant (and not merely a servant or agent), but on the understanding that his occupation may be terminated at any time at the will of either party. At common law, a tenancy at will is a personal contract between the parties; it is created without any formal agreement; and it does not grant any interest in land. It arises most frequently when a person enters into possession before a formal lease is entered into, as when a landlord is proposing to grant a new lease. "A tenancy at will, although called a **tenancy**, is unlike any other tenancy except a **tenancy at sufferance**, to which it is the next-of-kin. It has been properly described [in English law] as a personal relationship between the landlord and his tenant: it is determined by the death of either of them or any of a variety of acts, even by an involuntary alienation, which would not affect the subsistence of any other tenancy", *Wheeler v Mercer* [1957] AC 426, 427, [1956] 3 All ER 631, 634 (HL). However, unlike a **licence**, it has the characteristics of a proper tenancy, notably a right for the tenant to have exclusive occupation and the necessity for a valid notice to bring it to an end. A tenancy at will is brought to an end if either party commits an act that is inconsistent with the relationship, e.g. a denial of the landlord's title; a purported **assignment** or sub-letting; or an act of voluntary **waste**. However, upon a purported assignment or sub-letting of a tenancy at will, if the landlord recognises the new entrant, a new tenancy at will comes into existence. A tenancy at will is converted into a periodic tenancy if there is a payment of rent that is accepted by the landlord as an intent to create such a tenancy, absent any circumstances to the contrary.

In the US, the term 'tenancy at will' is sometimes used in a general sense to refer to any tenancy of an uncertain duration that must be brought to an end by either party by proper notice. In several jurisdictions, statute law requires a specified period of notice to terminate a tenancy at will. Depending on the jurisdiction, this notice period varies from three days to three months. In any event, the courts will normally allow a reasonable time for the tenant to vacate the premises. Also called an 'estate at will'. In the US, sometimes called a 'lease at will' or a 'general tenancy'. See also **agreement of a lease, use and occupation**.

tenancy by coparcenary   See coparcenary.

tenancy by curtesy   See tenancy by the curtesy.

tenancy by entirety or **tenancy by entireties**   See tenancy by the entirety.

tenancy by estoppel   A tenancy that comes into existence where a person is unable to grant a lease because he does not have the form of title to the land that would enable him to grant the particular lease, but he still purports to create that lease. By virtue of the doctrine of **estoppel**, the grantor cannot deny to his 'tenant' that he has not created a contract of tenancy so that "[e]ven though it is apparent to the parties that the landlord's title is defective [subject to an exception if the tenancy be estoppel arises by deed], both they and their successors in title will be estopped from denying that the grant was effective to create the tenancy that it purported to create", Charles Harpum, *Megarry & Wade. The Law of Real Property*. 6th ed. London: Sweet & Maxwell, 1999, p. 801. In the US, the term 'tenancy by estoppel' is not generally used, although the same principle arises from an **estoppel by deed**; a grantor is estopped from denying the title of the person to whom he has granted an interest in land and, if he subsequently acquires the title he purports to have, his grantee has the benefit of that 'after acquired title'. Where applicable, may also be referred to as 'estoppel by lease' (American Law Reports, *Annotations and Cases*, Anno: 51 ALR2d 1238: Estoppel by Lease). See also **after-acquired title**.

tenancy by succession[Eng]   See assured tenancy, statutory tenancy.

tenancy by sufferance[US]   See tenancy at sufferance.

tenancy by the curtesy   A common law right to a property that has been acquired by a husband and wife together and which falls to the husband in the event of the prior death of his wife.

In particular, a tenancy by the curtesy gives the husband a right to a life interest in his deceased wife's property, if she dies intestate and before him, but leaves a child who would have inherited an **entailed estate**. This right has been abolished under English law (AEA 1925, s. 45(1)).

In the US, some states still recognize the right of curtesy. However, in most of those states where it subsists, the husband's right has been restricted to a one-third interest in the real estate owned by the wife. Also, in most states that recognize the right of curtesy, the requirement that a child must have been born to the couple, before a right of curtesy can be obtained, has been abolished. Curtesy is terminated on divorce. Also called an 'estate by the curtesy'. cf. **dower**.

tenancy by the entirety or **tenancy by the entireties**   A form of property ownership that arose when property was conveyed to a husband and wife without any words expressing the intent to create a different estate. The property was conveyed to the parties as if they were a single fictitious entity, with equal unity of time, title, interest, possession and unity of control over the whole property so that, on the death of one spouse, the other took the entire property to the exclusion of any heirs or other claimants. A tenancy by the entirety is now virtually obsolete. Also called a 'tenancy by entirety', 'tenancy by entireties', 'estate by entireties', 'estate by the entirety' or an 'estate in entirety'. cf. **homestead**. See also **community property, marital property**(US), **matrimonial home**(Eng).

tenancy determinable with a life   See **tenancy for life**.

tenancy for a fixed term or **tenancy for a fixed period of time**   A **tenancy** for a fixed period of time or, at least, for a period that is capable of being fixed in time – the maxim being *id certum est quod certum reddi potest*, 'that is certain which can be rendered certain'. A tenancy for a fixed term does not have to be brought to an end by **notice to quit**; it automatically determines at the end of the fixed period (unless the tenant is entitled to remain in possession by virtue of some statutory provision). It is intended to end by effluxion of time; although it may be terminated by **forfeiture, surrender, merger, enlargement** and possibly **frustration**. cf. **periodic tenancy**. See also **fixed-term tenancy, term, term of years**.

tenancy for a term of years(Eng) or **tenancy for years**(US)   An interest created under a lease, or agreement for a lease, that grants possession of land for a fixed and definite period of time. Strictly, a **tenancy** for a minimum of two years' duration. However, a tenancy for a fixed period of one **year**; a period of less than a year; or parts of a year (or even a week); may be called a tenancy for years or a **term of years**, provided the commencement and termination dates of the tenancy can be ascertained precisely when the lease comes into operation, and provided it is not a **periodic tenancy**, i.e. it is not one that continues from period to period until terminated by notice. A 'tenancy for a term of years' is synonymous with 'tenancy for a fixed term' except that the former has reference to a year or a fixed portion of a year or years. A tenancy for a fixed term comes to an end upon expiration of the term and need not be terminated by notice, unless there is a statutory requirement to the contrary.

In English law, a tenancy for a term exceeding three years must be in **writing** and signed by the person creating the tenancy (or the authorised agent), otherwise it only has the force and effect of a **tenancy at will** (LPA 1925, s. 54).

In the US, in most jurisdictions (based on the requirement of the **Statute of Frauds**), a lease for more than one year (or in some jurisdictions more than three years) must be in writing and signed by the party creating the lease, or by their agents, otherwise it is unenforceable in law (but not necessarily in equity), or it takes effect only as a tenancy at will.

Also called an 'estate for years', or sometimes a 'fixed period tenancy' or a 'fixed period estate'; or a **lease for years**. cf. **tenancy from year to year**. See also **estate for years**(US), **term of years absolute**(Eng).

tenancy for life or **tenancy determinable with a life** 1. The **estate** held by a **tenant for life**, i.e. freehold tenure limited in duration for the life or lives of some person (whether the holder of the estate or another). Such an interest is not strictly a tenancy in the sense of the creation of a relationship between a landlord and tenant, but an 'estate' in land granted for a life. See also **joint tenancy**, **life estate**. 2.(Eng)A **tenancy** for a period fixed according to a person's (or persons') life, whether the life of the tenant, or the life of another (*pur autre vie*). Such an interest (as well as any tenancy for a term of years determinable with a life or lives or on the tenant's marriage), if granted at a rent or for a fine (or premium), is converted automatically into a lease for a term of 90 years. The lease may continue after the death of the tenant (or tenants) for the residue of the 90 year period, but after the death can be terminated by either party giving one month's notice on a quarter day that is appropriate to the tenancy, or if there is no quarter day applicable to the tenancy, a 'usual **quarter day**' (LPA 1925, s. 149(6)). Such tenancies are rarely created in English law. Note: if there is no rent or fine payable, the interest is a right to hold a freehold for a life, i.e. a **life estate** or 'life interest', in other words the interest held by a **tenant for life** as in 1. above (SLA 1925 s. 20(1)(iv). A tenancy that is granted for a term, but determinable before the end of the term in the event of the death of the tenant is not affected by these provisions, but is a tenancy for that term subject to a condition subsequent.

tenancy for one year certain and thereafter from year to year See tenancy from year to year.

tenancy for years(US) See tenancy for a term of years.

tenancy from month to month See month-to-month tenancy.

tenancy from week to week See weekly tenancy.

tenancy from year to year A tenancy that continues for one **year** and then another, for an indefinite number of years, until brought to an end by the landlord or the tenant serving a valid **notice to quit**, usually to expire at the same time of the year as it started. A tenancy from year to year is treated as a tenancy for a minimum duration of one year and if it is not brought to an end after the first full year, a tenancy for another year comes into existence. The rent need not be payable yearly, provided the basis on which it is calculated is related to a year. A rent of 5,000 *per annum*, payable monthly or quarterly implies a tenancy from year to year and not one from month to month or quarter to quarter. However, if the rent is fixed by reference to a shorter period, it creates a tenancy for that period. A tenancy from year to year does not come to an end upon the death of either party, nor by the mere alienation by either party; in this respect, it can be distinguished from a **tenancy at will**. Nonetheless, the tenancy from year to year must be determinable by proper notice given by either party, in this respect it is granted for a certain term (*id certum est quod certum reddi potest*).

At common law, a tenancy from year to year, or a 'yearly tenancy' (unless there is an agreement or statutory requirement to the contrary) may be terminated by notice given **half a year** before the anniversary of the commencement date.

In English law, it has been held that a tenancy 'for one year certain, and thereafter from year to year' cannot be terminated by notice to quit until it has run at least *two* full years, and cannot be terminated until the end of the third year or any subsequent year (*Re Searle* [1912] 1 Ch 610). Also, a yearly tenancy that starts on January 1 may be terminated by notice given on or before June 30 to expire on December 31, unless there is anything expressly to the contrary; literally construed, the end of a 'year' is midnight of the day before the anniversary of the day on which the tenancy commenced. However, a notice to quit that expires on the anniversary date itself is normally just as good.

In the US, in the absence of any agreement, express or implied, many jurisdictions follow the common law and require not less than six months notice of termination; although a few jurisdictions provide by statute that a tenancy from year to year does not need to be terminated by notice. In some states, there are statutory requirements that a tenancy from year to year must be terminated at the end of a calendar year and many states prescribe periods for the termination of such tenancies generally ranging from 30 days to six months. Also called a 'year-to-year tenancy' or in the US, an 'estate from year to year'. See also **agricultural tenancy**[(Eng)], **periodic tenancy, waste**.

tenancy in common A form of co-ownership that arises when two or more persons have distinct but undivided ownership rights to the same property; ownership that may be separately and freely disposed of by grant or devise. (The word 'tenancy' in this context has nothing to do with the relationship of landlord and tenant as created by a lease, but is derived from **tenure** denoting a right to 'hold' or 'own' land.) A tenancy in common is normally created by **words of severance** which indicate, to whatever extent, that each owner is to have an 'undivided share' in the property. Unlike a **joint tenancy** there is no *jus accrescendi* 'right of survivorship' (or 'coalescence of interests'), between the owners, so that on the death of any one owner his interest passes to his personal representative and not to the surviving owner(s). Thus, the owners may be said to have 'sole and several' interests in the property as against the other owners.

A tenancy in common does not require three of the four unities essential to a joint tenancy. It does not require 'unity of time': each owner can hold the land for a different duration; as when one has a fee simple interest and the other a life interest; nor 'unity of title': each owner can come by his interest by separate documents, e.g. a grant to one and a devise to another; nor 'unity of interest': for example one owner can have a quarter interest and the other a three quarter interest in the property and each owner can convey or mortgage his share separately. But, there must be **unity of possession**, i.e. any one of the owners must have the same rights over each and every part of the property as any other.

"The only fact which brings them into co-ownership is that they both have shares in a single property which has not yet been divided among them. While the tenancy in common lasts, no one can say which of them owns any particular parcel of land", Charles Harpum, *Megarry & Wade: The Law of Real Property.* 6th ed. London: Sweet & Maxwell, 1999, p. 480 (*City of London Building Society v Flegg* [1988] AC 54, [1987] 3 All ER 435 (HL); 4A *Powell on Real Property*, § 601). A tenancy in common, as a rule, is construed to exist when there is joint ownership and the intention is to preclude the right of survivorship; or when the owners are granted separate shares in a property but without the 'four unities' that are essential to a joint tenancy; or when the express intention is to create a tenancy in common, especially when 'words of severance' are used such as "to be divided between A and B equally" or "to be held by A and B respectively".

In English law, unless there is evidence to the contrary, it is generally considered that joint ownership of real property takes the form of a tenancy in common when: (i) money is advanced under a mortgage by two or more persons as co-mortgagees, in that case the money belongs to the mortgagees as tenants in common (LPA 1925, s. 111); (ii) the money to purchase the property is provided in unequal shares; (iii) land is held by a partnership – *jus accrescendi inter mercatores, pro beneficio commercii locum non habet* – 'for the benefit of commerce, there can be no place for the right of survivorship' (the Partnership Act 1890, ss. 20, 21 provides that any property brought into the business, or brought with money belonging to the business, is prima facie partnership property and thus is held as a tenancy in common); or (iv) the property is held for the several individual business purposes of the co-owners.

In English law, a tenancy in common (or, as it is referred to by statute, an estate "in undivided shares") cannot exist as a **legal estate** (LPA 1925, s. 1(6)), but must be held upon **trust for sale**, i.e. the legal estate is held by trustees who ultimately have a duty to sell the property and distribute the proceeds to the tenants-in-common, although this duty may be postponed. Thus, the 'joint owners' have no more than a beneficial or **equitable interest** in the land.

In the US, in most jurisdictions, when property is conveyed or devised to two or more persons, a tenancy in common is presumed to be created, unless it clear that the intention is to create a joint tenancy.

A tenancy in common may be brought to an end by: (i) **partition** – whereby the right to the property is divided severally by agreement of the co-owners; (ii) sale – so that there is no longer any unity of possession and all the purchasers take the property free of the co-owners; or (iii) the unity of the beneficial interest in one person – whether by express grant or, when all the shares come into the hands of one co-owner, by operation of law.

In the US, also called an 'estate in common' (as in effect it is an estate and not a tenancy) and in some jurisdictions a **cotenancy** (although that term may refer also to the holder of joint tenancy). See also **constructive trust**, **coparcenary**, **matrimonial home**(Eng), **resulting trust**, **severance**.

tenancy in coparcenary(US)   See **coparcenary**.

tenancy in partnership(US)   A tenancy held in the name of a **partnership**. Historically, a partnership, having no legal status, may not contract *per se* for a tenancy – the partners must be co-owners in their respective names. However, all states, except Louisiana, have adopted the Uniform Partnership Act that permits a partnership, subject to the observance of strict rules, to enter into a tenancy as if it were a corporate entity. Under a tenancy in partnership the partners have the same right to possession for the purpose of the partnership; they have no interest that they may assign as individuals (except to another partner); and, on the death of one partner, his or her interest vests in the other partner or partners (subject to payment of due compensation to the deceased partner's estate). See also **joint tenancy**.

tenancy in severalty   See **several estate**.

tenancy in tail   See **entailed estate/entailed interest**.

tenancy in tail after possibility of issue extinct   See **estate in tail after possibility of issue extinct**.

tenancy on sufferance   See **tenancy at sufferance**.

tenancy upon special limitation(US)   See **determinable interest**.

tenant   Derived from the Norman French *tenaunt*, 'holder'. One who holds or possesses real estate by any kind of right. In particular, one who holds land from another (**landlord**) for a determinable period of time or at will, in return for a payment called rent. A person who, under the terms of a contract of **tenancy** (termed a **lease**), is permitted with the consent of another to hold a possessory interest in land, where that other has an interest in the same land for a longer duration. In its primary and historical significance, a tenant is anyone who has a right to possession of land whether as a fee interest, or for life, or for a term of years, or at will, or for any certain period of time. In common usage, a tenant is anyone who has been granted a lease, or an agreement for a lease or similar right or anyone who takes over the rights of an original grantee, whether as an assignee, a subtenant or otherwise. The tenant is entitled to (a) **exclusive occupation** of the leased property, which may take the form of a right to actual occupation, or he may forego that right in return for a right to rents and profits; and (b) **quiet enjoyment**. Thus, the tenant has the full use and enjoyment of the demised property for the duration of the lease, but he must surrender possession to the landlord upon expiration, or prior legal determination, of the lease (unless he is protected by statute from having to surrender possession). 'Tenant' is commonly used interchangeably with **lessee**, although the latter is strictly someone who is a party to a formal lease. cf. **licensee**, **lodger**. See also **landlord and tenant, lessee, tenant for life, tenure**.

tenant at sufferance or **tenant by sufferance** See **tenancy at sufferance**.

tenant at will See **tenancy at will**.

tenant by curtesy See **tenancy by the curtesy**.

tenant contributions Any cost that a tenant pays towards the expense of the leased property, excluding the contract rent. See also **operating expense**(US), **service charge**(BrE).

tenant cooperator(US) See **cooperator**.

tenant fixture See **fixture, trade fixture**.

tenant for a term of years or **tenant for years** One entitled to possession of land under a **tenancy for a term of years**. Sometimes called a 'termor'.

tenant for life 1. The holder of a **life estate** (or **life interest**) in land, i.e. a freeholder who has the right to possession of land for his life or the life of another. When the length of the interest is determined by the life of a person other than the holder of the estate in land, the former is called the *cestui que vie* and the holder of the estate is called a tenant *pur autre vie*. (In this context the word 'tenant' is used to refer to a person who has **tenure**, i.e. 'holds', land; it is not used in the sense of a person who is a party to a contract of tenancy.) The interest of a tenant for life ceases on his or her death and does not pass to the holder's personal representative.

Unless expressly restricted to the contrary, a tenant for life or 'life tenant' may take the annual profits from land, but he must not take or destroy anything that is part of the inheritance or do permanent injury to the inheritance. "He is entitled to fruits of all kinds, but must leave unimpaired the source of the fruits", E. H. Burn,

Cheshire and Burn's Modern Law of Real Property. 16th ed. London: Butterworths, 2000, p. 294. Thus, he is entitled to **emblements**, annual crops that he has sown but which ripen after the life interest has ended and to reasonable **estovers**. He must not commit voluntary **waste**, unless made unimpeachable for such waste, and thereby impair the interest of the person who comes after him and he must carry out ordinary repairs to the property during his lifetime. However, he is not liable for permissive waste, such as not repairing a roof damaged by storm, unless expressly made responsible for such repairs and strictly need not insure any buildings on the property for the benefit of the reversioner or remainderman. A tenant for life may sell his interest (which is of value only for as long as he, or the *cestui que vie*, survives); grant leases; or mortgage the land for all or part of his life, although he may require consent to such actions; but he may not create any interest or enter into any commitment beyond the life or lives that determines the length of the estate, unless so empowered by the holder of the fee. In the US, more generally called a 'life tenant'. 2.(Eng)In the case of **settled land**, the tenant for life is "the person of full age who is for the time being beneficially entitled under a settlement to possession of settled land for his life", SLA 1925, s. 19(1). If there is no one who meets this definition, the 'tenant for life' is any person of full age who has an "estate or interest in possession" and the power to manage and eventually dispose of the settled land. This statutory definition includes: a tenant in tail; the holder of a fee simple or term of years absolute whose interest fails if there is no longer an issue; a person entitled to a base fee or determinable fee; a tenant for a term of years determinable on life (provided he does not hold the settled land merely under a lease at a rent); and various other persons considered to have the powers of a tenant for life in respect of the settled land (SLA 1925, ss. 20, 117(xxviii)). If there is no tenant for life of settled land, nor anyone who qualifies under the above definitions, then the legal estate and powers of administration are vested in a **statutory owner**. There can be only one tenant for life for the purpose of the SLA, but the 'tenant' may be constituted by two or more persons of full age acting as joint tenants for life (SLA 1925, s. 19(2)).

A tenant for life holds the **legal estate** in the settled land; has extensive powers over the settled land; and is effectively a trustee for all the parties entitled under the settlement; and must "have regard to the interests of all parties entitled under the settlement", SLA 1925, s. 107(1). However, the exercise of these powers must be exercised in the manner prescribed by statute and cannot be exercised for a collateral advantage. Also the tenant for life may not commit voluntary **waste**, unless made unimpeachable for such waste; and is not liable for permissive waste, unless made responsible expressly for repairs. These powers are usually subject to the prior approval of a court or the trustees of the settlement and the money arising therefrom will have to be treated, wholly or partly, as **capital money**, i.e. invested in securities authorised by the settlement or used for such purposes as the repairs to buildings on the settled land. See also **emblements, estate owner, mansion house, registered proprietor, vesting document**.

tenant for years   See **tenant for a term of years**.

tenant from month to month   One who holds a **month-to-month tenancy**. See also **month, periodic tenancy**.

tenant from year to year   One who holds a tenancy from year to year. See also **periodic tenancy, year**.

tenant improvement (TI) allowance(US) A sum of money or concession granted to a tenant by a landlord to cover the cost, in whole or in part, of preparing leased premises for occupation. This allowance covers the cost of such items as partitions, false ceilings, carpeting, electrical installations, etc. The allowance may be expended directly on the demised premises by the landlord or may be paid to the tenant as a cash sum (usually on provision of evidence of expenditure on the leased premises) or sometimes in the form of an offset against rent. Also called a 'construction allowance', or in the UK a 'fitting-out allowance' or 'fit-out allowance'. Sometimes called a 'reverse premium', as it is a form of premium payable by a landlord to a tenant as an effective reduction in rent. See also **fixture, rent concession**.

tenant improvements   (TIs)(AmE) Improvements to leased premises carried out by the tenant. In particular, improvements paid for by the tenant. Also called 'tenant-paid tenant improvements'. See also **fixture, improvement, tenant improvement allowance, trade fixture**.

tenant in common   The holder of a **tenancy in common**.

tenant in fee   See **fee**.

tenant in fee simple   See **fee simple**.

tenant in occupancy(US)   See **occupancy**.

tenant in possession   See **possession, take possession**.

tenant in sergeanty   See **sergeanty**.

tenant in severalty   One who has the sole ownership of a property. A **sole tenant**, as distinguished from a tenant in common. See also **several estate**.

tenant in tail   One who is entitled to an **entailed interest**, whether as an immediate or future right to possession. See also **estate in tail after possibility of issue extinct, fee tail**.

tenant in tail after possibilities   See **estate in tail after possibility of issue extinct**.

tenant-like manner(Eng)   When a tenant is required to use a house in a 'tenant like manner' he "must take proper care of the place ... he must do the little jobs about the place which a reasonable tenant would do. In addition, he must not, of course, damage the house wilfully or negligently; and he must see that his family and guests do not damage it; and if they do, he must repair it. But, apart from such things, if the house falls into disrepair through **fair wear and tear** or lapse of time, or for any reason not caused by him, the tenant is not liable to repair it", *Warren v Keen* [1954] 1 QB 15, 20, [1953] 2 All ER 1118, 1121 (CA). This obligation is, therefore, less onerous than **tenantable repair**; it is the form of obligation imposed as an **implied covenant** upon a weekly tenant of a dwelling-house. A requirement to use premises in a **husband-like manner** conveys a similar obligation on an agricultural tenant. See also **waste**, **weekly tenancy**.

tenant mix   The manner in which units in a **shopping center** are allocated to tenants. The way in which retail stores are leased to different trades according to the size of the store, the type of merchandise, the size and drawing power of the store, the pedestrian flow, the rental level of each store and other associated factors. A well-balanced distribution of uses in a shopping center is considered a prerequisite to the success of the center in terms of its ability to draw and keep consumers, and as a means of insuring healthy competition between retailers without causing friction between competing or conflicting users. See also **user clause**.

tenant-paid tenant improvements (TPTIs)(AmE)   See **tenant improvements**.

tenant *pur autre vie*   See **tenant for life**.

tenant right   1.(US)A right that a tenant may have to a renewal of a tenancy.   **2.** See **tenant-right**.

tenant-right   1.(Eng)The right of an outgoing tenant to compensation from his landlord for **improvement** or **amelioration** left to the landlord's benefit. In particular, the right of a tenant of agricultural land to claim compensation, upon the termination of a tenancy or upon quitting a farm, for the benefit of work expended on cultivating, sowing, and manuring land. This right was originally founded on **custom** or agreement (based on the principle that it was usual to grant a new tenancy to an existing occupier in preference to a stranger and, therefore, an outgoing tenant should be paid for any benefit that might accrue to an incoming tenant) (*Faviell v Gaskoin* (1852) Exch 273, 155 Eng Rep 949). However, this right is now governed by statute. See also **compensation for improvements**.   **2.**(Ire)A form of tenancy by which the holder was entitled to (i) a permanent tenancy of land as long as he paid his rent and performed his obligations; (ii) sell his interest without restraint by the landlord; and (iii) a right to payment of compensation on eviction or termination of the tenancy. A right that originated in Ulster and was extended to the rest of Ireland (Landlord and Tenant (Ireland) Act 1870). This right has generally been superseded by subsequent legislation.

tenantable repair   Such repairs as a tenant might reasonably be required to carry out by virtue of the fact that he has been granted a right to use and occupy another's property and it is not expected that he should be permitted to return the premises at the end of the tenancy in an unduly deteriorated state. The type of **repair** that an incoming tenant would expect an outgoing tenant to have carried out; "'Good tenantable repair' is such repair as, having regard to the age, character and locality of the house, would make it reasonably fit for occupation of a reasonably-minded tenant of the class who would be likely to take it. ... The house need not be put into the same condition as when the tenant took it; it need not be put into perfect repair", *Proudfoot v Hart* (1890) 25 QBD 42, 52 (CA) (*United Cigar Stores Ltd v Buller* [1931] 2 DLR 144, 147 (Can)). In that case the lease was granted for three years, so a stricter interpretation may well be applicable to a longer lease (and conversely a lesser obligation to a shorter lease). Even though premises are in a very poor state at the outset, a tenant is not absolved from carrying out 'reasonable repairs'. Words such as "repair reasonably and properly", "keep in good repair", "sufficient repair", and "tenantable repair" all convey similar meanings. "The tenant must when necessary restore by reparation or renewal of subsidiary parts the subject matter demised to a condition in which it is reasonably fit for the purposes for which such a subject matter would ordinarily be used", *Anstruther-Gough-Calthorpe v McOscar* [1924] 1 KB 716, 729 (CA). However, all such words should be interpreted in the context of the lease and with due regard to the condition and locality of the property at the start of the lease. A tenant is not required to redecorate completely (a requirement to "redecorate completely" would normally be an express covenant in a lease) if an incoming tenant would be happy to take the premises without complete redecoration, providing there would be no undue adverse effect on the rent the incoming tenant might pay. A tenant is not obliged to repair or restore that which has worn out by age, but he should carry out such work as painting the woodwork to preserve it. The tenant is not responsible for **fair wear and tear**; but he must not commit **waste**.

In the US, the terms 'tenantable repair' or 'good tenantable repair' are not commonly used in leases; the more usual term being **good repair**, or 'good order and condition'. However, when the term is used, it carries a similar connotation to that referred to above (American Law Reports, *Annotations and Cases*, Anno: 45 ALR 12, 13-17: Tenant's Covenant to Repair IIIc Good order and condition). cf. **tenant-like manner**. See also **good repair**, **wear and tear**[AmE].

tenantry[US]   1. Property occupied by tenants. 2. A body of tenants.

tenants' association   See **merchants' association**.

tenant's contribution   See **escalation clause**[AmE], **service charge**[BrE].

tenant's default insurance   An insurance policy taken out to indemnify a landlord against a loss of rent in the event of the tenant's default; for example, on the liquidation or bankruptcy of the tenant. Also called 'tenant's insurance' or 'lease insurance'. cf. **rent-loss insurance**.

tenant's fixture   See **agricultural tenant's fixture**[Eng], **fixture**, **trade fixture**.

tenant's improvement   An improvement to a property made at a tenant's expense. See also **compensation for improvements**, **fixture**.

tenant's insurance   See **tenant's default insurance**.

tender   1. An unqualified **offer** of goods or services to fulfil a demand or obligation. Thus "one *tenders* from a prudential motive in order to serve specific purposes", George Crabb, *Crabb's English Synonyms*. 1816. Reprint, London: Routledge, 1982. 2. An actual proffering of the exact amount of money required to pay a debt at the time and place where the obligation is due, especially in order to avoid a penalty or forfeiture or a right. A tender represents an expression of willingness to pay a debt or discharge an obligation. It is a means by which a penalty, or the forfeiture of a right, may be avoided; but it does not discharge the debt or obligation that is accomplished only by payment or complete performance. See also **bid**, **bilateral contract**, **legal tender**, **rent**. 3. A response to an invitation to supply goods or services. Usually a tender constitutes an **offer**, which the invitor is at liberty to reject or accept. However, whether the party who calls for a tender is obliged automatically to accept the offer made by the tenderer depends on the language of that invitation. See also **invitation to trade**[AmE]/ **invitation to treat**[BrE].

tenement   1. Derived from the Latin *tenere*, 'to hold', or *tenementum*, 'creating a holding'. That which can be the subject of **tenure**; land or real property. Any permanent incorporeal right to land that can be held (2 *Bl Comm* 17). 'Tenement' includes the right to anything that issues out of or is a part of land, such as rent, commons, estovers, or other profits, provided it is permanent. Anything that is connected with or savours of realty. "In popular language 'tenement' means a house or part of a house capable of separate occupation, and is sometimes so used in statutes; and, where the language or the purpose of the statute so requires, the expression is restricted to property capable of visible and physical occupation, and does not include incorporeal rights", 39(2) *Halsbury's Laws of England,* Real Property, 4th ed. Reissue, para. 78. The term 'tenement' is used frequently in conjunction with **hereditament** and the terms may be considered as synonymous. However, 'hereditament' refers more particularly to that which is capable of inheritance and 'tenement' to any right to land. See also **dominant tenement, servient tenement**. **2.** A house or land that is the subject of tenure. A dwelling or place in which to live, especially a room or apartment in an old and run-down building. See also **tenement building**.

tenement building   **1.** A house divided and let as separate dwellings. A building that contains a number of dwellings that are leased separately. A term applied commonly to any residential building that contains a number of rooms, flats, or apartments, with a common access from the street. In particular, a tenement building is one that contains rooms or flats that are significantly over-crowded and have substandard amenities, or shared facilities and where the occupiers are deprived of many of the essentials of privacy, decency, and good health. In the US, a similar type of building may also be called a 'community house'. See also **apartment house**[(AmE)]. **2.**[(Scot)]"A single or individual building, although containing several dwelling-houses, with, it may be, separate means of access, but under the same roof, and enclosed by the same gables of walls", Frank Worsdall, *The Tenement: A Way of Life*, 1979, p. 1. The individual dwelling areas or spaces are held in separate ownership,

with the entrance areas, passages, stairways and similar areas, held in common with the other individual owners, or held and managed by the local authority.   **3.** In a lease, a 'tenement house' is a large house let in parts to a number of tenants with each part also called a house; "part of a house so structurally divided and separated as to be capable of being a distinct property or a distinct subject of a lease", *Russell v Coutts* (1881) 9 R 261, 19 Sc LR 691 (Scot).

tenement factory   **1.**[(Eng)]A **factory** situated in a building that contains similar premises at different levels.   **2.** See **flatted factory**.

tenendum[(Lat)]   **1.** 'To hold'; 'to be holden'. Land held from a superior lord. A word used "to signify the tenure by which the estate granted was to be holden", 2 *Bl Comm* 298, 299.   **2.** A clause in a deed that sets out the kind of tenure that was to be held. In a lease, the 'tenendum' indicates the interest held by the tenant. In practice, the tenendum is usually combined with the **habendum** and starts with the phrase "to hold", or in a phrase that combines both meanings, "to have and to hold". See also **conveyance, tenure**.

tenets of rating[(Eng)]   See **rateable occupation**.

tenor or **tenour**   **1.** Derived from the Latin *tenor* 'the act of holding' or Old French '*tenér*' 'to hold'. The general meaning or process of thought. The import or general sense of a document. An executor of a will 'according to the tenor' is one who is appointed by constructive interpretation rather than by an exact provision. See also **words**. **2.** The exact words. A copy of an instrument or deed that sets out the precise words and figures.

tenure   A right to hold property, especially land. The term or mode by which a right or title is held. In particular, the word tenure is a vestige of the **feudal system** whereby all land was held subject to the acknowledgement of a superior right. Under the feudal system of land tenure all land was held of a superior lord and ultimately from the

Sovereign, subject to the rendering of a service or the making of a payment for the privilege. The Sovereign was the only person who had an absolute right to the ownership of land and 'tenure' signified that land was held or possessed from another; it implied that one man held in an inferior position to another. Most forms of feudal tenure were abolished or converted to free and common socage from 1660 (Tenures Abolition Act 1660). In modern usage, tenure means the manner in which land is held and may be qualified by being 'freehold' or 'leasehold'. The term may also be used synonymously with 'tenancy', which signifies in the same way that land is held from another. (Strictly, the terms 'tenure' and 'tenancy' have different origins, the former being a right to land held against another – to exclude another's seisin; the latter being a contractual right to the **exclusive occupation** of land for a certain duration, in return for a payment called rent.)

In the US, land may be considered to be held under an **allodial system**, whereby a holder of the fee estate holds in his own right and not by virtue of any sovereign authority, other than the sovereign right to limit the use of land by **police power**. See also **doctrine of tenure, gavelkind**(Eng), **manor, security of tenure, tenant for life**.

term 1. A word or phrase used in a particular sense. A word or phrase that has a fixed or known meaning in a science, art or profession. "Every *term* or *expression* is a word [or words], but every *word* is not denominated a *term* or *expression*. ... Usage determines *words*; science fixes *terms*; sentiment provides *expressions*", George Crabb, *Crabb's English Synonyms.* 1816. Reprint, London: Routledge, 1982. See also *ejusdem generis, noscitur a sociis*, **term of art, words**. 2. A part of an agreement that relates to a particular matter. A **condition, warranty**, or **limitation** in an agreement. The word 'term' has no legal import, although it is commonly used in contradistinction to refer to any clause or part of a contract that falls short of a condition and which, if breached, would not give rise to a right to terminate the contract. Also, a term may be classified as a 'material' term (usually called a 'condition') or a 'non-material' term (usually called a 'warranty'). See also **covenant, express term, implied term, terms and conditions**. 3. A fixed or prescribed period of **time**. A specified **duration**, or length of time, for which something is permitted to endure. The **quantity** or duration for which an estate or interest in land may exist, especially a fixed period for which a lease is granted. The period for which a right to use and occupy land may be enjoyed. The word 'term' may be qualified in order to signify the time for which a lease or estate may last, assuming that it will run the full period for which it was granted, e.g. a 'term of years' or a 'life term' or 'life estate'. See also **habendum, tenancy for a fixed term, termination, unexpired term**.

term and reversion method(BrE)   The conventional method of assessing the capital value of a property that will generate a variable income. Each tranche of income is capitalised for the term for which it is receivable and these capital values are summated. For example, if a property is let at a rent of £10,000 per annum for 3 years and then it is estimated that the income will revert to a market rent of £15,000 per annum, the capital value may be assessed as:

'term rent'	£10,000 p.a.	
years' purchase (YP) for 3 years at 5%	<u>2.72</u>	
		£27,232
'reversion' to capitalised in perpetuity at 6½%	£15,000 p.a. 15.38	
deferred 3 years at 6½%	× <u>0.83</u>	
	<u>12.77</u>	
		<u>£191,481</u>
Total capital value		£218,713

(Note: The 'term rent' is considered a more secure income and, therefore, is capitalised at a lower rate of interest or higher capitalisation rate than the market rent.) Sometimes called the 'block-income approach'. cf. **hardcore method**.

See also **income method of valuation**.

term contract   A contract that is made for a fixed period of **time** and does not automatically continue at the end of the specified term. See also **installment land contract**[US], **long-term insurance agreement**, **term loan**, **term of years**.

term date   The date on which a **tenancy for a fixed term** comes to an end by effluxion of time. See also **unexpired term**.

term day   See **quarter day**.

term for years   See **term of years**.

term loan   1. See **standing loan**.   2. A medium-term loan granted to a corporation, as distinguished from a loan made through the capital market (such as debenture or capital stock). A term loan usually requires amortisation of part of the capital with a significant balloon payment upon redemption. Term loans generally require the borrower to meet strict operating requirement, such as the maintenance of specified working capital ratios and restrictions on the pledging of assets.

term of art   See **word of art**.

term of years   A lease granted for a fixed and definite period of time that relates to a **year**. Strictly, a term of, or for, years is a term of not less than two years; "if a Man makes a lease for Years, without saying how many, this shall be a good Lease for two years certain, because for more there would be no Certainty, and for less there can be no sense in the word", *Bishop of Bath's Case* (1605) Co Rep 34b, 35b, 77 Eng Rep 303, 305-6. However, a 'term of years' or an 'estate for years' may be intended to be for a duration of only one year; and, in most contexts, a lease for a fraction of a year may be considered a 'term of years', the phrase meaning a term of fixed duration that has reference to a period of a year or part of a year. The essential requirement is that the duration is fixed and that it has reference to a year, years, or part of a year.

In English law, in the definition of a **term of years absolute**, a term of years includes a "term for less than a year, or for a year or years and a fraction of a year or from year to year", LPA 1925, s. 205(1)(xxvii) (LRA 2002, s. 132(1)). However, in relation to the provisions of the L&T Act 1954 s. 38(4), which provide for the exclusion of a **business tenancy** from the other provisions of that Act, a tenancy for a term of twelve months and thereafter from year to year, subject to determination by the landlord giving 12 months' notice, has been held not to be a tenancy "granted for a term of years certain" *Nicholls v Kinsey* [1994] EGCS 9 (CA).

In the US, an estate for a 'term of years' is defined as an estate that lasts for a "fixed and computable" period of time. It is "fixed" when the lease specifies a beginning and end date, and "computable" when there is a means to determine those dates (The American Law Institute, *Restatement Second, Property (Landlord and Tenant)* § 1.4, Comment *c* (1977); United States v. First Nat'l Bank, 74 F.2d 360 (5th Cir 1934)). The 'term of years' may be longer or shorter than a year (The American Law Institute, *Restatement of Property* § 19 (1936)). See also **estate for years**[US], **tenancy for a term of years**[Eng], **tenancy for life**[Eng], **tenancy for years**[US].

term of years absolute[Eng]   A lease granted for a fixed and ascertainable duration; which may include a **periodic tenancy**, provided the periods are fixed and are of ascertainable duration. "'Term of years absolute' means a term of years (taking effect either in possession or in reversion whether or not at a rent) with or without impeachment for **waste**, subject or not to another **legal estate**, and either certain or liable to determination by notice, re-entry, operation of law or by a provision for cesser on redemption, or in any other event (other than the dropping of a life, or the determination of a determinable life interest); but does not include any term of years determinable with life or lives or with the cesser of a determinable life interest", LPA 1925, s. 205(1)(xxvii). A 'term of years absolute' does not include a lease that is "not expressed to take effect in **possession** for 21 years after the creation thereof"; but the expression "term of years" does include a "term for less than a year, or for a year or years and a fraction of a year or from year to year" LPA 1925, s. 205(1)(xxvii). However, neither a **tenancy at will** nor **tenancy at sufferance** can be a term of years, because their duration is wholly uncertain. The word **absolute** indicates that the term cannot be qualified by prior determination on the ending of a life or lives, or the prior determination of a determinable life interest; but it can be determinable by notice to quit, a right of re-entry, operation of law, or (as in the case of such a lease granted as a form of charge) a provision for cesser on redemption. A term of years absolute is one of the two interests in land that can exist as a "legal estate" (LPA 1925 s. 1(1)(b)), provided it is created by the required formalities (in most cases by deed). See also **legal lease, tenancy for a fixed term, term**.

term of years certain(Eng)   See **term of years**.

term policy   See **long-term insurance agreement**.

terminable interest   An interest in land that will come to an end on the occurrence of a specified event or on a specified date, e.g. a tenancy for a life or a tenancy for a term of years. In the US, sometimes called 'terminable property'. cf. **periodic interest**. See also **term**.

terminal equity   The value of an investor's interest, or **equity**, in a property at the end of an assumed period of ownership or at the time when all loans or debt capital will have been repaid. See also **equity build-up, redemption value**.

terminable property(US)   See **terminable interest**.

terminal capitalization rate   The capitalisation rate(BrE)/capitalization rate(AmE) applied to the net operating income for the last year of the actual or anticipated holding period of a property. Terminal capitalization rate may be expressed by the symbol R_T. Also called a 'residual capitalization rate'. cf. **going-in capitalization rate**. See also **internal rate of return, redemption value**.

terminal value   See **redemption value**.

termination   The coming or bringing to an end, as with a contract, lease or interest in land. In particular, the act of bringing to an end by mutual agreement, by effluxion of time, or by the exercise of a right of one of the parties. 'Termination' may have a transitive or intransitive meaning, according to the context. It may mean the act of coming to an end, or the action of being brought to an end, by whatsoever means. It may also be used to refer to the bringing of an agreement to an end as a matter of right, or in accordance with a condition in the agreement; as well as an ending of the contract as a result of a deliberate breach by one party amounting to a repudiation of the whole contract. "'Terminate' is an ambiguous word, since it may refer to a termination by a right under the agreement or by a condition incorporated in it or by a deliberate breach of one party amounting to a repudiation of the whole contract", *Bridge v Campbell Discount Co* [1962] AC 600, 620 (HL).

In relation to a lease, 'termination' may have a similar duplicity of meaning; "termination of a lease occurs (1) where it expires, upon the passage of time, according to its terms; (2) on the happening of a condition subsequent and re-entry or conditional limitation; (3) by operation of law, as in the case of the merger of the tenancy into a reversion in the same person; or (4) by cancellation by the act and with the consent of the lessor and the lessee or by a rescission by the lessee in a proper case", 49 Am.Jur.2d., L & T, § 215. (The latter instance is more commonly a result of an 'option to cancel'.) However, the term is more commonly used in the active sense of bringing the tenancy to an end by notice, especially when that occurs before the expiration of the expected **term** whether by agreement of the parties or by the exercise of one of the parties remedy due to the default of the other.

In English statute law, in relation to an **agricultural tenancy**, termination means "the **cesser** of a contract of tenancy by reason of effluxion of time or from any other cause", Agricultural Holdings Act 1948, s. 94. cf. **rescission**. See also **determination, disclaimer, expiration, forfeiture, frustration, merger, notice to quit, satisfaction, surrender, time is of the essence**.

termination clause   A clause that permits either party to nullify or terminate a contract. A clause that provides for a contract to be brought to an end by mutual agreement, e.g. by service of **notice to quit**, or when one party is in **breach of contract**. Also called a 'cancellation clause', especially when the cancelling party has a right to compensation for non-performance of the entire contract or an unperformed balance. See also **revocation, termination**.

terminus(Lat)   1. 'A limit'. A **boundary line** or limit.   2. 'A term'. An **estate** for a term of years. *Terminus* "does not only signify the limits and limitation of time, but the estate and interest that passes for that time", 1 *Co Litt* 45b.

terms and conditions   The express provisions of a **contract**. The essential points or stipulations that make up and constitute the agreement contained in the contract, e.g. the subject matter, consideration, date of commencement, quantity of property, etc. See also **condition, proviso, term**.

terra(Lat)   'Earth'; 'soil', **land**.

terra firma(Lat)   'Dry **land**', especially as distinguished for the sea.

terra nullius(Lat)   Land that has no owner. Land that has never belonged to any state, or land over which there was no right of sovereignty. Such land was available for claim, and sovereignty over the land could be acquired by the occupation and control of the first possessor. Early colonists used the principle behind *terra nullius* to deny the rights of any original occupants on the land who did not exercise their rights over the land in a manner akin to the European concept of ownership. As a result, the new settlers claimed the land for the ruler of the colonising country and subsequent settlement by its migrants. This view now has limited validity in international law and does not override the established rights of an indigenous people (*Western Sahara Case* 1975 ICJ 120). See also **native title**.

terrace   A row of interconnected houses of similar design that are situated on raised ground or along a sloping site. See also **terrace house**.

terrace house(BrE)   A house annexed to another house on two sides, forming part of a row of similar houses that have frontage onto a public road or public place. cf. **back-to-back house, semi-detached house**. See also **party wall, row house**(AmE)**, town house**.

terre-tenant   1. One who has actual possession and enjoyment of land, as distinguished from one who has a future or conditional right to possession. Also called a 'land-tenant'.   2.(US)In certain jurisdictions, one who purchases a property subject to the prior right of a mortgage or lien, especially land that is still subject to the rights of a judgement debtor.   3. One who had the power to dispose of land on behalf of a *cestui que use* or beneficiary; the forerunner of a modern trustee of a legal estate – a *feoffee to uses*. See also **feoffment**.

terrier   A register used for setting down a schedule of land boundaries and interests in land as held by a person or body. An official register of real property – historically as maintained by a parish church.

testament   A written statement specifying the desired arrangement for the transfer of a person's property on his death; "the true declaration of our last will, of that we would be done after our death", *Termes de la Ley*. A testament may be distinguished from a **will**, as historically the latter dealt only with real property, whereas a testament dealt with personal property. However, in modern usage a will may be used to transfer both personal and real property. Thus, in this context 'testament' is now seldom used, except in the phrase 'last will and testament' which is used as an introduction to a will. In effect, therefore, the words 'will' and 'testament' are interchangeable, and 'testament' may include a **codicil**.

testamentary disposition   A disposition of property, by will or deed, that does not take effect until after the grantor's death. See also **testament**.

testamentary trust   A **trust** established under the provisions of a **will**.

testate   The condition of a person who, at the time of death, has left a valid **will**.

testator (f. testatrix)   One who makes a will. A deceased person who, having made a valid will, is said to die testate.

testatum(Lat)   'Testified'. That part of a **deed** or **conveyance** that starts with such words as "Now this deed [this indenture] WITNESSETH …". Such words may be used as an introduction to the **operative part** of the deed. cf. **testimonium**.

testimonial clause(US)   See **testimonium**.

testimonium or **testimonium clause**
The formal introduction to the final or **attestation clause** in a deed; the clause that precedes the signature of the parties and the effective date thereof. A testimonium starts with words such as "IN WITNESS whereof the parties …" or "this will was signed by me on … at …". Also called the 'witnessing clause' as this clause contains the signature of the witnesses. In the US, sometimes called the 'testimonial clause'.

testing clause(Scot)   A testimonium clause.

the legal(US)   See **legal description**.

thing   A permanent object that may be perceived through the senses; the object of a right. That which has existence or may be considered to have an existence. In common usage, a 'thing' is that which is tangible, being the object of property; but in legal usage it means any of the rights to **property** whether tangible goods, chattels, land, etc. – or intangible – estates, interests, rights, claims, patents, etc. "By this word is understood every object, except man, which may become an active subject of a right", *Code du Canton de Berne*, art. 322.

In common law, things are divided into *real* things and *personal* things. "The objects of **dominion** or property are *things*, as contradistinguished from *persons*. … Things *real* are such as are permanent, fixed, and immovable, which cannot be carried out of their place; as lands and tenements: things *personal* are goods, money and all other movables; which may attend the owner's person wherever he thinks proper to go", *2 Bl Comm* 16. In the civil law (as in Roman, French and Scots law), things are classified broadly as corporeal property or incorporeal property; and movables or immovables (heritable).

Things may also be classified as: (i) land or real property; (ii) goods or 'choses-in-possession', i.e. movable and tangible property; (iii) 'choses-in-action', i.e. movable and intangible property; (iv) money, including legal tender, cheques or other readily acceptable means of exchange; and (v) funds, e.g. capital of a company or money held in trust being something which retains its identity but may change in content. cf. **effects**. See also *ejusdem generis*, **moveable**.

thing in action   See **chose**.

third party   **1.** A party who is a stranger to a contract, or action, but may be affected by it. One who is intended to benefit from a promise in a contract, but is not a party to that contract. Any party other than one of the principal parties to a contract. A feature of real estate is that, more often than not, it is affected by rights held by parties other than the ostensible owner; such rights being enforceable against real estate itself rather than owner, e.g. the rights of a mortgagee or the beneficiary of a trust; the rights appertaining to an easement or restrictive covenant. Such rights may benefit or burden those who are not parties to the contract by which they were created; for example, a purchaser of land affected by a mortgage or an assignee of a lease. See also **escrow, legal estate, lien, notice, overriding interest, privity, public liability insurance**.   **2.** A lender that was not the original party to the loan; in particular, a bank or institution that acquires the benefit of a loan with the intention of resale or **syndication**.

third-party liability insurance   See **public liability insurance**.

third possessor(US)   A term of Louisiana law for someone who purchases a property that is subject to a mortgage, but does not accept any obligation to pay the mortgage, i.e. a 'third party' to the mortgage. A person who buys real estate as third possessor assumes the responsibility only to "either give up the property, or pay the amount for which it was mortgaged. He is limited to one or the other alternative. This is the full extent of his responsibility as a purchaser", Thompson v. Levy, 50 La Ann 751, 23 So 913 (1898). See also **assumption, subject to mortgage**.

third schedule rights(Eng)   See **planning assumptions**.

thorough repair   A requirement in a lease that requires the same standard of repair as would be required by a requirement to maintain a property in **tenantable repair**.

thoroughfare   A **highway, street, bridleway,** or **footpath** used by the public; especially a 'throughway' that is subject to constant and regular use. A major highway or a way from one part of a town to another. A way along which traffic does or can pass. A street or path that is open at both ends for the free flow of traffic. cf. **cul-de-sac**.

three monthly   Every three months. Once in three consecutive periods of one months' duration; as a rule, three periods of one calendar **month**. For example, on January 20, April 20, July 20 and October 20. cf. **quarterly**. See also **month**

thrift association or **thrift institution**(US)   An organization that specializes in accepting deposits from individuals and making loans or providing financial services to its depositors or members, including a **savings and loan association** or a **mutual savings bank**. Called a 'thrift' for short. See also **financial institution**.

thrift shop(US)   A retail store that sells used goods.

throughput method(BrE)   A method of valuing petrol filling stations, based on the volume of sales achieved. See also **profits method of valuation**.

tidal land   Land that is covered and uncovered by ordinary tides. See also **foreshore, shore**.

tied accommodation(Eng)   Residential accommodation provided to an employee as part of his or her terms of employment; especially accommodation that is provided to enable a person to better perform his or her duties of employment. In general, an occupier of tied accommodation is granted a contractual right to remain in occupation only as long as the employment subsists; the employer reserving the right to put an end to the arrangement if the occupier leaves or is dismissed from the employment. However, in the case of a 'qualifying agricultural worker', if the right of occupation existed prior to January 15, 1989 he or she may be a **protected occupier**; and, if the right is granted on or after that date, he or she may have an **assured tenancy**.

tied cottage(BrE)   A cottage maintained by an employer, especially a farmer or owner of a large estate, for occupation by an employee. See also **tied accommodation**.

tied house(BrE)   A public house which, by virtue of a franchise or control over its ownership (in the form of outright ownership or a mortgage), may sell only those alcoholic or other beverages supplied by a particular brewer or distiller. A term that may be applied also to any business house that is obliged to purchase its goods from a particular concern (Finance Act 1998, s. 41). See also **equity of redemption, solus agreement, tied accommodation**.

tied loan or **tied mortgage**   A loan that is granted subject to a tie or commitment to some other business relationship. For example, a loan granted on condition that the borrower purchases goods or services that are supplied by the lender. See also **equity of redemption, solus agreement**(BrE), **tying agreement**(AmE).

tier(US)   See **government survey system**.

timber   In general, a growing **tree** or wood therefrom, especially wood that may be used for building, carpentry or joinery. The traditional common law view is that 'timber' could only be derived from an oak, ash or elm, any of which had to be over twenty years old, and it had to be sufficient to make a good post. However, it is now more generally accepted that timber can be derived from any species of tree, provided it can be put to a similar use. In some instances, a local custom may dictate that 'timber' can only be derived from the species of tree mentioned above; or from beech, hornbeam, lime, whitethorn, blackthorn, aspen or horse-chestnut. Also, in some cases, 'timber' is only considered to be wood derived from a tree that has reached certain size, e.g. a minimum diameter of six inches, a girth of two feet, or a height of ten feet. In English law, larch, willow and fruit-trees have been held not to constitute timber.

In the US, in most states, a grant or conveyance of "timber", made without qualification, includes trees that are suitable for the manufacture of lumber that can be used for building or similar construction. Thus, saplings, brush, fruit trees, and trees that could be used only for ornament or firewood, are not normally classified as 'timber'. See also **estovers, waste**.

timber rights   See **profit à prendre**.

time   A measure of change; the relative occurrence, or reoccurrence, of something. A period of existence. In common law, time runs, as a rule, from the end of the **day** specified as the starting point and continues throughout the day specified as the finishing point, there being no fractions of a day (3 *Co Inst* 53). The word 'from' may be inclusive or exclusive according to the context and the subject matter (*Pugh v Duke of Leeds* (1777) 2 Cowp 714, 717, 98 Eng Rep 1323, 1324). As a rule, unless there is an indication to the contrary, an agreement that starts 'from' a particular **date** excludes the first day, because in common law the day is not normally divided into parts or fractions (3 *Co Inst* 53); and lasts during the entirety of the anniversary day from which it was granted (*Ackland v Lutley* (1839) 9 Ed & El 879, 894, 112 Eng Rep 1446). Thus, a lease for four months 'from' November 10 starts at the beginning of November 11 and ends at midnight on March 10. However, if the date has a particular significance, such as the first of the month, it is more likely that the parties intended to include the first day and exclude the last, especially if the rent is payable on the first of the month. Nonetheless, it is preferable to express 'from' as 'from and including', or as 'commencing on' the particular date, if that is what is intended.

When performance of a contract is required 'not later than' a specified date, generally the period for performance expires at the end of that day, unless the nature of the required obligation clearly dictates that it should be completed on the date preceding that date, as when a building is required for occupation on the specified date. A requirement to perform an obligation 'by' a specified date normally gives the whole of that day to complete the performance of that obligation. The same rule applies to a requirement to perform 'on or before' a specified date; clearly with the additional option for the obligor, or debtor, to perform, or discharge, the duty at any time before the required date. Similarly, 'at or before' would include the day specified. 'Within' a given period of time (days, weeks, months, etc.) generally delimits a period inside which certain events may happen or an action must be taken, with the last day also allowed for performance. In particular, 'within' refers to a duration and is used ordinarily to restrict that which precedes from that which follows. Thus, 'within' generally excludes the first, but includes the last day, being intended primarily to limit the period beyond which an action can no longer be carried out. Similarly, a requirement to carry out an action within a specified period 'after' a designated day excludes that day but includes the last day of the permitted period. As a rule, 'until' includes the date it qualifies – until January 20 includes the entirety of the 20th, but no longer. However, 'till' and 'until' can be equivocal and can be construed to include or exclude a specified date. Thus, such words should be qualified accordingly, e.g. 'until and including December 21', 'until but excluding January 3, 1984'. 'During' the term of a lease means the entire period for which the tenant has a right of tenancy.

In English law, the use of such expressions as 'commencing with', 'commencing on', or 'beginning with' a stipulated date have been held to include that date. On the other hand, commencing on the date set by receipt of a notice would exclude that date and would effectively start the next day, leaving the entire date for the notice to be received. 'Commencing three days after receipt of a notice' refers to the end of the third clear day after the day during which the notice is received.

In English law, a year-to-year lease, 'from' March 25, with the rent payment due on that date, starts on that date (especially as that is one of the 'usual' quarter days on which rent is customarily payable for most commercial leases) and the lease would terminate at midnight on March 24 of a subsequent year (or at midnight before one of the other quarter days, if appropriate), unless there is a clear intention to the contrary. See also **abandonment, adverse possession, half a year, limitation, month, prescription, term, time is of the essence, week, year**.

time bargain   A contract to sell a stock at a certain price at a future date. A dealing in a future right to property. See also **future, option**.

time immemorial   See **appendant, prescription**.

time is of the essence   An expression inserted in a contract (either by these words, or similar terms which denote clearly or precisely that the same effect is intended) to indicate that performance of the contract within or by a specified time is essential to the contract; it makes time a **condition** of the contract, not a mere **warranty** for the better performance of the contract. Time may be expressed to be of the essence of a contract at the outset; or it may expressly be made a condition after reasonable notice has been issued to that effect. In the latter instance, the consequences of any further delay must be seriously detrimental to the proper performance of the contract and the need for the time limit must stem from the construction of the contract at the outset or from the nature of the subject matter; it is not possible to make time of the essence merely because a breach of contract may arise, or has arisen. Even if time is stipulated to be of the essence of a contract, equity may look at the whole scope of the agreement and decide that the intention of the parties was only that the contract should be performed within a reasonable time.

As a rule, time is of the essence in the case of a unilateral contract, such as an **option**, that requires one party to take action by a certain date in order that the other party is put under an obligation, or when one party is put under disability (as with being unable to sell a property elsewhere). Similarly, time is of the essence for the service of a notice to terminate a lease.

In English law, time has been said, "in short", to be of the essence "if such is the real intention of the parties and an intention to this effect may be expressly stated or may be inferred from the nature of the contract or from its attendant circumstances. By way of summary it may be said that time is essential first, if the parties expressly stipulate in the contract that it shall be so [*Hudson v Temple* (1860) 29 Beav 536, 54 Eng Rep 735], secondly, if in a case where one party has been guilty of undue delay, he is notified by the other that unless performance is completed within a reasonable time the contract will be regarded as at an end [*Stickney v Keeble* [1915] AC 386 (HL); *Ajit (Chintamanie) v Joseph Mootoo Sammy* [1967] 1 AC 255 (PC)]; and last, if the nature of the surrounding circumstances or of the subject matter makes it imperative that the agreed date should be precisely observed. Under this last head, it has been held that a date fixed for completion is essential if contained in a contract for the sale of property which fluctuates in value with the passage of time, such as a public house [*Lock v Bell* [1931] 1 Ch 35]; business premises [*Harold Wood Brick Co v Ferris* [1935] 2 KB 198] a reversionary interest [*Newman v Rogers* (1793) 4 Bro CC 391, 29 Eng Rep 950]; or shares of a speculative nature liable to considerable fluctuation in value [*Hare v Nicoll* [1966] 2 QB 130, [1966] All ER 285 (CA)]", M. P. Furmston, *Cheshire, Fifoot & Furmston's Law of Contract*. 14th ed. London: Butterworths, 2001, p. 614). A contract for the sale of land (except in one of the special situations stated above) must be completed within a reasonable period of time from the date set for completion and the contract normally cannot be repudiated if completion is fairly delayed beyond a stipulated time; although in such a case there may still be a right to damages. What is reasonable is a question of fact, taking account of such matters as investigation of title, searches and preparation of the requisite documents.

In the US, where time is expressed to be of the essence in a contract for the sale of land, it is generally enforced as such, unless a reasonable extension of time is unlikely to lead to a loss, or the parties by their actions indicate that they have waived this strict requirement. If no period of time is fixed for performance, time is not of the essence, but the law will imply that a reasonable period is allowed, based on all the circumstances. However, time may always be made of the essence by notice given in accordance with the terms of the contract, or if time for performance has been extended by making that time of the essence. Although, in the latter instance, some jurisdictions consider that the time allowed for performance must be reasonable.

In a building contract, when work should be completed by the stipulated time, there is no implied covenant that a longer time is permitted, unless the employer renders it impossible or impracticable for the contractor to do his work within the stipulated time. In the latter event, the work must be completed in a reasonable time – "that is, as a rule, the stipulated time plus a reasonable extension for the delay caused by his [the employer's] conduct. [*Dodd v Churton* [1897] 1 QB 562]", *Trollope and Colls v North West Metropolitan Regional Hospital Board* [1973] 1 WLR 601, 607, [1973] 2 All ER 260, 266 (HL) (Carter v. Sherburne Corp., 132 Vt 88, 315 A.2d 870, 874 (1974)).

In English law, when applied to a **rent review clause** in a lease, the provision therein is usually a form of machinery for reviewing the rent and the times stipulated for the service of notices are not of the essence. If there are no express words, nor extraneous or surrounding circumstances, time is not of the essence of a rent review. However, the exact wording may well affect the interpretation of the lease provision. When a tenant has a right to bring the settlement of a rent review to fruition, for example by serving notice of a wish to refer the matter to an independent expert in accordance with a provision in the lease, then he may make time of the essence by exercising that right. If he does not take any such action, he cannot later declare that the landlord has been unreasonable in delaying the service of notice of an intention to increase the rent, unless the delay is inordinately prolonged. See also **abandonment, act of God, laches, offer, rescission, specific performance, waiver.**

time loan   A loan that is fixed until a specified future date and cannot be terminated before that date by either party. See also **term loan.**

time out of mind   See **prescription.**

time ownership   See **timeshare.**

time sale   See **installment sale.**

time-share   See **timeshare.**

time value of money   See **future value, present value.**

time-weighted rate of return (TWR)   An **internal rate of return** that is calculated in order to give due weight to the time at which capital investments are made, or repaid. Thus, greater weight is given to the capital value at the time that an investment is acquired than to capital expenditure subsequently incurred on improvements. The most common means of time weighting is to weight capital according to a geometric progression.

timeshare or **time-share**   A right to the use of property that is granted to a succession of persons so that each person has a series of similar and exclusive rights to use or occupy a property for a period of time. Generally, the timeshare owner has an ownership interest in the property (which may be equivalent to a fee ownership, or a right for life, for a term of years, or for shorter intervals). However, the right may be no more than a **licence** – a 'vacation licence'. Time sharing is most commonly used for resort or vacation property to enable the users to have a legal interest in the property and a right of user for a period of time, without having to acquire the property outright. The most common structures for time sharing are: (i) 'timeshare' or 'time-span'

ownership (TSO) where the owners have a **tenancy in common** in the property and each is granted a right of exclusive use for a period of time; (ii) 'interval ownership' where successive leases are granted to each occupier, e.g. two weeks each year or a lease is granted to each party for a term of years, with a limited right of occupation and, in some cases, the owners have a remainder interest in the property by which they all become tenants in common after a specified period of years; (iii) 'condominium interest' with each 'owner' holding a joint **condominium** ownership of the particular unit, together with the grant of occupational lease to each owner for specified periods of the year; (iv) ownership of entire property is held by a separate entity (corporation, trustee, partnership, etc.) which grants each timesharer a right to use and occupation for a period of time, and the timesharers may also have an interest in the owning entity. Under most structures the timesharers may have a right to vary the period of use by an exchange with other timesharers and, in some cases, a right to exchange their use right with timesharers in other projects.

In many countries, separate laws have been enacted to govern the structure, management and rights of the timesharers. In the US, several states have adopted the Uniform Real Estate Time-Share Act that regulates the rights and obligations in respect of this form of ownership.

In the UK, a purchaser of "timeshare accommodation", or a person who enters into a "timeshare credit agreement", is given a right to cancel the agreement of purchase, or the credit agreement, within 14 days (Timeshare Act 1992). In this respect, 'timeshare accommodation' is any living accommodation used for leisure, within a pool of such accommodation, for intermittent periods of short duration (1992 Act, s. 1).

Conroy, Kathleen. *Valuing the Timeshare Property.* Chicago: Appraisal Institute, 1981.

Jenkins, Colin, and Paul Dean. *International Timeshare Law and Practice.* London: Butterworths, 1999.

Suchman, Diane R., et al. *Developing Timeshare and Vacation-Ownership Properties.* Washington, DC: Urban Land Institute, 1999.

tithe 1. A term derived from the Old English *teogotha*, 'a tenth'. A form of due, payable to an established Church, which was based on one tenth of a person's income or the yearly profit from land. "The tenth part of all fruits, praedial, personal and mixt which are due to God, and consequentially to his churches' ministers for their maintenance", *Cowell's Law Dictionary* (c. 1600) (*2 Bl Comm* 24-32). Tithes were abolished by the Finance Act 1977, s. 56. 2. Any levy that amounts to one tenth of the value of a property or service.

tithe redemption annuity See **tithe**.

title Derived from the Latin *titulus*, 'a label'; a cause of acquiring a right. The right to or the evidence of **ownership**. The foundation of ownership. Title, if proven, is the means by which a person recovers or retains just **possession** and enjoyment of his property. It constitutes all the elements that make up ownership: possession, a right to possession and a right to property. 'Title' may be used in two senses; it may refer to ownership – a vendor's right to a property; or it may be used to refer to the evidence supporting the claim to the ownership – the proof or facts that support a right of ownership. 'Title' may be used: (i) to represent the link between a person and property; (ii) to signify a right to enter and take possession of property; (iii) as a representation of a right to ownership of property; or (iv) to indicate the means or capacity by which the right comes about.

Title to real estate may be acquired by descent, by purchase, by adverse possession, or by gift. Title may be considered to start as mere possession – actual occupation; progresses through a right to possession, even if physical possession is held by another; and arrives at the point when complete title arises – when the right and physical possession are combined. Title may be defective due to: (i) uncertainty as to whether it satisfies the law; (ii) doubt as to the view the law might take when considering its validity; or (iii) doubt on a matter of fact; or a combination of any of those reasons. cf. **lien**. See also **absolute title, abstract of title, cloud on title**(US), **color of title**(US),

defect of title, good leasehold title(Eng), **good title, land registration, marketable title, possessory title**(Eng), **qualified title**(Eng), **root of title, title deed, title insurance**.

title assurance(US) See **title insurance**.

title binder(US) See **binder**.

title block A space on a drawing, usually in the bottom right hand corner, that is used to set out the title of the document, the scale, the author (usually the architect), the date, a reference number and brief description (e.g. third floor plan).

title by accretion See **accretion**.

title by adverse possession See **adverse possession**.

title by descent See **descent**.

title by occupancy or **title by occupation** Title to property that arises as a result of being the first to lay claim to the property – especially property that belonged to nobody. See also *jus possidendi*, **possessory title**, *res nullius*.

title by patent See **title of record**.

title by prescription See **adverse possession**.

title by purchase See **purchase**.

title by record(US) A title that is derived from the state. A title that is based on a judicial or other public sale. See **title of record**.

title by survivorship See **joint tenancy**.

title certificate See **certificate of title, land certificate**.

title closing(US) See **closing**.

title cloud See **cloud on title**.

title commitment(US) A preliminary report issued by a title insurance company, which provides a statement of the status of the title to a property and sets out the steps required prior to the transfer of the title. Also called a 'title report'.

title covenants 1.(Eng)See **beneficial owner, covenant for title**. 2.(US)See **covenants of title**.

title deed A deed that is part of the **chain of title**. In particular, a deed that transfers the legal right to title to land. Deeds, or one of a number of deeds or other documents, that are sufficient to substantiate a person's legal right to land. Title deeds or "evidences" may be called "the sinewes of the land", 1 *Co Litt* 6a.

In English law, on completion of the sale of an unregistered title to land, the title deeds are normally retained by the purchaser, unless: (a) the vendor retains any part of the land to which a document relates (LPA 1925, s. 45(9)); (b) a document relates to a subsisting trust; or (c) if there is a mortgage charge, the deeds are usually retained by the mortgagee. See also **abstract of title, deed of title**(US), **forgery, title document**.

title defect See **defect of title**.

title document A document that evidences the right or **title** to the ownership of land. A document used as evidence, or proof, of title to property. For real property a document of title, or strictly a **deed of title**, is any evidence in writing of a title to that property and may include any deed, map, roll or recorded document. For goods, a document of title, in particular a **negotiable instrument**, may be used as a means for transferring the right to control those goods.

In English statute law, the expression 'documents of title to lands' has been defined to include "any **deed**, map, roll, register, instrument in writing being or containing evidence of the title or any part of the title to any land or any interest in or arising out of any

land, or any authenticated copy thereof", Forgery Act 1913, s. 18. See also **certificate of title, deed of title**(US), **land certificate**(Eng), **title deed**.

title guarantee or **title guaranty** 1. See title insurance. 2.(Eng)full title guarantee, limited title guarantee.

title guaranty policy See title insurance policy.

title holder One who holds a **title**; an **owner**. See also **tenure**.

title insurance or **title insurance policy** A contract of insurance provided to indemnify a purchaser, mortgagee, or any other party with an interest in land, against an unknown **defect of title** or against a loss due to any encumbrance, lien, etc., that is defective or has not been disclosed when a property is acquired or mortgaged. The contract (or 'insurance policy') usually covers such matters as defective or lost documentation, mistakes, maladministration, forgeries, lack of capacity to contract (as with minors), etc., but does not indemnify a purchaser who fails to make proper inquiries prior to purchase.

As a rule, title insurance is intended to provide compensation in the event that an unknown defect impedes the use or subsequent sale of the property, together with an agreement by the insurer to defend lawsuits arising as a result of a defective title. Unlike most other forms of insurance, title insurance protects the policyholder against an event or act that has already occurred, rather than one that may occur in the future; it is not a policy of guaranty; and usually entails a one-time premium. A title insurance policy is normally personal to the insured and is not assignable nor does it run with the land. A title insurance policy, like any other insurance policy, contains exclusions and exceptions. In particular, a title insurance policy is likely to exclude liability of the insurer for such matters as condemnation; governmental regulations; changes in zoning ordinances or similar regulations; most developments on adjoining property or changes to a public highway (unless they affect an existing easement); non-recorded mechanic's liens; tax reassessments or special assessments made after the policy is issued; the rights of those in possession of the property and not shown on the public records (including the rights of an adverse possessor); matters that are apparent from a physical inspection of the property (such as easements) and shown by the public records; defects known to the insured but not recorded or notified to the insurer; non-recorded encroachments, boundary disputes, etc. that would be ascertained from an accurate survey of the property; and matters that the insured expressly assumes or agrees to exclude; or matters arising from the insured's misconduct, fraud, lack of good faith, etc. However, the owner or mortgagee may be able to acquire an 'extended insurance policy' to cover some of these risks.

Title insurance is normally taken out at the time of a purchase of property by the new owner (an 'owner's policy'); or, where applicable, when a new mortgage loan is made (a 'lender's policy'). Such a policy may be issued by the same company that has prepared the **abstract of title** (sometimes called a 'lawyer-title' policy as it is issued by the insurance company based on the information provided by the lawyer's abstract and not the independent investigation of the insurance company), or it may be based on an abstract prepared by an independent lawyer or an approved abstract company, in either case it provides protection against errors and omission arising during the preparation of the abstract. Occasionally the insurance company may issue the policy based only on an examination of the most recent transaction documents and accept the risk of prior defects of title. The majority of policies are based on forms produced by the American Land Title Association (ALTA) (except California, which uses the California Land Title Association (CLTA) policy for homeowner and non-institutional lenders, and New York and Texas which have developed their own policy forms).

The policy is generally issued by one of the companies established in the applicable state.

Sometimes called 'fee insurance' when the policy is intended to indemnify the insured if his title turns out not to be a fee simple interest but is, in some way, limited or qualified. A title insurance policy may also be called a 'title guaranty policy' or a 'guaranty title policy'. Title insurance is not required in a state that has adopted the **Torrens title system**, or a variant thereon, as under that system the title is verified and guaranteed by the state after recordation. See also **certificate of title**, **constructive notice**, **contingency insurance**, **marketable title**, **title report**(US), **utmost good faith**.

Gosdin, James. *Title Insurance: A Comprehensive Overview.* Chicago: American Bar Association, 1996.

title of record(US)   **1.** A **title** to land that is evidenced by documents that are all entered on the public land record. A title that is recorded with a record going back to a government grant or a grantor in possession. A person who contracts for 'good record title' does not need to accept a title that is dependent on a claim that is dependent on adverse possession that has not been recorded on the public records. See also **record title**.   **2.** A term used in Kentucky and Virginia for a title derived from the issue of a **patent** from the commonwealth before the Constitution became effective. Sometimes called a 'title by patent'. See also **title by record**.

title opinion(US)   See **certificate of title**.

title paramount   See **paramount title**.

title plant(US)   The place, or record room, at which a title insurance company maintains a complete record of properties in its area. Title plants contain private records, although they may contain duplicates of the public records for the area.

title policy   See **title insurance**.

title recording(US)   See **land recording**.

title registration(Eng) See **land registration**.

title report(US) A preliminary report on an owner's title to land obtained for the purpose of **title insurance**. A title report shows the status of the title at the time it is issued, together with details of such encumbrances as unpaid taxes, mortgages, liens and easements. A title report is generally issued by a title insurance company and is used to set out the terms and conditions upon which the company is prepared to issue a full policy. However, a title report is not binding on the company until the policy itself is issued. The 'preliminary' title report (or 'prelim') is issued when escrow is opened, or before closing, and is intended primarily to disclose any clouds on title or other issues that are to be resolved before completion of the relevant transaction. cf. **abstract of title**.

title search 1.(US)An examination of the title records to a parcel of land and a search of the public or other judicial records prior to the preparation of **abstract of title**. A title search is made usually after a binding contract of sale has been executed and before the completion of the transfer of title to the subject land. The work is normally undertaken by a title company or abstractor who specializes in such work, or sometimes by the attorney for the purchaser. See also **bring-down search, certificate of title, chain of title, title insurance**. 2.(Eng)In the case of unregistered land, an investigation to ascertain the validity of a vendor's title, which includes examining the title documents and submitting a set of written questions to the vendor's solicitor (or any other interested party, e.g. a mortgagee), in order to verify that there is a **good title** to the property. See also **abstract of title, searches**. 3.(Eng)See **official certificate of search, official search certificate**.

title theory(US) See **mortgage**.

titled land(US) Land situated within the boundaries of a **patent** from the state. Land is said to be 'titled' when a patent is issued, which, on its face, is evidence that the state has parted with its right and conferred it on the patentee.

titulus est justa causa(Lat) See **title**.

to have and to hold See **habendum, tenendum**.

toll 1. A price or a fixed charge paid for a service rendered or privilege granted. In particular, a sum payable for the use of another's land as with a toll road. 2. A sum payable for a right to offer goods for sale at a **market** or fair. See also **franchise, stallage**. 3. To abate. To stop the running of a statutory period of time, as in a period of **limitation**. See also **Statutes of Limitation**. 4.(Eng)A right of a lord to levy a tax against a villein tenant. See also **villeinage**.

tone of the list(Eng) A phrase used in **rating valuation** to indicate that, when making an assessment for the purpose of an entry in the **rating list**, rateable values are to be assessed on a 'uniform basis', as at the date that the valuation is made, but having regard to the physical characteristics and other circumstances at the later date when a property (**hereditament**) is entered in the list, or a **proposal** is made to alter the list. A principle that is not easily adopted when (as frequently happens in rating valuations) a value is to be based on prevailing values several years before and when any comparable property may subsequently have changed in character. In essence, the current statutory provisions require that the **rateable value** is ascertained at the "antecedent **valuation date**", but account is to be taken of "relevant factors" such as the actual "mode or category of occupation" (taken as a general rule not a specific rule, i.e. occupation as a shop, but not as a butcher's shop); as well as the "physical state or physical enjoyment", or the "physical state of the locality" of the property, as it exists, at the date that the hereditament is being entered into the list or a proposal is being effected to alter the rateable value (General Rate Act 1967, s. 20; Local Government Finance Act 1988, s. 121, Sch. 6, para.

2(5)-(7)). In summary, the physical state of the property and its locality are taken to be as when a proposal is made, but the value is to be based on comparable information adjusted to reflect, as far as possible, the values prevailing at the 'antecedent valuation date'. See also *rebus sic stantibus*.

tonnage royalty or **tonnage rent**   A royalty calculated by reference to the tonnage of mineral extracted from a mine or quarry, or manufactured articles produced from such minerals, or by reference to any similar system. cf. **dead rent**. See also **mining lease**.

top-line, bottom-line commitment(US)   A commitment to provide a loan on the basis that part of the funds will not be advanced until a property has achieved a minimum occupancy rate or a stated level of income return (the bottom-line) and the balance will be retained until the property is fully-leased or has reached an agreed level of income (the top-line). See also **ceiling loan, floor loan**.

top loan   See **ceiling loan**.

top out   See **topping off**.

top-slice income   A portion or slice of the **net income** from a property investment over and above a stipulated level. In particular, the amount of income, if any, available after a **priority yield** has been paid. For example, if a property produces a return of 9% on an investment of $2m, i.e. $180,000, and it is agreed that an investor will receive a priority yield of 7%, i.e. $140,000, then the top-slice income is $40,000. See also **equity participation, hardcore method, overage, profit rent**(BrE).

top-slice lease   A lease that provides for the lessor to receive a share of the income receivable by the lessee above an agreed level. Sometimes called a 'horizontal lease'.

top-slice participation   1. A form of **equity participation** whereby the partners in an

investment project or joint venture share in different levels of cash flow received from the investment or venture. For example, the passive investor may receive the first share of the cash flow until his return equals an agreed percentage – a **priority yield**; the next share may go to the active or managing partner up to an agreed percentage; and any additional cash flow is shared equally. Also called 'horizontal-slice participation'. cf. **side-by-side participation**. See also **slice, top-slice income**.   2. See **equity**.

topographical surveying   The art, or science, of producing maps, charts or other graphical representations of natural or manmade features such as rivers, lakes, towns, roads, together with contours to delineate relief. A topographical map is intended primarily to show the relative position of objects on the earth's surface, in a horizontal and vertical plane. See also **plan, surveying**.

topping off   The completion of a new building up to the stage of enclosing the main structure: usually an event calling for a minor celebration. In British English called 'topping out'.

topping out   See **topping off**.

topping-up clause   A clause in a loan agreement that provides for the borrower to provide additional **security**, if that is required to maintain the margin between the total amount borrowed and value of the property held by the lender as security for the loan.

Torrens certificate of title   A certificate issued under the **Torrens title system**, which is a copy of those parts of the land register that relate to the proprietor's land. The certificate identifies the person who owns the title being recorded upon first registration or the new owner; describes the estate held; contains a description of the land; contains details of any easements, encumbrances, leases (normally those over three years), options, mortgages, liens or charges affecting the land. The certificate represents confirmation of the recordation or transfer of title and is the equivalent to deeds of title for unregistered land. The certificate does not by itself confirm all interests in the referenced land; these have to be obtained from the other records that form a part of the title recording system.

In Australia, such a certificate may be called a 'certificate of title' or a 'certificate as to title'. It is issued by the Registrar of Titles or the Registrar-General for the State and is identified by a volume and folio number. The certificate may be issued in respect of an absolute title, or in respect of a qualified or limited title. The certificate of title is normally issued to the registered proprietor, or a registered mortgagee or chargee. In some States it must be issued as soon as a new title is recorded, in others the certificate is only issued when requested. See also **land certificate**(Eng).

Torrens title system   A system for the registration of titles to land, originally introduced into South Australia in 1858 by Sir Richard Torrens, an Irish emigrant to Australia, who devised a system for the registration of titles to land based primarily on the method used to record ownership interests in ships as used by the British Ship Registry. The system is based on the principle that title to a parcel of land cannot pass, and no encumbrance can be enforced, unless it is noted on a land register; registered title is then deemed to be absolute and indefeasible, i.e. it is guaranteed or effectively insured by the State. The Torrens system, or any similar system, provides for the registration of land titles, as distinguished from other systems that merely provide for the recording of evidence of title, and all encumbrances that restrict title, in order to act as a form of **notice** to any third party who may take an interest in the land. Under the Torrens system the actual transfer of title is effected by registration, i.e. the cancellation of the old certificate and the issuing of a new certificate in the name of the new proprietor. Title deeds are replaced by the official record of the land ownership. This record is evidenced by a **Torrens**

certificate of title (or simply a 'Certificate of Title') issued to the land owner by the 'Registrar of Titles'. The system also provides a means for recording in a systematic way all liens (public or private), court orders, easements, restrictions, encumbrances, leases and rights and claims of third parties (especially those in possession) that affect every recorded parcel of land. As a rule, any item that is not recorded, and therefore not noted on the certificate of title, is not binding on a **bona fide purchaser** of the registered land; although most recording Acts provide for exceptions in the case of minor interests such as short-term leases.

In Australia, although the Torrens system has been adopted in every State, it is by no means uniform and there are significant differences between the States on such matters as forms of co-ownership; the effect of forgery; the treatment of volunteers (those who receive property by gift); the recognition of claims based on adverse possession; the division between the requirements for registration of formal and informal lease; and the recognition of implied easements and restrictive covenants. cf. **old system title**. See also **land recording**(US), **land registration**(Eng).

Shick B.C., and I. Plotkin. *Torrens in the United States.* Lexington, MA: Lexington books, 1978.

Stein, Robert T. J., and Margaret A. Stone. *Torrens Title.* Sydney: Butterworths, 1991.

Stone, M. A. *Torrens Title.* Charlottesville, VA: Michie, 1991.

Whalan, Douglas A. *The Torrens System in Australia.* Holmes Beach, FL: Gaunt; Sydney: The Law Book Company, 1989.

tort   Derived from the Latin *tortus*, 'twisted' or 'crooked'. In general usage, any wrong or misdemeanour. In law, a private or civil wrong, independent of any contractual obligation or trust, whereby one person, by act or omission, causes injury to another person, or to his property or reputation, without any legal authority. At common law, a tort requires three essential elements: (i) a breach of a **duty of care** owed by one person to another; (ii) injury or loss which arises as a reasonable consequent of that breach, i.e. the

damage must not be too remote; and (iii) the act or omission must not be authorised by law. The injury does not arise as a result of a breach of contract or breach of trust, although there may be a relationship of contract or trust between the parties. A tort may arise, for example, from: (i) wrong to the body of a person, e.g. assault; (ii) wrong to a reputation, e.g. libel; (iii) interference with another's goods, e.g. **conversion**; (iv) interference with another's right over real property, e.g. **trespass, nuisance, waste**; or (v) failure to take reasonable care in one's actions as they affect other people thereby causing injury, i.e. **negligence**. The remedy for the wrong is an action at common law for **unliquidated damages**. See also **injunction, strict liability, vicarious liability**.

Dugdale, A. M. *Clerk & Lindsell on Torts*. 18th ed. London: Sweet & Maxwell, 2000.

tort-feasor or **tortfeasor** One who commits a **tort**.

tortious In the nature of a **tort**. Constituting a tort.

total cost See **acquisition cost**.

total equity See **equity, net worth**.

touches and concerns land See **covenant running with the land, positive covenant, restrictive covenant**.

town and country planning A term applied to any form of planning directed, in the interests of the community, towards controlling the free and unimpeded use of land; especially the establishment of a system of laws, rules and guidelines to govern the **development** of land and the intensification of its use. In particular, a means of allocating the scarce resource of land, taking account of all social and economic factors that affect society as a whole, rather than any particular sector of society. Town and country planning is concerned with guiding and regulating the growth and change of cities, towns, villages and rural areas. It goes beyond the physical form and arrangement of buildings, streets, parks, utilities or other specific parts of the environment. It combines these aspects with considerations of aesthetics, general harmony of design, economic planning, communications, demography, and future development or redevelopment proposals, in a given area or district, in order to try and achieve a degree of harmony with the natural and man-made environment. In particular, town and country planning covers such aspects as: (i) the lay-out of sites and the inter-relationship of land uses; (ii) the balanced distribution of buildings, open spaces, roads, etc., in terms of size and scale; (iii) the arrangement of communications in order to ensure the most efficient circulation of traffic; (iv) the housing, health, educational and recreational needs of a community; (v) the provision of adequate land for the agricultural, horticultural, commercial and industrial needs of a society, as well as general **amenity** or the overall environmental 'quality of living'.

Modern western planning has tended to move away from the early grand design that was adopted in Haussman's Paris, Wren's London, L'Enfant's Washington, Peter the Great's Petersburg, to the consideration of each individual proposal for development within a set of government rules and ordinances, with the supervisory role being taken away from the architect and entrusted to a specialist called a 'town planner', 'urban planner', or to an engineer. In the US, the terms 'urban planning', 'town and city planning', or 'city and regional planning', are more commonly used for this form of planning. See also **conservation area**[(Eng)], **development plan**[(Eng)], **garden city, land-use planning, planning authority**[(Eng)], **planning permission**[(Eng)], **public participation, zoning**[(US)].

town center management programme[(BrE)] See **business improvement district**.

town green[(Eng)] See **green**.

town house or **townhouse**   **1.** A house in the town, as distinct from a house in the country. **2.** A **house** of two, or sometimes three or four stories, that is connected in a row to other similar houses by a common or **party wall**. A townhouse is normally a single-family residence. See also **row house**(AmE), **terrace house**(BrE).

town planning   See **land-use planning**, **town and country planning**.

township(US)   **1.** An area comprising a square of six miles on each side, being thirty six square miles which forms part of the **government survey system** (43 USC § 751). See also **section of land**.   **2.** A territorial or political subdivision of a state or county, especially one that is a quasi-corporate entity and has been given express powers over a particular district.

townsite or **town site**(US)   An area of **public lands** that had been settled by a number of persons who wished to establish the area as a town or city. The right to establish new townsites has been largely repealed by the Federal Land Policy and Management Act of 1976 (43 USC §§ 711-738).

tract   **1.** A **contiguous** area of land. An expanse or **parcel of land**. A large undefined expanse or stretch of land, especially a large contiguous area of land owned by one claimant. Any large **lot**, piece or parcel of land may be referred to as a tract, although a tract is generally not precisely defined, surveyed or sectioned off, but refers to an area of land that is held contiguously. Sometimes used to refer to an area of water or an air space. See also **section of land**.   **2.**(US)A parcel of land that has been referenced and recorded at the office of the County Recorder. See also **plat**.

tract index(US)   A master index or record kept by a Recorder's Office showing the location, boundaries and owners of land in a county and the deeds and other documents of title affecting each recorded parcel of land. See also **grantor-grantee index**, **mortgagee-mortgagor index**.

tract loan(US)   A loan secured on a large area or **tract** of land that is to be subdivided and sold as smaller lots.

trade   An occupation. A commercial way of life. A means of making a profit from the buying and selling, or manufacture for sale, of goods. A **business** or employment carried on principally by a skilled worker. A means of earning a living that requires a training or skill but does not necessarily demand the same level of education and training as is required by a **profession**. Trade is a word of extensive meaning and may be broadly used to refer to: (i) an occupation or business conducted by a group of people; (ii) the barter, exchange, buying and selling of goods for profit; or (iii) a skilled form of employment. It is not essential that the aim is to make a profit, although this is a common objective; in that respect a trade may be distinguished from a business. However, trade is concerned primarily with buying and selling; it may include manufacture, especially when skill is required and the ultimate intention is the resale of the manufactured goods.
In English law, in the case of a **business tenancy**, taking in lodgers and making only a meagre profit is not a "trade, profession or employment" within the meaning of s. 23(2) of the L&T Act 1954. See also **custom**, **goodwill**, **retail**.

trade area   See **catchment area**.

trade custom   See **custom**, **implied term**, **usage**.

trade cycle   See **cycle**.

trade fixture   A **fixture** that is necessarily installed for, and related directly to, a lessee's business, trade or manufacturing. "An item installed by a tenant for the convenience or relative to [his] trade", *Poole's Case* (1703) 1 Salk 368, 91 Eng Rep 320. As a rule, an item that is affixed to a property by a tenant, becomes a part thereof, and may not be removed at the end of the lease. However, a 'trade fixture' is an exception to that rule and may be removed at the end of the lease, unless it is so incorporated into the real property that it is clearly not intended as an adjunct to the business, but has become a part thereof and can only be removed by causing considerable damage to the landlord's property. A trade fixture may be considered primarily to be any item that is installed for the convenience of use as part of the trade or business, rather than as an addition or appendage to the leased property. For example, dispensing equipment in a bar and shelves and counters in a retail store. In common law, an agricultural fixture is not considered a trade fixture. However, in the US, most jurisdictions do not follow this common law view, but consider any such item like any other trade fixture and allow its removal at the end of a lease, unless it is permanently fixed to the land; is clearly intended as an integral part of a farm; and would cause considerable damage if removed.

A lease may provide that a tenant cannot remove any fixture at the end of his lease, but in order for the tenant to lose his ordinary right to remove a trade fixture, the items that cannot be removed must be clearly and expressly agreed. In cases where a tenant has the right to remove a trade fixture, he must do so before the end of the lease, or at least within a 'reasonable' time thereafter. See also **agricultural tenant's fixture**(Eng), **distress**.

trade property   See **business property**.

trade usage   See **custom, usage**.

trading area   See **catchment area**.

trading estate(BrE)   **1.** An **industrial estate**. In particular, an industrial estate where the main occupants are involved in manufacture.   **2.** A form of industrial estate first established by the government in Britain in the 1920's to provide cheap land and buildings in order to encourage industrial expansion, especially in areas of high unemployment. See also **development area**.

trading on the equity(AmE)   **1.** Increasing the rate of return on the equity invested in a property by borrowing funds at a rate of interest that is lower than the return provided by the existing or projected net income from the property. The result is sometimes called 'upside leverage'. See also **convertible mortgage, leverage**.   **2.** The **assignment** of a contract for the sale of land, especially when the property is worth more than when the agreement was entered into, i.e. the equity value has increased. See also **sub-sale**.

traditio(Lat)   'Delivery'; 'handing over'; 'transfer of possession'. In Roman or the civil law, the delivery of **possession** (*animo et corpora*) of a corporeal property combined with a cause or reason that supports the act; *traditio* being a means to secure the conveyance of goods.

trailer   An unpowered vehicle, or one of a series of such vehicles, that is designed to be hauled or towed behind another vehicle that is motorised. A trailer is normally an item of personal property, unless it has been fixed onto land in such a way that it has become a part thereof, i.e. it has become a **fixture**. In that case it is no. longer strictly speaking a 'trailer', but a permanent home. On the other hand, if it still retains its basic characteristic of being designed to be hauled it can still be considered a 'trailer'. In the US, when such a vehicle is designed for living in it is commonly referred to as a 'trailer home' or a 'house trailer'. See also **mobile home**.

tranche   A slice, instalment, or portion. An instalment on a loan facility that has been actually borrowed or 'drawn-down'. See also **collateralized mortgage obligation, top-slice participation**.

transfer   **1.** The passing of a legal right or title from one person to another in order to vest that right or title in the other. The act of conveying or making over possession or control from one person to another. The process by which real or personal property is delivered from one person (transferor) to another (transferee) with the intention of passing ownership to the latter. A change in the party who has possession or title to a property. In general use, transfer is an all embracing term and may include any means of disposing or parting with property or an interest in property, including a **conveyance**, sale, mortgage, gift, devise, or a grant or creation of a lien or encumbrance or otherwise. A transfer may be direct or indirect, conditional or unconditional, voluntary or involuntary. A direct transfer takes place from one party to another. An indirect transfer takes place through the aegis of a third party, such as an agent or trustee, or by a transfer to one party and then an onward transfer to the final owner. An unconditional transfer is effected at the date of the passing of ownership or title, but a conditional transfer does not normally take place until the condition has been satisfied. A voluntary transfer may arise by way of sale, exchange or settlement. An involuntary transfer may arise by expropriation, condemnation, compulsory purchase, requisition or confiscation. An involuntary transfer may also arise by operation of law, as when a person is declared bankrupt; dies intestate and without heirs; or it may arise by any other form of judicial proceeding. A transfer may take place *inter vivos*, between living persons, or on death (either by will or by the laws of intestacy).

In the United States Bankruptcy Code, 'transfer' is defined as "every mode, direct or indirect, absolute or conditional, voluntary or involuntary, of disposing or parting with property or with an interest in property, including retention of title as a security interest and foreclosure of the debtor's equity of redemption", 11 USC § 101(54). In a lien theory state, a grant of a mortgage of a leasehold interest may not be considered as a 'transfer', but it is likely to be construed as such in a title theory state. cf. **subrogation**. See also **assignment, assumption, bill of sale, cession, deed, delivery, donation, grant, subject to mortgage**[US]. **2.**[Eng]A conveyance of registered land; such land being transferred by the execution of an instrument in the statutory form and by an entry of the change of ownership on the land register (LRA 1925, s. 18(2), 21(5)). See also **dealing, disposition**. **3.**[Aus/NZ]A formal document (a certificate or record of a computerised file or folio) that shows the registered owner of a parcel of land, and any encumbrances or caveats affecting that land, as issued under the **Torrens title system**. The term 'transfer' may be used to refer to any alienation or disposition of property, but it is specifically used to refer to an assurance of land under Torrens title or a disposition of title to **Crown land**.

transfer deed   A deed or instrument that is used to effect a **transfer** of a right to property from one party to another. A term more commonly used with reference to a transfer of securities or shares in a company. See also **conveyance, delivery**.

transfer fee   1. Any fee charged for the transfer of ownership or title to property. See also **closing costs**. 2.[US]A fee charged by a mortgagee to cover the expenses involved in substituting one mortgagor for another, as when the mortgaged property is sold. See also **assumption fee, subject to mortgage**.

transfer inter vivos   A transfer of property 'between living persons'. cf. **devise**. See also **conveyance**.

transfer rights   The rights of a property owner to **transfer** his interest in the property to a third party. In particular, the limitations on the rights of a mortgagee or mortgagor, or a landlord or tenant, to transfer their interest without the consent of the other party. See also **alienation, assumption, due-on-sale clause, restraint on alienation, subject to mortgage**.

transfer stamp[US]   See **stamp tax**.

transfer tax   A tax payable on the **transfer** of property, whether corporeal or incorporeal property, frequently in the form of a **stamp duty**[Eng] or **stamp tax**[US]. Unless defined by statute in a particular way, the term is generic and includes any tax or duty payable as a result of the transfer of property, or an interest in property, from one person to another.

In the US, 'transfer tax' refers especially to a state

tax on the value of real property transferred by deed. See also **conveyance tax, estate tax, inheritance tax, registration duty**.

transferable development right (TDR)[US] A right to the development of **land** that may be transferred from one area of land to another. A right to develop property in accordance with the zoning ordinances may be considered as a marketable item and may be sold by the owner of one parcel of land to another to enable the new owner to develop his land to a greater density. In particular, if an owner of a site is restricted in his right to develop his property, as for example, where a development would require the demolition or alteration of an historic building, then the right to add additional floor space may be transferred to an adjoining site thereby enabling that site to be developed to a higher density, provided the overall zoning proposals for the surrounding area are not unduly affected. In most jurisdictions, the right of transfer is restricted to the adjoining block or the same 'transfer district'. Also called an 'air right' being the right to use the air space over a building. See also **air rights, windfalls and wipeouts, zoning**.

Costonis, J. *Development Rights Transfer and Landmark Preservation* (1975), 9 Urb.L.Ann., 131.

Pruetz, Rick. *Saved by Development: Preserving Environmental Areas, Farmland, and Landmarks with Transfers of Development Rights*. Marina Del Rey, CA: Arje Press, 1997.

transferee One to whom something is transferred. See also **transfer**.

transferor One who makes a **transfer**.

transitional use[US] A permitted land use that acts as a buffer or transition between areas of different intensities or development or types of land use. Generally, a transitional use is set down in a zoning regulation to separate two incompatible land uses.

transmission 1. The devolution of property by will, intestacy or by operation of law. See also succession, transfer. 2.[Eng] The passing of a title to registered land to a new proprietor on the death or bankruptcy of the existing proprietor.

transparent investment An investment that is made on the basis that the income receivable is paid directly in proportion to the beneficial interest held by each investor.

treasure trove Derived from the French *trésor*, or the Greek *thesauros*, a 'store laid up'; and the French *trouvé*, 'found'; or from the Latin *tresaurus inventus*, 'treasure hidden'. A treasure that has been buried or hidden in a secret place; is lost to the true owner; and, when found, is incapable of having an ascertainable owner. "Money or coin, gold, silver, plate or bullion found hidden in the earth or other private places, the owner thereof being unknown", 1 *Bl Comm* 295. In common law, such treasure belonged to the Crown. Treasure trove does not belong to the Sovereign unless no one knows who hid it and it is the hiding, and not merely the abandonment of the property, that entitles the Crown to it (*A-G v British Museum Trustees* [1903] 2 Ch 598).

In common law, treasure trove may also be defined as that which occurs "when any gold or silver, in coin, plate or bullyon hath been of ancient time hidden ... [3 *Co Inst* 132]", *A-G of the Duchy of Lancaster v GE Overton (Farms) Ltd* [1982] Ch 277, 288 (see pp. 287-293 for detailed history of the term by Lord Denning, M.R.). Also, the coin should contain a "substantial amount of gold or silver", *ibid.* at 291-292. If the treasure is found in a secret hiding place or is buried it is presumed to have been hidden, and the finder must rebut the presumption that it is treasure trove (however, if it is not treasure trove and is found *in* or *under* the land, and the true owner cannot be found, it belongs to the land owner). It is an offence at common law not to disclose treasure trove when it is discovered.

In English law, in the case of any 'treasure' found on and after September 24, 1997, whatever the place in which it was found or whatever the circumstances in which it was left, such property vests in the 'franchisee', if there is one, or otherwise in the Crown (Treasure Act 1996, s. 4). In this context, 'treasure' has now been given a broader meaning and covers basically any object that is at least 300 years old (but not a single 'coin' that has metallic content of which at least 10% by weight is precious metal); or in certain defined cases, any object that is at least 200 years old (Treasure Act 1996, s. 3).

In the US, "'Treasure-trove' is usually defined as any gold or silver in coin, plate, or bullion found concealed in the earth, or in a house or other private place, but not lying on the ground, the owner of the discovered treasure being unknown, or the treasure having been hidden as long as to indicate a probability that the owner is dead. It has been further defined as property in which no one can prove any rights, regardless of where it is found. If the owner of the property is known, or if it can be ascertained who is the owner, the property is not treasure-trove. It seems to be generally considered that the treasure must be either gold or silver, coin or bullion; but treasure trove has been held to include paper representatives of gold and silver, especially when they are found hidden with both of these precious metals", 36A C.J.S., Finding Lost Goods, § 1. In the absence of a statute to the contrary, treasure trove may be retained by the finder, unless the true owner can be ascertained. However, many jurisdictions provide by statute that treasure trove, if unclaimed, passes to the state. cf. *res nullius*.

treasurer's deed[US]   See **tax deed**.

treat   To deal, negotiate or consider terms for a bargain. See also **invitation to trade**[AmE]/ **invitation to treat**[BrE], **negotiation, notice to treat**.

tree   A woody perennial plant that has a single main stem, generally with few branches on its lower part, but with a head of branches that spring from the stem or trunk.

A tree is part of the **land** (i.e. it is a **fixture**). Thus, unless expressly excluded, it passes upon the grant of a right to land as an integral part thereof. A tree is also the property of the landlord at the end of a lease; except in the case of a nursery where such items would normally be classified as trade fixtures. In common law, for this purpose, a woody perennial that was suitable for building was considered to be a 'tree', i.e. it suitable for conversion into **timber** or lumber (1 *Co Litt* 53a; *Bullen v Denning* (1826) 5 B & C 842, 851, 108 Eng Rep 313; United States v. Schuler, 27 Fed Cas 978, 982 (1853)). However, a tree that is ornamental, planted for protection or shade, or whose removal would change the nature of the demised property, is likely to be considered a fixture.

A tree that stands on the boundary between two parcels of land that are in separate ownership is, as a rule, held as the common property by the owners of the parcels, i.e. it is held under a **tenancy in common**, and neither may cut or damage the tree without the consent of the other. However, where the base of a tree is situated entirely on one parcel of land, but close to the border of another's land, the owner of land upon which a tree is situated usually has a right to remove the tree or otherwise prune or maintain it. On the other hand, he is responsible for any **encroachment** or **trespass** onto adjoining land, or for any forms of **nuisance** caused by the tree, excluding natural growth or decay that causes no damage or injury. Thus, a branch of a tree that overhangs another's land does not, of itself, constitute a trespass; but a landowner may cut such branches (but not lop the tree) without prior notice to the owner of the tree, provided he does not need to venture onto the adjoining land or does not create a breach of the peace. Similarly, as a rule, a person may cut roots of trees on his own land, even if that kills a tree on a neighbour's land, provided his action is not done with malicious intent and the tree is not serving as a boundary protection. However, any landowner has a duty to maintain his trees so as not to cause nuisance or damage to his neighbour. Fruit from trees are the property of the owner of the tree even if they overhang or fall on neighbouring land. See also **coppice, forest, monument, strict liability, tree preservation order**[Eng]**, waste, wood**.

Mynors, Charles. *The Law of Trees, Forests and Hedgerows*. London: Sweet & Maxwell, 2002.

tree preservation order (TPO)(Eng)   An order made by a local planning authority for the purpose of preserving a **tree**, a group of trees, or an area of woodland (TCPA 1990, ss. 198-202). The order may specify that a tree or certain trees, as defined on a map attached to the order, may not be cut down, lopped, topped, uprooted or wilfully damaged or wilfully destroyed, without the authority's consent. There is no statutory definition of 'tree' for this purpose and an order may be made to cover trees that are smaller in size to those defined as such at common law; but bushes, shrubs, and trees in a woodland under six inches in girth and under ten feet in height, are not normally covered by a TPO, although a hedgerow may well be covered. The order does not prevent thinning and it may be made to cover a **coppice**, even though by definition a coppice must be thinned out and pruned. Such an order is made "in the interests of **amenity**" and the authority is not required to consider the economic value of the tree or trees. The order does not prevent the cutting of a tree that is dying, dead or dangerous; when it is necessary to prevent or abate a nuisance; or when required under a statutory obligation. However, this does not sanction wilful damage to a tree that is included in a TPO and any tree that is cut down in defiance of an order must be replaced, unless the authority waives that requirement. Consent to fell a tree included in a TPO is obtained in much the same way as planning permission and the consent may be granted conditionally, e.g. felled trees must be replaced by similar trees elsewhere on a site, or unconditionally. There is a right of appeal to the Secretary of State against a refusal of consent to fell a tree, or against a condition imposed on such consent. Contravention of a TPO is an offence punishable by a fine (TCPA 1990, s. 210). Compensation may be payable for a refusal of consent, or the grant of consent subject to a condition, to fell a tree covered by a TPO, although such compensation is limited normally to the timber value of the tree (TCPA 1990, ss. 203-205). See also **conservation area**, **local land charge**, **planning condition**, **purchase notice**.

trespass   An actionable wrong or transgression against a person or property. An unlawful act or transgression that interferes with a person's property or rights, including an act that causes injury to a person or to his or her reputation, but does not constitute a crime. Trespass may be to the person or his or her property, real or personal. However, the term is more commonly used to refer to trespass on land of another. "Our law holds the property of every man so sacred, that no man can set his foot upon his neighbour's close without leave; if he does he is a trespasser, though he does no damage at all; if he will tread upon his neighbour's ground, he must justify it by law", *Entick v Carrington* (1765) 2 Wils KB 275, 291, 95 Eng Rep 807, 817.

Trespass to property may be instigated by taking physical, i.e. *de facto* **possession**, or by taking away a legal right to possession, including taking away goods without consent. Trespass may be in person, or may be committed by something under a person's control; as by beast or animals, or by the incursion of an object, vegetation, building work, or part of a building, onto another's land, or in such a way as to interfere with a use or enjoyment of land or a right over land. In addition, a person may be liable for trespass if he authorises or excites such an act by another, whether as an agent, servant, employee, or one acting in a similar capacity.

Trespass to **land** (or buildings) may be committed on, over or under the land. It includes destroying anything attached to land, or placed on land or placing anything on, over or under land; as well as any act or omission that interferes with possession of land, e.g. flooding land. A person may commit an act of trespass, even though he has an unrestricted right to enter land (or buildings), if he abuses his right or acts recklessly when in possession of land (*R v Jones, R v Smith* [1976] 3 All ER 54 (CA); 87 C.J.S., Trespass, § 14). He may also commit an act of trespass if he enters an area open to the public and then engages in an act, such as blocking of entrance, that would revoke the implied consent of the owner. A person may become a trespasser if he strays beyond the limits to which his right to possession was constrained in terms either of space or time; especially if he refuses to leave when required to do so.

A trespass may occur on the surface, in the space above land, or in the ground underneath – the maxim being that land extends *ad coelum usque ad inferos*, 'from the heavens to the center of the earth'. However, this maxim is limited to a height above the ground that is reasonable for the proper enjoyment of land or a height above the land that does not affect the reasonable use of the land. Thus, an aircraft flying above such a limit does not necessarily constitute a trespass (although persistently flying over an area of land may create a **nuisance**).

An object that projects or swings over adjoining land may constitute a trespass. The English or Commonwealth courts have found the following to constitute a trespass: the running of power cables over land (*Barker v Corporation of the City of Adelaide* [1900] SALR 29 (Aus)); a neon sign that projected into adjoining air space (*Kelsen v Imperial Tobacco Co Ltd* [1957] 2 QB 334, [1957] 2 All ER 343); the swinging of the jib of a crane over neighbouring land (*Woollerton and Wilson Ltd v Richard Costain Ltd* [1971] 1 WLR 411, [1970] 1 All ER 483); and the cross-arms of a power line stay (*Didow v Alberta Power Ltd* [1988] 5 WWR 606 (Alta. CA Can). The US courts have considered the following to be acts of trespass: the suspending of wires across another's land (Butler v. Frontier Tel. Co., 79 NE 716 (NY 1906); shutters that swing over adjacent land (Homewood Realty Corp. v. Safe Deposit & Trust Co., 160 Md App 457, 154 A 58, 78 ALR 8 (1931)); the encroachment of the eaves of a "leaning building", Zerr v. Heceta Lodge No 111, I.O.O.F., 523 P.2d 1018 (Or 1974).

In common law, a person who enters land lawfully and then exceeds his authority, or refuses to leave when properly requested to do so, may be liable for the consequences of his trespass *ab initio*, 'from the beginning' (*Six Carpenters' Case* (1610) 8 Co Rep 146a, 77 Eng Rep 695; The American Law Institute, *Restatement Second, Torts* § 214, Comment *e* (1977)). However, in the US, this doctrine has now generally been rejected as an ancient fiction, at least for the period during which the possession was exercised with the consent of the owner or whilst the act of purported trespass does not exceed the occupier's authority. Trespass is actionable *per se*, without the necessity of proving damage or financial loss. Thus, a person who brings an action for trespass may recover the property *in specie*, i.e. the object itself, or possession of land and not just damages, or he may obtain an **injunction** to prevent a further trespass on land without needing to prove a continuing financial loss.

In common law, a trespasser may be requested to leave by a person who is otherwise entitled to possession, and if he refuses to leave the person in possession may use reasonable force to remove him. Alternatively, the owner of the land may issue proceedings in a court of law to recover possession.

In English law, trespassing on residential property after being requested to leave by a "displaced **residential occupier**" or by a "protected intending occupier" is now a criminal offence (Criminal Law Act 1977, ss. 6-11, 13(1)).

An owner or occupier of land owes no true **duty of care** to a trespasser, especially if the trespasser's presence on the land is unknown; but he must not act callously or maliciously; for example, by setting man-traps or spring guns. He should take reasonable steps to alert anyone who may stray onto his land of any potential danger or any inducement to injury. In addition, he should take special care of the possibility that children may enter on his property (called the 'attractive nuisance doctrine'); "the presence in a frequented place of some object of attraction, tempting him [a child] to meddle where he ought to abstain, may constitute a trap, and in the case of a child too young to be capable of contributory negligence it may impose full liability on the owner or occupier, if he ought as a reasonable man to have anticipated the presence of a child and the attractiveness of the peril of the object", *Latham v Johnson (Richard) and Nephew Ltd* [1913] 1 KB 398, 416 (CA) (Sioux City & Pacific Railroad Co. v. Stout, 17 Wall 657, 84 US 657, 21 L Ed 745 (1874); *British Railways Board v Herrington* [1972] AC 877, 907, [1972] 1 All ER 749, 765 (HL)). In the US, it has been said that "although the attractive nuisance doctrine takes many forms, its essence may be stated in the following terms: One who maintains upon his or her premises a condition, instrumentality, machine, or other agency which is dangerous to children of tender years by reason of their inability to appreciate the peril therein, and which may reasonably be expected to attract children of tender years to the premises, is under a duty to exercise reasonable care to protect them against the dangers of the attraction", 62 Am.Jur.2d., Premises Liability, § 272, p. 606.

In English law, an **occupier** has a **strict liability** for any dangerous item kept on his land. In addition, he must "take such care as is reasonable in all the circumstances" to see that a trespasser does not suffer injury while on his property by reason of any danger that is known to the 'occupier' of the land. In particular, an occupier must take care to afford protection against the risk posed by any danger that exists on his property, when he knows or has reasonable grounds to believe that there may be a trespasser who may come within the vicinity of the danger, unless the trespasser knowingly and willingly accepted the risk when he entered the land (Occupier's Liability Act 1984, s. 1; *Ratcliffe v McConnell* [1999] 1 CL 472 (CA)). cf. **adverse possession, conversion**. See also **air rights, damage feasant, ejectment, encroachment, forcible entry, negligence, recovery, right of access, self-help, squatter, squatting, tenancy at sufferance, tort, tree,** trespass *quare clausum fregit.*

75 *Am.Jur.2d.,* Trespass, §§ 1-225.
87 *Cor.Jur.Sec.,* Trespass, §§ 1-165.
Birts, P. W. *Remedies for Trespass.* London: Pearson, 1990.
Elvin, David, and Karas, Jonathan. *Unlawful Interference with Land.* London: Sweet & Maxwell, 1995.
Thomas, David (editor-in chief). *Thompson on Real Property, Second Thomas Edition.* Newark, NJ: LexisNexis, 1994 with cumulative supplements, Ch. 68 "Trespass".

trespass *quare clausum fregit* (*q.c.f.*)
Trespass 'wherefore he broke the close'. Derived from "the language of the writ, which commanded the defendant to show *quare clausum querentis fregit* why

he broke the close of the plaintiff", John Burke (editor), *Jowitt's Dictionary of English Law.* 2nd ed. London: Sweet & Maxwell, 1977, 2nd imprint 1990, p. 1476. An ancient action used to recover damages when an owner of land considered that another had entered on his land using an element of force to technically 'break the surrounding protection or close' (1 *Co Litt* 4b). cf. **trespass to try title**[US].

trespass to try title[US]   A form of action that is authorized in a few states (Alabama, South Carolina, Texas) as a substitute for **ejectment** when there are rival claimants to title to land. Unlike the ancient action of **trespass** *quare clausum fregit*, which was brought to show that a party had unlawfully entered onto land, the action 'to try title' requires that the claimant must prove title to the land.

trespass *vi et armis*   See **trespass**.

trespasser   One who commits an act of **trespass**.

triple A rating   A financial standing of the first order, derived from the highest form of credit rating that can be given by a rating agency. See also **blue chip, covenant, credit rating**.

triple net lease[AmE]   A lease that requires the tenant to pay all expenses of property ownership, so that the landlord receives his rent clear of all expenses and outgoings or, at least, the three major expenses namely, taxes, insurance and repairs. A term used to refer to a lease that is more tightly drawn than a **net lease** or **net-net lease**, in order to place a greater contractual responsibility on the tenant for real estate outgoings. The tenant accepts responsibility for a property as if he were the owner; except, of course, that the landlord retains a **reversionary interest**. The landlord may remain responsible for structural repairs, and is almost always responsible for latent defects that might arise in the building. A ground lease, or a lease to a major shopping center tenant (a pad tenant), usually takes the form of a triple net lease and such leases are normally granted for a long term (over 50 years). Also called a 'net-net-net lease', or sometimes an 'absolute net lease', 'fully-net lease', or a 'bond net lease' as to the landlord the lease is more like a bond. See also **full repairing and insuring lease**[BrE].

triplex[AmE]   A building divided into three separate dwelling units or apartments each with its own separate entrance. One of the units in a building that contains three family units or apartments. cf. **duplex**.

trophy building   1. A building that is acquired or held more for its prestige value than for its value. A 'trophy building' is usually one that has been acquired by a foreign investor who wants to display pride or a symbol of ownership. It is generally situated in a prestige location and has a prestige appearance, as with the Dorchester Hotel in London or the Rockefeller Center in New York. See also **Class A office building**, **prime property**.   2.[US]See **landmark property**.

true effective rate   See **effective annual interest rate**.

true interest rate   See **annual percentage rate**, **effective annual interest rate**.

true net yield[US]   See **net yield after tax**.

true owner   A person who is the **owner** of property notwithstanding a right, charge or claim of another. In particular, in bankruptcy, a person who has acquired the beneficial interest in personal chattels; to be distinguished from a vendor, mortgagor or grantor who has been allowed to retain possession and, therefore, to act as the apparent or **reputed owner**.

In the US, the term 'true owner' is used in statutes relating to a **mechanics' lien** to refer to the owner of property, who is entitled to notice of such a lien. In that context, the 'true owner' has been held to includes the owner of a leasehold estate and the holder of whatever interest the employer had in the property at the time the work was done or the materials were furnished. See also **beneficial owner**, **legal owner**, **trust**.

true rate of return   See **internal rate of return**.

true rent   See **virtual rate**.

true rental rate   See **effective lease rate/ effective rental rate**.

true value   The **market value** of something when assessed on a cash basis. In particular, 'true value' may refer either: (i) to the value as determined in arriving at the amount of **just compensation** payable on condemnation, especially as used in Louisiana (La CC, § 2633) to refer to the assessed value in the event of 'expropriation'; or (ii) to the value as determined for the purpose of levying an assessment. In either case, 'true value' is synonymous with 'market value' based on the estimated value in a cash sale made in good faith.

true yield   1. See **effective rate of return**. 2.[BrE]See **equated yield**.

trust   1. Derived from the Old English *tryst*, 'support or confidence'. The confidence that one person imports to another. In particular, the confidence or security that is granted to another in respect of the holding of property or the performance of a duty. See also **agency**, **fiduciary**. 2. An arrangement by which real or personal property is transferred or vested in one person, a **trustee**, to be held for and on behalf of the true owner or **beneficiary** (or *cestui que trust* – 'he for whom the trust is held'). A **fiduciary** relationship that is created, or comes into existence, when a person is compelled or required to hold or deal with property, over which he has control, on behalf of another in such a way that the benefits to be derived from the property accrue not to the trustee, but to the beneficiary. The principle features of a trust are: (i) a clear intention that the person who holds the trust property is to hold it for the use or benefit of another; (ii) the subject matter of the trust is ascertainable and capable of forming the subject of a trust; (iii) the trust property is transferred, expressly or by operation of law, so that it can be held by the trustee; (iv) the trustees are able to administer the trust in accordance with the terms by which it was created; (v) the trust is workable within the law, so that it can be 'policed' by the courts; and (vi) there is certainty as to who is intended to benefit from the trust and clear arrangements for the profit and use to remain with the beneficiaries.

A trust may be created expressly or may arise by implication of law. It may be created expressly either: (i) by the trustor or settlor transferring the property to another and declaring that the intention is that it will be held on trust; or (ii) by the settlor or trustor declaring that he himself will hold property on trust for a particular purpose. An express or 'declared' trust must be a present and irrevocable disposition of property, even though the benefits do not accrue until a future time. It may be created between living persons, *inter vivos*, or by a testamentary disposition, i.e. a **will**. An express trust may be created by words even though they do not demonstrate clearly that the aim is to create a trust, provided it is apparent that a trust was intended; the maxim being "equity looks to the intent rather than the form". An **implied trust** (or a **constructive trust** or **resulting trust**) arises when it is clear from the surrounding circumstances or actions that there should be a trust. For example, when one person takes title to a property on the tacit understanding that it is to be held for the benefit of another or when one person acquires title to property with another's money. A trust may also be implied by statute, sometimes called a **statutory trust**.

A trust may be 'private' when the beneficiaries are individuals; or 'public' when the object is general welfare, i.e. a charitable trust. It may be partially constituted when the trust property remains to be vested in the trustees; or it may be completely constituted. It may be 'executed' when it is completely and finally declared, and no further instrument is required; or it may be 'executory' when some instrument remains to be completed to define the interest to be held in trust. It may be a 'dry', 'simple', or **passive trust**[US] (also called a **bare trust**[Eng] or 'naked trust'), when the trustee does not have any responsibility for the active management of the property, or is required to do no more than hold the trust property, leaving the beneficiary with effective control and power over the property. It may be an **active trust** whereby the trustee has active and substantial duties and powers in relation to the management, control and disposal of the trust property in accordance with the grantor's intentions or as dictated by law. It may also be a 'spendthrift trust' or **protective trust** when the trustee has extensive control over the property in order to safeguard the beneficiaries' interest.

A trust may be distinguished from a **power** in that the holder of a power has no direct interest in the property in respect of which he is required to deal and has a discretion in dealing with the subject property (although that discretion may only be exercised in a directed manner); whereas a trustee generally has particular obligations or responsibilities in respect of the trust property. Thus, the court may compel the performance of a trust, but will never compel the exercise of a power. A trust may be distinguished from **agency**, as although both create a fiduciary relationship, an agent has no title or right to hold the principal's property; an agency relationship is purely personal; the agent is governed entirely the terms of his or her appointment; and the agent seeks to represent, and establish contractual relationships for, the principal. An agent may have possession of the principal's property, but title is not vested in the agent. A trust may be distinguished from **bailment** by which there is a delivery of goods to be held on trust, but bailment applies only to personal property; the bailor retains legal title to the property in question; and a bailee (unless he is a factor) normally cannot pass a good title to a third party without first acquiring title himself. Also bailment is recognised at common law, whereas a trust is only recognised in equity. Unlike a **contract**, the beneficiary of a trust need not be a party to the transaction that creates the trust; and, as a rule, a third party to a contract cannot enforce rights or obtain benefits from that contract. In addition, a contract cannot be enforced unless there is consideration, or it is made under seal; whereas a trust may be enforced by a party who has given no consideration, provided the trust is properly constituted. An **escrow** is a form of contract and the person entitled to the property that is held in escrow usually does not have use or physical possession of the property. See also **discretionary trust, executed trust, executory trust, special trust, statutory trust for sale**(Eng), **writing**.

Hayton, David J. *Underhill and Hayton: Law of Trusts and Trustees*, 15th ed. London: Butterworths, 1995, Article 1 "Definitions of trust, trustee, trust property, beneficiary, and breach of trust".

3. A form of business organisation established when a number of persons entrust money to a manager for the purpose of investment. The investors or beneficiaries retain the right to the capital and all profit or income to be derived therefrom; but the management and administration of the organisation is left entirely to the managers. As with any other form of trust, the managers have a **fiduciary** responsibility to the beneficiaries and their powers and duties are strictly controlled by a deed of appointment. The managers may receive a commission or fee for performing their duties, but may not share in the profits or proceeds of sale of the investments. cf. **partnership**. See also **housing trust**(Eng), **investment trust, Massachusetts trust**(US), **real estate investment trust**(US), **unit trust**(BrE). **4.** A combination of firms operating together, in the same line of business, for the purpose of securing the same ends, especially creating a monopoly or defeating competition.

trust agreement   See **declaration of trust, deed of trust**(US), **trust deed**.

trust beneficiary   See **beneficiary**.

trust company(US)   An organization that is responsible for administering trusts and settling estates. "A corporation formed for the purpose of taking, executing, and administering all such trusts as may be lawfully committed to it, and acting as testamentary trustee, executor, guardian, etc.", *Black's Law Dictionary*, 6th ed., 1990, p. 1513. A trust company is frequently a subsidiary of a bank or similar financial institution that also specializes in acting as a trustee for the administration of property.

trust corporation   **1.** A corporation established for the purpose of accepting, holding, and administering trusts.   **2.**(Eng)The Public Trustee, or a corporation either appointed by the court or entitled by statute to act as the Public Trustee (LPA 1925, s. 205(1)(xxviii); SLA 1925, s. 117(1)(xxx), as amended; AEA 1925, s. 55(1)(xxvi); Trustee Act 1925, s. 68(18); Supreme Court Act 1981, s. 128). A trust corporation is appointed when a situation arises that requires two or more trustees and none has been so appointed. A 'trust corporation' may also be the Treasury Solicitor, the Official Solicitor, any other official prescribed by the Lord Chancellor, as well as a trustee in bankruptcy, trustees of a deed of arrangement and various other local or public authorities who administer charitable, ecclesiastical or public trusts (LP(A)A 1925, s. 3).

trust deed   **1.** A **deed** by which a **trust** is established. See also **debenture, declaration of trust, trust instrument**(Eng), **vesting document**(Eng).   **2.**(US)A **deed** used to transfer property to be held in trust for a lender who has an interest in that property as security for a loan. A document that has a similar purpose to one that is used to create a **mortgage**. "A trust deed is similar to a mortgage in that it is given as security for the performance of an obligation. However, a trust deed is a conveyance by which title to the trust property passes to the trustee. Upon default, the trustee has power to satisfy the trustor's debt to the beneficiary", First Security Bank v. Banberry Crossing, 780 P.2d 1253, 1256 (Utah 1989). In most jurisdictions, such a document is called a **deed of trust**.

trust deed mortgage(US)   See **deed of trust**.

trust estate   See **trust property**.

trust for sale   1. An arrangement by which property, especially real property, is held on **trust** for another with express or implied instructions from the creator of the trust (settlor or testator) that the property must eventually be sold. See also **conversion**.   2.(Eng)A form of **settlement** that is created, or arises, when property is devised to one or more persons on the basis that they are intended only to enjoy a right to the proceeds of sale; rather than, as with a **strict settlement**, the benefit of using the property itself. Although the beneficiaries may be granted a right to occupy land held under a trust for sale, that is not the primary intent. Unlike a strict settlement there does not even have to be an element of succession, property can merely be held upon trust for sale for one person, or number of persons, absolutely. Property is generally held on trust for sale when there are concurrent interests, although it may be created for successive interests. A trust for sale, in relation to land, means "an immediate binding trust for sale, whether or not exercisable at the request or with the consent of any person, and with or without a power at discretion to postpone the sale; 'trustees for sale' means the persons (including a personal representative) holding land on trust for sale; and 'power to postpone' means power to postpone in exercise of a discretion", LPA 1925, s. 205(1)(xxix); AEA 1925, s. 55(1)(xxvii).

A trust for sale may be created expressly or may arise by virtue of a statutory provision. An express trust for sale is created when a settlor specifically vests land in a trustee to hold 'on trust for sale' with instructions that the trustee is to provide an income for the beneficiary or beneficiaries of the settlor's estate (usually for members of his family). It is usually created by two instruments, a 'written assent' which vests the **legal estate** in the trustees and a **trust instrument** which expresses the settlor's intentions for the distribution of the proceeds of sale. However, unlike a strict settlement, it may be created by one instrument alone, e.g. by a **will**.

When a trust for sale arises under a statutory provision, it is then called a **statutory trust for sale** (or sometimes an 'implied trust for sale', the trust arising by implication as a result of the statutory provision). The most common instances when a statutory trust for sale arises are when a **joint tenancy** or **tenancy in common** is created, or in the case of **intestacy**. If a land is left by way of **succession** and a trust for sale is not created expressly, a strict settlement arises (SLA, s. 1(1)). A trust for sale is generally created by the use of words such as "to sell the land and hold the proceeds of sale for the benefit of ..."; although there may well be a provision to defer the sale. A trust for sale may be established so that the beneficiaries can, usually at the trustees' discretion, take occupation of the property in lieu of receiving rents and profits – such a trust for sale is called an 'occupation trust'. When there is no intention that occupation should be taken, the trust may be referred to as a 'distribution trust'.

Since January 1, 1996 any land that is to be held in trust, whether in the form of a trust for sale or otherwise, is held as a **trust of land** and no new strict settlements can be created, although an existing strict settlement can continue as long as there is settled land that remains unsold (Trusts of Land and Appointment of Trustees Act 1996, s. 2). See also **overreached interest**, **trustee for sale**.

trust indenture(US)   See **indenture**, **trust instrument**.

trust instrument   1.(US)An **instrument** that creates a **trust** and contains details of the powers of the trustees and the rights of the beneficiaries. Also called a 'trust indenture'. See also **deed of trust**.   2.(Eng)The document or instrument that declares the existence of a **strict settlement** (statutorily called "the trusts affecting the **settled land**" or the "settlement"); appoints or constitutes the trustees of such a settlement; sets out the powers, if any, to appoint new trustees and stipulates any powers or duties that are an extension of those provided by statute; as well as bearing any *ad valorem* stamp duty in respect of the settlement (SLA 1925, s. 4(3); 1st Schedule, Form No 3). "'Trust instrument' means the instrument whereby the trusts of the settled land are declared, and includes any two or more such instruments and a settlement or instrument which is deemed to be a trust instrument", SLA 1925, s. 117(1)(xxxi). The purpose of a trust instrument is to set out the terms on which the settlement is made and the rights of the beneficiaries, but to leave details of the land that forms the subject of the settlement (the settled land) to be described in a separate **vesting deed**. Thus, a purchaser of the settled land can obtain title by reference to the vesting document without requiring access to the terms of the settlement as set out in the trust instrument (which sets out the interests of the beneficiaries). The separation of these rights is referred to as the 'curtain principle' of a strict settlement. When a strict settlement is made by **will**, the will is deemed to be the trust instrument, because it sets out the intended rights of the beneficiaries. The testator's or settlor's personal representative is then required to execute a vesting document (called a 'vesting assent') in order to transfer title to the settled land to the **tenant for life** or **statutory owner**.

A 'trust instrument' may be used to create an express **trust for sale**, although there is no statutory definition of a trust instrument as used for the purpose of creating a trust for sale; the 'curtain principle' not being an inherent part of a trust for sale. See also **overreachable interest**.

trust mortgage(US)   See **deed of trust**.

Trust Number(US)   See **land trust**.

trust of land(Eng)   A form of **trust** that came into effect after January 1, 1997 when land is to be held on behalf of a beneficiary, whether concurrently or successively. A trust for land is defined as "any trust of property which consists of or includes land", Trusts of Land and Appointment of Trustees Act 1996, s. 1(a); but excluding land that is already held as **settled land**, or land held in trust for a university or college under the Universities and College Estates Act 1925. A trust for land is now the sole form of trust for holding land and it replaces the **trust for sale** and the **strict settlement** A trust of land may be expressly created; or it comes into effect when a 'trust for sale' is, or has been, created, but is not expressed to remain as such. An existing strict settlement can continue, at least whilst any of the land remains unsold. However, subject to a few exceptions, no new strict settlement can be created and all land that is held in trust must be held as a 'trust of land' (1996 Act, s. 2). A trust in this context may be any form of trust (whether express, implied, resulting, or constructive), including a trust for sale and a bare trust, and a trust created or arising before January 1, 1997 (1996 Act, s. 1(2), 27(2)).

Under a trust of land the trustees have wide statutory powers to deal with the trust land, which are applicable unless expressly excluded by the will or deed of settlement creating the trust (1996 Act, ss. 6, 7, 8). The trustees can delegate their functions to a **beneficiary** of full age who is entitled to possession of the land, including the power to sell the land (1996 Act, s. 9). However, unlike a strict settlement, the entitlement to possession is not held as of right, but it is granted only at the discretion of the trustees.

trust power   See **power of appointment**.

trust property   Property held under a **trust**. Property that has been vested, i.e. the title thereto has been transferred to a trustee to hold for and on behalf of a beneficiary. See also **trust deed**, **trust for sale**.

trustee   A person to whom a property is entrusted to be held on behalf of another (the **beneficiary**). One who deals with a property as a principal or owner, but is under an equitable obligation to account to another: a *cestui que trust* or beneficiary. As a rule, the beneficiary retains the use or right to the profits from the property and the trustee has a **fiduciary** obligation to account to the beneficiary for any income derived for the property.

In general, any person may be a trustee provided he has the legal capacity to hold property. Also a corporation can act as a trustee. A trustee may be appointed: (i) by a settlement or will (as a rule, if there is no declared trustee, the person in whom the trust property is vested is considered to be the trustee); (ii) by an express provision in a **trust instrument**; (iii) under a statutory provision, especially when an existing trustee is unable or unwilling to act; or (d) by a court. A trustee has a duty to take care of the property entrusted to him; to carry out the terms of the trust; and may be controlled by statute law or power entrusted by a court as to the manner in which he conducts his responsibilities, powers and duties. cf. **executor**. See also **strict settlement, tenant for life, trust corporation, trustees of a settlement**(Eng).

trustee for sale(Eng)   A person appointed to administer land held on **trust for sale**, including a personal representative when a person dies intestate; "the persons (including a personal representative) holding land on trust for sale", LPA 1925, s. 205(xxix). A trustee or trustees for sale have similar powers and management responsibilities to a **tenant for life** under a strict settlement, such as the right to grant leases, accept surrenders of leases, or to raise money to pay for improvements by mortgaging the land. The trustee for sale also has the power to postpone the sale of the trust property, unless there is a contrary intention (LPA 1925, s. 25). The trustee for sale has wide powers for dealing with the trust property. In the case of a **statutory trust for sale**, the trustee for sale has an obligation to consult with the beneficiaries of full age and may have an obligation to consider the wishes of the beneficiaries if so required by the instrument that created the trust.

trustee's deed(US)   A deed of conveyance executed by a trustee.

trustees of a settlement(Eng)   The trustees who are responsible for the administration of a **strict settlement**, including the trustees with the power of sale of the **settled land** (whether as a present or future power of sale) or those properly appointed as such by the beneficiaries or by the trust instrument (SLA 1925, s. 30(1)). See also **estate owner, tenant for life**.

trustor(US)   1. One who creates a **trust**. Also called a 'settlor', or 'donor' or 'grantor' of the trust property, depending on the means by which a property is placed in trust. See also **testator**.   2. A person who creates a **deed of trust** in which he is also nominated as a beneficiary.

trusty process(US)   See **garnishment**.

turbary(Eng)   See **right of turbary**.

turn-around sale   A conveyance of property by a borrower to a lender and then a simultaneous transfer back to the lender. Such a transaction may be used as a means of increasing the cost to the borrower, or charging an "upfront fee", in order to try and circumvent usury laws.

turnkey contract or **turn-key contract** 1. A building contract by which a developer or builder undertakes to complete a building up to the stage where the key is in the door. The contractor accepts the risks and responsibility for completing the project. Usually the entire contract price is payable on completion. However, unlike a **design-and-build contract**, the contractor owns the building and on completion contracts to dispose of the entire project. Sometimes also called a 'design-and-management contract'. However, the term 'turnkey contract' can be used to refer to a variety of forms of construction contract where the contractor accepts most, if not all, the responsibility of the building work. See also **entire contract, build-to-suit contract**. 2.(US) In the oil and gas industry, a contract whereby a driller of a well undertakes "to furnish everything and does all the work required to complete the well, place it in production, and turn it over ready to 'turn the key' and start the oil [or gas] running into the tanks", Retsal Drilling Co. v. C. I. R., 127 F.2d 355, 357 (5th Cir. 1942).

turnkey lease   A lease that provides for the landlord to be responsible for the completion of the fitting out of the leased premises to the tenant's specification, so that the tenant can take possession and start business from the commencement date of the lease. cf. **shell lease**.

turnover   **1.** The rate at which properties are sold or resold in a given market.   **2.** The rate at which tenants move in and out of a leased property.   **3.** The value of business done in a given period. The total value of sales by a retailer in a stipulated period (day, month, quarter or year). The value may be stated in absolute terms or based on the amount of space occupied, i.e. dollars or pounds per square foot or square meter. Sometimes called a 'productivity level'.

turnover lease   See **percentage lease**.

turnover rent   See **percentage rent**.

turnover vacancy(US)   The **vacancy rate** in a building that arises for the movement of tenants, as distinguished from the 'general vacancy' rate that includes all vacant space.

turpis causa(Lat)   An 'immoral cause'. See **illegal contract**.

twelve months   A period of twelve consecutive months or one **year**. In common law, a lease for twelve-months was taken to be one for twelve lunar months, or 12 periods of twenty-eight days (*Catesby's Case* (1607) 6 Co Rep 61b, 77

Eng Rep 346; 2 *Bl Comm* 141). However, in modern usage a **month** normally means a calendar month, unless there is something express or clearly implied to the contrary. Nonetheless, 'twelve months' can lead to some misunderstanding, so it is preferable to refer to a 'year', 'twelve calendar months', or to set out the start and finish dates of the intended span of **time**.

twilight area or **twilight zone**   An area of urban decay. An area where buildings are in an advanced state of deterioration, especially a predominately residential area that is in a state of transition so that many of the buildings have been adapted to a different and generally inferior use to that for which they were originally constructed. See also **slum**, **unfit for human habitation**(Eng), **urban development area**(Eng), **urban renewal**.

two-family house(AmE)   See **double house**.

two funds doctrine(US)   See **marshalling**.

tying agreement(AmE)   An agreement by which a seller of goods or provider of services agrees to supply those goods or services provided the purchaser undertakes to purchase other products from the supplier, or agrees to buy all supplies or a particular commodity from one source. In many instances, such an agreement may be illegal as an unreasonable restraint of trade (Sherman Act of 1890, as amended by Clayton Act of 1914, s. 3 (15 USC § 14)). In the UK, a similar form of agreement is called a **solus agreement**. See also **list-back agreement**(AmE), **tied house**.

U

uberrima fides(Lat) 'utmost good faith'.

uberrimae fidei(Lat) 'Of the **utmost good faith**'. See also **insurance**.

udal ownership Ownership without need of writing (as an acknowledgement to another). Absolute or allodial ownership. A term used in Scots law, especially in Orkney and Shetland, which did not succumb to the feudal system of landownership but adopted instead the allodial ownership of Scandinavia. See also **allodial system**.

ulterior estate(US) See **remainder**.

ultimate title(Aus) See **radical title**.

ultra vires(Lat) 'Outside the scope'; 'beyond the **power**'. An act of a public authority, company, or a person acting in a fiduciary authority, may be *ultra vires* if it is outside, or goes beyond, the powers entrusted to that party; although the act may not necessarily be illegal or contrary to public policy. For example, a zoning ordinance or planning regulation may be *ultra vires* if it is not applied in accordance with the legislation that authorises the making of such ordinances or regulations. See also **ratification**, **restitution**.

umbrella insurance **1.** Insurance that provides cover for an amount, or for risks, not covered by any other insurance policy. Also called an 'excess liability policy'. **2.** Insurance that combines the indemnity of **comprehensive insurance** and **public liability insurance**, i.e. an insurance policy that covers all or most insurable risks associated with the ownership of a property.

umbrella lease(US) A lease, granted to a key or **anchor tenant** in a shopping center, in which the rent is based on the normal market rental value, plus a contribution to the landlord's debt service. In return, the tenant obtains a right to a share of the net cash flow receivable from the center. See also **equity participation**, **triple net lease**.

umbrella partnership REIT (UPREIT) A **Real Estate Investment Trust** (REIT) that does not own properties directly, but holds an interest in an umbrella partnership that in turn acquires and operates the properties. Generally, an UPREIT is created by an owner or developer who contributes properties to an umbrella or 'operating partnership' and, in return, receives partnership units that can be exchanged at a future date for stock in the REIT. The REIT is a **general partner** of the operating partnership and holds a majority interest in that partnership. In most cases, no tax liability arises until the stock in the REIT is acquired, or the partnership assets are sold. UPREITs are commonly created prior to an initial public offering of the stock in the REIT as generally the historic cost basis is maintained on the properties contributed to the operating partnership, which would not be the case if the property was transferred direct to the REIT. If REIT owns a substantial amount of property directly and the holding in the umbrella partnership is a small part of the REIT's holding the REIT is called a 'downREIT'.

umpire A person who acts to settle a dispute that cannot be resolved by two or more arbitrators. One who has authority to arbitrate and make a final decision. See also **arbitrator**.

unaccrued sum A sum of money that is not yet due, but against which a payment has already been made, e.g. rent paid before the due date (but not rent paid properly in advance). See also **rent in advance/rent in arrears**.

unadjusted rate of return See **average annual return**.

unalienable See **inalienable**.

unavoidable   That which cannot be prevented even by reasonable care and forethought although it may result from a human act. An act that results from *force majeure* may be considered unavoidable. See also **act of God**, **time is of the essence**.

unconditional offer   An offer that is not subject to any condition, restriction, qualification or limitation. cf. **counter offer**. See also **sealed offer**.

unconscionable bargain
or unconscionable contract   A bargain that is outside the limits of what is reasonable or acceptable. A bargain or contract that is so unfair or unreasonable that no one in his right mind would enter into it; or, no honest person would entertain it. In particular, a contract made when the bargaining power of the parties is so patently unbalanced that one of the parties cannot be said to be acting of his own volition, or when one party is clearly advantaged by special or technical knowledge that is used to the detriment of an unsuspecting party. An unconscionable bargain is entered into usually when a person is in dire need; because "necessitous men are not truely free men but, to answer a present exigency, will submit to any terms that the crafty will impose on them", *Vernon v Bethell* (1762) 2 Eden 110, 113, 28 Eng Rep 838 (United States v. Bethlehem Steel Corp., 315 US 289, 62 S Ct 587, 86 L Ed 855, 877 (1941)). An unconscionable bargain may result also from **undue influence** or **duress**.

In English law the courts have an equitable power to examine any **mortgage** transaction to decide if it is unconscionable or oppressive, although this power is exercised only in exceptional cases. "[E]quity does not reform mortgage transactions because they are unreasonable. It is concerned to see two things—one that the essential requirements of a mortgage transaction are observed, and the other that oppressive and unconscionable terms are not enforced. Subject to this, it does not … interfere", *Knightsbridge Estates Trust Ltd v Byrne* [1939] Ch 441, 457, [1938] 4 All ER 618, 626 (CA), aff'd [1940] AC 613, [1940] 2 All ER 401 (HL).

In Canada, each province has a statute that permits the court to annul or modify an unconscionable transaction and these laws are applicable to mortgages of real property.

In the US, the courts may grant relief in cases of unconscionable mortgages, particularly in cases of expectant heirs or reversioners, or where the lender is taking advantage of the borrower's weakness. The Uniform Residential Landlord and Tenant Act, which has been adopted by a number of states, provides that the court has a discretion to refuse to enforce any unconscionable tenancy agreement. Also, the Uniform Commercial Code, which has been adopted in whole or in part by all the states, as applying to commercial transactions (but not to most real estate or lease transactions), provides that if the court finds a contract, or any clause of a contract, unconscionable it may refuse to enforce the contract or limit the enforceability of part of the contract (UCC § 2-302). Sometimes called a 'catching bargain'. See also **constructive trust**, **equity of redemption**, **estoppel**, **fraud**, **penalty**, **undervalue**.
Deutch, Sinai. *Unfair Contracts, the doctrine of unconscionability.* Lexington, MA: Lexington Books, 1977.

under seal   See **seal**.

under the hammer   See **auction**.

underground room   See **basement**.

underimprovement   An **improvement**, or construction of a building on land, that does not represent the highest and best use of the land. cf. **overimprovement**.

underinsurance   See **average**, **co-insurance**, **insured value**.

underlease   See **sub-lease**.

underlessee   See **sub-lessee**.

underlessor   See **sub-lessor**.

under-let   See **sub-let**.

underlying lien or underlying mortgage
1. A lien, or mortgage, that has **priority** over another lien, or mortgage, granted on the security of the same property. An underlying mortgage may be a **first mortgage** or any mortgage that takes priority over another mortgage. cf. **junior mortgage**.   **2.**(US)A mortgage that is covered by a **wraparound mortgage**, i.e. the 'in-place' mortgage.

underpinning clause(Aus/NZ)   See **ratchet clause**.

under-tenant or under tenant   See **sub-lessee**.

undertaking   **1.** An agreement to perform an act or provide a service. A **promise** to do or to refrain from doing something. For example, an agent or broker may undertake to use his best endeavours to find a purchaser **ready, willing and able** to buy a property. An undertaking may have the force of a binding contract; or it may represent no more than an expression of intent – binding only morally or by a code of conduct. See also **commission, letter of intent**.   **2.** A willingness to undertake a business enterprise or accept a risk.

undervalue   To value at less than the real worth. To assess the value of a property at a figure well below its true worth or **market value**. Generally, to be undervalued, a property must be significantly below the just or proper value – everyone is permitted a reasonable tolerance in making an assessment of value. See also **fraud, fraudulent conveyance, mistake, mortgage value, negligence, power of sale, undue influence**.

underwriter   **1.** One who signs their name on a document and thereby accepts the risks inherent in that document, such as an agreement to subscribe for shares or an insurance policy.   **2.** One who agrees to subscribe or contribute a certain sum of money to a venture or financial obligation

(as with a mortgage loan or stock of a company).   **3.** An insurer. A person who enters into an insurance policy for compensation.   **4.** A person, bank or syndicate that agrees to subscribe for or purchase an issue of security on a given date and at a specified price. An underwriter may undertake to purchase securities that are offered for sale to the general public, or a group of investors, but are not purchased from the issuer at the date of the initial offering, generally with a view to a subsequent resale. In such cases, an underwriter accepts the risk of a loss if the price that he undertakes to pay is more than the market value the time of issue, or he may profit if he is able to sell the securities latter at a price that is above his underwriting price.
Precept Corp. *Handbook of First Mortgage Underwriting*. Washington, DC: Urban Land Institute, 2001.

undeveloped land   See **raw land**.

undisclosed agency   An agency where the agent does not disclose that he is acting for another. If someone who is dealing with an agent knows, or has good reason to believe, that the agent is clearly representing a third party or principal, but the third party's identity is kept confidential by the agent, the '**undisclosed principal**' is liable on the contract. On the other hand, if the agent, at the time of making a contract, fails to disclose his agency and the identity of the principal, he may be liable for the contract as if he were the principal, especially if his identity is material to the contract. He cannot subsequently say that he was only the agent and has no more to do with the commitments arising from the contract. In the US, when it is known that there is an agency, but the identity of the principal is unknown, the principal may be called a 'partially disclosed principal'.

undisclosed principal   A **principal** whose existence or identity has not been disclosed by his **agent**. A principal who may be known to exist, but whose name has not been disclosed in an agreement. (In English law, the latter is generally called an **unnamed principal** to whom the 'doctrine of undisclosed principal' described below is not strictly applicable.)

The doctrine of 'undisclosed principal' arises when an agent acts in such a way that he leads the party with whom he is dealing to believe that he (the agent) is the principal. If an authorised agent makes a contract in his own name, without disclosing that he is merely a representative, he may sue or be sued upon the terms of that contract, even if the other party to the contact has reason to believe that there may be a principal (*Saxon v Blake* (1861) 29 Beav 438, 54 Eng Rep 697; Albany & Rensselaer v. Lundberg, 121 US 451, 7 S Ct 958, 30 L Ed 982 (1887)). Under the 'doctrine of undisclosed principal', the principal, when his existence is made known, may intervene also as a party to the contract, provided the result is not unduly detrimental to the third party to the contract. The principal is invested by the authorised act of the agent with the benefit and burden of the agent's actions. On the other hand, an undisclosed principal (i.e. one whose existence was never made known by the agent) may not normally intervene if the agent has manifestly indicated that he (the agent) is acting alone; nor can the principal later seek to benefit from an executory contract where the third party to the contract proves that he intended to deal with the agent personally, believing him to be the party with whom he was contracting. As a general rule, the third party to the contract may sue the agent or the principal, as and when he is disclosed, but he may not sue both, he must make an **election** for one or the other. In the US, although this election rule is followed in many jurisdictions, in some jurisdictions action may be taken against both parties; although satisfaction may only be obtained once. See also **agency, agency of necessity, estoppel, ratification**.

undivided fee(US)   See **undivided interest**.

undivided interest(US)   **1.** An interest in land as held by a co-owner. An interest that has not been segregated. The holder of an undivided interest has no right to any specific part of the property, but has a 'fractional' right to possession of the whole in common with others. An undivided interest in a property may be equal, as with a **joint tenancy** or a **tenancy by the entirety**; or unequal, as (usually) with a **tenancy in common**. Also called an 'undivided fractional interest' or, if the title is a fee interest, an 'undivided fee'. See also **partition**.   **2.** An interest in the **common areas** of a **condominium**.

undivided property   See **co-ownership**.

undivided share   See **tenancy in common**.

undue influence   Such influence as destroys a person's freedom to act at his own volition. Any form of moral or unreasonable pressure exerted by one party on another, which may take the form of coercion, deceit, force, or superiority of will or mind. In particular, an inequality of bargaining power that is used to persuade or entice another to enter into a contract. Any conduct that amounts to over persuasion, or artful or fraudulent contrivance, to such a degree that a person's free will to act is destroyed, may amount to undue influence. In particular, undue influence is likely to be a factor when the result can be described as a "manifestly disadvantageous transaction", *National Westminster Bank plc v Morgan* [1985] 1 AC 686, 707 (HL). On the other hand, undue influence does not arise merely from a desire to gratify the wishes of another; it must be affirmative and decisive. Undue influence does not arise from the reasonable level of trust that is required during normal business dealing and it does not arise simply because one party uses fair argument or reasoned persuasion. On the other hand, undue influence may arise if a person uses a threat to disclose confidential information; plays upon another's fears or foibles; offers exceptional favours or gifts; or if a professional adviser exerts pressure on his client in order to coerce that party to enter into a contract. Normally, a presumption of undue influence requires some form of special relationship between the parties, e.g. parent and child, doctor and patient, attorney and client, banker and borrower, one co-owner over another. However, undue influence does not arise merely from the existence of that special relationship, but from its misuse to the advantage of the user. In certain relationships – trustee and beneficiary, guardian and ward, doctor and patient, lawyer and client – a presumption of undue influence may well arise from the nature of the relationship placing the onus on the proponent to show an absence of any such influence. In particular, if there is a "disadvantage sufficiently serious to require evidence to rebut the presumption that in the circumstances of the parties' relationship, it was procured by the exercise of undue influence," *Royal Bank of Scotland plc v Ettridge (No. 2)* [2002] 2 AC 773, 799, [2001] 4 All ER 449, 460 (HL) (*National Westminster Bank plc v Morgan, supra* at 704).

A contract that results from undue influence is voidable at the instigation of the influenced party, because any agreement depends on free consent. An **agent** (or a **trustee**) is expected to be able to demonstrate that he has not used his unique position to induce or coerce his principal (or a beneficiary) to enter into a contract. Once a presumption of undue influence arises, it continues until positively rebutted, usually by showing that the 'influenced' party acted of his own free will. Any transaction for valuable consideration that results in a benefit to one party out of all proportion to the amount of valuable consideration so given, may be set aside on the basis that there was undue influence, even if the person who benefited by the transaction is different from the one who exerted the influence. cf. **duress**. See also **fraud, rectification, unconscionable bargain, undervalue, voidable contract**.

unearned increment   An increase in the value of a property brought about by natural causes, such as the growth in the population; by favourable changes in the neighbourhood; by a grant of consent to carry out new development; or a change of use or a rezoning; rather than by any intrinsic change in the property. An increase in the value of land arising from any cause other than an action of the owner. See also **accretion, betterment**.

unencumbered   Free of any **charge** or **burden**. A totally unencumbered property is free of any private condition, easement, restrictive covenant, mortgage, lien, servitude or other **encumbrance**; although it may be subject to a lease or licence, and any public law that affects its use or alienability. However, the term is more commonly used to refer to a property that is free of any charge, mortgage, lien or similar financial obligation. In American English, sometimes spelt 'unincumbered'. See also **beneficial owner, vacant possession**.

unenforceable contract   A contract that cannot be enforced in a court of law. A contract that cannot be enforced by any of the parties through direct legal proceedings, but one that may still create an obligation between the parties. For example, a contract may be unenforceable because: (i) there is a lack of a requisite formality, as when it is not evidenced in **writing** and signed so as to meet requirements of the **Statute of Frauds** (which has particular application to real property contracts and leases); (b) the right of action is barred by a **Statute of Limitations**; or (c) it is made with a foreign sovereign or his ambassador. Apart from such a defect the contract is valid in all other respects. An unenforceable contract is not void and may be enforceable if the defect is cured, although the term may be considered a contradiction in terms as a contract that is not enforceable may be considered not to be a true contract. cf. **voidable contract**. See also **agreement for a lease, specific performance, void contract**.

unexhausted manurial value or **unexhausted value**(Eng)   See **tenant right**.

unexpired term   The period of a lease that, at any point in time, remains until the lease terminates by lapse of time, especially the remaining term of a **tenancy for a term of years**.

unfair contract term See **duress, exclusion clause, misrepresentation, rescission, unconscionable bargain, undue influence**.

unfit for human habitation(Eng) Unsuitable for living in by a human being; not reasonably suitable for occupation as a place of residence by reason of the state or condition. "If the state of repair of a house is such that by ordinary use damage may naturally be caused to the occupier, either in respect of personal injury to life or limb, or injury to health, then the house is not in all respects reasonably fit for habitation", *Summers v Salford Corp'n* [1943] AC 283, 289 (HL). A local authority is required to carry out an annual assessment of the condition of housing in its area to determine details of houses that may be "unfit for human habitation" and the appropriate ways of dealing with the problem. A house is "unfit" if it fails to meet one or more of nine statutory criteria and "by reason of that failure it is not reasonably suitable for occupation", HA 1985, s. 604. These criteria include structural stability, serious disrepair, dampness that is prejudicial to health; inadequate supply of such facilities as lighting, heating, ventilation, food preparation facilitates, a supply of hot and cold water, proper drainage and sanitary facilities (HA 1985 Act, s. 604(1); Housing Grants, Construction & Regeneration Act 1996, s. 97). cf. **fit for human habitation**. See also **clearance area, closing order, demolition order, furnished tenancy, repairs notice**.

unfit for occupancy(US) A term that may be used in a lease, or a statutory provision, to express a state of the demised premises that would relieve the tenant of an obligation to pay rent, as when the premises have been damaged by fire or a similar calamity. Such premises may also be said to be **untenantable**. See also **frustration, warranty of habitability**.

unidentified principal See **unnamed principal**.

Uniform Building Code(US) A national code of building standards published by the National Council of Building Officials and adopted as the basis for the building codes in a large number of municipalities, especially in western states.

Uniform Business Rate (UBR)(Eng) A tax fixed by central government based on the annual value of non-domestic property. UBR is popularly referred to as 'rates' and, as from April 1, 1990 the 'general rate' on all properties was replaced by the Uniform Business Tax, in respect of non-domestic properties and **Council Tax**, in respect of domestic properties. The Uniform Business Rate is based on the annual or **rateable value** of all non-domestic property and is payable by the occupier or, if there is no occupier, the owner of the individual property or **hereditament**. The amount of tax payable by each owner or occupier is based on a rate in the pound that is applied to the rateable value of each individual property. The resultant is payable to the local authority to finance part of the cost of its services. This rate is determined separately for England, for Wales, for the City of London, for the Isles of Scilly, and for Scotland and increased annually in line with inflation. Notionally the UBR is pooled so that there is a single tax amount which is then redistributed to each local authority according to its population. Any amount expended by the local authority over and above that received from UBR is financed by the Council Tax or grants form central government. Also called the 'National Non Domestic Rate' (NNDR). See also **rateable occupation, rating list**.

Askham, Phil, and David Mackmin. *Rating Law and Practice.* London: Sweet & Maxwell, 1995.

Uniform Standards of Professional Appraisal Practice (USPAP)(US) Uniform standards of appraisal practice developed and published by the Appraisal Standards Board (ASB) of the **Appraisal Foundation**. Such standards are used by local, state and federally regulated agencies, as well as being required by many professional appraisal associations and clients' groups, both in the US and in many other countries. These standards are based on the original Uniform Standards of Professional Appraisal Practice developed in 1986-87 by the Ad Hoc Committee on Uniform Standards and were copyrighted by the Appraisal Foundation. Title IX of the Financial Institutions Reform, Recovery and Enforcement Act (FIRREA), which has been established to protect federal financial and public policy interests in real estate related transactions, and took effect from August 1989, specifically recognized USPAP as the generally accepted standards for such real estate appraisal activities. USPAP is updated and released on an annual basis. USPAP is enforced by the states, as well as by the member organizations of the Appraisal Foundation. See also **market value**, **self-contained appraisal report**, **restricted appraisal report**, **summary appraisal report**.

Appraisal Standards Board. *Uniform Standards for Professional Appraisal Practice (USPAP)*. Washington, DC: The Appraisal Foundation, 2004 edition.

unilateral contract   A contract by which only one party is bound. A promise or promises made by one party only, and usually assented to by the other. A unilateral contract creates rights in one party only and duties in the other; it is an 'if' contract—"if you provide … then I will, or I undertake to", or "If I wish to … then you will agree to"; "a promise on one side is exchanged for an act (or forbearance) on the other", P.S. Atiyah, *An Introduction to the Law of Contract* (5th ed. 1995), p. 42 (*Carlill v Carbolic Smoke Ball Co* [1893] 1 QB 256 (CA)).

Instances of unilateral contracts include: an offer of a reward for the return of stolen goods; the grant of an **option** to purchase a property (at least until the option is exercised); the appointment of an agent or broker to find a prospective purchaser for a property, provided his remuneration is based entirely on success (but not in respect of other duties he may be required to perform, such as working on a marketing campaign); and the making of a **promissory note**. Also, an **executory contract** may sometimes be referred to as unilateral, when one party has performed his

obligation (as by delivering the subject property), but the other's obligation remains outstanding (such as the payment of the price). cf. **bilateral contract**. See also **contingency fee**, **deed poll**, **open offer**, **open listing**, **synallagmatic contract**.

unilateral mistake   See **mistake**.

unimpeachable for waste   See **waste**.

unimproved land   Land that has not been tilled or cultivated. Land upon which no improvement or building has been placed or constructed. In particular, land that would be suitable for development, but that has not been opened up by roads, services or utilities. In British English, a site that comprises unimproved or undeveloped land may also be referred to as a 'green field site' and in American English as **raw land**. See also **brownfield site**.

unimproved value   The value of land excluding any improvements or additions that have been made; the value of land in its virgin state. Used mainly for rating or taxation purposes. See also **site value**.

unincumbered(US)   See **unencumbered**.

uninsurable title(US)   See **unmarketable title**.

union mortgage clause or **union-mortgage clause**(US)   A clause in an insurance policy taken out by a mortgagor that provides for any payment that may be due to the mortgagee to be assessed as if the mortgagee had contracted directly with the insurer. The mortgagee becomes not only a party interested in the insurance policy (as in a **mortgagee insurance clause** or 'open mortgage clause') but, in the event of a payment under the policy being due to the mortgagee, his rights are to be considered independently of, and are to be unaffected by, the rights, claims, acts or omissions of any other party, in particular the mortgagor or owner of the property. Also called a 'standard mortgage clause', 'standard mortgagee clause', or a 'mortgagee loss clause'. cf. **loss-payable clause**.

unit 1. A single property. A residence, office or other property unit in a building that contains several other such units. See also **condominium, planning unit**(Eng), **standard unit, unit cost**. **2.**(NZ)A parcel of land, or a part of a building, that is subdivided into similar units that are owned by individual proprietors, as with a parcel of land on a subdivision, an apartment unit in a building. "'Unit', in relation to any land, means a part of the land consisting of a space of any shape situated below, on, or above the surface of the land, or partly in one such situation and partly in another or others, all the dimensions of which are limited, and that is designed for separate ownership", Unit Titles Act, 1972, s. 2 (NZ). See also **unit entitlement**(Aus).

unit assessment(US)   An **assessment** placed on one property out of two or more properties owned by the same person.

unit entitlement(Aus/NZ)   In a **strata title** building the proportion of the building allocated to an individual unit owner in respect of expenses, levies, rates and taxes. The unit entitlement is generally based on the proportionate floor area that the unit bears to the total. See also **strata plan, unit**.

unit cost or **unit value**   The cost, or value, of a property related to an area or to a volume of measurement, e.g. dollars per acre, euros per square metre, pounds sterling per square foot. The cost or value allotted to a given unit of property, e.g. the value of a standard unit. The average cost of a building expressed as a rate per unit area or unit volume.

unit-in-place method or **unit method**(US) A method of assessing the cost of a development project or the replacement cost of a building by determining an appropriate unit cost for each component of the property and applying the appropriate unit cost, such as the estimated cost per square foot, to the number of components or units that make up the property. Also called the 'comparative unit method' or the 'segregated cost method'. See also **quantity survey method, reproduction cost**.

unit method(US)   See **unit-in-place method**.

unit mortgage(US)   A mortgage secured on one unit in a **condominium** property together with the rights of the owner of the unit over the common areas, as distinguished from a mortgage secured on the entire building.

unit owner   The owner of an individual unit in a **condominium** property. A unit holder holds title to the area within the confines of the 'unit' (apartment, office area, etc.) and an undivided interest in the common elements.

unit ownership   See **condominium**.

unit rule(US)   A rule that is adopted when assessing the amount of **just compensation** in eminent domain proceedings whereby a property is valued as a whole, even though there may be separate interests in the same property. The principle of this rule is that the condemnation action is *in rem* – 'against the property', and not against the individual claimants (Bogart v. United States, 169 F.2d 210 (10th Cir. Kan 1948)). The amount of the award is subsequently apportioned among the claimants as part of a separate proceeding.

unit trust(BrE)   A form of **trust** established to enable persons with funds for investment to join together in order to acquire a diversified block of stocks, shares or other forms of investment and thereby spread their risks. "Any arrangement made for the purpose, or having the effect, of providing facilities for the participation by persons, as beneficiaries under a trust, in profits or income arising from the acquisition, holding, management or disposal of securities or any other property whatsoever", Prevention of Fraud (Investments) Act 1958, s. 26(1); Charging Orders Act 1979, s. 6(1) (these statutes provide that such a trust must be authorised by the Department of Trade and Industry). A unit trust is constituted by a deed that sets out the terms of the trust, appoints the manager or trustees, and stipulates the permitted forms of investment. Units in the trust are not transferable but are bought and sold through the trustees or managers, and the price of those units is based on the underlying value of the investments (less a difference between the unit buying and selling price to cover the costs of administering the trust, including remuneration for the managers). The beneficiaries receive an income based on the return from the invested funds. A unit trust is similar to a **mutual fund** or **open-end investment company**. cf. **investment company**, **investment trust**. See also **mutual fund**[US], **property unit trust**.

unit value   See **unit cost**.

unitary development[US]   See **planned unit development**.

unitary development plan[Eng]   See **development plan**.

unities of time, **possession**, **title**, **and interest**   See **joint tenancy**.

unitisation[BrE] **or unitization**[AmE]   1. See **syndication**, **unit trust**[BrE].   2. The bringing together of all or parts of two or more oil or gas producing reservoirs into a common producing reservoir.   See also **pooling clause**.

unity of interest   See **joint tenancy**.

unity of possession   1. A right to the same undivided **possession** of the whole of a property, as held by co-owners. A co-owner of land has unity of possession as he is entitled to possession and enjoyment of the whole; but he has no right to preclude any other co-owner from the land, because he cannot point to any part of the property as his own to the exclusion of the other co-owners. If he could there would not be **co-ownership** but separate ownership. See also **joint tenancy**, **tenancy in common**.   2. A temporary form of unity of a right to land that arises when an owner of a **dominant tenement** (land benefiting from an easement or restrictive covenant) acquires a lease or some other temporary right to possession of the **servient tenement** (the land burdened by the easement or restrictive covenant). During the term of that right of possession, the easement or restrictive covenant is of no effect as it is held by one person against himself, but it is re-established when the possession terminates and the tenements are again in different hands. If the right to the dominant and servient tenement comes into possession of the same person permanently (i.e. there is effectively joint ownership), there is said to be unity of **seisin** and the interest is extinguished.   3. Joint possession of two interests in land held by the same person. A situation that arises, for example, when a person who holds a lease of land then acquires the reversionary interest and thereby extinguishes the lease.

unity of seisin   See **seisin**, **unity of possession**.

unity of time   See **joint tenancy**.

unity of title   See **joint tenancy**.

universal agent   An **agent** who is authorised to do all the acts that his principal could do himself. As a rule, a universal agent can delegate the powers entrusted to him to another. Such a form of agency is rarely granted; it is more than likely that the agent will be appointed as a 'general agent' authorised to carry out duties within a particular area of business.

unjust enrichment   A legal doctrine that seeks to grant **restitution** when a person in enriched at another's expense. The principle is applied where there is no contract, but a person unjustly or unfairly obtains money or property for which he should expect to pay. The doctrine of unjust enrichment creates a fictitious, or **quasi-contract**, in order to ensure a just and equitable payment for a benefit received. Unjust enrichment may be considered as a relative of *quantum meruit*, both of which are implied in law. Unjust enrichment is that which is obtained and *quantum meruit* – 'as much he deserves' – is a measure of the liability arising from such a contract. Unjust enrichment is a cause of action that the law implies to remedy a wrong, but should be distinguished from an **implied condition** which the law implies, or reads into a contract, to give proper effect to the intention of the parties.

Klippert, George W. *Unjust Enrichment*. Toronto: Butterworths, 1983.

Symposium: Restitution and Unjust Enrichment (June 2001) 79 Texas L. Rev.

Virgo, Graham. *The Principles of the Law of Restitution* (1999), Part II "Unjust Enrichment". Oxford: Oxford University Press, 1999.

unlawful detainer   The retention of possession of property by someone who originally had a legal right of possession but which is now no longer valid, as with a tenant who is holding over at the end of a lease and has been requested to vacate by the landlord. An action for unlawful detainer may be brought to regain possession, but unlike an action for **ejectment** does not determine any question of title or legal right to an estate. In English law unlawful detainer (which has been abolished) was used in respect of goods and not the retention of possession of land. See also **holding over, summary possession proceedings**.

unlawful eviction   See **eviction, harassment, security of tenure**.

unlawful user clause   See **user clause**.

unlimited mortgage   See **open-end mortgage**.

unlimited policy   An **all-risks insurance** policy that sets no ceiling on the amount of cover provided for the insured; the insurer provides an indemnity to cover the actual loss sustained by the insured. See also **blanket insurance, unvalued policy**.

unliquidated damages   **Damages** that have not been fixed or determined. In particular, damages that are not specified in a contract but, in the event of a dispute, are left to be decided by a court of law or arbitrator. cf. **liquidated damages**.

unmarketable title(US)   A title to property that is so far defective that it would expose a purchaser to the risk of litigation, or would reduce substantially the market value of the property. A title may be treated as unmarketable if there is a reasonable doubt as to its validity and it would not be accepted in the ordinary course of business. The title may not be totally defective, but it is considered unmarketable if there is sufficient doubt as to its validity so that there is a risk of litigation if the purchaser were to accept it. An unmarketable title may also be referred to as an 'uninsurable title' if the title is so far defective that a title insurance company would refuse to provide **title insurance**. Also called a 'nonmerchantable title'. cf. **marketable title**.

unnamed principal   A **principal** whose identity is not revealed to a third party by an agent, although unlike an **undisclosed principal**, one whose existence is made known by the agent. As a rule, an agent is not liable for a contract made for an unnamed principal, provided there is a principal who can consummate the transaction when called upon to do so (either directly or through the agent). However, an agent may be liable when he does not disclose the identity of his principal if the custom of the trade dictates, or if the nature and intention of the contract or the surrounding circumstances so dictates. See also **ratification**.

unoccupied   Not inhabited or used for its intended purpose. An property may be kept ready and available for **occupation**, e.g. by being furnished, but it is unoccupied if it is not used as such. An unoccupied property lacks human occupancy, as distinguished from a **vacant** property which is also devoid of all furniture or personal property.

In connection with a liability of an insurer for vacant and unoccupied premises, 'unoccupied' implies that no actual use is being made of the premises by anyone physically present or in possession. It may be distinguished from **vacant** which implies that the property is empty, deprived of contents, without inanimate objects. Vacant implies entire **abandonment**, non occupancy for any purpose. A residential property is unoccupied (and, therefore, probably not insured) when it has ceased to be used as a dwelling or place of abode. On the other hand, a property may still be considered as 'occupied' if it has been merely left unattended for a short period. Whether a person has left a property unoccupied depends on the intention of the person who has the right to take up occupation; if a person leaves premises and takes up residence elsewhere the indication is that he has left the premises unoccupied (or ceded occupation to another).

unpaid vendor's lien   See **general equitable charge, lien, overriding interest.**

unreasonably refuse consent   See **improvement, restraint on alienation.**

unreasonably withhold consent   See **improvement, restraint on alienation.**

unreasonable restraint on alienation   See **restraint on alienation.**

unsecured debt or **unsecured loan**   A debt or loan that is not protected by any form of **security,** other than the personal liability of the borrower. A loan that is not secured by **collateral.** Sometimes called a 'straight loan'. cf. **secured loan.** See also **lien, mortgage, non-recourse mortgage.**

unsecured ground rent   A ground rent

receivable for a site upon which no building has yet been built. cf. **secured ground rent.** See also **security of ground rent.**

unsightly land   See **derelict land, waste land.**

untenantable   A condition in which a leased property cannot be considered suitable for the purpose for which it has been let, especially when the lease specifies a purpose for which the property is intended to be used. See also **constructive eviction, unfit for human habitation**[Eng]**, unfit for occupancy**[US]**, warranty of habitability**[US]**.**

until   See **determinable fee simple, determinable interest, time, words of limitation.**

unusual covenant[Eng]   A **covenant** that one would not commonly expect to find in a lease of a particular type of property, but would only be entered into by express agreement. An 'unusual' covenant may be expressly inserted in a lease, but it cannot be implied in any way. Covenants that have been held to be 'unusual' include a covenant by a tenant to insure the demised premises or to repair or rebuild after fire; a covenant not to carry on a particular trade; a proviso for re-entry on bankruptcy. In particular, an 'unusual covenant' is one that would not be inserted in a lease except by express stipulation, especially one that would negate the other provisions of the lease. cf. **usual covenant.** See also **express term.**

unvalued policy   An insurance policy in which the value of the insured property is not specified but, in the event of a claim, is left to be determined on the basis of the actual loss suffered, i.e. any payment made under the policy is based on the strict principle of **indemnity.** Any sum that is referred to in an unvalued policy is intended merely as an upper limit to the insurer's liability, not as a representation of the amount for which the insured is covered. Real estate insurance policies are generally unvalued policies. A **blanket insurance** policy, which covers a number of properties, is usually 'unvalued', with the upper limit of indemnity varied as and when properties are added or removed from the policy. Also called an 'open policy'. cf. **valued policy**.

up on[US] A term used to describe a **commitment fee** that is payable in two stages; the first payment being due upon the signing of the commitment and the balance is due when the loan is granted.

uplift factor[Eng] An allowance applied to the value of a property to reflect a special feature of that property, e.g. a factor applied to the value of a tenant's interest in a property to reflect the fact that the rent is fixed for a long period and, therefore, protected against inflationary increases. cf. **quantity allowance**. See also **constant-rent factor, equated yield**.

upon 1. At the time of. 'Upon' or 'on' the occurrence of a particular event or act may mean immediately before, simultaneously with, or immediately after the event or the act, according to the context and the subject-matter of the document. Usually 'upon' means commencing with and includes the **day** to which it may refer. However, it is a word that is imprecise as to time and should be avoided in contracts. See also **time**. 2. On the occurrence of a **condition**, especially a **condition precedent** In this context 'upon' is synonymous with 'on condition that' or 'upon the occurrence of (a stipulated event)'. "In a statute which provides for one event 'upon' some other contingency, the word 'upon' is a word of variable meaning. It may mean 'at the time of' or 'with little or no interval thereafter'. On the other hand, it may mean 'in consequence of' or 'on condition of', without implying contemporaneity", Walsh v. Board of Admin., 4 Cal App.4th 682, 705, 6 Cal Rptr.2d 118, 133 (1992).

upset bid[US] See **upset price**.

upset-cost contract[US] See **cost-plus contract**.

upset date[US] A date by which a contract, in particular a building contract, must be performed. After the 'upset date' if the contract is not substantially completed, it may be rescinded. See also **substantial performance**, 'time is of the essence.

upset price[US] 1. The minimum price set by a court above which a property can be acquired at a **judicial sale**. Also called the 'upset bid'. 2. The minimum price that must be bid at an auction sale before the property that is on sale will be sold or 'knocked down'. See also **reserve price**[BrE]/ **reserved price**[AmE]. 3. A price agreed under a building contract as the maximum for the payment of a performance bonus. Under such a building contract, if the final cost is below the 'upset price', the builder will receive a share of the savings.

upside leverage[US] See **trading on the equity**.

upwards-only rent review[BrE] A provision in a **rent review clause** that the rent can only remain at the same level or increase. If the rental value determined at the time of the review is less than that currently payable the rent remains at its existing level and does not decrease. See also **ratchet clause**.

upzoning[US] A change of a **zoning ordinance**, or **zoning classification**, in order to widen the use to which a property may be put. cf. **downzoning**.

urban From the Latin *urbanus*, 'of a town [or city]' or 'belonging to a town'. Forming part of a town or city; a densely populated or built up area. cf. **rural**. See also **suburb, urban region**.

urban easement[US] See **urban servitude**.

urban development area (UDA)[Eng] An area of land in a metropolitan district or in an inner London Borough, that the Secretary of State has designated as an area for **urban renewal** or "regeneration" by "bringing land and buildings into effective use, encouraging the development of existing and new industry and commerce, creating a new environment and ensuring that housing and social facilities are available to encourage people to live and work in an area", Local Government, Planning and Land Act 1980, s. 134. The Secretary of State may create an 'urban development corporation (UDC) to be responsible for this task. The role of a UDC is "to secure the regeneration of its area ... by (a) bringing land and buildings into effective use; (b) encouraging the development of existing and new industry and commerce; (c) creating an attractive environment; (d) and ensuring that housing and social facilities are available to encourage people to live and work in the area", Local Government, Planning and Land Act 1980, s. 136(2).

urban development corporation (UDC)(Eng) See **urban development area**.

urban development grant(Eng) Financial assistance provided for a development project in a deprived or declining urban area. Urban development grants are provided by a local authority (a "designated district authority" who reclaims 75 per cent of the cost from central government) and such grants normally take the form of top-up aid to meet part of the cost of a development project that would not otherwise be viable. Grants may be made also towards the cost of improving the amenity of the area (Inner Urban Areas Act 1978, ss. 5, 6). See also **inner urban area**.

urban enterprise zone(US) See **enterprise zone**.

Urban Regeneration Agency (URA)(Eng) An agency established in 1993 (Leasehold Reform, Housing and Urban Development Act 1993, s. 158) to secure the regeneration of areas of need through the reclamation, development or redevelopment of land and buildings. The URA works especially with local and regional partners (both private and public) to encourage housing, industrial, and commercial development. The Agency has extensive powers, including power to acquire, manage, improve land, plant, equipment and other property; to assemble, plan and service sites; to carry out development and redevelopment; and to lend financial support to encourage others to carry out development of vacant, unused and derelict land. In particular, the Agency aims to clean up and use contaminated, neglected and unsightly land and to encourage development in areas of urban deprivation or high unemployment (LRHUDA 1993, ss. 159-176). The URA has now been incorporated within the **English Partnership**. See also **Scottish Enterprise**, **Welsh Development Agency**.

urban region A town or city region, comprising an area of continuous and highly condensed development which includes, but extends beyond, the confines of a single town or city. A term that may also be used to refer to a group .or cluster of towns or cities that have a degree of unity in terms of trade, population, communications, etc. An urban region is similar to, but generally smaller than a **megalopolis**, and is larger than a **conurbation**. See also **metropolitan area**.

urban renewal The **renovation** or **rehabilitation** of a run-down area or district of a town or city by a series of measures designed to improve and remodel the existing buildings, but at the same time to conserve the environment. A process that may include improving the communication system; repairing the existing fabric; rebuilding certain buildings to a significantly higher standard; and landscaping or augmenting the landscape. The intention of urban renewal is to preserve, as far as possible, the basic character of the area rather than to carry out comprehensive redevelopment. 'Urban renewal' may be used synonymously with **comprehensive development**; especially to refer to any combined activity designed to prevent urban decay, or blight, and to eliminate slum property. Urban renewal may be carried out by private landowners or by bringing land, wholly or partly, into public ownership.

urban servitude 1. In Roman, the civil and Scots law, a 'real' **servitude**. In particular, a servitude that affects a building (wherever situated) and one that runs with the building so as to burden or benefit (as appropriate) a future owner of the building, e.g. a right of light, eavesdrop, drainage onto another's land, or a right of support. See also **easement of eavesdrop**. 2.[US]A right to enjoy certain easements that are appurtenant to a building that abuts a street. In particular, a right of light to windows facing the street, and the right to the free flow of clean air and an unimpeded right of access. Also called an 'urban easement'. See also **easement of necessity**, **natural rights**. 3.[US]A right to use the streets of an urban area for the purpose of laying sewers, and gas and water pipes.

urbanisation The conversion of a rural area to an urban area. The process by which an area grows into a city. A significant increase in the concentration of the population in a particular district so that it takes on the characteristics of a town or city.

urbanity The state or condition of being part of a town or city; possessing the character of an **urban area**. A word in English town and country planning jargon used to describe a well-ordered and controlled development. See also **town and country planning**.

usable area 1. The area that a tenant or occupier may actually use for the purpose for which he is occupying a building. The area from which an occupier can effectively derive benefit. Typically, the usable area is measued between the internal face of the perimiter walls, or the window line if appropriate, less any vertical penetrations such a stairwells and elevator shafts. If the area is being computed for a multi-let floor, the measuement is made to the mid-point of the dividing wall. The floor area taken up by columns, perimeter ventilation units, cupboards, etc. that are leased to the tenant may be included in the determination of the usable area because the tenant is considered to have an exclusive right to that part of the floor. Although the term 'usable area' is not normally used for the measurement of lease space as it is too subjective. Also called the 'net occupiable area'. See also **effective floor area**[BrE], **loss factor**, **net internal area**[BrE], **rentable area**[US]. 2. In a building that is let to a number of tenants, the area that each tenant occupies exclusively, as distinguished from the **common areas** (or common parts) that are available for the joint use of two or more tenants.

usable value[AmE] The value that may be derived from the use and occupation of a property, especially as distinguished from the **rental value** that may be derived therefrom. A term that may be used in relation to the **damages** payable as a result of a nuisance.

usage A habitual practice or **use**. A long and well established practice. A notorious, but legal, reasonable practice that is adopted and accepted by those in a particular form of trade or business. "Usage may be broadly defined as a particular course of dealing or line or conduct generally adopted by persons engaged in a particular department of a business life or entering into a common type of contract, or more fully as a particular course of dealing or line of conduct which has acquired such notoriety that, where persons enter into contractual relationships of the particular kind, or in the particular place, to which the usage is alleged to attach, those persons must be taken to have intended to follow that course of dealing or line of conduct, unless they have expressly or impliedly stipulated to the contrary", 12(1) *Halsbury's Laws of England*, Custom and Usage (4th ed. Reissue), para. 650, p. 203. A practice that is so well accepted in a particular line of business, or in a particular context, that it need not be expressed in writing. A practice that is more than a mere trade practice accepted between some parties in their dealings. 'Usage' may encompass **custom** or **prescription**, although it differs from both; for if custom and prescription lose their being usage fails (*Coke's Complete Copyholder* 33 (1673)). cf. **user, enjoyment**. See also **implied term**.

usance   1. The period of time allowed for the payment of a **bill of exchange**, excluding any days of grace.   2. Interest payable for the use of money, especially a usurious rate of interest. See also **usury**.

use   1. Derived from the Latin *opus*, or Norman French *oes*, 'work' or 'benefit'. The act of employing something for a purpose, especially a continuous or profitable purpose. The **enjoyment** or **benefit** to be derived from holding, occupying or manipulating something. In the case of land or buildings, use means particularly occupation and enjoyment of the fruits and profits to be derived therefrom.

An owner of land or real estate may retain the use entirely for himself or he may transfer that use, in whole or in part, to another. Such a transfer may be by gift, sale, lease, or **licence**. If a person is given the 'use' of land, and nothing more, he is granted a mere licence. A covenant in a lease prohibiting a tenant from letting any other person 'use' the demised premises, prohibits almost any activity on the property by another person, except a visitor or casual interloper.

In the civil law, a person may obtain the use of property by being granted the **usufruct** therein. However, usufruct is the right of enjoying something and the usufructuary may take and enjoy all the fruits and revenues that the property can produce, whereas 'use' is the "right given one to make a gratuitous use of such portion of the fruits of a thing as is necessary to supply his personal wants, or those of his family", Strause v. Elliott, 43 La Ann 501, 9 So 102, 103 (1891)). cf. **occupation**. See also **established use, exclusive use, existing use, highest and best use, use and occupation, user clause, utility**.   2. The purpose to which a property is put. Any activity, occupation, business or purpose to which a building or a plot of land is put or intended to be put.

In English planning law, with reference to a **discontinuance order**, "'use' means activities that are done in, on, or around land even if they do not interfere with the physical characteristics of land", *Parkes v Secretary of State for the Environment* [1978] 1 WLR 1308, 1311 (CA). See also **certificate of lawfulness, material change in the use, nonconforming use**.   3. To put something into practice, to put into action or service. To follow a practice or **custom**, especially as a matter of habit. A regular use or practice may well establish a custom. See also **usage**.   4. The legal enjoyment of property, especially the benefits or profits arising in favour of a person other than the legal owner. In particular, an ancient term employed to indicate that a property was to be transferred to one person to be held 'on behalf of' (or *ad opus*, *ad oeps* or *ad eops*, 'to the use of') another. See also **beneficiary, shifting interest, trust**.

use and occupancy insurance(AmE) **or use and occupation insurance**(BrE)   1. Insurance to cover an occupier of property against the cost of renting alternative premises in the event of fire or any other specified casualty to his property. Sometimes called 'rental value insurance'. cf. **rent-loss insurance**.   2. See **consequential loss insurance**.

use and occupation   1. A form of action by which an owner of land claims that another has had the benefit of occupying and enjoying his land, with permission, but that no form of payment has been made for that benefit. An action for use and occupation may be brought when someone has enjoyed the same rights and benefits from land as can be enjoyed by a tenant, but when there has been no lease or agreement for a lease and, therefore, no formal liability to pay rent. The person bringing the action seeks damages or compensation for a loss of the right to 'use and occupy' the land, but acknowledges that he had not gone so far as to create a tenancy. A claim for use and occupation is based on the doctrine of *assumpsit*, whereby there is an implied or tacit contract to pay for the use of the land. It does not represent a claim against a trespasser or illegal occupant. Thus, a tenant who remains on demised premises after a writ has been served for ejectment is not liable for 'use and occupation', although he may be liable for **mesne profits**. Where a verbal contract to grant a lease has been made and the intending tenant has taken possession, he may be liable for 'use and occupation' and the amount of compensation payable is fixed usually at the level of the agreed rent.   **2.** The combined benefit derived from the **use** and the **occupation** of land. "'As occupation is a kind of user, it is difficult to envisage occupation of land or building which is not also a user. The reverse does not apply. Not every use is an occupation, and obviously many things capable of being used are incapable of being occupied. The words are not fully interchangeable but only interchangeable in some contexts", *Land Reclamation Co Ltd v Basildon DC* [1978] 2 All ER 1162, 1166-7, aff'd [1979] 2 All ER 993 (CA).

use and occupation insurance(BrE)   See **use and occupancy insurance**(AmE).

use classes(Eng)   See **Use Classes Order**.

Use Classes Order(Eng)   An order made under the provisions of the TCPA 1990, s. 55(2), which sets out a number of categories of 'use classes' within which a change of use may take place without there being **development** and, therefore, a need for planning permission. A change of use may be made to "any other purpose of the same class", unless such a change would amount to a breach of a planning condition. The purpose of the order is to avoid the need for planning permission when there is merely a change from one similar use to another.

The Town and Country Planning (Use Classes) Order 1987 sets out sixteen use classes. Thus, certain retail uses are included in one class, various industrial purposes in another, offices that are not in the retail class in another, and dwelling houses in another. Each Class contains a number of notable exceptions, but if the change falls strictly within the same use class it may be made without a need for planning permission.

A Use Classes Order should be distinguished from a **General Development Order**, as the former lists changes that do not constitute 'development', and the latter lists activities that are 'development', but do not require planning permission. Thus, a change from a grocer to a butcher, or a cloths shop to a shoe shop, does not constitute development; but a change from a restaurant to a grocer is development, although it is 'permitted development' (Town and Country Planning (General Permitted Development) Order 1995 Class A). Similarly, a change from assembly of radios to the assembly of computers is not development; but a change from a use in Class B8, storage and distribution, to Class B1, business, is 'permitted development'; although the reverse is not 'permitted'. See also **planning unit**.

use clause or **user clause**   A clause or covenant in a lease limiting the use to which the demised property can be put; e.g. a clause that requires a tenant "to use the premises only for the sale of shoes and footwear", or a clause that prohibits certain uses of the premises, such as "not to use the premises for the storage of toxic or hazardous materials" or "not to use the premises for any illegal or immoral purpose". The tenant's freedom to use the premises is usually restricted, by the user clause, to a limited number of uses or to a limited number of specified purposes, unless the landlord's consent is obtained to a change of use. If there is no express or implied restriction on the use to which the leased property may be put the tenant can make what use of the premises he wishes, within the confines of the law and the design and construction of the property. However, a tenant must not use the premises in such a way as to clearly damage the value of the owner's interest in the property; is bound by any **restrictive covenant** that affects the use of the freehold, because such covenants 'run with the land'; and should not use the premises in any way that might prejudice the landlord's interest or cause **waste**. A use clause may be inserted in order to protect the value of the leased property or to protect the value of other property owned by the landlord. A use clause may provide that the tenant will not use the premises for any purpose that increases the insurance risk of the demised premises or in violation of any building code or other statutory regulation. As a rule, a clause in a lease which specifies that the demised premise are to be used for a particular purpose does not preclude a similar use or a use that is compatible with the area; unless the lease states clearly to the contrary.

Use clauses are particularly important in shopping center leases as a means of regulating and controlling the **tenant mix**. "Leasing of space in these centers differs from the usual treatment of commercial property in that the 'center' concept denotes a unified complex of stores. The individual leases must complement one another in order to foster the goal of multi-purpose or 'one-stop' shopping", Richard R. Powell and Patrick J. Rohan, *Powell on Real Property*. San Francisco: Matthew Bender, Looseleaf, 1949, § 24. **2.** In such cases several courts in the US have held that the lessee is restricted to the precise use stipulated in the lease.

In English law, any provision that prohibits the tenant from changing the use of the demised premises, without the landlord's prior licence or consent (provided the change does not involve a structural alteration of the premises), does not permit the landlord to demand a **fine** for granting such licence or consent, except for a payment to cover the landlord's legal expenses or other reasonable expenses of granting the licence, as well as a reasonable payment in respect of any damage to the value of the landlord's premises or neighbouring premises of the landlord (L&T Act 1927, s. 19(3)). This section does not apply to agricultural or mining leases (L&T Act, s. 19(4)). cf. **non-competition clause**. See also **change of use, continuous operation clause**.

use density　The ratio of the number of building units used for a particular purpose (dwellings, retail outlets, warehouses) to a given unit area of land, e.g. dwellings per acre or retail units per hectare. See also **residential density**.

use district(US)　An area of a town or city within which the use of land and buildings is regulated by law. See also **zoning**.

use value　**1.** The **value** of a property for a particular **use**, as distinguished from the value for the **highest and best use**. The **utility** to be derived from something. See also **existing use value, usable value**(US). **2.** The **reinstatement cost** of a property, especially as used to value a special-purpose building. Also called 'value-in-use'.

use variance(US)　See **zoning variance**.

use zoning　See **land-use planning, zoning**.

useful life　See **economic life**.

user　The continuous **use**, or the enjoyment of a right to property; the actual exercise or enjoyment of any right or interest. An essential element of the right to property. cf. **usage**. See also **prescription**.

user as of right　See *nec vi nec clam nec precario*.

user clause　See **use clause**.

usque ad coelum(Lat)　'To the heavens'. See **air rights, land**.

usque ad medium filum aquæ(Lat)　See *ad medium filum aquæ*.

usual covenant　**1.**(Eng)A **covenant** that is deemed to have been inserted in a lease, either because an **agreement for a lease** specifies that the lease when formally granted will contain 'usual covenants', or when the agreement is silent as to the covenants to be included in the lease, but it is reasonable to expect that certain covenants will be imposed on the parties. In the later instance, the usual covenants are implied by law. What is a usual covenant is a question of fact and not of law, based on the type of property, the duration and other terms and conditions of the lease. Unless there is anything expressed to the contrary, the 'usual covenants' on the part of the tenant (what one would expect in any lease) are: (i) to pay **rent**; (ii) to pay the rates and property taxes (except those that are imposed on the landlord by statute); (iii) to keep and deliver up the premises in reasonable **repair**; (iv) to permit the landlord upon reasonable notice to enter the demised premises to view the state of repair; and (v) to permit the landlord a **right of re-entry** for non-payment of rent, but not necessarily for a breach of any other covenant. On the part of the landlord, there is a usual covenant that he will grant the tenant **quiet enjoyment** and to pay such taxes as are imposed directly on him. It may be usual also to consider that a lease should contain some form of covenant as to responsibility for insurance; as to the permitted user or restrictions on user; not to create a nuisance; not to make structural alterations without the landlord's consent; and possibly in a modern office lease, a restriction on assignment or sub-letting without the landlord's reasonable consent. However, although these and many other covenants are usually inserted in a lease, they are not deemed to be 'usual' in the technical sense of the word unless, based on precedent, **custom** or trade **usage**, they are clearly usual for the type and duration of tenancy created. Thus, what is a usual covenant depends to some degree on the nature of the property, its location and the may be based on the precedents from other similar lettings. Accordingly, a covenant providing for re-entry for breach of covenant (other than for non-payment of rent) is not necessarily a "usual covenant", but is 'usually' inserted in a well-drawn lease. Sometimes called a 'common covenant'. cf. **implied covenant**. See also **beneficial owner**, **recital**. 2.(US)See **covenants of title**.

usual quarter days(Eng) See **quarter day**.

usufruct; **usufructuary right** A right to the use and enjoyment of the fruits or profits of another's property, without fundamentally changing its substance. "In order to define usufruct it is necessary to introduce two other characteristics: (a) first, usufruct is a *temporary* right, and in the majority of cases, for a life [of a person or a corporate entity, which is restricted to 30 years] ... (b) also usufruct is a real right ...", Patrice Jourdain et al., *Droit Civil, Les Biens*. Paris: Dalloz, 1995, p. 103. Usufruct grants the right to use the property and receive the fruits therefrom. Without the right of usufruct, there is the complementary right called 'bare ownership' and when the usufruct is extinguished the bare ownership reverts to absolute ownership. Usufruct comprises two of the rights to property as recognised in Roman law, the right of user and the right of enjoyment of the fruits or profits, but does not include the right to destroy or 'abuse' the property (*abusus*), this latter right is only available to the absolute owner.

Unlike a lessee, the **usufructuary** takes and accepts the thing as he finds it, but is obliged to return the subject matter as he found it originally or to provide equivalent value. Although, if the property wears out through normal use, as with most goods, the usufructuary is not responsible for such degradation. The grantor or bare-owner is responsible primarily for major or structural and the usufructuary for maintenance, but not for deterioration due to **wear and tear** or damage caused by *force majeure*.

A usufruct may come to an end: (i) at the end of the life of the grantee; (ii) at the end of a set period of limitation; (iii) upon the expiration or exhaustion of the thing granted; (iv) after a period 30 years of non-user; or (v) by renunciation, merger or subrogation. It is a right that may be mortgaged, charged or otherwise alienated, unless there is a prohibition to the contrary in the terms of the grant.

Usufruct is recognized in a few jurisdictions in North America, notably in Quebec (Quebec CC, arts. 1124-1171); Louisiana (La. CC, arts. 533-645); and other states that came under French or Spanish jurisdiction: "Usufruct is a right of using and enjoying and receiving the *profits* of property that belongs to another. ... Three types of usufruct exist. First, there are the *natural* profits produced by the subject of the usufruct. For example, the profits produced spontaneously by the earth or animals, such a timber, herbs, fruits, wool, milk, and the young of cattle are natural. Second, there are *industrial* profits, which are profits produced by cultivation, such as crops of grain. Third, there are *civil* profits, which are rents, freights, and revenues from annuities and from other effects and rights", Marshall v. Marshall, 735 SW.2d 587, 598 (Tex Civ App 1987)). See also **use**.

usufructuary   **1.** A person who has a right of **usufruct**, i.e. a right to use (*usus*) property and reap profit (*fructus*) therefrom, provided he does not alter its substance.   **2.** Of or relating to the right of **usufruct**.

usurpation   **1.** The unauthorised assumption of and exercise of power. In particular, the unlawful use of another's authority or property, as with the **encroachment** on another's land. See also **prescription acquisitive**.   **2.** The use of a royal **franchise** without authority.

usury   Charging of **interest** for the use of money, or charging an amount of interest that is excessive, illegal, unconscionable, inordinate or malicious. Any contract by which interest, or any other charges, are levied in excess of a stipulated legal limit. Usury is no longer considered to be a common law offence, although it may be in breach of statute law. For example, in the case of a loan to an individual it is usually necessary to spell out the full terms of the loan. In English law, the courts have power to review credit agreements (which may include mortgage loans) to ensure that they do "justice between the parties", CCA 1974, s. 137, and do not constitute 'extortionate credit bargains', i.e. the loan is not "grossly exorbitant" or "grossly contravenes ordinary principles of fair dealing" CCA 1974, s. 138(1). In the case of a mortgage loan, the court can set aside an agreement that is considered to constitute an **unconscionable bargain**; as well as an agreement that has been entered into as a result of **undue influence** by the lender or a related party. On the other hand, the court does not upset mortgage transactions simply because they may appear unreasonable, but were entered into after due legal advice and consideration and were made as arms' length transactions (*Knightsbridge Estates Trust Ltd v Byrne* [1939] Ch 441, [1938] 4 All ER 618, 626 (CA), aff'd [1940] AC 613, [1940] 2 All ER 401 (HL)).

In the US, several states have laws that fix the maximum rate of interest that can be charged on a loan, especially a consumer loan or loans in the secondary mortgage market. Thus, all 'federally-related' loans secured by conventional first mortgages on residential property are excluded from state usury laws (including provisions regarding discount points and other finance charges), unless the state has passed a law overruling such legislation (Depository Institutions Deregulation and Monetary Control Act of 1980, 12 USC § 1735f-7). However, federal and state laws requiring clear disclosure of the terms and conditions of mortgage loans to private individuals and small businesses, and to protect the borrower from money lenders or 'loan sharks', have become more prevalent. In particular, the Consumer Credit Protection Act of 1968 which requires certain disclosures concerning interest and finance charges and the Real Estate Settlement Procedure Act of 1974 which requires disclosure of settlement charges on loans. In addition, the courts may revise or strike out 'unconscionable bargains' or loans made where there has been 'undue influence' (54A Am J2d., Mortgages, § 15). See also **annual percentage rate**, **compound interest**, **customary interest**[US], **legal rate of interest**, **penalty**, **settlement statement**[US].

usus[Lat]   'usage'. See **usufructuary**.

utilities   See **public utilities**.

utility   **1.** Capable of, or the quality of, being of use. The ability of property to satisfy a particular need or want, especially in a given situation and over a given period of time. Capable of being used beneficially either directly or as a substitute. See also **value**. **2.** See **public utility**.

utility easement(US) See **easement in gross**.

utility room(US) A room in a dwelling house used as a laundry, for storage of maintenance equipment, or for a similar purpose.

utmost good faith A principle which demands that the parties to certain types of contract should act openly and in all good conscience to one another. A party to a contract of utmost good faith, *uberrimae fidei*, must not suppress facts that are material to the contract, nor fail to disclose facts that subsequently are known to have an adverse effect on the essential terms of the contract. The requirement of 'utmost' good faith goes beyond the need for **good faith** as expected of many contracts. It demands a complete disclosure of facts or circumstances that are known to only one of the parties and might have influenced the other party's decision to enter into the contract. Contracts of **insurance** are the most important contracts of utmost good faith. It is inherent to a contract of insurance that the insured party makes a full and fair disclosure of all the information that he or she might be aware and that might have an impact on the risk accepted by the insurer. After all it is only the insured who may be cognisant of facts affecting the subject property at the time the policy is entered into or at any stage that the policy is in force.

A contract with a broker is generally considered to be one that requires utmost good faith because the broker has a **fiduciary** relationship with the party or parties he represents. The broker should not make secret profits at the expense of his principal; nor secretly deal with property in which his principal has or, as a result of the broker's activity, may have an interest; and a broker should reveal to his principal all information that he obtains or has knowledge of in respect of the property with which he is dealing. He should also reveal any material information that he may have regarding a prospective purchaser; as well as any fee-splitting or fee-sharing arrangement entered into with another broker directly involved in the transaction (unless he is acting purely as a middleman). A contract that requires such disclosure is voidable at the option of the 'deceived' party, but it is not automatically void. Contracts to subscribe for shares in a newly floated corporation; contracts between partners; contracts by which a party acts as surety; and contracts involving arrangements between members of a family or other closely related parties, require a degree of honesty of intent that makes them akin to contracts of utmost good faith. See also **misrepresentation, voidable contract**.

$\mathcal{V}$

vacancy allowance An allowance or discount made when estimating the projected income from a property investment, or a proposed development, to take account of the anticipated loss of income due to vacant, but rentable, space. This allowance may be expressed as a ratio or a percentage of the total projected income. Also called a 'vacancy factor'. cf. **vacancy rate**. See also **effective gross income**.

vacancy allowance ratio See **vacancy allowance**.

vacancy clause A clause in an insurance policy that enables the insured to leave a property **vacant** for a stipulated period of time without prejudicing the insurance cover. Also called a 'vacancy permit', especially when such a right is granted after the policy has been effected.

vacancy factor See **vacancy allowance**.

vacancy permit See **vacancy clause**.

vacancy rate The ratio of the number of vacant units, or the area of vacant space, to the total number of units or total area of the property available, normally expressed as a percentage. The vacancy rate may express the vacancy in a particular building or in a particular market. When such vacancy is the result of tenants relocating, rather than space that has not been leased, the result may be called 'frictional vacancy'. Sometimes called the 'vacancy factor', although that term is best reserved for a 'vacancy allowance' that is allowed when estimating the income available form a property. cf. **occupancy rate**, **vacancy allowance**. See also **turnover vacancy**.

vacant Empty; devoid of all use and occupation. A vacant property is generally one that has been left empty for a reasonable period of time, especially when all the furniture and personal goods have been removed. In an insurance policy that precludes coverage of a 'vacant' building, that normally means that the property is empty of all (or virtually all) contents; devoid of animate and inanimate objects; and may be distinguished from **unoccupied** which refers to the absence of animate use or the lack of the habitual presence of human beings. cf. **unoccupied**. See also **vacant possession**.

vacant land Land without buildings, or land that is not put to any use. See also **unimproved land, waste land**.

vacant possession A term used primarily in English law to refer to the right to the unimpeded enjoyment of physical or actual **possession**. Vacant and available for use and occupation for an intended purpose, without burden or impediment. "[W]hen solicitors and laymen alike refer to delivering 'vacant possession' of a house they are referring to a house free of household furniture and effects as well as animate occupancy. See also 34 Hals., 3d ed., p. 259. Vacant possession means not only the ejectment of tenants and trespassers but also, subject to the *de minimus* rule, the removal of goods", *Burke v Campbell* 87 DLR (3d) 427, 432 (Can). "An estate which has been abandoned, vacated, or forsaken by the tenant. The abandonment must be complete in order to make the possession vacant, and therefore, if the tenant have goods on the premises it will not be so considered. 2 Chitty, Bail. 177; 2 Stra. 1064 [*Savage v Dent* 93 Eng Rep 1034]", *Black's Law Dictionary*, 6th ed., 1990. A purchaser of real property should be given vacant possession of the property upon completion of the sale, unless there is a clear agreement to the contrary. The possession should be such as would enable the purchaser to use and enjoy the property for the purpose intended (*Topfell Ltd v Galley Properties Ltd* [1979] 1 WLR 447). 'Possession' of land may be satisfied by the receipt of the rents and profits; but the phrase 'vacant possession' is generally used in order to make it clear that what is being sold is not an interest in reversion, i.e. it is not subject to any form of tenancy, and that the property is clear of any user or rights that are evidence of the previous owner's or user's possession.

vacantia bona(Lat)   See *bona vacantia*.

vacation home(US)   See **second home**.

vacua possessio* or *vacuo possessio(Lat) 'vacant possession'.

vadium(Lat)   In the civil law, a **pledge** or security. A pawn or pledge of a chattel, especially by **bailment**.

VA-loan(US)   See **Veterans Administration loan**.

valid agreement or valid contract   See **contract**.

valid planning consent(Eng)   See **planning permission**.

valuable consideration   **Consideration** that is sufficient to enable a promise to be enforced. Something that is real and is given as an element in the creation of a **contract**. "Some right, interest, profit or benefit accruing to one party, or some forbearance given, suffered or undertaken by another", *Currie v Misa* (1875) LR 10 Ex 153, 162, aff'd (1876) 1 App Cas 554 (HL) (*Fleming v Bank of New Zealand* [1900] AC 577, 586 (PC); The American Law Institute, *Restatement Second, Contracts* §§ 17(1), 71 (1981)). In common law, valuable consideration is that which is required for a valid contract (unless the contract is under seal). Valuable consideration may be pecuniary, or even the consideration of a future marriage; it need not be adequate or sufficient, provided it can be estimated by the recipient in terms of value and represents some loss to the grantor or gain to the recipient. It may include a surrender of a right or claim, or the exchange of mutual promises and, in certain instances, may even be nominal, e.g. $1, £1, ¥1, €1, etc.

In English statute law, in connection with a fraudulent conveyance of land that has subsequently been registered, valuable consideration "includes marriage, but does not include a nominal consideration in money", LRA, s. 3(xxxi). In connection with a transfer of registered land, "valuable consideration does not include marriage consideration or a nominal consideration in money", LRA 2002, s. 132(1). cf. **good consideration**, **sufficient consideration**.

valuable improvement   An **improvement** to a property that adds permanent value, as distinguished from temporary work or a minor improvement that does not provide any benefit to the property or that can readily be removed. In the event that an improvement made to a property is claimed as an act of **part performance**, in general, that improvement should be substantial and add value to the property to which the claim relates. See also **compensation for improvements**.

valuation   The act or process of determining the **value** or **worth** of something. An **assessment** of the **market value** of a property, at a given point in time. The provision of a written opinion as to value of an interest in property. A valuation is normally accompanied by associated information, assumptions or qualifications. However, it may simply provide the opinion, without anything further. Valuation is a process normally carried out by an **expert** or **valuer** using his or her skill, experience and objective view of the subject property. (Valuation differs from placing a price on a property in that the latter does not always afford a true measure of value, whereas the former is intended to do so.)

A valuation of a property may be made for a number of purposes, such as: (i) investment; (ii) sale by private treaty; (iii) compulsory purchase; (iv) insurance; (v) probate; (vi) rating assessment or property tax levy; (vii) an estimate of the going-concern value of a company; or (viii) mortgage security reasons. The value may differ depending on the purpose for which it is required. An insurance valuation may assess the cost of reinstatement of a property, whereas a valuation for sale may assess the market value.

A valuation may be made using a number of methods or approaches, including: (i) the comparative or **comparison method**; (ii) the income or **investment method**; (iii) the replacement or **reinstatement method**; (iv) the **residual method**; or (v) the **profits method**. More than one method of valuation may be used for any given property and the method used may vary depending on the purpose of the valuation. In the US, the term valuation is usually used to refer to the assessment of value for taxation purposes; otherwise the term **appraisal** is used. See also **assessment, before-and-after method, compensation, rating valuation, valuation report**.

Johnson, Tony, et al. *Modern Methods of Valuation of Land, Houses and Buildings.* 9th ed. London: Estates Gazette, 2000.

Millington, A. F. *An Introduction to Property Valuation.* 5th ed. London: Estates Gazette, 2001.

Murdoch, John, and Paul Murrells. *Law of Surveys and Valuations.* London: Estates Gazette, 1996.

Scarrett, Douglas. *Property Valuation: The Five Methods.* London: E. & F.N. Spon, 1991.

valuation by abstraction(US)   See **abstraction approach**.

valuation certificate(BrE)   A formal certificate, signed by an expert or qualified **valuer**, stating the estimated value of a property. The certificate may be a separate document, or more usually it is incorporated into a formal **valuation report**. In either case, the certificate should state the valuer's qualification; outline details of the subject property; and state any factors that have a direct bearing on the valuation, such as planning or zoning consents. See also **appraisal report**(AmE), **certificate of valuation**.

valuation date   1.(BrE)The date at which a valuation is placed on a property, i.e. the date applicable to a **valuation certificate**. This is the date the valuer specifies as the date at which the value was fixed (the 'value date') and does not necessarily correspond to the date of the formal report, i.e. it may be specified after allowing a reasonable period of proper marketing of the property. See also **appraisal date**(AmE).   2.(US)The date in condemnation proceedings at which a property is to be valued for determining the amount of **just compensation**. There is no uniform date for determining the valuation but, as a rule, the date is that of the 'taking'. In the case of a 'declaration of taking', the valuation date is the day of the declaration, or as close as it is reasonably possible to assess the value (with no account being taken of the change in the value of the property after the valuation date), or the date of the authority's entry into possession, whichever is the earlier (United States v. Dow, 357 US 17, 78 S Ct 1039, 2 L Ed.2d 1109, 1113-1115 (1958)). In the case of 'straight' condemnation (without any declaration of taking), the amount of compensation is determined as the date the authority tenders payment to the owner of the land, or the date of the trial to determine the amount of compensation (Kirby Forest Industries, Inc. v. United States, 467 US 1, 104 S Ct 2187, 81 L Ed.2d 1, 14-15 (1984)). **3.**(Eng)The date at which the value of a property is determined for the purpose of assessing **compulsory purchase compensation**. When **market value** is the basis for the assessment of compensation, the date is either: (a) the date when compensation is agreed or the date of a Lands Tribunal award; or (b) the date the acquiring authority takes possession, whichever is the earlier. When cost of **equivalent reinstatement** is the basis, the valuation date is the earliest practicable date at which reinstatement is possible or the date the authority takes possession of the property that is being acquired, whichever is the earlier (*Birmingham Corporation v West Midland Baptist (Trust) Association (Inc.)* [1970] AC 874, [1969] 3 All ER 192 (HL)). See also **notice to treat**. **4.**(Eng)In English rating law, the date on which the **rateable value** is effectively determined. This date is before the date the rating list comes into effect and is known as the 'antecedent valuation date' (AVD). Thus, the rateable value is determined at the AVD, but on the basis of the property as it physically exists on the date the list comes into effect (currently two years after the AVD) or, if appropriate, the date that an alteration is made to the list or the date of a proposal to alter the list (Local Government Finance Act 1988, Sch. 6(2)(3)). This difference is intended to provide time to carry out the valuation work before the rating list comes into effect. See also **tone of the list**.

valuation list(Eng)   See **Council Tax**, **rating list**.

valuation officer (V.O.)(Eng)   An employee of the Valuation Office Agency (VOA) who, *inter alia*, assesses the rateable value of properties for local authorities to enable the authority to collect rates on those properties. The valuation officer is responsible for the preparation and amendment of the **rating list**. A valuation officer may also be called to give evidence as an **expert witness** before a local valuation court or the Lands Tribunal on the rateable value of a property in the officer's area of responsibility. The valuation officer is also responsible for the determination of capital value for the purpose of the **Council Tax** and for that purpose the local valuation officer is called the "Listing Officer".

valuation report(BrE)   A statement of the facts and opinions that have guided a **valuer** when assessing the worth of a property. The report sets out details of all data and information collated by the valuer, as well as setting out the basis for his opinion of value. In particular, it provides (at least) details of location; communications and amenities; socio-economic facts; a description of the property: its dimensions (with the basis of measurement), age, state of repair, type, use, accommodation, condition and any such factor that especially affects its value; tenure, easements, encumbrances, licences, and any other rights affecting the property; services or public utilities; permits and consents (or lack or breaches thereof), town planning, highway, environmental and other statutory details; rating or other applicable taxation information; and especially for an investment property, details of tenants and occupiers, rental income, outgoings, etc. In effect, the report is a statement of the information collected by the valuer, especially as a result of his inspection of the property, presented in sufficient detail to advise the client of all circumstances that might impact on the valuation. The report should also state the name of the party to whom it is addressed; the purpose of the valuation, any special instructions, assumptions or omissions that have been taken into account; provide market and comparable valuation information; and conclude with the date of the valuation and a **valuation certificate** signed by the valuer. In addition, the report may include details of plant and machinery, usually in the form of a separate detailed valuation. See also **appraisal report**(AmE).

The Royal Institution of Cratered Surveyors. *Appraisal & Valuation Standards*. 5th ed. London: RICS Books, 2003.

valuation tables   A mathematical table that sets out a number of different factors to be used in the **investment method of valuation**. These tables provide figures for such factors as an **amount of one**; an **amount of one per period**; a **present value of one**; a **present value of one per period**; a **years' purchase**; a **mortgage constant**; an **equated yield**; an **Ellwood factor**; and life expectancy. See also Appendix C, **Financial Formulae**.

valuation tribunals(Eng)   Tribunals established to replace local valuation courts in England (including the Isles of Scilly) with the function of hearing appeals at first instance on disputes on property rating matters, including any disputed **completion notice** (Local Government Finance Act 1988, s. 136, Sch. 11, as amended; Valuation and Community Charge Tribunal Regulations 1989). Similar tribunals were established in Wales in 1996 (Valuation Tribunals (Wales) Regulations 1995). The tribunal normally sits with three members and may hear evidence (usually in public) as submitted by the appellant, the valuation officer, the owner or occupier, the local (billing) authority or an objector to the proposal who has a superior interest in the property. The evidence submitted may be written or oral, and may be based on matters of fact, or law, as those issues may impact on the valuation of the property. Such evidence may also be submitted by an **expert witness** called on behalf of one of the parties appearing before the court. There is a right of appeal to the **Lands Tribunal** against a decision of a valuation tribunal on a matter of valuation, and a right of appeal to the High Court solely on a matter of law.

valuator(US)   See **appraiser**.

value   1. Derived from the Latin *valere*, or the Old French *valoir*, 'to be worth'. That which is good or desirable, or the result of owning or using something that is good or desirable in itself. The relative benefit or satisfaction to be derived from something, either: (a) by use or possession – its intrinsic good or usefulness; or (b) by exchange for something else– its extrinsic advantage or **price**. A subjective assessment of the merit, desirability, **worth** or **utility** of a property at any point in time. The estimated price that could be achieved if a property is sold in the open market. "'Value' expresses an economic concept. As such it is never a fact but always an opinion of the worth of a property at a given time in accordance with a specific definition of value. in appraisal practice, value must always be qualified – for example, market value, liquidation value, or investment value", Appraisal Standards Board. *Uniform Standards for Professional Appraisal Practice (USPAP)*. Washington, DC: The Appraisal Foundation, 2004 edition,' Definitions'.

The word 'value' has a variety of meanings according to the context. In economics, value is given two meanings; it "sometimes expresses the utility of some particular object, and sometimes the power of purchasing other goods which the possession of that object conveys. The one may be called 'value in use' the other, 'value in exchange'", Adam Smith, *Wealth of Nations* (1776), Book I, Ch. 4. The value in use may be considered equivalent to the 'worth' to the user. The value of something

at any point in time, is a function of four factors: (i) utility – its ability to satisfy human wants or to be of use to someone (especially 'marginal utility', i.e. the extra benefit to be derived from one more unit of the commodity, which in turn is a function, but normally an inverse function, of how much we possess already); (ii) scarcity – the inadequacy of the available quantity to meet demand, i.e. the supply relative to the desire for it; (iii) taste – the total quantity of that which is desired or preferred; (iv) transferability – the ease with which an alternative can be made available. Value may also be considered a function of: (i) demand, which depends on the amount a consumer wishes to pay (the price), the price of substitutes, the total level of consumer income, and consumer tastes or preferences; and (ii) supply, which depends on the profitability and the price of the factors of production (i.e. the cost of land, labour and capital) required to produce more of the same, the ability to produce substitutes, and producer tastes or preferences. In essence, value is not dependent on any one factor, nor on an interaction of objective and subjective, intrinsic and extrinsic, and determinable and determining factors. To a home owner it may be measured in comfort, convenience and congeniality. And to a modern real estate investor it is primarily a function of the total income or return that can be obtained from a property in the future; or the power that the ownership of the property represents for use and occupation; or its use as a medium of exchange, either for other property or for **money**.

The intrinsic factors that may affect the value of real estate include topography, soil, plot size and shape, improvements, utilities or services, title, property rights and interests. The extrinsic factors include accessibility, location, climate, zoning or land use planning, taxation, building restrictions, consumer preferences. When considering the 'value in use', the intrinsic factors may dominate; when considering the 'value in exchange', the extrinsic factors may dominate. In the final analysis, the value of a plot of land or building, at any point in time, depends on the interaction of these factors as assessed by individual wants and needs. A plot of land may be readily accessible, level, zoned for offices and in a tax free area, but have little or no value if no one needs it. On the other hand, it may be irregularly shaped, unsuitable for building, be held on a short lease, but have premium or **nuisance value** because it provides access to a site that is suitable for immediate development.

Value may have different meanings, even for the same property, according to the context or the use of the word. For example, to a landowner it may mean **market value**, or **replacement value**; to a mortgagee, **loan value**; to a tenant, **rental value** or **annual value**; to an insurer, **insurable value**; to a shareholder of a company, **asset value** or **going-concern value** and to an occupier who is liable for a property tax, **assessed value**(US) or **rateable value**(Eng). However, unless qualified or varied by the context, value in real estate normally means 'market value'.

In the US, for taxation purposes or when assessing **just compensation** value is generally taken to mean **fair market value**. See also **actual cash value, book value, capital value, cash value, collateral value, current use value, economic rent, existing use value, hope value, intrinsic value, investment value, leasehold value, marriage value**(BrE), **mortgage value, net asset value, net present value, open market rental value, open market value**(BrE), **par value, present value, real value, residual value, reversionary value, valuation.** **2.** Valuable **consideration**; something of economic value that is given to support a simple contract.

In English law, in the phrase 'purchaser for value', 'value' means "any consideration in **money** or **money's worth** ... or marriage", Charles Harpum, *Megarry & Wade: The Law of Real Property*. 6th ed. London: Sweet & Maxwell, 1999, p. 139. Value can be given even if the amount is nominal (e.g. £1); or not equivalent to the full worth of that which is received (*Midland Bank Trust Co Ltd v Green* [1981] AC 513, [1981] 1 All ER 153 (HL)). Good consideration (e.g. natural love and affection) or a promise made in respect of a past marriage is not value and, therefore, will not make a promise enforceable.

In the US, a few jurisdictions accept that a 'purchaser for value' may pay any amount, however nominal, to enjoy the protection accorded to one who will not be affected by an unrecorded interest in land. However, most jurisdictions require an amount that bears a fair relation to the property being transferred, although that amount need not be equivalent to the market value. See also *bona fide* **purchaser**.

value added tax (VAT) A tax charged on the goods and services on the basis of the value added by each process of supply or production. In particular, a form of sales tax charged on the taxable supply and importation of goods and services. VAT is payable on the supply of goods and services in the course or furtherance of any business, unless the supply is relieved from such liability. It is levied at each stage of the manufacturing, producing or selling of goods, or the provision of services, by way of a percentage of the increased value of the goods or services brought about by the business activity. VAT is levied in such a way that the tax is paid ultimately by the final 'consumer' as a percentage increase on the purchase price of the goods or services. The person adding value at each stage is the effective collector of the tax because that 'taxable person' charges tax on the increased value of goods or services supplied by him in the course of business and then accounts to the appropriate authority. *Butterworth's Orange Tax Handbook*, Annual, "Value Added Tax".

Hincks, Barry, and Ron Gould. *VAT for the Property Professional*. Welwyn Garden City: EMIS Professional Publishing, 1996.

Slater, Brian. *VAT on Property Transactions*. 2nd ed. Bristol: Jordans, 1999.

Soares, Patrick C. *VAT Planning for Property Transactions*. 8th ed. London: Sweet & Maxwell, 2002.

value before-and-after taking(US) See **before-and-after method**.

value center(US) **1.** A retail store that sells branded or quality merchandise at prices below those in department stores or regular main street stores.   **2.** A shopping center that specializes in retailers that sell at a discount or at prices that are below those offered in department or main street stores.

value-cost contract   See **cost-plus contract**.

value date   The date upon which a transfer of money becomes effective or a credit instrument becomes available for use as ready cash. From a given value date, the recipient is able to earn interest on the money or use the cash.

value engineering   A process by which all the components in a construction or development project are analysed, in order to ascertain the most cost efficient means of carrying out that project within a prescribed budget. Value engineering seeks to save money, reduce time, improve quality, reliability and performance of the project. The process considers the materials used, as well as the means by which the project is carried out and assesses these components against the final standard required of the project. Value engineering is an ongoing process that continues until a project is complete.
Dell'Isola, Alphonse. *Value Engineering, Practical Applications*, Kingston, MA: R. S. Means Company, 1997.

value-in-use   See **cost-in-use**, **use value**, **value**.

value policy   See **valued policy**.

valued policy   An **insurance policy** in which the amount to be paid in the event of total loss is an agreed sum as stipulated in the contract, usually without any assumed allowance for depreciation or appreciation. The stipulated figure is taken to be the true value of the subject matter of the policy, i.e. **liquidated damages** are payable in the event of loss. "A valued policy is one in which the measure of the value of the property insured is agreed upon by both parties to the contract, so that in the case of total loss it is not necessary to prove

the actual loss. Indeed it has been said that it is the uncertainty of the amount which distinguishes an open from a valued policy. Such a valuation is in the nature of a contract for liquidated damages", John Alen Appleman and John Appleman, *Insurance Law and Practice*. St Paul, Minn.: West, 1981, § 3827. The value placed on the subject-matter is binding between the parties and the insured does not have to prove the figure (except in the event of fraud, gross overvaluation or mistake), although he has to prove a loss. In the event of partial loss, the insurer only pays for the actual loss suffered. Real property insurance policies are generally not valued policies. Sometimes called a 'value policy'. cf. **unvalued policy**. See also **first-loss insurance**.

value received   Words used in a written instrument to indicate that **consideration** has been paid. The words are sometimes used to confirm that proper and sufficient consideration has been paid.

valuer   A person whose business is to estimate the worth of property. An **expert** who assesses the **value** of property. An acknowledged expert in a particular field of **valuation**. "The term 'Valuer' (with a capital 'V' at any rate) is used nowadays to denote a member of a recognised profession comprising persons possessed of skill or experience in assessing the market price of a property, particularly real property", *Sudbrook Trading Estate Ltd v Eggleton* [1983] 1 AC 444, 477, [1982] 3 All ER 1, 5 (HL). A valuer's ultimate conclusion as to the worth of a property is a matter of opinion; he may be optimistic or pessimistic and accordingly be permitted that degree of latitude which is commensurate with the nature of the task. "The law does not require any man, valuer ... or any other expert agent to be perfect ... there is no absolute rule as regards the proper methods of ascertaining the value ... [if the methods of ascertaining the value in a particular case] are not perfect, if they are not the best, if they might have been improved upon, still [they] are methods which a man of position, endeavouring to do his duty, might fairly adopt without being said to be wanting in reasonable care and skill", *Lowe v Mack* (1905) 92 LTNS 349, 350. A valuer "cannot be faulted for achieving a result which does not admit some degree of error", *Singer and Friedlander Ltd v John D. Wood and Co* (1977) 243 EG 212, 213. (It has been suggested that a latitude of ten per cent is reasonable, but twenty per cent leaves something to be desired.) However, a valuer of real property must assemble all those factors – planning, building construction, legal constraints, area measurements, special situations, and any other relevant matters – that might have a bearing on his final figure; such facts as he ought to know or have ascertained; and he should draw his client's attention to these factors, and any other matters that have affected his opinion of value (*Old Gate Estates Ltd v Toplis* [1939] 3 All ER 209). In particular, "familiarity with the local market in which the subject property is situated and experience in valuing property of a type similar to the subject property is highly desirable ...", Ruaraidh Adams-Cairn & Jonathan Nash, *Adjudicating Valuation Claims*, (1993) 9327 EG 109.

In the US, this person is usually called an **appraiser** or sometimes a 'valuator'. (In common usage, an appraiser may be distinguished from a valuer as the former not only assesses the price or value of a property but may also assess its quality, worth or excellence.) See also **chartered surveyor, mortgage value, professional negligence, registered valuer**[(Aus/NZ)], **valuation report**; Appendix A, **Real Estate Associations**.

Joyce, Lindsay, and Keith Norris. *Valuer's Liability*, 2nd ed. Sydney: The Australian Institute of Valuers and Land Economics, Inc., 1994.

A. Loke. *The valuer's liability for negligent valuation*, 19 Legal Studies, March 1999, 47-67.

variable-amortization mortgage (VAM)[(AmE)]   See **variable-payment mortgage**.

variable annuity   See **annuity**.

variable operating expense[(US)]   An **operating expense** that is directly related to the use and occupation of the building to which it relates, e.g. the cost of most utilities, general cleaning and daily maintenance. cf. **fixed expense**.

variable-payment mortgage (VPM)   A mortgage loan in which the repayments of **principal** vary during the term of the loan. In particular, a mortgage that provides for reduced repayments during the initial years of the loan; especially when the payments are below those required by an **amortization mortgage**. Generally, later payments are increased to make up the deficit and ensure repayment of the entire principal over the term of the loan. Although the payments of principal vary, the interest rate may be fixed for all or part of the loan term. The term **variable-payment mortgage** is commonly applied to a mortgage on a residential property when repayments of principal are reduced in the early years to assist first-time buyers. In particular, the mortgage may provide for the payment only of interest in the initial years.

When the payments of capital are increased at fixed stages, or by fixed amounts, this form of mortgage may be termed a 'graduated-payment mortgage'. Also called a 'variable-amortization mortgage', or a 'flexible-payment mortgage', especially when the capital repayments in the initial years are reduced to reflect the borrower's ability to pay, or the income generated by the mortgaged property. An alternative form of variable-payment mortgage is the 'graduated-payment adjustable mortgage loan', which provides for one rate at which the borrower actually pays interest (the 'debit rate') and another higher rate at which interest on the loan is accrued (the 'payment rate'). The payment rate may be fixed, but the debit rate is variable and may increase after one or two years to make up for any negative amortization that arises during the initial term of the loan. cf. **adjustable-rate mortgage**. See also **deferred-payment mortgage, flexible loan insurance plan**[(US)].

variable-rate mortgage (VRM)   See **adjustable-rate mortgage**.

variable rent or varying rent A rent that may be changed by one of the parties (usually the landlord), or a rent that varies according to a predetermined formula, during the term of a lease. See also **graded rent**, **graduated rent**, **indexed rent**, **rent review**, **turnover rent**.

variance 1. The difference in a project or scheme between a standard or budget cost and the actual cost incurred. 2.(US)See **zoning variance**.

variation See **accord and satisfaction**, **discharge**, **estoppel**, **variation order**, **waiver**.

variation order (VO) or **variation instruction**(BrE) A form of **architect's instruction** issued in accordance with the terms of a building contract that requires a change or alteration to the quantity or quality of the work, or a condition under which the work is carried out. The order is normally given by the **architect**, on behalf of the employer, and may enable the contractor to request a modification of the contract price. A properly executed and written variation order should be the only means of altering any part of a building contract. A variation order may be made verbally, but should be confirmed by a written order submitted at the earliest date thereafter and this order should be copied to all professional advisors directly concerned with the contract. See also **change order**(AmE), **waiver**.

variations See **change order**(AmE), **variation order**(BrE).

variety store(US) A retail store, usually on one level, that sells a wide variety of merchandise, such as groceries, take-out food and drink, household supplies, stationery supplies, and sometimes items of clothing. A variety store aims to sell at low prices and is normally a self-service store. Such a store usually has a selling area between 10,000 and 100,000 square feet. Sometimes called a 'bazaar store'. cf. **department store**, **specialty store**. See also **convenience store**, **discount store**.

varying rent See **variable rent**.

vault An enclosed space covered by an arched roof, especially such space that forms part of a **cellar** that is used for the storage of materials that require cool and dark conditions, such as wine, or such a space, as in a bank, that is used for the safe keeping of valuables.

vendee One who acquires property, especially real property. More commonly called a 'buyer' (of goods) or a 'purchaser' (of land). See also **purchase**.

vendition The act of selling.

vendor One who sells property or offers property for **sale**. Although 'vendor', **grantor**, and **seller** may be used interchangeably to refer to a person who transfers title or ownership of property to another, a vendor sells property, especially real property for value; a grantor transfers or cedes property by any means, including by gift; and a seller gives up property for money or valuable consideration. (A **lessor** is not *prima facie* a vendor, but is an assignor or cessor.)

vendor and purchaser covenant See **restrictive covenant**.

vendor and purchaser summons(Eng) A document issued by the High Court requiring a party to a contract for the transfer of an interest in land to answer questions arising out of, or connected with, that contract. The summons may relate to such matters as sufficiency of title, sufficiency of answers to requisitions, the construction of the contract, matters of compensation relating to the contract or rights of rescission (but not a question relating to the validity or existence of the contract). It may be requested by the vendor or purchaser (LPA 1925, s. 49(1)). See also **deposit**, **specific performance**.

vendor's lien See **lien**.

venture capital Capital that is invested to

assist with the start-up of a new business or venture, especially one that is to provide an untested product or will serve an unproven market. See also **risk capital**.

verba accipienda sunt secundum subjectam materiam(Lat) 'Words are to be interpreted according to the subject matter'. See *ejusdem generis*.

verba chartarum fortius accipiuntur contra proferentem(Lat) 'The **words** of deeds are to be take more strongly against those who chose them'. See *contra proferentem*.

verba ita sunt intelligenda ut magis valeat quam pereat(Lat) 'Words should be so understood so that the object may be carried out and not be null'.

versus(Lat) 'Against'. Abbreviated to *v*. In English law, when used in the name of a civil case *v* should be referred to as 'and', not *versus*.

vertical lease See **side-by-side participation**.

vertical privity(US) The relationship that exists between those who are in a direct chain to the parties to an original agreement that relates to an estate in land. For example, the original landlord and an assignee of his tenant; or the purchaser of land and the owner of an adjoining lot that has the burden of an easement over the land or a covenant that restricts the development of the land acquired. Thus, for there to be vertical privity, for example between a party who now holds title to land that is burden by a covenant and the other original party to the agreement, there needs to be a continuous succession of conveyances between the original covenantor and the party now sought to be burdened. cf. **horizontal privity**. See also **covenant running with the land**, **privity**, **privity of estate**, **real covenant**.

vertical-slice participation See **side-by-side participation**.

vest 1. To bestow or endow with an immediate and fixed right, privilege or authority. To confer a legal right on someone. In particular, to grant or bestow an estate, interest or right to land, but not so that it is subject to any contingency. For the purpose of the **rule against perpetuities**, the word 'vest' means to give an immediate, fixed right of present or future enjoyment, and it grants an interest in land that is ascertainable and can be transferred or 'alienated' without limitation. In order to satisfy the rule against perpetuities, an estate or interest is said to be or to become vested when "(1) the person or persons, corporation or body to whom or to which it is limited is or are ascertained and in existence and capable of being an alienee; (2) the quantum of the estate and interest is ascertained; and (3) all other events have happened to enable the estate or interest to come into possession at once, subject to the determination at anytime of the prior estates and interests", 35 *Halsbury's Laws of England*, Perpetuities and Accumulations, 4th ed. Reissue, para. 1019. An estate is not vested as long as it remains subject to the occurrence or non-occurrence of some uncertain or contingent event. See also **vested interest**, **vesting declaration**. 2. To give **seisin**; to deliver **possession**. See also **alienation**.

vested estate See **vested interest**.

vested-in-interest See **vested interest**.

vested-in-possession See **vested interest**.

vested interest or **vested estate** 1. An interest, or estate, in land that is held unconditionally. A right to possession of land that is not dependent on any contingent or uncertain event. A right that has accrued to, or is vested in, a determinate person; as distinguished from a right that is accompanied by an uncertainty as to whether it may or may not be acquired by someone, or an uncertainty as to who will acquire that right. An interest (or estate) may be created at present, but the right to possession is restricted to a future determinable period. Thus, the date that possession will occur may be uncertain, but that it will occur is certain, as with death. For example, if an estate is conveyed "to A for life, remainder to B in fee simple", then A has a vested interest in possession (a right that is said to be 'vested-in-possession') and B a vested interest that comes into possession on the death of A. B has an interest that during A's lifetime is said to be 'vested-in-interest' or a 'vested remainder', i.e. the beneficiary is known and there are no prior conditions to be satisfied, and on A's death B's interest 'vests in possession'. When used by itself 'vested interest' means primarily an interest 'vested-in-interest'. An essential feature of a right that is 'vested-in-interest' is that the person or persons entitled to the interest has been ascertained, but that, although the interest may be ready to take effect forthwith, it does not take effect until the determination of the preceding estates and interests. An interest held under a class gift cannot be vested until there can be no possibility that the class can continue to increase or decrease. At common law, a holder of a vested interest has an interest in land that can be alienated or devised; as distinguished from the holder of a **contingent interest** who has an interest that may never arise or may be lost if the contingency arises upon which the interest depends. cf. **inchoate interest**. See also **defeasible, remainder, rule against perpetuities, vest.** **2.** An interest in a property, affair, or business, where the holder has a personal commitment, or is likely to produce a pecuniary benefit from that interest. An involvement with a thing, person or body that is likely to produce a pecuniary benefit as a result of the actions of a third party. See also **arm's-length transaction, undue influence.**

vested remainder   See **vested interest.**

vested right(US)   A right to carry out development or construction work pursuant to a valid building permit. A valid building permit or licence cannot arbitrarily be revoked, especially when the owner has incurred significant expenditure in reliance thereon. Such a right is normally considered to exist after substantial work has been carried out on a project, even if the development or building has not been completed. In the event that a vested right is established, any restraint on the subsequent completion of the project may constitute a 'taking' of private property and entitle the landowner to **just compensation**. See also **grandfather clause, non-conforming use, vested interest.**

vesting assent(Eng)   See **vesting deed.**

vesting declaration(Eng)   **1.** A declaration, contained in a deed to the effect that an estate or interest in trust property is to **vest**, i.e. be transferred, to the new trustees. A vesting declaration avoids the necessity for a separate conveyance for the trust property; except in the case of a mortgage, shares in a company, and a leasehold interest held subject to a covenant against assignment (Trustee Act 1925, s. 40). See also **general vesting declaration.** **2.** A deed by which a local authority adopts a private sewer in order to enable the authority to carry out its responsibility for the proper provision of sewage facilities (PHA 1936, s. 17). See also **adoption.**

vesting deed(Eng)   A deed, order of a court or assent that transfers the **legal estate** in **settled land** to the tenant for life or the statutory owner. In other words, a formal instrument that transfers land to the person who is to hold the 'paper title' when there is a **strict settlement**. In most cases, a strict settlement of land is created by two deeds, a vesting deed (or in the case of registered land a 'vesting transfer') and a **trust instrument**. The former provides details of the title to the land and the latter sets out details of the settlement. Without this evidence of separation there cannot be a strict settlement (SLA 1925, s. 4). The purpose of having separate documents is to enable a future purchaser of the land to obtain a valid title without concerning himself with the terms of the settlement – known as the 'curtain principle'.

When the settlement is made *inter vivos* (between

living persons), the legal estate is conveyed by means of a 'vesting deed'. If the settlement is made by **will**, the will acts as the trust instrument and the personal representatives, after having paid debts or death duties, are required to execute a 'vesting assent' which is a simple written document, signed by the personal representatives, that has the same effect as the vesting deed (SLA 1925, ss. 6, 8(1)). When settled land is vested in the tenant for life or statutory owner by order of a court, that order is called a 'vesting order'. A vesting deed, vesting assent, or a vesting order (provided the land remains settled land when the order has been made) may each be referred to as a 'vesting instrument' (SLA 1925, s. 117(1)(xxxi)).

A vesting deed (referred to in the SLA 1925 as the "principle vesting deed") must describe the settled land; state that the settled land is vested in the person or persons to whom it is conveyed; name the trustees of the settlement; name the persons entitled to appoint new trustees; and describe any powers conferred on the tenant for life by the trust instrument beyond those provided by the Act (SLA 1925, s. 5; First Schedule, Form No 2). The deed must contain also a statement "that the settled land is vested in the person or persons to whom it is conveyed or in whom it is declared to be vested", SLA 1925, s. 5(1)(b). A vesting deed or vesting assent is like any other **conveyance**, except that it states that there is a settlement affecting the land, and sets out such details of the settlement, but no more, as may be required by the person to whom the land is conveyed. If the settlor divests himself of all interest in the settled land, the vesting deed conveys the **legal estate** to the tenant for life. Alternatively, the vesting deed may state that the settlor holds the legal estate as tenant for life under the settlement. The vesting deed signifies to a purchaser of the land that the purchase money must be paid to the trustees of the settlement. If additional land is to become the subject of the settlement, it is conveyed to the tenant for life by a 'subsidiary vesting deed' (SLA 1925, s. 10).

vesting document(Eng)   See **vesting deed**.

vesting instrument   See **vesting deed**.

vesting order(Eng)   An order made by a court by which an interest in land is vested in such a person as the court considers appropriate as if a transfer of the interest had been made by a **conveyance**. A vesting order made for the purpose of vesting, conveying or creating a **legal estate** has the same effect as if it were made by the estate owner of the interest to which it relates (LPA 1925, s. 9). The Trustees Act 1925, ss. 44-56 sets out a number of instances in which the High Court may make such an order: for example, when it is necessary to transfer a legal estate to trustees because land has been granted as security for a mortgage to an infant or a person under a disability; when there is no personal representative of a deceased trustee; or in any other case where a court appoints, or has appointed, a trustee. See also **vesting document**.

vesting transfer(Eng)   See **vesting deed**.

vesture of land   Everything (other than trees) that is growing on **land**. The right to a "vesture of the land" is the right to the surface, "the corne, grasse, underwood, sweepage and the like", 1 *Co Litt* 4b. See also **seisin**, **trespass** *quare clausum fregit*.

Veterans Administration (VA) **loan**(US)   A loan for the purchase of a single-family home that is guaranteed by the Veteran's Administration and is granted to any "eligible veteran", or to an unremarried widow or widower of a veteran who dies in service. Generally, an eligible veteran is one who has served a minimum of 181 days active service between September 16, 1940 and September 7, 1981, or two years active service after September 7, 1981. The Veterans Administration (VA) was established as a federal agency in 1930 to provide benefits for those who had served as enlisted men or women or as commissioned officers in any of the Armed Services, as well as their dependents. Since 1989, the VA has become the cabinet level Department of Veterans Affairs, although it is still referred to as the Veterans

Administration. Lenders designated by the VA may make home loans (including loans for the purchase of a townhouse or condominium in a VA-approved project and mobile homes) to eligible veterans upon terms that are more favorable than those that are available to other borrowers. For example, the veteran may be able to obtain loans that are granted (a) without the need for a down payment; (b) up to 100% of the VA-established reasonable value (although loans are generally limited to $203,000); (c) at or below market interest rates, for up to 30 years, with a choice of principal repayment plans; (d) as assumable loans; (e) without any penalty on repayment of the principal; (f) without any mortgage insurance premium to pay; or (g) the veteran may be able to pay lower closing costs on the cost of the loan. See also **no bid**.   (**www.va.gov/vas/loan**).

vi, clam, precario(Lat)   See *nec vi, nec clam, nec precario*.

vi et armis(Lat)   'By force of arms'. See **trespass**.

viability study   See **feasibility analysis**.

vicarious liability or **vicarious responsibility**   An indirect legal liability. A liability for the acts of another. The liability for a **tort** committed by another, even though the person made liable is not the direct cause or is not a party to the tort. Vicarious liability may arise: (a) where there is a relationship between the parties that is sufficient to justify the imposition of the liability; and (b) the tort can be related to that relationship. For example, vicarious liability may well arise from the relationship of employer (or master) and an employee (or servant) because the servant's acts, when carried out as part of his duties of employment, are considered as the acts of the master – *qui facit per alium facit per se*. (The employee may be liable also for his acts, but a wronged person may prefer to claim against the employer, or against both parties.) A person is liable for the tort of another if the former is able to control the method by which the latter performs

his duties; but, in general, there is no similar liability for the acts of an **independent contractor**, provided the contractor is left free to control and direct the manner in which he performs the job entrusted to him and the employer does not condone the contractor's deficiencies (The American Law Institute, *Restatement Second, Torts* § 409 (1965); *D & F Estates Ltd v The Church Commissioners for England* [1989] AC 177 (HL)). A similar liability may arise between a **principal** and his **agent**, the principal being liable if a relationship akin to master and servant exists, as where the agent is acting under strict instruction or authorisation; but not, as a rule, if the relationship is that of employer and independent contractor and the agent is not controlled as to how he exercises his duties, or if the agent is acting (expressly, apparently or ostensibly) outside his authority (*Lloyd v Grace, Smith & Co* [1912] AC 716 (HL); The American Law Institute, *Restatement Second, Agency* § 220 (1958)). A **partnership** may be vicariously liable for the acts of one of its partners when that partner is acting in the ordinary course of the business of the firm. In the US, sometimes called 'imputed liability'.

vicarious performance   1. The **performance** of all or part of a contractual obligation by a person who is not a party to a contract, e.g. by a subcontractor. See also **main contractor**, **privity of contract**.   2. An action carried out by a company using a human or mechanical agent. A company, being an intangible entity, must act through a tangible body, i.e. it acts vicariously; and thus may be 'vicariously liable' for it actions. See also **vicarious liability**.

vice   A defect or fault in something; an imperfection. See also **inherent defect**.

vicinage   An adjoining area; part of a neighbourhood. In English law, a right *pur cause de vicinage* was a form of **profit à prendre**, being a **right of common** by which cattle that were rightfully on the common land of one manor were permitted to stray and feed on the unfenced common land of an adjoining manor. "Common *because of vicinage*, or neighbourhood, is where the inhabitants of two townships which lie contiguous to each other, have usually intercommoned with one another: the beasts of one straying into the other's fields without any molestation from either", 2 *Bl Comm* 34 (*Tyrringham's Case* (1584) 4 Co Rep 36b, 76 Eng Rep 973; *Newman v Bennett* [1981] QB 726, [1980] 3 All ER 449, 452).

videlicet [*viz.*]^(Lat)   'That is to say'; 'namely'.

view   To take notice by eye; but not to go as far as to survey. See also **access**, **easement**, **right of light**, **right to view**, **valuer**.

vigilantibus, non dormientibus, jura subveniunt^(Lat)   'Law aids those who are vigilant, and not those who sleep on their rights'; 'law aids the vigilant, not the indolent'. See also **laches**.

village green   See **green**.

vindictive damages   See **damages**.

virtual rent   The **rent** paid under a lease plus the **annual equivalent** of any improvement to the leased property carried out at the tenant's expense, i.e. the true annual cost of the property itself, excluding property taxes or similar impositions. Also called 'sitting rent or 'true rent'. cf. **effective lease rate**, **improved rent**. See also **cost-in-use**, **occupancy cost**.

vis major^(Lat)   'A greater or irresistible force'. A force of nature or man that cannot be avoided by reasonable diligence, or by the exercising of prudence and care. For example, a storm, a riot or a governmental act arising from the necessities of war. *Vis major* is sometimes used as synonymous with **act of God**, although the term is more akin to *force majeure*. A person is not normally liable for a breach of contract caused by *vis major*.

visibility clearance^(AmE)   An area of land on a corner lot upon which no building, structure or other item is permitted in order to ensure visibility at the intersection of two highways. The area is generally a triangle of land (a 'sight triangle') that permits a line of sight of at least 45°. The restriction on the use of the land commonly takes the form of an **easement** (a 'line-of-sight easement') granted by the landowner to the highway commission. See also **vision splay**^(BrE).

vision splay^(BrE)   An area of land at the junction of two highways, or at an access point to a highway, which must be kept free of buildings or obstructions to afford adequate visibility for motor vehicles crossing or entering the highway. A highway authority may require a landowner to maintain a vision splay as a condition for authorising a development that could increase the volume of traffic entering a highway. See also **building line**, **planning condition**, **visibility clearance**^(AmE).

visitor   One who enters on land, or into a building, with the leave and at the invitation of the owner or occupier, usually for a particular purpose, but with no intention to stay. A person who enters onto property for business or pleasure and is not expected to stay for an extended period.

In English law, an occupier of land owes a "common **duty of care**" to his or her visitors; that is, a "duty to take such care as in all the circumstances of the case is reasonable to see that the visitor will be reasonably safe in using the premises for the purposes for which he is invited or permitted by the occupier to be there", Occupier's Liability Act 1957, s. 2(2). A duty that is higher in the case of a child, but is not necessarily owed to a trespasser (although see **negligence**). In this context "a person is a 'visitor' if at common law he would be regarded as an **invitee** or **licensee**; or be treated as such, as for instance, a person lawfully using premises provided for use of the public, e.g. a public park, or a person entering by lawful authority, e.g. a policeman with a search warrant. But a 'visitor' does not include a person who crosses land in pursuance of a public or private right of way. Such a person was never regarded as an invitee or licensee, or treated as such", *Greenhalgh v British Railways Board* [1969] 2 QB 286, 293, [1969] 2 All ER 114, 117 (CA) (1957 Act, s. 2(6)). See also **negligence, trespass**.

vitious dispossession(Scot) Literally 'vicious' dispossession. The dispossession of an occupier of land without consent and without judicial authority. A person who is vitiously dispossessed is entitled to immediately reclaim the original right to possession. See also **spuilzie**.

vitium reale(Lat) 'Inherent defect'.

viva voce(Lat) 'By word of mouth', e.g. an oral testament.

void contract A **contract** that is completely 'null' and cannot give rise to any legal right, duty, effect or obligation. An agreement that is devoid of legal effect, usually because it lacks an essential element (such as a competent party or an ascertainable subject matter). A contract that is invalid and unenforceable and of which the court will take no account. A void contract may arise because the agreement is illegal or immoral; induced by fraud; or one of the parties does not have the capacity to contract. A void contract follows the rule *non est factum*, 'it has not been made' and, therefore, unlike a **voidable contract**, it is not a contract at all; it never came into existence as such. A void contract may be one that is of no force or effect, it may be void as it is illegal, or the term may be used loosely to refer to a contract that is voidable at the instigation of one of the parties. Whether an agreement is null and void, or 'voidable' at the option of one of the parties, does not depend on the express provision of an agreement, but on the nature of the agreement. It may also be used inaccurately to refer to a contract that was valid but has ceased to have effect before its normal expiry, either automatically, or by **election** of one of the parties after breach. Strictly, 'void contract' is a contradiction in terms, because

an agreement must have legal effect to constitute a contract. cf. **illegal contract**. See also **equity of redemption, rectification, solus agreement**.

void trust A **trust** that cannot be enforced because it is against the policy of the law, e.g. a trust that offends the **rule against perpetuities**. See also **resulting trust**.

voidable contract A contract that appears valid but, due to some defect or vitiating factor, may be repudiated or avoided by one or more of the parties, although it has not been so declared. A voidable contract, unlike a **void contract**, has legal effect but it may be avoided, or accepted as valid, by the **election** of one or other of the parties. A voidable contract may arise from **misrepresentation, mistake, duress, undue influence**, when there is a breach of a requirement for **utmost good faith**, or when one of the parties is legally incapable of contracting (due to drunkenness, age, soundness of mind or statute). A voidable contract remains valid until the party who has the power to negate or aver it takes the appropriate action to rescind it, to have it set aside in a court of law, or to affirm it. If it is not rescinded within a reasonable time, or if a benefit is accepted from it, the contract may cease to be 'voidable'. cf. **unenforceable contract**. See also **estoppel, ratification, rescission**.

volenti non fit injuria(Lat) 'To a willing person a wrong cannot be done'. 'That to which a man consents cannot be considered an injury'. An action for damages arising from a tort may be defeated when it can be shown that the injured party expressly or impliedly assented, in whole or in part, to the act that caused the injury, i.e. is contributorily negligent, as by "voluntarily and rashly exposing himself to injury", *Smith v Baker and Sons* [1891] AC 325, 355 (HL). However, merely being aware of a risk, or a willingness to take a risk, is insufficient to support this defence; there must be full and free consent to accept the risk entailed – actual and not constructive knowledge. See also **contributory negligence, negligence, waiver**.

voluntary conveyance   **1.** A conveyance or other transfer of real estate made without the transferor receiving any 'valuable' **consideration**. A **deed of gift** (but not a marriage settlement, because, in common law, marriage is valuable consideration for a transfer of property). A conveyance made for valuable consideration, where the parties are closely related, may be considered as a voluntary conveyance. Also called a 'voluntary disposition' or in the US a 'voluntary deed'. See also **fraudulent conveyance**.   **2.** A transfer of mortgaged or secured property, by the mortgagor to the mortgagee, in order to extinguish an outstanding debt without the need to resort to **foreclosure** or a public sale. See also **deed-in-lieu of foreclosure**.   **3.** See **voluntary sale**.

voluntary deed(US)   See **voluntary conveyance**.

voluntary disposition   See voluntary conveyance.

voluntary improvement   An **improvement** that is made without obligation or that adds nothing to the value of a property. An improvement made purely for adornment. cf. **repair**.

voluntary lien   See lien.

voluntary settlement   A **settlement** that is not made for money or money's worth or in consideration of a future marriage, i.e. a settlement that is not made for 'valuable' **consideration**.

voluntary sale or voluntary transfer   A **sale** or **transfer** made when there is no constraint on the owner of the thing sold. A sale or transfer made without **duress** or compulsion. cf. **compulsory purchase**(Eng), **involuntary transfer**. See also **market value, willing seller**.

voluntary trust   A trust made voluntarily during a person's lifetime. A **trust** that arises from a confidence placed in another and voluntarily accepted, as distinguished from an involuntary trust which arises by operation of law. A voluntary trust may be distinguished from a **gift**, in that the former passes legal title to a third party and the beneficiary retains an equitable interest, whereas a gift passes absolute title to the donee. cf. **constructive trust, resulting trust**.

voluntary waste   See waste.

volunteer   **1.** A person who acquires property without paying valuable **consideration**. One who acquires a right or interest in real or personal property as a **gift**. See also **voluntary conveyance**.   **2.** One who without a duty or obligation pays the debt of another.

voucher plan(US)   A method of financing construction work by which the lender advances funds directly to those who have provided labor or materials based on orders (vouchers) received from the employer or a principal contractor.

W

wait and see rule   See **rule against perpetuities**.

waiver   Derived from the Old French *gaiver*, 'make a *waif* of' or 'to abandon'. The act of voluntarily giving up, or of intentionally relinquishing, a known right, claim, benefit or interest. The unilateral renunciation or repudiation of a remedy against a tort, or a right under a contract. Waiver arises especially when one party to a contract unilaterally indicates that he will not insist upon the **performance** of some or all of its stipulations or provisions. Waiver requires that a person intends to give up a right; that he communicates his intention to the person who might benefit from it; and that the other person relies on the waiver. Waiver applies only to a right and not to property *per se* and in that way differs from **abandonment**; although a waiver may result in the abandonment of a right or claim.

In common law, a landlord may waive his right of forfeiture or termination of a lease, when a tenant is in **breach of covenant**, if he *knows* (directly or through an agent) of the breach, but accepts rent; issues a demand, sues or distrains for rent; or does some unequivocal act recognising the continued existence of the lease. The acceptance of rent is evidence that the landlord acknowledges that the tenant has complied with the conditions of his lease; even if the acceptance is stated to be 'without prejudice', or the rent is accepted and retained by an authorised agent by mistake. A receipt of part of the amount due from a tenant may not amount to a waiver of the landlord's right of possession, if it is clear that the landlord is continuing to insist on payment in full.

Waiver may be express or implied. An express waiver (which resembles a **release**) is given normally in **writing**. In particular, it must be in writing when the contract, or the condition of the contract that is waived, is in writing. A lease commonly contains a provision that it may not be waived, amended, or modified unless there is written evidence to that effect. An implied waiver may arise from an act that is inconsistent with the continuance of the right or benefit that might be claimed, or an act that indicates that a person no longer intends to rely on the right or benefit – provided the act is made knowingly, positively and intentionally. An implied waiver is closely analogous to **estoppel**; although strictly speaking a waiver is a surrender of a right, a voluntary and intentional act, whereas estoppel is a failure or inhibition to assert a right after something has happened as a consequence of an action or inaction by the other party. Nonetheless, in the US, the terms are sometimes used interchangeably, especially in the context of insurance.

'Waiver' is used also to refer to an **election** whereby one right is forgone by adopting an alternative, but inconsistent, course of action; although when an alternative right is 'waived' it is preferable to refer to the 'election' of that which is accepted (*Kammins Ballrooms Co Ltd v Zenith Investments (Torquay) Ltd* [1971] AC 850, 873, 883, [1970] 2 All ER 871, 886, 894 (HL)). Waiver may refer also to the loss of a right by **laches**, i.e. an unreasonable delay in asserting or enforcing a right. However, a waiver can only extinguish a right or claim, it can never act as a basis for a claim.

In the US, most jurisdictions follow the common law principle that a landlord's right of forfeiture of a lease may be waived expressly or by implication. Thus, the acceptance of rent with knowledge of the breach may be considered as an affirmation of the existence of the lease and a consequent waiver of the right of **forfeiture**. However, in the case of a continuing breach or a subsequent reoccurrence of a breach, or if the landlord has no knowledge (actual or constructive) of the breach, there is no such waiver. Also, some jurisdictions do not accept that if a landlord accepts rent he waives his right to forfeit the lease on the grounds of consistent late payment of rent. See also **discharge, imputed notice, non-waiver clause, rescission, surrender**.

28 *Am.Jur.2d.*, Estoppel and Waiver, §§ 197-227.
31 *Cor.Jur.Sec.*, Estoppel and Waiver, §§ 67-89.

waiver clause A clause in an insurance policy that provides for the insurer to have the right to take such action as is necessary to minimise his loss. For example, a clause that permits the insurer to demolish a dangerous building after a fire. See also **non-waiver clause**, **subrogation**.

waiver of defenses(US) See also **estoppel certificate**.

walk in, walk out sale(Aus) A sale of a rural property as a going concern. A sale of a business with the stock, equipment and fittings.

walk-up apartment house(AmE) An **apartment house** with two or more stories and without an elevator. A 'walk-up' may refer to an apartment above ground floor level, especially an apartment that is reached only by an external flight of stairs.

walking possession See **distress**.

walkway A passageway intended for walking, i.e. a **footpath** or **sidewalk**. In particular, a way that links a number of buildings at ground or upper levels. See also **right of way**.

wall An upright structure made of a hard and durable material, such as brick, stone, masonry, wood, that acts as a boundary; holds back earth, water or any other substance; or forms part of the structure of a building in order to frame the exterior or divide the interior. An embankment of stone, concrete, masonry or other hard material constructed to retain land or restrain the erosion of land by a sea or river. See also **fence**, **partition wall**, **party wall**.

warehouse A place where goods, wares or merchandise is stored. A building, usually of considerable size, used for receiving, storing and distributing merchandise, raw materials or goods in bulk; but not one used primarily for processing or manufacturing goods and merchandise. In particular, a building where goods, which are not immediately needed for sale or manufacture, are stored in large quantities. A warehouse may incorporate the ancillary use of receiving tradesmen, or even limited public access to inspect goods for wholesale. As a rule, a warehouse is a covered area, so an open yard used for the same purpose is not strictly speaking a warehouse. cf. **factory**. See also **industrial building**.

warehouse loan(US) A loan secured by means of a number of mortgages held by the same borrower. The borrower (usually a mortgage bank) is holding or 'warehousing' the mortgages until they can be sold in the secondary mortgage market. See also **mortgage-backed security**.

warehousing See **warehouse loan**.

warrandice(Scot) A guarantee by a transferor of property, usually in a disposition of a heritage, that the title conveyed will be effectual. A warrandice may be express, but is implied into any contract for the sale of land, although the guarantee is personal to the parties.

warrant 1. Derived from the Old French *guarant*, 'be a guarantee for'. A document that authorises someone to do something, especially to pay or receive a sum of money, or to deliver or receive goods. 2. A tradable security that gives the holder the right (but not the obligation) to buy or sell a financial instrument (such as an equity stock or a fixed-income security) during a stipulated period of time and upon certain conditions, usually at a predetermined price. A warrant may be a 'call' if the holder has the right to buy the underlying stock, or a 'put' if it gives the right to sell the stock. 3. A certificate delivered under seal, or an authority in writing, authorising or requiring an action; especially an action that would not otherwise be permitted. A document by which an officer of the law is authorised to enter premises and conduct a search thereon, when that would otherwise be an act of trespass. 4. To guarantee the security or condition of a property. See also **warranty of habitability**, **warranty of title**.

5. Something given as a **pledge**, **guarantee** or assurance. **6.** A **receipt** for deposited goods.

warrant of distress(US)   See **distress**.

warranties of title(US)   See **covenant for title**.

warrantor   One who gives a **warrant**.

warranty   **1.** A **promise** or assurance, express or implied, to the effect that a certain fact is true or that a property is in a stipulated condition. In particular, a statement that induces a person to enter into a contract and comes to form part of the terms upon which the contract is created. "In essence a warranty is an assurance by one party to an agreement of the existence of a fact upon which the other party may rely; it is intended precisely to relieve the promisee of any duty to ascertain the facts for himself. Thus, a warranty amounts to a promise to indemnify the promisee for any loss if the fact warranted proves untrue", Clearwater Forest Industries, Inc. v. United States, 227 Ct Cl 386, 650 F.2d 233, 238 (1981).

In the traditional sense, warranty meant to 'give one's word', but "during the last hundred years, however, the lawyers have come to use the word 'warranty' … to denote a *subsidiary* term in a contract as distinct from a vital term which they call a **condition**", *Oscar Chess, Ltd v Williams* [1957] 1 All ER 325, 328 (CA). Accordingly, if there is a breach of a condition, the damaged party may treat the contract as discharged; whereas the breach of a warranty merely gives a right to claim damages. However, whether a term of a contract is intended as a warranty or as a condition depends on what the parties intended. In the final analysis, whether it is intended to create a warranty or a condition is a matter for the courts. 'Warranty' when used in relation to the transfer of property may be used to refer to the condition of the title, or to refer to the physical condition of the property. 'Warranty' is used commonly, but incorrectly, as synonymous with **guaranty**. cf. **puffing**. See also **implied warranty, pledge, proposal, repair, security**. **2.** A **covenant** by which the seller of real property undertakes that he will convey the estate that he has specified in a deed and undertakes to pay compensation for any loss suffered by the buyer as a result of any defect of title. See also **covenant of warranty, warranty deed**. **3.** An **indemnity** against loss. In common usage, a contract, or any term of a contract, that guarantees the quality of a property or the suitability of work or of a product. An undertaking, express or implied, that a statement that forms part of, or is incidental to, a contract is true or is as represented.

In insurance, warranty is used when the insured gives an undertaking that a particular fact does or does not exist or that something will or will not be done and in that circumstance the warranty constitutes a fundamental **term** or **condition** of the contract of insurance. On the other hand, warranty may be distinguished from insurance as the former promises indemnity against defects, whereas **insurance** provides payment to cover loss or damage resulting from that which arises outside of the defect in the article itself. See also *caveat emptor*, **covenant**.

warranty deed(US)   A **deed** that contains **covenants of title**. A deed by which a grantor of land guarantees that he has **good title** to the land and gives an undertaking as to the quality of the title being granted. In several jurisdictions, the use of a warranty deed and the inclusion of such words as "convey and warrant" or "warrant generally" implies the common law 'usual covenants of title', i.e. the **covenant of seizin**; **covenant of warranty**; **covenant against encumbrances**; and **covenant of quiet enjoyment**. In a few jurisdictions, the covenant of quiet enjoyment is not implied and in others only the covenants of seizin and against encumbrances are implied. In some jurisdictions, the covenants of title are set out in full, whereas in others the use of certain words, such as "by, through or under the grantor", "warrants particularly" or "warrants specially", implies the 'usual covenants of title'. A warranty deed does not guarantee that the vendor has the title he claims (the buyer should make his own searches in this respect), but if that which has been warranted is false, it gives the right for the purchaser to take an action to recover damages for the loss suffered. Such a deed may also be called a 'general warranty deed', or sometimes a 'full covenant and warranty deed', especially where the grantor undertakes to defend against "all lawful claims of title to the land" and there is a **covenant for further assurance**, i.e. the grantor undertakes to secure the execution of such other deeds or instruments as are necessary to perfect the title against third party claims. In some jurisdictions, a 'general warranty deed' requires, in particular, that the grantor convey the property free of any encumbrances.

The deed may be called a 'special warranty deed' if the grantor (who in such instances is usually acting in a special fiduciary position, e.g. a trustee) covenants only against certain claims, or the claims of certain persons, especially claims arising directly from the grantor's own acts or the grantor's own rights and persons claiming through such rights – sometimes called a 'covenant against claims and demands of the grantor'. A special warranty deed may also contain a covenant to the effect that the grantor has not himself encumbered the property, or will accept responsibility for acts arising "by, through or under the grantor" while the grantor held title to the land (but not while the land was held by a predecessor). The deed may also be called a 'limited warranty deed' if the warranties are granted only for a specified period of time, or if they cover only the period during which the grantor held the title. In some states, a special warranty deed is called a 'grant deed'. The warranty deed grew out of the common law 'bargain and sale deed', and transfers similar rights – except, as a rule, the covenant for further assurances – to those implied in English law in the case of a sale by a **beneficial owner**. Thus, it should be distinguished from the uniquely American **quitclaim deed**. See also **grant**.

warranty of habitability(US)   A requirement that rented residential property is free from any latent defect or conditions that render the premises uninhabitable for residential purposes, and that they will remain reasonably fit for residential purposes during the entire term. A warranty of habitability carries with it an implied duty to repair. At common law, there is no implied covenant in a lease that the demised premises are fit for habitation (*Smith v Marrable* (1843) 11 M & W 5, 152 Eng Rep 693; Franklin v. Brown, 118 NY 110, 23 NE 126 (1889); Posnanski v. Hood, 46 Wis.2d 172, 174 NW.2d 528 (1970)). However, there may be an implied term that arises as a result of the nature of the letting and, if the tenant is unable to use the premises because of a severe impediment, such as vermin infestation, or is unable to enjoy the property as intended, that may amount to **constructive eviction**, or that may constitute a breach of the landlord's covenant for **quiet enjoyment**. Also, many jurisdictions have accepted, or imposed statutes to the effect, that there is an implied warranty of habitability in a lease of residential property. The degree of this warranty varies from a requirement that the property complies with all building codes to a requirement that the demised premises are safe, sanitary and fit for habitation. On the other hand, some jurisdictions do not accept that there is any implied covenant or warranty by the landlord that the premises are fit for occupation, but have statutory provisions to similar effect which apply to multi-unit dwellings (*viz.* NY Real Property Law § 235-b). See also **fit for human habitation**(Eng), **fit for the purpose**, **habitable**, **implied warranty**, **set-off**.

warranty of title(US)   See **covenant of warranty**.

waste   1. An action that results in loss or deterioration, whether from use, misuse or neglect. Spoil or destruction that results in a marked and lasting alteration to the nature or condition of land (including any building or fixture thereon), sometimes for better, but usually for worse. In particular, an act or omission by someone in legal possession of property in order to alter or impair its value to the detriment of a person who will come into possession in the future, such as the reversioner or remainderman who follows a tenant for life or the landlord when he regains the property at the end of a lease. Unlawful damage caused to land and buildings by a tenant whereby the value of property is depreciated to the detriment of the person who is entitled to the immediate **reversion** or **remainder**, especially the fee simple, following a lease, or a fee tail (or entail), following a life interest. Waste may be distinguished from **trespass** as the former is an act committed by one who is rightfully in possession, whereas trespass is a wrongful act of possession.

Waste may be classified as: (a) 'permissive' waste (in the US also called 'negligent' or 'passive' waste) – failure to do that which ought to be done, as by negligence, or an omission to make necessary repairs, so that a property is permitted to fall into a state of decay, e.g. not repairing a roof damaged by storm or allowing decay to continue due to a lack of protective paint; (b) 'voluntary' or 'actual' waste (in the US also called 'affirmative or commissive waste')—making a deliberate change to a property, but an act that falls short of wanton damage or destruction, e.g. pulling down a house; altering or destroying part of a building, even if the work could be considered an improvement; converting woodland, meadow or pasture into arable land; cutting down **timber** (except on a timber estate, where such actions may be permitted by local **custom**, or when the timber is considered as an **estovers**); or opening up a new **mine** or **quarry** (but not working one that is already open nor opening one to use the produce for the reasonable repair of the property, unless expressly prohibited; (c) 'ameliorating' or 'meliorating' waste—an act of voluntary waste that has the effect of improving property, e.g. restoring a dilapidated building or changing the method of husbandry in order to improve the profitability of the land; and (d) 'equitable' waste—wanton or malicious damage or destruction; "that which a prudent man would [definitely] not do in the management of his own property", *Turner v Wright* (1860) 2 De GF & J 234, 243, 45 Eng Rep 612 (*Storey's Equity Jurisprudence* (14th ed. by W.H. Lyon. 1918), § 1242). Examples of equitable waste are cutting down trees that are clearly meant to be ornamental

or taking away elements (roof, windows, floor boards, etc.) from a sound building. Waste is considered as a form of **conversion** (not a breach of any contract between the tenant and the person who follows him), and a reversioner or remainderman who is prejudiced by an act of waste may obtain damages for the depreciation in the value of his reversion or remainder, or may recover the equivalent to the monies received as a result of the sale of a severed item; or he may seek an injunction to restrain the act (except in a case of permissive waste). In the US, in a few jurisdictions, a tenant for life may forfeit his lease for waste. However, in English law, the 'writ of waste', which provided such a remedy, has been abolished (Real Property Limitation 1833, s. 36).

A **tenant for life** (whether a tenant for his own life or for the life of another) is not liable for permissive waste (unless he is made responsible for repairs as a condition of his holding the estate (*Woodhouse v Walker* (1880) 5 QBD 404, 406-7), except as may be necessary to prevent further deterioration to the property. On the other hand, he is liable, or 'impeachable', for voluntary waste, including opening new mines or drilling for **oil**. In many cases, a tenant for life may be granted consent to commit what would otherwise be waste, e.g. cut timber on a non-timber estate or open new mines, and he is then said to be 'unimpeachable' for waste; although he is generally restrained from committing equitable waste (*Vane v Barnard (Lord)* (1716) 2 Vern 738, 23 Eng Rep 1082; The American Law Institute, *Restatement of Property* § 141, Comment (a) (1936)).

In common law, a **tenant for a term of years** is liable for voluntary and permissive waste (unless excused by agreement or by the consent of the landlord). A short-term periodic tenant (especially one from week to week, and probably one from month to month or even year to year), although liable for voluntary waste, is not liable to repair the demised premises (unless expressly committed thereto) and, therefore, the doctrine of voluntary and permissive waste has little application to such tenants. Nonetheless, in common law, a **weekly tenant** is required to maintain the premises in a tenant-like manner. A **tenant at will** is not liable for permissive waste, but an act of voluntary waste automatically terminates his right to continued occupation and he is liable for the consequential damage. A **tenant at sufferance** is liable for voluntary waste, but usually not for permissive waste. All such tenants are responsible for equitable waste. With regard to meliorating waste, although technically such acts are waste, a court is unlikely to restrain or grant damages for a reasonable improvement (especially for a life tenant or if the lease has a long unexpired term), because a landowner must show that he has suffered financial loss to his reversion or that the nature of the land has changed to his detriment (*Doherty v Allman* (1878-79) 3 App Cas 709, 733-735 (HL); Melms v. Pabst Brewing Co., 104 Wis 7, 79 NW 738, 739 (1899), see also pp. 739-740 for review of the history of the law of waste in England and the US in 19th century; cf. Prudential Ins. v. Spencer's Kenosha Bowl, 137 Wis.2d 313, 404 P.2d 109 (Wis App 1987)—no longer recognizing a distinction between 'active' and 'passive' waste). An action cannot be waste if it is authorised by the terms of the lease; nor if the action is one that accords with local **custom** or **usage**.

In common law, a **mortgagor** is responsible for equitable waste, but (unless he has agreed to the contrary – which is the case in most mortgage deeds) he may permit the property to fall into disrepair and may do acts, such as cutting timber, that alter the character or diminish the capital value of the mortgaged property. However, it may generally be considered that a mortgagor should not do anything that may impair the capital value of the security, especially if the action results in a reduction in the value of the security below the amount of the debt.

In the US, the cutting of timber and similar acts when in the interests of 'good husbandry' or 'reasonable use' of the land is not considered as waste, especially where new land was opened up for use and occupation (5 Am.L.Prop., § 20.5). Most jurisdictions follow the common law rule in considering the opening of a new mine as an act of waste (5 Am.L.Prop., § 20.6 n. 1), although an

open mine may be worked to exhaustion, unless there is an express prohibition. On the other hand, a few jurisdictions do not consider the opening of a new mine as an automatic act of waste.

In the US, a mortgagor is generally considered to have an obligation to safeguard the value of the mortgagee's security. In particular, in those jurisdictions that consider a mortgage as merely a lien on the property ('lien theory' states), waste is based on any injury to the value of the mortgagee's security, not physical damage to the property. cf. **fair wear and tear**[BrE], **improvement**, **wear and tear**[AmE], See also **assart, dilapidation, estovers, grounds for possession, implied covenant.**   **2.** See **wasteland**.

waste land[Eng]   See **manor**.

wasteland   An area of open and uncultivated, barren or unproductive land. Unoccupied and unused land. Land that is no longer used and has now become derelict.

In England and Wales, if it appears to the local planning authority that the **amenity** of part of their area, or of an adjoining area, is adversely affected by the condition of land in their area, they may serve on the owner and occupier of the land a notice requiring steps to be taken to remedy the condition of the land (TCPA 1990, s. 215). If the notice is not complied with, the authority has power to impose a fine on the owner or occupier (TCPA 1990, s. 216). A reasonable time must be given to remedy the condition and there is a right of appeal against the notice to the local magistrates' court, or subsequently to the Crown Court (TCPA 1990, ss. 217, 218). Also, local authorities have extensive statutory powers to require the tidying up of wasteland on the grounds of danger to public health, or to abate a public nuisance (Public Health Act 1931, ss. 92-100, Public Health Act 1961, s. 34). cf. **derelict land**. See also **nuisance**.

wasting property   Property with a limited or predictable **economic life** or property that is intended to be consumed or used up. Any form of property, or an interest in property, that diminishes in value due to time, as with a leasehold interest; due to obsolescence or wearing out, as with a buildings, plant, machinery; or due to use or depletion, as with a mine, oil well and quarry. Also called a 'depleting asset'. See also **depreciation**, **sinking fund**.

water gavel Rent paid for a right to water, or to take fish from water. See also **gavel**.

water rights A right to take water on or below, or running on or below, **land**. In particular, a right to take water from a river or stream for general or specific purposes.

At common law, water cannot be reduced to ownership, it can only be converted to a temporary right of user – water is considered to be *publici juris* (public property). However, water may be owned as *"land covered with water"*, 2 *Bl Comm* 18. Thus, water on land, as in a natural pond or lake, is part of the land and belongs to the owner of the land (1 *Co Litt* 4a). The owner of land may use the water thereon without limit (subject to any restriction or limitation that may be applied to the land on which it stands) and provided such use does not impact another landowner.

Water may also be appropriated in certain circumstances. The common law permits a landowner to use or divert water flowing in an undefined channel, especially water that percolates underground (unless there is a malicious intent to cause damage to an adjoining landowner or the extraction is restrained by statute law) and, therefore, no landowner can claim a right to a continuous flow of water that percolates to his land along an undefined path (unless he has the benefit of an **easement**; or a **restrictive covenant** – negative covenant – has been imposed on the upper riparian owner for that purpose). However, in most states in the US, the upper riparian owner's right to divert water is no longer regarded as absolute and is generally restricted to reasonable (and usually domestic) use, or is restricted by licensing or permit requirements.

In common law, water flowing in a clearly *defined* bed or channel (which it is unlikely to do underground) must be left to run without alteration as to its character or quality, so a riparian owner may have a right of redress against an upper riparian owner if the **stream** is dammed or diverted or the quality of the water is changed (*Swindon Waterworks Co Ltd v Wilts and Berks Canal Navigation Co* (1875) LR 7 HL 697 (HL); *John Young & Co v Bankers Distillery Co* [1893] AC 691, 698 (HL) (Scot)—although a right to dam or divert the stream may be acquired as an easement or negative covenant. However, there is a common law right for a person whose land is intersected or bounded by water flowing in a defined channel to use that water for 'ordinary use' connected with the land itself (which generally means reasonable domestic use and watering animals that are used to work the land), even if this has the effect of exhausting the supply to a landowner down stream.

In addition, under common law, a riparian owner may extract water for 'extraordinary' purposes in any quantity (but not in order to significantly interrupt the supply of water to other property), provided it is restored substantially in volume and unaltered in character. This right only applies to use in connection with the adjoining land (within the common ownership or 'watershed') and does not permit the taking of water for resale or use elsewhere (*Swindon Waterworks Co Ltd v Wilts and Berks Canal Navigation Co* (1875) LR 7 HL 697 (HL)).

In the US, in many jurisdictions, the rights of water extraction have been substantially modified by statutes enacted to restrict and control the use of water in a modern urban industrialized society, based, in most jurisdictions, on an extraction permit system. However, the common law rules are generally adopted in disputes between adjoining landowners, although there are many local variants, especially in the application of a 'reasonable use' doctrine designed to ensure a fair distribution of rights to water.

In the arid and semi-arid states west of the one-hundredth meridian, the rights of a landowner to extract water from a river or stream that passes across or alongside his land is largely governed by statutory regulation based on prior **appropriation**. These regulations vary considerably from state to state. Essentially this system allows for the use of water according to its prior or customary usage (as may have been practised by the original settler, especially for mining or milling purposes). This right is then limited by a requirement that the water may only be applied to 'beneficial use' (which need not be on the adjoining land). In ten states (including California and Texas), a hybrid system has developed, combining recognition of the 'reasonable use' doctrine and acceptance of prior 'appropriation rights', but taking into account the purpose of the water usage. In a few states, the prior appropriation system has effectively transferred the regulation of water usage to the state government so that a permit is required for all water extraction, such permits being granted according to the use to which the water is applied and the effect on other users. In Louisiana, following the civil law rule that a lower riparian owner has a **servitude** to receive a natural flow of surface water, a person is not permitted to interfere with the natural flow of water in order to affect another's use and enjoyment of his land (La CC, arts. 657-8). Although this civil law rule has been modified to take account of modern urban needs and changes to land use.

In the England and Wales, the common law rights to extract water have been substantially modified by statute, so that, without an 'abstraction licence from the **Environment Agency**, water can only be extracted "from any source" in relatively small amounts (Water Resources Act 1991; Environment Act 1985). See also *ad medium filum aquæ*, **conveyance**, **correlative water rights**[US], **dereliction**, **foreshore**, **general words**[Eng], **littoral rights**, **overriding interest**[Eng], **profit à prendre**, **right of support**, **right to fish**, **riparian rights**, *res nullius*, **strict liability**.

Fisher, D. E. *Water Law* [Australia]. Pyrmont, NSW: Lawbook Co., 2000.

Gould, George A., and Douglas L. Grant. *Cases and Materials on Water Law.* 6th ed. St Paul, MN: West, 2000.

Howarth, William. *Wisdom's Law of Watercourses.* 5th ed. Crayford, Kent: Shaw & Sons, 1992.

watercourse or **water course** The passage that carries water over land, in a more or less defined channel, e.g. between walls or banks, including a **river**, **stream**, creek or ditch. A well-defined channel in which water normally flows, especially in times of heavy rain or snow melt. The channel formed may be man-made or naturally formed as long as water flows continuously, or regularly (e.g. seasonally). The term 'watercourse' may be used to refer to the water, the channel in which it runs (even when dry), or the land over which the water flows. "It is difficult to define the term 'water course' in language that is uniformly applicable, since the topography and surrounding conditions which contribute to its existence may vary. In general terms it has been said to consist of a running stream of water following a regular course or channel and possessing beds and banks. It is a channel through which the water of a particular district or watershed usually or periodically flows. While it is ordinarily defined as a stream, containing a definite bed, banks and channel, which flows into some other river, stream, lake or sea, none of these characteristics is an absolute fixed factor. A water course may exist even though it serves as a mere channel by means of which a particular watershed is drained, and although it may be dry in certain seasons, or despite the fact that it may not empty into any other river, stream, lake or body of water, but, on the contrary, even though it terminates in some sandy basin where it disappears from sight. (See 25 Cal. Jur. 1032 secs. 31-38)", Costello v. Bowen, 80 Cal App.2d 621, 182 P.2d 615, 619 (1947). Although a watercourse may be dry some of the time, or for extensive periods during the year, when wet it is a regular flowing stream of water and not merely an area that is inundated by water from melting ice or snow.

In English law, 'watercourse' is defined as "all rivers, streams, ditches, drains, cuts, culverts, dykes, sluices, sewers and passages through which water flows, except mains and other pipes which—
(a) belong to the Authority or water undertaker; or
(b) are used by a water undertaker or any other person for the purpose only of providing a supply

of water to any premises", Water Resources Act 1991, s. 221(1) (Water Industry Act 1991, s. 219).

A watercourse may form an **easement** if it exists by virtue of a right to receive water from one person's land for the benefit of another's land. See also **drain, foreshore, highway, meander line**(US)**, quasi-easement, right to fish, riparian rights, water rights**.

Howarth, William. *Wisdom's Law of Watercourses*, 5th ed. Crayford, Kent: Shaw & Sons, 1992.

waterfall   The priority by which the cash flow from a **mortgaged-backed security** is distributed to the bondholders. The highest ranked securities are normally paid first and then holders of lower-rated bonds are paid according to their rating.

way   See **easement of necessity, highway, right of way, road, street**.

way of necessity   See **easement of necessity**.

way-going crop   An annual crop that has been sown or planted during the course of a tenancy that has been granted for a fixed term, but which will not ripen until after the termination of the tenancy. Generally, **custom** permits a tenant to a single harvest of such crops, after the expiration of the tenancy, unless there is an agreement to the contrary. Also called 'away-going crop' or sometimes 'off-going crop'. See also **compensation for improvements**(Eng)**, emblements**.

wayleave   1.(US)A **right of way** over or under adjoining land for the purpose of accessing a mine or quarry, or for the purpose of carrying away extracted minerals. See also **easement in gross, outstroke, wayleave rent**.   2.(BrE)A **right of way** over, under, or across land, used as a means for laying a conduit or transferring material; including a right for the passage of wires, cables, ducts, pipes, sewers, as well as coal or other minerals from a mine. Normally a wayleave is a species of **easement**, although in the case of a public utility easement the dominant and servient tenements may be some distance apart. However, a wayleave may be a mere

licence for the passage of such a conduit or, in some cases, a right granted by **lease** permitting the exclusive use of the land over which the conduit passes for as long as the right is exercised.

Poole, R., and Poole, P. M. *The Valuation of Pipeline Easements and Wayleaves*. London: Estates Gazette, 1962.

wayleave fee or **wayleave rent**   1. A fee, or rent, paid for the right to a **wayleave**.   2.(US)A payment for the use of a right of way to or from a mine or quarry. See also **outstroke**.

wealth   Derived from Middle English *welthe*, health, well-being or prosperity. In modern usage, an abundance of worldly goods or possessions; that which contributes to a well-being, even to the extent of opulence. The total value of all that is possessed, whether by an individual, an association, or a nation.

wear and tear(AmE)   Physical deterioration that arises as a result of normal and reasonable use. The gradual deterioration of premises resulting from use, lapse of time, and the action of the elements, but not the negligent care or use of the property by the tenant. A tenant is not liable for wear and tear that arises during the period of his occupation of the demised premises (unless there is an express condition that requires the tenant to put the property back exactly as it was at the start of the lease). A lease may also expressly exclude a tenant's liability for such repairs as 'normal', 'reasonable', or 'usual', 'natural' or 'ordinary wear and tear', and such wording precludes responsibility for deterioration from the use of the premises over time. See also **fair wear and tear**(BrE)**.

week   Any period of seven successive days, from midnight to midnight. In most commercial contexts, a week runs from Sunday through Saturday – from midnight between Saturday and Sunday to midnight of the following Saturday (*Bazalgette v Lowe* (1855) LJ Ch 368; Leach v. Burr, 188 US 510, 23 S Ct 393, 47 L Ed 567, 568 (1902)). However, in many situations in the western world, a week runs from midnight Sunday to midnight the following Sunday; or in the case of a 'working week' from midnight Sunday to midnight the following Friday (or in some businesses midnight Saturday). See also **day**, **time**, **week-to-week tenancy**.

weekly tenancy(Eng)   See **week-to-week tenancy**.

weekly tenant   The holder of a **weekly tenancy**.

week-to-week tenancy(US) or **weekly tenancy**(Eng)   A **periodic tenancy** that continues for a **week** and thereafter from week to week, until terminated by proper notice to quit. In English law, and in most jurisdictions in the US, a weekly tenancy is terminable by not less than seven clear days notice that expires at the "end of the current period". If a tenancy is terminable by 'one week's notice', then, as a rule, there must be seven *clear* days between the day the notice is given and the day from which it takes effect, i.e. the notice should be delivered to the tenant before twelve o'clock at night to expire by twelve o'clock at night on the subsequent corresponding day (unless some other hour has been agreed upon or is fixed by local law or custom).

As a rule, a 'weekly tenancy' or 'tenancy from week to week' runs from midnight on Saturday until the end of the following Saturday, unless there is an express agreement to the contrary, or it can be implied that the tenancy runs from a different day, as when the tenancy started and rent is payable on a different day of the week. Notice to terminate a weekly tenancy should be given so as to exclude the day of the notice, but to include the day upon which the period is to end, unless the tenancy states to the contrary. However, to avoid doubt a notice may be given in such a form that it expressly terminates the tenancy at the end of the requisite weekly term, (or, if a number of weeks notice is required at the end of the next completed week (or weeks). The notice should expire on the last moment of corresponding day—Friday midnight for a tenancy that starts on Friday, Saturday midnight

for one that starts on Saturday, and so on.

Unless there is evidence to the contrary, a letting at a rent that is payable weekly is a tenancy from week to week.

In the US, in those states that have adopted the Uniform Residential Landlord and Tenant Act, a tenancy from week to week must be terminated by written notice given at least ten days before the termination date specified in the notice (§ 4.301(a)).

English statute law provides that a weekly tenancy of a **dwelling-house** may not be terminated except by written notice given not less than four weeks before the date on which it is to take effect, which does not count the day on which it is given (Protection from Eviction Act 1977, s. 5(1)(b)). See also **rent book**(Eng), **waste**.

weighted aggregate index   An index that reflects relative changes in a number of cost or expenditure items. These items are weighted to take account of their relative importance in the overall index. For, example, a cost of construction index may be compiled from the cost of labour and materials, in order to reflect their relative importance in a building contract. If materials are considered to account for 2/3 of the total cost and labour 1/3 of the total cost, then materials would be allocated a weight of 66.66 and labour 33.33. Expenditure of 10,000 on materials and 5,000 on labour would produce a weighted cost of $(10,000 \times 66.66) + (5,000 \times 33.33) = 833,250$, so that if materials increased by 25% and labour by 10%, the weighted cost or index would increase to $[(10,000 \times 1.25) \times 66.66)] + [(5,000 \times 1.1) \times 33.33)]$ = 1,016,565, or by 22%.

A formula for calculating such an index is:

$$\frac{P_i \times w}{P_0 \times w}$$

Where:

P_i = new price
P_0 = old price
w = appropriate weight attached to each price.

See also **indexation**.

weighted average cost of capital (WACC) See Appendix C, **Financial Formulae.**

weighted average life (WAL) The average life of a **mortgaged-backed security** loan from the date of issuance to the time when it is expected that the principal will be repaid in full. The WAL is based on assumptions as to the date at which, on average, the principal of each underlying loan will be repaid. The average payment date is weighted according to the size of the loan, and may be based on the scheduled date or assumptions as to early repayment.

weighting The relative importance given to a specific factor. In particular, the relative importance given to the value of a **comparable property** when applying it to the subject property.

Welsh Development Agency (WDA) Established by the UK government in 1976 the WDA is responsible for regenerating economic activity in Wales in the wake of decline in heavy industry in the late 1970's and early 1980's. The Agency functions include "acquiring land in Wales which in its opinion needs to be made available for development and disposing of it to other persons (for development by them)", Local Government, Land and Planning Act 1980, s. 102(1), Sch. 18. The Authority is constituted similarly to a local authority; it has compulsory purchase powers; and it may carry out infrastructure work on land it has acquired in order to make the land more suitable for sale or development. WDA's program has resulted in some 8,000 hectares of land being restored for recreational and commercial use. WDA is not a planning authority, although it may offer advice in this field to a county or district authority and it collaborates with Unitary Authorities to ensure that regional initiatives are used for the benefit of Welsh development. (**www.wda.co.uk**).

wetlands An area of land that is inundated or saturated with water of a sufficiency to support vegetation that is typical to saturated soil conditions (United States v. Ciampitti, 615 F Supp 116, 119 (D NJ 1984); 20 C.F.R. § 230.41(a)). A permanent or semi-permanent swamp, bog or marsh, especially an area of land that cannot be developed without artificial drainage. 'Wetlands' are characterized by aquatic plants, hydrophilic vegetation, hydric soils and hydrology. In particular, the term is applied to areas that are considered worthy of conservation, or should not be used for new development, due to the uniqueness or rarity of the vegetation and plant life. Prior to filling in an area of wetlands, a permit must be obtained from the Army Corps of Engineers (Clean Water Act of 1977, Sec. 404; 33 USC § 1344). See also **inverse condemnation.** Keating, David M. *The Appraisal of Wetlands.* 2nd ed. Chicago: Appraisal Institute, 2002.

white bonnet(US/Scot) See puffer.

white elephant Something that has lost the high esteem in which it was held by its owner. An investment made with high expectations, but one that has turned out to be a financial disaster or fiasco. A building erected at considerable expense that has lost its attraction to potential users or occupiers. Something acquired by a speculator whose crystal ball has turned frosty. The term is derived from a rare species of albino elephant found in India, Sri Lanka, Burma and Thailand. Such an animal was acquired at considerable expense by P.T. Barnum of Barnum and Bailey's circus; but it drew few extra people to the circus, proved expensive to keep and subsequently was difficult to dispose of.

white land(Eng) An area demarcated on a statutory **land use plan**, or development plan, to remain as agricultural land or to remain undisturbed: the area is left white (or uncoloured) on the plan. The type of land use plan that uses this form of designation is now almost obsolete; although the term may be used to refer to any urban land that has not been designated, or is not intended, for development. See also **certificate of appropriate alternative development.**

white rent   Rent that is reserved or payable in silver, as distinguished from rent payable in the form of a base metal.

whole loan sale(AmE)   The sale of a loan in its entirety by the lender as opposed to the sale of a loan as part of a **mortgage-backed security**.

wild animals   See **game**, *res nullius*, **strict liability**.

wild deed(US)   A **deed** that has been recorded, but cannot be found in the index of recorded instruments because of some defect in recording a previous instrument in the **chain of title**.

wilful waste   See **waste**.

will   An valid instrument by which a person expresses what he or she desires to be done after death, in particular a document that expresses the maker's intentions for the disposition of his or her property after death. A will, although valid at the time it is made, is an 'ambulatory' declaration; that is, it does not take effect until after the death of the person (testator or testatrix) who made it. A will may be revoked or changed at any time during a person's life, but if still valid it is applicable to the situation that exists at the time of the maker's death. In that respect, it may be distinguished from a **deed** which makes a lifetime transfer of property and once executed effects the transfer without an option of revocability. Also, a will may have the effect of transferring property that is acquired by the testator after it is made. Historically, a will was used to express a person's intention for real property and personal property was dealt with in a **testament**. This distinction is still recognized in a few jurisdictions in the US, but generally a will is now used to deal with real and personal property.

In English law, a will is not valid unless it is in **writing** (whether typed, printed, photocopied, either in whole or in part), signed by the testator (who must be of sound mind and of age) or on his behalf by some other person in the presence of the testator. It must appear that the testator intended by his signature to give effect to the will and the signature must be made or acknowledged by the testator in the presence of two or more witnesses present at the same time.

In the US and Canada, most jurisdictions require that a will is made in writing and attested by two witnesses (and in Vermont, three witnesses). Some jurisdictions specify that the testator's signature must be placed at the end to make a valid will.

The term 'will' may also be used to refer to a **codicil** to a will, although 'will' usually signifies a document that is complete in itself and any subsequent document is called a codicil; thus a codicil may be referred to as a **supplementary instrument**. cf. **settlement**. See also **attest**, **devise**, **holographic will**, **nuncupative will**, **signature**, **tenancy at will**, **words of limitation**.

willing buyer or **willing seller**   One who is motivated, but not under any obligation, duress or pressure to contract for the purchase or sale of a property. A person who has a reasonable time to conclude a settlement; has time to negotiate the best terms; and, if necessary, may await changes in market conditions that favour the buyer's, or seller's, best interests.

In the context of **market value**, a 'willing buyer' is "one who is motivated, but not compelled to buy. This buyer is neither over-eager nor determined to buy at any price. This buyer is also one who purchases in accordance with the realities of the current market and with current market expectations, rather than in an imaginary or hypothetical market which cannot be demonstrated or anticipated to exist. The assumed buyer would not pay a higher price than the market requires. The present property owner is included among those who constitute 'the market'", The Royal Institution of Chartered Surveyors, *Appraisal & Valuation Standards*. 5th ed. London: RICS Books, 2003, PS 3.2.4. The "willing seller" is "neither an over-eager nor a forced seller prepared to sell at any price, nor one prepared to hold out for a price not considered reasonable in the current market. The willing seller is motivated to sell the asset at market terms for the best price attainable in the (open) market after proper marketing, whatever that price may be. The factual circumstances of the actual asset owner are not a part of this consideration because the 'willing seller' is a hypothetical owner", The Royal Institution of Chartered Surveyors, *Appraisal & Valuation Standards*. 5th ed. London: RICS Books, 2003, PS 3.2.5.

In the US, when determining of the **fair market value** as when assessing **just compensation** upon the exercise of the power of eminent domain, such value is to be ascertained on the basis of a 'willing buyer' and a 'willing seller. When assessing the 'fair market value' of property for estate tax purposes, it has been said that such a value is based on the price at which the property would change hands "between a willing buyer and willing seller, neither being under any compulsion to buy or sell and both having a reasonable knowledge of the facts. Reg. § 20.2031-1(b)", United States v. Simmons, 346 F.2d 213, 217 (5th Cir. Ga 1965).

In English law, when considering a claim for **compulsory purchase compensation**, anyone who is selling an interest in property to the acquiring authority is assumed to be a "willing seller" LCA 1961, s. 5(2). "A willing seller means one who is prepared to sell, provided a fair price is obtained under all the circumstances of the case. I do not think it means only a seller who is prepared to sell at any price and on any terms and who is actually at the time wishing to sell. In other words, I do not think it means an anxious seller", *Inland Revenue Commissioners v Clay and Buchanan* [1914] 3 KB 466, 478 (CA).

A willing buyer does not have to purchase a property unless he can obtain it at what he considers a fair price; although if he wishes to purchase, he only does so on terms that are reasonable having regard to the conditions of the market at a given point in time.

willing seller   See **willing buyer**.

willing to purchase   See **ready able and willing**.

wind and water tight(BrE)   Words that may be used in a lease which are intended to require a tenant to repair and maintain the skin or fabric of a building to an extent that is sufficient to keep out the elements, e.g. to cover up holes in windows; replace roof titles; repair external doors; patch up gaps around a window frame; or replace a chimney pot. However, it is a term of uncertain definition and "I [Lord Denning] think that the expression 'wind and water tight' is of doubtful value and should be avoided. It is better to keep to the simple obligation 'to use the premises in a **tenant-like manner**'", *Warren v Keen* [1954] 1 QB 15, 20, [1953] 2 All ER 1118, 1121 (CA). cf. **tenantable repair**. See also **waste**.

windfall   A **tree**, or fruit therefrom, blown down by the wind. Generally these belong to the owner of the land from whence they came.

windfalls and wipeouts(AmE)   Extraneous or unexpected gains or losses in the value of land, especially when these arise from the activities of a public authority. A windfall or a wipe-out may have a direct or indirect effect and it may arise as a result of a positive activity, e.g. the construction of a new highway, a grant of planning or zoning consent; or as a result of a negative activity, e.g. a refusal of planning permission, closure of vehicular access to a site. Also referred to, especially in British English, as **betterment** and **worsenment**. See also **transferable development right**.

winkling   Seeking to evict or dispossess a person from property. In particular, seeking out property to be acquired in order to secure a site for development or redevelopment or to resell at an immediate profit. Commonly applied to harassing an owner or tenant in order to entice him or her to sell or vacate a property. See also **harassment**.

wipeouts(AmE)   See **windfalls and wipeouts**.

wired lease   A lease of a landlord's internet portal. For example a lease of space on a portal provided by a landlord of a shopping center that includes information and sales facilities for other tenants in the center.

with recourse   See **recourse**.

withholding tax   A tax on income deducted at source.

within   See time.

without impeachment for waste   See waste.

without notice   See *bona fide* purchaser, notice.

without prejudice   Without intending to be bound or committed, especially when one does not intend to sacrifice a right or claim. Without intending to suffer any consequential injury. In particular, when used in correspondence these words mean that the correspondence is not intended to create a binding commitment. The term 'without prejudice' is commonly used (especially in English legal practice) to indicate that negotiations are being conducted on the basis that the content of such negotiations (especially any correspondence or draft agreement) will not be used in a court of law or in any quasi-judicial proceedings, unless the parties concerned give their consent, or when disclosure of details of the negotiations is the only way to ascertain whether a binding agreement has resulted therefrom. The purpose of holding without prejudice discussions, or marking a letter or document 'without prejudice', is that, as a matter of public policy, every effort should be made to negotiate a settlement prior to the submission of a dispute to subsequent proceedings. In other words, "before bloodshed let us discuss the matter, and let us agree that for the purposes of this discussion we will be more or less frank; we will try to come to terms, and that nothing that each of us says shall be used against the other so as to interfere with our rights at war, if unfortunately, war results", *Kurtz and Co v Spence and Sons* (1887) 57 LJ Ch 238, 241. The words 'without prejudice' are not intended to totally exclude the use of the text to which they refer; nor do they apply in respect of a document which, from its character, may prejudice the person to whom it is addressed (*Unilever plc v The Procter and Gamble Company* [2000] FSR 344—which sets out eight instances where the rule does not prevent evidence being admitted into court). Also, if there is no dispute between the parties, the use of the words 'without prejudice' has no legal effect. Thus, an offer made 'without prejudice' is capable of being accepted and forming the subject of contract—it does not, as is sometimes thought, have any semblance to the result of using such words in English law as '**subject to contract**' (B. Beaumont, *Arbitration & Rent Review* (2nd ed. 1993), pp. 22-26)). On the other hand, a proposal of a revised rent, put forward under the provisions of a lease, when made 'without prejudice' may be devoid of effect, because the subject matter is capable of dispute and the proposal amounts to an equivocation. In the same way, a notice of an intention to rescind a contract may be void if it is marked 'without prejudice'. An agreement reached, or negotiations held, 'without prejudice' remains so, unless or until the parties express their intention to waive or concede this reservation. 'Without prejudice' letters or documents are not intended to be admissible if a dispute is submitted to **arbitration**, but it is not certain in English law whether legally they may be submitted to an expert or valuer for his consideration (although the submission of 'without prejudice' negotiations or correspondence without the consent of both parties to the dispute could be considered as a breach of a professional institution's rules of conduct).

In the US, the words 'without prejudice', or 'without waiver or prejudice' may be used in particular when a claim is dismissed, but in contemplation of other proceedings; or when money is paid by one party to another without any intention of having a legal effect between the parties, so that they may continue negotiations as if the money had not paid. cf. **waiver**.

without recourse 1. The use of the words 'without recourse' (or the French equivalent *sans recours*) by the drawer, or an endorser, of a **negotiable instrument** precludes that person's own liability to any subsequent holder of the bill, in the event that the bill is not paid when it matures. However, the endorser is not thereby absolved from liability for a failure of warranties in the instrument, such as that the grantor had good title. See also **non-recourse mortgage.** 2.(US)The sale of a loan or obligation without any obligation on the part of the seller. In particular, the use of the words 'without recourse' indicates that the seller does not intend to repurchase the loan.

without reserve The sale of a property at auction when there is no **reserve price** fixed and, therefore, it is intended that the property will be sold to the highest bidder. "When a property is offered for sale without reserve the meaning, and the only meaning that can be attached to it, is that of the bidders – the public – who choose to attend the sale, whoever bids the highest shall be the purchaser", *Robinson v Wall* [1847] 2 Ph 372, 375, 41 Eng Rep 986.

In common law, if an auctioneer does not stipulate that a sale is subject to a 'reserve price', or that the property is being sold 'with reserve', it is generally considered that the auctioneer cannot withdraw a property after a *bona fide* bid has been made. The auctioneer implies that he is making a public offer, when he sets the property up for sale 'without reserve' or, strictly, that he will be bound to accept any **offer** made. However, he is at liberty to withdraw the property up to the last moment set for auction, or even up to the time immediately before the first bid is made. After that the property cannot be withdrawn once a clear and genuine bid has been made.

In the US, in a few jurisdictions, the view is taken that the auctioneer is merely soliciting offers and, as with any other offer, the property can be withdrawn at any time until the prospective purchaser's 'offer' is accepted by the auctioneer. The words 'without reserve' merely indicate that a minimum price has not been set by the seller.

A vendor of property being sold at auction 'without reserve' cannot bid or employ anyone else to bid at the sale; the presumption is that the auctioneer will offer it without constraint or interference to anyone who cares to bid and will accept the highest *bona fide* bid. If a sale is not expressed to be "without reserve", it is probable that there is a reserve price and a prospective purchaser should make inquiry of the auctioneer. In the US, a sale at auction 'without reserve' is referred to sometimes as an 'absolute auction'.

witness 1. To subscribing one's name to a deed to indicate that a **signature** is genuine or that the signature was placed with a free will.

In English law, most real property contracts do not require a witness; with the notable exception of a **will**; a Form for the **transfer** of title to registered land; or when a contract has to be made by **deed**.

In the US, in most jurisdictions, where only a mark is made on a document, two witnesses are required to authenticate it. For a will, most jurisdictions require that it be signed and attested in the presence of two witnesses (normally with the attesting witnesses signing at the end of the will), and a few jurisdictions require three witnesses. Many states prescribe the form to be used for attesting a will. See also **acknowledgment, attest.** 2. One who gives evidence under oath at a hearing. See also **expert witness.**

witnessing clause See **testimonium/testimonium clause.**

wood 1. An area of land that is covered with a substantial number of mature trees. A group of trees growing together in an area that is larger than a **coppice**, but smaller than a **forest**. In a deed of conveyance (including a lease), the transfer of 'woods' includes the land under the trees (1 *Co Litt* 4b). See also **waste.** 2. The main substance of a **tree**. The trunk, roots or branches of a tree, whether growing, cut down or fashioned into another object, but remaining as the same basic substance. See also **estovers, timber.**

woodland   Land used primarily for growing trees. An area of land covered with trees or substantially covered with wood vegetation; especially an area where trees are grown for the production of timber, as compared with a coppice which is intended to be cut and pruned after a short period of time. See also **afforestation, agriculture, estovers, forestry, open country**(Eng), **right of common, tree preservation order**(Eng), **waste**.

word of art   A word (or term) that has a meaning in a legal or technical context that may be different from, or more precise than, the meaning in common usage; "by a term of art is meant one which is used in a particular field with a precise technical meaning. 2 Sutherland, Statutory Construction, 3rd ed. (1943), p. 437", Suwannee Fruit & Steamship Co. v. Fleming, 160 F.2d 897, 899 (Em App 1947). A word of art in law is interpreted strictly, normally based on precedent, and as a rule, it is not altered by the context. In many documents, certain words or phrases may be capitalised to indicate that for the purpose of that document they are words (or terms) of art and have a defined meaning as set out in the document. See also *ejusdem generis, noscitur a sociis*, **words**.

words   1. In law 'words' generally refers to a term or phrase as used in a technical sense. In the interpretation of a statute, a word is normally given its ordinary or literal meaning in its context, unless there is a definition assigned to the word in the statute. Thus, it has been said in the English House of Lords that "it is only when that meaning leads to some result which cannot reasonably be supposed to have been the intention of the legislature that it is proper to look for some other permissible meaning of the word or phrase", *Pinner v Everett* [1962] 3 All ER 257, 258 (HL). However, a word has to be looked at in the context and time of its use; a word is not "a crystal, transparent and unchanged; it is the skin of living thought, and may vary greatly in color and content according to the circumstances and the time in which it is used", Oliver Wendell Holmes in Towne v. Eisner,

245 US 418, 425, 38 S Ct 158, 62 L Ed 372, 376 (1918). See also *ejusdem generis*, **interpretation clause, word of art.   2.** See **general words.   3.** See **operative part/operative words**.

words of conveyance(US)   Words of a **deed** that describe its character, such as "grant, bargain and sell" or "release and forever quitclaim". See also **operative words**.

words of demise   The words in a lease by which the lessor undertakes to transfer to a lessee an exclusive right of possession of the demised premises for a determinable period of time. See also **demise**.

words of grant(US)   The words in a deed for the transfer of property that express the present intention to transfer the grantor's interest. "In order to transfer title, an instrument must contain apt words of grant which manifest the grantor's intent to make a present **conveyance** of the land by his deed, as distinguished from an intention to convey it at some future time", 23 Am.Jur.2d., Deeds, § 19, p. 91. No particular form of words is necessary, as long as there is a clear expression of intention to pass title. Such words as **grant**, 'convey' 'transfer', and 'give' are all commonly accepted words of grant, although the use of such words alone may not be sufficient if there is not a clear intention to transfer title. See also **grant, grant bargain sell and convey, operative words**.

words of inheritance   See **words of limitation**.

words of limitation   Words used in a deed or instrument to mark out or define the limit or **quantity** of an estate that is granted or settled. In particular, words used in a conveyance or will by the holder of a **freehold** estate to indicate that the entire interest is not to be transferred, but that it is to be cut down in some way. For example, a conveyance or testamentary grant to 'A for life and thereafter to B', limits A's interest by the words of limitation 'for life'. Words of limitation may be of 'direct' limitation, e.g. 'for life'; or of 'determinable' limitation, e.g. 'until A marries'.

In English law, since 1837, a will without any words of limitation passes a fee simple, or the testator's entire estate, unless a contrary intention appears in the will (Wills Act 1837, s. 28). A **conveyance** of freehold land also passes a fee simple estate, or the entire estate of the grantor; unless, in either case, there are express words of limitation to the contrary (LPA 1925, s. 60). Thus, words of limitation are now used to indicate that an estate of limited inheritance, an **entailed interest**, is to pass. Prior to 1881, it was necessary in English law to use the words 'heirs' to convey a fee simple, i.e. to indicate that the estate was not to be cut down; the use of the words such as "and his assigns" or "and his successors" alone only created a life interest. However, since 1881, the use of the words 'in fee simple' are sufficient to pass a fee simple without the need for such reinforcing words as 'and his heirs' or 'and his descendants', and 'in fee tail' or 'in tail' is sufficient to pass an entailed interest (Conveyancing Act 1881; LPA 1925, s. 60(4)). If the intention is to create a life estate, whether as a conveyance or by devise, the words 'to A for life' should be used to indicate the contrary intention from a grant of a fee simple or the grantor's entire estate.

In the US, in most jurisdictions, words of limitation are no longer necessary as the grant of a 'fee' or a 'fee simple' transfers a fee simple estate without limitation, unless there is a clear and decisive indication to the contrary. The addition of the words 'absolute' or 'absolutely' may serve to confirm that there is to be no defeasance of the estate. Sometimes called 'words of inheritance' or in the US 'succession words'. cf. **words of purchase**. See also **heir, limitation, qualified estate**.

words of procreation Words used to designate the person or persons entitled to an **entailed interest** in land, e.g. "to A and the heirs of his body", "to A and the male heirs of his marriage to B". An entailed interest cannot be created without words of procreation. The words indicating who shall receive land after the grantee are sometimes called 'words of inheritance'. See also **heir, words of limitation**.

words of purchase Words that indicate that a person is to acquire property by any means other than descent. A slight misnomer, as the word 'purchase' does not have the significance normally ascribed to it. The words in a contract (including a gift or will) for the transfer of an interest in real property, defining who shall take the interest. For example, if a grant is made "to A in fee simple" or "to A and the heirs of his body", "to A" are words of purchase indicating who shall take the property; and the words "in fee simple" or "the heirs of his body" are **words of limitation**. The former indicating that the estate is unlimited and the latter places a limitation on the grant so as to create a fee tail. On the other hand, if a grant is made by a lease to A for 20 years and on expiration of the lease "to A's heirs" those words are words of purchase as they indicate that the estate is to pass to A's heirs, but subject to the lease. See also **habendum, purchase**.

words of severance Words used to indicate that joint owners of a property are to take distinct or specific shares in the property, e.g. "in equal shares", "equally", "to be divided between", "amongst". The use of such words is intended to demonstrate that there is no 'unity of interest' between the parties and, therefore, that a **tenancy in-common** is to be created and not a **joint tenancy**. See also **severance**.

work letter An addendum or schedule to a lease (or an agreement for a lease) setting out details of the works to be carried out by the landlord or tenant at the commencement of the contract. In particular, work to be carried out at the landlord's expense.

working capital Liquid assets available for the day-to-day running of a company or for meeting immediate liabilities. The monetary difference between current assets and current liabilities; the 'net current assets'. Working capital is defined to include stocks (inventories) plus debts (accounts receivable) and cash, less creditors (accounts payable). cf. **fixed capital**. See also **floating capital**.

working drawing   A drawing, or large scale plan, containing details of a proposed building, or proposed changes to an existing building; especially one of the drawings prepared by an architect, setting out sufficient details for the workmen on site. Working drawings may show all or part of the building or may show the detailed design of a component of the building.

working interest(US)   An interest in an oil or gas exploration as held by the party that bears the expense of exploration, drilling and production, as distinguished from a **royalty interest** which is merely the right to share in the proceeds of production. The working interest is similar to a 'leasehold interest' and is generally held by the lessee, whereas the royalty interest is usually held by the lessor or landowner, or merely as a contractual arrangement between the operator and the landowner and the operator.

working-up   A process in **quantity surveying**, that follows **taking-off**, by which the total quantity of materials required for the performance of a building contract is added up. This total is then used to ascertain the price of these materials. "The traditional preparation of a bill of quantities divides itself into two distinct stages: (1) the measurement of the dimensions and the compilation of the descriptions from the drawings and specifications. This process is commonly called *taking-off*. (2) The preparation of the bill. This involves the calculation of volumes, areas, etc. (known as *squaring the dimensions*). Traditionally, this was followed by entering the descriptions and squared dimensions on an abstract to collect similar items together and present them in a recognised bill order. From this abstract the draft bill was written. This process is commonly known as *working-up*", Andrew Willis and William

Trench, *Willis's Elements of Quantity Surveying*. 9th ed. Oxford: Blackwell, 1998, p. 3. With the use of computers, these step-by-step processes are now much more integrated.

workout agreement   An agreement between a borrower and a lender by which the parties modify the terms of a loan primarily to allow more time for payment when the borrower is in default, or is likely to default. Usually the agreement establishes a new repayment schedule, a 'rescheduling agreement', and possibly revises the loan interest rate or the property to be held as security. When the lender merely agrees to defer any rights to foreclosure, the agreement is generally called a 'forbearance agreement' – the lender forebears or gives more time for payment.

workshop   A small building or establishment where goods or products are manufactured or a craft is conducted, usually with the objective of producing, repairing, altering, maintaining, finishing goods or adapting them for sale. See also **factory, garage, industrial property, shop**.

worldly estate or **worldly goods**   The total **estate** or all the **goods** owned by a person. "All my worldly *goods*" does not necessarily include real estate, unless the context so admits.

worsenment or **worsement**   A reduction or depreciation in the value of a parcel or plot of land caused by an external factor; in particular, by the activities or decisions of a public authority, e.g. by the construction of an airport or sewage works. cf. **betterment**. See also **blight, injurious affection, nuisance, windfalls and wipeouts**.

worth   relative **value** of something. The esteem or value placed on something by the possessor, or someone who aspires to something. That for which something may be sold or exchanged. In particular, worth is "that 'value' which is acknowledged; it is … something more fixed and permanent [than value]: we speak of the *value* of external objects which are determined by taste; but the *worth* of something as determined by rule. The *value* of a book that is out of print is fluctuating and uncertain; but its real *worth* may not be more than what it would fetch for waste paper", George Crabb, *Crabb's English Synonyms*. 1816. Reprint, London: Routledge, 1982. See also **price, wealth**.

wrap(US)   See **wraparound mortgage**.

wraparound mortgage(US)   A special form of second or junior mortgage granted against security of a property (usually commercial property) that is already mortgaged, whereby a new mortgagee assumes (that is, takes over) the obligation to pay interest and principal on the existing or 'in-place' mortgage (without assuming or extinguishing that mortgage, which retains its priority) and makes a further 'wrap-around' advance to the mortgagor. "A junior mortgage that secures a promissory note with a face amount equal to the sum of the principal balance of an existing mortgage note plus any additional funds advanced by the second lender. Wraparound mortgages may be used in several forms. ... Typically, however, wraparounds are either *purchase-money* mortgages, where the wraparound lender is either the real estate seller or a third party, or *refinancing* or *non-purchase-money* mortgages, where the lender is either the same lender that holds the first mortgage or a third party. See Arditto, *The Wrap-Around Deed of Trust: An Answer to the Allegation of Usury*, 10 Pac LJ 023 (1979), for a discussion of various types of wraparound mortgages", Mitchell v. Trustees of U.S. Mutual Real Estate, 144 Mich App 302, 375 NW.2d 424, 428 (1985). The face value of the wraparound mortgage is equivalent to the amount outstanding on the 'in-place' mortgage, plus the additional funds advanced. The mortgagor undertakes to make payments to the new or subordinate mortgagee that are sufficient to cover that mortgagee's cost of servicing the existing mortgage, plus the interest on the new advance. In turn, the wraparound mortgagee undertakes to make all payments to the first or in-place mortgagee. A wraparound mortgage may be taken out when an in-place mortgage is held at a favourable interest rate and, therefore, the mortgagor does not wish to refinance the entire mortgage arrangements and there is substantial equity in the property. The interest rate, or 'blended rate', on the wraparound mortgage is fixed usually at a rate between the in-place mortgage rate and the rate that would be charged if an entirely new advance was to be made. Sometimes called an 'overriding mortgage', an 'overlapping mortgage', an 'all-inclusive mortgage'; or, if the loan is made by means of a deed of trust an 'all-inclusive deed of trust'. See also **assumption, purchase money mortgage**.

writ   A formal written document. In particular, an order from a court or an officer of the court, commanding the person to whom it is sent to do, or to refrain from doing, something. In modern English law, a writ is a summons in the name of the Crown submitted, in civil proceedings, by a plaintiff to a defendant or defendants, requiring the named party or parties to answer an alleged case. It is the document used to start an action. The summons is first sealed by Supreme Court in London, or a District Registry in the Provinces, and then served on the defendant's solicitor. There is no longer a need for a special form of writ, i.e. the 'form of action' does not have to be named, the same form can be used for any action, thus leaving a plaintiff free to state the claim in his own words. In the US, 'writ' generally refers to a judicial writ, including the writs of *mandamus, certiorari* and prohibition as issued by a court of law. See also **action, attachment, ejectment, *fieri facias*, Land Charges Register**(Eng), **real action, replevin, service, warrant**.

writ of assistance   "A summary proceeding by which a court of equity will enforce its decree determining the title or right of possession of real estate, without compelling the party entitled to resort to a court of law to recover the same", Rooker v. Fidelity Co., 196 Ind 373, 145 NE 493, 495 (1924). See also **writ of possession**.

writ of attachment   See **attachment**.

writ of distress   See **distress**.

writ of ejectment   See **ejectment**.

writ of entry   A writ used to enable a person to go on land in order to assert a legal right to possession of that land. Abolished in English law by the Real Property Limitation Act 1833. In the US, the writ of entry is still in use in a few states. See also **forcible entry and detainer, foreclosure, recovery**.

writ of entry and possession[US]   A writ that may be obtained from a court in some of the New England states to enable a mortgagee to enter into property and take possession in the event of a default by the mortgagor. The mortgagee is entitled to receive the rents and profits from the mortgaged property and to apply the proceeds for repayment of the debt, either until the mortgagor is able to make good or redeem the loan or until the end of a statutory period at which time the property must be sold. See also **foreclosure, writ of possession**.

writ of execution   A court order or writ instructing an official or sheriff of the court to implement a decision of the court, e.g. regain possession of property or levy a judgement against property of a judgement debtor.

   In English law, there is no writ of execution as such, but the term may be used to refer to a number of writs by which the judgement or orders of a court of justice are enforced by a public office, including a writ of *fieri facias*, of possession, of delivery, of sequestration and various related writs (Rules of the Supreme Court Order 46, r. 1). See also **attachment, judgment lien**[US]**, judicial sale**.

writ of *fieri facias*   See *fieri facias*.

writ of possession   1.[US]Historically, a 'writ of *habere facias possessionem*' used to enforce a writ of ejectment. A decree or order from a court

directing possession to be given or authorizing a sheriff to reclaim possession of land (28A C.J.S., Ejectment, §§ 131-135). Sometimes used as synonymous with a **writ of assistance**.   See also **ejectment, possessory action, writ of execution**. 2.[Eng]A writ issued by the High Court to the sheriff of the court to the effect that a judgement or order has been made to give a claimant possession of land. The writ may also authorise the sheriff to seize goods to pay a debt. See also **possession order**.

writ of waste   See **waste**.

write down   To reduce in value an amount specified against an asset in a financial statement, e.g. to reduce the book value. cf. **write up**. See also **depreciation, write off**.

write off   1. To depreciate or write down an asset to nil in a book of accounts. See also **depreciation**.   2. A cost that may be set off against a tax liability.   3. A debt that has been accepted as uncollectible and is so recorded in a book of accounts.

write up   To increase the value of a property, as shown in a financial statement, usually to its **market value**. cf. **write down**. See also **revaluation**.

writing   The forming of letters on any suitable surface. "The expression of ideas by letters visible to the eye. The giving an outward and objective form to a **contract, will**, etc., by means of letters or marks placed upon paper, parchment, or other material substance", *Black's Law Dictionary*, 6th ed., 1990. In English statute law, 'writing' is defined to include "typing, printing, lithography, photography, and other modes of representing or reproducing words in visible form", Interpretation Act 1978, Sch. 1.

   A requirement that estates or interests in land should be created or transferred in writing to enable them to be enforced in a court of law was first introduced by the **Statute of Frauds** 1677, s. 4. to discourage fraud, falsehood and deceit. This provision did not make an oral contract void or invalid, but meant that it was unenforceable in a court of law; although it may still be enforceable in a court of equity. Thus, if an oral contract is made for the sale of land and a deposit is made, normally the seller can keep the deposit if the buyer defaults because there is no contract upon which the buyer can bring an action at law. On the other hand, this provision did not prevent a contract being enforced in equity if there is an adequate act of **part performance** (37 C.J.S., Frauds, Statute, § 166; *Steadman v Steadman* [1976] AC 536, 2 All ER 977 (HL)). In English law, on or after September 27, 1989, "a contract for the sale or other **disposition** of an interest in land can only be made in writing and only by incorporating all the terms which the parties have expressly agreed in one document, or where contacts are exchanged, in each", LP(MP)A 1989, s. 2(1). The terms of the contract may be incorporated by being actually set out in the document, or "by reference to some other document", LP(MP)A 1989, s. 2(2). "The document incorporating the terms or, where contracts are exchanged, one of the documents incorporating them (but not necessarily the same one) must be signed by or on behalf of each of party to the contract", LP(MP)A 1989, s. 2(3). This provision does not apply to: (a) a contract to grant a lease for a term not exceeding three years as mentioned in the LPA 1925, s. 54(2) (see below); (b) a contract made in the course of a "public **auction**"; or (c) a contract regulated under the Financial Services Act 1986 (such as a contract to form a unit trust which incorporates interests in land); nor do these provisions affect the creation or operation of a **resulting trust**, **implied trust** or **constructive trust** (LP(MP)A 1989, s. 2(5)(c)). As a rule, these provisions only apply to 'true' contracts for the sale of real property. Thus, they do not necessarily apply to: (i) the exercise of an **option** to purchase land (but they do apply to an agreement to grant an option; (ii) a collateral contract (including a **lock-out agreement**; or (iii) an agreement that is supplemental to a contract. This provision does not apply to the creation of a **parol lease** that (a) takes effect "in possession", i.e.

immediately; (b) is for a term not exceeding three years; and (c) is created at the **best rent** reasonably obtainable without the payment of a **fine** or **premium** (LPA 1925, s. 54). With the exception of such a parol lease "no interest in land can be created or disposed of except by writing signed by the person creating or conveying the same, or by his agent thereunto lawfully authorised in writing, or by will, or by operation of law", LPA 1925, s. 53(1)(a). Further, a disposal of an **equitable interest** must be in writing and be signed by the person disposing of the same, or his agent authorised in writing, and a **declaration of trust** (but not an implied, resulting, or constructive trust) cannot be enforced in a court unless it is evidenced in writing and signed by the person declaring the trust (LPA 1925, s. 53(1)(b)(c)). A surrender of any lease that granted a **legal estate**, even one created orally (except a surrender by operation of law or a lease that need not be surrendered in writing), should be made by deed (LPA 1925, s. 52). A declaration of trust that relates to land, or any interest therein, and is created by a transfer *inter vivos* must be "manifested and proved by some writing signed by some person who is able to declare such a trust, or by his will", LPA 1925, s. 53(1)(b)) (If the trust is created by will, it must be created with the due formalities of a will.)

In Canada, most provinces have enacted statutes based on the Statute of Frauds and in those provinces that have no specifically enacted legislation the original statute is treated as being in force. In Australia, all the States have statutes that contain similar provisions to the Statute of Frauds (e.g. Law Reform (Miscellaneous Provisions) Act 1955, s 52 (ACT); Conveyancing Act 1919, s 54 A (NSW); Law of Property Act, s 62 (NT); Property Law Act, s 59 (Qld); Law of Property Act 1936, s 26 (SA); Conveyancing and Law of Property Act, s 36 (Tas); Instruments Act 1958, s 126 (Vic)); and in Western Australia the original statute remains in force (as amended by the Law Reform (Statute of Frauds) Act 1962). In New Zealand, similar language to the Statute of Frauds has been adopted by the Contracts Enforcement Act 1956, s. 2.

In the US, most states have adopted the Statute of Frauds, in its original or a modified form. Thus, most real estate contracts, or some note or memorandum confirming such a contract (other than, in most jurisdictions, a lease for less than one year), must be made in writing and the writing must refer to the property, the parties, contain all the essential and material terms of the agreement, and must be duly signed by the parties or a properly authorised agent. Any lease that must be in writing to satisfy the Statute of Frauds must be surrendered in writing, unless the surrender operates by law, as when the tenant abandons the premises and the landlord retakes possession. In some jurisdictions, any lease must be surrendered in writing, even if it was not originally made in writing. A failure to comply with the Statute of Frauds may render the contract unenforceable, or it may limit the remedies available to the parties. See also **assent, bill of exchange, bond, conveyance, covenant, declaration of trust, deed, escrow, guarantee, instrument, legal assignment, listing agreement, notice to quit, signature, surrender, unenforceable contract.**

written contract　　See **express contract, writing**.

written statement(Eng)　　**1.** A document that accompanies a **development plan** (a "structure plan" or "local plan") and sets out the future planning proposals for the area covered by that plan, as well as the reasoning behind the proposals in the plan (TCPA, ss. 31(2), 36(2)).　　**2.** A submission that a local planning authority propose to put forward at a planning inquiry; including a list of all documents it intends to submit to the inquiry.

wrong　　An action that is unjust, inequitable or injurious. An illegal or immoral act. An infringement or violation of the legal rights of another, either the rights of an individual – a private wrong or **tort**; or of the community – a public wrong or crime. See also **breach of contract, forcible entry and detainer, void contract.**

wrongful conversion　　See **conversion.**

Y

yard **1.** Derived from the Old English *geard*, 'fence or enclosure', the Middle English *yeard*, the Dutch *gaard*, or German *garten*, 'garden'. An area of land, usually enclosed, that adjoins or surrounds a building and is used in conjunction with the building, either for domestic use (as with a 'back yard' of a house) or for commercial purposes (as with a builder's yard or junk yard). In American English, 'yard' commonly refers to an enclosed area of land immediately surrounding or adjacent to a private house that may be hard surfaced, or covered in whole or part by lawns, shrubbery, and other plantings (an area that in British English would be called the **garden** of a house). In British English, a yard is generally paved or hard surfaced and is situated at the rear of a house or forms a service area for an industrial building. See also **curtilage**. **2.**(US)See **setback**. **3.**(US)The grounds of a public building, especially a college campus.

year The period of just over 365 consecutive solar days required for the earth to make one revolution around the sun. In common law, a period measured by the Gregorian calendar which has 365 clear days in a common year and 366 days in a 'leap year'. A year is normally twelve calendar and not lunar months (*Bishop of Peterborough v Catesby* (1608) Cro Jac 166, 79 Eng Rep 145; *Black's Law Dictionary* (6th ed. 1990)). A 'calendar year' is normally considered to be one that runs from January 1 to December 31 inclusive, unless an alternative start date is designated (Calendar Act 1751; 86 C.J.S., Time, § 5). However, if the context so admits a calendar year may run from the end of any day to the start of the corresponding day of the following year (thus in the UK, for the assessment of income tax, the tax year runs from April 6 to April 5). As a rule, when subdividing a leap year, the 29th of February is treated as an extension of the 28th, unless the period is by reference to a number of days less than a year (2 *Bl Comm* 140; Am.Jur.2d., Time, § 8). In English law, a 'year' in the case of a **weekly tenancy** has been held to span 52 weeks and not 365 (or 366) days (*Lamb v Boyden* [1961] CLY 4906). See also **half year, per annum, quarter year, tenancy for a term of years, tenancy from year to year, time**.

year capped(AmE) The year in which an income is capitalized. In particular, the year in which the net operating income is capitalized in order to ascertain the residual price or value of the reversion when calculating the **internal rate of return**.

year certain and thereafter from year to year See **tenancy from year to year**.

year-to-year tenancy See **tenancy from year to year**.

yearly tenancy See **tenancy from year to year**.

yearly value See **annual value**.

years' purchase (YP) A sum of money which if invested now will produce an annual return of one unit of value for a given number of years. The present capital value of the right to receive one unit of value per annum over an appropriate term at a required rate of return, i.e. the **present value of one per period** (or **per annum**). When the appropriate period is indefinite, i.e. the income is deemed to be receivable in perpetuity, the years' purchase is equivalent to the reciprocal of the required rate of return expressed as a decimal. Thus, a years' purchase at: $5\% = 100/5 = 20$; at $6\% = 100/6 = 16.66$. A years' purchase is usually applied in reverse, i.e. as a **capitalisation factor**, so that capital value = income × years' purchase; the income then provides the requisite return on that capital value. In the US, the equivalent to a years' purchase is called a 'present worth factor' or **Inwood factor**. See also **dual-rate capitalization factor**(AmE)/**dual-rate years' purchase**(BrE); See also Appendix C, **Financial Formulae**.

Yellowstone injunction(US)   A specialized preliminary **injunction** that may be granted in landlord and tenant proceedings to toll the running of the tenant's cure period and stay the expiration of the lease, pending a determination of the landlord's claim that the tenant is in default and should forfeit the lease. Such relief is granted on the basis that an injunction is an equitable remedy and should be granted only when it is reasonable. In order to obtain such an injunction, the tenant has to be able to demonstrate that he has the desire and ability to cure the alleged default by any means short of vacating the premises (First Nat'l Stores v. Yellowstone Shopping Center, Inc., 290 NYS.2d 721, 237 NE.2d 868 (1968)).

yield   1. The net income or profit from an investment expressed as a percentage of its cost or the capital invested, usually calculated at an annual rate. The actual **rate of return** on capital. The yield from an investment in real estate is primarily a function of: (i) the comparative return on alternative forms of investment; (ii) the type of property, e.g. office, retail, industrial, hotel; (ii) the security and regularity of income; (iii) the risk of loss of capital; (iv) the liquidity of the investment and the costs of transfer; (v) the cost of management and upkeep; (vi) political and taxation risks and (vii) specific risks associated with a particular investment, e.g. risk of earthquake, expropriation, planning or zoning restrictions, lease restrictions. See also **all-risks yield, capitalisation rate, cash-on-cash yield, dividend yield, earnings yield, equated yield, equity yield rate, initial yield, investment yield, net yield, redemption yield, reversionary yield, running yield, yield to maturity.**   2. To perform or yield services as an incident to land tenure. In old English law, to pay a sum to the lord of the manor. Thus, in a lease the words 'yielding and paying' are followed by the amount payable for the right to occupy the demised premises, i.e. the **rent**. See also **cede, incidents of tenure.**   3. To give up, give way or **surrender**. In particular, the surrendering of possession of property. 4. To produce or earn, as farm land yields crops.

yield-back clause(US)   See yield-up clause.

yield capitalization(AmE)   The assessment of the capital value of a property by discounting all estimated future income to a single **present value**. The conversion of future income into a single present value by applying an appropriate capitalization rate. See also **annuity capitalization, discounted rate of return.**

yield gap   The difference between the rates of return on two alternative forms of investment, or between the immediate and long-term returns from the same investment. 'Yield gap' may refer to: (i) the difference between the yield on long-dated fixed interest government securities and an equity investment, whether in corporate stock (a dividend yield) or an investment in real estate; (ii) the difference between the return from an equity investment in a real estate (**equity yield**) and the cost of servicing the debt used to purchase that investment; or (iii) the difference between the **initial yield** and the **redemption yield** on a given investment. Where the yield on one form of investment is historically higher than on another (as with government securities over equity shares) and the situation reverses, the difference may then be referred to as the 'reverse yield gap. See also **deficit financing.**

yield on average life   The average yield over the 'assumed' life of a **mortgage-backed security**. For example, in the case of a pool of 30-year mortgages, the average yield on the securities may be calculated on the assumption that the average life of the mortgages is twelve years (i.e. on average the mortgages are repaid or redeemed within 12 years).

yield rate   The return on an investment. See also **equity yield rate**(US), **free and clear return.**

yield to maturity (YTM)   The yield on a bond on the basis that it is held to maturity, i.e. until the entire capital is repaid. The yield on an investment based on the current cost or purchase price and bringing into account all income and expenditure until the investment is sold or written off. See also **redemption yield**.

yield-up clause(US)   A clause in a lease which provides that the tenant must peacefully vacate the premises and leave them in a good state of repair at the end of the lease term. The covenant may read, for example, "to peacefully yield up and vacate the demised premises at the expiration of the lease term … and to leave the premises in the same condition and repair as the same were at the commencement of the lease"; thereafter follows any exceptions such as damage by wear and tear or damage by fire or other casualty. Sometimes called a 'yield-back clause'.

yielding and paying   A term used in a lease to indicate that the language that follows is the amount of **rent** to be paid; in effect the introduction to the covenant to pay rent. See also **implied covenant, reddendum, yield**.

zero-coupon bond A bond that does not pay interest, but is sold initially at a price that is substantially below its face value so that the return is paid in capital appreciation.

zero-lot line(US) A **building line** that corresponds on at least one side to the **boundary line**. In particular, a line prescribed under zoning ordinance that allows a building to be constructed up to the lot line, without the need for any **setback**. The location of a building on a plot of land so that one or more sides of the building butt up against the **lot line** may be referred to as creating a 'zero-lot line'.

zero-rated See **value added tax**.

zone 1. An area of land that has been designated for a specific use. In particular an area or district within which certain uses of land and buildings are permitted and certain others are prohibited. A district established for a particular type of use or purpose under a **zoning classification**. See also **simplified planning zone**(Eng), **zoning**. 2. An area or district set aside for a different purpose from the surrounding area. See also **zoning variance**.

zone A(Eng) See **zoning method**.

zone *non aedificandi* See **building line**, *non aedificandi*.

zoning 1. A means of land use planning by which different areas or districts of a town or city are allocated, or zoned, on an official map for different uses, either to indicate the present use or proposed future use. Zoning is concerned primarily with controlling or restricting the use and development of land by setting down density controls, rules for the height, size, type and shape

of new buildings and the grouping together of complementary land uses. In particular, zoning aims to limit or exclude any incompatible use (a **non-conforming use**); to group compatible uses together according to the resources available to accommodate new development; and to guide the use and development of land without unduly fettering the scope for individual expression in terms of new building design.

In the US, zoning forms the basis of development control in most states and cities and is considered part of the **police power** available to a municipality to restrict the type of uses to which property may be put within a particular 'zoning district', unless the actions of the municipality have "no foundation in reason and is a mere arbitrary or irrational exercise of power having no substantial relation to the public health, safety, morals, or general welfare", Nectow v. Cambridge, 277 US 183, 48 S Ct 447, 72 L Ed 842, 844 (1928) (Village of Euclid v. Amber Realty Co., 272 US 365, 47 S Ct 114, 71 L Ed 303, 314 (1926)).

Although the term 'zoning' and '**planning**' are closely related processes, zoning is part of the planning control of an area or district, but planning may be carried out with or without the more defined means of 'zoning'. See also **cluster development, comprehensive plan, conditional zoning, contract zoning, density zoning, downzoning, exclusionary zoning, floating zone, incentive zoning, inclusionary zoning, master plan, partial zoning, rezoning, special-use permit, spot zoning, zoning classification, zoning ordinance, zoning variance**.

Anderson, Robert M. *Anderson's American Law of Zoning*. 5 vols. 4th ed. Deerfield, IL: Clark Boardman Callaghan, 1996 with annual supplements.

Mandelker, Daniel R. *Land Use Law*. 5th ed. Newark, NJ: LexisNexis, 2003.

2.(BrE)See **zoning method**.

zoning board of appeals(US) See **board of adjustment**.

zoning certificate(US) See **certificate of occupancy, certificate of zoning compliance**.

zoning classification(US) A system of designation given by a planning commission to indicate the permitted use for an area of land or 'use district'. Commonly used designations are (A) – agriculture; (C) – commerce; (I) general industry; (M) – manufacturing or heavy industry; (P) – parking; (R) – residential. A numeric designation limits the use more strictly, e.g. (M3) – heavy industry; (R1) – single-family residences; (R5) – residential with a floor area ratio of 5.0. The area so designated may also be called a 'zoning district'. See also **zoning**.

zoning commission(US) A body vested with powers to regulate the application of zoning laws. See also **zoning board of appeals**.

zoning district(US) See **zoning classification**.

zoning exception(US) See **zoning variance**.

zoning map(US) See **comprehensive map, zoning ordinance**.

zoning method(BrE) A method of analysing or assessing the rental value of a retail store. The zoning method is based on the principle that the rent a trader will pay for retail premises is highest at the front of the property and decreases the greater the distance from the street frontage. Accordingly, a shop is divided into notional areas or zones for which it is assumed different rental values will be paid.

To apply the zoning method of analysis the front area of the shop, or 'Zone A', is given the value of x, the next zone half that value, the next a quarter and so on as necessary: a process called 'halving back'. Ancillary or non-retail space is normally excluded from the analysis and assessed separately and the halving process is normally discontinued after the third zone. The depth of each zone is commonly taken as 15, 20 or 25 feet (or 5, 7 or 9 metres), the width corresponding to the actual width of the premises. Then the total area of the shop is reduced to a factor of x and by dividing the rental value of the shop by that factor the quotient represents the rate per square foot (or per square metre) appropriate to the 'zone A' area, i.e. it represents the 'zone A rate'. For example, if a shop has a rental value of £49,500 p.a., a frontage, and width throughout, of 25 feet and a depth of 52 feet, the 20 ft 'zone A' rate would be:

$$20 \times 25 \times x = 500x$$
$$20 \times 25 \times \tfrac{1}{2}x = 250x$$
$$12 \times 25 \times \tfrac{1}{4}x = \underline{75x}$$
$$825x$$

so that, $x = 49{,}500 \div 825 = £60$ per sq. ft for zone A. This rate may be applied to assess the rental value of a shop that is considered of comparable value but has different dimensions. Thus, if the shop being valued has a frontage of 18 feet and a depth of 65 feet, based on the zone A rate of £60, its rental value is $(20 \times 18 \times 60) + (20 \times 18 \times 30) + (25 \times 18 \times 15) = £39{,}150$ p.a. The particular zone A depth used in the analysis is not of considerable importance, provided that same depth is used when assessing the value of another shop – "as one analyses so should one value". When adopting this method of valuation to a corner plot it is assumed that the zone 'A' extends the same depth from each frontage. See also **comparison method of valuation, quantity allowance**.

zoning ordinance(US) An **ordinance** that governs the permitted use or development for a given area of land. A zoning ordinance normally comprises a text containing: (i) regulations for the use of land and buildings thereon; and (ii) a 'zoning map'. The zoning map delineates the boundaries of various permitted uses; as well as showing areas for new development; areas for special uses (such as schools or hospitals); and areas that will be required for proposed new highways, open spaces, or similar public uses. The 'zoning regulations' may be divided into two classes: "(1) those that regulate the height or bulk of buildings within certain designated districts – in other words, those regulations which have to do with structural and architectural designs of the building; and (2) those which prescribe the use to which buildings within certain designated districts may be put. Both modes of regulation have received the sanction of the Supreme Court of the United States", Miller v. Board of Public Works, 195 Cal 477, 234 P 381, 384, 38 ALR 1479 (1925). Under the ambit of such regulation, ordinances may specify such matters as density limits ('density zoning'), **zoning classification**, parking standards, landscape requirements, building or improvement lines, etc. A zoning ordinance may also be referred to as a 'bulk zoning' when it controls the overall envelope or 'bulk' of the building permitted on a site, in order to control the intensity and scale of development (including such aspects as the size and height of a buildings on a lot, location of exterior walls, site coverage, the **floor area ratio** and open space requirements). A zoning ordinance should be made in accordance with state statutes that authorize the making of such ordinances and, as a rule, a zoning ordinance should be prepared in accordance with a comprehensive plan that applies to the entire municipality and, therefore, does not unduly favor one land owner over another. A zoning ordinance should substantially relate to public health, safety, morals, or general welfare and should not be arbitrary or unreasonable (Village of Euclid v. Amber Realty Co., 272 US 365, 47 S Ct 114, 71 L Ed 303 (1926); Nectow v. City of Cambridge, 277 US 183, 48 S Ct 447, 72 L Ed 842 (1928)). cf. **master plan**. See also **zoning variance, zoning**.

zoning permit(US)   1. See **building permit**. 2. See **certificate of zoning compliance**.

zoning regulation(US)   See **zoning ordinance**.

zoning variance(US)   A change in a **zoning ordinance** permitted in special circumstances, such as in cases of undue hardship. In that respect it differs from a **special-use permit** or 'special exception', which allows for a use that is compatible with the existing ordinance. A zoning variance is intended to provide flexibility in zoning to allow for special circumstances, such as retaining an existing, but strictly non-conforming, use in order to allow a business to expand. A zoning variance may take the form of an 'area variance' by which the dimensional requirements of the ordinance are altered or waived (including such matters as density regulations and off-street parking, especially when the changes deal with practical difficulties), or a 'use variance' by which a different use is permitted (especially to avoid economic hardship). A 'use variance' may be considered an authorized use of land that is otherwise proscribed by the zoning regulations; whereas an 'area variance' permits deviations from restrictions upon the construction and placement of buildings and structures that are employed to serve the permitted statutory use. Any zoning variance or exception should be in line with the provisions of the comprehensive plan for the area; unless, in some cases, the variance is required to allow for changing conditions in the surrounding area. Sometimes called a 'zoning variation'. See also **cluster development, spot zoning**.

APPENDIX A

This Appendix provides a short summary of the principal National and International Real Estate Organisations and Professional Associations.

More details are available on: **www.deltaalpha.com**

PROFESSIONAL ASSOCIATIONS

APPENDIX A

CANADA

UNITED STATES

APPENDIX A

OTHER ORGANISATIONS INVOLVED IN REAL ESTATE

APPENDIX A

AUSTRALIA AND NEW ZEALAND

Australia Property Institute (API)

www.propertyinstitute.com.au

The premier property organisation in Australia whose members include valuers, professional property advisors, analysts, lawyers, bankers, fund managers, academics and accountants.

New Zealand Property Institute (NZPI)

www.property.org.nz

Founded in 2000 by the amalgamation of the New Zealand Institute of Valuers, the Institute of Plant & Machinery Valuers, and the Property & Land Economy Institute of New Zealand. The new Institute is the major association of real estate professionals in New Zealand.

Property Council of New Zealand

www.propertynz.co.nz

A not-for-profit organisation that represents commercial, industrial and retail property funds and multi-unit residential property owners.

Real Estate Institute of Australia Ltd. (REIA)

www.reia.asn.au

The national professional association for the real estate industry in Australia. REIA works to represent the real estate industry interests and to provide advice to the Federal Government and the public on a wide range of issues.

Real Estate Institute of New Zealand Inc. (REINZ)

www.reinz.co.nz

Members of the Real Estate Institute of New Zealand include all licensed real estate agents throughout New Zealand. The REINZ operates under the Real Estate Agents Act 1976 and is responsible for the professional standards of its members.

Royal Institution of Chartered Surveyors Australia

www.rics.org.au

Headquartered in Sydney, the Australia region of the **Royal Institution of Chartered Surveyors** (RICS) represents chartered surveyors in Australia, New Zealand, Fiji and Papua New Guinea.

APPENDIX A

EUROPE

British Institute of Facilities Management (BIFM)

www.bifm.org.uk

The BIFM's objectives are to develop high standards of professional conduct in facilities management; to support the practice of facilities management with training, education, information and research; and to generate awareness of the value of the effective use of facilities management.

Chartered Institute of Building (CIOB)

www.ciob.org.uk   www.constructors.org

The leading professional body worldwide for managers in the construction industry. CIOB is an educational charity, governed by Royal Charter, that provides a multi-disciplinary technical management based qualification.

The European Group of Valuers' Association (TEGOVA)

www.tegova.org

A pan-European association of valuation professionals that develops and promotes European Valuation Standards and certification standards for valuers.

European Confederation of Real Estate Agents
Confédération Européenne l'Immobilier

www.web-cei.com/cei

One of Europe's largest professional organisations of estate agents, bringing together property agents and advisors from thirteen European countries.

European Public Real Estate Association

www.epra.com

An association of European public real estate companies.

European Real Estate Society (ERES)

www.eres.org

An organisation that was created in 1994 to provide a structured and permanent network between real estate academics and professionals across Europe.

Fédération International des Géomètres (FIG)
International Federation of Surveyors

www.fig7.org.uk

A non-governmental federation of national associations that is the only international body that represents all surveying disciplines.

Fédération Internationale des Professions Immobilières (FIABCI)
The International Real Estate Federation
www.fiabci.com

An independent association that is the largest international association of companies and persons practising the real estate profession.

Fédération Nationale de l'Immobilier (FNAIM)

www.fnaim.fr

A professional association of property agents and advisers that represents the property profession in France at national (parliament, government and administrative) and at local (commune and regional) levels.

Institute of Revenues, Rating and Valuation (IRRV)

www.irrv.org.uk

The preeminent professional body in the UK concerned with local taxation and property valuation.

The International Real Estate Federation (FIABCI)

See *Fédération Internationale des Professions Immobilières.*

International Valuation Standards Committee (ISVC)

www.ivsc.org

A non-government organisation that works with member states and other organisations (such as the World Bank, OECD, the International Federation of Accountants and the International Accounting Standards Board) to formulate and publish valuation standards and procedural guidelines for the valuation of assets for use in financial statements. These standards are published as the *International Valuation Standards* (6th ed. 2003).

Irish Auctioneers & Valuers Institute (IAVI)

www.iavi.ie

The leading real estate body in the Republic of Ireland representing the vast majority of qualified auctioneers, estate agents, valuers and other property professionals.

National Association of Estate Agents (NAEA)

www.naea.co.uk

The largest professional organisation in the United Kingdom dedicated to estate agents involved in sales and letting.

National House-Building Council (NHBC)

www.nhbc.co.uk

A not-for-profit organisation whose mission is to assist the house-building industry construct good quality new homes that meet the reasonable expectations of homebuyers.

Ordre des Géomètres-Experts

www.geometre-expert.fr

The official organisation of *géomètres-experts* (land surveyors) in France.

Property Consultants Society

A society whose principal objects are to provide a central organisation for quantity surveyors, architects, valuers, auctioneers, land and estate agents, master builders, and constructional engineers, who practice as consultants in their branches of the profession.

Royal Institute of British Architects (RIBA)

www.riba.net

The principal body for architects in Britain. Founded in 1834 to promote "the general advancement of Civil Architecture and for promoting and facilitating the acquirement of the knowledge of various Arts and Sciences connected therewith".

Principal Professional Designations:
Associate of the Royal Institute of British Architects (ARIBA)
Fellow of the Royal Institute of British Architects (FRIBA)

APPENDIX A

The Royal Institution of Chartered Surveyors (RICS)

www.rics.org

One of the largest professional associations in the world, with four main responsibilities to the public and its members: ensuring high standards of education and training; the maintenance of standards of conduct; professional advice to governments; and the provision of information to and about the profession itself.

Principal Professional Designations:
Associate of the Royal Institution of Chartered Surveyors (ARICS)
Fellow of the Royal Institution of Chartered Surveyors (FRICS)

Royal Town Planning Institute (RTPI)

www.rtpi.org.uk

An independent organisation whose objective is to advance the science and art of town planning for the benefit of the public.

Principal Professional Designations:
Member of the Town Planning Institute (MRTPI)
Fellow of the Town Planning Institute (FRTPI)
Legal Associate (RPTPI)   *Technical Member* (TechRTPI)

Society of Chartered Surveyors (SCS) (Ireland)

www.scs.ie

The professional body for Chartered Surveyors practising in the Republic of Ireland. SCS maintains strong links to **The Royal Institution of Chartered Surveyors.**

FAR EAST

All Japan Real Estate Federation

www.zennichi.or.jp

A federation of members who are private individuals or corporations possessing a license under the Building Lots & Buildings Transaction Business Law, private individuals who have an interest in real estate, corporations and organisations which support the business activities of the federation as supporting members, as well as honorary members who possess learning and experience in real estate.

Thai Appraisal Foundation

www.thaiappraisal.org

A non-profit organisation that is responsible for valuation education in Thailand. The Thai Foundation conducts research on property appraisal and urban studies and acts as an education centre conducting regular valuation and research courses.

APPENDIX A

CANADA

Appraisal Institute of Canada (AIC)

www.aicanada.org

The national society of professional real estate appraisers. The Appraisal Institute of Canada is a sponsoring organisation of The **Appraisal Foundation**.

Principal Professional Designations:
Canadian Residential Appraiser (CRA)
Accredited Appraiser Canadian Institute (AACI)

Building Owners and Managers Association of Canada

www.bomacanada.org

A federation that represents the Canadian commercial real estate industry on matters of national concern. BOMA Canada is closely associated with the **Building Owners and Managers Association (BOMA) International**.

Canadian National Association of Real Estate Appraisers (CNAREA)

www.cnarea.ca

A national, non-profit, independent appraisal association. The Association is dedicated to raising the standards of the profession in Canada; maintaining the professionalism of its members as qualified appraisers; and to protecting the consumer. CNAREA is a member of **The Appraisal Foundation**.

Canadian Real Estate Association (CREA)

www.realtors.mls.ca/crea/

A national organisation that represents the real estate interests of its members and the public, enhances members' professionalism, competency, and profitability. One of Canada's largest single-industry trade associations.

UNITED STATES

Accredited Review Appraisers Council, Inc. (ARAC)

arac.lincoln-grad.org

A professional association that provides current, relevant educational opportunities for its members. ARAC aims to keep its members up to date and knowledgeable of the latest changes in the industry.

Principal Professional Designations:
Accredited in Appraisal Review (AAR)

APPENDIX A

American Escrow Association

www.a-e-a.org

A national trade association of settlement (escrow) industry professionals.

American Institute of Architects (AIA)

www.aiaonline.com

The principal association for professional architects in the United States.

Principal Professional Designations:
Architect Member (AIA)
Associate Member (Assoc. AIA)
International Associate Member (Int'l Assoc. AIA)

American Land Title Association (ALTA)

www.alta.org

A national trade association that represents the interests of the land title industry ALTA members search, review, and insure land titles to protect real estate investors, homebuyers, mortgage lenders, and other investors in land. Associate members include attorneys, builders, developers, lenders, real estate brokers, surveyors, consultants, educational institutions and related national trade associations.

American Planning Association (APA)

www.planning.org

A professional association of city planners and zoning officials. The APA brings together the professional planner and the citizen member of a board or commission; the elected official and the member of the community group; planners for big and small cities, states, regions, and rural areas; and practitioners, students and teachers.

Principal Professional Designations:
Certified Planner (AICP)

American Real Estate and Urban Economics Association (AREUEA)

www.areuea.org

A non-profit association that provides information and analysis in the fields of real estate development, planning and economics. The Association fosters the exchange of information and opinions between academics and professionals, as well as those in government, who are concerned with urban economics and real estate issues.

APPENDIX A

American Real Estate Society (ARES)

www.aresnet.org/ares

A society that serves the needs of leaders in the real estate industry and real estate professors and practitioners at colleges and universities throughout the United States and the world.

American Resort Development Association (ARDA)

www.ari.net/arda

A trade association representing the vacation ownership and resort development industries.

American Seniors Housing Association (ASHA)

www.seniorshousing.org

A professional association for those involved in the senior housing industry. ASHA is concerned with legislative and regulatory matters and promotes research among those involved in senior housing.

American Society of Appraisers (ASA)

www.appraisers.org

An international non-profit, independent appraisal organization. ASA is the oldest appraisal organization in North America and it represents all disciplines in the appraisal of real and personal property. The ASA is a sponsoring organization of **The Appraisal Foundation**.

Principal Professional Designations:
Accredited Member (AM)   *Accredited Senior Appraiser* (ASA)
Fellow of the American Society of Appraisers (FASA)
Master Gemologist Appraiser® (MGA)

American Society of Farm Managers and Rural Appraisers (ASFMRA)

www.agri-association.org/asfrma

An association of professional appraisers, comprising independent appraisers, managers and consultants, employees of financial institutions, government agency representatives, farm management firms, rural appraisal firms, and other institutions. The American Society of Farm Managers and Rural Appraisers is a sponsoring organization of **The Appraisal Foundation**.

Principal Professional Designations:
Accredited Farm Manager (AFM)   *Accredited Rural Appraiser* (ARA)
Accredited Real Property Review Appraiser (RPRA)
Accredited Agricultural Consultant (AAC)

APPENDIX A

American Society of Home Inspectors®, Inc. (ASHI)

www.ashi.com

A not-for-profit professional society whose volunteer membership consists of private, fee-paid home inspectors. ASHI's objectives include promotion of excellence within the profession and continual improvement of its members' inspection services to the public.

The Appraisal Foundation

www.appraisalfoundation.org

"A not-for-profit educational organization founded to foster professionalism in appraising through the establishment and promotion of appraisal standards and appraisal qualifications". The Foundation was first established in 1987 and was empowered by the Financial Institutions Reform, Recovery and Enforcement Act of 1989 and is authorized by Congress as the Source of Appraisal Standards and Appraiser Qualifications (12 USCA §§ 3345, 3350). The Foundation is directed by a Board of Trustees, which appoints two independent Boards: the 'Appraisal Standards Board' (ASB), which promulgates the generally accepted standards of the appraisal profession, and the 'Appraisal Qualification Board' (AQB), which establishes the minimum education, experience and examination criteria for the state certification of appraisers and sets minimum standards for practising appraisers. The Board of Trustees has also appointed The Appraisal Foundation Advisory Council (TAFAC) which is composed of 55 non-profit organizations that represent appraiser, users of appraisal services and regulators; most of the federal real estate lending institutions of the United States; as well as the Internal Revenue Service, the Office of Thrift Supervision, the U.S. Department of Army (Corps of Engineers), the U.S. Department of Housing and Urban Development, the U.S. Department of the Interior (Bureau of Land Management and Fish & Wildlife Service), the U.S. Departments of Veterans Affairs, and the U.S. Department of State.   See also **Uniform Standards of Professional Appraisal Standards**.

Appraisal Institute (AI)

www.appraisalinstitute.org

A non-profit organization that is the leading association for professional real estate appraisers. Through its extensive educational programs, the Appraisal Institute's members are skilled in the current methods of real estate valuation for commercial and residential properties. Members of the Appraisal Institute are required to adhere to a strict Code of Professional Practice.

Principal Professional Designations:
MAI for commercial appraisers
SRA for residential appraisers

In addition, the Appraisal Institute recognizes its members who hold the RM, SREA, and SRPA professional designations.

APPENDIX A

Association of Appraiser Regulatory Officials (AARO)

www.aaro.net

A national organization that promotes communication between state appraisal licensing and certification officials.

Association of Foreign Investors in Real Estate (AFIRE)

www.afire.org

The official voice of the foreign institutional real estate industry. AFIRE members have a common interest in preserving and promoting international real estate investment.

Association of Real Estate License Law Officials (ARELLO)

www.arello.org

A not-for-profit association made up of entities involved in licensing and regulating the practice of real estate. Members of ARELLO are real estate commissioners and real estate administrators who come from all the 50 states, the Canadian provinces, US Territories, South Africa, Hong Kong, the Philippines and other selected jurisdictions outside North America.

Building Officials and Code Administrators (BOCA)

www.bocai.org

A trade association for professionals involved in building code enforcement. BOCA publishes model building codes.

Building Owners and Managers Association International (BOMA)

www.boma.org

An international federation of professional organizations that own and manage downtown and suburban commercial properties and facilities in North America and abroad. BOMA is also recognized for its *Standard Method of Measuring Floor Area in Office Buildings*. BOMA also publishes statistics on office buildings.

CCIM Institute

www.ccim.com

The Certified Commercial Investment Member (CCIM) Institute is a network for developing real estate business with local chapters throughout the United States and Canada, and relationships with other real estate organizations nationally and internationally. The CCIM Institute is an affiliate of the **National Association of REALTORS®**.

Principal Professional Designations:
Certified Commercial Investment Member (CCIM)

Commercial Real Estate and Secondary Market Securitization Association (CSSA)

www.cssacmbs.org

An international trade association that promotes the issues involved with commercial real estate capital markets, including commercial mortgage-backed securities.

Congress for New Urbanism (CNU)

www.cnu.org

A non-profit organization that works with architects, developers, planners, and others involved in the creation of cities and towns, to promote and implement the principles of the New Urbanism.

CoreNet Global

www.corenetglobal.org

An organization that was formed in 2002 by the merger of Nacore International and the International Development Research Council. Members are real estate professionals engaged in the management of real estate for major corporations worldwide.

Principal Professional Designations:
Master of Corporate Real Estate (MCR)

APPENDIX A

Counselors of Real Estate (CRE)

www.cre.org

A not-for-profit international association of high profile professionals including members of prominent real estate, financial, legal and accounting firms as well as leaders of government and academia who provide expert, objective advice on real property and land-related matters. CRE is affiliated with the **National Association of REALTORS®**.

Principal Professional Designations:
Counselor of Real Estate (CRE)

Foundation of Real Estate Appraisers (FREA)

www.frea.com

The Foundation of Real Estate Appraisers was founded in 1992 in response to changes in the appraisal industry resulting from Title XI of the Financial Reform Enforcement Act of 1989 (FIRREA). FREA offers a package of benefits and education for its members, including an errors and omissions insurance policy.

Institute of Real Estate Management (IREM®)

www.irem.org

The professional association for real estate managers, asset managers and management firms involved with all types of real estate. The largest affiliate of the **National Association of REALTORS®**.

Principal Professional Designations:
Certified Property Manager® (CPM®)
Accredited Residential Manager® (ARM®)
Accredited Management Organisation® (AMO®)

International Association of Assessing Officers (IAAO)

www.iaao.org

An educational and research association of individuals in the assessment profession and others interested in property taxation. A sponsoring organization of The **Appraisal Foundation**.

Principal Professional Designations:
Certified Assessment Evaluator (CAE)   *Cadastral Mapping Specialist* (CMS)
Personal Property Specialist (PPS)   *Residential Evaluation Specialist* (RES)

International Council of Shopping Centers (ICSC)

www.icsc.org

The trade association of the shopping center industry. The association is a not-for-profit organization with members in over 70 countries, including shopping center owners, developers, managers, marketing directors, leasing specialists, retailers, lenders, consultants and professional advisors, as well as academics and public officials.

International Facility Management Association (IFMA)

www.ifma.org

A not-for-profit, incorporated association dedicated to serving the **facility management** profession. Members of the Association are divided into five classes, namely Professional, Associate, Student, 'Lifetime' and 'Honorary'.

International Real Estate Federation

www.fiabci-usa.com

See *Fédération Internationals des Professions Immobilières* (FIABCI)

International Real Estate Institute (IREI)

www.iami.org/irei.html

The largest international association of real estate professionals with members in over 100 nations. Members specialize in finance, development, property management, valuation, and other related real estate work.

International Right of Way Association (IRWA)

www.irwaonline.com

The professional membership association for individuals who perform services as right of way agents. Right of way agents are involved with the acquisition and valuation of land used for highways, pipelines, airports, telecommunications and numerous other projects.

Principal Professional Designations:
Senior Member Right of Way Association (SR/WA)

Mortgage Bankers Association of America (MBA)

www.mbaa.org

The Mortgage Bankers Association of America represents the professional needs and interests of mortgage lenders and allied professionals in real estate finance. MBA is a sponsoring organization of **The Appraisal Foundation**.

National Apartment Association (NAA)

www.naahq.org

A federation of local and state associations of owners, builders, investors and managers of rental property.

Principal Professional Designations:
Certified Apartment Manager (CAM)
Certified Apartment Maintenance Technician (CAMT)
Certified Apartment Property Supervisor (CAPS)
National Apartment Leasing Professional (NALP)

National Association of Home Builders (NAHB)

www.nahb.com

A federation of more than 850 state and local homebuilder associations throughout the United States. The mission of this trade association is "to enhance the climate for housing and the building industry, and to promote policies that will keep housing a national priority. NAHB's goal is to provide and expand opportunities for all Americans to have safe, decent and affordable housing".

National Association of Independent Fee Appraisers (NAIFA)

www.naifa.com

A professional organization for real estate appraisers who are in large part self-employed. NAIFA is a sponsoring organization of The **Appraisal Foundation**.

Principal Professional Designations:
Independent Fee Appraiser (IFA)
Senior Independent Fee Appraiser (IFAS)
Independent Fee Appraiser and Counselor (IFAC)

National Association of Industrial and Office Properties (NAIOP)

www.naiop.org

An association of owners and developers of industrial, office and related property.

National Association of Master Appraisers (NAMA)

www.masterappraisers.org

A national professional association for those interested in the profession of real property appraisal. The National Association of Master Appraisers is a sponsoring organization of **The Appraisal Foundation**.

Principal Professional Designations:
Master Residential Appraiser (MRA)
Master Farm and Land Appraiser (MFLA)
Master Senior Appraiser (MSA)

National Association of Mortgage Brokers (NAMB)

www.namb.org

A not-for-profit organization committed to promoting the highest degree of professionalism for its members and providing ethical and professional standards against which mortgage brokers can be measured.

National Association of Real Estate Appraisers (NAREA)

www.iami.org/narea.html

A professional organization founded to make available highly qualified Real Estate Appraisers to those who require Professional Appraisal Reports. The Association provides a special professional designation for Real Estate Owned (REO) appraisers. Members must be State Licensed or Certified Appraisers. NAREA is an affiliate of the **National Association of Real Estate Brokers** and a sponsoring organization of **The Appraisal Institute**.

Principal Professional Designations:
Certified Real Estate Appraiser (CREA)
Certified Commercial Real Estate Appraiser (CCRA)
Certified Real Estate Owner Appraiser (CREO)

APPENDIX A

National Association of Real Estate Brokers (NAREB)

www.nareb.org

The oldest minority trade association in America. NAREB seeks to unite those engaged in recognized branches of the real estate business, including Brokerage, Management, Mortgage Financing, Appraising, Land Development, Home Building, and allied fields in the United States of America and Canada, for the purpose of effectively exerting a combined positive influence upon matters affecting real estate.

Principal Professional Designation:

Realtist

National Association of Real Estate Investment Trusts, Inc. (NAREIT®)

www.nareit.com

The national trade association for REITs and publicly traded real estate companies. Members are real estate investment trusts (REITs) and other businesses that own, operate and finance income-producing real estate, as well as those firms and individuals who advise, study and service those businesses. NAREIT maintains statistics on all Real Estate Investment Trusts.

National Association of REALTORS® (NAR)

www.realtor.com

The largest real estate organization in the world. NAR members include salespeople, brokers, property managers, appraisers, counselors, and others engaged in the real estate business. NAR has several affiliated groups including, the **Commercial Investment Real Estate Institute**; **Counselors of Real Estate**; **Investment Real Estate Institute**; **Institute of Real Estate Management**; **REALTORS® Land Institute**; Realtors National Marketing Institute; the Real Estate Securities and Syndication Institute; **Society of Industrial and Office Realtors**; **Women's Council of REALTORS®**; and the American Chapter of the **International Real Estate Federation (FIABCI)**.

National Association of Review Appraisers and Mortgage Underwriters (NARAMU)

www.iami.org/nara.html

A non-profit organization dedicated to maintaining professional standards and promoting ongoing education in the fields of Appraisal Review and Mortgage Underwriting. Members represent international corporations, banks, thrifts, insurance companies, law firms and private real estate lenders.

National Auctioneers Association (NAA)

www.auctioneers.org

A professional organization for auctioneers, although the association is not limited to those who specialize in real estate auctions.

National Council of Real Estate Investment Fiduciaries (NCREIF)

www.ncreif.org

An association of institutional real estate professionals who share a common interest in their industry. The Council publishes the NCREIF Property Index, which is used by many institutions as a benchmark for measuring real estate portfolio performance.

National Society of Real Estate Appraisers

www.nareb.com/affiliates/society_appraisers.shtml

A national association that represents and supports minority professionals involved in appraisal work.

Real Estate Educators Association (REEA)

www.holonet.net/realed

An association that promotes education, communication and professionalism among individuals involved in real estate education and training.

Principal Professional Designations:
Designated Real Estate Instructor (DREI)

REALTORS® Land Institute

www.rliland.com

An association of real estate professionals that are involved in land brokerage and agribusiness.

Society of Industrial and Office REALTORS® (SIOR)

www.sior.com

An affiliate organization of the National Association of REALTORS® that represents those who specialize in industrial property and property that is associated with industrial property.

Urban Land Institute (ULI)

www.uli.org

An independent non-profit education and research institute whose mission is "to provide leadership in the responsible use of land to enhance the total environment". The Institute acts as a forum that facilitates the open exchange of ideas, information and experience among local, national, and international industry leaders and policy makers dedicated to creating better places.

Women's Council of REALTORS (WCR)

www.wcr.org

An affiliate organization of the National Association of REALTORS® that provides members with a referral network and promotes the skills of professional women in real estate.

OTHER ORGANIZATIONS INVOLVED IN REAL ESTATE

American Bar Association (ABA)

www.abanet.org

The largest professional association in the world. ABA is the national representation of the legal profession.

American Institute of Certified Public Accountants (AICPA)

www.aicpa.org

The national professional association of Certified Accountants.

The Institute of Chartered Accountants in England and Wales

www.icaew.co.uk

The largest professional accountancy body in Europe.

National Association of Securities Dealers (NASD)

www.nasd.com

A private, not-for-profit organization that provides financial regulatory services for securities firms doing business in the US.

The Law Society

www.lawsoc.org.uk

The representative and regulatory professional body for solicitors in England and Wales.

The Law Society of Scotland

www.lawscot.org.uk

The governing body for solicitors in Scotland.

Mortgage Insurance Companies of America (MICA)

www.privatemi.com

A non-profit trade association that represents the private mortgage insurance industry.

Further up-to-date information and links to these Professional Organisations and Associations is available on: **www.deltaalpha.com**

TABLE OF MEASUREMENTS
OF LENGTH, AREA AND VOLUME
including Metric/Imperial Conversions

LAND LINEAR MEASURE

Imperial/US measurements

12 inches (in or ")	= 1 foot (ft or ')	
3 feet	= 1 yard (yd)	
1,760 yards	= 1 mile (mi)	= 5,280 feet =320 rods
5½ yards	= 1 rod (rd), pole or perch	= 16½ feet
40 rods	= 1 furlong (fur)	= 220 yards
22 yards	= 1 chain	= 4 rods, poles or perches
220 yards	= 10 chains	= 1 furlong
8 furlongs	= 1 mile	= 80 chains

Metric measurements

10 millimetres (mm)	= 1 centimetre	
10 centimetres (cm)	= 1 decimetre	
10 decimetres	= 1 meter$^{(AmE)}$/metre$^{(BrE)}$	
10 metres	= 1 decametre/dekametre	
10 decametres	= 1 hectometre	= 100 metres
1,000 metres	= 1 kilometre (km)	
10,000 metres	= 1 myriametre	

Surveying measurements

7.92 inches	= 1 link (Gunter's or surveyor's chain)	
100 links	= 1 chain	= 4 rods = 66 feet
80 chains	= 1 statute mile (mi)	= 5,280 feet
12 inches	= 1 link (Engineer's chain)	
100 links	= 1 chain	= 100 feet
52.8 chains	= 1 mile	= 5,280 feet

APPENDIX B

Imperial/US to Metric Conversion

0.3937 inches	= 1 centimetre (cm)
39.37 inches	= 1 metre (m)
3.28084 feet	= 1 metre (m)
1.0936 yards	= 1 meter[AmE]/metre[BrE]
0.621371 miles	= 1 kilometre (km)
2.5400 centimetres	= 1 inch
0.3048 metres	= 1 foot
0.9144 metres	= 1 yard
1.609344 kilometres	= 1 mile
1 kilometre	= 0.62137 miles

LAND AREA MEASURE

Imperial/US measurements

1 square inch (sq in)	= 0.006944 square feet
144 sq inches	= 1 square foot (sq ft or ft^2)
9 sq feet	= 1 square yard (sq yd or yd^2)
4,840 sq yards	= 1 acre (ac)= 43,560 square feet
10 acres	= 1 square furlong
160 acres	= one quarter US section
640 acres	= 1 square mile (sq mi) = 1 United States Section

Metric measurements

100 sq millimetres (mm^2)	= 1 sq centimetre (cm^2)
100 sq centimetres	= 1 sq decimetre
100 sq decimetres	= 1 sq metre
100 sq metres	= 1 are (a)
10,000 sq metres	= 1 hectare (ha)
100 ares	= 1 hectare
100 hectares	= 1 sq kilometre (km^2)
1,000,000 sq metres	= 1 sq kilometre

Surveying/Land measurements

30¼ sq yards	= 1 square rod (rd^2), pole or perch
160 sq rods	= 1 acre
625 sq links	= 1 sq rod, pole or perch
16 poles or perches	= 1 sq surveyor's chain
16 sq rods	= 1 sq surveyor's chain
40 sq rods	= 1 rood
1 rood	= ¼ acre
4 roods	= 1 acre = 10 sq surveyor's chains
100 perches	= 1 arpent = 0.85 acres (approx.) (or between 5/6 and 1¼ acres)
1 vara	= 33.33 inches (Texas)

Imperial/US to Metric Conversion

0.1550 sq inches	= 1 sq centimetre (cm^2)
10.764 sq feet	= 1 sq metre (m^2)
1.19599 sq yards	= 1 sq metre
0.3861 sq miles	= 1 sq kilometre
2.47107 acres	= 1 hectare (ha)
6.452 sq centimetres	= 1 sq inch
0.0929 sq metres	= 1 sq foot (sq ft)
0.83613 sq metres	= 1 sq yard
2.590 sq kilometres	= 1 square mile
1 sq kilometre	= 247.105 acres
0.40468 hectares	= 1 acre

VOLUME MEASURE

Imperial/US measurements

volume

1,728 cubic inches	= 1 cubic foot (cu ft)
27 cubic feet	= 1 cubic yard (cu yd)
128 cubic feet	= 1 cord
5.8 cubic feet	= 1 bulk barrel

capacity

1.7339 cubic inches	= 1 fluid ounce (Brit.)
4 gills	= 1 pint
2 pints	= 1 quart
8 pints	= 1 gallon
4 quarts	= 1 gallon
2 gallons	= 1 peck
4 pecks	= 1 bushel
4 bushels	= 1 sack
8 bushels	= 1 quarter
36 bushels	= 1 chaldron/bulk barrel
277.42 cubic inches	= 1 Imperial gallon
6.2288 cubic feet	= 1 Imperial gallon
231.04 cubic inches	= 1 US gallon
7.4794 cubic feet	= 1 US gallon
1 Imperial gallon	= 1.20094 US gallons

APPENDIX B

Metric measurements

volume

1,000 cubic millimetres	= 1 cubic centimetre
1,000 cubic centimetres	= 1 cubic decimetre
1,000 cubic decimetres	= 1 cubic metre (m^3)
1,000 cubic metres	= 1 cubic decametre
1,000 cubic decametres	= 1 cubic hectometre
10 cubic metres	= 1 decastere
1,000,000 cubic centimetres	= 1 cubic metre

capacity

10 millilitres	= 1 centilitre
10 centilitres	= 1 decilitre
10 litres	= 1 decalitre
10 hectolitre	= 1 kilolitre
1000 litres	= 1 cubic metre

Imperial/US to Metric Conversion

1 cubic inch	= 16.387 cubic centimeters	
1 cubic foot	= 0.02832 cubic meters	
1 cubic centimeter (cm^3)	= 0.061024 cubic inches (cu in)	
1.7598 pints (Brit.)	= 1 litre$^{(BrE)}$/liter$^{(AmE)}$	
2.1134 pints (US)	= 1 liter	
0.879 quarts (Brit.)	= 1 litre	
1.0567 quarts (US)	= 1 liter	
4.5460 litres	= 1 gallon (Brit.)	
3.7853 litres	= 1 gallon (US)	
1 **acre foot**	= 43,560 cubic feet	= 325,693 US gallons

APPENDIX B

WEIGHT OR MASS

Imperial/US measurements

16 ounces	= 1 pound (lb)
14 pounds	= 1 stone
2 stone	= 1 quarter
4 quarters	= 1 hundredweight
20 hundredweights	= 1 ton
2,240 pounds	= 1 ton
1 ton	= 1,016 kilograms
2.2046 pounds	= 1 kilogram (kg)
100 pounds	= 1 short hundredweight
112 pounds	= 1 long hundredweight
1 short ton	= 20 short hundredweights = 2,000 pounds
1 long ton	= 20 long hundredweights

Metric measurements

1,000 milligrams	= 1 gram (g)
10 grams	= 1 decagram
1,000 grams	= 1 kilogram (kg)
10 decagrams	= 1 hectogram
10 hectograms	= 1 kilogram
100 kilograms	= 1 quintal
10 quintals	= 1 tonne

APPENDIX B

Imperial/US to Metric Conversion

1 gram	= 0.0353 ounces
1 ounce (oz.)	= 28.35 grams
1 pound	= 454 grams
1 ton	= 1,016 kilograms
1 kilogram	= 2.204623 pounds
1 short ton (2,000 lbs)	= 0.9072 metric tons/tonnes
1 long ton (2,240 lbs)	= 1.01605 metric tons/tonnes
1 degree Celsius	= x 9/5 (+32) degrees Fahrenheit
1 kilometre/hour	= 0.62137 miles/hour

Measures of Angles and Arcs

1 degree	= 0.01745 radians
60 seconds	= 1 minute
60 minutes	= 1 degree
90 degrees	= 1 quadrant
180 degrees	= half circle
360 degrees	= 1 full circles

Areas and volume calculations

Area of circle	$= \pi r^2$ where: $\pi = 3.14159265$ r = radius
Area of parabola	= base x 2/3 altitude
Volume of cylinder	$= \pi r^2$ x height
Volume of pyramid	= base length x height $\div$ 3
Volume of sphere	$= 4/3 \pi r^3$

APPENDIX C

FINANCIAL FORMULAE

APPENDIX C

Amount of One or Future Value of $1, £1, ¥1, €1, etc.

The future worth of one (unit of money) when invested for a specified period of time with **compound interest**. Calculated by the formula:

$$A = (1+i)^n$$

Where:
A = the value of one unit of monetary value, invested for

n = periods of time (or n years), at

i = interest rate, expressed as a decimal

If the interest is compounded more than once during the given periods of time (or more than once per annum), then the amount of one is given by the formula:

$$[1 + (i/m)]^{mn}$$

where m represents the number of times that the interest is credited per period of time (or in a year). Thus, if $1,000 is invested for 8 years at a nominal rate of 9% p.a. and interest is credited to the principal (and compounded) monthly, then it will accumulate to

$$1,000 \times [(1+(0.09/12)]^{12 \times 8}$$

$$= \$2,050 \text{ at the end of the period.}$$

Present Value (or Present Worth) of $1, £1, ¥1, €1, etc.

The inverse of the **Amount of One**. The value today of one unit of value that is receivable at the end of a given time. Alternatively, the Present Value of One is the sum of money that, if invested now at a stated rate of compound interest, will be worth one unit of value at the end of the given period of time (as at the end of a nuber of years).

Calculated by the formula:

$$V = \frac{1}{(1+i)^n}$$

Where:
V = the value today of one unit of value

n = the number of periods of time (or years)

i = the interest rate

Thus, if $1,000 is receivable in 5 years and is assumed to reduce in 'real value' at the rate of 12% per annum *at present* that sum is worth:

$$1,000 \times \{1/[(1 + 0.12)^5]\} = \$567.40$$

Alternatively, if $567.40 is invested today at a compound interest rate of 12%, that sum will be worth $1,000 in 5 years. Called also the 'payment to amortiseone unit of value'. In the US, also called a 'reversion factor'.

APPENDIX C

Amount of One per Period or Future Value of One per Period

The amount to which a *series* of deposits, or payments, of one unit will accumulate in a given period (or number of years), at a stated rate of compound interest.

Calculated by the formula:

$$A_n = 1 + (1+i) + (1+i)^2 + (1+i)^3 + \cdots + (1+i)^{n-1}$$

$$= \frac{(1+i)^n - 1}{i}$$

Where :
A_n = the sum accumulated
n = the number of periods of time
i = the interest rate

Thus, if $10,000 is invested every year for 15 years with interest compounded annually at 6% the amount accumulated will be $10,000 x [(1.06^{15}-1)/0.06] = $232,760.

Called also an 'annuity factor', the 'future annuity of 1 per period' or, sometimes in the US, a 'sinking fund accumulation factor'. cf. **sinking fund factor**.

Present Value (or **Present Worth**) of One per Period

The sum of money that might reasonably be paid today for the right to receive a series of future deposits, or payments, of one unit of value, which are invested at a stated compound interest rate over a given period of time (or number of years); or, the discounted value of a future level income, i.e. of an annuity certain.

Calculated by the formula:

$$P_n = \frac{1}{(1+i)} + \frac{1}{(1+i)^2} + \frac{1}{(1+i)^3} + \frac{1}{(1+i)^{n-1}} + \cdots + \frac{1}{(1+i)^n}$$

$$= \frac{1 - \dfrac{1}{(1+i)^n}}{i}$$

Where:
P_n = the value today of a right to receive one unit of value
n = periods of time (or years)
i = the interest rate

In the US, the Present Value of One per Period is also called a 'present worth factor', an '**Inwood factor**' or an 'Inwood coefficient'. In the UK, it is commonly referred to as a **years' purchase**. See also **capitalization factor, internal rate of return, net present value**.

944

APPENDIX C

Sinking-Fund (s.f.) Factor

The inverse of the **Amount of One per Period**. A number of equal periodic payments that will accumulate to one unit of value when invested with compound interest.

Calculated by the formula:

$$S_n = \frac{s}{(1+s)^n - 1}$$

Where: S_n = the periodic payment or 'sinking fund factor'

n = number of periodic payments

s = compound interest rate or sinking fund rate

See also **dual-rate capitalization factor**.

Annuity One Will Purchase

An annual return, or **annuity**, receivable, over a given number of years, from an investment of one unit of value. That sum of money which if paid in annual instalments, over the period of a loan, will repay one unit of that loan, together with interest thereon; i.e. an 'annuity factor' which provides a sinking fund to recoup the principal amount of the loan and also repays interest on the outstanding balance. The factor is given by the formula:

$$a_n = i + S_n = i + \frac{i}{(1+i)^n\ 1}$$

$$= \frac{i}{1 - \frac{1}{(1+i)^n}}$$

Where: S_n = **sinking fund**

i = interest rate per annum (or per period), expressed as a decimal

n = number of annual (or regular) loan repayments (during the term of the loan)

a_n = the annuity

This annuity figure is most commonly calculated in order to determine the level periodic instalments that will amortise a loan, i.e. to calculate a **mortgage constant**. For example, if a loan of $100,000 is taken out for a period of 25 years, then the constant annual amount required to repay the loan together with interest at 9% per annum is:

$$100,000 \times 0.09 / [1 - (1.09^{25})^{-1}] = \$10,180.63$$

The annuity one will purchase is the reciprocal of the **Inwood factor**, i.e. of the **Present Value of One per Period**.

APPENDIX C

The previous formulae may be expressed as a function of the
Amount of One/Future Value of One $A^n = (1+i)^n$ so that:

Present Value of One
$$= \frac{1}{A^n}$$

Amount of One per Period
or Future Value of One per period
$$= \frac{A^n - 1}{i}$$

Present Value of One per Period
or Inwood factor/Years' Purchase
$$= \frac{1 - \dfrac{1}{A^n}}{i}$$

Sinking-Fund Factor S_n
$$= \frac{i}{A^n - 1}$$

Annuity One Will Purchase
$$= i + \frac{i}{(A^n - 1)}$$

APPENDIX C

Dual-rate Capitalization Factor(AmE) or Dual-rate Years' Purchase(BrE)

A **capitalization factor** or **years' purchase**, used to capitalize income from a depreciating investment (e.g. a leasehold interest or a wasting asset), that incorporates a mathematical adjustment so that the capital value obtained is comparable to a similar, but non-depreciating, investment. The capital value obtained by applying this factor to a projected income from an investment is such that the investor receives both (i) a **remunerative rate** of return which is comparable to a permanent investment; and (ii) a notional **sinking fund**, which is set aside at a 'safe' or **accumulative rate** of return, to replace the original cost of the investment at the end of its useful or anticipated life. A dual-rate factor is 'adjusted' to notionally set aside extra income to replace the capital cost of the original investment, with the result that the capital value of the declining income is reduced so that the net return to the investor is comparable to the level achieved by an investor who acquires a permanent, or non-depreciating, asset. The factor may be calculated by the formula:

$$r = \frac{1}{\text{interest rate} + \text{sinking fund factor}}$$

$$\text{or} \quad \frac{1}{(i + S_n)}$$

$$= \frac{1}{i + \dfrac{s}{(1+s)^n - 1}}$$

Where:
r = capitalization factor
i = remunerative rate
S = sinking fund factor
s = accumulative or sinking fund rate
n = number of income receipts during the term of the investment (assumed in arrears)

Thus, if a wasting asset is acquired for P and produces an income of v per annum, such that $P = rv$, then the investor will receive a return on his cost of i per annum, which is less than v throughout the term of n years, with the difference between v and i notionally invested at a rate of interest of s in order to accumulate to the capital sum P to replace the wasted asset; in other words, hypothetically, to perpetuate the income. (With a single rate **capitalization factor** there is a notional sinking fund, but it is deemed to accumulate at the same rate as the remunerative rate, i.e. $i = s$.) The dual-rate capitalization formula only provides for the replacement of the original capital cost and makes no allowance for inflation or tax on the sinking fund element. (For a discussion of the alternatives and a bibliography on approaches to the valuation of declining investments see J. Ratcliffe and A. Trott. *Valuation - Demand and Techniques* (1980) 255 EG 435 & 529.) In the US, this factor is called also the **Hoskold factor**, the 'Hoskold approach', or the 'Hoskold premise'. See also **internal rate of return**.

APPENDIX C

Capitalisation^(BrE) or Capitalization^(AmE)

Capitalisation for a limited period of time may be expressed by the formula:

$$C_v = \frac{a_1}{(1+r)} + \frac{a_2}{(1+r)^2} + \frac{a_3}{(1+r)^3} + \cdots + \frac{a_n}{(1+r)^n}$$

Where:

C_v = the capital value

$a_1, \ a_2, \ a_3 \ \ldots \ a_n$ = the income or cash flow receipts in each period of time.

r = capitalisation rate, expressed as a decimal

n = number of periods of time (or years)

When the income is constant, straight capitalisation produces a capital value = a/r, where a = income and r = capitalisation rate.

Internal Rate of Return

The rate of interest that discounts a series of future cash flows or income returns to make them equal to the total cost or outlay on the investment that generates those cash flows or income returns; the one rate of interest at which the **present value** of all expenditure on an investment equals the present value of all receipts from that investment (i.e. the discount rate when the **net present value** is zero). The internal rate of return may be calculated solving for r in the formula:

$$P_0 = \sum_{i=1}^{i=n} \frac{R_i}{(1+r)} + \frac{P_n}{(1+r)^n}$$

Where:

P_0 = initial cost

R_i = income during period i (or per annum), in arrears

P_n = value of reversion

or **redemption value** in period n (or the scrap value after n years)

n = number of periods (or years)

r = internal rate of return

Thus, if P_0 is the price paid for an investment, which produces a periodic (or annual) income in arrears of R_i for n periods (or years), and the investment is sold at the end of that period for P_n then the equivalent annual return over the life of the investment is r. Under this formula, it is assumed that all income received from the investment is reinvested during the term of the investment at the same rate. The rate calculation may be 'adjusted' by applying a lower or safer rate to the income received throughout the term of the investment.

APPENDIX C

Net Present Value (NPV)

The net present value of the **net income** receivable from an investment is equivalent to the **capital value** of that investment and may be obtained from the formula:

$$\text{NPV} = \sum_{t=0}^{T} \frac{CF_t}{(1+r)^t} = CF_0 + \frac{CF_1}{(1+i)} + \frac{CF_2}{(1+i)^2} + \frac{CF_3}{(1+i)^3} + \cdots + \frac{CF_n}{(1+i)}$$

Where:

CF_t = the cash flow at time t

CF_0 = the initial cash flow or outlay

CF_1, CF_2, CF_3, CF_n = net cash flows from the investment at periods 1, 2, 3, etc. or years 1, 2, 3, etc. up to the final period or year n

i = discount rate or cost of capital

n = number of periods of time (or years)

If $NPV = 0$, then i = the **internal rate of return**. In other words, NPV represents an 'absolute' measure of value, whereas IRR is a 'relative' rate of return.

Weighted Average Cost of Capital (WACC)

The average cost of capital (whether equity or debt), taking into account the relative proportions of each source of capital. For example, if $1.5m is provided as equity capital on the basis of an expected dividend yield of 5%, and $5m is provided as debt capital at an interest rate of 12%, the weighted average cost is: $[(1.5/6.5) \times 5\%] + [(5/6.5) \times 12\%] = 10.38\%$. A generalised formula for calculating the weighted cost of capital is:

$$k = \sum_{i=1}^{i=n} w_i k_i$$

Where: w_i is the weight of the ith type of capital and k_i is the cost of the ith component. If the firm has one class of debt, preference shares and equity, k would be found as:

$$k = w_b k_b + w_{ps} k_{ps} + w_s k_s$$

This latter equation can be expanded to encompass short-term debt, long-term debt, convertibles, etc. See also **composite rate**, **gearing**.

FINANCIAL FORMULAE

BIBLIOGRAPHY

UNITED STATES

Akerson, Charles B. *Capitalization Theory and Techniques: Study Guide (with financial tables, including J and K factor tables)*. 2nd ed. Chicago: Appraisal Institute, 2000.

AIREA. *Financial Tables, edited and compiled by James J. Mason*. Chicago: Appraisal Institute, 1981.

Ellwood, L. W. *Ellwood Tables for Real Estate Appraising and Financing*. 4th ed. Cambridge, MA; Ballinger Publishing Co., 1977.

Fisher, Charles E. *Mathematics of Real Estate Appraisers: an Appraisal Institute Handbook*. Chicago: Appraisal Institute, 1996.

Sindt, Roger P. *Real Estate Investment: Analysis and Applications*, Upper Saddle River, NJ: Prentice-Hall, 1997, Ch. 3 "Real Estate Investment Mathematics".

Wiley, Robert J. *Real Estate Accounting and Mathematics Handbook*, 3rd ed. New York: Wiley, 1993.

UNITED KINGDOM

Bowcock, Philip. *Excel for Surveyors*. London: Estates Gazette, 2000.

Bowcock, Philip. *Property Valuation Tables*. London: Macmillan, 1978.

Johnson, Tony, Keith Davies and Eric Shapiro. *Modern Methods of Valuation*, 8th ed. Ch. 8 "The Mathematics of Valuation Tables". London: Estates Gazette, 2000.

Davidson, A. W. *Parry's Valuation and Investment Tables*, 12th ed. London: Estates Gazette, 2002.

Enever, Nigel and David Isaac. *The Valuation of Property Investments*, 5th ed. London: Estates Gazette, 1995, Ch. 6. "The Mathematics of Valuation and Finance".

Rose's Property Valuation Tables, constituting the 34th edition of INWOOD'S TABLES, reconstructed and explained by J. J. Rose. Oxford: The Freeland Press, 1975.

Royal Institution of Chartered Surveyors. *Commercial Investment Property: Valuation Methods, An Information Paper*, London: RICS Books, 1997, Ch. 2 "Appraisal Mathematics".

APPENDIX D

ABBREVIATIONS & ACRONYMS

A

A	Atlantic Reporter (USA)
A.2d	Atlantic Reporter, Second Series, 1983-date (USA)
AAA rating	triple A rating
AACI	Accredited Appraiser Canadian Institute (see Appendix A)
AAR	Accredited in Appraisal Review (see Appendix A)
	average annual return
ABS	asset-backed security
a/c	air conditioning
AC	Law Reports, Appeal Cases, 1890-date (Eng)
(ACT)	Australian Capital Territory
ACRS	accelerated cost recovery system
ADC loan	acquisition, development and construction loan
Adm'r	Administrator
Admin.	Administrat[ive, ion]
ADR	alternative dispute resolution
	average daily room rate
AEA	Administration of Estates Act (Eng)
aff'd	affirmed
AFFO	adjusted funds from operations
A-G	Attorney-General
AGI	adjusted gross income
AHA	Agricultural Holding Act (Eng)
AI	all inclusive
AIA	American Institute of Architects (see Appendix A)
AIC	Appraisal Institute of Canada (see Appendix A)
AIREA	American Institute of Real Estate Appraisers (see Appendix A)
AIRR	adjusted internal rate of return
AITD	all-inclusive deed of trust
AJA	Administration of Justice Act (Eng)
Ala	Alabama; Alabama Supreme Court Reports

All ER Rep	All England Law Reports, Reprinted, 1558-1935
All ER	All England Law Reports, 1936-date
ALR	American Law Reports Annotated, 1913-1947
	Argus Law Reports, 1895-1973 (Aus)
	Australian Law Reports, 1973-date, formerly Argus Law
ALR3d	American Law Reports Annotated, Third Series, 1965-1980
ALR4th	American Law Reports Annotated, Fourth Series, 1980-1991
ALR5th	American Law Reports Annotated, Fifth Series, 1992-date
ALTA	American Land Title Association (see Appendix A)
Alta. CA	Alberta, Court of Appeal (Can)
Am Rep	American Reports
Am.Jur.2d.	American Jurisprudence, second edition (see page 975 n.1)
Am.L.Prop	American Law of Property
AMC	Agricultural Mortgage Corporation(Eng)
	Asset Management Company
AMI	alternative mortgage instrument
AML	adjustable-mortgage loan
Anno	Annotation
ANSI	American National Standards Institute
AONB	area of outstanding natural beauty (Eng)
APA	American Planning Association (see Appendix A)
App Cas	Law Reports, Appeal Cases (House of Lords and Privy Council) 1875-1890 (Eng)
App Div	Appellate Division (New York Supreme Court), 1896-1955
app. den.	appeal denied
app. dism.	appeal dismissed
app./appr'n	appreciation
APR	annual percentage rate
ARELLO	Association of Real Estate License Law Officials (see Appendix A)
ARES	American Real Estate Society (see Appendix A)
AREUEA	American Real Estate and Urban Economics Association (see Appendix A)
Ariz	Arizona; Arizona Supreme Court Reports, 1866-date
Ark	Arkansas; Arkansas Report
ARM	adjustable-rate mortgage
ARR	all-risks rate

ARR	average rate of return
ARV	aggregate retail value
ARY	all-risks yield
ASA	American Society of Appraisers (see Appendix A)
ASB	Appraisal Standards Board [US]
a.s.f.	annual sinking fund
ASHI	American Society of Home Inspectors, Inc. (see Appendix A)
ASREC	American Society of Real Estate Counselors (see Appendix A)
Ass'n	Association
AST	assured shorthold tenancy [Eng]
ATCF	after-tax cash flow
(AUS)	Australia
AUV	alternative use value
AVD	alternative valuation date [Eng]
AVM	automated valuation model

B

B & Ad	Barnewall and Adolphus's King's Bench Reports (109-110 ER), 1830-1834 [Eng]
B & Ald	Barnewall and Alderson's King's Bench Reports (106 ER), 1817-1822 [Eng]
B & C	Barnewall and Cresswell's King's Bench Reports (107-9 ER), 1822-1830 [Eng]
Beav	Beavan's Rolls Court Reports (48-55 ER), 1838-1866 [Eng]
BFP	bona fide purchaser
BID	business improvement district
Bing NC	Bingham's New Cases (131-3 ER), 1834-1840 [Eng]
Bing	Bingham's Common Pleas Reports (130-1 ER), 1832-1834 [Eng]
Bl Comm	Blackstone's Commentaries on the Laws of England [see page 975 n.2]
Black	Black's Supreme Court Reports (66-7 US) 1861-2
BOMA	Building Owners and Managers Association (see Appendix A)
Bos & PNR	Bosanquet and Puller's New Reports Common Pleas (127 ER), 1804-7 [Eng]
BPN	building preservation notice [Eng]
Bro CC	Brown's Chancery Reports (28-9 ER), 1778-1794 [Eng]
Bro PC	Brown's Cases in Parliament (1-3 ER), 1702-1800 [Eng]
Bros.	Brothers
Brownl & G	Brownlow and Goldesborough's Common Pleas Reports

(123 ER), 1569-1624 [Eng]

BRR	book rate of return
Burr	Burrow's King's Bench Reports (97-8 ER), 1757-1771 [Eng]

C

c.	chapter (Act of Parliament, Eng)
c.	mortgage co-efficient [US]
(CA)	Court of Appeal [Eng]
CA	commonhold association [Eng]
CA#	Court of Appeals, no. of Federal Judicial Circuit
CAD	cash available for distribution
Cal App	California Appellate Reports
Cal App.2d	California Appellate Reports, Second Series
Cal App.3d	California Appellate Reports, Third Series
Cal App.4th	California Appellate Reports, Fourth Series
Cal CC	California Civil Code
Cal Rptr	California Reporter
Cal	California; California Reports
Cal.2d	California Supreme Court Reports, Second Series
Cal.3d	California Supreme Court Reports, Third Series
CAM	common area maintenance
(Can)	Canada
CAP rate	capitalization rate
CBA	cost-benefit analysis
CBD	central business district
CC	Civil Code
	County Council [Eng]
CCA	Circuit Court of Appeals [USA]
CCS	commonhold community statement [Eng]
CD	certificate of deposit
CERCLA	Comprehensive Environment Response and Liability Act [USA]
cert. den.	certiorari denied
Cf./cf.	'confer', compare with
CFAT	cash flow after tax

CFBT	cash flow before tax
C.F.R.	Code of Federal Regulations [USA]
CGT	capital gains tax [Eng]
Ch Cas	Cases in Chancery (22 ER), 1660-1698 [Eng]
Ch D	Law Reports Chancery Division, 1875-1890 [Eng]
Ch	Law Reports Chancery Division, 1891-date [Eng]
Ch./Chs.	chapter/chapters
C.I.R.	Commissioner of Inland Revenue [USA]
Cir.	Circuit Court of Appeals (Federal)
C.J.S.	Corpus Juris Secundum [US] (see page 975 n.3)
Cl & F	Clark & Finnelly's House of Lords Cases (6-8 ER), 1831-46 [Eng]
CL	Current Law, 1947-date [Eng]
CLR	Canada Law Reports, 1923-date
	Commonwealth Law Reports, 1903-date [Aus]
CLRA	Commonhold and Leasehold Reform Act [Eng]
CLY	Current Law Year Book, 1947-date [Eng]
CM	construction management
CMA	comparative market analysis
CMBS	commercial mortgage-backed security
Cmnd	Command Papers [Eng]
CMO	collateralized mortgage obligation
CMSA	consolidated metropolitan statistical area
CNAREA	Canadian National Association of Real Estate Appraisers (see Appendix A)
Co Inst	Coke's Institutes (see page 975 n.4)
Co Litt	Coke on Littleton (see page 975 n.4)
Co Rep	Coke's King's Bench Reports (76-7 ER), 1572-1616 [Eng]
CO	certificate of occupancy
Co./*Co*	company
Colo App	Colorado Court of Appeal Reports
Cor.Jur.Sec.	Corpus Juris Secundum (see page 975 n.3)
COREA	construction operation and reciprocal easement agreement
Corp./*Corp'n*	Corporation
Cowp	Cowper's King's Bench Reports (98 ER), 1774-8 [Eng]
CPA	Compulsory Purchase Act [Eng]

CPA	critical path analysis
CPD	Law Reports, Common Pleas Division, 1875-1880 (Eng)
CPI	consumer price index
CPM	critical path method
CPO	compulsory purchase order (Eng)
CRA	Canadian Residential Appraiser (see Appendix A)
CRE	corporate real estate
CRV	certificate of reasonable value (US)
Ct App NY	Court of Appeals of New York
Ct Cl	United States Court of Claims
	Court of Claims Reports, 1863-1982/United States Claims, 1982-1992
CTT	capital transfer tax (Eng)
Cush	Cushing's Massachusetts Reports (55-6 Massachusetts)
CUV	current use value

D

D Del	United States District Court for the District of Delaware
D NJ	United States District Court for the District of New Jersey
DC	District Council (Eng)
DC Ark	United States District Court, Arkansas
DC Cal	United States District Court, California
DC Mass	United States District Court, Massachusetts
DC Pa	United States District Court, Pennsylvania
DC	District of Columbia
DCF	discounted cash flow
DCR	debt-coverage ratio
De GF & J	De Gex, Fisher and Jones's Chancery Reports (45 ER), 1860-1862 (Eng)
Del	Delaware; Delaware Reports
dep./depr'n.	depreciation
Dict.	Dictionary
DIM	deferred-interest mortgage
DINK	dual income, no kids
DLR (2d)	Dominion Law Reports, Second Series, 1956-1968 (Can)
DLR (3d)	Dominion Law Reports, Third Series, 1969-1984 (Can)

DLR (4d)	Dominion Law Reports, Fourth Series, 1969-date [Can]
DLR	Dominion Law Reports, 1912-1955 [Can]
DOE	Department of the Environment [Eng]
DPM	direct-payment mortgage
DRC	depreciated replacement cost
Drew	Drewry's Chancery Reports (61-2 ER), 1852-1859 [Eng]
DRM	direct reduction mortgage
DRT	development rights transfer [US]
DSCR	debt-service cover ratio

E

E & O insurance	errors and omissions insurance
E.O.E.	Errors and omissions excepted
E.O.M.	End of the month (as with payment due under a contract)
EA	environmental assessment
East	East's Term Reports, King's Bench (102-4 ER), 1800-1812 [Eng]
EBIT	earnings before interest and tax
EBITDA	earnings before interest, taxes, depreciation and amortization
ECAT	expendable cash after tax [Aus]
Econ.	Economist
ECV	effective capital value
ed.	edition; editor
Eden	Eden's Chancery Reports (28 ER), 1757-1766 [Eng]
EFRV	estimated future rental value
EG	Estates Gazette, 1858-date [Eng]
EGCS	Estates Gazette Case Summaries [Eng]
EGD	Estates Gazette Digest of Cases, 1902-date [Eng]
EGI	effective gross income
EGIM	effective gross income multiplier
EGLR	Estates Gazette Law Reports [Eng]
EIA	environmental impact assessment
EIR	environmental impact report
EIS	environmental impact statement
El & Bl	Ellis and Blackburn's Queen's Bench Reports (118-120 ER), 1851-1858 [Eng]

Em App	Emergency Court of Appeals (US)
Eng Rep	English Reports, 1220-1865
EPA	Environmental Protection Agency (US)
EPRA	environmental property assessment (US)
ER	English Reports, 1220-1865
ERISA	Employee Retirement Income Security Act (US)
ERP	estimated realisation price
ERRP	estimated restricted realisation value (US)
ERV	estimated rental value
ESA	environmental site assessment
Esp	Espinasse's Nisi Prius Reports (170 ER), 1793-1807 (Eng)
esp.	especially
et seq.	*et sequentes, et sequitor*, 'and those following'
EUV	existing use value
Ex CR	Canadian Exchequer Court Reports
ex rel.	*ex relatione*, 'on the relation of'
Exch	Exchequer Reports (154-6 ER), 1847-1856 (Eng)
EZ	enterprise zone

F

F Supp	Federal Supplement, 1932-1998 (US)
F Supp.2d	Federal Supplement, Second Series, 1998-date (US)
F	Federal Reporter (US)
F&B	food and beverage
F.2d	Federal Reporter, Second Series
F.3d	Federal Reporter, Third Series
FAD	funds available for distribution
FADA	Federal Asset Disposition Association (US)
FAMC	Federal Agricultural Mortgage Corporation (US)
Fannie Mae	Federal National Mortgage Association (FNMA) (US)
FAR	floor area ratio (US)
FASIT	financial asset securitization investment trust
FDIC	Federal Deposit Insurance Corporation (US)
Fed. Cir.	United States Court of Appeals, Federal Circuit

APPENDIX D

Fed.	Federal
FF & E	furniture, fixtures and equipment
FFLS	Federal Farm Loan System [US]
FFO	funds from operations
FHA	Federal Housing Administration [US]
FHFB	Federal Housing Finance Board [US]
FHLBB	Federal Home Loan Bank Board [US]
FHLMC	Federal Home Loan Mortgage Corporation (Freddie Mac) [US]
FIABCI	*Fédération Internationale des Professions Immobilières* (see Appendix A)
FIFO	first in, first out
FIG	*Fédération International des Géomètres* (see Appendix A)
FIRPTA	Foreign Investment in Real Property Tax Act [US]
FIRREA	Federal Institutions Reform, Recovery, and Enforcement Act [US]
Fla	Florida; Florida Supreme Court Reports, 1846-1948
FLIP®	flexible loan insurance plan [US]
FM	facility management
FmHA	Farmer's Home Administration [US]
FMV	fair market value
FNAIM	*Fédération Nationale de l'Immobilier* (See Appendix A)
FNMA	Federal National Mortgage Association (Fannie Mae) [US]
FPM	flexible-payment mortgage
FRA	Fines and Recoveries Act [Eng]
Freddie Mac	Federal Home Loan Mortgage Corporation (FHLMC) [US]
FREIT	finite life real estate investment trust
FRI lease	full repairing and insuring lease
FRM	fixed-rate mortgage
FRN	fixed-rate note
FRT	federally-related transaction [US]
FRV	full rental value
FSA	Financial Services Act [Eng]
FSBO	for sale by owner
FSG	full service gross (lease)
FSI	floor space index
FV	future value

G

Ga	Georgia; Georgia Supreme Court Reports
GAAP	general accepted accounting principles [US]
GBA	gross building area
	gross built area
GDP	general development plan
GDPO	General Development Procedure Order [Eng]
GDS	General Depreciation System [US]
GEA	gross external area
GEM	growing-equity mortgage
GIA	general improvement area [Eng]
	gross internal area
GIC	guaranteed investment contract
GIM	gross income multiplier
Ginnie Mae	Government National Mortgage Association [US]
GIS	geographic information systems
GLA	gross lettable area/gross leasable area
	gross living area
GNMA	Government National Mortgage Association (Ginnie Mae) [US]
GOI	gross operating income
GPAML	graduated-payment adjustable mortgage loan
GPDO	General Development Procedure Order [US]
GPM	graduated-payment mortgage
GPS	Global Positioning System
GRA	General Rate Act [Eng]
GRM	gross rent multiplier
GRMM	gross rent monthly multiplier
GSA	General Services Administration [US]
GSE	Government Sponsored Enterprise (such as Fannie Mae or Freddie Mac) [US]
GSP	guaranteed sale program
GST	goods and services tax [Aus/NZ]
GVD	general vesting declaration [Eng]

H

HA	Housing Act (Eng)
HAA	Housing Action Area (Eng)
HAT	Housing Action Trust (Eng)
HECM	home equity conversion mortgage
HEL	home equity loan (US)
HELCPA	Home Equity Loan Consumer Protection Act (US)
HELOC	home equity line of credit (US)
HKC	Hong Kong Cases
(HL)	House of Lords (Eng)
HL Cas	House of Lords Cases, 1847-1866 (9-11 ER)
HLR	Housing Law Reports, 1967-date (Eng)
HMDA	Home Mortgage Disclosure Act (US)
HMO	house in multiple occupation (Eng)
HMSO	Her Majesty's Stationery Office (Eng)
HOA	homeowners' association/home owners' association (US)
Howard	Howard's Supreme Court Reports, 1834-1843 (US)
HUD	Department of Housing and Urban Development (US)
Hun	Hun's New York Supreme Court Reports
HVAC	heating, ventilation and air conditioning

I

IAAO	International Association of Assessing Officers (see Appendix A)
IBA	industrial building allowance
ICSC	International Council of Shopping Centers (see Appendix A)
Idaho	Idaho Supreme Court Reports, 1866-date
IFMA	International Facility Management Association (see Appendix A)
Ill App	Illinois Appellate Court Reports
Ill	Illinois; Illinois Supreme Court Reports, 1819-date
ILSFDA	Interstate Land Sales Full Disclosure Act of 1968 (US)
in perp.	in perpetuity
Inc.	Incorporated
Ind	Indiana; Indiana Supreme Court Reports

Indus.	Industr[y, ies, ial]
Ins.	Insurance
Int'l	International
Inv.	Investment
IO	interest only (security)
I_0	net operating income
Iowa App	Court of Appeals of Iowa
Iowa	Supreme Court of Iowa; Iowa Reports, 1855-1968
IR	Irish Reports, 1838-date
IRA	individual retirement account [US]
IRC	Inland Revenue Commissioners [Eng]
IRC	internal revenue code [USA]
IREF	International Real Estate Federation (see Appendix A)
IREI	International Real Estate Institute (see Appendix A)
IREM	Institute of Real Estate Management (see Appendix A)
IRR	internal rate of return
IRS	Internal Revenue Service [US]
ISVA	Incorporated Society of Valuers and Auctioneers
IVSC	International Valuation Standards Committee

J

JCT	Joint Contracts Tribunal [Eng]
Johns & Hem	Johnson and Hemming's Chancery Reports (70 ER), 1859-1862 [Eng]
JPL	Journal of Planning and Property Law, 1954-1972 [Eng]
	Journal of Planning and Environmental Law, 1973-date [Eng]
Jur	The Jurist, London

K

'k' factor	mortgage factor; mortgage constant
Kan	Kansas; Kansas Supreme Court Reports, 1862-date
KB	Law Reports, King's Bench Division, 1901-1952
Ky Ct App	Court of Appeals of Kentucky
Ky	Kentucky; Kentucky Supreme Court Reports, 1879-1951

L

(Lat)	Latin (or in this book more usually 'law Latin')
(LT)	Lands Tribunal (Eng)
L Ed	Lawyers' Edition United States Supreme Court Reports
L Ed.2d	Lawyers' Edition United States Supreme Court Reports, Second Series
L&T Act	Landlord and Tenant Act
L&T	Landlord and Tenant
L.S.	*locus sigilli,* 'place of the **seal**'
L/C	letter of credit
L/V ratio	loan-to-value ratio
LA	Limitation Act (Eng)
La	Louisiana; Louisiana Reports, 1830-1841, 1901-1972
	Louisiana Supreme Court Reports, 1901-1972
LCA	Land Charges Act (Eng)
LcompA	Land Compensation Act (Eng)
LCR	Lower Canada Reports, 1850-67
Lev	Levinz's King's Bench and Common Plea Reports (83 ER), 1660-97 (Eng)
LGHA	Local Government and Housing Act (Eng)
LGRA	Local Government Reports of Australia, 1956-date
LHA	local housing authority
LIBOR	London Interbank Offered Rate
LIFO	last in, first out
Lit.	Litigation (Eng)
LJ Ch	Law Journal, Chancery, New Series, 1831-1946 (Eng)
LJ	Law Journal, 1866-1965 (Eng)
LLCA	Local Land Charges Act (Eng)
LP(MP)A	Law of Property (Miscellaneous Provisions) Act (Eng)
LPA	Law of Property Act (Eng)
LRA	Land Registration Act (Eng)
	Leasehold Reform Act (Eng)
LT	Law Times Reports, 1859-1947 (Eng)
	Law Times, Scranton, Pennsylvania, 1873-85 (US)
LTV	loan-to-value ratio

LUI	land use intensity (system) (US)
LVT	Local Valuation Tribunal (Eng)

M

M & E	mechanical and electrical
M & W	Meeson and Welsby's Exchequer Reports (150-3 ER), 1836-1847 (Eng)
M.R.	Master of the Rolls (Eng)
MA	metropolitan area
MARCS	modified accelerated cost recovery system
Mass	Massachusetts; Massachusetts Reports, 1967-date
MBA	Mortgage Bankers Association of America (see Appendix A)
MBB	mortgage-backed bond
MBO	mortgage-backed obligation
MBS	mortgage-backed security
Md App	Maryland Appellate Reports, 1967-date
Md	Maryland; Maryland Supreme Court Reports
Me	Maine; Maine Supreme Court Reports (USA)
MFLA	Master Farm and Land Appraiser (see Appendix A)
MGIC	Mortgage Guaranty Insurance Corporation (US)
MIC	mortgage insurance certificate
Mich	Michigan; Michigan Supreme Court Reports, 1847-date (USA)
Minn	Minnesota; Minnesota Supreme Court Reports (USA)
MIRR	modified internal rate of return
Misc	Miscellaneous Reports (New York)
Misc.2d	Miscellaneous Reports, Second Series (New York)
Miss	Mississippi; Mississippi Reports, 1851-1966
MLP	master limited partnership
MLS	multiple listing service
Mo	Missouri; Missouri Supreme Court Reports, 1821-1956
Mo App	Missouri Appeals Reports, 1876-1954
Mont	Montana; Montana Supreme Court Reports
MPC	master planned community
MPLR	Municipal and Planning Law Reports (Can)
MPTB	mortgage-pass-through bond

MRA	Master Residential Appraiser
	(see Appendix A, National Association of Master Appraisers)
MRA	multiple regression analysis
MSA	Master Senior Appraiser
	(see Appendix A, National Association of Master Appraisers)
MSA	metropolitan statistical area [US]
MUD	mixed-use development
MV	marriage value

N

n.	note; sub-note
NAA	National Apartment Association (see Appendix A)
NAHB	National Association of Home Builders (see Appendix A)
NAIFA	National Association of Independent Fee Appraisers (see Appendix A)
NAMA	National Association of Master Appraisers (see Appendix A)
NAR	National Association of Realtors® (see Appendix A)
NARAMU	National Association of Review Appraisers and Mortgage Underwriters (see Appendix A)
NAREB	National Association of Real Estate Brokers (see Appendix A)
NAREIT	National Association of Real Estate Investment Trusts (see Appendix A)
Nat'l	National
NAV	net asset value
NC Ct App	Court of Appeals of North Carolina
NC	North Carolina; North Carolina Supreme Court Reports, 1968-date
NCC	Nature Conservancy Council [Eng]
NCREIF	National Council of Real Estate Investment Fiduciaries (see Appendix A)
NE	North Eastern Reporter [USA]
NE.2d	North Eastern Reporter, Second Series [USA]
Neb	Nebraska; Nebraska Supreme Court Reports, 1860-date
NH	New Hampshire; New Hampshire Supreme Court Reports, 1816-date
NHBC	National House-Building Council (see Appendix A)
NHPA	National Historic Preservation Act [US]
NIA	net internal area
NIBR	net income before recapture

NIM	net income multiplier
NJ Eq	New Jersey Equity Reports, 1830-1948
NJ	New Jersey; New Jersey Supreme Court Reports, 1948-date
NLA	net leasable area/net lettable area
NNN	net, net, net or **triple net**
NOA	net occupiable area
NOI	net operating income
NPL	non-performing loan
NPV	net present value
NRV	net realizable value
(NSW)	New South Wales [Aus]
(NT)	Northern Territories [Aus]
NW.2d	North Western Reporter, Second Series [US]
NY	New York Court of Appeals Reports
NY.2d	New York Court of Appeals Reports, Second Series
NYS	New York Supplement, 1887-1937
NYS.2d	New York Supplement, Second Series, 1938-date
(NZ)	New Zealand

O

O&M	operations and maintenance
OCR	overall capitalization rate
ODP	office development permit
OE & T	operating expenses and taxes
OEO	Office of Equal Opportunity [US]
OER	operating expense ratio
OILSR	Office of Interstate Land Sales Registration [US]
OIRO	'offers in the region of'
O.L.&T.	owner's, landlord's and tenant's public liability insurance policy
OLA	Occupiers Liability Act [Eng]
Or	Oregon; Oregon Supreme Court Reports, 1953-date
OR	overall return
ORE	owned real estate
OREO	other owned real estate

ORR	overall rate of return
OTS	Office of Thrift Supervision (US)
Otto	Otto's United States Supreme Court Reports (91-107 US)
OWN	Ontario Weekly Notes (Can)

P

P & CR	Planning (Property from 1968) and Compensation Reports, 1949-date (Eng)
P	Law Reports, Probate, Divorce and Admiralty Division, 1891-1971 (Eng)
p & i	principal and interest (payment)
P&L	profit & loss
p./pp	page(s)
P.2d	Pacific Reporter, Second Series (USA)
p.s.f	per square foot
P/E ratio	price-earnings ratio
Pa Cmwlth	Pennsylvania Commonwealth Court Reports
pa	per annum
Pa	Pennsylvania; Pennsylvania State Reports, 1845-date
PAA	Perpetuities and Accumulations Act
Pac LJ	Pacific Law Journal (USA)
PAC	planned amortization class
PAM	pledged account mortgage (US)
para./paras	paragraph/paragraphs
(PC)	Privy Council (Eng)
pc sum	prime-cost sum
PCB	polychlorinated biphenyls
PCD	planned commercial development
PD	Law Reports, Probate Division, 1875-1890 (Eng)
PEA	Protection from Eviction Act (Eng)
perp.	perpetuity
PERT	project evaluation and review technique
Pet	Peters' United States Supreme Court Reports (26-41 US) 1828-42
PGI	potential gross income
PGIM	potential gross income multiplier
Ph	Philip's Chancery Reports (41 ER), 1841-1849

PHA	Public Health Act (Eng)
PHA	Public Housing Administration
PI	profitability index
PID	planned industrial development
PILOT	payment in lieu of taxes (US)
piti	principal, interest, taxes and insurance
PLAM	price-level-adjusted mortgage
P(LBCA)A	Planning (Listed Building and Conservation Areas) Act (Eng)
PLSS	public lands survey system (US)
PMDT	purchase money deed of trust
PMI	private mortgage insurance
PMM	purchase money mortgage
PMSA	primary metropolitan statistical area
pmt	payment/periodic payment
PO	principal only (security)
POB	point of beginning
POE	post-occupancy evaluation
pp	per pro/per procuration
PPM	parts per million
PR	Pacific Reporter (USA)
	profitability ratio
PRD	planned residential development
Prec Ch	Precedents in Chancery (T. Finch) (24 ER), 1689-1722 (Eng)
PSA	Property Services Agency (Eng)
psf	per square foot
PSI	positive spread investment
PTCF	pre-tax cash flow
Pty.	Property
PUD	planned unit development
PUT	property unit trust
PV	present value
PW	present worth

Q

q.v.	*quod vide*, 'which see'
QB	Law Reports, Queen's Bench Division, 1891-1901, 1952-date (Eng)
QB	Queen's Bench Reports (Adolphus & Ellis, New Series) (113-8 ER), 1841-52
QBD	Law Reports, Queen's Bench Division, 1875-1890 (Eng)
Qd R	Queensland Reports (Aus)
(Qld)	Queensland
Quebec CC	Quebec Civil Code (1981)
qv	*quod vide*, 'which see'

R

r	basic rate
	correlation coefficient; coefficient of correlation
R	capitalisation rate
R	*Rex* (King) or *Regina* (Queen)
r./rr.	rule/rules
R.R.	Railroad
RA	Rating Appeals (Eng)
	Rent Act (Eng)
RAM	reverse annuity mortgage
RAP	Rule against Perpetuities
R_B	building capitalization rate
R_E	equity capitalization rate
REA	reciprocal easement agreement
Real Prop.Prob.& Tr.J.	Real Property Probate & Trust Journal (USA) 1966-date
REC	real estate commission
REEA	Real Estate Educators Association (see Appendix A)
REIT	Real Estate Investment Trust
REMIC	Real Estate Mortgage Investment Conduit
REMT	real estate mortgage trust
REO	real estate owned
REOC	real estate operating company
RESPA	Real Estate Settlement Procedure Act of 1974 (US)

RIBA	Royal Institute of British Architects (see Appendix A)
RICS	Royal Institution of Chartered Surveyors (see Appendix A)
R_L	land capitalization rate
Rly/Ry	Railway
R_M	mortgage constant; loan constant; mortgage coefficient
R_N	terminal capitalization rate
R_O	overall capitalization rate
ROI	return on investment
ROM	roll-over mortgage
rr.	rules
RRM	renegotiable-rate mortgage
RSL	registered social landlord [Eng]
RTC	Resolution Trust Corporation [USA]
RTPI	Royal Town Planning Institute (see Appendix A)
RULPA	Revised Uniform Limited Partnership Act
Russ	Russell's Chancery Reports, 1823-1829
RV	rateable value
r/w	right of way

S

(SA)	South Australia
(Scot)	Scotland
S&L	savings and loan association
S Ct	Supreme Court Reports [USA]
s.	section
s.f.	sinking fund
S.S.	Steamship
S.T.C.	subject to contract
Salk	Salkeld's English King's Bench Reports (91 ER), 1689-1712 [Eng]
SALR	South Australia Law Reports, 1865-1892, 1888-1921
SAM	shared-appreciation mortgage
Sask. CA	Saskatchewan, Court of Appeals [Can]
SASR	South Australian State Reports, 1921-date
Saund	See Wms Saund [Eng]

SBS	sick-building syndrome
SC (HL)	House of Lords Session Cases [Scot]
SC Can	Supreme Court of Canada
Sc LR	Scottish Law Reports, 1865-1924
SC	Session Cases, 1907-date [Scot]
	South Carolina Supreme Court Reports, 1868-date
Sch.	Schedule
SCLR	Scottish Civil Law Reports, 1987-date
SCR	Reports of the Supreme Court of Canada
SD	South Dakota Reports
	Supreme Court of South Dakota
SD Ind	United States District Court of the Southern District of Indiana
SD NY	United States District Court of the Southern District of New York
Sec.	Securit[y, ies]
sec./secs.	section/sections
SEC	Securities and Exchange Commission [US]
s.f.	sinking fund
	square foot
SFD	single-family detached
SFR	single-family residence
SI	Statutory Instrument [Eng]
SLA	Settled Land Act [Eng]
SLE	substantive lessor entity
sm	square metre
SMBS	stripped mortgage-backed security
SMSA	standard metropolitan statistical area
SNDA	subordination, nondisturbance, and attornment agreement
SNH	Scottish National Heritage
So	Southern Reporter [USA]
So.2d	Southern Reporter, Second Series (USA)
SOYD	sum of the years' digits
SPC	special-purpose corporation
SPE	special-purpose entity
SPV	single-purpose vehicle

SPZ	simplified planning zone (Eng)
ss.	sections
SSSI	site of special scientific interest (Eng)
Stra.	Reports by Sir John Strange (d. 1754), M.R. 1st ed. 1755 2 vols. Reprinted from 1795 ed. in 93 Eng Rep.
SW.2d	South Western Reporter, Second Series (USA)
SW/SW Rep	South Western Reporter (USA)
SYD depreciation	sum-of-the-years' digits depreciation

T

TAB	total assets of a business
(Tas)	Tasmania
Taunt	Taunton's Common Pleas Reports (127-9 ER), 1808-1819 (Eng)
TCPA	Town and Country Planning Act (Eng)
TDR	transferable development rights
Tel.	Telegraph/Telephone
Term/Term Rep	Dunford and East's Term Reports (99-101 ER), 1785-1800 (Eng)
Termes de la Ley	*Les Termes de la Ley* (see page 975 n. 5)
Tex Civ App	Court of Civil Appeals of Texas
Texas L. Rev.	Texas Law Review
Thomp & C	Thompson & Cook's New York Supreme Court Reports, 1873-75
TI	tenant improvement (allowance)
TIA	total intangible assets
TIF	tax increment financing
Times	The Times, Law Reports (Eng)
TLR	Times Law Reports, 1884-1952 (Eng)
TPL	third party liability
TPO	tree preservation order (Eng)
TPTIs	tenant-paid tenant improvements
TRO	temporary restraining order
TROL	tax retention operating lease
TWR	time-weighted rate of return

U

UCC	Uniform Commercial Code (US)
UCC-1	Uniform Commercial Code financing statement
UDA	urban development area (Eng)
UDC	Urban District Council (Eng)
UDP	unitary development plan (Eng)
ULI	Urban Land Institute (see Appendix A)
ULPA	Uniform Limited Partnership Act (US)
UPA	Uniform Partnership Act (US)
UPC	Uniform Probate Code (US)
UPREIT	umbrella partnership real estate investment trust (US)
URA	Urban Renewal Administration (US)
URLTA	Uniform Residential Landlord and Tenant Act (US)
US	United States Supreme Court Reports, 1790-date
USC	United States Code
USCA	United States Code Annotated
USPAP	Uniform Standards of Professional Appraisal Practice (US)
UXB	unexpended balance of established development value (Eng)

V

v	*versus* (stated as 'and' in English law)
v.	versus (roman case with period indicates United States citation in this book)
V.O.	valuation officer (Eng)
VA loan	Veterans Administration loan (US)
Va	Virginia Supreme Court Reports
VAM	variable-amortisation mortgage
VAP	variable-payment mortgage
VAT	value added tax (Eng)
Vaugh	Vaughan's Common Pleas Reports (124 ER), 1665-1674 (Eng)
V_B	building value
V_E	equity value
Vern	Vernon's Chancery Reports (23 ER), 1680-1719 (Eng)
Ves Jun	Vesey Junior's Chancery Reports (30-4 ER), 1789-1817 (Eng)

(Vic)	Victoria
V_L	land value
VO	variation order [Eng]
V.O.	valuation officer [Eng]
VPM	variable-payment mortgage
VRM	variable-rate mortgage
Vt	Vermont; Vermont Supreme Court Reports, 1826-date

W

W Va LQ	West Virginia Law Quarterly
(WA)	Western Australia
WACC	weighted average cost of capital
WAL	weighted average life
Wall	Wallace Reports [US]
Wash App.2d	Washington Appellate Reports, Second Series
Wash	Washington; Washington Supreme Court Reports
Wash.2d	Washington Supreme Court Reports, Second Series
Wheat	Wheaton's United States Supreme Court Reports (14-25 US) 1816-27
Wils KB	Wilson's King's Bench Reports (95 ER), 1742-74 [Eng]
Wing.	Wingate's Maxims, 1658 [Eng]
Wis	Wisconsin Supreme Court Reports
Wis.2d	Wisconsin Supreme Court Reports, Second Series
WLR	Weekly Law Reports, 1953-date [Eng]
Wms Saund	Williams' Saunders' King's Bench Reports (85 ER), 1666-73 [Eng]
WN	Law Reports, Weekly Notes, 1866-1951 [Eng]
WWR	Western Weekly Reports, 1912-1950 [Can]

Y

Y	yield rate
Y_E	equity yield rate
Y_O	overall yield rate
YP	years' purchase
YTM	yield to maturity